LIVING WITH DYING

END-OF-LIFE CARE: A SERIES

SERIES EDITOR: VIRGINIA RICHARDSON

We all confront end-of-life issues. As people live longer and suffer from more chronic illnesses, all of us face difficult decisions about death, dying, and terminal care. This series aspires to articulate the issues surrounding end-of-life care in the twenty-first century. It will be a resource for practitioners and scholars who seek information about advance directives, hospice, palliative care, bereavement, and other death-related topics. The interdisciplinary approach makes the series invaluable for social workers, physicians, nurses, attorneys, and pastoral counselors.

The press seeks manuscripts that reflect the interdisciplinary, biopsycho-social essence of end-of-life care. We welcome manuscripts that address specific topics on ethical dilemmas in end-of-life care, death, and dying among marginalized groups, palliative care, spirituality, and end-of-life care in special medical areas, such as oncology, AIDS, diabetes, and transplantation. While writers should integrate theory and practice, the series is open to diverse methodologies and perspectives.

Joan Berzoff and Phyllis R. Silverman, *Living with Dying: A Handbook for End-of-Life Healthcare Practitioners*

Virginia E. Richardson and Amanda S. Barusch, *Gerontological Practice for the Twenty-first Century: A Social Work Perspective*

LIVING WITH DYING

A HANDBOOK FOR END-OF-LIFE HEALTHCARE PRACTITIONERS

Edited by Joan Berzoff and Phyllis R. Silverman

COLUMBIA UNIVERSITY PRESS / NEW YORK

COLUMBIA UNIVERSITY PRESS
Publishers Since 1893
New York   Chichester, West Sussex
Copyright © 2004 Joan Berzoff and Phyllis R. Silverman

Library of Congress Cataloging-in-Publication Data
Living with dying : a handbook for end-of-life healthcare practitioners /
edited by Joan Berzoff and Phyllis R. Silverman.
p. cm.
Includes bibliographical references and index.
ISBN 978-0-231-12794-3(cloth : alk. paper)
1. Social work with the terminally ill.
I. Berzoff, Joan.   II. Silverman, Phyllis R.
HV3000.L58   2004
362.17′5—dc22
2004043850

∞

Columbia University Press books are printed
on permanent and durable acid-free paper.

Printed in the United States of America

c 10 9 8 7

To Babsie, and to her children, Sarah, Katie, and Zach,
so that others may suffer less

CONTENTS

CONTRIBUTORS

TERRY ALTILIO, ACSW
Beth Israel Medical Center
New York, New York

STEPHEN ARONS, JD
University of Massachusetts
Amherst, Massachusetts

LISA ARONSON, MSW, PHD, JD
University of Virginia School of Medicine
Charlottesville, Virginia

MERCEDES BERN-KLUG, MSW
University of Kansas Medical Center
Kansas City, Kansas

JOAN BERZOFF, MSW, EDD, BCD
Smith College School for Social Work
Northampton, Massachusetts

SUSAN BLACKER, MSW, RSW
St. Michael's Hospital
Toronto, Canada

DAVID BROWNING, MSW, BCD
Education Development Center
Newton, Massachusetts

ESTHER CHACHKES, DSW
New York University Medical Center
New York, New York

NANCY CINCOTTA, MSW
Mount Sinai Medical Center
New York, New York

ELIZABETH J. CLARK, PHD
National Association of Social Workers
Washington, D.C.

ELLEN PULLEYBLANK COFFEY, PHD
Berkeley, California

YVETTE COLÓN, MSW, ACSW, BCD
American Pain Foundation
Baltimore, Maryland

INGE B. CORLESS, RN, PHD
MGH Institute of Health Professions
Boston, Massachusetts

ELLEN CSIKAI, MSW, MPH, PHD
The University of Alabama School of Social Work
Tuscaloosa, Alabama

PENNY DAMASKOS, CSW
New York University Medical Center
New York, New York

BARBARA DANE, MSW, PHD
New York University
New York, New York

JENNY DAWES, BA
Adelaide, Australia

JOHN DAWES, MSW, PHD
Flinders University
Adelaide, Australia

NORMA DEL RIO, MSW
San Francisco Department of Public Health
San Francisco, California

THOMAS R. EGNEW, EDD, LICSW
University of Washington School of Medicine
Seattle, Washington

KIM ELLIS, LBSW
The Sweet Life at Rosehill Skilled Nursing Facility
Shawnee, Kansas

SHEILA R. ENDERS, MSW
University of California
Davis, California

LUCILLE ESRALEW, PHD
Statewide Clinical Consultation and Training
of Trinitas Hospital
Cranford, New Jersey

ANNALU FARBER, MBA
Tacoma, Washington

STUART FARBER, MD
University of Washington School of Medicine
Seattle, Washington

IRIS COHEN FINEBERG, MSW, PHD
University of California
Los Angeles, California

ZELDA FOSTER, MSW, CSW
New York University
New York, New York

LES GALLO-SILVER, CSW-R, ACSW
New York University Medical Center
New York, New York

SUSAN GERBINO, MSW, PHD
New York University School of Social
Work
New York, New York

SHELLEY HENDERSON, CSW
Jansen Memorial Hospice
Tuckahoe, New York

ROBERTA HOFFMAN, LICSW
Children's Hospital
Boston, Massachusetts

ELIZABETH HURWITZ, CSW
Mount Sinai Hospital
New York, New York

CHRISTIAN ITIN, MSW, PHD
State University of New York
Brockport, New York

CAROLYN JACOBS, MSW, PHD
Smith College School for Social Work
Northampton, Massachusetts

BARBARA JONES, MSW, CSW
Albany Medical Center
Albany, New York

ALICE RAINESS JORDAN, MSW, LCSW
Palm Harbor, Florida

WENDY A. KARGER
Delray Beach, Florida

BETTY J. KRAMER, MSW, PHD
University of Wisconsin
Madison, Wisconsin

ALLEN LEVINE, MSW
Barrier Free Living
New York, New York

DANIEL LIECHTY, ACSW, LCSW, PHD
Illinois State University
Normal, Illinois

JOHN F. LINDER, LCSW
University of California
Davis, California

SUSAN J. MCFEATERS, LCSW-C, PHD
University of Maryland School of Social
Work
Rockville, Maryland

PATRICE K. NICHOLAS, DNSC, MPH, RN, CS
MGH Institute of Health Professions
Boston, Massachusetts

ILLENE NOPPE, PHD
University of Wisconsin
Green Bay, Wisconsin

PATRICIA O'DONNELL, DSW, LICSW, ACSW,
CCM
Inova Health System
Springfield, Virginia

SHIRLEY OTIS-GREEN, ACSW, LCSW
City of Hope National Medical Center
Duarte, California

MARY RAYMER, MSW, ACSW
Acme, Michigan

DONA REESE, MSW, ACSW, PHD
University of Arkansas School of Social Work
Fayetteville, Arkansas

IRENE RENZENBRINK, MS
Griefworks International
Sydney, Australia

CHRISTIAN B. RUTLAND, MD
City of Hope National Medical Center
Duarte, California

PHYLLIS SILVERMAN, MSW, SCM, PHD
Women's Studies Research Center of Brandeis
   University
Waltham, Massachusetts

JUNE SIMMONS, MSW
Partners in Care Foundation
Los Angeles, California

GARY L. STEIN, MSW, JD
New Jersey Health Decisions
Verona, New Jersey

AMANDA L. SUTTON, CSW
Cancer Care, Inc.
New York, New York

SUSAN TAYLOR-BROWN, MPH, ACSW, PHD
Nazareth College
Rochester, New York

BRUCE THOMPSON, MSW, PHD
Roger Williams University
Bristol, Rhode Island

NEIL THOMPSON, PHD
Avenue Consulting
Wrexham, Wales, UK

SUE THOMPSON, MA
Avenue Consulting
Wrexham, Wales, UK

**KATHERINE WALSH-BURKE, MSW,
   PHD**
Springfield College
Springfield, Massachusetts

FELICE ZILBERFEIN, MSW, PHD
Mount Sinai Medical Center
New York, New York

ACKNOWLEDGMENTS

THIS BOOK would not have been possible without the generous support of the Open Society's Project on Death in America Social Work Leadership Award, through which I have been able to develop the End of Life Post-Masters Program for Social Work at Smith College, which has served as the springboard for this book.

Neither this book nor the program, however, would have ever reached fruition were it not for the tireless efforts of two people in the Center for Innovative Practice at the Smith College School for Social Work. There, Georgina Lucas has offered consistently outstanding administrative leadership, support, and thus the infrastructure to allow this creative work to take place. Her extraordinary efforts and attention to the large picture and to the details have been seamless and invisible, and they are gratefully acknowledged. Donna DeLuca, our research assistant, also deserves much recognition for her outstanding organizational skills, her humor, her tireless energy, and her capacity to track multiple drafts of more than forty-six chapters with élan and great skill. Donna has been a consummate professional who has helped to bring all of the pieces together in ways that have enriched this book.

It goes without saying that this book is the stronger, the deeper, and the wiser for the absolutely high standards, skills, knowledge and expertise of my coeditor, Phyllis Silverman, whose tireless energy, to my amazement, outstrips my own. She has been a wonderful collaborator in the truest sense of the word: a colleague, a teacher, a friend and an adversary with whom I could differ respectfully.

This book has also received support from Acting Dean Carolyn Jacobs, who found the resources to ensure its completion and afforded me the time to do the same.

Many of these chapters have been written by those who have taught in the End of Life Certificate Program at Smith or have been recipients of PDIA Leadership Grants themselves. They are wonderful practitioners and scholars who have made a tremendous contributions to the field, who are able to convey their work with enormous respect for the patients and families with whom they have worked. They represent what is best about the social work profession: in their unswerving commitments to at-risk populations, ethical practice, patient-centered care, advocacy on behalf of those least able to advocate for themselves, and creative approaches to theory and to practice. Among the authors in this book are also lawyers, psychologists, nurses, and physicians whose scholarship, practice experiences, leadership, and personal narratives embody social work values: dignity and respect for the dying and their families. They were initially invited to contribute to this book because of particular areas of expertise outside of the field of social work, but their compassion, empathy, knowledge, and skill represent what we consider to be the best kind of social work care at the end of life. I am grateful to each of the contributors, then, for upholding the values and ethics of the profession and for allowing us, the readers, into the rich and complex contexts in which they live and work.

I am also very grateful to those who have supported me so that I could complete this book. Once again my boys, Zeke and Jake, have been wonderfully supportive despite their shared view that their mother's distraction might become a permanent state. They have been funny, comforting, and distracting too, and I am deeply grateful to them both. My dear husband, Lew Cohen—my soulmate, my colleague, and my friend—has, as ever, created the space for me to work creatively and provided the resources to do so, as well as the intellectual rigor that contributed so much to my thinking.

My dear friends have done it again, seeing me through another book and tolerating my lack of availability while they offered theirs. Special thanks go to my dearest friend, Jaine Darwin, to my sister, Emily Entress, and to Wendy Salkind, Merry Nasser, Cathy Hanauer, Vivienne Weiss, Kathryn Basham, Adin Delacour, Andrea Ayvazian, Bob and Cynthia Shilkret, Sandra Weiner and Donald Andrew, Anne Lown, and Patty Kates, to name only a few. I also thank my bereaved and grieving patients, who have taught me a lot about themselves, and about myself.

One of my greatest sources of support has been my mother, Myra Berzoff, who has taught me about ways to handle death and dying. It has been wonderful to have her continual presence: helping out, assuring me of my strengths and capabilities, and sharing her own.

I would be remiss were I not to mention the incredible support I have received from Stella Marsh, who, on the home front, has, all these years, held it altogether, in her endlessly cheerful and caring ways for me, my family and my home.

I thank my colleagues at the School for Social Work who have tolerated my absence to complete this book, and the many students in the End of Life Program and in the Doctoral Program who have contributed so much to my thinking and learning about the field of end-of-life care. And finally, as ever, I thank my sister, Barbara, and her children, Sarah, Kate and Zach, from whom I have learned so many sad lessons about living and about dying.

—Joan Berzoff

I want to thank Joan Berzoff for inviting me to join her in editing this book. It proved to be an exciting and stimulating collaboration. We started by identifying all our differences and ended realizing that we had learned a great deal from each other. The gap between us has narrowed considerably, and we are proud of what our combined efforts and energy has produced. In this process, she also brought me back to my social work roots and helped to reestablish my connection to my alma mater, Smith College School for Social Work. I am also grateful for the opportunity this work presented to test out how some of my thinking fits into end-of-life care.

I must add my husband and my daughter. My husband knew when to take me to dinner as we pushed to meet deadlines and helped get references that seemed obscure and out of reach. My daughter, Gila, edited my copy to ensure that I was making sense. I also want to thank Lu Farber for doing a final reading of my history chapter. This was beyond her family obligations as my cousin's wife.

I have advocated for writers to have a support group to give them encouragement, help them clarify ideas, and review their work critically. The Writer's Study Group at the Women's Studies Research Center at Brandeis University is mine. Members of the group read my chapter on bereavement and carefully contributed to making my writing clearer and easier to understand. I appreciate this help, but even more important to me was the approbation they gave me for my relational approach to grief.

Several of my friends and colleagues from the Association for Death Education (ADEC) and the International Work Group for Death, Dying and Bereavement (IWG) responded to my invitation to contribute to this book. They gracefully shared their breadth of knowledge, their international perspective, and experience in the chapters they wrote.

My four other children and grandchildren are always on my mind. They have learned that since I "failed retirement," my time is often taken up with projects like this book. Thank you for understanding.

—Phyllis Silverman

FOREWORD

THOMAS R. EGNEW

BENJAMIN FRANKLIN long ago observed that in this world nothing is certain but death and taxes. Though taxes may be a source of stress, this hardly matches the distress surrounding death and the processes of dying in contemporary American society. The sorrow of death is as old as humanity, and it cannot be evaded. Although our medicine can support life at its biological edges, it will never overpower the planned obsolescence that is part of our genetic programming (Nuland 1994). We are born with the seeds of our death, and, in light of the potential of medicine to manipulate its timing, the decisions we make around the reality of death are important and far-reaching for ourselves, for those we love, and for our nation.

For ourselves, we want respect for our values, preferences, and attitudes regarding how we prefer to live until our death. We would like those providing care for us and our families and coordinating the services involved in our dying to be caring, professional people. We would likely want some sense of control, some voice in the process of dying, and an opportunity to bring closure to what is important to us. For our families, we would hope that they were well supported during our dying and that our estates were not depleted paying for care that extends our lives without any meaningful quality. And for our nation, facing an onslaught of end-of-life care for an aging baby-boomer generation, we need a care system that can competently and compassionately provide these services without bankrupting the country.

The death of a family member invariably involves suffering, the resolution of which requires multidisciplinary interventions (Seaburn et al. 1996). Systems supporting quality end-of-life care have evolved as multidisciplinary entities, including social workers as essential members of palliative care teams. Yet, the requisite skills and knowledge in palliative care are unevenly taught and poorly integrated with theoretical concepts and research in schools of social work. Christ and Sormanti (1999) note that social work preparation for work in end-of-life care is woefully inadequate. Some schools of social work offer an elective course on death and dying, and only recently has any continuing social work education in end-of-life care been offered. At the organizational level, the National Association of Social Workers has issued a policy statement on end-of-life care (NASW 1994), stressing client self-determination. However, this policy offers no practical steps for social workers to assist in resolving myriad end-of-life care ethical issues (Csikai and Bass 2000) and may be confusing regarding the ethical priorities of the social worker (Wesley 1996). Social workers are therefore inadequately prepared to provide care to dying persons and their families at the BSW, MSW, and postgraduate levels.

None of these policies and only a few of these educational programs address what is described in this volume as a respectful death, let alone the social worker's role in palliative care. What prescribed set of attitudes, skills, and knowledge do social workers need to support dying persons and their families professionally and competently? What roles—and there are many—do they play in supporting such a death? What working conditions influence how these roles are enacted? In other words, for social workers participating in end-of-life care, what are the implications of supporting a respectful death?

This book addresses the theoretical knowledge necessary for working with the dying and their families. Social workers need to know how to adapt social work skills to the end-of-life environment. They need the knowledge and skills to be effective interdisciplinary team members and a mastery of the values and attitudes needed to fulfill their roles. And, perhaps most important, they must have a passion for the personal connection that relieves suffering. Proficiency in these areas can help assure that social workers functioning in end-of-life care settings are adequately prepared to discharge their duties competently and professionally.

THEORETICAL KNOWLEDGE

Death is one of the most powerful of human experiences. As such, it has been a source of fascination to philosophers and theologians, artists and scientists throughout the ages. The ways in which physical, social, psychological, ethical, and spiritual issues interact in death and dying demand that those working in end-of-life care have a broad understanding of the issues related to death and dying (see chapters 5, 6, 7, 9, 10, and 13). The knowledge required by professionals on the palliative care team is shaped by the roles played in the support of the dying and their families. For example, physicians direct and administer medical treatments whose theory and practice are beyond the scope of the social worker. Conversely, social workers provide material support and referral and counseling services that are beyond the purview of the physician.

The role of the palliative-care social worker is shaped by the nonmedical goals set by the palliative care team, the systems requirements to meet these goals, and the expectations of all involved (Monroe 1993). Nonmedical goals involve the expression of emotional pain and the exploration of spiritual pain. "Dying people," Monroe observes, "want to explore: 'Why, why me, why now, for what purpose'" (1993:565). The answer to these questions is crucial to learning the patient's and family's story and thereby understanding the unique values, meanings, and perspectives that must be reflected in the care that supports what they consider a respectful death. Exploration of these questions requires considerable insight into the human condition and theoretical knowledge of a variety of related topics.

Palliative-care social workers must understand theories of death, dying, and bereavement to explore and interpret the experience of the dying and their families thoughtfully. They must be cognizant of ethical theory to appreciate the balance between self-determination and the family common good when discussing care options (Wesley 1996; see chapter 9, this volume). They must understand the personal and familial impact of pain, disability, and chronic illness across the life span and be able to integrate physiological data pertinent to a particular case (Sieppert 1996; Egan and Kadushin 1999; see chapters 6 and 13, this volume).

Social workers must also appreciate how particular settings—residential settings such as nursing homes or prisons—profoundly affect ways of dying (see chapters 31 and 32). They must understand national policies, funding, and other systems variables that affect the care effort (Yagoda 2002). Social workers are generally knowledgeable about advance directives (Baker 2000; see chapters 37 and 38, this volume), but they must be careful that their own values regarding the care they would prefer do not unconsciously influence the choices of the dying person and family.

Palliative-care social workers must understand psychodynamic, developmental, and relational theories and be knowledgeable about spirituality. This knowledge helps the social worker to shape a death experience that respects the values of the dying patient and family amid the complex personal, social, and systems contexts in which dying occurs (see chapters 6, 7, 8, 12, and 13).

Practically, dying persons and their families want help with the process of dying, the support of which requires an interdisciplinary team that shares common goals and expectations of care. Social workers must therefore understand team dynamics to help coordinate the team's efforts to meet the needs of all involved—patient, family and caring system—while supporting a death that reflects the patient's and family's values (see chapter 8). By employing an ecological perspective focusing on persons, their environments, and the interactions therein, social workers contribute valuable perspectives to help insure "safe passage" for dying patients (Rusnack, Schaefer, and Moxley 1988; see chapters 7, 28, and 29, this volume).

An appreciation of the person demands that the focus of care originate from the perspective of the dying patient who is best understood in the contexts of not only family but also community and time. Within these contexts, numerous forces determine those interventions that best support that patient's and family's conceptions of a respectful death. Social workers, trained in relational skills and a systems focus, are well suited to be productive members of the palliative care team and to help assure that the client and family have experiences of death that respect their desires. Given the complexity and emotionality of death and dying, the breadth of theoretical information informing palliative-care social work is formidable. This volume addresses many of the theoretical topics that are essential for orienting social workers to end-of-life care and has summarized much of the pertinent knowledge social workers need in palliative-care settings.

SKILLS

Palliative-care social workers commonly provide counseling, case management, and advocacy services (Christ and Sormanti 1999). These traditional social work activities, in the palliative-care setting, are highly influenced by the expectations and attitudes of patients and families, colleagues, and society. Flexibility is necessary to fit services to the needs of a particular patient and family facing an end-of-life situation. Promoting self-determination and acting as a liaison between healthcare providers and the patient and family are essential palliative-care social-work activities (Csikai and Bass 2000). In a respectful death, self-determination is best realized when the dying person and the family have authorship of their story of their time left together and when the care dispensed supports the values and desires they define (see chapters 1, 2, 3, and 13).

The principal palliative-care social-work task "concerns the social and psychological health of the patient and family before and after death" (Monroe 1993:566) and requires skills in both assessment and intervention. An ecological assessment involves the patient as an individual, the family as a unit, and the social and physical resources available to support the care effort. Accordingly, this book emphasizes advanced skills in patient-centered interviewing (Steward et al. 1995; Laine and Davidoff 1996) that focus on the patient's experience. Such an approach helps assure that the care plan developed centers on the story of the dying person and family. Only after hearing the story that embodies the values and preferences of the dying person and the family may the interventions that reflect their wishes be determined and the actions that support them initiated. Social workers must therefore know how to develop therapeutic alliances with dying persons and their families to facilitate incorporating discussion of advance directives with assessment (Rosen and O'Neill 1998; Baker 2000; see chapters 37 and 38, this volume) and provide personal support. The sensitive, in-depth end-of-life discussions accompanying a respectful death require that the social worker be an extremely skilled interviewer who is very comfortable with the emotional aspects of death and dying (see chapters 14, 15, 16, 17, 24, and 44).

The social worker must also be highly skilled in the assessment of psychiatric distress and be alert for the same. Dying patients commonly experience anxiety, depression, and cognitive disorders (Jacobsen and Breitbart 1996; see chapter 18, this volume), which can compromise their abilities to complete any unfinished emotional business that may be a part of their particular story. Appropriate diagnosis and treatment can alleviate many troublesome symptoms, freeing energy for possible closure activities. Most terminally ill persons suffer troubling thoughts and concerns about death (Cherny, Coyle, and Foley 1994). There are unfortunately no generally accepted methods for assessing the existential distress of dying patients (Jacobsen and Breitbart 1995), but chief among these are fears of intractable pain and abandonment (Cassell 1976; see chapter 19, this volume). Determining the fears and hopes of dying persons and assessing their psychiatric status are essential to helping patient and family to have a respectful death experience.

The patient's family must be assessed as well. The strengths and liabilities of the family system, general family functioning, and the existence of any vulnerable individuals within the family should be ascertained, which requires skills in family group interviewing. The family is most often the basic source of support for the dying patient (see chapter 28). The physical and emotional burdens of being a caregiver are major sources of suffering for family members (Jacobsen and Breitbart 1996; Ramirez, Addington-Hall, and Richards 1998), and social workers possess skills to provide emotional support while advocating for material assistance (Luff and Blanch 1998; Oliver and Gallagher 1998; see chapters 25, 28, and 32, this volume).

After the desires and wishes of the patient and family have been determined, the physical and social resources available to support their perceptions of a respectful death must be assessed. Does the family have adequate financial resources, and is housing adequate? Are resources available to address unmet physical needs such as ramps in the home or meal services? What types of formal and informal systems for support of the patient and family are on hand? What ethnic, cultural, and religious influences affect the patient and family and shape the illness/death trajectory (see chapters 21, 22, 23, 25, and 34)? The palliative-care social worker must be both knowledgeable about community resources and skilled at effecting referrals and arranging care. At times this involves creating programs that provide services not currently offered but necessary to meet the unique needs of the dying person and the family (Rusnack, Schaefer, and Moxley 1988; see chapter 33, this volume). Skilled assessment of the social and community resources available to support the patient and family encourages a care plan that reflects their wishes and values (see chapter 12).

Palliative-care social work interventions include the provision of information, the facilitation of communication, and bereavement services (Monroe 1993). The social worker must be a highly skilled communicator, capable of imparting sensitive information in both a vocabulary and venue that promote an accurate understanding for the dying person and the family (Buckman 1992). The sharing of feelings and information is crucial for the dying person and the family to resolve the problems that death brings (Monroe 1993). The social worker must therefore be a highly skilled facilitator of communication among family members to help create the harmony that helps them to come together in their desires for the time remaining between them (Csikai and Bass 2000; see chapters 17 and 24, this volume). Interventions require skills in many arenas, but a "key task" is listening and talking (Monroe 1993:570), for through listening and talking are the relationships forged and the values and preferences determined that define a death considered respectful by a particular client and family (see chapters 34, 35, and 36).

Palliative-care social workers must also be skilled in understanding developmental issues for the dying child, adolescent, or adult. They need knowledge about traumatic and unanticipated deaths and the unique issues that families face in light of them. They need to understand a range of disease entities and the meaning to the patient and family of each disease and treatment. The social worker also needs to know that death is inevitable, and that when we talk of death occurring "out there" and to someone else, we must always be aware that we are also talking about ourselves (see chapters 15, 16, 17, 31, and 32).

Bereavement services are interventions provided to patients and families throughout the process of dying and after death. For these to be effective, social workers must develop a strong therapeutic alliance with dying persons and their families. Both patient and family must mourn the losses accompanying the progression of disease. Allowing the dying to discuss their concerns helps them become aware that their fears often involve the process of dying more than the actual death (Spiegel and Glafkides 1983), an insight that is comforting when the concerns about the dying process are addressed. Methods of effecting closure can be explored and developed so the dying person and family may have some control by setting goals and objectives for the time they share before death. The existential suffering of the dying regarding past regrets, present losses, and impending death must be addressed (Cherny, Coyle, and Foley 1994). After death, family members need support while adjusting to their loss. These services are instrumental in the safe passage of patient and family through the dying process and require palliative-care social workers to be highly skilled bereavement counselors (see chapters 12, 13, 26, 27, and 29).

As the authors in this book indicate, the complex nature of a respectful death requires a multidisciplinary care effort, and this necessitates specific skills for palliative-care social workers as well. In reality, all disciplines within the team provide psychosocial services (Monroe 1993; Rusnack, Schaefer, and Moxley 1990; Oliver and Gallagher 1998), and thus palliative care teams are considered interdisciplinary rather than multidisciplinary (see chapter 8). Collaboration among team members pools their expertise and yields a better understanding of both client needs and the resources available to support a respectful death (Abramson and Mizrahi 1996). To be effective palliative-care team members, social workers must be highly skilled collaborators who can communicate between disciplines and across systems (Christ and Sormanti 1999; see chapter 20, this volume) to advocate a care plan focused on the patient's and family's desires rather than the professional values of the care team.

Confidentiality must be respected, and considerable clinical judgment is needed to determine what information must be held confidential and what should be shared with other team members (Monroe 1993). The potential for role competition, confusion, and turf battles is considerable owing to the differences in the professional socialization of the various team members (Abramson and Mizrahi 1996; Mizrahi and Abramson 2000). Successful collaboration therefore not only requires an appreciation for the culture of the other professions (Seaburn et al. 1996) but also must ensure that the decisions that are enacted are not so medicalized that they no longer reflect the desires of the patient and family.

Shepherding the respectful death experience that this book promotes requires social workers to be highly skilled in a variety of professional activities. Utilizing traditional social work responsibilities such as counseling, case management and client advocacy, the social worker must be highly skilled in the assessment of and intervention in end-of-life scenarios. This requires exceptional interviewing skills to determine the values and preferences of dying persons and their families concerning the impending death, and extraordinary collaborative skills to assure that the interdisciplinary team supports the same. Failure to develop and maintain high skill levels risks compromising the abilities of the dying person and family to determine the values and preferences reflected in the care provided them.

ATTITUDES

Palliative-care social workers must also possess the values and attitudes that allow them to engage therapeutically with those experiencing loss, death, and suffering without rushing to fix problems or eventually burning out (Ramirez, Addington-Hall, and Richards 1998). Indeed, social workers experienced in end-of-life care must examine their own values regarding end-of-life issues (Csikai and Bass 2000; see chapters 15, 16, 23, and 36, this volume). Such insight is important to assure that the starting point for services is defined by the dying person and the family, and not by the professional role or cultural, religious, and spiritual beliefs of the social worker (Monroe 1993; see chapters 10, 21, 22, and 23, this volume).

It is crucial for the social worker to come to terms with any personal fears of dying and death and any previous losses, for we "cannot listen properly to the loss of others if our own losses, actual or feared, are unexplored and unresolved" (Monroe 1993:570). Palliative-care social workers must therefore make peace with their personal losses and become reconciled to their mortality to reduce any psychiatric morbidity concomitant to providing end-of-life care. On the other hand, having gained perspective, the stress of caring for the dying can be balanced by the personal satisfaction of assisting dying persons and their relatives to experience a peaceful death reflective of their hopes and dreams (Ramirez, Addington-Hall, and Richards 1998). But this always requires the "relentless self-care" that Irene Renzenbrink describes in chapter 44.

The palliative-care social worker must also be comfortable in the presence of suffering. Suffering comes from perceptions of a threat to the integrity of the self (Cassell 1982). Suffering is an inherently unpleasant emotional experience that is an enduring psychological state reflecting perceptions of helplessness (Chapman and Gavrin 1993). A common response is to rush to action in an attempt to be instrumentally helpful somehow. This is rarely productive, for its impetus lies in *our* emotional response to the situation, rather than being centered on the needs and desires of the dying person or the family. To be present to those who are suffering, it is important for the palliative-care social worker to cultivate what Dass and Gorman (1985:67) call a "Witness" that "gives us a little room" in which to be naturally compassionate while not detaching from the patient or family.

Allowing the dying and their families to share their suffering reduces it by addressing the isolation and abandonment that dying persons fear. But staying engaged also means sharing the experience rather than being a detached problem solver, as many chapters of this volume illustrate. Palliative-care social work cannot be done at arm's length, behind the protection of a professional role that focuses on the provision of services. Rather, it must be done through a personal connection. "Recovery from suffering," Cassell has noted, "often involves help, as though people who have lost parts of themselves can be sustained by the personhood of others until their own recovers" (1982:64). There is power in being present to suffering, and sharing the suffering of another is an honor that helps make a respectful death a reality.

The personal assessment and clarification of values that accompanies work in palliative care should be ongoing (Csikai and Bass 2000), inasmuch as numerous ethical dilemmas concerning self-determination, access barriers for services, advance directives, and issues of mental competence arise in home care settings (Egan and Kadushin 1999). Balancing patients' and families' rights to self-determination can be difficult, but is essential in the promotion of a death that respects their values and preferences. Mental competence erodes as dying persons become increasingly ill (Cassell, Leon, and Kaufman 2001), which poses ethical dilemmas in decision making. The personal nature of the decisions made in end-of-life care requires palliative-care social workers to be therapeutically present to those who are suffering without withdrawal, needless action, or burnout. Having clarified one's values and cultivated a capacity to witness suffering, the palliative-care social worker can be present to dying persons and their families and reap the rewards of assisting them in an experience of living until dying that reflects their values and preferences. In light of the pain and suffering that accompanies the death of a family member, the honor of assisting the dying person and the family to experience a respectful death is extremely fulfilling.

By now, the reader may have ascertained that palliative-care social work is both challenging and rewarding. The complex work of shepherding the dying and their families challenges the best of one's intellectual, relational, and emotional resources. It holds the reward of "seeing people make something good of a tough situation," as Dame Cicely Saunders, the founder of St. Christopher's Hospice, has observed (Egnew 1995:104). This book fills a void in the literature for social workers wishing to work in palliative care. Its chapters provide a rich framework for understanding the theoretical knowledge, attaining the requisite skills, and developing the appropriate attitudes to provide compassionate, professional palliative-care services. These pages can decidedly aid the reader to appreciate the contexts in which dying occurs. They warn the reader of the socioeconomic, cultural, and oppressive conditions that can undermine care to our most vulnerable populations—and we are all vulnerable to the helplessness that accompanies death. The stories told herein attest to the personal nature of this work, which is neither for the faint of heart nor for those who wish a social work practice that does not deeply touch them. As such, this volume is invaluable to social workers who wish to assume the mantle of palliative-care social work competently and professionally and is a substantial contribution to a field that holds the potential for tremendous personal and professional satisfaction.

REFERENCES

Abramson, J., and T. Mizrahi. 1996. When social workers and physicians collaborate: Positive and negative interdisciplinary experiences. *Social Work* 41(3): 270–281.

Baker, M. E. 2000. Knowledge and attitudes of health care social workers regarding advance directives. *Social Work in Health Care* 32(2): 61–74.

Buckman, R. 1992. *How to Break Bad News.* Baltimore: Johns Hopkins University Press.

Cassell, E. J. 1976. *The Healer's Art.* Cambridge, MA: MIT Press.

———. 1982. The nature of suffering and the goals of medicine. *New England Journal of Medicine* 306(11): 639–645.

Cassell, E. J., A. C. Leon, and S. G. Kaufman. 2001. Preliminary evidence of impaired thinking in sick patients. *Annals of Internal Medicine* 134(12): 1120–1123.

Chapman, C. R., and J. Gavrin. 1993. Suffering and its relationship to pain. *Journal of Palliative Care* 9:5–13.

Cherny, N. I., N. Coyle, and K. M. Foley. 1994. Suffering in the advanced cancer patient: A definition and taxonomy. *Journal of Palliative Care* 10:57–70.

Christ, G. H., and M. Sormanti. 1999. Advancing social work practice in end-of-life care. *Social Work in Health Care* 30(2): 81–99.

Csikai, E. L., and K. Bass. 2000. Health care social workers' views of ethical issues, practice, and policy in end-of-life care. *Social Work in Health Care* 31(2): 1–22.

Dass, R., and P. Gorman. 1985. *How Can I Help.* New York: Knopf.

Egan, M., and G. Kadushin. 1999. The social worker in the emerging field of home care: Professional activities and ethical concerns. *Health and Social Work* 24(1): 44–55.

Egnew, T. R. 1994. On becoming a healer: A grounded theory. Ph.D. dissertation, Seattle University.

Jacobsen, P. B., and W. Breitbart. 1996. Psychosocial aspects of palliative care. *Cancer Control* 3(3): 214–222.

Laine, C., and F. Davidoff. 1996. Patient-centered medicine. *Journal of the American Medical Association* 275:52–56.

Luff, G., and M. Blanch. 1998. Carers of patients receiving palliative care: Social workers bring specialist skills to care of carers. *British Medical Journal* 316(7140): 1316.

Mizrahi, T., and J. S. Abramson. 2000. Collaboration between social workers and physicians: Perspectives on a shared case. *Social Work in Health Care* 31(3): 1–24.

Monroe, B. 1993. Social work in palliative care. In *Oxford Textbook of Palliative Care*, ed. D. Doyle, G. W. C. Hanks, and N. MacDonald, 565–574. London: Oxford University Press.

National Association of Social Workers. 1994. Client self-determination in end-of-life decisions. In *Social Work Speaks: NASW Policy Statements*, 58–61. Washington, DC: NASW Press.

Nuland, S. B. 1994. *How We Die.* New York: Knopf.

Oliver, D., and D. Gallagher. 1998. Carers of patient receiving palliative care: Specialised psychosocial care may be needed for carers. *British Medical Journal* 316(7140): 1316–1317.

Ramirez, A., J. Addington-Hall, and M. Richards. 1998. ABC of palliative care: The carers. *British Medical Journal* 316(7126): 208–211.

Rosen, A., and J. O'Neill. 1998. Social work roles and opportunities in advanced directives and health care decision-making. www.socialworkers.org.

Rusnack, B., S. M. Schaefer, and D. Moxley. 1988. "Safe passage": Social work roles and functions in hospice care. *Social Work in Health Care* 13(3): 3–19.

———. 1990. Hospice: Social work's response to a new form of social caring. *Social Work in Health Care* 15(2): 95–119.

Seaburn, D. B., A. D. Lorenz, W. B. Gunn Jr., B. A. Gawinski, and L. B. Mauksch. 1996. *Models of Collaboration: A Guide for Mental Health Professionals Working with Health Care Practitioners.* New York: Basic Books.

Sieppert, J. D. 1996. Attitudes toward and knowledge of chronic pain: A survey of medical social workers. *Health and Social Work* 21(2): 122–130.

Spiegel, D., and M. S. Glafkides. 1983. Effects of group confrontation with death and dying. *International Journal of Group Psychotherapy* 33:433–447.

Steward, M., J. B. Brown, W. W. Weston, I. R. McWhinney, and T. R. Freeman. 1995. *Patient-Centered Medicine*. Thousand Oaks, CA: Sage.

Wesley, C. A. 1996. Social work and end-of-life decisions: Self-determination and the common good. *Health and Social Work* 21(2): 115–121.

Yagoda, L. 2002. End-of-life care for older clients: What social workers should know about the Medicare hospice benefit. www.socialworkers.org.

LIVING WITH DYING

INTRODUCTION

JOAN BERZOFF AND PHYLLIS SILVERMAN

THE NEED for this book evolved after the death of Joan Berzoff's sister, an experience that pointed Joan's career in a new direction. We therefore begin this book with the story of Barbara. In doing so, we honor her memory, and we honor her children with the hope that the book that follows will prevent others from suffering as Barbara and her family did.

JOAN WRITES: I can still remember the dull heaviness I felt when, at the age of thirteen, I heard the news that President John F. Kennedy had been shot. I felt it again when his brother, Robert, was killed, and yet again when Martin Luther King was gunned down. I remember the small details of places I occupied at the time: the crowded train station, the city street, the TV room of a friend whose family I was visiting far from my own. I remember what I was wearing and the crying around me. I remember feeling an inconsolable sadness, a sense of injustice, of impossibility. My world lacked a moral compass; it felt empty, without meaning.

I was seventeen when my father, sick for two years with lymphoma, lay dying in the intensive care unit. In my last visit to him, I feigned good cheer. I remember my mother's voice, later that night, when the call came that he had died. A health fanatic, a man who walked five miles a day, my funny, caring, irreverent, and devoted forty-nine-year-old father no longer existed. The dullness, the lost compass again: he came to occupy a large empty place in my heart. I pined for him, I yearned and searched for him: among the men who commuted home each day from the city or, in later years, on the streets of Paris, or in Israel, where so many other middle-aged men looked like him.

I was preparing a course in a busy summer at the Smith College School for Social Work when I received a call from my sister, Barbara, my closest friend and confidante. I remember the stickiness of the time of day, the early summer's smell, her voice, my voice, when my assumptive world changed again. While I chirped on about wanting to conceive a second baby, and, being the consummate little sister, asked her how I could ensure I'd have a girl, her silence became ominous, and I was afraid. She had

had a biopsy, she told me. She had breast cancer. She would be having a mastectomy, and then chemotherapy. Her voice was remote and dull. I began to lose her on that day. She was forty-two years old. I was forty.

In fact, I did become pregnant that year, and my sister, with whom I had spoken daily for most of my life, stopped calling me. I wanted to scream at her, to punish her, but I willed myself not to. I tried to force myself to live in her shoes: three children, a primary identity as a mother, a bad marriage, a low-paying career as a social worker, and the reality that she too might soon cease to exist. Why should she celebrate my life?

When she was forty-seven and her breast cancer was seemingly cured, and after we had long ago reestablished our relationship, this time at an even deeper level, she came up to the country, where I live. We had always spent a month in the country together, she with her three children, and me in a frenzy of teaching full time and parenting my own two boys. She was relaxed; I was always on the edge. She was the comforter, and I the frenetic, overextended, nutty professor.

She had a cough that would not remit, so she tried treating it with acupuncture. It got increasingly worse, although she minimized it. It was not her nature to complain. But when she got so weak that she couldn't walk up a low hill, she reluctantly visited my internist. He hospitalized her. I arrived at dinnertime with two frozen yogurts in hand (our favorite flavors, no less) and cheerily breezed into her room. My internist asked to see me. I left the yogurts and my sister, and he bluntly gave me the news. Her diagnosis: myelodysplastic syndrome. She had less than two years to live.

I can remember the color of his tie. I can remember the smell of the hospital hallway. I can remember the squeak of shoes, and I remember feeling that this time the world could never right itself. This was the sister who was like my twin: we shared the same humor, the same sensibilities. We both lived in Victorian houses; we were both married to doctors; we shared a history that only she could remember. She had been my constant companion and my most honest friend. I could not lose her.

The next day we took off for the city to meet with her oncologist, who was about our age. The oncologist barely looked at us. She was cold, clinical, factual, and anxious to have the meeting end. She had known the diagnosis for a while but had not told my sister. She told us that the only option for my sister was a bone marrow transplant, and that my sister had better have it fast. She gave my sister a 30 percent chance of survival if she had the transplant. Without it, she had none.

So two sisters who looked like twins, my other half and I, went out to a fancy bistro, dined next to Anthony Hopkins, and checked into a fabulous hotel. As she slept, I wrote. This was one loss I thought I could not withstand. My sister, my friend, who held the light for me, who went first into every life experience, was going to die.

What followed were the frantic calls to all of the medical acquaintances that we knew. The experimental protocols, the alternative medicines, the desperate measures one takes to hold onto life, became daily routine. One spring day, as we walked around the reservoir in her city, I remembering suddenly keening, unable to go forward. I couldn't envision a world without her: this beautiful, bountiful other.

We ended up at the most prestigious cancer hospital in her city. It was April, and a year had passed. She was getting transfusions every day so that she could continue to work with the children in her clinic and with the families in her private practice, be present at her own children's games, events, and play dates, still have the stamina to take short walks. Her first contact was with the hematological oncologist, not with a social worker. My sister recounted her medical history: the lump she had found ten years ago, the doctor who ignored it, the diagnosis of breast cancer two years later, the cure for the breast cancer, the death sentence from the cure. I felt the familiar dullness, yearning, and injustice.

She was hospitalized immediately and had her spleen removed. But that did not help to change her platelet levels, which hovered dangerously between six and four thousand. She was told that she would be dead within months without bone marrow transplantation. She might be dead sooner with one.

My sister was ambivalent about this highly touted cure. She believed she was going to die, and she did not want a high-tech death. She did not want to die alone; she did not want to die in a research hospital. More than anything, she did not want to die physically immobilized or cognitively impaired. She did not want her children to witness her suffering or pain. She did not want her family of origin to become her primary caregivers. She did not want to depend on others; she did not want to be in the complete isolation that the procedure required. She was not sure she wanted to undergo a treatment whose purpose was to bring her to the brink of death and back.

When she expressed her ambivalence to the chief of the Bone Marrow Transplantation Service, his response was quick and imperious. He told her to leave; he had a line of people desperate for his services, and if she didn't want them, she was wasting his time.

Neither he nor his transplant coordinator, however, had elicited her psychosocial history. Had a social worker done so, it might have revealed that my sister had lost a father to lymphoma at the same age that she was now. A social worker might have learned that when our father died, he left three children, exactly the ages of my sister's children. No social worker noted that her husband was absent from all of these meetings and that this might suggest marital difficulties and additional psychosocial stresses. No one asked, and therefore no one knew, that she was the primary and absolute caretaker for her children and the designated caregiver in her community of friends. No social worker talked with her about who would take over in her absence. Without a psychosocial history, and without a social worker to interpret her ambivalence to the team, she was viewed by the surgeon as a noncompliant and ungrateful patient.

Ultimately, my sister decided to undergo the transplantation, not because she felt it would save her, but because she felt that by not doing so she might leave a legacy for her children that she had not tried every means to stay alive. Not surprisingly, I was a perfect match as her donor.

She entered the hospital with a number of concerns. First, she did not want to experience the crippling anxiety that had become her constant companion. Second, she did not want to be kept alive if there was no hope for her survival and if life supports were the only means of living. Third, she wanted most of all to protect her children, at all cost, from the reality of what she would encounter. Had there been a social worker present, a psychopharmacology consult might have been called. A social worker might have recognized my sister's hopelessness and helped her to find a group, or made a referral to a mental health professional. A social worker might have initiated a conversation with my sister about advance directives. A social worker might have inquired about the ways she was trying to cope, and some of the ways that shielding her children might not serve them best. A social worker might have thought through with her the children's different developmental needs and how best to address them. A social worker might have suggested a family conference. A social worker might have empathized with my sister as she left her job, terminated her private practice, and wrote letters to her children in preparation for her death.

Had a social worker been available, she might have addressed my sister's concrete needs: Who would pay for this procedure? Who would take care of her should she leave the hospital? She might have inquired about her spiritual needs: Where did she find comfort and solace and how could it be provided? The social worker might have anticipated her physical needs, her family's psychological needs, and my needs as the donor.

It might have made a difference to her survivors, after she died, to have had a social worker present to let the team know that when the bone marrow transplantation "failed," it was the procedure and not the patient that had failed.

On every level—individual, couple, group, family, systemic—it would have been important to have a social worker who could have intervened. But my sister was a social worker, and anyone who worked with her would have to look mortality in the eye, face some of their own existential issues around dying, and be able to bear a range of feelings that would arise, simply by being present.

When our father lay dying, we did not discuss it. In fact, it was considered bad taste, grossly insensitive, to mention death. It was as if by naming death, we would be responsible for it happening. When our father was in the ICU, I remember asking his physician about his chances for survival. I was seventeen and I needed to know. At that time, physicians and medical caregivers did not tell adolescents that their parent was dying. The prevailing view was that neither the patient nor the family member could handle the news and that the adolescent was too young to know. When he told me that my father had a fifty-fifty chance, I knew that he was lying. My father was dying and there was no one in that hospital to tell me the truth, let alone to help me process it.

Now my sister's children were in the same situation. Unwittingly, my sister and I, two social workers, and two children of a dead parent in adolescence, were complicit in shielding them from the pain of her likely death. She wanted her eldest daughter to go back to college, free of the dread and fear she had felt at the same age. Her sixteen-year-old daughter had stopped eating. She wanted to ease her psychological pain and to protect her from more. Her ten-year-old son was just so young. He didn't really need to know, did he? Hence when her children came to the hospital to see my sister, and when she was so wasted that she could no longer sit up at all, my mother, the nurses, and I arranged her body to look as if she was sitting, knitting, or sewing. We could not bear the truth. There was no social worker to help her children, or us, to face it, let alone metabolize it.

Within days of the first bone marrow donation, my sister bled into her lungs and was sent to the ICU, where she depended fully on a respirator. One kind nurse took my other sister and me aside, and in a broom closet told us that no bone marrow transplant patient ever survives after such a bleed. But to the world, to the assembled guests in the ICU waiting room, to her children, to our mother, we put on a brave face, acted as if we had hope, and quietly bore the despair, and the dullness, that the world had once again been shattered.

As for being a donor, it would have been useful to have a social worker involved. I lived three states away. I had two young children. I worked full time, and the transplant had been scheduled during my most demanding season: the summer. I needed someone with more expertise than I to help me anticipate not only my physical needs but also my psychological ones. I needed someone to help me size up my commitments and make my sister the first priority. When the first bone marrow transplant failed, I needed to give platelets every other day. This meant finding a driver to take me to the city and finding a place to stay. When bone marrow was extracted from me a second time, no one told me how I was to get across the street after surgery without the wheelchair that I had to relinquish at the door of the hospital. While unrelated donors routinely receive psychosocial counseling, none existed for related donors.

Five months passed in isolation. Every visitor to my sister's room was gowned and gloved. Our facial expressions were obscured, and our ability to touch, skin to skin, was made impossible. Weeks and months dragged on, and summer turned to fall. My sister never left her room, except for three trips to the ICU. After two bone marrow failures, the team decided that they would send my sister home. They did not say she was going home to die, just that the good news what that she was ready to go home. She was entirely dependent on platelets. She had inadequate physical and emotional support at home. She had no round-the-clock caregivers in place. But no referral to hospice was made, and the opportunity to die with her family and friends around her, dealing with the reality before them, in a safe setting where her physical and psychological needs would be met, never occurred. No social worker was present to advocate to the team on her behalf. Three days later, always anticipating the needs of others, she kindly suffered a stroke that would mean she would never go home. Although the stroke solved the problem of inadequate physical care, it also left her paralyzed and cognitively impaired. She developed a reflex where she repeatedly lifted her arm over her head, smiled a bizarre and clownlike smile, and patted her head. She was diapered; she no longer recognized her children. Her worst fears had been realized. What would it have been like to have had a social work professional to help them, and us, with our grief and loss?

After my sister died, her hematologist wrote the family a lovely letter, as did the bone marrow coordinator. As there had been no psychosocial services prior to her transplant and during the months that she was dying, there were none after she died. Her greatest fears—that she would die cognitively impaired, that she would die without a plan in which her children would be adequately cared for, that she would be paralyzed and kept on life supports—had been realized. Her children's grief went unacknowledged. My own guilt about not being able to save her life was something

I carried alone. There was certainly no bereavement follow-up care for her donor or her family.

⁂

JOAN'S STORY about her sister Barbara in many ways sets the stage for how we approach this book. What we learn from Barbara's death and her children's bereavement brings together the personal and the professional. In her death and dying, as in her family's subsequent bereavement, there were so many moments when a social work intervention might have made a difference. This book is about the differences that social workers can make in the lives of the dying and bereaved every day.

One theme resonates throughout the rich and multifaceted contributions that make up this book: The authors have emphasized the importance of their own lived experiences in ways that are not always considered in other practice settings. As we worked with their contributions, we came to appreciate even more that there is something in end-of-life care that makes it difficult for workers in this field to leave their own selves at the door. And this is as it should be.

Death is not something that will happen only to others, but something that all of us will encounter. We may not die at a young age, we may not die after a long illness, we may not die as a result of a violent or traumatic death, but we will all die. As we get close to people as their lives end, it quickly becomes clear that we are talking about something that will happen to us too. We will all know grief, as well, as long as we are involved with others about whom we care. We are not talking about "them"; we are talking about all of us. How does this change who we are when we work with the dying?

To be effective, we are forced not only to look at but also to use our own attitudes, values, and fears and feelings about death. We cannot simply adopt a removed or neutral clinical perspective. How do we deal with our common humanity and still be available to help those we are there to serve?

As we tried to answer these questions, we were faced with a need to visit contemporary views of social work theory, practice, and policy. Traditionally, we had been taught that it is important for the well-trained social worker to maintain boundaries between herself and her clients, to be sure that the personal and the professional do not mix. But this work is always personal, and it requires that we examine our practice with a different lens. This is one of the goals of this book.

OUR GOALS

This book is directed to social work practitioners and social work students working in end-of-life care settings. The focus is on practice in settings that are devoted to caring for terminally ill people and their families. However, all social work practitioners need to know about end-of-life care. People come to social workers at various times in their lives, and many will be dealing with dying and grief, even when it is not in the forefront at that moment. Those who work with bereaved children in foster care or in schools, those who work in mental health, those who work with the elderly, to name a few, routinely encounter end-of-life issues. We hope that this book raises practitioners' consciousness, improves their practice, and provides much of the knowledge, values, skills, and attitudes needed to effect changes in our systems of social work care. We hope that this book helps the practitioner in her micro practice, and in being an agent of change in larger systems. We hope that this book encourages social workers to take major leadership roles in the field of end-of-life care: as practitioners, educators, consultants, agents of change, and researchers.

We asked, as we invited practitioners and scholars to contribute to the book, several questions to focus their writing. We wanted to know what in their own clinical experiences informed their practices. We wanted to know about the theories and perspectives that were most useful to those working with individuals, families, and groups at the end of life. We wondered how clinicians who work with the dying and their families sustained hope, worked successfully as members of teams, maintained their clients' dignity, facilitated communication, and provided access to services, whether those clients were young or old, single or partnered, straight or gay. We asked each of our authors to use examples from their practices, from their own lives as practitioners. What were the settings in which they worked, and what were the issues that must be attended to? What are we already doing in the field of end of life care that is exemplary? Where are the gaps? Who benefits from the current system, and who is disenfranchised on the basis of culture, race, gender, sexual orientation, ability, age, or social status?

Joan's sister's experience points to some of the profound gaps in the service delivery system. In the years since Barbara's death, has anything changed?

Sadly, according to a report from the Robert Wood Johnson Foundation of November 2002 on the state of the art for end-of-life care, not much has. In 1995, that foundation produced the SUPPORT (Study to Understand Prognosis and Preferences for Outcomes and Risks of Treatments) Report and found that the majority of Americans die alone in institutions, in pain, attached to machines against their wishes. The 2002 report looked to see what had changed since. Although some progress is being made, end-of-life care in this country is still mediocre, at best. Some of the key findings were:

- Seventy percent of Americans say they want to die at home, but only 25 percent of them do.
- Half of all deaths occur in hospitals, but less than 60 percent of hospitals offer specialized end-of-life services.
- There are serious reimbursement issues for hospice, palliative care, and pain management services.
- Most states have only fair hospice use — 12 to 25 percent of deaths include a hospice stay.
- In any given state, at least 25 percent of nursing home residents have pain for at least two months without appropriate pain management.

- Only 33 percent of U.S. physicians are certified in palliative care. The average percentage of nurses certified in hospice and palliative care is 0.44 percent.
- Even though ICU care is often unwanted, 16–37 percent of deaths among Medicare recipients include ICU hospitalization in the last six months of life. A study of cancer patients in ICUs found that 75 percent had pain, discomfort, anxiety, sleep disturbance, and unsatisfied hunger or thirst.
- Half of all dying people experience severe pain.
- Demographers predict that with increasing numbers of elderly people the burden of chronic illness will increase.
- Emotional and spiritual care for families and patients that respects their cultures and traditions are essential parts of the dying experience but are not generally available.

As we study these findings, we see the importance and value of being knowledgeable in the psychological, social structural, and policy domains. We see the need for social workers trained to provide emotional and spiritual care needed at this time in people's lives. It may not be enough to improve clinical practice. It may require social workers' using all of their skills and talents to take leadership in changing policy and practice in this field.

Hence another goal of this book is to expand the reader's perspective about practice beyond the individual person who is dying. The findings from the Robert Wood Johnson Foundation remind us that we cannot simply look at an individual who is dying in isolation from her larger community. Every individual is a member of, a participant in, and a by-product of his or her family and community, with a set of beliefs and values that reflect who the person is and how she came to be that way. The social worker needs to understand the dying person in the larger context in which the person lives: his or her spiritual life, economic reality, and cultural life. Every dying person is a member of a larger community that either affords or blocks access to quality care, based on factors such as class, race, gender, age, ability or sexual orientation, and/or political philosophy as exemplified by the ways healthcare is financed and delivered in this country. Many of those who are dying are marginalized in our society. Prisoners, certain racial and ethnic groups, those for whom literacy is impaired, those with reduced cognitive functioning, those who carry a mental illness, a cognitive or physical disability, a stigmatized status, immigrants for whom English is not their language, children who are bereaved from ravages of the AIDS epidemic, those traumatized by disasters—all of these groups are at the heart of social-work priorities and practice. As social workers in end-of-life care, we must always try to know who a person is in the context of all of these factors and be prepared to advocate on behalf of the most vulnerable clients.

We also need to consider the attitudes, the resources, and the organizational structures of the institutions in which we work. Much of end-of-life care in the United States takes place in hospice programs, many of which are freestanding nonprofit organizations. Some are parts of medical settings and others are for profit. All of these programs rely on a specific reimbursement scheme: the Medicare Hospice Benefit, enacted by Congress in 1982. This benefit can be accessed only by those whom a physician certifies to have a life expectancy of six months or less. Hospice also refers to a philosophical approach to care for the dying that is holistic and family centered. In Canada hospice-like programs are referred to as palliative-care programs. Palliative care is an approach to care that extends hospice philosophy and practice to a wider range of healthcare settings earlier in the process. Palliative care seeks to prevent, relieve, reduce, or soothe the symptoms of disease or disorder without effecting a cure. It is not restricted to those who are dying or enrolled in a hospice program. It does not preclude the provision of curative treatments. Palliative care provides comprehensive management of the physical, psychological social, spiritual, and existential needs of people with life-limiting illnesses or who are suffering from chronic pain. The needs of children with life-limiting and incurable conditions for palliative and hospice care are now being recognized. Programs that address the child's/adolescent's needs within the context of the child's/adolescent's physical condition, developmental stage, family, and community are proliferating. Palliative care and hospice can be seen as part of a continuum of care providing the same interdisciplinary practice, values, and attitudes regardless of the setting. How social workers provide these services forms the nexus of this book.

The quality of clinical practice can never be divorced from the institutional contexts that make the rules and regulations and that control the resources, all of which effect accessibility and the quality of end-of-life care to those whom it potentially serves. This book seeks to help social workers become knowledgeable about who gains access to healthcare in America: Who is included, and who (such as the homeless or substance abusers) is excluded from receiving adequate pain management or Medicaid reimbursements for hospice care? To address this situation, we not only need to be clinicians, but we also must sharpen our skills as advocates of policy change, educators, and consultants. We need to develop a range of roles to be spokespersons for the most at-risk populations as part of the interdisciplinary team that makes and implements policy decisions. We need to become leaders in making systems changes. This is part of our early social work history and mission, and one that must be reclaimed in end-of-life care. In order to understand where we are going, we need to look at where we have been, and the readiness of the profession to grow into this new work.

We must also see that there are adequate curricula to prepare social workers to do the difficult work of end-of-life care, at the BSW, MSW, and post-master's levels. This includes including content on transference/countertransference, on uses of self, and on the intersubjective spaces between client and clinician. Social workers need to know how to work in a range of settings: bereavement, palliative care, medical social work, nursing homes, prisons, family bereavement camps. Social workers need to be exposed to content on a range of biological diseases. They need to be able to assess and therefore treat the clients whom they meet. They need to learn to be present for the spiritual, existential, and intimate moments in this work. They need to be able to be present to another's suffering, which requires some attunement to one's own.

In the first draft of the chapter on the concept of a "Respectful Death," by Stuart and Lu Farber and Tom Egnew, Egnew wrote a review of the role of the social worker in palliative care. The content of this section so paralleled material we were writing for this book that we asked his permission to make this aspect of his contribution to their chapter the preface to the book. In it, Egnew critically examines the core competencies and values that social workers need to provide end-of-life care. He looks at practice and at professional education. Rather than paraphrase what he wrote, we encourage the reader to read the preface, for it lays out the important knowledge, values, and skills for the profession of social work in end-of-life care.

Tom Egnew's review of the state of the profession reminds us of the urgency and importance of listening to the client. We need to recognize that every client is in a process of change, and that the dying person and his or her family need to learn to collaborate with those who care for them, just as we, in the role of caregivers, need to learn to collaborate. Phyllis Silverman's experience provides us with an example of how this happened for her.

❇

PHYLLIS WRITES: My own life as a child and young adult was checkered with many deaths, ranging from the death of a child on our street to the death of grandparents and the death of a dear friend. However, they were always one step removed from me, and I was away from home when the later deaths occurred. My parents worked very hard to shelter me from experiencing their impact. They did not take me to funerals, and they delayed sharing the news of the deaths with me for as long as they could. This is what was considered appropriate at that time.

A question I often ask my students is to think about when they first knew that they would die. Many cannot remember; others feel that in a way they always knew. Others did not think about it until they were teenagers. I asked with whom they could share this. Not all, but many, felt that their parents listened and the conversation was comforting and reassuring. I was eight years old when I first realized that I, too, would die. I was so fearful that I couldn't sleep for several nights. There was no one to talk to. My solution was to close my eyes when I went by cemeteries, and in many ways I did not open them until I began my work with the widowed in the mid-1960s.

When Joan asked me to join her in editing this book, she saw me as an expert in bereavement with more experience in the death-and-dying world than she had. However, this is only partly true, and then only in a theoretical way. My research, my work in program development, and my clinical experience largely derive from looking out from what I call the other side of the door. I know a good deal about how people die, and about who they were, but I have learned about them by listening to their surviving relatives. I began to appreciate that there was no one good way to die. As a researcher, I learned that the bereaved have profound strengths that they can offer to one another through self-help. What involved me was not the tragedy of their loss, but the opportunity this work created for me to look at people's ability to cope, to move in new directions, and to find new ways of living in the world without the deceased. I almost did not take the job of working with the widowed because I wasn't sure I could deal with death and bereavement. To have become involved was probably one of the most important decisions I ever made. While it doesn't stop hurting when I experience other people's pain, I can live with it and be there for them, for my family and for myself. I find that I am always learning. This began early on in my relationship with the widowed I met in my work.

When I first began my work with the widowed, they taught me a very important lesson. In 1965, bereavement as described in the clinical and research literature was seen as something that people got over and would get on with their lives in a period of six weeks to several months. When the widowed women I recruited to work with me on the widow-to-widow experiment heard this, they couldn't stop laughing. They said, "If in two years you have your head turned around so you can look ahead, you are doing well." It became very clear to me that they were going to be my teachers, and this has guided me in my work ever since. I saw that when a theory is not supported by the real world, there may very well be something wrong with the theory, not the world. Whenever I think I have it all together or become too confident as a professional, I hear the laughter at that meeting and I am reminded that I always need to listen. My professional colleagues have challenged me many times about the importance I place on what the bereaved can do for each other and themselves, but this point of view has enabled me to look differently at what I was hearing from the bereaved and in analyzing my research data. In my work I try to hear what people tell me and teach me about their situations.

I came to this work with a background in both social work and public health, having just earned a second master's degree. I had learned about population patterns in the need to understand the incidence and prevalence of a problem or disease as we considered appropriate ways of reaching those who might be in need. This meant that for any one client seen in an agency there could be many in the community who might not need "treatment," but who needed some attention and perhaps a "little bit of help from a friend." The widow-to-widow program that we developed was successful because we were reaching women in their own homes and the help provided was offered by another widow whose experience was immediately relevant to the newly widowed. I talked to my colleagues in agencies about services for the widowed that they might provide. They assured me that they were providing these services as demonstrated by the one or two cases they were seeing. I also learned that the majority of the widowed I interviewed did not see themselves as needing counseling or therapy in spite of the pain they were experiencing. I learned that my social-work training did not provide me with a view of the larger community and the tools to become aware of those people whose needs the agency could not appropriately meet. My work was guided by a public-health approach that included a wider range of interventions than might be provided in any given clinic, among them an acceptance of experiential knowledge—that is, knowledge gained from lived experience (Silverman 2001). This was another way of "knowing" that added a new dimension to what I understood as help and challenged the role of the professional as the expert. I also began to differentiate between the range of mental-health problems people brought to social agencies and those created by life-cycle events that all of us must experience. I am constantly reminded that these are adversities that none of us will escape and that we all need to be experts in how we manage these periods in our lives and that we will learn from each other.

I don't think we ever become immune to the pain in the people whom we meet or to our own vulnerability. When I wrote my book on children's reactions to death, I included a section on how parents and siblings react to the death of a child. I cried my way through each of these chapters. At first I was apologetic that after all these years I should react so personally. The keyboard was a bit moist as I began to understand that unless I could begin to experience some of their pain, I could never hope to offer these people anything. I came to accept my tears as I also realized that I was an observer who was most thankful that I didn't really understand.

As I worked on the chapters for this book, I became involved in the stories that so many gifted authors have contributed, and I have experienced the pain, the sadness, and the vitality of those who are beneficiaries of their services. I am drawn to this work in a new way, so that my learning and, I hope, my personal growth continue.

ORGANIZATION OF THIS BOOK

This book, then, brings together the three aspects of practice highlighted so eloquently in the preface: theory, skills, and attitudes, to which we add personal narratives and the social and contextual issues of policy, research, and leadership. In addition, we have been deeply committed to developing curricula for training for social workers who work in death, dying, and bereavement. Much of this book is based on what social workers need in their training to provide excellence in end of life care.

DEVELOPING CURRICULUM

In 1999, the Project on Death in America announced its first Social Work Leadership Award to improve the psychosocial quality of dying in America. Joan was then a teacher of psychodynamic theory and practice and wondered what she knew about death or dying that might contribute to the field. Her husband, himself a PDIA scholar, pushed her to use her lived experience of her father's and sister's deaths, and she began to map out both an educational program and a textbook for post-master's advanced training for social workers in end-of-life care.

G. H. Christ and M. Sormanti had already documented the woefully inadequate preparation that social workers receive in their masters' programs in end-of-life care. Joan was then given a PDIA Social Work Leadership Award to offer a post-master's training program in end-of-life care at the Smith College School for Social Work that would address social workers' needs to attend to psychological, social, and cultural factors and ethical issues in hospice, palliative, and bereavement care. She also began the outline that has now become this book.

The End of Life Certificate Program is in its fourth year, training post-master's social workers from the United States and Canada in theory, practice, ethics, hospice and palliative care, bereavement, uses of self, cross cultural issues, issues for gay and lesbian clients, spirituality, and legal issues and in leadership in end-of-life care. In addition to two intensive weeks of coursework over two summers at Smith, every participant completes an eight-month internship and receives clinical supervision in her workplace telephonically, integrating into practice the academic content learned during the summer. Every participant also produces a final paper, some of which are included in this book. Every participant is expected to run a group and to take leadership in the field. Although we wish we had been able to publish many more of their innovative papers, many of the students have already published in journals, presented at national conferences, and taken leadership roles in their end-of-life care settings.

In part, then, this book follows the structure of Joan's program. We have brought together the voices of those who have taught in the program, those who have studied there, those who are already leaders in the field, and those who have been practitioners whose lives and work have been shaped by personal losses. We have supplemented many of the chapters with scholars and practitioners who are also social-work leaders in the Open Society's Project on Death in America, supported by the financier George Soros. Additionally, we have solicited many chapters from a range of other outstanding practitioners/scholars in the fields of death, dying, and bereavement, many of whom are affiliated with the International Work Group on Death, Dying and Bereavement.

The book begins with an important aspect of the attitude we bring to our work that focuses on combining the personal and the professional.

THE IMPORTANCE OF THE PROFESSIONAL AND THE PERSONAL

We begin the book with four narratives that are similar to Joan's, written by professionals in the field who faced extraordinary losses and found ways to give special meaning to them. We begin the book with narratives because we believe that meaning making is an essential part of dying. Creating a coherent narrative is one of the best adaptations to grief and to loss that people make. The contributions of these four authors provide wonderful ways of teaching us about living, and about dying. We begin with David Browning's reflections on the death of his mother and his own suffering. David is able to reflect upon his own career and his gifts that emerged from that profound trauma. We move to Roberta Hoffman, who was a social worker on the hospital unit where her son was diagnosed with cancer, and where he ultimately died. She talks about the distance her colleagues created, and about, as in Joan's story, her son's death, which was seen as the patient's failing, not the service's failing him. Ellen Pulleyblank Coffey, a psychologist, writes about making the decision *not* to terminate her husband's life support and about the joys and agonies of family life that ensued over the next five years with her husband on a respirator. Les Gallo-Silver and Penny Damaskos, both social workers from New York City, write about being practitioners and people when the World Trade Center collapsed, again reminding us that in living and dying we are all human: sometimes uncertain and often afraid. Each narrative chronicles the role of social worker in end-of-life care. Each story reminds us that dying can be capricious, traumatic, and out of our control. Each narrative offers hope: that out of loss we gain something: a link to the person(s) we have lost, and to our own humanity. Each story reminds us of how we continue our ties to the dying as we return to living fully, and often with a new focus. Each story is about loss of hope and its restoration. Each story presents the intersection of empathy and compassion that derives from each of our vulnerabilities. By reading these narratives, we experience bearing witness to suffering, and the ways in which facing loss may allow us to be more present. Most of all, these narratives remind us that we cannot fix or take away pain, but we may act as guides and collaborators for those who suffer.

THE THEORIES THAT INFORM OUR WORK

The second section of the book encompasses a more theoretical and historical approach to practice in end-of-life care. If we are to bring about change, we need to understand the historical and theoretical lenses that have influenced current practice. We need to know about the theories from psychology, ethics, spirituality, sociology, and even organizational behavior that influence death and dying in America.

We begin this section with a chapter by Stuart and Lu Farber and Tom Egnew, who have developed the concept, not of a "good death," which runs the risk of romanticizing death, but of a "respectful" death. They look at how social workers and physicians learn from each other in the service of their patients or clients. They tell us of core competencies for physicians and for social workers, and they set the tone for a basic approach that we hope to maintain throughout this book: that of learning from the patient and the family. Phyllis Silverman next looks at death and bereavement as universal human experiences over time. Mary Raymer and Dona Reese help us to understand what influenced the development of the hospice movement and the role of the social workers in this development. Carolyn Jacobs integrates psychodynamic and spiritual perspectives in her chapter on the social worker's journey with the dying. Patricia O'Donnell adds the ethical dimensions of end of life care to the discourse. Inge Corless and Patrice Nicholas provide a scholarly view of the complexity of interdisciplinary teamwork and its centrality in end of life care. Patricia O'Donnell examines ethical issues that surround all end-of-life decision making. Illene Noppe considers, from a social-psychological perspective, the ways in which gender and death intersect. Phyllis Silverman offers complementary developmental models on loss and bereavement, and Joan Berzoff offers a historical view of psychodynamic theories in grief and bereavement, looking at how inner life is shaped by and transformed by loss.

SKILLS: THE BASIS OF GOOD PRACTICE

In the next section on practice, we hope to convey the ways in which the social worker works within a range of modalities, over the trajectory of illness, in a range of settings and with diverse populations. We have sought contributors who explain their clinical work from experience-near perspectives. Our authors use themselves and their stories in ways that bridge the gulf between self and other, to encourage writing in the first person, to model an approach in the field of end-of-life care that we consider essential to quality social work.

We begin the practice section with Wendy Karger and Allan Levine's chapter on the trajectory of illness that looks at the impact of diagnosis on every aspect of an individual and family's life. Felice Zilberfein and Elizabeth Hurwitz's chapter on clinical practice with individuals at the end of life artfully integrates the biological, psychological, spiritual, and social dimensions in a person who is dying, with the experiences of the social worker. Nancy Cincotta moves the lens to the inner lives of children and their families and how they intersect with the personal and professional aspects of the social worker. Neil and Sue Thompson look at complementary issues in old age. We still read these chapters with great sadness. This is as it should be, because if we are not moved by the work we do, we are likely not fully in it.

A crucial part of providing skilled end-of-life care requires excellent assessments. We hear from Katherine Walsh-Burke on making an assessment that includes mental-health issues: depression, anxiety, or other disorders. Terry Altilio examines how to assess pain and use the skills of the social worker to participate in provision of symptom management. Because pain and symptom management are only a part of quality palliative care, Susan Blacker discusses the multiple roles of the social worker in providing palliative care. Another aspect of quality palliative care is spiritual care, and Barbara Dane provides a clinical view of spiritual practices at the end of life.

Social work practice and palliative care must always be directed toward the most disenfranchised in our society. Hence a number of chapters follow that look at populations at risk who are dying or bereaved. Norma del Rio turns our attention to those whose disenfranchised status based on culture or race may interfere with receiving quality end-of-life care. Shirley Otis Green and Chris Rutland consider dying from the perspectives of the disabled, the homeless, and the addicted, all marginalized at the end of their lives. Bruce Thompson and Yvette Colón introduce the psychosocial concerns of lesbians and gay men at the end of their lives. Gary Stein and Lucille Esralew consider both clinical and legal issues for the disabled, who are often unable to speak for themselves. We know of no other book that has elicited the voices of the disenfranchised dying and bereaved.

With Amanda Sutton and Daniel Liechty's chapter on groups, we shift the lens to consider a number of modalities: group and family work in end of life care. Sutton and Liechty write about group work with the dying and bereaved; Yvette Colón extends the model, writing about innovative group techniques such as telephone and Internet groups. Susan Blacker and Alice Jordan further expand upon clinical practice in discussing work with families facing life-threatening illnesses in medical settings.

We move the lens again, in a chapter by Phyllis Silverman, to consider bereavement, an essential part of palliative care, to look particularly at what we mean by helping. We also consider, in a chapter by Susan Gerbino and Shelley Henderson, the question of end-of-life bioethics in clinical practice.

Quality palliative care takes place in many settings and requires specific clinical skills. These may include international settings where disasters have occurred, as discussed by Lisa Aronson. Quality clinical social work care may take place in prisons (Sheila Enders), nursing homes (Mercedes Bern-Klug and Kim Ellis), or in bereavement camps for children and families with AIDS (Christian Itin, Susan McFeaters, and Susan Taylor-Brown).

Disease processes also have trajectories that are different, and challenges in each of their treatments. Iris Cohen Fineberg helps us experience the world of bone marrow and hematopoietic cell transplantation units and the psychosocial challenges for patients and their families there. John Linder's chapter on working in oncology offers a window into palliative care with patients who have cancer. We end with his chapter because he provides such a clear intersection of race, class, and gender with individual, group, and family practices in palliative care, again in a voice that is subjective, not objective.

CONTEXT AND LEADERSHIP

In the next section, we examine what else social workers need to know to provide quality clinical care to persons at the end of their lives. Social workers are often on the front lines for making ethical decisions and need to be knowledgeable about legal and ethical issues at the end of life. Both Stephen Arons and Ellen Csikai offer the reader ways of understanding current policies related to advance directives, autonomous decision making, and the right to die. John and Jenny Dawes examine the policies of prisons, in which significant end-of-life care occurs. June Simmons adds the financial contexts to death and dying in America to the discourse.

We go on to examine future directions for social work. Here we have gathered the voices of leaders, and scholars in end of life care to discuss the state of the research in end-of-life care for social work (Betty Kramer and Mercedes Bern-Klug) and the necessity of taking leadership in this field (Esther Chachkes and Zelda Foster). Social workers cannot simply be practitioners: they must become consumers of research, and producers of research. They must take on roles as consultants, educators, and spokespersons for the dying and their families. They must advocate for policy changes, within their institutions and nationally. They must develop new curricula in end of life care. They must be activists and change agents in their settings and for their clients.

How do they do this, without burning out? Here we hear from the current president of National Association of Social Workers, Elizabeth Clark, about the future of social work in end-of-life care. But there is another dimension to thriving in and sustaining oneself in this work. We deliberately chose to have our last chapter address self-care for the social worker because we think that this work requires "relentless" self-examination and care. Irene Renzenbrink writes beautifully about her own experiences as a novice in the field of end-of-life care and about the ways in which this work is always personal and demands care of ourselves and of our souls. She embodies the philosophy of the book in suggesting that who we are is crucial to the work that we do, and that we must always attend to replenishing ourselves, through education, supervision, and collegiality, in order to be effective and authentic.

We invite the reader into the lives of so many people: professionals who have suffered major losses and made meaning of them, social workers who work with people dying from particular diseases such as cancer or hemopoetic diseases, social workers who have tried to integrate psychological and spiritual practices, social workers who work with the most disenfranchised, social workers who practice with those at the beginning of their lives or those who are ending their lives. We introduce the reader to the many roles of social work: in interdisciplinary care, in pain and symptom management, in palliative and hospice care and in bereavement care. We introduce the voices of social workers that have developed innovative programs, such as the Family Unity Camp for families and children dealing with AIDS.

But we also introduce the reader into the lives of people who are dying alone in prisons, on inpatient units, in nursing homes. We introduce a range of very articulate people who teach us about dying: about cultural differences, about existential fears, and about strength and hope.

It is the voices of the dying and bereaved that we hope emerge above the rest. They are our teachers, and as social workers we always learn from their experiences. Many contributors to this book discuss how working with the dying is a privilege. Work with the dying means encountering suffering, mystery, and complexity. Working with the dying compels us to live, and live fully. It requires the best of our knowledge, our skill, our self-awareness, and our appreciation of the multiple contexts in which people live and die.

We hope that this book offers many windows into the worlds of the dying and their families and, of the utmost importance, provides ways to intervene with respect for the ways they have lived, the ways they die, and the legacies they leave behind.

REFERENCES

Christ, C., and M. Sormanti. 1999. Advancing social work practice in end of life care. *Social Work in Health Care* 30(2): 81–89.

Silverman, P. R. 2001. It makes a difference. *Illness, Crisis and Loss* 9(1): 11–128.

PART I

NARRATIVES IN END-OF-LIFE CARE

1

FRAGMENTS OF LOVE: EXPLORATIONS IN THE ETHNOGRAPHY OF SUFFERING AND PROFESSIONAL CAREGIVING

DAVID BROWNING

> Let the fragments of love be re-assembled in you;
> only then will you know true courage.
> —*Hayden Carruth*

WHEN I was thirteen, my mother died. There was no room for grief in a household of three boys and a father who, in his own encounter with mourning, set the best example he knew: you pull yourself together, you get on with life. I remember little in the way of emotion or consolation, but I do remember the numbness. The embodied memory I hold of the months following her death is one of floating in a cloud of gray gauze: alone, desolate, but cushioned from pain.

Twelve years later, in the consulting room of a therapist who conveyed by his warmth that he would suffer with me whatever pain was uncarthcd, thc numbncss gave way to a deep mine of emotions. Soon after the excavation began, I began to reestablish what had been a long-interrupted communication with my mom. The conversation commenced with fury. I wrote the following poem on May 9, 1977, my twenty-fifth birthday:

ON VISITING MY MOTHER'S GRAVE

If I could snatch you from your grave
If I could shake you from your slumber
If I could speak with you for five minutes
If I could hold your hand
If I could have your love
If I could only feel it
If it could only guide my days
If I only had it to fall back on
If you could be there when I need you.

Your death was vicious—and senseless.
They had no right
You had no right

To leave me alone.
You took away my bearings
And I have been detached
From people
From living
From myself.

I have been afraid to live or to love.
You took my joy with you
And if I dare to live or love again
To do so with abandon
I again take the risk
Of my joy being snatched away
Recklessly
To be buried in a box.

Safer to exist cautiously.
To not risk my love on living
Or risk my life on love.
Better to construct my own world
Of maximum security.
A maximum security prison
Where the only one
That can be dangerous to me
Is myself.

How is my personal story relevant to an understanding of the ethnography of suffering? What insight does it bring to my encounters with the dying and the bereaved? I believe that when we, as professional caregivers, accompany others through tragic life events, our own experiences with suffering, and the sense that we make of those experiences, constitute both the starting and ending points of these explorations.

THE ETHNOGRAPHIC LENS

Ethnography, a practice borrowed from anthropology, is a tradition of looking, listening, and responding to human beings as an avenue toward understanding and helping. The person who is trying to understand and to help is an integral part of the process. The knowledge that emerges between caregiver and client is collaborative and mutual. The ethnographic approach provides access to culture, broadly defined. This broad definition of culture assumes fluidity between one's inner experience and the outer world. It views people as contextual beings, influenced by gender, age, class, race, ethnicity, sexual orientation, and religion/spirituality, as well as a myriad of additional variables that shape identity. Culture thus defined is a process of meaning making that occurs both internally, in conversations within the self, and externally, in conversations between the self and the other. Ethnography provides a holistic and inclusive perspective that can accommodate the richness and complexity of both "external" and "internal" processes that occur both between and within caregiver and client in the clinical encounter. Several authors have argued for adopting an ethnographic perspective as a productive route toward understanding in psychotherapy and the helping professions (Andersen and Goolishian 1992; Falicov 1995; Klass 1999; Laird 1998). For the purposes of this chapter, ethnography provides a framework for understanding the many levels of meaning at work in the encounter between caregiver and a client in the throes of suffering. Central to this framework is the lived experience of caregiver/ethnographer and client: "The ethnographer's focus moves back and forth. The task is to interpret patterns of meaning within situations understood in experience-near categories; yet, ethnographers also bring with them a liberating distance that comes from their own experience-near categories and their existential appreciation of shared human conditions. That means that ethnography, like history and biography and psychotherapy, holds the possibility of a way of knowing more valid to the dialectical structure and contingent flow of lived experience than reductionistic forms of knowing which by definition distort the existential conditions of life" (Kleinman and Kleinman 1991:278).

In my social work practice, I often work with clients who are grieving traumatic losses. I know that who and how I am with my grieving clients, and who and how they are with me, will form the foundation from which new understandings will emerge. My clients' suffering has the potential to teach me something. My own suffering has the potential to teach something to my clients. As I sit with them in their anguish, I am acutely aware that the starting point in my effort to engage with and understand them is my own repertoire of personal experience, which dates back to a time in my life when I judged it "better to construct my own world of maximum security" than to "risk my life on living" or "risk my life on love." I know at least something about the fragmentation of love that suffering creates; I know at least something about the isolation, detachment, anger, and depression that can follow.

In this chapter, I will explore several fundamental issues relevant to an appreciation of human encounters in end of life and bereavement care: (1) the ethnography of suffering in the context of religion, history, and medicine; (2) the ethnography of professional caregiving, suffering, and meaning making; and (3) the caregiver's encounter with suffering.

THE ETHNOGRAPHY OF SUFFERING IN THE CONTEXT OF RELIGION, HISTORY, AND MEDICINE

The word "suffering" derives from the Latin verb *sufferre*, which means "to bear," "to undergo," or "to carry." Suffering can be defined as a state of severe distress that occurs on a biological, psychological, spiritual, and/or sociocultural level, and that is associated with events that threaten the sense of intactness of the person. Suffering often poses the existential challenge of the loss of meaning and purpose. With suffering at the end of life, there is a loss of personhood itself, a process that occurs repeatedly and progressively up until the time of death.

RELIGION

Historically, religion has been the custodian and arbiter of suffering at the end of life. All world religions attempt to understand and explain the meaning and purpose of suffering. The following examples discuss suffering in the context of Buddhism, Christianity, and Judaism.

In the Buddhist tradition, suffering is considered the "stuff of existence." It arises from a person's attachment to the world—physical pleasures, material possessions, personal accomplishments and failures, relationships of love and hate, and ultimately attachment to the self. The Buddhists are fond of saying that we all suffer from a terminal case of "somebody-ism." That is, we all tend to become self-absorbed and attached to ourselves in ways that bring about suffering. Consider the following exchange between the African American scholar bell hooks and Pema Chodron, a Buddhist nun:

> HOOKS: It seems so much of our longing to escape suffering arises from the sense that the closer we are to suffering, the closer we are to death.
> CHODRON: For me, the spiritual path has always been a lesson in how to die. I don't mean just the death at the end of this life, but all the falling apart that happens continually. The fear of death—which is also the fear of insecurity, of not having it all together—seems to be the most fundamental phenomenon we have to work with: because death is an ending, and endings happen all the time. Things are always ending and arising and ending. But we are strangely conditioned to want to experience just the birth part and not the death part. (HOOKS 1995:26)

In the Christian tradition, suffering is also understood as an inevitable part of human life. The Christian orientation holds that the release from suffering lies not in this world but in the hereafter. Based on the example of Jesus, there is an emphasis on "offering up" one's suffering for those in distress, and as repentance for sin. A frequently spoken prayer in Christian liturgy is "Lord Jesus, I offer to you my prayers, works, joys, and sufferings of this day for all the intentions of your sacred heart, in reparation for my sins and the sins of the world" (Byock 1996:238).

C. S. Lewis, the Christian author and theologian, focused on what he called "the problem of pain." He professed that the ultimate good in life is in consciously surrendering oneself to God. Without suffering, human beings would remain focused on their own goals and desires and on the worries of the world. God gives suffering to us out of love, so that we might be made perfect by surrender. Lewis was sorely tested in his beliefs when his wife, the American poet Joy Gresham, died very soon after their marriage.

> Talk to me about the truth of religion and I'll listen gladly. Talk to me about the duty of religion and I'll listen submissively. But don't come talking to me about the consolations of religion or I shall suspect that you don't understand. (LEWIS 1961:28)

Aren't all these notes the senseless writings of a man who won't accept the fact that there is nothing we can do with suffering except to suffer it? Who still thinks there is some device (if only he could find it) which will make pain not to be pain? It doesn't really matter whether you grip the arms of the dentist's chair or let your hands lie in your lap. The drill drills on. . . . (LEWIS 1961:38)

The Jewish perspective, rather than embrace the view of suffering as sacrifice, stresses the promise of humility and insight inherent in pain. The lesson of suffering depends on one's capacity to recognize the limitations of human knowledge. Whenever human words and human knowing are stretched to their outer limits, there is the potential for insight. The modern poet David Rosenberg exemplifies this outlook when he gives these words (1977:25) to the biblical Job in response to the "friends" who provide too-facile reasons for Job's extreme suffering:

> you are all plasterers
> you think you are doctors
> but it's only broken walls before you
>
> you smear them over
> with a whiteness of lies
> a color you take for truth itself
>
> you should shut up before them
> and your silence becomes
> a road to wisdom.

Job rejects his friends' shallow and self-serving efforts at consolation and explanation. He knows how profoundly insufficient they are. Job suggests here that sometimes the most fitting response to human suffering can be a respectful and attentive silence.

HISTORY

Over the past four hundred years, our understanding of suffering at the end of life has shifted substantially (Walter 1994). In the sixteenth and seventeenth centuries, end-of-life concerns revolved around the dying person's confirmation or rejection of faith. Last-minute repentance from sin could change the course of one's potential destiny, as could apostasy, the renunciation of one's faith. Lethargy, delirium, and excruciating pain often prevented the dying person from uttering these final words, but strict believers saw this as a spiritual, not a physical, failure.

During the sixteenth and seventeenth centuries, published accounts of deathbed words and behavior were often published postmortem as a way of defining the person's life. There was special interest in women's words, since women were never allowed to speak in other religious settings while they were alive. Notorious criminals were also watched very carefully on their deathbeds, to see if there might be any last-minute repentance or acceptance of faith. The deathbed was the scene in which one's beliefs were put to their final test; the requirement of confirming one's faith at the end of life applied even to atheists. Recantation invalidated an atheist's life.

In the eighteenth and nineteenth centuries, and into the twentieth, the growing authority of medicine undermined the centrality of religion. There was a shift from a concern that the priest be present to elicit faith to a concern that the doctor be present to administer opium. By the time we moved into the twentieth century, we were more likely to ask "Did she die in pain?" or "What was the cause of death?" than we were to ask "Did she die affirming her faith in God?" Medical accounts of the dying process became more central throughout the twentieth century.

In the last third of the twentieth century, and moving into the new millennium, we have seen a psychological/personal-growth version of suffering develop alongside the medical model. Now, in addition to the question "Was he in pain?" we want to know "Did he make his peace with his wife/mother/children? Was everything said that needed to be said? Was the "unfinished business" attended to?" So in the present social context, we approach the last chapter of life with an emphasis on finishing personal business in the context of a relatively pain-free death.

MEDICINE

In our modern, secular, Western point of view, we tend to see suffering as negative and devoid of value. It should be avoided or, if unavoidable, eliminated as quickly as possible. In our largely white North American perspective, we live in "a society . . . where to bear or endure hardship for most of its members seems to run counter to the now dominant secular text of a world without pain or suffering" (Kleinman and Kleinman 1991:291). The word "patient" is derived from the Latin *pati*, which means "to suffer." Sufferers in our culture routinely enter the medical arena, where suffering is subsumed within the paradigm of Western medicine's mission to cure.

Two powerful assumptions determine how suffering is seen and understood within the medical context. The first is the separation of mind and body. In medicine, the body is objectively understood to operate on the basis of universal principles. The mind (which is understood to include the spirit, society, and morality) is seen as disconnected from the body. The second is that the individual is a sovereign being who functions independently of family, society, and culture. Sickness is seen as resid-ing in the individual and in individual physiology. Thus suffering is understood most often as limited to the physical domain, occurring within a body divorced from mind and spirit, within an individual divorced from culture and society. Is it any wonder that the modern individual who suffers often does so alone, alienated from others and herself?

Fortunately, there are at least a few countertrends in health care that attempt to resolve the longstanding Cartesian dissection of the human by viewing individuals in a holistic framework. One helpful way to think about human suffering is in terms of the loss of personhood. Personhood includes everything we associate with being hu-man: personality, character, a past, life experiences, family, cultural background, roles, relationships with others, relationship with self, political being, unconscious (aspects of self outside of awareness), habitual behaviors, a secret life, a perceived future, a transcendent dimension, a body (Cassell 1991). Any of these aspects of the person are susceptible to damage or loss throughout the lifespan. If the injury is sufficient, the person suffers. The suffering continues until the threat or injury has passed, or until the integrity of the individual can be restored in some other manner. In the context of the end of life, the loss of personhood includes the progressive dissolution of each and every aspect of the person up until the time of death.

Ira Byock (1996), a prominent leader in hospice and palliative care, adds to this perspective in his theory of dying as a stage of the human life cycle, which he sees as comparable to infancy, childhood, adolescence, adulthood, and advanced age. He argues that when physical pain is properly controlled, the dying process can be conceived of as a developmental stage with a set of tasks, occurring in the context of a transforming personhood. These tasks include

- sense of completion with worldly affairs
- sense of completion in relationships with community
- sense of meaning about one's individual life (e.g., life review)
- experienced love of self
- experienced love of other
- sense of completion in relationships with family and friends
- acceptance of the finality of life—of one's existence as an individual
- sense of a new self beyond personal loss
- sense of meaning about life in general
- surrender to the transcendent, to the unknown—"letting go" (Byock 1996:251)

In hospice and palliative care, the dying and their families may be able to work on these tasks. As a dying person addresses them, the personhood of the individual may become less complex, as some spheres of self fall away and others are released. The release from suffering often involves surrender to a new sense of reality. As the person is stripped away, layer by layer, some individuals discover a core of their being that can ease the transition from life to death.

Although the shift to a more holistic view of the person at the end of life is heartening, the danger exists for the philosophy of the "good death" to become romanticized in ways that are not sufficiently respectful of the myriad ways in which individuals traverse the dying process (Silverman 1999). There is a risk that practitioners will adopt a new ideology that approaches the "necessary tasks" of dying in a prescriptive manner, rather than supporting individuals and families to find the path that is right for them. A great challenge of the new millennium for the hospice and palliative care movement will be its capacity to employ an ethnographic sensibility that is responsive to the great diversity of meaning-making practices engaged in by individuals and families at the end of life.

THE ETHNOGRAPHY OF PROFESSIONAL CAREGIVING

There is a crisis in caring for persons that cuts across the boundaries of the helping professions. Patients in hospitals feel depersonalized and processed, students suffer from inadequate attention, clients wonder if therapists really care about them, and parishioners feel unknown in their places of worship. Caregivers are rewarded for efficiency, technical skill, and measurable results, while their concern, attentiveness, and human engagement go unnoticed within their professional organizations and institutions. (PHILLIPS 1996:1)

Care work is devalued; care is also devalued conceptually through a connection with privacy, with emotion, and with the needy. Since our society treats public accomplishments, rationality, and autonomy as worthy qualities, care is devalued insofar as it embodies their opposites. . . . To recognize the value of care calls into question the structure of values in our society. Care is not a parochial concern of women, a type of secondary moral question, or the work of the least well off in society. Care is a central concern of human life. It is time that we began to change our political and social institutions to reflect this truth. (TRONTO 1994: 117, 180)

Ours is not an easy time to care, especially to do so for a living. Words like "vocation," "service," "calling," and "caring" are seen by many in the contemporary context as self-serving and suspect. At best, caring practices are relegated to the sidelines of the public consciousness, distorting any thoughtful examination of their centrality to the functioning of the culture. Caring has been incarcerated by a market economy and marginalized as a commodity of debatable value. The language of professional training, in its growing embrace of cost-efficiency and expediency, interferes in our ability as caregivers to experience, understand, and reflect thoughtfully upon the ways in which we care for others who are suffering.

Any meaningful discussion of our response to suffering must acknowledge these social forces that have shaped and commodified our caregiving practices. In addition, we must be cognizant of the various lenses through which we view and understand human suffering and the ways in which those lenses shape our interactions. Returning to the principles of ethnography, we must be careful not to package, pasteurize, or homogenize human suffering in ways that may serve our own needs for security and clarity, but that may do violence to the experience of those we are trying to help. If our task is to observe, listen, and respond to *this* suffering person at *this* moment in time, it may be helpful to heed two "ethnographic guidelines."

1. *Be wary of the potential for diagnostic categories or theoretical frameworks to reify the experience of our patients.* When I sit with a father who comes to see me after the drowning of his toddler daughter, whom he left in the bathroom for a few minutes while he ran to answer the doorbell, I must be vigilant not to view him or his situation more through the lens of "post-traumatic stress disorder" or "traumatic grief" than from the ethnographic standpoint of needing to connect to the horrific experience of losing a beloved child due to a momentary lapse in judgment. (Do I dare to imagine the magnitude of pain I would be feeling as a parent if I made this mistake with my one of my own daughters when she was a baby?) I am not arguing that diagnostic assessment and treatment strategies that derive from them have no useful place in this work. I am arguing, however, that we must be vigilant to hold this knowledge lightly

in our consciousness, in such a way that it does not interfere with our bearing witness to the full humanity of our patients. The psychiatrist and anthropologist Arthur Kleinman makes a strong case for this point of view: "The professionalization of human problems as psychiatric disorders . . . causes sufferers (and their communities) to lose a world, the local context that organizes experience through the moral re-sounding and reinforcing of popular cultural categories about what life means and what is at stake in living. We are far along in this process of inauthenticating local moral worlds, of making illegitimate the defeats and victories, the desperation and aspiration of individuals and groups that could perhaps be more humanly rendered not as representation of some other reality (one that we as experts possess special power over), but rather as evocation of close experience that stands for itself" (Kleinman and Kleinman 1991:293).

As the anthropologists might say, we need to bring fidelity to the data. When we are faithful to the lived experience of our patients, our theory is more likely to be "grounded theory" (Glazer and Strauss 1967), in which we ask ourselves, "What do we really know, and how do we really know it?" We must be wary of the understandable proneness to falling back on "ungrounded" theories and methodologies at those times when we feel most helpless or anxious. We must struggle to move toward rather than away from our suffering clients. To be fully empathic with a client at a time of over-whelming anguish, we must be capable of, in Martin Buber's words, "a bold swinging, demanding the most intensive stirring of one's being, into the life of the other" (Margulies 1989:18).

2. See ourselves as an integral part of the story we are trying to understand. We must be cognizant of how the suffering of the other connects to our own suffering in ways that reveal clues to understanding ourselves, and how understanding ourselves con-nects to our engagement and response to the other. Who and how I am with my clients, and who and how they are with me, is central to what we are trying to com-prehend. This principle is important in terms of the self-knowledge we bring to our work regarding our personal experiences with suffering, as well as the perspective we bring in terms of our own cultural narratives. Bringing an ethnographic stance to the caregiving relationship is about "figuring out how, when entering the experience of another individual or group of individuals, to be as unfettered as possible with one's own cultural luggage—how to leave at home one's powerful cultural assumptions and to create the conversational spaces wherein the voices of the 'other' can emerge" (Laird 1998:30). We must leave at home the professional judgments and cultural assumptions that may distance us from our client, while carrying along with us the self-knowledge and personal connection to suffering that can enable us to move closer.

SUFFERING AND MEANING MAKING

The relief of suffering comes most often by changing the meaning of the experience for the sufferer and restoring the disrupted connectedness of the sufferer with herself and with those around her. Indeed, modern medical practice, by focusing so exclu-

sively on bodily pain and ignoring the multiple aspects of personhood and personal
meaning, may inadvertently increase suffering while seeking to relieve it.

(H. BRODY, IN HAUERWAS 1990:118)

To suffer is to be shut in, to be locked up by grief in a world without light. A pane
opens when sorrow is somehow voiced, shared, spewn out of the closed world of the
individual in pain. When others respond to the voice of the sufferer . . . with truthful
attentiveness, the window of insight becomes broader still. The echo of genuine responsiveness gives meaning to personal grief, heartens one to say more, to probe further
a wound that might have festered in silence otherwise. (SCHWARCZ 1997:128)

In human life, the experience of suffering is mediated by the meaning and belief
system of the sufferer. When I am working with a bereaved client, I find useful the
constructivist principle that asserts that "grieving is the act of affirming or reconstructing a personal world of meaning that has been challenged by loss" (Neimeyer 1999).
Consider the following narrative of a sixty-five-year-old nurse referred to me six weeks
following the sudden death of her forty-year-old daughter from an undiagnosed heart
condition. In the past two years, she had experienced multiple losses: her husband,
two siblings, her remaining parent, her best friend, and now her daughter. Notice the
oscillation between helpless despair and the struggle to make sense, to find meaning
in the face of profound suffering and a personal world that has been shattered:

With the other deaths, I was so sad. I grieved and I grieved. But this time it's different.
This time my soul hurts. It's so deep inside. You see all those people out there, selfish
people, people who don't care at all about others, and they get rewarded for it. I've
tried to be a good person all my life. . . . I don't understand. Nothing makes sense. I've
worked all my life. The security was so important. Now, none of that matters. So many
people have died.

You never know what might happen. You can't be sure how much time you have.
Every moment is precious. I need to do whatever is most important, while I still have
time.

The people I would have looked to for support are gone: my husband, my daughter,
my parents, my friends. . . . I can't do this alone. I feel jealous of all the people that
have so much support around them. I used to have that. Now it's all gone.

I don't want you to take this the wrong way, but I wouldn't care if I died tomorrow.
Then I'd be with the people I love. A widow friend of mind keeps saying she has
nothing left to live for, she just wants to be with her husband. I understand how she
feels. It's not that I'm suicidal. I just miss them all so much.

There's one thing, though, all those deaths taught me. They died, I had so much pain,
but each time I got through it. There's no easy way through this. It's going to take a
long time. But I'll survive. I really don't have any choice. I can't let myself become,
what's the word for it, a victim.

As these statements suggest, we can see the usefulness of bringing a perspective to suffering that pays attention to the loss of meaning that is inherent in bereavement and end-of-life concerns, where our primary tasks as caregivers attempt to create a context for our clients in which they may work toward a new worldview, a new construction of meaning. We can heed the words of the humanistic psychologist Gordon Allport: "If there is a purpose in life at all, there must be a purpose in suffering and in dying. But no man can tell another what this purpose is. Each must find out for himself, and must accept the responsibility that his answer prescribes. If he succeeds he will continue to grow in spite of all indignities" (Allport 1984).

Allport offers three insights into suffering and the caregiving relationship. First, if we believe there is purpose and meaning in life, then there must be purpose and meaning in suffering and dying as well, since they are inherently part of life. Second, we cannot *prescribe* to another the purpose or meaning they ascribe to their own suffering. Third, if a person succeeds in finding meaning or a purpose out of suffering, he or she is likely to become stronger and continue to grow.

Yet a question arises from these insights, one that it is critical to address. What do we do as caregivers when meaning is not to be found, when our clients are either not inclined or not capable of finding new meaning or purpose from their suffering? This challenge is so fundamental to our work as caregivers that it bears exploration. Consider the comments of Nicholas Wolterstorff in *Lament for a Son,* the diary of a grieving father whose son was killed in a mountain-climbing accident. Wolterstorff, a devout Dutch Calvinist, struggles with the meaning of his son's death and how or why God would allow it:

> I cannot fit it all together by saying, "He did it," but neither can I do so by saying, "There was nothing He could do about it." I cannot fit it together at all. I can only, with Job, endure. I do not know why God did not prevent Eric's death. To live without the answer is precarious. It's hard to keep one's footing. . . .
>
> To the "why" of suffering we get no firm answer. Of course some suffering is easily seen to be the result of our sin: war, assault, poverty amidst plenty, the hurtful world. And maybe some is chastisement. But not all. The meaning of the remainder is not told us. It eludes us. Our net of meaning is too small. (HAUERWAS 1990:74)

The grieving father strives for a way of understanding his son's death, but no explanation provides meaning. What he achieves, however, is substantial: he endures.

In recent years, theory building in the fields of end-of-life care and bereavement has increasingly emphasized the centrality of meaning making in the processes of dying and mourning. As part of this evolution, ideas of "transcendence" and "transformation" have entered the therapeutic lexicon, and newer paradigms of mourning have included these ideas as goals or phases in the mourning process (see chapter 13). For example, at a recent professional conference that marked the anniversary of the tragic warehouse fire in Worcester, Massachusetts, in which four firefighters lost their lives, one of the keynote presentations was entitled "Coping with Catastrophe: Surviving and Transcending Trauma" (Rando 2000). In the presentation outline, transcendence is defined as "to rise above or go beyond," and it is suggested that one attribute of those individuals most likely to have their bereavement foster growth will be to "choose to transcend the experience life handed them and employ psychological traits to withstand the repercussions of the event, integrate the experience within their own unique life story, and live healthily with the scars." In line with the emphasis on meaning making, two of the "appropriate goals of healthy mourning" are listed as "making 'sense' out of the loss" and to "transcend loss, not merely survive it" (Rando 2000).

The potential for transformation and transcendence in the aftermath of traumatic loss is a testament to the wonder and resilience of the human spirit. As professional caregivers, we should be open at all times to this potential in our clients, and be prepared to support and bear compassionate witness to its unfolding. However, we must be wary of seeing these as goals of the mourning process or as necessary attributes of "healthy mourning." As caregivers, we must be watchful of the manner in which our own need for meaning and a sense of transcendence may function as a method of managing the feelings of anxiety and horror that can accompany our bearing witness to suffering that is unrelieved, or damage to psyche and spirit that cannot be undone. The theologian Wendy Farley reminds us that "once human suffering is possible, nothing restricts its range so that the kindest, or the weakest, or the most admirable people will be magically protected from it. Nothing limits suffering, in its intensity, from driving people to despair through grief, pain, or cruelty. Once suffering is posited as an essential component of human existence, radical suffering threatens every person. No one is protected from suffering that is so terrible that it breaks the human spirit" (Farley 1990:29). Farley argues for a "tragic vision" in which we recognize the potential of tragic events to damage the sufferer severely. Such events can have the power to destroy any effort to transcend, transform, or make sense out of suffering. "A tragic vision is branded by suffering, but the mark of tragedy is defiance rather than despair. . . . As such, it is an ethical (and ultimately theological) response to suffering: it begins and ends in compassion" (Farley 1990:37).

The caution I have expressed regarding the rush toward meaning making and transcendence is especially warranted when we encounter instances of massive social suffering such as those that throughout the twentieth century and into the twenty-first: the extermination of Jews in Germany, the murder of millions by enforced famine in Stalinist Russia, the recent destruction of whole civilian populations in Yugoslavia and Rwanda, or the mass murder of thousands of Americans in the terrorist bombing of the World Trade Center. Lawrence Langer, who has documented countless Holocaust testimonies, argues the need for an "alarmed vision" in response to these terrifyingly recurring forms of social suffering, setting aside the more comforting or hopeful images of reconciliation or redemption (Langer 1997). Langer argues that "the Holocaust and subsequent large-scale atrocities exist in an orbit void of the usual consoling vocabulary. . . . [These] atrocities have invaded our sense of stable living and normal dying, leaving us a legacy that colonizes the future with nightmares of frustration rather than dreams of fulfillment" (Langer 1997:54). Consider this excerpt of testimony from a former inmate of the camps at Auschwitz and Plaszow:

We never knew . . . who would come back from roll call. Those who were "selected" for the "action" had to first dig their graves, then after stripping and placing everything they were wearing on the ground (in proper order: clothes on one side, underwear on the other), they had to kneel at the edge of the ditch and wait for the bullets in the back. Bullets that the Germans made the Jewish "leaders" of the camp pay for. Economizing on ammunition meant that the work was often botched, and cries rose from the ditches for hours after the execution. During large "actions" things moved too fast. There was no question of burying the bodies, they were simply covered with sand, so you could no longer tell whether you were walking on bones that were old or recent. Everything happened so fast that you didn't even have time to see your mother or sister vanish. We were no longer capable of suffering, or of being scared or surprised. Death is only frightening to the living. We hadn't been that for a long time. (LANGER 1998:54)

The discussion of such horrific instances of social suffering may appear to be irrelevant to the clinical context of bereavement and end-of-life care, but it is not. In our effort as professional caregivers to respond to the suffering of individuals who have experienced severe trauma and loss, we often reach for diagnostic categories of posttraumatic stress disorder or traumatic grief, and treatment approaches organized around working through or transcending traumatic loss, without any social or political framework to inform our efforts. Such strategies have been implemented with client populations as diverse as Holocaust survivors, Vietnam veterans, and, more recently, survivors of the September 2001 World Trade Center attack.

It would help to be able to call this condition a treatable trauma, but if the testimonies of hundreds of Holocaust survivors are to be trusted, that clinical formula simply will not serve the truth of their ordeal. As we shall see, their memories are not symptoms, nor in telling their tales do they seek some form of reintegration into their community—a goal they have long since achieved. Well-intentioned intervention after the fact is no substitute for strong action to prevent atrocities from occurring. Painful memories are not always disabling, and narratives about them—at least this is true of Holocaust testimony—rarely "liberate" witnesses from a past they cannot and do not wish to escape. For them, forgetting would be the ultimate desecration, a "cure" the ultimate illusion. As for renewal or rebirth, such monuments to hope cannot be built from the ruins of a memory crammed with images of flame and ash.

(LANGER 1998:54–55)

The ethnographic perspective challenges caregivers to be faithful to the lived histories of our clients, and faithful to our own lived histories in our meetings with clients. "What the ethnographer experiences matches how individuals encounter the flow of experience. They do not dominate it, or invent it, but rather are thrown into the stream of lived interactions" (Kleinman and Kleinman 1991:277). We are asked to confront the question of what is at stake for the client in her life situation and in the clinical encounter, and what is at stake for ourselves. What is at stake may lead the therapeutic process down numerous paths. These paths may end in transformation or transcendence; they may also lead to a defiant stance, an alarmed vision, or to the simple but profound commitment to endure.

THE CAREGIVER'S ENCOUNTER WITH SUFFERING

I have argued that in our work as professional caregivers, we must first validate and reclaim our vocations of caring from the dictates of a market economy and healthcare system driven by cost-efficiency and profit. Second, we must be careful not to allow our diagnostic and treatment paradigms to overshadow or distort the human encounter that is at the core of our work. Third, we must see our personal knowledge of suffering as integral to the collaborative healing process between our clients and ourselves. Fourth, as we respectfully accompany our clients in their efforts to make meaning out of traumatic life experiences, we must simultaneously be prepared to bear witness to suffering that may not be transformed or transcended, but rather endured.

What are the personal and professional qualities that we can cultivate to engage with the suffering of others, and to remain engaged in this process over time? The remainder of this chapter will explore the two central qualities: compassion and empathy.

COMPASSION

The word "compassion" derives from the Latin root *pati* (to suffer) and *com* (with). Compassion is our capacity to suffer together with others. Compassion operates on the level of universality. That is to say, although we cannot presume to understand fully the experience of another person who is suffering, we *can* connect to that person from the place within us that knows suffering, from a position of universality. In the presence of your suffering, I can convey by my presence a knowledge of human suffering. In the presence of your vulnerability, I can respond from a place that knows my own vulnerability. It is not easy to stay connected to our vulnerability as we join with our clients. Sometimes, when we do stay connected, it can feel as if the ground is falling out beneath us. Pema Chodron comments on this process, a process that can occur for client and caregiver alike: "When the bottom falls out and we can't find anything to grasp, it hurts a lot. . . . This is where tenderness comes in. When things are shaky and nothing is working, we might realize that we are on the verge of something. We might realize that this is a very vulnerable and tender place, and that tenderness can go either way. We can shut down and feel resentful, or we can touch in on that throbbing quality. There is definitely something tender and throbbing about groundlessness" (Pema Chodron as cited in hooks 1995:27).

The late theologian and pastoral counselor Henri Nouwen wrote wisely about vulnerability in his description of the wounded healer. The term "wounded healer" comes from a story that originally appeared in the Hebrew Talmud:

> Rabbi Yoshua ben Levi came upon Elijah the prophet while he was standing at the entrance of Rabbi Simeron ben Yohai's cave. . . . He asked Elijah, "When will the Messiah come?"

Elijah replied, "Go and ask him yourself."

"Where is he?"

"Sitting at the gates of the city."

"How shall I know him?"

"He is sitting among the poor covered with wounds. The others unbind all their wounds at the same time and then bind them up again. But he unbinds one at a time and binds it up again, saying to himself, 'Perhaps I shall be needed: if so I must always be ready so as not to delay for a moment.'" (NOUWEN 1979:81–82)

Because it is the healer's task to help others, we must first bind our own wounds carefully, in anticipation of the moment when we will be needed. Because we are in the business of caregiving, we need to understand and be attentive to our own wounds in order to respond to the wounds of others. Nouwen reminds us that we are all broken, we are all suffering; hope begins when we do not run away, but instead accept this reality. Compassion includes the recognition of our own helplessness, our human limitations. Acceptance of our own limitations opens the door to surrendering in our helplessness to God, or, if we do not think in terms of God, to a power that is outside of and larger than ourselves. Nouwen promises that in our shared vulnerability with others, we can mobilize our mutual suffering into a common search for life.

Built into the concept of the wounded healer is the recognition that it is not the healer's job to take away pain. Healing occurs not because the healer takes away the pain and loneliness of the other, but because she invites the other to recognize her loneliness on a level where it can be shared. Healing is seen as an invitation to recognize our mutual mortality and brokenness, so that we might take a step together on the road toward liberation.

An important aspect of staying with compassion is the ability to be comfortable with not having answers, and with not imposing our own answers on others. This connects to the ethnographic stance that in order to be successful in our caregiving responses to suffering, we need to cultivate an attitude of "informed not-knowing" (Shapiro 1995) in our approach to the other, and a "disciplined self-awareness" (Klass 1999) in relation to ourselves. Professional training tends to do a poor job in nurturing either of these orientations. Compassion involves the capacity to be empty and to be willing to listen carefully, to create the conversational space in which the other may emerge. The times when it seems as though we are doing nothing can potentially be the times when we are doing the most.

This vital lesson about what we can and cannot offer as caregivers was brought home to me by a nine-year-old girl who was referred to me for counseling about four months following the death of her twelve-year-old brother, who died suddenly and unexpectedly from an undiagnosed medical condition. She was normally a happy, sociable child who did very well in school. Since her brother's death, however, her grades had dropped considerably, she had stopped spending much time with friends, and she had become depressed, to the point of talking repeatedly of her wish to die and to join her brother in heaven. She was an unusually verbal and articulate child who came to the first appointment with a list of five questions: (1) How do kids handle this when they're alone? (2) Do some kids start support groups? (3) Could kids go to someone else they could talk to besides a counselor, like another kid? (4) Do some parents donate their kid's arms and legs? (5) Do some kids actually kill themselves?

I met with this child for only twelve sessions. I worked to create a context for her to express her thoughts, feelings, and questions about her brother's death, and to honor his memory through telling stories, sharing photographs, and constructing dialogues with him in heaven. Within about six weeks, her depression lifted, her grades were improving, and her thoughts about death had subsided. At about the tenth session, she came in and announced that she was feeling better and was ready to end her sessions with me.

I was a bit taken aback. I felt quite attached to her by this point, and I had the expectation that she would want to be in counseling for a longer period. She pulled out a poem she had written about two buckets, and asked me to read it. I couldn't understand it very well, so I asked if she could explain what the poem meant to her. She said that it was about a little girl who was carrying a small bucket and a large bucket. Both buckets had been full of tears, and the girl had been carrying them for a while. But now the small bucket was empty and she only had to carry the large bucket.

At some point in our discussion, she acknowledged that she was the girl in the poem, and that it was because of the love and caring she had experienced from her parents, teachers, and me that the smaller bucket was now empty. Though I was happy to hear that the small bucket was empty, I hoped that the large bucket could be emptied as well, and that I could help her to empty it. I knew the isolation and despair of a child's grief from my own childhood experience, and I wanted to give her more parental insight and compassion than had been available to me.

But this was her bereavement narrative, not mine. She looked at me sympathetically and said, "No, you can't help me with the large bucket. That's the bucket I need to carry with me as I get older. . . . But it's okay, because I'm feeling better. I'm ready to go ahead with my life now. And you helped me to feel strong enough to carry that bucket."

EMPATHY

The word "empathy" is a translation of the German word *Einfühlung,* a word introduced in 1903 by the German philosopher Theodor Lipps to describe the process of aesthetic empathy in art, or feeling oneself into the object (Clinchy 1996). Expanded into the interpersonal realm, the term has come to mean "the ability of one person to come to know firsthand, so to speak, the experience of another"; "inference, judgment, and other aspects of reasoning thought" are as central to the process as affect (Clinchy 1996:224). As applied to the caregiver's response to suffering, empathy can be understood as an active imagination of the other, an effort to place one's self into the head and heart, as well as the shoes, of the other. In contrast to compassion, which occurs on the level of universality, empathy exists on the level of particularity and uniqueness. Empathy requires the body, mind, and spirit: it is not simply a feeling.

Martin Buber describes this process as making the other present, or as boldly swinging into the life of the other.

The paradox of this bold swinging into the life of the other is that it does not require leaving home ground. Empathy is an experience of separateness within connection, a process in which the self simultaneously remains intact and is transformed. Many cognitive developmental theorists (Clinchy 1996; Loevinger 1976; Mead 1981) and object relation theorists (Winnicott 1965; Mahler 1995) have addressed how connection requires the capacity for separateness. Fully connected knowing (Clinchy 1996) depends on a well-developed capacity to understand the self. If the other person is to be more than a screen for our projections, we must know ourselves well. Without such self-awareness, we cannot clearly identify the real similarities between our own experience and the experience of the other, nor can we fully preserve the otherness of the other. Connected knowing with the self, or empathy with the self, and connected knowing with the other, or empathy with the other, are reciprocal processes (Clinchy 1996). Intersubjective theorists (Aron 1996; Mitchell 1988; Ogden, 1996) have elucidated this process as well.

Buber adds an additional insight to this perspective. He uses "confirmation" to describe the aspect of the healing relationship that involves accepting the whole potentiality of the other person. Thus, integral to the process of my accepting you as you are is the process of my accepting you as you are meant to become. Howard Thurman, the African American theologian who was a mentor to Martin Luther King Jr., called this "double vision," by which he meant the capacity to see and accept the other in her brokenness and potential wholeness simultaneously.

The challenge to the clinician to be empathic, compassionate, and engaged in the midst of great suffering is exemplified in the case narrative of a young woman who came to see me approximately two months following the disappearance of her pre-adolescent son. She had given her son a ride to soccer practice, dropping him off at the entrance to the local athletic fields. At some point in the one hundred yards between the road and the soccer field, he vanished. The police assumed from the available evidence that he had been abducted. The following are excerpts from my client's description of her experience, followed by an account of my internal experience during the hour.

CLIENT

As a parent, you think that something like this happens to other people. You know, you see those pictures on the milk carton, and you feel so bad for those parents. But you never imagine it could happen to you. You don't want to imagine it; you can't let yourself imagine it. You know, it's just too horrible a thing to get yourself around.

The police won't tell you this, but after thirty days they don't have much hope of finding him alive. After thirty days they assume he's dead.

We have to have hope, even though our minds tell us he is probably is gone.

My mind goes back and forth a thousand times a day. Is he alive, is he dead? I pray all day long that he's alive and we'll find him.

But I know that if he's alive, he could be terribly hurt. Someone would be holding him, maybe torturing him. Then I think it's selfish to want him alive, and . . . I hope he's dead. Then I would know he's safe . . . he'd be in Heaven, with my mother and his aunt and uncle.

Then I just pray that we find the body, so we'll know he's not being hurt, that he's at peace.

He came to me in a dream. . . . He told me, tell Papa I love him. He's very close with my husband. That would seem to say that he's passed on, and he's okay. But I'm not sure. . . .

I know I have to prepare myself for the worst, so I'll be able to survive. We miss him so much, we just miss him so much.

There's really nothing we can do. . . . All we can really do is pray. That's all we can do.

CAREGIVER

What I remember: the need to breathe deeply, repeatedly. The physical experience of trying to get bigger, of keeping myself open. The paradox that I must do my best to "get myself around" this pain, while knowing that I can't really succeed. As my client says, it is "just too horrible a thing to get yourself around."

I struggle to allow the framework of my own experience with suffering to create a space in which her suffering can exist and be expressed. I am allowing my awareness of my own wounds to be of service to her, even though my own losses suddenly seem small in this context. My own experience with loss *does* help me to connect to my vulnerability, and most of all my utter helplessness.

I am outraged at the undeserved nature of this trauma, at the injustice. This is a good person, a loving and devoted mother, a caring family. How could this type of thing be allowed to occur?

It is so overwhelmingly clear that there is very little to say, that words are not of much use. It is even clearer that this suffering is bigger than she can handle, and bigger than I can handle. It is bigger than both of us. I dig down for my own sense of connection to God; none of us can carry such a burden alone. I work at surrendering the pain to God, as she is so vigilantly trying to do.

How can I be empathic? How do I stay present? To be present, I have to imagine the horror. I drift to imagining what the horror would be like if I were in her shoes. I have children myself. I can't allow myself to imagine.

I remind myself that my job is to imagine what it must be like to be in *her* shoes. To use Buber's words, my challenge is to swing boldly into the life of this person. I am unable to be bold, but in small doses, I allow myself to connect to the dreadfulness and impossibility of her experience.

I have to imagine what it's like to know your child is gone, but not know whether he is alive or dead

I have to imagine the importance of hope even when there is little reason to hope.

I have to imagine the fearful vision of a son being held captive or tortured.

I have to imagine how it might feel selfish to wish your own child alive in this context that it would be more reassuring to have him dead, and safe in Heaven, than to have him suffer.

I have to imagine the sickening irony that in this context, the hope of finding your son alive slowly shifts into the fervent wish to find him dead, that the retrieval of a body becomes the center of your survival.

I have to wonder how well a faith in God can possibly hold up under this kind of emotional and spiritual assault.

In the midst of all this suffering, I am acutely aware that as my client takes strength from being able to share her suffering with me, I will be taking strength from my client's remarkable struggle to endure.

Fundamental to the qualities of compassion and empathy is the capacity to provide, in Winnicott's words, a "holding environment" for our clients. When deep suffering is shared with us as caregivers, we must be capable of a kind of elasticity or expansiveness within our hearts and souls. In my clinical practice, I experience this quite literally as the need to "get bigger." As I accompany a client into a place of deep pain, I am conscious of breathing deeply from the diaphragm as a way of expanding the spiritual and emotional space in which to witness this pain. I am also acutely conscious of how imperfect my effort is in the face of this suffering. In my imperfection I am aided once again by the reassurance Winnicott directed at the mothering process. I don't need to be perfect; I need only endeavor to be "good enough." The quality of expansiveness I am discussing here is well captured in the following story:

An aging Hindu master grew tired of his apprentice complaining, and so, one morning, sent him for some salt. When the apprentice returned, the master instructed the unhappy young man to put a handful of salt in a glass of water and then to drink it.

"How does it taste?" the master asked.

"Bitter," spat the apprentice.

The master chuckled and then asked the young man to take the same handful of salt and put it in the lake. The two walked in silence to the nearby lake, and once the apprentice swirled his handful of salt in the water, the old man said, "Now drink from the lake."

As the water dripped down the young man's chin, the master asked, "How does it taste?"

"Fresh," remarked the apprentice.

"Do you taste the salt?" asked the master.

"No," said the young man.

At this, the master sat beside this serious young man who so reminded him of himself and took his hands, offering, "The pain of life is pure salt; no more, no less. The amount of pain in life remains the same, exactly the same. But the amount of bitterness we taste depends on the container we put the pain in. So when you are in pain, the only thing you can do is to enlarge your sense of things. . . . Stop being a glass. Become a lake." (ANONYMOUS 2000)

CONCLUSION

I began this chapter with the proposition that, in our effort as caregivers to respond to the suffering of others, it behooves us to understand our personal reservoirs of suffering. Our experiences with suffering, and the sense we have made of them, constitute both the starting and ending point of our caregiving endeavors. As the ethnographic perspective teaches us, when we encounter a client fully and authentically, we bring a faithfulness to the other's lived experience and a faithfulness to our own. As my young poet/client taught me, we as caregivers cannot empty the buckets of tears our clients carry in their lives, much as we may wish to do so. In the most basic human sense, when we sit with another who is suffering, the only thing we truly have to offer is our own knowledge of suffering, our own wounds, our own broken hearts. Paradoxically, as we recognize our mutual vulnerability, we may help our clients find the strength to carry their buckets, as they help us find the strength to carry our own.

At the age of twenty-five, when I first began to be conscious of the reservoir of grief I had carried since my mother's death, I poured out my anguish into the poem that begins this chapter. Twenty years later, when I reached the same age as my mother when she died, I wrote a second poem. By this point, my own personal life lessons, enriched by the profound teachings of my clients, had prepared me to loosen the emotional and spiritual grip in which I held my mother's soul. I was able to "deprivatize" the alchemy of sweetness and melancholy created by my mother's death and to commit myself more fully to the lives and loves that comprise my contemporary world. Piece by piece, I could begin to allow the fragments of love, which had been so thoroughly shattered some thirty years ago, to be reassembled within me. Piece by piece, I could begin to know true courage.

IT'S TIME

When you died, I wasn't ready.
I had to freeze you in time and space.
Like a child, grasping a popsicle,

Unwilling to acknowledge
The certitude of its melting.

Now it's time
(*Did we know it could take so long?*)
Thanks for staying frozen for me
(*What mothers will do for their sons!*)
But the meltdown is long overdue.

Today it is clear:
There are more pressing things to do
Than to deny our spirits their destinies.
I must get on with living;
You must get on with death.

Me, I intend
To free my heart
For . . . who knows what?

You, dear mother,
I imagine rising . . . rising . . .
And doing whatever it is
Angels need to do

REFERENCES

Allport, G. 1984. Preface. In V. Frankl, *Man's Search for Meaning*. New York: Simon & Schuster.

Andersen, H., and H. Goolishian. 1992. The client is the expert: A not-knowing approach to therapy. In *Therapy as Social Construction*, ed. S. McNamee and K. Gergen, 25–39. Newbury Park, CA: Sage.

Anonymous. 2000. *Unity Magazine* 7:37.

Aron, L. 1996. *A Meeting of the Minds: Mutuality in Psychoanalysis*. Hillsdale, NJ: Analytic Press.

Byock, I. 1996. The nature of suffering and the nature of opportunity at the end of life. *Clinics in Geriatric Medicine* 12:237–252.

Cassell, E. J. 1991. *The Nature of Suffering and the Goals of Medicine*. Oxford: Oxford University Press.

Clinchy, B. 1996. Connected and separate knowing: Toward a marriage of two minds. In *Knowledge, Difference and Power*, ed. M. Belenky, B. Clinchy, N. Goldberger, and J. Tarule, 205–247. New York: Basic Books.

Falicov, C. J. 1995. Training to think culturally: A multidimensional comparative framework. *Family Process* 34:373–388.

Farley, W. 1990. *Tragic Vision and Divine Compassion: A Contemporary Theodicy*. Louisville, KY: Westminster/John Knox Press.

Glazer, B., and A. Strauss. 1967. *The Discovery of Grounded Theory: Strategies for Qualitative Research*. Chicago: Aldine.

Hauerwas, S. 1990. *Naming the Silences: God, Medicine, and the Problem of Suffering*. Grand Rapids, MI: Eerdmans.

hooks, b. 1995. An interview with Pema Chodron. *Inquiring Mind* 12:26–29.

Klass, D. 1999. *The Spiritual Lives of Bereaved Parents.* Philadelphia: Taylor & Francis.

Kleinman, A., and J. Kleinman. 1991. Suffering and its professional transformation. *Culture, Medicine and Psychiatry* 3:275–301.

Laird, J. 1998. Theorizing culture: Narrative ideas and practice principles. In *Re-Visioning Family Therapy: Race, Culture, and Gender in Clinical Practice*, ed. M. McGoldrick, 20–37. New York: Guilford.

Langer, L. 1997. The alarmed vision: Social suffering and holocaust atrocity. In *Social Suffering*, ed. V. Das, A. Kleinman, and M. Lock, 47–65. Berkeley: University of California Press.

———. 1998. *Preempting the Holocaust.* New Haven, CT: Yale University Press.

Lewis, C. S. 1961. *A Grief Observed.* London: Faber.

Loevinger, J. 1976. *Ego Development: Conceptions and Theories.* New York: Jossey-Bass.

Mahler, M. 1995. *Oneness and Separation: From Infant to Individual.* New York: Simon & Schuster.

Margulies, A. 1989. *The Empathic Imagination.* New York: Norton.

Mead, G. H. 1981. *Selected Writings.* Chicago: University of Chicago Press.

Mitchell, S. 1988. *Relational Concepts in Psychoanalysis: An Integration.* Cambridge, MA: Harvard University Press.

Moffat, J. 1992. *In the Midst of Winter: Selections from the Literature of Mourning.* New York: Random House.

Neimeyer, R. 1999. Meaning reconstruction and the experience of loss. Workshop, San Antonio, TX.

Nouwen, H. 1979. *The Wounded Healer.* New York: Bantam.

Ogden, T. 1996. *Subjects of Analysis.* New York: Jason Aronson.

Phillips, S. 1996. Introduction. In *The Crisis of Care: Affirming and Restoring Caring Practices in the Helping Professions*, ed. P. Benner and S. Phillips, 1–16. Washington, DC: Georgetown University Press.

Rando, T. 2000. Paper delivered at the Catastrophe: Community Impact and Healing conference, Worcester, MA.

Rosenberg, D. 1977. *Job Speaks.* New York: Harper & Row.

Schwarcz, V. 1997. The pane of sorrow: Public uses of personal grief in modern China. In *Social Suffering*, ed. V. Das, A. Kleinman, and M. Lock, 119–131. Berkeley: University of California Press.

Shapiro, V. 1995. Subjugated knowledge and the working alliance: The narratives of Russian Jewish immigrants. *In Session: Psychotherapy in Practice* 1:9–22.

Tronto, J. 1994. *Moral Boundaries: A Political Argument for an Ethic of Care.* New York: Routledge, Chapman and Hall.

Walter, T. 1994. *The Revival of Death.* New York: Routledge.

Winnicott, D. 1965. *Maturational Processes and the Facilitating Environment: Studies in the Theory of Emotional Development.* New York: International Universities Press.

Wolterstorff, N. 1987. *Lament for a Son.* Grand Rapids, MI: Eerdmans.

2

THE SYMPTOM IS STILLNESS:
LIVING WITH AND DYING FROM ALS

ELLEN PULLEYBLANK COFFEY

STILLNESS

My symptom is stillness.
My body feels normal with usual sensations,
but I never move.

Sitting still, a quiver of muscles around my jaw,
Like the disease's first symptom, a slight cool shudder,
shivering everywhere, subtle, but persistent.

My lungs no longer take breaths, they accept them.
Totally passive, they receive air,
in the unchanging rhythms of a ventilator.

Sometimes my mind slips off into a clear fresh water lake.
Rising out of the water, moving through the water on the force of my arms,
slipping into coolness with each stroke.

When I return to my body it is still, completely still.
This is true now. It will be true in an hour, a day, a week,
and forever, just completely still.

—*Ronald Pulleyblank, 1989*

ALS AFFECTS the nerve cells or neurons that carry messages from the brain to the muscles under voluntary control. As these motor neurons die, the brain loses its ability to direct muscle movement. The unstimulated muscles weaken and atrophy.

Typically victims become progressively weaker and unable to walk, swallow, speak and move their arms and hands. Respiratory function can also become impaired. However bladder and bowel control, the five senses and the mind—the abilities to think clearly and to feel—are generally unaffected.

Life expectancy can vary greatly: three to five years is typical, but some victims have remained active for a decade or two after diagnosis. In a few cases symptoms may temporarily disappear.

At present the most common form of ALS has no discernible underlying factors. It can strike anyone, anywhere. Experts speculate that people who develop it have some sort of predisposition that is activated by exposure to some environmental factor or to a virus. (JANE BRODY, *NEW YORK TIMES*, 21 MAY 1986)

INTRODUCTION

On January 13, 1993, in our family living room, a doctor disconnected my husband, Ronald Pulleyblank, from the ventilator that had kept him alive for seven years. He lived with, and finally died from, amyotrophic lateral sclerosis (ALS), commonly known as Lou Gehrig's disease after the famous New York Yankees baseball player, who died of it in 1941. Like Lou Gehrig, Ron was in the prime of his life when the disease struck. Gehrig was known for never missing a game in fourteen years. Ron was known for never missing a day at work. He became ill in 1985 when he was forty-two; within fourteen months his condition deteriorated to the point at which he could not breathe on his own. Completely paralyzed, dependent on the ventilator for every breath, he lived at home for seven more years. During much of that time, with the help of specially equipped computers, he continued to do research as a Hewlett-Packard Laboratory engineer. My daughters and I, our friends and family, lived through an experience that taught us more than we wanted to know about life, illness, and death, and about the importance of family and friends. We are only recently able to look back on those years and reflect on what we learned.

In a culture that values individual choices above responsibility to others, we had to learn when to make decisions as a family, when to decide alone, when to listen to others about what to do, and when to listen only to each other. We learned about suffering and how to bear it when there was no relief. After the ventilator extended Ron's life, we worked to maintain quality of life for him and for the rest of our family. We were ordinary people living under extraordinary circumstances, pushed up against significant social, political, and medical issues. We fought legal battles with a medical system that could save lives in the emergency room but wouldn't provide care for the living. We learned how to build a community of support with our friends and family and how to find humor and love in unexpected places.

In my work as a therapist with other families facing catastrophic illness, we grapple with the same issues. Our stories are not always inspirational; they are sometimes as much about despair as about courage. They tell about the day-to-day struggles, successes, and failures of family life under duress. In a culture that fears death, many of us are not taught how to face the tragedy of chronic illness and death. We learn instead that if we avert our eyes, we will keep illness and death from our door. We are afraid to feel grief, let alone talk about it. We believe that if we talk about these experiences they will consume us. We are therefore often compelled to remain silent about the most difficult parts of our lives. Families and patients, discouraged from expressing rage when someone is ill or discussing suicide when there appear to be no better choices, keep quiet and stay to themselves. Yet it is in these experiences of vulnerability that we learn what it means to be human, learn about our capacities and limitations as human beings. It is in finding ways to speak of these experiences and to share them with those who stay with us as we go through what often feels unbearable, that we survive. Providing opportunities for such difficult conversations is the role that social workers can play in working with chronically ill patients and their families.

Before Ron's illness, my work as a family therapist had been based on the Western assumption that in taking responsibility for ourselves we find positive choices in our lives that avoid future pain. Our family tragedy taught me that even if we take responsibility for ourselves, sometimes all possible choices might be painful.

This chapter addresses family issues connected to a catastrophic progressive illness. The first section describes how repeated crises affect family life. The second section describes ways in which therapeutic, spiritual, and community resources can help address the problems associated with a catastrophic illness. The third section examines the process of conscious death and dying and its effect on the family. Following the conclusion, I include a review of suggested practices for social workers, who with families wrestle with the social, ethical, psychological, and spiritual dilemmas often connected to catastrophic illnesses.

MANY CRISES

In his book *Holocaust*, Lawrence Langer distinguishes between two kinds of time: chronological time and durational time. He says that we expect a life in chronological time, made up of a past, present, and future. When crises become the norm of life, durational time sets in. This is time without past or future, with a recurring, disturbing present that is difficult to organize, express, or forget. Langer writes that because durational time cannot overflow the blocked reservoir of its own moment, it never enters what we usually experience as the stream of time. Living with a disease like ALS creates such an experience of time. Up until three years after Ron died, our story continued in my mind as a jumble of feelings and thoughts often experienced as if it was still going on in the present. In writing about these experiences, I have placed those years back into the linear stream of time.

THE FIRST CRISIS: THE DIAGNOSIS

We had been a family of good fortune until our story changed early one summer morning in Paris. We were on vacation in France before we went to the Netherlands for a year's sabbatical. Our car was parked on the Rue du Buci, a busy street on the Left Bank. We carried down our baggage, and Ron got busy tying it to the roof of the car. We were in a loading zone. A truck honked and the driver yelled for us to get going. I was annoyed with Ron. As always, he was doing this perfectly, and it was taking too long.

"Hurry up," I shouted.

"I am hurrying, but I'm having trouble tying the knots. I can't get my hands to work," he said in a strained voice. Finally he secured the baggage and got into the car. He looked pale. I noticed that his shoulder was pulsing.

"Why is your shoulder throbbing?" I asked.

"I've had spasms in different parts of my body for awhile," he replied briskly, and then said no more, as if too intent on his driving. As he had often done before, he found his way out of the city by instinct, winding confidently through unfamiliar streets. When we were out of the city, I asked him lightly, "Why didn't you tell me about the spasms in your shoulders?"

"I didn't want you to worry. I think it's just stress," he replied.

That was our first conversation about what became the central issue of the remainder of our life together.

✠

IN mid-September Ron's symptoms were worse, and we made an appointment with a neurologist at the teaching hospital in Rotterdam. As soon as Ron took off his shirt, the doctor immediately noticed the spasms that ran all over his upper body. I watched the doctor closely, searching for every nuance of meaning. I saw his grim look. I was so afraid that I barely listened to him when he said to Ron, "There is something weakening your muscles. What it is and how it will progress is unclear. You need a muscle biopsy, blood tests, a CAT scan of your brain, and a spinal tap. We are trying to rule out MS, vertebrae pressure, inflammation of the spine, and a subdural hematoma. Can you come into the hospital tomorrow? You'll need to stay overnight."

We made plans for Ron's stay in the hospital. Little else was said. Ron was already changed. His walk had slowed down, his gait was uneven, and he looked painfully thin. What I noticed most was a difference in his eyes. Ron's eyes were deep green, and he had always looked directly at the world around him. Now there was a tentativeness in his gaze, as if he was not so sure about what he was seeing.

Ron went into the hospital for tests in the last week in September. Reluctantly, I left him there. People often seem normal in a crisis. They pay attention to what needs to be done. It is as if they are pulled through the most difficult moments in life by the most mundane details. Reflection, emotion, or any kind of understanding has to wait until questions are answered. When a state of crisis continues for a long time, it is the details of everyday life that may keep people sane when the uncertainty of their circumstances pushes them toward insanity.

I left the hospital, went home, and fixed dinner for the girls and myself. We chatted about their day and reassured each other about Ron. We played a game of Scrabble before bedtime, and I tucked them in as always. This part of our day went as if things were as they had always been.

After Ron came home we had to wait another week before meeting with the doctor. At this visit he confirmed Ron's diagnosis.

He bluntly said, "You have ALS, and it is a fatal disease. Many people, however, live for eight or ten years with it. You should just go on with your life as normal and do as much as you can. I am sorry to tell you, but there are no cures or treatments for the disease. You might want to consider going back to the United States to be near your family. I'd like to see you again in about a month."

Like children, we sat and listened to what we were told. When we left his office we walked along the Rotte, a beautiful canal near our village. It was so peaceful—windmills, thatched cottages, long open fields running along the water. We walked, talked, and cried. I thought that perhaps we should go home, but Ron was adamant that he wanted to stay in the Netherlands. "I don't want to change anything I don't have to. We don't even know what's going to happen. I can't believe right now that I'll die in a year, and if I do, I want to keep doing what I can as long as I can," he said.

It is not just human nature that works to keep things the same. In Africa, the large red ants that build tall mud anthills work in this same way. When the hill is disrupted, ants come together in a central place and begin to work madly at repairing what is in front of them without even assessing the damage.

Because I did not know what I thought or felt, I followed Ron's sense of what to do. Before this, we made decisions together, often struggling over my way or his, but always in a fair fight because we each held our own. In this situation, from the beginning, I believed that I had to do things Ron's way because it was his life that was threatened.

After we decided to stay put, we told the girls and then our family and friends. With each person, especially the girls, we tried to sound calm and reassuring. No one knew anything about the disease and no one could believe that Ron was really terminally ill. Oddly, the telling did not relieve us, but created an aura of unreality as we tried to calm everyone and ourselves in the midst of great confusion. Good fortune had lulled us into believing that we could control our lives. Now we had to face the horror of devastating illness and death. We were not prepared and had no passport for entering into this incomprehensible world.

In many middle-class American families, I believe, illnesses are often hidden, and many of us are unprepared when they occur. With childlike innocence, we believe that what might happen to someone else will not happen to us. The public conversation about illness and death is slowly bringing more of us into the realization that serious illness can and will happen to many of us or to those we love. This conversation is helping us prepare, but when catastrophic illness hit our family in 1985, few people we knew were having that conversation.

This first crisis was what John Rolland (1994) calls a "framing event" and was only one of an ongoing series. Unlike other illnesses that have a predictable progression, ALS moves in different ways and at different rates, although it always worsens. In Ron's case, the disease moved rapidly, with one crisis following on the heels of another, and the disease progressed in such a way that we never caught up with it.

THE SECOND CRISIS: THE VENTILATOR

Within a year of his diagnosis, after we returned home to California, Ron was increasingly weak and began to have difficulty breathing. At first, I was sure that if we worked hard enough, we could figure out how to keep life going on as usual. Nevertheless, as more and more decisions needed to be made, we scrambled to make sense of situations that we knew little about. The crisis accelerated one night at home when Ron could not breathe. We rushed to the emergency room at the nearest hospital. I did not call anyone. I went to the hospital alone. After a short time, Dr. A., our neurologist in California, came into the room where I was sitting and asked me if I wanted him to put Ron on a ventilator. He explained that without the ventilator Ron would die that night. Without a second thought, I told him to put Ron on the ventilator. I then sat there through the night alone and terrified, not knowing what this meant and what would happen to us.

Eleven years after that night and four years after Ron died, I went back to Dr. A.'s office. Everything in the waiting room looked the same as on the first day that Ron and I went there. This time I was meeting with the doctor during his lunch hour, and there were no other patients waiting. Sitting there, I found it hard to believe that Ron was not well and with me.

Dr. A. opened the door and greeted me warmly. He still had a youthful friendly face, though the lines around his eyes had deepened and his hair had thinned. He seemed pleased to see me again. Taking him a bit by surprise, I told him how often I had thought about the night that he had put Ron on the ventilator and how unprepared I was to make the decision at the time. He said that his notes showed that at Ron's last appointment, before he was hospitalized, we had discussed the issue of life support. I told him that he had been vague at that appointment, only implying that Ron might need a ventilator or some other breathing support at some time. We had no idea that Ron might end up on a ventilator in order to stay alive. After that appointment we had begun to investigate what it meant to be on a ventilator and what other options might be available, but the crisis in Ron's health happened before we got a grasp of the situation. I wanted him to know how crucial it is to have more than one conversation before any family can make such decisions.

Dr. A. said that he was certain that Ron wanted to be placed on a ventilator. I asked him, if he was so sure, why he had come out of the emergency room to ask for my permission.

"It was just routine," he said.

"What do you think about life support for ALS patients?" I pressed.

"I don't think life support makes sense for ALS patients, but you never can know what is right for someone else. I know many people who say that they want to die, but when the moment comes, they choose to live. I know how devastating ALS is, but I am not sure what I would have done if I were in Ron's situation. It wasn't my job to give you advice on what to do. The decision was up to Ron." Dr. A. began fiddling with Ron's file, opening and closing it. He no longer looked directly at me. He had stopped smiling, but I continued.

"Was it really just up to Ron? Can a decision to be so dependent be an independent one? Is such a decision just up to an individual, or should it include the family and other important people? Isn't it a decision that needs to be discussed and weighed before a crisis? No one talked to us about the costs, physical, financial, and emotional. Nor had anyone given us information about what is known about living on a ventilator.

Why didn't you help us talk to each other about it and help us seek advice from others?"

Dr. A. looked impatient. This interview was over for him.

"I thought I did tell you what you needed to know. In our medical system, a doctor can't say what he thinks you should do. It is up to the individual. If I made that decision in the emergency room without your permission I could be sued." Now the interview was mostly over for me too, but with one last outburst I said: "I don't doubt that we would have made the same decision, but we would have had some idea of what we were deciding. What we did not know was this: if you decide to turn a ventilator on, you will eventually need to decide to turn it off. This decision affects everyone in a family and a community. It is supported by a healthcare system that protects life in the emergency room, but has no means of providing ongoing care. You could have prepared us, helped us to think about how to keep Ron at home, given us time to contemplate the enormity of our decision."

"Ellen," he said, "most people who are sent home on ventilators only live for a month or so. We send them home to have some time with their families and get their affairs in order. Rarely does anyone survive for seven years on a ventilator at home. It amazed me how you kept him alive."

I am no longer angry with this doctor. I realize that he believed that he had no choice but to proceed. He had been shaken by Ron's age, so close to his own. His distress about a disease for which he could do nothing had made his keeping Ron alive the one thing that he believed that he had to offer. He had to act without the counsel or the support of his colleagues and did what was expected of him. Unfortunately, without systems in place that help doctors, social workers, and patients contemplate complex situations, there are few choices.

ONGOING CRISES

Pauline Boss (1999) offers the concept of ambiguous loss. She describes two kinds of losses. In the first, a member of a family may be physically absent but psychologically present, and it is unclear whether the person is alive or dead, as in the case of a prisoner of war. In the second, a person is physically present but psychologically absent because of a psychological or neurological condition. Ron's case offers a third type of ambiguous loss in which he was both physically and mentally present, but his physical capacities continually diminished and it remained unclear from day to day if he would live or die. From Boss's point of view, people who experience extreme uncertainty with loss often become frozen with grief. Normal decisions and actions may become extremely difficult under these circumstances. This was certainly true in our case.

As Ron's illness progressed, it took an army of friends, family, nurses, social workers, lawyers, and psychotherapists to keep him at home and to keep us all well. Crises occurred regularly with the ventilator so that Ron would be left gasping for breath. Insurance companies refused to pay for his care. Much of our energy was spent advocating for his physical and emotional needs. Each of us went in and out of depression, and our family splintered and reconfigured many times. It soon became clear that we needed help from others if we were to manage our situation.

SENDING OUT THE CALL:
BUILDING INTERNAL AND EXTERNAL RESOURCES

Before Ron's illness, I had witnessed families in therapy feel shame when difficulties overwhelmed them. Even illness, which no one could blame them for, produced profound humiliation and a sense that illness was a private matter not to be foisted upon others. When working with these clients, I often challenged their desire for isolation and encouraged them to reach out and create a wider circle of support. After Ron became ill, I was surprised at how much I shared this desire for isolation.

This craving for isolation was not because others were not concerned, but in part came from a belief that we should be able to manage things on our own. From the time of Ron's diagnosis until he turned off the ventilator, almost everyone who knew and loved us was on red alert, ready to help. At first I resisted their efforts, and then I tried accepting their spontaneous acts of kindness, but ultimately I had to admit that even these were not enough. We needed to develop systems that would consistently help us make difficult decisions, manage our home care system, and raise money to pay for Ron's care.

In order to get the help we needed, I finally asked a group of friends to meet with me once a month. I thought if we created a group mind for problem solving, I could get more done. They were eager to help. One friend said that by offering help she felt some relief about our situation. At last, she could do something. It reassured her to think that if she ever had the need, others would be there to help her. At our meetings, I spoke about what was happening in our family. I raised issues about the nurses, the children, Ron's care, and even my distress about the changes in our relationship. My friends gave me the gift of their time and made suggestions that I had overlooked. Sometimes it was awkward shifting the balance of these friendships. As friends before, we had equally exchanged the stories of our lives. During Ron's illness I asked them to give me extra time and attention. They were more than generous, but we often had to sacrifice the easy flow of friendship and instead become a working body. In the long run they raised money to help keep Ron at home and helped us wage a legal battle against our insurance company as it tried to institutionalize Ron. Social workers often provide many of the functions of group process that we developed independently. They need not only to offer support for families, but also to convene a wider circle of friends and family who will help and to advocate for families in a managed care environment.

Even with the help of friends and extended family, the four of us in my immediate family struggled with depression at different times. Over the years of Ron's illness we were fortunate to work with a number of caring therapists as individuals, as a couple, and as a family. We did best with therapists who were able to tolerate the hopeless aspects of our situation while at the same time helping us sort out normal difficulties that we could address. We all believed that Ron was deeply ill in that we saw no end in sight except death. According to Arthur Frank (1998), most people want to tell "restitution stories," ones in which someone will be cured. These are also the stories that family members and therapists most want to hear. The stories that are not told and that others often do not want to hear are what Frank calls "chaos stories." These stories reflect the confusion of what earlier I spoke of as durational time. They have no beginning, middle, and end. One way to live with and move through a chaos story is for it to be witnessed by someone who is not overwhelmed by the pain of the story. Because ours was a chaos story, we found that social workers who had experienced their own chaos and could speak of it with us were most helpful. We were also encouraged by some to draw upon our spiritual practices as well as our psychological resources. This helped us enormously.

I learned that when a family is treated by multiple medical systems, all members of the team need to be part of any solution. This was particularly true of our home nursing team. From the beginning of Ron's illness I was acutely aware of the changes in Ron and the changes in our relationship. In order to feel close to Ron, I needed to be able to talk to him about this part of my experience. Ron often focused on what was the same; especially his internal thoughts and feelings, and he wanted me to pay attention to how we could still be the same with each other. These different perceptions and priorities often stood between us. The nurses lined up around Ron, making it that much more difficult for us to remain close. They hadn't known Ron before he was ill. They fully accepted him as he was. They thought I should be able to do the same. It is helpful for a practitioner to leave space in conversations for a couple to speak about their different experiences of illness.

In addition to working on how to fit with our family, the nurses constructed a system of their own. They needed to feel some control and guarded their territory, trying to take charge of what Ron did and did not do. Because they often did not agree with each other about how things should be done, their conflicts were playing out in our household. Occasionally I was forced to intervene and hold a nurses' meeting in which I tried with my best therapeutic skills to help them work out agreements, but because they often saw me as part of the problem, we would have benefited from an outside resource. The therapists we saw missed the significance of these disruptions on our family life, and they were never fully addressed. As Ron's condition worsened, these conflicts greatly added to our distress. In the work that I do with families who have caregivers, I include them on a regular basis in family sessions. Family boundaries that have worked in less stressful times often need to be reexamined and reconfigured in families struggling with catastrophic illness.

CONSCIOUS DEATH AND DYING: A QUEST STORY

In addition to restitution and chaos stories, Frank describes what he calls "quest stories." These are stories in which illness offers opportunities for learning for a patient and can also be useful to others. In my experience with ALS, I learned many lessons, but the most valuable came from Ron's decision in 1993, eight years after his diagnosis, to turn off his ventilator. Ron began this process by talking with our daughters and me about his increased thoughts of dying. After informing us, he wrote a letter to our families telling them that he had begun to think about dying. It had become almost impossible for him to use the computer. He was losing all speech. We were in financial jeopardy and our children had their lives on hold. He had begun to see that it was more and more difficult for us to provide him with a quality of life and also take care of ourselves. From that time on, he had many conversations with family, friends, spiritual teachers, and our psychotherapist. Ron had been holding onto life, but at this time he began to let go. He grew clearer about his wish to die. He went toward this decision with a sense of purpose, as if on a quest for him and with us. We followed his lead and learned from him how to move with him through his dying process.

At one point he was distressed about whether turning off the ventilator was a kind of suicide and discussed this with a well-known biomedical ethicist. He helped Ron come to the decision that in his situation he had the choice to allow his life to end naturally if he wished. Ron's physician also spoke with him about this decision over a number of months, assessing whether or not he was making this decision of his own accord and from a place of clarity and not depression. Finally, it was important to Ron that the larger community understood and approved of his decision. At Stanford University, a biomedical ethics committee made decisions in cases such as his. I attended a meeting of that group and presented Ron's wishes. Everyone in the group, though saddened, fully supported his choice.

Once he made his final decision, he began to say goodbye in one halting conversation after another. By then very few people could understand him, but it was very important to him to say goodbye in his own words. Because I could still hear his words, I sat with him through each of these conversations, making sure that he was understood.

When it was time, Ron, our daughters, the doctor, one of Ron's nurses, a close woman friend, and I sat in our living room. As the doctor hesitated, Ron nodded to him to begin. The doctor then gave him a small dose of morphine so he would relax. Ron wanted to die naturally without tubes or drugs. The doctor first removed the gastrostomy tube that had fed him, and then the ventilator. As soon as the tubes were gone, Ron's face changed. The strained, frozen look on his face melted away, and my handsome husband returned for a few brief moments. Then we sensed his leaving us with gentle ease. For all its sadness, it was an uplifting moment.

In work with ill clients, it is essential to talk with them and their families about death and dying. As with our family, spiritual beliefs and family practices of prayer need to be explored. It is important that ethical issues such as discontinuation of life supports be fully discussed in the light of shared values and religious practices. Dying has become an acceptable topic for exploration, allowing people to examine their fears and their wishes.

CONCLUSION

My witnessing Ron's illness and working with families living with ALS and other catastrophic illnesses have greatly affected my work as a therapist and as a teacher of therapists. In situations in which families are facing more than normal human beings are expected to bear, or have the resources to address, several questions may arise for therapists. They might include:

What do I have to offer in this situation?
What does healing mean for this family?
How might therapy, spirituality, and community interface to be helpful?

These are some of the questions that I ask the families that I work with who live with catastrophic illness. For myself, as a therapist, I now know that there is often very little I can do to help people change their situation. Instead, I offer my willingness to witness their suffering and to listen to their experience, without expecting change. In order to do this in situations that are often hopeless, I have learned to spend much more time helping clients focus on bearing pain by paying attention to it; witnessing the suffering of others by staying present and doing only what is possible; knowing that rational explanations don't explain the unexplainable; letting go control of the uncontrollable; and balancing responsibility to themselves with what they have to offer to others.

What I do in a more active way is to work with families to create a collaboration in which we search for spiritual, psychological, and social resources that might sustain them. In doing this we often call together extended family, friends, and other social supports, including social workers. This group works with the family to provide networks of support. I also bring my personal story to them, one of the most helpful parts of that story being that after Ron died, I found a way, step by step, to go on. I wrote about this a year after his death. I include it here to give a sense of how personal stories may help survivors call upon their resources.

A LONE WALK ON THE BEACH—ONE YEAR AFTER RON'S DEATH

I drove to Limantour Beach just at sunset. The night was foggy, but the sky was still streaked with the fading sun. There were very few cars in the parking lot. I took the path above the beach, the path along which we had pushed Ron's wheelchair, when we were still compelled to keep it all going, no matter what. I came to the small trail leading to the bluff above the beach and I vividly saw us placing those plastic sheets, one in front of the other, so his wheelchair could go up the path and not get stuck in the sand. How easy it was now just to walk up the path and how alone.

I climbed down from the bluff and struck out onto the beach, keeping my eyes on the faint streaks of sunlight. I got caught up in the beauty of the shapes and shadows, the birds flying and then feeding in the waves. I kept checking on the receding sun, counting on it to light my way. I found myself feeling slightly mad, singing "Amazing Grace," "Swing Low Sweet Chariot," and Hebrew songs that had only come to me as an adult during the nights when I walked the girls, as babies.

After a while, I turned back to return to my car, but whatever light there was had disappeared. I could barely see two feet in front of me and I was afraid. Suddenly I remembered years ago, on a huge lonely beach, just Ron and I alone. He was ecstatic. He ran into the water and came out shouting, chasing me, wanting to make love, wanting to sleep out under the stars. I was terrified at the vastness of the beach and ocean. Girls like me, from Jersey City, weren't used to big open spaces and I desperately wanted to withdraw back into the warm familiar indoors. I begged Ron to take me back to the house we had rented with friends. Since I was trembling and even though he didn't understand, we went back. There were other times. Early on in our marriage, on one of our first camping trips in Yosemite, I hid from the bears in our VW Bug. Ron slept outside close by. I spent most of the night watching over him, as if I could keep him safe.

He kept heading out and I kept holding on and now he was truly gone and I was alone, on another vast beach. I saw shadows moving. I thought about murderers and rapists without any help in sight. How stupid I was to be out alone in a deserted place! I felt panic rising in my throat. If Ron were there, I would have turned to him, leaned on him and had him lead me back to safety, but he wasn't there.

How could he leave me? We had agreed to go through this life together and he left me little bit by little bit. So now not knowing what else to do, I kept going back alone, one foot in front of the other. I felt terrified all the way back to the parking lot. Finally, when I saw the outline of my car, I realized that I was going to make it. For a moment I was excited, even elated with a glimmer of something new. Maybe, just maybe, this Jersey City girl would climb mountains, swim in cold rivers and head out on her own.

Living alone was a hard lesson for me, and it took many years for me to learn it. This is often hard for others. Sometimes it can help if we share our stories with each other as we face hard times.

APPENDIX: SUMMARY OF SUGGESTED THERAPEUTIC PRACTICES FOR SOCIAL WORKERS WORKING WITH FAMILIES FACING CATASTROPHIC ILLNESS

DIAGNOSIS

DILEMMA: MAINTAINING THE FAMILIAR WITH RADICAL CHANGE

1. Providing a safe container for the expression of intense shock and disbelief.
2. Facilitating conversations about the diagnosis with children and extended family members.
3. Bearing with the family the ambiguity of not knowing the outcome.
4. Searching for ways to maintain the normal everyday of life, especially for children.
5. Shifting anxiety about not knowing to finding out information from others.
6. Discussing ways that other family members and/or friends can participate in the crisis.
7. Helping families make and/or face medical decisions and prepare questions for meetings with doctors.
8. Advocating for families in their dialogues with medical and insurance systems.

ONGOING CRISES

DILEMMA: SUSTAINING HOPE WITH CONTINUING LOSS

1. Normalizing a distorted sense of time and feelings of anxiety and depression as predictable responses to ongoing crises.
2. Including your experiences with catastrophic illness and death.
3. Looking out for and treating overwhelming depression or anxiety in the patient and family members.
4. Facilitating conversations about the meanings of illness and death in the family and in the wider social context.
5. Searching out underlying values, beliefs, and family history that have led to these meanings.
6. Looking for stories and practices in the family and in the wider culture that offer other possible meanings and responses to illness and death.
7. Bearing and talking about the ongoing pain with the patient and the family as they witness the illness worsen.
8. Finding creative ways for the family to spend good times together within their limited circumstances.
9. Allowing for the different experiences and needs of the patient and family members.
10. Facilitating dialogues and planning that take into account these differences.
11. Convening a wider circle of friends and family to facilitate ongoing support networks.
12. Bringing nursing, medical, spiritual, and social-service providers together with the family to assess ongoing needs and to provide coordinated services.

CONSCIOUS DEATH AND DYING

DILEMMA: KNOWING THE UNKNOWABLE

1. Providing openings for conversations about death and dying.
2. Tolerating and experiencing intense grief with family members.
3. Exploring beliefs, meanings, and family stories about death and dying.
4. Participating with families in discussions about the economic, ethical, social, and spiritual implications of life-support systems.
5. Offering opportunities for friends, family members, and spiritual teachers to participate in these conversations.
6. Discussing desired rituals and practices in preparation for dying and death.

REFERENCES

Boss, P. 1999. *Ambiguous Loss.* Cambridge, MA: Harvard University Press.
Frank, A. 1998. Just listening: Narrative and deep illness. *Families, Systems & Health* 18(3): 197–212.
Hanh, T. N. 1975. *The Miracle of Mindfulness.* Boston: Beacon Press.

Johnson, F. 1996. *Geography of the Heart.* New York: Scribner.

Langer, L. 1975. *The Holocaust.* New Haven, CT: Yale University Press.

Levine, S. 1987. *Healing Into Life and Death.* New York: Anchor.

Lewis, C. S. 1976. *A Grief Observed.* New York: Bantam.

McDaniel, S., and T. Campbell. 1997. Training health professionals to collaborate. *Families, Systems and Health* 15(4): 353–360.

Polin, I. 1994. *Taking Charge: How to Master Common Fears of Long-Term Illness.* New York: Times Books.

Pulleyblank, E. 1996. Hard lessons. *Family Therapy Networker* 1:42–49.

——. 2000. Sending out the call: Community as a source of healing. *Families, Systems and Health* 17(4): 473–481.

Rolland, J. 1994. *Families, Illness and Disability: An Integrative Treatment Model.* New York: Basic Books.

Spiegel, D. 1993. *Living Beyond Limits.* New York: Fawcett Columbine.

3

THE LOSS OF A CHILD TO CANCER:
FROM CASE TO CASEWORKER

ROBERTA HOFFMAN

There is a wholeness about a person who can give himself away, who can give his time, his money, and his strength to others. — *Harold Kushner*

I **WORK** in a large pediatric teaching hospital, where for many years I have counseled acutely and chronically ill children and their families. I thought I was an empathic listener, sensitive to the pain and suffering that chronic and life-threatening illnesses bring to children and their families. I thought I was in touch with the intense feelings of sadness, rage, frustration, helplessness, and fear that parents experience when their children are sick. Nothing in my personal or professional life, however, adequately prepared me for the world that my family unwillingly entered in mid-August 1989, when our healthy fourteen-year-old son Aaron was diagnosed with osteosarcoma, bone cancer. Every assumption about life was shattered; every day raised new fears about Aaron's survival and ours, and many questions about my work with sick and dying patients. Aaron's illness taught us more than we ever wanted to learn about loss, about living in the shadow of death, and about battles that take place on many fronts. More than that, it taught us about ways the medical system can isolate the patient and family, almost making them untouchables, as if the contagion of the illness extended to acknowledging one's vulnerability or grief.

Aaron's diagnosis came only ten days after the first symptom, a dull pain below his right knee, which was thought to be and was initially diagnosed as a sports-related injury. The treatment for osteosarcoma in 1989 was a combination of radical surgery: either a below-the-knee amputation or a leg-sparing bone graft, which carried high risk for infection, along with intensive physical therapy, lifelong restrictions on physical activity, and at least a year of debilitating chemotherapy with potential risk for life-threatening infections and damage to vital organs. Most of the treatments were done in the hospital over several days, with innumerable outpatient appointments in between. Still reeling from the diagnosis, we had to make decisions quickly, beginning with choosing a treatment center. Although it seemed obvious that it should be through the outpatient pediatric oncology program affiliated with the hospital where I worked, it was not a simple choice for me because of anticipated privacy and confidentiality issues with patients, staff, and even friends who worked in the system. That would be my own burden, not Aaron's, and because we considered this the premier pediatric oncology center in the area, there really was no choice.

The next decision was whether to have surgery or chemotherapy first, the former assuring that the tumor would be removed up front but possibly allowing it to seed elsewhere, the latter offering the hope of saving his leg by reducing the size of the tumor significantly so that a new piece of bone could be placed. No one, least of all a child whose extracurricular life centered on competitive sports, should be faced with such a choice. Armed with the most current data and a cautiously optimistic surgeon, we chose chemo first to save Aaron's leg. He was due to start high school in two weeks, and we made an eleventh-hour decision to send him to a small private school close to our house, where several of his friends were enrolled. This was unquestionably one of the better decisions we made.

Walking into the cancer clinic the first time was simply terrifying. Symbolically and literally, we crossed from the healthy and secure world, as we had known it, into a world of suffering, uncertainty, and fear. A close friend had come with us, and we were very grateful for her support. Nevertheless, her presence was a stark reminder that this was catastrophic. Never before had we experienced a situation that we could not handle on our own. In the clinic were two large murals depicting underwater scenes from *Pinocchio*. In one, Pinocchio was tied at the waist to a huge boulder, which weighted him down. He looked terrified as he struggled to pull himself toward the surface. In the second, Pinocchio rode an enormous fish. His eyes were bulging as he propelled himself forward in a valiant attempt to escape. I was horrified by these images. For me, each poignantly symbolized the sheer terror and helplessness we were experiencing and the enormity and ferocity of the disease we faced. How could anyone think that these paintings were in any way cute or reassuring? Over the course of Aaron's illness, I commented about these murals many times, but each time I was met with a shrug, chuckle, or blank stare. How could they be so clueless? My second observation was that one of the nurses had beautiful blond hair that fell below her waist. She wore it in a headband, Alice in Wonderland style. It was clearly her most prominent feature, and she frequently fluffed it and adjusted the headband. What was she thinking? Did she ever consider the impact this had on her young patients who had lost even some basic thing that they assumed was their birthright, like hair?

Dr. Jerome Groopman, a renowned physician, researcher, and author, writes in *The Measure of Our Days* about the struggle and turmoil of both doctor and patient in fighting life-threatening illness and the despair surrounding it; about how he understands the sacredness of the doctor-patient relationship; and about the journey they must embark on together. He talks about how hard it is to give patients bad news, how essential it is to give hope, and how important it is to understand a family's strength in order to help fortify them and create a holding environment in the face of catastrophic illness. "After you give the bad news . . . you mobilize your resources to fight to save this person. You look hard into the eyes of the family and search for the core of their inner strength. You need to find this . . . nurture it. . . . You need to understand this inner strength, where it comes from and how deep and resilient it is. Once you find it, you try to take it into your hand and fuse it with your own, because together this creates the unified force required to sustain the patient through the hell that awaits, and carry him back to normal life" (1997:91).

The attending physician met with Aaron, my husband, Ken, and me. In the room were two oncology fellows. They did not speak, although we learned that one would be Aaron's "fellow," the oncologist in training who would follow him. The attending was factual and blunt, and delivered his message in a rote, stylized manner as though he was reading a warning label on a bottle of pills. He told us that osteosarcoma is aggressive, its treatments toxic and damaging to the heart, kidneys, liver, and lungs; that Aaron would likely lose his leg (even though the orthopedic surgeon had given us a great deal of hope that the leg could be saved). He repeatedly used the word "poison" to describe the chemotherapy. By definition, poison means any substance that can cause injury or death, and children are taught from an early age that poisons are dangerous and lethal. Poisons do not cure; medicines might. What message did he think this conveyed to a child and to two frightened parents? We heard about statistics and protocols, but not a word about coping. I don't remember much in the way of a personal outreach other than a few words about his awareness that we had friends in common, including some of his colleagues, and a question about how we wanted to handle that vis-à-vis confidentiality. Most of the conversation was directed toward Ken and me. Aaron was silent but tearful when he learned he would lose his hair, would never play sports again, might lose his leg, and would need at least one year of treatment. We looked to the doctor for signs of his strength, his commitment to embark on this journey with us, and his ability to provide a holding environment to support us. He spent little effort getting to know Aaron or us. His overall message was that this was a bad disease and that our lives would be changed forever. Although we saw him many times over the next four and a half years and considered him an expert in the field and a good and decent man, his bedside manner and style never changed. He never seemed to understand what it meant to connect to or comfort patients or share grief the way Jerry Groopman does. He never seemed to understand the power of words or the power and negativity of his delivery. In actuality, we had more in common than not. We shared ethnic, religious, educational, and socioeconomic backgrounds, came from the same community, and had friends in common. He and I were "colleagues," and we later learned that he had a daughter Aaron's age. Our hope was that this would connect us in some personal way, would perhaps make him more invested or would help to transcend some of the traditional boundaries between doctor and patient, but it never did. Throughout Aaron's treatment he remained distant, scientific, and objective. Taking refuge in science and research seemed to protect him from becoming "wounded" or affected by our suffering.

The oncology fellow had a very different style, which was distressing and anxiety-provoking in a different way. He was devoted to his patients and worked tirelessly on their behalf, for which we were all extremely grateful, but he hovered, and he bound his own anxiety by bombarding families with far more scientific detail and medical data than we needed, wanted, or could handle. He did this with me more than others because I was an "insider" and a colleague, and it was a constant struggle to keep him from doing it with Aaron and Ken. He wore his anxiety on his sleeve, and this served to heighten ours, especially mine. Having worked in a medical system for many years, I knew enough about elevated creatinines and low platelet counts to know when these might be signals of serious complications. Many patients relapsed and many died during the course of Aaron's illness. We sensed that the fellow struggled with this on his own, inasmuch as there appeared to be rigid professional norms about being either vulnerable or "too involved" and nothing built into the system in the way of supervision, psychoeducation, or counseling to support staff to help them deal with their awesome responsibilities or their grief.

If we experienced the fellow as anxious and hovering, the clinic nurses and some of the inpatient nurses were the opposite. The outpatient nurses were businesslike and flip. There was a disconnect between how they behaved and what was happening in the infusion room. Patients often vomited through treatments, screamed through painful spinal taps, or sobbed quietly under the covers, but the nurses often joked and carried on in a perfunctory, detached way, as though they were performing routine car maintenance. Some staff members were wonderful and able to comfort anxious parents and children; others seemed to have little patience to wait for children to stop crying or vomiting. Some of the inpatient staff did better, but not all.

Throughout the year, Aaron struggled to keep weight on without the support of any professional nutritional guidance, which, shockingly, was not built into the program. Neither was any form of alternative or complementary therapy. We were too frightened to seek it out on our own because it was devalued by the doctors. Another glaring omission was the lack of a consulting psychiatrist in a program where probably 75 percent of the patients were depressed and some may have benefited from a short course of medication. We quickly learned that the attending physician was in charge of the protocol for osteosarcoma but not for the patient. We saw him mostly for quick check-ins during rounds, or, more pointedly, when things were not going well and a change in protocol was needed. There was a different oncologist attending every month, each of whom was an expert in a different childhood cancer, but not osteosarcoma, so most of the time the doctor in charge did not know the patient or his or her disease-specific issues. This was compounded by a young, inexperienced staff of inpatient residents on their first or second oncology rotation who provided frontline care. Unless he was "on service," Aaron's fellow had no authority to write orders or make treatment decisions. Half the time we felt as if there was no one in charge.

The treatments were horrible, isolating, and fraught with complications, delays, and debilitating side effects. Aaron vomited through most treatments and was given sedatives to make him sleep, which sometimes he did for most of the admission. Nurses gowned and gloved to protect themselves from bodily exposure to the toxic chemicals, which ran through his veins. During his first treatment, the chemo was set to run at double speed, a mistake that could have had devastating consequences, and once I discovered that a "rescue" drug to protect Aaron's bladder was given six hours late. One of the most frightening complications occurred when Aaron had thrombocytopenia with a platelet count so low that he could have bled to death at any moment. Despite this emergency, it took a week for a senior hematologist to send the blood to a special lab for analysis. I knew enough to be alarmed, and enough to know how the system protects itself when "errors" occur. Things like this made me hypervigilant and afraid to leave the bedside.

Aaron hated every treatment. He brought his own linens and pillow as he quickly developed an aversion to the smell of everything "hospital." He wore old clothes and arrived armed with tapes, joke books, and any diversion he could think of to while away the time. Mostly he preferred to sleep through treatments, though the amount of Ativan he regularly got slowed him so much that he couldn't shake it for days. He didn't want friends to make hospital visits. He didn't want to be known that way. Nothing in his childhood prepared him for the sick role, and he struggled to define himself, especially in a new school. Everything about having a chronic, much less life-threatening, illness is an assault on the tasks of adolescence. On the brink of burgeoning independence and rapid physical and emotional growth, Aaron was faced with life-altering changes in every aspect of his being, in his ability to set or reach goals or separate from his parents, whom he needed for protection, advocacy, and support. One of us stayed with him every night he was in the hospital. We had promised this to him when he got sick, and he wanted it. Our lives were insane. We slept and showered at the hospital, worked when we could, went home only to take care of household tasks or to spend time with our seven-year-old son David, who was often farmed out to friends because we do not have immediate family in Boston. We were always exhausted, and we lived in constant fear of a relapse.

Self-disclosure and exposure continued to be issues for me at work. I often encountered my patients and families at night and on weekends, and I wondered what they thought. Sometimes they saw me with Aaron, and some asked about it. I shared information selectively, and when appropriate I asked advice from medical and other staff whom I trusted. Sometimes I shared cases with doctors who had rotated through the oncology service and knew Aaron. It was awkward for me, and more so for them. With some families the disclosure connected us in a mutually supportive way, with others not so. One mother lambasted me when I suggested that she and her husband communicate more openly with their sixteen-year-old daughter, who was very frightened about a serious complication of her transplant. She would not allow the doctors to share any medical information with the girl or allow her to meet with our child psychologist, stating that I should know better because of Aaron, and if I didn't, I should not be giving her advice. I had a very different experience with another mother. Her three-year-old daughter and Aaron had surgery on the same day, and we found ourselves side by side in the surgical family waiting area. This traditionally dressed Moslem woman, whose English was extremely limited, took my hand and, with tears in her eyes, told me she would pray for my son. When her child died several months later, she wrote thanking me for all I had done for her family over the years, and ended the note with "I hope your son be well. I pray." I am Jewish, with family and a strong attachment to Israel. She is an Arab, with most of her family and roots in Lebanon. We met, by chance, in a Boston hospital, with me in the professional role of providing emotional support to her family, and ended as two wounded parents desperately fighting for our children's lives, able to reach out to one another beyond linguistic, political, and cultural barriers in a most human and compassionate way.

Our son David came to the hospital all the time at first, but over time he resisted it because it was too hard and too scary to see Aaron so sick and miserable. Our daughter, Danya, was in college 750 miles away. She was very close to Aaron and did the best she could long-distance. We were a very close family, and we all felt helpless.

It was hard for friends and family, and for Aaron's peers. Some family and friends were outstandingly there for us; others, who should have been, incredibly and disappointingly, were not, even those who should have known better. Patients and families I work with often say the same. We represent every family's worst fear, and those not touched by illness or catastrophe are often not able or willing to put themselves at emotional risk, so simply flee, justifying it by saying that they don't know what to do or how to help. We found that professional mental-health clinicians didn't do much better. A social worker was assigned to us, and a psychologist was assigned to Aaron through the clinic. His job was to support Aaron; her job was to support the rest of us. The social worker was a pleasant woman, but singularly unhelpful. I never knew if she was intimidated or limited by the fact that she and I were colleagues and did the same work, but she seemed totally at a loss as to how to handle it and never raised the issue. At no point did she sit down with me to acknowledge it or to ask how she could best support us. Neither, even more concretely, did she provide any kind of road map, psychoeducation, or model about how to get through this. We did not need housing, meal coupons, or transportation and were not a dysfunctional family, so she seemed to have little to offer. I asked her to call Ken and Danya many times, but she didn't, and looked to her to advocate for us, but she couldn't, so after a while it was simpler just to avoid her. Aaron worked with a male psychologist. He was an armchair sports enthusiast, and they connected first and foremost on that level. Initially, we were skeptical of his laid-back style, but eventually we came to respect greatly his clinical skills, despite the limitations of the system. For a long time, during Aaron's illness and after, we used him as a barometer for how we were doing, and, more specifically, how the children were doing.

Like others in the program, we struggled to compartmentalize the cancer in whatever way we could. We all knew we had children who could die. None of us was in denial about that, although every time we got frustrated or upset, we were seen as angry parents. It was easier to label us difficult than to acknowledge our suffering or how intractable the system was. We had to interface with two separate institutions that were ostensibly a combined program but did not even share a blood-results reporting system, much less other systems to make even one admission or discharge simpler. Children are not supposed to get cancer. They are not supposed to experience chronic pain and invasive, disfiguring procedures or suffer the humiliation of baldness and bodily scars. They are not supposed to miss half of high school, school trips, and the prom. They are not supposed to live in the shadow of death. When children are sick, spiritual wounds run deep, and children facing life-threatening illness need reassurance, encouragement, hope, and spiritual sustenance. They need answers to tough questions that often cannot be articulated, much less answered, by medical providers or the family. Sometimes these questions are best addressed by clergy. The Jewish chaplain was a retired rabbi who had no formal hospital chaplaincy training. He was a gentle and soft-spoken man, but, remarkably, he never seemed to remember us or Aaron's diagnosis or progress, despite seventy hospitalizations over four and a half years. He made little attempt to ascertain our level of Jewish education, involvement, or observance, to get to know Aaron, or to engage in any kind of meaningful religious or spiritual discussion with him or with us. Had he just scratched the surface, he would have learned we were suffering an acute crisis of faith, another profound loss for each of us.

At the end of the year, Aaron resumed a reasonably normal life. He appeared on a TV commercial for the clinic, finished his freshman year on the honor roll, volunteered at the hospital that summer because he wanted to give something back, and participated in an educational day at the clinic to teach schools how to support students with cancer. Sixteen months off treatment, in November of his junior year, on the last CT scan on the protocol, a nodule was found on the edge of his lung. The relapse was almost worst than the initial diagnosis. The first time we didn't know what we faced. This time we did. Aaron faced another year of intensive treatment, but with a diminished chance of cure. We learned at this juncture that Aaron had had a 95 percent chance of cure after the end of the first year of treatment, and that his doctors were genuinely shocked. Undergoing more surgery and twelve months of chemotherapy was more horrific than the first time, and I do not know how we got through it. Our daughter moved home for the year after graduation and experienced the daily turmoil she had seen only episodically while she was in college.

Encouraging Aaron, who was by nature upbeat and optimistic, to adopt a positive attitude a second time around was enormously challenging. He often left school in tears because he was overwhelmed and distressed about missing so much academically and socially. During one admission while his psychologist was on vacation, we asked for someone to see him because we had never seen him so depressed. He refused to talk to us or to start chemotherapy. The head psychologist from the clinic came to the floor. Despite my plea, she refused to see him "because they did not have a therapeutic relationship." She told me that she would let his psychologist, whom she supervised, know when he returned—in a week. She simply refused to get involved. This was the response to a parent and child crying out for help. This was the response to a colleague who worked in the hospital next door, who was trained to identify crisis, to know how to ask for and use help. This was the response from the director of the psychosocial unit, who set the standard for mental-health services and psychoeducation to staff. We had already felt that the program was more focused on research and science than on patient care, and that there was little fusion between the medical and mental health sides, and we now understood how limited the role of mental health really was. Why it was so didn't matter. What mattered was that we were in crisis and there was no response.

After this encounter, we found a psychologist in the community whose expertise was in chronic and life-threatening illness. He was considered one of the most respected family therapists in the area. He was warm, personable, and empathic and truly seemed to "get it." He had trained in the clinic and understood and validated its limitations. He cried with us, and even Ken, who was a skeptic, felt supported. The overriding message was that we were doing everything "right," and, in light of the situation, were doing remarkably well. Three months later he abruptly announced he could no longer see us because he had a full schedule of teaching, lecturing, writing, and seeing patients, and that Aaron's treatment schedule was so unpredictable that it was not "convenient" for him to hold an open slot. It wasn't "convenient" that Aaron had cancer either, or that we had so little control over our own lives. He told us we could call him from time to time, but when we did, it was clear that he was not willing to reengage or flex his schedule. Like the oncology attending, we had much in common. He had children around our children's ages, lived in our community, and belonged to our synagogue. Without much warning and without a plan for follow-up, he simply abandoned us.

The drugs the second time around were more toxic, the complications more life-threatening, and the prospect that Aaron may not make it hung over our heads daily. Nonetheless, he completed a whole year without a relapse. His doctors were guardedly hopeful, and they told him that he still had a fighting chance, although sometimes their facial expressions and behavior belied this. Three months off treatment, Aaron relapsed in the pelvis. That marked a decided turning point, and coincided within two months with Danya's engagement and, a month later, my father's death. We were too frantic and numb to deal with the death other than to perform perfunctory religious rituals for the week of Shiva (mourning). It was like a rehearsal. Aaron had always been resolute and determined, but from this point on, he became even more so. He tried to protect everyone in our family even when he didn't have the strength to do so, as if blanketing us with his courage and strength could shield us from pain and him from harm. His first response whenever a drug did not work was, "What's the plan? What's next?" And there always was another plan. By now we had trained the fellow not to convey messages like "Aaron didn't meet the challenge" or "the patient failed the treatment" (both referring to not responding to a drug or treatment modality), though this is common medical parlance and was charted as such. Aaron responded extremely well to some new drugs, but unfortunately his heart could not handle them. Another defining moment—he had had some heart damage from the cumulative chemotherapy. During that summer we interviewed a psychiatrist who could not get past our collective loss history and onto the crisis at hand, and eventually we found a psychologist, who was recommended by friends who had a family member who died of cancer. It was December 1993, two months before Aaron died. We were desperate, and we conveyed this to the therapist, recounting being abandoned before. He reassured us that he would not do so, but astoundingly, less than a month later, he did, also citing his busy schedule as to why he could not accommodate ours, which was increasingly chaotic and unpredictable given Aaron's medical complications and emergency appointments. More astonishingly, he never called us despite Aaron's condition. Two months after Aaron died, he saw us in the community, and after a perfunctory word of condolence (somehow he had known of Aaron's death), told us that if we wanted to see him, we knew how to reach him. What was he thinking?

Aaron graduated from high school and was accepted at seven excellent colleges. This was an important confirmation of his extraordinary performance in high school despite missing about half of it, and he looked forward to attending the University of Michigan in the fall. Our last hope was an experimental drug, which was supposed to stop the blood flow to tumors. This class of angiogenesis drugs received international attention the past few years, and continues to show great promise. Dr. Judah

Folkman, a preeminent researcher and surgeon at the hospital where I work, developed it, and he thought Aaron might respond because of his response to interferon. This drug was being tested and showed promise at other cancer centers, but the clinic was not willing to pursue this for Aaron even though we had had reassurance that if we could get it released from the National Cancer Institute, Aaron could get it on a compassionate-use basis. We used every connection we had at the NCI and at the company that manufactured the drug. The program was not behind this, although no one told us this directly. We believe we were deceived about the availability of the drug at the center, where it was slated to be tested in a few months, and believe the program stonewalled the NCI as well. Suddenly, we found ourselves not only fighting for Aaron's life but also fighting the center itself, caught in a battle of institutional jealousies and vicious medical politics. We received a call from the NCI informing us that the drug would be made available to Aaron beginning on a Saturday. When the fellow tried to arrange it, he was informed this was not possible because the clinic was closed. The program was unwilling to administer it on the oncology unit of the hospital where Aaron always went on weekends for blood tests and for all inpatient treatments. This was unacceptable to the NCI. We don't know what took place behind the scenes, but the drug was started the next day. For several weeks it appeared to be holding the cancer at bay, and the hope was that it would buy Aaron time until the next generation of the drug and the next phase of testing became available. Dr. Folkman was present for each treatment and spent hours getting to know us and talking about his work. He brought other doctors to meet Aaron and encouraged him to keep a journal and to think of himself as a pioneer. He said he had seen too many miracles in his forty-year career not to believe in them, and that somebody was always the first. We learned so much from him about healing and hope and about his long struggle to develop a new class of drugs. We learned about his efforts to develop an innovative approach to a deadly disease despite discouraging odds, brutal competition for research funding, ridicule and skepticism from colleagues who relied on time-tested but often ineffectual treatments, and the dark side of medical and commercial politics, which limit patient access to new treatments. We learned about patience and persistence, and about Dr. Folkman's never-ending commitment to educating colleagues and patients. In his book *Dr. Folkman's War*, Robert Cooke writes, "The most basic skill of the physician is the ability to have comfort with uncertainty, to recognize with humility the uncertainty inherent in all situations, to be open to the ever present possibility of the surprising, the mysterious, and even the holy, and to meet people there" (2001:350). Dr. Folkman travels and lectures extensively and is said to carry around a long list of patients who have contacted him for new treatments. He is reported to call at least ten of them every night to offer them encouragement and whatever "humble" advice he can. It is hard to describe what it is like to sit with this man, who many experts say will someday be nominated for a Nobel Prize for his work. He is a brilliant clinician who has dedicated his postsurgical career to biomedical research, but whose compassion, humility, and connectedness are so healing and "real" that it is like being in the presence of G'd.

Unfortunately, for Aaron, even this was little and too late. Many experts believe that angiogenesis therapy, perhaps in conjunction with other innovative therapies will someday make cancer a chronic rather than life-threatening disease and will supplant the more traditional toxic treatments of chemotherapy, radiation, and surgery. Angiogenesis therapy was tested and has been approved for use in exponentially more powerful doses than existed in 1994, including at the center where Aaron was treated.

Aaron died in February 1994, three months shy of his nineteenth birthday and what should have been his second semester in college. His last hospitalization was a travesty. He was transferred to different floors six times in eleven days so that there was never one doctor or one team in place for long. He was admitted because of congestive heart failure but was not seen by a cardiologist for three days after being moved to the oncology unit. A week before he died, an epidural was placed for pain management. It was a delicate procedure, and his blood pressure dropped to dangerously low levels. A surgical resident came to the bedside in the recovery area. Without acknowledging the situation, or us, he thanked the senior anesthesiologist for letting him observe the procedure with a simple, "Thanks so much. That was a lot of fun." Fun? Aaron's doctor, who stood next to us, flinched, but no other clinician seemed to take note. Throughout the last week, Aaron was breathless and could not talk, but when he did, he made it clear that he had not given up and did not want to stop treatment. No one told him or us that we had exhausted all options or that he would never make it home. Angiogenesis treatments continued until the last weekend. Hardly anyone from the clinic, and few from the inpatient unit, came to our room, and there appeared to be considerable team conflict around his management. We were already alienated and isolated, and we became more so. Dr. Folkman and the fellow were still actively engaged, almost lone players on the team. The resident on service the last weekend had never met us before. She made virtually no effort to do so now. She challenged Dr. Folkman's recommendation about using lasix and, from our perspective, remained totally detached, relying on a standard cookbook approach to "managing the dying patient," a task she seemed to find time-consuming and annoying. Our own rabbi and close friends, including two staff physicians, helped us make end-of-life decisions and encouraged us to hold on to hope for as long as we could. Aaron was not ready to die, and was outraged by the prospect of being deprived of life when on the threshold of starting college. He had been doing reasonably well on the new treatment, and believed he had time on his side. I think the fellow did as well. In the end he was in a double bind, and he almost fell apart: caught between a rigid medical establishment that did not allow him to get too involved, and one more desperate family that begged him to. I am grateful that Aaron was too sick and too medicated to know what struggles ensued, and that he died thinking everything possible was being done for him. He knew that we could never have done less, nor would he have wanted us to.

Jerry Groopman writes, "Choice is an assertion of courage and dignity. Dignity for a person with an incurable illness is created by the capacity to remain a person, with a will, to make choices, even when life offers such brutally limited options" (1997:57). Aaron maintained a sense of humor and dignity throughout his illness, never relinquished control, and demonstrated a spirit and will to live that were compelling. His psychologist at the center recognized this and reassured us (and the team) that we had not pushed Aaron into any treatment, and that he was determined to do everything he could to stay alive.

Kitchen Table Wisdom is an inspirational collection of vignettes about life's lessons, healing, and spirituality written by Dr. Rachel Naomi Remen, a pioneer in the field of mind-body health and healing. She writes: "Sometimes our vulnerability is our strength, our fears develops courage, and our woundedness is the road to our integrity." In his eighteen years, Aaron knew more about love, devotion, compassion, and strength of character than many learn in a lifetime. His death was not one that should make either the hospital or the oncology program proud. It is not an overstatement to say that as he became sicker, we were abandoned not only by two respected psychologists in the community trained to work with sick and dying patients, but also, apart from a few (including Aaron's psychologist at the center), by a program that considers itself the gold standard of pediatric oncology. What was so distressing was the refusal and inability of so many trained professionals to acknowledge or share in any meaningful way their own loss, or the all-consuming sadness and tragedy of ours. Some never even had the decency to send a condolence card.

Ken Doka and the contributors to his anthology (1989) write about disenfranchised grief and compassion fatigue, where clinicians who work with traumatized and dying patients, who are exposed to loss on a daily basis, learn to protect themselves from burnout by becoming numb to the pain and suffering around them. Most of the loss remains unacknowledged, unresolved, and ungrieved, sanctioned by systems like this one whose message is "don't feel," "be strong," and "move on to the next patient." Rachel Remen (1996) believes that this approach is an assertion that someone can die in front of us without its touching us—but one, she adds, that denies one's humanity and makes no sense. Some doctors and nurses who treated Aaron still avoid eye contact with me in the halls; others mumble a quick hello and keep walking. Few have ever asked how we are. After Aaron died, we met with high-level hospital administrators and with the chief of medicine to discuss our experience, and specifically the last eleven days. The chief of medicine defended his resident and told me that some doctors don't learn. We told him it was his mandate to make sure they did. We also participated in a lengthy multicenter end-of-life care study, which I think revealed serious flaws in the center's practice, and I actively participated in an effort to improve the quality of pastoral care to Jewish patients and families.

There has not been a day since the diagnosis that I have not thought about what it is like to continue to work with sick and dying patients. There is not a morning that I walk into the hospital that I do not think about Aaron, and some days I wonder why I have not left to sell real estate or do something more uplifting. This is what I am trained to do, and I could not continue if I did not find it important, challenging, inspiring, and rewarding. More than most, I understand the value of this work. I work in a good program that recognizes and respects teamwork and the role of social work. During Aaron's illness, I derived most of my own support from the team and from my social-work colleagues, who were my personal barometer and cheerleading squad. They could "talk the talk" and were willing to accompany me on "the walk," sharing and validating the experience as few others could.

Shortly after Jerry Groopman's first book was published, I attended a talk he gave. He said, "When we cope with catastrophic illness we don't have many choices. We must accept the reality of what is happening, and must move forward . . . that many aspects of illness are filled with more dread than what is seen under the microscope, namely fear, isolation and the loss of the spiritual self." Statistics are meaningless. A 95 percent chance of survival means nothing if you are in the other 5 percent; and a 1 percent chance of survival is everything if you are in that 1 percent. Every patient hopes to be that 1 percent and could not go on without that hope. Not all patients are willing to endure what Aaron did, but because he insisted on pursuing every avenue of hope, so did we. I learned that while being realistic, we must never give up. Dr. Sidney Farber, for whom the Dana Farber Cancer Institute is named, had a sign on his desk that read something like: "As long as the patient is alive there is hope he can be cured." Dr. Folkman passionately believes that the first rule of care is to give patients hope, but even when a cure is ultimately not possible, there is always hope for dignity, peace, and spiritual healing. Those who provide bedside care must be spiritual as well as physical healers. The more we learn about the connection between mind and body, the more we learn about the physical consequences of despair and the benefits of hope and a positive outlook. There is a powerful prayer in Judaism called the Mi Sheberach that recognizes both. The prayer is recited in the synagogue by a family member or friend of someone who is sick to ask for healing. Freeman and Abrams (1999) discuss this in their book on illness and health in the Jewish tradition: "Let your spirit rest upon all who are ill and comfort us. May we soon know a time of compete healing, a healing of the spirit, a healing of the body" (1999:102). *Refuat ha nefesh; refuat ha guf:* Some believe that healing comes from the soul, and in this prayer the soul is mentioned first. At a minimum there is a need to nourish the spirit as much as the body. Therese Rando writes, "Hope is an essential requirement for existence to continue, for the threat of demise to be confronted, and for life's meaning to be sustained" (1993:270). There is nothing glamorous or sexy about end-of-life care. No one is going to win a Nobel Prize for sitting at the bedside of a dying patient, but it could be the most important work we do.

I have not written about our lives before Aaron got sick. Suffice it to say we were happy, healthy, and blessed. Nor have I written much about the "good" and compassionate caretakers sprinkled throughout Aaron's treatment. Of course there were some, and we were grateful for each of them. But they were in the minority, and what continues to reverberate for us is how vulnerable we were and how isolated we became within a system that prided itself on being able to provide total patient care. Ours is not a culture that readily embraces sickness and death, especially when it comes to children. Counseling families facing these challenges is extremely demanding and emotionally laden, and it evokes powerful countertransference issues, which are much easier to suppress than to face. Rachel Remen observes that doctors pay a terrible price for their hard-won objectivity. It prevents them from being able to cry, accept comfort, or find meaning. She adds that sometimes there is a suffering so unspeakable, a vulnerability so extreme that it goes beyond words, beyond explanation, and even beyond healing. In the face of such suffering, all we can do is to bear witness so no one need to suffer alone. The doctors, nurses, and mental health professionals who treated Aaron "looked like us." We mirrored back to them their lives and their families. Instead of reaching out, opening their hearts, and acknowledging this unspeakable tragedy, our vulnerability and theirs, instead of staying the course, they dismissed us. They wanted families like us, who had "failed their treatment" to take our children home to die. We were unwelcome reminders of the limitations of science, of their repetitive losses, and of the illusion that any family is safe.

Ken Doka, a well-known teacher and author on life-threatening illness and bereavement, spoke several years ago at a national bereavement conference sponsored by the New England Center for Loss and Transition. He spoke about the hospice movement, his work, and three requests that are most often articulated by sick and dying patients. These resonated with me and should be the foundation of the work we do with sick and dying patients. The first request is for *help*: helping patients and families take those difficult first steps after hearing the diagnosis: help them learn about the illness, assist them in making treatment, career and family decisions, and helping them to identify strengths and coping strategies that will enable them to adjust to the illness and regain some modicum of control in their lives. The second request is to *stay*: to stick by them literally and emotionally as they struggle through changes in their lives, losses, and uncertainty. Harold Kushner, the author of *When Bad Things Happen to Good People* (1981), tells a story of a mother who sends her young son out on an errand. He is gone a long time, and when he returns she asks him where he was because she was worried. He tells her about meeting a boy down the road who was crying because his bicycle was broken, and that he had offered to help him fix it. The mother asks what he knows about fixing bicycles. The boy replies "Nothing, but I sat down with him and helped him cry." In describing her own medical training, Rachel Remen says there were not many opportunities to learn compassion. The message in her medical training was that in order to serve, you had to be strong, never vulnerable. She writes, "Doctors are taught to fix pain but not share it" (2000:209). On a daily basis, those of us who work in health settings are exposed to sadness and catastrophe. Clinicians are taught to manage the dying patient and to recognize grief—but not to share it. Too often we hide behind protective hardware and justify this in the name of maintaining professional distance. Remen says that "the way we distance ourselves from loss is the way we distance ourselves from life." Even when there is nothing else to do, we can sit with our patients and cry. Tears link us to each other, to our humility, and to our humanity.

The third request is to *listen*: to listen to what patients and families have to say and are experiencing, to be willing to tolerate the intense feelings of rage, sadness, fear, and the like that come from traumatic life experiences. Being able to say and mean "I'm sorry" is a powerful entree to developing a meaningful and mutually respectful relationship. I had a fifteen-year-old patient who was newly diagnosed with a brain tumor. Her parents were biochemists with impressive credentials. They spent the first few days in the hospital challenging every diagnostic test, every treatment decision, and intimidating everyone on the floor, frequently reducing staff to tears. Out of desperation I was called in to "do something," that is, fix it. Initially, they rejected the notion that they needed emotional support, challenged my competency, and tried to intimidate me as they had done to others. After twenty minutes of listening to them rail about every aspect of the experience thus far, and what they already had researched, I reached over, touched them lightly, and quietly said, "I am really sorry about your daughter. You must be so frightened." They stopped short and started to cry. We spent the next two hours talking about the death of their first child at the age of three, how they could ever face potentially losing another child, how helpless and scared they were, and how they would ever be able to trust "strangers" with their daughter's life. We talked about their coping style and why this might not work for them over the long run, and about ways to begin to establish a working relationship with medical providers in whose hands they were placing their precious child. I met with them several times before they were transferred to the oncology service, and at the last meeting, they thanked me for being able to sit with their pain. There are many times when you do more for patients by opening up your heart, and being willing to absorb and share some of their pain than by anything fancier or "more clinical." It has worked for me with even the most defensive and angry patients and parents.

David Browning is a social worker who does bereavement counseling at Safe Passages in Cambridge, Massachusetts. He tells a story about a twelve-year-old girl who had been referred to him because of major depression following her brother's death (see chapter 1). In the course of therapy she told him she had had a dream where she was carrying two buckets, a large one and a small one. Both were filled with tears. After many sessions she told him that her small bucket was empty and she wanted to end therapy. He felt there was much more to do, and he tried to convince her to stay in treatment. When he reminded her that the big bucket was still full, her reply was that she would always carry that bucket. Some buckets are heavier than others, and some will never be emptied. We unloaded a small bucket in family grief counseling after Aaron died, but we will always carry the heavy one, the one that is filled with sadness, disappointment, and anger about the injustice of Aaron's suffering, and at a system that embraced "success" and abandoned those who "failed."

Mental health professionals and other caregivers have a unique role to play in a patient and family's struggle with life-threatening illness. Ken Doka likens that role to a candle that provides warmth and light along a dark path. He writes, "Caregivers can provide that light through a sometimes scary and treacherous path. The journey might still be dark, but the light can make it less terrifying" (1993:288). Our job as social workers is to help patients and families develop the strength and tools to illuminate and guide their way. As medical social workers we have a unique role in supporting both patients and staff, in providing psychoeducation to them about the illness experience, and in modeling empathy and respect. In social work, unlike medicine, there is a built-in system of support through supervision, which teaches and encourages self-searching and self-awareness in addition to clinical skill. This helps us understand the powerful transference and countertransference, and helps us learn how to use ourselves differentially. What many of us learned in traditional social-work training about neutrality and professional boundaries does not work in all situations.

More than anything else, patients and families need to know that people care. In the end, that is what matters.

There is a story whose origin I do not know. It was given to me as a student, and I give it to my students. It is about an old man who walks on the beach day after day, picking up beached starfish and tossing them back into the ocean. One day, he is approached by a young man who asks him why he does this. He replies that if he does not do it, the starfish will die in the morning sun. The young man ridicules him, telling him not to waste his time because there are thousands of starfish and thousands of beaches, and he could not possibly make a difference. The old man walks on and carefully picks up another small starfish. He gently throws it gently into the sea and says, "I make a difference to this one." It is easy to be overwhelmed and numbed by the sheer volume and catastrophic nature of the situations we see, but we must remember that at the very least, we can make someone's day or last days more full of compassion and caring than they would have been without us. The power of the human spirit is remarkable, and our patients' stories are compelling. If we can find it within ourselves to tolerate the painful feelings evoked by the suffering of others, to reach out in a compassionate and "real" way, if we can find ways to nurture and fortify ourselves on the job, then we can help our patients discover new strengths, meaning, and peace, and can be enriched personally as well. I continue to do this work because I think I make a difference.

REFERENCES

Cooke, R. 2001. *Dr. Folkman's War: Angiogenesis and the Struggle to Defeat Cancer.* New York: Random House.

Doka, K. J., ed. 1989. *Disenfranchised Grief: Recognizing Hidden Sorrow.* New York: Lexington.

Freeman, D., and J. Abrams. 1999. *Illness and Health in the Jewish Tradition.* Philadelphia: Jewish Publication Society.

Groopman, J. 1997. *The Measure of Our Days: New Beginnings at the End of Life.* New York: Viking.

Kushner, H. 1981. *When Bad Things Happen to Good People.* New York: Schocken.

Rando, T. 1993. *Grief, Dying, and Death.* Champaign, IL: Research Press.

Remen, R. N. 1996. *Kitchen Table Wisdom: Stories That Heal.* New York: Riverhead.

——. 2000. *My Grandfather's Blessings: Stories of Strength, Refuge, and Belonging.* New York: Riverhead.

4

SEPTEMBER 11: REFLECTIONS ON LIVING
WITH DYING IN DISASTER RELIEF

LES GALLO-SILVER AND PENNY DAMASKOS

"**H**AVE A good day." "Be careful." "I love you." These words are part of the morning ritual that I share with my wife, addressing my own struggles with separation anxiety. These are the words we share each day at the bus stop she uses to go to work near Wall Street as I head uptown to New York University Medical Center. Many couples, families, and friends went through their own morning rituals on September 11, 2001. No one realized that this would be a significant day in the history of New York City and for the nation as a whole. No one realized that, for some, the person they said goodbye to on that warm, breezy morning would not be coming home to them. Thankfully, no such loss darkened my life, but I would soon become acquainted with many people who were not as fortunate as I.

This is my story and the story of my friend and colleague Penny Damaskos. Both of us are oncology social workers, and neither of us realized on that day that in the days and weeks that followed we would be using our skills of helping people manage loss and trauma in a way that pushed us to our emotional and physical limits.

The attacks on the World Trade Center found the mental health community in the area searching for some sort of similar event to provide a context to help their injured community. The bombing of the federal building in Oklahoma City and the earlier terrorist bombing of the World Trade Center offered some, but not comparable, models of potential interventions (Morgan 1995; Nightingale 1997; Ofman, Mastria, and Steinberg 1995; Tucker et al. 2000). The enormity of the attacks, the loss of life, and the ensuing war made it difficult to transfer what had been learned from previous experiences to September 11. Mental health professionals were given the task of creating services and programs for a high-density urban area in crisis with little time for contemplation or self-examination (Gallo-Silver et al. 2002). Hospitals, hospice programs, and community agencies providing services to people with cancer, HIV/AIDS, or other life-threatening illnesses were inundated with requests for mental health professionals who could provide support services to people confronting potential loss and death (Gallo-Silver 2001; Gallo-Silver et al. 2002). Penny and I, and the many others who left their daily work routine to assist a community in crisis, struggled to cope with our own fears of death and loss.

I often write in a journal when I am feeling particularly sad and vulnerable, and the attacks prompted an increased need to externalize my thoughts and be able to examine them by writing them down. In college I was privileged to study poetry in a class taught by Audre Lorde. She helped me find the confidence to express my rawest emotions and longing by composing my own poems. The poetry helped me to process what I witnessed and absorbed throughout the experience of helping, and to manage this extraordinary disaster. In this chapter, I will share my poetry, which functions as a type of process recording in dialogue format of my experience of the trauma of September 11 (Ackerman 2002; Fox 1997; Galea et al. 2002).

Social workers involved in end-of-life care became a crucial resource, and they naturally assumed both a leadership and a coordinating role in the provision of clinical and practical services (Gallo-Silver 2001). Penny and I learned how being comfortable with the issues related to death, dying, bereavement, and recovery served as the nucleus for the confidence we needed in order to develop new skills. We also needed to learn intervention techniques to provide a psychosocial response to the terrorist attacks (Andrykowski et al. 2000; Kelly et al. 1995; Kwekkeboom and Seng 2002; Meeske et al. 2001; Rando 1996). We share our experiences using a diary format that demonstrates the unfolding journey of learning by doing under duress.

TUESDAY, 9/11/2001, 8:55 A.M., LES

"A plane crashed into one of the World Trade Center towers," my wife told me over the telephone from her office three blocks away. Soon the entire pediatric-oncology outpatient clinic staff was huddled around the small televisions in the chemotherapy treatment area, viewing the burning tower. Like many, we thought it was one of those terrible accidents that happen, often involving a small private plane. Soon a second plane hit the other tower, and we wondered if we were under attack. The attacks ignited each individual's "flight or fight" response (Salamon 2002; Spiers 2001). Once the attacks were recorded on live television and scenes of people fleeing the collapse of the towers were indelibly replayed, a sense of crisis typified the emotions of many in the city that day and for weeks thereafter (Galea et al. 2002; Salamon 2002). As medical providers, we were unsure of our own safety and what other targets might be destroyed in the city. A few families and children had started to arrive at the clinic. Our patients and families were the primary concern, but we were acutely distracted by the need to locate our own family and friends (Gallo-Silver 2001). Helping parents remain calm helped their children feel less threatened. Instinctively we knew that it would be traumatizing to allow the children (most were preschool age) to watch events unfold on the television. Until I knew my wife had succeeded in walking back to our apartment, braving the panic and the air thick with ash, I was barely able to concentrate on planning for patients who needed temporary housing because they were unable to return home.

At the NYU Medical Center, where we work, a few miles north of Ground Zero, thirty-six relatives of the staff who worked near the attack or were members of the uniformed workers who responded to the attack were missing and feared injured or dead. We provided comfort to our coworkers, who were confronting their and our worst fears.

We saw it in her cheeks,
as the color left her face.
We sensed it in an instant,
because we felt it in his gaze.
We calmed her.
We soothed him.
And hid our own relief.
That we were not to be them.
Our hearts were still intact.
Safe for now,
however brief.
Safe for now?
Safe from grief?

In the days and weeks following the attack, we struggled with a sense of being unsafe, worried about our loved ones, and yet followed our daily routines (Gallo-Silver et al. 2002). Each new warning or alert activated a similar if less acute response. The fear of potentially being "next" was all too real. It was this sense of personal physical vulnerability, during and following September 11, that ignited the "flight or fight response." The most frequently selected "fight response" was to be actively engaged in helping in any way possible. That response continued to separate me from my wife as I used my work to cope with my own fear and sadness.

TUESDAY, 9/11/2001, 8:40 A.M., PENNY

On Tuesday mornings, I have a private client whom I see before I go to work, and as I walked up Sixth Avenue to the subway, I remembered seeing the mayoral hopefuls greeting children at the local elementary school. I finished my session at 8:30; the roaring planes and the crash into the buildings had not yet taken place. The towers were there, intact and still gleaming behind my back as I walked up the street, marveling at the perfect day with my artist's eye, assessing the New York autumn light. Once I got to my office, an outpatient oncology clinic near NYU Medical Center, a colleague burst in and said the words that were echoing all over the city (and perhaps the world by now): "Have you heard that a plane flew into the World Trade Center?" I hadn't. I ignored the flashing light on my machine that indicated I had messages, and followed her into the conference room, where much of the staff looked shocked as the building burned on TV.

I am ashamed to remember that I had no concept that there were people in those buildings. I saw buildings; I saw one on fire, but did not connect to the humanity that was inside. It was a building in a city, in a neighborhood, on TV.

We watched as the second plane flew in and exploded, and when the picture went blank, I left immediately to call my partner, whose office was just several blocks from the site. She was calm. She had seen the first plane crash and watched the second from her expansive conference-room widows with an unobstructed view onto the buildings. Neither of us had a full understanding of what was happening. We said that we would be in touch. We said goodbye. We made no plan. We took it for granted that we would be okay. The minute we hung up it hit me that that was crazy. I called her right back and all lines were dead, the cell phones were jammed, the e-mail was out. It was just minutes past nine in the morning, and I felt as if I had just willingly let go of her hand and watched her float away into a vast, gray sea. I felt, and fought, a full body chill and did what so many people did: I used every defense mechanism I could muster and helped the people at hand.

It was chaotic. Some staff cried, some fainted, some mobilized into action to take care of patients. We had a full clinic, which can average several hundred people, that day. I helped calm people and used the skills I use for counseling oncology patients; I helped them to compartmentalize, taught them to be task-oriented and focused. I did rounds on the patients and found that people were either crying or disconnected from the events. One patient had family members in both towers and the Pentagon; others were primarily concerned about treatment-related hair loss or plagued by thoughts of recurrence.

As I spoke with people, TVs were everywhere, and in the background I heard one event after another: the Pentagon was hit; the president gave a speech; there were nine planes hijacked and missing; the buildings collapsed. Time was warped and multidimensional. It moved slowly: I felt every minute with acuity while at the same time events unraveled too fast, dizzying and overwhelming. If I took it all in I would fall apart. I kept thinking: "Deal with the tasks at hand, manage the crisis that is here."

Patients who lived in the neighborhood came to be with us because they felt safe. Family members and friends who had been at the site had made their way to our offices. People trickled in every fifteen or twenty minutes. Some semblance of stability was being restored. I had still heard nothing from my partner. I kept listening to the message that she had left on my machine describing the first crash. I still couldn't get through. I had given myself a deadline: If I had not heard from her by noon, I was going to find her because waiting and not knowing was too unbearable.

I kept working, supporting people, staff and patients alike. It was 11:30 before I heard anything—she was at home. I could hear the fear in her voice. We were able to stay in close contact while I stayed at the office and worked.

When I walked home to my apartment beneath Fourteenth Street, I was hit by the acrid smell of plastic and fuel. I knew that the dust particles that floated down from the sky were likely composed of all aspects of matter destroyed by the attacks—buildings, people, glass, paper. . . . My throat became scratchy, and I became queasy.

That night, and for the rest of the week, I slept with my shoes and clothing by the bed in case a gas explosion caused us to vacate our apartment, or in case there was another attack. Nothing could be taken for granted. Hypervigilance was the norm.

TUESDAY, 9/11/2001, 11:00 A.M., LES

Once all of the pediatric patients and families were in secure environments and the clinic was closed, I reported to the emergency room. The generic institutional disaster plan often calls for psychosocial support professionals to assist in the emergency room, managing family/visitors and tending to the concrete needs of the treated and released patients (Gallo-Silver et al. 2002). The emergency room at the NYU Medical Center treated survivors, who walked the almost three miles from Ground Zero, as well as injured uniformed service workers (particularly firefighters and EMS personnel). Cardiopulmonary, muscular/skeletal, and ocular problems were the most frequent presenting medical problems. My role, as one of many social workers, was to attempt to establish telephone contact with the family and friends of the "civilian" survivors. This was a role given to social workers by the patients themselves. At times, patients delayed or refused triage medical services until someone agreed to try to contact their loved ones and tell them that they had survived (Gallo-Silver 2001). I helped uniformed service workers locate their injured colleagues. I had to provide social-work quick response and psychosocial first aid in waiting rooms and hallways, establishing a sense of privacy and an opportunity to obtain emotional relief.

One survivor I worked with that day was Ms. Z. She was visiting New York City with her church group, staying in a hotel near the World Trade Center. She waited while her friend received treatment for minor injuries in the emergency room, when she overheard the news about the sudden collapse of her hotel. At that moment she realized that her pastor, who had remained in the hotel, might have been killed. Guilt about not having protected the pastor overwhelmed Ms Z. She struggled to understand the meaning of her survival and what her pastor might think about it. Was she still a "good Christian?" Focusing on her relationship with her church and her pastor, and helping her recall his words urging her to care for herself and love herself (Alexander 1990; Spiers 2001), was a way of supporting her.

> I left him.
> He said: "Go on ahead."
> "Find out what's happening out there."
> "I'll be safe here in my bed."
> "I'll keep the door locked."
> "Now take your key."
> "If there's trouble,
> Y'all can come back for me."
> Did he die
> because I let him be?
> The cloud of smoke and ash,
> chased me to your door.
> A sprained ankle,
> a broken wrist,
> that, and nothing more.
> But I left him.

Role-playing interventions also helped Ms. Z. practice how she would respond to her friend's questions about their pastor. The discussion they shared was painful to listen to, and I unashamedly became tearful as they clung to each other for comfort and forgiveness. Ms. Z. required follow-up mental health services, but her emergency room experience increased her willingness to seek further professional assistance (Goode 2001).

WEDNESDAY, 9/12/2001, 5:30 A.M., LES

On September 12, 2001, many families realized that their loved ones were not among the people who escaped the Towers, nor were they in any of the area hospitals treating the severely burned and seriously head injured patients. Before dawn on that day, families began cueing by the New York City Medical Examiner's Office, hoping to gain more information and to file the necessary missing persons report (Gallo-Silver 2001). The crowd was soon too large for the small office, and the first staging area for the Medical Examiner's Office was set up within the nearby NYU School of Medicine, a part of my hospital's overall complex. We were contacted by Social Work Administration to report to work between 5:00 and 6:00 A.M. I remember walking through the silent, empty streets, seeing National Guard troops being transported downtown. It was the first time I noticed the smell of burning plastic and chemicals. I shuddered at the thought that the air was intermingled with human remains. This scent would linger for days at a time. I am not sure when it ended, but it was impossible to ignore.

The numbers of families and friends waiting to file their reports and obtain more information built throughout the morning. Some of us helped the families fill out the missing-persons report forms. I was among the social workers actively assisting the police while they interviewed the families and friends. The police were overwhelmed by the sadness of their task. They were not cool or stoic; the sadness registered in their voices, in their faces, and in their eyes glistening with unshed tears. My own countertransference was obviously a factor in my choosing to focus on the men reporting their lost wives.

Can you please help me?
My wife is named Marie.
We kissed goodbye and went on our way.
I don't remember what she wore that day.
I put posters everywhere, in case someone would see,
An injured woman, who is named Marie.
Should I pray for peace?
Should I scream for war?
When the numbness ends,
Will it hurt much more?
God, why have you abandoned me?
To the emptiness of not knowing
What has happened to Marie.
Is it possible to help me?
My wife was named Marie.

My husband was named Jose.
My mother was named Sharda.
My father was named Tyrell.
My daughter was named Li-Jin.
My son was named Anthony.
My sister was named Rachel.
My brother was named Hakim.
My grandmother was named. . . .

In the days and weeks following the attack, the reporting center was moved several times to different and larger staging areas. In addition, the American Red Cross, the Salvation Army, and other social service/mental health organizations began to deploy their workers fully in response to the families' enormous emotional and practical needs. Cancer Care, Gilda's Club, the Visiting Nurse Service of New York, and the Federation Guidance and Employment Services extended counseling services to their neighborhoods, the larger community, as well as to affected businesses. But on that first morning, the social workers with experience in end-of-life care from NYU Medical Center were those who comforted the families and assisted them through the process of reporting a person as missing, presumed seriously injured, or dead. As we worked, we began to develop informal intervention criteria that targeted people who were alone, pregnant, families with young children, and older adults (Gallo-Silver 2001).

Many of the families were dazed and numb. Some chatted nervously with the other families who were also waiting on the long lines. Families often presented intense emotions while being interviewed by the police. A few wept silently; others hid their sadness and fear, reacting angrily toward the police and the social workers. Many social workers experienced the desperate anger of families as they struggled with impending loss. None of us was prepared for the huge number of frightened families grieving in a small, crowded space. We feared that individual anger would ignite the crowd, and we knew we did not have enough staff to provide direct comfort to everyone. Some families wanted to view the bodies that had been discovered at Ground Zero. Neither the social workers nor the police were able to share with the families the horrific condition of the remains. There would be very few instances of visual identification of the deceased. Tragically, many families would not have any human remains for burial, truncating funeral rituals and diminishing the healing nature of these ceremonies (Roberts 2002; Sella 2001; Worth 2002). Our inability to provide any concrete information or any validation of hope left us feeling that this necessary reporting process caused additional pain to the families and friends of the missing.

Just show me his body.
Just show me his face.
Just tell me it's over.
Just don't make me another case.
I've given you the details.

The photo you have.
See, his eyes are green.
There's the beauty mark he has.
He plays the piano.
His fingers are long.
I'm carrying his baby,
I'm five months along.
Just show me his body.
Just show me his face.
Just tell me it's over.
I'm just another case.

As in our daily medical social work practice, the family's anger was met with a respectful presence and active listening. Families needed for their emotional pain to be heard, recognized, and validated (Figley 1999; Hedlund and Clark 2001; Rando 1996; Worden 1983). We modeled this approach for the police officers, demonstrating how permitting a few moments of silence and slowing down the question/answer process gave families an opportunity to compose themselves.

I have no illusions.
I know that she's gone.
I'll go through the motions,
For the sake of her mom.
No, I don't need any counseling.
No, don't say any prayers.
I'm fine, keep your tissues.
Just please, don't notice my tears.
Let me go through the motions,
And fill out those forms.
I have no illusions.
I know that she's gone.

This intensity often caused emotional and physical exhaustion. Most people who initially presented as angry found themselves apologizing for their outbursts, and they shared the stress they were experiencing in words rather than in behavior. This became an opportunity for further on-site intervention and ultimately for referrals to the counseling services implemented by the American Red Cross, NYU Medical Center, Bellevue Medical Center, St. Vincent's Medical Center, Beth Israel Medical Center, New York Presbyterian Medical Center, Safe Horizon, and the Jewish Board of Family and Children Services.

WEDNESDAY, 9/12/2001, 8:00 A.M., PENNY

The next morning, as I walked to work, I ran into several people I knew. We hugged and briefly told our stories. We all were in shock and wanted to help. The city was suddenly made smaller by this tragedy, where neighbors helped each other, gave food, money, and blood if needed. We all lived close and lovingly. It all felt very surreal.

I reported to the main hospital, where the family counseling was taking place. The space could no longer accommodate the amount of people. When a new location was found, chaos, anger, and confusion reigned. There were long lines of people who were weary and dehydrated. They were refugees or victims of war, and they looked small and cold. I was assigned to talk with people on the line and to give them information. One woman begged me to help her get into the building so that she could fill out the forms for missing sister. She cried that she had waited all night, had already done the paperwork required, and now had to redo that process. I told her that she had to stay in line, but asked her to give me her name so that I could ask whether she could move forward. I was able to help facilitate her moving through the line and into the medical examiner's office to begin the task of filling out the paperwork a second time. As she moved out of the line and into the building, she held my hands tightly and looked into my eyes. The grief and pain were blinding.

Later, I sat with the police as they assisted families in the completion of paperwork. The processing rooms had many tables and chairs and looked strangely like elementary classrooms. The police had the most recent lists of those people located at the hospitals and those confirmed dead. They pored over them as intently as did the family members; everyone was looking for a name that they recognized. The boundaries between "victim" and "official" were blurred, and my role as support extended to them as well. Family after family came to our table and went through the painstaking task of recounting every detail of the missing person's body—teeth, toenails, ties.

The families were from every socioeconomic level. We processed paperwork for a president of a large company. Several of his adult children and their spouses were there. One sibling was in acute shock and alternated between hysterical crying and a blank, unmovable stare. Between answering questions I supported the family members, who had formed a circle around her and made suggestions for care that included additional medical and emotional support. They coped by staying together as a group, each with designated roles. Some were task-oriented while others cried. As they described what their father was wearing, a watch or a tie, they would segue into stories and memories about the articles they were listing. They laughed, which then startled them back into tears and grief.

This was a very painful experience to watch. The process of identifying the body offered solace as family members would recount memories, but the reality of why they were there would return as a sharp slap in the face. I tried to help them negotiate the discomfort and pain by acknowledging their sadness and by being receptive to the stories. By witnessing their terror and stories, I tried to create a human connection in a process that was grueling and bureaucratic. For the social workers, we knew that people were not "missing." "Missing" was the only acceptable word anyone could utter, and it was the only kind of form the government had to use in this instance. There was not a form for "complete annihilation." Those missing-person forms gave rise to the missing-person posters that began to appear all around the city. Those forms were the first way to conceptualize what was inconceivable. After spending many hours helping family after family in the same way, I walked back to my office and found myself weeping. I sat on a curb and wept, crying out the grief and horror I had witnessed and absorbed. This was only the second day, and it was still achingly, beautifully clear in hell.

When I returned home to my neighborhood, I had to show identification to get into my block because the National Guard had sectioned it off to all but residents. There was no food in the shops, and no cars allowed in or out of this part of town. Later that week, I remember eating dinner at a local restaurant and watching the WTC site debris snow down onto people's food as they sat outside and ate. They didn't seem to notice. Nothing seemed strange anymore.

THURSDAY, 9/13/2001, 10:00 A.M., PENNY

In the days immediately following September 11, the American Red Cross set up emergency relief centers around the city for the families and coworkers of the people missing in the attacks. Walking through the city en route to the relief center was like tracing a path into a war zone. The United Nations was barricaded off by trucks filled with sand and surrounded by National Guard and Army personnel. Rapidly and effortlessly, familiar images of the city were usurped by those of war that, for me, were at once comforting and profoundly frightening.

I was dispatched to a five-star luxury hotel. With typical New York City flair, the hotel owners donated a grand ballroom where the families and coworkers of a company that had lost more than six hundred people in the attacks could gather, comfort one another, and wait to hear news about relief efforts. When I entered that arena of extreme opulence, I saw that it had been transformed into a welcoming safe haven. When I walked into the ballroom, I thought of an enormous faith-based bereavement ritual—without acknowledgment that a death had taken place. Groups of people gathered around tables that were scattered throughout the massive space. There were additional tables overflowing with food, and a steady murmur of voices, broken up by intermittent wailing, which filled the room. Along the sides on each wall were the pictures of the missing from ceiling to floor, and they were scorchingly beautiful images of young people caught in life: on vacation, in their back yards, holding their children, each and every one smiling. Demographic identifiers framed these photos: weight, height, hair color, and place of employment. This was a vigil to hope, and it was in stark contrast to the mood of the people that looked at them.

Our role as "counselors" ranged from listening to the details of the tragedy to helping family members with resources. I was assigned to a section of the ballroom where families had placed the posters. I stood with people as they found their friends or loved ones in the sea of faces that lined the walls of the hall. Sometimes I spoke with people; sometimes people spoke to me. I remember feeling exhausted by the hours of maintaining the emotional balance of being present but not intrusive, supportive but not overwhelming. I spoke with people who had survived the attacks and had come to the hotel to "help others." One woman said that she was outside the towers on her way into work when the buildings were hit. She saw people falling and dodged flaming debris, but she could not see that she had been traumatized because she was "alive." She needed to connect with others because she felt isolated and because her family and friends could not understand her feelings. We went through the photos together. She pointed to faces she recognized, cried as she spoke about the people she worked with, and intermittently held my hand as we talked. I asked her how she was caring for herself and helped her with self-care strategies. We talked about how her feelings were "normal," not "crazy," as she had thought, and about how there were many people who felt as she did, especially those who had survived. She eventually moved on from our conversation and joined a group of people she recognized at a nearby table.

As I stood by the photos, a woman came up to me and said, "Do you remember me?" I stared at her but could not recognize the face in front of me. Then she said, "You helped me yesterday in the line." That moment seemed so many years and so many stories ago. Again she grabbed my hand, but this time her eyes reflected back dull and quiet.

While I stood alongside the wall of photos, a mother and sister of a missing person began a conversation with me. The mother delivered her story in detail but was often distracted and would interrupt her narrative with random thoughts and tangents. I listened for a long time and eventually normalized her feelings and gave her information about expected reactions to trauma as a way to help her gain some measure of control. I did not ask too many probing questions because I did not want to overwhelm her and cause more anxiety than relief. I told her that she was showing some of the symptoms of trauma such as difficulty concentrating, decreased memory, confusion, hypervigilance, intrusive images, disorientation, decrease in appetite, difficulties breathing, and decrease in sleep and fluid intake (Scott and Stradling 1972; Watts 1997; NCPTSD 2001). The rest of our interactions focused on self-care instructions that emphasized the need for food, sleep, and fluid intake. Through our conversation, I learned that her family had experienced a previous loss with her father's sudden death several years ago. When they learned that their father's loss contributed to the intensity of their current reactions, they expressed a sense of relief through understanding the intensity of their current feelings. By normalizing reactions, I gave people an understanding of what was happening to them that led to additional interviews with the family that mobilized their natural support network. After meeting additional family members, I was able to identify the strengths within the family structure and reinforce them with educational interventions, support, and concrete suggestions on how to use the family's natural healing abilities.

I returned to the hotel for the next few days, and the mood in the room shifted from shock and hope to anger and fervent denial. With each hour came the realization that fewer and fewer bodies would be found. In fact, only one person was rescued and survived after the first day (MMWR 2001). The first day there was shock, grief, sadness, denial, hope, and hypervigilance. During the third day following the attacks, irritability and anger intensified as the need for information increased. People expressed self-blame and agitation and talked about using alcohol and medications to numb their feelings. With time, the inability to deny the death of the missing brought with it a more palpable articulation of sadness, grief, and loss.

I joined a large round table with a group of employees who had survived the attacks by several means. Using my group work skills, I facilitated a discussion between the employees. When one said, "I wish I could have done something," another would reply, "There was nothing any of us could have done" or, "You do so much all the time." Within the course of the discussion, the minimization of feelings was frequently demonstrated: "I'm okay. I just want to help everyone else because there are so many other people who are suffering more than me." I used an educational intervention to remind them that everyone suffered from the enormity of these attacks. I stated that there was no hierarchy of those worthy of grief and feeling and those not worthy. Our task as counselors was to provide support through facilitating discussions between family members and coworkers and to build a healing sense of community in which the less fragile could actively comfort the more emotionally wounded in the room. Empowering the surviving coworkers and those who were not at work on the day of the attacks to reach out to the families of the missing supported the coping abilities of both groups.

As I provided support to the family members and workers directly affected by the attacks, I felt a sense of privilege in being able to share their space and help them better understand what had happened and guide them to a place with some comfort and moments of peace. This work, of course, helped me to do the same thing for myself. Watching people move through intense feelings and awaken to the reality of the tremendous loss and slowly move through it helped me to transform the profound sadness of this "moment in time" to a sense of hope. I marveled at the strength and kindness of humanity. I felt a sense of purpose that I had never felt before and saw that this was important work that mattered. That clarity was addicting, and I knew, ironically, that it signaled the beginning of burnout. I realized I had to pace myself, that I belonged to a community of people who were helping too, and that I needed to return to my life for replenishment. If I continued to keep going at this rate without retreating, I would not be of any help to anybody.

THURSDAY, 9/13/2001, 3:30 P.M., LES

Some families and friends continued to visit the emergency rooms throughout the city, hoping that an unidentified survivor had been admitted to the hospital. Many of the families retold mythic stories of people having been found under debris after an earthquake or mudslide, saved by an air pocket and found days later by a diligent search effort. Sometimes these stories of survivorship took place in Mexico or Colombia, occasionally in Turkey or Armenia. There were air pockets under the debris of the World Trade Center, but the air was fueling the fires that burned for many days after the buildings collapsed. It was perhaps too brutal for the families to put that information together with their desperate hopes that more survivors would be found. Some members of the B. family believed that their son, who had an appointment at the World Trade Center on September 11, was trapped but alive under the debris. They came to the NYU Medical Center Emergency Room, hoping to find him or someone with more information about survivors in other hospitals. The police and the Medical Examiner's Office kept updated lists of survivors, but no one was added to the list after the first twenty-four hours following the attacks. The B. family had checked the most recent list of survivors and, not finding their oldest son, continued to search. Families and friends often did not integrate and accommodate sad and frightening information at that same rate or in the same way. This caused feelings of isolation within typically healthy and loving families. At times a family member considered to be out of synchrony with the rest of the family was seen as coping poorly rather than coping in his or her own healthy manner (Rando 1996; Worden 1983). The younger son of the B. family did not share his family's hopes that his older brother had survived. His father and uncle accompanied this younger brother, twenty-one years old, to the emergency room. His family decided to seek a psychiatric evaluation for him, as they were concerned about his frequent crying while the rest of the family was busy searching for his older brother. They indicated that his distress had worsened after he completed the missing-persons process at the Medical Examiner's Office. I interviewed him, and he said that he "knew" his brother had been killed at the World Trade Center. In addition, he was struggling to cope with his family's continued hope that his brother was alive, trapped under the rubble and sustained by an air pocket. I encouraged him to share his emotional experience as well as his thoughts and impressions at the Medical Examiner's Office, where he had donated his own DNA and brought his brother's toothbrush (Chen 2002; Lipton 2002). A family session helped to normalize his and his family's portrayal of various coping styles as healthy. The younger Mr. B. needed reassurance that his intense grief was not a sign of mental illness.

> He took a swab of my cheek.
> And every night since,
> I spend my time feeling the spot
> with my tongue.
> Sometimes it helps me feel.
> Sometimes it helps me sleep.
> He took a swab of my cheek.
> And that's how I knew,
> My brother was dead.
> Dad will find out soon,
> That inside my cheek,
> is the only place,
> my brother still lives.

It was important for the younger Mr. B.'s family to recognize the additional trauma he experienced at the Medical Examiner's Office. This gave them an opportunity to comfort him without feeling they were agreeing with him that his older brother was dead. I shared with him that he demonstrated considerable maturity and sensitivity in allowing his family to come to terms with his brother's loss in their own time, even though it prevented them from comforting him. This young man and his family were referred to a local mental health program for follow-up services.

WEDNESDAY, 9/19/2001, 10:00 a.m., PENNY

The emergency room closest to Ground Zero at the NYU Downtown Hospital received not only some of the most seriously injured survivors but also the frightened and frail members of the surrounding downtown residential community. The hospital's emergency room and other public areas served as a sanctuary, similar to how a fort or castle functioned in times of war when villagers sought protection within their walls. The heightened emotionality of the situation presented a need for the kind of respectful, paced, and subtly worded interviewing skills that social workers have developed during family conferences about advanced directives. This mixture of validating the emotional connection and commitment, with the need to obtain information is a basic end-of-life social work skill (Figley 1999; Hedlund and Clark 2001; Worden 1983). The "refugees" from the surrounding community required comfort and practical assistance similar to the types of interventions used to help extended family members of dying patients.

Hospital workers experienced secondary trauma while managing victims and their families in their institutions (Duckworth 1986; Jenkins 1997; Kelly 1997; Schorr et al. 1998). In massive psychic and physical trauma, the psychosocial and practical needs of the staff need to be addressed to maximize their effectiveness, to support their physical and emotional stamina, and to assist their eventual return to routine institutional functioning (Galea et al. 2002; Gallo-Silver 2001; Gallo-Silver et al. 2002). Developing counseling programs for staff to come and talk was part of our overall response to these needs (Gallo-Silver et al. 2002). We disseminated information on post-traumatic stress disorder (PTSD) to staff throughout the hospital. Some hospital staff participated in Critical Incident Debriefing (CISD) sessions because many employees experienced difficulty managing their feelings while at work and/or at home (Everly 2000; Irving 2001).

CISD debriefings were first developed during wartime to help prevent the development of the symptoms of PTSD (NCPTSD 2001), and were designed for people exposed to severe trauma. It is usually conducted in a group format and follows a structured series of stages. CISD is primarily a defusing process designed to allow people to emote and share their feelings, gain some new understanding of the event, and feel relief as a result. It is most successful when people attend more than one session. As a result of the September 11 tragedy, the overall long-term benefit of this intervention has been questioned because often people only attended one session, and when it occurs in isolation from comprehensive follow-up services it is much less effective (Irving 2001). Comprehensive follow-up services are often necessary as the emotions and thoughts provoked by the traumatic event resurface with renewed intensity many months after the actual event (Everly 2000; Irving 2001; Spiers 2001). CISD is thought to be most effective if conducted immediately after the trauma to help people verbalize their feelings and reactions as close as possible to the experience.

It is not designed as a longer-term intervention, for repeated verbalization of the trauma can be retraumatizing for some people. Although I was aware that there were other interventions being used around the city, I did not use any interventions other than the CISD model.

The CISD debriefing follows structured stages, but these do not necessarily need to occur sequentially. Leaders can be flexible in what is covered and when, as long as all areas are discussed. There are many similarities in the CISD approach to the techniques social workers use in bereavement support groups. Like the bereavement and psycho-oncology groups, the CISD sessions provide a combination of education and a structure within which participants can emote sadness and loss. Both groups provide a safe space where members provide support and mutual understanding not available in other areas of their lives. However, these groups do not have the same goals. The CISD is designed to elicit feelings quickly and defuse them immediately, while the oncology groups are less focused on the trauma of diagnosis than on the articulation of coping strategies and on the assimilation of the cancer experience into one's life. With CISD, people learn that what they feel is based on what happened in the past; with the oncology groups, people learn to cope with an ongoing condition and situation.

With the hospital chaplain, I led CISD debriefing for the professional staff that worked in the operating room at a hospital that received numerous casualties. During the group, the staff recounted the events of the morning and day of the attacks. They described the billowing smoke and the instantaneous darkness that occurred as a result of the collapse of the buildings. They then remembered how smoke and dust came through the windows, and their concerns about the integrity of the hospital building. They described the horrors and extreme injuries of the casualties that came into the operating room. The group shifted to a stage in the CISD model: the reaction stage. It was in this segment that some staff members confessed that they left their posts. They shared how the panic and fear caused them to retreat, with administrative permission, to a sleeping residence adjacent to the hospital. Some closed the curtains and hid in bed for several hours before returning to work. Feelings of guilt, remorse, and recrimination filled the group room. The leaders focused on the humanity of the responses. Other group members said that they, too, wished that they had retreated to a "safe spot." Some of the staff spoke about their inability, even now, several days later, to feel grief or to cry. In contrast, some group participants cried and others comforted them.

Some participants verbalized feelings of alienation outside of work, citing that on numerous occasions people outside their neighborhood seemed untouched and detached from the impact of the attacks. This was deeply disturbing to the group inasmuch as all of the participants feared being isolated and alone with their intense feelings. This helped the group focus on a sense of appreciation and solace in their colleagues' understanding and shared experience. They also learned the limits of what they were able to do as individuals, and the experience reinforced their connections to the hospital with a renewed sense of community. The group leaders educated the group about the well-documented symptoms of PTSD and handed out literature from the American Red Cross listing self-help and self-care activities. Many staff members experienced anxiety when they heard a loud noise or when a plane flew overhead. Many were unable to sleep and eat. They were hypervigilant and ready for another attack. They had flashbacks of the event and some reported shortness of breath. The group ended with the leaders summarizing the group experience and leading the group through a short breathing/prayer exercise. Following the group, it was essential for the leaders to debrief one another because the leaders had witnessed and absorbed powerful feelings and horrible images from the group's experiences. I found the debriefings very helpful because they gave me a chance to understand what had taken place and examine my feelings about what I had witnessed. It ultimately helped with the transition from being a part of a group to being in the present.

FRIDAY, 9/14/2001, 11:00 P.M., LES

The close proximity and relationship of the Medical Examiner's Office to the NYU Medical Center exposed social workers to the ongoing suffering of the families of the missing, but also offered the opportunity to provide psychosocial support services to the ME staff and to the police officers assisting in the securing and cataloguing of personal effects of the casualties (Jones 1985). The social workers led small informal support and education groups during the dinner service provided by the NYU School of Medicine from 5:00 P.M. until midnight. Social workers sensitively joined groups of Medical Examiner's Office workers and police officers and offered them an opportunity to share their feelings, thoughts, and fears. Many of the social workers and medical examiners were working double shifts and were unable to receive or provide support to their own families. Creating a community of mutual support during the dinner breaks helped to diminish the isolation they were experiencing. People who ate in silent groups and people who elected to eat alone were targeted for enhanced services. Often the silence and the choice to be alone seemed to be part of a desperate effort to keep feelings of anger and sadness under control. Many of the Medical Examiner's Office workers and the police feared that they would be unable to protect their families from the emotional intensity of their work. Some of the workers indicated they were inundated by requests from neighbors who learned of their roles at the Medical Examiner's Office and hoped that they could obtain information about their loved ones for them. All of these pressures needed to be voiced, mourned, and validated within the human process of counseling and sharing, thereby being relieved in some small way.

> The foot was from someone's grandmother,
> I could tell from the type of shoe.
> A watch, a wallet, a comb,
> All some type of clue,
> To the name of someone loved.
> Sifting through all of what is left,
> Sifting through all of the regret,

Of things unsaid and undone.
Searching through the sadness.
Trying to avoid the madness.
Hoping to be able to get home.
But first, I have to try,
and wash the horror off.

SATURDAY, 9/15/2001, 1:30 P.M., LES

Extraordinary work was accomplished by social workers at the NYU Downtown Hospital, St. Vincent's Medical Center, New York Presbyterian Medical Center in Manhattan, Long Island College Hospital in Brooklyn, and St. Barnabas Medical Center in New Jersey where many of the most severely injured survivors were treated. Sadly, some of the survivors ultimately died of their injuries. The social work staff at the NYU Downtown Hospital required additional assistance during the weekend after the attacks. Many of those seriously injured in the attacks were evacuated before the weekend as the hospital was using its emergency generators. Several patients were too unstable to be moved. While the weekend social worker concentrated on the complexities of discharging patients who wanted to return home even though the city was still struggling with power and telephone outages, I focused on assisting the intensive care unit staff with the most injured survivors that remained in their hospital. It was there I met Mr. C.

Mr. C. was brought to the hospital unconscious from a serious head injury. He was intubated and transferred to the intensive care unit following surgery. He had been hit by debris while helping others to safety when the first tower collapsed. He was identified by the contents of his wallet. An identification card listed his home telephone number. Also inside were pictures of a woman and three small children. One of them was an infant. The social worker called Mr. C.'s home telephone number and left several messages before she left the hospital for the weekend. The Saturday following the attacks, Ms. J. came to the hospital and identified herself as Mr. C.'s cousin. I accompanied her to Mr. C.'s bedside and comforted her as she wept. She related that her cousin had come to the United States as a legal immigrant fleeing religious persecution in his country. She had helped to sponsor him. Mr. C. visited his wife once every year, helped support his family, his parents, and her parents. He was hoping to sponsor his wife and children to enter the United States. I facilitated a meeting between Ms. J. and Mr. C.'s physician where she learned that her cousin was unlikely to survive. I had participated in meetings similar to this one for many years, and yet I felt sadder and more helpless than usual. Trying to maintain the focus on Mr. C. and Ms. J., and not on myself, was harder. Lack of sleep, working long shifts, and my own fears and sadness made managing my countertransference more difficult. Ms. J. returned to her cousin's bedside and I instructed her on how to touch his brow without disrupting the respirator and how to speak to him softly near his potentially unaffected ear. Ms. J. needed help in strategizing about what to say to his wife once she reached her, a process that would take several days. Once alone with Mr. C., I talked to him about how brave the police and firefighters considered him, how many people he had saved, and about his devotion to his wife and family. Perhaps he heard me, and my voice and affect provided some comfort. Perhaps I did this to help myself feel that there was something I could do to honor this brave man. Mr. C. deteriorated that evening and died after a five-day admission.

MONDAY, 9/17/2001, 10:00 A.M., LES

Social workers providing services to the medically fragile became aware of their patients' increased sense of vulnerability. Their lives were "full of danger" before the attacks; the current reality intensified their sense of vulnerability and emotional struggle (Christ 1993). In addition, we were acutely reminded that the emotional challenges of our patients left them little emotional energy to cope with the impact of the attacks (Dewan 2001). Some patients felt more isolated by their inability to focus on the difficulties in the city and the active mourning of the community around them. One of my patients needed considerable reassurance that her problems and concerns still mattered to me and that I had the interest and the energy to help her.

> It didn't register at first.
> His cancer is out of control,
> It means he will die.
> I feel so lost.
> I feel so weak.
> I just couldn't feel for them.
> Forgive me.
> So many missing,
> So many dead,
> So much sadness
> But I couldn't feel for them.
> Forgive me.
> I don't want anyone to know.
> Am I coldhearted?
> Am I halfhearted?
> I'm too brokenhearted
> to feel for them.
> Forgive me.

Extraordinary complex existential issues challenged the medically fragile who were in close proximity to the attacks and were evacuated from the Financial District (Dwyer et al. 2002; Fullerton et al. 1999). They presented increased difficulty in managing their illnesses as the world changed around them. This further complicated the clinical work that they were engaged in before the attacks. One of my patients who had previously demonstrated passive suicidal thoughts struggled with issues of life and death in an even more acute fashion than before September 11.

He required more frequent sessions and became less resistant to participating in a psychiatric evaluation.

> Down countless flights of stairs cane in hand,
> Feeling the breath of those behind me,
> Trying, struggling to get down quickly.
> I'm so sorry so many got caught behind the cripple.
> Why did I bother? I live alone. I have cancer.
> I don't expect to survive.
> Anyway, who would miss me?
> And yet, I walked down all those stairs,
> With every step I moaned.
> the clouds of dust made me choke,
> So many young people died,
> This must be one of God's sick jokes.
> Why did God bother?
> I live alone. I have cancer.
> Who would miss me?
> And yet, I survived.

MONDAY, 9/17/2001, 9:00 A.M., PENNY

After September 11, many found themselves floating in confusion, anxiety, and psychic distress (Haberman 2002). Many social workers who participated in new programs developed to manage the aftereffects of the attacks observed the gradual development of their own symptoms of PTSD (Kershaw 2002). Others reported continued hyper-vigilance, especially in the wake of the anthrax attacks, a heightened sense of vulnerability, interrupted sleep, binge eating, or lack of appetite. Smoking and drinking behaviors seemed to increase, as did intense crying episodes. One person characterized these episodes as large "grief-burps."

Some had difficulty returning to work and continuing their daily routines. I ran several support groups for staff who reiterated the same issues: they were terrified of their commute into work, and sometimes felt overpowered by their anxiety. Staff were afraid of the subways, buses, and bridges. They reported elaborate transportation routines to minimize their anxiety and to help them select the "safest" route into work. For others, the attacks highlighted their isolation and disconnection from others and dissatisfaction with their present situations. I connected these people to counseling outside of work to help them cope better, and strategized with them about ways to reduce isolation.

In my clinic, I followed a woman undergoing chemotherapy for a recurrence of her ovarian cancer. Ms. L. lived in an apartment in Chinatown, a high-density neighborhood adjacent to the attacks. She spoke and read little English, but sought me out for assistance following the attacks. She recounted her experiences in meticulous detail; how she heard the plane crashes, saw people jumping from the WTC towers, heard the powerful crunch of the buildings' collapse followed by a loss of telephone and electrical services. Her neighborhood was sectioned off by police order. As she spoke, I could see her anxiety increasing. I felt powerless to help her, but as I listened, I saw that the act of recounting her feelings alleviated some of her stress and fear. For me, it was clear that the aftereffects were going to be felt for a long time, not just with this patient, but also with many.

Ms. L. was required to show identification whenever she left or returned to her building. Even though she was medically fragile and emotionally overwhelmed, she coped by connecting with her neighbors and family as well as by knitting and sewing clothing. These had helped her cope with her cancer and treatment. We worked on her adjustment to the trauma, her restricted living conditions, and issues of control and anxiety. I also offered her concrete services. Ms. L. asked for assistance with letters for air purifiers and vacuums provided by the Federal Emergency Management Agency (FEMA), and information on financial assistance. Through counseling sessions, we addressed her continued sense of helplessness and vulnerability from the attacks and the fear of contamination from the fumes and dust. Ms. L.'s anxiety diminished as her environment gradually became more stable and as she felt more distance from the attacks.

LOOKING TOWARD THE FUTURE: LES

The role of the social worker in the weeks and months after September 11 expanded drastically as the aftermath of the attacks rippled into all segments of society. Social workers found themselves on an expanding front line where they helped people who continued to feel the affects of the attacks. Several support programs were developed through "Project Liberty," funded primarily through FEMA and administered through the New York State Office of Mental Health. Through this project, people now receive individual or group counseling free of charge (Dewan 2001).

The development of new services permitted us to return to our own work with patients struggling with serious illness. However, none of us, nor our patients and their families, returned to "normal." We have all been changed by trying to absorb the shock of being attacked and by struggling to establish a sense of physical and emotional safety. Even now, over a year later, I find myself poring over the lists of the casualties, searching for the names of people I met through their family and friends who were searching for them, and making sure that the names were spelled correctly. Ultimately, the tragedy is not about the social workers, but those who lost a sense of hope, security, and connection to loved ones.

REFERENCES

Ackerman, D. 2002. The Morse code of the heart: Poems foster self-discovery. *New York Times*, 3 June.

Alexander, D. 1990. Psychological intervention for victims and helpers after disasters. *British Journal of General Practitioners* 40:345–348.

Andrykowski, M. A., M. J. Cordova, P. C. McGrath, et al. 2000. Stability and change in post-traumatic stress disorder following cancer treatment: A one-year follow-up. *Psycho-oncology* 9:69–78.

Chen, D. W. 2002. Grim scavenger hunt for DNA drags on for September 11 families. *New York Times*, 8 February.

Christ, G. 1993. Psychosocial tasks throughout the cancer experience. In *Oncology Social Work: A Clinician's Guide*, ed. N. Stearns, M. M. Lauria, J. F. Hermann, and P. Fogelberg, 7–100. Atlanta: American Cancer Society.

Dewan, S. K. 2001. Beyond calamity: Death goes on; grief unrelated to terror takes on a broader context. *New York Times*, 17 October.

Duckworth, D. H. 1986. Psychological problems arising from disaster work. *Stress Medicine* 2:315–323.

Dwyer, J., E. Lipper, K. Flynn, J. Glanz, and F. Fessenden. 2002. Fighting to live as towers died. *New York Times*, 26 June.

Everly, G. S. 2000. Crisis Management Briefings (CMB): Large group crisis intervention in response to terrorism, disasters and violence. *International Journal of Emergency Mental Health* 2(1): 53–57.

Figley, C. R. 1999. *The Traumatology of Grieving: Conceptual, Theoretical and Treatment Foundations*. London: Taylor & Frances.

Fox, J. 1997. *Poetic Medicine: The Healing Art of Poem Making*. New York: Tarcher.

Fullerton, C. S., et al. 1999. Disaster related bereavement: Acute symptoms and subsequent depression. *Aviation Space Environmental Medicine* 20:902–909.

Galea, S., J. Ahern, H. Resnick, et al. 2002. Psychological sequelae of the September 11th terrorist attacks in New York City. *New England Journal of Medicine* 346(13): 982–987.

Gallo-Silver, L. 2001. Adapting skills for a community in crisis. *Association of Oncology Social Work* 17(1): 1–3.

Gallo-Silver, L., E. Chachkes, D. Rosenstein, et al. 2002. Healing in the midst of crisis: Creative clinical program development following the WTC attack. Abstract. Second Annual Congress of Disaster Psychiatry, Mount Sinai Medical Center, New York.

Goode, E. 2001. Treatment can ease lingering trauma of September 11th. *New York Times*, 20 November.

Haberman, C. 2002. You've been warned, now, get on with your life. *New York Times*, 23 May.

Hedlund, S. C., and E. J. Clark. 2001. End of life issues. In *Social Work in Oncology*, ed. M. M. Lauria, E. J. Clark, J. F. Hermann, and N. Stearns, 299–316. Atlanta: American Cancer Society.

International Critical Incident Stress Foundation. 1996. CISM Information Pamphlet & the CISD Team. Information sheet.

Irving, P. 2001. Stress debriefing: Does it work? *Counseling and Psychotherapy Journal* 1:18–21.

Jenkins, S. R. 1997. Coping and social support among emergency dispatchers: Hurricane Andrew. *Journal of Social Behavior and Personality* 12(1): 201–216.

Jones, D. R. 1985. Secondary disaster victims: The emotional effects of recovery and identifying human remains. *American Journal of Psychiatry* 142:303–307.

Kelly, B., B. Raphael, M. Smithers, et al. 1995. Psychological responses to malignant melanoma: An investigation of traumatic stress reactions to life threatening illness. *General Hospital Psychiatry* 52:1048–1060.

Kelly, R. E. 1997. Trauma counseling of emergency service workers: Contact with deceased victims and the use of reverent acts to gain cognitive mastery. *Dissertation Abstracts International, Section B: The Sciences and Engineering* 57(12–B): 7732.

Kershaw, S. 2002. Even six months later, "Get over it" just isn't an option. *New York Times*, 11 March.

Kwekkeboom, K. L., and J. S. Seng. 2002. Recognizing and responding to post-traumatic stress disorder in people with cancer. *Oncology Nursing Forum* 29(4): 643–650.

Lipton, E. 2002. The toll: The cold numbers, a census of the September 11th victims. *New York Times*, 9 April.

Lipton, E., and J. Glanz. 2002. DNA science pushed to the limit in identifying the dead of September 11th. *New York Times*, 22 April.

Marotta, S. 2000. Best practices for counselors who treat post-traumatic stress disorder. *Journal of Counseling and Development* 78(4): 492–495.

Meeske, K. A., K. Ruccione, D. R. Globe, and M. L. Tuber. 2001. Post-traumatic stress, quality of life and psychological distress in young adult survivors of childhood cancer. *Oncology Nursing Forum* 28(4): 481–489.

Morbidity and Mortality Weekly Report. 2001. Vol. 51: 1–5.

Morgan, J. 1995. American Red Cross mental health services: Implementation and recent developments. *Journal of Mental Health Counseling* 17(3): 291–300.

National Center for PTSD. 2001. Effects of traumatic stress in a disaster situation. www.ncptsd.org/facts/disasters/fs_effects_disaster.html.

Nightingale, A. S. 1997. Counseling and support services for civil emergencies and major incidents: Psychodynamic reflections. *Psychiatric Bulletin* 21(8): 486–488.

Ofman, P. S., M. A. Mastria, and J. Steinberg. 1995. Mental health response to terrorism: The World Trade Center bombing. *Journal of Mental Health Counseling* 17(3): 312–320.

Rando, T. 1996. Complications in mourning traumatic death. In *Living with Grief After Sudden Loss: Suicide, Homicide, Accident, Heart Attack and Stroke*, ed. K. Doka, 139–159. Washington, DC: Hospice Foundation of America.

Roberts, S. 2002. When history isn't something that happens to other people. *New York Times*, 24 April.

Salamon, J. 2002. Reliving 9/11: Too much? Too soon? *New York Times*, 12 May.

Schiraldi, G. R. 2002. *The Post-Traumatic Stress Disorder Source Book: A Guide to Healing, Recovery and Growth*. Lincolnwood, IL: Lowell House.

Schorr, J. K., et al. 1998. The relationship between perceived social support and psychological distress: Oklahoma City firefighters two years after the Alfred P. Murrah Federal Building. Paper presented to the International Sociological Association.

Scott, M. J., and S. G. Stradling. 1972. *Counseling for Post-Traumatic Stress Disorder*. London: Sage.

Sella, M. 2001. Missing: How a grief ritual is born. *New York Times Magazine*, 7 October.

Spiers, T., ed. 2001. *Trauma: A Practitioners Guide to Counseling*. Bristol, PA: Brunner-Routledge.

Tucker, P., et al. 2000. Predictions of post-traumatic stress response systems in Oklahoma City, exposure, social support and peri-traumatic responses. *Journal of Behavioral Health Sciences Research* 27:406–416.

Watts, R. 1997. Trauma counseling and rehabilitation. *Journal of Applied Rehabilitation Counseling* 28(1): 8–10.

Worden, J. N. 1983. *Grief Counseling and Grief Therapy*. London: Routledge.

Worth, R. F. 2002. 800 Victims may not be identified, City says. *New York Times*, 13 July.

PART II

THEORETICAL ASPECTS OF DEATH AND DYING

INTRODUCTION: THEORY

THE OBSERVATION that social workers have not been trained or prepared to work with people who are at the end of their lives or with the bereaved has been made several times already in this book. The chapters in this section were chosen to provide the theoretical perspectives that we consider crucial to informing social work practice more effectively. They assume that the reader is building upon basic social work knowledge. However, as we look at social workers' personal experiences in dealing with death and how this influenced their practices, we feel justified in asking if we can ever be fully "trained or prepared" to engage with others in our role as professional helpers? If we thought this before, we are now more certain, after reading the narratives in the first part of the book as well as the chapters in the other sections of this book, that this work cannot rely only on our cognitive or intellectual abilities alone. But to be an effective helper in the context of the work that we do, we cannot rely exclusively on our own experience and feelings, either. There is a body of knowledge, much of which builds on what we have already learned in our training as social workers, that is essential to being effective in work with people at the end of their lives. In a sense we need to work from both sides of our brains: the cognitive and the affective.

In this section we bring together a number of chapters that focus on various domains of theory, by no means inclusive, that will add to our knowledge base and have immediate relevance for social worker practice in end-of-life care. We think of these chapters as providing both conceptual and theoretical frameworks that are the underpinnings of good practice in end-of-life care. These are the ideas that can and do direct, inform, and justify what we do. They help us move beyond the individual case to see common patterns in our practice and help us select from a variety of perspectives about where to put the emphasis in our relationships with those we are serving.

Yet in many ways we cannot move beyond the individual case. Dying is a very personal and individual matter. Dying is something every person does alone. But people die in many settings—at home, in hospitals, in prisons, in nursing homes, under traumatic circumstances. By default, others are involved with the dying process, and many religious traditions are clear that people should not die without others at their side. Social workers need to know about the contexts in which death occurs and the influence of these contexts. Each context has values, attitudes, beliefs, and traditions that need to be understood and the differences between them recognized. These values and attitudes influence how society constructs particular views of the human experience, including how the individual is valued and finds meaning. How the individual constructs his or her death emanates from these values and attitudes. These attitudes and values also influence the kind of resources available in any given community as well, and the kind of care the person receives that is consistent with the ethical and moral approaches to care and the institutional settings this society supports. To this we add the behavioral, cognitive, and relational factors that affect how the individual dying person and family came to their way of approaching dying and mourning.

We frame some of our understanding in the question: "What is their story?" How people put together their stories involves, as well, the cultural, socioeconomic, and spiritual milieus that have informed their lives. This multifaceted perspective reflects multiple theories, informs how these needs are defined and how these needs are met, and contributes to our making sense of what is happening to the dying person and her family. Thus the chapters in this section provide various contexts or lenses for understanding how any given individual comes to view living and dying: psychologically, relationally, spiritually, and ethically.

In this modern and postmodern world, there is a new appreciation for the range of acceptable human behaviors, making each person's story richer and taking in a broader view of their lived experiences. We see the value of examining their behaviors from many points of view to which we add, for example, ethnic, cultural, interpersonal, developmental, and intrapsychic lenses. We recognize that dying may differ based on sexual orientation, social class, and gender as well.

Very little about dying is universal except that all of us will die. We need to recognize that much of how we look at dying is socially constructed, changing over time. In this book, we focus throughout on what is involved in creating environments that respect the needs of the dying and their families. The values and attitudes that promote a respectful death must be reflected in our individual practices and in the institutional settings in which we work. Death, in the end, is inevitable, an experience over which we have no control and less understanding. In some ways theories, as described in this section of the book, about what we do at this time, provide us with ways to feel grounded when faced with this mysterious and unknown terrain.

What do we mean by theory? From a modern, positivist approach, theories provide hypothetical explanations for observable phenomena. For a theory to be accepted as true it would need to be studied and tested. As we look at human experience, at the very fact of life and of death—how they stay constant and how they have changed over time—we develop many theories for explaining what we observe that cannot be tested. We turn to philosophy, to religion, to history, to the arts, to psychology, to life experience to provide us with ways of understanding living and dying.

It is also essential that in considering various theories, we learn to critique them as well: to recognize their limitations. Most of the time, when dealing with life and death, the only certainty we have is that death happens. In looking at these aspects of human experience, we need to accept uncertainty, ambiguity, and our inability to understand and control all that is happening to our clients, and ultimately to ourselves.

Our authors represent various schools of thought, some of whom may sound certain about absolutes in death, dying, and bereavement. It is important to be able to hold the uncertainty of any theory while trying to learn it at the same time. We have tried to present a variety of perspectives in the hope that the reader will test them out against her own practice and take from each what serves her or his clients best, recognizing and tolerating the uncertainty and ambiguity of what we do not know.

The chapters in this section represent the work of researchers and practitioners. Many of them are works in progress as the authors explore what they have learned from their practice and from research. They are works in progress because it is impossible to bring closure to the study of dying that has such unclear boundaries, and for which universal explanations are impossible. They are works in progress because good practitioners are always learning from those they serve and need to be open, in each encounter, to the unexpected. Carolyn Jacobs, for example, describes this very well. Her own journey as a practitioner concerned with the spiritual life of those she serves began as a result of an encounter with a client. These chapters are works in progress because views are always changing, and we are participating in making these changes by our own work in this book. In the process, we have become increasingly aware of aspects of the human experience that until recently were not attended to, such as the impact of gender, race, and sexual orientation on dying. Do we stigmatize people for their race, for their gender, even for the fact that they are dying? What are the forces that separate people and their common experiences from each other? How do we recognize each other's differences and recognize our common humanity?

Good practice has to be responsive to the needs of those we serve. The paradigm for research presented here, that interfaces with and informs practice, is exemplified in Farber, Egnew, and Farber's chapter on a respectful death and in the findings of Silverman's research with the widowed and with bereaved children. A qualitative approach to research may be most relevant for this work (Silverman 2001). It does not test hypotheses, nor predict outcomes. It focuses on what people are experiencing at this time of their lives, accurately describing it and allowing the voices of clients or other people to energize and give direction to practice.

We also see the importance of thinking critically about the application of these ideas to practice. In a sense, every clinical interview is a small qualitative research project. Information is gathered about the client or family and a plan is made, based on an analysis of themes and a conceptualization of the problem is proposed. If the assessment and intervention(s) prove to ameliorate the problem or help people cope more effectively, then there is some reason to consider the hypothesis correct. If the intervention fails, then it is essential to develop new categories for understanding. We must always be ready to challenge and revise our theories based on our clients' experiences. Often we say that if a theory does not apply, it is the client who is at fault. We blame the victim. Practitioners in this field need to be able to say if the theory does not apply, then it is *not* the client but the theory that is at fault.

This section contains eight chapters. It begins with Phyllis Silverman's, describing how our views of dying, death, and bereavement have changed over the past millennium and how these changes have led to the current practices, attitudes, values, and institutions that are evolving today.

Seeing dying as a medical failure has led to a focus on curative medicine. Most healthcare professionals have difficulty facing that some of their patients will not live to see the end of the year and are reluctant to consider palliative or comfort care. In so doing they most often ignore the individual and his story and his preferences in this matter. The chapter on a respectful death that follows Silverman's personalizes and humanizes the dying process. Stuart Farber, Tom Egnew, and Lu Farber describe how the concept of a respectful death evolved from their own research. We no longer talk about "patients" but "people" who are more than equal partners in deciding what care they need and can get. In reading this chapter we need to consider what is needed to implement the kind of respectful care advocated in this book. Most people do not want to die in the hospital or alone. In the past, hospitals were not prepared to provide palliative and comfort care. New settings were needed. What began as a grassroots effort, in part emulating the hospice program in Great Britain, has grown and become institutionalized as hospice and palliative care in the United States. Mary Raymer and Donna Reese, in their chapter on the history of social work in hospice, describe the growth of hospice as an innovative means of providing dying people with more humane care in their own homes or in institutional settings. Hospice is more of an approach to care than a service tied to one setting.

Hospice care and most end-of-life care emphasize the importance of care by a team. No one has all of the requisite skills to provide both the required medical care as well the psychosocial and spiritual care of people at this point in their lives. Rather, a team of care providers seemed called for: a physician, a nurse, a physical therapist, a social worker, a clergyperson, a home health aide, a dietitian, a speech pathologist are all parts of the team. People who are ill in a hospital or at home often feel confused by the number of people wearing white coats who come to help and who are indistinguishable one from the other. Most people are neophytes in knowing how dying works and what professions, other than a physician and a nurse, are involved in their care. In their own homes, most people feel as if they have a bit more control over who comes and goes, whom they attach to, and who cares for them and about them. How is the team defined, then, for the dying person? How does the team define itself? How do they divide roles and responsibilities, help each other distinguish their areas of expertise, deal with the gray areas, resolve differences in expertise and what they do? Inge Corless and Patrice Nicholas, both nurses with extensive experience in end-of-life care, use a sociological lens to examine the issues that can interfere with team development, such as, for example, control and power. Social workers are generally not socialized to practice as part of a team, although in practice, especially in a medical setting, they often occupy a subordinate role. They need to consider how to collaborate, to share information, to learn from each other, and in the end to recognize that the patient or client not only is a member of the team but also should be the captain.

When we begin to focus on the needs of people who are dying, we open the door to another aspect of conflicting and competing viewpoints, this time between what healthcare personnel may think is best for the client and what the client wants for himself. Ethical dilemmas permeate all end-of-life practice and by using ethical principles, differences may be reconciled between medicalized and patient-centered care. Patricia O'Donnell describes factors that contribute to the rise of ethical issues in the end-of-life care and how they are mediated by finding ways of dealing with conflicting principles and values.

What are the factors that move people at this time in their lives, that inform their attitudes and values? One key factor is how we make meaning out of what is happening to us. This takes us to the realm of spirituality and religion, areas of human experience that have not typically been part of social work discourse. Some people have faith systems that help them think about life and death and provide them with customs and rituals that give direction to this experience. Although not the same as a faith system, many people find this a time when their quest for meaning is important, and the social worker has to be prepared to join them on their quest. Carolyn Jacobs brings us on a spiritual journey directed by her colleague and clients. She provides a framework for adding questions about a client's faith and spiritual beliefs into the interview. She begins to develop her thinking about how fluid the boundaries are between the social worker and her client and the importance of being present in the situation and of listening to what is being said rather than trying to force data into a theoretical framework.

Other factors that inform values and attitudes at the end-of-life include race, social class, gender, and ethnicity. Illene Noppe, using research data, opens a dialogue about the similarities in how women and death have been neglected in our society. She describes what it means to live in a gendered society. Her analysis forces us to examine how we treat one another and to acknowledge that our research designs, for all their espoused objectivity, often ignore or minimize these important differences.

The last two chapters of this section look at interpersonal and intrapsychic factors that influence how people think about themselves and how they act when they are bereaved. They both focus on how the bereaved are transformed by the loss and how they grow and change. Phyllis Silverman, building on her research, points to how the bereaved build new relationships with the deceased. She focuses on grief as a life-cycle issue that people live through and are changed by. Joan Berzoff's chapter on psychodynamic theory offers a historical and theoretical view of bereavement, following Freud's theories and those who wrote after him. Using concepts of identification, internalization, and introjection, she points to ways in which the bereaved take in aspects of the lost person that can be transformative, thus producing psychological growth.

Theories are valuable as they can be applied in practice, and we invite readers to apply, critique, and develop new theories based on both their practice and research. To do so is to begin to take leadership in end-of-life care.

REFERENCES

Silverman, P. R. 2001. Research, clinical practice and the human experience: Putting the pieces together. *Death Studies* 24:469–478.

5

WHAT IS A RESPECTFUL DEATH?

STU FARBER, THOMAS EGNEW, AND ANNALU FARBER

APPROACHING DEATH provides an opportunity for individuals, families, and health professionals to experience something profound and respectful. Within the modern culture of medicine, a positive concept toward death is relatively recent. Phyllis Silverman discusses death from a social and historical context in the following chapter. This chapter explores similar issues from an individual and family context. How do we as individuals, family members, caregivers, and clinicians make sense of death? How do we shift from Avery Weisman's middle knowledge to the reality that we or someone we know will die soon? Are there any universal experiences that will help social workers and other health-team members assist patients and families to have a more positive experience? We will present a research-based model for a respectful death, discuss the implications of this model for social work practice, and share the field experience of Pat and Kristin, social workers who practice exclusively in end-of-life care.

"A GOOD DEATH"

The phrase "good death" is increasingly used to describe the option for positive possibilities at the end of one's life. The concept of a good death certainly contrasts with the idea that death in any form is bad and the result of medicine's failure to cure. A good death acknowledges the inevitability of death and provides values upon which to judge more positive experiences. An example of well-accepted values for judging a good death are supplied in Ira Byock's book *Dying Well* (1997). Byock describes essential elements of a good death, including a safe environment where basic human needs of shelter, food, and nurture are provided; physical symptoms, especially pain, are aggressively managed to minimize physical suffering; and the opportunity to pursue issues of human development appropriate to the end of life are supported. He describes basic developmental tasks of value to patients and their families. These include affirmation (I love you; do you love me?), reconciliation (I forgive you; do you forgive me?), and saying goodbye.

Although few would argue the inherent value of Byock's elements for judging a "good death," they are by no means universally accepted. Anyone with personal and clinical experience in caring for seriously ill patients has experienced cases where affirmation, reconciliation, or saying goodbye were not part of either the patient's or family's experience or, in some cases, their agenda. In fact, there is grave danger that such values start to become prescriptive and seen as a formula for the successful or good death. "If only she would tell her husband that she loves him." "If he would just take his pain medicine as prescribed his dying would be so much better." "She is not safe in her apartment. She's going to fall and hurt herself. She needs to be living in a safer environment." Such statements are frequent in most hospice team meetings. The judgments are sound but are often diametrically opposed to the values, goals, or abilities of the ill person and family.

The concept of what is "good" is value-laden and implies a judgment by someone. Determining who that someone should be is not always easy. Given the high value placed on patient autonomy by our society and healthcare teams, should that someone always be the patient? What role does the caregiver have in deciding what is good, especially when he or she is worn thin by long hours of caring and is now expected to do even more? What about the social worker and other healthcare professionals who have extensive clinical experience and wisdom to share? What should clinicians do when they witness patients and families making decisions that they deeply grieve because they are certain patients and families will only add to their combined suffering? In the clinical context, these competing points of view make determining what is "good" an ephemeral task.

A RESPECTFUL DEATH

As an alternative to "a good death," we propose the term "a respectful death." In choosing the word "respect," we wish to emphasize a nonjudgmental relationship between parties. A relationship that acknowledges differences and allows for a shared process of integrating differences into as coherent a whole as possible. This shared point of view allows patients, families, and health-team members to make judgments and simultaneously embrace differences as valid and worthwhile. The challenge becomes weaving these differing perspectives into a whole cloth that supports as many of the common values as possible for all parties. Respect guides all participants to act within a tight community where the patient, family and clinicians act upon, as well as with, each other. For respect to flourish, each member must be mindful of the others and strive to understand their values and goals. It is particularly important for health team members to understand the values and goals of the highly vulnerable patient and family dealing with incurable illness who are almost always novices navigating a frightening road through the powerful culture of medicine.

PROCESS VS. PRESCRIPTION

What we wish to propose is a process of respectful exploration of the goals and values of patients and families at the end of life rather than a prescription for successfully achieving "a good death." This proposal, while ambitious, is well supported by four decades of literature. Researchers, educators, and social critics have explored how health professionals provide end-of-life care (Feifel 1959; Glaser and Strauss 1968;

Kübler-Ross 1969; Weisman 1972; Becker 1973; Corbin and Strauss 1988; Charmaz 1991). All reflect this common theme: the need to provide care based upon the unique illness experience and values of the patient and family. That we are still striving to provide such care forty years later speaks to the challenges of doing so in our present healthcare systems. The medical culture is incredibly powerful and defines the human experience in a way that easily ignores individual experience. There is little language, time, or ritual for patients and caregivers to conceptualize, let alone express, their values and goals in the battle against disease and death until death is the only possible outcome. Only then does the medical culture allow for something else to fill the void.

All of us are trained to identify problems that the patient and family experience. Once the problems are identified, we typically offer prescriptive solutions from our professional experience. How often do we *mindfully* listen to the lived experience of our patients and families as they struggle with loss and grief (Langer 1990)? How often do we mindfully hear their stories and understand them as singular experiences at one of the most mysterious and challenging points in the life cycle? How often do we act from both our professional experience and our human experience to offer creative solutions that allow our clients to live the best lives possible, based on their values and goals, before attempting to solve their problems? Coming to death is an inevitable event to be lived and not a problem to be solved. Like all living, we propose, it is an ongoing process occurring within a community. Our job is to help each member of that community—patients, families, and ourselves—live the best quality life possible while a singular life comes to an end.

Our model will describe a process for exploring a respectful death for patients, families, and health-team members. The first step in this process is discovering the individual values, meanings, and goals of the central players. The core group includes the patient, family, and clinicians. Eric Cassell (1991) describes this process as understanding stories. He particularly emphasizes understanding the patient's story. Storytelling is a way that we make sense of our lives, provide continuity, and gain a sense of identity (Kaufman 1986). By voicing and understanding all the stories being told, the community has the opportunity to create a common story in which the lived experiences of the patient and family are at the center. This common story increases the opportunity for patient and family values and goals to drive healthcare decision making, thus increasing the opportunity for medical care to support the life that patients and family want to live rather than supporting life continuance at all costs.

A RESEARCH-BASED MODEL

The editors asked us to describe the history of the model we are about to share with you. In particular, Stu Farber, from the perspective of a physician, was asked to recount how this model developed and the consequences of working with an interdisciplinary research team that included a social worker colleague, Tom Egnew, and a nursing colleague, Jan Herman-Bertsch. The journey began in 1995 when Stu Farber was awarded a Project on Death in America Scholar's grant. His project was to create a curriculum in end-of-life care for eighteen family-practice residency programs affiliated with the Department of Family Medicine at the University of Washington School of Medicine. During the initial needs assessment it became clear to Stu that most faculty would greatly improve both their clinical practice and teaching with a well-developed end-of-life curriculum. The faculty, however, felt that they provided excellent end-of-life care to their patients, did a good job of teaching it to residents, and had no time to add new elements to their already crowded curriculum.

In an effort to bridge these different perspectives, one of the research projects that developed our model of a respectful death was born. The process was a thoughtful, deliberative, and collaborative process, but how it actually occurred was a mixture of planning, creativity, and luck. Phyllis Silverman was an important consultant and mentor as Stu formulated the research project. With her firm and persistent counsel, a qualitative study was devised. The goal was to explore the issues important in end-of-life care to family-practice residency faculty and the patients and families they served. With over a decade of hospice and palliative care experience, Stu understood the highly interdisciplinary nature of end-of-life care and the importance of a research team that paralleled this interdisciplinary process. Therefore three crucial disciplines from the hospice team: social work, nursing, and medicine were recruited to the team. (Those interested in the design, methodology, and results should refer to Farber, Egnew, and Herman-Bertsch 1999; Farber et al. 2002; and Farber et al. 2003.) What we will discuss here is how the physician, nurse, and social-work perspectives influenced each other and enriched development of this model.

Stu reflects on several key benefits that come from collaborating with his nurse and social-work colleagues. First, both Tom and Jan used qualitative methodology in their doctoral dissertations, including ethnographic interviewing and grounded theory. Second, each team member brought a unique set of perspectives and abilities to the project; some from our personal experiences, and others were from our professional training. We still look back with gratification on how we were able to work together collaboratively, each of us informing the others, often challenging each other's basic assumptions, and frequently providing new ways of understanding our data based on our professional backgrounds. Tom's social work perspective allowed him to provide a deeper understanding of the psychosocial issues embedded in our research. An example was his introduction of Engel's biopsychosocial model, which greatly expanded our ability to understand the data more deeply (Engel 1977). Jan's nursing perspective helped focus us on the concept of caregiving. For example, her introduction of Mayeroff's (1990) philosophy on caring allowed us to understand more deeply the information family caregivers provided.

As we honed our working relationship with respect for each other's contributions, we also developed the common purpose of giving voice to the clinician, patient, and family caregiver experience at the end of life. Working together in a nonhierarchical, respectful, and interdisciplinary manner allowed us to understand what our subjects voiced more deeply and to develop a model to describe these experiences that was richer and more complex than what each of us could have done independently. It was a creative, satisfying, and rewarding experience.

As with any team, ours still had its limits. We felt confident that our collaborative efforts produced a rich understanding of the clinician experience. But we struggled to integrate the patient and family experience into the model we had developed from the clinician's voice. As a team we felt we needed additional help. Again respecting the value of the interdisciplinary process, we invited a cultural anthropologist and another physician experienced in qualitative research and clinical decision making to join the team. The addition of these new perspectives allowed the expanded team to develop richer ways of understanding the data and the eventual development of the seeds of our model for a respectful death. Put simply, the research process that produced this model parallels the process we are asking you to explore in assisting the patients and families you serve and in assisting your clinician team to support a respectful death.

During the same period, Stu Farber was also the lead investigator for a research project at our local cancer center. This second project focused on enhancing the patient-centered healing environment throughout the center. Surviving family care-givers of patients who had been treated at the center were invited to participate in open-ended interviews to share their experiences with and insights about what worked well, what could have gone better and what was missing for them altogether. The cancer-center research team gathered and assessed a rich pool of data that eloquently spoke to the missing component in health care—integrating the emotional and spiritual experiences of those living with cancer. In other words, we were told that medical teams weren't paying attention to the daily experiences, goals, and values of the patients and families that they were serving.

This research team decided that patients and families needed a tool that would help them reflect on their life values, meanings, and goals as they related to their illness, a tool that would amplify their voices into the medical system. Using the very words of the surviving caregivers, we began to craft a workbook for patients and families who were experiencing life-threatening illness. Lu Farber was invited to take on the project of writing, testing and implementing the workbook (Farber and Farber 2001). She brought to this work a passion for the intent of the tool, business management experience, and specific expertise in developing client-centered communications and service systems.

As the workbook concept grew into a tangible tool, it became clear that we were missing a critical voice. Lu noted that, while we had a wealth of insights from family caregivers, "we were missing the voice of cancer patients as they lived with their illness." So we initiated a pilot study of the workbook with twenty patient volunteers from the cancer center. Each participant was asked to read and complete the workbook based on his or her personal experience, then to participate in one or two focus-group feedback sessions.

The feedback from these focus groups gave us deeper and broader insights into the experience of living with cancer. We began to appreciate the value of making space for the ill person to share his or her story. Two of the most profound outcomes of these focus groups were the gratification and validation expressed by participants at having been asked about their personal values, goals, and experiences. They appreciated both the very circumstance of being asked and the opportunity to share with others who understood what they were going through. While all care team members can function in this dual role of bringing knowledge of the experience of the ill person and creating a safe place for the person to tell his or her story, we believe that social workers are uniquely trained for this task.

Lu was particularly affected by the first focus group session, which was a complete immersion into the world of those living daily with life-threatening illness. Each of the participants had been living with cancer for a significant period of time (ranging from one and a half to eight years). About forty-five minutes into the discussion, Lu was struck by the fact that no one in the room, outside herself, was likely to be alive in a year. She reflected, "This thought nearly incapacitated me, I was so overwhelmed with the grief that accompanied it. Then I realized that, for the care of those present and the good of the project, I had to stuff away these thoughts and deal with them at another time. The next day I made time to process my grief. This experience brought home to me the importance of professional care team members being aware of, acknowledging, and processing the suffering and grief that they experience as they work daily in end-of-life care."

By using the workbook, we were asking people living with cancer to consider the importance of this experience as it related to their personal values, goals, and life objectives. As the workbook became a reality, Lu worked with the cancer-center management team to develop protocols for its use in their care system. Pilot-study patients and families had told us how valuable the workbook was to their experience, and they also warned us that if we intended to give this tool to families living with serious illness, the medical system had better to be prepared to integrate their information into its care planning.

The foundation of our implementation plan is an intensive two-day workshop designed to educate all of the members of an interdisciplinary care team that focused on patient-centered care planning and communication. The workshop is highly interactive and participatory. Learners reflect first on their personal values and goals, then learn and practice the attitudes and interviewing skills necessary to bring out the story of the patient and family and establish the foundation for a respectful end-of-life experience. Social workers, nurses, and doctors alike struggle with the attitudes and skills needed to be a "listening presence" to the ill person rather than a "fixer."

The social workers that attend our workshops often recognize the seeds of their training in the attitudes and skills that we teach. They acknowledge the ease with which they become myopic and task-oriented as they pursue their work. The difficulty in true patient-centered communication is learning to begin with a blank slate and to be open to surprise. It takes concentrated effort to suspend our preconceived notions and listen deeply to the story of the "other" before we create a plan. Through research, practice, and feedback, the interdisciplinary team members, patients, and families have all helped to develop this model for respectful caring.

WHEN TO BEGIN THE DISCUSSION

When is it appropriate for social workers and other healthcare professionals to have conversations acknowledging that people are entering the end stage of their lives?

Another way of phrasing this question is, "When do you believe that your patient is at the end of her/his life?" In our work, we ask this question often of physicians, nurses, and social workers. The typical answer focuses on prognosis. Certainly a patient is at the end of life when he or she has a serious illness and all known treatments are likely to be ineffective. The problem with using prognosis in defining end of life is that we aren't very good at it (Fox et al. 1999). Using prognosis as the guide will lead to end-of-life discussions occurring in the last days or weeks of life when death is the only possible outcome. Conversely, discussing the possibility of end of life when the risk of dying is very small is equally problematic. Focusing on the possibility of dying with an otherwise healthy seventy-five-year-old who is contemplating a hip replacement may prevent that person from having a valuable surgical procedure.

Despite our limited prognostic ability, clinicians acknowledge that they do know when death is a likely outcome, though it may not be the only outcome. The typical question that innovative palliative care programs and end-of-life researchers use with clinicians to identify end-of-life patients is, "Do you have any patients in your practice that, if they died in the next year, you wouldn't be surprised?" (Farber et al. 2003). By removing the need to be certain that the ill person will die, you open up the opportunity of having more than one outcome. They may well die or they may outlive you, but the understanding that they have a significant chance of dying makes the conversation a possibility.

Those experienced in geriatric care have evolved another definition of the end of life. The end of life is that period in the life cycle where the person can expect a future of loss and diminishment on the physical and/or cognitive level. Depending on the disease process and individual experiences, the end-of-life period can be brief or prolonged. An otherwise healthy woman who dies of a massive heart attack may have an end-of-life experience that lasts no more than three minutes. On the other hand, a man who develops Alzheimer's dementia is likely to have an end-of-life experience lasting many years. Because the dementia progresses each time he has a major life-threatening complication, it could be the end of his life or not. This depends on the decisions his family and healthcare team makes on his behalf. A bout of pneumonia, a fall causing a fractured hip, or the loss of the ability to swallow food can either be seen as opportunities for a natural end to a life well lived, or for medical interventions to sustain life until the next serious illness occurs.

We propose that end-of-life discussions should be considered whenever there is a serious medical illness that threatens a person's life or when health-team members believe that death is one of many significant possible outcomes in the foreseeable future (Would you be surprised if this person died in the next year?).

CROSS-CULTURAL PERSPECTIVES

One way of understanding and integrating the differing perspectives of seriously ill people, their families, and the healthcare team is to view each medical encounter as a cross-cultural experience. Although these participants have in common that they are dealing with the end of life, each is doing so from his or her unique perspective.

Our research describes three "cultural" perspectives—the ill person, the family caregiver, and the healthcare team (Farber et al. 2003). We identified four domains common to each of these participants when dealing with far advanced, life-threatening illness:

- *Awareness:* The process of interpreting and embracing the impact of terminal illness on life experience.
- *Management/Coping:* The necessary regimen or tasks the patient and family must accomplish in order to get through each day.
- *Relationships:* Bonding through time with self, others, and the environment.
- *Personal experience:* The individual's living through the dying process.

Although each participant is dealing with these common domains, they are doing so from their differing and unique perspectives.

THE ILL PERSON

The ill people in our research emphasized the personally overwhelming impact of serious illness. Whether consciously acknowledged or not, the awareness of impending death infused every moment of their lives. This became the context in which each day was lived. Coping with the physical, financial, psychosocial, and spiritual challenges of illness; maintaining relationships in the light of change, conflict, and potential growth; and experiencing suffering, loss, spiritual growth, reconciliation, uncertainty, and physical discomfort became primary tasks. The ultimate task of the ill person was to accommodate to "my death," inevitably leaving this world and all his or her attachments to it.

THE FAMILY CAREGIVER

Family caregivers also described the overwhelming impact of serious illness, emphasizing subtle but significant differences from their loved one who was ill. Family caregivers are dealing with "my loved one's death" as opposed to dealing with "my death." The potential loss of their loved one challenged them to continue to meet their usual daily obligations while assuming the new and ever changing responsibilities of caregiving. Family members are not preparing to leave this world; instead they are living in forever-changed circumstances. The family needs to maintain stamina in order to provide caregiving; to garner appropriate community resources to provide care; to accommodate change and the loss of relationships; to experience suffering, loss, spiritual growth, reconciliation, uncertainty; and to advocate physical comfort for their loved one. The ultimate task for the family is to remain close to the ill person and support him or her and at the same time accommodate themselves to the pain of losing their loved one and constructing a new life, forever changed after the death of their loved one.

THE HEALTHCARE TEAM

Social workers, physicians, and nurses are trained to be experts in identifying problems and providing solutions from the perspective of their professional expertise. The medical perspective places the initial focus on reaching consensus with the ill person and family on the diagnosis (you have a serious disease, do you know what it is?), the prognosis (your disease is incurable and will likely cause you to die prematurely [Farber et al. 2003]), and the plan (here is the set of actions medicine recommends and here is the medical team that will provide them to you based on your disease). Clinicians described the difficulty of developing this consensus in light of the unpredictability of the disease course for any individual patient (Farber, Egnew, and Herman-Bertsch 1999).

The objective world of Western medicine upon which the diagnosis, prognosis, and plan is based is an enormously powerful view of the world of the sick. Diagnosing, prognosing, and treating define the comprehension of an illness experience that is understandable and controllable and offers the hope of actions that can prolong life. Appreciation of the personal values and goals of the ill person and family may be acknowledged but generally interpreted from a disease perspective. The lived experience of the patient and family cannot be seen without going beyond the borders of disease and its treatments. This includes awareness of death, coping with illness on a daily basis, maintaining relationships, and experiencing suffering, loss, spiritual growth, reconciliation, uncertainty, and physical discomfort.

BRIDGING THE CULTURAL GAP

Given the differing cultural perspectives, it becomes easier to see why it is so difficult to integrate an ill person's and family's perspectives into medical decision making and caring. The experience of the patient and family in their own cultural context of illness must become as real and engaging to the healthcare team as the disease that is being treated through the powerful lens of medicine in order for end-of-life care based on the values and goals of the patient and family to occur. All those involved in the patient's care must strive to bridge the cultural gap between the dominant medical culture and that of the patient and family.

One concept on which all parties—ill persons, family members, and healthcare team members—strongly agree is the importance of the presence of a therapeutic relationship (Farber, Egnew, and Herman-Bertsch 1999, 2002). This concordance provides the most effective avenue of overcoming these cultural gaps. Clinicians identified the following domains as necessary for a therapeutic relationship:

- *Commitment:* Stressing she/he will care for the patient and family through and beyond death.
- *Connection:* Creating a special relationship that allows any topic of importance to the patient and family to be discussed regardless of whether or not it is medical. This

aspect of relationship is similar to Carl Roger's concept of unconditional positive regard (Rogers 1951).

- *Consciousness:* Understanding the patient's and family's personal experience as well as the personal and professional meaning for the clinician within the ever-changing context of illness.

With definitions unique to their perspective, ill people and their families identified the same domains (Farber et al. 2003):

- *Commitment:* Actions that demonstrate commitment beyond traditional medical care; receiving help out to the car, a home visit, special foods while in the hospital, or a call between visits were perceived examples of commitment.
- *Connection:* Empathic/supportive clinicians who listen and allow the patient and family to express their personal concerns. They also spoke about clinicians who do not listen or ignore their personal concerns in strongly negative terms. Family members especially appreciate being listened to and having their perspective elicited and valued.
- *Personal Caring:* Patients appreciated clinicians who treat them as "persons" and not as "diseases." Communicating a sense of caring and openness to the ill person's experience was a fundamental need expressed and universally valued.

A PROPOSED PROTOCOL FOR EXPLORING A RESPECTFUL DEATH

1. Meet the ill person and family in a quiet setting.
2. Include all of the important participants, both from the family and the healthcare team.
3. Make sure you have adequate time and that all beepers, cell phones, etc. are turned off.
4. Create a safe environment through a therapeutic relationship. You will be discussing difficult and distressing issues and your demeanor and presence should reassure the ill person and the family that you will listen to any concerns they wish to explore, that you are committed to caring for them through the end of life, and that you will provide the information and context from your professional experience that they need to make sense of their situation.
5. Explore the ill person and family's story by asking open-ended questions. Such questions are:
    What do you think will happen to you in the next weeks? Months?
    What do you fear most?
    What do you hope for most?
    What would you like to accomplish in the rest of your life?
    What are your past experiences with serious illness and loss?
    Where do you draw your strength in times like this?
    Is there anything else I should know about you and your beliefs?

6. Listen fully, resisting the need to identify problems or suggest solutions. As you hear the story unfold, ask deeper questions that will encourage the ill person/family member to go more deeply into their own experience and will allow you to gain a better understanding of their stories (see the appendix to this chapter).

7. Once you have gained an understanding of their stories, verify what you understand by using reflective statements. Clarify the shared values and goals that are at the core of the ill person and family stories. Acknowledge differences where they exist.

8. Emphasize your commitment to integrate these values and goals into the medical context that you understand and share your professional experience on how medical/social resources can best support the patient's and family's goals and values.

9. Develop a plan of care that supports the ill person and family's story using their values and goals as the driving force in decision making, whether around medical or psychosocial support.

10. Acknowledge that suffering and loss are a part of the end of life and be a compassionate witness when no solutions are possible.

RESPECTFUL-DEATH CASE STUDIES

In our workshops we find that clinicians readily understand and embrace these concepts in theory; however, most are challenged to apply them in practice. Why is this? Participants describe many barriers, but two significant hurdles were frequently mentioned: the difficulty of identifying what we do automatically and reflecting on its value, and the uncertainty inherent in practicing something new. The second obstacle moves us from the comfortable position of "expert" to the uncomfortable one of "novice." To help the reader better grasp the attitudes and skills needed to put this respectful death model into action, we will present two case studies based on clients served by Pat and Kristin, the palliative-care social workers mentioned in this chapter's introduction.

Pat was educated as a social worker and then pursued advanced training in bereavement and spiritual counseling. She has been caring for ill people for nearly thirty years; the last fourteen have been dedicated to end-of-life care. Pat's calling has been that of a spiritual guide—listening, counseling, teaching, and being present to patients, families, and coworkers.

Kristin began her social-work education later in life, after having been a school counselor for many years. Both her life and professional experience prepared her well for social work. Kristin was drawn to end-of-life work by some unique experiences during her training, beginning with her practicum at a mental health center in a low-income community. She observed, "It seemed that whatever they [clients] were coming in for—abuse, depression, whatever—at the base of it was grief and loss." Kristin also elected to take two interdisciplinary courses, Spirituality and Medicine and The Hospice Training course, both cofacilitated by Stu Farber. These courses influenced her decision to enter end-of-life care. Kristin has been a hospice social worker in our community for two and a half years.

We will begin with the client and family stories that Pat and Kristin shared with us, then follow these cases as we explore the implications for social workers of practicing the respectful-death care model. In this way we will emphasize the diversity and challenges that social workers face when caring for clients and their families at the end of life. The names used here are not the real names of these clients.

CASE EXAMPLE: SUSAN

Pat recalled a specific experience with a woman named Susan who was admitted to our local hospice during the time that Pat was the bereavement counselor and chaplain for that team. At the team meeting Susan's husband from her second marriage was described as "very controlling" and her children were described as "extremely Christian." As Pat later listened to Susan's own story, she became aware of a woman who was "very spiritual with a more universal view of the Divine." She noted that different dimensions of this family's dynamics hooked different people on the hospice care team.

One of the nurses, whose theology was similar to the children's, sympathized with them. The children were worried about their mother's spiritual salvation and they wanted to help care for her as well, but Susan's husband would not allow them to share in their mother's care. Another of the hospice nurses worked actively to encourage the aggressive use of pain medications in support of Susan's husband's agenda. Susan said she wasn't afraid to suffer, especially if not taking medication allowed her to do the things that she wanted to do. She told the team that she could manage her pain with meditation and other complimentary therapies.

CASE EXAMPLE: TRUDY

Kristin and a hospice nurse visited Trudy in her home at the trailer park three times before Trudy trusted them enough to allow limited support services. Trudy's goals were to live independently and to have control over the decisions that affected her daily life. She was reluctant to share information or talk about what the future held.

Eventually Trudy began to tell Kristin about her childhood, problems among siblings, a strained relationship with her mother, stormy relationships with her own children, and her three marriages. Trudy also shared that she had worked in a nursing home for a while and was adamant that she not end up in one. The meaning that shaped Trudy's values and therefore her decisions became clearer as her story unfolded. Her desire for absolute control of daily activities and her uneven moods began to have some context.

As Trudy's illness progressed, both her son and her sister began to reconcile their differences with her. Her son was even ready to be Trudy's caregiver, but during one of her dramatic moods swings, Trudy lashed out him and he withdrew his offer. As Kristin put it, Trudy "had one egg in her basket and she broke it."

IMPLICATIONS FOR SOCIAL WORK PRACTICE

We have said that a respectful death involves helping patients and their families realize the end-of-life care that supports the life that they choose to live until death. Thus a relational emphasis in end-of-life care giving can bring out the values, preferences, and attitudes that support how the patient prefers to live until death, while also being attentive to similar issues for the family and coordinating those services that compassionately and respectfully support all involved. Yet, what does a respectful death mean for social workers serving dying patients and their families? What personal and professional skills are required of the social worker?

We noted at the beginning of this chapter that social workers are not well trained in the required attitudes and skills to support a respectful death. Therefore, most social workers need further preparation in order to be prepared adequately to provide care to the seriously ill and their families. This challenges each social worker who is engaged in the palliative care field to obtain education that builds professional skills and competency in (1) understanding the roles that we play when assisting a respectful death, (2) self-knowledge to facilitate appropriate role performance, (3) an appreciation for the healing power of the story of the ill person and family members, and (4) a capacity to witness suffering. Proficiency in these areas helps assure that social workers functioning in end-of-life care settings are adequately prepared to competently and professionally orchestrate a respectful death experience for dying patients and their families.

THE ROLE OF THE SOCIAL WORKER IN END-OF-LIFE CARE

Our research-based model indicates that quality end-of-life care is organized around relationships, meaning, and roles (Farber, Egnew, and Herman-Bertsch 2002). While the subjects of the original research were physicians, patients, and family-member caregivers, our patient-centered care workshops have demonstrated that the knowledge, attitudes, and skills drawn from this research are readily generalizable to social workers and nurses as well.

The social-worker role is shaped by the nonmedical goals set by the patient, the family, and the palliative-care team, the systems in place to meet these goals, and the expectations of all involved (Monroe 1993). Nonmedical goals include the expression of emotional pain and the exploration of spiritual pain. The values, meanings, and goals expressed as clients reflect on these issues are integral to the unique story that defines the hopes and dreams for the time left to the patient and family. Using the questions in our model as a process for learning these stories begins to establish a personal relationship with them. Therefore, the clinician attending a respectful death is not a detached bystander providing professional services, but rather becomes part of the fabric of the story and of the end-of-life process.

Seeing oneself "in relationship" with the ill person and family may test the traditional role that the social worker plays. This model for facilitating a respectful death challenges the standard professional and personal boundaries of relationship that clinicians create, as illustrated by Susan's story:

All participants in this story—the husband, the children, and the individual hospice team members—focused on their own goals and their own ways of problem solving. Susan often seemed to struggle against the team. She had a clear path that she wished to follow which was different from the agendas of her husband, her children or some of the hospice team members.

One day the hospice nurse that sympathized with the children made a home visit and listened to Susan describe a recurrent dream that she was having about snakes. The nurse became alarmed and called Pat out to the home to "take care of this." The nurse feared that this was some horrible satanic imagery, and she was concerned that this indicated that Susan was in great distress.

By acknowledging that the social worker cannot separate her/his personal and professional self from the shared story of the client and family, significant tension may arise. If we become personally overwhelmed by sharing in the client and family's grief and suffering, our ability to offer them professional support may be impaired. Conversely, if we distance ourselves to prevent being overwhelmed, we run the danger of being so detached that we are unable to truly share in the patient and family's experience to gain an understanding of their story.

In our research we describe three roles that clinicians often assume in developing effective relationships with patients and families when facilitating a respectful death: the consultant, the collaborator and the guide (Farber, Egnew, and Herman-Bertsch 2002). We will explore these roles and the implications for palliative-care social workers as they become actors in the patient and family story. More important than the role labels themselves are the attitudes and skills adopted in each role.

The consultant provides expert information to the dying patient and family, based on their particular diagnosis and stage of disease. This requires an appreciation of a variety of personal and systems responses to death and dying. In this role social workers must understand the impact of pain, disability, and chronic illness on the ill person and the family, must integrate physiological data pertinent to a particular case, and must be aware of national policies, funding, and other systems variables that affect the care effort (Sieppert 1996; Egan and Kadushin 1999; Yagoda 2002). The consultant tends to remain more detached and be a provider of clinically significant information. Yet providing pertinent information and appropriate referrals can only occur after careful exploration of the family's values and goals in order to appreciate their understanding of the situation and provide the support they need. Effective consultation leads to referrals that alleviate troublesome symptoms and stressors, freeing the ill person and family's energy for achieving their personally defined goals.

More effective roles for an end-of-life practice that embraces the respectful-death model are those of the collaborator and the guide. As a collaborator, the social worker shares information with the patient and family to promote a common understanding of the end-of-life experience. This involves developing therapeutic relationships with patients and their families to provide personal support. Clinicians have knowledge of the medical environment and the resources available to treat and support the challenges of illness. But what significant knowledge do the patient and family bring to the discussion? They are experts in knowing how they live their lives, what is meaningful to them, and in defining their important goals. Using the questions outlined in the protocol earlier, we begin by determining the patient's understanding of the situation, his or her past experiences with illness that shape present responses, and the particular concerns of the patient and family that will affect the care effort. Effective collaborators elicit the special knowledge of the ill person and family, then weave this together with their expert knowledge of the end-of-life experience to recommend a plan of care consistent with the hopes, dreams, wishes, and values for the time left to them to share. Social workers, possessing relational skills and a systems focus, are particularly suited to be collaborators.

In the role of guide, the social worker may seek solutions for the patient based not only on professional expertise and the patient's values and preferences but also on the social worker's knowledge of the end-of-life context. Having determined that the end of a person's life is near and what is important to that person and his or her family at this time, the guide shows them "how to get there" (Farber, Egnew, and Herman-Bertsch 2002:155). In this role, the guide acts as both an advisor, promoting a treatment plan that is most appropriate for the dying patient's and family's unique situation, and an advocate, actively helping them to overcome obstacles and achieve their goals (Farber et al. 2000). The guide role is perhaps the most difficult and controversial for social workers due to its potential conflict with the social work value of self-determination. We believe that it may also be the most effective role for promoting a respectful death.

Self-determination is a core value that social workers are trained to promote particularly in cases of palliative care (Csikai and Bass 2000). Indeed, NASW (1994) has published a policy entitled "Client Self-Determination and End of Life Decisions." Yet the NASW policy has been criticized for stressing self-determination at the expense of the common good, and social workers are called to promote both (Wesley 1996). Let us look further at Trudy's situation:

Trudy's fierce independence often posed grave safety hazards. She used oxygen and she was a smoker, sometimes she would do both at the same time. When it became clear that Trudy was not safe and that no amount of counseling would change her behaviors, Kristin began to seek options for care that honored Trudy's goals. One day, when she came to Trudy's home for a scheduled visit, Kristin found Trudy in a coma. Kristin admitted Trudy to the hospital for a respite stay while the hospice team tried to figure out how best to care for her.

The only safe options for care appeared to be either a nursing home or an adult family home. Kristin knew that it was her job as the team's social worker to discuss these limited options with Trudy.

How does the social worker attending a respectful death act as a guide or collaborator for the dying patient and family without compromising self-determination? The answer lies in understanding the limitations of self-determination in the end-of-life scenario. The reality of palliative care is that the dying person and family have no choice in the impending death, only in the quality of life until death. With death looming, self-determination can be limited by a lack of information for considering options, compromised mental competency, external factors that limit choices, the values of the professionals involved in a particular case, or the legal requirements regarding interventions (Biesteck 1957). "Patients often can't make these [medical] decisions because they never have," Pat notes; "they live in the context of their families and communities. We are responsible to help them." In a respectful death, self-determination is best realized when the dying person and the family have authorship of the story of their time left together and are guided to care that supports the values and goals they define.

We earlier described the seriously ill patient and family as novices to the worlds of medicine and death. They often have little or no understanding of the medical and social systems that shape the process of dying. Thus, they are naive regarding the impact of their choices on the attainment of their goals and objectives. This renders them both dependent on those providing advice and vulnerable to unintended consequences from their decisions. Into this breach the social worker steps to usher the patient and family toward an end-of-life experience that respects their values. This is what Pat was able to do for Susan, her family and the hospice team:

At the request of the hospice nurse, Pat made her first visit to Susan's home. She sat with Susan and began to explore Susan's experience. "Do your dreams upset you? What do these dreams mean to you?" Susan answered that she hadn't been upset at all until the nurse and the kids had gotten so upset. In Susan's view of the world she had many ways of seeing the Divine all around her. She frequently drew on symbolism from mythology. A certain snake in mythology swallows its own tail, which begins the process of regeneration. She saw her dreams as a symbol of healing and rebirth, and she talked about the snakes intertwined on the staff of the healer—the age-old symbol for doctors of medicine.

"Each one of us," Sherwin Nuland notes, "needs a guide who knows *us* as well as he knows the pathways by which we can approach death" (1994:266). By bringing the special knowledge of the patient and family to care planning, by asking about their meanings, values, and goals and by grounding care decisions in this knowledge, the social worker guides the ill person and the family to decisions that will best fulfill their desires and helps to create a respectful death for all involved.

SELF-KNOWLEDGE

Death is a most personal and profound human experience. The combination of physical, social, psychological, and spiritual issues involved in death demands that those working in end-of-life care not only have a broad understanding of the issues related to death and dying, but also are personally comfortable with those issues. When we are able to achieve this balance, we may still be challenged. We wonder if we are accurate in our understanding of the client and family's story. Are our professional caring actions supporting their goals or are these actions merely our own projections of what we hope or wish for them or, perhaps, for ourselves? The skills of self-reflection, living with uncertainty, creativity, and flexibility become paramount for success. Our research found that attending to seriously ill patients means that clinicians are exposed to loss, incapacitation, disability, despair, and grief, which could be very stressful (Farber, Egnew, and Herman-Bertsch 1999). Adopting an attitude of unconditional positive regard helps the ill person to set the agenda so the social worker better can understand the client's story. Respecting the story of the client and family while presenting a medical context that may create distress and suffering requires a highly developed set of relational and communication skills.

Personal knowledge of one's own responses to loss, the professional confidence to be flexible in care planning, and collaboration with other professionals to promote therapeutic relationships with clients and families all support a respectful end-of-life experience. Having gained perspective, the stresses of caring for the seriously ill can be balanced by the personal satisfaction of assisting these people and their relatives in the experience of a death reflective of their hopes and values (Ramirez, Addington-Hall, and Richards 1998).

THE SYSTEM OF CARE

Palliative-care social work cannot be done by rote; each case is a unique creation meeting the distinctive needs of the patient and family for a respectful death. Neither can this work be done in a vacuum. Much of what we need to know is how to access and interpret the knowledge of the patient and family. Palliative care social workers must therefore be open to the uncertainty that comes with not owning all of the knowledge as well as have insight into their personal biases in order to maintain the flexibility required to assure that care plans reflect the desires of patient and family.

Our respectful-death model has significant implications for how social workers and other clinicians work together in providing appropriate care for the ill person and family. The same approach we use in developing relationships with the client and family—acknowledging their expertise, accepting differences, self-reflection, collaboration, building consensus, and providing care that supports the client and family's goals—should be brought to our work with fellow clinicians. Traditional multidisciplinary medical teams do not reflect this parallel process. Defined professional boundaries, hierarchical structure, communication limited to the medical chart, constrained appreciation for discipline-specific expertise restricts the ability of social workers and other clinicians to collaborate and support each other in the challenging work of caring for ill people and families at the end of life (Doyle, Hanks, and MacDonald 1998).

Interdisciplinary teamwork requires open communication, allowing team members to work together toward the goal of supporting patient and family values more effectively than individual efforts could achieve. The challenge of creating and maintaining such teams is significant but can be achieved by applying the same model of care that we propose employing for patient and family—discovering and understanding the values and goals of each teammate in an effort to enhance collaboration. Keeping team function or dysfunction from interfering with the intense end-of-life experience of clients is very important. Social workers often uniquely possess the attitudes and skills to facilitate team development while still advocating for a care plan that focuses on supporting their clients' values and goals. And an integral part of the care team is the family, especially as the patient's support needs increase.

Family, whether biological or "of choice," is most often the basic source of daily support for the seriously ill person. Family caregivers must be identified, prepared to do their jobs, and supported, since care plan implementation is "only as good as their primary caregiver" (Farber, Egnew, and Herman-Bertsch 1999:528). Imparting sensitive information to promote an accurate understanding is important to the patient and family being able to make informed decisions (Buckman 1992). Social workers should begin the exploration of available support systems early, in order to maximize preparedness in the event that the need for daily care arises. One who is seriously ill is often overwhelmed with the immediate circumstances of their illness, as is the family, so no one is projecting much beyond the current moment. The simple question, "Who would care for you if you were no longer able to care for yourself?" often helps the family prepare for this potential future outcome.

Another key social work task is listening to and helping the client and family share feelings and information to address the problems death brings, to raise awareness of differing values and objectives, and to facilitate the consensus-building necessary to help them achieve their desires for their time left together (Monroe 1993:570; Csikai and Bass 2000). Returning to Susan's story, her family was in great distress about her care and had not been guided to develop a consensus on the goals of care.

After meeting with Susan and coming to understand her goals, Pat asked the hospice social worker to join her in a conversation with the children. They began by asking the children what they valued most about their own religious beliefs. It took some time but the children were eventually able to articulate that they value, "God's love for each of us." Identifying this core value began to change their view of the situation. Pat asked them to think about how they could be most respectful of their mother. They decided that their role was to love their mother and to try to accept that Susan's values worked for her.

Pat and the social worker then had a separate meeting with Susan's husband. They began by acknowledging her husband's pain and asking how this situation was feeling for him. Pat asked him how he thought his decisions were affecting his wife. They helped her husband reframe his need for control and see that it was his way of loving his wife—he couldn't bear losing her, so he tried to control all that was going on.

To make space for such awareness and sharing, the social worker must master the role of being a listening presence in the company of the client and family, sometimes a difficult task in the face of all the suffering that accompanies palliative and end-of-life care.

THE IMPORTANCE OF STORY IN THE
SOCIAL WORK ASSESSMENT

The mark of a caring relationship is the intent to induce positive change (Mayeroff 1990). Yet, in a respectful death, who is to determine what change is positive? This can be discovered only by attending to the story that the client and family tell of their experience, for it is through their story that their suffering is voiced and the clues to its resolution revealed. Most clinicians are not trained to hear clients' stories and often seek to limit their storytelling in order to maintain diagnostic clarity, support efficiency, and avoid confusion and unpleasant feelings (Waitzkin 1991). In this process, the patient's story is neither heard nor honored. The social worker who would hope to orchestrate a respectful death must therefore have an appreciation of the power that story holds in caring for those facing serious illness and their families.

Becoming ill and dying calls for story in two senses: to address the damage to the sense of where one is and where one is going in life, and to convey this sense of being broken to those who inquire. As Frank explains, "The conventional expectation of any narrative, held alike by listeners and story tellers, is for a past that leads into a present that sets in place a foreseeable future. The illness story is wrecked because its present is not what the past was supposed to lead up to, and the future is scarcely thinkable" (1995:55). Indeed, there is a driving need for the individuals facing illness and death to make sense of and communicate their experience (Cousins 1979; Broyard 1992; Topf 1995). Often facing illness and death brings about major changes in how individuals perceive themselves, others, and life.

Suffering has been conceived of as arising from perceptions of a threat to the self (Cassell 1982). "Nothing so denies us and our stories," Amato has observed, "as the denial of our sufferings and sacrifices" (1990:210). The sharing of stories of suffering and sacrifice allows a seriously ill person to fashion a new sense of self with new meanings, essentially rewriting the story of the life that is being lived and is soon to end. The simple act of hearing the story helps the social worker develop a therapeutic relationship that is crucial to the care effort. "All of our interactions put us in relationship with the people that we are serving," Pat remarks. "When you see patients in a relational way. it can't help but impact you." From this relationship springs the seeds for crafting a life-end story that is respectful and meaningful, but only if the caring relationship is grounded in the patient's story, as in Susan's case:

Susan's end-of-life was not what many would consider a "good death." Susan chose to live the end of her life in a way that by others' standards might have appeared to include a lot of suffering related to her refusal of pain medications. It was often difficult for her family and hospice team members. The ending she chose, however, had meaning for her. As the family developed a better understanding of Susan's goals and their role in supporting her, they too came to a better place.

Care must be taken that the goals of professional assessment not take precedence over sharing the patient's and family's story. Assessment is a reorganization of the material contained in the story, rewritten in professional language to communicate to the care team what is necessary to support the care effort. Ideally, the assessment utilizes patient-centered interviewing techniques (Steward et al. 1995; Laine and Davidoff 1996), drawing on the full range of questions represented in the appendix to this chapter. Patient-centered interviewing focuses on experiences of illness in the context of clients' lives and considers treatment decisions as being collaborations toward common ground concerning the care to be dispensed. Still, an interview technique is not the same as sharing a story, for interviews focus on the collection of professionally pertinent data and stories are revealed through dialogue.

Dialogue is distinctive for its exclusive focus on understanding without judging or categorizing (Senge 1990). The drive to collect data in an interview can inadvertently squelch the telling of the story. Patient-centered interviewing techniques use open-ended questions and probe for meaning, values, and goals. Only after hearing the values and goals embedded in the stories of the client and family can a useful care plan, reflective of their wishes, be crafted. The story of the patient and family must first be woven into the assessment so that the care plan can reflect their story in a meaningful way and have healing power (Hunter 1991).

A respectful death is grounded in the values and goals of the client and family. Simply sharing in the story can be therapeutic for all, for it provides the context in which both patient and family can rewrite the story of their lives together to bring closure and meaning to the end-story. Ideally, a respectful death occurs when the care provided closely supports the authorship of the dying patient and family, with the clinician acting as editor rather than author in the process.

A WITNESS TO SUFFERING

In our research patients and families identified concerns about abandonment as in-fluential to their experiences and stressed the value of having a healthcare team committed to staying the course with them. Suffering occurs in the context of a perceived threat to the integrity of the self (Cassell 1982), loss of a perceived future and unresolved relational issues. In the face of such discomfort, to rush to action and try somehow to "fix" things is tempting. This is often counterproductive, for the locus of action stems from our own anxiety and professional training rather than being centered on the needs and goals of the client or the family. In the face of suffering, it is better to "just stand there" rather than to "do something" aimlessly or precipitously.

To be present to those who are suffering, it is important for the palliative care social worker to cultivate what Dass and Gorman call a "Witness": "What's required is to cultivate a dispassionate Witness within. This Witness grows stronger, can see precisely how we jump the gun in the presence of pain. It notices how our reactions might be perpetuating denial or fear or tension in the situation, the very qualities we'd like to help alleviate. The Witness catches us in the act, but gently, without reproach, so we can simply acknowledge our reactivity and begin to let it fall away, allowing our natural compassion to come more into play. The Witness gives us a little room" (1985:67). The development of such a presence in the face of suffering enables the social worker to stay engaged without rushing to relieve that which may not be relievable. We see this in Trudy's case:

As Kristin made several attempts to discuss safe care options over the course of two days, Trudy became deeply resentful and accused Kristin of not having been honest with her. On the third morning Kristin went to Trudy's room again, very uncertain about how to resolve the situation. Trudy met her with intense anger.

Kristin sat quietly with Trudy, then began by observing that this was a tough situation with no easy solutions. She reviewed some of the things that had occurred leading up to this decision point then, she said, "Trudy, this is such a hard situation. What do you think the solution is?" Trudy thought for a while, then responded, "I guess it's time for me to go to a nursing home." Kristin was amazed at this response and noted the immediate change in Trudy's demeanor: "She came back to her old self again and began to make the best of a really horrible situation. Once she was listened to and not pushed, she was able to come to her own decision, which gave her the power that she wanted." Kristin had taken the time to understand what made life meaningful for Trudy. Because of the safety issues Hospice was unable to honor Trudy's desire for autonomy and independent living, but Kristin was able to respect Trudy's need to make decisions for herself and retain a sense of control.

Staying engaged helps reduce suffering by allowing the ill and their families to share their suffering, thereby addressing their fears of isolation and abandonment. Staying engaged means sharing the patient's and family's experience, not being a detached problem solver. It requires becoming comfortable with silence, something with which professionals, taught to be instrumental and in control, often struggle

(Monroe 1993). Staying engaged creates a safe space for those suffering to come to terms with their real and impending losses. Kristin did something for Trudy that was very powerful: she sat with Trudy's suffering, fully committed to staying the course with her, until Trudy could come to her own resolution. There is therapeutic power in being present to suffering.

SUMMARY

Social workers are not well prepared by their professional education to provide end-of-life care services, but they do come with knowledge and skills helpful to ill people, their families, and the palliative care teams that support them. Pat and Kristin both stressed the value of learning the client's story—what they value, what gives them meaning and strength—and discovering the client's personal goals. Kristin observed that the value of this respectful death model is that "it puts the patient in the center of the system, across the system." It informs the development of the plan of care and the resources that social workers bring to support the family.

In years of caring for and learning from the families she has served, Pat noted that often "how we try to 'save' people can be abusive." She added that we must work to be present out of our "giftedness rather than out of our own need." Both of these palliative-care team members believe deeply in the need to recognize and separate their own values and discomfort from those of the ill person and family. Pat explains, "I must acknowledge first what is going on with me. I must name my own discomfort before I can be a witness to your suffering." Here is where we begin to work with the ill person and their family in a meaningful way. This requires learning the deeper techniques of open questioning, listening, and being present to the client, the family, ourselves, and our coworkers on the clinical team.

APPENDIX: SUGGESTED QUESTIONS TO EXPLORE PATIENT/CAREGIVER PERSPECTIVES

PATIENT	CAREGIVER
AWARENESS	
My Death	**My Loved One's Death**
Many patients with this condition tell me they think about the possibility of dying. They have questions about this. Do you?	Many families caring for a person with this condition tell me they think about the possibility of their loved one dying. They have questions about this. Do you?
You say you will beat this illness. Is there any time, if only for a few moments, when you are not so sure?	You/your loved one says (he/she) will beat this illness. Is there any time, if only for a few moments, when you are not so sure?

How does your cultural tradition approach a serious illness like yours? What traditions, beliefs or rituals should we be aware of?

How does your cultural tradition approach the end of life? Are there any traditions, beliefs, or rituals we should be aware of?

My Life Has Changed

How has your life changed since you began caring for your ill loved one?

Uncertainty

When you think about getting very sick, what worries you the most?

Uncertainty

When you think about getting very sick, what worries you the most?

MANAGEMENT/COPING

Coping: Physical

How do you cope with the physical limitations and challenges of your illness?

Coping: Stamina

How do you maintain the energy to care for your loved one and at the same time renew your own physical, emotional, and spiritual strength?

Coping: Financial

How do you cope with the financial demands resulting from your illness?

Coping: Financial

How do you cope with the financial demands resulting from (his/her) illness?

Coping: Psychosocial/Spiritual

As you think about your current condition, what are the hardest issues for you?

Coping: Psychosocial/Spiritual

As you think about your loved one's current condition, what are the hardest issues for you?

Coping: Resources

Do you have all the resources you need to care for your loved one? If not, where do you need help?

RELATIONSHIP

Continuity

What roles and responsibilities do you want to maintain?

Continuity

What roles and responsibilities do you want your loved one to maintain?

Change

What roles and responsibilities have you had to give up?

Change

What roles and responsibilities have you had to take on/give up because of your loved one's illness?

Conflict	Conflict
How do you deal with changes in the way you relate to your relative or caregiver caused by your illness?	How do you deal with changes in the way you relate to your loved one caused by his or her illness?

Growth	Growth
Has this illness increased your appreciation of your abilities or potentials?	Has caring for your loved one increased your appreciation of your potentials?

PERSONAL EXPERIENCE

Suffering	Suffering
As you think about your current condition, what is the hardest thing for you? What do you fear the most?	As you think about your loved one's current condition, what is the hardest thing for you? What do you fear the most?

Loss	Loss
What are the hardest losses you have experienced with this illness?	What are the hardest losses you have experienced while caring for your loved one?

Spiritual	Spiritual
From what sources do you draw your strength?	From what sources do you draw your strength?
What role does spirituality play in your life?	What role does spirituality play in your life?

Reconciliation	Reconciliation
If you died tonight, is there anything you would leave unsaid or you would regret?	If your loved one died tonight, is there anything you would leave unsaid or you would regret?

Physical Discomfort	Physical Discomfort
Are you suffering physically in any way? Afraid of anything?	Are there symptoms your loved one is experiencing that cause you to suffer?

Note: Questions may be asked of the patient and caregiver alone or together.

Source: Farber, Egnew, and Herman-Bertsch 1999.

REFERENCES

Amato, J. A. 1990. *Victims and Values: A History and a Theory of Suffering.* New York: Praeger.

Becker, E. 1973. *The Denial of Death.* New York: Free Press.

Biestek, F. 1957. *The Casework Relationship.* Chicago: Loyola University Press.

Broyard, A. 1992. *Intoxicated by My Illness.* New York: Potter.

Buckman, R. 1992. *How to Break Bad News.* Baltimore: Johns Hopkins University Press.

Byock, I. 1997. *Dying Well.* New York: Riverhead.

Cassell, E. J. 1982. The nature of suffering and the goals of medicine. *New England Journal of Medicine* 306(11): 639–645.

——. 1991. *The Nature of Suffering and the Goals of Medicine.* New York: Oxford University Press.

Charmaz, K. 1991. *Good Days, Bad Days: The Self in Chronic Illness and Time.* New Brunswick, NJ: Rutgers University Press.

Corbin, J. M., and A. L. Strauss. 1988. *Unending Work and Care: Managing Chronic Illness at Home.* San Francisco: Jossey-Bass.

Cousins, N. 1979. *Anatomy of an Illness as Perceived by the Patient.* New York: Norton.

Csikai, E. L., and K. Bass. 2000. Health care social workers' views of ethical issues, practice, and policy in end-of-life care. *Social Work in Health Care* 31(2): 1–22.

Dass, R., and P. Gorman. 1985. *How Can I Help.* New York: Knopf.

Doyle, D., G. W. C. Hanks, and N. MacDonald, eds. 1998. *Oxford Textbook of Palliative Medicine,* 2d ed. New York: Oxford University Press.

Egan, M., and G. Kadushin. 1999. The social worker in the emerging field of home care: Professional activities and ethical concerns. *Health and Social Work* 24(1): 44–55.

Engel, G. L. 1977. The need for a new medical model: A challenge to biomedicine. *Science* 196:129–36.

Farber, S. J., T. R. Egnew, and J. L. Herman-Bertsch. 1999. Issues in end-of-life care: Family practice faculty perceptions. *Journal of Family Practice* 49(7): 525–530.

——. 2002. Defining effective clinician roles in end-of-life care. *Journal of Family Practice* 51(2): 153–158.

Farber, S. J., T. R. Egnew, J. L. Herman-Bertsch, T. R. Taylor, and G. Guldin. 2003. Issues in end-of-life care: Patient, caregiver and clinician perceptions. *Journal of Palliative Medicine* 6(1): 19–31.

Farber S. J., T. R. Egnew, J. Stempel, and J. Vleck. 2000. *End-of-Life Care.* Kansas City, MO: American Academy of Family Physicians.

Farber, S. J., and Farber, L. 2001. My care guide: A plan for personal health care. Unpublished manuscript.

Feifel, H., ed. 1959. *The Meaning of Death.* New York: McGraw-Hill.

Fox, E., K. Landrum-McNiff, Z. Shong, et al. 1999. Evaluation of prognostic criteria for determining hospice eligibility in patients with advanced lung, heart or liver disease. *Journal of the American Medical Association* 282(17): 1638–1645.

Frank, A. W. 1995. *The Wounded Storyteller: Body, Illness, and Ethics.* Chicago: University of Chicago Press.

Glaser, B. G., and A. Strauss. 1968. *Time for Dying.* Chicago: Aldine.

Hunter, K. M. 1991. *Doctors' Stories: The Narrative Structure of Medical Knowledge.* Princeton, NJ: Princeton University Press.

Kaufman, S. R. 1986. *The Ageless Self.* Madison: University of Wisconsin Press.

Kübler-Ross, E. 1969. *On Death and Dying.* New York: Macmillan.

Laine, C., and F. Davidoff. 1996. Patient-centered medicine. *Journal of the American Medical Association* 275:52–56.

Langer, E. 1990. *Mindfulness.* Cambridge, MA: Perseus.

Mayeroff, M. 1990. *On Caring.* New York: HarperCollins.

Monroe, B. 1993. Social work in palliative care. In *Oxford Textbook of Palliative Care,* ed. D. Doyle, G. W. C. Hanks, and N. MacDonald, 565–574. London: Oxford University Press.

National Association of Social Workers. 1994. Client self-determination in end-of-life decisions. In *Social Work Speaks: NASW Policy Statements*, 58–61. Washington, DC: NASW Press.

Nuland, S. 1994. *How We Die*. New York: Knopf.

Ramirez, A., J. Addington-Hall, and M. Richards. 1998. ABC of palliative care: The carers. *British Medical Journal* 316(7126): 208–211.

Rogers, C. R. 1973. Client-centered therapy: My philosophy of interpersonal relationships and how it grew. *Journal of Humanistic Psychology* 13:3–15.

Senge, P. M. 1990. *The Fifth Discipline: The Art and Practice of the Learning Organization*. New York: Doubleday.

Sieppert, J. D. 1996. Attitudes toward and knowledge of chronic pain: A survey of medical social workers. *Health and Social Work* 21(2): 122–130.

Steward, M., J. B. Brown, W. W. Weston, I. R. McWhinney, and T. R. Freeman. 1995. *Patient-Centered Medicine*. Thousand Oaks, CA: Sage.

Topf, L. N. 1995. *You Are Not Your Illness: Seven Principles for Meeting the Challenge*. New York: Simon & Schuster.

Waitzkin, H. 1991. *The Politics of Medical Encounters: How Patients and Doctors Deal with Social Problems*. New Haven, CT: Yale University Press.

Weisman, A. 1972. *On Dying and Denying: A Psychiatric Study of Terminality*. New York: Behavioral Publications.

Wesley, C. A. 1996. Social work and end-of-life decisions: Self-determination and the common good. *Health and Social Work* 21(2): 115–121.

Yagoda, L. 2002. End-of-life care for older clients: What social workers should know about the Medicare hospice benefit. www.socialworkers.org.

6

DYING AND BEREAVEMENT IN HISTORICAL PERSPECTIVE

PHYLLIS R. SILVERMAN

Death is the only one of life's experiences we cannot share . . . nor can we impart to others what its lessons truly are, how it feels and is. The only lesson we can pass on to our fellows is the example of living decently and dying well. —Cyrus Sulzberger, My Brother Death

THIS CHAPTER will briefly look at how attitudes, beliefs, and practices that affect how we approach dying, death, and bereavement have changed over time. For social workers who want to help both people at the end of their lives and the bereaved, it becomes critical to understand that there has been little constancy over the centuries in how death is viewed and how grief is understood. How we live out the end of our lives and how we mourn must be looked at contextually: that is, it cannot be separated from the attitudes, values, and beliefs of the society in which we live. The view presented in this chapter is that how we make meaning of death, and how we deal with this fact of life, is the result of socially shaped ideas and assumptions subject to historical and cultural changes (Charmaz 1994; Stroebe et al. 1996; Walter 1999; Rosenblatt 2001). The concept of social construction suggests that these values, attitudes, and behaviors, while evolving from past experiences reflect the time, place, and context in which they are occurring. This point of view leads us to recognize that there may be no right way to live the end of life or to mourn, that how this is done may relate to many other factors that influence how we behave. Only with this broader understanding is it possible to grasp what is required to be effective helpers.

Rosenblatt (2001) reminds us that in a world where everything is relative, it is difficult to find the universal aspects in human behavior. However, the fact that everyone dies is not socially constructed; we all have this in common. Nor is the notion that people react to death socially constructed. *How* we react and how we experience these events are socially constructed. This is clearly reflected in that every society and faith system has developed some way of integrating the reality of death into their belief systems and ways of life. As we will see later in this chapter, these systems and beliefs have changed considerably over the centuries. Thus, the attitudes and values of the society we live in provide direction for how we understand illness and health, how we define our purpose and place in the world, and how death fits into this picture. These attitudes and values affect how we relate not only to ourselves but to others as well, and how we give our experiences meaning. To understand any one person's or society's thoughts, feelings and attitudes about death, we need to recognize that these ways of making meaning are not isolated personal variables but are effected by the historical, social, and economic context of the time. Another way of saying this is to ask: What voices influence this culture and what do they have to say?

Explaining human behavior around death and bereavement is no longer the prerogative of philosophers and clergymen. For the most part, contemporary views of grief are framed by modern psychological theories, and it is the voice of the psychologist that we hear. During the twentieth century we have witnessed what Meyer (1988) called the creation of the modern psychological individual. He sees the qualities that define this individual as related to the complex social changes taking place in Western economic, cultural, and political systems that foster the ideology of individualism. Psychological theories, following this view of reality, focus on the individual's responsibility for his or her own inner psyche, as well as that of his or her children. In this view of human behavior, the influence of the social and community context is minimized as a mediator of how people cope with their dying and with their grief. When we frame the needs of the dying and the bereaved in psychological terms, which can be helpful in understanding people's adequacies, inadequacies, and needs in dealing with these situations, we focus primarily on the inner life of an individual. This limited view can stand in our way of seeing the fullness of what is happening. Our view, whether limited or expansive, influences the support and care that we make available at this time in people's lives. Helpers in each generation have to be sensitive to changing cultural views that may require new forms of support and intervention.

Although I do not think that it is always possible to make a true dichotomy of what happens when someone is dying and the grief of those who survive the loss, there seems to me to be sufficient difference to divide what follows into two sections. The first deals with how death is viewed, and the second with the mourning process that follows. Although the first may influence the second, these are in many ways two different experiences. When someone is at the end of his/her life, the focus is on this dying person's needs, support, and the care they require during this process. This is a time-limited process that ends with death. Grief is an intimate part of this process. As death approaches, the dying person loses more and more and mourns these losses. As family and friends grieve with the dying person, they also begin to anticipate what it will be like without this person, and there is grief in this experience as well. However, as long as the person at the end of his or her life still lives, the energy of those involved is focused on that life and on continuing that relationship, regardless of how it is changed by the end-of-life circumstances. Another kind of grief begins once the door is finally closed and the loved one is gone. We need to understand this difference.

Mourners face the silence of the grave. Part of the difference comes in the sense of time: There is finality to a death, an end. Grief, on the other hand, may seem endless, and time gets measured in a different way as people find their way through their grief. The division into two sections allows me to focus on the unique experience of the dying and then of the bereaved. Where I do not succeed, I leave it to the reader to bring the pieces together.

ON DEATH AND DYING

GIVING DEATH MEANING

It is a biological fact that we all die, a fact with which we must learn to live. Weissman (1972) wisely pointed out that if we spend all our energies anticipating that at some point our life will end, the life that we have to live will become untenable. We all live with what he calls "middle knowledge," implying that while we know what the ultimate reality is, our daily actions avoid and ignore this fact. We thus construct a world that allows us both to move toward this reality and to move away from it. To do this effectively, we must both face death and construct a view of it that frames this middle knowledge.

Staton, Roger, and Byock (2001) observe that one can tell a lot about a society by the way it deals with death and cares for its people who are nearing life's end. Without exception, all societies have rituals to guide the dying, rules for disposal of the body, and a system of beliefs about what happens after death. These beliefs and rituals were often quite prescriptive until the beginning of the twentieth century.

WHEN DEATH WAS A FREQUENT AND FAMILIAR VISITOR

Throughout history, death was an everyday occurrence in most communities, and people experienced it as an expected part of their lives. Such killers as the plague and infectious diseases were constant companions, and in many parts of the world this is still true. Children were often not named during the first year of their lives, waiting until it was clear that they would survive. People usually died at home and were readied for burial there. The body was prepared by members of the family as part of their accepted obligation to the deceased.

Most people felt prepared for the inevitability of death. Basic religious faith provided structure for people to be ready to "meet their Maker" and to accept their fate or destiny. Walter (1999) observes that in the nineteenth century, when someone was dying people asked if they were being sustained by their faith. This is in contrast to the question common in the late twentieth and early twenty-first centuries: "Was it a pain-free death?" A family diary from the 1850s reports a conversation between a minister and a dying young woman. The minister asks if the woman is ready to meet her Maker. She answers that she is and quietly awaits her end (Edmonds 1847–99). Given the limitations of medicine at the time, there was little else that could be done but to provide a comforting environment and wait for the inevitable.

Ariès (1981), focusing on specific historical periods over the past millennium, describes the various ways death was viewed in Western, Christian cultures. His analysis provides us with an overview of how attitudes and values toward dying and death have changed. He identified five historical periods, each with their unique qualities: Tame Death, Death of Self, Remote and Imminent Death, Death of the Other, and Death Denied or Forbidden Death. Corr, Nabe, and Corr (1997) point out that these periods overlap, and even today it is possible to identify aspects of each of these approaches in contemporary behaviors and traditions.

A TAME DEATH. During this period, from approximately 400 C.E. to 1100 C.E., the dying and their communities knew what was expected of them. The dying person was usually at the center of a group of people who followed prescribed behaviors, known to them all, including how she should place her body in preparing for the expected end. It was often the dying person who knew how long he had to live and could tell others when it was "time." Death was constructed as sleep, awaiting the second coming of Christ. The dying, having confessed their sins, felt they were assured a place in the world to come. People tended not to fear what awaited them and understood that "we shall all die" (De Spelder and Strickland 2002). Most people were buried in common graves. The most undesirable death was one that was sudden and solitary, not leaving time for the dying person to prepare with confession and prayer. A sudden death was sometimes associated with shame, seen as the wrath of God in disguise, spoiling the expected order in the world. During this period the dead were not feared and mourners did not avoid the body.

DEATH OF SELF. Patterns associated with the death of self began around the twelfth century C.E., when people began to express anxiety about death. Ariès observed that people showed signs of deferring and avoiding the ultimate confrontation with the inevitable, and they worried about what would happen to them after death. Personal biographies were documented as a record of what people had done in their lifetimes. They understood that they were to be judged on the quality of their adherence to Christian values and behaviors, and they worried if their actions were sufficient for salvation. Were they going to heaven or doomed to hell? It was understood by Christians that those who were not baptized in Christ would be damned. Following Christian doctrine, people began to see their lives as a body of facts that could be itemized and summarized in a book. The importance of the sense of self was growing. People of prominence were now being buried in individual graves that were marked in some way. Commoners continued to be buried in common graves.

Ariès saw this period as connected to a "tame death" but with the seeds of movement in a new direction from the community to the individual. Changing religious attitudes (this was the period of the Protestant reformation), led to a growing anxiety about death. The authority of the Church was being challenged by new discoveries about the nature of the universe. Efforts to keep death at a distance increased with people's growing belief that the time and place of dying could be shaped by human behavior rather than by divine order. At the same time there was a fascination with death and a growing interest in examining the cadaver, and people kept relics of the deceased body as a sign of their love.

The tradition of *Ars Moriendi* (The Art of Dying) began during this period of the Death of Self and reached a high point in the fifteenth and sixteenth centuries. This tradition was based on a series of manuals of the same name designed to give guidance to the individual on how to orchestrate his or her death. From these books, people learned the craft of dying that would help control their fear and anxiety. The artwork pictured in these books was macabre, often showing the cadaver, with or without a coffin, in various states of decay. Sometimes biblical figures were represented fighting over the dying person's soul. Other books on dying, such as *The Book of Hours*, were written to provide the reader with a guide for making the transition from this world to the next. Guides included instructions for proper behavior for those who were observing the death as well as for those who were actively dying. Confession, recanting sins of omission and commission, prepared people for a heavenly destiny. Because there were few cures for illnesses or treatments for the mortal wounds of war, prayer was valued, and people prepared themselves in positions of repose until death took them (Lofland 1978).

REMOTE AND IMMINENT DEATH. Coinciding with the Renaissance and continuing into the seventeenth century, the influence of *Ars Moriendi* continued but became a category of pious literature for the devotions of everyday life. The growing sense of anxiety about death became more intense and people looked for ways of pushing its reality into the background of their lives. The fact that people died was never very far away from their consciousness, but understanding the consequences of death on how they lived their daily lives became a part of one's daily religious practice. Ariès writes about the process of dying being pushed to what he saw as a remote and prudent distance. He associates these changes with the growing differences between Catholicism and Protestantism, as well as with the changing economic and world conditions. People were also trying to soften their fear of the harsh qualities of judgment that they believed would occur at or after their death. Llewellyn (1991) described English funereal rituals of the time, including images intended to remind people of their mortality found in all kinds of public and private situations. These were largely commissioned for members of the upper class or royalty. It was becoming common to find images of "the deceased" on graves, designed and built long before one's actual death.

THE DEATH OF THE OTHER. The nineteenth century view of death was dominated by how people reacted to the death of others. Accordingly, Ariès saw in this period the focus shifting from concern with how people died to how people mourned. He called this the period of a beautiful death. Mourners were concerned with what they lost when a relationship was broken by death. Queen Victoria, after the death of Albert, personified and in some ways set the standard for the mourner of this period in her extensive mourning practices and in continuing to find a place for Albert in her life. There was a growing recognition of the grief that mourners experienced, and it was acceptable to express one's grief in dramatic ways. Mourners found consolation in the certainty that the deceased had gone to a better place, and that they would meet again one day (Silverman 1997). There was a greater emphasis on the separation of the body from the soul. Often the spirit of the dead person was thought to continue to be present in this world.

The idea that the dead could rise as spirits became prominent at this time, and a good deal of energy was spent on trying to communicate with the dead to overcome the separation. A romantic view of death evolved as a way of dealing with the mourner's sorrow. Graves were individually marked, tombstones became more elaborate memorials to the deceased, and cemeteries became parks or gardens that attracted visitors who were not mourners. The cemetery at Gettysburg, developed during and after the Civil War, is a good example of the movement to make cemeteries into parks to honor the dead. In the background of this romantic tradition was the growing influence of science on how life and death should be viewed that was to become so important in the twentieth century.

DEATH DENIED. In the past 150 years, philosophical and theological perspectives have been informed by the growing influence of science and medicine. Science has provided us with unimaginable means of mass destruction as well as treatments and cures for many previously untreatable diseases. We now have more control over sickness and health. Life expectancy has been extended to a point that could not have been imagined a century ago; many of the infectious diseases of childhood have been eliminated; families no longer have numerous children with the expectation that many of them will not survive childhood. Although we do not have cures for diseases such as AIDS, modern medicine has limited the debilitating consequences of many of the common diseases of our past.

In a technological world, where logic and reason prevail, it is possible for death to be neither seen nor heard. Death has come to be viewed as "the failure of medicine," and to a large extent it is still seen that way. In the Western world of the twentieth century we were no longer comfortable talking about death, and we were less comfortable talking about our reactions after a death occurred. In many instances, rituals and traditions that guided our behavior and feelings fell into disuse or were given a minor role in community life. Ariès (1981) calls this the period of the Invisible Death, and Fulton refers to it as a time of Denying of Dying (1965). Gorer (1965) characterizes the treatment of death in the mid-twentieth century as a new pornography. Death, as he saw it, was as taboo a subject as sex once was. Gorer noted that the rituals that once identified a person as a mourner, such as flowers on a front door or a black armband, were no longer in use, and he was concerned about the isolation of the dying as well. Others noted that the fact that death had moved out of the home and into the hospital made it even more invisible (Glaser and Strauss 1965; Krulik, Holaday, and Martinson 1987).

MAKING DEATH VISIBLE

By the mid-1960s, researchers began to develop a body of knowledge documenting the negative consequences for end of life of trying to avoid the fact that death happens (Fulton 1965; Feifel 1959; Glaser and Strauss 1965, Benoliel 1994). Glaser, Strauss, and Benoliel studied how terminally ill patients were treated in the hospital. Their study identified various trajectories of dying. They found that people died for the most part in hospitals in a closed, isolated setting where death was not discussed and the care was minimal. Feifel (1959) was the first to break through the silence surrounding death with his research at the Veterans Administration hospitals. Like Elisabeth Kübler-Ross a decade later, Feifel found that terminally ill people were very eager to talk about what was happening to them. The work of these pioneers helped reframe some of how death was viewed, opening the dialogue about how seriously ill people were treated in the healthcare system.

By the late 1960s we were witnessing a period of intense social change. The growing consumer movement was challenging social authority in a range of domains. For example, the merits of the war in Vietnam were questioned, as was the authority of the medical professional to control how our society dealt with birth and death (Silverman 1978; Corless 1985). But the main energy behind the spreading interest in how people died and the programs that followed came from volunteers, who often were dissatisfied with the care a dying family member or friend had received (Corless 1985). The discussion of death in our larger society was popularized with the publication of the work of Kübler-Ross (1969). Although the stages of dying that she proposed are no longer considered the best way of characterizing the dying process, she made it easier to relate to dying people and normalize their experience. There was a readiness in the larger society for this kind of information. Ill people were encouraged to talk about their impending death, and once again it became acceptable to face death openly. Whereas only a few years earlier information about dying would have been withheld from the ill, caretakers in this period often became somewhat insistent that the dying face what was happening to them. This almost prescriptive approach was meant to assure the ill person of reaching the last stage of Kübler-Ross's paradigm before death: acceptance.

Observers such as Ariès (1981), Weissman (1972), and Lofland (1978) point to the dangers of focusing only on the final act of dying. Lofland describes what she calls "the happy death movement," which, she argues, was creating a "romance with death." Most of the energy, as Lofland sees it, is invested in helping people die. She believes that modern technological advances allow us to assign people to the role of "dying person" long before death occurs, an approach that leaves people living as nonpersons for long periods of time. Having gone through the stages of dying to a place of acceptance, an individual could be left quite alone and isolated as he or she waited to die, while others went on with their lives, sometimes becoming impatient with the waiting.

Weissman (1972), reacting in part to the fact that both healthcare professionals and consumers were taking Kübler-Ross's stages too literally, observes that we cannot live with the fact that we will ultimately die as a constant awareness, even if we are suffering from an illness from which we will not recover. He notes that death is "not a terminal illness" and that the dying do not always follow an orderly progression. Rather, he describes the goal as providing options for people to achieve what he calls an appropriate death, that is, a death that they can live with. People need the opportunity to create a reality suitable for themselves until the end comes. Lofland suggests that those working with the ill need to shift their focus. She advocates acceptance of the fact that people's lives may end soon, and she emphasizes the importance of helping people remain involved in living in spite of the constraints of their illness or disability. This critique suggests that we look at the quality of living the end of life rather than at the quality of dying. The modern hospice movement has created opportunities for this to happen.

In the latter half of the 1960s Dr. Cicely Saunders, who came to medicine from social work, opened St. Christopher's Hospice in London, England, an inpatient facility with an accompanying home care program. St. Christopher's was the inspiration for the modern hospice movement. This program demonstrated that pain could be reasonably controlled to enable people to die with dignity, often in their own homes (Kastenbaum and Kastenbaum 1989; Saunders 1994; Lattanzi-Licht, Mahoney, and Miller 1998; Connor 1998). Hospice has grown into an international movement. In the United States, it is now governed by federal guidelines and funded by Medicare and most insurance companies. In 1974, Florence and Henry Wald founded the first hospice in the United States in Branford, Connecticut (Connor 1998; see chapter 7, this volume).

HOW WE DIE: THE LIMITS OF SCIENCE

The experience of the hospice movement led to expectations that the dying should receive more humane treatment and that there should be a place for death in our view of life. However, today death is still seen as a failure of modern medicine, an obstacle to be overcome (Feifel 1986). Healthcare and other institutional systems in our society continue to support the delusion that death can be avoided. Roberta Hoffman (see chapter 3) points to an experience she had on a hospital ward in which staff said in a patient's hearing that he "failed the treatment." Rather than saying, "I can't help," the health professional blames the patient. In another example, a mother reported that when the doctor came to tell her that her child had died, he was so upset that he kept repeating, "It shouldn't have happened, it shouldn't have happened." The mother understood that there had been little hope for her child, and now it was left to her to reassure the doctor who could not accept the fact that he was unable to sustain this life. The science and reason that guided his practice gave him a false sense of control. But this is not an unusual experience; the burden is often placed on the patient or the family (Silverman 2000). Worse still is the family sent away from the deathbed so that the healthcare professionals can do their "work." In reality we can defer death and make it possible for some people to live longer, healthier lives, but we cannot remove death from the human experience.

The prolongation of life as a result of modern technology can sometimes make the process of dying more terrifying than death itself. Ethical issues about artificial life supports have raised the question about the right to choose how and when we die. Often people are hooked up to machines that will keep them alive physically, though they are not living in any meaningful way. On admission to the hospital, people are now required to designate a surrogate who can act on their behalf if they are incapacitated. Whether it is a parent who assumes this role for a child or an adult serving another adult, this need to designate a surrogate brings the subject of how and when to die to the forefront. It often stimulates discussion about choices and options, only made possible by our new technology. The situations of Karen Quinlan and Nancy Cruzan opened the door to questions of when a person has the right to die and who has the responsibility to discontinue life support and allow people to die a natural death (De Spelder and Strickland 2002). In this setting, it is not uncommon to learn that healthcare providers ignore a patient's advance directive. The physician's unwillingness to comply with the wishes of the patient and family can leave people in vegetative states regardless of their careful planning to avoid such situations. These ethical issues could not have been imagined a hundred years ago (see chapter 39).

We tend to think that end-of-life decisions apply primarily to the elderly, but the right to die without the aggressive intrusion of medicine applies to children as well (Field and Behrman 2002). This is probably one of the most difficult decisions a physician and family have to face. One mother had to tell the doctor what they all knew: medicine could not cure her teenage daughter's cancer, which had spread throughout her body to the brain. She wanted her daughter to die at home with as little pain as possible. The girl's doctor admonished the mother, saying, "I do not understand you; when a house is on fire you do everything to put out the fire. How could you suggest that we no longer treat this young woman? There are still drugs to try." The mother reminded him that these treatments were intrusive, debilitating, and experimental, albeit giving the doctor a sense that he was doing something. The mother had finally come to accept that there was nothing medicine could offer her daughter. The family could not avoid the pain of the loss; all they could realistically hope for was that their daughter's death would bring her peace and an end to pain (Silverman 2000). Science could not help; instead, it significantly hindered the natural process of this death. The doctor's inability to accept his own helplessness added to the parents' distress because they felt that they were going against medical advice. Science cannot offer answers to the sorrow and pain of caregivers and families. The rush of activity, trying to do something to prevent death, leaves no room for coming to a quiet time of acceptance of the inevitable or to focus on how to live the time left to them.

In this discussion of what happens when people are ill and death is anticipated, we need to keep in mind that not all deaths occur in the hospital or after an illness (Nuland 1994). There are accidental deaths, sudden deaths, and, in spite of the emphasis on good pain management, deaths where the pain cannot be controlled.

INTO THE TWENTY-FIRST CENTURY

We are witnessing a significant transition in how death is dealt with in our society. This book, expanding how social workers think about their role in end-of-life care, is one example. At the cutting edge, there is a growing awareness of the reality of death as a part of life, of the limits of science, and of patterns of treatment and care of the dying that are inadequate. There is an effort to focus on the whole person, with physical, emotional, and spiritual needs. This process of change is slowly leading to greater visibility and more humane care for the dying (Lattanzi-Licht, Mahoney, and Miller 1998; Field and Cassel 1997). In 1997 the Institute of Medicine issued a report reviewing the state of the art in end-of-life care and making suggestions for improvements. Many books written to educate and inform the general population have also appeared (Nuland 1994; Byock 1997; Lynn and Harrold 1999). The focus is now on people in the end-stage of their life, with the emphasis on living. The nature of what Kastenbaum and Kastenbaum (1989) call our "death system" is slowly changing, and consumers are becoming more and more engaged in the discourse. There seems to be an increasing readiness in the population as a whole to hear, as evidenced in the written press, television, and radio, where we find extensive coverage on dying and about mourning. Bill Moyers's series of programs on end-of-life care stimulated community discussion groups and coalitions to improve services within their communities. There has been active debate about euthanasia and assisted suicide that has led to legislation in several states and an appeal to the Supreme Court of the United States, *Washington v. Glucksberg.*

There is also a growing interest in the psychosocial and spiritual needs of the person who is dying, a recognition that, as people approach death from an illness, a degenerative disease or a trauma, the emphasis must change from cure to palliation (symptom relief) and comfort care. Ira Byock (1997) reminds us that our medical model, which focuses on healing, recovery, and cure, is ill suited to caring for someone at the end of life. It is very difficult for the healthcare system to relinquish this emphasis on cure and to value palliation and comfort care. It has been noted that medical education must train physicians to make this transition (Farber, Egnew, and Bertsch 1999). However, it is the full healthcare team, social workers in particular, that needs this additional training.

In 1995, the Robert Wood Johnson Foundation issued a report documenting the gap between what is known about dying and what is done in the healthcare system. Not only were physicians and other members of the healthcare system not dealing well with end-of-life issues, but families were also equally uncomfortable bringing up questions regarding when treatment would no longer be helpful and how to manage pain. Neither the healthcare system nor those who utilize it were comfortable with the inevitable fact that people die or that medicine cannot fix everything. One conclusion of the RWJ report was that if people want control over their own end-of-life care, they must leave the hospital. As resources continue to develop in the community this may become standard practice. A product in part of this study, the Missoula End-of-Life Demonstration Project has worked since 1995 at involving an entire community in the provision of appropriate and accessible services to the dying and the bereaved (Staton, Roger, and Byock 2001).

From his experience as a hospice physician and initiator of the Missoula End-of-Life Demonstration Project, Byock has developed the concept of "dying well." Byock writes that "the concept of dying well and the related notion of wellness in dying preserves the subjective nature of the personal experience and can be understood as a subjective experience of personal growth. This can involve a renewed—or enhanced—sense of meaning and purpose and a sense of completion" (1997:246). While embracing the opportunity for growth at life's end, he cautions against becoming prescriptive in how we think people should behave when they are dying.

The Robert Wood Johnson study was reported widely in the print media, raising readers' consciousness about the end of life and the options that might be available at this time in their lives. In another initiative, the Open Society Institute of the Soros

Foundation began the Project on Death in America. Through its faculty scholars program, a new generation of physicians and nurses are being provided learning and mentoring opportunities to improve end-of-life care in their communities. In 2000 the Open Society Institute also sponsored a program for social-work leaders with the goal of expanding the role of social workers in end-of-life care. In addition, the Open Society funded the work of individual practitioners who were using the arts and humanities in end-of-life care and community programs for the bereaved, and provided grants for institutional development to agencies and schools concerned with end-of-life care. We see then that change has generated more change, and we are on the cusp of a new era in Western society of caring for the dying and of how we look at death.

ON BEREAVEMENT, MOURNING, AND GRIEF

As our views on death itself have changed over time, so too have our views on grief and bereavement changed. The way in which a society views death informs and influences its expectations of appropriate behaviors for mourners (Stroebe et al. 1996; Walter 1999; Stroebe et al. 2001; Rosenblatt 2001). Gorer (1965), as noted earlier, points to how mourning traditions have disappeared over time. In addition, he notes that the focus for mourners is on restraint, making the pain and sadness associated with loss a personal and private matter. Thus, as death became more invisible, so did mourning. Nonetheless, the price we pay for being involved with others, for caring and for loving, is that we experience the pain of loss when these relationships end (Parkes 1996). Was there ever a time when personal pain after a loss was absent from the human experience? From early recorded history there are stories of how various mourners have dealt with their loss and how various faith systems guided this grief. Some traditions made room for public mourning and others were more private.

Until the twentieth century, religious faith and ritual played an important part in helping people give expression and direction to their grief, including ways to mediate between the living and the dead. In some societies, rituals respond to a fear of the dead coming back as a ghost (De Spelder and Strickland 1996; Rosenblatt, Walsh, and Jackson 1976). For example, Australian aborigines do not mention the name of the deceased for two years after his or her death so as not to interfere with the dead's passage to the "other side." A community's grief is invariably framed in a language compatible with the belief system of that society. Arnold Van Gennep (1960), an anthropologist writing in the early twentieth century, described mourning traditions in the communities he studied. He identified a several-stage process of mourning, marking a rite of passage separating the living and the dead. Van Gennep observed that the initial focus was on the burial of the dead, mourners then visualize the dead person at rest in the land of the deceased from which there is no return, and finally there is a severing of ties with the deceased—a cessation of the role obligations that kept the deceased's involvement with the living alive.

In some societies the obligation to one's ancestors is ongoing. In Japan, for example, the deceased are worshipped in family rituals, usually at home, and are consulted about family decisions, remaining part of the family's life (Klass 1996). Still other societies have ways of memorializing the dead that are part of communal rituals visible in that society (Walter 1999). A good example comes from a Jewish tradition, more than a thousand years old, that dictates that no one should die alone. After a death, a quorum *(minyan)* of ten people is required to say the mourner's prayer along with the mourners, whose obligation is to recite this prayer for approximately eleven months after the death. The community is obligated to visit and care for mourners immediately after the death; there are rituals that guide a mourner's behavior over the first year of bereavement and a cemetery ritual for the stone marking the grave (Lamm 1969).

In many societies, the rituals of mourning differentiate the duties of the mourner from those who are not mourning. For the mourner, daily routines are interrupted and behavior changes are legitimated. In due time there are rituals of reentry or reintegration into the community. Participating in these rituals shows solidarity with the social group of which the mourner is a part. Rosenblatt, Walsh, and Jackson (1976) identify a person, in communities they studied, who is designated as a "ritual specialist," whose task it is to guide the mourner through his or her mourning to a different place in society. These rituals all have their roots in the faith systems of the communities, but there are many other ways that we see grief and mourning depicted in various societies.

The arts have provided outlets for expressing grief through the ages (Bertman 1979–80, 1991; Morgan 1999). Poetry, music, and painting become ways for mourners to tell their story and provide vehicles for memorializing the deceased. In Greek legend, as presented by Sophocles in his play *Antigone*, we see the importance for Antigone of fulfilling her filial obligation to provide a proper burial for her brother. She believes that only when she has completed this ritual, at the risk of her own life, can both she and her brother rest in peace. Another example is the famous *Pietà* of Michelangelo, which depicts Mary's grief at the death of Christ. In sharing her pain, the statue has comforted many mourners over the years. Jan Kochanowski (1995), a fifteenth-century Polish poet, wrote a series of laments about the death of his four-year-old daughter that can resonate with any bereaved parent today:

> The void that fills my house is so immense
> Now that my girl is gone. It baffles sense
> We are all here, yet no one is I feel:
> The flight of one small soul has tipped the scale.

Philippe Ariès (1981) describes bereavement practices in nineteenth-century Western society, when grief was very public, as a continuation of earlier practices. In a sense the arts were reflected in the kind of clothes mourners, particularly women, could wear. Even the fabric and the design were prescriptive. There were clothes worn shortly after death, then often a change in fabric, color, and design could take place as the mourner entered a period of what was called half mourning (Llewellyn

1991). By the nineteenth century, all social classes in Great Britain had adopted these practices.

During the Age of the Beautiful Death, public rituals acknowledged loss, making the mourner's status apparent to all. Visiting the grave became common, and people wore dark clothes for an extended period of time to identify themselves as mourners (De Spelder and Strickland 2002). Conversely, in India and China, white is the color of mourning. Stroebe et al. (1996) describe how mourners maintained an active connection to the deceased. Pieces embroidered by children hung in the home, and there was the continuation of earlier practices where portraits of the bereaved were painted that included a representation of the deceased as well. With the advent of photography, it was not unusual for people to take pictures of the dead. We begin to appreciate that there is no right way to mourn, and we cannot understand the way people react to a death or how they cope without understanding the social context in which they are embedded. We also see the importance of religion in mourning ritual and that people have a sense of the changes in the intensity of mourning as mourners moved away in time from the time of death.

TWENTIETH-CENTURY CONTEXT

We have moved from a time when communal rituals and practices and religious beliefs framed the mourner's behavior to a time when the focus is almost solely on the individual and his or her inner feelings and personal reactions. In contemporary Western society both the physical and the social sciences have had an important impact on religious philosophy and where it fits into people's lives. Belief in an afterlife was pushed to the background and the value of ritual was minimized (Parsons 1994), so that neither played an active role in consoling or guiding the behavior of the bereaved any longer. Viewing death as a medical failure began to frame our understanding of grief. Like death, grieving was separated from the normal life cycle and became something to fear. By the middle of the twentieth century, mourning had become sanitized, and mourners were sent away to the clinician's office to be "healed." This is the age of the psychological person, and the mental health professional and the physician have been assigned the role of "ritual specialists" for the bereaved.

Most of the earlier research in the twentieth century was conducted by psychiatrists working with mourners who came for psychiatric help. These patients became their research subjects (Furman 1974; Volkan 1981), and the problems they presented were then generalized to the larger population of bereaved people. Their problematic behaviors, the pain and tumult following a death, were labeled as symptoms, implying they are pathological and a sign of illness. It was thought that if the "correct" form of mourning was followed, these "symptoms" could be prevented.

Many contemporary psychological theories of grief are based on the works of Sigmund Freud (1961). Freud's early characterization of grief pointed to the necessity of detaching one's memories and expectations from the deceased. He felt that the work of grieving was to let go of the deceased—once emotional investment was removed from the relationship to the deceased, the mourner's emotional energy would be freed for new relationships. From his personal letters it is clear that Freud's own experience did not support this view of the trajectory of grief (Silverman and Klass 1996; see chapter 13, this volume). Nonetheless, his view of how grief ends has dominated most thinking about bereavement in the twentieth century.

In 1944, Erich Lindemann, studying the grief of survivors of the Coconut Grove nightclub fire in Boston, identified the three tasks that composed the "grief work" of these mourners: (1) emancipation from the bond to the deceased; (2) readjustment to the environment in which the deceased is missing; and (3) formation of new relationships. He also observed intense guilt in survivors of the fire in which hundreds were killed (Lindemann 1944). These feelings are not unlike those described by Holocaust survivors, who often have difficulty reconciling their own survival with the death that surrounded them (Frankl 1972, 1978; Valent 1994). Today, guilt is invariably looked for in mourners, and when it is not found, the observer often reports that the mourner is repressing or avoiding his or her feelings. Lindemann, influenced by Freud, saw grief as ending when the mourner severed his relationship to the deceased. He recognized that the bereaved had to adjust to an environment without the deceased and proposed that the way to do that was to "let go" of the relationship to the deceased.

Multiple theories of grief developed in the last half of the twentieth century. Stroebe et al. (2001) observe that most research during this period focused on the prevention of physical or emotional ill health that was associated with the death of a loved one and was not guided by an integrative theory of grief. They divided the research into two schools of thought. The first, the psychoanalytic school of thought, evolved from Freud's writings about depression. Aspects of depressed behavior were associated with loss and were seen as the symptomology of grief, which supported the view of grief as a purely psychological process. The second focused on stress theories, examining coping strategies and their impact on the mourner's adaptation to the loss. Research in this area found that the most stressful events people experienced were first the death of a child and second the death of a spouse (Holmes and Rahe 1967; Dohrenwend 1973). The larger context in which people mourn came into focus and the widowed, in particular widowed women, were the primary focus of research during this period (Silverman 1966; Glick, Weiss, and Parkes 1974; Parkes 1972; Lopata 1973). Lopata was particularly interested in the widows' behavior in social context, how the role and status of women shifted with the death of their husbands. There is also now a rising interest in how children process loss.

John Bowlby, a psychiatrist with a psychoanalytic orientation who was interested in research that would test the validity of psychoanalytic theories of human behavior current at the time, studied children who were sent away from their families during the London Blitz in World War II and their reaction to the separation and loss that followed. He published a paper describing the grief he saw in these children as a time of transition (Bowlby 1961). In it, he observes how the children changed emotionally as they moved away from the time of the loss. He identifies a period of shock, numbness, and disbelief that the loss occurred, after which the children gradually accepted the impossibility of a reunion. He also observes a phase of yearning and searching, typical of young children, when they tried to find the lost person and be reunited with them. Bowlby notes that there was a strong tendency to keep a clear visual memory of the deceased, but that the intensity of this memory diminished over time. Following a phase of disorganization and despair, which occurs as the mourner realizes that the deceased will not return, comes a phase of reorganization in which the bereaved lets go of ties to the deceased and establishes new relationships.

Bowlby's work had a critical impact on how grief in children was understood, and his research (1981) established that children do grieve. Bowlby described grieving behavior as observable in all mammals who attach to a primary maternal figure that facilitates their growth and ability to thrive (Osterweis, Solomon, and Green 1984). The source of this "attachment behavior" emanates, he hypothesized, from an instinctual need to be close to a mothering figure. When this relationship is lost there is sadness, weeping, and a threat to the child's sense of well-being. He saw the grief in the children who were evacuated from war-torn London as a form of separation anxiety, which, unlike after an actual death, could be rectified by a reunion with their mothers, or prevented in the first place by limiting the separation. Bowlby's work has been reframed to emphasize the importance of the child's attachment to critical caregivers. Researchers of attachment theory have described types of attachments, but only recently have they begun to talk about issues of loss (Noppe 2000).

Furman (1974) worked with preschool children who were in a clinical program for disturbed children at the time that one of their parents died. Furman identifies three tasks that confront a mourning child: (1) to understand and come to terms with the reality and circumstances of the death, (2) to mourn, and (3) to resume their lives. She saw acceptance of the death in these young children coming only after a struggle between disbelief that the death had occurred and confusion about why the deceased was not coming back. Mourning, Furman writes, involves mastery of this process that comes with loosening ties to the deceased. Mourning ended when the children identified with a part of the deceased, thus allowing them to keep aspects of their lost parent with them forever. Furman also emphasizes the importance of the process of detachment that occurs when the deceased does not come back and children need to withdraw their emotional investment in what is no longer there. Her findings reflect the dilemma faced by clinicians who recognize that people, children and adults, do not detach from the deceased but were themselves committed to a theory that insisted that this letting go was necessary to "recover." Attitudes toward grief that develop in this context emphasize the individual's inner ability to cope. Bereavement is not seen as a communal issue, but as an individual one. Time-limited and contained within the emotional life of the mourner, grief is characterized as something the mourner will get over. Pathology, it was hypothesized, resulted from not grieving as prescribed (Parkes 1996).

The impact of grief was the subject of a good deal of the research during this period (Osterweis, Solomon, and Green 1984). The focus was on identifying how grief negatively affected the physical and mental health of mourners and interventions were sought that could prevent these negative consequences. Factors such as age, role in the family, and relationship to the deceased were identified as possibly leading to ill health and problem behavior. Because of diverse research approaches, there is still little consensus about which factors are most critical to which outcome (Berlinsky and Biller 1982; Stroebe et al. 2001). Nonetheless, outcome studies have remained one of the key concerns of bereavement research, with much less focus on understanding the grieving process itself.

Bowlby's view of mourning as a time of transition was very useful in looking at the grieving process, particularly in understanding the grief of widows and of children (Silverman 1966, 1986; Parkes 1972, 1996; Neimeyer 1999). The concept of transition helps to describe accurately what the bereaved go through with the death of a spouse as they adapt to the loss and reorganize their lives finding new roles for themselves. This concept facilitated looking beyond the individual to see grief as a life-cycle issue, including family, belief systems, and community values (Marris 1974). Parkes talks about the changes people experienced in their assumptive worlds, pointing to their need to find a new place for themselves in the world and a new identity. (Chapter 29 of this volume elaborates on this from a developmental and relational point of view.) In a sense, this work led to understanding the nature of the change that the bereaved experience and seeing change as part of the grieving process. It became possible to talk about the bereaved developing a new narrative about themselves and their place in the world (Silverman 1989).

The narrative approach is a tool used by Neimeyer (1999) as he focuses on the need of the bereaved to give meaning to death and to the life once lived. He reminds us of the importance of a constructivist perspective. This directs our thinking away from a single model of grief for all to the importance of family history and culture, as well as the personal qualities of the mourner, in understanding one's grief and the direction it is going.

Rubin (1981, 1996, 2000) has observed that parents who have lost a child to sudden infant death follow what he calls a two-track model of grief, thus pointing to the importance of the larger social context in the way they cope. He focuses on the need to construct a relationship to the deceased, on understanding the personal qualities of the bereaved and the attitudes and resources in the community in which they live. Worden (1982), following on the work of Lindemann and Furman, discusses the tasks to be dealt with if people are to cope with their grief successfully. He differentiates grief counseling, supportive help that most people need as they deal with their grief, from grief therapy, which might be required by a minority of people with more extreme emotional problems. Wolfgang and Margaret Stroebe have provided us with two major resources about bereavement and research in this area in the *Handbook of Bereavement* (1993, 2001). As the Institute of Medicine report provided a guide for needed research twenty years ago, so these volumes are providing direction for the current generation.

DETACHMENT REVISITED

The view of grief as something people get over, and the accompanying psychologization of grief were compatible with the value placed on individual independence and autonomy in Western society. Dependency on others was seen as a negative quality (Miller 1986). Relationships with others were viewed instrumentally—in terms of having one's needs met—and the focus of individual development was on separation and individuation. Thus, when a relationship ended, as with a death, it was appropriate to consider how to sever these ties. In this view, by implication, people were seen as having sequential relationships, as if it was possible to have only one close relationship at a time. Different kinds of relationships were not accounted for. Over the years there were questions raised by researchers as they look at their data from bereaved families (Rubin 1981; Silverman 1986; Klass 1986; Silverman, Nickman, and Worden 1992; Silverman and Klass 1996; Stroebe et al. 1996; Walter 1999). The data pointed to how the bereaved remained involved and questioned the merit of the concept of detachment.

Stroebe et al. (1996) and Walters (1999) observe that historically mourners have found ways of continuing their bonds with the deceased. For example, Victorian women lived in companionship with the dead for a long time. In that society the widowed were not expected to let go and get on with their lives, and for most of the twentieth century this was still true. Silverman and Klass (1996), in their review of the recent bereavement research, conclude that there is significant evidence that most bereaved people do not experience the relationship to the deceased as ending at death. Most bereaved people report that letting go of the deceased was not consistent with their experience. The relational and contextual part of their lives need to be included to understand their reactions (Silverman and Klass 1996; Silverman 2000; Klass and Walters 2001). This view challenges the use of the language of recovery that suggests that grief is an illness from which mourners must recover.

IS GRIEF AN ILLNESS? Parkes (2001), in a historical review of theories of grief, notes that as early as 1657 Robert Burton, in his book *The Anatomy of Melancholy*, observed that grief or sorrow are the chief causes of melancholia. Today this might be called clinical depression. Raphael, Minkov, and Dobson write that "research and the study of bereavement phenomenology, including reactions from different kinds of deaths, has made it quite clear that for the majority of people, grief, although psychologically painful and distressing, is a normal process reflecting both the strengths and value of human attachments and the capacity to adapt to loss and adversity" (2001:587).

There is a tension that still exists between those who focus on grieving behavior as symptoms of psychiatric problems and those who see mourning as an expected life-cycle transition, the pain that is to be expected under the circumstances. The former is consistent with a worldview that emphasizes psychological well-being and understands behavior to reflect the intrapsychic construction of the individual personality. Yet, when grief is seen as a life-cycle event, the larger social and interpersonal context is brought into consideration. People's responses are legitimated by their communities, which provide them with support as they learn to live with the pain, accommodate to feelings of loss, and adjust to the changes in their lives that follow the death.

The view of grief as an illness permeates into many layers of society (Jacobs 1999; Prigerson and Jacobs 2001) as a continuation of the invisible death Ariès describes. Grief is taken to the "doctor's office," where it can be contained and controlled and will not intrude on the life of the community. Like an illness that can be treated with a little "penicillin," the grief is seen as something that can be diagnosed and cured. The community does not deal with the fullness of the way that people's dying changes the world.

Robert Lifton (1974) reminds us that we cannot accept death without dealing with mourning, which in its way is a constant reminder that people die. We see heroic stories in the media about how people die, as in the tragedy of September 11, 2001. When the subsequent pain is discussed, the emphasis is on how to limit and control it, and ideally, make it go away. The predominant discourse speaks of the need of the bereaved to find closure rather than helping them live through it and learn new ways of coping with this horror.

Stroebe et al. (2001) remind us that most bereaved people cope well with their grief and find new and constructive ways of dealing with the changes in their lives. I am not ignoring the small percentage of people who after a death do not adapt and seem to develop psychiatric problems. It is important to understand their needs, and it is important to consider that their problem may not be caused by the death itself but may relate to earlier difficulties in their lives. They may well need professional care and attention. These people, however, are not representative of the general bereaved population. We need to change our question as we look at the pain of the mourner to ask what is right with them, given the circumstances, not what is wrong. The bereaved do need comfort, support, and help as they deal with their grief and find a new direction for their lives. I go back to the research of "ritual specialist" Rosenblatt and ask: Who should that helping person be in our postmodern society—grief counselor, therapist, clergy, family, and/or friend?

THE BEREAVED TALK FOR THEMSELVES

The consumer movement that was important in the development of more humane care at the end of life has also played an important role in how we understand bereavement. Since the late 1960s there has been a growing network of mutual-aid organizations that are run by the bereaved for the bereaved. The pioneers that provided the impetus for these organizations came from my own work with the widowed (Silverman 1966, 1969, 1974, 1979) and from England, where bereaved parents organized Compassionate Friends (Stephens, 1973) to help each other after a child died. These groups organized based on the finding that the most helpful person to the newly widowed or newly bereaved parent was another bereaved person. These programs began to challenge existing views of grief and facilitated another perspective to what grieving people experience (Silverman 1966, 1986, 1988; Klass 1986).

The work with the widowed is being carried on in the Widowed Persons Service, a program of the American Association of Retired Persons. Such groups have served as models for other self-help organizations dealing with other kinds of death, such as Mothers Against Drunk Driving. Representatives of these organizations are now included in planning services for the bereaved in many communities nationally, and their influence is affecting our theoretical formulations about the nature of grief.

CONCLUSION

In part, our difficulty with grief comes from the way human behavior has been described by the dominant psychological sciences of the past century. We characterize behavior in linear terms, as if one experience can only lead to one outcome. However, people can rarely be put into a simple cause-and-effect model (Bruner 1990). We are beginning to recognize the complexity of the human condition and human relationships. In recent decades, we have witnessed a shift to a more realistic view of how we live, appreciating that we are very interdependent. This shift was propelled in some ways by the women's movement. Women observed the importance of relationships in people's lives, and that the goal of development was not independence but interdependence (Gilligan 1993; Miller 1986). We now acknowledge that relationships with others frame our sense of self and how we live our lives.

These relationships frame how we organize and think about death, that is, how we make meaning of this aspect of our lives. As we try to understand the relational world of the mourner, we must include their relationships with the deceased. We are moving toward what I call a relational view of grief, language also used by Weiss (2001) as he describes what is lost for the bereaved.

We are participating in a changing system that increasingly looks at the complexity of human relationships and makes invisible deaths impossible. We are moving toward a view of the world that understands that there are things that science can do for us, but that reason can only take us so far on this life journey. We are at a place where former ways of doing things are no longer sufficient. Though new ways have not yet developed, we have to recognize that we cannot control death and that we do have choices about how we react to it. This is not an event that will happen to others—all of us need to be expert in coping, in making meaning out of death and the grief that will follow.

REFERENCES

Ariès, P. 1981. *The Hour of Our Death.* New York: Knopf.

Benoliel, J. Q. 1994. Death and dying as a field of inquiry. In *Dying, Death, and Bereavement: Theoretical Perspective and Other Ways of Knowing*, ed. I. B. Corless, B. B. Germino, and M. Pittman, 3–13. Boston: Jones and Bartlett.

Berlinsky, E. B., and H. B. Biller. 1982. *Parental Death and Psychological Development.* Lexington, MA: Heath.

Bertman, S. L. 1979–80. The arts: A source of comfort and insight for children who are learning about death. *Omega* 10(2): 147–162.

———. 1991. *Facing Death: Images, Insights and Interventions.* New York: Hemisphere.

Bowlby, J. 1961. Childhood mourning and its implications for psychiatry. *American Journal of Psychiatry* 118:481–498.

———. 1980. *Loss: Sadness and Depression.* New York: Basic Books.

Byock, I. 1997. *Dying Well: The Prospect for Growth at the End of Life.* New York: Riverhead Books.

Charmaz, K. 1994. Conceptual approaches to the study of death. In *Death and Identity*, ed. R. Fulton and R. Bendickson, 28–79. Philadelphia: Charles Press.

Connor, S. 1998. *Practice, Pitfalls and Promise.* Washington, DC: Taylor & Francis.

Corless, I. B. 1985. The hospice movement in North America. In *Hospice Care: Principles and Practice*, ed. C. Corr and D. Corr, 335–351. New York: Springer.

Corr, C., C. M. Nabe, and D. M. Corr. 1997. *Death and Dying: Life and Living*. Boston: Brooks/Cole.

De Spelder, L., and A. Strickland. 2002. *The Last Dance: Encountering Death and Dying*. 6th ed. New York: McGraw-Hill.

Dohrenwend, B. S. 1973. Life events as stressors: A methodological inquiry. *Journal of Health and Social Behavior* 14:167–175.

Edmonds, M. E. 1847–99. Unpublished family diary.

Farber, S., T. Egnew, and J. Bertsch. 1999. Issues in end-of-life care: Family practice faculty perception. *Journal of Family Practice* 49(7): 525–530.

Feifel, H., ed. 1959. *The Meaning of Death*. New York: McGraw-Hill.

Field, M. J., and R. E. Behrman, eds. 2002. *When Children Die: Improving Palliative and End-of-Life Care for Children and Their Families*. Washington, DC: National Academy Press.

Field, M. J., and C. K. Cassel, eds. 1997. *Approaching Death: Improving Care at the End of Life*. Washington, DC: National Academy Press.

Freud, S. 1961. Mourning and melancholia. *The Standard Edition of the Complete Psychological Works of Sigmund Freud* 14:243–258. New York: Basic Books.

Frankl, V. 1972. *The Doctor and the Soul: From Psychotherapy to Logotherapy*. New York: Knopf.

——. 1978. *The Unheard Cry for Meaning: Psychotherapy and Humanism*. New York: Simon & Schuster.

Fulton, R. 1965. *Death and Identity*. New York: Wiley.

Furman, E. 1974. *A Child's Parent Dies: Studies in Childhood Bereavement*. New Haven, CT: Yale University Press.

Gilligan, C. 1993. *In a Different Voice: Psychological Theory and Women's Development*. 2d ed. Cambridge, MA: Harvard University Press.

Glaser, B., and A. Strauss. 1965. *Awareness of Dying*. Chicago: Aldine.

Glick, I. O., R. S. Weiss, and C. M. Parkes. 1974. *The First Year of Bereavement*. New York: Wiley.

Gorer, G. 1965. *Death, Grief and Mourning in Contemporary Britain*. London: Cresset Press.

Holmes, T., and R. Rahe. 1967. The social adjustment rating scale. *Journal of Psychosomatic Research* 11:213–218.

Jacobs, S. C. 1999. *Traumatic Grief: Diagnosis, Treatment and Prevention*. Philadelphia: Bruner/Mazel.

Kastenbaum, R., and B. Kastenbaum. 1989. *Encyclopedia of Death*. New York: Avon.

Klass, D. 1988. *Parental Grief: Solace and Resolution*. New York: Springer.

——. 1996. Grief in an eastern culture: Japanese ancestor worship. In *Continuing Bonds: New Understandings of Grief*, ed. D. Klass, P. R. Silverman, and S. L. Nickman, 59–70. Washington, DC: Taylor & Francis.

Klass, D., and T. Walters. 2001. Processes of grief: How bonds are continued. In *Handbook of Bereavement Research: Consequences, Coping and Care*, ed. M. S. Stroebe, R. O. Hansson, W. Stroebe, and H. Schut, 431–448. Washington, DC: American Psychological Association.

Kochanowski, J. 1995 [1580]. *Laments*. Trans. S. Baranczak and S. Heaney. New York: Farrar, Straus & Giroux.

Krulik, T., B. Holaday, and I. M. Martinson. 1987. *The Child and Family Facing Life-Threatening Illness: A Tribute to Eugenia Waechter*. Philadelphia: Lippincott.

Kübler-Ross, E. 1969. *On Death and Dying*. New York: Macmillan.

Lamm, M. 1969. *The Jewish Way in Death and Mourning*. New York: Jonathan David.

Lattanzi-Licht, M., J. J. Mahoney, and G. W. Miller. 1998. *The Hospice Choice: In Pursuit of a Peaceful Death*. New York: Fireside.

Lifton, R. J. 1974. Symbolic immortality. In *The Patient, Death, and the Family*, ed. S. B. Troup and W. A. Greenberg, 21–33. New York: Scribner.

Lindemann, E. 1944. Symptomatology and management of acute grief. *American Journal of Psychiatry* 101:141–148.

Llewellyn, N. 1991. *The Art of Death: Visual Culture in the English Death Ritual c. 1500– c. 1800*. London: Reaktion Books.

Lofland, L. 1978. *The Craft of Dying: The Modern Face of Death*. Beverly Hills, CA: Sage.

Lopata, H. Z. 1973. *Widowhood in an American City*. Cambridge, MA: Schenkman.

Lynn, J., and J. Harrold. 1999. *Handbook for Mortals: Guidance for People Facing Serious Illness*. New York: Oxford University Press.

Marris, P. 1974. *Loss and Change*. London: Routledge and Kegan Paul.

Meyer, J. W. 1988. The social construction of the psychology of childhood: Some contemporary processes. In *Child Development in a Life-Span Perspective*, ed. E. M. Hetherington, R. M. Lerner, and M. Perlmutter, 47–65. Hillsdale, NJ: Lawrence Erlbaum Associates.

Miller, J. B. 1986. *New Psychology of Women*. Boston: Beacon Press.

Neimeyer, R. A. 1997. Meaning reconstruction and the experience of chronic loss. In *Living with Grief when Illness Is Prolonged*, ed. K. J. Doka and J. Davidson, 159–176. Washington, DC: Taylor & Francis.

——. 1998. *Lessons of Loss: A Guide to Coping*. New York: McGraw-Hill.

——. 2001. *Meaning Reconstruction and the Experience of Loss*. Washington, DC: American Psychological Association.

Noppe, I. C. 2000. Beyond broken bonds and broken hearts: The bonding theories of attachment and grief. *Development Review* 20:514–538.

Nuland, S. B. 1994. *How We Die: Reflections on Life's Final Chapter*. New York: Knopf.

Osterweis, M., F. Solomon, and M. Green, eds. 1984. *Bereavement: Reactions, Consequences and Care*. Washington, DC: National Academy Press.

Parkes, C. M. 1996. *Studies of Grief in Adult Life*. 3d ed. New York: Routledge.

——. 2001. A historical overview of the scientific study of bereavement. In *Handbook of Bereavement Research: Consequences, Coping and Care*, ed. M. S. Stroebe, R. O. Hansson, W. Stroebe, and H. Schut, 25–45. Washington, DC: American Psychological Association.

Parsons, T. 1994. Death in the western world. In *Death and Identity*, ed. R. Fulton and R. Bendickson, 60–79. Philadelphia: Charles Press.

Prigerson, H., and S. Jacobs. 2001. Traumatic grief as a distinct disorder: A rational, consensus criteria and a preliminary empirical test. In *Handbook of Bereavement Research: Consequences, Coping and Care*, ed. M. S. Stroebe, R. O. Hansson, W. Stroebe, and H. Schut, 613–637. Washington, DC: American Psychological Association.

Raphael, B. 1982. *The Anatomy of Bereavement*. New York: Basic Books.

Raphael, B., C. Minkov, and M. Dobson. Psychotherapeutic and pharmacological intervention for bereaved persons. In *Handbook of Bereavement Research: Consequences, Coping and Care*, ed. M. S. Stroebe, R. O. Hansson, W. Stroebe, and H. Schut, 587–612. Washington, DC: American Psychological Association.

Rosenblatt, P. 2001. A social constructivist perspective on cultural differences in grief. In *Handbook of Bereavement Research: Consequences, Coping and Care*, ed. M. S. Stroebe, R. O. Hansson, W. Stroebe, and H. Schut, 285–300. Washington, DC: American Psychological Association.

Rosenblatt, P., R. P. Walsh, and D. A. Jackson. 1976. *Grief and Mourning in Cross-Cultural Perspective*. New Haven, CT: HRAF Press.

Rubin, S. 1981. A two-track model of bereavement theory and application in research. *American Journal of Orthopsychiatry* 51:101–109.

——. 1992. Adult child loss and the two-track model of bereavement. *Omega* 24(3): 183–202.

——. 1996. The wounded family: Bereaved parents and the impact of adult child loss. In *Continuing Bonds: New Understandings of Grief*, ed. D. Klass, P. R. Silverman, and S. L. Nickman, 217–234. Washington, DC: Taylor & Francis.

Rubin, S., R. Malkinson, and E. Witztum. 2000. An overview of the field of loss. In *Traumatic and Non-traumatic Loss and Bereavement: Clinical Theory and Practice*, ed. R. Malkinson, S. Rubin, and E. Witztum, 5–40. Madison, WI: Psychosocial/International Universities Press.

Saunders, C. 1994. Foreword. In *A Challenge for Living*, ed. I. B. Corless, B. B. Germino, and M. A. Pittman, xi–xiv. Boston: Jones and Bartlett.

Silverman, P. R. 1966. Services for the widowed during the period of bereavement. In *Social Work Practice*, 170–198. New York: Columbia University Press.

——. 1978. *Mutual Help Groups: A Guide for Mental Health Workers*. Washington, DC: U.S. Government Printing Office.

——. 1986. *Widow to Widow*. New York: Springer.

——. 1988. In search of new selves: Accommodating to widowhood. In *Families in Transition: Primary Programs That Work*, ed. L. A. Bond and B. Wagner, 200–219. Newbury Park, CA: Sage.

——. 2000. *Never Too Young to Know: Death in Children's Lives*. New York: Oxford University Press.

Silverman, P. R., and D. Klass. 1996. Introduction: What's the problem? In *Continuing Bonds: New Understandings of Grief*, ed. D. Klass, P. R. Silverman, and S. L. Nickman, 3–27. Washington, DC: Taylor & Francis.

Silverman, P. R., and S. L. Nickman. 1996. Children's construction of their dead parent. In *Continuing Bonds: New Understandings of Grief*, ed. D. Klass, P. R. Silverman, and S. L. Nickman, 73–86. Washington, DC: Taylor & Francis.

Silverman, S. M. 1997. Justice Joseph Story and death in nineteenth-century America. *Death Studies* 21:3997–3416.

Staton, J., S. Roger, and I. Byock. 2001. *A Few Months to Live: Different Paths to Life's End*. Washington, DC: Georgetown University Press.

Stephans, S. 1973. *When Death Comes Home*. New York: Morehouse-Barlow.

Stroebe, M., M. Gergen, K. Gergen, and W. Stroebe. 1996. Broken hearts or broken bonds. In *Continuing Bonds: New Understandings of Grief*, ed. D. Klass, P. R. Silverman, and S. L. Nickman, 31–58. Washington, DC: Taylor & Francis.

Stroebe, M. S., R. O. Hansson, W. Stroebe, and H. Schut, eds. 2001. *Handbook of Bereavement Research: Consequences, Coping and Care*. Washington, DC: American Psychological Association.

Stroebe, M. S., W. Stroebe, and R. O. Hansson. 1993. *Handbook of Bereavement: Theory, Research and Intervention*. Cambridge: Cambridge University Press.

Sulzberger, C. 1961. *My Brother Death*. New York: Harper & Brothers.

Valent, P. 1994. *Child Survivors of the Holocaust*. New York: Bruner-Routledge.

Van Gennep, A. 1960. *The Rites of Passage*. Chicago: University of Chicago Press.

Volkan, V. D. 1981. *Linking Objects and Linking Phenomena*. New York: International Universities Press.

Walter, T. 1999. *On Bereavement: The Culture of Grief*. London: Open University Press.

Washington v. Glucksberg. 1997. 521 U.S.702,117 S.Ct. 2258,138 L.Ed.2d 772.

Weiss, R. 2001. Grief, bonds and relationships. In *Handbook of Bereavement Research: Consequences, Coping and Care*, ed. M. S. Stroebe, R. O. Hansson, W. Stroebe, and H. Schut, 47–62. Washington, DC: American Psychological Association.

Weissman, A. 1972. *On Dying and Denying: A Psychiatric Study of Terminality*. New York: Behavioral Publications.

Worden, J. W. 1991. *Grief Counseling and Grief Therapy: A Handbook for the Mental Health Practitioner*. New York: Springer.

7

THE HISTORY OF SOCIAL WORK IN HOSPICE

MARY RAYMER AND DONA REESE

THE INSTITUTE of Medicine broadly defines hospice as (1) an organization or program that provides, arranges, and advises on a wide range of medical and supportive services for dying patients and their families; (2) a discrete site of care in the form of an inpatient hospital, nursing home unit, or freestanding facility; and (3) an approach to care for dying patients based on clinical, social, metaphysical, or spiritual principles (Field and Cassel 1997). These definitions, although correct, leave out one of the most distinguishing features of hospice that represents the core social work value of self-determination. Hospice care was designed to be driven by the patient and the family, not by professionals. The focus is on helping people live as fully as possible until they die in the manner in which they choose to live. Another distinguishing core value of hospice is that care is provided by an interdisciplinary as opposed to a multidisciplinary team.

Hospice is a specialized form of palliative care, but not all palliative care is hospice care. The World Health Organization defines palliative care as "the active total care of patients whose disease is not responsive to curative treatment. Control of pain or other symptoms, and of psychological, social and spiritual problems is paramount. The goal of palliative care is achievement of the best possible quality of life for patients and their families" (World Health Organization 1990). The ideal of palliative care, similar to the vision of many of the early hospice leaders, is to facilitate holistic, interdisciplinary care on all points of the continuum of care. In other words, hospice philosophy is taken "upstream" in the disease process in an attempt to transform care across all healthcare settings.

Where have we come from and how far have we come? This chapter will look at the development of the hospice movement and social work and will identify some of the strengths and future challenges of hospice care.

THE HISTORY OF SOCIAL WORK AND HOSPICE

The good social worker doesn't go on helping people out of a ditch. Pretty soon, she begins to find out what ought to be done to get rid of the ditch.
—*Mary Richmond*

Dame Cicely Saunders, an Englishwoman trained as a social worker, nurse, and physician, began to "get rid of the ditch" when she established St. Christopher's inpatient hospice in London in 1967. Her passion, making hospice care a reality, was fueled during her first job as a social worker. She worked with a forty-year-old terminally ill man named David Tasma, a Polish Jew who had escaped from Poland during World War II. He was a stranger in a strange land, and it was clear that traditional hospital routine and structure was not conducive to helping him sort through the psychosocial and spiritual issues he needed to address before he died. Together they talked for hours about the need for a place of healing and support where dying people could receive specialized and holistic care. When David died, he left five hundred pounds to Saunders as the first donation to help make an inpatient hospice home a reality for others.

The word "hospice" is derived from the Latin *hospitium,* meaning guesthouse. It was originally used to describe places of shelter and rest for tired and/or sick travelers on religious pilgrimages. At St. Christopher's the term was used to describe both a special concept of care and a place designed to provide comfort and support to terminally ill patients and their families when cure was no longer possible. Hospice distinguished itself from the more traditional medical model by embracing the care of both the patient and her family or significant others as well as by pursuing aggressive symptom management in the physical, social, psychological, and spiritual arenas.

When discussing how her social work training affected her, Saunders writes, "in many ways it was the years as a Medical Social Worker (or Lady Almoner) from 1947–1951 that helped me to see patients as a part of a whole family network, best known as individuals in their own home setting" (Corless and Foster 1999:2). There is no doubt that her training also strongly influenced the other hallmarks of hospice care, such as the need for an interdisciplinary team, empowerment of the patient, and a psychosocial/spiritual focus, as well as aggressive symptom and pain management. In fact, McDonnell aptly describes the entire hospice movement as an "embodiment of social work values, principles, and practice" (1986:225). The core values of social work, such as service, social justice, the importance of human relationships, integrity, and competence, were considered crucial guidelines for the development of hospice both in England and in America.

The evolution of hospice began in America when Saunders visited Yale University in 1965. She lectured on the concept of holistic hospice care to a group of medical students, social workers, nurses, and chaplains. The idea caught on quickly. Florence Wald, then dean of the Yale School of Nursing, took a sabbatical to work at St. Christopher's and returned to develop the first hospice in America in Branford, Connecticut, in 1974. Nationally, hospices quickly began to take form. Initially, most were volunteer efforts, supported almost entirely by donations and grants.

The American hospice movement, unlike the development of hospice in England, was more of a grassroots community movement. It grew during a time in history when many traditional beliefs and institutions were being challenged. Social and individual empowerment fostered the development of such patient-focused healthcare practices as home births and self-help literature. Faced with the strife of the Vietnam War, people actively questioned what gave life "meaning." Many community members and healthcare professionals alike were disenchanted with a healthcare system whose focus was increasingly on technology and not on the individual.

Healthcare technology advanced more rapidly than the necessary ethical debates, and increasingly life was being prolonged at all costs whether there was quality of life or not. Terminally ill individuals and their families were all too often ignored and abandoned once it was clear that there was no hope for cure. In fact, they were often treated as symbols of shame by the traditional medical model. Denial of death and dying was prevalent. Many people were not told the full truth regarding the serious nature of their diseases, and, as a result, were not aware of palliative-care options. People were often literally treated "to death." Truth-telling in any form was largely viewed as fatalistic and predictive. Social workers in hospitals were frequently put in the uncomfortable position of answering questions and talking to people about their limited prognosis for the first time because many physicians avoided the issue. In this situation, idealistic practitioners came together to reject the status quo and to transform the dying experience into a more humane and crucial stage of life. Social workers, nurses, clergy, and many others denounced the lack of compassion and expertise in the dominant healthcare model, where death was the enemy and the dying were considered "failures." There was a great deal of collaboration and energy in the 1970s, and hospice leaders saw themselves as social activists as much as healthcare providers.

Hospices in America were as unique as the communities in which they developed. In many communities, hospices were started by nurses; in others they were organized by social workers; and in yet others they were initiated by spiritual caregivers or lay people. The common denominator was that practitioners came together as change agents who challenged the traditional medical model and advocated for the terminally ill and their families. The initial emphasis of hospice in America was on caring for the terminally ill person at home, as opposed to the English practice, where the first step was the use of an institution. Early hospice providers demanded that anyone caring for the terminally ill view their charge as a serious commitment to enhancing quality of life as defined by the individual and their family via an interdisciplinary team. Hospice made liberal use of lay and professional volunteers to provide respite, errands, and simple, caring human services in addition to the more traditional physician, nurse, nursing aide, social work, and clergy services. At first, hospice was mostly viewed as a radical movement of "do-gooders" who were on the outside of the medical establishment and therefore marginal, even suspect. Much of the early hospice work was classic community organization; empowering community members to mobilize resources to care for "their own." As it developed, however, the hospice movement had a profound impact on the field of medicine in America. In 1972, the American Hospital Association developed a "patient's bill of rights" providing for the patient's right to make treatment choices, terminate treatment, and access all available comfort measures as well as the right to know the truth of his or her condition. Such professional standards were followed by the enactment of laws addressing these same patient rights. Once the Medicare Hospice Benefit came into being, hospice emerged as the first true managed care program and a solid part of the healthcare payment system.

Despite the fact that hospice embodied social work values and that in many communities individual social workers were often key players in hospice, the profession of social work as a whole did not take a leadership role in hospice in the 1970s. That reticence has subsequently hurt the profession in end-of-life care. Social work has been a step behind other disciplines until quite recently in end-of-life care research, development of professional competencies, and macro-level advocacy efforts.

Although social work was identified as a mandatory core discipline when the Medicare Hospice Benefit was enacted in 1982, the ensuing years have seen disturbing trends that dilute the role of social work in hospice. In 1996, the Health Care Financing Administration (now CMS) proposed changing the Medicare requirement for social work from a social worker with a degree from an accredited school of social work to a person with a "social work–like" degree. This proposal (ultimately rejected, but only after an extensive lobbying effort) was partly in response to hospice administrators who reported having difficulty finding degreed social workers. They were also juggling increasing costs of care and looking for places to reduce labor costs. More important, this proposed change indicated a serious and pervasive misunderstanding of the field of social work and its knowledge base, values, and skills.

In the early days, hospice social workers, nurses, chaplains, community members, and many others worked respectfully side by side with relatively few "turf" issues. A common goal and perhaps a common "enemy"—that is, the traditional medical model—enhanced a strong spirit of teamwork and camaraderie. Many volunteered their time or worked for minimal pay because of their passion and commitment to changing society. All disciplines addressed various aspects of the human experience according to the clients' immediate needs—the physical, psychological, social, and spiritual. Roles of team members were "blurred" at times, but members were able to respect the limits of each other's practice and utilize each other to enhance their mutual expertise. Weekly interdisciplinary team meetings kept teamwork functioning and communication flowing. For a social worker, hospice work was and remains a rich and profound field of practice. At the end of life every intervention, whether environmental, psychological, or spiritual, takes on a new level of importance precisely because time is limited. Unfortunately, in many cases, salaries have been too low to attract the most experienced social workers. A master's level social worker was typically paid the same amount or less than a bachelor's level nurse (Reese, Raymer, and Richardson 1998). Additionally, social work education had not kept pace with the field of practice and had failed to provide adequate end-of-life-care training for social workers entering the hospice field (Csikai and Bass 2000; Kovacs and Bronstein 1999; Kramer 1998). Social workers have graduated with little or no training in any aspect of death and dying and yet were expected to provide appropriate interventions on the job upon graduation. This was especially problematic given that in most hospices social workers were supervised by nurses, and too frequently did not acquire their own clinical social work supervision or mentoring. As a result, too many inexperienced social workers were limited in their understanding of their own roles on the team. Far too often they could not effectively articulate their roles and functions to the other disciplines. This led to a devaluation of the role of social work on the team. Role "blurring" all too often began to mean that other disciplines, typically the nurse (Reese 1995–96; Sontag 1996), saw themselves providing most of the psychosocial care. To compound matters, social workers were not conducting research or performance improvement efforts in order to document their impact on hospice outcomes.

The advent of managed care and increasing costs have meant that hospice administrators have felt pressured to make decisions based on fiscal realities rather than on the original hospice vision of holistic care (Mahoney 1997). The growing perception of psychological disciplines as "ancillary," that is, "nice but not necessary," encouraged too many hospice administrators to diminish social work services in order to lower costs. By 1996 it was clear that, all too frequently, other disciplines did not understand the role of social work, and, sadly, many felt that it was easily replaced.

A CALL TO ACTION

In 1996, Mary Raymer, then leader of the Social Work Section of the National Hospice and Palliative Care Organization (NHPCO), called a special meeting of the section members in Chicago to discuss these problems. Members developed a three-pronged strategy for improving the state of social work in hospice. The first priority was to document, through a national research project, social work outcomes in hospice care as well as social work's role on the team. The section also prioritized the development of a competency-based approach to social work continuing education in addition to designing a tool to measure the effectiveness of hospice social work intervention on an ongoing basis.

SOCIAL WORK OUTCOMES IN HOSPICE

A preliminary review of the literature revealed an appalling lack of outcomes data in the field of hospice social work. The only existing studies were ones independently conducted by three social workers in their individual hospices (Cherin 1997; Mahar, Eickman, and Bushfield 1997; Paquette 1997). These social workers had all implemented pilot programs in which social work involvement was increased through participation in the intake interview as well as through making early and frequent social work visits. Measures were taken before the new programs began and then again at the end. In all three cases, the social workers found beneficial differences between their pre- and post-test measures.

Results of these studies indicated that with more intensive social work services, patients were hospitalized less frequently, required fewer after hours visits, needed fewer IVs, and did not require as much pain medication. Additionally, they required fewer nursing visits, and in general, had better quality of life and client satisfaction scores. Nurses and physicians also reported increased job satisfaction, and there was a decrease in staff turnover. All of these benefits translated into lower costs for hospice programs.

Although these results were exciting, they were little known and only documented in three individual hospices. The NHPCO Social Work Section then built upon this research by conducting the National Hospice Social Work Survey, the first national survey regarding social work outcomes. Social workers in sixty-six randomly selected hospices across the nation offered their support to the survey by completing questionnaires and reviewing a total of 330 patient charts. Hospice directors also helped by completing questionnaires about social work involvement and outcomes in the hospice.

Results of the national survey documented similar relationships between social work services and hospice outcomes. The survey emphasized the importance of social work participation in the intake interview along with frequent, continuing client contacts. These authors reasoned that social workers are skilled in preventing crises, due to the ability to assess potential difficulties as well as to assist clients in adjusting to a terminal illness and hospice services. It confirmed that clients should not be referred to the social worker only after a crisis has occurred, but initially and regularly throughout the course of the illness.

Other findings indicated that the qualifications of the social work staff were important. Social workers with more experience and master's degrees had better client outcomes. It was also critical for social workers to be clinically supervised by a social worker to enhance outcomes.

Hospice staffing and budgeting policies also made a difference. Hospices that provided more social workers and paid them higher starting salaries had better outcomes. The data also indicated that it was important not to assign the clinical social worker additional duties outside of the social work position—coordinating bereavement activities, volunteer activities, and so on. This promoted the social workers' abilities to address more issues with the interdisciplinary team and therefore help to enhance team functioning. Other beneficial outcomes related to increased social work services included fewer hospitalizations, fewer home health aide visits to patients, fewer nights of the continuous-care portion of the hospice benefit, and better client satisfaction scores. Additionally, social workers rated the problems in the cases that they worked with as less severe when there was more social work involvement. All of this, as in the previous three studies, resulted in lower costs for the hospice programs.

The results of this study helped to provide hard data to address the waning priority placed on social work services by some administrators and by the Health Care Financing Administration at the time. It addressed the problem of low salaries by linking higher salaries with beneficial outcomes. Supervision by a social worker rather than by a professional from a different discipline was related to enhanced patient outcomes. The finding that perhaps had the most impact was the strong evidence that increasing, rather than decreasing, social work services reduces costs in hospice care.

THE ROLE OF THE HOSPICE SOCIAL WORKER

Historically, social workers have differed from other disciplines in health care by bringing the concepts of patient self-determination, "person in environment," and a strengths perspective to the table. This orientation to addressing the whole person matches the core values of the hospice philosophy. The roles of social work in hospice are diverse. Social workers engage in assessment, diagnosis, and screening. They manipulate the environment, stimulate internal and psychosocial strengths/coping skills, and provide specific pain and symptom relief. They enhance patient and family self-worth and advocate for the individual/family within the system. In addition, hospice social workers facilitate healthy teamwork and serve as bereavement counselors and program coordinators or CEOs. Finally they provide education and training for the community at large as well as for fellow team members.

Results of the National Hospice Social Work Research Survey indicated that the majority of hospice social workers provided input to the team on psychosocial, cultural, and spiritual issues. They also promoted team awareness of an ecological perspective, advocated within the team for client self-determination, and provided emotional support and counseling to other team members. The majority of the social workers reported that they had helped the team to resolve conflicts regarding differences between disciplines in values, boundary, self-determination, and turf issues. Finally, the majority reported fulfilling educational roles in the areas of volunteer training, public education, and outreach to the medical community.

The second strategy of the Social Work Section was to develop a monograph to address competency-based education for social workers. Topics included definitions of competency-based education, a review of the Joint Commission on Accreditation of Healthcare Organization (JCAHO) and the National Hospice and Palliative Care Organization standards related to social work continuing education, an exploration of appropriate learning methods and appropriate steps for competency-based education programs.

The third strategy of the Social Work Section was to document and improve social work outcomes by developing a tool to measure them. In order to implement this strategy a researcher-practitioner coalition developed the Social Work Assessment Tool (SWAT). The SWAT is based on social work theory and research documenting the major psychosocial and spiritual variables affecting social work outcomes (Reese and Orloff 2002). The social worker uses it to rate client progress on these variables after each social work session. Future plans are for the SWAT measure to be completed as part of the ongoing performance review of hospices nationally. It is expected that use of the SWAT will serve as a guideline leading to improved performance. Social work outcomes will be routinely documented, thus addressing the problem of lack of evidence based practice. In addition, data will be collected for a national research database on hospice social work outcomes. Calculating national averages will allow for the development of benchmarks for social work outcomes. Examining service approaches in hospices with higher performance scores can then identify best practices. National dissemination of this information will contribute to improved social work practice in hospice care. These strategies have and will continue to assist both social workers in the field as well as colleagues in other disciplines to better understand and therefore value the role of social work in hospice.

LOOKING AHEAD

Clearly, there are challenges to the profession of social work both in hospice as well as in other forms of end-of-life care. The future effectiveness and growth of social work depends on the development of effective curriculum, theory, practice models, research, publications, community organization, macro-level advocacy, interdisciplinary education, and collaboration. Hospice social workers serve a critical but largely undocumented function in end-of-life care. In many ways social work appears to be a victim of its own values and its diversity of roles. Other professionals and the public alike often do not understand the unique roles of social work. Increasingly other professions are embracing the values of the social work profession but are unaware that these are and always have been the core values for social work. In order to be effective, the profession of social work, as well as individual social workers, must meet the following challenges:

1. Define and articulate the role and functions of social work in end-of-life care in a consistent manner across all settings.
2. Address negative public and professional perceptions of social work internally and externally.
3. Identify and articulate specific and unique contributions of the social work profession in end-of-life care.
4. Facilitate and promote end-of-life social work research that demonstrates the utility and efficiency of social work in hospice.
5. Facilitate collaborative advocacy at the macro level to ensure access to quality interdisciplinary end-of-life care for all people.
6. Actively challenge shortsighted cost-saving initiatives that minimize the psychosocial and spiritual components of care for patients and families.
7. Develop standards for effective models of practice in end-of-life care.

Many Americans are increasingly able to articulate what they want at the end of life. According to a public opinion survey conducted by the National Hospice Foundation in 1999 (NHF 1999), 83 percent want someone to make sure their wishes are known and honored; 85 percent want good pain control, a choice of care options, a team of professionals to carry out their choices, and emotional and spiritual support for themselves and their loved ones. A 1997 Gallup poll revealed that 70 percent of American citizens preferred "relieving pain and discomfort as much as possible, even if that meant not living as long," to "extending life as much as possible even if it meant more pain and discomfort." In addition, 70 percent of the respondents stated that they preferred to die at home.

In fact, these are the very wishes that hospice was designed to facilitate. Too many people, however, still have not even heard of hospice care. In the same National Hospice Foundation survey, 80 percent of respondents did not know the meaning of the term hospice, and 90 percent did not know that Medicare pays for hospice. Despite the dominant culture's concurrence with the basic tenets of hospice philosophy, and the wide availability of hospices, only 25 percent of Americans died while under the care of a hospice in 2000 (National Hospice and Palliative Care Organization 2001). Because most patients become aware of hospice when their physicians present it as an option (Gordon 1995), it appears that the medical profession as a whole is still oriented toward curative rather than palliative care. A number of authors have written about the lack of preparedness of physicians to provide end of life care (Carron, Lynn, and Keaney 1999; Field and Cassel 1997; Lynn and Harrold 1999). In addition, these survey results reveal that the field of hospice has a long way to go in the arena of public education.

There have also been significant difficulties surrounding the actual Medicare Hospice benefit. Under the benefit, hospices are paid a per diem rate and are expected to cover all costs, including durable medical goods, pharmaceuticals, respite care, and a full interdisciplinary team including bereavement services for the family after the death. Although the benefit originally solidified the role of hospice in the healthcare system and other reimbursement systems for hospice were modeled from it, reimbursement rates have not kept up with the cost of hospice care. With increasingly shorter lengths of stay, expensive startup costs, and soaring pharmaceutical expenses, many hospices are struggling. In 1994, the Office of Inspector General (OIG) audited some of the larger hospices in five different states. Among other things, the audits questioned the validity of the six-month terminal prognoses of hospice patients. This regulatory auditing exacerbated the problem of late referrals to hospice. Physicians, afraid of being accused of fraud, now often wait until the last days of life to refer to hospice programs. These late referrals are expensive for hospices but also cheat patients and families of a longer stay where more optimal planning, evaluation, and treatment could enhance the quality of life. In the early days of hospice, stays of six months or longer were not uncommon. Today stays of one to three days are all too frequent. The Medicare Benefit requires that all patients admitted to hospice be certified as having a life expectancy of six months or less. What then becomes of people who are dying but have more than six months to live? What about the people who know they are dying but want curative treatment? Increasingly, these are issues that create serious barriers to transforming end-of-life care in America. Most Americans, including many medical professionals, still believe that any curative treatment attempt is better, no matter what the cost or how limited the effectiveness. In this environment, hospice is often viewed as "giving up." The recent growth of palliative-care programs is in response to these serious limitations. Currently, however, many initial palliative-care programs do not embrace social work services. These are crucial arenas for social work involvement.

Hospice began as a mostly white, middle-class movement. To this day, the vast majority of people opting for hospice are still white and middle class. This is another serious flaw in hospice practice that has only recently begun to be addressed. Social workers need to play key roles in advancing cultural competence and sensitivity to insure that underserved populations have the same access to end-of-life care that meets their needs. Hospice care must look different for each family or it is not living up to its mission to provide patient- and family-driven care.

Social work advocacy in the public policy arena surrounding access issues, reimbursement issues, and informed consent is urgently needed. Social workers who are in the trenches working with patients and families have important stories to tell and research to complete. There is no doubt that the dying experience unfolds quite differently when there is time to individualize care as opposed to a twenty-four-hour rush to address symptoms as quickly as possible before death occurs. Hardcastle, Wenocur, and Powers tell us that "social workers whose indignation as well as compassion quotients run high are primed for professional advocacy" (1997:347). Hospice must return to and promote its original mission of client self-determination. People want choice and control at the end of life, and not just in the last six months. According to the data, they do not want their care dictated or defined by others. They want their values, rituals, and cultural belief systems and needs to be respected. In Michigan, the Michigan Partnership for the Advancement of End-of-Life Care, funded by a Robert Wood Johnson Foundation grant, conducted focus groups with underserved populations in the state. Conclusions drawn from these focus groups indicate that the availability of websites, videos, pamphlets, and other resource material can promote informed choice at the end of life for all cultures to a degree, but that in diverse communities that were studied the messages are often not received via these modalities. Information is generally accepted by word of mouth. Regardless of the modality, the issue of trust was also crucial. The interviewed community members stated that they needed and desired access to information about caring for their aging and dying, but often did not know what questions to ask or even where to go for answers. The majority of participants reported being intimidated by medical jargon and the healthcare professionals delivering care. The confusion about what hospice and palliative care are was pervasive.

The most obvious common thread in each group was the desire for human connection when seeking information and support as opposed to impersonal and often culturally insensitive materials. The report concludes, "Participants may be unable to communicate their end of life needs, but know that they prefer to stay within their own family and cultural practices at such intimate times. Participants want advisors and providers who they can talk with, who appreciate and respect their culture, heritage, belief system, and family" (Raymer, McKinney, and Gelfand 2000:4).

CONCLUSION

The model of hospice is a powerful template for effective end-of-life care, but hospices must become more flexible and reach out to more and different populations with messages that fit their diverse needs. Social workers within hospice programs need to take responsibility for advocacy, effective social work practice, and participation in research that enhances the care of the dying, not just in hospice but also in all models of end-of-life care.

As social workers, we are held to a code of ethics that emphasizes our responsibility to the broader society. By strengthening end-of-life care in all of its various forms, we will help to build a more decent and humane nation where compassionate interdisciplinary and expert end-of-life care is the norm instead of the exception.

REFERENCES

Carron, A., J. Lynn, and P. Keaney. 1999. End-of-life care in medical textbooks. *Annals of Internal Medicine* 130(1): 82–86.

Cherin, D. 1997. Saving services: Redefining end-stage home care for HIV/AIDS. *Innovations* 26–27.

Corless, I., and Z. Foster. 1999. *The Hospice Heritage: Celebrating Our Future.* Binghamton, NY: Haworth.

Csikai, E., and K. Bass. 2000. Health care social workers' views of ethical issues, practice, and policy in end-of-life care. *Social Work in Health Care* 32(2): 1–22.

Field, M., and C. K. Cassel, eds. 1997. *Approaching Death: Improving Care at the End of Life.* Washington, DC: National Academy Press.

Gallup International Institute. 1997. *Spiritual Beliefs and the Dying Process.* Princeton, NJ: Nathan Cummings Foundation.

Gordon, A. K. 1995. Deterrents to access and service for blacks and Hispanics: The Medicare hospice benefit, healthcare utilization, and cultural barriers. *Hospice Journal* 10(2): 65–83.

Hardcastle, D. A., S. Wenocur, and P. R. Powers, eds. 1997. *Community Practice: Theories and Skills for Social Workers.* New York: Oxford University Press.

Kovacs, P., and L. Bronstein. 1999. Preparation for oncology settings: What hospice workers say they need. *Health and Social Work* 24(1): 57–64.

Kramer, B. 1998. Preparing social workers for the inevitable: A preliminary investigation of a course on grief, death, and loss. *Journal of Social Work Education* 34(2): 1–17.

Lynn, J., and J. Harrold. 1999. *Handbook for Mortals: Guidance for People Facing Serious Illness.* New York: Oxford University Press.

Mahar, T., L. Eickman, and S. Bushfield. 1997. Efficacy of early social work intervention. Paper presented at the National Hospice and Palliative Care Organization Management and Leadership Conference.

Mahoney, J. 1997. Hospice and managed care. *Hospice Journal* 12(2): 81–84.

McDonnell, A. 1986. *Quality Hospice Care: Administrative, Organization, and Models.* Owings Mills, MD: National Health Publishers.

National Hospice Foundation. 1999. National Hospice Foundation survey. www.nhpco.org.

Paquette, S. 1997. Social work intervention and program cost reduction outcomes. Paper presented at the National Hospice and Palliative Care Organization Management and Leadership Conference.

Raymer, M., B. McKinney, and D. Gelfand. 2000. *How Do Community Members Seek Information About End-of-Life Care?* Lansing: Michigan Partnership for the Advancement of End-of-Life Care.

Reese, D. 1995–96. Testing of a causal model: Acceptance of death in hospice patients. *Omega: Journal of Death and Dying* 32(2): 81–92.

Reese, D., and S. Orloff. 2002. The social work assessment tool (SWAT): Development and use in practice. Paper presented at the Joint Clinical Conference, National Hospice and Palliative Care Organization.

Reese, D., M. Raymer, and J. Richardson. 1998. National hospice social work survey: Plan and preliminary results. Paper presented at the National Hospice Organization Annual Symposium and Exhibition.

Schneider, L. 2001. *Social Work Advocacy: A New Framework for Action.* Belmont, CA: Wadsworth/Thompson Learning.

Sontag, M. 1996. Hospices as providers of total care in one western state. *Hospice Journal* 3:71–94.

World Health Organization. 1990. Definition of palliative care. www.who.int/dsa/justpub/cpl.htm.

8

THE INTERDISCIPLINARY TEAM: AN OXYMORON?

INGE B. CORLESS AND PATRICE K. NICHOLAS

IS THE concept of an interdisciplinary team an oxymoron? Is a team multidisciplinary by definition? Is the expectation that one discipline will be in charge—the captain, as it were—with the other disciplines serving as the crew? Interdisciplinary collaboration is difficult for many reasons, including the idiosyncrasies of socialization into the professions, distinctions in roles, and differences in moral reasoning perspectives. In this chapter we will examine a number of these issues, including what is meant by discipline, disciplinary education, disciplinary approaches to patient care, goals of service, ethical approaches, occupational role relationships, interdisciplinary education and practice, role blending, and multidisciplinary vs. interdisciplinary approaches.

We begin by examining the concept of discipline. *Discipline* is a term with different meanings depending on the perspective of the viewer. *Webster's New World Dictionary* defines it as "1. a branch of knowledge or learning; 2. training that develops self-control, character, or orderliness and efficiency; 3. the result of such training; self-control; orderly conduct; 4. acceptance of or submission to authority and control; 5. a system of rules or methods, as for the conduct of members of a monastic order; 6. treatment that corrects or punishes."

Each discipline attempts to demonstrate that it has a distinctive branch of knowledge that is foundational to its work. Indeed, professions engage in research to enhance the scientific foundation for their practice. Disciplines also engage in special education that prepares the recipients for practice values, knowledge, and skills. Such education has been termed *training*. In nursing, the early programs were entitled training programs. In medicine, as well, medical school graduates seek training programs to engage in the primarily experiential phase of their education where theoretical knowledge previously learned is combined with "on the job" experience buttressed by clinical science. Medicine developed a four-year program of university-based medical education with subsequent hospital-based training, moving away from an apprenticeship-only model decades before that would occur with nursing education. Social work training also requires internships as well as two years of didactic learning. For any of the professions, training focuses on knowledge, but the implicit emphasis is also on the self-control, character, orderliness, and efficiency with which the knowledge is employed. The outcome of training is the professional who demonstrates the effect of disciplinary education both in expertise and in conduct.

The term *profession* has been used in explicating the domain of the term *discipline*. What is their relationship? One of the meanings of "profession," according to *Webster*, is "a vocation or occupation requiring advanced training in some liberal art or science, and usually involving mental rather than manual work, as teaching, engineering, writing, etc.; especially medicine, law or theology (formerly called the learned professions)." Professions require discipline in the many meanings of the term.

Professions are governed by legitimate and illegitimate assertions of authority. The demarcations of authority and responsibility are defined by state boards, which govern who may and may not practice as a professional in a given discipline. The state boards of the professions underscore the rules of practice learned in the educational programs of each of the professions. The state boards also provide the "treatment" that corrects or punishes the deviant behavior of individuals certified as members of a given profession.

Why this lengthy and perhaps pedantic explication of the term *discipline*? It is only if we understand the total meaning of what is it meant by discipline that we can proceed to consider what we mean by *multidisciplinary* and ultimately *interdisciplinary*, and whether interdisciplinary approaches are indeed possible and to what degree by custom and law.

Henneman (1995), in a consideration of nurse-physician collaboration, cites the work of Michel Foucault (1975), who links discipline with power. Disciplinary organizations are associated with the acquisition, maintenance, and expansion of power for their members. Foucault identifies three mechanisms: examination—for both entrance into and legitimation of requisite knowledge; normalizing judgment—as a means of assuring conformity to the mores of the discipline; and hierarchical observation—both within and between disciplines. In essence, what is at stake is control over practice, the development of scientific knowledge, and the legitimated access to institutional resources, as well as decision making about individual health care with the implication that well being, if not life and death, hang in the balance. That exemplifies disciplinary power, not only over individual health care but also the manner in which health and illness care are provided and by whom. And, as Mendez, Coddou, and Maturana state, "A claim to objective knowledge is an absolute demand for obedience" (1988:170).

Given that in the Western practice of medicine the physician has such power, what incentive is there to relinquish this power and the resultant status in a hierarchy of healthcare providers? The remainder of this chapter will attempt to provide an answer to this question. To begin with, it behooves us to examine how physicians use the term *discipline*. For physicians, a professional of another discipline is a physician whose specialty differs from their own. Thus, a urologist and an obstetrician are members of different disciplines. And while it may appear so, given the specialized knowledge and professional organizations generic to each specialty, in reality each physician has received similar core knowledge prior to specialty practice. Indeed, were it the specialty knowledge that defined a discipline, then individuals with differing core knowledge bases but similar specialty education and experience might be considered members of the same discipline. These disciplinary distinctions within medicine offer the potential for "disciplinary" associations among professions. More will be said about this later in this chapter.

Sir Cyril Chantler has a broader view of the concept of discipline than many of his peers. In discussing his work with children with chronic renal failure, he observes, "success depends on numerous people from different disciplines working together with the child and family" (1998:317). Aside from the centrality given to patient and family, Chantler includes "not just paediatricians and surgeons but also dieticians, psychologists, social workers, laboratory scientific staff, technical staff, secretarial staff, play therapists, urologists and orthopaedic surgeons. But particularly important are the nurses and the relationship between the nursing and medical staff" (1998:317). What is important here is that Chantler has a vision of what constitutes a team and that vision incorporates professionals from disciplines other than medicine. Chantler is also aware of the breadth of knowledge required of physicians. He states, "Teamwork, management, ethics, and law and the behavioural and social sciences are now represented in the curriculum. The basic understandings required of a newly qualified doctor should in my opinion include cell biology, molecular genetics, communication skills, and informatics, which are introduced early and reinforced throughout the course. We do not neglect evidence-based medicine, but we bear in mind that many patients do not have evidence-based illnesses and most illness has a genetic, an environmental, a social and a psychological context" (1998:317–318). The wit and wisdom of Chantler will reverberate when consideration is given next to education and interdisciplinary relationships.

Sarah Shannon (1997) contrasts the focus and training of doctors, nurses, and social workers. She observes that for clinical judgment, Edmund Pellegrino notes that physicians emphasize the generalities of the case. "Diagnosing physical illness involves considering physical signs and symptoms, results of diagnostic tests, and knowledge of disease patterns. The doctor seeks diagnostic closure on what is wrong with a patient through reasoning that relies heavily on certain rules of clinical prudence" (17). Shannon contrasts this with nurses' being "taught never to assume the obvious. The exception is the rule when it comes to patient eccentricities around responses to medications, coping mechanisms, interpersonal skills" (17). In similar fashion, "Social workers learn that if a problem or solution looks simple or straightforward, one should look again. Social and family situations are more complex than they appear. Furthermore, there is always more than one answer to a question and more than one solution to a problem. The expert social worker never bases a judgment on only one side of the story but gathers information from a wide variety of sources" (18). In essence, and simplifying the situation, in examining an issue the physician looks for the "elegant" solution, the nurse looks at the nuances and details for idiosyncrasies, and the social worker looks at the complexities.

Each profession claims to be the patient's advocate, and each profession is—in different ways. The physician's claim "stems from the fiduciary nature of the doctor-patient relationship, in which vulnerable patients must be able to trust that their physician will make recommendations based on their best interests rather than the physician's interests (such as financial or job security), profits for stockholders of the health care plan, or a family's financial or other interests" (Shannon 1997:23). Nurses assume "patients need an advocate to protect them from the highly technologic environment of health care. Patients are vulnerable to a loss of rights because they have inadequate knowledge and decreased personal power when hospitalized" (22). Social workers give allegiance to the principle of patient autonomy and keep that uppermost in mind for patients. "For social work, acting as the patient's advocate means actively supporting the patient's choices for health care, living arrangements, and other expressions of self-determination" (24). This allegiance to autonomy may put social workers in conflict, in particular in this instance, with physicians whose role it is to advocate for what is medically most beneficial. Appreciating these differences can be helpful to these professions and other members of the healthcare team.

In advocating for the patient, each of the professions manifests an aspect of caring for the patient. The claim to "caring," whether by hospice providers to oncologists or by nurses to doctors, emphasizes the differences in the focus of care and cure by obfuscating the commonalities. Cure is achieved by the "identification of pathophysiology, leading to a diagnosis, and reduction of symptomatology through the treatment of pathology" (Baumann et al. 1998:1040). Care is a more elusive concept "often measured by maintenance of a satisfactory level of functioning in several dimensions, rather than by attainment of a particular outcome (e.g., decreased blood pressure)" (Baumann et al. 1998:1041). Compassion, empathy, and respect are often considered central to care and caring and to the role of nursing where there is an emphasis on the responses of the client to health care and the illness experience. That does not make it absent from the diagnostic process or the work of the social worker who, whether in making financial, housing, or custodial arrangements, or in providing mental-health care, also exhibits these behaviors. It is more evident in "person" work than in technical activities, whether those are the ordering of tests for a differential diagnosis, maintaining the patency of intravenous medication lines, or securing placement post–hospital discharge. Empathy is not absent from the work of the physical therapist or the dietician. Indeed it is often the manner in which the activities are discharged rather than the activities per se that identifies the presence of caring. It is the emphasis on the biopsychosocial well-being of the patient that is indicative of caring. A foray into ethics may bring additional clarity to this discourse.

Two ethical principles widely used in healthcare decision making are the ethics of justice and the ethics of care. These poles of moral reasoning, while wholly legitimate, can cause conflict when members of an interdisciplinary team view the world from different perspectives. The distinctions between these two principles mirror some of those between cure and care when these are viewed simplistically. As Botes states, "The ethics of justice constitutes an ethical perspective in terms of which ethical decisions are made on the basis of universal principles and rules, and in an impartial and verifiable manner with a view to ensuring the fair and equitable treatment of all people. The ethics of care, on the other hand, constitutes an ethical approach in terms of which involvement, harmonious relations, and the needs of others play an important part in ethical decision-making in each ethical situation" (2000:1071). Using a concept analysis, Botes cites the defining attributes of justice as fairness, equality, verifiable and reliable decision making based on universal rules and principles, autonomy, objectivity, impartiality, and positivistic rationality (1072). Using the same methodology, Botes found the defining attributes of the ethics of care to be care, involvement, empathy, maintaining harmonious relations, holistic, contextual, need-centered, and communicative rationality (1072). Botes states, "It is suggested that the ethics of justice and the ethics of care represent opposite poles. If the members of the health care team were to use only one of these two perspectives in their ethical decision making, certain ethical dilemmas would be likely to remain unresolved" (1075). The solution she proposes is the use of both approaches. Implicit in this response is a further challenge. Whereas the ethics of justice are implemented by adherence to universal principles, the ethics of care demand consensus as to the best approach in a given situation. How is this to be achieved without cumbersome, lengthy decision making? And by whom? Where standardization and quality control would appear to demand application of universal approaches diminishing the individualistic considerations of the case, the push for accountability for the individual case countervails this seeming neglect.

Further complicating the situation is the history of occupational role relationships. An example of this is the history of medical omnipotence and nursing subservience and the resultant indirect mode of communication exemplified in what was first characterized by Stein (1967) as the doctor-nurse game. The sex-role aspects of the game have diminished with the advent of female doctors and male nurses. And the enhanced role of nursing and fallibility of physicians has lead to an improvement of relations (Stein 1990), but the ghosts linger. Although, as Sweet (1995) notes, this may vary by whether the nursing transpires in a general or specialty unit. And collaboration is more important to nurses than to physicians (Baggs et al. 1997; Mohammadreza et al. 2001).

The role of handmaiden to medicine has included social work as well. Little has been written, however, about this phenomenon. In large part this may be because these roles are concerned with different spheres of activity. The requirement of graduate preparation for a career in social work has also supported the status of the field and the view of social workers by their physician colleagues. That is not to say there are no problems. Abramson and Mizrahi (1996), in a study of social worker–physician collaboration, suggest, "Social workers who grasp the action and outcome orientation of many physicians as well as the emphasis they place on communication will stress these aspects when collaborating" (Huntington 1981:208). Unfortunately, for social workers and other professionals, "given traditional physician socialization, the majority of physicians are unlikely at present to offer the degree of shared responsibility and mutuality that many social workers seek" (Abramson and Mizrahi 1996:280). They suggest that social workers look to other reference groups for validation of their performance and support for themselves. The move from episodic care to ongoing care will require collaboration for effective patient care. This should serve as a countervailing force to physician dominance. More about this shortly.

Although there is no social worker–nurse game per se, that is not to say there are not areas of potential friction. Social workers and nurses may overlap in some aspects of patient/family counseling that may make for competitive relations between members of the two disciplines. The extreme of this is the notion that social workers' activities can be subsumed into the roles of other colleagues. The impetus for this is not professional jostling for sphere of influence but rather bottom-line bean counting. This thrust is no different from the introduction of patient care associates to assume aspects of the nurse's role, thereby reducing the complement of registered nurses. These financial decisions about the composition of the cadre of professional caregivers add to the stress of the professionals so affected and their colleagues.

Differences in professional perspectives can be attributed to the differing professional ideologies, the ethical principles that govern the work, and some of the organizational constraints on the disciplines. Another source of potential dissension is the dysfunctional patient and family who often align themselves with different caregivers, creating misunderstandings among the caregivers (Groves and Bersein 1998). It is a maxim that when there is dissension in the team beyond differences of opinion, look to the family (or patient) for dysfunctional relationships. The assumption, of course, is that the team is not dysfunctional which may or may not be the case.

How can we achieve better interdisciplinary care? Richards et al., after examining the literature on physician, nurse, and other professionals' relationships and subsequent health care, conclude that "more equitable and less hierarchical models of multi-professional teams working in primary care will be most successful" (2000:185). But that is primary care and that is the English experience; what other evidence is there? Larson (1999) comes to much the same conclusion, noting both the unhealthy work environments and the poor patient outcomes that result from a lack of collaboration. Zwarenstein and Bryant (2000), in a structured review of the literature, found that increasing collaboration reduced length of hospital stay and cost of care and resulted in greater staff satisfaction and understanding of patient care. In another study of collaboration in three intensive care units (ICU), "medical ICU nurses' reports of collaboration were associated positively with patient outcomes" (Baggs et al. 1999: 1991). Controlling costs, improved patient care, and feeling better about the job were three outcomes of another study of medical ICU personnel (Baggs et al. 1997; Baggs and Schmitt 1997).

The importance of collaboration and the interdisciplinary team was stressed in the rehabilitation field in 1945 by Howard Rusk and Alice Morrissey, whose emphasis on holistic care guided practice in this field (Morrissey 1951). Thus it comes as no surprise that the long-term care venue of the nursing home is another site for interdisciplinary teamwork (Tremethick and Wallace 1999).

An attempt to implement collaborative practice on a general surgery service in a university hospital underscored differences in emphasis of the participants. "The medical students believed the purpose of the rounds was to instruct, and guide them in the principles and practice of surgical medicine. The nurses viewed rounds as a means to discuss the key needs of the patients with the resident staff. The resident staff viewed rounds as a time to make patient care decisions. There was some tension between the conflicting priorities of teaching as a teaching institution mission and providing care as another aspect of the service mission of the hospital" (Felten et al. 1997:124). How else might this teaching occur?

Laura Blickensderfer (1996) examines strategies for enhancing collaboration. She notes Claire Fagin's (1992) call for nursing and medical-school curriculum changes. Blickensderfer states that Fagin "challenges us to examine the total separation of the two curricula, asking how nurses and physicians are to learn collaboration when they have never learned anything together" (1996:130), a theme echoed by Smith, Barton, and Baxter (1996). Blickensderfer notes that professionals have not "heard collaboration encouraged by their teacher role models, or seen it displayed by the people they respect most while in school." She suggests "joint nurse/physician classes [and] professor exchanges" (1996:127–131).

Collaboration by all members of the team requires widespread interdisciplinary education (Cunningham 1997). This interdisciplinary education needs to include all of the members of the healthcare team, including doctors, nurses, physical and other therapists, social workers, and chaplains. The literature indicates that interdisciplinary education for student health professionals has had an impact on student knowledge, skills, and beliefs about professional roles and teamwork (Cooper et al. 2001). Georgetown University has an interdisciplinary curriculum in clinical ethics developed by the nursing and medical faculty (Cloonan, Davis, and Burnett 1999). Although this is a step in the right direction, it is imperative that this model be expanded to include professionals in training from other disciplines. Pharmacists are also interested in such education and professional experiences (Kepple 1999).

A family practice center in Wisconsin has developed a collaborative educational model for social work, medical, and nursing students (Lough et al. 1996). The objectives are for students to be able to "articulate the values and focus of one's own profession to other members of the interdisciplinary student team; describe the expertise of each other's disciplines; develop interdisciplinary healthcare plans that involve clients as members of the team; participate in the development of healthcare programs that are responsive to the needs of an essentially underserved community; and deliver health services using a collaborative approach" (Lough et al. 1996:29). The idealistic motives that animate the development of interdisciplinary education and practice opportunities such as the Georgetown and Wisconsin programs will likely expand. They will also be joined by interdisciplinary approaches motivated by enhancing management outcomes (Warren, Houston, and Luquire 1998). These outcomes are concerned with the quality markers by which institutions are assessed by regulatory agencies. Whatever the motive, the broader implementation of interdisciplinary approaches that are a core facet of hospice care is a welcome occurrence. What can be learned from the hospice experience?

Hospice programs have assumed that the interdisciplinary team is a key aspect of the approach to care. In the early days of the hospice movement, there was much discussion about the differences between multidisciplinary and interdisciplinary with the latter the preferred model. Note that multidisciplinary might be likened to parallel play, whereas interdisciplinary connotes collaboration without hierarchy. The focus in the interdisciplinary team is on the knowledge and expertise possessed by each of the team members as well as their personal talents (Ryan 1999). The "captain" of the team is decided by the needs and wishes of the care recipient. The captain and team work collaboratively to meet patient and family concerns and needs. Leadership here implies shared responsibility and not hierarchy.

What is termed "role blending" indicates the degree to which professionals do what needs to be done with less attention as to which discipline is responsible for what. That is not to say that social workers write prescriptions for medications. Rather, the social worker, while engaged in discipline-specific activities, also will observe responses to medications and report back to the team for further discussion. This experience is common in hospice care. The concern has been expressed that the new institutionally based palliative-care movement is less likely to exhibit the characteristics of the interdisciplinary team (O'Connor 1999). The drive to legitimate the palliative-care approach as a part of the medical school curriculum has lead to a reification of disciplinary boundaries. A sign of hope, however, is the incorporation of an interdisciplinary palliative-care experience by McMaster University in Canada for nursing, occupational therapy, physiotherapy, medical, radiation, and divinity students (Latimer et al. 1999).

Does this examination of the terms *multidisciplinary* and *interdisciplinary* matter with regard to patient care? Ina Cummings, who has had long experience in hospice and palliative care, clarifies the distinctions between these terms. She contrasts the differences between multidisciplinary and interdisciplinary teams. In a traditional multidisciplinary team, "individuals are known first by their professional identities and only secondarily by their team affiliation. They share information using the vehicle of the medical record, and the leader is the highest ranking member" (1988:19). How such ranking is determined is not stated. It may be by profession or by organizational position. She continues, "As the team is not the primary vehicle for action, the interaction process is not of primary importance." This is a stunning observation. Multidisciplinary activities are, as noted previously, parallel play. The comparison with interdisciplinary teams is striking. "Here the identity of the team supercedes individual personal identities." Here, we would hope that Cummings also includes professional identities. She notes that information is shared and that goals are developed by members working interdependently. "Leadership is shared among team members depending on the task at hand." The idea that leadership varies is not solely profession-dependent but also, in the context of team, skill-dependent. Those skills include not only the interests and personalities of the professionals but also the *je ne sais quoi* of the relationships with patient and family that make for a valued bond. Last, "Because the team is the vehicle of action, the interaction process is vital to success." Interaction process refers here to the communication process of the team. Integral to effective communication is the absence of secrets among team members. Information is not privileged in the sense that some team members have access to relevant information whereas others do not. Information is privileged among the team so that it can be shared as a basis for the development of common goals. The distinction of the team as the unity rather than the separate parts distinguishes what the meaning of *interdis-*

ciplinary is. The process of interaction based on respect, information sharing, and shared decision making is the hallmark of the interdisciplinary team.

Is the concept of the interdisciplinary team an oxymoron? For most professional education and practice, the standard of care to date has been mostly multidisciplinary parallel play. By way of contrast, in practice sites such as hospice, interdisciplinary team is not an oxymoron. Indeed, it is the gold standard. Were it so everywhere!

REFERENCES

Abramson, J. S., and T. Mizrahi. 1996. When social workers and physicians collaborate: Positive and negative interdisciplinary experiences. *Social Work* 41(3): 270–281.

Baggs, J. G., B. G. Baggs, M. H. Schmitt, et al. 1997. Nurse-physician collaboration and satisfaction with the decision-making process in three critical care units. *American Journal of Critical Care* 6:393–399.

——. 1999. Association between nurse-physician collaboration and patient outcomes in three intensive care units. *Critical Care Medicine* 27(9): 1991–1998.

Baggs, J. G., and M. H. Schmitt. 1997. Nurses' and resident physicians' perceptions of the process of collaboration in an MICU. *Research in Nursing and Health* 20:71–80.

Baumann, A. O., R. B. Deber, B. E. Silverman, and C. M. Mallette. 1998. Who cares? Who cures? The ongoing debate in the provision of health care. *Journal of Advanced Nursing* 28(5): 1040–1045.

Blickensderfer, L. 1996. Nurses and physicians: Creating a collaborative environment. *Journal of IV Nursing* 19(3): 127–131.

Botes, A. 2000. A comparison between the ethics of justice and the ethics of care. *Journal of Advanced Nursing* 32(5): 1071–1075.

Chantler, C. 1998. Interdisciplinary relationships. *Journal of the Royal Society of Medicine* 91(6): 317–318.

Cloonan, P. A., F. D. Davis, and C. B. Burnett. 1999. Interdisciplinary education in clinical ethics: A work in progress. *Holistic Nursing Practice* 13(2): 12–19.

Cooper, H., C. Carlisle, T. Gibbs, and C. Watkins. 2001. Developing an evidence base for interdisciplinary learning: A systematic review. *Journal of Advanced Nursing* 35(2): 228–237.

Cummings, I. 1998. The interdisciplinary team. In *Oxford Textbook of Palliative Medicine*, ed. D. Doyle, G. W. C. Hanks, and N. MacDonald, 19–30. Oxford: Oxford University Press.

Cunningham, W. F. 1997. Postgraduate education for general practitioners: Interdisciplinary education would help improve teamwork. *British Medical Journal* 315(7121): 1543.

Fagin, C. 1992. Collaboration between nurses and physicians—no longer a choice. *Nursing and Health Care* 13:354–363.

Felten, S., N. Cady, M. H. Metzler, and S. Burton. 1997. Implementation of a collaborative practice through interdisciplinary rounds on a general surgery service. *Nursing Case Management* 2(3): 122–126.

Foucault, M. 1975. *Discipline and Punish.* New York: Vintage.

Groves, J. E., and E. V. Bersein. 1998. Difficult patients, difficult families. *New Horizons* 6(4): 331–343.

Henneman, E. A. 1995. Nurse-physician collaboration: a poststructuralist view. *Journal of Advanced Nursing* 22(20): 359–363.

Kepple, S. R. 1999. Pharm. D. student takes interdisciplinary path to career goals: Interdisciplinary practice model begets opportunities, questions. *American Journal of Health-System Pharmacy* 56(1): 12, 14–16.

Larson, E. 1999. The impact of physician-nurse interaction on patient care. *Holistic Nursing Practice* 13(2): 38–46.

Latimer, E. J., A. Deakin, C. Ingram, L. O'Brien, M. Smoke, and L. Wishart. 1999. An interdisciplinary approach to a day-long palliative care course for undergraduate students. *Canadian Medical Association Journal* 161(6): 729–731.

Lough, M. A., K. Schmidt, G. R. Swain, et al. 1996. An interdisciplinary educational model for health professions students in a family practice center. *Nurse Educator* 21(1): 27–31.

Mendez, C., F. Coddou, and H. R. Maturana. 1988. Bringing forth of pathology. *Irish Journal of Psychology* 9:144–173.

Mohammadreza, H., T. J. Nasca, M. J. M. Cohen, et al. 2001. Attitudes toward physician-nurse collaboration: A cross-cultural study of male and female physicians and nurses in the United States and Mexico. *Nursing Research* 50(2): 123–128.

Morrissey, A. B. 1951. *Rehabilitation Nursing.* New York: G. P. Putnam's Sons.

O'Connor, P. 1999. Hospice vs. palliative care. In *The Hospice Heritage: Celebrating Our Future*, ed. I. B. Corless and Z. Foster, 123–137. New York: Haworth.

Pellegrino, E. D. 1979. The anatomy of clinical judgements: Some notes on right reason and right action. In *Clinical Judgement: A Critical Appraisal*, ed. H. T. Engelhardt Jr., S. F. Spicker, and B. Towers, 169–194. Dordrecht: D. Reidel.

Richards, A., J. Carley, S. Jenkins-Clarke, and D. A. Richards. 2000. Skill mix between nurses and doctors working in primary care-delegation or allocation: A review of the literature. *International Journal of Nursing Studies* 37(3): 185–197.

Ryan, J. W. 1999. Collaboration of the nurse practitioner and physician in long-term care. *Lippincott's Primary Care Practice* 3(2): 127–134.

Shannon, S. 1997. The roots of interdisciplinary conflict around ethical issues. *Critical Care Nursing Clinics of North America* 9(1): 13–27.

Smith, M., J. Barton, and J. Baxter. 1996. An innovative, interdisciplinary educational experience in field research. *Nurse Educator* 21(2): 27–30.

Stein, L. 1967. The doctor-nurse game. *Archives of General Psychiatry* 16(6): 699–703.

Stein, L., D. T. Watts, and T. Howell. 1990. The doctor-nurse game revisited. *New England Journal of Medicine* 322(8): 546–549.

Sweet, S. J., and I. J. Norman. 1995. The nurse-doctor relationship: A selective literature review. *Journal of Advanced Nursing* 22(10): 165–170.

Tremethick, M. J., and D. C. Wallace. 1999. Interdisciplinary teamwork for hip fracture prevention. *Geriatric Nursing* 20(6): 293–296.

Warren, M. L., S. Houston, and R. Luquire. 1998. Collaborative practice teams: From multidisciplinary to interdisciplinary. *Outcomes Management for Nursing Practice* 2(3): 95–98.

Zwarenstein, M., and W. Bryant. 2000. Interventions to promote collaboration between nurses and doctors. *Cochrane Database of Systematic Reviews* 4. www.cochrane.org.

9

ETHICAL ISSUES IN END-OF-LIFE CARE: SOCIAL WORK FACILITATION AND PROACTIVE INTERVENTION

PATRICIA O'DONNELL

O PTIMAL CARE at the end of life requires not only a comprehensive assessment of the patient and family's physical, social, psychological, and spiritual needs, but also understanding and managing the complex ethical challenges encountered by the patient, family, and professional caregivers. Social workers have had a traditional role in facilitating communication between the patient and family and care team in health care. This role is critical at the end of life, and particularly in managing the ethical dilemmas associated with end-of-life treatment and care decisions. This chapter explores the ethical issues that relate to end-of-life care and the role of social work in facilitating the resolution of these issues.

INFLUENCES AND TRENDS IN CURRENT END-OF-LIFE CARE

McCormick (1984) summarized the cultural factors that have influenced and changed the provision of health care and the perspective of its providers at both the individual and institutional levels. The most influential factors include (1) the increasing complexity of problems related to the rise in technology and an increased ability to offer miracle care; (2) the expanded options available to the patient, family, and physician complicated by issues of best interests and self-determination; (3) the professional's fear of litigation if all options for treatment are not provided on demand; (4) the influence of values held by not only the physicians but by the patient and others in reaching clinical decisions; (5) the emergence of patient autonomy over the traditional paternalism in physician-patient relationships; (6) the view that health is a commodity to be managed and sold as a market good; (7) the potential conflict of religious convictions with individual and institutional values of healthcare providers; and (8) the impact of multiple outsiders on previously private decisions between the physician and patient.

These factors have also contributed to the rise of ethical issues in end-of-life care. Innovations in technology and treatments have transformed catastrophic illnesses into chronic illnesses with accompanying questions related to the quality of life. Other questions such as should it be the patient or the physician who makes the decisions to withhold or withdraw treatments arise from the growth of consideration of patient autonomy over physician benevolence or paternalism. The plurality of cultures in the professional and patient populations demand extended knowledge of and sensitivity to value conflicts in end-of-life decision making especially in the areas of communication and disclosure.

In the Education for Physicians in End of Life Care (EPEC) overview of the current state of end-of-life care, the authors state that the source of the problems with end-of-life care is that death is no longer seen as a natural outcome of illness and disease but as a phenomena that can be controlled (AMA 1999). The process of death has been medicalized. As a result, patients fear that their dying will be a process characterized by loss of control and of personal dignity, unrelieved pain and isolation, and increased emotional and financial burdens to their families. Callahan (2000) identifies the desire for meaning in one's death as the most common wish expressed by patients. In addition, patients want to be treated with respect and dignity, to have their deaths matter to others, to have private time with their loved ones, to present no undue burdens (either emotional or financial) to their families, to avoid a prolonged death, not to be in coma, to live in a society that supports survivors and accepts death, to be alert, and to have their pain and suffering managed. Callahan further notes that advances in technology have transformed previously fatal illnesses into chronic illnesses that can be treated, often blurring the line between life and death. Death is seen as something that must be controlled. The goal of treatment moves from care at the end of life to a life-extending process. In addition, choices that were previously unavailable now complicate treatment decisions that combine consideration of the possible benefits of science and technology in relation to personal and societal values.

SOCIAL WORK PARTICIPATION IN BIOETHICS

Social workers are increasingly involved in the identification and resolution of biomedical ethical issues (Reamer 1985). Social work is a values-based profession and is particularly suited to addressing the value-laden decisions that patients and families face in modern health care. These decisions include the use and allocation of technology, the right to live, the right to die, the limits of intervention, and quality of life. As patients and families struggle with understanding the parameters of care and accepting the limitations of intervention, they turn to social workers to help them resolve these difficult issues and manage their consequences. Jennings (1987) described the ethical duties of the social worker as extending beyond the realm of service to the public interest into the realm of service for the common good, that is, to make a difference not only in people's lives but also in society's perspectives. He identifies social work as a vocation as it involves a "calling" that is driven by social work values of altruism, social justice, mutual aid, and public welfare. The public duty of the profession is to "make the invisible visible." Social workers have assumed leadership roles in forming and chairing ethics committees, ethics consultation, policy development and implementation, and education (Skinner 1991; Furlong 1986; Joseph and Conrad 1989; Csikai 1997).

Social work values and principles cited in the preamble of the National Association of Social Workers (NASW) Code of Ethics (1999) direct social workers to support patient, family, and staff values and preferences by exploring all points of view, by respecting the individuals involved, and by using the professional relationship to promote the goals of all. To achieve these goals, social workers need a foundation in ethics that includes knowledge of the process of ethical analysis and decision making. This includes an understanding of ethical perspectives from philosophy, ethical principles, the influence of professional and personal values, legal and regulatory obligations, and the guidance offered by professional Codes of Ethics. The more difficult and complex the issue the more important it is to be able to define the ethical aspects and reflect conflicting principles and values (Reamer 1985; Joseph and Conrad 1989).

MODELS OF ETHICAL DECISION MAKING

To help social workers identify, examine, and resolve the ethical issues and conflicts that are the source of ethical dilemmas in social work practice in healthcare settings, social work scholars have developed several models for ethical decision making. The models have much in common, but include some variation in guiding the process. Joseph (1983), building from the biomedical models, begins with the need to clearly define the dilemma. The definition process includes describing the setting, identifying all of the parties involved, and including all of the details of the problem that have given rise to the dilemma. Ethical dilemmas usually are centered on competing and/or conflicting obligations. Supporting the interests of the patient may conflict with obligations to the care team or the institution.

A review of both the social work and ethics literature will provide precedents established in similar cases, a complete range of the ethical issues involved, and justify why the resolutions offered were selected. The second advantage of the literature review is that previous reviews will inform future deliberations. Applying bioethical principles of autonomy, beneficence, nonmaleficence, and social justice as well as understanding of the ethical frameworks such as the deontological, teleological, and utilitarian perspectives will help the social worker reflect on the ethical factors of the dilemma and its resolution. Each of these philosophical perspectives will offer different directions in evaluating a course of action. For example, in making a decision related to truth telling, the deontological perspective would direct that the truth must always be told regardless of the consequences as the rightness of the act lies in the act itself. The teleological perspective would allow consideration of the consequences of telling the truth in a particular situation. The utilitarian perspective would direct the decision maker to consider how the act of truth telling would maximize the benefit for and the values of the majority of the involved parties. Professional codes of ethics, such as the NASW Code of Ethics (1999), provide guidance on the expectations of the profession for ethical practice. It is also important to consider the codes of ethics of other professionals involved in the case. There are occasions when the guidelines provided in other professional's codes differ from the directions for action outlined in the NASW Code of Ethics. A review of the values of all parties, including the institution and community, will help establish a hierarchy to measure the impact of each of the options for resolution. An examination of inherent biases on the part of the decision makers brings an awareness of and sensitivity to their influence on the potential options for resolution. The final step involves listing the range of options and justifying each for examination. The decision maker then selects the option that best meets the inherent obligations and values associated with the dilemma.

The Joseph (1983) model serves as the exemplar for social-work ethical decision making. Other social work–ethics scholars have added further refinements to the model. Reamer (1990) suggests that rules against basic harms to necessary preconditions of actions (life, shelter, health, food) take precedence over other rules. For example, a social worker may break the rule of confidentiality to protect their client's life. Lowenberg and Dolgoff (1992) use a similar template of obligations to prioritize protection of life over obligations to clients, colleagues, and employers.

BIOETHICAL PRINCIPLES AND ASSOCIATED OBLIGATIONS

Thomasma and Graber (1990) delineate the duties of the professional caregiver to the dying to include care aligned with the patient's values not on what therapy can be offered; to assess and relieve physical, social, psychological and spiritual pain and suffering; to understand the patient's perception of quality of life and reassess the care plan as appropriate; and to provide full information on risks, benefits, and alternatives of treatments including palliative measures and the option to not treat. Bioethical principles serve as the grounding principles for defining the parameters of the ethical dilemma as well as one of the components for evaluating options for resolving ethical dilemmas. These principles include autonomy, beneficence, nonmalifecence, and justice (Beauchamp and Childress 2001). Autonomy encompasses two conditions: (1) liberty or independence from controlling influences, and (2) agency or capacity for intentional action. The healthcare professional's duties that arise from autonomy are to tell the truth, respect privacy, protect confidentiality, obtain consent, and help others with decisions when asked. Beneficence requires that the healthcare provider promote the good or interests of the patient. It calls for self-effacement of personal interests over the interests of the patient in all aspects of the professional relationship in health care. This may result in extensions of self that result in personal sacrifice such as extra time to provide information and reassurance. Professional integrity based on the principle of beneficence is critical to patient trust in the professional's judgments and recommendations.

Nonmaleficence, simply stated, requires that no intentional harm be inflicted on the patient. Healthcare providers' decisions often call for a balancing between the benefits and harms of proposed treatments. Associated obligations are not to kill, not to cause pain and suffering, not to incapacitate, or to deprive others of goods of life. Justice guides decisions at the individual and institutional levels on fairness and equity in access to care and allocation of resources. These principles apply to all medical care but assume greater importance when caring for people at the end of life as their vulnerability to discrimination is greatly increased.

ETHICAL ISSUES IN END-OF-LIFE CARE

Researchers have identified the most common ethical dilemmas that challenge social workers as end-of-life issues. Other healthcare professionals including physicians and nurses also identify end-of-life issues as their most difficult bioethical dilemmas (DuVal et al. 2000; Ferrell et al. 2000). End-of-life issues such as Do Not Attempt Resuscitation (DNAR) orders; confusion or conflict about advance directives; withdrawal or withholding of treatments such as artificial nutrition and hydration, dialysis, and mechanical ventilation; physician-assisted suicide; and futility are the most frequently cited (Foster et al. 1993; Proctor, Morrow-Howell, and Lott 1993; Miller, Hedlund, and Murphy 1998; Csikai and Bass 2000; Landau 2000; Manetta and Wells 2001).

The key concern in many of these cases involves the patient's capacity for decision making and the patient's best interests (Egan and Kadushin 2001). It is has been established by the Supreme Court that patients with decisional capacity have the right to refuse any treatment including life-sustaining treatment (Burt 1997). Beauchamp and Childress (2001) define decisional capacity as the ability to understand the information presented and to discern the decision to be made as well as the risks, benefits, and alternatives of all of the options for treatment, including no treatment. The second feature of capacity is whether the person can make the decision free from undue or interfering influence (Beauchamp and Childress 2001). Patients may make a decision based on what they think others expect or want of them. They may be unwilling to risk harming or losing a relationship by choosing what they really want. There may be other familial, social, or financial concerns that are influencing the patient's choice (Emanuel et al. 2000). Reflecting the patient's decision against previously stated values and beliefs can clarify if the current decision is truly what the patient wants.

If a patient does not have decisional capacity, a surrogate decision maker may act on the patient's behalf. Controversy may arise on the status and capacity of the surrogate and whether he or she is acting in the best interests of the patient. Surrogates should represent and support the patient's written or verbal preferences made before he or she lost the ability to participate in the decision-making process. If a patient has not shared his or her preferences with the surrogate or others involved in the decision, then the decision makers base their choice from available options on the patient's best interests, defined as those that relieve suffering, offer opportunity to preserve or restore function, and sustain the extent and quality of life (Fletcher et al. 1997).

ADVANCE DIRECTIVES

Advance directives are written and verbal statements of the patient's designation of a surrogate decision maker and statement of preferences for treatment. Patients are encouraged to create advance directives inasmuch as they will provide that: (1) the patient can maintain control over what happens to him/her when he/she cannot participate in decision making due to physical or mental capacity; (2) guidance is accessible to the decision makers especially in relation to life sustaining treatments; (3) immunity is available for healthcare providers from civil or criminal liability when advance directives are honored in the face of objections from family and surrogates. Each state has developed its own legislation and set of regulations for advance directives. Most advance directive documents include a living will and durable power of attorney for healthcare decisions. The living will describes the life sustaining treatments that the patient does or does not want in the face of a terminal illness with a defined limited prognosis. The durable power of attorney for healthcare decisions appoints a surrogate decision maker when the patient cannot participate in decision making. The patient's condition need not be terminal and the surrogate's authority is relinquished when and if the patient's capacity is restored. There are times when the advance directives may not serve as an adequate guide for care providers. Statements that are too broad or too narrow leave room for conflict in interpretation by surrogates, family members, and healthcare providers (AMA 1999). The central ethical issues related to advance directives include the absence of written or verbal statements of preferences to guide difficult decisions, questions of the capacity of the patient or surrogate, and disagreements about what the advance directive actually means.

Social workers can enhance patients' choices and desire for control, and address their concerns about burdening their families with difficult decisions by first educating themselves and, then patients about advance directives. Social workers should facilitate completion of the documents; ensure that the documents are shared with appropriate parties, including the designated decision maker, physician, and care team; and document the patient's verbal wishes in the medical records.

WITHHOLDING AND WITHDRAWING TREATMENTS

The patient or family may be asked or suggest themselves that treatments or interventions such as mechanical ventilation, cardiopulmonary resuscitation, dialysis, and/or artificial nutrition and hydration be withheld or withdrawn. The decision should be guided by the patient's stated preferences, the patient's estimation of an undesirable quality of life, consideration of the burden of the treatment versus the benefits of the treatment, and the patient's expressed wish for a natural death free of extraordinary care. The decisions are made in collaboration with the care team, the patient or surrogate, and the family. Difficulty arises when there is disagreement or different perceptions about the patient's wishes, what constitutes quality of life, the acceptable burden level of treatment, and a belief that life must be preserved at all costs including physical, emotional, and social costs (Meisel, Snyder, and Quill 2001).

Withholding and withdrawing treatment decisions have become more common as technology can sustain life in the face of overwhelming disease and illness. Often technology is clinically developed and established well before there has been any consideration of its bioethical implications related to questions of defining quality of life and when life actually ends. Mularski and Osborne (2001) note that life may be extended, but with increased pain. Healthcare providers witnessing the suffering of the patient in the face of an inevitable death are torn between providing the care that will alleviate the patient's suffering and the family's or other care providers' desire to maintain life at all costs. Some of the reluctance to withhold or withdraw treatment is based on moral and legal myths. Many believe that withdrawal of life support is equated with murder and suicide. Others believe that once a treatment is initiated, it cannot be discontinued. If they believe it is acceptable to withhold or withdraw treatment, they falsely assume that it is required that the patient's condition be terminal. Education on the legal and moral contexts of withholding and withdrawing treatments is the second step of the withdrawal decision process once the question of withdrawing treatment has been raised. The President's Commission for the Study of Ethical Problems in Medicine and Biomedical Research, the Supreme Court of the United States, and state-based legislation support the moral and legal rights of patients to decide what treatments they will or will not accept (Campbell 1998; Meisel, Snyder, and Quill 2001). Etchells et al. (1999) affirm that consent involves disclosure, capacity, and the voluntary quality of the consent. This applies to both acceptance and refusal of treatment and is grounded in the ethical principle of autonomy. Care providers are thus obligated to educate patients and families/surrogates on all their options.

Brody et al. (1997) suggest that physicians and nurses may be reluctant to withdraw aggressive treatment owing to a lack of knowledge of the technical process, previous negative experiences, fear of causing suffering, and lack of counseling and emotional support for patients, families, and staff during the withdrawal process. Incorporating the palliative-care perspective into the acute-care setting will help healthcare providers remain focused on the total goals of care for the patient. It will also enhance more effective communication, build trust with families toward meeting the total care needs, and sensitize all involved to consider cultural beliefs and values that influence these difficult decisions (Danis et al. 1999; Faber-Langedon and Lanken 2001).

Social workers should be able to focus on overall goals of withdrawing treatment that promote the comfort of the patient and family, withdraw treatments judged to be particularly burdensome, or allow death to occur with rapidity or certainty. Social workers are not as focused on individual treatments as some care team members may be, but instead can focus on the overall goals of care as stated by the patient and family. Clinicians feeling frustration, loss, and emotional exhaustion associated with caring for critically ill patients benefit from the same emotional support that is routinely offered to patients and families by the social worker. Helping the care team shift its focus from aggressive treatment to aggressive comfort care is a key role for social work.

PHYSICIAN-ASSISTED SUICIDE

Physician-assisted suicide (PAS) refers to the act of providing the means to commit suicide knowing that the recipient plans to use the means to end his or her life. Provider-assisted suicide specifically refers to a provider making available medications or other interventions with the understanding that a patient plans to use them to commit suicide and subsequently does so (AMA 1999). It is differs from euthanasia in that in euthanasia someone other than the patient commits an act with the intent to end the patient's life. The patient may or may not be aware of the act and consent.

PAS is legal only in the state of Oregon in the United States. Physicians may provide the patient with a prescription for medication to end the patient's life after the patient completes a screening and approval process regulated by the state. The law was enacted in 1997. The average number of prescriptions written has been double the number of patients who have actually committed suicide. The majority of patients who commit suicide have had a cancer diagnosis, are divorced female college graduates, and express concerns about loss of control, an inability to participate in enjoyable activity, and losing control of bodily functions (State of Oregon 2002). The American College of Physicians Position Paper on PAS authored by Snyder and Sulmasy (2001) does not support legalization of PAS. They argue that it is incompatible with sound medical practice for the following reasons:

- Physician skills are not used to alleviate suffering
- Their code of ethics forbids intentionally causing a patient's death
- PAS compromises the trust in the patient-physician relationship
- Patient autonomy is not an absolute value
- The physician has an obligation to protect the most vulnerable patients
- There is a large potential for misuse and abuse

The association strongly supports overall improvement in end-of-life care for patients and families, reflecting Burt's (1997) comments on the Supreme Court decision that individuals do not have a constitutional right to assisted suicide but that the federal and state legislatures need to remove artificial and arbitrary barriers to palliative care.

Emanuel (1998) and Tulsky, Ciampa, and Rosen (2000) recommend a stepwise approach to requests for PAS. They suggest a process that begins by identifying and treating the root causes of the requests. Patients have the right to be free of unwanted intervention related to autonomy that assures bodily integrity and freedom from assault rooted in ethics and law. One of the root causes may be depression. A thorough assessment for depression includes differentiating between the normal distress associated with terminal illness and clinical depression (Block 2000). Despite the extensively documented prominence of depression in the chronically ill population, clinical depression remains underdiagnosed and undertreated. Depression can be treated with medication and supportive therapy. If the patient has been cleared of clinical depression and is capable of making decisions, the physician should directly assess the patient's concerns. These concerns may include fears of dying in pain, of being a burden to family, and of losing personal dignity. Efforts should be focused on relieving sources of distress with the help of other care team members and regularly reassessing the care plan. The patient should understand the legal and moral constraints against PAS.

The National Association of Social Workers (NASW 1993) issued a policy statement entitled "Client Self-Determination in End-of-Life Decisions." According to this document, social workers should work to enhance the client's quality of life, to explore all options and choices, and to assure the client is capable of making a choice. Additionally, the social worker should be open to discussions about means to end-of-life care but should not promote suicide. If the social worker is uncomfortable with discussing PAS, then the client should be referred to another counselor. The social worker cannot participate in or witness PAS. This position is grounded in the principle of autonomy, that is, the right of the client to determine what is best for themselves without undue influence or interference. However, those opposing the policy believe that supporting PAS without other considerations may sacrifice social work's duty to the common good (Callahan 1994; Wesley 1996).

Miller, Hedlund, and Murphy (1998) present a set of guidelines to assess the patient's request for assisted suicide. The components include an understanding of the presenting concerns such as diagnosis, symptoms, support, and care needs; the meaning of illness in his or her cultural history; and psychosocial factors for both the patient and family. They are careful to emphasize that the assessment is a complex, interactive, and ongoing process not a mere list of tasks. Listening skills and critical thinking are essential to successful intervention and support for the patient and family.

The Association of Oncology Social Work (1999) suggests that the social worker's obligation to the patient in relation to PAS requests is not to facilitate or judge the requests. It is suggested that the social worker seek to understand patients and their difficulties and to assist them in their search for meaning and solutions. AOSW believes that the majority of the requests for PAS lie in the failure of the health system to respond to the needs of the dying patient. The NASW Code of Ethics (1999) supports the social worker's duty to address social policy and services that will improve available care.

MEDICAL FUTILITY

Medical futility is a common referral for ethical consultation and often identified as the most difficult to resolve because of the question of what constitutes futility and who defines futility (Orr 2000). Futile treatment is commonly defined as treatment that will not alter the natural course of the disease and, in fact, may be adding additional physical, social, and/or emotional burdens to the patient (Schneiderman, Jecker, and Jonsen 1990). At the heart of the issue are the relief of the patient's suffering and the avoidance of secondary costs to the family, care team, and the institution that mandates that futility cases be resolved. A review of the literature related to futility falls into two categories: how to define the criteria for futile treatment and who the determiner of futility should be.

Rubin (1998) identifies a number of conflicts associated with the definition and establishment of criteria for futility. Questions persist as to who has the requisite expertise. Should the healthcare professional or the patient/family select the goals of treatment that may be judged futile? Additionally, how does one choose which criteria for futility should be used? The lack of a uniform set of criteria to define futility leaves room for confusion and for the focus of the ethics consultation to shift from quality patient care to financial costs and social prejudice (Lantos 1994). Schneiderman, Jecker, and Jonsen (1990) have adapted a science-based approach to set quantitative and qualitative measures for criteria to define futility. The quantitative criteria are derived from empirical data or from clinical experience where the physician notes that in one hundred cases the treatment brought no physical improvement. The qualitative criteria for definition of futility include treatment that merely preserves unconsciousness or fails to end total dependence on intensive medical care. They recommend that any treatments that meet either quantitative or qualitative criteria should be regarded as nonbeneficial and therefore futile. Rubin (1998) notes that even when conflicts of definition and criteria are resolved, conflict may arise about when the criteria apply to particular treatments for a particular patient.

The President's Commission for the Study of Ethical Problems in Medicine and Biomedical and Bioethical Research (1983) suggests that consideration of the burdens that the treatment imposes on the patient is a reasonable criterion for evaluating the futility of treatments. Pellegrino (2000) utilizes the concepts of benefit and burden of the treatments to develop a moral algorithm for withdrawing treatment in cases related to questions of futility. He outlines a collaborative process between the physician and patient to make decisions on withdrawing treatment. The algorithm considers the physician's clinical evaluation of the probability of beneficial outcomes of the treatment in conjunction with the patient's estimation of the physical, social, and financial burdens associated with the treatment.

Younger (1994) proposes that the evaluation of the worth of the goals of treatment serve as the measure for defining futility. He identifies the use of life-sustaining treatments for patients diagnosed as in persistent vegetative state (PVS); or the use of chemotherapy for patients with end-stage metastatic cancer as two examples of futile treatment because the ultimate course of the patient's illness will not be reversed as a result of the treatments. Others may argue that the goals of gaining time for the family to reach closure or for the patient to receive palliation from pain through chemotherapy would exempt the treatments from Younger's definition of futility. The question to be answered is whose values and goals are given priority—the patient, the family, the care provider, the physician—and why? This is especially critical in our current pluralistic society where the values of individual parties may be in absolute conflict with each other, weakening the fit between medical practice and public values (Callahan 1994). The conflict can lead to difficult interpersonal relationships among the patient, family, care team, and physician and result in an increased complexity in decision making for the best interests of the patient. Truog, Brett, and Frader (1992) argue that the best interest of patient, not rules and standards, may be the best approach to resolve futility issues. But again, conflict may arise as to who (physician, staff, or patient/family) should determine the best interests of the patient.

The second controversy associated with futility begins with who determines that the treatment is futile and should be withdrawn. How do we balance the autonomy of the patient with the moral rights of the care providers? Concerns related to the physician or other care providers serving as the determiners of futility include several unacceptable results.

- Will the patient's status as an individual be diminished?
- Will the determiner substitute her values for the patient's?
- Will the best interests of society replace the best interests of the patient?

In their review of futility, Swanson and McCrary (1994) found both physicians and non-physicians were concerned that if physicians unilaterally decided that a treatment is futile there could be many other consequences.

- Would a patient's rights to make decisions be violated?
- Would futility become a tool for cost control denying critical care for some patients?
- Would futility be applied to patients for social not medical reasons?
- Could agreed-on criteria for futility ever be established across a variety of practitioners and settings?
- Would physicians advance their own values over the patients' values?

The importance of preserving the patient's trust in their physicians based on the power imbalance inherent in the relationship is key to the patient-provider relationship (Lantos 1994). Physicians who offer ineffective treatments or misrepresent expected outcomes of treatments diminish their integrity (Brody 1994). Asch (1995) reported that 14 percent of physicians in adult intensive-care units had withheld or withdrawn treatment they considered futile without informing the patient's family. More than 80 percent had withdrawn treatment over the family's objection. Smith (2001) believes that futility policies are being developed to ration treatments, but not to promote quality care.

If the patient and family are the sole determiners of futility, the result may be a decrease in the role of the professional, violations of the professionals' ethical obligations to the patient, and increased disadvantages to others as a result of patients' choices. Veatch and Spicer (1992) argue that the patient should have access to any available treatment if the treatment is funded and desired by a competent patient. Troug (2000) believes that in pediatric cases, priority should be given to parental wishes. He justifies this course based on the contractual relationship between the patient, family, and physician; on the priority of the value judgments of the family; and on the fact that the family will live with the memory of their decisions for the balance of their lives. This is especially true in cases where decisions are made to withdraw treatments that result in allowing a child's illness to progress toward a natural death. He does add that clearly established goals of care will promote cooperation and understanding in the treatment process and when difficult decisions must be made.

Each case merits individual assessment. The assessment should include an overview of the patient's overall health status and their ability to achieve meaningful life goals. Rubin (1998) proposes that if the treatment will not further the patient's goals then it should be considered futile. The best interests of the patient are met when the intent of withholding or withdrawing any treatment is to allow the natural course of the illness to continue, not to hasten death. Patients, families, and care providers want reassurance that the goal of care remains on comfort and palliation throughout the final stages of the illness. Alpers and Lo (1999) suggest that physicians may refuse to continue treatments considered futile but have the moral obligation to negotiate decisions with families and surrogates maintaining the focus on the patient's best interests. Physicians also have an obligation to be culturally sensitive and compromise as appropriate. They may apply the ethical principles of beneficence and nonmalefi-cence to justify not providing treatments that will harm patients without a correspond-ing benefit. For example, recent studies have shown that the artificial nutrition and hydration in the dying patient actually contribute to the patient's suffering (increased edema, skin breakdown) without providing any nutritional or comfort care benefits.

The American Medical Association (1999) identifies several common myths asso-ciated with futility referrals that increase the difficulty and complexity of the cases. First, the urgency conveyed in the referral is seldom as acute as portrayed in the referral. In most cases, there is adequate time to work through to a mutually agreeable resolution. Second, the factors contributing to the referral for futility are never as black and white as presented. Third, a belief may exist among family members, staff, and physicians that once a treatment is begun, it cannot be discontinued for any reason. Younger (1994) suggests that the ethics of prevention may be the most effective way to avoid futility issues. The ethics of prevention begin with an early recognition of situations likely to result in an ethics consultation for futility. Problems inherent in futility involve consideration of the issues of patient autonomy and capacity, the pa-tient's best interests, withholding and withdrawing treatments, and the moral well being of the professional caregiver in addition to the stated concern of futility. Issues related to communication failures, poor understanding of the facts and outcomes related to the diagnosis and treatment, and unrealistic expectations are often clarified and addressed by social workers after evaluation and consultation with all parties. This provides an opportunity to implement a partnering among the physician, staff, and patient/family for the best interest of the patient (Weil and Weil 2000).

Glajchen and Zuckerman (2001) suggest a protocol for social workers toward re-solving conflicts by confirming the facts, evaluating the decision makers, determining patient wishes, convening a family meeting, and determining best interests. The social worker is a key professional in establishing a common ground and gaining commit-ment from all parties to resolve the conflict. Exploring the patient and family story by the social worker and, then sharing it with the care team including the physicians is another important social work intervention. The story must be inclusive of all parties involved in the case including extended family members and significant others. Un-resolved conflicts and losses may generate requests for treatment that others judge as of no benefit to the patient. The family may be trying to buy some time for resolution and/or reconciliation. Members of minority cultures may have experienced previous denial of access to care or unequal care themselves or in their extended family. There may be a distrust of the care team, institution, and healthcare system based on per-ceptions of neglect and discrimination. Recent immigrants from disadvantaged pop-ulations, who can now have access to state of the art medical care, may have unrealistic expectations of what can be accomplished. Attentive listening, clarification of percep-tions and beliefs, and offering of unconditional support on the part of the social worker reassures the patient and family that their stories are heard and understood. The social worker can help the patient and family share with the physician and care team their feelings, concerns, and cares. The physician and care team can present information in such a way that is inclusive and addresses their needs. Understanding the meaning attached to a treatment can shape acceptance of the information by the patient and family (Teno et al. 2001). In a retrospective study of family members, Jacob (1998) found positive interactions with physicians and the care team helped family members find peace in decisions made during their loved ones' terminal care.

CRITICAL SOCIAL-WORK SKILLS

Improving communication is cited as a continuing need in improving end-of-life care. Communication failures among care providers as well as with patients and families exacerbate the complexity of the ethical issues in end-of-life care. Physicians have developed a number of protocols to guide physicians in their information sharing with patients and families (AMA 1999; Baile et al. 1999; Balaban 2000). Roter et al. (2002) find that physicians who can address psychosocial issues and incorporate lifestyle discussions and questions into information sharing build stronger partnerships with their patients. Learning to be less verbally dominant, to probe for the patient's values and experience, and to elicit the patient's plan, while providing support in the decision making process are skills that social workers can model and train other professionals to use in their conversations with patients and families. Weil and Weil (2000) and Abbott et al. (2001) found that there was significant decreased family conflict regarding treatment withdrawals when there was improved communication, when physicians were more available, provided more information, and used more support staff. Problems arose when physicians and other care providers attempted to soften the blow of difficult information by focusing on the positives of the patient's condition, which reinforced the patient's and family's denial (Hanson, Danis, and Garrett 1997; Teno et al. 2001). In other cases, the language used to present the information may be so technical and complex that the patient and family cannot understand what is being said. They may not question or ask for clarification out of fear of appearing ignorant. Patients and families may turn to the social worker for help in understanding what information has been presented and what decisions need to be made. Early social work intervention in improving communication patterns and assuring patient and family understanding can prevent the miscommunication that fosters ethical issues.

RECOMMENDATIONS FOR SOCIAL WORK

Bern-Klug, Gessert, and Forbes (2001) note that social work skills in values clarification, emotional assessment, crisis intervention, goal setting, decision making, active listening, bereavement counseling, advocacy, and interpersonal communication are well suited for intervention in addressing ethical issues. In particular—because they are process-oriented—communication, clarification of values, and advocacy help to facilitate ethical decision making. Social workers have a bridge role in explaining the context of care to patients and the concerns of families to staff. The majority of studies related to social work involvement in ethics and end-of-life care have called for education and training focused on increasing social work participation and comfort in these areas of practice.

Joseph and Conrad (1989) found that social workers who had a discrete course in ethics were better prepared to participate as presenters of the psychosocial content related to ethics cases and interpreters of ethical information to patients and families. Foster et al. (1993) found that discussing futile treatment of the irreversibly ill was identified by social workers as an area for further ethical training. The respondents specifically noted their training needs needed to be based in bioethics not in psychosocial practice skills. Christ and Sormanti (1999) found that 78 percent of social workers in healthcare settings felt poorly prepared to recognize and manage the ethical issues related to end-of-life care. Additionally, social workers felt they needed more training in communication skills across the disciplines. Csikai and Bass (2000) surveyed social workers to assess their challenges in working with patients and families at the end of life. Social workers identified activities related to ethical problem solving and examining their own values in relation to end-of-life care as areas for increased educational training.

Focus in ethics education at the graduate level as well in ongoing training opportunities is essential to improve social work's contribution to improving care for patients and their families at the end of life. This mandate is reflected in the mission and values statement identified in the NASW Code of Ethics (1999) to improve the lives of all people especially vulnerable populations. Actualizing social work's core professional values of service, social justice, the dignity and worth of the person, the importance of human relationships, integrity, and competence ensures that the needs of the dying patient and their family will be managed in the caring and compassionate manner that the profession espouses.

REFERENCES

Abbott, K. H., J. G. Sago, C. M. Breen, A. P. Abernathy, and J. A. Tulsky. 2001. Families looking back: One year after discussion of withdrawal or withholding of life-sustaining support. *Critical Care Medicine* 29:197–201.

Alpers, A., and B. Lo. 1999. Avoiding family feuds: Responding to surrogate demands for life-sustaining interventions. *Journal of Law, Medicine, & Ethics* 27:74–80.

American Medical Association. 1999. *Education for Physicians in End of Life Care.* Chicago: American Medical Association.

Asch, D. A., J. Hansen-Flaschen, and P. Lanken. 1995. Decisions to limit or continue life-sustaining treatment by critical care physicians in the United States: Conflicts between physician's practices and patients' wishes. *American Journal of Respiratory Critical Care Medicine* 151:288–292.

Association of Oncology Social Workers. 1999. Position paper on active euthanasia and assisted suicide. www.aosw.org/mission/euthanasia.html.

Baile, W. F., G. A. Glober, R. Lenzi, E. A. Beale, and A. P. Kudelka. 1999. Discussing disease progression and end-of-life decisions. *Oncology* 13(7): 1021–1028.

Balaban, R. B. 2000. A physician's guide to talking about end-of-life care. *Journal of General Internal Medicine* 15:195–200.

Beauchamp, T. L., and J. F. Childress. 2001. *Principles of Biomedical Ethics.* 5th ed. New York: Oxford University Press.

Bern-Klug, M., C. Gessert, and S. Forbes. 2001. The need to revise assumptions about the end of life: Implications for social work practice. *Health and Social Work* 23(1): 38–47.

Block, S. D. 2000. Assessing and managing depression in the terminally ill patient. *Annals of Internal Medicine* 132:209–218.

Brody, H. 1994. The physician's role in determining futility. *Journal of the American Geriatrics Society* 42:875–878.

Brody, H., M. L. Campbell, K. Faber-Langedoen, and K. S. Ogle. 1997. Withdrawing intensive life-sustaining treatment: Recommendations for compassionate clinical management. *New England Journal of Medicine* 336(9): 652–657.

Burt, R. A. 1997. The Supreme Court speaks: Not assisted suicide by a constitutional right to palliative care. *New England Journal of Medicine* 337(17): 1234–1236.

Callahan, D. 1994. Necessity, futility, and the good society. *Journal of the American Geriatrics Society* 42:866–867.

——. 2000. *The Troubled Dream of Life: In Search of a Peaceful Death.* Washington, DC: Georgetown University Press.

Callahan, J. 1994. The ethics of assisted suicide. *Health & Social Work* 19(4): 237–244.

Campbell, M. L. 1998. *Forgoing Life-Sustaining Therapy: How to Care for the Patient Who Is Near Death.* Aliso Viejo, CA: American Association of Critical Care Nurses.

Christ, G., and M. Sormanti. 1999. The social work role in end-of-life care. *Social Work in Health Care* 30(9): 81–99.

Conrad, A. P. 1988. Ethical considerations in the psychosocial process. *Social Casework* 69:603–610.

Crawley, L. M., P. A. Marshall, and B. A. Koenig. 2001. Respecting cultural differences at the end of life. In *Physician's Guide to End of Life Care*, ed. L. Snyder and T. E. Quill, 35–55. Philadelphia: American College of Physicians.

Csikai, E. L. 1997. Social workers' participation on hospital ethics committees: An assessment of involvement and satisfaction. *Arete* 22(1): 1–13.

Csikai, E. L., and K. Bass. 2000. Health care social workers' views of ethical issues, practice, and policy in end-of-life care. *Social Work in Health Care* 32(2): 1–22.

Curtis, J. R., D. L. Patrick, S. E. Shannon, et al. 2001. The family conference as a focus to improve communication about end-of-life care in the intensive care unit: Opportunities for improvement. *Critical Care Medicine* 29(2), Supplement: N26–N33.

Danis, M., D. Federman, J. J. Fins, et al. 1999. Incorporating palliative care into critical care education: Principles, challenges, and opportunities. *Critical Care Medicine* 27(9): 2005–2013.

DuVal, G., L. Sartorius, B. Claridge, G. Gensler, and M. Danis. 2000. What triggers requests for ethics consultations? *Journal of Medical Ethics* 26:1–5.

Emanuel, E. J., D. L. Fairclough, J. Slutsman, and L. L. Emanuel. 2000. Understanding economic and other burdens of terminal illness: The experience of patients and their caregivers. *Annals of Internal Medicine* 132:451–459.

Emanuel, L. L. 1998. Facing requests for physician-assisted suicide: Toward a practical and principled clinical skill set. *Journal of the American Medical Association* 280(7): 643–647.

Etchells, E., G. Sharpe, P. Walsh, J. R. Williams, and P. A. Singer. 1996. Bioethics for clinicians: Consent. *Canadian Medical Association Journal* 155:177–180.

Faber-Langendoen, K., and P. N. Lanken. 2000. Dying patients in the intensive care unit: Forgoing treatment, maintaining care. *Annals of Internal Medicine* 133:886–893.

Ferrell, B., R. Virani, M. Grant, P. Coyne, and G. Uman. 2000. Beyond the Supreme Court decision: Nursing perspectives on end-of-life care. *Oncology Nursing Forum* 27(3): 445–455.

Field, M. J., and C. K. Cassel. 1997. *Approaching Death: Improving Care at the End of Life.* Washington, DC: National Institute of Medicine.

Fletcher, J. C., F. G. Miller, and E. M. Spencer. 1997. Clinical ethics: History, content, and resources. In *Introduction to Clinical Ethics*, ed. J. C. Fletcher, P. A. Lombardo, M. F. Marshall, and F. G. Miller, 3–20. Hagerstown, MD: University Publishing.

Foster, L. W., J. Sharp, A. Scesny, L. McLellan, and K. Cotman. 1993. Bioethics: Social work's response and training needs. *Social Work in Health Care* 19(1): 15–29.

Furlong, R. M. 1986. The social worker's role on the institutional ethics committee. *Social Work in Health Care* 11(4): 93–100.

Glajchen, M., and C. Zuckerman. 2001. Resolving conflict and making decisions. *Journal of Palliative Medicine* 4(2): 221–225.

Goold, S. D., B. Williams, and R. M. Arnold. 2000. Conflicts regarding decisions to limit treatment: A differential diagnosis. *Journal of the American Medical Association* 283(7): 909–914.

Hanson, L. C., M. Danis, and J. Garrett. 1997. What is wrong with end-of-life care? Opinions of bereaved family members. *American Geriatric Society* 45(11): 1339–1344.

Jacob, D. A. 1998. Family members' experience with decision making for incompetent patients in the ICU: A qualitative study. *American Journal of Critical Care* 7(1): 30–36.

Jennings, B. 1987. The public duties of professions. *Hastings Center Report, Special Supplement*, 1–20.

Johnson, D., M. Wilson, B. Cavanaugh, C. Bryden, D. Gudmundson, and O. Moodley. 1998. Measuring the ability to meet family needs in an intensive care unit. *Critical Care Medicine* 26(2): 266–271.

Joseph, M. V. 1985. Ethical decision-making in clinical practice: A model for ethical problem solving. In *Advances in Clinical Practice*, ed. C. B. Germain, 207–217. Silver Spring, MD: National Association of Social Workers.

Joseph, M. V., and A. P. Conrad. 1989. Social work influence on interdisciplinary ethical decision making in health care settings. *Health and Social Work* 14(1): 22–30.

Kadushin, G., and M. Egan. 2001. Ethical dilemmas in home care: A social work perspective. *Health and Social Work* 26(3): 136–145.

Koenig, B. A. 1997. Cultural diversity in decision making about care at the end of life. In *Approaching Death: Improving Care at the End of Life*, ed. M. J. Field and C. K. Cassel, 363–382. Washington, DC: National Institute of Medicine.

Landau, R. 2000. Ethical dilemmas in general hospitals: Differential perceptions of direct practitioners and directors of social services. *Social Work in Health Care* 30(4): 25–44.

Lantos, J. D. 1994. Futility assessments and the doctor-patient relationship. *Journal of the American Geriatrics Society* 42:868–870.

Lowenberg, F. M, and R. Dolgoff. 1996. *Ethical Decisions for Social Work Practice*. 5th ed. Itasca, IL: F. E. Peacock.

Manetta, A. A., and J. G. Wells. 2001. Ethical issues in the social worker's role in physician-assisted suicide. *Health and Social Work* 26(3): 160–170.

McCormick, R. A. 1984. Ethics committees: Promise or peril? *Law, Medicine, and Health Care* 12(4): 150–155.

Meisel, A., L. Snyder, and T. E. Quill. 2001. Legal barriers to end-of-life care: Myths, realities, and grains of truth. In *Physician's Guide to End of Life Care*, ed. L. Snyder and T. E. Quill, 197–213. Philadelphia: American College of Physicians.

Miller, P. J., S. C. Hedlund, and K. A. Murphy. 1998. Social work assessment at end of life: Practice guidelines for suicide and the terminally ill. *Social Work in Health Care* 26(4): 23–36.

Mularski, R. A., and M. L. Osborne. 2001. The changing ethics of death in the ICU. In *Managing Death in the ICU: The Transition from Cure to Comfort*, ed. J. R. Curtis, 7–17. New York: Oxford University Press.

National Association of Social Workers. 1994. Client self-determination in end-of-life decisions. In *Social Work Speaks*, 58–61. Washington, DC: National Association of Social Workers.

———. 1999. *Code of Ethics*. Washington, DC: National Association of Social Workers.

Orr, R. D. 2000. Comment: Will futility policies make a difference? *Journal of Clinical Ethics* 11(2): 142–144.

Pellegrino, E. D. 2000. Decisions to withdraw life-sustaining treatment. *Journal of the American Medical Association* 283(8):1065–1067.

Proctor, E. K., N. Morrow-Howell, and C. L. Lott. 1993. Classification and correlates of ethical dilemmas in hospital social work. *Social Work* 38(2): 166–177.

Randall, R., and R. S. Downie. 1999. *Palliative Care Ethics: A Companion for All Specialties.* 2d ed. New York: Oxford University Press.

Reamer, F. G. 1985. The emergence of bioethics in social work. *Health & Social Work* 10:271–281.

——. 1999. *Social Work Values and Ethics.* 2d ed. New York: Columbia University Press.

——. 2001. *Ethics Education in Social Work.* Alexandria, VA: Council on Social Work Education.

Roter, D. L., S. Larson, G. S. Fischer, R. M. Arnold, and J. A. Tulsky. 2000. Experts practice what they preach: A descriptive study of best and normative practices in end-of life discussions. *Archives of Internal Medicine* 160:3477–3483.

Rubin, S. B. 1998. *When Doctors Say No: The Battleground of Medical Futility.* Bloomington: Indiana University Press.

Schneiderman, L. J., N. S. Jecker, and A. R. Jonsen. 1990. Medical futility: Its meaning and ethical implications. *Annals of Internal Medicine* 112:949–954.

Skinner, K. W. 1991. A national survey of social workers on institutional ethics committees: Patterns of participation and roles. Ph.D. diss., University of Pennsylvania.

Smith, W. J. 2001. "Futile care" and its friends. *The Weekly Standard*, 27–29.

Snyder, L., and D. P. Sulmasy. 2001. Physician-assisted suicide. *Annals of Internal Medicine* 135:209–216.

Society of Critical Care Medicine, Ethics Committee. 1997. Consensus statement of the Society of Critical Care Medicine's Ethics Committee regarding futile and other possibly inadvisable treatments. *Critical Care Medicine* 25(5): 887–891.

State of Oregon. 2002. *Fourth Annual Report on Oregon's Death with Dignity Act.* Portland: Oregon Department of Human Services, Office of Disease Prevention and Epidemiology.

Steinhauser, K. E., N. A. Christakis, E. C. Clipp, M. McNeilly, L. McIntyre, and J. A. Tulsky. 2000. Factors considered important at the end of life by patients, family, physicians, and other care providers. *Journal of the American Medical Association* 284(19): 2476–2482.

Swanson, J. W., and S. V. McCrary. 1994. Doing all they can: Physicians who deny medical futility. *Journal of Law, Medicine, & Ethics* 22(4): 318–326.

Teno, J. M., V. A. Casey, L. C. Welch, and S. Edgman-Levitan. 2001. Patient-focused, family-centered end-of-life medical care: Views of guidelines and bereaved family members. *Journal of Pain and Symptom Management* 22(3): 738–751.

Thomasma, D. C., and G. C. Graber. 1990. *Euthanasia: Toward an Ethical Social Policy.* New York: Continuum.

Truog, R. D. 2000. Futility in pediatrics: From case to policy. *Journal of Clinical Ethics* 11(2): 136–141.

Truog, R. D., A. S. Brett, and J. Frader. 1992. The problem with futility. *New England Journal of Medicine* 326: 1560–64.

Tulsky, J. A., R. Ciampa, and E. J. Rosen. 2000. Responding to legal requests for physician-assisted suicide. *Annals of Internal Medicine* 132(6): 494–499.

Veatch, R. M., and C. M. Spicer. 1992. Medically futile care: The role of the physician in setting limits. *Journal of Medicine and Philosophy* 18:15–36.

Weil, M. H., and C. J. Weil. 2000. How to respond to family demands for futile life support and cardiopulmonary resuscitation. *Critical Care Medicine* 28(9): 3339–3340.

Wesley, C. A. 1996. Social work and end-of-life decisions: Self-determination and the common good. *Health and Social Work* 21(2): 115–121.

Younger, S. 1994. Applying futility: Saying no is not enough. *Journal of American Geriatric Society* 42:887–889.

10

SPIRITUALITY AND END-OF-LIFE CARE PRACTICE FOR SOCIAL WORKERS

CAROLYN JACOBS

THIS CHAPTER defines spirituality and religion and discusses the importance for the clinical relationship to include attention to ritual issues during end-of-life care. The ideas are anchored in my own personal experience as friend and caseworker to give the reader a perspective on practice.

MEMORIES LOST

I'm writing this, but as yet I know not to whom
The course of my life has taken me through many valleys
And over the tallest of mountains . . . detours which
Lead nowhere. . . . Sometimes down dark lonely dead-end streets.

I now stand at a crossroads, thousands of miles from yesterday . . .
With its familiar sounds and faces
Which mirror themselves on a screen in my mind
Forms still vivid enough to reflect name, time, place and experience.

Occasionally, they disappear . . . as if someone
Had turned off a light in my head . . . I wondered
If this was how the medication plays games with memories
So we neither remember continuous joy nor pain.

Whatever the motive . . . I am left with only one choice . . .
to participate with each episode
Regardless of the outcome . . . be it win or loss
Laughter or tears. . . . Or even life . . . death.

I know even now . . . that someday, parts of yesterday I may not remember
    at all. . . .
There will be no Shadows or footprints leading back to
Lost love, promises not given . . .
And unfulfilled dreams.

When I gather myself unto my soul, I cannot hide
These words . . . without sound. . . . Thoughts without feelings.
For it is my soul who knows and remembers . . . all.

I bow in shame for holding on to what was.
Why should I try to create . . . today or a tomorrow
On bits and pieces of memories lost?
So let me stand in the Light . . . of now,
With my only friend and constant companion my soul.
                                        —*Tamu Imani*

Tamu Imani was diagnosed with breast cancer in the spring of 1987 and died in 1990 from complications of the cancer, which had spread to her lungs. I knew her for several years prior to her illness. When she was diagnosed with cancer, she chose to engage with me in focused discussions and through correspondence regarding her life and death. Her poetry was interspersed with her correspondence and our conversations. She gently demanded that our conversations not be limited to her psychological, family, and social issues but that they include her spiritual journey for exploring her concerns at end of life. "Memories Lost" was a poetic review of her life and an expression of the impact of struggling to reconcile difficulties with her family and to understand the impact of chemotherapy and radiation on her body and her spirit. I found that her poetry over the years of her illness was an important vehicle for communicating her experiences and reflections to family and friends and a way for us to talk about her life and death. My work with her encouraged me to seek training in spiritual direction.

As a social worker concerned with the place of spirituality and religious beliefs/practices in the lives of clients, I think it is important to explore ways that afford an appropriate synthesis of the spiritual and religious experiences in the development of the individual. Many programs provide training in spiritual direction, spiritual guidance, or spiritual companioning. These terms are used interchangeably in this chapter. I chose the Shalem Institute, located in Washington, D.C., because of its commitment to an ecumenical response to spirituality as expressed in the contemplative traditions of many religions. Training in spiritual guidance encourages an understanding and integration of spiritual practices into all dimensions of one's life through didactic materials on religious dogma and practices, ways of praying, discernment, and supervised internship experiences. It is an excellent preparation for exploring the synergy between spirituality, religious practices, and psychological or social issues. A good program provides frameworks for understanding when to refer the client for psychological treatment or for specific consultation, religious education, or rituals by ordained clergy. Because my own Catholic tradition provides a source of meaning making for me, I wondered about the use of spiritual and religious resources for others in times of crisis. I bring to this work a strong belief in a God or creative energy within and beyond religious traditions. I am grounded in my own tradition while open to others' experiences. Therefore, it was not surprising or unusual to find my social work practice moving toward a synthesis of spiritual and psychological understandings with an appreciation and respect for collaboration with therapists and religious leaders. I now have a small spiritual-direction practice and usually meet with individuals in my home office. When illness precludes individuals meeting me outside of their home, I am willing to meet with clients and their families in their homes or in their hospital rooms. I do not practice spiritual direction with my own family, friends, or colleagues, but there are moments when dying demands that I hold gently those boundaries and be open to responding to the moment.

The life and death of a dear colleague, Jerry Sachs, was a strong influence on my thoughts and work regarding end-of-life care. Jerry was a sixty-year-old social work educator who died after a two-year bout with colon cancer. We worked together at the Smith College School for Social Work for over fifteen years. During that time, we had had many discussions about the meaning, for individuals and communities, of religion and spirituality in social work practice. We shared a commitment to issues of justice borne out of our respective religious traditions. We also shared a deep respect for each other's religious beliefs and practices. For the last two years of his life, I served as acting dean of the school where we taught. As a result, my sharing of his journey included multiple roles of colleague, friend, and supervisor. All of these roles pale against the most important one—that of fellow human beings on our respective spiritual journeys.

One encounter that reveals the importance of understanding or at least accepting religious and spiritual meanings at the end of life was my visit to Jerry several weeks before he died. I came to this space, which I experienced as a sacred encounter, as an African American Roman Catholic who had just attended a Saturday vigil mass. Jerry came as a Jew who was terminally ill. He always reminded me that he did not believe in a transcendent God, and if that God existed, he asked, how could such a God allow pain, injustice, and death? In his tradition, grappling with that which one does not believe lends itself to arguments supporting and refuting God's existence and care about the inhabitants of this world. Thus, it was important for him to study the Hebrew Scriptures and to engage in the debate. When I arrived at his home, he was studying the scriptural reference (II Samuel 6:14–23) in an article in the Talmudic tradition that spoke of David, his wife Michal, and God's treatment of her when she spoke to David of his behavior. David was seen by women dancing before God while wearing only a linen apron. His dancing was meant as an expression of honor to God. Michal saw his dancing, while scantly clad, as a disgrace. The result of her confronting him was that she died childless. Jerry saw her not bearing children as God's punishing her unjustly for confronting David. How could God not recognize David's inappropriate behavior, especially in front of women? Why did God punish Michal and not David?

We both brought in our silence, words, tears, and deep affection for one another, our struggles about our God's relationships with people throughout history. I listened to many questions from him. Why are there suffering and death, and at this moment in time in our respective lives? Where was God's mercy for children who are left orphans, for the poor, for the vulnerable of our world, for Michal who after confronting

David's behavior was left barren? Why did God not repent for the evil that exists? Why did God, knowing our human limitations, demand so much of us? This sacred encounter was not destined to provide the answers to the questions of meaning and God's relationship with human beings. It was destined to provide a space in the days before Jerry died for the most irreverent yet reverent of questions, doubts, angers, and fears. It is a space where the fluidity of professional, spiritual, and friendship boundaries are open to the context of the other's dying. The process of dialogue in these relationships (both professional and personal) at the end of Jerry's life held us in joy and sorrow, in laughter and tears. It demanded of the social worker, the colleague, and the friend a transparency born of reflection on personal meanings, and practices.

Issues of spiritual and religious practices in end-of-life care are critical where elements of faith, religious or spiritual practices are part of an individual's development and cultural experiences. As with all dimensions of sound clinical practice, it is not the social worker's role to solve spiritual or religious problems, but rather to create an environment that enables clients to explore their concerns and to find meanings that move them towards a healthy resolution or a comfort with their questioning. Dealing with dying patients may raise spiritual issues for the social worker, such as coping with stress or witnessing suffering, which may challenge the social worker's basic beliefs. This requires that the professional deal with countertransference issues especially as they relate to suffering and death (Derezotes and Evans 1995; O'Connor 1993:136; Goldberg 1996; Cornett, 1998; Graham, Kaiser, and Garrett 1998; May 1987; Millison and Dudley 1992; Morgan 1993). Social workers also help to create a holding environment for the other.

DEFINING RELIGION AND SPIRITUALITY

Definitions of religion and spirituality abound in the literature that explores the integration of spirituality and mental health practices (Cornett 1998; Doka 1993; Hugen 1998; Kilpatrick and Holland, 1990; Lewandoski and Canda 1995).

It is important to distinguish between religion and spirituality. Religion offers social forms or shared beliefs and rituals. Spirituality on the other hand, provides personal experiences or themes of connectedness to others and the universe. Distinguishing between religion and spirituality allows for a deeper understanding of the impact of religious and/or spiritual practices on the individual's psychological functioning and on his or her way of making meaning out of life's circumstances (Canda and Furman 1999; Joseph 1987; Lovinger 1984; Lukoff, Lu, and Turner 1992).

Death is a motivator of spirituality. It is because life is finite, that one strives to connect with the infinite. The knowledge that suffering occurs moves people to seek meaning and comfort. It is because sometimes neither life nor death makes sense that one strives to find and to conform to a belief system in which the contradictions of living and dying, joy and terror, order and absurdity are reconciled (Wass and Neimeyer 1995).

Griffith and Griffith (2001) provide definitions of spirituality and religion that are most applicable to the discussions in this chapter.

Spirituality is a commitment to choose, as the primary context for understanding and acting, one's relatedness with all that is. With this commitment, one attempts to stay focused on relationships between one's self and other people, one's physical environment, one's heritage and traditions, one's body, one's ancestors, and saints, one's Higher Power, or God. Spirituality places relationships at the center of awareness, whether they are relationships with the world or other people, or relationships with God or other nonmaterial beings. (15–16)

Religion represents a cultural codification of important spiritual metaphors, narratives, beliefs, rituals, social practices, and forms of community among a particular people that provides methods for attaining spirituality, most often expressed in terms of a relationship with the God of that religion. (17)

Spirituality is essential to understanding meaning making in many cultures, such as Haitian or Puerto Rican spiritualists, religious healers such as Mexican *curanderos*, charismatic Christian groups found among rural Anglo-Americans and African Americans, and Pentecostals, who are represented in many ethnic groups. Spirituality can become increasingly important at specific stages of people's lives—births, coming of age rituals, celebrations, losses, terminal illnesses and deaths.

Experiences of loss create a need to make meaning of the loss or transition. How one defines the loss determines whether or not grief will begin and how it will be experienced (Martin and Elder 1993). The use of rituals, prayer, meditation, or scripture may elicit feelings of joy, comfort and peace, acceptance, and understanding as signs of healing in the grieving process. At the time of dying, prayers are often offered both spontaneously and according to specific traditions such as the sacrament for the sick in the Catholic tradition, which includes an anointing with blessed oil. In many traditions, touching or laying hands on the dying person provides both a physical and spiritual connection as he/she dies. In the Buddhist tradition, the body is not left alone until there is a sense that the person's spirit has finally exited. Sitting with the dying person is an important value across many cultures and religious traditions. Mortuary and burial rituals vary with religious traditions, ethnicity, and family preferences within traditions. For example, the social interactions and customs at a Catholic wake may be different for Irish Catholics and Hispanic Catholics. Cultural and religious groups vary regarding expectations for mourners to contribute and/or participate in a meal after the burial. Visiting, sending cards of condolences, and offering prayers have unique prescriptions for each group, which may be influenced by regional and class differences. Finally, expectations and public displays of grieving may be more culturally determined than based in religious dogma.

SPIRITUALITY AT THE END OF LIFE

It is always important to be aware of the patient and family's belief system. Impending loss and the reality of death may shake the foundation of the dying person and the survivors' faith. Impending death may leave the individual and the family with a sense of anger and hopelessness. Religious rituals may provide an outward sign of faith and hope; however, many religious people experience anger and abandonment that leaves the survivors questioning their beliefs and finding little solace. For atheists or agnostics, in the absence of firmly held religious beliefs, different struggles may occur as they attempt to make meaning of suffering and loss in their lives. What is true for both believers and nonbelievers is that human beings experience the reality of needing to make meaning of death as central to their experiences of grief and loss (Becvar 2001).

An awareness and appreciation of a client's spiritual orientation is essential to end-of-life care (O'Connor 1993). Caregivers and laypeople need not avoid spiritual material in clinical situations. Millison and Dudley's (1992) research findings confirm that listening to talk of God, sharing one's own spirituality, and exploring the meaning of life events are approaches used as often by the laity as by clergy. These findings support the earlier contention by O'Connor and Kaplan (1986) that spirituality is too critical an area to be left to clergy alone.

Life reviews offer opportunities to explore a person's religious dimensions as she interacts with end-of-life concerns. For adolescents and adults, life reviews can provide opportunities to resolve earlier conflicts with significant others and with God. In addition to the life review, a spiritual genealogy, which charts a client's spiritual family tree, can add to the life review for anyone facing death (Bullis 1996). Using one's earliest memory, one can identify those significant people, books, ideas, experiences that have nourished one's spiritual journey. The interweaving of ideas, people, and experiences gives vivid description of one's spiritual roots.

Spiritual suffering requires an ongoing assessment. It is not the social worker's responsibility to solve spiritual problems or concerns but to create a secure environment to nurture and support the client's exploration (Abram 1997; Applegate and Bonovitz 1995). Social workers and spiritual guides share a similar purpose in the goals of the clinical or spiritual relationship. It is to create a space where the clinician is informed of and aware of the importance of spiritual and religious beliefs and practices while attending to the psychological, physical, and social variables at play in the individual's life circumstances. For either the social worker or the spiritual guide, there may be a time where a religious leader, priest, rabbi, imam, or minister may need to be consulted with or invited into the session to provide those words and rituals, which carry particular import when administered by the ordained clergy.

We must always be aware of the sacred ground where as social workers we meet our clients in the struggle and hope of making meaning at end of life. It is also important that we do not cross boundaries in areas of spiritual and religious roles and responsibilities. Awareness of the differences and maintaining appropriate boundaries are important. When a worker has training in both social work and spiritual direction or guidance, he or she must be clear with clients which perspective and role each carries into the relationship. This does not mean that the awareness and knowledge of clinical issues or spiritual issues are dismissed from the relationship. It means that we explore the concerns that brought the client into the professional relationship and, when essential to the client's work and choice, we include and/or refer out for work in other dimensions of his or her life.

As we are aware, people respond to and perceive their environments according to their inner structures and levels of organization. At times, the presentation of that inner world is experienced in spiritual or religious language as much as in psychological language or meanings. It is in the dynamic process of listening for the different meanings and their contexts that we respect ways of knowing that come from spirituality and/or religious structures as well as ways of knowing that come from psychological structures.

ASSESSING SPIRITUALITY AND RELIGIOUS PRACTICES

A social worker's primary responsibility is to obtain as clear an idea of the client's inner structure as possible (Vaughn 1988). Spiritual assessment based on a strengths model of social work practices uses engagement, continuous collaboration, advocacy, and supportive disengagement when attending to the spiritual does not enhance the work to generate a holistic profile. It requires that the social worker actively engage in a relationship that positions the client as an expert on his or her life situation. With an emphasis on strengths and resources rather than on symptomology and problems, the pressing question is not what kind of life the client has had but what kind of life the client wants. It is now that spirituality emerges as a life force. Life strengths and support are not fixed, nor can they be evaluated once and then used as an ongoing standard. In the context of strengths assessment, spirituality often emerges as a stabilizing force that helps to maintain a person's sense of balance in the wake of change, difficulty, doubt, and death.

Assessment from a strengths perspective invites us to ask questions that provide definition to thematic life strengths and values that constitute a person's sense of self in the world.

Puchalski (2000) provides a useful and simple assessment tool for a spiritual history, "FICA: A Spiritual Assessment." FICA is an acronym that can be used to structure an interview:

F: Faith or beliefs (What is your faith or belief? Do you consider yourself spiritual or religious? What things do you believe in that give meaning to your life?)

I: Importance and influence (Is your belief important in your life? What influence does it have on how you take care of yourself? How have your beliefs influenced your behavior during this illness? What role do your beliefs play in regaining your health?)

C: Community (Are you part of a spiritual or religious community? Does this support you and how? Is there a person or group of people you really love or who are really important to you?)

A: Address (How would you like me, your healthcare provider, to address these issues in your health care?)

These questions are easily adapted for social workers working with clients at end of life. We may learn more by asking questions regarding what nourishes or supports a person's spirit, and by being open to hearing a range of responses including specific religious rituals as well as experiences of nature, music, poetry, and relationships.

Whatever the assessment tools or questions, the essential dimension is our capacity to be present to the client's spiritual quest for meanings at end of life.

SPIRITUAL OR RELIGIOUS PRACTICES AND A CHANGING SENSE OF SELF

Dombeck and Karl (1987) present a short Hasidic story that captures the assessment task: A student asks his teacher, "I have a question about Deuteronomy 6:6, which says, 'And these words, which I command you this day, shall be upon your heart.' Why is it said this way? Why are we not told to place them in our heart?" The teacher responds: "It is not within the power of human beings to place the divine teachings directly in their hearts. All we can do is place them on the surface of the heart so that when the heart breaks they drop in." The heart breaks in joy and in sorrow.

This particular story fits well with the theoretical orientation of object relations. Ana-Maria Rizzuto (1979) applies an object relation's framework for understanding the complexity of religious and spiritual experiences in individual development. The story of the family into which an individual is born comes with a perspective on the development of a God representation during the life cycle. This representation in the mind of the parents forms the mythology about the meaning of the child in the life of the primary caregivers. Often the birth of a child calls for a religious ritual (circumcision, baptism) thus physically and spiritually marking a child's relationship to God. Most children complete the oedipal period with at least a rudimentary God representation that remains constant as they continue to revise parent and self-representations during the life cycle. If the God representation is not revised to keep pace with changes in self-representation, it soon becomes asynchronous, may be experienced as ridiculous or irrelevant, or even threatening or dangerous. Each new life crisis or landmark—illness, death, promotions, falling in love, birth of children, catastrophes, wars—provide opportunities for remembering some once highly relevant or feared aspect of the God representation that will need to be renegotiated accordingly (Rizzuto 1979).

Developmental crises may bring about new encounters with both old and new God representations. Throughout the life cycle the individual will find herself in need of critical changes in self-representation to adapt to changing needs and possibilities as well as to new encounters with peers and parental representations. God—as a representation—may or may not be called upon to undergo his or her share in the changes. Finally, when death arrives, the question of the existence of God returns. At that point, the God representation, which may vary from a long-neglected preoedipal figure to a well-known life companion—or to anything in between—will return to the dying person's memory, either to obtain the grace of belief or to be thrown out for the last time (Rizzuto 1979).

God, psychologically speaking, is an illusory, transitional object. God comes into existence in transitional space. D. W. Winnicott says that religion is located in that illusory and intermediate area of experience that helps throughout life to bridge inner and outer realities. He defines that transitional domain as the space where art, culture, and religion belong. It is the place where people find the full relevance of relationships and meaning in their lives (Rizzuto 1979).

God, from an object relations perspective, has never been seen and cannot be proven to be real. Believers experience God as a fully intimate object who has total knowledge of them, even those deep dimensions of self that are not known to the individual or other people. The transitional space allows an unchallenged space of communication between the believer and his or her experience of God. Prayer becomes the way of communication and may be experienced in traditional and nontraditional ways (Rizzuto 1979; Winnicott 1982). Belief in God undergoes transformations in the course of life if it is to keep up with the transformations of the life cycle. If it loses its meaning, however, it can be set aside without being forgotten. "And it can recover its meaning at the time of a life crisis, either by a progressive new elaboration of the God representation or by a regressive return to an earlier representation or by repression when it becomes incompatible with psychic balance to the point that it cannot function as a transitional object" (Rizzuto 1979:202).

The following questions are used in a multifaceted model for taking a religious history that fits well with an object relation's perspective (Dombeck and Karl 1987). This model will be used in organizing Tamu Imani's personal religious history.

QUESTIONS FOR A RELIGIOUS HISTORY

While FICA provides a brief spiritual assessment tool that is compatible with a strengths perspective, Dombeck and Karl (1987) present a framework that allows for a more in-depth, dynamic approach to assessing a person's religious history and for placing that person within a religious community. They offer a way to understand personal meanings attached to symbols, rituals, beliefs, and divine figures, and a person's relationship to religious resources that allows one to build on the brief assessment provided by the FICA questions.

1. *Placement within a religious community.* What is the person's religious affiliation? Changes in religious affiliation? When did changes take place? What is the level of present involvement? What is the person's relationship with the religious or spiritual leader and the faith community? These questions focus on what is placed on the heart. They allow the practitioner to understand the person's particular belief systems and dogma that provide a context for understanding the various meanings of life events and human development.

For example, Tamu Imani was born into an African American family whose members were active in the African Methodist Episcopal Church. She converted to Catholicism when she married. She was actively involved in the Catholic Church until her divorce. Several years later, after travels to West Africa where she explored traditional African religious practices, she returned home to the Methodist Church of her family. Throughout these years, she participated in religious services and spiritual gatherings in the Catholic, African, and Methodist traditions.

2. *Personal meanings attached to symbols, rituals, beliefs, and divine figures.* This set of questions focuses on the spiritual resources that have been internalized by the

individual. What religious practices have been most meaningful? When and in what ways does the person feel close to the divine? What does one pray about? When? Where? What gives special strength and meaning? These questions center on what has dropped into the heart. They address that area of transitional space where the individual interacts with phenomena that can be used to organize responses and give meaning to life events.

Over the years, Tamu Imani's prayer life developed as she dealt with her feelings about a difficult divorce, her estrangement from her children, several affairs, and her role as caregiver for her terminally ill mother. She found solace in caring for her mother and in her development of an eclectic approach to spiritual practices. She found herself comfortably participating in prayer groups at the local Catholic parish while serving in a number of lay ministry roles in the Methodist Church that had been founded by her family. While she was often in conflict with the minister, she joined women's groups that were powerful influences in the life of the church. She developed family healing rituals that included prayers to saints, ancestors, and God.

3. *Relationship to religious resources.* This focuses on those internal objects that are used in understanding and making meaning of one's responses. What is the person's relationship with God? How does God feel about the person? How has the relationship changed? How is God involved in daily life? Does God help the person to find solutions to problems? Has there ever been a feeling of forgiveness? At this point in the religious history, the focus is on what heals or cripples the heart.

God was extraordinarily important as Tamu Imani's cancer developed and she found herself increasingly dependent on her family for financial, physical, and emotional support. The sense of God in her life as expressed through her writings and conversations with visitors was quite profound. While she was dying, I gave her a videotape of Sr. Thea Bowman, an African American Catholic nun who was herself dying of cancer and who movingly shared her journey of suffering and death. On the tape Sr. Thea exquisitely discussed her images and relationship with God and faith as a Catholic and as an African American. She described a God of joy and sorrow, who identifies with His oppressed people and gives them strength for living through life's crises, a God of one's ancestors, and a God of one's future. Tamu then insisted that all her visitors view the tape before seeing her. It proved to be a wonderful way of engaging her in conversations around the meaning of life, death, and faith, for her friends and her family. God and God's meaning for her life and suffering were well internalized. As she drew closer to death, she had a passionate commitment to have all those around her understand the ways she was making meaning of the experience and to struggle with their own understanding of her life, death, and the meaning of their lives. Through the experiences of prayer, by discussing her relationship with God and with others, and through her interweaving of Catholic, African, and African American Protestant understandings of a personal God, she was moved to engage in a healing of her family and other relationships. Spirituality for Tamu was a rich resource for negotiating and making meaning of her end of life.

In metaphorical language, Dombeck and Karl (1987) assess what has been placed upon the heart, what has or has not dropped in when the heart breaks, and what heals or cripples the heart in times of crisis. Tracing a wide concentric circle, they start with the person's placement within a religious community, with its social, cultural, and political contexts. Exploring personal meanings provides an opportunity to gain valuable information about cherished beliefs and spiritual practices. Next, by identifying the healing or crippling nature of one's relationship to religious and spiritual resources, a person is better able to assess the impact of his or her God representations on his or her own development and functioning. Here one explores the bond, range of affects, ambivalence, and important internal dialogues with God images, insight, questions, and feelings.

THE IMPORTANCE OF CLINICAL WORK DURING END-OF-LIFE CARE

We can make our minds so like still water that beings gather about us that they may see, it may be, their own images, and so live for a moment with a clearer, perhaps even with a fiercer life because of our quiet. (YEATS 1981:100)

This passage from the work of William Butler Yeats describes what is essential in our role as social workers who value the spiritual in end-of-life care. As social workers, our relationship with the client can also be described by Annette Garrett's quotation from a student's paper: "It is our goal and at the same time an art, to learn to enter into people's lives, to be helpful to them, to make no demand on them, and to be able to go out of their lives again when the time comes without hardship to them. To leave them with just that "trace of relationship" that makes their ego stronger by integrating what was positive in the relationship, to enrich them and one's self for another good human contact, and ask no more" (1954:104).

There are many influences on how I view myself as a spiritual companion to others. In listening for the sacred, what I seek is to bring the mind to stillness and to hear and see with the other the power of the transcendent present in the life of the other and in our time together (Guenther 1992). Guenther describes the spiritual companion, director, or guide as a midwife who is present and reflects back the journey of the other. Her description of the midwife as spiritual companion provides insight into how I am present to others on their journey. A lesser-known influence in my approach to spiritual direction is Mark Epstein's (1995) work on Buddhism and therapy, which I find invaluable. Epstein provides a thoughtful and engaging exploration of the synergy between psychodynamic, psychoanalytically oriented work that integrates Winnicottian thought with Buddhist psychology and practice. The importance of relationally based practice is stressed throughout his work. At the heart of practice is being fully present while being free to allow the relationship to develop.

Greenson (1981) discusses the real relationship between the therapist and client as being characterized by a realistic perception and reaction more or less uncontaminated by the distortions emanating from transference and countertransference. There is an authenticity, an openness, that is honest and not phony. It is the ability and willingness to be what one truly is in the relationship. In my opinion, a real therapeutic relationship is open to the presence of the transcendent. The sense of the transcendent that I am using in this chapter is not just a matter of the self's being transformed to a higher, more creative, or optimal level of being, but a transcendence that includes God as a reality. This also includes a sense of surprise, wonder, and not knowing.

I propose that the social worker with persons at the end of life be invited to be in the relationship as Epstein describes it:

> [What] I learned from Buddhism was that I did not have to know myself analytically as much as I had to tolerate not knowing. . . . Winnicott taught that to go willingly into unknowing was the key to living a full life. To develop the capacity to be alone: a faith, a trust in the relationship with the parent such that it is possible to explore the world outside of it. To simply be without worrying about keeping myself together. The experiences of unintegration . . . are experiences of letting go. They are feelings of losing oneself without feeling lost, hearing the self's innuendo rather than just its inflection. This is the space we create with the client or the person whose journey we share so that they are able to explore the sense of self. Not leaving the ego behind, but free to look around the edges. So, we hope to create a space where we can hear the innuendoes, the meanings that unfold in the relationship. (1999:17–20).

The clinical relationship that includes attention to spiritual development needs to elicit concerns about spirituality and one's relationship with God. It is a sacred situation in which a person may search for a fuller development of his or her spiritual self. The focus may be exclusively on spiritual matters or may include concerns of an emotional, physical, familial, financial, or career nature as they shape and influence the person's spiritual journey (Richards and Bergin 1998). Guenther (1992) identifies presence, patience, and waiting. These initial stages are often times for storytelling. They are times to explore ways of praying and relationships. This beginning of a spiritual journey ends in a period of transition when the old ways no longer serve. Images of God may change. What has been learned and diligently practiced may no longer help.

The next movement of a spiritual journey is the silent recognition that both social worker and client are on the same path, with different experiences while doing the same work of exploring, reflecting, and healing. The barriers between the therapist and client are fluid structures, erected for convenience, or perhaps they are completely illusory. The final movement is one of ending and termination. Here rituals of ending are important for the client and for the therapist.

The following case illustrates these processes for exploring the sacred in a social work setting.

SPIRITUAL ISSUES AT THE END OF LIFE WITH ADAM

Adam was a Caucasian male in his mid-fifties, married, with four children. He grew up in a large Roman Catholic family and was referred to me by his therapist, who felt Adam needed someone who could respond to spiritual issues he was facing at end of his life. Adam had an early history of emotional abuse from his father and carried into his adult relationships the fear of being seen as stupid and the fear of expressing emotions. He feared that expressing emotions meant being out of control. From his experience and perspective, it is not good to be out of control. As an adult he was fearful of being open, vulnerable to God and to others. He wanted to protect himself from rejection and emotional abuse. He struggled with his wife and children's attempts to close what he perceived as an emotional gulf. He spoke in both hope and anguish of the attempts by his son to touch him and be held.

Adam discovered that he was HIV-positive from a blood transfusion during a kidney transplant. He was diabetic and eventually had both legs amputated. The complications from subsequent treatments brought him close to death several times. I met with him for several months before his death due to renal failure. When he was able, he would write to me in between sessions. The following includes excerpts from our sessions and correspondence.

At our first meeting he expressed a longing for a relationship with God, a "disciplined" approach, a sense of focused prayer to understand why this had happened to him. As an adult, his clearest experiences of God were when he was singing at church and when he was totally engaged in a design project at work. He had experienced the presence of God, the emptiness of himself and God moving through him in the music and his work. He said he often tried to do his thing for God, not searching for what things God wanted of him.

Adam spoke of the first hospitalization as a time of stress and helplessness. He said,

> I had to rely on other people to help me get better, and that I can't get well right away is stressing me more. I believe that a lot of this has to do with my personal relationship with God (or lack of it). I internalize stress, and that's what makes me sick. I hold on to everything and try to take responsibility for everything, and it's too much. I need to realize the personal God, to cultivate my relationship with God. I need to gain a sense of God at whose feet I can lay the sick, broken, and imperfect parts of my life and myself, and receive unconditional love, acceptance, and healing in return. I need to learn how to pray. I'm not sure what holds me back, but I think that it may be a trust issue. . . . I don't want God to be just a subject of study; I want a personal relationship. I get glimpses of a personal encounter when I sing or during the mass. I know that it requires imagination, but it also requires commitment.

Over the months in which we met, Adam told me his story. In those times, he remembered, repeated, and worked through who God was for him. This was a time where he had a sense of creating what was there to be created: his life story as he knew it and wanted it to be heard, the reality of unconditional love and acceptance, and the acknowledgment that a miraculous return to full health might not happen. Accepting being a disabled person was scary for him. His loss of identity, from primary provider to disabled husband and father, along with his images of himself and perceptions that others had of him, plunged him into a psychological and spiritual crisis.

This became a turning point and an opportunity for him to engage in both psychological counseling and spiritual support. He began a journey to understand his images of himself, his family and of God and to realize how images influenced his experiences of who God was for him.

As Adam began this stage of his spiritual journey, he shared this with me:

Without really making a conscious choice, I went to the story of the rich young man in Mark 10:17–29. I read it over and over and really tried to put myself in the place of the man talking to Jesus. . . . Money and wealth have never had much of a hold on me. I had enough to care for my family and their future. Then I started to think about what Jesus was really asking for. He didn't ask the man to give up his wealth for the good of the poor (primarily) but for the good of his own soul.

Jesus said, "Go and sell all you have . . . *then come and follow me.*" And so I began to think. What is my treasure? What is it that holds me back from my ability to give myself fully and unselfishly? I'm sure that there are many things, but the one that came to mind, the one that the whole encounter seemed to focus on, was my craving for God's approval, for undivided attention from the hospital staff and the gift of good health. This desire of mine to bargain for the positive attention of people around me enters into all of my relationships. It limits these relationships and it limits me as a person, but it feels so precious to me. And when I see myself calling staff and begging for attention when I am not in crisis, I seem very small and weak. The unhealthy aspect of this attention seeking is what I feel Jesus was asking me to give up. So, I've been thinking about this and trying not to turn away from it, but I'm not quite sure how to progress. How to ask for the help I really need and not just for the attention I desire.

I became more directive in Adam's spiritual journey. I was very direct regarding scripture and in suggestion for ways to pray. In our conversations about interactions with staff and family, he began to see himself as unreasonably demanding. I served as a checkpoint for him as he tried new ways in his search for a discipline of prayer and reflection that was compatible with his sense of self and his health needs. As his medical problems became more complicated and he knew that he was terminal, Adam moved through a period of being stuck and feeling frustrated in a process of not knowing where he was in his relationship with God. He felt abandoned and had symptoms of depression. I felt the need to help him move forward in his work. I was aware that none of the usual techniques of changing prayer styles or exploring ways of reflecting were moving him out of being stuck.

Later Adam wrote,

Quite a lot has happened in the time since I've seen you, but I want to go back to something that you asked me at our last meeting. You asked who God was for me. I remember that the question caught me off guard. You asked me the same question awhile back and, the way my mind works, once you've covered something, you move on the next thing. But I now realize that it is the central question in spirituality. Now to my answer.

As I said, your question caught me off guard. I remember that I said something about my image of God as friend and lover, but I was not convincing to myself and I don't believe that I convinced you either. I think that it is a valid image for me; it is the image that I long for and even experience in brief glimpses. But mostly it is seen at a distance glimpsed in the future of my imagination. My day-to-day existential reality is quite different. God is still a demanding, wrathful, easily offended parent for me. I walk around carrying a large stone in my stomach that competes with my kidney failures for my attention. The stone is nothing other than my own sense of sinfulness. This is why I so rarely experience peace and stillness, even with the pain medication. I can no longer take care of myself and work to provide for my family. There is peace and security in the company of a friend or lover, but the way that I deal with God, the best that I can hope for is a pat on the head and a "good boy." I don't know how to change it and I don't know how to accept it. It has been exhausting to even write about it. I feel like I'm pulling some large tumor up out of my guts and out through my mouth.

I apologize for the unrelentingly dark tone of this letter. I must tell you that I am still praying. As a matter of fact, I'm praying more now than I have in many years. It gives me the feeling that I'm still connected with something that holds life and hope.

This session moved me to reflect on my own frustration with God in order to allow the space for the work to continue at its own pace for both of us. I felt forced to encounter my own struggles with God. I really felt that God had left Adam in the desert long enough. I used peer-group supervision to get in touch with my own struggles with God and with my issues of countertransference in my work with Adam. I felt that Adam, and thus I, had been abandoned by God to travel the desert of pain and suffering alone. I became in touch with my own experiences of being abandoned with the loss of my own father when I was the same age as one of Adam's children. It was a powerful experience of connecting and surrendering to the meaning of the loss of a parent for a child and of allowing for the work I needed to do to happen in the peer supervision group. As a result, I was able to shift to a deeper awareness and freedom to allow my self to move out of the way of the Spirit's direction with Adam. His transference to me was also powerful. His past experiences and displacement onto me of feelings, attitudes, and behaviors belonging rightfully to other significant relationships, and especially his relationship with God, provided an opportunity for a major breakthrough in our work together. This was a session of great intensity and ambivalence on his part. He risked sharing and did not experience my response of encouraging him to participate in the sacrament of reconciliation as condemning. I knew that this was a pivotal moment in Adam's life, inasmuch as he had a few months left to live and wanted to reconcile with his God and his family before he died. He went to confession and began the process of repairing those relationships that had been hurt. In the months before he died, his prayers gradually shifted to a peaceful, deeper intimacy with God.

CONCLUSION

Practitioners should be willing to examine their own spiritual development and their clients' experiences in the context of psychological developmental issues and theories. Concepts from psychological theories such as Winnicott's holding environment provide a context for exploring the meaning of religious and spiritual experiences at the end of life.

Creating a holding environment for Tamu, Jerry, and Adam, as each sought meaning in their respective religious traditions, was my professional and personal commitment to them. Their questions of "why me," their desires to reconcile conflictual family and other relationships, their spoken and unspoken questions of their relationships with God, permeated my relationships to them. Jerry was my colleague and my friend, and my relationships with Tamu and Adam were as their social worker who cared about their spiritual journeys. With all three, my goal was to be a caring presence who could tolerate and bear witness to their crises of faith and meaning making on their journeys toward death. Sharing joys and sorrows, listening for the shifts and unfolding of meaning at the end of their lives, was my primary role in the relationships. While their personal stories, poetry, and writings presented uniquely individual experiences, what was universal was the holding environment that allowed me to sit in compassion with the other's physical, emotional, and spiritual suffering.

To enter deeply into spiritual journeys at the end of life is both a challenge and opportunity for the social worker. Each story invites us deeper into our own mysteries, for we do our best work when we have faced the uncertainty and fear through our personal reflection. By being available to others on spiritual journeys and becoming a part of their healing, we may find the courage and freedom to engage and to witness our own existential crises of life and death.

REFERENCES

Abram, J. 1997. *The Language of Winnicott.* Northvale, NJ: Aronson.

Applegate, J. S., and J. M. Bonovitz. 1995. *The Facilitating Partnership: A Winnicottian Approach for Social Workers and Other Helping Professionals.* Northvale, NJ: Aronson.

Becvar, D. S. 2001. *In the Presence of Grief.* New York: Guilford.

Bullis, Ron. 1996. *Spirituality in Social Work Practice.* Washington, DC: Taylor & Francis.

Canda, E., and L. Furman. 1999. *Spiritual Diversity in Social Work Practice: The Heart of Helping.* New York: Free Press.

Cornett, C. 1992. Toward a more comprehensive personology: Integrating a spiritual perspective into social work practice. *Social Work* 37(2): 101–102.

———. 1998. *The Soul of Psychotherapy: Recapturing the Spiritual Dimension in the Therapeutic Encounter.* New York: Simon & Schuster.

Derezotes, D. S., and K. E. Evans. 1995. Spirituality and religiosity in practice: In-depth interviews of social work practitioners. *Social Thought Journal of Religion in the Social Services* 18(1): 39–56.

Doka, K. J., and J. D. Morgan. 1993. *Death and Spirituality.* Amityville, NY: Baywood.

Dombeck, M., and J. Karl. 1987. Spiritual issues in mental healthcare. *Journal of Religion and Health* 26(3): 183–197.

Epstein, M. 1995. *Thoughts Without a Thinker: Psychotherapy from a Buddhist Perspective.* New York: Basic Books.

———. 1998. *Going to Pieces Without Falling Apart: A Buddhist Perspective on Wholeness.* New York: Broadway Books.

Fleischman, P. R. 1990. *The Healing Spirit: Explorations in Religion and Psychotherapy.* New York: Paragon.

Garrett, A. 1954. Learning through supervision. *Smith College Studies in Social Work* 24(2): 104.

Goldberg, C. 1996. The privileged position of religion in the clinical dialogue. *Clinical Social Work Journal* 32(3): 125–136.

Graham, M. A., T. Kaiser, and K. J. Garrett. 1998. Naming the spiritual: The hidden dimension of helping. *Social Thought Journal of Religion in the Social Services* 18(4): 49–62.

Greenson, R. R. 1981. The real relationship between the patient and the psychoanalyst. In *Classics in Psychoanalytic Technique*, ed. R. Langs, 89–96. New York: Aronson.

Griffith, J. L., and M. E. Griffith. 2002. *Encountering the Sacred in Psychotherapy.* New York: Guilford.

Guenther, M. 1992. *Holy Listening: The Art of Spiritual Direction.* Boston: Cowley.

Hood, R. W., B. Spilka, B. Hunsberger, and R. Gorsuch. 1996. *The Psychology of Religion.* New York: Guilford.

Horton, A. L., and J. A. Williamson. 1988. *Abuse and Religion.* New York: Lexington.

Hugen, B., ed. 1998. *Christianity and Social Work.* Botsford, CT: North American Association of Christians in Social Work.

Joseph, M. V. 1988. Religion and social work practice. *Social Casework* 69:443–452.

Kilpatrick, A. C., and T. P. Holland. 1990. Spiritual dimensions of practice. *The Clinical Supervisor* 8(2): 125–140.

Lewandoski, C. A., and E. R. Canda. 1995. A typological model for the assessment of religious groups. *Social Thought Journal of Religion in the Social Services* 18(1): 17–38.

Lovinger, R. J. 1984. *Working with Religious Issues in Therapy.* New York: Aronson.

Lukoff, D., F. Lu, and R. Turner. 1992. Toward a more culturally sensitive DSM-IV psycho religious and psycho-spiritual problems. *Journal of Nervous and Mental Disease* 180(11): 673–682.

Martin, K., and S. Elder. 1993. Pathways through grief: A model of the process. In *Personal Care in an Impersonal World: A Multidimensional Look at Bereavement*, ed. J. D. Morgan, 73–86. Amityville, NY: Baywood.

May, G. 1987. *Will and Spirit: A Contemplative Psychology.* San Francisco: Harper & Row.

Millison, M., and J. Dudley. 1992. Providing spiritual support: A job for all hospices professionals. *Hospice Journal* 8(4): 49–66.

Morgan, J. D., ed. 1993. *Personal Care in an Impersonal World: A Multidimensional Look at Bereavement.* Amityville, NY: Baywood.

O'Connor, P. 1993. A clinical paradigm for exploring spiritual concerns. In *Death and Spirituality*, ed. K. Doka and J. Morgan, 131–141. Amityville, NY: Baywood.

O'Connor, P., and M. Kaplan. 1986. The role of the interdisciplinary team in providing spiritual care: An attitudinal study of hospices workers. In *Proceedings of a Colloquium: In Quest of the Spiritual Component of Care for the Terminally Ill*, ed. F. S. Wald, 51–62. New Haven, CT: Yale University School of Nursing.

Payne, I., A. Bergin, and P. Loftus. 1992. A review of attempts to integrate spiritual and standard psychotherapy techniques. *Journal of Psychotherapy Integration* 2(3): 171–192.

Plante, T. G., and A. C. Sherman. 2001. *Faith and Healing.* New York: Guilford.

Puchalski, C. M. 2000. FICA: A spiritual assessment tool. *Journal of Palliative Care* 3(1): 131.

Randour, M. L., ed. 1993. *Exploring Sacred Landscapes: Religious and Spiritual Experiences in Psychotherapy.* New York: Columbia University Press.

Reese, D. 1995–96. Testing of a casual model: Acceptance of death in hospice patients. *Omega: Journal of Death and Dying* 32(2): 81–92.

Reese, D., R. Ahern, S. Nair, J. O'Faire, and C. Warren. 1999. Hospice access and utilization by African Americans: Addressing cultural and institutional barriers through participatory action research. *Social Work* 44(6): 549–559.

Richards, P. S., and A. E. Bergin. 1998. *A Spiritual Strategy for Counseling and Psychotherapy*. Washington, DC: American Psychological Association.

Rizzuto, A. 1979. *The Birth of the Living God: A Psychoanalytic Study*. Chicago: University of Chicago Press.

Sanzenbach, P. 1989. Religion and social work: It's not that simple! *Social Casework: The Journal of Contemporary Social Work* 11:571–575.

Smith, E. 1995. Addressing the psycho-spiritual distress of death as a reality: A transpersonal approach. *Social Work* 40(3): 402–413.

Tice, C. Spirituality in the context of strengths assessment. *Society for Spirituality and Social Work Newsletter* 4(5): 1.

Vaughan, F. 1991. Spiritual issues in psychotherapy. *Journal of Transpersonal Psychology* 23(2): 105–119.

Wass, H., and R. A. Neimeyer. 1995. *Dying: Facing the Facts*. Washington, DC: Taylor & Francis.

Winnicott, D. W. 1982. *Playing and Reality*. New York: Routledge.

Yeats, W. B. 1981. *The Celtic Twilight*. Gerrards Cross, UK: Smythe.

11

GENDER AND DEATH:
PARALLEL AND INTERSECTING PATHWAYS

ILLENE C. NOPPE

I **BEGIN** this exploration of the significant interactions between gender and death with two examples. A 1997 study by Moss, Resch, and Moss considered the impact of parental loss on their middle-aged children. Although such loss in middle age is the normative experience of our culture, most of the bereavement literature suggests little about the experience of forty- and fifty-year-olds when their last surviving parent has died. Rather, the focus of such research has typically been on early widowhood or parental loss during the childhood years. Moss, Resch, and Moss (1997) looked at a number of factors that may influence the degree to which these surviving children reacted to the death in terms of the intensity of their grief, their acceptance of the loss, their sense of finitude (realizing the closeness of one's own death), continuing ties to the deceased parent, and the degree to which surviving children felt in control of their grief. Studying 212 middle-aged children, these researchers determined that gender accounted for most of the differences that were found. Daughters expressed a higher degree of emotional upset, fewer acceptances of the death, and a stronger continuing tie with their dead parent than sons, who did express a great sense of guilt for not helping take care of the parent before death. Why do these finding not surprise us? Is it because they conform to our expectations of how men and women in our society behave and are expected to act in contexts other than death?

Moss, Resch, and Moss's study exemplifies the adage, "Death is a mirror of life." In a gendered society, the behaviors, beliefs, and rituals around dying, death, and bereavement *reflect* social beliefs and prescriptions for gender. This may especially be true for death, because in situations that are highly charged with emotion, stress, and ambiguity, people tend to adhere more closely to stereotypes and social prescriptions (Walker 1982).

The second example points further to the relationships between gender and death, via an exploration of women, death, and art. Photographer David Robinson, in the course of photographing European cemeteries such as Père Lachaise, France, "soon became aware of women all around me" (Robinson 1995). In addition to noting that European women are the devoted caregivers of graves, where tending and socializing tend to commingle, Robinson found life-size sculptures of beautiful young (always) women, many evoking the mix of eroticism and beauty characteristic of the portrayal of women during this era. They often were shown in the anguish of grief, adorning the graves of men. Robinson has photographed literally hundreds of his "Saving Graces," which are suggestive of the romantic views of love, death, youth, and sex. These attitudes are frequently maintained in the images of popular culture of today.

Thus, death, the common denominator of all human existence, reflects the different experiences and perceptions of men and women. Although there has been significant progress in viewing social problems and issues through the lens of gender (Unger 2001), and despite the forward thinking of early pioneers in the study of death who acknowledged the significance of gender (see Stillion 1985), it is only of late that gender has taken a central role in the exploration of attitudes and responses to dying, death, and bereavement. Yet, if we are to understand death as a mirror of life, then it is necessary to be informed about how a gendered society influences the rituals and traditions as well as the processes of "meaning making" that are involved in dying, death, and bereavement. We therefore begin this exploration with a discussion of how theoretical and methodological traditions in the study of gender and in the study of death inform each other. Such parallels will be further illuminated by specific examples from the integration of these two fields of study, to be followed by implications for practitioners, who frequently will find it necessary to interpret their clients' reactions to a loss within the context of gender.

THEORY AND RESEARCH IN GENDER AND DEATH

Each area of scholarship has its own language and traditions of research and theory. The study of death and gender quickly reveals many compatibilities and ways in which their respective scholarly traditions enlighten one another. The two fields intersect both in paradigmatic, theoretical, and methodological ways. For example, both the study of death and the study of gender are inherently interdisciplinary, which helps us to appreciate a broader view of the different levels in which men and women deal with their losses. In order to understand the influence of gender in human interaction, it is necessary to study the biological basis of gendered behavior, conduct sociological analyses of institutions and power as they affect men and women, and understand the psychology of gender differences. Additionally, the history of women's movements in this country and abroad, the effects of different cultural traditions as these affect men and women, the relationship between women and the arts, are but a few of the myriad topics that need to be explored.

Thinking about death and gender and the relationship between the two is enriched by the contribution of many different disciplines, particularly when the relationship between gender and death is examined. For example, women's experiences with death reflect their biological propensity to live longer than men (which has enormous political, economic, and social implications), their capacities for giving life (birth) and death (miscarriage, abortion), and is affected by the medical profession's responses to men's and women's health issues. For example, AIDS is traditionally viewed as the killer of homosexual men, yet urban women of color, aged 25–44 years of age are more likely to die of AIDS than from any other disease (Anselmi and Law 1998, Sikkema, Wanger, and Bogart 2000). Depression further raises the risk of death in women, including depression related to the HIV virus (Gurung et al., in press). Conversely, gendered behavior may partially be to blame for men dying earlier than women. Playing out the traditional male gender stereotype of independence and strength can lead to a greater propensity for risk-taking behaviors, dismissal of early warning signs of illness, and reluctance to seek medical help. Furthermore, the traditional male gender role restricts men's opportunities to recognize and display their emotions, frequently leading to ineffective ways of dealing with stress (such as that associated with grief) and a greater likelihood of using alcohol and other drugs as a means of coping (Good, Sherrod, and Dillon 2000).

In death studies, we are just beginning to examine the historical and cultural bases of gender and death practices and rituals. The respective roles of men and women in funerary rituals and practices awaits exploration, particularly in terms of how these roles are affected by race and social class. Wisocki and Skowron (2000) aptly point out that there is great variation in the rituals and expression of grief across cultures. Cross-cultural analyses of death examine the degree of family and community involvement, the quality and quantity of expressed emotions, and the different functions of funerary and death rituals according to cultural tradition. However, there may be an important intersection of gender with cultural expectations. Cultural expectations for length of mourning and remarriage in the case of spousal bereavement may differ for men and women. In addition, in many cultures, women tend to cry and are expected to display physical manifestations of their loss (Leming and Dickinson 1998). Women may be expected to cut their hair, lacerate themselves, shave their heads, and cover themselves with ashes (Leming and Dickinson 1998). The Huichol women of Mexico are expected to engage in a great deal of wailing and crying or display suicidal gestures (Weigand and Weigand 1991). In the United States, it appears that African American, Puerto Rican, and Mexican American women are given greater latitude than men in the emotional expression of grief (Merdinger 1995). Chinese American parents who do not have a daughter are considered unlucky because she is the one who is expected to wail and cry in order to open the gates of heaven (Tanner 1995). Given that the United States is such a culturally diverse society, it is unfortunate that as of yet we have limited information about how the grieving rules of various ethnic groups may differ according to gender.

All students of the social sciences have experienced the warnings to avoid errors when designing research and when reading the research findings of others. Because both gender and death have traditionally been considered out of the mainstream of research, it is especially important to plan and evaluate research critically with an eye toward uncovering problems. Such concerns about methodology in gender research are also applicable to the research on dying and death. For example, we now know that it is important that researchers include both male and female participants, that gender as a variable typically is not a causal factor (leading to conclusions that gender differences are biologically based) but rather a descriptive one, that some research questions come out of inherently biased theoretical perspectives, and that meta-analytic studies, which estimate the magnitude of gender differences across a series of studies, are the standards of good social science (Anselmi and Law 1998; Halpern and Ikier 2002; Hyde 1994). Similar to the study of gender, the study of dying, death, and loss presents an emotion-laden arena of unquestioned assumptions, inherent biases, and pitfalls for the unwary consumer of research findings. The types of assessments (e.g., interviews or questionnaires) that are offered, for example, can affect how men and women report death-related experiences (Stroebe, Stroebe, and Schut 2001). Additionally, the inherent bias toward using women as the standard for how to grieve frequently leads to faulty generalizations in the research literature (Stroebe et al. 2001). Gender researchers have had to pursue a rather aggressive agenda for the inclusion of women in research design. However, the opposite may be true in bereavement research, inasmuch as women tend to live longer than men, tend to marry men who are older than they are, and tend not to remarry after the deaths of their spouses. With a ratio of widows to widowers reported to be 4:1, it is no small wonder that grief in widowhood has focused on the experiences of female participants (Stroebe, Stroebe, and Schut 2001).

In both areas of study, it is important to be wary of the "file-drawer" effect, or the tendency not to publish results when gender or sex differences are not found. Thus, it is possible that the finding of gender differences in death anxiety is exaggerated because the research reporting no differences has not made its way into print. Although meta-analytic literature reviews now contain a file drawer "fail-safe" value (Halpern and Ikier 2002), the research in dying, death, and loss has not been able to amass enough data to conduct many of these valuable studies that compare many findings in order to determine if the effect sizes are significant (Stroebe et al. 2001).

Examining theoretical assumptions and positing alternative perspectives for long-held beliefs has been a mainstay of the scholarship of gender. For example, the assumption that gender differences (e.g., aggression, verbal and quantitative abilities) reflected biological differences was questioned by feminist scholars who considered the significance of social experiences in such gender differences (McGillicuddy-De Lisi and De Lisi 2002). Out of such work has come the recognition that gender is a *socially constructed* phenomenon as well as a biological distinction (Sherif 1982). Thus, how men and women behave and what we consider "masculine" or "feminine" roles are strongly influenced by our cultural and individual efforts to make meaning out of these behaviors. Recently, this social cognitive perspective has also been used to understand bereavement. According to Neimeyer (2001, 2002) the symptoms of grief are most obviously physical (e.g., shortness of breath, restlessness, muscular tension, insomnia), but the significance of such loss is reflected in the effort to reconstruct and make sense of the world that must now encompass the loss of a figure of attachment. Such individual efforts at constructing a narrative about the loss, especially in terms of how it affects the sense of identity, should intersect with social understandings of gender. Thus, a woman in our culture (and many others) may approach her sudden widowhood with a different set of expectations and understanding of herself without a marriage partner than would a widowed man. Relearning the world with a new set of assumptions, and constructing a new narrative of the self without the physical presence of the person who has died, is affected by social conventions about male and female behavior in general, and male and female differences in grief in particular.

THE SOCIAL STRATIFICATION OF GENDER AND
THE SOCIAL STRATIFICATION OF DEATH

Our theme of death as a mirror of life is furthered by an examination of the social stratification of death. The sociology of gender recognizes that the lives of people are colored by factors of social status such as ethnicity, economic level, occupation, and educational background. In this culture, one of the most significant factors of social stratification is gender, which is reflected in differential treatment of individuals on the basis of their gender, gendered cultural symbols that reflect status positions, and correspondingly differential levels of power on the basis of gender. What evidence is there that such social stratification exists, even in death? Here are a few examples:

In the United States, gravestones for women tend to be smaller, and an examination of the early-twentieth-century records from a funeral home in Wisconsin revealed that they were less expensive than those for men. There also are significant differences by gender in the ways in which obituaries are constructed. Typically, more obituaries are written for males than for females, female obituaries are shorter in length, and rarely are they accompanied by a photograph. This has been especially true of white women (Spilka, Lacey, and Gelb 1979; Marks and Piggee 1998–99). Furthermore, the occupational status of the deceased is mentioned more frequently for men than for women, whereas social participation in organizations is most often mentioned for females. Further reflecting the mirror of social roles and expectations for men and women, Stillion (1985) observes that obituaries give greater recognition to women who were members of the helping professions, whereas men are afforded greater recognition in more competitive occupations such as business. Maybury (1995–96) found that a woman's obituary tends to be longer if she is a relative of a famous man. The obituaries of eminent psychologists also reflect gender differences, with men noted for the superior intellect and legacy-giving activities, and women for their humane behavior and ability to maintain families despite their demanding and successful careers (Radtke, Hunter, and Stam 2000).

In another example of gender and death reflecting social stratification, we note that women have a long history of being the caregivers of the dying; the men are more involved in legal, financial, and administrative issues involving the death. Even in hunting and gathering societies, the shaman or witch doctor, who drove out the source of the illness, was a role ascribed to men, but the caregiver of the sick was given to women (Benoliel and Degner 1995). At least as far back as the 1500s, the care and attendance of the sick and dying were associated with the work of women, although will making and distribution of wealth was the province of professional men (Hallam 1996). If we fast-forward to the modern-day hospice in the United States, where the emphasis is on palliative care, we find in a study of volunteers by the National Hospice Organization that 87 percent of the volunteers were female (NHO 1993). Perhaps the most striking example of the gendered social stratification in the treatment of the dying is seen in the allocation of duties among medical personnel. The nursing profession, a predominantly female occupation, has been most involved in caring for the dying and their families as it attempted to counteract the depersonalization of the dying process accompanying advances in medical technology (Benoliel and Degner 1995). It was nurses who made Elisabeth Kübler-Ross famous, as they sought out a guide for the humane caring of the dying, a task frequently passed on to them by doctors inadequately trained in the socioemotional needs of the dying. This tradition of women tending to the needs of sick and dying family members continues to the present, even for women who may also be employed full time outside of the home. Additionally, women are the bearers of cultural tradition and rituals surrounding death, and they often promote death education in formal and informal settings (Noppe 1999). Despite such active involvement with the care of the sick and dying, the positions of institutionalized power are predominantly male. For example, men are more likely to be funeral directors (in the United States, 93 percent, by recent estimates by the Funeral Directors Association), the makers of policy in the legal structure of our "death system," in the upper echelons of the medical hierarchy, and even the pall-bearers in American funerals!

RESEARCH FINDINGS RELATING GENDER
TO DEATH EXPERIENCES

There is a long tradition of examining gender differences in coping with widowhood, suicide, and death anxiety. Lately, the examination of gender differences in the grief process is appearing with greater frequency. Martin and Doka (2000), in a voice of irony, have pointed out that traditional standards of "healthy" or "normal" grieving are based upon the ways in which women handle their losses. How different this is from other standards of mental health! Thus, our idealized version of a "good" resolution to grief involves showing emotion, seeking social support, talking about the loss with others, and allowing time to grieve openly, and men typically fall "short" on these criteria (Cook 1988). In protest of this standard, Martin and Doka (2000) claim that the experience of grief may differ between men and women, where men are less expressive, deal with the loss as a problem to be solved, resort to activity as an expression of grief, and do not seek out social support. Cook's (1988) study of fifty-five men whose children died further revealed that the fathers' grief-management strategies encompassed vigilant monitoring of their thoughts, so that they either blocked out upsetting thoughts or reframed the death in logical and carefully reasoned ways. Martin and Doka (2000) suggest that the "masculine, or instrumental pattern" of grief may be equally valid to the "feminine, or intuitive pattern," but it is not recognized by the mental health community as an effective means of coping with loss. Of course, there is a continuum for both genders, but Martin and Doka (2000) perceptively argue that when individuals grieve in the patterns of the other sex, they are prone to social condemnation ("disenfranchised" grief). There is a double bind of bereavement for men, so that cultural standards of male stoicism in the face of devastating loss (as in the death of a child) come into direct conflict with cultural standards of "healthy" grieving. A man who is very emotional and talkative about a death may receive less tolerance from others than a woman who behaves in a similar fashion.

Further insight into the role of gender and the grieving process has come from studies on the bereavement experiences of widows and widowers. For example, Stroebe, Stroebe, and Schut (2001) have examined the differences in the mental and physical outcomes of loss for bereaved men and women. Their review of the research that has controlled for the generally higher depression levels of nonbereaved women, as compared to men, indicates that widowers tend to have higher depression scores, are more prone to alcohol abuse, and take longer to recover from the death of a spouse than widows (Glick, Weiss, and Parkes 1974; Stroebe, Stroebe, and Schut 2001). To some extent, this may be culture specific and linked to degree of social support, as widowed black men, whose extensive family network rally behind them, fare better than black widows in terms of the degree of their mental anguish (Williams, Takeuchi, and Adair 1992). Perhaps even more telling about the differential effects of bereavement on men and women is the relatively robust finding that men (both black and white) are at greater risk for their own death after the loss of their spouse than are women (Stroebe, Stroebe, and Schut 2001). Stroebe et al. (2001) are primarily interested in why spousal bereavement seems to be so much more detrimental to the health of men than to women. They suggest that the answer may lie in how two coping styles, emotion-focused coping and problem-focused coping, are differentially used by men and women. In emotion-focused coping, specific behaviors or cognitions are employed that help in the management of emotional responses to stress in order to avoid being overwhelmed by affect. Talking about the death, seeking social support, and reviewing and re-reviewing the circumstances of the death (ruminating) are aspects of such emotion-focused coping. This style of coping is reminiscent of the older notion that "grief work" is necessary in order to find a resolution to the loss. In problem-focused coping, stress is dealt with by attempts to modify or eliminate its sources. Stroebe et al. (2001) suggest that both styles are needed in order to "inoculate" against the outcomes of the stress associated with spousal bereavement. Women are more expert in making use of a number of opportunities to engage in their preferred style of coping, that is, emotion-focused coping, but they also must ultimately engage in problem focused coping because the relentless tasks of negotiating modern living forces them to do so. Men who engage in their preferred style of coping, problem-focused coping, however, can more easily avoid using the emotion-focused coping style, and thus do not benefit from attacking their loss-related issues in a dual mode. The problem-focused style, when used exclusively, can also present difficulties because it cannot be completely effective in eliminating the source of the stress, which ideally would be to restore the person who has died.

Suicide and death anxiety also offer interesting parallels with women's studies. For example, just as biased perspectives have perpetuated many false assumptions about women's and men's behaviors (see, for example, Taylor et al. 2000 on females' responses to stress), the same may be argued about women's suicidal behavior, which has frequently been interpreted on the basis of the experiences and behavior of men (Canetto and Lester 1995). For example, Canetto and Lester convincingly argue that the field of suicidology has focused on suicide mortality, which is relatively infrequent and typical of males, and from that has extrapolated to nonfatal suicidal behavior, which is more frequent and is more typical of females. These nonfatal behaviors have been referred to as suicidal failures, thus adding a negative evaluation to the phenom-enon in comparison to the completed or "successful" suicide. Women's suicidal be-havior has been studied in relation to the menstrual cycle, as if to imply that it is the cycle of hormones that lead to such pathological behavior. Yet, the incidence of suicidal behavior and male hormonal patterns has yet to be examined (Canetto and Lester 1995). And what of "she died for love and he for glory?" Canetto (1992–93) has reinterpreted suicide data to show that many women's suicidal behaviors are related to issues other than failed relationships, and that the role of relationships in men's suicidal behaviors may be unfairly diminished because of our gender stereotypes. In support of this claim, epidemiological studies have consistently shown that the risk of suicide is higher for unmarried and socially isolated men (Canetto 1992–93).

We can also turn to the research on death anxiety in order to uncover interesting gender differences. One of the most consistent and poorly understood findings in the thanatological literature is that women report higher levels of death anxiety than do men (Neimeyer and Moore 1994). Does this mean that women are more anxious, or that they are more apt to report their anxieties? Should we help women to be less neurotic, or should we encourage men to discuss their feelings more? Such questions, once again, resonate with our overall social constructions of gender. Kastenbaum (2000) offers an interesting interpretation that is more in support of the women-higher-anxiety hypothesis than the men-can't-admit-they-are-anxious hypothesis. He states that because women are the caregivers of the dying and promote death education, that they are the most sensitive to issues around death and loss. Women are socialized from early on to be the ones who provide care and comfort in these most difficult of situations, and thus they are more likely to think about and engage in discourse about death and dying. We would expect that even by statistically controlling for the ten-dency to self-disclose that the gender differences in death anxiety would be upheld, and that seems to be the case (Dattel and Neimeyer 1990).

NEWER THEORETICAL CONTRIBUTIONS AND THEIR RELATION TO GENDER

Consideration of the intersection between gender and death is enriched by relational theory, which proposes that human development involves the growth of the self within the context of relationships (Miller 1991; Spencer 2000; Surrey 1991). Relationships are growth-enhancing and serve to promote creativity, empathic capacities, and a sense of competence and self-worth. The idea of self-in-relation was posited as an alternative to the traditional psychological perspective emphasizing separation, autonomy, and individuation as the goal of human development. This prevailing model appears to capture the developmental experience of men more so than women. Rather than consider women deficient in their development because their sense of self continues to evolve in terms of what happens between themselves and others, relational theory suggests that this is the normative and psychologically healthy experience of women (Surrey 1991). The relational model asserts that disconnection and psychological iso-lation from others are sources of unhealthy psychological adjustment. This sense of self in relational context is actually present for both male and female infants, but our cultural beliefs translate it into a different life for a boy, who is steered away from situations in which reciprocal interactions with another are primary to those that emphasize independence and a style of relating that objectifies the other. Beliefs that such individuation leads to the attainment of one's full psychological potential have long pervaded psychological theory and practice, but Miller (1976, 1991) proposes that females develop a more articulated sense of self because of their growth within increasingly more complex relationships. The goal of development is not to reach individuation and autonomy, or to "grow out of relationships," but rather growth and active engagement within relationships (Miller and Stiver 1997). Recognition of the centrality of connections to others has also been the theme of Belenky et al. (1986), who saw cognitive development emerging out of relationships and their influence on women's ways of thinking and knowing about the world, as well as the work of Gilligan (1982), who used the relational approach to study moral and identity development.

This new view of human development as arising out of connections with others is paralleled by a paradigmatic shift in grief theory that has taken place over the past decade. Models of the grief process go as far back as the early 1900s with Sigmund Freud's *Mourning and Melancholia.* Glossing over the differences of a multitude of theories that have appeared since then, major themes of the grief process involve shock and denial, an extended period of depression and anxiety, and then recovery and reintegration. However, traditional concepts of grief can be criticized for their emphasis on disconnection in the same way as traditional theories of psychological adjustment have by relational theorists. Traditional grief theories have emphasized the necessity of detachment, decathexis, or the severing of bonds for effective recovery from bereavement. In this perspective, psychopathology emerges from the grief process ("complicated mourning") when the mourner does not "relinquish" the person who has died (Rando 1992–93).

Paralleling relational theory, contemporary grief theory has changed emphasis from a model of recovery that encourages disconnection and the detaching of the relationship to the deceased, to one that recognizes the efforts bereaved individuals engage in to maintain their relationships and connections with the deceased. Silverman (2000), Stroebe et al. (1992), and Noppe (2000) argue that earlier models of grief that value disengagement from the deceased stem from a twentieth-century social construction of grief that does not necessarily represent the grief experience of many people. It may be more typical of many to maintain their bonds with the deceased as they learn to renegotiate their lives without his or her physical presence (see Silverman and Nickman 1996). Such connections to the deceased have been observed in bereaved children (Normand, Silverman, and Nickman 1996), and the relationship continues to evolve as the child grows up: "We carry many relationships within us. A person does not always have to be present for us to feel connected. When the absence is the result of a death, it is necessary to change the nature of the relationship and find new ways of staying connected. As in life, relationships change shape and form as time passes but do not necessarily end" (Silverman 2000:105; see chapter 6, this volume).

Most of the scholarship on spousal bereavement and the maintenance of bonds are based on how women react to the loss of their husbands (Lopata 1996). Although yet to be studied, it also would be of interest to determine whether the "continuation of bonds" is more characteristic of women's grief than men's. Klass, Silverman, and Nickman (1996) suggest that both men and women remain connected to the deceased. What may differ, however, is the nature of this continued bond, whether such connections differentially affect men's and women's grief, and how the social support system interacts with an individual's need to remain connected to his or her deceased loved one. In particular, if for women, the self grows out of the relational context as is proposed by relational theory, it is important to explore how those relationships are maintained when one member has died, and how connections to the deceased and to living others can be growth enhancing in the face of loss.

As we recognize that there is no one set path in the journey of grief, we may learn that gender and ethnicity may also interact in the way in which continued connections with the deceased are formed. We know, for example, that many African Americans, Native Americans, and Asian Americans are intensely spiritual and meaningfully connected to their dead family members (Barrett 1993; Tanner 1995). Is it more important, from the family's perspective, for men or women to "speak" with the deceased, tend a memorial sanctuary, or keep the memory alive by recounting stories? Depending upon cultural beliefs, is it a taboo for either gender not to speak the name of the deceased? These all are important questions that must be answered if we truly are to recognize the diversity of grief responses in terms of the continuity of relationships with the dead.

DEATH AND GENDER: ISSUES FOR THE NEW MILLENNIUM

The events of the year 2001 are symbolic of a number of new challenges that face Americans as they are forced out of their death-avoidant complacency. Certainly trauma and grief take on new significance in the light of the tragic events of September 11. As a counterfoil to the startling reminders of our vulnerability to unexpected death, we as a society are faced with important end-of-life decisions such as caring for those with long-term illnesses and honoring requests for assisted suicide because of our ability to keep a person (or body) "alive" for an indefinite period of time.

It will take a long time to assess adequately the psychological consequences of the terrorist attacks on the World Trade Center and the Pentagon. In the days after the attacks, as commentary sped across the Internet, one popular email discussed how men were finally receiving their overdue recognition for acting in a manly manner— the heroism of the firemen, policemen, and those men who brought down the airplane in Pennsylvania were applauded as true expressions of masculinity. Times of great stress and confusion promote adherence to culturally defined belief systems that serve as a buffer for death anxiety (Pyszczynski, Greenberg, and Solomon 1997). Yet, these newer issues also present problems and issues that demand traversing uncharted waters toward resolution, and gender must be taken into consideration for many of these issues. Some of our newer, contemporary concerns that must consider gender in relation to dying and death are death in the workplace, assisted suicide, and trauma and sudden death.

The workplace presents a context in which both productive tasks and social interactions are central. The meaning and nature of work has changed radically during the past century, with one of the most dramatic changes being the increase in the number of women who work outside of the home. The higher numbers of women workers also include an increase in the number of women in positions of leadership, medicine, and other occupations once the province of men (United Nations 1991), but it does not mean that the workplace has achieved full equality. Rather, the workplace represents one of the most gender-segregated and gender-stratified arenas of adult daily life (Bose and Whaley 2001). Within this context, we must acknowledge that death does not stay away. Workers contending with the death of their colleagues, the loss of their family or friends, life-threatening illnesses, or the balance of work with caregiving responsibilities for seriously ill family members are a few of the instances in which death intrudes upon the workplace. Although there are a number of humane workplace environments that attend to the needs of their grieving workers, there also are many where employees experience insensitivity to their losses, expectations of former levels of productivity and interpersonal interactions, and a lack of social support (Hofsess 2002; Lattanzi-Licht 1999). The responses to these situations are equally as varied. With respect to grief, some people use work as a distraction from their sadness by vigorously plunging into projects, whereas others may find it difficult to concentrate and be productive (Doka 1999). What we have limited knowledge of is whether or not men and women react to such situations differently, and whether or not their social interactions and employer expectations are modified by gender. For example, do bereaved women get more social support in the workplace, or are they viewed with disdain if they remain in an emotion-focused coping strategy for longer than an employer and coworkers can tolerate? Are men expected to be task-oriented or "professional," even the day after a significant loss, the social context making it very difficult to express their grief (Lattanzi-Licht 1999)? Perhaps men use immersion in work as a primary coping strategy, as Cook found in her study of bereaved fathers: "Work was an escape. When I was at work I could put this part out of my mind, because I had to concentrate on what I was doing. I could get away when I was at work. . . . You try to tie into it and forget about things. . . . It kept my mind occupied" (1998:298).

Furthermore, if more women than men are expected to be the caregivers of their ailing family members, how tolerant is the workplace when conflicts arise? As Merdinger (1995) notes, the increased time and responsibilities of women at work has not decreased the amount of time that women spend caregiving for the terminally ill, adding to their burdens in the "second shift." For many women, the balance between the intense emotional investment of their caregiving at home and the demands of the job is a precarious one with any additional demand in either arena creating disequilibria and feeling that one is out of control (Stiver 1991). Women have a tendency in such situations to decrease the number of hours worked or to leave their employment altogether (Lattanzi-Licht 2002). Thus, in order to gain a more complete understanding of the impact of death within the workplace environment, it is important that gender be taken into consideration in terms of both research and policy.

Another issue facing the twenty-first century stems from our capacity to prolong life indefinitely. On an individual as well as societal basis, there has been a sense that the necessary ethical and moral decisions of end-of-life care have been far outpaced by medical technological advancements. The decisions that are required in these situations, such as whether to insert a feeding tube or withdraw life support, strike at the heart of the moral values underlying our personal philosophy of life. What sorts of cognitive processes are involved in such ethical decision making? Interestingly, one of the most generative theories of moral development comes from the work of feminist scholar Carol Gilligan (1982), who reconceptualized Lawrence Kohlberg's (1976) theory of moral development by examining the differing perspectives of men and women in their resolution of moral dilemmas. Her work came out of the concern that Kohlberg's highly influential theory suggested that women functioned at a lower level of moral decision making than men. Gilligan (1982) felt that the psychological reality of women centered on their connections to others. The moral dilemmas that women encounter and their moral decision making take on a modality that differs from that of men. According to Gilligan (1982; 1987), moral decision making can involve either an ethic/orientation of rights as reflected in a legalistic system of justice, or an ethic of care, in which the orientation is on the care and consideration of all who are involved in the moral decision. The former orientation is based on a separate view of self and other, as is characteristic of men. The latter, more common to women, emphasizes the role of self-in-relation to others, and an acknowledgement of the contextual complexities of interrelationships. For example, one of the most well known of Kohlberg's hypothetical moral dilemmas involves the case of Heinz, who stole a life-saving drug for his terminally ill wife. Whereas Kohlberg (1976) argued that the moral issues involved whether or not Heinz was obligated to uphold a social contract regarding theft, Gilligan argued that the moral dilemma also involved Heinz's obligation to care for the life of another. Empirical tests of Gilligan's theory have been equivocal (Walker 1995). The consensus is that men and women use both orientations in their decision making, with the modal domain expressed dependent upon the content of the moral dilemma presented. But it has also been found that men tend to find themselves more often in situations that involve issues of ethics of rights and responsibilities, and women in situations involving the ethics of care. It is apparent that gender issues in moral decision making have a direct parallel to the real-life moral dilemmas that men and women face in end-of-life decision making. Is it possible that men and women generally approach these issues from different perspectives? Do men view this as ultimately a question of whether or not one has a "right to die," or the social contractual view, and do women view such problems as involving a consideration of the needs of their families and an obligation not to be a burden, or the ethic of care view? Furthermore, is it possible that men and women are confronted with different concerns in their end-of-life decisions? For example, do more daughters serve as power of attorneys for heath care for their aging parents; do more men take on the lawyers when drawing up their wills and potential end-of-life treatments? Holding on to more traditional views of gender roles within the family, do men, as "heads of the household" or "family patriarchs" take on the ultimate responsibility for decisions about life-and-death treatment options in emergency situations (Cook 1988)? That people come to such important considerations with differing approaches, which may be tied to their gender socialization, must be taken into consideration in the education and counseling of individuals and families as they confront these issues.

Furthermore, concern over the needless prolonging of a low quality of life for those suffering from life-threatening illnesses has led to a more open debate about the ethical, religious, and legal validity of assisted suicide. There are many strong arguments both in favor of suicide with the assistance of another (such as a physician) and against such suicides. Thus far, only one state, Oregon, has passed legislation enabling, with many safeguards, assisted suicide. It is possible that gender may be a factor in individual decisions to use this end-of-life option. Concerns over the legalization of assisted suicide include the arguments that this would more likely be taken by the depressed (more common in women), those with minimal social support (more common in White elderly men), and those who do not wish to be burdens on their families (more women because they live longer). Assisted suicide may also look more appealing to women who typically do not resort to violent means of ending their lives (Kastenbaum 2001). Kastenbaum offers the suggestion that Jack Kevorkian, who sensationalized the thorny issues of assisted suicide, may have actually encouraged women in particular to seek out his "services." Currently we do not know how strong the gender bias may be and in what direction, although the latest report from Oregon (Oregon Department of Human Services 2002) indicates that for 2001, there was a slightly higher percentage of women than men who participated in the physician assisted suicide program.

Perhaps the most visible issue of today concerns the stress and trauma resulting from sudden and traumatic loss. Recent publications (Silver 2002) suggest that the events of September 11 may present serious challenges for individuals who reacted intensely to the tragic losses that occurred. For many, such as the bereaved family and friends and those involved in the rescue and clean-up efforts, the concern is that the long-term implications of these losses are yet to be seen. There is also concern that across the country signs of grief and mourning are still present from that terrible day. The unique losses of September 11, and many other types of losses from the sudden and traumatic death that accompanies deaths from violence, suicide, accidents, and natural disasters, place individuals at risk for complicated mourning (Rando 1996). According to Rando (1992–93, 1996) complicated mourning refers to the state in which the bereaved individual has difficulty accommodating the death in terms of recognizing the loss, experiencing the pain associated with grief and the memory of the deceased individual, and readjusting to the world without the physical presence of the deceased person. A number of factors have been identified that help to screen those at risk for complicated grief. These include the nature of the death, the support systems of the bereaved, the nature of the relationship of the deceased to the bereaved, the mourner's personal encounter with the death as well as perceived preventability. However, these factors have not been teased apart in terms of how gender may intersect with the responses to such deaths. For example, Martin and Doka (1996) point out that most models for treating people suffering from traumatic loss are based upon the "masculine" patterns of grief (i.e., problem-focused, regaining of self-control and early and short-term expressions of feelings). This is not surprising considering that many of these intervention programs were designed for individuals in high-risk situations such as the military, police, and firefighters, groups comprising mostly men. Thus, our views of complicated grief may be biased toward a male perspective, just as our views of "normal" grief may take on more of the coping strategies of females. However, Pine (1996) claims that social support is a major determinant of effective coping in such situations, yet grieving men typically do not seek out the comfort of others. The perception of preventability and the secondary losses associated with traumatic death, such as the loss of income or a mother for one's children, may also differentially affect men and women. Thus, it may be important to consider gender as a factor as we continue to consider the significance of theoretical and treatment models of the grief responses to these difficult situations.

GENDER AND DEATH: IMPLICATIONS FOR PRACTICE

In the preceding discussion of dying, death, and loss, a number of important inter-sections with gender have been explored. Because gender and death and dying are not only biological affairs, but human ones as well, both areas of study would be enriched were they to be more formally linked. Certainly there are "pockets" of mu-tuality at present, and these have tremendous implications for intervention, policy, and education.

Intervention efforts are most directly benefited when gender is considered. Because many models of intervention are either gender stereotyped, based upon one gender, or ignorant of gender differences, there is a great need to inform practitioners that modal responses may be more appropriate for one gender over the other. Without question, psychotherapeutic efforts are a way in which the translation into practice of research and theory on gender and on bereavement can have a direct and needed impact. It is not unusual that at some point during the course of therapy, loss issues emerge. Understanding how gender affects the process of coping can go a long way towards successful intervention. Consider, for example, what happened when Irene Stiver, a psychotherapist, supervised a psychology trainee who was working with "Jane," who requested help because she was having problems concentrating on the job: "She (Jane) thought her problems had something to do with the death of her mother, with whom she had been very close, over a year before. Jane became increas-ingly distraught and tearful. The trainee was very moved by Jane's story. At the end of the hour Jane asked if it would be possible for her to come to therapy twice a week" (Miller and Stiver 1997:13). Working from relational theory, Stiver was pleased that her trainee had set up a therapeutic context of mutual empathy, in which the loss was acknowledged, and relational connections between Jane and her deceased mother, and Jane and her therapist, were recognized. However, this approach was seriously questioned by another therapist, who viewed Jane as an "overly dependent person" whose difficulties in "separating from her mother may have resulted in an enmeshed relationship which contributed to her difficulties in adjusting to her mother's death" (Miller and Stiver 1997:13).

Although Miller and Stiver make the case that relational psychology may be applicable to both men and women, they draw upon their experiences with women in therapy to demonstrate how important relationships are to promoting psychological health and growth. The case of "Jane" aptly illustrates how bereavement counseling must take these efforts of connection with deceased loved ones seriously before any alleviation of the pain and distress of loss are to be attempted. Similarly, sensitivity to more "instrumental" or "problem-focused" styles of grieving must also be part of the psychotherapist's repertoire. A caseworker needs to understand that a grieving elderly man who has just lost his wife may have lost his only source of social support, that he may not feel comfortable presenting his emotions, and that his need to work in the garage may be his way of expressing his grief.

Peer support as a method of intervention has been shown to be very effective in helping those who have lost a spouse. At a time when grief counseling was nonexistent and relational theories emphasizing women's needs to form connections with others yet to be developed, Phyllis Silverman created the Widow-to-Widow program (1980, 1986) in which support was drawn from the members of the group who had similar experiences and were able to problem-solve within the context of mutual collaboration. Although women seem to be more inclined than men to use programs such as Widow-to-Widow, Silverman (1988) notes that when men do participate their responses are similar. (See chapter 12.)

Especially important is the recognition that caregivers in such emotionally charged situations also need support and understanding. Men and women who are hospice workers, in the medical field, and in social work need to be especially vigilant for signs of stress and burnout when working with the bereaved and/or traumatized. The common advice given to caregivers may also be more appropriate for women caregivers than for men. Caregivers are advised to seek out the support and encouragement of others, to avoid neglecting aspects of their lives besides work, and to accept their own helplessness in high-grief situations (Miller 1999). Certainly this advice may be of value to men as well, but it is also possible that alternative models of care, compatible with a more traditional "masculine" style, must be developed.

With regard to policy, it is imperative that the culture of the workplace become more sensitive to bereavement issues in general, and to the specific contexts in which men and women grieve in particular. Administrators and managerial staff need to have assistance in developing procedures and strategies that acknowledge that death will intrude upon the workday, that men and women may have to accommodate to different types of losses and cope with them in different ways, and that both genders are at risk of disenfranchisement if their individual responses are not responded to appropriately. The current legal and medical environment will continue to be presented with the complex ethics of the humane treatment of men and women at the end of their lives. It is important that those involved in the examination of these significant issues maintain a careful watch on whether men and women receive differential treatment for their degenerative illnesses, in the possible differences in the ways in which men and women frame their values in end-of-life decisions, and in how they respond to increasing pressures for the option for legalized assisted suicide. Finally, it is imperative that scholarly research on death be sensitive to gender and ethnic variations.

In addition to policy, there also are a number of educational implications in the study of death from the perspective of gender. Social workers who are interested in learning more about death and dying need to study this complex and significant dimension of life from a multidisciplinary perspective. Educating caregivers and interventionists that grief is socially constructed will promote understanding of the possible differences in the grief experiences of men and women, as well as on how grief is handled and understood in a social context. What needs to be taught is a greater appreciation of the *diversity* of ways in which men and women adapt to their losses (Silverman 1996). Furthermore, it is necessary to keep abreast of the latest theoretical understandings of responses to death as we continue to move away from earlier, simplistic notions of grief as a series of stages marching toward resolution. It is important that training in intervention encompass newer relational models of client-therapist interaction (Miller and Stiver 1997). Theoretical ideas about the continuing of bonds, and different styles of coping with grief, are enhanced when gender is factored into the equation.

Frequently, there is the admonition that we should not maximize the disparities between the sexes in the face of broad similarities. Certainly this is also true in men and women's experiences with death. Death and dying is a universal and unavoidable experience, and grief binds us all. It is imperative that we recognize the boundaries of our lives if we are to remain in touch with our basic sense of self (Feifel 1990). In many respects, the same also is true of gender. Yet, our understanding of death, and who we are as women and men, is also deeply rooted in the social constructions of place and time, and speak significantly to our collective and individual consciousness. And just as there may not be one "appropriate" way to be a man or a woman, despite the promotion of stages and phases, there may not be a one best way of "doing death" either (Feifel 1990).

REFERENCES

Anselmi, D. L., and A. L. Law, eds. 1998. *Questions of Gender*. Boston: McGraw-Hill.

Barrett, R. K. 1993. Psychocultural influences on African-American attitudes towards death, dying and funeral rites. In *Personal Care in an Impersonal World: A Multidimensional Look at Bereavement*, ed. J. D. Morgan, 216–230. Amityville, NY: Baywood.

Belenky, M. F., B. M. Clinchy, N. R. Goldberger, and J. M. Tarule. 1986. *Women's Ways of Knowing: The Development of Self, Voice, and Mind*. New York: Basic Books.

Benoliel, J. Q., and L. F. Degner. 1995. Institutional dying: A convergence of cultural values, technology, and social organization. In *Dying: Facing the Facts*, ed. H. Wass and R. A. Neimeyer, 117–141. Washington, DC: Taylor & Francis.

Bose, C. E., and R. B. Whaley. 2001. Sex segregation in the U.S. labor force. In *Gender Mosaics*, ed. D. Vannoy, 228–239. Los Angeles: Roxbury.

Canetto, S. S. 1992–93. She died for love and he for glory: Gender myths of suicidal behavior. *Omega* 26:1–17.

Canetto, S. S., and D. Lester, eds. *Women and Suicidal Behavior.* New York: Springer.

Cook, J. A. 1988. Dad's double binds. Rethinking fathers' bereavement from a men's studies perspective. *Journal of Contemporary Ethnography* 17:285–308.

Datell, A. R., and R. A. Neimeyer. 1990. Sex differences in death anxiety: Testing the emotional expressiveness hypothesis. *Death Studies* 14:1–11.

Doka, K. J. 1999. A primer on loss and grief. In *Living with Grief: At Work, at School, at Worship*, ed. J. D. Davidson and K. J. Doka, 5–12. Washington, DC: Hospice Foundation of America.

Feifel, H. 1990. Psychology and death: A meaningful rediscovery. *American Psychologist* 45:537–543.

Gilligan, C. 1982. *In a Different Voice: Psychological Theory and Women's Development.* Cambridge, MA: Harvard University Press.

———. 1987. Moral orientation and moral development. In *Women and Moral Theory*, ed. E. F. Kittay and D. T. Meyers, 19–33. Totowa, NJ: Rowman and Littlefield.

Glick, I., R. S. Weiss, and C. M. Parkes. 1974. *The First Year of Bereavement.* New York: Wiley.

Good, G. E., N. B. Sherrod, and M. G. Dillon. 2000. Masculine gender role stressors and men's health. In *Handbook of Gender, Culture, and Health*, ed. R. M. Eisler and M. Herson, 63–81. Mahwah, NJ: Lawrence Erlbaum.

Gurung, R. A. R., S. E. Taylor, M. Kemeny, and H. Myers. Forthcoming. "HIV is not my biggest problem": The impact of HIV, chronic burden, and SES on depression in women at risk for AIDS. *Annals of Behavioral Medicine.*

Hallam, E. A. 1996. Turning the hourglass: Gender relations at the deathbed in early modern Canterbury. *Mortality* 1:61–82.

Halpern, D. F., and S. Ikier. 2002. Causes, correlates, and caveats: Understanding the development sex differences in cognition. In *Biology, Society, and Behavior: The Development of Sex Differences in Cognition*, ed. A. McGillicuddy-De Lisi and R. De Lisi, 3–19. Westport, CT: Ablex.

Hofsess, R. 2002. Grief and loss in the workplace. *The Forum* 28:1–3.

Hyde, J. S. 1994. Should psychologists study gender differences? Yes, with some guidelines. *Feminism and Psychology* 4:507–512.

Kastenbaum, R. 2000. *The Psychology of Death.* 3d ed. New York: Springer.

Klass, D., P. R. Silverman, and S. L. Nickman, eds. 1996. *Continuing Bonds: New Understandings of Grief.* Washington, DC: Taylor & Francis.

Kohlberg, L. 1976. Moral stages and moralization: The cognitive-developmental approach. In *Moral Development and Behavior: Theory, Research, and Social Issues*, ed. T. Lickona, 31–53. New York: Holt, Rinehart and Winston.

Lattanzi-Licht, M. E. 1999. Grief in the workplace: Supporting the grieving employee. In *Living with Grief: At Work, at School, at Worship*, ed. J. D. Davidson and K. J. Doka, 17–26. Washington, DC: Hospice Foundation of America.

———. 2002. Grief and the workplace: Positive approaches. In *Disenfranchised Grief: New Directions, Challenges, and Strategies for Practice*, ed. K. J. Doka, 167–180. Champaign, IL: Research Press.

Leming, M. R., and G. E. Dickinson. 1998. *Understanding Dying, Death, and Bereavement.* 4th ed. Fort Worth, TX: Harcourt Brace.

Lopata, H. Z. 1996. Widowhood and husband sanctification. In *Continuing Bonds: New Understandings of Grief*, ed. D. Klass, P. R. Silverman, and S. L. Nickman, 149–162. Washington, DC: Taylor & Francis.

Marks, A., and T. Piggee. 1998–99. Obituary analysis and describing a life lived: The impact of race, gender, age, and economic status. *Omega* 38:37–57.

Martin, T. L., and K. J. Doka. 1996. Masculine grief. In *Living with Grief After Sudden Loss*, ed. K. J. Doka, 161–171. Washington, DC: Hospice Foundation of America.

——. 2000. *Men Don't Cry . . . Women Do: Transcending Gender Stereotypes of Grief*. Philadelphia: Brunner/Mazel.

Maybury, K. K. 1995–96. Invisible lives: Women, men and obituaries. *Omega* 32:27–37.

McGillicuddy-De Lisi, A., and R. De Lisi, eds. 2002. *Biology, Society, and Behavior. The Development of Sex Differences in Cognition*. Westport, CT: Ablex.

Merdinger, J. M. 1995. Women, death, and dying. In *A Cross-cultural Look at Death, Dying, and Religion*, ed. J. K. Perry and A. S. Ryan, 1–8. Chicago: Nelson-Hall.

Miller, J. B. 1976. *Toward a New Psychology of Women*. Boston: Beacon Press.

——. 1991. The development of women's sense of self. In *Women's Growth in Connection*, ed. J. V. Jordan, A. G. Kaplan, J. B. Miller, I. P. Stiver, and J. L. Surrey, 11–26. New York: Guilford.

Miller, J. B., and I. P. Stiver. 1997. *The Healing Connection: How Women Form Relationships in Therapy and Life*. Boston: Beacon Press.

Miller, J. E. 1999. If I am not for myself: Caring for yourself as a caregiver for those who grieve. In *Living with Grief: At Work, at School, and at Worship*, ed. J. D. Davidson and K. J. Doka, 213–223. Washington, DC: Hospice Foundation of America.

Moss, M.S., N. Resch, and S. Z. Moss. 1997. The role of gender in middle-age children's responses to parent death. *Omega* 35:43–65.

National Hospice Organization. 1993. *1992 Annual Report*. Arlington, VA: National Hospice Organization.

Neimeyer, R. A. 2001. *Meaning Reconstruction and the Experience of Loss*. Washington, DC: American Psychological Association.

——. 2002. Traumatic loss and the reconstruction of meaning. *Journal of Palliative Medicine* 5(6): 935–942.

Neimeyer, R. A., and Moore, M. K. Validity and reliability of the Multidimensional Fear of Death Scale. In *Death Anxiety Handbook*, ed. R. A. Neimeyer, 103–120. Washington, DC: Taylor & Francis.

Noppe, I. C. 1999. Death and women. In *Women's Studies Encyclopedia*, ed. H. Tierney. Westport, CT: Greenwood Press.

——. 2000. Beyond broken bonds and broken hearts: The bonding of theories of attachment and grief. *Developmental Review* 20:514–538.

Normand, C. L., P. R. Silverman, and S. L. Nickman. 1996. Bereaved children's changing relationships with the deceased. In *Continuing Bonds: New Understandings of Grief*, ed. D. Klass, P. R. Silverman, and S. L. Nickman, 87–111. Washington, DC: Taylor & Francis.

Oregon Department of Human Services. 2002. Fourth annual report on Oregon's Death with Dignity Act. www.ohd.hr.state.or.us/chs/pas/ar~smmry.htm.

Pine, V. R. 1996. Social psychological aspects of disaster death. In *Living with Grief After Sudden Loss*, ed. K. J. Doka, 103–116. Washington, DC: Hospice Foundation of America.

Pyszczynski, T., J. Greenberg, and S. Solomon. 1997. Why do we need what we need? A terror management perspective on the roots of human social motivation. *Psychological Inquiry* 8:1–20.

Radtke, H. L., M. Hunter, and H. J. Stam. 2000. In memoriam as in life: Gender and psychology in the obituaries of eminent psychologists. *Canadian Psychology* 41:213–229.

Rando, T. A. 1992–93. The increasing prevalence of complicated mourning: The onslaught is just beginning. *Omega* 26:43–59.

——. 1996. Complications of mourning traumatic death. In *Living with Grief After Sudden Loss*, ed. K. J. Doka, 139–159. Washington, DC: Hospice Foundation of America.

Robinson, D. 1995. *Saving Graces: Images of Women in European Cemeteries*. New York: Norton.

Sherif, C. W. 1982. Needed studies in the concept of gender identity. *Psychology of Women Quarterly* 6:375–398.

Sikkema, K. J., L. I. Wanger, and L. M. Bogart. 2000. Gender and cultural factors in the prevention of HIV infection among women. In *Handbook of Gender, Culture, and Health*, ed. R. M. Eisler and M. Herson, 299–319. Mahwah, NJ: Lawrence Erlbaum.

Silver, R. C. 2002. Grief after traumatic loss. *Facts of Life: Issue Briefing for Health Reporters* 7:2–3.

Silverman, P. R. 1980. *Mutual Help Groups: Organization and Development*. Beverly Hills, CA: Sage.

——. 1986. *Widow to Widow*. New York: Springer.

——. 1988. In search of new selves: Accommodating to widowhood. In *Families in Transition: Primary Programs That Work*, ed. L. A. Bond and B. Wagner, 200–219. Newbury Park, CA: Sage.

——. 1996. Introduction. In *Widower: When Men Are Left Alone*, ed. S. Campbell and P. R. Silverman, 1–16. Amityville, NY: Baywood.

——. 2000. *Never Too Young to Know: Death in Children's Lives*. New York: Oxford University Press.

Silverman, P. R., and S. L. Nickman, eds. 1996. *Continuing Bonds: New Understandings of Grief*. Washington, DC: Taylor & Francis.

Spencer, R. 2000. A comparison of relational psychologies. Paper presented at the Colloquium Series of the Stone Center for Developmental Services and Studies, Wellesley College.

Spilka, B., G. Lacey, and B. Gelb. 1979. Sex discrimination after death: A replication, extension and a difference. *Omega* 10:227–233.

Stillion, J. 1985. *Death and the Sexes: An Examination of Differential Longevity, Attitudes, Behaviors, and Coping Skills*. Washington, DC: Hemisphere.

Stiver, I. P. 1991. Work inhibitions in women. In *Women's Growth in Connection*, ed. J. V. Jordan, A. G. Kaplan, J. B. Miller, I. P. Stiver, and J. L. Surrey, 223–236. New York: Guilford.

Stroebe, M., M. M. Gergen, K. J. Gergen, and W. Stroebe. 1992. Broken hearts or broken bonds: Love and death in historical perspective. *American Psychologist* 47:1205–1212.

Stroebe, M., R. O. Hansson, W. Stroebe, and H. Schut. 2001. Future directions for bereavement research. In *Handbook of Bereavement Research*, ed. M. S. Stroebe, R. O. Hansson, W. Stroebe, and H. Schut, 741–766. Washington, DC: American Psychological Association.

Stroebe, M., W. Stroebe, and H. Schut. 2001. Gender differences in adjustment to bereavement: An empirical and theoretical review. *Review of General Psychology* 5:62–83.

Surrey, J. L. 1991. The self-in-relation: A theory of women's development. In *Women's Growth in Connection*, ed. J. V. Jordan, A. G. Kaplan, J. B. Miller, I. P. Stiver, and J. L. Surrey, 51–66. New York: Guilford.

Tanner, J. G. 1995. Death, dying, and grief in the Chinese-American culture. In *A Cross-cultural Look at Death, Dying, and Religion*, ed. J. K. Perry and A. S. Ryan, 183–192. Chicago: Nelson-Hall.

Taylor, S. E., L. C. Klein, B. P. Lewis, et al. 2000. Biobehavioral responses to stress in females: Tend-and-befriend, not-fight-or-flight. *Psychological Review* 107:411–429.

Unger, R. K. 2001. *Handbook of the Psychology of Women and Gender*. New York: Wiley.

United Nations. 1991. *The World's Women 1970–1990: Trends and Statistics*. New York: United Nations.

Walker, C. 1982. Attitudes to death and bereavement among cultural minority groups. *Nursing Times* 9:2106–2108.

Walker, L. J. 1995. Sexism in Kohlberg's moral psychology? In *Moral Development: An Introduction*, ed. W. M. Kurtines and J. L. Gewirtz, 83–107. Boston: Allyn & Bacon.

Weigand, C. G., and P. C. Weigand. 1991. Death and mourning among the Huicholes of western Mexico. In *Coping with the Final Tragedy: Cultural Variation in Dying and Grieving*, ed. D. R. Counts and D. A. Counts, 53–68. Amityville, NY: Baywood.

Williams, D. R., D. T. Takeuchi, and R. K. Adair. 1992. Marital status and psychiatric disorders among blacks and whites. *Journal of Health and Social Behavior* 33:140–157.

Wisocki, P. A., and J. Skowron. 2000. The effects of gender and culture on adjustment to widowhood. In *Handbook of Gender, Culture, and Health,* ed. R. M. Eisler and M. Herson, 429–447. Mahwah, NJ: Lawrence Erlbaum.

12

BEREAVEMENT: A TIME OF TRANSITION AND CHANGING RELATIONSHIPS

PHYLLIS R. SILVERMAN

THIS CHAPTER presents a view of bereavement that reflects some of the complexity of the grieving process, thus creating a broad framework for understanding how people cope with death. In the English language there are three words used to describe this process: grief, mourning, and bereavement. Grief typically refers to the ways in which people express the feelings that arise after a death: sadness, crying, despair. Mourning has been defined as the mental work following the loss of a loved one. Altschul (1988) defines mourning as the psychological process by which an individual adapts to the loss of a loved one. To this I would add a third element—the social process including the cultural traditions and rituals that guide behavior after a death. Bowlby (1980) emphasized these in his definition of mourning. Bereavement refers to the state of having experienced a loss. None of these words reflects the fullness of what a death introduces into the life of an individual, family, or community. This is why grief, mourning, and bereavement are words that are often used interchangeably, perhaps because one aspect of a person's reaction to loss cannot be understood fully without the other. Therefore, in this chapter I use these words interchangeably to describe effectively the mourning process and all that this involves as people cope with a death. The emphasis is on the larger context in which people are living and how this context frames and focuses their grief and provides them with support and guidance.

Grief is seen as a normal, expected period of transition in the life cycle that is associated not only with strong feelings but also with change. All of us who are engaged with and attached to others will experience grief. It is important when we speak of grief not to talk about "them" but about "us." Grief and loss touch every person's life. Loss is not simply something that happens to us. Loss is something that we must make sense out of, give meaning to, and respond to. When grief may seem to engulf us, we may feel that we have no control over what is happening. Grief is, in fact, something we live through and learn to deal with.

Looking at the grieving process, Tom Attig (1996) asks: How do we relearn the world? People who are mourning learn to cope not only with extreme feelings stirred in response to the absence of the deceased but also with a changed social context. When the deceased is no longer a living presence, we learn to construct another type of relationship with the deceased, as well as a new relationship with ourselves and the world. Each aspect of this process influences the others. Thus, when a person is grieving, change is a constant companion as well. Mourning does not end, we do not "recover." Rather, we adapt, accommodate, change. Making an accommodation is an active process directed at what, for some, can be seen as a new beginning (Silverman 1988, 2000).

Rarely is there a single mourner. There is the family, and there is the community, and all of these will affect how grief is expressed, understood, and experienced. To capture the fullness of the grieving process, this chapter is divided into three sections. Each interacts with the other. The first two sections focus on the relational and developmental aspects of grief that will help understand the nature and direction of the changes mourners experience. The third section explores looks at grief as a life-cycle transition.

THE RELATIONAL CONTEXT

We are social creatures. Our relationships frame and focus who we are and who we become. Charmaz (1994), using the theoretical perspective of symbolic interactionism, observes that society, reality, and the self are socially created through an interactive process. As an extension of this point of view, a relational paradigm of grief suggests that grief is an interactive process involving multiple mourners and others in the life of these mourners. People's worldviews need to be considered as well as how mutuality and interdependence are recognized and supported in this view. It is also critical to understand the bereaved person's relationship to the deceased, and what has been lost when this person died. Neimeyer (1997) describes a constructivist point of view, in which human beings are seen as meaning-makers, striving to punctuate, organize, and anticipate their engagement with the world by arranging it in themes that express their particular cultures, families, and personalities. How people construct meaning also relates to where they are developmentally, from both cognitive and emotional perspectives. Both cognitive and emotional development are processes that continue from childhood through old age to death and are important factors shaping how we understand and react to a death.

All of the parts in this interactive process of bereavement can be characterized as voices in the mourners' world. These voices, as they come together, influence how all the players react (those who are mourning as well as those who want to help). Voice is a metaphor for understanding a person's worldview, her place in it, and the influence of others (Gilligan 1993). Who are these voices? They include:

1.   The family with its various members, whose roles are changed with the death. It is important to consider their relationships to each other, both positive and negative, now as well as in the past. Age, developmental position, gender, and place in the family's life cycle make a difference in the roles that members adopt or are assigned. Individual characteristics (i.e., personality traits and character structure) make a difference in how family members relate to one another and what they experience as lost when the member dies.

2. The cultural or societal values, attitudes, and mores of the larger society in which family/mourners live frame and give direction to their grief.

3. A mourner's faith system directs how he or she gives meaning to death in general and this death in particular.

4. Community resources may provide support and care. The community also establishes values and attitudes toward bereavement that affect the resources that are available. Does the mourner's community see bereavement as an illness from which the bereaved must recover, or do they view grief as an expected life-cycle event to which mourners must accommodate?

5. The deceased's voice is present as well. The deceased's role in the family needs to be considered, as does his or her legacy and the relationship that is lost and its impact on the mourners.

The conversations between these voices give direction to the grief and are reflected in how mourners give meaning to their grief as individuals and as families. Some voices will have more status than others; some may be too timid to speak or too muted to be heard. Is the mourner aware of these "voices"? Do those trying to help pay attention to who speaks out, who is heard, who says what they mean, who is silent, and who is silenced (Belenky et al. 1996). For example, in the words of a widow of several years: "When my husband was alive, I deferred to him. Sometimes, as I look back on it now, it was as if I didn't have a voice. I'm not sure that's how he wanted it, but only now can I see that that was how it was. I guess that was how I saw my role in those days. Now I speak out and speak up and people listen in ways I hadn't expected."

Multiple voices present in any one mourner's life can be seen as the variables that need to be considered in understanding a particular person's reactions to a death. It is never a simple linear picture. The intensity and the nature of the mourner's responses will differ depending on who died, the mourner's relationship to that person, what is considered appropriate behavior in his or her culture, how he or she makes meaning of the death, and how family roles are defined and experienced. In considering the consequences of a death, it is important to recognize that, for any one mourner, there are always multiple losses involved. More than a life is lost. A relationship is also lost. A self in that relationship is lost and a way of living and relating to life has been is lost, as well.

RELATIONSHIPS IN A DEVELOPMENTAL CONTEXT

It is difficult to understand how people cope with death, how they make meaning out of the death and their loss, as well as the changes they make as they mourn without examining aspects of where they are developmentally.

What do we mean by a developmental perspective? Development can be seen as a life long, evolutionary process (Hetherington and Baltes 1988). Typically we associate development with children, where it is easy to chart emotional and cognitive movement with physical development. However, although not always as dramatic physically, in such a short period of time, for adults, it is a process that continues throughout the life cycle. It is important to look at the inner and outer motion of adults' lives and its direction. Where an adult is developmentally influences what he or she experiences as lost, how the lost relationship frames his or her sense of self, and how this self in relationship may change. In the words of a young widow: "I realize I love and am loved by many people. They have confidence in me and I in myself. Slowly I am trying to shed fear, guilt and overconcern about what other people think. I am working on many facets of what I hope will be changes in life style and personal growth" (Silverman 1988:232). This is an active, evolving process of change, leading to a new way of relating to themselves and to others.

Piaget (1954) observed how children change and evolve as they mature and develop, especially in terms of how they see themselves. A child's growing sense of self is intimately related to her growing ability to reflect on her own behavior and the role of others in her life. As their senses of self emerge and change, children develop different ways of organizing and making sense of their experiences, often revisiting them at different points in the life cycle. Scarr (1982) suggests that each person has her own developmental trajectory. This is supported by other research (Lerner 1989) that has demonstrated that the content and order of stages of development will be altered by the child's experiences and the context in which he lives. This is what leads to the child's individuality. This is equally true for adults. Nothing is set in stone.

Development is not something we do alone (Bruner 1989). The interaction of genetic dispositions and experiences, and the interaction of the individual with significant others and with her culture, all contribute to how this individual understands her experiences and what she may do with them. For example, members of a mutual-help organization for the widowed said that change took place as they learned how others coped and met people who could accept their tears and who gave them information that helped them find new perspective and direction (Silverman 1988).

Development implies movement, but one does not grow physically, emotionally, intellectually, spiritually, and socially in an even manner, or necessarily always follow the same patterns. Although developmental motion is often divided into stages or phases, individuals are not their stages of development. If we want to understand a given child or adult, we need to capture the direction of his or her movement, the meaning she or he makes out of this movement at this time, and the nature of the interaction between the person and his or her world (Kegan 1982). White (1959) wrote that the concern of children is not, as Freud suggested, to tame their impulses but to help them to learn to interact with the world in more and more complex ways. According to Piaget (1954), there is an ongoing conversation between individuals and their world that leads to a process of adaptation and assimilation. As children mature, their capacities to be aware of the environment that exists beyond their immediate view increases. At each stage children's understanding reflects not only an ability to observe the external properties of the world around them or their experience with it, but also the ability to observe the properties of their minds that help them compose order and make sense of their experience. This process applies to what the bereaved, who are not at the same development level, are experiencing. As they cope with a death and experience the need to change, this developmental process gives direction to how they will move to understand what needs doing now and how others fit into their lives.

Following Piaget's lead, Kegan (1994) sees development as a move toward greater complexity and coherence in the way both children and adults structure relationships between themselves and others. Both adults and children move in the direction of an increasing ability to grasp the relational complexity in his or her immediate world and in the world beyond. Children, adolescents, and adults develop cognitive skills that facilitate their developing a richer perspective on themselves and others. This allows them to move from an egocentric understanding in which the world revolves around them toward a perspective of greater mutuality. As adults we become more capable of negotiating and renegotiating our relationships. This is what the bereaved need to do. In the words of widower several years after his wife died: "I am more understanding of others. I am determined to live out my years in a mood of kindness to others" (Silverman 1988:232).

Children initially do not have the ability to differentiate themselves from others clearly (Kegan 1982). Their feelings and their motivations are subject to their limited ability to look in on their own behavior, to reflect on their feelings and thoughts and to understand others as people in their own right. For example, an eight-year-old did not want to go to school several months after his father's death. He explained to his mother that he hated his friend because his friend told him that if his father died he would be crying all the time. Our eight-year-old felt hurt and criticized until his mother explained that his friend was just trying to understand (Silverman 2000:54). He could not separate his experience from his friend's expectations. His solution was to withdraw. He and his friend did not yet have the cognitive reasoning that would help them deal with their differences. Many adults experience similar discomfort. They struggle to relieve themselves from the advice of well meaning friends that they feel obligated to follow. In the words of a father whose child had died: "We stopped seeing some people. They have advice and get upset when we don't agree with what they are suggesting. It is easier this way."

The role of others in the child's life changes as they move forward in this evolving process. Over time they develop an increasing ability to know that others have a point of view separate from their own, and that two points of view can coexist. By the time children reach late adolescence, they should be able to see the possibility of having more than one point of view at the same time. A fifteen-year-old reflected on the meaning of death after his father died, describing how he came to the decision that his father is in heaven: "I know some people don't believe that there is life after death. I was taught that there is. I've thought about this and I decided that I believe the soul lives on in heaven, and that's where my father is." He is able to reflect on these different belief systems and come to his own decision. For adolescents relationships with themselves and others can change in dramatic ways. However, not all adolescents have reached the point where they have these abilities, nor have many adults.

This developmental process becomes a key aspect of the mourning process, affecting how people seek meaning and direction in their grief. This movement is not so much hierarchical or even sequential in nature, but is a spiraling process (Kegan 1982).

What people experience as loss depends on how they see the role of others in their lives: not only the deceased, but also people in their family and in their community. Is everything seen as happening to them in an egocentric way: "She died on me"? Can they look at the larger, more complex picture, at their own sadness and at what the deceased lost as well? Can they negotiate their needs with the needs of another person? Can they see the complexity associated with the death and its meaning in their lives? These abilities bring with them a growing self-awareness or consciousness that leads to an increase in the mourner's ability to visit their own experiences, that is, to look in and reflect on what is happening to them, to be both the performer and the audience to their own performance (White and Epson 1990). In the words of a mother after her son was murdered: "Before this happened I was a quiet housewife. I would never say a word in public. I too was frightened to argue even when I knew someone was wrong. My husband asked, not long after our son was murdered, we have to decide: are we going to be part of the problem or part of the solution? Over the past few years I almost don't recognize myself. I realized that if I didn't speak out nothing would change. I found that I could make a difference. People listen, I listen. It's like I'm a new person."

This new sense of self can appear to be a more independent person. However, what we are looking at is a more interactive process based a new mutuality. Selman and Shultz (1990) define the capacity for autonomy as the ability to understand, coordinate, and negotiate one's own needs with the needs of another person. Autonomy is not defined as independence from others. Rather, it is the ability to recognize the need for others and the needs of others, and to participate in interdependent relationships that reflect newfound abilities to understand others as well as oneself.

While the ability to know the other may grow and change in a bereaved adult, it is more dramatic in children. As children mature physically and emotionally, the ways in which they experience and construct loss changes. As this changes, so does their relationship to themselves. Thus, over time they mourn a different loss and have a different capacity to do so. For example, a child of four who loses an older sibling may feel the loss of a playmate, of someone who did things with her that her parents would not do. She may even feel a bit of pleasure that she no longer has to share her parents' attention. By the time she is an adolescent, she will experience the loss in many new ways. She now understands that she lost someone with whom to share her life story; she lost a companion, a buddy, and a role model. She may also appreciate how much her sibling lost by dying so young. The child's ability to hold an image of the deceased will also change as the child changes. Dealing with death is not a static process. There is a constant interaction and change over time as the mourners deal with these experiences, as they mature, and as these developmental processes are affected by the death.

This view of development can also serve as a guide for looking at adult development. Many adults still have difficulty taking the point of view of others. They organize the world primarily to meet their needs or live on the other side of making deals as a nine or ten year old might (Kegan 1982). An older widower provides us with an example of someone who saw his wife's death as an abandonment. His sense of self did not include his being able to take care of himself, or see another person's point of view. Almost like a preteen, he saw others in terms of what they could do for him. Two years after his wife's death, he reflects on his life. He appears not to have moved: "My wife took care of me. My life is in chaos. I really counted on her, until she got sick and died on me. I'm not sure what to do. It's awful. My children say not to worry they will step in. My daughter brings me lunch every day. It's the least I can expect. Someone had the nerve to suggest that I could learn to cook."

Relational development is not tied to age. Some adults do not think abstractly, and they cannot generalize to see beyond their own immediate world. We see an example of this in adults who focus only on their own feelings and what they lost. They cannot see other people's grief or move beyond themselves to deal with a changed world. This becomes particularly problematic when there are bereaved children in a family and the surviving parent cannot appreciate that they are grieving as well (Silverman 2000).

Kegan (1983) describes the evolving capacity of the individual to author his own identity and organize his sense of self so that he feels empowered to deal with his own life. Empowerment may be a key concept here. For example, a high school senior described a new sense of self that she found after both her mother and her sister died in an automobile accident: "I had two choices and one was not even a choice. I could sit in my room for the rest of my life and cry 'poor me.' But I said no, I have to go on, in honor of them. I had to accept that I'm not going to have a sister. . . . I don't fight it anymore, it has really changed me" (Silverman 2000:163).

With this new sense of self a mourner can develop what Kegan calls "interpersonal mutuality." Sometimes new experience is assimilated into what Kegan calls the old "grammar," leading to one kind of accommodation. However, when it is impossible to assimilate the new experience into the old, then the accommodation leads to a new "grammar," or to what Piaget calls a "new schema" (Marris 1974; Silverman 1982). This conversation (often with ourselves) is marked by periods of stability and periods of dynamic instability. The time after a death is clearly a time of marked instability. The processes of assimilation and accommodation are essential parts of how we change and in many ways essential to the process of development over the life cycle. They are also a key part of the bereavement process. The ability of mourners to reflect on their own behavior and to understand the behavior of others will make a huge difference in how they cope with a death and their subsequent grief.

These relational and developmental views help to identify the direction of developmental change the bereaved are dealing with and the nature of that change that empowers them and facilitates their accommodate to the death.

A TIME OF TRANSITION

Grief has been characterized as a period of transition (Bowlby 1961; Parkes 1996; Silverman 2000). Marris (1974) called this a time of loss and change. This time of transition consists of many crises and periods of stress.

Strong and extreme feelings and reactions after a loss are appropriate. They should not be judged and labeled as problematic or symptomatic of an illness. The mourner's efforts to identify and respond to all the changes that he or she is experiencing are clear causes of stress. Mourners are often unaware that grief is so pervasive and so disruptive to the world they had known. Mourners need support and assistance from others, and they need to learn that they will not be "cured" of this "malady." There are bumps, derailments, disappointments, stressors, and bad moments in life that cannot be avoided or prevented, and this is one of them. Energy needs to be devoted to learning that adversity is also part of the life cycle and to learning how to manage this adversity.

There are some deaths that can be more distressing or traumatic for those who are grieving, than others. These include very sudden deaths, deaths caused by war and disasters, deaths that mutilate the body, and deaths that are self-induced. Altschul (1988) quotes Freud as saying that trauma is any experience that calls up distressing affects such as those of fright, anxiety, shame, or physical pain and that challenge the resources of the victims' ego. Van der Kolk, McFarlane, and Weisaeth (1996) define a traumatic event as one that disrupts and creates great stress in the individual where his or her own resources are inadequate to respond effectively. Almost any death, expected or unexpected, can be for the moment traumatic, even more so in a society where death is not accepted as a normal part of the life cycle and where there are few resources available to help the mourners cope.

The events of September 11, 2001, traumatized our nation and left a trail of mourners whose reactions we are just beginning to comprehend. This experience highlights the need to understand how trauma and grief come together in mourners. Perhaps, in the long run, mourners have more in common with each other than we realize, regardless of the cause of the death. There is no straight line between being bereaved and making an accommodation to the loss. It is impossible to take away the pain, although for most people as they learn to cope in new ways with the loss and the changes in their lives the intensity lessens with time. Over time mourners learn to make accommodations. To propose that they recover or get over their grief seems to be incompatible with their experience.

The concept of transition provides a way of mapping the experience of the bereaved as it changes over time (Bowlby 1961; Silverman 1966). When does the time of transition begin? We can say it begins with the death itself. When a death is anticipated there may be a preview or a foreshadowing of what life will be like afterward. Nonetheless, in reality, we cannot really deal with death until it happens. There is a quality of the unexpected in even the most anticipated death. The transition does not have an ending date because the bereaved continue to renegotiate the meaning of the loss for the rest of their lives. As part of this process, mourners develop new perspectives on their feelings and experience, reach a sense of how to live with the loss, and, depending on who died, live differently in the world.

The transition takes place on several levels, and not necessarily in any order. Individual mourners and their families find that they must develop resources and discover new capacities in themselves for dealing with changes in their feelings, in the way they live in the world and in their relationship to themselves and others. This can be described as developing a new sense of self and is a part of what happens to mourners over time. The bereaved also find that their relationship to the deceased does not end. They develop a continuing bond, keeping the deceased in their lives in a variety of ways. In the following sections, each of these parts of the transition— the developing a new sense of self, a continuing bond with the deceased, and another view of time—will be examined in more detail.

A NEW SENSE OF SELF

A period of transition always involves a turning point: a change in status, a role shift, a new sense of self, which, as noted earlier, often involves moving from one developmental place to another in order to live in a changed world (Silverman 1966, 1986, 1988; Lopata 1973). Parkes (1996) calls this a period of transformation. Assigned family roles often shift and new roles evolve as family members realize that the self that interacted with the deceased is lost.

There are many definitions of the concept of "self." Basch (1983) speaks of the self as the uniqueness that separates the experiences of an individual from those of all others, while at the same time conferring a sense of cohesion and continuity on the disparate experiences of that individual throughout his life. The self has the ability to process and connect experiences, to direct behavior, to know who we are and what we are doing. As noted in the section on development, it is clearly intertwined with how people define themselves in relationship to others and how they include others into their lives.

Mead (1930) said that we can only know ourselves as we know others, and as they know us and reflect back to us who we are. This way of looking at the self is important in understanding bereavement in a relational context as referred to earlier. A new self in new relationships evolves (Kegan 1982). Youniss writes, quoting Piaget, "There are no such things as isolated individuals. There are only relations. There is no self outside relations because the self can only know itself in reference to other selves. The child is said not to concentrate on discrete actions, per se. but to contend with interpersonal interactions. From the start, meaning is social rather than private" (1980:4).

Clinchy (1996) reminds us that the self is not something finished that one carries about from one relationship to the next. Selves-in-process are always being co-constructed and reconstructed in the context of new relationships. When someone dies, what is mourned are both the lost relationship and the self as reflected in that relationship. For example, a year after her husband died, one mother reflected on the multiple roles she had held, one of which was still intact: "I am John's mother, but I feel like I don't know who I am anymore now that Jim is dead. If I am not his wife, then who am I?" (Silverman 2000:46).

The part of herself that was embedded in her role as wife and therefore in her relationship to her husband needed to be constructed in a new way, in a new direction. She was at a place developmentally where she could see the problem and begin to understand what she needed to do. She continued to know herself as a mother, an active role in her life. However, she lost the self, as reflected in her feelings, purpose in life, and set of behaviors, that she knew in her relationship with her husband.

CONNECTING TO THE DECEASED

Letting go of the deceased, putting the past behind, has often been recommended as the preferred way to resolve grief in order to be able to invest in new relationships. In fact, this is a paradoxical situation. We cannot live in the past, and we cannot live as before, as if the deceased is still part of our life. However, as we listen to the voices of the bereaved, we realize that while death takes away the possibility of a living relationship with the deceased, both children and adults seem to find ways of constructing connections that are both comforting and sustaining (Pincus 1974; Klass 1988; Silverman and Silverman 1979; Silverman and Worden 1992; Rubin 1992; Normand, Silverman, and Nickman 1996; Klass, Silverman, and Nickman 1996; Silverman 2000). Mourning is what we do within ourselves to transform our relationship to the deceased (Attig 1996). Transformation is very different from detachment. These connections and constructions, in children and adults, change the mourners' identities over time after the death in ways that are consistent with the developmental trajectories described above (Silverman and Nickman 1996; Conant 1996).

Constructing a relationship to the deceased is typically part of an interactive process with other mourners, in the family and in the community (Silverman and Klass 1996). The support and shared memories of others help give the construction shape and direction (Nickman, Silverman, and Normand 1998). One father, after his son was murdered, described how the extended family and community played an integral role in this process: "Every Christmas we go to a shelter where we give presents to the children in our son's memory. Instead of shopping with the list he collected from all the relatives, we have a list from the shelter children. We feel close to him, and we talk about him with these children. Keeping his memory alive this way is very important to us."

Silverman and Nickman (1996) identified the elements from which children construct a relationship to the deceased. Children identified a place where the deceased could be found, such as in heaven; they experienced him/her in their dreams and as watching over them; they sensed his or her presence; they reached out to the deceased by visiting the grave, initiating conversations, thinking about him or her, and keeping things that belonged to the deceased. In fact, both parents and children utilize these same ways of constructing a bond with the deceased. From these patterns a relationship is constructed. In the words of a young widow: "I find it helpful to go to the cemetery and just go over the day with my husband and let him know how the children are doing. Sometime I complain about how tough things were and I ask him for advice."

Normand (1994) identified four clusters in the ways that the children she studied, ages twelve to fifteen, constructed a relationship to their deceased parents: seeing the parent as a visiting ghost; holding on to memories from the past; maintaining an interactive relationship; and becoming a living legacy. Normand demonstrated that these relationships were not constant but changed over time. She found that many children moved from one type of connection to another. A small group, by the end of the second year after the death, talked of themselves in what could be understood as their parent's legacy. A twelve-year-old said she acted in ways to please her father. He was still a part of her: "I try out things, at school and in sports. I am not as smart as he was. I like sports just to please him. I want him to be proud of me" (Normand, Silverman, and Nickman 1996:100).

Marwit and Klass (1996) identified how continuing bonds with the deceased influenced the lives of college students. The deceased served as role models, provided situation specific guidance, helped clarify values, and gave the survivors pleasure as they remembered them. In this way the deceased continued to play an active role in the lives of those who mourned them.

CHANGE OVER TIME

Responding to any loss takes place over time. It is with time that people mobilize and utilize their inner resources and the resources in the world around them. The question of how long grief should last is always present. If the mourners aren't asking, then those around them will ask, "Isn't it time you were over this?" It is important to appreciate that this stress will not go away in a short period of time. Duration is irrelevant if we see grief as a process of negotiation and renegotiation of the meaning of the loss, over the life cycle. As children mature, as adults change, their understanding and perspective on what was lost changes. People who experienced the loss of a parent in their early years have pointed to the fact that the deceased continues to be always be a part of their lives, not as unresolved grief, but as part of the way "things are" (Silverman 1987; Edelman 1994). For most people who lost critical relationships in their lives, such as a parent or a spouse, grief over time becomes less intense and all consuming, but it is still there.

Change occurs over time, and it can be divided into phases during which people do the "work" of the transition. The concept of tasks associated with grief has gotten a good deal of attention and is often talked about as the work of grief. Worden (1992) described four tasks, similar to those described by Furman (1974) and Lindeman (1944). However, tasks do not stand by themselves. They are things that people need to do in order to get from one place to another, relevant when anchored in time and place in a process. Attig (1996) raises critical questions about the use of the term "task." He notes that the dictionary defines these as circumscribable, modest in scale, and attainable, and thus the very word is inappropriate, implying something well defined that can be finished.

For example, one of the tasks frequently listed is accepting the fact of the death. When a mourner is initially numb and in shock, it may be totally impossible, at one level, to accept the reality of the death. Immediately after a death, a widow must get through the funeral, notify others of the death, learn about the family finances, deal with work, Social Security, pensions, insurance, and health care, and explain to the children and manage their issues, along with just getting through the day. Children may be busy learning about funerals, appropriate behavior, mourning, and what to do with their very strong and strange feelings. They know at one level that the death occurred. Is this acceptance? Or does acceptance come later on when they experience the new reality in a more intense and clearer fashion? We cannot therefore ask when the task is completed. Accepting the fact that someone has died is something that is done repeatedly over a lifetime.

It may then be best to abandon the word "task" and talk instead about issues and processes. This better reflects the negotiation and renegotiation that we do all of our lives as we deal with what is happening to us and what has happened to us. People are constantly in motion, and it is therefore impossible to delineate where one activity ends and another begins. It is more useful to note how responses change over time as mourners move in time away from the actual death and are dealing with different issues. It is helpful to divide the time into broadly defined phases or stages of transition. This division can help articulate the process of grief, but caution needs to be exercised that they are not looked at as if they follow in a clear and straight line. People move back and forth, and are simultaneously in more than one place at a time. Usually, this is a helix-like movement that is woven together by each person's own narrative.

INITIAL RESPONSES. The initial period after a death brings with it numbness, disbelief, a sense of moving on automatic pilot, a clouding or veiling of the mind that allows the bereaved to get through the rituals of burial and the early period of mourning. This ritual is the last social act in which the deceased has a part. Friends, family, and the community often surround the mourner at this time. Much of their immediate behavior is informed by the mores, values, and traditions of their religious and/or ethnic community. Sadness, crying, despair, searching for the deceased, and feeling forlorn may come in bits and pieces as if the human body has a way of protecting the mourners from the full impact of the death, which might overwhelm them. Those around them are often not aware of the underlying stress mourners may be experiencing. As a result of their numbness and almost reflexive behavior, mourners are able to maintain control and not put too many demands on others. In hindsight, most people report that they did not really feel in charge at this point. They were "on automatic pilot." All mourners, be they parents, children, widows, siblings, or friends, find themselves asking the same questions about the possibility of life, as they know it, continuing.

Stress at this time is expressed in the tension, anxiety, and awareness that nothing is the same. Sometimes these feelings are accompanied by a sense of being afloat— of losing direction. Slowly mourners become aware that their typical ways of coping are no longer effective. A sense of disorientation may follow when mourners learn that some of the ways they make meaning in the world no longer works. How do they define and understand what they are experiencing? Their sense of order in the world has been challenged. When their faith system provides an understanding of the place of death in life, they may see the deceased as having gone to a better place, but this may not suffice to comfort them at this time. In the long run, this faith system may help but they must also continue to live their lives on a day-to-day basis without the deceased that requires new skills and new ways of organizing their lives.

A NEW REALITY. This phase, sometimes called "recoil," refers to the time when the numbing lifts, sometimes in dramatic ways, as if a spring snapped. It now seems possible for the new reality to come into the full consciousness of the bereaved. These feelings may have emerged from time to time but been pushed aside. Each person finds his or her own way of visiting the fullness of the loss. This could be a time when people feel most depressed, especially if they were not aware of the extent of the numbness they were experiencing and that it would lift. For some there is a dramatic confrontation; for example, they may forget and set an extra place at the table or buy a toy that would have been suitable for their deceased child. The bereaved struggle with many forces that pull on them. They may explore various ways of coping to learn to live with their new reality.

Stroebe and Schut (1998) have identified loss-oriented responses and restoration-oriented responses in the bereaved. Loss-oriented behaviors help mourners face their grief and the sense of loss that follows a death. Restorative behavior includes keeping ties to the deceased alive, and these ties are welcome. As the bereaved cope, they alternate between these modalities. Most people use more than one way of coping and these are examples of two ways (Silverman 2000).

The mourners begins to recognize, in this period, that life is going to be very different than it was before, but they are seldom prepared, for the profundity of the changes is rarely talked about as part of the bereavement process. They may feel totally inadequate and be sure that they are going crazy, because six months to one year later people are asking why they are not over the loss already. Most of their friends and relatives will have returned to their own lives, and the bereaved can feel very alone. Often mourners themselves are unaware that the process may have only begun.

ACCOMMODATION. Over time mourners make accommodations to the death. This is not an end to grieving, but a time in which they have a sense of their own abilities to prevail, to deal with the pain, and to find new ways of living in the world. Stress can also lead to a positive outcome as well as to a deficit (Rutter 1983). As noted earlier we begin to see change associated with growth. Bereaved children often talk about feeling older than their peers. They begin to value the more intimate aspects of their relationships and take themselves and their lives more seriously (Silverman 1987, 2000). This is a continuing process. In the words of a teenager whose mother died several years before: "I feel older than my classmates. I have lived through something they do not understand yet. I am different and it is okay." The identity shift described earlier is consolidated at this time. The detours become part of what is now "normal" for people, influencing how they move on with their lives.

Most mourners seem to reach a point where grief no longer runs them. Rather, they run it. While they still feel some of the pain associated with the loss, it is no longer the driving force in their lives. There is always a place in their hearts and minds that feels the pain of the loss and is connected to the deceased. This is not an atrophied spot, but a place where a relationship with the deceased is constructed, nourished, and sustained, changing with time. Faith and religion often provide meaning and comfort that may elude mourners earlier (Cook and Wimberly 1983; Kushner 1989).

As part of their identity shifts, the bereaved can look in on themselves in different ways and relate to others from a different place. They find voices they did not have before, and are involved in relationships that give them a different sense of mutuality and exchange. A new self evolves (Silverman 1988). Mourners can recognize that this emerging self as an ongoing process that has altered the fabric of their lives in the present and will continue to do so in the future. In the words of a widow: "My friends find it hard to believe how I have changed since my husband died. I expect different things from people. I say things I never said before. I decide what is best for the family. If I was going to survive, that's what I had to do."

And, in the words of a bereaved mother:

> I have a different sense of strength and a clearer idea of where
> I want to go in my life. We all seem to be in a different place.

REFERENCES

Altschul, S. 1988. *Childhood Bereavement and Its Aftermath.* Madison, CT: International Universities Press.

Attig, T. 1996. *How We Grieve: Relearning the World.* New York: Oxford University Press.

Belenky, M. F., B. Clinchy, N. Goldberger, and J. M. Tarule. 1996. *Women's Ways of Knowing.* New York: Basic Books.

Bowlby, J. 1961. Childhood mourning and its implications for psychiatry. *American Journal of Psychiatry* 118:481–498.

———. 1980. *Attachment and Loss.* Vol. 3, *Loss: Sadness and Depression.* New York: Basic Books.

Bruner, J. 1990. *Acts of Meaning.* Cambridge, MA: Harvard University Press.

Charmaz, K. 1994. Conceptual approaches to the study of death. In *Death and Identity,* ed. R. Fulton and R. Bendickson, 28–79. Philadelphia: Charles Press.

Clinchy, B. 1996. Connected and separate knowing: Toward a marriage of two minds. In *Knowledge, Difference, and Power,* ed. N. Goldberger, J. M. Tarule, B. Clinchy, and M. Belenky, 205–247. New York: Basic Books.

Conant, R. D. 1996. Memories of the death and life of a spouse: The role of images and sense of presence in grief. In *Continuing Bonds: New Understandings of Grief,* ed. D. Klass, P. R. Silverman, and S. L. Nickman, 179–196. Washington, DC: Taylor & Francis.

Cook, J. A., and D. W. Wimberly. 1983. If I should die before I wake: Religious commitment and adjustment to the death of a child. *Journal for the Scientific Study of Religion* 22(3): 222–238.

Furman, E. 1974. *A Child's Parent Dies: Studies in Childhood Bereavement.* New Haven, CT: Yale University Press.

Gilligan, C. 1993. *In a Different Voice.* 2d ed. Cambridge: Harvard University Press.

Hetherington, E. M., and P. B. Baltes. 1988. Child psychology and life-span development. In *Child Development in Life-Span Perspective,* ed. E. M. Hetherington, R. M. Lerner, and M. Perlmutter, 1–19. Hillsdale, NJ: Lawrence Erlbaum.

Kegan, R. 1982. *The Evolving Self.* Cambridge, MA: Harvard University Press.

———. 1994. *In Over Our Heads: The Mental Demands of Modern Life.* Cambridge, MA: Harvard University Press.

Klass, D. 1988. *Parental Grief: Solace and Resolution.* New York: Springer.

Klass, D., P. R. Silverman, and S. L. Nickman, eds. 1996. *Continuing Bonds: New Understandings of Grief.* Washington, DC: Taylor & Francis.

Kuschner, H. S. 1989. *When Bad Things Happen to Good People.* New York: Schocken.

Lerner, R. M. 1989. Developmental contextualism and the life-span view of person-context interaction. In *Interaction in Human Development,* ed. M. H. Bornstein and J. S. Bruner, 217–239. Hillsdale, NJ: Lawrence Erlbaum.

Lindemann, E. 1944. Symptomatology and management of acute grief. *American Journal of Psychiatry* 101:141–148.

Lopata, H. Z. 1973. *Widowhood in an American City.* Cambridge, MA: Schenkman.

Marris, P. 1974. *Loss and Change.* London: Routledge and Kegan Paul.

Marwit, S. J., and D. Klass. 1996. Grief and the role of the inner representation of the deceased. In *Continuing Bonds: New Understandings of Grief,* ed. D. Klass, P. R. Silverman, and S. L. Nickman, 283–298. Washington, DC: Taylor & Francis.

Mead, G. H. 1930. *Mind, Self, and Society.* Chicago: University of Chicago Press.

Neimeyer, R. 1997. Meaning reconstruction and the experience of chronic loss. In *Living with Grief: When Illness Is Prolonged,* ed. K. J. Doka and J. Davidson, 159–176. Washington, DC: Taylor & Francis.

Nickman, S. L., P. R. Silverman, and C. L. Normand. 1998. Children's construction of a deceased parent: The surviving parent's contribution. *Journal of Orthopsychiatry* 68(1):126–134.

Normand, C. L. 1994. A longitudinal analysis of bereaved children's continuing relationships to their deceased parents. Ph.D. diss., Waterloo University.

Normand, C. L., P. R. Silverman, and S. L. Nickman. 1996. Bereaved children's changing relationship with the deceased. In *Continuing Bonds: New Understandings of Grief,* ed. D. Klass, P. R. Silverman, and S. L. Nickman, 87–111. Washington, DC: Taylor & Francis.

Parkes, C. M. 1996. *Bereavement: Studies in Grief in Adult Life.* New York: Routledge.

Piaget, J. 1954. *The Construction of Reality in the Child.* New York: Basic Books.

Pincus, L. 1974. *Death and the Family: The Importance of Mourning.* New York: Pantheon.

Rubin, S. S. 1992. Adult child loss and the two-track model of bereavement. *Omega* 24(3):183–202.

Rutter, M. 1983. Stress, coping and development: Some issues and some questions. In *Stress, Coping and Development in Children,* ed. N. Garmazy and M. Rutter, 1–41. New York: McGraw-Hill.

Scarr, S. 1982. Development is internally guided, not determined. *Contemporary Psychology* 27:852–853.

Selman, R. L., and L. H. Schultz. 1990. *Making a Friend in Youth: Developmental Theory and Pair Therapy.* Chicago: University of Chicago Press.

Silverman, P. R. 1966. Services for the widowed during the period of bereavement. In *Social Work Practice,* 170–198. New York: Columbia University Press.

———. 1982. Transitions and models of intervention. *Annals of the Academy of Political and Social Science* 464:174–188.

———. 1986. *Widow to Widow.* New York: Springer.

———. 1987. Impact of parental death on college-age women. *Psychiatric Clinics of North America* 10:387–404.

———. 1988. In search of new selves: Accommodating to widowhood. In *Families in Transition: Primary Programs That Work,* ed. L. A. Bond and B. Wagner, 200–219. Newbury Park, CA: Sage.

———. 2000. *Never Too Young to Know: Death in Children's Lives.* New York: Oxford University Press.

Silverman, P. R., and D. Klass. 1996. Introduction: What's the problem? In *Continuing Bonds: New Understandings of Grief*, ed. D. Klass, P. R. Silverman, and S. L. Nickman, 3–27. Washington, DC: Taylor & Francis.

Silverman, P. R., and S. L. Nickman. 1996. Children's construction of their dead parent. In *Continuing Bonds: New Understandings of Grief*, ed. D. Klass, P. R. Silverman, and S. L. Nickman, 73–86. Washington, DC: Taylor & Francis.

Silverman, P. R., and J. W. Worden. 1992. Children's reactions to the death of a parent in the early months after the death. *American Journal of Orthopsychiatry* 62(4): 93–104.

Silverman, S. M., and P. R. Silverman. 1979. Parent-child communication in widowed families. *American Journal of Psychotherapy* 33:428–441.

Stroebe, M., and H. Schut. 1998. The dual process model of coping with bereavement: Rational and description. *Death Studies* 23:197–224.

Van der Kolk, B., A. McFarlane, and L. Weisaeth, eds. 1996. *Traumatic Stress: The Effects of Overwhelming Experience on Mind, Body, and Society*. New York: Guilford.

White, M., and D. Epson. 1990. *Narrative Means of Therapeutic Ends*. New York: Norton.

White, R. W. 1959. Motivation reconsidered: The concept of competence. *Psychological Review* 66(5): 297–333.

Worden, W. J. 1992. *Grief Counseling and Grief Therapy*. New York: Springer.

Youniss, J. 1994. Rearing children for society. *New Directions for Child Development* 66:37–50.

13

PSYCHODYNAMIC THEORIES IN GRIEF AND BEREAVEMENT

JOAN BERZOFF

Remember me when I am gone away
Gone far away into the silent land
When you can no more hold me by the hand,
Nor I half turn to go, yet turning stay
Remember me when no more, day by day
You tell of our future planned
Only remember me; you understand
It will be late to counsel then or pray
Yet if you should forget me for a while
And afterwards remember, do not grieve;
For if the darkness and corruption leave
A vestige of the thoughts that once I had
Better by far you should forget and smile
Than that you remember and be sad.

WITH THESE lines from her poem "Remember," the romantic poet Christina Rossetti (1979:37) expresses the desire to be remembered not with sadness, but with a smile. Grief and bereavement are always a complex set of emotions that include sadness, anger, and distress but also humor, joy, and laughter. By a standard dictionary definition, grief is largely negative: "an intense emotional suffering caused by loss, misfortune, injury or evils of any kind . . . hardship, suffering and pain" (Webster 1979:801). But psychodynamic views of grief and bereavement suggest that grief, bereavement, and mourning are multidimensional, depending on the nature of the loss, the way the loss is metabolized, the meaning of the loss, who the mourner was before the loss (Rosenblatt 1993), how the loss is socially constructed (Neimeyer 2001; Klass, Silverman, and Nickman 1996), and the ways in which the loss may actually positively transform the mourner (Silverman and Klass 1996; Silverman 1986; Worden 1991). Although grief may leave the mourner with longing and regret, it may also allow the mourner to continue a relationship with the deceased (Klass, Silverman, and Nickman 1996) and grow from the experience.

This chapter will discuss a range of psychodynamic theories about grief and bereavement. I will examine the ways in which grief may be viewed as pathological, but will also discuss how people may be transformed in adaptive ways by their losses. I will look at a range of theories that explain how the deceased may become a part of the mourner's psyche through introjection, internalization, and identification, and how this may shape not only the mourner's ego but also his or her superego. I will look at why some grief is accompanied by self-blame, self-hatred, and even suicide, while other losses leave the mourner sadder but wiser (Loewald 1962). I will examine a number of different trajectories for grieving, while emphasizing that grief is always a unique phenomenon that differs based on multiple factors: preexisting losses, the mourner's personality, and the meaning to the mourner of who and what has been lost. Throughout, I will suggest that loss and mourning are ubiquitous to growth and development from childhood through old age. Because there is no universal experience of grief and the "resolution" of grief is a particularly Western concept, I will discuss why time limits for grief (Rosenblatt 1975; Silverman 1988) may interfere with grieving. Finally, I will also look at the ways in which grief, like any psychosocial phenomenon, is always socially constructed.

This chapter begins by examining those psychodynamic theorists who best contribute to our understanding of the ways in which grief and mourning shape the mourner's self and ideals. Using concepts from Sigmund Freud, Melanie Klein, D. W. Winnicott, John Bowlby, Margaret Mahler, E. M. Ainsworth, Vlamik Volkan, Gerald Kaplan, Erich Lindemann, Colin Murray Parkes, Hans Loewald, John Baker, Phyllis Silverman, Robert Neimeyer, and others, I also describe a number of sometimes competing, sometimes complementary lenses through which to see how losses can build upon or undermine psychic structure.

EARLY PSYCHODYNAMIC FORMULATIONS OF MOURNING

Perhaps one of Freud's most evocative papers, and certainly one of his most significant, was written in 1917. In "Mourning and Melancholia," Freud first distinguished between healthy and pathological mourning. From the start, he conceptualized mourning as not simply the loss of a loved object (and by this he meant person) but the loss of one's country, one's ideals, or one's home. Mourning itself, Freud thought, was not in and of itself a pathological state, though it might often feel that way.

In Freud's view, mourning feels like dejection, exhaustion, and depletion. In the process of grief, the mourner withdraws psychic energy from the outside world for a period of time. Freud described the ways in which the mourner is preoccupied with the loss, and, using a concept from physics, described how the mourner decathects, or withdraws energy from the outside world, while hypercathecting memories of the lost person. As Christina Rossetti suggested, the mourner is caught between letting go and holding near the object of the loss. The mourner tries to keep the person alive through telling her stories, wearing her clothes, playing her music, preparing the foods she loved, or visiting places that were shared. Nonetheless, the language of cathexis, decathexis, and hypercathexis that Freud employed to describe this phenomenon is off-putting, objectifying, and pseudoscientific (Bettelheim 1980).

Perhaps Ira Gershwin better describes hypercathexis when he writes, "The way you wear your hat / the way you sip your tea / the memory of all that / you can't take that away from me." Here he is demonstrating how, in mourning, each memory of the person who has died is full of meaning. The mourner keeps the person alive through tenaciously holding onto as many memories as possible. She may hold conversations with the dead person, visit the grave, set a place at the table, or ruminate about the events that surrounded the person's death.

No one, Freud wrote, ever abandons a libidinal position willingly, even when a substitute beckons. That is why we do not fall in love after a major loss. Grief takes energy. But with the passing of time, and with acceptance of reality, Freud expected that the mourner would slowly decathect energy from the person who had died, freeing up libidinal energy for new attachments. Taken literally, Freud maintained that the mourner must deinvest love for a lost person in order to love again.

In the same paper, however, Freud acknowledged that love may never be fully decathected and instead offered an alternative explanation for how the deceased may be given up in the interest of loving again. In the first object-relations concept to enter psychoanalytic discourse, Freud explained that lost objects, once loved, become internalized and ultimately set up inside of, and as part of, the surviving individual's ego or psychic structure. It is through identification with the lost object that aspects become part of the mourner's self. This is what makes mourning possible, bearable, and, ultimately, potentially transformative.

Unfortunately, Freud did not fully elaborate upon the concept of identification until he wrote *The Ego and the Id*, in which he argued that the oedipal situation bore great similarity to the state of melancholia. For the oedipal child, he writes:

> There quite often ensues an alteration of his ego which can only be described as a setting up of the object inside the ego, as it occurs in melancholia. . . . If one has lost an object or has been obliged to give it up, one often compensates oneself by identifying oneself with it and setting it up once more in one's ego. Since then we have come to understand that this kind of substitution is important in determining the form taken by the ego and that it makes an essential contribution towards building up what is called its character. (FREUD 1923:19)

Freud indicates that both mourning and melancholia feel alike. The mourner and the melancholic both feel dejected; both experience a loss of interest in the outside world, and both feel the lack of the capacity to love again. But whereas the mourner feels these things intensely, the melancholic feels something else in addition. The melancholic also experiences a disturbance in self-regard. The difference between the mourner and the melancholic, then, is that the latter feels bad about his or her own self. In fact, the melancholic suffers from what will later be called pathological grief. He or she feels self-critical and worthless and may experience problems with appetite or sleep.

How does identification with the dead create melancholia for some? Freud thought that unconscious conflicts (particularly unconscious aggression) toward the deceased made mourning difficult and often prolonged. Let me give an example.

CASE EXAMPLE

Ginny was thirty-five years old when she came to outpatient treatment. She suffered from headaches with no organic basis, and from a chronic depression. She was overweight, had unsatisfying relationships with men, and suffered some inhibition at her job as an associate vice president in a television company. She experienced herself as not worth others' attention, but maintained excessively high standards for herself.

Ginny had grown up in a family that from all outward appearances was enviable. Both parents had excellent careers and enjoyed financial success. When Ginny was five, however, her sister, age seven, became ill with pneumonia. Ginny's parents, frantic with their eldest daughter's high fever, rushed her to the hospital, but not before Ginny gave her sister a kiss goodbye. Her sister died overnight, and Ginny, with the magical thinking of a five-year-old, began to experience herself as the "kiss of death."

Her sister's pictures were removed from the mantle, and she was not spoken of again. Ginny felt somehow culpable, although unable to express her feelings, including her sorrow. She longed for a sibling to replace her sister, and so when her mother became pregnant when Ginny was six, she felt herself a major player in the conception. As many six-year-olds do in fantasy, Ginny imagined that this was her father's and "her" baby. But her newborn brother was born with Down's syndrome and, unconsciously, Ginny began to associate both her loving, sexual feelings and aggressive, angry feelings with loss and damage. She spent her childhood trying to "be good" and was an excellent student, a dutiful child who when angry would withdraw into a closet until her anger passed. At twelve, she wrote a birthday song for her brother. Her mother, who worked in the music publishing business, showed it to a colleague, who had the song published. It was an instant hit. But Ginny was confused. She was reluctant to take credit for this achievement and disavowed her success, as well as many other subsequent successes in work and love that she did not feel entitled to enjoy. Despite enormous talents, and a wonderful sense of humor, she experienced herself as inexplicably bad.

"When other children appear on the scene," Freud writes," the Oedipus complex is enlarged into a family complex. This . . . gives ground for receiving the new brothers or sisters with repugnance and for unhesitatingly getting rid of them by a wish" (1917:333). For Ginny, her aggressive wishes toward her siblings were of course unconscious. With her sister's death, however, these feelings had been turned against herself. Her lack of awareness of her own ambivalent feelings toward her sibling made the grief work irresolvable. "In mourning," Freud adds, "the world has become poor and empty. In melancholia, it is the ego itself."

Jane offers a second example of complicated mourning from a classically psycho-dynamic perspective.

CASE EXAMPLE

Jane, a seventy-five-year-old Italian Catholic woman, began to see me because she was profoundly depressed, having lost her husband of forty years eight years before. She visited his grave and talked with him daily, prayed with him in the morning, and at night. None of this would be pathological, except for the degree to which she referred to her home as her "tomb," was unable to feed herself, shop for herself, make any new relationships, or find any meaning in her life. She had lost twenty pounds and had driven her children away with a litany of complaints about them and about herself.

Jane had married at forty, having been the only one of seven siblings to live with and care for her aging and often abusive parents. She took care of all of her siblings' children, cleaned their homes, and did their laundry at considerable expense to herself. She denied any anger over forgoing college to take care of family members, and in fact, said, through clenched teeth, that she is never angry.

She had married a childhood friend, whom she had known, on some level, was homosexual. After conceiving three children, he moved into another bedroom and took a male lover who was twenty years his junior. Jane felt that her children blamed her for the disaffection between the couple, and did not remember, although each of her children report it, her murderous rage, during their childhoods, in which she would hit them with brushes, shoes, or her hands. Jane is a devout Catholic who sees herself and her God as all-loving. Her husband is described as nothing less than a saint.

During the course of our work together, Jane found, folded inside a drawer of her dresser, a journal she kept during the middle part of her marriage. In it, she confronted her loneliness, her fury at her husband, her disappointment in her life. During his illness and his death, however, these feelings were repressed, despite her husband, on his deathbed, telling her that he had never loved her and wished she were dead.

Why had Jane become so depressed, and even suicidal? In part, Freud would surmise, she had great difficulty acknowledging her anger toward the husband she had lost, and this threatened her ability to hold onto his memory. Second, her unconscious hatred for him had now been set up in inside of and directed against her ego. The third, and perhaps most difficult problem for Jane, from a dynamic perspective, was her need to maintain in fantasy what never actually existed in reality.

Freud writes, "One feels justified in maintaining that a loss has occurred, but one cannot see clearly what it is that has been lost. . . . The patient cannot consciously perceive what he has lost either. What gives rise to his melancholia is the sense that he knows whom he has lost, but not what has been lost in him" (1917:245). From Freud's point of view, pathological mourning often does not end. It is debilitating to internalize an unresolved and conflicted relationship. Melancholia is difficult to cure because of its unconscious and often denied roots.

In any situation of mourning, normal or pathological, Freud argued, the shadow of the object falls upon the ego. What a wonderful and evocative way of conveying how a mourner's psychic structure is always altered by the quality and nature of the relationship to the deceased! But when the mourner denies or cannot tolerate a negative relationship to the deceased, his or her own ego may be impoverished.

It needs to be said, however, that Freud revised his position on mourning many times, particularly with the death of his own daughter, Sophie. By the end of his career, and as a bereaved parent, himself, he recognized the impossibility of ever decathecting from a lost object, and wrote: "Although we know that after such a loss the acute stage of mourning will subside, we also know that we shall remain inconsolable and will never find a substitute, no matter what may fill the gap. And actually, this is how it should be. It is the only way of perpetuating that love which we do not wish to relinquish" (1960:210). In this statement, Freud foreshadows the idea that in mourning, one always maintains a continuing relationship with the deceased. Despite his recognition that the energy connected to lost objects is never extinguished, he did not revise his theory to include this insight (Silverman and Klass 1996).

Loewald (1962) added a further dimension to understanding how loss and mourning may alter psychic structure in transformative ways. He looked at the ways identifications with the deceased shape the mourner's superego. The superego normatively comprises identifications with valued others that shape one's conscience and ideals: who one wants to be and to become. When loss occurs, mourners inevitably identify with the lost person. For some, this can mean identifying with harsh, critical aspects of the other in ways that might result in a more rigid and inflexible superego. But loss also offers opportunities to expand the mourner's ego ideals.

CASE EXAMPLE

The Biehls lost their daughter Amy, aged twenty-two, in South Africa, when, as a Fulbright scholar working to end apartheid, she was murdered by four black South African men. Her parents returned to South Africa a year after her death to offer amnesty to her killers and publicly forgave their daughter's murderers. They created a legacy from her life as well as her death, and enabled her to live on, in memory, in the country to which she had devoted her life. For the Biehls, their daughter's murder altered their philosophy of how life might be lived (Biehl and Biehl 1998).

We commonly see superego development in those who are mourning. A mother who lost her daughter, a writer, to chronic obstructive pulmonary disease becomes a writer herself, educating others about the illness in order to help them. A senator's wife, widowed by her husband's plane crash, carries on his career but strives to change the lives of women in the process. A woman with breast cancer is compelled to work with other women to minimize their isolation and stigmatization, and this shapes how she feels about herself. A woman whose sister died in a bone-marrow transplant unit dedicates a part of her career to ensuring that others die with better psychosocial care.

OBJECT RELATIONS

KLEIN

While Freud and Loewald predominately theorized about the kinds of identifications with the deceased that led to changes in the mourner, Melanie Klein (1940) was interested in how grief and mourning may be experienced differently based upon the mourner's developmental level. She identified two kinds of anxieties that babies, early on, experience: annihilation anxiety at the most primitive level, and abandonment anxiety at a higher level. She also detailed the kinds of defenses that babies normatively employ to defend against these two anxieties. In her view introjection, rather than identification, helped the baby, or mourner, manage the intense anxieties that emerge under situations of dependency, loss, or frustration. She also noted that, under situations of loss, such anxieties are simply unbearable, and that the bereaved person who experiences them may need to deny their need for and dependency on the person who has died, taking flight into manic activity.

CASE EXAMPLE

Richard was a fifty-year-old lawyer and father of four when his wife became ill with colon cancer. Richard had never lived alone and was highly dependent on her to care for their children, home, finances, and bills and to manage his daily life. As her condition worsened, and during her first hospitalization, he placed ads in the local newspapers seeking a new girlfriend to replace her. By the time she died, he had a ready substitute, already installed in his house.

Klein would understand Richard's flight into manic activity as a function of his primitive level of psychological development. By denying his dependency on his wife and the meaning her loss had for him, he maintained an illusory independence from the person whom he so desperately needed. By seeking a new partner before his old one left him, he tried to manage his helplessness by convincing himself that his wife and his attachment to her were easily replaceable.

In Richard's early history, he had experienced a series of losses: his father died when he was eight, and his mother subsequently left him in the care of a sibling who was rejecting, while she moved to another country to be with her second husband. He saw dependency as a threat to his own psychological integrity inducing in him a kind of mania that represented some triumph over the dead, and over his earlier losses.

Klein described two normal positions in which babies (and sometimes mourners) predominately live when they are wholly dependent on others for their survival. The first is the paranoid/schizoid position, and the second is the depressive position. While it may sound crazy to think of babies or mourners as paranoid or depressed, Klein was trying to describe the inner world of a child who cannot yet see the world or others as whole. For the helpless baby, or for the mourner threatened by annihilation anxiety, others exist simply as need gratifiers who are good when they gratify and bad when they do not. In the world of an infant, the mother is the primary object and the source of all that is good when satisfying and of all that is dangerous when she is frustrating. In infancy, a mother's milk, and symbolically her love, are incorporated or introjected, and they become a part of the child's inner world, enabling him to feel good and worthwhile. Too much frustration, deprivation, or neglect, however, is experienced by the baby as bad and destructive, and in turn the baby feels himself or herself to be also bad. According to Klein, the baby's inner world is populated with good objects and persecutory objects. Good experiences with the mother restore the baby's sense of well-being and worth. Bad experiences with the mother that persist over time often contribute to an inner world that is both scary and dangerous. Many mourners, whose personalities have been undermined by excessive loss or deprivation, live in this shadowy and persecutory world where, when a new loss occurs, representations of the self and of the other are experienced as all bad. Where there has been a sufficient balance, however, between frustration and responsiveness, a baby, and later an adult, can begin to come to grips with the fact that the person she needs and loves is the same person who is frustrating and sometimes depriving. Klein refers to this as the depressive position, and it is a developmental achievement because it is simply sad to have to experience oneself and others as neither all good nor all bad. It is also just simply depressing to have to give up the belief in another person's omnipotence or destructiveness.

How then does loss threaten the adult's inner world? Klein suggests that when someone dies, the mourner regresses and loses not only the external relationship, but internally, may feel as if he has lost his good objects. If the mourner experiences annihilation anxiety, as Richard did, he is unable to restore a sense of internal goodness or well-being. When a mourner remains in the world of the paranoid/schizoid position, he may experience the death of another as his being robbed and punished. That is to say, feelings of persecution may dominate the mourner's inner world. The mourner's views of others as comforting and helpful are then thwarted by an inner world that is largely populated by bad and persecutory objects. But when a mourner has achieved the depressive position in which he or she sees others as both good and bad, grief can then be experienced without the fear of destruction to the self.

Klein writes that under the best of circumstances,

> The loss of a loved person leads to an impulse in the mourner to reinstate the lost object in the ego. . . . In my view he not only takes into himself (reincorporates) the person he has just lost but also reinstates his internalized good objects (ultimately his loved parents) who became part of his inner world from the earliest stages of development. The early depressive position is reinstated. Among all these emotions, (however) the fears of being robbed and punished by both parents are revived. That is to say, (for those in the paranoid schizoid position) feelings of persecution have also been revived in deep layers of the mind. (1940:353)

Klein's understanding of mourning is important in a number of ways. In working with people who are grieving, it is important to understand the mourner's internal world and to assess the mourner's capacity to see others as part objects or whole objects. Mourners who have achieved the capacity for depression may also be able to experience the loss without experiencing a simultaneous loss of self.

Winnicott (1960, 1965, 1971) offers a somewhat different but related understanding of how mourning is facilitated. Winnicott (1965) writes of the absolute and essential need, in infancy, for a mother to create a holding environment for her child: a place free from intrusion or impingement in which a child may begin to explore and develop his true sense of self (1960). A holding environment (1965) requires both the mother's presence and her absence in order to help a child to develop the capacity for solitude and aloneness. It is through a child's connectedness to the mother, and intermittent and incremental separations from her, that a child develops a sense of self (Winnicott 1960).

Loss is an inevitable part of any person's development and is managed through the infant's creation of an inner representation of the mother in her absence. Through illusion and through fantasy, the infant develops a sense of the mother, despite her lack of physical availability. The infant creates a space of imagination and of play that is neither the infant nor the mother (Winnicott 1971). This is a transitional space in which the baby may, for example, use a song, a blanket, or a teddy as a symbolic representation of the ministrations of his mother. Any one of these objects may symbolize the union of the two. When the mother is physically absent, then, the use of a transitional object may symbolize the union of two now separate things, baby and mother, at the point in time and space of the initiation of their separateness (Winnicott 1971).

Children, and by extension mourners, create transitional objects to deal with loss and separation. Transitional objects can thus be loved, but also mutilated. They serve a bridging function as symbolic representations of the person's experiences with the loved one's soothing and comfort. Under normal circumstances, babies eventually give up their pieces of blanket, or their teddies, the outside representations of the soothing and caring mother, because her functions become internalized. Hence separateness inevitably requires loss, but loss builds psychic structure through internalization. This process builds the capacity for mental representations of the lost object. When the mother has been too absent or too depriving, the transitional object becomes meaningless. Winnicott writes:

> If the mother is away over a period of time that is beyond a certain limit measured in minutes, hours, or days, then the memory of the internal representation fades. As this takes effect, the transitional phenomena become gradually meaningless and the infant is unable to experience them. We may watch the object becoming decathected. Just before a loss we can sometimes see the exaggeration of the use of the transitional object as part of denial that there is a threat of its becoming meaningless. (1953:15)

Hence when a loss occurs for an adult, it is important that the clinician assess the mourner's capacity to maintain an inner representation of the person who has died.

If an inner representation cannot be maintained, the person loses the capacity to soothe herself.

Normatively, we see mourners making use of transitional phenomena after a death. When the World Trade Center collapsed, or after the Oklahoma City bombing, mourners could be seen holding teddy bears, or posters, or photographs of the dead. Transitional phenomena link the mourner to the dead by helping the mourner to maintain a symbolic tie to the person who was lost. This is why so much grief work requires the use of transitional phenomena: photographs, diaries, real objects that represent memories of the dead that are suffused with meaning. These objects need to be recognized as ways of providing a soothing function for the mourner, which ultimately can be given up when internalized.

The capacity to maintain symbolic ties to the dead often reflects the nature of the mourner's inner representational world. There may be a connection between personality disordered individuals and pathological grief, since people whose self and object world are marked by insecurity and inadequacy are usually unable to see others or the self as whole are less able to grieve (Sanders 1988.)

MAHLER AND VOLKAN

Margaret Mahler (1975) notes the ways in which a child's inevitable separation (read loss) from her primary love object, her mother, facilitates psychological development. Every mother-child unity must encounter disruption, loss, and repair. Internalization of the mother becomes the way in which a child can separate while maintaining a mental image of the mother. In the course of normal development, a toddler begins to move away from her primary object. At the same time, the mother no longer holds or restrains the child and actively fosters more separateness. Through minute and incremental losses of the mother's presence, the toddler comes to internalize the mother's functions. Psychic structure, then, develops through internalizations (that continue to occur throughout the life cycle). Graduations, promotions, weddings, all evoke sadness, and often mourning. That is because they symbolize both loss and moving on (Carr 1993). Because loss in adulthood is inevitable, internalization can be seen as a lifelong process that builds character and psychic structure.

Internal object relationships are always complex. They include the person's image of the object, the feelings related to the object, and the feelings related to the self without the object. In mourning, it is possible to maintain a tie to the inner representation of the love object that also leaves room for investing in new loves, and new activities. Internal object relationships perform many functions: they soothe, they help in problem solving; and they help the mourner sort out her own identity in relation to the deceased (Baker 2001).

Vlamik Volkan (1981) discusses the ways in which transitional objects, which he calls linking objects (actual material objects of the dead), function to maintain a bridge with the lost person. For adults, linking objects provide a way to maintain contact with the dead, in which the physical objects (clothes of the dead, jewelry, photographs) allow the mourner to externalize elements of the self and internalize elements of the other. Linking objects are used to maintain the illusion of the lost person's aliveness. The mourner also uses the possessions of the dead to restore and to resolve some of the ambivalence that characterized the relationship with the deceased in life.

CASE EXAMPLE

Ann, a forty-seven-year-old internist, lost her forty-nine-year-old brother to lymphoma. He had been a highly successful lawyer, and their relationship, while loving, was not without rivalry. She remembers thinking, in the manic way that Klein describes, "At least, when he's dead, I'll get his music collection." For about five years thereafter, Ann played her brother's music often: in her house, in her office, and on any drive she took. Using the music as a linking object, she essentially carried him with her, but not without a note of triumph that she finally possessed a part of him, that she had always envied. At around the five-year anniversary, Ann noted that she no longer "needed" his music, and in fact, made tapes of some of his favorite songs, for his children. She began to change her taste in music as well.

While Volkan described linking objects as pathological, others (Satorsky 2000) have noted the ways in which linking objects maintain ties to the dead and build psychic structure. It is important to remember when we speak of introjection, internalization, or identification that these constitute a person's *inner* representations of others, not the actual person who has died.

BOWLBY

John Bowlby (1963, 1969–80) understood mourning to be directly related to a child's tie to the mother. He observed the ways in which children who were deprived of their essential ties to their mothers reacted to loss. Using children who had been institutionalized and abandoned as his subjects, he documented the ego disintegration among young children who were placed long term in institutional settings and without a primary caretaker. Bowlby (1963) first focused on the pathological consequences to the child of early loss, and demonstrated that the tie to the mother, or a primary caretaker, serves as the major organizer for the child's psyche. With the loss of that tie, a child experiences levels of separation anxiety that may undermine the ego. Bowlby noted a sequence of increasingly ego disorganizing behaviors when children are separated from their mothers. First, children expressed their anxiety through protest: a loud, angry crying and expression of pain, designed to bring the lost object back. In this view, the child's painful affects act as signals, and, under the best of circumstances, mothers or substitute caregivers respond to those signals with affection and love. A baby's protest cry is an active search to restore a lost object. But when the lost object or her functions were not restored in the course of separation, the hospitalized children became increasingly despairing: weeping, pining, searching, and yearning for the lost object. The final and perhaps most anguished state that he observed in infants was their detachment, a denial of the need for emotional ties altogether. A similar sequence has been noted in concentration camps, among prisoners of war, and among those who have been psychically overwhelmed by loss. Like the walking dead, such people may fall into a marasmus in which hope is extinguished.

Bowlby (1963) saw pathological mourning as akin to the first stage of healthy mourning: that of protest. Like the raging infant, an adult mourner for whom loss is permanent, may protest the loss and experience "anger and complaints that fester while love lies dormant" (Bowlby 1963:539). Unlike Freud, however, who viewed pathological mourning as a consequence of unacknowledged hate toward the lost object, Bowlby saw pathological grief as involving hostility and hate toward the self.

Bowlby (1963) described four kinds of pathological responses to grief: a persistent and unconscious yearning to recover the lost object; persistent and unconscious anger directed inappropriately toward others and the self; absorption in caring for someone else who is bereaved (projective identification); and denying that the object has been lost.

For more than a decade, Bowlby (1969–80) was particularly interested in the internal working models that children develop through their real relationships to their primary caretakers. For infants in settings where there was both maternal rejection and neglect and no substitute objects for maternal caretaking emerged, permanent and irreversible ego damage could be the consequence. However, he may have confounded the effects of institutionalization with the effects of loss, so that where substitute care was offered consistently, the long-term consequences of personality disturbances were less likely (Eisenberg 1975).

Bowlby further thought that children experience pathological or chronic mourning that can look like depression. The opposite side of pathological mourning may be total detachment from loved objects that can look like the absence of grieving. Bowlby described four stages of grief:

1. Numbing: Initially the griever is numb and unable to feel the impact of the death.
2. Yearning and searching: there is pronounced separation anxiety that prompts the mourner to try to find and recover the lost object. Repeated failures to restore the lost object may lead to the next stage.
3. Disorganization and despair
4. Reorganization

In reality, people do not grieve in such linear ways. Furthermore, many (Bonnano 2001; Schucter and Zisook 1993; Stroebe and Shut 1987) have questioned Bowlby's emphasis on protest, anger, and the expression of negative affects as important and normative aspects of the mourning process. In fact, minimal expression of negative emotion directed at the bereaved may reflect a healthy form of dissociation, in which the mourner moves in and out of awareness of the loss. In contrast to Bowlby and Freud, then, a number of the more contemporary researchers (e.g., Bonnano) have found that a *minimizing* of emotion is linked to reduced grief over time. This finding calls into question the degree to which the abreaction of emotion is necessary or desirable in grief and mourning.

Bowlby's work has been further elaborated through research on attachment (Ainsworth, Waters, and Wall 1978). Not all losses are the same; rather loss is always mediated by the internal working models that constitute any individual's attachment style. Ainsworth, Waters, and Wall described a range of attachment styles that characterize children and adults as mourners. Those who have secure attachment styles are able to maintain clear and coherent memories of others. Those with less secure attachment styles fall into three groups. The first are those who are avoidant of attachment, or in adulthood, are dismissive. They tend to suppress the need for others. The second are those with anxious or preoccupied attachment styles. They may be highly expressive but unable to cope with and maintain coherent memories in the absence of the other. The last group is referred to as "disorganized attachment" and includes those who cannot create an organized narrative of the other in her absence. The latter two attachment styles are often found in people who have been traumatized and are very important to assess in trying to understand the range of capacities for mourning. Death is the loss of an attachment, and grief and loss will look different, depending on the mourner's attachment style.

Grief requires the capacity to maintain an inner representation of the deceased, but there are ways in which the deceased continue to change, inside the mourner, while the mourner's relationship to the deceased also changes (Baker 2001).

ADAPTATION TO LOSS

In 1942, fire broke out in Boston's Coconut Grove nightclub, and almost five hundred people were killed. Erich Lindemann (1944) a psychiatrist and pioneer in grief and mourning research, worked with the survivors of this trauma and the family members of those killed in the fire. He was the first to describe acute grief as a psychological syndrome, and he also enumerated the symptoms of normal grief, as distinguished from pathological or complicated grief. Drawing upon previous concepts from drive, ego psychology, and object relations, Lindemann included in his description of normal grief the expression of physiological symptoms, preoccupation with the image of the deceased, guilt feelings related to not having done enough for the deceased, hostility for other professionals who had not rescued the deceased, and changes in patterns among the bereaved (e.g., restlessness and irritability, as well as difficulty in organizing activities and conducting social relationships). What he considered to be pathological, or complicated, grief reactions included the development of symptoms that represented an incorporation of the lost person; overactivity or manic behavior; marked hostility without sadness or apathy; or self-destructiveness. Lindemann (1944, 1979) also introduced the concept of anticipatory grief, suggesting that those facing a loss or death may go through all the phases of grief, which may protect the mourner or undermine the mourner's capacity to grieve. Lindemann's views on complicated grief, however, have been challenged, on the basis that it may not be at all pathological for the bereaved to express emotion and and/or crying for long durations (Zisook, DeVaul, and Click 1982).

Colin Murray Parkes (1972, 1993) also suggested that "normal" grief and loss may protect the mourner's ego. After a death, Parkes noted, the mourner first experiences shock, which may be accompanied by cries of extreme distress. To a large extent, numbness shields the mourner from unbearable psychological pain. Gradually numbness turns into pain, in which the mourner experiences distress that includes a restless hyperactivity, difficulty concentrating, a loss of interest in the outside world, and a pining for the deceased. The mourner may seek connection to the lost person through transitional objects and phenomena: looking to objects of the dead, or photographs, all of which serve as ways of searching for the lost object. When the mourner cannot restore the lost person through pining or searching, apathy may accompany despair and a kind of disorganization may be the consequence.

He viewed different sequences for the "pathological mourner" and identified three forms of pathological grief: "chronic grief," in which the mourner experiences prolonged grief with exaggerated symptoms; "inhibited grief," in which there appears to be an absence of emotion; and "delayed grief," in which the mourner's emotions are avoided until a later time. Bereavement researchers, however, have questioned whether delayed grief, and its longer duration, predicts pathological grieving. In fact, the question of whether bereavement leads to pathology or reflects preexisting pathology continues to be central to bereavement research. So many variables: the mourner's capacity for ambivalence, preexisting capacity for mental representation, the ways in which the object is experienced in the mourner's internal object world (Baker 2001), personality organization, internal object world, attachment style, capacity to tolerate ambivalent feelings, all, in addition to sociocultural factors and social supports effect how any individual grieves (Middleton et al. 1993) No one theorist has yet been able to integrate them all.

CONSTRUCTIVIST VIEWS

Until now, this chapter has addressed ways in which grief may be pathological and/or transformative, depending upon who the mourner is, her capacity for self and object representations, and the kinds of identifications and introjections that either foster or undermine the mourner's psychological structure. Much of the psychodynamic literature on bereavement, however, has overly emphasized the negative consequences of loss and bereavement, and viewed mourning, depression, or complicated grief, as functions of previous difficulties: for example, early losses, insecure attachment patterns, personality disorders, excessive aggression, poor adaptation, dependency, or detachment without examining the ways in which people make meaning out of their losses.

A postmodern view of mourning sees grief as neither universal nor essential. There are no fixed stages in which mourners move in lock step. Instead, persons who are grieving are always active participants in the process. Grieving offers the mourner an opportunity to create a new narrative about the death and its meaning (Neimeyer

2001). All individuals construct meanings—personal, familial, cultural, and somatic— that are highly variegated. The view that grief is an ongoing process of making meaning also suggests that grief is a process in which new roles, adaptations, and assumptions are created in relation to the person who has died.

Stroebe (1992–93) and others have shown that loss may actually benefit bereft individuals because they are forced to learn new strategies for coping and living. Caplan (1964) notes how loss may lead to a changed sense of self, a changed sense of relationships, and a changed philosophy of life. Loss may produce existential and spiritual growth and contribute to a sense of resilience in the mourner. That death may be transformative calls into question a worldview that suggests that death should be overcome.

A postmodern perspective also deconstructs the ways in which particular values are embedded in our theories of mourning. For example, in a Western culture in which autonomy, independence, and separation are the goals, it is not surprising that mourning is viewed as an inevitable series of separations. But some mourners maintain ongoing relationships to the deceased (Klass, Silverman, and Nickman 1996) that promote resilience and strength in the mourner. Continuing bonds to the dead, instead of representing denial or unresolved mourning, may represent strengths and contribute to creating an ongoing dialogue and a coherent narrative about the person who has died. For example, children who have lost a parent maintain an internal bond to the person who has died. Memories of the parent do not stay fixed or static; they are active and ever-evolving internal representations that change over time (Normand, Silverman, and Nickman 1996). Merwit and Klass (1996) studied adolescents who had lost a parent, and examined the role the deceased continued to play in their lives. Adolescents, like younger children, maintain relationships to the dead in which the deceased act as (1) a role model with whom the adolescent might identify, (2) a source of guidance in specific circumstances, (3) someone to help the adolescent clarify values, and (4) a memory of someone who brought feelings of comfort to the individual (Baker 2001). Silverman and Nickman (1992) provide other dimensions along which children construct continuing bonds with their dead parent. Clinicians who conceptualize their work as helping the mourner to achieve autonomy from the person who has died may miss the importance of the mourner's maintaining ongoing connections to the deceased that lead to positive changes in the mourner.

Rather than be passive recipients of death experiences (Neimeyer 2000), bereavement offers mourners opportunities to construct new meanings about themselves and others. The view that grief is constructed also suggests that grief is a lifelong process in which new roles, adaptations, and assumptions are created in relation to the person who has died. Constructivist views of grief decenter the individual self and see the griever as multiple selves in the context of the individual, family, culture, and community. In this view, depression, denial, and anxiety are no longer seen as pathological by-products of the grief experience, but instead as affects and defenses intrinsic to the mourner's processes of constructing new meanings (Silverman 2000; Baker 2001; Bonnano 1996; Normand, Silverman, and Nickman 1996; Merwit and Klass 1996; Stroebe et al. 1993).

Grief, when treated like pathology, contains a prescription that there is a right way to grieve, and an optimal time frame for bereavement. Grief becomes something to be "worked through" or "resolved" (Stroebe and Shut 1999; Worden and Silver 1989; Klass and Silverman 1996) instead of a process that is ongoing. In this view, depression, denial, and anxiety are not pathological by-products of the grief experience, but instead may represent the mourner's processes of reconstructing new meanings (Silverman 2003; Baker 2001; Bonnano 2003; Normand, Silverman, and Nickman 1996; Merwit and Klass 1996).

Additionally, most mourners do not hold an either/or view of the person who has died, but rather experience mixed feelings that are normative. While Freud maintained that ambivalence could be problematic, and Klein noted that inability to maintain ambivalence represented an early developmental failure, healthy mourning always involves views of the deceased that are flexible and ever-changing.

Stroebe and Schut (1999) have suggested that people cope with grief through a dual process. "Long-term adjustment to loss requires the capacity to move back and forth between expressing grief and living life. For people who cannot move between those two positions, complicated grief is often the result. The idea that death may be transformative calls into question a worldview that suggests that death should be overcome. The idea that death offers new meaning and narrative incorporates dying as a part of living" (199).

CULTURAL CONSIDERATIONS

The Western literature on grief and mourning, like so many psychological theories, developed within a white, middle-class, Eurocentric worldview. It is therefore important to recognize the degree to which the values of that context are embedded in ideas of what is "normal" or what is "pathological." For example, in Western cultures, the emphasis on separation and individuation leads, not surprisingly to the view that grief is an event to be worked through, and resolved, so that the griever can become free (read autonomous) to love again. In many Western cultures, the presence of the dead or communication with the dead is seen as pathological. But other cultures may express and work through their grief in ways where interconnectedness, not autonomy, is the end point. Grief and bereavement are not universal constructs. They always represent the underlying values of the mourner's point in history, and are socially and culturally constructed.

Western cultures place a great emphasis on talking cures, while other immigrant populations and some American subcultures do not value a verbal, introspective, or intellectual approach to grief. People grieve in multiple multicultural ways that often represent transitions between cultures and therefore cannot be stereotyped.

A multicultural perspective needs to respect the multiple ways of dealing with loss. In addition, not every loss or death requires clinical intervention. For example, it was assumed that all survivors of the World Trade Center needed mental health counseling, and many were "treated" as if they did. Grief was also "pathologized" by providing mandatory services to survivors and families without regard to need, or culture.

Every culture has specific idioms and methods for dealing with death. Each culture and society has specific ways of expressing distress and emotions. These may include the time frame through which loss is to be dealt with, and the ways in which the loss is experienced in the body rather than the psyche.

For example, it is well known that in Asian cultures, people rarely present with "grief" as the presenting complaint after a loss, but are much more likely to experience the loss as a somatic symptom: a pain in the belly, or a wind in the heart. For Hispanic cultures, grief is often seen as a part of life, and deaths are accepted with the expectation that the mourner be strong. In Hispanic cultures, however, the loss of a family member may also be seen as a threat to the interdependence of the family (McGoldrick et al. 1991), and when a child dies, death may be viewed as tragic. Latina clients may also experience bereavement somatically, experiencing attacks that may look like seizures but that express a high degree of emotion. Aboriginal tribes may tear out their hair or mutilate their bodies (Stroebe and Stroebe 1987). African Americans, whose worldviews are influenced both by Christianity and African philosophy, may view death as God's will. In this context, death can be seen as emancipation from further suffering on earth and as inaugurating a new life in another form. A life not dying for is a life not worth living (McGoldrick et al. 1991). At African American funerals, however, stoicism is considered pathological (Imber-Black 1991).

For many cultures, grief work is not about resolving the loss as much as it is about assuring that the fate of the soul of the dead will be honored. Many African Americans, Puerto Ricans, and Caribbean Islanders believe that the soul will not enter an afterlife until issues are resolved with the dead. Therefore, at the end of life, the grief work is concentrated not on pulling away from the dead nor on resolving unconscious conflicts, but on preparing the soul for an afterlife. The mourner invests in saying goodbye, and even pays off debts so the deceased may enter the spirit world (Corwin 1995; Braveheart-Jordan 1991) Many cultures believe in ghosts and communicate with the dead accordingly. In many cultures, parts of nature are understood to embody aspects of the dead in the form of spirits that act as intermediaries between God and the living. Many Native American, African, and Indian subcultures encourage contacting the dead for help and counsel. Most cultures outside of a Eurocentric perspective see the goal of mourning, not as one of severing ties to the dead, but rather maintaining a sense of spiritual involvement with the dead. Hindu cultures believe in the transmigration of the soul. Sacrifice is an essential part of bereavement, and offerings are made from birth to death to ensure the dead's entrance into Nirvana. Here one does not talk about the person who has died. In fact, it is honorable to separate emotions about the deceased from everyday life (McGoldrick et al. 1987).

There are vast cultural differences in mourning practices as well. In Jewish culture, mourning begins as a full week of commemoration for the dead person. In this tradition, the family comes together, a part of their garments is torn, and they sit on low wooden chairs. Some mourners wear no leather. Mirrors are covered in cloth to discourage focusing on appearance. Men do not shave for the first month after a death, and women wear no makeup. During this week of Shiva, mourners await the presence of friends, neighbors, and other extended kin who arrive with food and stories, that are told, and retold. After thirty days, the mourner returns to life but recites the Kaddish, or prayer for the dead, daily, for a year. At the end of eleven months, the deceased is commemorated by unveiling a headstone, which signals the end of the mourning period. These rituals encourage the mourner to immerse himself or herself in the loss for a carefully prescribed period of time. In Jewish cultures, suffering is a shared value. One rails against the unfairness of a death, and the orientation at this time is not to the future, but to the present.

Native Americans may deal with loss and dying by attending sweat lodges where a person who has difficulty in mourning may be expected to sweat out bad memories of the deceased. Where there are symptoms such as nightmares or anxiety, sitting in the nude, and sweating, may promote the release of an old identity and the creation of a new one.

CONCLUSION

Grief and mourning are obviously complex psychological and social phenomena that are neither linear nor universal. Each individual is a product of her culture, gender, race, ethnicity, social class, and environment. While psychodynamic theories offer rich ways of entering into the individual's psyche to explore the degree to which loss undermines or transforms character and identity, they do not suffice to explain universally how grief, loss, trauma, and mourning are experienced. Freud was central in beginning the discourse on how loss could not only affect but also actually change the mourner, sometimes leading to internalization of the lost object as a part of the self. Under the best of circumstances, this could enrich the ego. Where the relationship with the lost object had been problematic, internalization could lead to depression or complicated mourning. Klein (1940) and Winnicott (1951) provided ways to understand behavior in light of the loss of a real object, not only through death but also through separation. Bowlby (1969–80) offered ways of understanding a range of reactions to loss and separation, by emphasizing the primacy of attachment to loss, and helping to elucidate the yearning and searching aspects of grief and mourning. Lindemann (1944) and Caplan (1961) offered ways to understand the adaptive nature of grief and mourning by looking at how the mourner might make sense of traumatic circumstances that shake one's confidence in the stability of everyday life. Jacobs, Mazure, and Prigerson (2000), Parkes (1974), and Lindemann (1944) have suggested that deaths may lead to psychiatric sequelae manifesting as PTSD and depression. Others (Neimeyer 2001; Engel 1961; Silverman 2000) have called into question the medicalization of grief and pointed to the complex ways in which death and loss require individuals to maintain ongoing relationships with the deceased, leading to a new and more coherent life narrative.

Grief can undo the mourner, resulting in persistent self-hate or self-blame. Grief can be traumatic, resulting in a range of symptoms. Grief can undermine psychic functioning. But grief can also change the mourner: through identification and internalization, through the internal representations of those who were lost, and through maintaining continuing relationships with the deceased. The mother who lost a daughter who had been a writer and became a writer, the widow whose husband died during a political campaign and took on his career by advocating for women's rights, the sister who lost her sister and began an end-of-life program and wrote a book, the parents whose values changed in the act of forgiving their daughter's murderers: all demonstrate ways in which grief and mourning may change the mourner (Silverman 2000). Not everyone runs for the Senate, becomes a writer, or begins an end-of-life program, nor should they. But grief can be transformative in ways that promote psychological growth. Grief may heighten our appreciation for living. Adversity and loss may change who we are and how we see ourselves in relation to the deceased.

Anne Morrow Lindbergh observed, "I do not believe that sheer suffering teaches. If suffering alone taught, then all the world would be wise, since everyone suffers. To suffering must be added mourning, understanding, patience, love, openness and the willingness to remain vulnerable" (1973:212). While none of us ever welcomes grief or bereavement, both are inevitably parts of living and in this way will always shape the mourner.

REFERENCES

Ainsworth, M, E. Waters, and S. Wall. 1978. *Patterns of Attachment: A Psychological Study of the Strange Situation.* Hillsdale, NJ: Lawrence Erlbaum.

Baker, J. E. 2001. Mourning and the transformation of object relationships. *Psychoanalytic Psychology* 18(1): 55–73.

Bettelheim, B. 1980. *Freud and Man's Soul.* New York: Basic Books.

Biehl, L., and P. Biehl. 1998. The story of Linda and Peter Biehl: Private loss and public forgiveness. *Reflections* 3:11–22.

Bonanno, G. A. 1988. Emotional dissociation, self deception and adaptation to loss. In *The Traumatology of Grieving,* ed. C. Figley, 89–105. Washington, DC: Taylor & Francis.

——. 2001. Grief and emotion: a social-functional perspective. In *Handbook of Bereavement Research,* ed. M. Stroebe, R. Hansson, and H. Schut, 493–515. Washington, DC: American Psychological Association.

Bowlby, J. 1963. Pathological mourning and childhood mourning. *Journal of the American Psychoanalytic Association* 11:500–541.

——. 1969–80. *Attachment and Loss.* 3 vols. New York: Basic Books.

Braveheart-Jordan, M. 1991. The return to the sacred path: Healing the historical trauma and historical unresolved grief response among the Lakota through a psychoeducational group intervention. *Smith Studies in Social Work* 68(3): 287–305.

Calhoun, L., and R. Tedeschi. 2001. Post traumatic growth: the positive lessons of loss. In *Reconstruction and the Experience of Loss,* ed. R. Neimeyer, 157–172. Washington, DC: American Psychological Association.

Caplan, G. 1961. *An Approach to Community Mental Health.* New York: Grune & Stratton.

——. 1964. *Principles of Preventative Psychiatry.* New York: Basic Books.

Carr, A. 1975. Bereavement as a relative experience. In *Bereavement: Its Psychosocial Aspects,* ed. H. C. Shoenberg et al., 3–9. New York: Columbia University Press.

Corwin, M. 1995. Cultural issues in bereavement therapy: The social construction of mourning. *Session: Psychotherapy in Practice* 1(4): 23–41.

Eisenberg, L. 1975. Normal child development. In *Comprehensive Textbook of Psychiatry II,* ed. A. Freedman, H. Kaplan, and B. Sadock, 2:2036–2054. Baltimore: Williams & Wilkins.

Engel, G. L. 1961. Is grief a disease? *Psychosomatic Medicine* 23:18–22.

Freud, S. 1917. Mourning and melancholia. *The Standard Edition of the Complete Psychological Works of Sigmund Freud* 14:237–258. London: Hogarth Press.

——. 1923. *The Ego and the Id*. London: Hogarth Press.

——. 1960. Letter to Binswanger (Letter 230). In *Letters of Sigmund Freud*, ed. E. L. Freud. New York: Basic Books.

Imber-Black, E. 1991. Rituals and the healing process. In *Beyond Loss: Death in the Family*, ed. F. Walsh and M. McGoldrick, 207–223. New York: Norton.

Jacobs, S., C. Mazure, and H. Prigerson. 2000. Diagnostic criteria for traumatic grief. *Death Studies* 24:185–199.

Klass, D. 1997. The deceased child in the psychic and social worlds of bereaved parents during the resolution of grief. *Death Studies* 21:147–175.

Klass, D., P. Silverman, and S. Nickman, eds. 1996. *Continuing Bonds: New Understandings of Grief*. Washington, DC: Taylor & Francis.

Klein, M. 1940. Mourning and its relation to manic depressive states. In *Contributions to Psychoanalysis 1921–1945*, ed. John D. Sutherland, 34:311–338. London: Hogarth Press.

——. 1946. *Notes on Schizoid Mechanisms*. New York: McGraw-Hill.

Lindemann, E. 1944. Symptomatology and the management of acute grief. *American Journal of Psychiatry* 101:141–148.

——. 1979. *Beyond Grief: Studies in Crisis Intervention*. Northvale, NJ: Jason Aronson.

Loewald, H. 1962. Internalization, separation, mourning and the superego. *Psychoanalytic Quarterly* 31:453–504.

Mahler, M., F. Pine, and A. Bergman. 1975. *The Psychological Birth of the Human Infant*. New York: Basic Books.

McGoldrick, M., et al. 1991. Mourning in different cultures. In *Living Beyond Loss: Death in the Family*, ed. F. Walsh and M. McGoldrick, 176–205. New York: Norton.

Merwit, S. J., and D. Klass. 1996. Grief and the role of inner representation of the deceased. In *Continuing Bonds: New Understandings of Grief*, ed. D. Klass, P. Silverman, and S. Nickman, 297–309. Washington, DC: Taylor & Francis.

Middleton, W., B. Raphael, N. Martinek, and V. Misso. 1993. Pathological grief reactions. In *Handbook of Bereavement: Theory, Research and Intervention*, ed. M. Stroebe, W. Stroebe, and R. Hansson, 62–77. New York: Cambridge University Press.

Neimeyer, R. A. 2001. *Meaning, Reconstruction, and the Experience of Loss*. Washington, DC: American Psychological Association.

Normand, C. L., P. Silverman, and S. Nickman. 1996. Bereaved children's changing relationships to the deceased. In *Continuing Bonds: New Understandings of Grief*, ed. D. Klass, P. Silverman, and S. Nickman, 87–111. Washington, DC: Taylor & Francis.

Parkes, C. M. 1972. *Bereavement*. Madison, CT: International Universities Press.

——. 1993. Bereavement as a psychosocial transition. In *Handbook of Bereavement: Theory, Research and Intervention*, ed. M. Stroebe, W. Stroebe, and R. Hansson, 102–112. New York: Cambridge University Press.

Rosenblatt, P. 1975. Uses of ethnography in understanding grief and mourning. In *Bereavement: Its Psychosocial Aspects*, ed. H. C. Shoenberg et al., 212–224. New York: Columbia University Press.

Rossetti, C. 1979. *The Complete Poems of Christina Rossetti*. Ed. R. W. Crump. Baton Rouge: Louisiana State University Press.

Sanders, C. M. 1988. Risk factors in bereavement outcome. *Journal of Social Issues* 44:97–112.

Satorsky, D. 2000. Comprehensive examination. Unpublished manuscript.

Shucter, M., and S. Zisook. 1993. The course of normal grief. In *Handbook of Bereavement: Theory, Research and Intervention*, ed. M. Stroebe, W. Stroebe, and R. Hansson, 23–44. New York: Cambridge University Press.

Silver, R. L., and C. B. Wortman. 1980. Coping with undesirable life events. In *Human*

Helplessness: Theory and Applications, ed. J. Garber and M. Seligman, 279–340. New York: Academic Press.

Silverman, P. S. 1988. In search of new selves: Accommodating to widowhood. In *Families in Transition: Primary Prevention Programs That Work,* ed. L.A. Bond and B. M. Wagner, 200–220. Newbury Park, CA: Sage.

Silverman, P. S., and S. Nickman. 1992. Detachment revisited: The child's construction of the dead parent. *American Journal of Orthopsychiatry* 62:93–104.

Silverman, P. S., and J. Worden. 1993. Children's reactions to the death of a parent. In *Handbook of Bereavement: Theory, Research, and Intervention,* ed. M. Stroebe, W. Stroebe, and R. Hansson, 317–300. New York: Cambridge University Press.

Stroebe, M. 1992–93. Coping with bereavement: A review of the grief work hypothesis. *Omega* 26(1): 19–42.

Stroebe, M., and W. Schut. 1999. The dual process model of coping with bereavement: Rationale and description. *Death Studies* 23:197–224.

Stroebe, W., and M. Stroebe. 1987. *Bereavement and Health.* New York: Cambridge University Press.

Volkan, V. D. 1972. The linking objects of pathological mourners. *General Psychiatry* 27:215–221.

——. 1981. *Linking Objects and Linking Phenomena.* New York: International Universities Press.

Warwick, M., B. Raphael, and V. Misso. Pathological grief reactions. In *Handbook of Bereavement: Theory, Research, and Intervention,* ed. M. Stroebe, W. Stroebe, and R. Hansson, 44–62. New York: Cambridge University Press.

Webster. 1979. *Webster's New Twentieth Century Dictionary of the English Language Unabridged.* New York: Collins.

Winnicott, D. W. 1951. *Transitional Objects and Transitional Phenomena.* London: Hogarth Press.

——. 1960. *Through Pediatrics to Psychoanalysis.* London: Hogarth Press.

——. 1965. *The Maturational Process and the Facilitating Environment.* New York: International Universities Press.

——. 1971. *Playing and Reality.* Middlesex, UK: Penguin.

Worden, J. W. 1991. *Grief Counseling and Grief Therapy: A Handbook for the Mental Health Practitioner.* New York: Springer.

Wortman, C. B., and R. C. Silver. 1989. The myths of coping with loss. *Journal of Consulting and Clinical Psychology* 57:349–357.

Zisook, S., R. DeVaul, and M. Click. 1982. Measuring symptoms of grief and bereavement. *American Journal of Psychiatry* 139:1590–1593.

PART III

CLINICAL PRACTICE ISSUES IN
END-OF-LIFE CARE

INTRODUCTION: CLINICAL PRACTICE

IN THE previous sections, we have emphasized the importance of the clinical social worker's having respect for, and an appreciation of, the patient who is dying, and of the family and community who accompany the patient on the journey. We have made clear the need for theories that explain the biopsychosocial domains of dying and of bereavement. We have underscored the importance of theory about interdisciplinary work, ethical issues, and psychological and spiritual practices.

In this section, on clinical practice, we continue to realize a goal that is consistent throughout this book: one that fosters a respectful death, whether working with a dying child, an adult, or a person who has lived a long life. The social worker may meet with the patient and family once, at a point of diagnosis or in the event of a traumatic death, or may work with the family and patient over the long term of the illness and through bereavement. Dying may take place at home, on the streets, in a hospice, hospital, prison, nursing home, or bone-marrow transplant unit. Dying people and their families may seek support from social workers for creative solutions to illnesses, losses, and bereavement: in groups, in family work, or in family camps that help them deal with loss. Dying people and their families have a range of human concerns—psychological, financial, spiritual, cultural, and ethical—and the clinical social worker in end-of-life care must try to help the family and client meet their needs, with dignity and with some degree of choice.

In this section on practice, however, we have chosen not to attempt to discuss every illness nor every end-of-life setting, because this would require another book and because many of the principles of excellent clinical care with the dying and the bereaved generalize to a range of settings, populations, and illnesses. Hence, our division of these very rich and compelling clinical practice chapters is finally somewhat arbitrary, given the overlapping roles of the social worker and the needs of patients and families in every setting and with every disease and stage of the life cycle.

In this section we offer many exemplars of excellent clinical practice in a range of settings and with a range of populations. What, ultimately, do we mean by excellence in clinical practice? What requisite social-work skills enable patients and families to have respectful deaths?

Foremost, the clinician needs to be able to create authentic relationships with patients and families in which he or she is prepared to be present with both her heart and her mind. Clinical social-work practice needs to be flexible, because the social worker carries multiple roles: case management, counseling, advocacy, and as a liaison between the patient, family, team, and community. Social work practitioners need to learn anew from every patient and family: who they are, how they came to be that way, their history with death, dying, and bereavement and with medical care, and their inclusion or marginalization in larger social systems. Excellent clinical care requires attending to the meanings of loss for each individual and family. Quality clinical care requires knowing oneself—one's fears about death, loss, and mortality—in order to "be present" for others who are dying or bereaved. While death is a universal event, it is also universally feared, avoided, or dreaded, and so much of what constitutes excellence in clinical practice is the capacity to stay connected, to be willing to enter into a family or patient's journey while also maintaining perspective, hope, and humor. Excellent clinical practice is client-centered and promotes a patient's and family's choices about the right ways to die. Death, dying, and bereavement are often isolating and often lonely processes, made more so when the disease is stigmatizing or the setting is punitive. The social worker has an obligation to stay in the work: to stay connected to patients and families and to help them maintain connections to their communities of caring. Excellent clinical social work care helps patients and families to advocate for themselves, to make choices, and to make decisions that are consistent with how the dying person has lived.

Hence quality clinical social-work care attends to a range of biological, psychological, and social issues that patients, families, and children regularly face. Psychologically, people who are dying may experience a loss of self-esteem, anxiety, depression, guilt, loneliness, hopelessness, conflicts over dependency and independence, and fears of suffering, abandonment, or being a burden. Quality social-work care creates safe and supportive environments to elicit these fears, to hear them, and to respect their expression. Quality clinical social-work practice requires recognizing a patient's and family's cultural values, religious practices, need for privacy, financial, and psychological resources, and connections to friends and the community. Quality clinical practice attends to practical issues: who will care for dependents and provide transportation or household care? Quality clinical social-work care helps those who are dying deal with the end of their lives through legacy building, life closure, rites, rituals, celebrations, funerals, and services. Clinical social workers also help families to survive their grief, loss, and mourning. Clinical social workers attend to the physical aspects of death and dying: the management of pain and the management of a range of symptoms. In every case, the social worker responds to who the patient and family are: their values, beliefs, developmental stages, strengths, levels of literacy, competence, disabilities, gender, race and ethnicity, and sexual orientation (Ferris et al. 2002).

Every patient and family has wishes and preferences about dying with dignity and these must be elicited anew. Every patient and family carries a range of affects—anger, sadness, hopelessness, or hope—and these must be borne within the larger contexts of the family's history with loss and bereavement. Many deaths are out of sequence, traumatic, or simply tragic, and the social worker must be able to share a patient and family's suffering because she is able to bear her own. A clinical social worker needs most of all to be able to work with an open heart because she has faced loss, mortality, and the unknown herself.

We begin this section on clinical practice with three particularly powerful and evocative chapters; the first addresses the trajectory of illness, the second looks at working with individuals who are dying, and the third focuses on working with children who are dying. Each of these three chapters approaches end-of-life care from an experience-near perspective. Allen Levine and Wendy Karger show how, from an initial diagnosis onward, the newly diagnosed person and family embark upon a journey not of their own making, not within their control, and certainly not of their own choice. This chapter asks the reader to look mortality in the eye, drawing the practitioner to examine the ways in which an initial diagnosis changes a person's relationship to herself and to others as well as to the medical community. A diagnosis may be followed by a series of normative losses: of role, of function, of body change, of disfigurement, of autonomy. A diagnosis and an ensuing illness may lead to a range of intense feelings, a changed self-concept, a loss of faith, or of hope. The reader smells, tastes, and feels the fear and foreignness that accompany the trajectory of illness toward death, an event each of us encounters only once alone.

The chapter by Felice Zilberfein and Elizabeth Hurwitz on the dying individual further sets the context for dying with respect and dignity. In every stage of the life cycle, and in every setting, the social work practitioner needs to create a caring, responsive holding environment aimed toward reducing a client and family's suffering. Zilberfein and Hurwitz refer to this clinical stance as working with "an open heart," and, like a "respectful death," it is a stance that we advocate for all practitioners who work with those at the end of their lives. These authors make clear that an open heart is not an empty heart. An open heart bears witness to a range of feelings—fear, sadness, anger, hope, surrender—without having to "fix" or change them. An open heart listens, but can be silent. A practitioner whose heart is open knows a great deal about a range of developmental issues, disease processes, affects, needs of the family, and resources in the community, but also is able simply to be present. This is only possible when the practitioner knows herself well.

Perhaps nowhere is the practitioner challenged to be more present, more authentic, than in working with dying children, and their families. Nancy Cincotta, in her chapter on working with dying children and their families, takes the reader into the last part of the lives of dying children who must come to terms with their life-threatening illnesses and make meaning of them. For the practitioner, working with dying children can be daunting, and even unbearable. But Cincotta identifies the profound rewards that are possible when practitioners can remain emotionally and physically present to the dying child and her family. The social worker's capacity to represent the child's best interests during a shortened lifetime may profoundly influence the child and family's ability to die with the highest possible quality of life. While new parents can usually learn about parenting from a book or a course, Cincotta reminds us that there is nothing that prepares parents for their children's life-threatening illnesses or deaths. Using the words and wisdom of dying children and their parents and siblings, Cincotta grounds her clinical assessment and practice in "the data" of children's and their family's lives, underscoring the unique culture in which dying children must live.

Having lived a long life is very different from dying when one's life has hardly begun, and Sue Thompson and Neil Thompson, in their chapter on working with older people at the end of life, argue that good palliative care, regardless of age, has universal principles: care for the individual and family that restores dignity and self-determination. The elderly are also often a stigmatized and isolated group, their common humanity ignored. They are often lumped together, as if their concerns, needs, and wishes are all the same.

To open one's heart fully to another's suffering, the clinician must also be able to assess a range of factors that affect the dying or bereaved individual and the family. The social work clinician must be able to assess a family's strengths and vulnerabilities as well as those of their community, using a bio-psycho-social-spiritual perspective. As we have maintained throughout, dying is not in and of itself pathological. Yet many factors are brought to bear in any death that may strengthen or may undermine the last chapter of a life. There may be psychological difficulties such as anxiety or depression that may need treatment. Dementias or other cognitive impairments need to be assessed when a patient's competence is at stake. There may be a history of major mental illness that if assessed and treated may add quality to the end of a life. Kathy Walsh-Burke's chapter on psychiatric assessment discusses the psychological variables of the bio-psycho-social-spiritual equation. How to differentiate anxiety, depression, and adjustment reactions when death threatens can be very challenging.

Persons who are dying may also suffer unduly and unnecessarily based on their physical pain. Pain is always subjective, and always carries a range of meanings for the patient and the family. Pain may, for some, represent redemption; for others, it may represent punishment. A person's levels of pain, and its associated meanings, must always be elicited, understood, and addressed. Terry Altilio's chapter on pain and symptom management makes clear the social worker's role in accurately identifying the sources and nature of physical, spiritual, and psychological pain, which may be different based on culture, gender, and race. The social worker plays an essential role in advocating for pain and symptom relief with the palliative care or hospice team, the family, and the community, as well as in providing pain management using cognitive techniques, relaxation, and guided imagery.

Susan Blacker's chapter on palliative care considers all of the factors in the bio-psycho-social-spiritual equation and discusses what social workers do to reduce suffering, work with the patient and family to ensure that their wishes and needs are represented, and serve as a liaison to the team. Palliative care addresses all of the physical, psychological, practical, and spiritual needs of patients and families; it helps them to prepare for a self determined life closure, cope with loss and grief during illness and bereavement, and promote meaningful opportunities for personal and spiritual growth and self-actualization. Any patient or family living with a life-threatening disease, with any prognosis, regardless of age and at any time, is appropriate for receiving palliative care (Ferris et al. 2002).

Barbara Dane expands upon the role of the social worker in integrating spirituality and religion in palliative care and on the ways in which the practitioner elicits the patient and family's spiritual practices and beliefs, while being aware of the practitioners' own spiritual countertransference.

The social work practitioner, whether as a member of a palliative care team or not, has an equally important role in advocating for the client and family based on a thorough assessment of the family's culture and history of oppression, especially within healthcare systems. For example, depending on whether the family comes from an individualist or collectivist culture, " truth telling" or "patient autonomy" have completely different meanings. Some groups may seek the most aggressive treatments, based on a history of exclusion from health care, while other groups may seek no treatment at all. Some groups may be denied access to pain medication based on their race, ethnicity, or the community in which they live, and other groups may view Western medicine with doubt and suspicion and choose to use complementary and native healers exclusively. Here Norma del Rio's chapter on culturally sensitive theory and practice in end-of-life care helps the practitioner to recognize cultural differences and the ways in which race, culture, and oppression interact, and to intervene at the micro, mezzo, and macro levels in providing culturally competent care.

Nowhere is this more germane than in working with underserved individuals and families at the end of life. Shirley Otis-Green and Chris Rutland examine the particular challenges of working with those who are addicted or mentally ill, who may also be homeless. They address the cognitively impaired and the disenfranchised patients and families who have limited resources and a lack of access to prescription drugs. They look at those whose culture, language, and social status is stigmatizing and isolating. For those most marginalized and stigmatized, it is incumbent upon social workers to recognize their concerns, advocate for their support, and uphold the core values of our profession in working with them at the end of their lives.

The clinician must also elicit and try to understand who constitutes the family, whether it is a group of friends, a same-sex partner, a multigenerational family, or a community. The clinician needs to know about the client's and family's past history with illness and whether medical care been viewed as helpful, or whether the patient and family has encountered racism, homophobia, or cultural discrimination within the healthcare system. Bruce Thompson and Yvette Colón address the unique needs of patients with AIDS, who die from a highly stigmatized disease. While some of the tasks are similar to any person who is dying, there are also different needs that clients and families face as they deal with the burden of the illness such as having been closeted, estranged, or oppressed on the basis of the disease.

How does the social worker advocate for those who have been traditionally disenfranchised by the nature of their disease, their ability, their sexual orientation, their social class, their cognitive, or physical limitations, with dignity and respect? Gary Stein and Lucille Esralew turn the lens again to consider the needs of the disabled and the cognitively impaired at the end of their lives: for autonomous decision making, for education, for the right to withdraw treatments. Social workers who work with the disabled need to be able to assess individual's abilities, offer a range of modalities (counseling, behavioral, and psychopharmacological), and be prepared to help and to advocate for patients making healthcare decisions that allow them choice, dignity, and access to hospice and palliative care.

Once an individual's, family's, and larger community's needs and resources have been assessed (and this is always an ongoing process), a range of help may be provided that includes group work, family work, consultation, and education, as well as mobilizing natural supports within the larger community. Social workers need flexibility in taking on roles that have always been part of the social work tradition, but are too often lost as we focus too narrowly on the individual. In clinical work with the dying and with the bereaved, social workers act as facilitators, innovators of new practice, team members, educators, advocates, and teachers.

One powerful intervention that a social worker can make is in leading or referring a patient or family member to a group. Here patients, parents, grandparents, children, caregivers, and siblings are able to express, in supportive and safe contexts, a range of feelings and experiences that afford them a sense of sameness, ways to solve problems, a sense of belonging, and a place for feeling less alone. Groups offer a place where hopelessness may be expressed and strengths may be identified. Amanda Sutton and Daniel Liechty's chapter on group work in end-of-life care and Yvette Colón's chapter on technology-based groups demonstrate the power of eliciting people's stories and their unique ways of coping. Sutton and Liechty's chapter pays particular attention to the role of the leader, the stages of group formation, the importance of confidentiality, as ways of providing holding and support in face to face groups on dying or bereavement. Colón's chapter discusses the ways in which in telephonic and online support groups may enhance self-disclosure, provide outreach, offer support, and provide a range of information to those caregivers and patients who might otherwise not be able to access help. Susan Blacker and Alice Jordan conclude this subsection with an important discussion of the role of family work and family conferencing in end-of-life care.

Phyllis Silverman's chapter moves the practitioner to the terrain of bereavement. Her chapter on Helping reminds us that there are a range of helpers for the bereaved, including clergy, funeral directors, and health professionals. Social workers need to collaborate and as appropriate, to make referrals. They need to be what Silverman calls "ombudsmen" or "ritual specialists." Every individual or family has, regardless of their age or position in the family, their own energy and imagination. Often the bereaved find creative solutions and ways of being in the world that they would never have imagined for themselves prior to the death, and social workers need to help them to find their own solutions. Silverman emphasizes the natural helping networks that can destigmatize the bereaved.

The social worker also needs to help the patient and family to express their own wishes through the use of advance directives or healthcare proxies. Every social worker encounters conflicts between the wishes of the patient that may differ from those of the family, or from the service. The social worker is often in the position of helping the patient, the family, and the team come to terms with competing values and aims. Sometimes this means helping each simply to understand each other's behaviors and points of view. Often this requires participation in ethical decision making. Susan Gerbino and Shelley Henderson discuss the complex ethical dilemmas that are often a part of social work practice.

In every setting there are challenges that may be specific to that setting. Patients in prisons encounter isolation, the loss of dignity, and a decided lack of support. Here living is devalued, and so is dying. In fact, in prisons, death with dignity is an oxymoron. Sheila Enders, in her chapter on dying in prisons, takes the reader to one of the most dehumanizing settings in which dying occurs: where prisoners may be shackled to their beds or be seen as deserving of only punishment, not care. The social worker working in a nursing home also may encounter clients in dehumanizing conditions and must be able to elicit the joy and the hope that are a part of a long life lived. Nursing homes are also places in which clinical, legal, ethical, and spiritual issues converge in the provision of a respectful death. Mercedes Bern-Klug addresses the biopsychosocial issues of this often neglected population.

Bereavement work is a core function of social work, and so we have included two other chapters that address creative settings for bereavement work. Chris Itin, Susan McFeaters, and Susan Taylor-Brown, in their chapter on a family unity camp for families who have AIDS, combine individual, family, and group work skills that foster both activity and reflection as part of living with dying. Their chapter also identifies the very creative roles that social workers play as program developers. Lisa Aronson's chapter on international disasters brings in another set of clinical skills for traumatized people in international settings. Cross-cultural competencies, consultation, and bereavement skills are discussed therein.

The last two chapters in this section take the reader to the bone-marrow transplant unit, where a life-threatening disease is treated by an equally life-threatening cure, and to the oncology unit, which in many ways serves as a template for excellence in palliative care. We end with these chapters because they capture the complexity, the conflicting roles and responsibilities, the practice methods, and the consultative and teaching roles that every social worker who works with the dying needs to play. We end with these chapters, too, because, like so many chapters in this section, they convey a sense of awe and wonder about the practitioner's own reactions to issues of death, dying, and bereavement as they interact with the clients and families whom they serve. John Linder poignantly describes the tasks of the social worker working with patients with cancer and seamlessly identifies the challenges for the patient and family within the palliative-care setting. Iris Cohen-Fineberg beautifully enumerates the particular issues that bone marrow transplant patients face: isolation, aggressive and debilitating treatments, the loss of dignity and control, and the use of treatment that treats the disease but not the person in her environment with the disease.

Both authors, and indeed all of the authors in this section, have interwoven into their practice the concerns of the disenfranchised and underserved. All of the authors have stressed the importance of assessment: of developmental, spiritual, cultural, psychological, and physical issues and their convergence. Many of the authors make use of a range of creative modalities that include individual, group work, family work, pain and symptom management, spiritual work, play, and expressive therapies consultation and ethical decision making.

Because we are mortal and will all face death, end-of-life care is always subjective and intersubjective. The social worker is shaped by his or her own experiences with loss, as well as frustrations, beliefs, values, and ethics in relation to this work. The worker is challenged to discover or to rediscover parts of himself or herself in working with the dying. Because patient, family, and caregiver are human, they are always influencing one another. The clinician who strives to be objective or the "expert" is not likely to be open to learning about living and dying from the patient or the family anew. There are very few objective "truths" in this work, as we try to practice with the dying and bereaved. There are fewer absolutes, and "prescriptions" for dying need to be left out of the discourse altogether.

But the social worker does have skills: the capacity for empathy, for listening, for bearing witness, for reflecting upon what the client and family may be saying, for support and for insight, for helping patients and families become aware of the ways in which they may be repeating past losses, not hearing one another, scapegoating family members, shutting down, or tuning out. The social worker has the skills to identify the patient's and family's strengths in coping with the current crisis, past losses, and past adversities.

Every clinician has reactions, feelings, and moments of "not knowing" in this work. These are inevitable and important. In the past, social work clinicians were trained to rid themselves of their reactions and feelings, of their "countertransference" to achieve clinical objectivity. Not only can we never be "objective" about the feelings and experiences that end-of-life care evokes, but our subjective states—confusion, sadness, anxiety, existential angst—also influence the work we do always. Authentic attunement involves the capacity for engaging multiple subjectivities: that of client and family as well as the worker as they interact with each other about physical, psychological, existential, and spiritual pain. The social worker can only do this when she listens anew to each patient and family's stories about: how they construct the meaning of illness, hospitalization, or hospice care. In work with the dying, or the bereaved, the social worker needs to be aware of the institutional setting's influence— how its practices, values, and attitudes may or may not promote a respectful response to the patient and family—and to consider how to effect change in the large system.

We hope that the reader will take away from this section the complexity, the conflicting and creative roles and responsibilities, the developmental and life-cycle issues, the innovative practice methods, and the consultation and teaching roles that every social worker engaged in work with the dying must do. Most of all, we hope that the reader will keep a sense of awe and of wonder about their own reactions to issues of death, dying, and bereavement and those of the clients and families whom they serve. In the next section, Irene Renzenbrink speaks of relentless self-care. In providing care for the dying and bereaved, however, we argue that that the social worker must be relentless in applying all that she knows to those facing the last chapters of their lives.

REFERENCES

Ferris, F. D., M. M. Balfour, K. Bowen, et al. 2002. *A Model to Guide Hospice and Palliative Care, Based on National Principles and Norms of Practice.* Ottawa: Canadian Palliative Care Association.

14

THE TRAJECTORY OF ILLNESS

ALLEN LEVINE AND WENDY KARGER

THE PHONE rings. Tina, a thirty-six-year-old divorced mother of twins, rushes down the hall to her office, certain it will be that terrific guy she met at the health club. But her breathless "hi" is answered, instead, by the nurse from her primary care physician's office. Apparently, one of the blood tests, from her checkup last week, is showing a slight irregularity. When can she come in and repeat the test?

Which test? What does this mean? The voice on the other end reassures her that it's probably a lab error; that's been known to happen. But the doctor just wants to be sure.

Tina takes a deep breath and flips through her appointment book. How about a week from Tuesday?

She is more than a little unnerved when the nurse gently insists that she really shouldn't wait that long. How about three o'clock tomorrow?

WHEN DOES THE "END OF LIFE" ACTUALLY BEGIN?

Concepts have changed dramatically from a stage-related end-of-life process to a broader understanding of the complex, subtle and more diverse elements involved. But even with these new realizations, a very important piece of the picture is often not acknowledged.

The tendency is to equate the end of life with the end-stage of a *disease*, rather than the end of the *experience* of life as it had always been—before "cancer," "HIV," "Parkinson's," "Alzheimer's," "ALS," or some other serious diagnosis turned that life upside down.

Perhaps it even starts before the moment of diagnosis, with a phone call about a questionable test result, a suspicious lump discovered one morning in the shower, a tremor that suddenly makes it difficult to hold a cup of coffee, or perhaps, just a vague sense that something doesn't feel quite "right."

For Tina it began with that call. It took several months of tests to pin down the diagnosis: multiple sclerosis. There is no specific course of treatment for her at this early stage, and to date she has hardly been aware of any symptoms beyond the sporadic and inexplicable bouts of weakness and fatigue that triggered her appointment for a checkup.

And yet, suddenly her entire life has been invaded by an unpredictable disease she has barely heard of, but that may or may not ultimately disable her. Even if the symptoms never become any more pronounced than they are right now, it will cast a permanent shadow over the rest of her life.

This is where the trajectory of illness actually begins. In this chapter, we will examine the journey from these initial events forward, keeping the following concepts in mind:

• Even when a remission or complete recovery occurs, the reality of everyday life is forever altered, coloring any future dreams, decisions, relationships, financial considerations and personal priorities.
• Illness doesn't happen in a vacuum. Rather, it is one more thread that is now going to be woven into the entire fabric of that person's life—along with all the other problems that were there prior to its onset.
• The effects on the patient and the ripple effects on that patient's "universe" will take a variety of forms, including the social, financial, spiritual, emotional, and, of course, physical.

These ramifications will be illustrated as we follow several different patients on their journeys through the labyrinth of illness and treatment.

DIAGNOSIS AND DECISION: THE FIRST LEG OF THE JOURNEY

In an overly air-conditioned consultation room, Migdalia and Juan sit huddled in their chairs waiting to hear the results of her cervical biopsy. The oncologist explains the seriousness of her situation while peering alternately at her test results and then over the rims of his reading glasses at the two of them. He senses he is not getting through.

Migdalia is in her mid-twenties, but she looks much older. She is raising her three children in a new country with a strange language and foreign culture. She and her husband have little education and very little money. A religious and extremely modest woman, Migdalia had been particularly traumatized when two young medical students had been invited to observe as her biopsy was being performed. But because she was so intimidated, as well as self-conscious about her limited ability to express herself in English, she said nothing at the time.

In Colombia, she had given birth to her children at home with the aid of the village midwife who had been a trusted friend of the family since her childhood. Even when it was difficult and painful, she always felt safe and lovingly cared for. Now she is being told that she will have to have an operation, which will make it impossible for her to have any more children. But she is a young woman! Yes, she has had three children, but they are all girls and they were hoping to have a boy—maybe more than one. She is from a culture where the birth of a male child is considered essential in order to continue the family name.

Realizing that he is not communicating his message, the doctor asks for a Spanish-speaking nurse to come in and translate. There is a malignancy that requires immediate surgery, but it is not yet clear whether, or to what extent, it may have metastasized. Migdalia will also need chemotherapy after her surgery, and it would be wise for her to arrange for help taking care of her family for the duration of treatment. She is given several referral slips and some instructions printed in Spanish, regarding different tests that will be needed prior to her surgery. She is reassured that she should consider herself very lucky because, with this surgery and chemotherapy, there is a 70 percent probability that she will live at least five years.

THE INITIAL JOLT

Suddenly, Migdalia's everyday life is unceremoniously scooped up and dropped into a complex medical matrix. Like a piece on a game board, she is being shuttled from one remote corner of the hospital to another, where she is left to sit in a heavily trafficked hallway wearing nothing but a hospital johnny that is completely open in the back.

There are so many complicated, rushed instructions, which would be hard to comprehend even for those who speak the same language!

Like Alice in Wonderland, she has somehow stepped through the looking glass and feels herself quickly and uncontrollably descending into a world where nothing is remotely familiar. And from here on, she will depend on these strangers in lab coats who now, very literally, hold her life in their hands. The people who provide her care will become as central to her day-to-day experience as her family. But, unlike all the other relationships in her life, they will know the most intimate details about her, but she will know next to nothing at all about them, beyond their specific roles in her treatment.

As this ominous journey progresses, the people and issues from the patient's "real" life won't just wait in suspended animation. Practical issues, such as finding appropriate substitutes to take over family responsibilities, work, and other commitments during a course of treatment, can be further complicated when there is no clear picture of exactly how long this might be necessary.

In the wake of all this confusion, patients also begin to wonder about the longer-term implications of their diagnoses. What will be the ultimate impact of the unanticipated interruptions that will now be necessary to accommodate treatment? And how will the effects of the disease and treatment impinge upon everything else that matters? How will it affect their professional goals, financial status, social standing, and the constellation of other significant people who are dependent on them: family, friends, coworkers, and others in their community?

No one can provide these answers, but from this point forward, the intervention of an understanding and knowledgeable social worker can be the most likely source of practical help and comfort.

THE UNIQUE ROLE OF THE SOCIAL WORKER
IN ADDRESSING THESE ISSUES

Of all the professionals participating in a treatment team, the social worker has a unique perspective that can have a tremendous impact at every stage of illness, which we will soon begin to look at in detail. There are two areas where your intervention is key:

1. The psychological: Because of your specialized training, you can detect important signs and signals from the patient that other members of the treatment team might overlook. While the physicians and nurses are watching the patient's physical vital signs, you're there to understand and interpret the more subtle, emotional effects of the treatment process, and this awareness can be of great help to the patient, the family, and the medical team.

2. The practical: You are the one person on the treatment team who has the knowledge, the network, and the capabilities to intercede and relieve the patient and family of some of the practical obstacles to treatment. You can help them find and arrange for services that will ease their burden substantially.

UNDERSTANDING THE SPECIFIC IMPLICATIONS
FOR DIFFERENT PATIENTS

At thirty-seven, Rick is proud of his reputation for remarkable dexterity in the construction company where he has worked for thirteen years. He's the guy they depend on to carry out the most delicate maneuvers from precarious heights or tight spaces. And his younger colleagues look up to him as a craftsman and a role model.

In his spare time, Rick spends countless, pleasurable hours building intricately detailed miniatures. He has just about finished putting together a magnificent dollhouse for his daughter, Katie, complete with all the furniture, including a tiny slip-covered couch and an electrical system with lights in every room.

But over the last several months he's begun to notice a certain unsteadiness, which he had attributed to just being tired and "not a kid any more." Then one morning, about six weeks ago, he could barely button his shirt because his hands were shaking so uncontrollably that he couldn't grasp the individual buttons. In his panic and frustration, he became dizzy and lightheaded and could hardly keep himself from falling down. What if he'd been up on a girder when this had happened?

Now, diagnosed with Parkinson's disease, Rick feels like his whole world has just collapsed. What will he do with himself if he can't go back to work, or even finish building Katie's dollhouse? How will he explain that to her—or to himself?

His doctor suggests the possibility of a new surgical procedure for which, it seems he is an ideal candidate. The results of this procedure, thus far, have been very encouraging, although there are always risks. But no one seems to understand that, right now, Rick isn't sure he would even want to live if he can't go back to the life he knows and the things he lives to do! What would be the point?

THE "WHERE" FACTOR

The site of a disease, and the specific physical limitations it may impose, can have a profound effect, depending on how it is linked to an individual's perceived self-image.

Even if he may not appear to be obviously handicapped after successful treatment, someone like Rick may feel irreparably betrayed by a body that was so much a part of his total persona. To him, the idea of not being able to complete his daughter's dollhouse is tantamount to losing a part of himself, where, to another patient, a similar setback might be experienced as little more than an annoying inconvenience.

SIMILAR DIAGNOSES/DIFFERENT REVERBERATIONS

There are instances where the same disease, affecting the same area of the body, may be perceived very differently by different patients.

Lynn's mother had died of breast cancer at age fifty-eight. As she herself approaches her mid-forties, Lynn has become assiduous about getting her yearly mammograms and checkups. Having fairly large, cystic breasts has made this precaution even more crucial, and there were several times when vaguely suspicious tissue on both sides had been biopsied, just to be safe.

She would jokingly say that they ought to "just put in a zipper" to save them the trouble of having to open her up each time. But beneath her lighthearted banter is a very real fear, which has now increased since she learned that she has precancerous tissue in both breasts and needs to consider her options. One might be a prophylactic bilateral mastectomy.

Both she and her husband, Rob, agree, without skipping a beat, that to lose her breasts would be preferable to the risk of losing her life. They are told that reconstructive surgery can be performed during the same operation, but until her doctor brings it up, Lynn is not even thinking about the cosmetic implications. All that she and Rob want to know is how soon it can be done, even when it is explained that waiting a few weeks until she sees the plastic surgeon and schedules the procedure will not put her at any further risk.

That same day, Diane, a forty-three-year-old real estate broker, is diagnosed with a malignancy in her right breast. Six months ago she had broken up with the man she'd been living with for several years after discovering that he'd been having an affair with a younger woman. She has just reached the point where she is starting to date again. After losing fifteen pounds and undergoing plastic surgery to remove the puffiness under her eyes, she has rewarded herself with some beautiful new clothes. She was finally beginning to get her life back on track.

Because there is no history of breast cancer in her family, it comes as a total shock when the suspicious shadow on her routine mammogram is confirmed with a biopsy. To Diane, the idea of a mastectomy is unthinkable in her current situation. Even a lumpectomy would be somewhat disfiguring. And the option of chemotherapy would probably make her hair fall out! Isn't there anything they can offer that won't destroy her life in order to save it?

A CLOSER LOOK AT THE IMPLICATIONS
OF THE SITE OF AN ILLNESS

The name of a disease, like cancer, only begins to tell the story. No two cancers are going to be experienced in the same way. There are several factors involved, starting with the specific area of the body effected by the illness.

1. The physical effects: How will the disease and the treatment impinge upon an individual's capacity to perform his or her activities of daily living? We've seen the example of how Parkinson's disease will challenge Rick's ability to earn a living as a construction worker. Another example might be a person who lives in a two-story home and develops emphysema.
2. The psychological effect: What symbolism or meaning does that part of the body have to a particular individual? We have seen that both Lynn and Diane have the same part of the body affected, yet respond very differently.

The social worker needs to assess both the physical and the psychological effects on the individual patient, and explore the meaning of the losses that could occur, both short-term and long-term.

A CLOSER LOOK AT THE IMPLICATIONS
OF BEING SERIOUSLY ILL

In addition to the area of the body where the illness strikes, other elements contribute to an individual patient's reaction to a diagnosis.

• The patient's age at the onset of illness: An older patient may be more able to accept the possibility of illness, disfigurement, diminished capacity, and mortality than a younger person like Migdalia or Tina.
• The emotional support system available to the patient: While someone like Lynn is happily married to a man whose feelings toward her will not change if she loses her breasts, Diane is particularly vulnerable because she has already been rejected for a younger woman. To someone in her position, the scarring of a breast would represent the worst possible scenario at a time when her sexual attractiveness and self-image are already a major concern in her life.
• The literal support system: Who will be there to hold the bucket when a cancer patient who lives alone, like Diane, is vomiting after a round of chemotherapy?
When a patient is unable to take care of his or her needs, yet no longer requires hospitalization, who will be there to help? For Diane, it is economically feasible to hire a companion, but that is not the case for many patients, especially when the need for assistance is protracted. Yet a nursing home or rehab facility would mean the loss of independence and privacy, which can feel equally unacceptable.
• The practical and financial ramifications of long-term loss of mobility or function: For someone like Rick, whose occupation as a construction worker is so dependent on his physical agility, even a minimal loss of function will have a direct and imme-

diate impact on his ability to support his family, in addition to the extreme emotional repercussions.

• Cultural influences: A major part of Migdalia's reaction is centered on her inability to bear more children. She is from a large, religious family and has been brought up to view motherhood as her primary role in life. Other women would also mourn this loss, but perhaps not to the same degree.

• Historical events from the patient's past: Lynn's immediate decision to have a bilateral mastectomy, even when there was no urgency, was triggered by the memory of her mother's long struggle and eventual death from breast cancer. Diane had no experience to influence her decision in that way.

THE "WHY?" FACTOR

Making decisions about the course of treatment may seem clear-cut to the medical team whose sole focus is finding a solution that will save the patient's life. In many instances, by avoiding or delaying treatment, a patient can significantly lower the chances of a successful outcome. So it becomes especially difficult, and often extremely stressful for healthcare providers, when a patient in serious need of treatment is not responding to the urgency of the situation.

Cyril is a successful, twenty-nine-year-old high-fashion designer. He has come a long way from his childhood in a ghetto housing project, where the neighborhood kids used to call him "Mr. Clean" because he had no interest in drugs, girls, or "hanging out." At one point, when he was seventeen, he had caved in to peer pressure and gotten a small tattoo on his upper arm. In all likelihood, this was probably when he contracted hepatitis C.

To watch Cyril in action, one would never suspect he has a potentially fatal disease, and it was only discovered because he had volunteered to donate blood when a friend was having surgery. Because he is asymptomatic, Cyril is in no hurry to begin treatment, even though his ALT levels are nearly twenty times higher than normal and he has been told that the chances of arresting the disease would be nowhere near as favorable at a later stage.

But, for Cyril, the potential side effects of treatment with drugs like interferon, and the impact it might have on his life, are simply not worth it. In fact, if anybody in his business were to find out about his illness, it could spell the end of everything he has worked so hard to achieve. So, in spite of his doctor's urging, Cyril has made the firm decision simply to take his chances. He's "had this thing" in his system for twelve years now and didn't even know it was there! And besides, he's confident that there are going to be new options with fewer side effects sometime down the road—if he ever gets "really sick."

THE "I CAN'T AFFORD TO BE SICK!" FACTOR

It is now going on three months since Harry began experiencing shortness of breath and sudden bouts of extreme fatigue for no apparent reason. At seventy-four, he had assumed that these symptoms are just a normal part of aging. He was quite surprised, and a little put off, when his golf buddy, Phil (who happens to be an internist), responded with such alarm, insisting he should see a cardiologist—right away.

As a retired Army pilot who had been decorated in World War II, Harry knows how to recognize a real life-and-death situation, and this, he is sure, is not one of them. His biggest mistake was mentioning his shortness of breath to Phil! All this fuss over cholesterol tests and stress tests. . . . Phil went on relentlessly when it was clear to Harry that there really was no need! But he finally acquiesced, although he still argues that he has never had any reason to worry about his health.

It's his wife, Corrine, who has had a number of serious illnesses, including a stroke two years ago, from which she never fully recovered. There are some days when she depends on him for help with even the simplest things, like dressing herself, and she has become increasingly fearful of being left alone. He hasn't mentioned "this heart business" to her at all because it would just be upsetting.

But just this morning, Harry got a call from the cardiologist about scheduling more tests. Apparently, he suspects some significant blockage. And he urges Harry not to delay. Essentially, according to his preliminary results, Harry could be "a walking time bomb," and going in for an angiogram is the only way to know for sure.

But still Harry is adamant. He has to put it off until one of his daughters can come down and stay for a week or two to "take care of mother" so he can go into the hospital with peace of mind. Of course, he hasn't mentioned it to either of his daughters yet, because "there hasn't been a good time" when Corrine wouldn't overhear.

A CLOSER LOOK AT THE BARRIERS TO ACCEPTING TREATMENT

There are numerous reasons why patients postpone or resist treatment which, in their view, loom larger than the potential consequences of delay or going untreated. Some of these reasons have been illustrated in the cases we've been discussing, including

- Denial of the urgency (Migdalia's, Harry's, and Cyril's cases)
- Fear of the visibility and resulting social stigma of an illness (Cyril's case)
- Fear of disfigurement or side effects of treatment (Diane's and Cyril's cases)
- Primary responsibility for another dependent family member (Harry's case)

Other commonly stated reasons for postponing or resisting treatment include

- "Bad timing," when treatment interferes with professional responsibilities or when a patient wants to wait until after an important family or social event
- Financial considerations, such as an insurer who refuses to pay for a proposed treatment, or the inability to afford the other ancillary costs such as babysitters, transportation, special supplies, or services not directly related to medical care (such as help with housekeeping or having meals delivered)
- Religious and cultural conflicts: when the treatment goes counter to a patient's beliefs
- Distrust of the medical profession because of experience or negative family mythology
- Confusion or depression that totally immobilizes a patient, resulting in virtual inaction

At this juncture, the intervention of a social worker can help a patient distinguish when a decision against treatment is actually being made as a choice on the basis of a side issue that might be resolved with appropriate assistance. Arranging for home care after surgery or providing information about available childcare or transportation to and from the hospital for treatments are examples of where you can supply the kind of practical advice that could tip the balance.

Just by making sure the patient understands all the options and is basing his or her decision on solid information, you will have performed an invaluable service, regardless of the patient's ultimate decision.

CRISIS WITHOUT WARNING

There are some instances when there's no warning—and no choice. It could be an accident, a fire, or some other life-and-death emergency, or a sudden onset of illness that precipitates the trajectory.

It is the Sunday afternoon of the week between Christmas and New Year's. Eleven-year-old Jeff is rushed to the emergency room by his parents after he's had an apparent seizure while playing a computer game with his nine-year-old brother, Doug. Nothing like this had ever happened before, and there is no history of epilepsy or any related disorder in the family.

But Jeff had been complaining of headaches lately, and his teacher had called several weeks ago to report sudden outbursts of anger that were "not like him at all." Jeff is a good student, a terrific athlete, well liked—an all-around "great kid." Something, obviously, is terribly wrong. But what?

Jeff's terrified parents are told to have a seat in the waiting room while he is examined by several residents, who are now huddled in a corner trying to decide what to do next. A neurology consult? A CT scan? It is decided that both are indicated. And after several hours of tests, Jeff is admitted, still with no definitive diagnosis, but there is now evidence of a small mass in his left frontal lobe. The question is whether it is malignant. An oncologist is now added to the team.

It is determined, after a few more days and many more tests, that there is only one way to find out. Surgery is scheduled for the following day. The whole time, his younger brother, Doug, wonders in silence whether this had anything to do with the fight that the two of them had the week before—when Jeff hit his head against the wall.

It isn't long before they are told that Jeff does in fact have a malignancy. And even though Doug is pretty sure that cancer doesn't result from a fistfight, he becomes increasingly tortured with guilt and spends more and more time by himself, unwilling to talk or even be in the same room with his anguished parents.

TREATMENT: THE NEXT PHASE

The beginning of treatment is loaded with expectations—both good and bad. There's the hope of a cure on the one hand, and the fear of it not working on the other. There's the anxiety about side effects on the one hand, and fear that if they do not occur, it means the treatment may not be powerful enough to succeed. And there's a range of raw feelings that come up about the disease and treatment that are often hard for the patient and family to reconcile:

- The anger, either spoken or unspoken, about, "Why is this happening to me?" coupled with the idea of having one's privacy invaded—starting with the prospect of being confined to a hospital.
- The fears about permanent bodily changes, physical limitations, and pain are often overwhelming, especially when a patient is afraid that she or he will not be able to tolerate it "gracefully" or "like a man."
- The anxiety about who will be there to take care of the patient, and what their reactions might be, both in the beginning and over the long haul
- The depression that can come when the patient begins to consider the long-term aftereffects—financial, social, psychological, and spiritual, as well as the physical ramifications.
- The underlying fear of mortality, which the patient and family may or may not acknowledge.

Discussions around these themes can provide the social worker with important cues to help evaluate the particular type and degree of support that individual patients will require to help them through their medical procedures. And, here again, your role can be pivotal because of the special relationship and level of trust that can develop between you, the patient, and the family.

But, what, specifically *is* your role? Aside from providing information and helping to arrange for practical help, what can you actually *do* to help alleviate the suffering?

CONTAINMENT

When a patient is able to put all of his or her feelings and fears into words, it makes him or her more accessible and less charged. Your lack of shock upon hearing the patient, and your reassurance and validation, can take a tremendous "load" off the patient and family. By helping to universalize and normalize the patient's and family members' thoughts and feelings, it reassures them that they're not "going crazy." And in giving these feelings over to you, it means they no longer have to bear them alone. Now *you* become their "container."

ASSESSMENT

As you consider each situation, these other factors are also key:

- How did the patient respond to the idea of illness prior to this instance?
- What family dynamics are there that will have an impact—positive or negative?
- What are the patient's past and present coping mechanisms, and how are they likely to come into play?

- How great is the patient's capacity to understand and to make appropriate decisions?
- What developmental processes and roles are being affected by the disease and treatment?
- Are there cultural or spiritual conflicts that need to be addressed?
- What are the ramifications of the *specific illness* to this particular patient, and what types of support might help the patient acclimate more successfully?

ANTICIPATION AND DENIAL WEAR MANY FACES

HOPE

The night before her surgery, Lynn's friends and family can hardly believe how calm and collected she seems on the phone. She actually compares her upcoming bilateral mastectomy to having a bad tooth pulled! Sure, it won't be easy, but it's a lot easier than living with the ever-present dread of breast cancer.

She had watched her mother die a miserable death and is determined not to let that happen to her. And the disfigurement from the surgery is not as big an issue for Lynn as it might be for other women who don't have such supportive husbands. As for her looks, Lynn never really liked her figure very much, anyway. And now she's even being given a choice about how they will "resculpt" her! She's opted for small, B-cup implants, so that after surgery, she'll actually look more like a "normal person" and be able to wear clothes she would never have considered before. In fact, she's already planning a shopping trip on the day she's scheduled to drive in to Chicago for her follow-up with the plastic surgeon!

RESIGNATION

That same week, in San Diego, Diane has opted for a lumpectomy. Her tumor is small, and its location is not in an area where lymph node involvement would be most likely. If they can get it all out, then it will be over and done with. The scar will be small, which is good because she's "not ready for anything too extreme." Chemotherapy may not even be necessary. Radiation, perhaps, but at least that won't make her hair fall out. However, she is reminded that nothing can be certain until they go in and make sure the tumor is as small and as localized as they now suspect.

ANGER AND DEPRESSION

Saturday afternoon in West Palm Beach, Harry experiences another episode of breathlessness during a golf tournament at his club. This time he has chest pains too. Now he can no longer deny there's a problem. Phil has already alerted Harry's daughter, Jenny, who appears almost instantaneously from Virginia. She'll stay as long as she's needed to take care of her disabled mother.

Harry is furious with his "golfing buddy," Phil, for interfering when he was handling everything so well himself. He would have called Jenny when *he* had decided the time was right!

Already he has lost control of his affairs and he hasn't even gone into the hospital yet! He sees Jenny and Phil talking in hushed tones in the next room. Why is *he* not being included in the decisions being made in his own house? It never occurs to him that this is exactly the way Corrine has felt at times when he has discouraged her from doing things for herself or participating in important decisions.

Harry has become very morose and despondent, and has spent the few days before going into the hospital making sure all his papers are in order and arranging for full-time nursing care for Corrine, "in case anything should happen" to him.

ASSIGNING BLAME

Migdalia and Juan have gone back to Colombia. Maybe her sickness was caused by coming to America! They left the children with a relative in the Bronx so that they could continue going to school, while she and Juan decide what to do. She's been told that putting off the surgery might significantly increase her risk, but she and Juan are not convinced. Before they agree to anything, they must first seek the counsel and advice of their family, friends, and spiritual advisor at home.

But now, she has apparently had a change of heart and notified her doctor in New York that she is coming back to have surgery. She's learned that she had been shielded from the fact that several women in her family had died of ovarian cancer—sisters of her mother whom she never met or does not remember because she was so young when they died.

Migdalia's mother is also coming up from Colombia to be with her and will stay at her bedside for as much time as she is allowed while her daughter is in the hospital.

AMBIVALENCE

Rick has grudgingly agreed to undergo some tests to see whether he would be a good candidate for a new surgical procedure for Parkinson's disease. So far, the results have been promising, but the down side is that, although most patients respond well initially, the long-term results are still unknown. He needs to understand that going in. Rick doesn't like the idea of being a "guinea pig," and he's never been "big" on uncertainty. He doesn't even like to try a new restaurant unless he's sure he's going to like it.

Rick's wife, Annie, has insisted that he go into counseling to help relieve his anxiety and depression. But she is as terrified as he is, wondering how *she* is going to be able to cope with what she fears will lie ahead for Rick and the rest of the family.

It can be particularly frustrating for the medical team when forces, other than the patient's medical prognosis, factor into decisions regarding treatment. Often the team is not even aware of these other issues, especially when they are not emanating directly from the patient himself. In this case, Annie's lingering impressions from a negative past experience may become a major impediment, should the team recommend surgery for Rick.

Although, on one hand, Annie seems to be encouraging him, she is actually giving Rick mixed messages about whether to sign up for the treatment if it turns out that he is an appropriate candidate. And he is responding by becoming even more hopeless and depressed and less likely to make a rational decision.

When Annie was about the same age as their daughter is now, her father was diagnosed with colon cancer and was treated with what was then an "experimental" procedure. She remembers how he was in and out of the hospital, growing sicker and more debilitated and finally dying a painful death. It was a very scary experience, which she doesn't want to go through again. Of course, it was a different time and a different disease, and her father had never been physically strong to begin with. Perhaps that was one of the reasons she had been so attracted to Rick. His physical strength made her feel safe.

But here again, she finds herself looking down what feels like the same mine shaft. And, unchecked, Annie's fears could literally stand in the way of saving Rick's productive life if that becomes the basis for his decision. The hospital social worker, upon learning of Annie's fears, can help her verbalize and work them through.

LOSING CONTROL

Rick's doctor decides that the best way to proceed is to admit him for three or four days, even though the testing is usually done on an outpatient basis. But because Rick and Annie live a good forty-five miles from the hospital, his doctor senses that the logistics could easily become a convenient reason for Rick to opt out.

There are official visiting hours, but they are not strictly enforced, so Annie goes to the hospital every afternoon and stays for several hours. The nurses are often happy to see family members, especially when patients like Rick have nothing to do but wait all day to be taken down for tests. Visitors can help take the edge off and keep patients comfortable and occupied.

But today, as she's walking down the hall, Annie hears someone screaming and ranting in expletives, threatening to get dressed and go home. She can barely believe that it's Rick, who is usually so reserved and mild-mannered! In seven years of marriage, she has never seen him like this, except for one isolated incident when he had come home drunk from a night out with the boys.

No one knows exactly what set him off. But apparently, situational episodes of "hospital psychosis" are not that uncommon. After all, there could hardly be a more stressful situation. There he is, "in captivity," unable to sleep with all the constant commotion. The patient in the next bed is hard of hearing and has the TV turned all the way up. There are lights on, noises in the hallway, and nurses and aides constantly walking in and out of the room and being paged on the loud speaker. And, of course, there is the underlying uncertainty about what is in store for him.

Under other circumstances, he might have been given an antianxiolytic, but in this case the residents are hesitant to prescribe anything that could compromise his test results. Seeing Annie helps calm him down, and the social worker is summoned and reassures them both that this is not a symptom of anything more than anxiety.

A CLOSER LOOK AT THE QUESTION OF CONTROL

Regardless of the disease, the type of treatment, or the long-term effects, loss of control, to some degree, is an almost unavoidable part of the trajectory of illness. The word "trajectory" itself connotes a course and speed that is determined by forces outside of an individual's control. The process takes over and the patient becomes an unwilling passenger.

Many factors will influence how the patient handles this aspect of the trajectory, as well as the anxiety of facing the unknown. Let's review some of the variables we have touched upon and see how they figure in the cases we've been discussing.

- How central is the concept of control to a particular individual?

Being in control is more of an issue to some people than others—and therefore, more of a threat when it is taken away, even temporarily. We talked earlier about the fact that illness does not occur in a vacuum. And a person's response to the loss of control, to whatever degree, during hospitalization, treatment, and a protracted illness, is very much predicated on who he or she was *before* the onset. Among our cases, Harry and Diane are two who define themselves as being chief decision makers— Diane in her successful real estate business and Harry in his role as caretaker at home. Both are especially unnerved by the prospect of others, whom they feel are not as capable, taking charge.

- How reliable is the support system?

Who will be there—and for how long? And are they up to the task? In Harry's case, both daughters live in other states and his wife is incapacitated. But he will probably not require help for long, unlike someone with long-term needs like Rick. After months and years of dealing with a chronic illness, even the most dedicated caretaker (like Rick's wife, Annie), will feel the effects of physical and emotional burnout.

Today, many diseases, like HIV, which not long ago were considered terminal, are treatable as chronic illnesses. The good news is obvious. But the flip side is the wear-out factor, exacerbated by social and financial consequences, which we will see in more detail later on.

- How predictable is the pattern of the disease? Is the particular disease generally gradual or precipitous? How much success has there been in treating it? What symptoms are likely to surface—and when?

Uncertainty is among of the most troubling aspects of many chronic illnesses. Rick's Parkinson's disease, Cyril's hepatitis C, and Tina's MS all will be erratic. And, in all three cases, none of the limited treatment options presently available have been successful in curing, only in treating symptoms, and with mixed results.

- What is the probable prognosis? When there is the specter of the ultimate loss, control issues become that much more charged. The content may shift from control over one's career and social interests to deciding whether the green pill or the white pill should be taken first. It all revolves around the same universal human need—to maintain dignity and have one's wishes count.

For all patients, the loss of control is a major stumbling block. It is not just the treatment that might make them dependent on others, even if only temporarily, but also the unmistakable signal that something bigger than themselves is now threatening to usurp control of their lives—namely *the disease*.

POSTSURGERY

To date, Harry, Migdalia, Lynn, Diane, and Jeff have all undergone surgery. Harry had successful bypass surgery and is in a special rehab unit connected with the hospital. His other daughter, Melanie, has come down to Florida to help him adjust to this first phase of recovery. His wife, Corrine, has become less fearful and more independent since Harry has been in the hospital, which no one would ever have predicted!

Migdalia will be in the hospital in New York for at least another week. She has needed two transfusions and is in serious condition. There is now some doubt that she will be strong enough to tolerate the chemotherapy, and without it, her prognosis is guarded at best. But, unable to grasp the reality of her condition, she worries that she will not be able to take her children to a movie they've been looking forward to seeing. Juan promises her that she will be home before the movie has gone and that they won't go to see it without her.

Lynn has gone home and expects to return to work within a few weeks. She is amazed at how little pain she is experiencing, although she needs a lot of rest and has been told not to lift anything until her stitches are removed.

Diane is not faring well at all. They had to remove her entire right breast, and there were lymph nodes under her arm that had also tested positive. She will now have to undergo chemotherapy. Rather than counting on people she knows for help during her treatment, she has decided to hire LPNs or companions as she needs them. It will cost a small fortune, but she would rather pay than risk disappointment or rejection by friends or family who have their own lives. And although it has now been several weeks, she has not told most of her clients or even her friends. As far as they are concerned, she is "traveling."

But the worst-case scenario is Jeff's. Although some of his tumor was removed, the location made it impossible to get it all. He is now undergoing an aggressive course of chemotherapy. He seems to be responding well so far, but the prognosis is far from hopeful.

Jeff's parents are doing everything they can to put on a positive face, and he is looking forward to going back to school, although he has some apprehension about how his friends will react to his hair loss. Generally, baseball caps are not allowed in school, but his parents have called the principal and were assured an exception can be made for Jeff.

His nine-year-old brother, Doug, has recently been exhibiting some odd behavior. He often "disappears" for hours at a time and doesn't tell anyone where he's going. And when he's home, he seems to be spending more and more time locked in his room with the stereo blasting.

THE UNMARKED PATH OF CHRONIC ILLNESS

Rick has been told that he is not a good candidate for the new surgical procedure after all. So he has been receiving a mix of medications, and is responding very well. In the early part of the day, before he becomes tired, he appears to be the same as always. During this window of opportunity, his movements are not quite as fluid as before, but he has no tremors and his balance is fine. He cannot go back to work, of course, but he has been able to work on finishing Kate's dollhouse, and he is very happy to be able to spend so much time with his family. The only thing that worries him is his inability to make a living. But Annie has gotten a part time job as a hair-dresser, which is what she did before they met. And he is eligible for disability benefits, so they will be all right.

Curiously, Cyril has been experiencing recurrent bouts of abdominal pain and weakness in the last few weeks, but he is chalking it up to anxiety and refuses to give in to it.

Tina has begun a relationship with that fellow, Sean, from her health club. It was his call she was expecting when that ominous call came from her doctor's office three months ago. He did call after all, and things are going so beautifully that she cannot bring herself to spoil it all by telling him she has MS.

In fact, she has not told anyone, and it isn't easy carrying around this dreadful secret. She has toyed with the idea of mentioning it to her best friend, but changed her mind because, with all her good intentions, Stephanie has never been great at keeping mum. And she certainly can't tell her children, or her parents. It would only worry them. Also, if her ex were to find out that she is sick, he might use it as a way to get custody of the twins. Right now, nothing is happening, anyway! And it might never be a problem that she can't handle. Lots of people have MS and don't become visibly incapacitated, and she's determined to be one of them.

BUMPS IN THE ROAD BACK TO NORMALCY

In the context of a life-threatening or chronic illness, "normalcy" has a somewhat looser meaning. After treatment is over, in the case of a disease like cancer, or once a regimen has been found to be effective, as with Rick's medications, there is hope that life can resume at a level that's as close as possible to what it was like before, allowing for some necessary adjustments and modifications.

If you were to map out the trajectory of an illness, this juncture would be the first of many plateaus in an uneven series of steps going down. In the beginning, the "landings" are longer and flatter. But as the illness progresses, the plateaus become shorter in duration and each step down becomes a steeper drop, while the succession becomes more and more rapid.

The more active a person was before the onset of illness, the more unsettling these disruptions and losses can feel. A person who used to be agile and athletic, like Rick, will experience a physical change much more profoundly than someone who had been more sedentary before a disease like Parkinson's set in. So it is almost impossible to assign a universal meaning to any specific limitation of movement, like the sudden inability to climb a ladder and remain steady.

But, in general, "normalcy" represents a plateau that has been achieved as a result of successful treatment, and which the patient hopes will remain the norm from that time forward.

For Rick, it has meant continuing to schedule his daily activities around his "window of opportunity," which, for him, is early in the day. He is now able to take Kate to kindergarten in the morning, do the grocery shopping, and take care of other errands while he still has the energy. Sometimes he needs to take a short nap on his return, but not always. There have even been days when he feels strong enough to go to a construction site where his old buddies are working to say hello, and sometimes even join them for a sandwich.

Only, as the months have gone by, he finds that there is less and less to talk about, since he's not really part of the crew any more. And then, there are those awkward pauses. One of the guys might say something that would be funny under ordinary circumstances, but now it makes them all feel uncomfortable. Rick senses their uneasiness about his whole situation but doesn't know how to handle it. They always ask him how he's doing, but lately he thinks that maybe they really don't want to hear about it.

The other thing that is really depressing Rick is the avalanche of bills coming in. His insurance covers most of his medical expenses now, but that will only last so long, and COBRA is very expensive. Without his being able to work, he is really getting scared about how they're going to manage. SSD will only go so far, and there's a six-month wait from the date of acceptance. In the meantime, he can't even bring himself to finish filling out the application forms. He was supposed to have done that three weeks ago, and Annie has offered to help him, but every time he thinks about it, he either gets a headache or has to take a nap.

NORMALIZATION "JET LAG"

The whole concept of normalization is fairly new. Not that long ago, relatively few people with life-threatening illnesses would have had the expectation of living "normal" lives again. But, as with most quantum leaps into a new era, there are often unexpected, new problems that come along which are hard to resolve. Let's examine a few of them.

- While you were gone . . .

As critical as the patient's role might have been in the office or in social and family situations, life goes on. It can be extremely upsetting for patients to find that, while they were missed, eventually someone else stepped in to handle their functions. Upon return, it may be difficult for a patient to reclaim his or her former role and status. There also may have been other substantial changes during the patient's absence, especially if it spanned several months.

- Why aren't you happy?

A welcome back party is supposed to be a joyous occasion! But the patient may not be ready to celebrate quite yet. Maybe it's the fear of being vulnerable without the support, care and monitoring of the medical team. On the one hand, there is the relief of not having to go through any more treatments, side effects, and inconvenience. But without all the old safety nets, it doesn't feel entirely safe.

- We thought you were better!

Sometimes it isn't only the patient who expects just to step right back in without skipping a beat. Others often don't understand that after surgery or chemotherapy, a person's energy level is not what it was. As much as he or she may *want* to keep up at the expected pace, it might be very difficult or impossible for the returning patient, and that can create resentment—on both sides.

- You can lift now . . . so why aren't you doing the laundry?

After all the fanfare, the family and coworkers have an expectation that the patient, who is now in remission or symptom-free, will simply step in and take over his or her former tasks! But, for the patient, there is often a lag time in accepting wellness. During the diagnosis and treatment phases, the patient is living on adrenaline. Now that it's all over, the entire experience can come crashing down like a ton of bricks.

And then, there's also the worrying, waiting and watching for symptoms to reappear. It often takes a considerable period for this to pass, and can cause confusion and tensions among all those involved.

- Patients vs. civilians

When a patient has been through a traumatic illness, it is very much like a soldier returning from battle. Everything has a different meaning when viewed from this new perspective. Others can't possibly understand because they haven't experienced it, and they may even feel uneasy around someone so odd and depressing

- Handling the cosmetics

People can't wait to say, "Hey, you look great!" But when the person standing before them is wearing a wig and has no eyelashes, it can be an awkward scenario. And that can make it even more difficult for the patient to simply fold back into the mainstream.

- Being treated like everyone else

Even when they know that an illness, like cancer, is not contagious, people may shy away from someone who has obviously been ill. They may feel awkward and not know whether to pretend not to notice. Especially if the patient appears frail, it can be difficult for coworkers or neighbors simply to treat him or her exactly as they had before.

ONE STEP FORWARD . . .

CONGRATULATIONS! YOU'RE ON YOUR OWN!

Harry's progress is better than expected. After four months, he's not yet able to play golf, but he and Corrine take walks together every day. It's important for both of them.

And now they even walk at just about the same pace, due to the pain in Harry's leg where they had to take a vein to use in his bypass surgery. And he still tires easily, but that seems to be improving with time.

One thing that annoys Harry comes as a real surprise. As much as he had discouraged people from "hovering" when he first got home from the hospital, he now resents the fact that, since everyone assumes he's "out of the woods," neither Phil nor his daughters are calling every day. In fact, Phil and his wife, Nan, are going on a cruise in a few weeks, and although there are other neighbors Harry could call on for help if he needed to, he almost feels as though Phil is "abandoning" him! He is becoming very anxious as the cruise date draws nearer, although, of course, he would never mention it.

NEW WAVE

Jeff has gone back to school. His two best friends have shaved their heads and a couple of other kids are thinking about following suit. The school has also relaxed its policy about wearing caps. The only problem came when Marty, Jeff's dad, took the boys to a Red Sox game and it came time to sing the national anthem. When Jeff didn't remove his cap, somebody two rows back started yelling at him about respecting his country until Marty straightened him out, insisting he apologize to Jeff for his ignorance.

Doug had considered shaving his head, too, but quickly decided against it, since most of the kids in his class are not particularly aware of Jeff's cancer, and it feels safer for Doug not to talk about it. Some kids might even think it could be catching and avoid Doug! So why risk that?

Also, the more time he spends thinking about other things, the more normal his own life is beginning to seem. He has joined both the drama club and the soccer team, although neither activity particularly interests him. But it gives him something to do two days a week after school, so he doesn't have to go home. And the other days, he often hangs out at his friend, Donny's house. Donny is one of four brothers, so his mother doesn't mind having one more for dinner and has invited Doug to stay over many nights. This makes Eileen and Marty feel a little uncomfortable, since they can't return the favor, but Donny's mom has assured Eileen that she is glad to have him around. Donny has never had such a good friend.

OVER AND DONE WITH!

Lynn has gone back to work. She's a regional sales rep for a pharmaceutical company and has a hectic schedule involving quite a bit of traveling to appointments each day, some as much as forty or fifty miles away from home. Even though she only had to heal from her surgery and didn't need chemotherapy or radiation, her energy level is not back to where she feels it "should be," and that worries her. She's also terrified that other people will notice her fatigue, and in a field as competitive as hers, there's "just no room for that!"

She's been having an incredibly difficult time getting up and out of the house every morning, and her husband, Rob, has become increasingly concerned. He has even gone so far as to suggest she take a six-month leave of absence. He can easily support them and she can do whatever she wants—just relax or, perhaps, take a course. She's always wished she had time to pursue her painting. But she continues to insist there's nothing wrong with her and cries whenever he talks about it. She feels like she's failing on all fronts. And she didn't even have cancer!

In fact, in the hospital, when the American Cancer Society volunteers came around to visit all the other women who'd had mastectomies, they skipped her. She wasn't going to have to go through treatment and lose her hair and feel sick and be scared to death that she wouldn't make it . . . so she guessed they felt she wasn't worth their time. But it made her angry, because even though her surgery was, technically, "elective," it wasn't in fact. If she had waited another six months, she would have had full-blown cancer in both breasts!

Before her surgery, Lynn had had a hard time convincing the insurance company that it wasn't a "cosmetic" procedure! They finally saw the light when she pointed out that if she waited until it was "real cancer," it would end up costing them a lot more for her subsequent treatment!

But now, with the worse of it behind her and everything to look forward to, she can't understand why she isn't feeling the elation she thought she would when the surgery and the prospect of breast cancer were over. In fact, she's never felt more sad and insecure. And she's been crying a lot, for apparently no reason.

The other day she started to weep uncontrollably in the supermarket when she couldn't decide what to make for dinner. She found herself wheeling her shopping cart around and around the store, putting items in and then taking them back out again. She began to feel like people were staring at her, even though she knew it probably wasn't true. She could barely breathe and just needed to get out of the store. So she left the cart there, in the middle of the aisle, and flew out the door to her car, where she sat with her head in her hands and cried.

When she finally regained control of herself and put her key in the ignition, Lynn suddenly realized she didn't know which road to take to get home. She knew this was ridiculous, but she just couldn't remember! So she grabbed her cell phone and called Rob to come and get her.

She is now seeing a social worker to work through her intense survival guilt about "getting away with" living when her mother died. In addition, her male social worker wonders why she continues to deny mourning the loss of her breasts. He has also referred Lynn to a psychiatrist for antidepressant medication. She was told it would take four to six weeks before she would experience the full benefit. In the meantime, she's just trying to "keep the lid on," and get back to normal. After all, she's free now . . . isn't she?

YOU CAN'T MAKE IT GO AWAY. SO WHAT CAN YOU DO?

How do you help a patient adjust to having an illness—or no longer having an illness but still carrying the emotional scars? Basically, you can help them recognize what they *can* do and what they *can't*. And you can assist them in finding ways to acclimate and accommodate their lives to their new reality—at whatever stage.

Earlier, we had talked about containment and assessment. Let's take a moment to define further what each entails, and some of the many "hats" a social worker wears in the process.

- As a conduit: you can assist the patient in telling his or her story

  All of it—the sights, sounds, smells, pain and fear. They've been through a lot, and a lot of it was not fit to share with anyone else. As long as it goes unexpressed, the patient might be stuck with the guilt, anger, shame, sadness, mortality issues and other strong emotions that have had no other outlet. By encouraging and supporting ventilation of the full range of affective expression, you begin to help them work through it.
- As a mirror: you can focus the patient on insight and reflection

  By helping patients understand their feelings—past and present—and helping them recognize their past and present coping mechanisms and strategies, you can help them to see the arsenal they already have, so the fight back can feel a lot less daunting. Also, exploring the role that cultural and spiritual beliefs and supports can play can further help a patient regain his or her feeling of readiness to cope and move forward.
- As a guide: you can educate the patient about other available supports

  Providing information about useful resources and, when appropriate, referring patients to support groups dealing with similar issues can be tremendously helpful. This will also help to reinforce the feeling that patients are not alone, and that others are there to help make the transition easier.
- As a trusted ally: you can be there when they need you

  Just knowing you're a phone call away is probably the biggest relief of all. Patients are able to confide in you and rely on your honest feedback and support. At a time when nothing else seems certain or worthy of their trust, including their own bodies, your support can help them find the strength and will to cope.

A SURPRISE SILVER LINING

Diane's chemotherapy is finished and it seems to have accomplished its goal. She, too, is back at work. But she feels a little skittish about being on her own, without the constant monitoring and support system of the hospital and the "Wednesday Club."

Wednesdays at ten, no matter where she is, she finds herself thinking about the other women sitting in that row of almond-colored vinyl seats that reminded her of an old-fashioned beauty parlor. Only here, instead of sitting under helmet-shaped hair dryers, these women had IVs in their arms. Jan and Theresa still had a few more treatments to go. But Kathy and Diane had finished at the same, and they promised they would stay in touch, yet somehow it never quite feels like the right time to call.

Then yesterday Diane had an idea. The hospital has volunteers who come to talk about where to buy wigs and prostheses and give patients makeup tips. She could definitely do that! And it would give her a way to stay connected without actually being a patient any more.

Diane had never understood why people would want to volunteer when they could be out spending that same effort making money. But this is completely different. And she's now made the necessary calls. She'll go for a six-week training seminar and then she'll be ready to start. It feels like the best idea she's ever had in her life! Although she has lost her breast as a result of her cancer, she has discovered another side of herself she might never have known was there. She will now have a chance to make a real difference in the lives of others and inspire them to feel better about themselves.

A TURN FOR THE WORSE

Jeff, Rick, and Cyril have all had recent setbacks. In Jeff's case, the medical team has known it was only a matter of time, even though everyone hoped against hope. And he did have several good months before the metastasis resumed.

But Jeff's parents refuse to take no for an answer and are frantically trying to enroll him in a clinical trial in Houston. They decide not to even wait for an answer, but to just get on a plane and fly down to the hospital with Jeff. Clearly, they are desperate. How can these people keep putting them on hold and telling them to call back tomorrow when there might not *be* a tomorrow?

They will leave Doug behind in his grandmother's care so he can continue school. He has become more withdrawn, is having terrible nightmares, and is failing every subject except math, but that can be dealt with later.

For Rick, the effectiveness of his medications had started to decrease after only a few months. Other combinations were tried and would work temporarily. But he was unable to sustain his improvement. With some drugs, he would suddenly develop a tolerance, which would necessitate a higher dose that brought on severe side effects, and with others there would be little response at all. He now has tremors and tardive diskinesia, his speech is often slurred, and some days he has trouble dressing and feeding himself because his coordination has decreased so drastically. His window of opportunity is a lot narrower now, and on some days it barely exists at all.

Cyril's "imagined" symptoms have turned out to be very real. It was the jaundice that finally convinced him that he needed help. But, after an exhaustive battery of tests, it has been determined that his hepatitis C has, unfortunately, progressed to liver cancer.

LAST STOP: CLINICAL TRIALS

Diane was doing so well. And she had found a whole new purpose in her volunteer work. But when she went for her yearly checkup after the end of her chemotherapy, two small lumps were discovered under her other arm. Biopsies brought more bad news. And because the metastasis has occurred so soon after her first treatment, it is clear that a much more aggressive regimen is going to be needed.

Diane is determined not to take this news lying down. This setback is just that—a setback! And just the way the first round of chemo had worked, she is determined that this one will, too.

She wonders whether any of the other women who were in her "Wednesday Club" the first time around have had this new treatment. But she doesn't see any familiar faces and nobody seems to know. Uta, her favorite nurse, stops by to see her, but will not be involved this time. And Diane senses a certain remoteness, although she can't quite put her finger on it.

Maybe she's reading things into it, but the whole experience feels different this time. The "Wednesday Club" felt much more positive. Even though it was a difficult time, they had all gone through it together and knew they were going to get better. They joked and encouraged each other. Diane had almost looked forward to it, in a strange way—except for the actual treatment and the nausea that would follow. But her memories of that part were overshadowed by the strength of the "sisterhood."

However, this clinical trial group is not like that at all. It almost feels like she's in a different hospital! The actual treatment is a lot harsher, so the other patients are hardly in the mood to chat. Some start throwing up even before it's over. And others look as if they can barely hold their heads up.

There is no levity of any kind in this group. No cheerleading. No new makeup tips or discussions about how everybody's doing. These patients barely acknowledge each other. And Diane notices that most are too sick even to bother with wigs or makeup or trying to appear confident. It's all very matter-of-fact. And she's almost afraid to get too close to some of these women, because she has an eerie feeling that they may not be there long enough to get to know—either because the side effects from the treatment are becoming more than they can tolerate, or worse.

Cyril had no prior experience with which to compare his clinical trial treatments. Although he sometimes has moments where he is angry with himself for having waited this long, the other part of him is glad that he had had that "extra time" of what seemed to be a normal, productive life. So he is convinced that he would make the same decision again, even if he knew it would eventually come to this.

In the meantime, Jeff has started treatment in Houston, but the doctors are not giving his parents any false hopes. The social worker assigned to the unit is providing a lot of support, filling in the information gaps when Marty and Eileen are unclear about what they've been told. Sometimes it's hard to take it all in, especially under these circumstances. And in addition, they are far away from the familiarity of their home base in Boston, which makes it that much harder. But the biggest task ahead for the social worker now will be to help them accept the most difficult news of all.

WHEN DOCTORS HAVE NOTHING MORE TO OFFER

When it becomes clear that even these aggressive new treatments aren't working, the doctors must tell the patient and the family that medical science has nothing else to offer that can cure, or even stem the tide of the disease. This is the point when the patient enters the phase that is truly the "end of life."

From here on, it is up to the medical team—and in many cases, a hospice team— to make the patient as comfortable as possible.

The role of the social worker now shifts to helping the patient and the family prepare for the patient's death with as much dignity and as little suffering as possible. There are several specific tasks involved in this process:

- Giving "permission" for the patient to acknowledge pain

  Even during the last days of life, many patients try to hide or "tough out" their pain because they are afraid of appearing "weak." However, with all of the drugs now available to control pain, and without the concern, at this stage, about addiction, it is not necessary for these patients to suffer.

  The idea that suffering is dignified needs to be replaced with the notion that a human being who is loved and respected *deserves* to die in peace, without pain! And the social worker is someone who can give the patient the "permission" not only to acknowledge the level of pain but also to verbalize it in specific terms in order to get the relief they need as they need it.

- Helping the patient to describe the pain and interceding when necessary

  There is specific language that will help the medical team determine how much pain the patient is experiencing, what type of pain it is and, therefore, how best to control it. The social worker can help the patient describe his or her needs to the medical team and intervene on the patient's behalf to make sure these needs are understood and treated appropriately. There may be times, when there is intractable pain, and the social worker may need to be more aggressive to get it handled.

- Helping the patient define and express his or her final wishes

  Without forcing the issue, the social worker can talk with the patient about his or her imminent death and what arrangements should be made. The patient may want to compose a letter or videotape for the family, especially if he or she is finding it difficult to talk to them in person. It is critical to be the "container" now, and to be careful not to interject your own values system. The patient will provide cues for you to follow, either verbally or nonverbally. If the patient is not alert or in a coma, just sitting by the bedside with the family allows you to help them through anticipatory grief.

- Helping to stave off dissonance

  This is not an easy time for the family, especially when there are differences of opinion about final arrangements or whether or not to sign a DNR order. But this, literally, is the patient's last chance to discuss and resolve his or her unfinished business. The social worker can become an invaluable conduit at this juncture. By providing support, encouraging the patient to express his or her feelings, and helping to minimize hostilities, you can help to facilitate resolution, so the patient can die in peace.

The rest of this book will take you through the many issues that occur when a person experiences a range of illnesses in the context of his or her culture, pain experience, decision making, age, developmental stage, spiritual concerns, mental health issues, and family issues. The follow chapters will also focus, in depth, on bereavement and follow-up care for families.

15

CLINICAL SOCIAL WORK PRACTICE AT THE END OF LIFE

FELICE ZILBERFEIN AND ELIZABETH HURWITZ

SOCIAL WORK practice with individuals facing the end of life requires that the clinician begin to come to terms with his or her own mortality. This is no small task, and one that social workers, like the rest of society, are inclined to avoid and deny. But to engage in the process of deeply knowing these patients with an open heart, the practitioner should address denial and work it through to whatever extent possible. Many clinicians who find themselves drawn to this work have already looked closely at death owing to significant personal loss and have emerged much less afraid. Consider the effort it takes to be an empathic presence in the face of simultaneous physical, psychological, and spiritual suffering. To survive and flourish as a professional demands a high degree of self-awareness, a supportive work environment, and an effective yet manageable self-care plan.

Most good clinicians can cope with seeing one or two dying patients, but when the practice primarily comprises patients at the end of life, the ability to tolerate loss after loss becomes a prerequisite. "Death is a natural part of life" becomes not a trite statement of the obvious, but an accepted part of the life cycle that is fully appreciated and even respected. When this work is undertaken without some level of death awareness, the clinician is vulnerable to becoming depressed, overwhelmed, or numb in order to dissociate from daily exposure to nonexistence.

The essential work at the end of life is to accompany the patient side by side on a journey that has no clear destination. The journey is never the same for any two who set forth. Because there is so much that cannot be known in advance, and because nonexistence is a daily threat, the professional clinician would do well to have carefully examined his or her own beliefs, attitudes, fantasies, and fears about death. It is important to derive some personal meaning from the dying and loss process, a framework that helps the clinician make sense out of each individual loss and the collective losses as a whole. Whatever surfaces during the labors of self-reflection will not be wasted, for it will likely be of use somewhere on the journey, this time or the next. There is the potential for significant personal growth along the way for the patient, the family, and the social worker, which is perhaps one of the greatest rewards of the journey itself. There is no more hopeful experience than this. We are fortunate that we can begin to understand what dying is like by engaging in this work. To understand dying after all, is to understand how best to live.

This chapter divides social work practice at the end of life into five sections: how patients face the challenge of death; what is meant by dying with dignity; the role of hope in end-of-life care; developing a holding environment; and implications for practice. Case vignettes are provided throughout the chapter to illustrate the major themes. The practice settings discussed here are a rural home-hospice program and an urban academic teaching hospital.

FACING THE GREATEST PSYCHOSOCIAL CHALLENGE: DEATH

"The primitive dread of death resides in the unconscious—a *dread that is part of the fabric of being*, that is formed early in life before the development of precise, conceptual formulation, a dread that is chilling, uncanny, and inchoate, a dread that exists prior to and outside of language and image," writes I. Yalom (1980:45). Death anxiety is our fear of death; it is a multifaceted concept and can include fears about the process of dying, death itself, and what happens afterward. We have found that many people have an idea of the ideal death: one that involves no pain, happens at a very old age while we are still in relatively good health with our physical and mental capacities intact, and occurs when all family conflicts are resolved. Most people know that this seldom happens, which is a great source of anxiety. Nowhere is death anxiety seen more clearly than in patients suffering from terminal or potentially terminal conditions. Facing one's own mortality is a frightening experience that one cannot totally prepare for. It is a process of both the unknown and the known. The dying may experience both the fear of what they already have experienced and the fear of entering the unknown. Both qualities of dying are potential objects of fear. One of the frequently expressed fears about dying concerns the possibility of chronic pain that will increase every day and may become intolerable. Another fear sometimes associated with death is that of dependency. Losing control and needing help from others in life's basic tasks can be frightening and humiliating. The pain of dying, is not only physical, "it is based in the patient's psycho-emotional-spiritual-familial reality" (Rando 2000). It comes from the incomprehensible idea of no longer existing.

"What is the fate of our body and mind?" asked one patient. The fear of what lies ahead in the afterlife concerns many. A thought that plagues many is: Will I be punished for my sins the next time around? And with dying comes the fear of isolation and separation from loved ones. Psychologically, the patient may experience intense anxiety when imagining all of these unknowns of death. Helping a patient to deal with the anxiety of death means carefully assessing the patient's fears of dying and trying to address them thoroughly and creatively.

CASE EXAMPLE

Dina was a forty-year-old woman who was facing death for the second time in her life. She had nearly died from cancer ten years before, and now she had relapsed and found herself to be "unbearably anxious." She spoke freely about her earlier experience with cancer, the pain involved in both the disease and the treatments intended to help. She remembered the anxiety she experienced when she saw the fear and sadness in the eyes of her parents and sister. Her own experience, and others known to her, increased her anxiety in what felt like insurmountable ways. But when she spoke of the unknown, her death, her concerns were: "Where will I go? Will I go anywhere? Who will be there? Will anyone be there? Where is there?" She did not know which was worse, the anxiety of the known or the anxiety of the unknown.

❋

DEATH ANXIETY contains many emotions, including anger, sadness, and guilt. Anger is a common emotion experienced in the dying process. Anger may exist as a normal reaction to an illness or loss. Initially anger can be protective and can provide the necessary energy needed to cope in the face of the dying process. When it lingers, however, it can negatively affect close relationships. Excessive experiences of anger during one's illness, dying, or death by either the patient or the loved one may be expected to complicate relationships. Closure with loved ones is often forfeited at the expense of anger. If anger exists partially because of unfinished business, it will be important for the social worker to provide vehicles for resolving it. If the condition of the patient precludes resolution, the social worker can still be of help to a family member.

CASE EXAMPLE

Mr. C. was a thirty-year-old man hospitalized with metastatic lung cancer. He did not want to talk about his condition or his impending death. He was angry and dismissed any attempt to help him. He experienced rage, hopelessness, and fear. I and other staff made many unsuccessful attempts to engage him. His mother, who visited him daily, revealed that the two had had a very tumultuous relationship for much of their lives. This began with the divorce of his parents when he was seven years old. He blamed his mother for the divorce, and over the years they grew farther and farther apart. During the past years, the two were completely estranged. Now, his mother wanted to heal the rift with her son. She had so much to say to him and wanted to express how sorry she was for all the years of bitterness. However, he dismissed her as he did the hospital staff. In this situation, I suggested that his mother write a letter to express her feelings and unresolved conflicts, keeping in mind that he might choose not to read it. She was able to do this, and Mr. C. did indeed refuse to read the letter. The mother said that while she naturally felt disappointed, she also felt relief at having had an opportunity, albeit less than ideal, to express her own feelings.

During an illness, anger and associated hostility may be expressed in many different ways—for example, negative outbursts, aggressive behavior, intolerance, withdrawal, passive aggressiveness, withholding behaviors as seen in the case above. Anger can be directed at the self, a loved one, or caregivers. Often, anger is expressed without conscious knowledge of it or the intent to harm.

In our society, many people continue to have significant problems contending with anger as an acceptable emotion. Social workers and other healthcare professionals must convey their recognition of the normalcy of this emotional response under the conditions of life-threatening illness. People need permission to ventilate charged feelings and to channel these feelings in an appropriate way. We must recognize that some repetition in processing and expressing anger may be required in order for the patient or family member to work through the emotion. In the end, it is not the person with the "bag of tricks" that is helpful, but rather the person who can listen, who is patient, who cares enough to remain open, and is unafraid of the emotion of anger who can be helpful. Feelings of sadness frequently underlie aggressive feelings and behaviors.

A dying person may appear sad and depressed. The depression may not be due solely to the approach of death. For many, the dying process reactivates unresolved problems from both the near and distant past. Depression may be a sorrowing over past losses and may be a sorrowing over the great loss yet to come. When the dying person is mourning her own death, it is helpful for someone to be close by to hear what is expressed (Pattison 1978).

CASE EXAMPLE

Mrs. E. was a sixty-five-year-old woman dying of cancer and talking about the sadness she felt when thinking about dying. She had a thirty-year-old daughter with whom she was very close, "probably to the point of too close." Mrs. E. talked a great deal about the losses she was experiencing in addition to the loss of her own self. She was not going to have the opportunity to see her daughter marry. She would not have the opportunity of becoming a grandmother, something she very much yearned for. She would not be there for her daughter through these happy events. This deeply saddened her.

Guilt may develop from interpersonal conflicts that often arise during a serious illness, when anxiety, frustration, and sadness are pervasive. Guilt is stimulated by loss and trauma. Guilt may accompany the recognition of other feelings that preexisted before the illness. Long-term family dynamics have a significant impact on the level of guilt. Guilt is not uncommon in family members of a dying patient when they feel responsible for the illness in any way, because they failed to protect the loved one from the illness, or because they will survive the loved one. Some believe that the closer the relationship, the more likely it is that guilt will be part of the response (Grollman 1974). Parkes (1986) identifies feelings of guilt as one of the high risk factors in predicting poor bereavement outcomes. Many feel guilty for simply being alive, or may become obsessed with ways they failed their loved ones. Guilt, like anger, can also serve in a protective manner. People use guilt to protect themselves from other sometimes more painful emotions such as sadness and anxiety.

CASE EXAMPLE

Craig was a twenty-seven-year-old man diagnosed with leukemia two years before I met him. He had already undergone two unsuccessful bone marrow transplants. Helen, his thirty-two-year-old sister, came to see me as she "needed help coping with the impending death" of her brother. Craig and Helen's father had died of melanoma when they were very young, their mother remarried soon after. Helen disclosed that Craig had been physically abused as a child by his stepfather and neglected by their mother. Helen spent much of her early life trying to protect and save Craig from the cruelty of their stepfather and has spent the last two years of her adult life trying to save Craig from leukemia. Slowly she began to talk about how losing Craig felt almost like losing a son. Dreams emerged where Craig appeared as her son, distressing Helen, but forcing her to deal with her emotions. She became aware of her guilt about having been protected from her stepfather and spared from a cancer diagnosis while Craig had suffered from both. It became clear that Helen was more comfortable with blaming herself for her brother's misfortunes than she was imagining life without him.

DYING WITH DIGNITY

Dignity is defined as "the quality or state of being worthy, honored or esteemed." Dignity involves self-control, style, caring, and free choice. To experience a sense of dignity, one must feel a sense of worth both in who one is and in what he or she is doing. If, in the process of dying, one sees oneself as empty of giving or empty of a role that previously gave one a sense of worth, then dignity is compromised. Dignity is socially constructed through belief systems, experiences, and culture and is often represented as autonomy, self-worth, or physical capacity (Street 2001). Dignity means different things to different people.

Dignified dying is afforded to the patient when that person is continually regarded as a responsible individual capable of clear thinking, honest relationships, and purposeful behavior despite physical decline. At the end of life, the quality of one's relationships continues to influence dignity critically. Loving care for a terminally ill person from a devoted family member and friends can be associated with self-worth and meaning. A sense of personal worth is nurtured through the sensitivity and choice of words used in communicating to the dying person. In the following case, issues of self-worth, roles, privacy, choice, and sexuality all play into a dying person's sense of dignity.

CASE EXAMPLE

Mr. J. was a fifty-five- year old man, married for twenty years, with two adult children. Mr. J. developed viral cardiomyopathy and was in need of a heart transplant. After waiting eighteen months, and becoming progressively ill, he received a transplant. During this waiting time, I had the privilege of getting to know and work with both Mr. J. and his wife. During the waiting process, they struggled with the unknown, and

Mr. J.'s physical decline. After the transplant, Mr. J. had one additional year of, in his words, "his old life," but then he was diagnosed with cancer. Mr. J.'s cancer had already metastasized, and there was little that could be done to prolong his life or the quality of his life. Over the next six months and until his death he was hospitalized many times. He had to give up his business. This forced his wife to return to work for the first time since their marriage. In addition, his illness took away his sense of himself as a "strong, big, and handsome man." Mr. J. had always taken pride in his appearance. He was particularly attractive, with great stature. He lost a significant amount of weight, causing him to appear small and meek. He also expressed losing his sense of himself as a sexual person. His wife "neglected to realize how important touch was." It was assumed that he no longer had any sexual feelings or desires, which he indeed did but was unable to fulfill independently. Roles were reversed. He no longer brought home the money and felt that he "was not able to take care" of his family. He felt demoralized and talked openly about his feelings of worthlessness. Mr. J. expressed how his "dignity was quickly slipping away." To compound the situation, he was frustrated with the way the hospital staff treated him. Staff stopped talking directly to him, but talked about him. They approached his wife with information, decisions, and consent. He felt as if his self-control was lost. During this time, he also felt robbed of his privacy. Staff did not knock on his door; friends did not call to ask if he wanted visitors. Nurses' aides bathed him with little regard to modesty, at times leaving him naked while they attended to another patient. I intervened by educating the nurses aides about the emotional impact of this on the patient and by consulting with staff on ways to treat him with the dignity he deserved.

How is it possible to die with dignity? Some of the effects of a terminal prognosis cannot be altered—for instance, losing weight, physical decline, or loss of bodily functions. However, others (for example, privacy, treatment by others, decision-making rights, and a sense of oneself as a sexual being) can be adjusted and maintained. The dying patient may need help expressing his or her needs. By this I refer to the social worker's ability to identify that a patient has the need to talk about the loss of dignity. The social worker can help a patient navigate the hospital system.

CONTROL, CHOICES, AND DECISION MAKING

In Western cultures, being in control of one's life is very important. Many patients want to be participants in decision making. Gravely ill and hospitalized, a person is often left out of the decisions to have certain tests, procedures, and treatments. Physicians and other medical staff fly in and out of their rooms/lives with little regard for their opinions. Decisions are made, perhaps with consent, but not always with full participation. Staff members look to family members to assist them in decision-making processes, and families, in an attempt to protect their loved ones, make decisions that may inadvertently diminish the patient's sense of self-control. Sophisticated new medical technology can constitute a threat to the physical and intellectual integrity of the individual, minimizing the degree of control and choice over his or her own life (Sampaio 1992). Technology can keep individuals alive when their conditions of life can hardly be described as human. Patients, families, and medical staff often find it a challenge to resist the temptation of new technology. Whenever possible, the social worker should focus on the patient as the primary decision maker.

SEXUALITY

One of the myths of the dignified death is that it a sexless death (Street 2001). Sexual desire is treated as if it does not exist, and often the sexual and sensual needs of the dying are denied. When a social worker openly talked to Mr. J. about sexuality, he was relieved to talk about his feelings and dispel the sense of shame that he felt. This helped him to broach the issue with his wife. Many loved ones need to relinquish their caretaking tasks in order for both the patient and the partner to maintain sensual feelings toward one another. It may be important to lie with and stroke a loved one instead of engaging in caregiving tasks such as handling incontinence, which can undo sexual desire.

ROLE CHANGES

Illness in a family can be expected to result in the reassignment of power, role, and functions within that system. This is an attempt to restore homeostatic balance lost as a result of the ill person's inability to fulfill roles or obligations that he or she had previously carried. Negotiating and adapting to such role reversals and changes are seen as primary aspects of anticipatory mourning. The promotion of as much normalcy and appropriate interpersonal interaction among loved ones is critical to maintaining a dignified dying process. One must reassign responsibilities and functions carefully (Rando 1986). Although a terminally ill patient may not be able to return to work, there are other functions that they can retain (such as financial affairs) that can be helpful to and at the same time contribute to the patient's sense of self-worth.

CASE EXAMPLE

Mrs. W. was a forty-seven-year-old married woman and mother of three children under the ages of nine. She had metastatic breast cancer. She was now bedbound and unable to participate in many of her previous, much loved responsibilities, such as taking children to baby classes and nursery school, changing diapers, and feeding. Her husband took over these functions when it was time. Mrs. W., however, maintained many of her other functions that gave her a sense of self-worth and purpose. She was able to sing lullabies to her children, hug and kiss them, and, most important, talk with them. She continued to hold on to these important functions until she died. Her husband was consoled by the fact that she was able to have what he called, "meaning and satisfaction in her life up to her very time of death."

THE ROLE OF HOPE

Maintaining hope throughout the dying process is very important. Without hope, self-cohesion may be jeopardized, often in advance of the physical body (Garrett and Weisman 2001). In the absence of hope, medical, social, psychological, and spiritual interventions mysteriously lose their potency and may have little or no impact. Even so, promoting hope at the end of life has not gained universal support among helping professionals. In fact, hope has been blamed for feeding denial, and thus preventing a more realistic dying process. The persistence of hope may be identified as resistance when a social worker exits a hospital room exasperated by thwarted efforts to get a patient or family to focus on the choice between aggressive comfort care and aggressive treatment. Another example of this is the family's insisting on the possibility of a different outcome in spite of what they have been told. When the family clings to hope over time, some professionals may see it as rejection. He or she may feel like a failure in the effort to "break" through denial.

Hope can make the dying process more tolerable. It can create fertile ground for personal growth. It can present an ongoing ability to derive meaning from life events and interpersonal relationships. In the context of hope, the focus at the end of life shifts from the attainment of long-term goals to the subjective meaning that can be derived from each remaining moment (Herth 1990). This is why some dying patients have reported an unexpected increase in their quality of life once the quantity of their life has been clearly limited.

On the other hand, the medical profession has traditionally relied on promoting the type of hope that tends to impede rather than encourage progress in the psychosocial process of dying (Herth 1990). Well-intentioned physicians may give the impression that attending to end-of-life concerns would be premature in advance of one last treatment attempt, but time is a commodity that many patients with advanced illness cannot afford to waste.

Some physicians still try to protect their patients from the truth of the diagnosis, which is thought to be in the patient's best interest. On the contrary, this approach serves the unconscious interests of the physician by shielding him or her from the reality of the patient's mortality and his or her own. This paternalistic approach essentially prevents patients from making decisions about their care because they do not have the needed information. This kind of hope thrives on the promise of advanced technology and the possible development of "miraculous" cures. Patients are encouraged to keep on trying one more episode of chemotherapy, radiotherapy, or surgery in the service of maintaining hope even beyond the real possibility of cure while reducing quality of life (Ruddick 1999). This is not a patient-centered approach because as the physician continues to recommend treatments, there is the reassurance that medical science always has something to offer and that the physician is never helpless in the ongoing battle against disease. In this way, physicians routinely support patients' false hopes, often with family collusion and vague, euphemistic diagnoses and prognoses, and sometimes overt lies (Yates 1993). The ensuing dance among the healthcare team members and the team and the family about what can and cannot be said to the patient is fraught with anger, misunderstanding, and frustration.

The issue of medical paternalism came into question in the 1960s, when telling the whole truth to "terminally ill" patients became more common. Social forces such as the civil rights movement, feminism, and the autonomy movement in medicine supported this push to empower patients with full disclosure (Parker-Oliver 2002). The hospice movement, which was then becoming an alternative to the medical approach to death, was the first effort to recognize death as the normal and natural conclusion to the life cycle. Hope was understood as being independent from cure. However, Medicare reimbursement for hospice services required that patients be fully informed of their doctor's prognosis of six months or less, as criteria for their admission to the program. Hospice philosophy has a natural conflict with the overt paternalism of the medical approach and the exigencies of reimbursement that demand that people give up hope.

Keeping silent about vital information or overwhelming the patient with too much information ignores individual preferences and variations in coping ability. A third approach is patient-centered and identifies the starting point of care as the patient's subjective experience, not the healthcare professional's personal belief system or clinical opinion. The patient-centered approach encompasses the other two approaches and relies on direct patient/family feedback to regulate the flow of information. The "flow" is determined by a combination of the patients' expressed wishes and carefully assessing coping style and the possible effects of the information to be shared. In advance of divulging sensitive medical information, patients can and should be asked what and how much they would like to know regarding their medical situation. A decision to refuse information must be respected to the same degree as a decision to be kept fully informed. This decision is apt to change over time depending on where the patient is on the dying trajectory and the patient's individual personality style. A life-limiting diagnosis is usually digested bit by bit over time. As the idiosyncratic meaning assigned to the diagnosis is more fully absorbed, priorities, needs, and hopes may shift dramatically.

CASE EXAMPLE

Bill was a thirty-five-year-old, fourth-generation Vermonter. He and his wife, Doris, lived with their three children, ages three, five, and nine, on their dairy farm in northern Vermont. He and Doris worked long hours seven days a week. His wife had several siblings living nearby. The family was very connected to their church, which they attended regularly. Bill was diagnosed with lung cancer about two months before the family was referred to hospice. No one in the family was surprised about the diagnosis since he had been smoking two packs of unfiltered cigarettes a day since he was twelve and had started spitting up blood several months earlier. At that time he had been given a six-month prognosis.

The doctor referred the case to home hospice. During the intake interview, Doris spoke on behalf of Bill, who was dozing at the table where we sat drinking coffee.

"We're waiting to hear from the doctor about this experimental drug that might contain the tumor and keep it from spreading. We're putting our hopes in that even though doctors around here don't have much positive to say about it. . . . We know that there is a possibility that Bill won't live much longer but we're still praying for a miracle," she said matter-of-factly. As the discussion focused on cure, Bill perked up and declared that he intended to live beyond any guess that his doctor could make. It would not be easy to admit this family to hospice because of their intent to pursue active treatment. But because the family could clearly benefit from hospice services, the decision was made to present the case to the admissions committee. Bill was accepted following a lengthy admissions discussion, which included reassessing the probability that additional aggressive treatment would actually be offered. Some hospice programs, especially the larger ones, can afford to admit families like this one, even when Medicare reimbursement is not guaranteed.

The initial treatment plan recommended weekly social work visits to introduce and discuss death and dying issues (end-of-life care was referred to as death and dying in the 1980s). This family was not interested in discussing death and dying in spite of gentle social work encouragement and in direct contrast with the identified plan of care. They preferred instead to focus on hope and recovery. Clinical encounters took place with Bill and Doris separately and together. The children were a constant presence when visits took place after school hours. Doris was able to easily verbalize her concerns and wishes, and she worried about being able to manage the farm on her own and raising their children as a single parent. She had married Bill at eighteen, moving out of her family's home and directly into his. She wondered about her capacity to be independent without Bill's quiet presence at her side.

Bill, on the other hand, was a man of few words. Typically, sessions were punctuated with long silences during which he would gaze wistfully out the parlor window at his herd grazing in the pasture. These periods of contemplation usually were extremely fruitful although finding the words to reflect on his life and express his concerns did not come easily or naturally to him. He felt that Doris should automatically know what he was thinking without his having to spell it out. He said that he was not afraid to die but that he was simply not yet ready to go. He had always imagined living to a ripe old age, working his farm, and watching his children marry and have children of their own. Bill believed God was not ready to "take him home yet," but wondered about the specific details of the plan God had in store for him.

Bill and Doris repeatedly rejected any discussion of the dying process, which they felt God might interpret to be evidence of a lack of their faith. As the hospice team attempted to encourage them to accept what they believed was inevitable, an end-of-life process unfolded entirely in the absence of any overt discussion of death. Being in counseling was unfamiliar territory to them; finding the words to express their sorrow was an impossible request, but they could readily tell their stories, which evolved into their process of life review. They shared their personal narratives proudly and as the relevant material emerged, end-of-life issues were explored in the context of hoping for a longer life. Any attempts to inform them about the dying process itself were greeted with hostility and repeatedly rejected. When a threshold of trust was reached,

Bill and Doris were able to do the financial planning, which helped Doris to feel more secure about her future responsibilities. Together they were able to create a legacy for Bill to leave for their children. There were no goodbyes exchanged because Bill remained steadfast in his belief that it was not his time to be "called home." Attention to these practical matters gradually shifted to more interpersonal concerns. During his last month of life, as Bill's condition continued to deteriorate, he was able to express his deep love for his family.

The agenda that hospice had developed in the initial treatment plan of care was modified in order to meet the needs of this family better. The social worker adopted a more empathic presence, which created the opportunity for increased self-expression. During this process, Bill continued to derive profound meaning from his daily routine, which he altered only because of increased infirmity. Every task he undertook was intimately linked with past generations of his family, who had engaged in similar daily activities. Bill knew his place in the world and as long as he could wake up each morning, see his beloved Green Mountains off in the distance, and tend to his herd, he felt at peace.

Bill's family never considered the option of his spending any part of his illness anywhere other than at home. Had he needed to be hospitalized or sent to a nursing home, his quality of life would have been seriously compromised. For Bill, the source of meaning was unusually transparent, which is not typical of many cases where finding out what sustains adequate meaning may require the painstaking sifting through of defenses before it can be successfully identified. Bill died at home three months later, surrounded by his family, with an increased level of acceptance and with Bill being much more at peace.

Bill never gave up hoping for his miracle, but this did not prevent him from putting his affairs in order, as might have been predicted. Anchored by his faith, Bill was unaware of the intrinsic conflict his position implied. He prayed repeatedly for a long life and to remain with his family while at the same time he prepared to accept God's will regardless of the outcome. This family never lost hope, a hope that had been fortified by daily exposure to the healing effects of the Green Mountains of Vermont. In her grief, Doris redefined the "miracle" they had been seeking as the last months they spent together as a whole family.

THE ROLE OF HOPE IN THE INTERDISCIPLINARY TEAM

Bill and his family taught the healthcare team about the role of hope at the end of life. The fact that our society perceives every death as a failure weighs heavily on a team whose mission it is to accompany patients on their final journey. It is difficult enough for hospice/palliative care professionals to go against the grain of mainstream medical science by actively supporting a patient's right to a comfortable death without having a dying patient challenge this hard-earned position in the process.

Initially there was concern that Bill's refusal to accept his prognosis would prevent them from getting the services they needed. The social worker was dispatched to confront the denial and assist the family to accept Bill's imminent death. The social worker was unsuccessful in this task and subsequently faulted for not getting them to accept the prognosis in the face of clear medical evidence. The nurses in the agency defined the social work role as counseling the couple through their resistance. The team interpreted Bill's inability to reconcile these obviously conflicting viewpoints as evidence of his denial. However, the social worker helped the team to understand this phenomenon as adaptive as Bill struggled with the threat of annihilation. Although Bill spoke energetically of life, his behaviors clearly demonstrated preparation for the end of life. Essentially, he simultaneously believed that he would survive and that he would perish.

The team, already feeling uneasy with the case, was urged to focus on Bill's behaviors and not on his expressed beliefs, which they discounted as his hyperreligiosity. Team members had reacted to Bill's unwillingness to participate in a dying process that better conformed to their expectations. The team believed that "a good death" should adhere to a defined course. When patients veer too far astray, discomfort surfaces among the team members. This unmanaged countertransference can lead to a rupture that does not usually result in termination of care, but can lead to impatience and indifference toward the patient and family. Because this team had a history of working well together, and because they genuinely respected one another's competence and commitment to the work, the social worker was able to help members differentiate between their hopes and beliefs and those of Bill and Doris. It is also worth noting that Bill and Doris played a significant role in assuring the success of their care: as most team members agreed, it simply felt good to visit them.

Some members of the hospice team, like many in American society, understand "hope" and "life-limiting illness" as being mutually exclusive. After all, how could hope exist for those who know they are dying? Dying was thought to engender the complete absence of hope. Family members and significant others worry that the dying will give up all hope if they know they will die, resulting in a hastened, more depressed demise (Hunt 1992). Yet in order to remain engaged in life in the face of an uncertain future, it is essential to remain hopeful.

External expectations of how the patient is "supposed" to behave frequently influence the dying process. Healthcare professionals working in end-of-life care can sometimes grow overly secure with their knowledge of the death trajectory and become too attached to one option or another, which may result in unnecessary conflict with patients and their families. Sometimes family members may insist on continuing treatment that doctors judge as merely prolonging the dying process. Although doing so is generally not seen as being in the patient's best interests, there may be circumstances where the family views it differently. It is important to make sure the family understands the choices at hand, but once this has been assured, the choices should be respected and supported. When there is a clear divergence between the team's recommendations and the family's preferences, the team should carefully reexamine its thinking. Team members tend to focus on the most rational choice because of their presumed emotional detachment, but hopeful families are not always concerned with the most rational choice and may focus on possibilities, not on evidence or probabilities. Maintaining a keen awareness of the team's agenda as distinct and apart from the patient's and family's will help answer the question: Whose death is it anyway?

HOPE AND REALITY

Hope can also be described as a reality-based belief that a positive future exists, but the ever-present possibility of a less optimistic outcome is acknowledged (Parker-Oliver 2002). This can include a full acceptance of the prognosis, or, as in the case of Bill, the patient can continue to profess a will to live, but at the same time, without intra-psychic conflict, speak vividly about anticipating death and taking care of the business necessary to complete his life.

Hope is also the expectation of good in the future and is not dependent on one's belief in immortality for its existence. Bill was aware that death was inevitable; he just felt it was his duty to stay in the race until the finish line was crossed. Although many social workers and other healthcare professionals may find it hard to comprehend, when all seems to be lost, hope may actually be stronger than ever before. Physicians generally hold onto the hope of cure much longer than their patients, who may, for obvious reasons, be more connected to the dying process (Ruddick 1999). Patients experience from the inside what bodily deterioration, loss of function, and autonomy that shows no sign of improvement over time feels like. The war that physicians sometimes wage against the disease process disregards the patients' central role. Social workers who regularly attempt to negotiate a cease-fire can find themselves exhausted, demoralized, and ready to reassess this aspect of their role.

HOPE AND THE DENIAL OF DEATH

It is essential to distinguish between the denial of death, which may exist for defensive psychodynamic reasons, and the unshakable presence of hope (Schechter 2000). The hopefulness outlined here does not deny death; it simply expands the parameters to encompass the patient's own subjective experience of it. With patients who are death-denying, there is limited ability to engage in active end-of-life-work. A patient's level of hopefulness looks very different depending on where along the dying trajectory the patient is encountered. The time of the initial diagnosis of life-limited illness is the optimal point to begin clinical work. However, in most cases, contact with a social worker begins either at the terminal diagnosis, when the patient is referred to a hospice program, or during an acute episode of illness in a hospital, when a referral to palliative care is made. It is particularly difficult to begin cultivating hope in patients at this advanced stage of their disease processes.

THE ROLE OF HOPE IN THE SOCIAL WORK CLINICIAN

Schechter (1999) suggests that in order to be a hopeful clinician one must have an emotional tolerance for the reverse, "a sense of the tragic" in life and the capacity to move past it. The capacity to tolerate the psychic pain and despair of others is an important aspect of the empathic self that can expand in the course of training and experience. To expand the capacity of the empathic self, high-quality, consistent clinical supervision must be available, with a supervisor who has experience in end-of-life care. Lacking sufficient supervision and training, it is unlikely this critical capacity will develop or be sustained. This work always evokes past losses, fear of future losses and requires the willingness to examine one's own death anxiety. Without self-examination, such anxiety becomes a chronic stressor and leads to job dissatisfaction (Parry 2001).

Hope rests on the meaning that can be derived from each clinical encounter, apart from an outcome of extended life. In this context each death is not unexpected but inevitable, not hopeless but filled with hope regarding the time that is left and how it is used. The job as seen in this light is emotionally challenging but not overwhelmingly burdensome. There is opportunity for success in each case, which is the focus for pride and reward in the work. It is the process, not the outcome, that determines satisfaction. Clinicians without hope have much greater vulnerability to depression, compassion fatigue, and decreased job satisfaction.

A safe place to debrief, analyze cases, manage countertransference, and get support is essential, especially because personal family and friends are rarely able to welcome the discussion of end-of-life topics into casual conversation after work. Social workers are generally drawn to this work out of a personal or family history of loss and have a vested interest in learning more about this profound and inevitable human process.

DEVELOPING A HOLDING ENVIRONMENT

Winnicott (1965) proposes that the mother's nurturing relationship to her baby provides a psychological scaffolding for the infant to develop internal psychic structures. The "holding environment" is later replicated in psychotherapy through the patient's relationship with the therapist. In therapy, the client's internalization of the therapeutic relationship serves as the scaffolding for the client's development of psychological structure. This is generally an extended process in the context of long-term psychotherapy, where it provides the necessary level of safety in all dimensions for clients to give expression to their inner life and to the development and testing of new or reworked interpersonal skills.

Developing and maintaining a holding environment is as crucial at the end of life as it is at other stages of human development. However, most of the patients encountered at this stage are not in a traditional psychotherapeutic relationship where the development of a holding environment has been a goal. Dying patients who are not already engaged in psychotherapy are unlikely to begin at this juncture. Hospice and palliative-care patients do not visit their social worker in a quiet, nicely furnished office somewhere removed from distraction and interruption from real life. The first social work encounter generally occurs in a medical setting or at home. In the hospital, interviews may be conducted in the midst of the hustle and bustle of alarms and beeps, doting or hostile family members, the blaring of overhead PA systems, unexpected visitors, and parades of physicians and their trainees. Finding time alone with the patient is sometimes impossible, and yet a relationship must be established in order to make it possible to connect with these patients on a deeper level. When social workers are able to be present with their patients, the "not knowing" that accompanies the existential plight of the dying patient can be better tolerated. The patient must feel secure in order to examine his or her experience of dying. Understanding and empathy are the tools used to create a holding environment, which can be accomplished (not in the classic sense) even under these difficult circumstances (Garrett and Weisman 2001).

CASE EXAMPLE

Carlos was a twenty-six-year-old single Puerto Rican man who worked as a chef and lived with his parents and extended family in their apartment in New York City. At twenty-five, Carlos developed severe viral cardiomyopathy and was told that without a heart transplant he would die within the year. Soon after diagnosis, Carlos was admitted to the hospital to await a transplant. He stayed in the hospital for nine months and died before receiving a new heart.

Carlos grew up in New York City with his parents, four siblings, and grandparents. He was highly identified with his family, which he described as close-knit and loving. Carlos said his family doted on him because he was "the baby." He described how much he enjoyed their special attentions. He talked about the meaning his home provided him, that he always felt more connected and safe when he was there. His home was filled with the sights and sounds of his closest family members and the smells of his mother's home cooking. His room held special meaning, but was only a designated space within the larger room that he shared with his brother and sisters. It was a mirror of his inner self. His "room" contained all of his sports paraphernalia, trophies, cookbooks, even toys from his childhood that he continued to cherish. His walls were covered with posters of his favorite Latin musicians, and his CD player was perpetually on.

Initially Carlos had been reluctant to talk about how he was feeling about his medical situation. He was not generally inclined toward self-reflection and did not see any benefit to discussing his condition. He hoped that a heart would be available soon and that he would then make a full recovery. Instead, Carlos's condition worsened and his mood deteriorated. Going home was not an option for him, so the social worker encouraged Carlos to make his hospital room feel homier. Carlos enthusiastically engaged in room redecoration by requesting that specific personal treasures be brought in from home. During this period, the unit was filled with the delightfully uncharacteristic aroma of home-cooked yellow rice and beans. One family member slept on a cot beside him every night. His little room within a room was successfully re-created over the next few weeks, which significantly decreased Carlos's anxiety about his uncertain future. The process of re-creating the room and the outcome of having the vastly improved space to live in was an attempt to provide him a holding environment. It had a profound effect on Carlos.

Once the room was suitably personalized, and the menu familiar and lovingly prepared, Carlos began to improve psychologically. He felt less helpless and more in control of his daily routine. He started to care more about how he looked and even accepted visits from some of his women friends. He established relationships with other transplant patients on the unit. After drifting into a passive patient role, his felt his personhood had been restored, and he enjoyed a quality of life he had not thought possible.

Carlos never complained about pain. When he became short of breath, meetings with the social worker were ended or postponed. When he was feeling well enough, Carlos spoke about his experience of loss. He realized that he was resentful of other men his age who were contemplating marriage and fatherhood instead of clinging to a hospital bed wishing for a new heart. He felt cheated out of his youth and wondered about the tenuousness of his future. In his empty hospital room, he had been unwilling to explore these concerns.

Carlos and his family had a strong Puerto Rican identity that formed the context for his life. Although Carlos spoke English well, he would immediately switch to Spanish when his family arrived, always seeming more animated and at ease communicating this way. His mother, who was the matriarch of their extended family was "in charge" of his care. There was an ongoing battle between the nurses and her about what was appropriate to feed him and what was deemed medically contraindicated. She seemed suspicious of the women who were assigned to take care of her son. She was certain her home cooking could restore her son's health better than standard hospital fare. Faith in church and family were seen as the primary source of strength and fortitude needed for Carlos to survive until the transplant.

IMPLICATIONS FOR PRACTICE

A social worker cannot medicate pain, dress wounds, or offer the appropriate religious rituals. She constitutes the member of the team who is trained to see the patient as part of a family system with a past, present, and future from within a cultural context, as well as to help the family to cope with the patient's severity of illness and impending death. The social worker has many roles within end-of-life care in hospital and hospice-based practice.

The privatization of the American healthcare system is in conflict with the provider's and patient's perception of care. In the current climate, where decreasing healthcare reimbursement forces institutions to emphasize the "bottom line" of care rather than its comprehensiveness, social work has had to work hard to maintain its identity and, in many medical institutions, to justify its continued existence. One result has been a significant cutback in social work staff, and thus fewer patients with biopsychosocial needs are seen by social workers. In many instances, social work services have been limited to patients facing discharge and their immediate needs on their return home or into other institutional arrangements.

In the case vignettes and discussions in this chapter, we explored several different strategies in working with patients and families in the dying process. Although a large part of the dying process is a very personal and subjective experience, social workers can take an active role in helping people manage optimally in many ways.

Social work in end-of-life care is multifaceted. Although social workers have many roles, each one and each task is accomplished with the use of clinical expertise. Whether it is arranging for a patient to have a hospital bed at home or talking with someone about her impending death, a social worker utilizes clinical skills to assist the patient and the family. Although there is significant overlap between all components of the social work role, the framework outlined here attempts to highlight those functions that correspond most directly to each.

COUNSELING

The social worker helps the patient and the family make sense of their coming loss and regain meaning. This is done by preserving hope, ensuring a dignified death, and encouraging the expression of related feelings. When one is imminently facing death, he or she, along with loved ones, experiences a wide range of emotions. The truly therapeutic experience mandates "a delicate balance among the mutually conflicting demands of simultaneously holding onto, letting go of, and drawing closer to the dying patient" (Rando 1986). The social worker assists patients and families by helping them to understand the meaning behind what they are holding on to and how difficult it is to let go.

The ability to develop a trusting relationship with patients in end-of-life work is essential. The development of a holding environment fosters a level of safety that can allow the patient to share their dying process. Providing an empathic presence demonstrates both attunement and a concern for the patient's inner world.

Social workers also help to facilitate communication between patients and their family members at the end of life. There is a daunting array of clinical variables to consider in situations where family members are coming together to talk about the mortality of one of their own. Supporting the expression of appropriate feelings and opportunities for continued interacting and communication with the dying person and providing the space for a chance to make amends with any existing problems in the relationship is critical (Sheldon 2000). This helps minimize unfinished business, premature separation, and poor communication and interaction with the dying loved one, each of which is associated with poor bereavement outcomes (Parkes 1986). This is all the more complicated where illicit drug use and alcohol are factors, where family is estranged, where there are other ill family members, where young children are in the home, and where family resemblance is undeniable; staring into the face of death and recognizing yourself is a particularly threatening experience to the self.

Because it is not always possible to know the most culturally sensitive intervention, the social worker must be willing to take clinically sound risks in order to develop and maintain the therapeutic relationship. The social worker always considers culture in her assessment and treatment.

BIOPSYCHOSOCIAL SERVICES

One important role for the social worker is to help the patient access the biopsychosocial services needed. Social workers act as advocates to patients and families to help them through this arduous process. This involves completing biopsychosocial assessments that are periodically updated to assure that patient and family needs are being addressed. It is the responsibility of the social worker to assure equality of access to services for all patients. The social worker ensures the continuity of care across practice settings. Social workers make referrals in the community that are responsive to the specific needs of the patient. Information is provided to patients and families about insurance coverage, benefits, and entitlements. Social workers assist patients in addressing the legal and ethical concerns including the understanding and completion of advance directives (Monroe 1994; Christ and Sormanti 1999).

INTERDISCIPLINARY COLLABORATION

The social worker on the interdisciplinary team must have sufficient self-esteem to thrive in an environment where all team members see themselves as "counselors" (see chapter 8). There is value to each member of the team taking a therapeutic, nonjudgmental, and "listening" stance. However, social work education, training, and clinical supervision foster a set of skills that makes the social worker uniquely suited for interdisciplinary collaboration. The social worker is trained to be self-reflective, have a high degree of self-awareness, and provide crisis intervention with family members. Clinically trained social workers are aware of transference/countertransference, maintain strong boundaries, understand the patient and family from the biopsychosocial and cultural context, and, perhaps most important, are skilled in the therapeutic use of self. Other team members have their defined roles, and while their sensitivity to the patient's behavior and attitudes is critical, it is the combination of the social worker's clinical skills that makes the social worker both unique and indispensable to interdisciplinary teams (Sheldon 2000).

The social worker helps negotiate tensions within the team that can result from role overlap or unclear role expectations. When working with the team, the social worker defines the social work role and its interdependence with the other disciplines. Educating others about the social work role is accomplished formally via structured presentations and case conferences, and informally by modeling various aspects of the role.

The social worker interprets the patient and family's behavior to the team that may seem abusive, out of character, or passively life-threatening, such as chronic noncompliance with the medical regimen. These interpretations can help resolve the discomfort that may arise from delivering care under confusing, frustrating, or threatening circumstances. When the team is invested in a plan of care that the family does not agree with, the social worker can reframe the predicament to gain a greater understanding of all perspectives involved and to achieve an acceptable resolution.

The team social worker has a role to play in the promotion of comfort and assurance of adequate pain control. As with all team members, the social worker is careful to assess the level of pain before focusing on other concerns. Assessments are done throughout the course of treatment to identify suffering that may have a psychological component as well as to identify psychological suffering that has arisen as a result of chronic pain. Interventions are designed to reduce the effects of these psychological components, which improve quality of life and can contribute to positive outcomes in these challenges to pain management.

EDUCATION

The social worker provides education and support to staff on a wide range of topics pertaining to end-of-life care as well as on general topics such as stress reduction, interdisciplinary team-building, and effective communication. Trainings may be structured as lectures, workshops, or impromptu case-based discussions.

The social worker facilitates small groups where designated staff may be helped with managing multiple patient losses, stress reduction, and maintaining strong boundaries between personal and professional concerns. These groups are designed to increase coping skills, provide a forum for communication, and foster mutual support. They are generally requested in response to observed changes in morale, increased absenteeism, and decreased energy levels and mood that seem subsequent to recent or serial loss over time.

CLINICAL SUPERVISION

Working with patients and families facing the end of life is challenging, but rewarding. The social worker's self-awareness and insight into her own death anxiety are pivotal in this work. Although clinical supervision is taken to be an important and unique enabling social work process, only thirty empirical articles have been published over the last three decades on this topic (Tsui 1997). This is a reflection of the wide gap between practice and research on supervision. It is critical for social workers in end-of-life care to have supervision, yet it is increasingly difficult to access. (See chapter 44.) Providing clinical supervision in end-of-life-care work should be mandatory.

The boundary between the processes of therapy and the development of case-related self-awareness in supervision must be understood and maintained. Ambiguities that are inherent in working toward self-awareness can be overcome where the supervisor has a clear concept of the supervisory process and can thereby maintain a clear focus, with appropriate boundaries (Lewis 1988). The following are some essential issues to address in clinical supervision. Fear of one's own mortality, if not confronted, can affect competence in various ways. Countertransference is a phenomenon that must be addressed in the supervision of social workers in end-of-life care. The unanalyzed expression or acting out of the countertransferential feelings will impede treatment (Greenberg and Mitchell 1983).

Donna, a social worker in a hospital, recounted an experience that forced her to address some of her own death anxiety in supervision:

> I was working as a social worker in a hospital when I was asked to see a 25-year-old woman (my own age) who was in the surgical intensive care unit following rare and unexpected complications from a routine surgical procedure and was anxious about

the possibility that she would die. She was on a ventilator and could only communicate by writing. Although I had been working at the hospital for nearly a year, this was the first patient I was referred to who was a contemporary. I went into the intensive care unit and immediately felt uncomfortable. As I approached the patient I began to feel unusual symptoms, i.e., heart racing, lightheadedness, tingling in my fingers. I immediately left the unit without seeing the patient. I felt grateful that I did not faint and soon the symptoms subsided. I wondered about the cause of these symptoms and ultimately convinced myself that it must have been hunger. When the same symptoms occurred the next day and actually intensified, I began to see that there may be an emotional connection.

In supervision, Donna spoke about this experience and quickly began talking about her own fears of death and how this particular patient forced her to be in touch with them. We identified the similarities she and the patient had—age, sex, cultural background. The patient was facing the possibility of death, and the social worker was deathly afraid. Talking about this in supervision enabled her to return to the unit and talk with the patient. She also realized that she would benefit from individual therapy to explore these issues more profoundly.

Social workers often feel inadequate working with patients in end-of-life care. A social worker reported the following incident in supervision:

I was working with Mr. M., who was a 65-year-old man dying of end-stage cardiac disease in the cardiac intensive care unit. He had for several days been critical, but stable, until yesterday when he began to quickly deteriorate and the team reported that death was imminent. He was in bed surrounded by his large family and I made the decision that they did not need me at that time—rationalizing that his family was there and quite supportive. Perhaps, I was right, however upon retrospect, I made that decision because I felt inadequate and could not imagine what I could have said or done at that time.

Many social workers are afraid of not knowing the right thing to say with dying patients. It is our hope that with ongoing experience and supervision, and with the points highlighted here, social workers will begin to develop the skills and confidence for this work.

The concepts of maintaining hope, creating a holding environment, dying with dignity, and expressing feelings are crucial in supporting patients and families through the dying process. Sometimes when social workers intervene with dying patients, they feel disappointed that they cannot do more. It is important to develop an understanding and appreciation of what it is you are doing with patients and families when you feel as though you are not doing anything. Often these accomplishments are not concrete and could be easily overlooked by the social worker. So it is recommended that at the conclusion of each case, these less tangible benefits, such as providing an empathic presence, cultivating meaning, and helping to facilitate the expression of feelings, be identified and fully acknowledged.

Another dimension of this work is the recognition of the social worker's own grief. Because this work can be very intimate, close relationships sometimes form between social workers and their patients, which makes the loss more powerful. Finding ways in which social workers can personally grieve over the death of patients is pivotal to remaining effective. As we attend to our patients' grief, so must we attend to our own.

REFERENCES

Christ, G. R., and M. Sormanti. 1999. Advancing social work practice in end-of-life care. *Social Work in Health Care* 30:81–99.

Garrett, C., and M. G. Weisman. 2001. A self-psychological perspective on chronic illness. *Clinical Social Work Journal* 29:119–132.

Greenberg, J. R., and S. A. Mitchell. 1983. *Object Relations in Psychoanalytic Theory.* Cambridge, MA: Harvard University Press.

Grollman, A. 1974. *Concerning Death: A Practical Guide for the Living.* Boston: Beacon Press.

Herth, K. 1990. Fostering hope in terminally-ill people. *Journal of Advanced Nursing* 15:1250–1259.

Hunt, R. 1992. Sources of hope in chronic illness. *Oncology Nursing Forum* 19:443–448.

Lewis, S. 1987. The role of self awareness in supervision. *Australian Social Work* 40(2): 19–24.

Monroe, B. 1994. Role of the social worker in palliative care. *Annals of the Academy of Medicine* 23:252–255.

Parker-Oliver, D. 2002. Redefining hope for the terminally ill. *American Journal of Hospice & Palliative Care* 19(2): 115–120.

Parkes, C. M. 1986. *Bereavement: Studies of Grief in Adult Life.* Harmondsworth, UK: Penguin.

Parry, J. K. 2001. *Social Work Theory and Practice with the Terminally Ill.* Binghamton, NY: Haworth.

Pattison, E. M. 1977. *The Experience of Dying.* Englewood Cliffs, NJ: Prentice-Hall.

Rando, T. A. 1986. *Loss and Anticipatory Grief.* New York: Lexington.

Ruddick, W. 1999. Hope and deception. *Bioethics* 13:343–357.

Sampaio, L. 1992. To die with dignity. *Social Science Medicine* 35(4): 433–441.

Shechter, R. A. 1999. The psychodynamics of a clinician's hope: A delicate balance. *Clinical Social Work Journal* 27:371–382.

Sheldon, F. M. 2000. Dimensions of the role of the social worker in palliative care. *Palliative Medicine* 14:491–498.

Street, A. F. 2001. Constructions of dignity in end-of-life care. *Journal of Palliative Care* 17(2): 93–101.

Tsui, M. 1997. Empirical research of social work supervision: The state of the art (1970–1995). *Journal of Social Service Research* 23(2): 39–54.

Winnicott, D. W. 1965. *The Maturational Processes and the Facilitating Environment.* Madison, CT: International Universities Press.

Yalom, I. 1980. *Existential Psychotherapy.* New York: Basic Books.

Yates, P. 1993. Towards a reconceptualization of hope for patients with a diagnosis of cancer. *Journal of Advanced Nursing* 18:701–706.

16

THE END OF LIFE AT THE BEGINNING OF LIFE:
WORKING WITH DYING CHILDREN AND THEIR FAMILIES

NANCY CINCOTTA

JANICE, a fifteen-year-old whom I had known for quite some time, was dying in the hospital. Without the knowledge of the professional staff, she had asked her aunt if she could be "laid out" in a fetal position. Her aunt said that this would not be possible, "because coffins are standard widths, so everyone has to be buried in the regular position or they would have to break all of your bones to fit you in." When I heard this, I asked some of the nurses how they would have responded to Janice. They each concurred that they would have told her she could not have been buried in that way. I was unclear, as I am not convinced that burial in that position is precluded. In addition, I would have entered into a discussion about why Janice was asking.

I then asked the nurses what they would have said had Janice asked if she had to do homework or take tests in heaven. They responded that they absolutely would have told her that she did not have to do these things. When I asked why, their answer was the same as mine would have been: they knew that Janice would be comforted by the response. How could they feel comfortable offering this certainty when they would not have offered Janice the assurance as to how she could be placed in the coffin? I was able to discern (after much soul-searching) that they felt that the child (or rather her spirit) was still somehow present at the wake and would be able to see that they had not told her the truth. There would be no such check about the activities in heaven. In reality, it was they who could see that they had told an untruth at the wake, but as far as activity in heaven goes, they would not be witness to it.

❋

CHILDHOOD generally serves as a barrier to the profound impact that death has on adults and to the philosophical and complicated thinking about it that can characterize adult life. Embodied in childhood is a natural curiosity about life, of which death is a part. Children's conceptualizations of death play a role in their adaptation to the loss of significant attachments, in managing age-appropriate death anxiety, and in those instances when they are faced with their own mortality.

When a child is diagnosed with a life-threatening illness, the homeostasis of the family is challenged, the natural order threatened. The profound sense of loss that begins with diagnosis continues throughout the course of the child's illness (Rosof 1994). The responses to a child's life-threatening illness have been well characterized, most notably in the case of childhood cancer, which can serve as a model for other similar and fatal illnesses (Cincotta 1993; Christ and Adams 1984; Ross 1978).

Several authors have described specific tasks for social workers working with children with life-threatening illnesses and their families within the context of the particular stages of medical treatment (Lansky 1985; Christ and Adams 1984; Ross 1978; Kagen-Goodheart 1977). The stage of illness; the child's age, personality, and cognitive ability; the family's stage of development; and cultural, religious, and societal factors will all affect the way the patient adapts to a severe illness and death. Stage-appropriate interventions enable the family to "(1) reduce uncertainty, (2) gain and maintain some control of the situation, (3) maintain and protect self-esteem, and (4) reduce negative feelings" (Van Dongen-Melman 1986).

For children to cope with life-threatening illness, and ultimately death, they need tremendous support from their families. For parents, anticipation of a child's death can be overwhelming and immobilizing. Death in childhood seems incongruous. Dealing with the stark reality that as a parent you are unable to protect your child from a life-threatening illness, and that ultimately you cannot protect her from death, can seem unbearable. Upon learning that a child has a fatal illness, the greatest challenges for a parent are to remain emotionally and physically available to the child, to work in the child's best interests during the child's lifetime, and to provide the child with the highest possible quality of life (Lauria 2001).

Before diagnosis, it is quite common for parents to protect their children, to censor what they should watch or hear, and to monitor their experiences. There is often the feeling that children do not understand death, that they would have difficulty coping with the knowledge of the severity of their illness, or that they should not be forced to face reality. These factors can create an atmosphere of "constricted communication" in families of children with life-threatening or fatal illnesses.

There are many anxieties, myths, and misperceptions about working with children who are going to die regarding their capacity to understand, their capacity to grieve, and their capacity to grow (Wolfelt 1996). The reality is that children often know much about what is happening to them, regardless of what they have been shielded from or formally told (Sourkes 1995; Bluebond-Langner 1978).

It is striking to me how much children understand about their illness. For instance, in a group work program I run for children with an ultimately fatal illness and their parents, I am stunned by the consistency with which children talk about very "real" issues (e.g., "We know we are going to die" or "I know I need a bone marrow transplant"). At the same time, their parents are talking about what their children know and do not know and what they should and should not discuss with them. It is a most significant intervention when I get permission from the children to tell parents that their children are talking among themselves about issues that the parents are unsure they should even mention.

In a recent discussion group among children who are HIV-positive and who had not been formally told their diagnosis, the conversation again went to what information they should share with their caretakers. Clear, honest communication about illness makes the experience easier for children (Spinetta and Maloney 1978). Dealing with difficult information in an age-appropriate manner expends less emotional energy than holding on to "untruths," "secrets," or withholding information. Trust is a dominant issue in personal and professional relationships with children, particularly those who are physically and emotionally vulnerable. Most of the time children create a realistic picture of their own medical situation from what they are told, from what they are not told, from what they hear from other children, from what they overhear, and from their own bodily changes. When medical information is shielded from them and they learn it "coincidentally," they can begin to distrust the information they are being given about their illness and other aspects of life.

ISSUES FOR PARENTS OF DYING CHILDREN

After having a child, it is not uncommon to take a parenting course or be given a book about being a new parent. There is no course on how to be the parent of a child with a life-threatening illness, much less a dying child (see chapter 3). Parents can benefit from the collective wisdom derived from other parents and professionals who have traveled on this journey.

DEALING WITH SHOCK AND DISBELIEF

"Is this really happening to me?"
"Even though I heard the doctor say this could happen, I never really believed this day would come."
"He made it through so many other things. I thought he would make it through this."

Even if a child has been ill for an extended period of time, the news that there is nothing more that can be done for the child is devastating. Overcoming the shock and dealing with the reality of the tasks and emotions at hand is a tremendous effort for parents who are about to lose their child. The "normal" world may otherwise stop in order for a family to attend to the needs of their dying child. During this time, families do whatever needs to be done to get through the moment; it will be weeks, months, and years before they learn to find a place in the world without their child.

One mother told me at a bereavement group that her strongest memory was of the doctor sitting with his arm around her telling her that her child was going to die, and crying with her.

REMAINING CONNECTED TO WHAT THE CHILD NEEDS: MAINTAINING ATTACHMENTS

It is natural to be overwhelmed with grief and distracted when one's child is dying, or to retreat into one's own sorrow. Alternatively, it is also easy to become "obsessed" with the child's every need and to want to spend every moment with him. Staying focused on the child, identifying, understanding, and meeting the child's physical and emotional needs help parents when their child is dying. Remaining cognizant of who the child is, what the child likes, and to whom the child is connected provides a structure for the whole family. Although this is a very serious time, children are often not serious by nature. Nurturing their playful, imaginative qualities can help them relax and be more comfortable.

CASE EXAMPLE

A five-year-old who was in the hospital dying, but still eager to be playful, realized that the doctor was coming in every day to see her. She wanted to do something to acknowledge his visits. So from the minute he left, until he came the next day, she would work on a different costume and assume a different identity. These costumes became the legacy of her final days.

Being able to have an experience that gives your child pleasure, even for a brief time before the child dies, is more desirable than never having had the experience at all. For example, if there had been a plan to buy a pet, many families will purchase one at this time. Children are good at verbalizing their wishes and wish programs are good at actualizing them. Having a trip, an event, or a camp program on which to focus distracts families from the process of dying and generally affords some relief and joy. Happy memories created in those weeks or months before a child's death perpetuate themselves throughout the bereavement period when the family needs to remember that their child did enjoy some time at the end of his or her life.

Social workers can enable and assist parents in being available to their children (for example, to help parents recognize the value of this time and to encourage them to accept help from others in order to free them to be with their child), and in reconnecting with simple activities that bring pleasure and comfort (reading, watching television, playing games).

MAINTAINING FAMILY INTEGRITY: FOSTERING INTIMACY IN THE PARENT-CHILD RELATIONSHIP

Families have private lives, routines, and rituals. That unique rapport is often interrupted when a child requires hospitalization, aggressive treatment, or palliative care. Working with families to maintain the integrity of their family life and to create routines that can feel normal or parallel old routines can make this intolerable time more tolerable. Celebrating holidays in the hospital or in hospice care contributes to enabling the whole family to function as a unit while the child is dying.

CASE EXAMPLE

One mother talked openly about the week her daughter was dying. Her extended family was there. The hospice nurse was there. The mother felt claustrophobic and she asked them all to leave. She wanted to have the freedom to close the door and be alone with her child, to lie on the bed, to share a cup of tea, and do things they had done hundreds of times alone. She did not want her child's death to be a public thing, even within her own family. She said that she felt quite selfish, but what she needed was to be alone with her daughter.

IDENTIFYING TASKS FOR CHILD AND FAMILY

What are the physical and emotional tasks for the family? Are there issues that need to be resolved?

CASE EXAMPLE

One parent, whose son had died of an infection several months after bone marrow transplantation at a center a thousand miles from home, continued to have one regret. When things started going poorly, she really did not think that her son would die and did not make arrangements for her daughters to see him before he died. She and his sisters continue to be remorseful that they did not have a chance to say goodbye.

The decision to leave siblings or spouses behind must not be taken lightly, as they may have implications for family relationships for years to come. A bereaved sibling remarked: "[My mother] went away for almost a year. Then she came back and wanted everything to go back to how it was before. There was no way that was going to happen. She left me. I'm not going to depend on her."

The emotions and tasks associated with a dying child include maintaining comfort; alleviating anxiety and pain; expressing intense emotions: love, anger, and remorse; acknowledging primal issues of attachment and separation; feelings of grief; and fear of the unknown and the unknowable. Pediatric pain is often underestimated. If a child dies in pain and parents perceive that this could have prevented, they will feel angry, resentful, and guilty (Contro et al. 2002).

Dying children often help their families during this time by raising issues, by setting the tone, and by establishing the ground rules (e.g., who they want around, what they want to do, what they want to wear). This is a time to validate the lives of these children, their strengths, and their unique role in the family.

The process of coming to terms with the situation, of understanding that one will need to let go of one's child but not letting go while the child is emotionally or physically present, is arduous. Separations between parents and children for things such as kindergarten, college, and marriage are complicated, but they are anticipated and normal developmental milestones. When a child is dying, a parent begins to plan for a final separation, which comes without a "road map," without developmental gain, and at a terrible cost. Yet there can be spiritual and emotional growth for both the parent and child. Living with dying often engenders emotions that have not been experienced before and allows for emotional intimacy unparalleled at other stages in life.

Once an illness is diagnosed, after feeling completely helpless, parents usually begin to cope by accepting the illness, reframing their thinking, and focusing on a cure. When cure seems impossible, there is always hope for prolonging life and for a miracle. Ultimately, parents still perceive that they can protect their child from dying. At the point when death becomes inevitable, so do feelings of inadequacy, disappointment, confusion, loss of control, and loss of vision in life. The death of a child symbolizes the ultimate failure of parenting and results in a sense of vulnerability that is unequaled. One method of coping with this feeling of helplessness is to try to achieve the "best death possible" for one's child.

Allowing mothers and fathers to carry on parenting functions at the end of their child's life affords them the ability to maintain their roles in caring for their child. Parents may need permission and support to provide physical care for the child at the end of life, particularly if the child is hospitalized.

CASE EXAMPLE

One mother was quite expressive, feeling that it was a privilege to have been able to bring her child into the world and having been there to care for him while he was dying, and usher him out. This was her second child to die and she had not had that opportunity the first time.

Another mother stated that the worst thing she ever had to do (and there was no way she would not do it) was to watch her child, in her arms, painfully take her last breath . . . and have given her permission to do so.

MAKING CHOICES: FOSTERING DECISION-MAKING SKILLS

Parents of children with life-threatening illnesses often report that people ask them, "How do you do this?" The answer is that they do this because they have to, not because they want to, not because they are skilled at it but because it is what life imposes on them.

Using available resources, researching the disease, contacting experts, and making sound decisions allow parents the ability to develop expertise in dealing with expected and unexpected outcomes. This learned skill is essential as parents are forced to make choices during their child's illness and dying process. It is imperative for them to feel that they have made the best possible decisions. These can ultimately include things such as participating in an experimental protocol, starting a morphine drip, or opting for no additional treatment.

The issue of "do not resuscitate" (DNR) orders is complex in pediatrics. A DNR order means giving up on treatment and hope, which is a critical emotional juncture for parents as they recognize that their child is dying. If a child is in pain and has a disease that is unremitting, a parent is forced to face the reality of the child's "dying" before he or she dies. A DNR order may seem to be in the best interests of the child, and a parent may actually be relieved after agreeing to the order. If a child is in no apparent pain and the disease course, although terminal, is not as evident, it is more difficult for parents to enter into the discussion of DNR orders. When a situation arises in which there is a sudden change in the status of an illness that renders the disease incurable, it is especially difficult for parents to consider DNR status. Coping is often sequential, with parents needing time to adapt to the reality of the current circumstances before making the next decision.

A child's developmental level will be a strong indicator as to whether or not the concept of DNR is broached with the child. Older children and children who have seen their friends suffer may have their own wishes to have a DNR order. These are intimate discussions, not for large teams or medical staff who are not well known to the child and family. At times professional staff and either the child or the family will have differing opinions about DNR status. Staff members may feel that a child is being kept alive and in pain unduly. For children or their parents to move forward with DNR orders, they must have knowingly accepted the reality of the child's ultimate death. This is difficult to achieve, and not always achievable.

CASE EXAMPLE

One family wanted their child to be resuscitated time and time again, and after much discussion, their wishes were followed a number of times. There was eventually a point at which the parents were asked to examine whether they were doing this for their child or for themselves. Ultimately the parents were able to recognize that resuscitating her again and again served no purpose. This was such an uncomfortable time for the family that years later they returned to talk about it, to try to understand what happened that day. They were still unsure of their decision.

One child made me promise that she would not be intubated and forced to live on a ventilator. I could not do this without involving her mother in a painful conversation, but it was a conversation that had to occur.

Families face the decision about where their children should die. This is a matter of family preference with practical considerations, including the availability of support, the ages and number of children living in the home, the family's rapport with death, and the child's wishes.

HOPE AND ANTICIPATORY GRIEF

Hope is a dominant theme in the work with parents at the end of life—not unrealistic hope, not denial, but hope that parents have for their child's survival that exceeds some parameters of realistic expectation. They hope beyond hope, and pray for a miracle, that sometimes does happen.

CASE EXAMPLE

Matt's leukemia relapsed after bone marrow transplantation. At that point, it was rare to undergo a second transplant, especially for a four-year-old. Matt's mother insisted that he undergo the procedure. When the original transplant center refused because of the high risk, his mother persevered and found another center, which agreed, with "no promises." Matt remains alive eighteen years later.

Can you ever be prepared for the death of your child? When talking to parents after their child has died, it is notable to hear them say that you can never be completely prepared for your child's death, because you can never completely give up hope. At the same time, for the parent of a child with a fatal illness, the process of anticipatory mourning begins at the time of diagnosis and continues throughout the course of the disease. The negative emotions encountered during the period of anticipatory grief may be offset by experiencing life in the context of the moment or the task at hand (Hedlund and Clark 2001).

"The experience of anticipatory loss involves a range of intensified emotional response that may include separation anxiety, existential aloneness, denial, sadness, disappointment, anger, resentment, guilt, exhaustion, and desperation. Emotional expression often fluctuates between these more difficult feelings and others, such as a heightened sense of being alive, life's precious nature, intimacy, appreciation for 'routine' daily events, and hope" (Rolland 1991:145). Conceptualizing anticipatory grief as a process by which parents begin to anticipate emotionally the loss of their child does not capture the part of the process in which parents simultaneously cling to the child's life, hoping for a miracle. Maintaining a parallel focus on living in the moment and in anticipation of the future is complicated and burdensome.

CASE EXAMPLE

Mrs. K knew her son was not going to survive bone marrow transplantation. Although the doctors and her son were optimistic, she was not. She chose not to share her feelings with other staff members or her family. She wanted to seem only hopeful to the medical staff, as this was her son's only hope for survival. She did however buy a cemetery plot in the town cemetery prior to the transplant and was grateful to have done so after her son died.

There is a natural tendency for parents to hope for the future for their children. Parents hope that death does not come, but if it does, they may hope for a good death. For many, the hope of communicating with their children after death exists as a very real (and comforting) possibility, regardless of religious affiliation (Klass 1992–93). Many parents remain in "ongoing communication" with their children after their deaths (Sormanti and August 1997).

Children and families can derive comfort by staying focused in the present, valuing the moment, and connecting with the concept of being part of a larger universe in which there is a natural order to things. If a child is no longer mobile, simple moments, such as bringing snow indoors, catching the rain or a butterfly in a jar for the child to touch, all serve to transcend the isolation that may be experienced as a child moves toward death, and can bring moments of joy.

TALKING AT THE END OF LIFE

The dialogue between adults and children at the end of life is not always in words. Sometimes it is about a work of art made by a child, the story he tells, a conversation among stuffed animals about heaven, or the description of a dream. The use of metaphor is a gentler and often a more age-appropriate way for children to gather information, to construct reality, and to integrate it in an acceptable and understandable manner.

CASE EXAMPLE

The mother of a child with AIDS felt that her child was unaware of her illness, the tenuousness of her situation, and its implications. Then her child began to draw a series of pictures of birds flying over the house. Those that would pass the chimney would then fall to the ground dead.

After breakfast one morning, after the child had already drawn a series of these pictures, the child asked her mother whether they would meet up with each other in heaven. The mother was so stunned that she could not answer. She came in and talked to me about what to say. She talked about what she truly believed happened after you died. She did believe that she would be reunited with her child, so she went back to her daughter (and with a little coaching) was able to say to her daughter that in fact they would meet up in heaven. After that the little girl stopped drawing the pictures of the dead birds and seemed content.

Photograph albums and journals are useful in allowing children to chronicle their lives. In the cases of dying children, they also serve as a gift to the family from the child. Some children enjoy making videotapes and "telling their story" (of their illness, of their lives), while other children enjoy taking a "theme" and capturing that component of their lives such as "my days at the beach." For younger children handprints from different ages serve as wonderful artwork and are invaluable should the child go on to die.

If a child is working with a counselor, what thoughts the child would like shared with the parents must be established. It is never the professional's role to displace parents. Some children talk more freely with "strangers"—social workers, nurses, doctors, and other professionals—than with parents. If they do so, parents may need help in understanding that children may not always express their fears or concerns to them, not because they do not love them, but because they do. Children feel the need to protect their parents at times. Alternatively, many children will seek out their parents as "confidants" if they perceive that their parents are able to hear them. Regardless, when they are feeling intense emotions such as anger, it will be their parents to whom they direct their anger.

For most parents, this is the first time they are experiencing the death of their child. Clinicians with expertise in working with dying children can be true assets, as they try to negotiate this emotional challenge.

In a number of situations I have had children tell me that I can share information with their parents. If the child does not make this explicit, I will directly ask if I can share it. In other cases children and I have discussed things they want their parents to know after they die (e.g., "I will be okay," "I want you not to cry," "I played hooky on this day"). One adolescent knew the tombstone she wanted, because it was just like one her friend had. Initially, she did not want to have that conversation with her mother, but she wanted her mother to know.

All parents respond differently in crisis. It is however unlikely that a parent will change dramatically when their child is dying. Patterns of communication around death and dying will parallel previous patterns of communication.

ISSUES DURING THE DYING PROCESS

There are a series of losses faced by families as they reframe their reality to live with the uncertainty of their children's futures. When adults are dying, there may be tasks they complete privately. When children are dying, for the most part, they do so in the presence of their parents. Most parents will not leave their children during this time, grieving for them, with them. It becomes a parallel process for the adult and the child. It is not until after their children die that parents must contend with their feelings alone, absent from the safety of their child's presence. Partializing the magnitude of the situation, dealing with only what one has to deal with today, enhances families' abilities to function.

ALLOWING FOR A RANGE OF FEELINGS AND FOR SPIRITUAL AND EMOTIONAL GROWTH

This is a time to help parents to reaffirm their strengths, understand what they have been able to do for their child, and begin to reflect. The intensity of emotions they feel—grief, anger, loneliness, fear, and isolation—should have an avenue for expression.

Watching and attending to your dying child is painful. Families remember the moments around their child's death forever. They replay these last scenes over and over again as they learn to cope with the reality of their child's death.

One mother told me how angry she was at all of us on the staff the night her daughter died. It was Christmas Eve, and we had stayed late. A few of us joined at the nurses' station (about a hundred feet from the child's room) before we left for the evening. Months later, the mother recounted to me how angry she was to see us talking there. She felt as if we had been talking about her and that we belonged to a club of which she was not part. After having just spent many intimate hours with her awaiting her child's death, she felt very connected to us and felt that we had excluded her.

Throughout illness and dying, allowance should be made for parents' dialogues with God. This is a time for exploration of their beliefs, which may or may not be different in the face of this crisis. The hope for a miracle, salvation, and eternal peace for a child are often based in religious doctrine. There is a relationship with religion and spirituality throughout this dying period. After the death of a child, anger, or at least feelings of "betrayal" or "confusion" toward God may surface.

Mother after mother has told me, "If God only gives you what you can handle, than let's tell Him that I can't handle this." Statements such as "Your child was chosen to be an angel" or "God needs him" are often felt by parents to be useless (for example, one mother replied, "God doesn't need him. I need him and he needs me").

Reliance, belief, and faith in God give some families the support they need to survive while their child is dying. In a pilot survey of thirty-five parents of children with cancer, when asked the question "Do you pray?" the overwhelming majority made it very clear that they prayed about many things, including, but not limited to, their child's illness. God was very prevalent in the survey, and should be present in the work as religion and spirituality relate to each individual family.

ANTICIPATING AN EXISTENTIAL CRISIS

During the course of their child's illness, many parents work to keep intrusive thoughts about their child's potential death out of their minds. When their child is dying, they can no longer block out these thoughts and the concomitant feelings. They become overwhelmed with emotion, often near tears or in tears. They experience an impending sense of role confusion. They still have much to do for their child, but they begin to think about life without them.

"Am I no longer a mother?"
"How many children will I say I have?"
"My life is meaningless without her."
"I am losing the only person I truly love."

In the middle of the crisis of dying, parents will begin to struggle with finding "meaning" in their lives and in understanding their child's death (Miles and Demi 1983–84). Who will they be after their child is dead? What happens to the child after she dies? A child's dying is a time of singular focus for parents. When it is over, they are lost, forced to redefine who they are. As one mother said, "I just got fired from the single most important job of my life." From the point that parents learn that their child is dying until long after the funeral, it is a struggle for them to regain control over their emotional lives.

Although it may not occur until the bereavement period, I have had mothers make peace conceptually with their child's death and say things such as, "I am not happy that he died, but if you ask me if I would have chosen never to have met him, or not to have had those twelve years with him to not feel the pain, absolutely not," "He was my teacher about so many of the important things in life," and "I am no longer afraid to die."

Parents can feel so intensely connected to their children that they never want to let go. Choices may be made to prolong the child's life, because it is too difficult to do otherwise. Some children feel incredibly guilty about dying and leaving their parents behind. Even though a dying child will ultimately die, there is a feeling that children respond to parents' "giving them permission," making the suggestion that it is acceptable for the child to die. This allows parents to do one last thing for their child.

ANTICIPATING FUNERAL PREPARATIONS

For some parents, part of the adaptation to their child's impending death involves detailed planning for the child's funeral. Once they have worked out those details, they feel more relaxed and able to attend to the needs of their child. For others, even allowing such thought would feel as though they were giving up on their child. There are other parents who are aware of the reality, but do not choose to plan for it, while others would feel that planning for a funeral while their child was still alive wound be an anathema.

CASE EXAMPLE

A few months before Vanessa died, her mother bought her a beautiful dress to wear to her funeral. Staff thought this was the most unusual and unkind thing that they could imagine. However, Vanessa and her mother were both quite pleased with the purchase. A child's funeral is the last act of visible parenting, the final emotional obligation that parents make to their child: to take care of that child always.

TIME OF DEATH

The moment a child dies is a private one. When it happens in a public setting, it already defies that sense of privacy. Respecting a family's wishes and allowing them as much time as they need to have with their child are significant pieces of "ending work." Parents may not have anticipated the emotion of actually leaving their child's body for the last time. When the child dies in the hospital, the family leaves the body. When the child dies at home, the body leaves the family. This may seem a subtle distinction, but these actions may provoke different responses.

Offering suggestions that allow parents to have either a task or ritual upon leaving the body (whether it is being the person to take the other children home, or going to the hospital chapel) can facilitate an element of closure to this transition. Some families need a time limit and encouragement to say goodbye, because they cannot bring themselves to leave.

There was one mother who we anticipated would have a real problem when her child died. The mother and child had a "symbiotic" (that is, enmeshed) relationship. The child had been sick her entire fifteen-year life, and her mother had been with her every minute and would complete her sentences. When the child died in the middle of the night, several of us on the team came in from home and had planned an intervention with the mother. It was very directive and consisted of very clear statements: "She is dead," "She is no longer in her body," "You are no longer with her," "You can't stay with her body," "Her spirit is with you, but it is gone from the body." To the outsider this may appear to have been too harsh, but this enabled this mother to leave the hospital.

Who their children might have been and who their children were at the time of their death remain forever embedded in their parents' minds.

AUTOPSIES

Autopsies serve a medical purpose and are sought by physicians. This conversation can occur before the critical moments of a child's death or afterward. As with other difficult medical conversations, having a social worker available to the family after the physician leaves allows them to ask more personal questions and express emotional responses. From an emotional point of view, the autopsy can answer many questions for families as to the exact cause of death, the extent of the illness, and answers to past medical questions. Although autopsies can be inconclusive and the theoretical cause of death may be known prior to the autopsy, they still serve a purpose. If a family is not given the choice to have an autopsy performed or chooses not to have one, they must understand that there are questions that will remain unanswered.

THE CONTEXT OF WORKING WITH DYING CHILDREN

A major component of social work with children who are dying and their families is to help children live life to the fullest in periods of uncertainty, illness, or health. If successful, at the end of the day, parents who face bereavement can do so knowing that they did the most they could for their child, not just physically, but also emotionally.

In the case of adults who are dying, the primary focus of social work is often with the patient. In pediatrics the work may be with the child (individually or in groups), the parents, the siblings, and the medical staff. The work with the child may be verbal or nonverbal, utilizing modalities that are comfortable and engage the child.

Beginning with the time of diagnosis there is an art to delivering difficult information in an honest, compassionate, clear, and age-appropriate manner. Consistency, honesty, and developmental sensitivity are the hallmarks of trusting clinical relationships with children. At each age, death takes on new meaning. As these children continue to grow, they need ongoing education and information concerning each new stage of their illness in developmentally appropriate language. How the "reality" of children's conditions is presented to them can affect how they cope subsequently.

One mother talked with me about her son, who had had two bone marrow transplants. At the first transplant center the physician was honest with the child but had always presented new information to the parents first, and then in a very sensitive manner to the child. The family went to a different center for his second transplant. In this case the new doctor chose to tell her son, at the same time he was talking with her, that his chances for survival were less than 10 percent and that even if the transplant was successful, he was still unlikely to survive. This direct imparting of information has had a long-term negative effect on this eleven-year-old child. He is now eighteen months past transplant. Regardless of how well he is doing, he is clear that he is going to die and is struggling to embrace life.

Children's beliefs often reflect those of their parents, both in living with their illness and about dying. If parents approach death comfortably, discuss it openly, and have a belief system about what happens after one dies, children are likely to follow in that belief system. The work consists of reflecting on what the family and child believe, responding to what children are talking about, and being physically and emotionally available to them. As a child, if you are embarking on a journey and the adults around you are too frightened to go there, then you envision the journey to be frightening and undesirable. The most terrifying thing is to be alone on this journey.

Children who are dying are children first, and their needs and desires revolve around how they feel and what they want to do. They are spontaneous and can easily learn to live day to day. Children are event-focused; they want to live to do things. After surgery, they want to play. After throwing up, they want pizza. Their spirit is admirable. Children are by emotional design narcissistic, which helps them focus on their needs. What children understand about dying and how they approach death are two critical factors in this work.

Throughout development children struggle to assert themselves and define themselves independently. As they begin to lose function during the dying process, they need to be supported for what they can do and recognized for their accomplishments. Their lives are multidimensional, a combination of many stories, of which illness and death are only one chapter.

Play and art therapy can be used for distraction, expression, exploration, and fun. *Dramatic play* can take on many forms, whether acting out a scene from "the medical world," to acting out plots with good guys and bad guys, good cells and bad cells, sometimes seeking comfort in how the story ends, at other times allowing the story to express emotions that would be too painful to express otherwise. Adults can learn tremendous amounts about what children are experiencing by watching or becoming involved in their play. For some children, acting or other expressive activity will be effective, whereas for others more reflective, private activities will be appropriate. *Medical play* is a unique outlet for expression and may be utilized throughout the course of the child's illness. Play is a child's work; it can be focused or unstructured. Children learn new things, in this case medically and illness-oriented, and master them. Even mastery over death-related issues can offer a child great satisfaction.

Young children will instinctively go to a medical play area and act out things that have been done to them. When they see the toy replicas of familiar medical tools, they may easily take on the role of the doctor and seek out a patient to treat.

CASE EXAMPLE

Gregory set up a play hospital bed with characters. Once he set up the scene, he would throw a little boy and the toys out of the bed, as if to discard them. I would place them back in the bed and he would throw them out. He told me that, "After things die, they get thrown away." I explained that sometimes things get thrown away, but not people. People are loved forever. This is a conversation that could never have been had in the first person.

The use of syringes filled with finger paint makes a potentially threatening item fun. That pleasurable component carries over to experiences with the same syringe in its other environment. (Once you have seen something in a less threatening context, it is difficult to see it as threatening again.) It familiarizes children with the "tools" of the trade, gives them positive connotations, allows them to work through issues, and affords those who make conscious connections an opportunity to ask questions. As the child grows more gravely ill, these familiar tools can now serve as a safe avenue for expression of emotions related to illness and death.

Even adolescents can indulge in variations on medical play:

CASE EXAMPLE

At seventeen, Juanita never chose to talk directly about the fact that she was dying, but she was very eager to watch soap operas such as *General Hospital* and focus on the problems of the characters. When she was more playful, she would write wonderful stories, placing her doctors and nurses into the script and doing horrible things to them so they would be "dealing with fates worse than death."

Preparatory play allows children to become familiar with medical equipment and be given age-appropriate descriptions of what they will in fact experience. They can feel more in control, and the entire experience can seem more manageable, minimizing the negative impact. For example, when children learn that the taste of a sedating medication will be "bubble gum," they are comforted when they go to the procedure and encounter the familiar taste.

When a child's physical abilities become limited, encouraging other compensatory activities facilitates adaptation. Children continue to develop until they die, and achievements, of whatever magnitude, are important. They can learn about math through medication doses; they can practice subtraction by measuring the amount of fluid remaining in their IV bags. Children perfect drawing skills, use computers, and continue to make intellectual gains, even as their bodies fail. Intellectual mastery, learning a new word, or simple joy can continue to bring a sense of accomplishment to children and their parents. Games are also a resource, in that they allow for the mastery of rules, can be competitive, enjoyable, pass time, and are distracting. During a game children can be in control, which they may not otherwise experience if their disease cannot be contained. In all types of play there is value in looking at themes that present themselves, as well as the affect of the child.

Another interesting activity is to ask children what advice they would give their parents about taking care of a child with an illness like theirs. Most children have a tremendous amount to say and it allows them to be experts about their own needs and how they should be met.

When children are dying, every effort should be made to help them achieve their desired goals, whether attending a prom, writing a journal, continuing their growth, or allowing for regressed behavior—for example, rereading favorite books from earlier ages. Children want and expect to have certain experiences, but their illnesses do not always cooperate. One child really wanted to go to camp. Because she was quite ill, she was able to get there and stay for only a short time. She died three days after returning home.

Affording children the opportunity to achieve or experience the things they want allows them to continue to want to live, experiencing life rather than waiting for death to come.

CASE EXAMPLE

Just before heading off for a risky medical intervention, a young adolescent had met someone to whom she was very attracted. When she learned she had to have her treatment delayed because of a very serious complication, she was eager to return home to have the opportunity to experience her first kiss.

LIFE REVIEW/PREVIEW

Children may be encouraged to reflect on the achievements in their lives, and confirm their connections with loved ones. Children find solace in these activities. Their accomplishments may differ from those of adults, but in each instance, the life is complete for its length. Children seek to know and feel comfort in the life they have lived and the love they have known. They continue to want to live, play, and experience life with the support of their families until the day they die.

Some of my work with adolescents has been in discussing what life might have been. I would call this "Life Preview," as opposed to "Life Review." For children who will not be able to have certain experiences, it is often helpful for them to project about "what would have been." The sense of completion of a life preview exercise has helped some adolescents to find peace with where they are. Having had this opportunity seems to allow them to embrace the present and to begin to let go of the future.

A dying adolescent's parents were getting a divorce. She envisioned what her role in her family would have been after her parents separated. What would she have done? With whom would she have lived? Would she have been a mediator?

ACKNOWLEDGING LOSSES, CLARIFYING REALITY, AND PROVIDING INFORMATION

Children can be very concrete about their experiences and their bodies. At times they will need to acknowledge various losses, both large and small. Things such as not being able to go to a dance, losing a limb, receiving a new liver, or going bald, may seem remarkably dissimilar, but to a child may hold comparable meaning. Children are proud to show off their scars, and are happy to have adults available to see and remark about them. Some procedures that may not seem significant to adults are especially problematic for children. For example, if a child has already undergone major surgery, a minor procedure may be emotionally traumatic. Understanding and connecting to the significance of each event helps children feel recognized and valued.

CASE EXAMPLE

Glynnis was comfortable talking to me about anything. When she was in extreme distress, she would always ask the nurse to call for me. Once when I asked her why she thought she could talk to me, she said, "You are the only one who is comfortable enough to come in and sit down and not be afraid to get close to me." (This was a child who had had her leg amputated.)

Children find it difficult to perceive why this all happened, looking for reasons they can justify in their own developmental understanding. They need clarification as to the lack of culpability on their part or anyone else's. Children have different levels of tolerance for information, but will eagerly tell you how much they want to know.

"It is my body. I want to know everything."
"I want to know everything, but I don't want to know too much at one time."
"I would prefer not knowing until five minutes before something is going to happen."

Many children do not want to have direct conversations about the things that are going to happen to them. All styles of coping are appropriate; not everyone has to talk about their illness or death.

GROUP WORK

Children thrive in groups and use other children for points of reference. They are comfortable with their peers and find great solace in the company of others going through the same experience. At times parents may be reluctant to introduce their children to others with the same prognosis, fearing that they will establish a relationship and that it would be painful if one of the children were to die. Most children will tell you that they are glad to have had the opportunity.

Support groups give voice to the many concerns children experience, such as their parents being overly protective and their ability to manipulate adults. In groups, what children talk about ranges from the silliest of details to the most profound of thoughts. Children recognize that they are not alone and often use these forums to work through very difficult issues. Groups can be conversational or activity-focused. This does not mean that every discussion group is profound, but even in the most mundane of groups, the camaraderie of knowing you are "in the same boat" as others meets a primal human need. (For another example of the value of a camp experience, see chapter 33.)

I worked with a young man who grew up with a fatal illness and lived into his twenties, longer than most people with the disease were living at that time. As he got older, he got very involved in family support programming and he would meet with parents' groups and talk to them about his experiences. For many he was an inspiration, a source of hope. One day he volunteered to meet with a group of twelve- to eighteen-year-olds. That evening, he told me that he had gone back to his room and cried after the group, both in reaction to issues they had discussed and because of his own memory of going up to his room and crying at night, feeling very alone as a child.

TALKING ABOUT DEATH

It is sad and painful to listen to children's thoughts about death, but it is comforting for them to be able to talk and feel that people are not afraid of them. Children become curious about what happens after death. Their concerns, and not those imposed by the adults around them, should be the dominant themes in the work with dying children.

Children are inquisitive by nature. They ask questions such as:

"What does it feel like to die?"
"What happens after you die?"
"Where do you go when you die? What do you think it is like there?"
"Have you ever talked to anyone who has died?"
"Do you need a toothbrush?"
"Do you have to do homework in heaven?"
"How is it that you know that you can be helpful to me?"

When children ask questions, it is necessary to assess what the child is asking and reflect back the child's thinking. Children are often seeking confirmation of their own impressions. If their concerns are realistic, there is importance in validating their feelings. In other situations, the child's perceptions may be much more alarming than reality (for example, when the child perceives that the person who is coming into the room "to take his blood" is going to remove all of the blood from his body).

I was in a room with a physician to tell an adolescent that his treatment was not going well. He asked her, "Am I dying?" She thoughtfully responded, "Not now." He was satisfied with that answer. It behooves the professional or the parent to present information in a manner understandable to the child. When dealing with details that are already known to the child, it is imperative to respond in a manner consistent with the family's philosophy and beliefs. When a child is dying, the work done with the child is most often done in close partnership with the child's parents.

In a program serving large numbers of sick children, children become exposed to the death of peers. When children go to specialized camp programs with children with the same diagnosis, they meet other children who later go on to die. In their own minds, children come to understand that other children like themselves die. Although they may not consciously see this as something that prepares them for the potentiality of their own death, it brings death closer to their sphere of reference.

CASE EXAMPLE

A thirteen-year-old with osteogenic sarcoma was hospitalized at the same time that a three-year-old she knew well died. In the neighboring room she was quite struck by the reality that you can be alive one minute and dead the next. Although of an age commonly associated with mature death concepts, being party to the death of her friend made death all the more real and threatening for her. It is hard to believe that this type of experience would not change your perception of death, whether you are an adult or a child. Although she had a well-developed concept of what happened when you died, the reality that life and death were a moment apart startled her. Seeing a child younger than herself die, someone who she felt protective of, forced her to deal with issues with which she did not want to deal.

CASE EXAMPLE

Karen was dying. On morphine for the last few weeks of her life, she told me story after story of her past life, interspersed with information about her current college courses. One day, after she had been talking for about thirty minutes, she sat up abruptly and looked at me and asked, "Am I boring you?" She needed her life to feel important, to be of value, and not to be boring. At many times during those sessions she worried about not having been important enough. She was seeking to find the intrinsic meaning of her life and sought to find it in the details of her day-to-day activities.

Children may communicate though the use of metaphor. In the face of life-threatening illness, even older children may choose to work indirectly, with concerns cloaked in a different way. An older adolescent who was aware that she was dying said that she envisioned death as a party in one place and that she was in another place and could not get there. The clinical work then focused on the adolescent working within that metaphor, while working on other issues in her life, to get more comfortable where she was. At a memorial balloon launch, I have watched children who know they have a fatal illness write detailed notes on balloons to friends who had died of the same disease, telling them how much they love them and how important they were to them. They find comfort in knowing that their deceased friends were loved, honored, and remembered.

It is a normal developmental phenomenon beginning in the latency period for children to hide some private thoughts and feelings from their parents. However, when these thoughts concern their own deaths, the motivation for withholding discussion is often that they do not wish to upset their parents. As protective of children as parents are, children also learn to be protective of their parents. Being protective is a family affair.

At a sleepaway camp for children with cancer, where the goal was "fun" and not discussion, a group of adolescent girls chose to braid my very long hair. Once in the process they began a discussion about who would take care of their parents after they died. They talked about what they wanted on their tombstones and how they thought their parents would do, and what they would need for help. They kept me captive long enough to express their thoughts. When they were ready to move on, my hair was done. Each of these children went on to die (after which I did share their discussions with their parents).

Children who are gravely ill still prioritize life within the context of their stage of development. One boy fell in love with another patient, but his love was unrequited, so much so that after he died, and before she died, her greatest worry was that he would continue to pursue her in heaven.

SIBLINGS

When working with dying children, their siblings need to be recognized as a most vulnerable population. Sibling relationships are intense at every age. During the course of the illness and dying process, the needs of the sibling may be overlooked while the family is investing their energy in the interests of the ill child. Even when family members are acutely aware of the needs of their healthy children, they may feel ill prepared to deal with them, depleted of energy and time. There is an unspoken sense that you can catch up with the other children, whereas you will never have that time again with the child who is dying.

Of particular interest, when healthy children become forced to be more autonomous because their parents are involved with their ill sibling, they remain independent afterward. The process of growing up has changed irrevocably for them and for their parents. Bereaved children express feelings of needing to get to know their parents again and establishing new routines.

In a sibling bereavement group, one child very angrily told the story of how hard it was for her that her brother died, and how difficult the funeral had been for everyone in the family. Her mother had not returned to work, her father took a family leave, but for her the expectation was that she would return to school the next day, and that her performance would be at a superior level.

In another sibling bereavement group I was stuck by the dominant theme in the group of siblings: "We did not die." Children of all ages, at all stages need attention and support.

One sibling whose sister was dying said, "I know it's selfish, but I need my mother, too."

DEVELOPMENTAL CONSIDERATIONS

One might suggest that dying children have a more "mature" perception of life after death than the adults around them were willing to concede. How development affects dealing with life-threatening illness and dying is complicated, because the understanding of death, particularly your own, is not exclusively a cognitive concept, but also a spiritual, cultural, and emotional one.

Personal life-threatening illness has been found to correlate with premature knowledge of death (Bluebond-Langner 1978; Spinetta 1974; Waechter 1971a). Bluebond-Langner concluded that terminally ill children had a heightened awareness of death and increased comprehension independent of age or level of development. She noted that children's awareness of the terminal nature of their disease was directly related to their experience and exposure to children in similar situations. When children are exposed to the death of a peer, they may have an increased awareness of death, but may also misperceive the proximity of their own deaths. When a seven-year-old child in a special education class died, I wanted to talk with the class to facilitate their coping and adaptation to the child's death. What I learned was that this group of children held the perception that all children in special education classes die. They were not alarmed, but rather resigned.

Brunnquell and Hall identified factors that may challenge the severely ill child's normal development, particularly issues related to control, competence, and separation and loss. (Brunnquell and Hall 1982) There is actually less written than one would expect about the commonly held belief that these children are wise "beyond their years," because of the challenges they face.

Are children's abilities to formulate concepts of death changed if their own deaths are imminent? It has been observed that even two-year-olds can understand death when faced with a significant death experience (Bluebond-Langner 1978; Childers and Wimmer 1971; Nagy 1948). This can be contrasted to the experience of a thirty-month-old whose brother had died. Even after numerous explanations that he had gone to heaven, he continued to save things for him and awaited his return. Another three-year-old, verbally aware that her brother had died, insisted on saving candy for him, still maintaining that he could eat it.

When preschool-aged children become aware of their own impending deaths, they will often ask their parents, "When I die, will you come with me?" or "Can we die together?" or "Can we be buried together?" They are concerned with their own needs and wish to have their parents present. Day to day, children's fears are often exaggerated beyond the reality of the circumstance. Experiences in this age group are within the context of the child's comprehension. For example, children approaching surgery for a brain tumor may misperceive that the surgeon is going to cut off their heads. It cannot be expected that children will cope beyond their level of cognitive functioning. "The child of, say, three to seven years has therefore begun to appreciate some facts about death, such as not breathing, being buried, and not returning. They also have fantasies about death, and fact and fantasy mingle, with the facts adding terror to fantasy" (Yudkin 1967:38).

CASE EXAMPLE

Vicky, age five, asked innocently when she learned from her mother that she would be going to heaven to be with grandma, "Do I need to bring another dress? Do I have to brush my teeth in heaven?" She told me that she knew that people did not live forever, that she would go to heaven, and that people she knew would be there with the angels. Then she asked, "Where do you go after heaven? When you die there, where do you go?" She saw heaven as one step in a continuum of lives with successive deaths.

Making meaning of every day is a reality that parents of children with life-threatening illnesses come to. Even if their child's life is going to be short, it should be full and rich with experiences. Parents will remark that although their child was seven years old, he touched more people's lives than many eighty-year-olds.

Some theorists perceive that terminally ill children less than six years of age rarely experience death anxiety, as it is said that they react primarily to the separation and painful treatment regimens imposed by hospitalization and to the changed family relationships that occur as death approaches (Spinetta and Maloney 1978). Bluebond-Langner's early work was significant in pointing out that these are primarily perceptions of staff and parents that are attributed to the child. Share suggests that it is parental denial and reluctance to communicate about the illness, coupled with the child's acceptance of that lack of interaction that results in an increasing discrepancy between the child's experience and adult perceptions (Share 1972).

Nagy concluded that rather than worrying about their own deaths, terminally ill six- to ten-year-olds were more concerned with those aspects of their environments that caused them pain and discomfort, so-called "mutilation anxiety." More recent work suggests that terminally ill elementary school children experience more anxiety during hospitalizations than their chronically ill peers (Spinetta 1974; Spinetta, Rigler, and Karon 1974; Waechter 1971b). Whether this is because they are aware of their own imminent deaths or reacting to different cues from their families is not clear. Children, even if they have not been told, often know the serious nature of their illness because of changes in their parents' behavior. This is in keeping with Susan Harter's conceptualization that younger children, unable to comprehend more than one emotion at a time, will feel confused by and responsible for such changes (Harter 1983), feeling that they have done something wrong.

Lee and coworkers interpreted the responses of Chinese children with leukemia on a measure of apperception to indicate themes of isolation, of difficulty in dealing with uncertain situations in which they found themselves, and of having to solve difficult problems on their own. Children with leukemia used significantly more denial and isolation defenses, displayed a detached attitude, and exhibited twice as much fear and diffuse anxiety as controls. Because death in childhood is unthinkable in China, "the sick child is left to his or her own devices as to how to interpret parental behavior which often results in misinterpretation. Expressions of worry on the part of the parent can be mistaken to mean parental dislike of the child" (Lee et al. 1983–84:289).

Spinetta and colleagues used projective measures to elicit stories from hospitalized children and found that fatally ill children aged six to ten years were significantly more preoccupied with threats to their body integrity and function and expressed a greater degree of anxiety on a standardized instrument than did chronically ill controls (Spinetta, Rigler, and Karon 1973). In another study, fatally ill children aged six to ten years who were perceived not to know their prognosis were found to be much more anxious and alluded to death frequently (Spinetta, Rigler, and Karon 1974). The anxiety of not knowing what is going on, and a feeling that their parents are withholding information, creates a very tenuous emotional climate for the child.

Bluebond-Langner warns against drawing any conclusions based on a single session with a child in this "continuum of dying." Terminally ill children surrounded by other patients become part of another culture. It is within that world that they come to know death and create an adaptive reality to it. Discovering the intimate nature of your beliefs about death is the culmination of life's work, regardless of how many years your particular life is.

In the case of an older adolescent who had not been exposed to family deaths prior to her own diagnosis of cancer, the knowledge and experience of the deaths of her peers came as a rude awakening. In one discussion, it was my role to inform her of the death of a friend. She was able to react with appropriate remorse and then speculated that perhaps the reason she had come to know children who died was so she would "know people when she got there," after her own death.

Children's concepts of death differ from those of adults. We can also speculate that adults' concepts of death or life after death may differ dramatically from one another. Although there is perhaps a finite number of ways that each adult perceives what happens to an individual after death, there are certainly numerous opinions, couched with much ambiguity. Children often find comforting ways to depict what they believe happens after they die. They look toward adults to support their conceptualizations.

Adolescents who are dying are unique, as their stage of illness completely defies their developmental stage in life; feelings of immortality are lost. One young man had been told he would not be able to have a child because of his treatment. He became quite ill and was determined that he would try to have a child. He was, in fact, successful (regardless of what the medical team had perceived). He felt it was his legacy to leave behind a child, which allowed him to die peacefully. (Obviously, this raised many other issues for his partner.)

Teenagers who are dying often challenge their parents beyond the scope of normal adolescent development. Dying adolescents sometimes decide that they want to do things they would not otherwise live to do, such as drinking, using illicit drugs, and engaging in sexual activity. They need to learn to coexist with their parents, to compromise and be at peace with one another.

Adolescents are capable of reaching for meaning and understanding their lives in an abstract way in which younger children are not; they can be quite expressive.

"I like myself the way I am, disease and all; I don't know myself any other way,"
"I want people to accept me for what I am, not what I might have been."

CASE EXAMPLE

Abigail was an adolescent from whom there was much to learn. While being treated, she did everything that she thought she should be doing for her age. She went to parties with her friends; she manipulated her father; she continued experimenting sexually (which included having "pubic" hair tattooed on). Adolescents may be mature in some ways, but are able to use the wisdom of childhood to help them cope with emotions that may seem beyond their reach.

CASE EXAMPLE

Denise had been sick for many years. At the time of her death, she was a teenager and had come to know many people who had died before her. She planned her funeral and what she would wear. She seemed wise beyond her years and was able to do things that many adults could not do. At the same time, she assured her father that she would send him a postcard from heaven.

Adolescents seek immortality in different ways when they are dying. They want to be remembered. They want to continue to live on in some way.

CASE EXAMPLE

A dying adolescent wrote a letter and a poem, which she gave to her mother to give to me after her death. Her message was, "Don't worry about tomorrow, because tomorrow may never come." She knew that I did a lot of public speaking and she wanted me to have stories to tell about her, to keep her memory alive.

CASE EXAMPLE

An adolescent to whom I was very close went for bone marrow transplantation in Iowa. She mailed me a T-shirt on Wednesday and died on Friday; I received it on Saturday. I had the feeling from her note that she knew I would receive it after she died. It was the only time in my life that I have received mail from someone who was no longer alive. It almost could have you believe that you could get mail from heaven.

Are children who perceive you can get to heaven with a ladder different from adults who perceive that you can get there through prayer? Many of the questions that children grapple with are similar to those of adults; they are simply expressed differently.

DEATH ANXIETY

Death anxiety may appropriately heighten in children when faced with their own mortality. "A few writers, mostly Kleinians, have argued that death anxiety derives from the danger arising from the inner working of a hypothetical death instinct. Other authors, within the framework of object-relations theory, have associated death anxiety with both dread of symbiotic envelopment on the one hand, and the fear of individuation on the other. And finally, the existentialists have claimed that death anxiety, or the dread of imminent Nonbeing, is built into the ontological structure of human existence and hence is omnipresent and at the core of every fear" (Stolorow 1974:351). Death anxiety may manifest itself in many different ways. For instance, why and for whom do adults use euphemisms when speaking to children? Avoidance of the words "death" and "dying" can be confusing. The adult's fear of death is provoked by the child's concerns and they may try to avoid this subject. When discussion is unavoidable, the adult may move quickly to reassure the child rather than deal with the feelings (Janssen 1983). The actual words can offer children a better understanding than euphemisms. When death is likened to sleep, children may have problems going to bed or falling asleep.

It strikes me how very aware children are of their diagnoses and prognoses and how expressive they are when they choose to be. I think for children (and probably adults) to be able to be in control of what they say and to whom they say it regarding issues of their own mortality is perhaps one of life's last autonomous acts.

SOCIAL WORKERS REACT TO THE WORK

Social workers new to this type of work often worry about the questions children will ask them about their illness. The reality is that children ask questions to their own tolerance. Social workers work with medical staff and therefore should not find themselves in the position of giving information about diagnosis or prognosis. The work is to ascertain what children know and assist them in coping with that information. It is also social work's role to help children and parents learn to ask questions, and to understand what it is they want to know.

Some of the questions children ask during this period are not answerable. However, children rarely ask social workers questions they cannot answer. Children want reassurance about many things in life, and there are many individual things that dying provokes. However, all children want to know that they will be not be alone and many want to know that whatever happens after this life, wherever they go, that they will be all right. These assurances can vary from family to family depending on spiritual, religious, and cultural beliefs.

The reactions of social workers to working with children with life-threatening illnesses play a significant role in their ability to work in this area (Cincotta 2000, 2001). The information below is derived from surveys of pediatric oncology social workers in 1992 and 1998 and is representative of some of their voices when asked to describe their most positive and negative work-related memories.

> The knowledge that I made a difference in a child's passage from life to death—that will last through time. It cannot be changed or corrupted in any way by others—it is a personal memory tucked away.

> Perhaps the most compelling reason to do this work is the knowledge that you can make a difference is someone's life.

> Noncompliance in a 16-year-old male with leukemia who pretended to take medication after a bone marrow transplant. . . . It was not detected by family or staff. His death provoked very ambivalent feelings in all of us who were involved in his life for two years.

There are challenges that come from working with teenagers, regardless of the setting. In the context of life-threatening illness, the developmental and emotional issues may play out during the course of the treatment. The treatment team will never know what the outcome would have been if this young man had been compliant. On some level they are aware of this and live with the ambiguity of the situation, which imposes a stress on the group.

> One time the whole team ignored a quiet nine-year-old's silent prayer for the team to stop being so positive and upbeat in her last days. I would . . . take her out alone and talk to her about how hard this is, validate, etc.

Social workers have the ability to step back and listen to the child, as well as to other family members. Sometimes this attribute can be useful in helping family members communicate with each other and medical staff. Sometimes the work is just to allow each individual to be heard.

Within an hour of the death of a 19-year-old patient I had known since he was 12, I went to another patient who was in the ICU. . . . My emotional strength spent, my thoughts were, "How can I get through the rest of the day?" I assumed my other patient was asleep following such a long surgery. As I was attempting to muster some support for his mom, he opened his eyes and called me to his bedside. I leaned over to hear him—he told me a wonderful knock-knock joke (it was a joke about death). He smiled and went back to sleep. And therein is the JOY.

Work with children who are dying may be intense and overwhelming at times, but it is not boring. Through the grief and sorrow, children are compelling and enjoyable and many maintain those attributes throughout their lives.

Actually it surrounds the death of an 18-month old child. She died on Halloween in 1992. Her parents knew she was dying and dressed her in her costume . . . an angel. When she died, she reached both arms up to Heaven as if being picked up. The amazing part of this is that she had been completely paralyzed by her brain tumor for the past month. The parents were so reassured and blessed by this.

There are many stories that parents tell of things their children did right before they died, and even after they died. The stories are part of the journey, the ways that parents can memorialize and begin to cope with the many ways in which their children are different, and will be forever different. As social workers, we carry these stories with us as well.

A 5-year-old sibling discussing the impending death of his older sister. He had been the donor for her bone marrow transplant—which was very successful. However, months later she was dying from infection. He questioned the physician about why he couldn't give his sister his breath (to make her breathe) the way he had given her his bone marrow to "make her blood work right."

When working with children the knowledge of their developmental level frames the work, but it is at times their simple understanding that brings profound meaning to very complex situations.

Having a teen write me a song and give it to his friend to give to me after he died. He wrote that I was a reliable adult in his life where no one was reliable.

Children find ways to give you gifts while they are dying and after they die. Some are tangible, some emotional; they are the types of gifts that give value to the work every day.

DEATH STORIES: SHARING THE JOURNEY

When asked the question, "What are your most positive memories of the work?" it was interesting that many of the responses of pediatric oncology social workers involved "death stories," including anecdotes regarding particular children; learning from children; respect, recognition, gratitude for the social worker's role at the time of death ("value my presence walking the journey"); and involvement after a child's death (eulogy, funeral).

Another component of the positive memories involved "sharing the journey" with families and included physical and emotional presence during the dying process; enabling family members to say goodbye; helping family members to communicate; sharing difficult emotions; talking about death; allowing children to die with dignity and respect; and facilitating dying wishes.

When social workers described their most negative memories about this work, among the things they mentioned were experiences with "bad deaths," such as a child's "bleeding out" or receiving inadequate pain control, as well as situations in which the family was angry with the social worker at the time of death. Team-related issues included physicians "failing to inform families," and "not working with the team." Of negative note were experiences in which social workers questioned their own competence, "I really think I could have been better," or issues related to being a new worker. They also noted negative experiences in which the family and staff were unprepared for a child's death. Another item that stood out was a category of "unnecessary deaths," in which the social worker perceived that a death was in some way avoidable or had occurred because of a physician's or a system error. Other death-related themes included the cumulative effect of too many deaths, the first death experiences, the helpless feelings when a child dies, and circumstances in which a child died alone.

It seems that death-related themes are a compelling component of the work with children with life-threatening illnesses and their families. Working with children who are dying is intense, and it can serve either to keep social workers engaged in it or to deter them from it.

When one tries to understand one's own commitment to working with children who are dying, it becomes clear that it is a privilege. What one learns as a professional on this journey is about the meaning of life. Its personal importance is unequaled.

REFERENCES

Bluebond-Langner, M. 1978. *The Private Worlds of Dying Children*. Princeton, NJ: Princeton University Press.

Brunnquell, D., and M. D. Hall. 1982. Issues in the psychological care of pediatric oncology patients. *American Journal of Orthopsychiatry* 52(1): 32–44.

Childers, P., and P. Wimmer. 1971. The concept of death in early childhood. *Child Development* 42:1299–1301.

Christ, G., and M. A. Adams. 1984. Therapeutic strategies at psychosocial crisis points in the treatment of childhood cancer. In *Childhood Cancer: Impact on the Family*, ed. A. E. Christ and K. Flumenhaft, 109–128. New York: Plenum.

Cincotta, N. 1993. Psychosocial issues in the world of children with cancer. *Cancer* 71(10): 3251–3260.

———. 2000. Reflections of our voices: A mission and a vision. Address delivered to the Association of Pediatric Oncology Social Workers, Houston, Texas.

———. 2001. Special programs for children with cancer and their families. In *Social Work in Oncology: Supporting Survivors, Families, and Caregivers*, ed. M. M. Lauria, E. J. Clark, J. F. Hermann, and N. M. Stearns, 169–191. Atlanta: American Cancer Society.

Contro, N., J. Larson, S. Scofield, B. Sourkes, and H. Cohen. 2002. Family perspectives on the quality of pediatric palliative care. *Archives of Pediatric and Adolescent Medicine* 156:14–19.

Dickinson, G. 1992. First childhood death experiences. *Omega* 25(3): 169–182.

Harter, S. 1983. Cognitive-developmental considerations in the conduct of play therapy. In *Handbook of Play Therapy*, ed. C. Schaefer and K. O'Connor, 100–125. New York: Wiley.

Hedlund, S. C., and E. J. Clark. 2001. End of life issues. In *Social Work in Oncology: Supporting Survivors, Families, and Caregivers*, ed. M. M. Lauria, E. J. Clark, J. F. Hermann, and N. M. Stearns, 299–316. Atlanta: American Cancer Society.

Janssen, Y. G. 1983. Early awareness of death in normal child development. *Infant Mental Health Journal* 4:95–103.

Jay, S. M., and C. H. Elliott. 1984. Psychological intervention for pain in pediatric cancer patients. In *Pediatric Oncology*, ed. G. B. Humphrey, L. P. Dehner, G. B. Grindey, and R. T. Acton, 3:123–154. Boston: Martinus Nijhoff.

Jay, S. M., M. Ozolins, C. H. Elliot, and S. Caldwell. 1983. Assessment of children's distress during painful medical procedures. *Health Psychology* 2:133–148.

Kagen-Goodheart, L. 1977. Reentry: Living with childhood cancer. *American Journal of Orthopsychiatry* 47(4): 651–658.

Kaplan, B. J. 1980. Understanding family disruption: The cognitive development of children. *Social Service Review* 12:414–422.

Kastenbaum, R., and R. Aisenberg. 1972. *The Psychology of Death*. New York: Springer.

Klass, D. 1992–93. The inner representation of the dead child and the worldviews of bereaved parents. *Omega* 26(4): 255–272.

Lansky, S. B. 1985. Management of stressful periods in childhood cancer. *Pediatric Clinics of North America* 32(3): 625–632.

Lauria, M. M. 2001. Common issues and challenges for families dealing with childhood cancer. In *Social Work in Oncology: Supporting Survivors, Families, and Caregivers*, ed. M. M. Lauria, E. J. Clark, J. F. Hermann, and N. M. Stearns, 117–141. Atlanta: American Cancer Society.

Lee, P., F. Lieh-Mak, B. Hung, and S. Luk. 1983–84. Death anxiety in Chinese children with leukemia. *International Journal of Psychiatry in Medicine* 13:281–289.

Miles, M. S., and A. S. Demi. 1983–84. Toward the development of a theory of bereavement guilt: Sources of guilt in bereaved parents. *Omega* 14(4): 299–314.

Nagy, M. 1948. The child's theories concerning death. *Journal of Genetic Psychology* 73:3–27.

Rolland, J. S. 1991. Helping families with anticipatory loss. In *Living Beyond Loss: Death in the Family*, ed. F. Walsh and M. McGoldrick, 144–163. New York: Norton.

Rosof, B. D. 1994. *The Worst Loss*. New York: Henry Holt.

Ross, J. W. 1978. Social work intervention with families of children with cancer: The changing critical phases. *Social Work in Health Care* 3(3): 257–271.

Share, L. 1972. Family communication in the crisis of a child's fatal illness: A literature review. *Omega* 3:3.

Sormanti, M. E., and J. August. 1997. Parental bereavement: An exploration of parents' spiritual connections with their deceased children. *American Journal of Orthopsychiatry* 67(3): 460–469.

Sourkes, B. M. 1995. *Armfuls of Time: The Psychological Experience of the Child with a Life-Threatening Illness*. Pittsburgh: University of Pittsburgh Press.

Spinetta, J. J. 1974. The dying child's awareness of death: A review. *Psychological Bulletin* 31(4): 256–260.

Spinetta, J. J., and L. J. Maloney. 1978. The child with cancer: Patterns of communication and denial. *Journal of Consulting and Clinical Psychology* 46(6): 1540–1541.

Spinetta, J. J., D. Rigler, and M. Karon. 1973. Anxiety in the dying child. *Pediatrics* 52(6): 841–845.

——. 1974. Personal space as a measure of a dying child's sense of isolation. *Journal of Consulting and Clinical Psychology* 42:751–756.

Stolorow, R. D. 1974. A note on death anxiety as a developmental achievement. *American Journal of Psychoanalysis* 34(4): 351–353.

Toews, J., R. Martin, and H. Prosen. 1985. Death anxiety: The prelude to adolescence. *Adolescent Psychiatry* 12:134–144.

Van Dongen-Melman, J., J. F. A. Pruyn, G. E. Van Zanen, and J. A. R. Sanders-Woudstra. 1986. Coping with childhood cancer: A conceptual view. *Journal of Psychosocial Oncology* 4(1–2): 147–161.

Waechter, E. 1971a. Children's awareness of fatal illness. *American Journal of Nursing* 71:1168–1170.

——. 1971b. Young children's concepts of death and dying. *American Journal of Nursing* 71:1171–1172.

Wolfelt, A. D. 1996. *Healing the Bereaved Child.* Fort Collins, CO: Companion Press.

Yalom, I. 1980. *Existential Psychotherapy.* New York: Basic Books.

Yudkin, S. 1967. Children and death. *Lancet* 7(480): 37–41.

17

WORKING WITH DYING AND BEREAVED OLDER PEOPLE

SUE THOMPSON AND NEIL THOMPSON

OLDER PEOPLE have specific needs in relation to death, dying, and bereavement. These needs arise not because of any factors associated with the biological changes associated with aging, but rather because of the discriminatory assumptions and stereotypes older people face as a result of the prevalence of ageism (Thompson 1996). It is therefore our aim in this chapter to highlight the role that ageist discourses play in perpetuating the assumption that older people experience loss and grief less keenly than their younger counterparts. Although it is certainly true that the older we get, the closer to death we are, and that losses of such things as personal relationships, status, physical and intellectual capabilities, and so on are likely to feature more often in old age than they do in the earlier stages of our lives, it is our contention that this should not be a justification for *equating* old age with a time of death, dying, and bereavement. Nor should we assume that these experiences are in any way normative or a necessary part of the experience of growing old.

We shall consider how ageism works as a set of social processes that portray older people as a class apart from other adults, in that they are perceived as being more accustomed to death and loss, and therefore somehow in need of less sensitivity, understanding, and therapeutic intervention. We shall argue to the contrary that to marginalize older people by treating them as a homogenous mass of people, defined only by reference to their age, is to disregard the uniqueness of each individual's experience of dying and bereavement. A comment from Moss and Moss continues to be apt: "Past losses constitute a pool of grief experienced over the lifetime. A death leads one to recall other losses in the recent as well as distant past. It may evoke despair and helplessness. On the other hand, successful mastery of past losses may lead to an affirmation of one's coping capacity" (1989:220–221).

We shall suggest that if practitioners fail to acknowledge that older people do not necessarily "get used to" loss, nor feel it less keenly each time they face an aspect of it, then they may fail to recognize it as a potentially traumatic event or process, and consequently fail to offer the older people with whom they work the help and support that they would afford younger adults in similar situations. In effect, they will be perpetuating a situation in which the experience of loss and the expression of grief in old age are not socially sanctioned—an aspect of what Kenneth Doka has described as "disenfranchised grief": "a loss that is not or cannot be openly, publicly mourned, or socially supported" (1989:4).

Because ageism is a key concept in our argument and the foundation against which other concepts will be discussed, the first part of this chapter will explore the main tenets of this form of discrimination and focus on some of the theoretical issues it raises. In the second part we move on to draw out some of the implications for social work practice, using practice scenarios to highlight that there are implications for policy makers, educators, and trainers, as well as for practitioners undertaking direct work with older people facing terminal illness or bereavement in their many forms.

LOSS IN OLD AGE

As we have argued elsewhere (Thompson and Thompson 1999), ageism is a form of discrimination that disempowers significantly large sectors of the population purely on the grounds of age, and without reference to any other aspects of identity or experience. It involves promoting the idea that older people are less worthy of either respect or resources than other members of society. This can apply to both ends of the age spectrum (Thompson 1997), but is more commonly used to refer to the marginalization of older people. Hughes and Mtezuka reflect this in their definition of ageism as "the social process through which negative images of and attitudes towards older people, based solely on the characteristics of old age itself, result in discrimination" (1992:220).

So, how does ageism operate? As with other forms of discrimination, such as racism, disablism, heterosexism, and sexism, ageism works to convince us that particular groups in society are "less than" others. Midwinter (1990) uses the term *postadults* to describe the way in which older people are conceptualized as a group apart from "real" adults, rather than as adults in their own right who have reached a somewhat arbitrarily chosen age, when they find themselves pushed to the margins of society and their experiences trivialized.

In his work on discrimination and oppression in social work (1995, 2001, 2003), Neil Thompson argues that discrimination can be seen to operate at three levels: personal, cultural, and structural. Ageism can also be seen to follow this pattern.

PERSONAL

This is the level of personal prejudice, attitudes, and behavior. Ageism can manifest itself at this level as a lack of respect—for example, through a tendency to laugh at, or draw attention to, such issues as slowness of movement, incontinence, or forgetfulness. Prejudicial actions and attitudes are not confined to younger members of society. They can be seen in the comments and actions of some older people themselves who have internalized the ageist messages around them and come to consider themselves as less deserving of resources than younger people experiencing loss. For example, it is not uncommon for friends and relatives of older people, and even the health and social-care workers with whom they come into contact, to make comments like "What do you expect at your age?" when the subject of failing health, approaching death, or the increasingly frequent loss of relatives and friends is raised. People who are constantly receiving intimations that they should not need help in coping with these issues are less likely to ask for it.

CULTURAL

This is the level of shared attitudes and meanings and the level at which stereotypes of old age operate. This can be illustrated by the use of language, a central feature of culture. Although racist and sexist references have been culturally vetoed to a large extent, demeaning terminology and images of older people as physically and intellectually frail still tend to go relatively unchallenged. Individuals may use terminology such as "old fogies" or "old dears" when referring to older people. The older population tends to be conceptualized in modern culture and political discourses as a burden rather than an asset—a process described as "welfarization," which serves to strengthen the association between old age and dependency (Fennell, Phillipson, and Evers 1988; Thompson 1995).

Another process associated with ageism is that of "infantilization" (Hockey and James 1993), whereby it is culturally acceptable for older people to be treated as if they are children who have not yet reached the stage of life where they should be able to command respect. For example, older people are often referred to by their first names without reference to their preference or permission. In relation to death and dying, this can be seen as particularly significant, as it means that the tendency for children to be excluded from matters relating to death (Wass 1995) may be transferred to older people—a factor that can further contribute to the notion of older people's grief as disenfranchised grief.

STRUCTURAL

The structural level relates to the way in which society is carved into social divisions, such as class, race, and gender, according to which power and life chances are distributed. It can be seen that age, too, is such a social division. That is, older people form a structural category in terms of power, a fact reflected in the discriminatory actions and attitudes at the personal level and stereotypes and assumptions at the cultural level. The structural level helps to explain why attitudes and practices at the other levels continue to be dominant (because they are intertwined with the structure of society). It also explains why it is not enough to challenge ageism only at the personal and cultural levels.

This very brief overview of ageism does not do justice to its complexities. However, it does enough, we hope, to highlight the contribution that ageist ideology and practices can make to the trivialization of issues affecting older people, and particularly to the experience of loss. One of its major effects is to "naturalize" death and dying in old age—to suggest that it is part and parcel of growing old, and therefore tolerable because of the frequency with which it is encountered. We would agree, however, with the views of Corr, Nabe, and Corr (1997), who argue that the view that accumulated loss experiences make them easier to bear is one that should be challenged.

Seymour and Hanson, writing about discrimination against older people in terms of palliative care, suggest that quality of life is often seen in terms of "a primarily functional framework" (2001:118), with an emphasis on practical rather than emotional and spiritual needs. We would suggest that this is yet another effect of ageist ideology—one that reifies older people and denies them an affective dimension to their existence.

A further effect is that of depersonalization, whereby a blanket approach to older people and their needs is deemed appropriate or sufficient. Terms that present older people as a homogeneous group and distance them from the rest of the population (such as "the elderly") are commonplace, as are assumptions that to be old is necessarily to enjoy dwelling on the past or to be resistant to change. This tendency to deny individuality and uniqueness in general will be exacerbated if there is also a blanket approach to loss issues in particular—one that assumes that everyone experiences loss and grief in the same way and to the same extent. As the work of Walter (1999) and others have shown, loss is something that is experienced differently by different people. There is no reason why this should not also be the case in old age.

What links these two tendencies, we would suggest, is a lack of focus on the meaning attached to individual life experience. For example, to some who have suffered intractable pain, or watched loved ones endure debilitating chronic conditions, death can sometimes be perceived as a positive and hoped-for event—a "merciful release." To others, bereavement or death might be perceived as being cruelly robbed of what Lustbader (1991) refers to as "unlived life." To refer to responses to loss without recognizing that the meanings attached to those losses are crucial is to oversimplify what is a complex and multilayered experience. The recent works of Neimeyer, Keesee, and Fortner (1998) and Neimeyer and Anderson (2002) on "meaning reconstruction theory" and of Stroebe and Schut (1999) on dual process theory also remind us of the uniqueness of grieving.

From the perspective of Neimeyer and his colleagues, grieving is seen not as "recovering," in that it is not possible to return to what was perceived of as normality before the loss, but as building a new "normality" that incorporates the person or thing that has been lost. They suggest that, in time, it may become possible to see life as a whole again after one's sense of reality has been shaken or shattered by loss, although it will be a new, or reconstructed, "whole." This process of reconstructing meaning is necessarily a very subjective experience, and should highlight how making spot judgments about the appropriateness of people's grieving patterns or methods can be misguided. We would ask you to consider the following two scenarios:

---

1. Frank is seventy-five years old and has lived with his older brother, Jack, all of his life. Their parents died while they were both adolescents, and the two brothers have continued to run the family business (a small food store) ever since. Neither married, and each is the other's only surviving relative. Frank has a learning disability and relies

on Jack to help him cope with looking after himself and to take the lead in managing the business. Customers are always remarking that they cannot remember ever seeing them apart, and that Frank would be lost without his big brother.

2. Frank is seventy-five years old. He has an older brother Jack, but he has only seen him two or three times since their parents died when they were adolescents. He says he probably wouldn't even recognize him now if they met. Following the death of their parents, Jack went off to seek work elsewhere. He did not want to take responsibility for the food store they had run as a family, nor for the welfare of Frank who has a learning disability and has never been capable of living independently. Before he left, Jack arranged for some friends to "look out for" Frank, who has remained part of their large extended family ever since. Jack kept in touch for the first few years, but since then Frank has heard nothing. He doesn't know where Jack lives, whether he has a family, or even whether he is still alive.

Imagine that both scenarios end with the news that Jack has died after a sudden heart attack. In both cases the loss event is, at an objective level, the same—the death of an only brother. However, at a subjective level, if we consider the meaning attached by Frank to the relationship and the implications of its loss, then we might expect very different grief reactions. To one, the death of his brother would probably be a hugely significant loss, and a life-changing event from which he might never recover. To the other, the news might have been unsettling for a while, but perhaps of less consequence to him than the death of one of his many pet dogs, or a member of the family who had given him friendship and support for most of his adult life.

Stroebe and Schut's (1999) dual process theory is another approach to our understanding of grieving, one that highlights its socially constructed and fluid nature. They suggest that, rather than working through stages (shock, denial, acceptance, and so on) in a linear fashion, bereaved people move backward and forward between mourning the loss (loss orientation) and adapting to the future (restoration orientation). Stroebe and Schut use the term "oscillation" to describe how people can experience a variety of emotions within a short time scale, moving between the two orientations, even within the space of a single day. For example, in adapting to the loss of a loved one, it is possible to feel reasonably positive about the future one morning but to sink into the depths of despair by the afternoon, after being reminded of the loss by a photograph or some other personal memento.

This approach suggests that there are two aspects of grief following bereavement. In the first "orientation," grief is the primary emotion we experience, and we tend not to want, or be able, to contemplate a future without the person or thing we have lost. In the second, we are able to focus more on putting the loss behind us and to accept that there is a future in which we can take part. It is likely that we will tend to focus more heavily on the loss aspect in the early days, weeks, or months, and to focus more heavily on adapting to the future in the later period, but Stroebe and Schut's argument is that we will still move between the two at any give time, sometimes experiencing both sets of emotions at virtually the same time.

Consider the following practice example.

CASE EXAMPLE

Indira is eighty-eight years old and moved to live in a care home so that she would not be separated from her husband, who was suffering from Alzheimer's disease and was unable to care for himself. They had been together for almost seventy years, and Indira wanted to stay with him, even though he often did not recognize her. When he died, Indira remained there, and the staff helped her to come to terms with the loss as best they could. After three years she still spent some time each day at a small shrine she had made, but for the most part she had come to terms with his death and had become more involved in the social life of the home. One day some of her grandchildren paid her a surprise visit, bringing a newly born great-grandchild for her to see. Indira became very distressed and took to rocking in front of the shrine, holding a photograph of her husband and weeping. This lasted for most of the day, and Indira's relatives were angry that the staff had not told them that their grandmother had still not got over their grandfather's death after all this time. The staff were surprised at this reaction and suggested that they should let her rest and return the next day. When they did so, they found Indira back to her old self. She explained to them that she had been reminded by the baby of the happy days she had spent in Sri Lanka raising their small children with her husband. The visit had made forgotten memories resurface and, for a short while, had made her feel his loss particularly keenly. After seeing Indira socializing with her new friends, and proudly showing them her new great grandchild, her family realized that she was missing her husband, as was to be expected, but adapting to a new life nevertheless.

The implication for practitioners of not taking Stroebe and Schut's analysis on board is that if they are assessing someone's ability to cope and rely on the snapshot image obtained from a single visit, then they may get a distorted view of how that person is coping with a loss and wrongly categorize them as experiencing "complicated" grieving.

What both the "meaning reconstruction" and "dual process" approaches bring to our attention is the process of adapting to the future. There appears to be nothing in either approach to suggest that their explanatory power is limited to any particular life stage or that they should not be applied to the understanding of loss in old age. We would return to our earlier point that loss in old age tends to be "naturalized." The implication of a process being conceptualized as "normal" or to be expected is that it therefore does not warrant being explained. Our argument has been that the experience of loss in old age *does* warrant academic enquiry, and has led us to consider that ageist stereotyping plays a part in denying older people a future aspect to their lives.

Thompson (1998) reminds us that Jean-Paul Sartre explained how we use the interplay between our experience of the past and our ambitions for the future to construct our sense of self in the present (the "progressive-regressive" method). If meaning reconstruction and dual process insights are to be applied for the benefit of older people by explaining and validating their loss and by providing the basis for therapeutic forms of intervention, then we must first challenge the ageist notion that there is no future for older people or that it is not important. As Sue Thompson puts it:

> For older people, the implication of denying that they need to adapt to their futures can therefore be seen as denying their identities and their very humanity. If we continue to conceptualize the suffering experienced by older people as a form of disenfranchised grief and to exclude them from the understanding and help that we would see as valid forms of intervention when working with younger bereaved or traumatized adults, then we run the risk of perpetuating what is, arguably, ageism's most demeaning process—dehumanization. If we accept that loss is indeed part of life, and we accept that older people are not a group apart from "adults," then surely to deny the impact of loss and grief in their lives is to treat them as if they were already dead. (2002:173)

THE POLICY DIMENSION

Before we even begin to look at what needs to be taken on board at a policy level, we would wish to make the point that there needs to be a policy at all. This may seem to be a rather obvious point to be making, but it is clear that death, dying, and bereavement as experienced in old age are not always on political and policy agendas. We would argue that it is not enough to take a commonsense approach and assume that matters such as adequate care provision, sensitivity to differing cultural practices and spiritual needs, and so on will happen automatically in a "caring" society. As our earlier discussion of the effects of ageism highlights, the assumption that older people are "less than" their fellow citizens is one that is embedded in both the cultural level of shared meanings and assumptions and the structural level of power relations and social institutions (health and social care networks, the education system, and so on), and will take more than the endeavors of individuals to challenge.

Antonio Gramsci's (1971) use of the concept of ideology is important here. He argued that the ideas of ruling groups become accepted as "common sense" or "accepted wisdom" and thus tend to be invisible to debate. This can be seen to be the case in relation to older people and the "commonsense" assumptions that, on closer inspection, reveal themselves to be ageist stereotypes. It is therefore important that the needs of older people at the end of life be put on the policy agenda in order to highlight them as issues that should not be trivialized or ignored altogether.

A doctor colleague of one of the authors commented that the best thing we can offer people who are dying or experiencing loss is the one we, as professionals, often find most difficult to give—our time and a willingness to listen (see also Lustbader 1991; Saunders 2002). Writing from a UK perspective, we are able to reflect the current debate among social workers in care-management situations (the major focus of social work with older people), which highlights an increase in bureaucracy and a decrease in the time available for face-to-face contact with those who could benefit from their skills (Postle 2002). Social workers are well placed in terms of their skills and value base to offer emotional support and therapy to those experiencing loss traumatically, but these interventions can be time-consuming. At a policy level, making this time available to social workers will involve commitment at both an ideological level (accepting that older people have the same rights as others to a range of services and support) and a strategic level (for example, looking at the skills mix in the workforce, and how social workers can be freed up to use their therapeutic skills most effectively).

The final point we would raise in terms of implications at the level of policy is that of giving consideration to the benefits to be gained from working in partnership with professionals in the fields of palliative and geriatric care. Seymour and Hanson (2001) remind us that the relationship between health and social-care agencies in terms of the responsibility for older people with palliative care needs is not always clearly defined. They comment on how a 1999 government inquiry in the UK identifies "a system of health and social care which is 'characterised by complexity and unfairness in the way it operates' and which 'contains a number of providers and funders of care, each of whom has different management or financial interests which may work against the interests of the individual client."

The following practice illustration highlights some of these issues, in particular, the importance of a coordinated response.

CASE EXAMPLE

Maude is eighty-seven years old and in the terminal stages of a progressive illness that has rendered her virtually immobile, with extremely low energy levels, no appetite, and little enthusiasm for the months she has left to live. Her only wish is to remain at home in her apartment for as long as she is able and, she hopes, to die there in the surroundings that have enriched her life this far. She is hopeful when she hears that support is available from specialist nurses who will be able to help her cope with the symptoms she is experiencing. She worries that the time may soon come when she is unable to be left on her own at all, and seeks reassurance from a social worker that care staff will be available to see to her needs, so that she will not have to enter a nursing home or hospital. Much as he tries, the social worker is unable to finance the level of care needed. Maude is told she has the option to use her own resources to employ a private carer to supplement the support provided by health and social-care services. Although Maude has the financial resources to cope with these arrangements, she finds that she does not have the emotional resources to cope with having different agencies to contact and worries about bills and timetables. Very quickly her health and mood deteriorate, and she is admitted to a nursing home in the absence of an available hospice place. Within a few weeks she dies.

EDUCATION AND TRAINING

In addressing social work with older people at the end of life, we are combining two areas that tend not to receive the attention they deserve in terms of education and training. Social work with older people has tended to be neglected in social work education in many settings at least (Thompson 1995). In conjunction with this, loss issues continue to be seen by many as a "specialism" rather than a topic which addresses a set of experiences that are a fundamental part of the experience of living and therefore relevant to all aspects of the social work education curriculum. If it were more fully appreciated that loss and grief are painful experiences that social workers can help people face and deal with (for example, illness or divorce), then it would be more likely that practitioners would recognize that losses will continue to be felt in old age. Therefore, when educators address the social work skills and knowledge base, it is important to include issues of loss and grief (Weinstein 2002).

Education and training therefore need to address not only loss issues across the life course, but also those that relate specifically to old age. Consider the following practice scenario.

CASE EXAMPLE

Ayesha was appointed to a post in which she worked with vulnerable older people in the community. She felt well prepared for the work as her training course had included aspects such as physical aging, interdisciplinary collaboration, management of risk, and the protection of vulnerable adults. However, the assumptions she had made about older people were challenged on her very first week in practice. On visiting a lonely and depressed man she discovered that he was an air force veteran and suggested that he meet up with old comrades so that they could discuss their common experiences. She was surprised when he became angry and told her that his memories held nothing but despair for him and that he found no solace in being reminded about the friends he had lost, nor the young wife who had been killed while he was on active service. He confided that he would not wish to meet up with comrades anyway, because he felt embarrassed by the debilitating effects of the series of strokes he had suffered in the last few years. Ayesha had not expected such an outpouring of grief and anger, but on reflection she questioned her own assumptions and was even more surprised that she had not considered how he might have felt about the losses he had suffered and was continuing to experience. She reflected on the curriculum for her training and realized that loss issues had hardly featured and that, far from feeling prepared, she had almost missed the significance of the losses he had suffered and the opportunity to work with him to address their effects.

PRACTICE IMPLICATIONS

Valuing uniqueness and difference form part of the underpinning value base of social work, and so it should not sit well with social workers to deny a diverse group of people a diverse range of responses. As we have discussed earlier, dying and bereavement hold different meanings for different people, and so to assume that this changes with age is to deny older people what makes them human — their hopes, fears, aspirations, and so on.

Helping people cope with change is another aspect of social work that is central to practice. Helping people come to terms with dying, losing loved ones or losing important aspects of their role or identity involves enabling people to find the personal resources to cope with difficult emotions and facilitating personal growth. We would argue that this is as relevant for older people as it is for their younger counterparts, and yet ageist ideology would have us believe that old age is not a time of continuing growth, but rather of stagnation or decline.

Of course, it is important to recognize that the potential for personal or spiritual growth does not stop at a particular age, and to assume that it does is to devalue the life left to be lived. Old age is a time of living, not a time of dying. As MacKinlay warns us, we must be wary of the "ageism that prevents people being open to the possibilities of continued spiritual development in aging" (2001:254). Similarly, Coleman et al. (2002) write of the important role of spirituality in helping older people deal with the loss of their life partner. This is clearly a dimension that we should not neglect, and so we should be prepared to challenge dominant ageist ideas that present old age in a grossly oversimplified manner, to the detriment of all concerned.

Assuming that older people experience dying and bereavement without too much trouble allows loss issues to remain something of a taboo subject, so that those who do experience these issues traumatically feel it is not acceptable to voice them or to seek help. Yet many have the need to discuss issues, such as where and how they will die, and whether their unique needs will be catered to, whether decisions about resuscitation will be made on their behalf by other people's conceptions of quality of life, whether their loved ones will receive support, and so on. If these matters are glossed over, then the very clear message that is given is that these things do not matter.

Biggs (1993) makes the point that caregivers can sometimes find it difficult to face up to the reality of death and may project their views on to older people in their care. This is a potentially very dangerous phenomenon, and one that needs to be handled carefully. This can especially be the case in residential settings (Sidell, Katz, and Komaromy 2000). As Thompson et al. argue:

> Older people in residential settings should not be denied the opportunity to know and openly discuss the deaths of fellow residents. Such denial and secrecy can be harmful and devalues the friendships developed among relatives and between caregivers and residents. It also eliminates any potential for open communication that may help older individuals cope with feelings of fear, doubt, and uncertainty. . . . Residents need to be offered the opportunity to participate in the decision making concerning how the deaths of residents are acknowledged and memorialized. They can help plan a memorial service or ritual to celebrate lives in ways that are acceptable to or chosen by the other residents. (2000:392)

These, then, are just some of the practice implications of adopting an approach to working with older people in end-of-life care that recognizes both the need to challenge ageist assumptions and structures and the importance of loss as a factor to be considered in old age.

CONCLUSION

In this chapter we have sought to raise awareness of the dangers of allowing ageist assumptions to lead us into forms of practice that neglect the grief-related needs of older people. We have challenged the ageist myths that older people "get used to" grief and that they form a homogeneous group who will face death and dying in uniform ways. In place of these myths, we have sought to emphasize the importance of loss and grief in the lives of older people and to acknowledge that the ways in which older people grieve and face death are just as diverse within this age group as they would be in any other.

As we have argued previously, "older people are, of course, our future selves—people at a certain stage in life rather than a separate or distinct social group. The tendency to see older people as a homogeneous group is a clear reflection of ageism, insofar as it fails to recognize the immense diversity of people in later life, thereby dehumanizing those who fall within the categories of old, elderly, or aged. To fail to recognize that experiences of crisis and loss occur in old age is to add insult to injury, to add a further layer of discrimination by neglecting the lived experience of real people" (Thompson and Thompson 1999:132).

We have provided practice examples in order to help establish that these issues are not just abstract theoretical principles, but rather basic elements of actual practice that have a significant bearing on the lives of those older people we seek to serve. We hope that, in tackling these important issues in this way, we will have provided not only food for thought but also a greater awareness of the dangerous tendencies to rely on ageist assumptions in general and to play down the significance of loss in the lives of older people in particular. We have not provided prescriptions for practice, nor do we think it is appropriate to do so. Rather, it is our intention that our contribution here should stimulate further thought, debate, and study in order to encourage a critically reflective approach to practice.

REFERENCES

Biggs, S. 1993. *Understanding Ageing: Images, Attitudes and Professional Practice.* Buckingham, UK: Open University Press.

Coleman, P. G., F. McKiernan, M. Mills, and P. Speck. 2002. Spiritual belief and quality of life: The experience of older bereaved spouses. *Quality in Ageing* 3(1): 20–26.

Corr, C. A., C. M. Nabe, and D. M. Corr. 1997. *Death and Dying, Life and Living.* Pacific Grove, CA: Brookes/Cole.

Doka, K., ed. 1989. *Disenfranchised Grief: Recognizing Hidden Sorrow.* New York: Lexington.

Fennell, G., C. Phillipson, and H. Evers. 1988. *The Sociology of Old Age.* Milton Keynes, UK: Open University Press.

Gramsci, A. 1971. *Selections from the Prison Notebooks.* London: Lawrence and Wishart.

Hockey, J., and A. James. 1993. *Growing Up and Growing Old.* Thousand Oaks, CA: Sage.

Hughes, B., and M. Mtezuka. 1992. Social work and older women: Where have older women gone? In *Women, Social Work and Oppression: Issues in Anti-Discriminatory Practice*, ed. M. Langan and L. Day, 220–241. London: Routledge.

Lustbader, W. 1991. *Counting on Kindness: The Dilemmas of Dependency.* New York: Free Press.

MacKinlay, E. 2001. *The Spiritual Dimension of Ageing.* London: Jessica Kingsley.

Midwinter, E. 1990. An ageing world. *Ageing and Society* 10:12–22.

Moss, M. S., and S. Z. Moss. 1989. Death of the very old. In *Disenfranchised Grief: Recognizing Hidden Sorrow,* ed. K. Doka, 213–227. New York: Lexington.

Neimeyer, R. A., and A. Anderson. 2002. Meaning reconstruction theory. In *Loss and Grief: A Guide for Human Services Practitioners,* ed. N. Thompson, 45–64. London: Palgrave Macmillan.

Neimeyer, R. A., N. J. Keesee, and B. V. Fortner. 2000. Loss and meaning reconstruction: Propositions and procedures. In *Traumatic and Non-traumatic Loss and Bereavement,* ed. R. Malkinson, S. Rubin, and E. Wiztum, 197–230. Madison, CT: Psychosocial Press.

Nolan, M., S. Davies, and G. Gordon. 2001. Integrating perspectives. In *Working with Older People and Their Families: Key Issues in Policy and Practice,* ed. M. Nolan, S. Davies, and G. Grant, 160–178. Buckingham, UK: Open University Press.

Postle, K. 2002. Working 'between the idea and the reality': Ambiguities and tensions in care managers' work. *British Journal of Social Work* 32(3): 335–352.

Saunders, C. 2002. The philosophy of hospice. In *Loss and Grief: A Guide for Human Services Practitioners,* ed. N. Thompson, 23–33. London: Palgrave Macmillan.

Seymour, J. E., and E. Hanson. 2001. Palliative care and older people. In *Working with Older People and Their Families: Key Issues in Policy and Practice,* ed. M. Nolan, S. Davies, and G. Grant, 99–119. Buckingham, UK: Open University Press.

Sidell, M., J. S. Katz, and C. Komaromy. 2000. The case for palliative care in residential and nursing homes. In *Death, Dying and Bereavement* (2d ed.), ed. D. Dickenson, M. Johnson, and J. S. Katz, 110–118. Thousand Oaks, CA: Sage.

Stroebe, M., and H. Schut. 1999. The dual process model of coping with bereavement: Rationale and description. *Death Studies* 23(3): 197–224.

Thompson, N. 1995. *Age and Dignity: Working with Older People.* Aldershot, UK: Arena.

——. 1996. Tackling ageism: Moral imperative or current fad? In *Ethical Issues in the Care of the Dying and Bereaved Aged,* ed. J. D. Morgan, 23–34. Amityville, NY: Baywood.

——. 1997. Children, death and ageism. *Child and Family Social Work* 2(1): 59–65.

——. 1998. The ontology of ageing. *British Journal of Social Work* 28(5): 695–707.

——. 2001. *Anti-Discriminatory Practice.* 3d ed. London: Palgrave Macmillan.

——. 2003. *Promoting Equality.* 2d ed. London: Palgrave Macmillan.

——, ed. 2002. *Loss and Grief: A Guide for Human Services Practitioners.* London: Palgrave Macmillan.

Thompson, N., et al. 2000. Death, dying, and bereavement in relation to older individuals. *Illness, Crisis and Loss* 8(4): 388–394.

Thompson, S. 2002. Older people. In *Loss and Grief: A Guide for Human Services Practitioners,* ed. N. Thompson, 162–173. London: Palgrave Macmillan.

Thompson, S., and N. Thompson. 1999. Older people, crisis and loss. *Illness, Crisis and Loss* 2(7): 122–133.

Walter, T. 1999. *On Bereavement: The Culture of Grief.* London: Routledge.

Wass, H. 1995. Death in the lives of children and adolescents. In *Dying: Facing the Facts* (3d ed.), ed. H. Wass and R. A. Neimeyer, 269–301. Washington, DC: Taylor & Francis.

Weinstein, J. 2002. Teaching and learning about loss. In *Loss and Grief: A Guide for Human Services Practitioners,* ed. N. Thompson, 193–207. London: Palgrave Macmillan.

18

ASSESSING MENTAL HEALTH RISK IN END-OF-LIFE CARE

KATHERINE WALSH-BURKE

Mrs. K. was barely able to keep her eyes open as she lay in her bed during the initial assessment interview at her home. Her thin frame constricted in pain as she shifted in vain to find some comfortable spot. A forty-three-year-old mother of three, she had agreed to a social work referral from her visiting nurse because she was concerned about the impact of her illness on her children. Several home-based counseling sessions with Mrs. K., her husband, and each of their three children and phone calls to the primary physician by the social worker revealed a complex picture. Formerly an efficient and respected accountant, Mrs. K had been diagnosed with inflammatory breast cancer following a biopsy that never healed. Electing aggressive treatment at a comprehensive cancer center two hours from her home with distant doctors directing her care, Mrs. K. had endured almost constant pain since the initial surgery, partly due to necessary dressing changes.

Pain management was complicated by Mrs. K.'s desire and need to be at home (often during the day alone) and as alert as possible with her family. When referred for social-work services, she was spending most of her time between hospital and clinic visits in bed. She was determined, however, to continue aggressive treatment in the face of devastating disease because so much "needed to be done" for her children. Not only was her medical situation complicated, but her psychological and social situation was as well. She had been estranged from her only sibling, a brother, after a disagreement regarding the settling of her parents' estate following their deaths. The relationship with her in-laws was ambivalent, as religious differences (she was Jewish, her husband was raised Catholic) had created conflict at the time of the marriage. Since her diagnosis, she had been unable to work and with what little energy she had, she was trying to direct other family members in the care of their home and finances, which she had always done independently but now was finding unmanageable. Her eleven-year-old daughter's grades were suffering, and her six-year-old son had begun evidencing regressive behavior—wetting the bed and clinging to his home and parents. Her husband expressed helplessness and fear and was spending long hours at work. Mrs. K. tearfully acknowledged loss of her self-esteem, discouragement, sadness, and anger directed toward both herself and her surgeon. She also evidenced insomnia, weight loss, and emotional lability. The nurses were concerned that these symptoms and her unwillingness to talk about her poor prognosis were signs of major depression, which she had also experienced in her college years. They, along with most of the people involved in Mrs. K.'s care, seemed overwhelmed and were eager for the social worker to help find solutions. Even the HMO case manager approved the requested social-work visits with unusual rapidity, stating, "Oh yes, this is just such a difficult situation!"

THIS CASE scenario will sound familiar to many social workers providing end-of-life care, particularly those of us involved in home-based or community-based care. An accurate assessment of Mrs. K.'s depressed mood, like that of many clients facing the end of life, was a major challenge in the context of so many biological, psychological, and social influences. It was unclear whether her symptoms were in reaction to biological and social factors that would be ameliorated through medical and family interventions or represented a recurrent major depression that required psychiatric management. Yet it was important to assess whether she was overwhelmed by persistent pain and very real psychosocial concerns or whether she was also clinically depressed. Ultimately, her plan included combined individual, marital, and family therapy sessions, augmentation of pain medication with antidepressant medication and self-hypnosis, and frequent consultation with the team members charged with her care. Through these interventions, Mrs. K. was able to move from isolation and anger to actively engaging in helping herself and her family cope with her illness and ultimately to prepare for her death at home. A spontaneous family embrace, initiated by her six-year-old son during a particularly emotional family session near the end of her life, remains a reminder to me of the unique rewards of this work, despite all of the challenges. It also illustrates why social work expertise is so essential in end-of-life care.

In every practice setting, social workers perform the essential function of assessing mental health risk as part of the comprehensive psychosocial assessment. However, the assessment of risk in clients who are facing the end of life is often more complex because so many aspects of clients' lives are affected by illness, injury, and death. As the primary mental-health professionals conducting psychosocial assessments in most health, mental-health, and social-service settings, social workers must be particularly knowledgeable about the impact of biological, psychological, social, and transpersonal (or spiritual) influences as well as the interactions of these factors. This is especially true in end-of-life care for two reasons: physical illness and death precipitate a range of psychological responses; and mood disorders or anxiety disorders may stem from illness or the medications used to treat illness.

The complexity of the assessment process is also increased because the individual diagnosed with a life-threatening illness is rarely the exclusive unit of focus of social workers providing end-of-life care. More often, in this arena of practice, the client family system is viewed as the unit of care. Interview data and other information may need to be gathered from multiple family members and significant others who are caring for the ill or injured individual and their mental health risk must also be assessed.

The psychosocial assessment provides the social worker, interdisciplinary team members, and clients with essential information to formulate a comprehensive treatment plan. The person-in-environment and strengths perspectives of social work are very important in assessing individuals and families facing end-of-life issues, as they are in assessing all social-work clients. Accurate identification of mental health risk is also essential in order to develop treatment plans that are effective in ameliorating distress.

Although not always used in community health settings, the Multi-axial Assessment of the *Diagnostic and Statistical Manual of Mental Disorders* (4th ed., 2000) is often included in the comprehensive assessment, particularly in outpatient mental health settings. The Multi-axial Assessment consists of the following:

Axis I: Clinical Disorders (such as Major Depression and PTSD)
Axis II: Personality Disorders and Mental Retardation
Axis III: Medical Conditions
Axis IV: Environmental Problems (Financial stress, lack of access to medical care)
Axis V: Global Assessment of Functioning Scale

The Multi-axial Assessment is most often used in making differential diagnoses of mental disorders.

RISK FACTORS OF PARTICULAR RELEVANCE IN END-OF-LIFE CARE

Results of empirical studies on adjustment to cancer and other life-threatening/life-limiting illnesses indicate the following factors that increase the risk of psychosocial distress in individuals and families facing the end of life:

- biological symptoms such as pain, dyspnea, and fatigue that create physical and emotional suffering,
- limited social support
- problems in family communication, relationships or functioning
- financial distress
- limited or inadequate access to medical and/or psychosocial services (including limited access due to lack of culturally competent care provision or language barriers)
- mental disorders (such as anxiety, depression, personality disorders, substance dependence, or other disorders whose symptoms may be exacerbated by the stress of serious illness or loss)

Studies have found that approximately 33–35 percent of clients with life-threatening illnesses such as cancer, heart disease, and neurological disorders experience significant psychosocial distress such as anxiety and depression (Popkin and Tucker 1992; Zabora et al. 2001). Although there are no definitive data to inform us about how many clients facing the end of their lives experience problems warranting psychosocial intervention, the clinical literature indicates that many clients evidence one or more of these identified risk factors. Social workers help to ameliorate these conditions with carefully selected interventions. These interventions are discussed in other chapters of this text and include individual and family counseling and cognitive-behavioral and stress-management techniques to help manage pain and other symptoms, as well as support groups, camps, and peer mentor programs. In addition, case management and advocacy are included in the treatment plan to assist in making maximum use of resources. For clients experiencing significant psychosocial distress, multimodal interventions such as psychotherapy combined with psychopharmacological treatment may be needed.

FACTORS OF SPECIAL SIGNIFICANCE IN END-OF-LIFE CARE

BIOLOGICAL INFLUENCES

Because a wide variety of medical conditions, accidents, and traumatic events cause death, the range of biological variables that influence individuals affected by these is very broad. It is essential for social workers to understand the common biological and psychosocial effects of each client's medical condition and the treatments used to address them. For example, many chemotherapy agents used in treating cancer, such as vincristin and interferon, have been associated with depressed mood. Awareness of this side effect is essential for both the patient and family coping with cancer, and for the treatment team. Similarly, many medications used in the treatment of heart disease and infectious diseases induce depressed mood. Changes in neurological functioning are common in brain tumors and many other medical conditions and are a recognized side effect of many medications, particularly when used for children and the elderly.

Changes in organ systems that are created by illness, injury, medical treatments, or aging can produce symptoms that are similar or identical to those of Axis I mental disorder diagnoses. Hepatic failure from liver disease, for example, can result in lethargy, impaired cognitive functioning, and depressed affect, among other symptoms. Impairment of the thyroid gland can produce symptoms that otherwise might be thought to be due to an anxiety or mood disorder. Failure to recognize these biological influences on psychological and cognitive functioning may result in inappropriate treatment aimed at symptomatic relief rather than effective treatment aimed at the biological cause. These biologically based conditions must be ruled in or out as part of the comprehensive assessment if an effective treatment plan is to be developed.

FAMILY HISTORY AND COPING

Family history and history of past coping are essential components of any comprehensive assessment and are essential in end-of-life care for two reasons.

The first reason is this: *The death (anticipated or actual) of an individual has a significant impact on other family members.* In this context, *family* is defined broadly to include all those that the client identifies as family, such as partners, godparents, and significant others.

In some ways, every family member facing the death of a loved one is at risk for distress owing to the strong emotions and the changes in family structure and functioning that accompany the anticipated or actual loss of a member. This is especially evident in the case of children facing a parent's death or an elderly dependent facing the death of a family caregiver. Social workers are often involved in directly helping families adjust to these changes or referring family members to appropriate resources to assist them. Conflicted or estranged family relationships can add significant distress to the impending death of a member (Coyle et al. 1999).

Even in families that have functioned effectively prior to serious illness, family members experience significant distress. Heart disease, pulmonary disease, and other serious illnesses such as Alzheimer's dementia cause changes in family members' identities, roles, and daily functioning. Studies document that spouses of cancer patients are as distressed as the patient and that spousal and patient distress are correlated (Blanchard, Albrecht, and Ruckdeschel 1997; Robinson-Whelen 2001).

Social workers routinely assess symptoms of distress such as depression and anxiety that are evidenced by individual family members. In addition, symptoms that indicate *family system* distress need to be identified. The following are some of the symptoms that family members and significant others may evidence when facing the end of life:

- Social isolation
- Communication difficulties
- Inability to carry out caregiving functions
- Anger, abuse, or violence
- Substance abuse or dependence
- Emotional cutoffs (isolation or scapegoating of a family member)
- Conflicts with or lack of access to professionals or organizational resources
- Anxiety
- Depression
- Anticipatory grief and bereavement

The second reason is this: *The family has a significant impact on the dying individual.* Families have a significant effect on the care and adjustment of the individual facing the end of life. If family members are not coping with impending loss, the needs of the individual who is dying may not be addressed effectively. It is equally essential to identify the strengths and resources upon which individual family members and the family as a unit can draw to cope effectively with the stress of illness and loss. Such strengths include:

- Flexibility in adapting to changes imposed by illness and loss
- Cohesion among family members
- Mutual support
- Communication of information
- Constructively expressed emotion and affection
- Effective use of internal and external resources and support

Understanding how families cope enables professionals to support their efforts effectively. The strengths perspective emphasizes this consistently and is one of the reasons that social work is so important at the end of life. Exploring family history in relation to past losses is especially important, as this history helps us to understand the current situation in light of how the family handled loss previously. Froma Walsh and Monica McGoldrick's *Living Beyond Loss* (1995) makes this explicitly clear, as they discuss the genograms of families such as the Kennedys and how succeeding generations are influenced by the reactions to loss of previous generations.

Yet another important reason for assessing family history is the genetic vulnerability for many conditions that is inherited by biological relatives. Risk for many mental disorders as well as medical conditions is genetically determined. A family history can help to identify genetic risks and contribute to accurate differential diagnosis, especially in the case of mood disorders.

It is very important in the assessment of families with diverse cultural and ethnic backgrounds to recognize how significant language and cultural factors are in the ways that family members respond to anticipated or actual death. Although it is not possible for individual social workers to be knowledgeable about every cultural group we encounter, cultural competence involves being aware of the limitations of one's own understanding and exploring with clients how their culture-based values, beliefs, and norms influence their adjustment. When clients are encouraged to share their beliefs and practices, professional caregivers reduce the risk of violating cultural norms or misdiagnosing client reactions. The cultural prescription against the discussion of a "terminal" diagnosis in some Asian groups, for example, can be misinterpreted as an indication of high anxiety and denial. A choice to pursue spiritually based interventions rather than medical intervention by clients of Caribbean or Indonesian background may be misinterpreted as a sign of depression or denial. One of the most important contributions that social workers make in this arena is to encourage client self-advocacy and to advocate for culturally competent care for vulnerable populations who may be less able to advocate for themselves.

DIFFERENTIAL DIAGNOSIS IN END-OF-LIFE CARE

Social workers perform a key function in helping both clients and interdisciplinary team members to determine whether symptoms such as anxiety or depressed mood fit the diagnostic criteria for a mental disorder. If the diagnosis of a mood disorder, anxiety disorder, or complicated bereavement is made, the treatment plan will need to include the offering of interventions such as psychotherapy and psychopharmacology in addition to case management and supportive counseling, which are a routine part of end-of-life care. Differential diagnosis is difficult, however, because psychological distress is an expectable response to the threat of death.

Therese Rando notes, "When a patient receives a terminal diagnosis, he is immediately thrown into the acute crisis phase of the living-dying interval. Annihilation anxiety arises. . . . The usual reaction is one of acute crisis anxiety. This escalates until it reaches a peak, after which the patient calls upon whatever psychological mechanisms are available to reduce the anxiety" (1984:210). Similarly, symptoms of depressed mood including sadness, loss of appetite, and loss of sleep are common reactions to learning of a terminal illness. It is essential for social workers to be able to differentiate between the expectable reactions to advanced illness, injury, or death that may require only brief or supportive interventions and those reactions that represent more serious biological, psychological, and/or social disturbances that require rapid and focused professional intervention. Failure to identify significant disturbance or risk for disturbance may result in increased suffering and even premature death.

The *Diagnostic and Statistical Manual of Mental Disorders (DSM-IV)*, compiled by the American Psychiatric Association and published in 2000, is the primary tool used by mental health professionals, including social workers, to make a differential diagnosis of a mental disorder. Several categories of diagnoses are most relevant in end-of-life care. The first category of relevant disorders is coded as both medical conditions (recorded on Axis III of the DSM-IV Multi-axial Assessment) and clinical disorders (recorded on Axis I). These include delirium and dementia.

Delirium due to a medical condition (293.0) is caused by a variety of biological conditions, including metabolic imbalances resulting from surgery or organ dysfunction and structural abnormalities such as brain tumors or vascular obstructions, and infections. (The medical condition is also recorded on Axis III.) It is "a transient organically based disorder that frequently mimics dementia. A person suffering from delirium may exhibit symptoms similar to dementia, such as mental confusion, impaired concentration, hallucinations, and erratic moods. The primary differences are that most delirious states develop rapidly and can be treatable. That is, the cognitive and emotional symptoms are often due to physical conditions in the body that, once identified, may be correctible. For this reason, delirium is sometimes referred to as reversible dementia" (McInnis-Dittrich 2002:120).

However, diagnosing and treating this condition in the context of end-of-life care can be challenging, since the organ failure that is part of the dying process can produce delirium and treatment decisions may be different when quality of life vs. quantity is the goal. Teamwork is essential, since medical professionals are equipped to determine whether infection or other biological processes are the cause. Social workers play a key role in helping patients and their loved ones to understand and cope with the changes in cognition as well as facilitate decision making. For example, many families utilizing hospice care express enormous relief when they learn that changes in cognition can be part of the expectable process in the last days of life and feel more comfortable with the decision not to aggressively treat but rather allow a natural death when they have the opportunity to consider and weigh all possibilities. Dementia is another biologically based dysfunction that is relevant in end-of-life care because it occurs in so many older persons whose life expectancy is limited. Unlike delirium, it is not yet reversible. The most common form is Alzheimer's dementia (recorded as 294.10 without behavioral disturbance, and 294.11 with behavioral disturbance, on Axis I). Some of the symptoms of dementia are similar to those of delirium and depression. They include loss of short-term memory, impaired orientation to time, space, and person, and difficulty with concentration and performance of complex tasks. The risk of Alzheimer's dementia increases with advanced age. The only way to diagnose this disorder definitively is through autopsy of the brain. However, computer-assisted to-mography (CAT scans) and magnetic resonance imaging (MRI), as well as PET and SPECT testing, can provide information about brain structure, cerebral blood flow, and abnormalities that can be helpful in making a differential diagnosis. Physical examination by a medical care provider is essential when symptoms of these biolog-ically based conditions are present. The social worker can play a key role in recog-nizing the need for neurological or neuropsychiatric evaluation as well as in ensuring that clients have access to adequate medical care for accurate diagnosis and treatment. A common error is for symptoms to be attributed to "dementia" when untreated depression or a metabolic disturbance is the cause of symptoms. Advocacy for com-prehensive assessment is a key contribution by social workers in these situations.

MOOD DISTURBANCE

The accurate diagnosis of a mood disturbance presents many challenges due to the complexity of biological and psychological factors influencing those facing the end of life. Depressed mood is one of the most common responses, in otherwise well-adjusted individuals, to a life-threatening illness or loss. In the psychological realm, depression "is another emotion experienced by the dying patient, as a natural reaction to the perception of imminent loss. It is both a symptom and a tool for the patient's preparation for the loss of all she knows and for coming to grips with the reality of demise. . . . In a preparatory or anticipatory depression, there will be times when it is necessary to focus on imminent losses. These need to be contemplated and worked through whenever possible" (Rando 1984:239).

Mood disturbances, however, can also be caused by biological factors and may be ameliorated through biological or combined biological and psychological interven-tions. When the symptoms of depression or anxiety occur in the context of end-of-life care, it is essential to identify biological influences that may be causing the reaction and insure that treatment for these is initiated.

Patients with anemia associated with chronic renal failure and certain chemother-apeutic agents can exhibit symptoms of depression such as lethargy, and hypersomnia and their behavior may resemble anhedonia in that they decrease or abandon activities from which they usually derive enjoyment. Patients and family members may inac-curately assume these symptoms indicate depression.

CASE EXAMPLE

Mrs. P. is a seventy-six-year-old mother of six and grandmother of fourteen grandchil-dren who has end-stage kidney disease but is not receiving renal dialysis. Despite learning that her illness is life-limiting, Mrs. P. has remained invested in her family and expressed deep interest in the activities of her children and grandchildren. Her visiting nurse requested social-work consultation when Mrs. P.'s daughter reported that her mother seemed to be increasingly depressed. She expressed concern that her mother had begun to sleep a good deal during the day, seemed to be avoiding family activities, and became tearful when her family prodded her. Her family suspected that knowledge of her terminal illness was causing her depression and wondered if anti-depressant medication might be indicated. As she completed the assessment, the social worker learned from Mrs. P. and her husband that while Mrs. P. very much wanted to spend time with her family, she was just "too tired" to keep up. She felt particularly discouraged and depressed about not being able to "enjoy the time" she had with her grandchildren. There was no individual or family history of mood disorder, and the main symptoms of depression that Mrs. P. was evidencing, including diminished plea-sure from activities that normally brought her pleasure and tearfulness, seemed related to fatigue.

After concluding that the majority of Mrs. P.'s "depressive" symptoms appeared to be directly related to the somatic symptom of fatigue, the social worker and the nurse consulted with Mrs. P.'s physician regarding treatment for the fatigue. Medication to boost red blood cells was initiated and the fatigue and hypersomnia diminished, en-abling Mrs. P. to derive increased participation in and satisfaction from interactions with her family.

When biological factors have either been ruled out or effectively managed and the diagnostic criteria for a mood or other mental disorder are met, these disorders are recorded on Axis I (for clinical disorders and other conditions that are a focus of clinical attention) and Axis II (for personality disorders and mental retardation) of the DSM-IV Multi-axial Assessment.

ADJUSTMENT DISORDER

Adjustment disorders are perhaps the most common diagnoses made in clients facing life crises or significant stressors. This diagnosis is made when a reaction to a stressor, such as life-threatening illness, is beyond that considered a "normal or expectable reaction." This, of course, is a subjective assessment, and some social workers may be uncertain about assigning this diagnosis when an intense emotional reaction is con-sidered by many to be a "normal" reaction to death or anticipated death.

According to Massie and Popkin, a characteristic response to news of life-limiting illness includes depression, anxiety, irritability, and disruption in appetite and sleep. They note, "Some patients continue to have high levels of depression and anxiety that persist for weeks or months. This persistent reactive distress is not adaptive and fre-quently requires psychiatric treatment" (1998:518). In such situations, the diagnoses of adjustment disorder (recorded as 309, with depressed mood, anxiety, or mixed anxiety and depressed mood, on Axis I) may be appropriate in either an individual facing death or in a significant other who is facing the anticipated death or actual loss of someone close to them. The diagnosis of an adjustment disorder is frequently made when symptoms cause significant distress but do not meet the criteria for another disorder such as major depression, generalized anxiety, or PTSD. The diagnosis is generally an indication that psychosocial intervention is needed and thus it is important to document it and develop an appropriate treatment plan that includes the provision of counseling.

MOOD DISORDER DUE TO A GENERAL MEDICAL CONDITION

Recent studies provide evidence that depression occurs in association with some medical and neurological illnesses (Lynch 1995; Nordin and Glimelius 1999). The prevalence of depression in patients with Parkinson's disease, Huntington's disease, and cerebral-vascular disease ranges from 30 to 50 percent. Similarly, prevalence is higher in patients with Cushing's syndrome, cancer, and coronary heart disease than in the non-medically ill population. "To what extent depression in the medically ill is a discrete entity, separate from depression arising in patients without co-morbid physical illness, remains a point of discourse" (Massie and Popkin 1998:522). This diagnosis may be made, however, according to the DSM-IV, when "a prominent and persistent disturbance in mood is judged to be a direct physiological consequence of a general medical condition.

The National Cancer Institute fact sheet on depression and cancer notes that, in the case of depression due to a general medical condition, "consideration should be given to obtaining laboratory data to assist in detection of electrolyte or endocrine imbalances or the presence of nutritional deficiencies. Clinical experience suggests that pharmacotherapy is more advantageous than psychotherapy alone in the treatment of depression that is caused by medical factors, particularly if the dosages of the causative agent(s), i.e., steroids, antibiotics, or other medications, cannot be decreased or discontinued."

Although the diagnosis of the medical condition is made by a physician, the social worker is often able to differentiate the symptoms of depression and, like with other types of psychosocial problems, plays a key role in providing counseling to both the patient and family as well as helping other professional caregivers understand the patient's distress. Mood disorder due to a general medical condition (293.83) is recorded on Axis I of the DSM IV, with the medical condition listed on Axis III.

SUBSTANCE-INDUCED MOOD DISORDER

This disorder is characterized by "a prominent and persistent disturbance in mood that is judged to be a direct physiological consequence of a drug of abuse, *a medication*, another somatic treatment for depression, or toxin exposure" (DSM-IV 346). Awareness of this diagnosis, similar to that of a mood disorder due to a medical condition, is important to social workers providing end-of-life care, inasmuch as many of the clients we assist are taking multiple medications. As the organs of the body become stressed and function decreases because of illness and treatment regimes, medication side effects may become more pronounced. A careful examination of the possible causes of depressed mood, including substance use or medication effects, is essential to avoid symptom exacerbation that can occur if the cause of the symptoms is not appropriately treated.

The DSM-IV also includes two additional categories of mood disorders that are relevant to end-of-life care: bipolar disorders (bipolar disorder I, bipolar disorder II, and cyclothymia) and unipolar depressive disorders (major depressive order and dysthymia).

BIPOLAR DISORDERS

Bipolar disorder, referred to in the past as manic depressive disorder, is frequently distinguished by periods of major depression alternating or intermingled with periods of elevated mood and energy that may suddenly turn into rage. Accurate assessment of mood changes and identification of clients with a previous history of mania or bipolar disorder is important in the context of end-of-life care, because symptoms may worsen as a result of medication changes and/or physiologic changes associated with illness and treatment of medical conditions. Close consultation between psychiatric and medical care providers is most important when a client with bipolar disorder is affected by a life-limiting illness. Careful monitoring and adjustment of medication is essential. Case management and supportive counseling for the patient and family help to ensure coordinated care.

It is also very important for social workers and other care providers to be aware that recent studies have shown that some patients, initially treated for unipolar depression with antidepressant medication, have subsequently developed refractory symptoms of bipolar disorder. Thus, great care in assessment, particularly related to family history of bipolar disorder, is essential before medication is used to treat depressed mood (Brown University 2002).

DEPRESSION

Accurate diagnosis of depression is one of the most challenging tasks for mental health professionals providing end-of-life care. In order to make the diagnosis of a major depressive episode (coded on Axis I as 296.2x for a single episode), the DSM-IV states that symptoms must include either depressed mood or loss of interest or pleasure in activities, in addition to at least four of the other identified symptoms such as feelings of worthlessness and changes in sleep and appetite; be present all or most of the day, every day, for at least two weeks; and cause significant distress or impairment.

Many practitioners in end-of-life care have learned that the first step in assessment is to rule out medical conditions and treatment effects as the primary causes of depressed mood (as in the example of Mrs. P. earlier in this chapter). It cannot be emphasized enough that the symptoms of pain, fatigue, and shortness of breath that accompany many medical conditions contribute to or cause serious levels of depression and anxiety as well as intense physical suffering. Yet it is surprising how often caregivers are tempted to attribute depressed mood to psychological causes before physical causes. If depression or anxiety is evidenced in the presence of untreated pain, fatigue, and/or dyspnea, these somatic symptoms must be addressed immediately. Not only can adequate management of these symptoms prevent or alleviate depression and anxiety, but inadequate management can also result in unnecessary suffering and early death. It is therefore essential that social workers be active advocates to ensure that these physiological symptoms are thoroughly assessed and effectively treated before a diagnosis of a mental disorder is made.

Once somatic factors have been ruled out or treated effectively, practitioners must inquire about how the client feels. Does he or she feel worthless? Is self-esteem significantly diminished? Thoughts of "wishing for death" or suicide as well as loss of feeling pleasure and expressions of guilt are signs of serious distress that suggest a diagnosis of depression is indicated and a psychosocial treatment plan should be implemented (Massie and Popkin 1998; Billings and Block 1995; Hedlund 2001).

Practitioners in some settings utilize screening instruments to identify clients with anxiety or depression. The Beck Depression Inventory-Short Form, the Zung Depression Scale, and the Brief Symptom Inventory-18 are some of the instruments that have been used effectively with nonmedically ill as well as medically ill clients (Zabora 1998).

Assessment and/or screening for depression is essential not only for the identified patient but for family caregivers as well.

CASE EXAMPLE

Mr. N. was a thirty-nine-year-old father of four who was diagnosed with metastatic sarcoma. Aggressive therapy was unsuccessful in achieving remission, and he was told his prognosis was very poor. He had a very strong affiliation with his church and drew on his faith in anticipating his death. He communicated openly with his family and care providers and expressed an interest in remaining at home with his family as long as possible. Aggressive treatment of his pain was initiated to make him as comfortable as possible, and he was anxious to participate in advance funeral and estate planning. In a referral to the hospital social worker, Mr. N.'s doctor reported that Mrs. N., Mr. N.'s wife of eighteen years, was "depressed." In individual interviews with Mr. and Mrs. N., the social worker learned that Mrs. N. was very discouraged and frightened by her husband's poor prognosis and felt very sad at the prospect of both losing her life partner and becoming a single parent. The social worker also learned that Mrs. N. had experienced episodes of "feeling blue" in the past and that both her father and her brother had been treated for depression and alcohol dependence. Low self-esteem had always been an issue for her, partly due to the alienating family environment she grew up in. She reported insomnia and loss of appetite, which she had experienced in the past, but attributed these to "reaction to the stress." Mrs. N. avoided both alcohol and medications, out of fear of dependence, but acknowledged that she was experiencing an increased sense of worthlessness as well as helplessness. Her primary physician had tested her for thyroid and other abnormalities and ruled them out. When asked how depressed she thought she was, she said, "It's getting more serious," noting she was having difficulty getting out of bed in the morning and engaging with her children. The social worker explained to Mrs. N. that because these symptoms did seem to be causing considerable distress and because there was a family history of depression, medication as well as counseling might be very helpful. A psychopharmacological consult was sought and weekly psychotherapy sessions utilizing cognitive and inter-personal techniques were initiated along with a short-term trial of antidepressant medication.

As is illustrated in this case, depression, when accurately diagnosed, is often most successfully treated with a combination of psychotherapy and psychopharmacologic agents. Medication can help to reduce symptoms so that clients can then make most effective use of insight and problem-solving strategies in therapy.

BEREAVEMENT

Another challenge to the clinician is differentiating between the diagnosis of depres-sion and bereavement in family members who are experiencing grief. Bereavement (V.62.82 recorded on Axis I) may be the more appropriate diagnosis when symptoms of depression are evidenced following the death of a loved one, yet we will often encounter grieving clients who are evidencing major depression that requires treat-ment beyond bereavement support. According to the DSM-IV, bereaved individuals may present with symptoms characteristic of a major depressive episode, including sadness, insomnia, poor appetite, and weight loss. These are all considered normal, expectable responses to a significant loss. Usually, social support provided through groups and informal networks is sufficient in helping bereaved individuals and families.

Again, the social worker's knowledge of cultural norms is extremely important in making accurate assessments, particularly because the norms for behavioral and emo-tional reactions to illness or loss vary tremendously in clients from diverse back-grounds. This is particularly relevant in differential diagnoses of anxiety and depres-sion vs. bereavement in individuals whose cultural norms regarding grief differ from those of the practitioner or the dominant culture. Professionals may misinterpret the intense and loud crying, keening, and wailing that are characteristic of Vietnamese Buddhists and Italian mourners as agitation associated with an anxiety disorder for example. The social withdrawal of a Hindu widow may be misdiagnosed as depression (Kagawa-Singer 1994). Berzoff, Flanagan, and Hertz (1996) eloquently point out how major errors can be made by practitioners who are unfamiliar with cultural norms, especially in assessing grief reactions. They describe a social work student's paying respects to the parents of a medical student who had committed suicide during a psychotic episode. The social worker, seeing the covered mirrors, ripped clothing, and unkempt appearance of this Jewish family sitting Shiva, assumed that the family members were also experiencing psychosis.

Misinterpretation of culturally prescribed grief reactions can result in very inappro-priate treatments and missed opportunities for the establishment of a therapeutic alliance. In the context of grief, treatment with prescription antidepressants or seda-tives may actually impede the process of normal grieving. It is also important to be aware that the Western view of grief as a phenomenon that people are expected to "recover" from within a year imposes expectations that can be problematic and inhibit the grieving process.

However, when symptoms cause prolonged distress and/or prevent the individual from completing the tasks of grieving, such as adapting to an environment without the deceased, then either complicated bereavement or depression may be an appropriate diagnosis (Worden 2002). The DSM-IV identifies morbid preoccupation with worthlessness, prolonged and marked functional impairment, and guilt about things other than actions taken or not taken by the survivor at the time of death as indicators that the bereaved individual may be experiencing a major depressive episode. Awareness of risk factors can also help the social worker in accurately identifying those in need of grief therapy. Risk factors include multiple stressors (such as financial distress, change in role, and becoming a single parent), ambivalent or conflicted relationship with the deceased, and a high degree of dependence on the deceased (Walsh-Burke 2000). The counseling needs of clients with these risk factors often require more than is provided in bereavement support groups and can be best addressed through more intensive intervention such as grief therapy.

CASE EXAMPLE

Ms. C. was a kindergarten teacher who reported continued symptoms of depressed mood at the three-month bereavement follow-up call by the hospice social worker. She had lived with her parents most of her adult life, and she and her mother had a close, mutually supportive relationship following her father's death ten years before the diagnosis of her mother's colon cancer. Ms. C. had begun taking Paxil when a stroke had necessitated her mother's nursing home placement six months before her death, and Ms. C. had managed all of the family and practical responsibilities effectively during the last months of her mother's life. She had a strong social support network and was much admired by colleagues and parents at her elementary school. During the follow-up call she reported this, but on further inquiry revealed that she felt melancholy and was experiencing guilt over placing her mother in a nursing home. She reported feeling that her life outside of her work had little meaning, and when asked if she had ever considered harming herself she avoided the question, stating that her religion (Roman Catholic) would not allow it. She asked whether a bereavement support group was available, but the social worker, concerned about the possibility of major depression, suggested individual counseling sessions instead.

Exploration of Ms. C.'s history revealed an alcoholic father whose drinking during Ms. C.'s childhood and adolescence had caused significant marital conflict, poverty, and verbal abuse of his wife and four children. None of this history had been revealed previously to anyone outside of the family. Ms. C. was the oldest daughter, had performed a caretaking role for her younger siblings as a child, and had assumed the role of primary caregiver for first her father and then her mother during their terminal illnesses. She derived her satisfaction in life through caring for others, but felt she never met the high expectations she had set for herself since childhood. A pattern of self-sacrificing behavior and negative self-talk, which contributed to low self-esteem, rapidly became evident. When these patterns were identified, Ms. C. acknowledged them with surprise, suggesting that these types of behavior were expected of her by others and she had just "lived with it."

Rather than focus primarily on Ms. C.'s feelings related to her mother's death, the emphasis in succeeding sessions was on helping Ms. C. develop insight into the roots of her self-sacrificing behavior and low self-esteem. She acknowledged having felt depressed much of her life and was then able to identify the ways in which her consistent accommodations to others' needs over her own reinforced her low self-esteem and depressed mood. The many positive aspects of Ms. C.'s relationships and interactions were identified, as were the ways in which she treated others better than herself. A positive transference developed as the social worker actively reflected Ms. C.'s strengths and provided reinforcement when Ms. C. expressed positive feelings about herself. She was also reminded frequently that her feelings and needs were valid, and should not be discounted—by herself or others—the way they had been when she was growing up. Scaling questions were used weekly in which Ms. C. was asked to assess how well she was caring for herself. Through these, she noted steady increases in her self-care and a consistent improvement in her mood. Significant others also remarked on the positive changes they observed in her, which helped to counteract her concern about being "selfish" or "too happy" following her mother's death. Ms. C. continued to experience sadness related to her mother's death and gave herself permission to express this, but she increasingly began to experience pleasure and self-satisfaction as well.

ANXIETY-RELATED DISORDERS

Any of us can imagine anxiety—even intense fear—as a first response to the news that we, or someone we love, will die. An accurate assessment of anxiety in the context of end of life, therefore, is as complex a process as assessment of depression. Many clients fear isolation, suffering, and separation related to dying and will benefit from social-work intervention to address these fears. However, while anxiety is considered an expectable response to anticipated death or loss, social workers play a key role in accurately assessing the various anxiety disorders described in the DSM-IV in order to offer effective treatment.

Clients who suffer from preexisting anxiety disorders are obviously at risk for increased distress in the face of a life-threatening illness or loss and should be offered intervention when identified. In addition, biological factors that may be causing anxiety must also be identified and addressed appropriately before the diagnosis of a mental disorder is made because anxiety and agitation can occur in clients who are using prescription and nonprescription drugs. These symptoms can also occur when medications, including opioid analgesics such as morphine, are withdrawn inadvertently or too rapidly. Caregivers may assume symptoms of anxiety are a psychological reaction to anticipated death, when in fact the agitation may be a result of medication effects or a withdrawal response. After identifying and treating biological factors that may be contributing to anxiety, the process of differential diagnosis includes ruling in or out the anxiety disorders described in the DSM-IV.

ADJUSTMENT DISORDER WITH ANXIETY

Like adjustment disorder with depressed mood, the diagnosis of adjustment disorder with anxiety (399.24 recorded on Axis I) is appropriate when the anxiety symptoms exceed those expected as part of the reaction to a life-threatening illness or loss but do not fit the diagnostic criteria for another anxiety disorder such as generalized anxiety disorder or PTSD. Often individuals with a life-limiting illness and/or their family members will request counseling or support when they themselves express that they are overwhelmed or "not coping well." The diagnosis of adjustment disorder is appropriate when the distress is significant enough to interfere with work or other daily routines. When an adjustment disorder diagnosis is made, clients will benefit from counseling (individual, family, or group) that identifies strengths and emphasizes communication, coping, and problem-solving strategies (Walsh-Burke 1992).

ANXIETY DUE TO A GENERAL MEDICAL CONDITION

Many medical conditions including metabolic imbalances due to sepsis, hypoglycemia, and certain types of tumors, as well as withdrawal from opioid analgesics are all associated with anxiety (Breitbart 1998). Shortness of breath that accompanies many pulmonary conditions can also create the sensation of suffocation, and anxiety is an expectable response. Biological treatments for these conditions are the first to be recommended, although in the context of a life-limiting illness, aggressive, life-prolonging treatments for these may not be elected by the patient. Palliative interventions, however, such as pain and anti-anxiety medication, focused breathing, guided imagery, and relaxation techniques, discussed in other chapters in this book, can be most effective in managing the anxiety that accompanies medical conditions. The diagnosis of anxiety due to a general medical condition is coded 293.84 on Axis I, with the general medical condition recorded on Axis III.

SUBSTANCE-INDUCED ANXIETY DISORDER

Restlessness, agitation, and sleep disturbances are all symptoms of anxiety disorders, but they are also side effects of many prescription medications such as steroids and neuroleptic medications that are used in treating cancer and neurological diseases. Anxiety and agitation are also symptoms of withdrawal from narcotics, barbiturates, and alcohol. A client with alcohol or other substance dependence may exhibit high anxiety and agitation during a prolonged or unexpected inpatient stay that causes withdrawal symptoms. Eliciting information about use of both prescription and non-prescription drugs from the patient and from significant others is an essential part of the assessment. When a substance-induced anxiety disorder is diagnosed, it is recorded on Axis I (292.89).

Frank discussions about the influence of substances is important, for seriously ill individuals and their caregivers may be better able to make decisions about care when they understand the effects of the medications used to treat medical conditions. Those individuals using nonprescription substances will require treatment for dependence or withdrawal. Although medical assessment and management of these effects is essential, social workers who identify anxiety symptoms can offer psychological and complementary interventions to help in the management of the distress that is experienced as anxiety.

POST-TRAUMATIC STRESS DISORDER
AND ACUTE STRESS DISORDER

According to the DSM-IV, the essential feature of post-traumatic stress disorder (PTSD) is the development of symptoms, including persistently reexperiencing the traumatic event, persistent avoidance of stimuli associated with the trauma, and persistent symptoms of arousal following an event that involves actual or threatened death or serious injury or witnessing an event that involves death, injury, or threat to the physical integrity of another person. The symptoms, such as hypervigilance, irritability, and intense psychological distress at exposure to internal or external cues that symbolize the trauma, are present for more than one month and cause significant distress or impairment. The symptoms of acute stress disorder are similar and are in reaction to the same type of extreme stressor, but this diagnosis is made when the symptoms occur during the first month following a traumatic event.

Some practitioners believe that the diagnosis of a life-limiting illness is an extreme stressor, threatening the bodily integrity of the person, which can precipitate symptoms of acute stress disorder (coded 308.3 on Axis I) or PTSD (coded 309.81 on Axis I). Following a particularly painful or distressing death, family caregivers may experience symptoms of PTSD. In such cases, the anxiety, irritability, insomnia, and other symptoms, whether due to acute stress or part of an adjustment reaction, are important to address through psychotherapy and complementary approaches, and are sometimes helped by anti-anxiety medication. More often, PTSD caused by trauma that predates the life-limiting illness becomes an issue in end-of-life care. Individuals with PTSD may evidence intense anxiety and avoidance when confronted with invasive diagnostic procedures or treatments. Social workers must be able to identify these symptoms as possible indicators of PTSD and can explore how past experiences are contributing to current distress, offering appropriate intervention and seeking psychiatric consultation, when indicated.

CASE EXAMPLE

Ms. T. is a forty-nine-year-old single woman receiving palliative care for metastatic lung cancer. She had completed the initial workup with great difficulty and was referred to the hospital social worker when she evidenced "panic" in the emergency department. Over the course of several sessions with Ms. T., the social worker learned that she had endured years of sexual abuse as a young child and early adolescent and, while never treated for PTSD, had experienced intense anxiety symptoms as a result of certain triggers and had avoided physical examinations and medical procedures throughout her adult life. The prospect of lying motionless with a large machine "descending on" or "surrounding" her was terrifying, as were thoughts of any other medical procedures. With this information, a comprehensive palliative-care plan was established that included relaxation and visualization training and that was used during all procedures along with medication and psychotherapy.

GENERALIZED ANXIETY DISORDER

According to the DSM-IV, the essential feature of generalized anxiety disorder is excessive anxiety and worry occurring more days than not for at least six months about a number of events or activities. The individual finds it difficult to control the worry and the anxiety is accompanied by additional symptoms such as fatigue, irritability, muscle tension, and disturbed sleep. As in all the other diagnoses discussed in this chapter, the diagnosis of this disorder is challenging in the context of end-of-life care because many medical conditions and treatment effects can produce similar symptoms. As with mood disorders, combined modality approaches such as psychotherapy using cognitive-behavioral and relaxation training along with medication can be very effective in reducing distress caused by the disorder in patients and family caregivers. This disorder is recorded on Axis I as 300.02.

CONCLUSION

In the assessment process, it is important for social workers to ascertain whether clients have been diagnosed with, or experienced the symptoms of, *any* mental disorders prior to a life-limiting illness because these symptoms are usually exacerbated by medical illness, treatments, or bereavement. Without accurate history and a complete assessment of factors contributing to symptoms of anxiety and mood disturbance, inappropriate or ineffective treatment can aggravate distress rather than alleviate it. Social workers are well prepared to complete these assessments. We also make a major contribution in helping other professional care providers as well as clients to understand the causes of distress and facilitate decision making regarding effective symptom relief. Advocacy is another primary intervention of social workers to ensure that clients have adequate access to diagnostic and ongoing medical care.

Whether due to preexisting disorders or in reaction to a life-threatening illness, many clients experience intense anxiety and depression related to uncontrolled pain, isolation, abandonment, and dependency that illness and anticipated loss precipitate. This distress is often best addressed through the establishment of a strong therapeutic alliance, the collaborative efforts of an interdisciplinary team, and effective psychosocial support to the patient and family.

As social workers, we are well equipped to assess the complex situations of patients and families facing the end of life, but we must bring to the assessment and intervention process all of our skill in effective engagement with vulnerable clients as well as our broad knowledge of biological, psychological, and social factors that contribute to psychosocial distress. Although we do utilize specialized expertise related to illness and grief, ultimately, in this arena of practice we draw on the same values, knowledge, and skills as in every other area of practice.

REFERENCES

American Psychiatric Association. 2000. *Diagnostic and Statistical Manual of Mental Disorders*. Washington, DC: American Psychiatric Association.

Berzoff, J., L. Flanagan, and P. Hertz. 1996. *Inside Out and Outside In*. Northvale, NJ: Jason Aronson.

Billings, J. A., and S. Block. 1995. Depression. *Journal of Palliative Care* 11:48–54.

Blanchard, C., T. Albrecht, and J. Ruckdeschel. 1997. The crisis of cancer: Psychological impact on family caregivers. *Oncology* 11(2): 189–194.

Brown University. 2002. Bipolar depression and rapid cycling: The latest pharmacologic strategies. *Brown University Psychopharmacology Update* 13(7): 1, 10–12.

Breitbart, W. 1995. Identifying patients at risk for, and treatments of, major psychiatric complications of cancer. *Supportive Care in Cancer* 3(1): 45–60.

Coyle, N., et al. 1999. Care of the terminal patient's physical and psychosocial needs. In *Oncology Nursing: Assessment and Clinical Care*, ed. C. Miaskowski and P. Buschnel, 359–382. St. Louis: Mosby.

Glajchen, M. 2003. Caregiver burden and pain control. In *Cancer Pain*, ed. E. Brucra and R. Portenoy, 475–481. New York: Cambridge University Press.

Hedlund, S. 2001. Assessment and management of depression. *Social Work and End of Life Care Curriculum* 1(3):14-20.

Kagawa-Singer, M. 1994. Diverse cultural beliefs and practices about death and dying in the elderly. *Gerontology and Geriatrics Education* 15(1): 101–116.

Lynch, M. E. 1995. The assessment and prevalence of affective disorders in advanced cancer. *Journal of Palliative Care* 11(1): 10–18.

Malmquist, C. P. 1983. Major depression in childhood: Why don't we know more? *American Journal of Orthopsychiatry* 53(2): 262–268.

Massie, M. J. 1989. Depression. In *Handbook of Psycho-Oncology: Psychological Care of the Patient with Cancer*, ed. J. Holland and H. Rowland, 283–290. New York: Oxford University Press.

Massie, M. J., and M. K. Popkin. 1998. Depressive disorders. In *Psycho-Oncology*, ed. J. Holland, 518–540. New York: Oxford University Press.

McInnis-Dittrich, K. 2002. *Social Work with Elders: A Biopsychosocial Approach to Assessment and Intervention*. Boston: Allyn & Bacon.

Moffitt Cancer Center and University of South Florida, Tampa. 1998. Multidimensional Fatigue Symptom Inventory, short form.

Nordin, K., and B. Glimelius. 1999. Predicting delayed anxiety and depression in patients with gastrointestinal cancer. *British Journal of Cancer* 79(3/4): 525–529.

Popkin, M. K., and G. J. Tucker. 1992. "Secondary" and drug induced mood, anxiety, psychotic, catatonic and personality disorders: A review of the literature. *Journal of Neuropsychiatric Clinical Neuroscience* 4:369–385.

Rando, T. 1984. *Grief, Dying, and Death: Clinical Interventions for Caregivers.* Champaign, IL: Research Press.

Robinson-Whelen, S. 2001. Psychological effects of caregiving. *Journal of Abnormal Psychology* 110:573–584.

Roth, A. J., and S. Passik. 1995. Is it drug-related akathisia, or anxiety? A diagnostic dilemma. www.cancernetwork.com.

Valentine, A. 2000. Depression, anxiety, and delirium. In *Cancer Management: A Multidisciplinary Approach* (4th ed.), ed. R. Pazdur et al. New York: The Oncology Group.

Velikova, G., et al. 1995. The relationship of cancer pain to anxiety. *Psychotherapy and Psychosomatics* 63 (3–4): 181–184.

Walsh, F., and McGoldrick, M. 1995. *Living Beyond Loss: Death in the Family.* New York: Norton.

Walsh-Burke, K. 1992. Family communication and coping with cancer. *Journal of Psychosocial Oncology* 10(1): 63–82.

———. 2000. Matching bereavement services to level of need. *Hospice Journal* 15(1): 77–86.

Worden, W. 2002. *Grief Counseling and Grief Therapy: A Handbook for the Mental Health Practitioner.* 3d ed. New York: Springer.

Zabora, J. R. 1998. Screening procedures for psychosocial distress. In *Psychosocial Oncology*, ed. J. Holland et al., 653–661. New York: Oxford University Press.

Zabora, J. R., K. M. Brintzenhofeszoc, B. Curbow, C. Hooker, and S. Piantadosi. 2001. The prevalence of psychological distress by cancer site. *Psycho-Oncology* 10:19–28.

19

PAIN AND SYMPTOM MANAGEMENT:
AN ESSENTIAL ROLE FOR SOCIAL WORK

TERRY ALTILIO

The fundamental principle of responsible medical care is not "do not hurt" but "do no harm." Harm occurs when the amount of hurt or suffering is greater than necessary to achieve the intended benefit. Here lies the basic ethical challenge to caregivers, since pain seems harmful to patients, and caregivers are categorically committed to preventing harm. . . . Not using all the available means of relieving pain must be justified.
— *Walco, Cassity, and Schechter 1994:541*

MULTIDIMENSIONAL pain and symptom management in the context of life-limiting illness can represent the best of clinical social-work practice, requiring an understanding of the symptom and illness as integrated by a unique person and family. A comprehensive, individualized approach to pain and symptom management respects the impact of the individual/family experience and present realities and perceptions, and recognizes that interventions have the potential to affect mood, function, and quality of life. The manner in which a family integrates the patient's death into the family narrative is often colored by the family's perception of the adequacy of symptom management along the continuum of illness and at end of life. Medical, biological, ethical, psychological, cultural, spiritual, social, economic, and policy issues converge in this important aspect of care, providing an opportunity for the social-work professional to intervene on multiple levels. Social-work roles as advocate, communicator, educator, clinician, mediator, and problem solver are all involved in identifying and seeking solutions to the issues that create conflicts and block the communication and understanding necessary to manage symptoms and associated distress. Management of pain and symptoms, while essential along the continuum of illness, is additionally meaningful at the end of life when suffering and feelings of helplessness are magnified for the patient, family, and staff, for time is limited and the quality of that time intensified by the reality of approaching death.

Each of us who has experienced a patient who is too fatigued to hold a grandchild, frightened from delirium, or in excruciating pain, needs only a single experience to be convinced of the responsibility to advocate for state-of-the-art treatment for symptoms. Each of us who has had a family member ask, "How can you let our mother starve to death?" or has witnessed a child terrified by a parent's uncontrolled pain is compelled to learn the ethical, medical, cultural, and psychodynamic aspects of pain management and medically provided nutrition and hydration at the end of life. It is often within the social-work relationship that these issues are raised, creating a mandate to establish competence and comfort to advocate and intervene in these profoundly important areas.

This chapter will focus on the management of pain as a model for the integration of biopsychosocial, spiritual, and ethical principles that are essential elements of palliative care. The model is transferable to other symptoms such as anxiety, delirium, depression, fatigue, insomnia, dyspnea, and anorexia. The evolution and presence of symptoms, whether physical or psychological, may signal a change in the status of a disease, providing an opportunity to reassess treatment choices and goals of care. Symptoms often have symbolic significance in the lives of patients, families, and staff, and therefore require understanding and interventions that affect multiple levels, including but not limited to physical management.

For the purposes of this chapter, family is defined as those individuals identified by the patient as their primary supports regardless of blood or legal ties. Family caregivers are those unpaid individuals who provide or arrange for essential assistance to a relative or friend who is ill (Levine 2000). Case examples will be used to exemplify the integration of multidimensional symptom assessment and intervention.

SYMPTOM PREVALENCE

Symptom prevalence studies and surveys attest to the presence of multiple, unpleasant symptoms associated with life-threatening illness and death. Symptoms may range from pain and dyspnea to depression and anxiety, delirium, weakness, and existential distress. Often symptoms present in combination. For example, uncontrolled pain may be associated with depression and dyspnea with anxiety (Vogl et al. 1999; Desbiens et al. 1996; see chapter 18, this volume). A national survey conducted by George H. Gallup International Institute for the Nathan Cummings Foundation and Fetzer Institute in 1996–97 investigated how and whether spiritual beliefs affect one's preparation and coping with death. Twelve hundred adults were surveyed and asked what worried them when they thought of their own death. Of these, 67 percent were concerned about the possibility of "great physical pain before death." The SUPPORT (Study to Understand Prognoses and Preferences for Outcomes and Risks of Treatment) study concluded that 40 percent of conscious patients had unrelieved severe pain (Desbiens et al. 1996). In advanced cancer, the prevalence of pain ranges from 50 to 90 percent (Vainio and Auvinen 1996; Mercadant, Armata, and Salvaggio 1994; Higginson and Hearn 1997). A survey of institutionalized elderly cancer patients indicated that between 25 and 40 percent of the patients had daily pain, and 26 percent received no analgesic agent (Bernabei et al. 1998).

Pain has long been identified as a prevalent and worrisome symptom, yet many medical practitioners have *acted as if* management of pain were a choice rather than an ethical mandate and an expected expertise among healthcare professionals. The creation of scientific standards and guidelines for the treatment of pain, revised JCAHO (Joint Commission on Accreditation of Healthcare Organizations) standards for improving pain management, litigation for failure to manage pain competently, and the emphasis on improving care at the end of life have created an environment of expectation and accountability for healthcare professionals across practice settings.

It is in this context that social work, as well, is mandated to extend its skills to this important aspect of patient and family care.

BARRIERS

In the setting of increased legal and regulatory accountability, it continues to be important to identify barriers that interfere in adequate management of pain. These barriers need to be understood, as they are often at the basis of a diagnostic formulation that guides interventions. In addition to a lack of knowledge, there is a range of attitudes, beliefs, values, and behaviors that influences the responses of systems, practitioners, patients, and family members to pain and pain-management efforts (Blum 1993; Ferrell et al. 1995; Glajchen 2001).

SYSTEM/PRACTITIONER BARRIERS

Historically, the lack of clinician knowledge and training in the assessment and management of pain has been tolerated by institutional and credentialing agencies. Physicians in the United States have feared scrutiny by regulatory agencies such as the Drug Enforcement Agency (DEA), which is charged with enforcing the Controlled Substances Act (CSA). The intent is to prevent diversion of controlled substances such as opioid analgesics that are mainstay pain-management drugs. However, many prescribing clinicians have felt threatened both from DEA activity and from increasing litigation that charges clinicians with the undertreatment of pain or inappropriate prescribing that results in hastened death or iatrogenic addiction (Jacox et al. 1994). Spurred by JCAHO standards and consensus guidelines, institutions, educational settings, and clinicians are creating curriculum and continuing-education programs designed to teach the art and science of multidimensional pain assessment and treatment. Evidence-based knowledge and practice has the potential to diminish perceptions of threat and to replace fear of causing addiction or hastening death with best clinical practices.

On a practice level, barriers may also be based in clinician lack of empathy and trust in the patient's report of the severity of his or her pain. A subjective experience, pain measurement relies heavily on patient report rather than on technical measurements as in the case of fever, blood counts, or blood pressure. This subjectivity can create a sense of uncertainty in clinicians, where inexperience, myths, bias, or prejudice affect the treatment relationship. For example, in minority communities or with adolescents, clinicians may have a heightened fear of addiction potential or diversion based on preconceived judgments rather than objective assessment. A request for a specific opioid medication may be misinterpreted as drug seeking associated with a diagnosis of addiction rather than the behavior of a patient in pain who is requesting a medication that has been helpful to him or her in the past. Impulsive drug use may be a sign of unrelieved pain, an untreated psychiatric disorder or confusion about the therapeutic regimen. The clinical task involves making a thorough multidimensional assessment so an appropriate treatment plan can be established (Weissman and Haddox 1989; Portenoy 2000).

Some patient groups are more vulnerable to undertreatment. Those with limited ability to communicate or advocate for themselves such as babies and children, the frail elderly, the cognitively impaired or demented, and those whose language, culture, or socioeconomic status differ from that of the professional caregivers are at increased risk. In the past, clinicians have practiced from the misperception that the elderly and babies do not feel pain. Racial and ethnic minorities are at greater risk for ineffective pain management (Bonham 2001), as are women (Cleeland et al. 1994). That these groups are especially vulnerable heightens the need for social-work advocacy and adequate clinician training. In the setting of fast-paced medical systems, there is a significant risk of inadequate assessment, misunderstanding, and undertreatment (Shapiro 1995).

Assessing the nature of clinician or systems barriers may also help to formulate immediate and long-term interventions and plans. For example, standards, guidelines, mentors and/or ethical guidance may help a clinician who is insecure in the use of opioids and who fears that medications may hasten death. In situations where fears of regulation or bias toward patient groups influence the adequacy of pain manage-ment, social workers, who are knowledgeable and aware of the comprehensive ele-ments of pain assessment, can encourage prescribing colleagues toward sound clinical judgment based in science and standards rather than in immobilizing uncertainty, fears, and myths. Practitioners who prescribe medications have a profound and unique responsibility that is not shared by social work clinicians. Respect for the importance of that responsibility must underlie any efforts to assist colleagues to identify and overcome the barriers that prevent optimum management of pain.

PATIENT/FAMILY/CAREGIVER BARRIERS

Patient/family barriers also interfere in the assessment and management of pain. These may be in the cognitive sphere of patient/family values and beliefs or in the emotional realm where fears, depression, denial, or distress may interfere (Fink and Gates 2001). Unrecognized barriers are often at the basis of communication problems that result in inadequate pain management and/or create frustration and helplessness in staff that may be expressed in the labeling of patients and families as nonadherent or pathological.

Values and beliefs that affect the pain experience of a patient and family may find their etiology in the familial, societal, cultural, or spiritual realm. Assessment skills are essential to partializing these factors to determine whether and when intervention is necessary. Many patients and families believe that pain is inevitable or necessary as a barometer of disease. Some maintain a stoic response to pain; some see suffering as part of life, to be endured, not treated, or relieved. Some view pain as sacrifice or redemptive in a spiritual sense, believing that their ability to endure pain may result in cure, expiate guilt or ensure a better afterlife (Steefel 2001; Die-Trill 1998; Lipson et al. 2000). In these settings, pain and treatment are symbolic of issues related to identity, self-esteem, and hopefulness and require assessment and interventions that go much beyond the physical management of pain. Social-work clinicians, intervening directly or as part of the team, need to validate the importance of these beliefs while suggesting alternate perspectives that might allow treatment. For example, where pain is viewed as redemptive, one might question, "How much pain is necessary for redemption?" "Is it possible that the suffering from the illness and related aspects is sufficient for redemption?" "Are there other ways one might attain redemption and demonstrate sacrifice?" Essential to all inquiry is a respect for and acceptance of the patient/family belief system and their right to choose or refuse interventions consistent with those values.

Patients may be reluctant to report pain, as they do not wish to bother or distract clinicians from working toward possible cure or remission of their disease. They may fear diagnostic procedures or be so distressed by the potential significance of the pain that they deny or minimize the degree of pain. For many, increased pain may be interpreted as a symbol of progressing disease, disability, and possible death. Avoidance or denial thus becomes a defense against the possible need to integrate the realities of their illness and life expectancy. In some situations, patients fear that reporting increased pain will create additional suffering for family members. For others, the experience of feeling pain equates with feeling alive. Ameliorating pain removes this barometer of continued physical life (Dar et al. 1992; Cleeland 1989; Von Roenn et al. 1993; Fink and Gates 2001).

The myths and misunderstandings surrounding pain and opioid analgesics have created barriers that are often reinforced in the larger society, in the world of politics, and in the popular media. The association of opioid analgesics such as morphine and methadone with addiction, hastening death, or intolerable side effects requires that social workers develop skills and knowledge to identify and to correct inaccurate information or to respond to exaggerated fears. Patients and families may refuse pain medications early on in the illness for fear that they will lose their effectiveness later in the disease, a phenomenon known as tolerance, which need not inhibit the early use of opioids (Portenoy 2000). Medication side effects such as confusion or sedation also affect one's sense of self and the ability to participate in life and with family. As clinicians, social workers need to be aware that the potential or realities of feared side effects extend beyond the physical self to aspects of one's identity and relationships.

Popular discussions of issues such as physician-assisted suicide, hastened death, and euthanasia have intensified the need to be knowledgeable about the ethical principles that guide decision making and vigilant in understanding treatment parameters, goals of care, and intent of interventions. These important aspects of care may be further complicated by a mistrust of clinicians and healthcare systems grounded in the history of ethical atrocities toward African Americans during public health studies at Tuskegee University and toward Jewish people during the Holocaust. In the setting of prior unethical institutional behaviors as well as the documented undertreatment of pain in the most vulnerable populations—minorities, women, and the elderly (Bernabie et al. 1998; Cleeland et al. 1994; Anderson et al. 2000)—it is necessary for social-work clinicians to assess whether mistrust is based in a historical context or in fact is generated or reflective of immediate institutional and clinician attitudes (Crawley et al. 2000). Additionally, marginalized groups such as gay men and lesbians or persons with disabilities, psychiatric illness, or substance-abuse problems may require increased advocacy and outreach to bridge the distance and isolation often experienced as a consequence of marginalization.

Identifying barriers that affect management of pain helps clinicians to direct interventions or to accept patient/family decisions that may be at variance with staff's recommendations.

CASE EXAMPLE

Monica is a fifty-five-year-old African American mother of five children, diagnosed with breast cancer widely metastatic to her bones. In addition to chemotherapy and radiation, she is followed by a palliative-care team, which has provided psychological and family interventions, continuity of care, practical support, and aggressive symptom management over the course of a two-year period. Most recently, Monica's pain has been managed at home with patient controlled analgesia (PCA), a portable battery driven pump that allows, within clinician-established limits, an ongoing infusion of opioid medication as well as bolus doses for breakthrough pain. Monica's disease is progressing, her pain is increased, and the team recommends a higher dose of morphine, which Monica refuses to accept. In exploring worries and beliefs about her pain, its symbolic significance, and the treatment recommendation, Monica reports that her friend works in a hospital and told her that morphine is the drug that doctors use to "kill" sick patients. She is reluctant to increase the opioid, fearing that she will become cognitively impaired. In the context of her increased pain that she perceives to be a symbol of advancing disease, she shares a level of fear and mistrust that was not expressed earlier. Her friend's perceptions, media attention to assisted suicide, and mistrust based in racist behaviors of medical systems have challenged Monica's trust in the intent of the team that cared for her for two years. In addition, her fear of becoming cognitively impaired is intensified by her sense of vulnerability to the intentions of her healthcare providers.

In order to help Monica accept changes in the pain-management protocol, her clinicians needed to acknowledge and explore her fears and encourage her to reflect on experiences with the clinicians, the drug, and the institution where she had received care for years. Advance-care directives and the assignment of a healthcare agent helped Monica to feel less vulnerable to the possibility of cognitive impairment or confusion, as the agent would be available to ensure that Monica's preferences regarding care were respected. Information and education regarding euthanasia, assisted suicide, tolerance, and respiratory depression helped counteract her fears and gave her an alternate understanding to share with her friend. With these interventions, Monica accepted a plan for a very gradual increase in morphine with a commitment to careful monitoring, twenty-four-hour telephone availability of her nurse practitioner, and an agreement that the treatment plan would be changed at Monica's request. The team also offered to meet or speak with Monica's friend and family to discuss treatment goals, rationale, and decisions.

The following practice points are important:

1. Barriers are important guides to the nature of needed interventions. Those based in misinformation may require an educational intervention, while those based in spiritual beliefs may in fact not be barriers at all, but rather aspects of a patient's value system that need to be supported rather than overcome.
2. Symptoms and medications have symbolic significance. For some, pain may be redemptive; for others, it may be viewed as a punishment. Pain that is a symbol of progressing cancer is interpreted differently from pain caused by a curative surgical procedure.
3. Racial and cultural variables affect perceptions, beliefs, and behaviors on the part of patients, family, caregivers, and staff. Social-work clinicians are skilled in assessing individual, family, and systems dynamics and share professional responsibility for understanding and intervening when racial or cultural variables affect treatment outcomes.
4. Education and information about symptoms and treatments often diminish conflict and mistrust and enhance collaboration and caring.
5. New or increasing symptomatology may create a crisis and opportunity to reformulate goals of care and to explore and express new or lingering fears and concerns.
6. Family, friends, and community perceptions need to be integrated into assessments in order to minimize barriers to treatment and maximize social supports.

PAIN AND SUFFERING: OPERATIONAL DEFINITIONS

Pain is defined as "an unpleasant sensory and emotional experience which we primarily associate with tissue damage or describe in terms of such damage" (Mersky and Bogduk 1994). Pain is a subjective experience. It is not measurable in the same objective way as temperature or blood counts, and any assessment begins with the patient's self-report. Clinicians' appraisal of a patient's pain is often incongruous with that of the patient, especially when the pain is most severe (Grossman et al. 1991). This same potential lack of congruence exists in patient and family caregiver appraisals and is important to consider when assessing quality-of-life and pain-related issues through the perceptions of family members. The judgments and observations of pain are filtered through the family member's own suffering, fatigue, and emotional and cognitive distress, with the result that pain may be minimized or magnified. By making a comprehensive assessment, the healthcare team respects and integrates patient and family reports and seeks to understand discrepancies such as when patient's behaviors or medical realities are inconsistent with verbal reports of pain. Symptom assessment is complex, as the degree of severity of pain does not necessarily equate with patient distress. It is often difficult to separate the distress and suffering of the patient from that of the staff or family. The clinical task is to partialize physical symptoms and

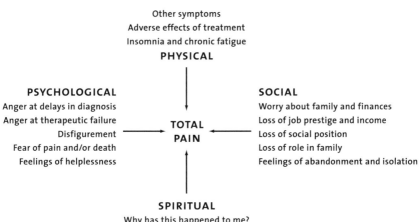

Other symptoms
Adverse effects of treatment
Insomnia and chronic fatigue
PHYSICAL

PSYCHOLOGICAL
Anger at delays in diagnosis
Anger at therapeutic failure
Disfigurement
Fear of pain and/or death
Feelings of helplessness

TOTAL PAIN

SOCIAL
Worry about family and finances
Loss of job prestige and income
Loss of social position
Loss of role in family
Feelings of abandonment and isolation

SPIRITUAL
Why has this happened to me?
Why does God allow me to suffer like this?
What's the point of it all?
Is there any meaning or purpose in life?
Can I be forgiven for past wrongdoing?

FIGURE 19.1 Factors Influencing the Perception of Pain
Source: Robert Twycross 2001. Reprinted with permission.

distress so that the interventions are directed in the most appropriate way and to the right person (Dar et al. 1992; Miaskowski et al. 1997; Redinbaugh et al. 2002).

In the setting of a progressive medical illness, the assessment of pain extends beyond the physical and sensory to a more global construct that has been called "total pain" (Twycross 1997). This includes the interface of physical, social, psychological, and spiritual dimensions (see fig. 19.1). Another valuable construct in the assessment of the pain experience is the concept of suffering, which E. J. Cassell defines as "distress brought about by the actual or perceived threat to the integrity or continued existence of the whole person" (1991:24). Like pain, suffering is a subjective experience that is individual and unique. Pain can occur without suffering, and suffering may or may not include pain. At times, the relief of pain is followed by an exacerbation of patient suffering, for pain can be a distraction from other sources of distress. For many, suffering relates to issues of individual meaning and purpose, which has a profound impact on the pain experience, and on the process of coming to the end of life. Existential pain or existential suffering is an additional area for exploration and relates to the discrepancy between one's belief of how the world should be and how life actually evolves (Otis-Green et al. 2002). Patients experiencing existential distress may feel unable to make sense of their lives and be immersed in feelings of despair and isolation.

ETHICAL CONSIDERATIONS

Every practitioner involved in symptom management needs a basic awareness of ethical and legal principles as they interface with the practice of medicine. These principles are not isolated concepts as in the practice setting; they interface with unique patient and family dynamics, culture, values, and preferences as well as the clinician's culture, values, and beliefs.

Social-work clinicians with a basic knowledge of ethical principles have a shared responsibility to initiate discussions that are often essential to solving conflicts, clarifying options, and making sound ethical decisions. The first step to resolving dilemmas is to identify when one exists and to consider which ethical principles apply. To this end, the following definitions and concepts are presented.

Clinical ethics is a "practical discipline that provides a structural approach to decision making that can assist healthcare professionals to identify, analyze and resolve ethical issues in clinical medicine" (Jonsen, Siegler, and Winsdale 1992; see chapters 9 and 31, this volume).

Autonomy relates to the individual's right to make decisions based on his or her values and beliefs. Individual autonomy is a concept of Western bioethics and not necessarily reflective of the multiculturalism of the United States and the world. Social workers need to identify those families in which decision making is a family or communal process to insure respect for individual differences. Just as persons can assert individual autonomy, they are also able to choose to share their autonomy with others or to delegate decision making to another.

Justice relates to fairness in application of care. Justice implies that patients will receive access to care equal to others and is violated when subgroups of patients such as minorities, women, and the elderly receive less adequate pain management (see chapter 39).

Beneficence requires that one *strive* to prevent or remove harm and promote good. Examples include aggressive management of symptoms, relief of suffering, and treating predictable pain related to procedures.

Nonmaleficence requires that one *strive* not to inflict harm or evil, either through active or passive behaviors. Violations of this principle might include the performance of painful procedures without premedicating, unnecessary or unwanted sedation, or uninformed withdrawal of treatment.

Do-not-resuscitate (DNR) discussions focus on the specific issue of whether the patient will be resuscitated in the case of a cardiac or respiratory arrest. Resuscitation is a medical intervention, and a DNR decision needs to be informed with an explanation of the procedure, risks, benefits, and potential outcomes. Resuscitation discussions often limit their focus to the treatments that will not be provided, such as intubation. It is important to articulate the treatments that will be provided, such as aggressive management of symptoms, support, and continuity of care. In some settings practitioners have begun to use AND (Allow Natural Death) orders, which reframes the discussion from one that focuses on withholding resuscitation (DNR) to one that allows the process of dying and ensures that active, aggressive comfort measures are provided (Meyer 2002).

The *principle of double effect* holds that a single intervention (giving medication for sedation or pain relief) with one intention (symptom control) may have two effects (one being pain relief and the second *possible* respiratory depression). The foreseen beneficial effect (symptom relief) must be intended and be equal to or greater than the foreseen harmful effect (*possible* respiratory depression). This is distinguished from euthanasia, where the direct intent is to end life (Coyle 1992). The principle of double effect is implicit in other areas of medicine where a single intervention may have two effects. For example, treatment with toxic chemotherapy agents to achieve the one goal of remission or cure of a disease (beneficial and intended effect) may have a second foreseen harmful consequence of side effects that may cause considerable pain and suffering. These cancer treatment decisions are based in an evaluation of risk and benefit and assessment of goals of care, as are decisions related to the aggressive treatment of symptoms in end of life.

Prescribing clinicians often fear that providing adequate doses of pain medications to manage pain or to reduce shortness of breath may hasten the death of a dying patient. Families may have the same fear, or, in some instances, may wish for death to be hastened. Increasing medication to manage symptoms has the primary beneficial *intent* of symptom control and a *possible* secondary effect of hastening death. Social workers can be instrumental in working with colleagues to articulate the basis for decisions, to explore the risk and benefit with patients and/or healthcare agents, and to insure that options are presented and that potential outcomes are identified and that the *intent* of the chosen intervention is discussed and documented clearly for the patient, family, and other staff members.

Palliative sedation in the imminently dying is the decision to induce unconsciousness without causing death in a setting where aggressive symptom management has been unsuccessful in controlling "refractory symptoms." This is a complex and controversial area that raises important questions. When is a symptom refractory? Should sedation be used to manage refractory psychological and existential distress? What is "imminent death" (Lesage 2000)? Should medically provided nutrition and/or hydration be continued during periods of sedation? Team members have a shared responsibility to raise questions for discussion as well as to evaluate the significance and potential impact on the family of a decision to sedate a patient. Once again, risk and benefit need to be explored, discussed with the patient and/or healthcare agent, articulated, and documented clearly.

Physician-assisted suicide involves actions by one person to contribute to the death of another by providing medications or other means with the knowledge of the patient's intention to end life. In assisted suicide, the patient is the agent of their death with means provided by another. Assisted suicide is only legal in Oregon consequent to the passage of the Death with Dignity Act in 1994 (see chapter 39).

Euthanasia is a deliberate intervention by someone other than the patient solely intended to end the life of a competent terminally ill patient who has made a voluntary and persistent request for aid in dying. The aggressive management of pain or dyspnea or the withholding of nutrition or hydration at the request of the patient who is dying is not euthanasia. Allowing death to occur is not euthanasia.

Involuntary euthanasia is a deliberate intervention to end the life of a person who is incapable of making a request to die or lacks decisional capacity (infant, demented, or comatose).

Social workers need to understand these concepts to be able to engage in interdisciplinary discussions of ethical issues. These dilemmas are always multifaceted and influenced by medical, emotional, familial, cultural, and spiritual factors as well as by the value systems of all who are involved, including staff. Clarity about facts, intent, and language and dispelling myths and misunderstandings are essential to reaching consensus and diminishing distress and suffering. It is important to recognize that the different professional roles of the healthcare team of necessity create different perspectives. Social workers do not prescribe, nor do they administer pain medications to patients. Sensitivity to this difference is vital if we are to work with our colleagues to clarify the intellectual, cultural, social, and emotional aspects of difficult decision making. The following case example illustrates the potential benefit of open discussion of family conflict, symptom management, and related ethical concerns.

CASE EXAMPLE

Rosa is a thirty-three-year-old Latina married mother of two preschool children diagnosed with metastatic cervical cancer. She is seriously ill, appears to be coming to the end of her life, and is admitted for management of pain, dyspnea, nausea, and vomiting. Rosa is unable to communicate. Based on prior discussions with Rosa, her aunt, the healthcare agent, has decided that Rosa will not be resuscitated and will receive aggressive symptom management but no intravenous fluids. Rosa's husband, sisters, and cousins accuse their aunt of "starving and killing" Rosa and "giving up hope" by refusing to hydrate her (hastening her death) and by establishing DNR status. A family meeting is held with the oncologist, palliative-care nurse, and social worker where conflicts and emotional issues are explored in the context of medical, physical, and ethical considerations. Rosa's physical condition includes a blockage that prevents urination. Hydration, which is perceived by family members of Rosa's generation to be helpful, would actually increase fluid retention, observable swelling, and shortness of breath, all of which would be harmful and cause additional suffering (Do No Harm).

In this context, all family members were able to accept that Rosa's cancer and its impact on her physical function precluded hydration's having a positive outcome. By exploring and discussing Rosa's positive but nonverbal response to morphine (given for both pain and shortness of breath), it became clear to her family that her medication was titrated to achieve symptom relief, not to hasten death. The family was helped to "reframe" their thinking that the aunt "was killing the patient" to an understanding that the cancer was the cause of her death, and that all symptom-management efforts were focused on comfort, not on hastening her death.

Rosa's aunt, the only available member of a parental generation, explained her decisions by sharing a spiritual belief system. She "reframed" the perception that she was "giving up hope" as she explained that she, too, believed in miracles and prayed for Rosa's recovery, but she also knew that "God did not need machines to perform a miracle." In this setting, love and caring for Rosa were reframed to include withholding interventions such as hydration, which would have exacerbated symptoms rather than enhance her comfort. The team's integration of the ethical, medical, familial, and spiritual factors assisted this family to move beyond conflict to support each other. Misunderstandings were corrected that would have influenced future bereavement, family conflict, and the family legacy surrounding the death of this young woman. Rosa's family was taught to participate in her care by moistening her lips and mouth, massaging her feet, and providing comfort through their presence, touch, and voices.

Rosa's case illustrates the following practice points:

1. Family meetings provide a setting to explore conflicts as well as the risks and benefits of treatments that may be acceptable to some and not to others. Social workers are trained to work with families and to recognize the power and potential in a family intervention. As such, our colleagues in medicine and nursing may count on social workers to maximize the potential of this intervention.

2. Symptoms are often objective representations of the need to reassess the goals of care and treatment options. An open discussion of objective physical signs of disease progression can help patients and families to integrate changing realities and consider difficult decisions (hydration). What may initially seem like harming the patient can be, as in the case of Rosa, reframed as helpful.

3. Family conflict and disagreement as to intent of interventions and decisions are often based in lack of information or misinformation.

4. Rosa's medical situation shows us that interventions that were initially beneficial (beneficent) can become unhelpful consequent to changes in physical condition. In her case as in many others, decisions related to management of symptoms such as pain, dehydration, and anorexia are best evaluated in the context of status of illness, goals of care, family dynamics, and symbolic significance of the symptom and the related treatments.

5. In Rosa's family, God, as conceptualized by Rosa's aunt, played a central and defining role in decision making and in helping the family to accept difficult choices. Cultural and spiritual beliefs often guide decisions and sustain patients and family beyond the illness and death of the patient and through the separation from the healthcare team.

6. Finally, family members and staff should be encouraged to comfort by their presence and their voices. When culturally and emotionally appropriate, integrative modalities such as music and massage can both help the patient and diminish helplessness of family.

HOW DOES THE SOCIAL WORKER ASSESS PAIN AND SUFFERING?

A complete pain assessment involves a multidimensional inquiry into the physical etiology and the psychosocial, spiritual, cultural, emotional, and cognitive factors that make up the unique person. Essential to any assessment of pain and suffering is the need for active inquiry and observation and a commitment to *accept the patient's report of pain.*

The process of assessment is, in itself, a beginning intervention. It implies an expertise and a willingness to listen, understand, and provide support and treatment, all of which have the potential to lessen the isolation and helplessness that often accompany uncontrolled pain in a person coping with life threatening illness. Assessment is an engagement process, which partializes the pain experience and implies that the patient's information and perceptions are valued. Although a multidimensional assessment is often the goal, a person in pain needs an immediate medical and pharmacologic evaluation and treatment plan. Psychosocial interventions are adjuncts to adequate medical management of pain, not a replacement for competent pain management.

Pain has physical (organic etiology), sensory (intensity, location, and quality), cognitive (beliefs, values, and attitudes), affective (mood, depression, anxiety, self-esteem), behavioral (pain behaviors, function), spiritual/existential (meaning, despair), and socioeconomic and cultural components (Fink and Gates 2001). A multidimensional exploration of pain and related issues is not a denial of the physical basis for pain, but rather an expression of interest, caring, and concern for the total person and his or her significant others. Medical management needs to be accompanied by efforts to understand beliefs, thoughts, behaviors, and feelings that may contribute to pain, suffering, and distress. As a patient's pain level is reduced, trust in the treatment team is established and additional aspects of concern and distress can be explored.

MULTIAXIAL FACTORS IN PAIN ASSESSMENT

CULTURE

A respect for patient dignity and self-determination involves knowledge of cultural differences (Kagawa-Singer 1996). Culture influences significant aspects of the patient/family and healthcare provider interface and impacts beliefs and behaviors related to pain, suffering, decision making, death, and grief. Clinicians and healthcare systems have their own cultures. In most American healthcare settings, Western philosophical and legal traditions emphasize such values as individualism, autonomy, open disclosure, desire for control, informed consent, and a future orientation—values that may be incongruous with the culture of the patient and family being treated (Koenig and Gates-Williams 1995; see chapter 23, this volume). Practitioners need to replace generalizations about cultural values and practices with a flexible, open, and observant inquiry into cultural content, generational and assimilation issues, values, and beliefs that shape the patient and family's individualized experiences. Sensitivity to cultural variation solidifies the patient/family and healthcare provider relationship and can prevent or reduce misunderstandings while keeping intact this important base of support for the patient and family at a time of crises.

Cultural factors affect the perception and expression of symptoms. For example, some groups will deny "depression," inasmuch as it is considered a psychiatric disorder that is shameful and a sign of weakness. Dyspnea and related anxiety may be exacerbated in the setting of a language barrier and may require proactive interventions to minimize the distress created by an inability to communicate with caregivers.

Cultural variations in the pain experience represent both a challenge and a richness when the care provided is responsive to and respectful of cultural difference (Lipson et al. 2000). For example, pain expression and description can range from direct, dramatic expressions to metaphoric descriptions that need to be understood by staff. Inquiry into the cause of pain is important. Some cultures interpret pain as internal disequilibrium or the effect of divine will or demonic forces. Treatment related behaviors might include an avoidance of medications, an inability to make direct requests, or a pattern of reporting pain to family and friends rather than bothering professional staff. Use of home remedies, healers, and complementary modalities may be important adjuncts to integrate and encourage (Die-Trill 1998; Kreier 2000; Crawley et al. 2002; Lipson, Dibble, and Minarak 1996).

CASE EXAMPLE

Soomatie is a forty-five-year-old woman with metastatic rectal cancer who had been referred to the Pain and Palliative Service for pain management. She was one of thirteen children, all of whom had emigrated from Guyana to America. Separated from her husband, she and her two adolescent daughters lived with her mother and sister. She did not report pain to the healthcare staff but would tell family members instead, leaving staff frustrated and family members worried that her pain went untreated when they were unavailable to advocate for her. During hospital admissions she would not consent to any diagnostic tests or changes in pain medication until she discussed the request with family members. This had considerable impact on the fast-paced hospital setting and was eventually interpreted to be a psychiatric disturbance diagnosed as a "dependent personality disorder." Upon discussion with the family, however, it became clear that this was consistent with her cultural norms that dictated family decision making. The family was ultimately responsible for the care of Soomatie's daughters should she die, and therefore any decision made that affected her illness and function was a family decision, not one based in the value of individual autonomy.

PHYSICAL/MEDICAL/SENSORY

An initial pain assessment should focus on identifying the etiology of the pain through a detailed history, physical examination, diagnostic workup, and psychosocial assessment, including the impact on important areas such as sleep, mood, and function. Sensory evaluation needs to include the location, intensity, and quality of the pain. Brief, easy to use assessment tools are helpful in documenting pain intensity and pain relief and relating these to other dimensions such as depression and anxiety (Jacox et al. 1994). There are pain scales based in numbers ratings and verbal descriptors as well as nonverbal scales that can be useful with children or the elderly or when verbal communication is impeded. In situations where the progression of disease, developmental issues, or cognitive impairment impedes direct patient report, assessment becomes more complex creating a potential for underreporting and undertreatment. Cognitive failure, delirium, and loss of consciousness are very common at the end of life, with the result that assessment often relies on the input of family and the competence, expertise, and involvement of staff and professional caregivers such as nurses and personal care attendants (McCaffery and Pasero 1999). The fears, subjective identification, and miscommunication that occurs when patients are unable to self-report symptoms can often be allayed by active, open, and repeated communication among the healthcare team, in the chart, and with the family, with particular emphasis on active sharing of the bases for treatment decisions.

Affective components of the pain experience include such reactions as depression, anger, anxiety, guilt, shame, loss of control, helplessness, and hopelessness. Emotional reactions may complicate assessment and influence interventions and treatment outcomes. At times, depression may have preceded the pain, affecting the patient's perception and coping ability. Anxiety may occur in anticipation of pain, as a consequence of pain, or be related to medications or physical and emotional issues that are distinct from the pain experience. The social worker may intervene using practice methods including cognitive behavioral techniques, supportive counseling, family meetings, environmental modifications, and spiritual counseling. Cognitive behavioral interventions are often useful in partializing and identifying sources of distress as well as impacting the cycle of anxiety, pain, and distress that often results in patients and families feeling out of control.

The *cognitive dimension* of pain assessment includes an understanding of the patient's and family's attitudes, beliefs, knowledge, and expectations. The social worker needs to inquire into the internal dialogue and symbolic significance of pain and treatment modalities, for this can create opportunities for interventions that are focused on minimizing distortions and catastrophic thinking while offering coping skills. The meaning of pain and the impact of pain on self-image and self-efficacy will influence both perception and coping ability of any patient (Barkwell 1991).

Social/economic variables, including demographics, need to be assessed from both an individual and a systems perspective, for they influence not only patients and families but also the biases and attitudes of healthcare professionals and healthcare systems. As stated previously, healthcare professionals may have preconceived fears about addiction in minority patients that affect prescribing practices. Often patients in lower socioeconomic neighborhoods worry about the use and misuse of opioid medications and have the additional barrier of pharmacies that choose not to stock opioid analgesics (Morrison et al. 2000; Kanner and Portenoy 1986). Economic disadvantage may also affect a patient's ability to obtain necessary medications as well as to access quality medical care. The social worker needs to assess distress related to such areas as insurance, finances, transportation, caregiver needs, roles, and family disruption. Knowledge of specific vulnerable populations should direct the focus of intervention. For example, the elderly may perceive pain as a normal part of aging and take a more passive role in decision making, increasing the need for advocacy and outreach on the part of healthcare professionals.

The *behavioral aspects* of the pain experience require clinicians to be cognizant of the patients' verbal and behavioral *expressions* of pain as well as the conscious and unconscious behavioral *responses* of patients in order to recommend interventions. Such behaviors might include grimacing, positioning, rocking, restlessness, crying, insomnia, tense body language, or nonadherence to a medication plan. The level and pacing of activities and verbal and nonverbal communications are all aspects of the pain experience that can be influenced by education, counseling, and problem-solving strategies that can enhance quality of life. In situations of cognitive impairment, interpretations of behavior become one of the important aspects of the team's assessment.

The spiritual/existential/religious dimensions may influence the pain experience as well as a person's preferences and acceptance of various treatment modalities. For example, Orthodox Jewish families may be very concerned about any pain interventions that they perceive may have the potential of shortening life; others may be highly distressed by any impact on consciousness that will preclude their ability to prepare for death (Abrahm 2000). Suffering and the meaning of pain are often related to spiritual and religious constructs, such as redemption, punishment, forgiveness, endurance, and abandonment by God. Social workers need to develop comfort in this area of inquiry, for this dimension of care is also a shared responsibility of the health-care team. Issues of meaning, suffering, despair, faith, and spiritual comfort are part of the human experience that include but are not limited to the specific chaplaincy role and the role of the community religious leader (see chapter 22).

The assessment of *environmental* aspects includes observing the physical environment as well as the behaviors of the staff, family, and friends that may be exacerbating pain and related distress. Staff behaviors that reflect differences of opinion, challenges to the credibility of the patient, hurried, harassed interchanges, or whispered conversations within earshot of the patient generally do not create a therapeutic environment. Environmental interventions may include creating quiet space, placing familiar items in patient's view, low lights, and providing care to the patient in a setting that is most responsive to their unique needs for comfort and security. For some, privacy is important. For others, being in the center of family activity or in a double room is more comforting. Both maintaining continuity of staff and preparing patients for interventions have the potential to enhance comfort especially in the setting of progressive illness and symptoms that make communication more difficult.

ASSESSMENT QUESTIONS AND CONSIDERATIONS

The assessment of pain in end of life care can be complicated by cognitive and sensory loss, cognitive impairment, and loss of verbal ability. All of these create the potential for unrecognized and unrelieved pain. A good pain assessment relies on patient self-report, and in situations where verbal report is problematic, patients and families must count on staff to adjust the assessment process to the patient's need. This adjustment may include observations of preexisting pain or treating based on the belief that most persons in a similar situation would experience pain. Family and staff who have known the patient historically may be important informants who can identify behaviors that signify that the patient is in pain and be helpful in assessing when the patient's ability to self-report is impaired. The assessment process may include eliciting nonverbal feedback such as blinking, nodding, or squeezing of hands or offering written materials or communication boards (Fink and Gates 2001). Modifications such as decreasing environmental stimulation, using large print, comforting communication, and consistent staff and frequent assessments can all maximize the potential for adequate assessment and the impact of resulting interventions (Stein 2001).

Where there are no barriers to verbal reports, the following assessment questions may assist the social worker and the team to partialize the pain experience and to differentiate components of pain and suffering. The nature and extent of inquiry is guided by the patient's condition and goals and the relevance to patient/family needs (Jacox et al. 1994; Abrahm 2000; Loscalzo and Jacobsen 1990). The language of assessment can be tailored to the patient who may use descriptors such as "ache" or "hurt" rather than "pain." In situations of language difference, professional translators or interpreters are preferable, as well-intended family will translate through their own feelings and opinions, generally with a lack of medical expertise.

As part of a pain assessment, the clinician needs to ask:

- Where is the pain? What does the pain feel like right now? What does the pain feel like at its worst?
- Can you describe the pain so I can understand how you experience it (size, weight, color, temperature, texture)?
- What makes the pain worse or better? What do you do to make the pain hurt less?
- What has been your past experience with pain? With pain medications?
- Do you feel you can be helped to deal more effectively with the pain? What do you think would help?
- If you did not have any pain, what might you be doing differently? What is the best part of your life right now? What was your life like before you started having the pain?
- What has been the effect of your illness/pain on family, function, religious/philosophical beliefs, self-image, and intimate relationships?
- How does your religion and/or culture view pain?
- What do you think is the cause of your pain? What has your doctor told you about the cause of your pain?
- What do you say to yourself about your pain? How do you express pain?
- What do you think your family (staff) thinks and feels about your pain? How does your family (staff) react when you complain of pain or demonstrate pain behaviors such as moaning, grimacing?
- What is your worst fear or fantasy concerning your pain?
- What would happen if your worst fear or fantasy was realized?
- Where do you feel safest and most comfortable?
- Can you create a pleasant or engaging experience in your imagination in which you can get emotionally involved? (Loscalzo and Jacobsen 1990:145–146)

These questions are often therapeutic in themselves as they empower some patients while allowing others opportunity for ventilation and validation. They elicit not only information but also feelings, thoughts, and worries that direct the focus of interventions.

INTERVENTIONS

MEDICAL/PHARMACOLOGIC

Primary medical interventions will likely be needed and involve pharmacologic management which may include a combination of opioid and non-opioid analgesics and adjuvant analgesics such as antidepressants, anticonvulsants, neuroleptics, oral anesthetics and corticosteroids. Other agents may be needed to treat or prevent side effects such as constipation, nausea, sedation, or confusion. Information and guidelines as to state of the art management of pain in medical illness are readily available and advocating for appropriate medical, anaesthetic, and pharmacologic interventions is the ethical and moral responsibility of the entire healthcare team.

CLINICAL INTERVENTIONS

Advocacy is an ongoing focus of social work. Patients' and families' needs change, distress varies, and skills of self-advocacy may be diminished by protracted symptoms and feelings of helplessness and hopelessness. Unrecognized and unrelieved pain, caregiver needs, the inability to secure medications, and misunderstandings within families and between patients, families, and staff are instances where advocacy skills are a primary intervention.

Family meetings are essential interventions over the course of an illness (see chapter 21). They may be planned or spontaneous and have the potential to create collaborative relationships of mutual respect and a valuable foundation for the important discussions that occur along the continuum of illness (Ambuel 2000). The potential purposes of family meetings are to clarify goals, problem-solve, and counsel (Miller and Walsh 1991). Although social workers have important skills for conducting family conferences, the leadership, focus, and attendees ought to be based on a careful assessment of the patient, family, and staff needs and the anticipated goals and outcomes. For example, where the focus of a family meeting is the concern about addiction or fear of side effects such as sedation, the physician or nurse may take the leadership role, with the social worker observing and responding to the family and group dynamics and to nonverbal communications.

Supportive counseling interventions, a core skill of social-work practitioners, include techniques of clarification, exploration, partializing, validating, and problem solving. When patients and family members are overwhelmed by pain and related distress, these interventions, along with aggressive medical management, establish a basis for trust and help identify additional areas of concern, strengths, and coping abilities of the patient and the family.

Education and information about pain, management techniques, and strategies to enhance coping can be very helpful. As the goals of care change and patients anticipate the end of life, their worries and anxieties may be exacerbated by clinician statements such as, "There is nothing more I can do for you." This message implies abandonment and helplessness that needs to be countered by the expression of an ongoing commitment to aggressive management of symptoms and a discussion of the risks and benefits of different treatments. In addition to education about specific symptoms, patients and families need to hear and experience the expertise and realistic confidence of the treating team to manage symptoms and provide multidimensional care throughout the course of illness.

Spiritual interventions may involve referrals to clergy for counseling or rituals such as prayer, readings, and sacraments. Social workers may identify and intervene in aspects of suffering and existential distress associated with pain and life-threatening illness. Just as psychological distress is often shared clinical work among team members, so are issues of meaning and suffering. Challenges to faith, hope, and feelings of despair may exacerbate pain and suffering, and members of the healthcare team need to explore and engage patients and families in discussions of spirituality, community supports, and areas of concern (see chapter 10).

Cognitive behavioral interventions and integrative modalities are useful adjuncts to medical management of symptoms and can be especially helpful to patients during procedures and diagnostic tests that often create distress and feelings of lack of control. Social workers can teach these interventions to individuals, or they may become an integral part of a group intervention. Their appropriateness is based in an assessment of the patient's physical, cognitive, and psychological condition as well as the goals of care. Patients who are debilitated, cognitively impaired, psychiatrically ill, or with limitation in communication may require adaptation or simplification of cognitive behavioral techniques and integrative modalities. In situations of metastatic bone disease or respiratory distress, muscle-tension exercises or focused breathing activities may need to be modified to avoid stressing fragile bones or limited respiratory capacity. Additionally, physical sensory modalities such as massage, cold or warmth, therapeutic touch, Reiki, and music that promote contact and comfort can be integrated into a holistic treatment plan and may be preferred techniques in the setting of cognitive impairment. Touch and sound are the primary senses that create feelings of safety and comfort in infancy; they are often the same senses that bring comfort and contact as patients come to the end of their lives. These therapeutic modalities are often shared skills among team members and are useful interventions for both patients and family members.

Family members may be highly distressed and are often helped by interventions that focus on education and information, support, enhanced coping and techniques (massage, breathing exercises) that minimize their feelings of helplessness. When the dynamics of the family relationships allow, and with the patient's permission, these interventions can be taught to family members who often value tasks that help minimize their feelings of helplessness and add comfort to the lives of their patients (McCaffery and Pasero 1999; Juarez and Ferrell 1999).

These modalities are not a substitute for analgesia, and their successful use does not imply that a patient does not have pain. They focus on the internal dialogue of patients and the relationship of body, mind, and emotion. They have the potential to affect pain-related behaviors and cognitions and restore a sense of calm, self-efficacy, and control. In the setting of life-limiting illness, it is helpful if new skills are taught early in the illness before the disease progresses and physical and/or cognitive functions are affected. Cognitive changes do not preclude the integration of cognitive behavioral strategies, but require modification such as slow pacing, extensive cueing, memory aides, and increased involvement of significant others (Carr and Addison 1994). These strategies can also be helpful to family members and caregivers who may experience emotional and physical distress as participants and witnesses to the distress of the patients (Gallo-Silver and Pollack 2000).

When assessing the appropriateness of cognitive behavioral interventions, it is useful to ask patients and family members how they have coped with distress in the past. Patients who use prayer, music, or reading to engage, comfort, or distract have given the clinician a beginning avenue for interventions. It is helpful to reinforce that many have a natural ability to distract themselves and engage in a mental activity to the exclusion of the painful stimuli. This does not mean that the pain does not exist or is "psychological." People can be helped to accept the relation between body, mind, and feelings when familiar examples are used. For example, Lamaze helps with labor pains, fear activates a physiologic response, and sexual fantasies create an emotional as well as a physiologic reaction. Distraction techniques and their relevance to pain can be compared with the experience of being involved in a good book or movie to the exclusion of other stimuli. When imagery is compared to daydreaming, the concept may become easier for patients to integrate.

Techniques such as *cognitive restructuring, coping statements, distraction, self-monitoring (diaries), and relaxation imagery* have the potential to minimize or correct distorted cognitions, diminish pain, distress and anxiety, promote sleep, and reduce feelings of helplessness and hopelessness (Loscalzo and Jacobsen 1990; Jacobsen and Hann 1998).

COGNITIVE RESTRUCTURING/REFRAMING

Cognitive restructuring involves examining and reevaluating a person's negative interpretation of events in order to reduce feelings of distress, helplessness, and hopelessness. Exploring a patient's internal dialogue isolates thoughts and feelings that worsen pain intensity and distress and provides opportunity to reinforce thoughts that enhance comfort and control (Beck et al. 1979).

CASE EXAMPLE

John is a forty-five-year-old married father of two daughters, ages seven and ten years. He has recurrent lung cancer that has metastasized to the ribs, causing considerable pain. While receiving active treatment for the cancer, he is aware of the serious prognosis and praying "for a miracle." He had originally been diagnosed four years earlier. In exploring the significance of the recurrence, John reviewed the four years since diagnosis and "reframed" his current reality. Rather than "waiting for a miracle from

God," he suggested that perhaps the "miracle" had already occurred, in that he had been given four years with his daughters to help them grow. He moved from an emotional posture of "waiting" to an active role of a father with time to prepare his children for the possibility of his death.

COPING STATEMENTS

Coping statements are internal or spoken statements designed to distract, enhance coping, and/or diminish the threatening aspect of a situation or experience (McCaul and Malott 1984). Catastrophic and defeating self-statements about pain can be replaced with internal dialogues that enhance coping and competence.

CASE EXAMPLE

A patient with intermittent sharp shooting pain in the ribs became anxious and frightened when the unpredictable pain occurred. While unpredictable, the pain was a recurrent experience, intense, but diminishing in a short time. The patient was taught the cognitive coping statement "I have had this pain before; while intense, I know it will go away. In the meantime, I need to focus on my breathing." The patient was able to combine a coping statement with a breathing exercise that promotes control both emotionally and physically.

DISTRACTION

Distraction involves refocusing attention and concentration to stimuli other than pain and to other aspects of self that might include mental activity (internal) such as prayer, reading, or a physical activity (external) such as breathing, rhythm, or engaging family or friend in conversation (Jacox et al. 1994; Turk, Meichenbaum, and Genest 1983). When the patient is sedated, confused, or frustrated, interventions might include massage or music when appropriate. The choice of intervention requires an assessment of the level of fatigue, cognitive status, and ability to concentrate and follow instructions. Family and friends can be encouraged to participate, if acceptable to the patient, through activities such as telling stories, sharing family albums, life reviews, music, prayer, and reading to the patient (McCaffrey and Pasero 1999; Beck 1991). The goal is to focus on another area that may have therapeutic value while at the same time reducing attention to pain or other symptoms.

RELAXATION TECHNIQUES

In the 1970s, research cardiologist Herbert Benson developed a simple relaxation technique that incorporates muscle relaxation and rhythmic breathing. The goal is to elicit a "relaxation response" that counteracts "fight-or-flight," the internal adaptive response of the body to threat. In this response, the body secretes catecholamines, stress hormones that prepare a person under threat to fight or flee. This response is essential when facing acute physical threats, but not helpful when stress is chronic, when faced with a CT scan or MRI, or when the threat is an internal experience of the patient's, such as pain or catastrophic thoughts. The relaxation response is characterized by changes in the sympathetic nervous system, producing a decreased heart rate, blood pressure, respiratory rate, and blood flow to the muscles (Benson 1975). Many patients can use breathing techniques with or without muscle relaxation to reverse the physiologic, emotional, and behavioral reactions to stress and pain. The choice of technique is related to the condition of the patient, but most exercises combine repetition of a word, phrase, or breath with or without imagery and are enhanced by a quiet environment and a physical position that is as comfortable and secure for the patient as is possible. The following exercise is a generic relaxation script that combines breathing, with relaxation and imagery and can be adjusted according to patient preference and condition. If taught and practiced early in the illness continuum, the conditioned response of relaxation can be established and more easily elicited when physical and cognitive changes occur (McCaffrey and Pasero 1999).

This sample script can be adapted and individualized by incorporating the person's name and using language appropriate to their understanding and circumstances.

"Let's start by getting as comfortable as possible. . . . Move around until you find the position that is most comfortable for you right now and when you are ready allow your eyes to close, or if you like just focus on a spot on the ceiling or the wall. . . . Begin by focusing your awareness on your breathing. . . . Pay special attention to breathing in breathing out. . . . You don't need to try to alter your breathing right now, simply become aware of it. . . . In fact, if you listen closely you might even be able to hear the sound of your own breathing.

You may notice the air that you exhale is a little warmer than the air that you inhale . . . and that with every breath you're becoming increasingly relaxed and calm. . . . You might imagine that you are inhaling feelings of comfort, relaxation and control; exhaling feelings of discomfort and distress. . . . Other thoughts or sounds may enter your mind but you can let them go; they are not terribly important right now. . . . Simply return your awareness to your breathing which is now slower, deeper, and more comfortable.

If you like, on every breath that you exhale you can silently repeat a word or a phrase that has special meaning to you. . . . It could be a word, a thought—or perhaps the word *relax*—so that you inhale deeply, exhale comfortably and repeat the word or phrase that you have chosen.

You may notice that your body is feeling more relaxed and comfortable as your breathing is easy, comfortable and comforting. . . . You may continue this as long as you need. . . . When you are ready allow your eyes to open slowly, easily, and you will remain calm and relaxed, yet alert.

(LOSCALZO AND JACOBSEN 1990:160–163; BENSON 1975:162–163).

HYPNOSIS

Hypnosis is a therapeutic technique that induces a state of heightened awareness and focused concentration that can be used to alter perceptions of pain, reduce the fear and anxiety that often accompany pain, and sometimes control the pain itself. This state is characterized by increased suggestibility that can improve some aspects of mental or physical functioning. Autogenic self-hypnosis uses techniques such as self-suggestions of warmth, heaviness, and relaxation sequentially through the body that can be associated with a decrease of pain and enhanced relaxation (Spiegel and Spiegel 1978; Schultz and Luthe 1969).

IMAGERY

Imagery is the use of mental representations to help control symptoms, to enhance relaxation and comfort, to create distance, or to give insight into a particular problem. Imagery often begins with a relaxation exercise to help focus attention. Visualization is the most common form, but many exercises can be enriched by involving the other senses, including taste, smell, sound, and touch. Images that are elicited from the patient have personal meaning and consequently have the potential to enhance the therapeutic impact of this intervention. Imagery can also be a useful modality for the mental rehearsal of activities or feelings that are threatening (Sheikh 1983; Graffam and Johnson 1987).

The following case narrative integrates relaxation, imagery, and coping statements to enhance the medical management of pain, depression, and anxiety.

CASE EXAMPLE

Jennifer is a fifty-three-year-old, white, divorced teacher, living alone. She is the mother of two adult children. Diagnosed with rectal cancer, metastatic to spine and bone, she was admitted with disabling and escalating buttock and paraspinal pain. The medical management included an epidural catheter as well as patient controlled analgesia (PCA). However, her anxiety consequent to pain and feelings of helplessness affected both her cognitive and physical functions. Additionally, her mood exacerbated her pain and despair. "I tend to get very uptight and nervous about things. I did not understand how I could have been broken into so many pieces. I felt as if I was removed from myself, my hands would shake, my knees would shake."

In collaboration with the patient, the social-work clinician combined a focused-breathing intervention with passive muscle relaxation and imagery. The patient selected the image of an English garden and was guided in an imagery experience that combined the colors, textures, sights, and sounds of the garden with related feelings of safety, calm, and comfort. This therapeutic use of imagery encouraged the patient's participation and ownership of the intervention and allowed for the integration of therapeutic suggestion related to her individual history and unresolved issues. The exercise was taped so the patient could use it independently, encouraging self-soothing consistent with maintaining and supporting her internal locus of control and enhanced self-efficacy.

"I began to listen to the tape. . . . If I followed that, I could sometimes have more control about what I was thinking and have more control about keeping myself from going to pieces. . . . I began to practice the breathing. . . . I wake up in the morning, be stiff, feel the rigidity coming on . . . put on the tape . . . and I've been able to keep myself so I don't become spun out thinking things can't be done. . . . It's all part of things where you can help yourself and not bother other people. . . . It made a tremendous difference in my being able to cope with waking in the night and feeling here's a pain coming on, what do I have to face tomorrow, I don't want to face tomorrow. . . . I truly amazed myself, by the end of the tape I found that I had gone back to sleep."

Audiotapes that are individualized for patients create an opportunity to personalize the dialogue and maximize and extend the comfort and therapeutic benefit that emanate from the relationship with the clinician. Similar to Winnicott's construct of a transitional object that comforts and contains aspects of the mother/child relationship, audiotapes and symptom diaries have the potential to provide support and become symbolic of an established therapeutic relationship (Winnicott 1953; see chapter 16, this volume).

SELF-MONITORING

Patients can receive enormous benefit from self-monitoring efforts such as diaries or journals. These allow for the objectifying of thoughts, behaviors, feelings, and fears while creating a historical record that may or may not be shared with others. Journals may help to identify maladaptive attitudes, thoughts, and beliefs. They may create an opportunity to redefine in part or in whole a threatening experience with the goals of decreasing anxiety and hopelessness. They are a flexible intervention, can be kept for a week or for months, written in telegram form or paragraphs, and have the potential to provide an ongoing link to the clinician, allowing for ongoing connectedness in the absence of frequent contact. The selection of a format is based on the purpose and the response of the patient or family member to the intervention. Diaries can be useful in understanding and intervening with the multidimensional aspects of many symptoms, including pain, insomnia, and depression. What follows is an example of the pain diary of a twenty-nine-year-old woman with metastatic breast cancer and multiple symptoms, including pain, depression, insomnia, and nightmares.

SEGMENTS OF A PAIN DIARY

March 22—2:10 AM; Didn't wake up from the pain, focused on it and couldn't sleep. Took it easy today because of pain in left lower back. But not upset about that pain since I walked two miles last night and clearly overdid it. [*Symbolic significance and etiology of pain affects emotional response.*] Was okay until found out my tumor markers were elevated again. Started to anticipate and focus on my ribs . . . watching and waiting for pain. [*Anticipation and preoccupation with pain causing distress.*] Keep reminding myself that it is how I feel that matters not what a test tells me to feel. [*Internal versus external locus of control.*]

March 24—4:00 PM; Went walking . . . had a pocketbook draped across my shoulder blade. After 15 minutes of walking this way—got sharp pain in left scapula. Feel like I did something to cause the pain to return. Feel out of control and like my life is at the mercy of this whimsical pain that comes and goes without warning. Also I waited too long to take the meds and the pain built up a lot. [*Changing how she carries pocketbook has potential to return semblance of control; emotional and cognitive adaptation required to shift her behavior from treating pain after it occurs to preventing pain by around-the-clock use of medications.*]

March 25—6:50 PM; Waited an hour but the pain is still there and feels even worse, although I don't think it's really worse. It's just that it won't go away and its driving me crazy. [*Partializing physical pain from the anxiety and distress caused by ongoing experience of pain and catastrophic thinking.*] I'm getting more and more upset and anxious as time passes. I'm thinking—"Is the pain from cancer? When will it go away?" [*Internal dialogue reinforces helplessness rather than self-efficacy and control.*]

March 28—1:00 AM; Mild pain but trying to see if it will allow me to sleep. [*Empowering pain as an objective entity outside of self may symbolize an untapped ability to create a therapeutic dissociation from the pain.*]

6:21 AM; Had a horrible nightmare. Still groggy but afraid to go back to sleep for fear of having another nightmare. [*Pain and nightmares empowered, decreases control and efficacy.*] Very mild pain, practically no pain when lying down. Here is an example of where I am taking pain meds not because of pain now but anticipating pain. [*Education regarding preventive use of medication being integrated into pain management behaviors.*]

March 29—11:00 AM; I had a relatively good nights sleep last night. When I woke up instead of putting the TV on, I tried to go back to sleep. I told myself I'd give it 15–20 minutes to try to sleep. Then I could get up or watch TV and I fell back to sleep both times. [*Integrating sleep hygiene techniques, which empower and diminish helplessness regarding sleep.*]

2:00 PM; Feeling very depressed because I was supposed to go out to dinner in the city but I cancelled because I feel so horrible. I'm also afraid that I'll be miserable in pain . . . that's why I cancelled. But now I'm feeling depressed because I feel like this pain has control over my entire life. [*Patient's catastrophic thinking and anticipation of pain controls behavior, exacerbating helplessness and distress.*]

April 8—4:30 PM; Feel really depressed about everything. The pain is making me feel like I'm dying. Not that it's that bad—it's not—it's actually pretty mild but I just feel overwhelmed by everything; the decisions I have to make. [*Patient differentiating pain, symbolic meaning of pain, and feelings and distress generated by pending decisions.*]

April 19—8:45 PM; Was walking around the city. Went to dinner, just got home. I'm now in an extreme amount of pain. I waited too long to take my pain meds. Now need more than usual. Was distracted and having fun tonight so every time I thought to take the meds, I thought I can wait a little longer. [*Identifying potential of distraction to divert attention from pain; integrating educational concept that delaying medication often results in a need for more medication.*]

April 22—6:00 PM; Took a long hot bath . . . the warmth of the bath seemed to help reduce the pain a bit. It loosened it up so I'm not bracing against the pain as much. [*Ongoing intervention of integrative methods for managing pain; discriminating pain from behavioral response to pain, i.e., bracing.*]

May 10—1:50 PM; Just finished yoga. This pain in my hip is not nearly as frightening to me now that I'm home, than it was in Hawaii. I felt very much alone with my pain there. I was scared and I felt like I was dying because of the intensity of the pain. Now the pain is much lessened and psychologically, the pain is more bearable. [*Ongoing integration of relationship of pain to emotions and existential distress; use of integrative techniques enhance self-efficacy and supplement medications.*]

May 24—3:10 PM; On my way into the city to go out. My low back pain is just starting to hurt a little bit . . . want to stop any pain before it builds up. This is one of the first times I've gone out alone to meet my friends in the city. I haven't done this in over a year because I would anticipate the pain I *thought* I'd be in. We'll see how it goes. [*Cognitive coping statement replaces catastrophic thoughts; engaging in developmentally appropriate behaviors.*]

June 2—10:00 PM; Friends came over. We watched a video. I was sitting up on the sofa. I feel good that I'm still doing things socially even when my pain increases a bit. [*Modalities of pharmacologic, integrative, supportive and cognitive behavioral interventions combine to assist patient toward age-appropriate activities that improve quality of life, return semblance of control in the setting of metastatic breast cancer.*]

CONCLUSION

Being alerted to reported or witnessed distress begs an appropriate response by the caregiver. —Frager 1997:892

A multidimensional approach to pain offers social-work clinicians a perspective that is transferable to other symptoms and allows a competent and compassionate response to "witnessed distress" along the continuum of life-limiting illness. Social workers are in a unique position to assess and advocate on an individual, family, and systems level, including political and health-reform activities designed to insure adequate pain and symptom management for the most vulnerable populations. Social work core principles of evaluating "person in environment" and "starting where the client is" are essential to enhancing the team's understanding of patient and family values, responses, beliefs, stresses, and goals. Patients and families need to count on the healthcare team and the unique skills of social workers to provide the best of medical, psychosocial, and spiritual interventions to manage pain and other troubling symptoms. It is the ethical and respectful thing to do.

REFERENCES

Abrahm, J. L. 2000. *A Physician's Guide to Pain and Symptom Management in Cancer Patients*. Baltimore: Johns Hopkins University Press.

Ambuel, B. 2000. Conducting a family conference. *Principles and Practices of Supportive Oncology Updates* 3(3): 1–12.

Anderson, K. O., T. R. Mendoza, V. Valero, et al. 2000. Minority cancer patients and their providers: Pain management attitudes and practices. *Cancer* 88(8): 1929–1938.

Barkwell, D. P. 1991. Ascribed meaning: A critical factor in coping and pain attenuation in patients with cancer related pain. *Journal of Palliative Care* 7:5–14.

Beck, A. T., A. J. Rush, B. F. Shaw, and G. Emery. 1979. *Cognitive Therapy of Depression*. New York: Guilford.

Beck, S. L. 1991. The therapeutic use of music for cancer-related pain. *Oncology Nursing Forum* 18(8): 1327–1337.

Benson, H. 1975. *The Relaxation Response*. New York: Avon.

Bernabei, R., G. Gambassi, K. Lapane, et al. 1998. Management of pain in elderly patients with cancer. *Journal of the American Medical Association* 279:1877–1882.

Blendon, R. J., L. H. Aiken, H. E. Freeman, and C. R. Corey. 1989. Access to medical care for black and white Americans, a matter of continuing concern. *Journal of the American Medical Association* 261:278–281.

Blum, D. 1993. Treatment of cancer pain: Cancer pain assessment and treatment curriculum guidelines. American Society of Clinical Oncology.

Bonham, V. L. 2001. Race, ethnicity and pain treatment: striving to understand the causes and solutions to the disparities in pain treatment. *Journal of Law, Medicine and Ethics* 29:52–68.

Carr, D. B., and R. G. Addison. 1994. *Pain in HIV/AIDS*. Washington, DC: Robert G. Addison.

Cassell, E. J. 1991. Recognizing suffering. *Hastings Center Report*, May/June, 24–31.

Cleeland, C. S. 1989. Pain control: Public and physicians attitudes. In *Drug Treatment of Cancer Pain in a Drug-Oriented Society*, vol. 11, *Advances in Pain Research and Therapy*, ed. C. S. Hill and W. S. Fields, 81–89. New York: Raven Press.

Cleeland, C. S., R. Gonin, A. K. Harfield, et al. 1994. Pain and its treatment in outpatients with metastatic cancer. *New England Journal of Medicine* 330:592–596.

Coyle, N. 1992. The euthanasia and physician assisted suicide debate: Issues for nursing. *Oncology Nursing Forum* 19:41–46.

Crawley, L. V., P. A. Marshall, B. Lo, and B. A. Koenig. 2002. Strategies for culturally effective end of life care. *Annals of Internal Medicine* 136:673–679.

Crawley, L. V., R. Payne, J. Bolden, T. Payne, P. Washington, and S. Williams. 2000. Palliative and end-of-life care in the African American community. *Journal of the American Medical Association* 284:2518–2521.

Dar, R., C. M. Beach, P. L. Barden, and C. S. Cleeland. 1992. Cancer pain in the marital system: A study of patients and their spouses. *Journal of Pain and Symptom Management* 7:87–93.

Desbiens, N. A., N. Mueller-Rizner, A. F. Connors, N. S. Wenger, and J. Lynn. 1999. The symptom burden of seriously ill hospitalized patients. *Journal of Pain and Symptom Management* 17:248–255.

Die-Trill, M. 1998. The patient from a different culture. In *Psycho-Oncology*, ed. J. Holland, 857–866. New York: Oxford University Press.

Ferrell, B. R., G. E. Dean, M. Grant, and P. Coluzzi. 1995. An institutional commitment to pain management. *Journal of Clinical Oncology* 13:2158–2165.

Fink, R., and R. Gates. 2001. Pain assessment. In *Textbook of Palliative Nursing*, ed. B. Ferrell and N. Coyle, 53–71. New York: Oxford University Press.

Frager, G. 1997. Palliative care and terminal care of children. *Child and Adolescent Psychiatric Clinics of North America* 6:889–909.

Gallo-Silver, L., and B. Pollack. 2000. Behavioral interventions for lung cancer-related breathlessness. *Cancer Practice* 8(6): 268–273.

Glajchen, M. 2003. Caregiver burden and pain control. In *Cancer Pain*, ed. R. K. Portenoy and E. Bruera, 475–481. New York: Cambridge University Press.

Graffam, S., and A. Johnson. 1987. A comparison of two relaxation strategies for the relief of pain and distress. *Journal of Pain and Symptom Management* 2:229–231.

Grossman, S. A., V. R. Sheidler, K. Swedeen, J. Mucenski, and S. Piantadosi. 1991. Correlation of patient and caregiver rating of cancer pain. *Journal of Pain and Symptom Management* 6:53–57.

Higginson, I. J., and J. Hearn. 1997. A multicenter evaluation of cancer pain control by palliative care teams. *Journal of Pain and Symptom Management* 14:29–35.

Jacobsen, P., and D. M. Hann. 1998. Cognitive behavioral interventions in psycho-oncology. In *Psycho-Oncology*, ed. J. Holland, 717–729. New York: Oxford University Press.

Jacox, A., D. B. Carr, R. Payne, et al. 1994. Management of cancer pain. Clinical Practice Guideline No 9 (AHCPR Publication No. 94–0592). Rockville, MD: Agency for Health Care Policy and Research, U.S. Department of Health and Human Services.

Jonsen, A. R., M. Siegler, and W. J. Winsdale. 1992. *Clinical Ethics*. 3d ed. New York: McGraw-Hill.

Juarez, G., and B. R. Ferrell. 1996. Family and caregiver involvement in pain management. *Clinic of Geriatric Medicine* 12:531–547.

Kagawa-Singer, M. 1996. Cultural systems. In *Cancer Nursing* (2d ed.), ed. S. B. Baird, R. McCorkle, and M. Grant, 38–52. Philadelphia: Saunders.

Kanner, R. M., and R. K. Portenoy. 1986. Unavailability of narcotic analgesics for ambulatory cancer patients in New York City. *Journal of Pain and Symptom Management* 1:87–89.

Koenig, B., and J. Gates-Williams. 1995. Understanding cultural differences in caring for dying patients. *Western Journal of Medicine* 163:244–249.

Kreier, R. 2000. Crossing the cultural divide. *American Medical News* 18:12–14.

Lesage, P. 2001. Ethical and legal issues in palliative care. www.stoppain.org/palliative_care/index.html.

Levine, C. 2000. The many worlds of family caregivers. In *Always on Call: When Illness Turns Families Into Caregivers*, ed. C. Levine, 1–17. New York: United Hospital Fund.

Lipson, J. G., S. L. Dibble, and P. A. Minarik, eds. 2000. *Culture and Nursing Care: A Pocket Guide*. San Francisco: UCSF Nursing Press.

Loscalzo, M., and P. Jacobsen. 1990. Practical behavioral approaches to the effective management of pain and distress. *Journal of Psychosocial Oncology* 8:139–169.

McCaffery, M., and C. Pasero. 1999. *Pain: Clinical Manual*. 2d ed. New York: Mosby.

McCaul, K. D., and J. M. Malott. 1984. Distraction and coping with pain. *Psychology Bulletin* 95:516–533.

Mercadante, S., M. Armata, and L. Salvaggio. 1994. Pain characteristics of advanced lung cancer patients referred to a palliative care service. *Pain* 59:141–145.

Mersky, H., and N. Boggduk, eds. 1994. *Classification of Chronic Pain*. 2d ed. Seattle: IASP Press.

Meyer, C. 2002. Allow natural death: An alternative to DNR. www.hospicepatients.org/and.html.

Miaskowski, C., E. F. Zimmer, K. M. Barrett, S. L. Dibble, and M. Wallhagen. 1997. Difference in patient and family caregivers' perceptions of the pain experience influences patient and caregiver outcomes. *Pain* 72:217–226.

Morrison, R. S., S. Wallenstein, D. K. Natale, R. S. Senzel, and L. Huang. 2000. "We don't carry that": Failure of pharmacies in predominately nonwhite neighborhoods to stock opioid analgesics. *New England Journal of Medicine* 342:1023–1026.

Nathan Cummings Foundation and Fetzer Institute. 1997. *Spiritual Beliefs and the Dying Process: A Report of a National Survey.* Princeton, NJ: George H. Gallup International Institute.

Otis-Green, S., R. Sherman, M. Perez, and P. Baird. 2002. An integrated psychosocial-spiritual model for cancer pain management. *Cancer Practice* 10:S58–65.

Portenoy, R. K. 2000. *Contemporary Diagnosis and Management of Pain in Oncologic and AIDS Patients.* Newton, PA: Handbooks in Health Care.

Redinbaugh, E. M., A. Baum, C. DeMoss, M. Fello, and R. Arnold. 2002. Factors associated with the accuracy of family caregiver estimates of patient's pain. *Journal of Pain and Symptom Management* 23:31–38.

Schultz, J. H., and W. Luthe. 1969. *Autogenic Therapy.* Vol. 1, *Autogenic Methods.* New York: Grune & Stratton.

Shapiro, B. S. 1993. Patient groups with special needs: Cancer pain assessment and treatment curriculum guidelines. American Society of Clinical Oncology.

Sheikh, A. A. 1983. *Imagery: Current Theory, Research and Application.* New York: Wiley.

Spiegel, H., and D. Spiegel. 1978. *Trance and Treatment: Clinical Use of Hypnosis.* New York: Basic Books.

Steefel, L. 2001. Treat pain in any culture. *Nursing Spectrum,* November.

Stein, W. 2001. Assessment of symptoms in the cognitively impaired. In *Topics in Palliative Care,* ed. E. Bruera and R. K. Portenoy, 5:123–133. New York: Oxford University Press.

Study to Understand Prognoses and Preferences for Outcomes and Risks of Treatment (SUPPORT). 1997. A controlled trial to improve care for seriously ill hospitalized patients. *Journal of the American Medical Association* 274:1591–1598.

Turk, D. C., D. Meichenbaum, and M. Genest. 1983. *Pain and Behavioral Medicine: A Cognitive-Behavioral Perspective.* New York: Guilford.

Twycross, R. G. 1997. *Oral Morphine in Advanced Cancer.* 3d ed. Beaconsfield, UK: Beaconsfield.

Vainio, A., and A. Auvinen. 1996. Prevalence of symptoms among patients with advanced cancer: An international collaborative study. *Journal of Pain and Symptom Management* 12:3–10.

Vogl, D., B. Rosenfeld, W. Breitbart, et al. 1999. Symptom prevalence, characteristics and distress in AIDS outpatients. *Journal of Pain and Symptom Management* 18:253–262.

Von Roenn, J. H., C. S. Cleeland, R. Gonin, A. K. Hatfield, and K. J. Pandya. 1993. Physician attitudes and practice in cancer pain management: A survey from the Eastern Cooperative Oncology Group. *Annals of Internal Medicine* 119:121–126.

Walco, G. A., R. C. Cassidy, and N. L. Schechter. 1994. Pain, hurt and harm: The ethics of pain control in infants and children. *New England Journal of Medicine* 331(8): 541–543.

Weissman, D. E., and J. D. Haddox. 1989. Opioid pseudoaddiction: An iatrogenic syndrome. *Pain* 36:363–366.

Winnicott, D. W. 1971. *Objects and Transitional Phenomena in Playing and Reality.* Harmondsworth, UK: Penguin.

20

PALLIATIVE CARE AND SOCIAL WORK

SUSAN BLACKER

IN ORDER to appreciate fully the scope and nature of the role of social work in palliative care, it is important to understand the context of how care is provided for the dying in the United States today. In recent years there have been heightened awareness of and concern about how individuals are cared for at the end of their lives. A number of factors have strongly influenced the dialogue about end-of-life care in the past two decades. The public and medical debates about both assisted suicide and the role of technology in prolonging life have led to an examination of opinions and legislation about the definition of a self-determined or peaceful death (Last Acts 2002). Criticisms about the current system of care, quality, and costs of care of the aged and the chronically ill living in long-term care facilities, including reports of poor pain control for nursing home residents, have alarmed the public. The baby-boom generation's parents' declining health and increased caregiving needs on their lives undoubtedly contribute to stronger support for examining the burdens faced by family caregivers and resources for the elderly.

Current understanding of the dying individual's experience recognizes that the physical, social, psychological, cultural, and spiritual dimensions of the patient and family's experience are interrelated variables of quality of life, as well as quality of death. Providing interdisciplinary care to individuals with life-threatening illness and their families, with the paramount goal of minimizing pain and other physical, psychosocial, and spiritual problems and achieving goals for quality of life, is known as "palliative care" (World Health Organization 2003).

This chapter examines current issues and gaps in care of those living with life-threatening illness, the ways that palliative care is presently delivered (including programs in hospitals and hospice care), important challenges within the field of palliative care, and the multidimensional role that social work plays in palliative care. Social work's ability to address the most complex of family and social systems in the face of crisis, to facilitate difficult decision making, to negotiate care transitions and resource acquisition, and to provide bereavement care is an essential part of the delivery of excellent palliative care (Taylor-Brown et al. 2001). As this chapter illustrates, social work is, and will continue to be, a critical part of the quest to achieve better care for the dying.

TRENDS AND ISSUES IN CARE OF THE DYING

Modern medicine, as we have come to know it over the past century, has changed the way in which we conceptualize life-threatening illness and the process of dying. The ability of medical technology to prolong life has also forced us to examine the dying experience more closely (Last Acts 2002; Hedlund and Clark 2001). Many illnesses that were once fatal are now amenable to curative and rehabilitative therapies (Field and Cassel 1997). Many diseases that once were expected to follow a sloping illness trajectory (predictable deterioration and ultimately death), such as many cancers and HIV/AIDS, are now more commonly experienced as chronic illnesses. As a result, living with these illnesses requires greater medical and other resources and challenges the family's ability to cope for much longer periods. Other illnesses, such as congestive heart failure (CHF) and chronic obstructive pulmonary disease (COPD), the cause of more than half of all deaths in America each year, follow a different illness trajectory. These illnesses more commonly involve episodes of serious and life-threatening symptoms requiring intensive care. Advance-care planning discussions are often avoided by healthcare professionals and patients. The disease is managed from crisis to crisis. Such diseases are not easily managed by the existing model of hospice care owing to their prolonged nature and to the challenge of identifying life expectancy or the end stage of the illness (Field and Cassel 1997).

The majority of Americans include the values of self-determination and choice in their definition of a "good" or "peaceful" death if life-saving measures or cures are not possible. Studies indicate that Americans generally believe that the end-of-life should not occur hooked up to machines (Last Acts 2002; American Health Decisions 1997). They are concerned that the current healthcare system does not support their ideal concept of dying (American Health Decisions 1997). In two Gallup polls, one in 1992 and a second in 1996, nine out of ten Americans said that they would prefer to be cared for at home if they were terminally ill (Field and Cassel 1997). An American Health Decisions study conducted in 1997 also revealed that the majority of Americans feel that it is important to plan for death and dying, but most are uncomfortable with the topic and resist taking action. Results showed that concern about creating family burden and protecting family finances is the primary concern of most individuals in making end-of-life decisions. Respondents indicated that they want to be surrounded by family and cared for by competent healthcare professionals, most often stating that they wish to be in their own homes in their final days. They want to be pain-free during the dying process. The majority of Americans are unsure about whom to contact with questions about end-of-life care (American Health Decisions 1997). Less well understood, however, are the differences between cultural/ethnic or faith communities and their specific values or ideals related to the end of life. A growing group of healthcare professionals and advocates are working to create standards for culturally sensitive and relevant models of care. A growing literature is developing in this area (del Rio 2002; Koening 1997; see chapter 22, this volume).

How and where does death occur? More than two and a half million deaths occur in the United States each year; 80 percent of those who die are Medicare recipients

(Last Acts 2002). Despite tremendous advances in medical technology and the amelioration of life-threatening conditions, fatal illnesses are responsible for the majority of deaths. The top three causes of death by disease are heart disease, cancer, and stroke (Field and Cassel 1997).

"Over the last century, death has moved out of homes and into institutions" (Field and Cassel 1997:39). Statistics illustrating where deaths occur in the United States show that about 50 percent of all deaths annually occur in the hospital. Most of these deaths occur on inpatient units, with a percentage occurring in emergency rooms and outpatient clinics. Approximately 25 percent of individuals die in a nursing home, and about 25 percent spent their final days in other settings, including their own homes (National Hospice Organization 1996) These statistics paint an important picture of where expert care at the end of life is most needed. They clearly illustrate the need for provision of multidimensional symptom management for the dying and specialized care for the bereaved, not only in the individual's home, but also within hospitals and long-term care facilities. The challenge has been incorporating quality and comprehensive end-of-life care into a highly technology-driven and cure-oriented healthcare system. This important challenge affects all disciplines involved in providing healthcare, including social work.

CHANGING THE CULTURE OF CARE: PALLIATIVE CARE

While a number of definitions of palliative care exist (including those by the World Health Organization and the National Hospice and Palliative Care Organization), the Canadian Hospice Palliative Care Association (CHPCA) has adopted perhaps the most progressive definition, with the broadest view of the integration of palliative care across the illness continuum:

> Palliative care as a philosophy of care, is the combination of active and compassionate therapies intended to comfort and support individuals and families who are living with life-threatening illness. During periods of illness and bereavement, palliative care strives to meet physical, psychological, social and spiritual expectations and needs, while remaining sensitive to personal, cultural and religious values, beliefs and practices. Palliative care may be combined with therapies aimed at reducing or curing the illness, or it may be the total focus of care.
>
> Palliative care is planned and delivered through the collaborative efforts of an interdisciplinary team including the individual, family, and caregivers. It should be available to the individual and his/her family at any time during the illness trajectory and bereavement. While many caregivers may be able to deliver some of the therapies that provide comfort and support, the services of a specialized palliative care program may be required as the degree of distress, discomfort and dysfunction increases.
>
> Integral to effective palliative care is the provision of opportunity and support for caregivers to work through their own emotions and grief related to the care that they are providing. (FERRIS AND CUMMINGS 1995)

The term *palliative care* was first coined by Dr. Balfour Mount when he brought the hospice movement, which began in the United Kingdom with Dame Cicely Saunders, to Canada. This term was acceptable in both English and French, based on the Latin root *palliare*, "to cloak or cover" (Ferris et al. 2002). The CHPCA definition has several important distinctions. First, it stresses that palliative care is "care that aims to relieve suffering and improve quality of life throughout the illness and bereavement experience, so that patient and families can realize their full potential to live even when they are dying." (Ferris et al. 2002:v). This challenges the notion that palliative care is limited to care at the very end of life, received only by those in their final days or weeks of life, and recognizes the proactive and integrated role that palliative care should play in acute, chronic, and bereavement care. Second, it highlights that care provided should be interdisciplinary in nature and that the patient and family should be integrally viewed as part of the team. Third, the specialty knowledge and skill needed for the expert provision of this kind of care is acknowledged. And finally, it notes that care and support of the caregiver, both familial and professional, is essential.

Palliative-care programs have typically developed within larger healthcare institutions, while hospice was a community-based movement, often beginning as a free-standing, volunteer-based program. Both movements are relatively young, with the history of each beginning in the early to mid-1970s. These two movements have now begun to converge (Ferris et al. 2002). Symbolically, both the National Hospice Organization and the Canadian Palliative Care Association have changed their names in recent years to include the other term. In 2002, the Canadian Hospice Palliative Care Association released a consensus document entitled "A Model to Guide Hospice Palliative Care: Based on National Principles and Norms of Practice." The model, based on a national consensus-building process spanning more than ten years, was developed in collaboration with individuals, committees, associations, and government. The comprehensive model, which promotes a standardized approach to hospice palliative care, is relevant to multiple domains: patient and family care, organizational development/function, educational competencies, accreditation standards, licensure standards, research, consumer advocacy, legislation and regulations, and funding (Ferris et al. 2002). This model is certain to influence efforts underway in the United States to develop similar norms and standards of practices and to legitimize and move the field forward.

How is palliative care provided in the present day? Palliative care, broadly, may be provided by a specialized team or program in a hospital, in the home or in other settings, like long-term care facilities. The core professions typically involved in palliative-care programs are medicine, nursing, social work, and pastoral care (Last Acts 1997). Many programs, especially those in the acute-care setting, also access expertise from psychiatry or psychology, pharmacy, nutrition, physical medicine and rehabilitation therapy, and child life therapy. Volunteers are well utilized by palliative-care programs and are often provided with specialized training to prepare them for their involvement.

The most recognized and common form of palliative care in the United States is hospice. As Mary Raymer and Dona Reese point out in chapter 7, "Hospice is a specialized form of palliative care, but not all palliative care is hospice." Hospice is typically referred to as a very specific model of care delivery (Byock 1998); the majority of hospice care is provided in the patient's home. Inpatient hospice units or facilities do exist in some communities, and hospice programs also provide care to some residents in long-term care facilities (NHPCO 2002). Hospice-hospital partnerships are also becoming increasingly feasible and more common, therefore increasing accessibility of palliative care. Palliative care has even evolved in some prison systems, such as the Angola Prison Hospice in Louisiana. In this innovative model, carefully selected inmates are provided with training and work alongside health professional staff to care for those dying in prison (Angola Prison Hospice 1998). Demonstration projects of innovative service-delivery models have increased in recent years.

CHALLENGES IN PALLIATIVE CARE

Making palliative care broadly available in all healthcare settings and systems, beyond the existing hospice model, is a priority in healthcare today. Much has happened in this arena over the past decade. Many national and international professional healthcare organizations are responding with studies and reports that scrutinized current care delivery. Major reports include the 1995 SUPPORT study, the Institute of Medicine's 1997 report *Approaching Death: Improving Care at the End of Life*, the National Cancer Institute's 2001 report *Improving Palliative Care in Cancer*, and the Institute of Medicine's 2002 report *When Children Die: Improving Palliative and End-of-Life Care for Children and Their Families*.

These reports have highlighted inadequacies in a number of areas, including the current systems of care delivery and healthcare policies, the professional training received by those caring for the dying, and the current empirical knowledge about clinical care and symptom management. The following list (summary of some of the key points from American Health Decisions 1997 and Field and Cassel 1997) summarizes some recommendations that have been generated for systemically improving care at the end of life.

IMPROVING END-OF-LIFE CARE: RECOMMENDATIONS

- Engage in public dialogue and education about care at the end of life
- Reestablish doctor-patient relationships and enhance communication
- Develop improved advance directive documents and implement advanced-care planning
- Overcome barriers to pain management
- Provide information to support informed decision making
- Expand hospice-type services to increase options for patients
- Respect cultural and religious differences
- Create systemic change in reimbursement/payment structures for care at the end of life
- Improve education for healthcare professionals at all levels of training

- Foster research in the area of end-of-life care, including symptom management, quality of life, and new methods of financing and reorganization care
- Address the language gap and current confusion about terms related to end-of-lifecare

Public and professional awareness has been heightened by initiatives led by grant-making foundations, such as the Robert Wood Johnson Foundation and the Open Society Institute's Project on Death in America, and organizations such as Last Acts, the Center to Advance Palliative Care, American Health Decisions, and Partnership for Caring. It is notable that social workers have been part of the work and leadership of many of these initiatives.

Undeniably, the palliative-care movement continues to grow and evolve in the United States. Palliative-care advocates continue to strive to heighten awareness about the barriers and limitations of the current systems of care and the need for better preparation of healthcare professionals and to offer suggestions for policy, reimbursement, and system change. Despite the many strides that have been made in the field of palliative care, challenges remain. This includes addressing a number of problem areas that exist within acute care, long-term care, and even hospice care-delivery systems.

Providing appropriate palliative care when and where patients need it is imperative. Given that hospitals are where the sickest patients in the United States are cared for, it is clear that this is a critical setting for palliative-care programs (CAPC 2002). Studies show that many patients with life-threatening illness spend a significant number of their finals days within the last six months of life in the hospital setting. This percentage is as high as 49 percent of all Medicare enrollees who died in some states (Dartmouth Atlas of Health 1999). As noted earlier, a high percentage of deaths (approximately 53 percent) occur in hospitals, therefore it is imperative for hospitals to be able to address effectively the needs of patients and families facing life-threatening illness and uncontrolled symptoms. Many institutions are responding to reports noting shortcomings in this area by developing palliative care programs. The American Hospital Association reports that 17 percent of registered community hospitals have palliative care programs, and at least 26 percent of U.S. academic teaching hospitals have either a palliative care consultation service or an inpatient unit (CAPC 2002). Some palliative care programs have developed an outpatient care component, such as pain and symptom management clinics. Palliative care programs have, in part, been highlighted in the hospital setting in recent years as they have helped a number of health-care systems to be recognized for meeting national standards of excellence in care at the end of life and other quality standards such as those put forth by the Joint Commission on Accreditation of Healthcare Organizations (JCAHO).

Innovative new initiatives are also emerging that see hospices actively working with hospitals and other healthcare systems to create programs specifically designed to address the gaps inherent in the current system, including the creation of designated inpatient "hospice" beds within a hospital. This represents a focus on bridging the gaps that have historically prohibited seamless care transitions and on identifying areas that need to be improved to insure continuity of care from ambulatory care to hospital to home or other settings (CAPC 2002). This is, in effect, the integration of the philosophy of aggressively managing symptoms, providing psychosocial support and proactively establishing a patient's wishes regarding their care and goals "upstream" to integrate it into all care settings providing services to those with life-threatening and advanced illnesses. Increasing healthcare professional training in symptom management and the principles of palliative care is also seen as essential. There is a strong movement to encourage all practitioners in medicine, nursing and medical social work, as well as other disciplines, to develop skills in this area and to integrate the principles of palliative care into their own practices.

Significant barriers exist in the realm of the current U.S. hospice-care system. Within the current model and parameters of hospice, there has emerged what is perceived by some as a conflict between goals of survival duration and provision of comfort care (Byock 1998). The concept of palliative care has evolved to see curative, life-prolonging therapies not necessarily as mutually exclusive of multidimensional symptom management and supportive care. Serving the patient, however, for whom "curative" or "aggressive, life-prolonging" therapies continue, has been an obstacle for hospices in the United States due to reimbursement mechanisms for hospice care, the costs of such therapies, as well as healthcare professional and patient perceptions. Significant to this discussion is also the Medicare Hospice Benefit eligibility criteria that requires that patients being admitted to hospice programs be certified by their physician as having a life expectancy of six months or less.

Patients and healthcare professionals are often seeking to achieve the goals of supportive care and prolonging life whenever possible. The potentially high costs and the often technology-intensive nature of care in the final months of life also present challenges to the current hospice model. There has been much debate about the adequacy of the Medicare Hospice Benefit and its eligibility criteria. Treatment of advanced cancer, for example, often includes palliative chemotherapy or radiation treatments with the goal of shrinking or slowing the growth of the tumor and decreasing symptoms of the cancer, such as pain. A patient who cannot swallow may receive artificial nutrition or hydration to meet nutritional needs, and halting this treatment may be unthinkable for the patient or family. A patient with a terminal illness may benefit from a course of intravenous antibiotics to deal with a treatable infection and eliminate the symptoms that it is causing. These therapies, which of course should be considered with careful weighing of the benefits and burdens that they offer the patient, are, however, expensive. The cost of these treatments can often exceed what an individual hospice agency can support given the significant reimbursement constraints that exist. A 2001 report on the cost of *routine* home care for Medicare hospice patients found that the cost of daily care ($117.10) was 10–20 percent more than Medicare reimbursement (NHPCO 2002).

For these reasons, among others, there is underutilization of hospice programs; hospice care is not utilized as often it could or should be. Even considering patient populations that do commonly receive hospice care (individuals with cancer, HIV/AIDS), hospices often receive referrals for patients very late in the trajectory of their illnesses. The national median length of service for patients receiving hospice care in 2000 was twenty-five days. Thirty-three percent of those served by hospice died in seven days or less (NHPCO 2002).

Healthcare professional practices, attitudes, and perceptions, as well as those of the patient and family, also influence the utilization of hospice. Misperceptions and misinformation along with personal views contribute to this picture of underutilization (Jennings et al. 2003). For many physicians, the transition to palliative care somehow reflects "failure" on their part to help the patient and they perceive that there is no longer a role for them in the patient's care once hospice becomes involved. Patients and families themselves are at times resistant to agreeing to a hospice-care plan for fear that this implies "giving up," "doing nothing" or that their physician is "no longer treating" the patient.

Referrals to hospice involve a process. The physician must determine that hospice care is appropriate for the patient and that the patient meets eligibility criteria. He or she then suggests that a referral to hospice is now an important part of the medical care plan. Finally, the patient must agree to this plan and accept the services of the hospice agency. This does not signal the end of the patient-physician relationship, but rather a revisiting of the goals of care. Problems, however, can arise at each point of this process. The following case illustrates such a situation.

CASE EXAMPLE

John S. was a forty-one-year-old, self-employed computer consultant with metastatic colon cancer. John and his wife had two children, ages six and nine years. In the course of eighteen months, John underwent two surgeries and two chemotherapy protocols. Despite these treatments, John's cancer reappeared and spread to other organs. He had been determined to minimize the impact of his illness on his family and managed to continue working through most of his treatments, despite experiencing fatigue and very significant weight loss. With the disease spread, he began experiencing increased pain. His local oncologist explained to John the seriousness of the disease spread and prescribed more effective pain medications. He informed him that there was nothing more that he could do for him in terms of cancer treatment but would be willing to follow him for pain management. He recommended referring John to a hospice program. John was angry at this response, saying, "I'm not ready to just give up and die." While John understood that his illness was terminal, he stated that he "did not want to give up" and was willing to pursue any therapy that might have a chance of prolonging his life. He refused the referral. His oncologist, surprised and unsure of how to respond, told him that he should take some time to think about it. John left the office abruptly.

In the next two weeks, John spent many hours on the Internet searching for both experimental cancer treatments as well as alternative forms of healing. He planned to travel for a consultation with a practitioner in California but became too ill to make the trip. Four weeks later, John's very frightened wife contacted his physician when John became too weak to sit up in a chair. His pain had suddenly increased, he was vomiting, and he was refusing any food or liquid. She needed guidance and wondered if she should bring John to the hospital. The children were frightened. Again the suggestion of a hospice referral was raised—and this time, at his wife's insistence, John agreed. Hospice quickly intervened and was able to decrease the intensity of his symptoms. John insisted he did not want to go to the hospital and was agreeable to a do not resuscitate order.

John died just three days after the local hospice agency first visited him and his family. Two years later, John's wife continues to express her feelings of frustration about the lack of support and information that she had access to during his final weeks of life and blames herself for not being more proactive about seeking help.

The misunderstanding, stigma, and resulting anxiety that John personally attached to the concept of hospice care created a barrier. Hospice, in his mind, was care that was given in the last days of an individual's life, when a patient would be kept heavily sedated and unable to interact with family or friends. In fact, the word itself conjured up an image of a large, cold wardroom filled with many dying patients. His misperception about hospice and what it would be able to provide him with at that point of his illness was the unaddressed issue. The need for education was paramount.

Obviously, the short length of time that hospice was able to be involved in his final, and most symptomatic days, created a less than optimal outcome for both John and his wife. In an ideal situation, John would have been able to access expert palliative-care services in a way that felt helpful to him, that support his goals for quality of life and even his search for other alternatives. Perhaps this might have occurred initially via an outpatient palliative-care clinic or via contacts with the hospice when he felt they were needed, maximizing his sense of control. Introducing the role of hospice and palliative care earlier, as opposed to raising it at a point of crisis, might have also made this transition easier and allowed for much more open dialogue about John's hopes and fears. In this scenario, his physician would have also been supported in helping John and his family. An interdisciplinary approach to John's care could have insured that the physical and emotional distress experienced in this family was addressed. This case points to the need for a flexible system of care delivery that can meet the needs of patients, family members, and healthcare providers alike. Public awareness of this special kind of care is also important.

Although much progress has occurred in the development and evolution of palliative care and hospice, many vulnerable populations continue to be underserved at life's end. Current models of care delivery do not serve all persons who are dying and have been criticized for their lack of cultural sensitivity and relevance. Many populations do not have broad access to appropriate care at the end of their lives, including prisoners, refugees and immigrants, those with severe physical and mental disabilities, and homeless persons. The need for well-defined models of pediatric palliative care for children who are dying has also been identified (Field and Behrman 2002). More than 55,000 children die each year (Last Acts 2002).

While hospice is the model of care most integrated in the community setting, it has not historically served a large proportion of nonwhite populations (Jennings et al. 2003). In 2000, the breakdown of hospice clients nationally revealed that 82 percent were white or Caucasian, 8 percent were African American, 2 percent were Hispanic, and 6 percent represented other ethnic and cultural groups (NHPCO 2002). Significant differences exist between cultural groups with respect to their philosophical, spiritual, and social approaches to dying and death. Similarly, the expectations about the family responsibility of caring for an ill family member, as well as the understanding of the role of hospice services and symptom management interventions, differ from cultural community to community. New models of delivering palliative care must consider the cultural differences and norms in their development and outreach strategies (Jennings et al. 2003).

The costs and demands of caregiving at the end of life are a significant issue, for individual families as well as for the healthcare system as a whole. Excellent care of the dying places demands on caregiving resources; this demand is experienced by both professional and family caregivers (Last Acts 2002). This has been particularly problematic in the model where care is provided in the patient's home. Even for those who are referred for hospice services in a timely manner, creating a care plan at home is not without logistical challenges. Many patients do not have family members who can or are willing to assume the role of being their caregiver, especially in the final weeks of life when having around-the-clock assistance is often necessary. Professional constant care is expensive and not always available as needed. The alternative to care at home may be receiving ongoing care in a freestanding hospice (if one exists in their community) or in a nursing home (in concert with a hospice program). The out-of-pocket costs associated are not financially feasible for many individuals without resources. Others may be reluctant to spend their family's inheritance on institutional care and therefore refuse to consider this option.

The numbers of patients that will require ongoing care as the elderly population increases, and the number of illnesses that have become chronic health problems as technology continues to emerge, will have a staggering impact on the healthcare system (Jennings et al. 2003). The number of skilled healthcare professionals that will be needed to provide excellent care at the end of life will also increase dramatically. This is of particular concern given shortages of nurses and other healthcare workers presently being experienced across North America.

How palliative care will become part of the care system, in a regulated or clear way, presently remains undefined. There is little consistency across the country, from institution to institution, regarding what "palliative care" looks like in practice. In 1998, Byock noted, "In one hospital the palliative care service may be identical to hospice, whereas in another medical center it may be a team composed of a part-time anesthesiologist and a nurse and a social worker, in yet another it may be a consult service run by a single, advance practice nurse. . . . Preexisting pain services in medical centers throughout the country have been relabeled palliative care services."

In settings where palliative-care consult services have been established, it is not uncommon for the majority of referrals received to be for those patients who are very near the end of their lives and requiring intensive symptom management. For palliative care to become a routine part of care of those with life-threatening illness, it will require broad accessibility, with the goal of intervention at any point it is needed in the trajectory of the illness. Earlier intervention would include advance care planning, patient and caregiver support and education and proactive, preventive symptom management. Norms and standards of practice need to be developed defining how palliative care should be integrated or provided in various settings.

The greatest challenge for the palliative care movement is to make the vision for better care of the dying a reality. To achieve this involves continuing to change culture and attitudes on multiple levels and to challenge the status quo: from individual healthcare professionals and institutions, to societal views and concepts of advance care planning and about death (Last Acts 2002).

SOCIAL WORK'S ROLE IN PALLIATIVE CARE

Social work has, and continues to play, an important role in the development and evolution of palliative care and its delivery. As clinicians, social workers effectively provide a bridge between the lived experience of the patient and the healthcare system. On a broader level, social work offers a unique and critical perspective to the field of palliative care and end-of-life care. It is the key discipline that intervenes with families in not only healthcare setting, but also where families live: in communities, in schools, in workplaces, through social service agencies, shelters, and crisis centers.

Social-work practice in palliative care draws on the expertise of a number of established arenas of practice and research, including medical social work (and specialized areas such as oncology and HIV/AIDS), hospice social work, and grief, loss, and bereavement counseling. The principles of palliative care are reflective of the core values of the social work profession. Viewing the individual in a holistic way, considering the family as the "unit of care," examining the client's experience across the continuum of care and building on the strengths of the family system are inherent to social work practice. Just as medicine and nursing have begun to create specialized practice in palliative care, social workers also have an expert role (Last Acts 1997). Social workers play a unique role on the palliative-care team in helping patients and families cope with complex medical, psychological, legal, social, and ethical issues associated with advanced illness. Social work's role in palliative care is multidimensional and dynamic, and involves clinical care, advocacy, education, administration, and research (Taylor-Brown et al. 2001).

Practice in palliative care includes completing psychosocial assessments, developing comprehensive treatment plans, participating as a member of the interdisciplinary team, and providing psychosocial intervention with individuals, families, groups, organizations, and communities (AOSW 1997; Taylor-Brown et al. 2001). These interventions include providing individual counseling and psychotherapy; family counseling and family therapy; facilitation of psycho-educational, support, and therapy groups; and crisis intervention (Taylor-Brown et al. 2001; Blum et al. 2001). Social workers in palliative care must also understand principles of bioethics (autonomy, beneficence, nonmaleficence, and justice) and how they relate to dilemmas that arise in end-of-life care (Csikai and Bass 2000). Social workers providing palliative care must be skillful at understanding the principles of multidimensional symptom management (see chapter 19) and contribute to this through the use of cognitive-behavioral and other strength-based approaches (Loscalzo and Jacobsen 1990). Case management, discharge planning, and resource attainment are core interventions, as are providing or referring for bereavement counseling and follow-up care (Taylor-Brown et al. 2001).

Social workers are fundamentally trained to practice from a "person-in-environment" perspective, and this theoretical view is invaluable to the team. The social worker possesses expert knowledge about navigating the medical and social systems that frequently present barriers to the client. Social workers are also experts in communication, both with families but also between the client and the healthcare team. Drawing upon knowledge of family systems and interpersonal dynamics, the social worker is able to examine the family's experience in a unique way and to guide the team in their interactions. Social work's view includes an appreciation of cultural and spiritual dimensions of the family's life. (See chapters 21 and 22 for further discussion.) As experts at helping individuals and families maximize coping in crisis, and at addressing the psychosocial domains of symptoms and suffering as well as the experience of grief and loss, social workers are able to provide intensive counseling for those confronted by life-limiting illness and the myriad of complex problems imposed by illness (Taylor-Brown et al. 2001).

Social work's role as patient advocate is also critical to palliative care. The social-work clinician often engages in advocacy work when linking clients to resources or assisting the patient, family, and team to negotiate goals of care. Social workers may be part of ethics committees or consult teams (Csikai 1997; Taylor-Brown et al. 2001). While the role of the social worker as advocate in palliative care certainly begins with the individual and family, it certainly extends to the institutional, community, and healthcare policy arenas as well (Csikai and Bass 2000). Upholding the principles of self-determination and autonomy, justice, and access for all within the care delivery system are important elements of social work advocacy. Social workers have played a critical role in many areas of healthcare policy creation and reform, and insuring access to quality care for the dying is an area for social action and advocacy.

Another important contribution that social work makes to the palliative-care team is expert provision of education for the patient and family. Imparting information about resources, advance care planning, caregiving tasks and supports, and normal grief response is common to social-work practice in end-of-life care (Blum et al. 2001; Hedlund and Clark 2001). The social worker commonly intervenes when barriers to understanding the complex medical information that is provided to the individual and family are identified, including language barriers, low literacy levels, and cognitive or memory deficits.

The role of the social worker as educator also extends to the provision of education to other social workers and healthcare professionals. It is noteworthy that many of the skills that have historically been unique to social work training, such as interviewing techniques and communication skills, are being incorporated in the training of the disciplines of nursing and medicine. This has created an opportunity for social work to participate in the training of other disciplines. This cross-fertilization of knowledge, values, skills, and attitudes will serve to enhance the functioning of teams and lead to truly interdisciplinary models of care. This multiprofessional education approach will also lead to the enhanced understanding of each discipline's unique knowledge base and skill set (Koffman 2001).

Finally, social workers in palliative care should be prepared to engage in practice evaluation, program development, administration, and supervision, as well as social change (Taylor-Brown et al. 2001; NHPCO 2001). Contributing to the evolving field of palliative care and the literature on care of the dying is a critical area for social workers to be involved in. There is a major area of opportunity for social work to participate in the empirical validation of specific interventions focused on reduction of distress and enhancement of quality of life (Clark 2001).

MOVING THE FIELD FORWARD

A striking example of social work's ability to contribute to moving palliative care forward has evolved out of the Project on Death in America developed by the Open Society. In 1998, the Social Work Leadership Development Award was created. This initiative has served to fund more than forty leaders in both clinical and academic settings to create innovative education programs, to generate critical research, and collectively to move the field forward. The sharing of knowledge and skills and refinement of expertise within this group has lead to much innovation.

An example of such collaborative work is the Social Work Leadership Summit on End-of-Life and Palliative Care, held March 20–22, 2002, in Durham, North Carolina. This meeting sought to formalize collaborative efforts within the social work profession that focus on palliative and end-of-life care. Leaders from national social-work organizations, schools of social work, hospices and hospitals, government agencies, and end-of-life care advocacy groups attended the meeting on behalf of more than thirty organizations. The groups in attendance represented more than 160,000 practicing social workers (Blacker and Christ 2002).

The purpose of the summit was to consider ways to build more capacity, better integrate and coordinate knowledge and skill development, and move social work in end-of-life and palliative care forward within the profession. During this meeting, participants designed a social-work agenda to improve care for the dying and their families. The agenda calls for organized professional leadership, standards of practice, and increased preparation at all levels of social work education. The summit, made possible through cosponsorship by the Last Acts Provider Education Committee, the Duke Institute on Care at the End of Life, and the Soros Foundation's Project on Death in America, was an important step in defining the broad impact that social work can have on the field of palliative and end-of-life care.

CONCLUSION

Palliative care offers many benefits to the healthcare system today. The expert symptom management it provides alleviates pain and other symptoms commonly experienced by patients with advanced illness. Palliative-care teams are highly valued for their ability to assist patients and families in difficult decision making and communication about treatment goals and quality of life. Tangible outcomes of palliative care in the hospital settings are being noted: palliative care boosts patient and family satisfaction, helps to create smooth transitions from one setting to another, and can greatly increase both referral rates and the length of stay in hospice programs (CAPC 2002).

As an integral profession in the palliative-care field, social workers are well poised to shape the future of care for those facing the end of life. In the clinical setting, social workers are expert at connecting patients and families to the services and care that they most need and in providing interventions to ameliorate psychosocial distress. At the policy level, social workers advocate tirelessly for patient rights, improved models of care, and resource allocation. Social workers are increasingly involved in educating and training a new generation of healthcare professionals and consumers. Building on the existing social work knowledge base and experiences, and by embracing new opportunities, social work in palliative care will most certainly continue to evolve.

REFERENCES

American Health Decisions. 1997. The quest to die with dignity: An analysis of Americans' values, opinions, and attitudes concerning end-of-life care. www.ahd.org/ahd/library/statements/quest.html.

Angola Prison Hospice. 1998. *Angola Prison Hospice: Opening the Door.* Documentary film produced by the Center on Crime, Communities & Culture and the Project on Death in America.

Association of Oncology Social Work. 1997. *Standards of Practice in Oncology Social Work.* Baltimore: Association of Oncology Social Work.

Blacker, S. 2000. Core competences for social work: Fellowship in palliative care. Unpublished manuscript.

Blacker, S., and G. Christ. 2002. Social work leadership summit on palliative and end of life care: Background information. Conference handout.

Blum, D., E. Clark, and C. Marcusen. 2001. Oncology social work in the 21st century. In *Social Work in Oncology: Supporting Survivors, Families and Caregivers*, ed. M. M. Lauria, E. J. Clark, J. F. Hermann, and N. M. Stearns, 45–71. Atlanta: American Cancer Society.

Byock, I. 1998. Hospice and palliative care: A parting of ways or a path to the future? *Journal of Palliative Medicine* 1(2): 165–176.

Center to Advance Palliative Care. 2002. The case for hospital-based palliative care. www.capc.org/content/165/index.html.

Clark, E. 2001. The importance of research in oncology social work. In *Social Work in Oncology: Supporting Survivors, Families and Caregivers*, ed. M. M. Lauria, E. J. Clark, J. F. Hermann, and N. M. Stearns, 194–211. Atlanta: American Cancer Society.

Csikai, E. 1997. Social workers' participation on hospital ethics committees: An assessment of involvement and satisfaction. *Arete* 22(1): 1–13.

Csikai, E., and K. Bass. 2000. Health care social worker's views of ethical issues, practice, and policy in end-of-life care. *Social Work in Health Care* 32(2): 1–22.

Del Rio, N., and M. Okazawa-Rey. 2002. *Cross-Cultural Social Work Assessment for Clients at the End of Life.* San Francisco: ACCESS to End of Life Care.

Ferris, F., H. Balfour, K. Bowen, et al. 2002. *A Model to Guide Hospice Palliative Care: Based on National Principles and Norms of Practice.* Ottawa: Canadian Hospice and Palliative Care Association.

Ferris, F., and I. Cummings. 1995. *Palliative Care: Towards a Consensus in Standardized Principles of Practice.* Ottawa: Canadian Palliative Care Association.

Field, M. J., and R. E. Behrman, eds. 2002. *When Children Die: Improving Palliative and End-of-Life Care for Children and Their Families.* Washington, DC: National Academy Press.

Field, M. J., and C. K. Cassel, eds. 1997. *Approaching Death: Improving Care at the End of Life.* Washington, DC: National Academy Press.

Hansen, P., P. Cornish, and K. Kayser. 2000. Live after death with dignity: The Oregon experience. *Social Work* 45(3): 263–269.

Hedlund, S., and E. Clark. 2001. End of life issues. In *Social Work in Oncology: Supporting Survivors, Families and Caregivers,* ed. M. M. Lauria, E. J. Clark, J. F. Hermann, and N. M. Stearns, 299–316. Atlanta: American Cancer Society.

Jennings, B., T. Ryndes, C. D'Onofrio, and M. A. Baily. 2003. *Access to Hospice Care: Expanding Boundaries, Overcoming Barriers.* Garrison, NY: Hastings Center.

Koening, B. 1997. Cultural diversity and decision making about care at the end of life. In *Approaching Death: Improving Care at the End of Life,* ed. M. J. Field and C. K. Cassel, 363–382. Washington, DC: National Academy Press.

Koffman, J. 2001. Multiprofessional palliative care education: Past challenges, future issues. *Journal of Palliative Care* 17(2): 86.

Last Acts. 2002. Means to a Better End: A Report on Dying in America. www.lastacts.org.

Last Acts Task Force. 1997. *Precepts of Palliative Care.* Princeton, NJ: Robert Wood Johnson Foundation.

Lecca, P., et al. 1998. *Cultural Competency in Health, Social, and Human Services.* New York: Garland.

Loscalzo, M., and P. Jacobsen. 1990. Practical behavioral approaches to the effective management of pain and distress. *Journal of Psychosocial Oncology* 8(2–3): 139–169.

Miller, P., S. Hedlund, and K. Murphy. 1998. Social work assessment at the end of life: Practical guidelines for suicide and the terminally ill. *Social Work in Health Care* 26(4): 23–36.

Munroe, B. 1993. Psychosocial dimensions of palliation. In *The Management of Terminal Malignant Disease* (3d ed.), ed. C. Saunders and N. Sykes, 174–201. London: Edward Arnold.

——. 1994. Role of the social worker in palliative care. *Annals of the Academy of Medicine, Singapore* 23(2): 252–255.

National Cancer Institute. 2001. *Improving Palliative Care in Cancer.* Washington, DC: National Academy Press.

National Hospice and Palliative Care Organization. 2001. *Competency-Based Education for Social Workers.* Arlington, VA: National Hospice and Palliative Care Organization.

——. 2002. NHPCO facts and figures. www.nhpco.org/public/articles/Facts&Figures-2002.pdf.

National Hospice Organization. 1999. *Facts and Figures on Hospice Care.* Arlington, VA: National Hospice Organization.

Soskis, C. 1997. End-of-life decisions in the home care setting. *Social Work in Health Care* 25(1–2): 107–116.

SUPPORT Principal Investigators. 1995. A controlled trial to improve care for seriously ill hospitalized patients: The Study to Understand Prognoses and Preferences for Outcomes and Risk of Treatments (SUPPORT). *Journal of the American Medical Association* 274:1591–1598.

Taylor-Brown, S., S. Blacker, K. Walsh-Burke, T. Altilio, and G. Christ. 2001. Care at the end-of-life. Society of Social Work Leadership in Health Care.

World Health Organization. 2003. http//:who.int/hiv/topics/palliative/Palliative Care.

Zabora, J., and M. Loscalzo. 1998. Psychosocial consequences of advanced cancer. In *Principles and Practices of Supportive Oncology,* ed. A. Berger, 531–545. Philadelphia: Lippincott Raven.

21

INTEGRATING SPIRITUALITY AND RELIGION

BARBARA DANE

HEALTH CARE for those approaching death has changed its focus from a disease model in which cure is the goal to one that focuses on comfort care to improve the quality of the end of life. In this latter orientation, holistic care is then provided for patients whose disease is not responsive to curative treatment with the expectation that they can achieve a death that is free from "avoidable suffering and pain." Emotional support from family and caregivers is essential that is consistent with the dying person's cultural, religious, and spiritual needs. Spiritual well-being and the reduction of psychological distress are critical parts of comfort care.

This chapter discusses distinctions between religion and spirituality and the role of religion and spirituality in social-work practice. It examines the role of rituals in bringing comfort and meaning to patients and families. It looks at how families convey and identify their spiritual beliefs. Finally, it explores the clinician's beliefs surrounding religion and spirituality as she grapples with her own mortality.

THE ROLE OF RELIGION AND SPIRITUALITY
IN END-OF-LIFE CARE

For many, death is the closing out of one form of being in hope of another. For others, death ends life. One goal of spiritual care of the dying is to help some to see themselves at a time of transition and others to find peace and acceptance.

The process of dying is unique to each individual. The symptoms experienced by dying patients reflect their underlying disease processes and organ systems involved, the presence of coexisting conditions, the medical interventions that are chosen, and patients' spiritual and emotional states (Paterson 1998).

For most, the mystery of death and dying defies imagination. What is seen of death is the finality of the physical body. But what is believed about the meaning of death, how it should be faced, and what happens after physical death varies by cultures and associated religions. All cultures help to make meaning about why the death has occurred at this time and in the ways many loved ones have died. For example, when a death occurs, religion and spiritual practices help with the expression of grief and with remembering the person who has died. Many cultures are rich in ritual; for example, Buddhist families chant at the temple during the dying process to facilitate a calm and peaceful atmosphere and help the dying person, and wailing has been noted among African Americans, people of Mediterranean descent, and others. One commonality of grief among cultures is crying as an expression of grief (Rosenblatt, Walsh, and Jackson 1976). Other cultures hold differing beliefs: Mexican Americans are likely to touch the body of the deceased, and Japanese Americans are likely to kiss the body. Families from the former Soviet Union who are Russian Orthodox or Catholic keep vigil over the coffin for several days (Kalish and Reynolds 1981). We look to our religions for advice on how to act. The culture prescribes rituals when a death occurs, and many people find comfort in them. Culture presents a structure within which death takes on meaning (DeSpelder and Strickland 1992; Johnson and McGee 1991).

Clinicians have long recognized the significance that religious and spiritual themes have with the dying and bereaved. Yet in a nation as religiously and culturally diverse as the United States, clinicians may feel inadequate to the task of addressing their clients' spiritual needs. Spiritual and religious beliefs may also have significant influence on the course of bereavement.

THE DISTINCTION BETWEEN RELIGION AND SPIRITUALITY

As we enter a third millennium, a new interest in religion and spirituality has emerged. The meanings of religion and spirituality have been a matter of controversy. Religion and spirituality affirm the power in "material" forms to reveal the presence of the divine—not only through "official" religious actions such as the liturgy or objects as sacred scripture, but also through the worlds of nature, music, and the visual arts (Webb 2001).

The concept of religion includes social institutions with rules, rituals, covenants, and formal procedures. Spirituality refers to an individual's personal experience of meaning making. For some, it is a connection to formal religion but spirituality is predominantly viewed as not associated with organized religion (Miller and Thoresen 1999).

Two related themes dominate the *Oxford English Dictionary*'s ten pages on the concept of spirituality. First, spirituality is concerned with life's most animating or vital qualities. Second, spirituality incorporates the more immaterial features of life. This is distinct from the body or other more tangible and material things, including our senses, such as sight, smell, touch, sound, and hearing (Simpson and Weiner 1989).

J. D. Morgan states that the term "spiritual" is identified with religion, but is not a term that has its roots in religion. "The word spirit comes from the Greek word 'pneuma' which means breath. As thought emerged, our ancestors identified the word spirit with living things; that is, those who had breath. It was not until Plato that the spiritual became identified with the immaterial" (Doka and Morgan 1993:3–4).

From ancient to modern times, various cultures have viewed health and disease as directly related to a variety of religious beliefs and practices that include prescriptions of certain diets, physical activities, and types of quiet reflection and prayer (Rosen

1993). Several spiritually focused books have gained prominence on the *New York Times* best-seller list during the last ten years. Some of these books, for example, are Thomas Moore's *Care of the Soul* (1992), Mitch Albom's *Tuesdays with Morrie* (1997), or Deepak Chopra's *How to Know God* (1999). They reflect a public need to connect health and physical functioning to religion and spirituality. Major news magazines such as *Time* and *Newsweek* have featured lead articles about spirituality and health, and special issues have been published in scholarly journals (e.g., *American Psychology, Annals of Behavioral Medicine, Journal of Health Psychology*, and *Health Education and Behavior*). Clearly, there is a strong movement among Americans to integrate both religious ritual and spiritual affirmation into their daily lives. The capacity for self-transformation and healing over the life span, and especially at the end of life, provides a process of finding meaning and purpose.

Thoresen, Harris, and Oman (2001:23) summarize the following assumptions about spirituality and religion:

• Religiousness and spirituality as concepts represent primarily functional or process-oriented phenomena (e.g., coping, social integration), not fixed structural characteristics (e.g., religious denomination). That is, religion-spirituality factors are concerned with the changing nature of what the person does, thinks, feels, and subjectively experiences within particular social and cultural contexts. They commonly are not fixed traits or unchanging characteristics.

• Both religion and spirituality are multidimensional in nature. Some dimensions can be easily observed (e.g., attending services), and some dimensions have latent (underlying or unseen) qualities that are not readily observed (e.g., feeling closeness to God). In this way they are much like the concepts of personality, health, and love. Just as personality is more than behavior, health more than blood pressure, and love more than sexual arousal, spirituality is more than feeling connected to life, and religiousness is more than attending church services.

• Religiousness and spirituality are not adequately assessed by questionnaires with one or a few items, nor are they comprehensively measured using just one mode of assessment (e.g., only questionnaires or only personal accounts or narratives). Unlike fixed traits, most spiritual and religious factors change with time and circumstances; therefore, multiple assessments appear more desirable than single assessments in representing these constructs.

Faith is commonly identified with a religious belief system. Some argue that religion is the more inclusive concept, with spirituality as its major focus: "Religion is a search for significance in ways related to the sacred" (Pargament 1999:11). Spirituality has been used as an even more inclusive term, where religion may or may not be included. Different terms emerge and overlap in meaning. Spiritual care, however, is to be based on a universal concept rather than only focusing on religious concepts. In summary, spirituality is the essence of one's human nature that can be expressed through religious practices or beliefs.

MEANING AND RITUALS

In every culture throughout history, mourning rituals have developed to help people accept the deaths of those close to them. In ancient Mesopotamia, tear vials, similar to bud vases, were found buried with the deceased in tombs. This simple act acknowledged the emotional significance of loss, the value of grieving, and—in burying those tears with the deceased—the importance of moving on with life (Walsh and McGoldrick 1991).

Some clinicians have used rituals to promote healing. Transforming a familiar ritual or creating a new ritual is a powerful intervention in healing, because a survivor can tailor the ritual to her individual experiences and needs. Healing is not a linear process, but a circular working and reworking. The rituals described by some clinicians show that they serve different functions and can be effective at different stages of healing. For example, a birthday celebration can help to commemorate a death, while photographs may be used to facilitate the process of reminiscing or to help break the silence around the taboo of AIDS. Through rituals and creative acts, clients are able to relive the wonderful and painful memories and affirm that they are now strong enough to go on. Clinicians have observed the similarities between psychotherapy and creative acts and suggest that therapy itself can function as a ritual process for clients (Dane and Miller 1992).

Although rituals can focus on a specific stage of healing or bereavement, they are often most effective if they explicitly affirm the developmental tasks and healing stages mastered previously by the client, and also initiate goals for the future. Individual, interpersonal, and communal levels are vehicles for healing and may be important for a survivor (Dane and Miller 1992).

Stories offer a natural language for children and adults. Stories that heal often exude optimism and hope, providing nourishment and encouragement about the possibility of change. It is best to avoid all verbal analysis or attempts to promote the children's conscious awareness of the underlying meaning of the stories. Children possess resilience, despite their emotional and spiritual pain related to death. Rituals provide a way to master cycles of disruption while remembering, integrating, and transforming the loss (Dane 2002).

Interpersonal contact is important for breaking through the feelings of isolation, shame, and secrecy caused by a death. Rituals can provide such interpersonal contact if they incorporate family, friends, and significant others who have a history with the deceased. A client may need to be encouraged to reach out to others as well as to strengthen her relationships to facilitate her grief (Dane and Miller 1992).

THE ROLE OF SPIRITUALITY IN SOCIAL WORK EDUCATION

Despite the lack of training in the social work arena and lack of explicit attempts to address spirituality, social work interventions with spiritual issues beneficially affect client outcomes. Reese (2001) further states that social work educators and field work supervisors should include the following as part of social work education: the definition of spirituality, identification of spiritual issues, models of practice that can be used to address these issues with terminally ill clients and families, diverse spiritual interventions, values about honoring diversity, proper documentation of spiritual interventions, values about the importance of addressing spirituality, awareness of personal issues of social workers that inhibit them from addressing spirituality, and approaches to address client difficulty in discussing spiritual issues.

Newman (1995:767) suggests the application of the following aspects of healing for educators:

- To incorporate learning opportunities for students to address their own healing process consciously in preparation for promoting the healing of their clients.
- To facilitate learning among students through self-reflection, self-discovery, and personal and professional development.
- To discuss the role of social supports as provided by and to family members and friends in the healing process.

Clients who are dying teach the clinicians lessons about life and death and healing more often than we teach them. The gift of exploring spirituality in times of adversity and suffering opens us to a world of transcending pain and surmounting the challenge of death.

THE ROLE OF RELIGION AND SPIRITUALITY IN SOCIAL WORK ASSESSMENT

Direct practice with dying patients and their loved ones easily triggers a universal anxiety, as clinicians are faced with an end of a life. Based on their beliefs, many clinicians may make efforts to retreat or they may make vigorous efforts to be aware of the threat of death anxiety. The social-work literature has recently begun to focus on religion and spirituality to understand work with individual and families and to tap into this resource of healing and growth.

In assessing clients at the end of life, clinicians need to attend to the client's formal religious and spiritual affiliations, beliefs, practices, and rituals. These provide useful information and communicate to the client the clinician's openness to discussing such concerns. Although the client's belief system may be different from the worker's, respect for those values and traditions needs to be communicated. Although many questions remain as to how to incorporate a spiritual perspective in intervening with clients at the end of life, the spiritual dimension of the work can no longer be overlooked. According to Hassed (1999), everyone has the capacity to question and make meaning. He suggests that the search for meaning seems to be a universal healing need that is taken for granted in our lives.

Merman (1992) outlines five probing statements that can be posed to clinicians working with person's approaching death:

1. Does life have meaning?
2. What is the patient's view of life after death?
3. What will it mean to "not be?"
4. How do we listen to seriously ill and dying patients?
5. What does it mean to be honest with the dying?

Clinicians need to understand how history, religion, and personal experience influence an individual's attitude toward the end of life. These experiences play out in how much patients trust healthcare providers, communicate treatment preferences, complete advance directives, favor euthanasia, and participate in organ donation. Clinicians need to be culturally sensitive to hear patients' fears in order to address their particular religious and spiritual concerns and to draw on them as resources.

CLINICAL EXAMPLES

The following cases will illustrate how patients, family, friends, and caregivers use "care of the soul" as an integral part of comfort care. Discussions and reflections often focus on questions of why, why me, why now, and for what purpose. These provide the opportunity for exploring and using people's faith systems and spirituality to help them at this time in their lives. Each of these vignettes illustrates another aspect of this process describing how the worker was helpful. The following vignette illustrates how a connection was made and maintained to the client through meditation and was then used to help her through this very difficult period in her life.

CASE EXAMPLE

Theresa, a fifty-six-year-old woman, met the clinician for a screening interview during her fourth hospitalization, asking "to set the last years of her life straight and be able to know she could die in peace." Five years ago, Theresa had been diagnosed with metastatic cancer from the breast to the spine. She was able to maintain her position at an investment bank. As her illness progressed, she spent more time at home, which caused her a great deal of distress. She went on disability. She tried to see the bright side of her situation, but until her pain was managed, she was in a stressful situation and could not resort to her rituals of healing. "Do you really want to get to know me?" she asked. Acknowledging my interest, Theresa said that what helped her most was daily meditation. "We could start our time together with five minutes of being quiet," she said. I agreed and encouraged her to take the lead. "If you pay attention to the breath," she said, "you feel aware of everything that is going on in the room." It was the best way she knew to relax. She said that before her divorce, she and her husband went on several religious retreats. This was something wonderful that she remembered and continues to practice. This reflection in time gave us an opportunity to discuss some unresolved feelings about her husband and her present thinking about having him visit her in the hospital. She also remembered him buying her Kabat-Zinn's tape on mindful meditation.

Listening to Theresa's story of her life through her discussion of meditation practice, as well as joining her each visit and beginning the session with a five-minute silent meditation, enabled her to voice her concerns and struggles of her life before her diagnosis. She reflected upon feelings of inadequacy in not having had children and how her life as a computer specialist in an investment bank, enabled her to "parent" younger people in the field. She acknowledged her accomplishments in creating animated program projects and in mentoring two women at her last job. This sense of closeness and accomplishment in her work life allowed her to discuss and explore her fears and feelings of loneliness and worry that her pain would be so severe that, "no one could help."

Listening attentively to her concerns on multiple levels: psychological, interpersonal, and spiritual, I asked who she would like to join her on her journey toward death. These discussions around emptiness and aloneness freed her to call on the two women she had mentored and upon her sister who was close to her at an earlier age. This connection, which began with the spiritual, was important in my listening for indications of significant relationships that might help her achieve a sense of relaxation—a form of meditation.

Over the next ten months until Theresa's death, her life was filled with the three women who surrounded her, providing her with comfort and peace. She taught them the meditation practice that we used in our clinical work. Her sense of humor resurfaced, and she discussed her burial arrangements. She requested that the three women scatter her ashes in the Sheeps Meadow section of Central Park, where she often attended the free concerts. As she lapsed into unconsciousness the week before her death, her sister and two colleagues took turns with her so she would not be alone. She died surrounded by her three loving women.

Mindful meditation practice and its clinical application began to draw attention in the 1970s as a way of understanding the connection between body and mind (Shapiro and Walsh 1984). Innumerable personal accounts exist regarding the positive impact of meditation on the ability to experience meaning, gain a sense of transcendence, and feelings of peace (Kabat-Zinn 1990; Shapiro and Walsh 1984). Cuthbert et al. (1981) have established that individuals previously unfamiliar with meditation could use it more effectively than biofeedback to lower their heart rates. This area of research has demonstrated the value of simple meditation techniques in assisting individuals to gain a state of increased relaxation. A challenge for clinicians is to integrate meditation as part of a therapeutic process to develop spiritual growth.

CASE EXAMPLE

Helen, a ninety-three-year-old Caucasian woman, suffered for three years before death with congestive heart failure. A devout and religious person, Helen prayed the rosary and novenas daily throughout her adult life. She was admitted to the nursing home from the hospital after a severe bout with pneumonia. Initially she felt this placement as a death sentence and longed to return home to live with her daughter and grandchildren.

However, three days after her admission to the nursing home, she was interviewed by the social worker to assess her psychosocial needs and her family supports. As the social worker entered Helen's room, she found her sitting on a rocking chair reading her novena prayers. Although she looked very frail, her smile radiated her countenance. She said she understood this was her time before she would die and be reunited with her parents, sister, brothers, and husband. Indeed, she was not in denial and was aware of her impending death. Helen talked about her daughters and their families' involvement in her life. "I never have to worry, they are always there." This elderly woman conveyed a sense of serenity and peace.

Over the next two years, Helen continued to deteriorate. She had difficulty ambulating with her walker and was confined to a wheelchair. She was able to voice her deterioration by stating, "I am closer to my Maker, inching my way to the end." Helen's conversing with God through prayer or her use of metaphors in describing her deterioration, seemed to provide her consolation in her connection with God. She did however, state quite emphatically that she did not want to be resuscitated and wanted to make sure her "living will and DNR orders were on her chart."

Sometimes it is hard to trust what medical personnel will do, in that so many workers come and go. The social worker, together with her daughters, reassured her that no extraordinary measures would be taken, but supportive care would be provided. It was at this time that hospice care was discussed and Helen agreed, again restating her wish for "dying in peace."

One day during a visit with her older daughter, Helen spoke of a visit from an angel. "The angel said, 'Your time is not up.'" Helen found this comforting.

Helen died surrounded by her family and nursing staff. Her rosary was linked between her fingers as she quietly died.

O'Connor states that "one does not change a lifetime of examining spiritual needs just because one is dying" (1988:33). It is important, therefore, that when assessing these needs, the social worker recognize the resources the patient has identified as having helped to meet these needs in the past. The process of assessment and re-assessment are frequent in order to identify spiritual needs. Many patients may have strong affiliations with religious institutions. Efforts to continue and bridge these connections are important. It is important to evaluate the patient's resources to enable him or her to meet psychosocial needs based on life patterns of behavior. This was illustrated in the case of Helen, who was involved in her religious traditions where she found solace and nurturing for her soul.

Burkhardt (1998) discusses approaches to dealing with spirituality in holistic clinical practice. Holistic practice requires attentiveness to the spirituality of both the clinician and client. This involves developing the awareness of oneself as a spiritual being and seeking to live in healing ways with oneself and others. Assessments require the art of "being with" another with the intent of coming to know who the person is and facilitating the person's coming to a fuller understanding of herself within the context of all of her life experiences. Considering questions such as what is sacred to the person, what brings joy or causes fear in living, where and with whom the person feels a sense of connectedness, and how a person understands God or if they have a sense of an Ultimate Other, are some ways of approaching making a spiritual assessment.

CASE EXAMPLE

Mrs. J. called to request an appointment with the social worker in the AIDS clinic when it became clear that her son's death was imminent. In her first interview, she told the worker that her major concern was her husband's steadfast refusal to allow John's longtime partner to visit him and his threats to exclude him and other friends from participating in the funeral. She described her sense of helplessness in the face of her husband's adamant stance and raised some minimal concerns about what she might have done to prevent John from leaving home.

The worker inquired about Mrs. J.'s feelings about her son's illness and the fact that he might die soon. Mrs. J. began crying as she told the worker about how promising John's life was from his earliest years of schooling through law school. She fully expected him to become a very important person and perhaps surpass his father's accomplishments as a lawyer. She described him as having an artistic flair, able to play the piano, and very good at social relationships. He had always had good relationships with his two sisters, who kept contact with him even while he was living in San Francisco.

She told me about how sad it was to see him so ill, suffering so much pain while still trying to respond to the interests and concerns of other family members. She knew that she would miss him a great deal, because they talked about so many different areas of life and have similar views about things. "He has been easier to talk with than my husband, at times."

I helped Mrs. J. understand how she was grieving John's death, even though he was still alive. We reviewed the range of emotions that Mrs. J. had been feeling: her anger at this untimely death, her feelings of guilt when she thought of what she might have done differently with John, and her disappointment about things that would never be, given that he would die before realizing his potential.

Mrs. J. called two days after she and her husband had visited John and wondered if we could have a family session. I wanted first to explore the request with John and would follow up on the request with the J.'s.

John welcomed the visit with his parents and felt a joint session would give him an opportunity to make peace with his family and relieve some of his guilt for hurting his parents, even though he said, "my life was a short party." It seemed that John wanted to seek forgiveness as he spoke of repairing the relationship with his parents in the short time he had left before his death. I explored this with John and he acknowledged that it was the next to the last hurdle he would have to master before he died. The other was having his loving partner be at his bedside and, if not welcomed by his family, at least be tolerated.

Forgiveness is described by religious scholars as a reflection of God's love, embodied in acts of reconciliation, renewal and reparation (Marty, 1998). Using this to guide my discussion with the J's, I arranged to have a family meeting. Mr. J. arrived for the first joint session with his wife in John's private room. He was visibly angry. I noted his emotional reactions and began to explore this with him. Mr. J. said that he was very upset because his wife and two daughters were angry with him because of his refusal to allow John's friends to visit him in the hospital. "They couldn't understand that I did not want a bunch of faggots parading around my neighborhood, and having my friends and neighbors talking about us."

The worker acknowledged his anger and his disappointment with John. Mr. J., fighting back tears, recalled his relief that John had moved away, coupled with his anger at "not having a son in my life." John cried initially and felt his father's pain but said he was relieved finally to hear his father's thoughts because he too had been in pain. The sessions revealed many previously controlled feelings, and I helped him to grieve over John's death and old unresolved wounds. Mrs. J. cried throughout the session but indicated that she felt relieved that they were at last talking. She requested follow-up sessions, and both John and Mr. J. agreed.

Mrs. J. began the second session, again expressing her pleasure regarding the work they had initiated. She commented that "for the first time this week, my husband and I began to really talk about John." Mr. J. responded, saying that "John's life-style has always been difficult for the family." He recalled that John had become aware of his sexual preference in high school and seemed determined to live a homosexual lifestyle openly. John refused to go to the prom and threatened the family that he would come out publicly. Mr. J. reported being scared that his partners in the law firm would become aware of John's homosexuality. "I was later concerned that our friends would also become aware of John's activities in the gay community and that the stigma would reflect on us. I was happy when John decided to relocate to San Francisco, since the move made it less likely that my colleagues and friends would hear about John and his activities. It also gave me a chance to be selective about what I revealed about John."

The worker acknowledged the societal stigma against gays and their families. This led to fuller exploration of Mr. and Mrs. J.'s experiences with being the parents of a homosexual. They each shared secrets that they had kept from the other, from friends and from their minister. Mr. J. stated that he felt uncomfortable about telling his minister and fellow parishioners about John. "I still have not revealed that John has AIDS." The worker explored the theme of stigma throughout the session, helping the couple to appreciate that they were not alone and to consider ways in which they might respond to others (Dane and Miller 1992).

For the J's, forgiveness was an interpersonal process that addressed the profound hurt and disruption that they had suffered. Reconciliation is a separate process from forgiveness, and thus defined as a two party action in which both the victim and injured work toward a resolution of their differences (Enright 1996).

Using a psychodynamic model of forgiveness, the focus is on internal readiness and the restoration of the symbolic function of the good object (Bloom 2001). In summary, how forgiveness should be addressed in treatment depends upon who the person is forgiving and how the disruption can be mediated. Forgiveness and reconciliation are often expressed in the spiritual domain.

THE THERAPIST'S SPIRITUAL COUNTERTRANSFERENCE

Social work practice with clients who are terminally ill presents unique issues for the clinician. When working with clients in the context of death and dying, issues of survivor guilt, the fear of death, and the existential meaning of life become integral parts of the work (Goldfinger 1990). Some of the underlying affects of fear, anger, guilt, grief, and denial parallel work with the client and clinician creating opportunities to grapple on both a personal and relational basis.

Farber (1994) notes the therapist's helplessness in working with patients diagnosed with HIV and AIDS. He defines helplessness as the experience of impotence, defenselessness, and powerlessness stemming from feeling a lack of control to change the situation and suggests that the clinician's self-doubt makes it difficult for her to offer effective treatment and to develop accurate empathy toward the client. There seems to be a parallel process in a worker's spiritual countertransference where imminent death raises existential issues for both client and worker. Questions arise about the worker's spiritual attitudes and belief systems. Van Wormer (1990) addresses social attitudes in Western cultures toward death, such as denial and escape through medical jargon, which makes it more difficult to acknowledge and examine one's spiritual needs.

Many clinicians have not recognized the value of religion and spirituality in their own lives and assessing the role of spirituality in a patient's life can be a challenge. The words "spirituality" and "religion" have different meanings and stir up responses that may affect treatment regardless of well-meaning intentions. It is also hard for clinicians to overcome the critics from the scientific world who do not see spirituality as part of a person's care. Due to these taboos, many clinicians feel discomfort in this area. Most clinicians have had little or no training in relation to religion and/or a person's spiritual needs. John T. Chirban states that before commencing treatment, the clinician should consider the following:

1. Clarify his or her approach to addressing religion and spirituality in therapy. It can be helpful to patients if, when asked, the clinician articulates his or her clinical approach to and treatment plan for addressing these issues.
2. Assess the degree to which his or her understanding of and interest in pursuing religious and spiritual material matches the patient's objectives. Additionally, when the clinician has a clear understanding of his or her objectives in addressing religion and spirituality, the ethical boundaries of treatment must remain focused.
3. Recognize his or her basic prejudices, biases, and values regarding the nature of "healthy" spirituality. It is important to identify one's own religious and spiritual values separate from those of the patient.

4. Modulate language so that it is genuine, professional, and in synchrony with the patient's. The clinician may need to clarify his or her use of terms and express sensitivity to the meanings that religion and spirituality hold for the patient (2001:284).

The following case example points to how the worker's countertransference interfered with her ability to help her client.

CASE EXAMPLE

Mrs. S. was a seventy-two-year-old widow who attended weekly sessions at the local senior center. Her husband had died of pancreatic cancer, ten months ago after a short illness. She cared for him during his illness and responded to the support of the hospice team. She felt close to Jo Ann, the social worker at the senior center. She felt Jo Ann was the daughter she always wanted. Jo Ann attended Mr. S.'s wake and the funeral and arranged for supportive intervention from Cancer Care. Mrs. S. also attended weekly services at the nearby Methodist church. She attended the coffee hour after the service and received support from some of the church elders.

During the last six weeks, Mrs. S. complained to Jo Ann about a pain in her throat especially when she swallowed. An appointment was made and a battery of tests was initiated. Ten days elapsed and Mrs. S. was diagnosed with cancer of the larynx. She openly voiced concerns over her fears of not being able to talk and the pain she may experience, and she wondered, based on her religious beliefs, if it was a punishment from God. Jo Ann reassured her that she would help with symptom management and negotiate with her doctor now and in the future so that Mrs. S.'s pain would be controlled. Mrs. S. felt some reassurance but continued to express her worries and concerns regarding her death and what would happen to her when she died. It was very difficult for Jo Ann to hear about her concerns of being punished by God since she was not raised in any religious tradition, and many times, she avoided the topic, feeling only that a dark cloud surrounded her. Jo Ann had no experience with religion or death in her family of origin since her paternal and maternal grandparents were still alive. Jo Ann also was not raised in a faith tradition, but felt connected spiritually to life's beauty: flowers, walks in the park, sunset cruises. Her only remembrance of death was that of Skippy, her dog, who died when she was five years old. She remembered how she came home from kindergarten one afternoon and her mother comforted her, saying Skippy was hit by a car. She cried for a few days. The following week, her father brought home a white kitten, Snowflake, who she did not like since the cat would bite her when she went to pet it. In supervision, she related this account, but did not connect her difficulty mourning Skippy's death with Mrs. S.'s ongoing discussions of her struggle to get up in the morning and difficulty sleeping at night. It was hard to explore her fear of dying alone.

In her supervisory conferences, Jo Ann was given permission to discuss her feelings of Skippy's death and draw the parallel of not saying good-bye, to her work with Mrs. S. She related her uneasiness when Mrs. S. talked about life after death and a punishing

God. Not having any ideas other than that the body no longer lives, she felt inadequate to explore Mrs. S.'s feelings and her religious beliefs.

During subsequent meetings, Jo Ann was able to explore Mrs. S.'s fears and began a "life review" of her losses and areas of accomplishment. She allowed Mrs. S. to express forgiveness, and an appreciation of her life and work with Jo Ann. Mrs. S. was able to seek legal help and get her affairs in order over the next six months. Ongoing adjustments were made to her medication and a referral to a "Doula" service was initiated. Jo Ann also began to ask Mrs. S. about her wishes when she died. Did she want to be cremated, or buried at the local cemetery? Jo Ann shared that her personal wishes were to be cremated and her ashes strewn round the six-acre park in the nearby town.

Jo Ann's initial fear created a blind spot in the work. Using her supervisor, personal therapy, and discussion with her family helped to connect to her undeveloped spiritual life, which contributed to initially "missing" the religious beliefs of Mrs. S.

This brief case vignette illustrates that a sense of comfort and peace can be initiated and worked through for the patient, if there is parallel work in supervision with the clinician's unresolved grief and attendance to the clinician's spiritual life.

CONCLUSION

Although the field of palliative care is in its infancy, social workers are attending more to end-of-life issues. Despite previous misconceptions and trepidations, social workers have begun to recognize the significance of the spiritual domain in the lives of their clients. A number of schools of social work are offering electives in spirituality, the Society for Spirituality and Social Work has recently emerged, and social workers have begun to adapt some relatively familiar methods and techniques to uses in exploring spiritual issues with their clients.

Although negative connotations about spirituality exist in the profession, education is a powerful medium to expose clinicians during their training and help them be comfortable with spiritual issues. As Scanlon and Chernomas (1997) note, reflection cannot occur without awareness, which is a need to know and to be curious about something. Self-reflection can be described as an event that occurs in the present moment, and can promote health, support a peaceful death, and provide insight and new perspectives.

Social workers face difficult discussions in their work with dying patients and their families. More than likely, they have belief systems that support a balance of their personal and professional roles through self-care. Caroline Myss describes healing as an "active and internal process that includes investigating one's attitudes, memories, and beliefs with the desire to release all negative patterns that prevents one's full emotional and spiritual recovery" (1996:48).

One of the important challenges for social work clinicians is to capture the many dimensions of clients, whether living or dying, that place emphasis on the interconnectedness of their expressions of healing. Forgiveness, hope, and a search for meaning are some concepts that offer a springboard to understand the extraordinary, complex, and multifaceted expressions of a client's culture. Social workers need to attend both to the positive and negative effects of a person's religion or spirituality and their link to the health and/or dying trajectory.

In summary, personal reflection enables us to gain insight into our experiences and understanding of life and death issues, and to develop a deeper understanding of who we are. Attention to our questions, wonderings, pain, joy, and struggles facilitates and shapes our healing (spiritual) presence with another (Burkhardt 1998) and can contribute significantly to helping our clients make meaning at the end of their lives.

REFERENCES

Albom, M. 1997. *Tuesdays with Morrie.* New York: Doubleday.

Bloom, S. 2001. In the shadow of the World Trade Center disaster: From trauma to recovery. *NASN New York State Chapter Update* 26(3): 5–9.

Burkhardt, M. A. 1998. Spirituality: An analysis of the concept. *Holistic Nursing Practice* 3(3): 69–77.

Chirban, J. T. 2001. Assessing religious and spiritual concerns in psychotherapy. In *Faith and Health: Psychological Perspectives,* ed. T. Plante and A. Sherman, 104–128. New York: Guilford.

Chopra, D. 2000. *How to Know God: The Soul's Journey Into the Mystery of Mysteries.* New York: Random House.

Cuthbert, B., et al. 1981. Strategies of arousal control: Biofeedback, meditation, and motivation. *Journal of Experimental Psychology: General* 110:518–546.

Dane, B. 2002. Bereavement groups for children from families with HIV/AIDS. In *Helping Bereaved Children* (2d ed.), ed. N. B. Webb, 226–241. New York: Guilford.

Dane, B., and Miller, S. 1992. *AIDS: Intervening with Hidden Grievers.* Westport, CT: Auburn Press.

Derezotes, D. 1995. Spirituality and religion: Neglected factors in social work practice. *Arete* 20:1–15.

DeSpelder, L. A., and A. L. Strickland. 1992. *The Last Dance: Encountering Death and Dying.* 3d ed. Mountain View, CA: Mayfield.

Doka, K., and J. Morgan, eds. 1993. *Death and Spirituality.* Amityville, NY: Baywood.

Enright, R. D., and the Human Development Study Group. 1996. Counseling with the forgiveness triad: On forgiving, receiving forgiveness, and self-forgiveness. *Counseling and Values* 40:107–146.

Farber, E. 1994. Psychotherapy with HIV and AIDS patients: The phenomenon of helplessness in therapists. *Psychotherapy* 31(4): 715–723.

Goldfinger, S. M. 1990. Psychiatric aspects of AIDS and HIV infection. *New Directions for Mental Health Services* 48:5–20.

Hassed, C. 1999. Spirituality and health. *Australian Family Physician* 28:387–388.

James, W. 1985. *Varieties of Religious Experience.* New York: Random House.

Johnson, C. J., and M. G. McGee, eds. 1991. *How Different Religions View Death and Afterlife.* Philadelphia: Charles Press.

Kabat-Zinn, J. 1990. *Full Catastrophe Living.* New York: Delacorte.

Kalish, R., and D. Reynolds. 1981. *Death and Ethnicity: A Psychocultural Study.* Farmingdale, NY: Baywood.

Kass, J. D., R. Friedman, J. Lesserman, P. C. Zuttermeister, and H. Benson. 1991. Health outcomes and a new index of spiritual experience. *Journal for the Scientific Study of Religion* 30:203–211.

Marty, M. E. 1998. The ethos of Christian forgiveness. In *Dimensions of Forgiveness: Psychological Research and Theological Perspectives*, ed. E. L. Worthington Jr., 9–28. Philadelphia: Templeton Foundation Press.

Merman, A. 1992. Spiritual aspects of death and dying. *Yale Journal of Biology and Medicine* 65:137–142.

Miller, W. R., and C. E. Thoresen. 1999. Spirituality and health. In *Integrating Spirituality Into Treatment*, ed. W. R. Miller, 3–18. Washington, DC: American Psychological Association.

Moore, T. 1992. *Care of the Soul*. New York: HarperCollins.

Morgan, J. D., ed. 1993. *Personal Care in an Impersonal World: A Multidimensional Look at Bereavement*. Amityville, NY: Baywood.

Myss, C. 1996. *Anatomy of the Spirit: The Seven Stages of Power and Healing*. New York: Three Rivers.

Newman, J. S., and K. I. Pargament. 1990. The role of religion in the problem-solving process. *Review of Religious Research* 31:390–404.

O'Connor, P. 1988. The role of spiritual care in hospice. *American Journal of Hospice Care* 5(4): 31–37.

Pargament, K. I., et al. 1999. The vigil: Religion and the search for control in the hospital waiting room. *Journal of Health Psychology* 4:327–341.

Paterson, M. 1998. Families experiencing stress: The family adjustment and adaptation model. *Family Medicare* 6(2): 202–237.

Raxxen, G. 1993. *A History of Public Health*. Baltimore: Johns Hopkins University Press.

Reese, D. J. 2001. Addressing spirituality in hospice: Current practices and a proposed role for transpersonal social work. *Journal of Religion in the Social Services* 20(1–2): 135–161.

Rosen, E. 1998. *Families Facing Death*. 2d ed. San Francisco: Jossey-Bass.

Rosenblatt, P., R. Walsh, and D. Jackson. 1976. *Grief and Mourning in Cultural Perspective*. New Haven, CT: HRAF Press.

Scanlon, J. M., and W. M. Chernomas. 1997. Developing the reflective teacher. *Journal of Advanced Nursing* 25:1138–1143.

Shapiro, D. H., and R. N. Walsh, eds. 1984. *Meditation: Classic and Contemporary Perspectives*. New York: Aldine.

Simpson, J. A., and E. S. Weiner. 1989. *The Oxford English Dictionary*. 2d ed. Oxford: Clarendon Press.

Thoresen, C. E., A. Harris, and D. Oman. 2001. Spirituality, religion, and health: Evidence, issues, and concerns. In *Faith and Health: Psychological Perspectives*, ed. T. Plante and A. Sherman, 19–35. New York: Guilford.

Van Wormer, K. 1990. Private practice with the terminally ill. *Journal of Independent Social Work* 5(1): 23–37.

Walsh, F., and M. McGoldrick. 1991. Loss and the family: A systemic perspective. In *Living Beyond Loss: Death in the Family*, ed. F. Walsh and M. McGoldrick, 259–274. New York: Norton.

Webb, G. 2001. Intimations of the great unlearning: Interreligious spirituality and the demise of consciousness wheels in Alzheimer's. *Crosscurrents* 51(3): 324–336.

Worden, J. W. 1991. *Grief Counseling and Grief Therapy: A Handbook for the Mental Health Practitioner*. New York: Springer.

22

A FRAMEWORK FOR MULTICULTURAL END-OF-LIFE CARE: ENHANCING SOCIAL WORK PRACTICE

NORMA DEL RIO

J UAN WAS a thirty-four-year-old Mexican man with end-stage AIDS. His wife Lola, also Mexican, was HIV-positive. They had two healthy HIV-positive daughters. Juan and Lola were both devoted Catholics. Juan was wheelchair-bound, and his right side was paralyzed. When Juan was informed that his condition was terminal and his prognosis was less than four months, he and his wife turned to what was known to them: faith healers. They found a faith healer, or *curandero*, who also practiced natural medicine. This person told them that to strengthen their immune system and fight the disease they had to change their diet to a natural diet, instructing them to start eating raw vegetables and to stop eating meat or any animal products. He even told them to stop using toothpaste and to use vinegar and water instead. The healer also instructed them to stop taking their medications because they were making them sicker. They followed his instructions. The faith healer would visit them and rub different oils on different parts of their bodies to remove what he believed was malicious contamination. Both Juan and Lola felt "better" the first few days of this treatment, but after a week they both became very ill. They both developed thrush in their mouths and esophagi. Eating became a painful experience for them. Lola developed an unusual skin condition and had to be hospitalized in isolation for seven days. Juan developed severe diarrhea and became dehydrated and weaker. He died three months after this episode. The diarrhea was an unresolved problem to the end. Lola went back on her medications, and she is alive and healthy today.

When we reflect on the story of Juan and Lola, the following questions emerge: Did they act "responsibly"? What would acting "responsibly" mean from their perspective? As a healthcare provider, what does acting "responsibly" mean? Was it the healthcare provider's responsibility to persuade them not to follow the healer's recommendations? If you were the social worker working with this family, what role should you have played in Juan and Lola's decision?

The true story described here is not an exception. Physicians, nurses, social workers, chaplains, and other healthcare providers face similar situations with their patients every day in this country. Similarly, many patients turn to what is most familiar to them, such as faith healers, as they search for a cure, answer, or explanation for their terminal illnesses.

As professionals working with the dying, we know that the threat of terminal illness often leaves patients, families, and caregivers with fear, frustration, anger, and hopelessness. For a person or family from an ethnic, religious, or cultural group different from that of the dominant culture, the experience can be even more devastating and disorienting. We all are vulnerable to diseases, and, as humans, we all share the common condition of death. But even though death is universal and inevitable, we all behave differently when we are sick. No one dies the same way. Many factors influence our physical, emotional, spiritual, and psychological responses to illness, death, dying and grief. And many of us, like Juan and Lola, when we are sick or facing an adverse situation, turn to what is familiar: our culture, religion, and/or spiritual practice to seek explanations, answers or meaning for our illness and suffering.

Our cultures also affect the way we express pain or suffering, and they determine what healing systems we may use to treat the illness. When we face the death of a loved one, we consciously or unconsciously look for advice, refuge, comfort, and strength in the rituals, traditions, practices, and behaviors that our culture provides. Culture not only affects healing and how we express our grief, but it also guides us through our bereavement process with directions for how to remember our loved ones (DeSpelder and Strickland 1992; Johnson and McGee 1991).

But the mystery of death is further complicated when the healthcare provider lacks the understanding, skills, knowledge and attitudes needed to provide end-of-life care in a multicultural environment and when the patient is caught up in the collision of medical, legal, ethical, scientific, technological, and bureaucratic tangles characteristic of our healthcare system (Braun, Pietsch, and Blanchette 2000). For people of color, the dying process is made more difficult by historical discrimination and lack of targeted medical research. Social and economic inequalities, language barriers, and the disproportionate access to health care further exacerbate the problem.

This chapter will discuss a conceptual framework for multicultural end-of-life care where ethnic and racial discrimination and culture are considered as they intersect with health care. I will then make recommendations about the use of cross-cultural assessments, cross-cultural communication, and the use of interpreters.

WHY IS A MULTICULTURAL FRAMEWORK TO END-OF-LIFE CARE NECESSARY?

As the United States becomes more multiethnic and multiracial, the provision of end-of-life care to diverse populations will become the norm rather than the exception. This is reflected in this country's demographics.

The population of the United States is changing rapidly. In 1950, 90 percent of the population of the United States was of white, European origin. As of the year 2000, over 25 percent of the population was composed of members of nonwhite ethnic groups. Experts in demographics project that by the year 2050, nonwhites will triple in population, with Asians representing 11 percent of the U.S. total, Hispanics/Latinos increasing from 9 to 21 percent, and African Americans increasing from 12 to 16 percent. It is expected that whites, who at the beginning of this decade (2000) comprised 75 percent of the population, will drop to 53 percent (U.S. Census Bureau 1999, 2000,

2001). In January 2002, a Harvard Graduate School of Education press release stated that "census projections suggest that in fifty years the United States will be the only major post-industrial democracy in the world with ethnic *minorities* [emphasis added] constituting nearly half of its population."

As the census points out, the West Coast is the most multiracial and ethnically diverse area in the United States (Ness 2001b). Recent statistics from the U.S. Census Bureau indicate that California's minority population became the majority in 1999. This is the first time that whites have not had a majority, at least since census data began to be collected in 1860. In 1990, non-Hispanic whites comprised 57 percent of California's populations; this population dropped to 49.8 percent in 2000, according to the U.S. Census Bureau.

In California, Latinos account for 31.5 percent of the state's population and Asians are just more than 12 percent. In addition, Asians and Latinos are the fastest-growing ethnic groups, with both populations increasing by nearly 35 percent between 1990 and 1999. The non-Hispanic white population was the only ethnic group to decline during this period, from 17 million in 1990 to 16.5 million in 1999. The population of blacks and American Indians increased slightly, with blacks accounting for 7.5 percent of California residents. California also has the most mixed-race people: 1.6 million, about three times the number in New York or Texas. Over one-quarter of Californians were born in another country, a level not seen since 1890. Nationally, the percentage of people born elsewhere has reached an estimated 11.2 percent, its highest point since 1930 (Verdin and Genaro 2000; Ness 2001a).

As these demographics show, the United States is becoming a pluralistic society. But while cultural differences existed in the first half of the last century, the goal was assimilation. The country was seen as a "melting pot" for these diverse communities. We are now moving toward a view of cultural pluralism that is more of a "cultural mosaic," where each piece of the mosaic preserves its distinct color and characteristics but at the same time forms part of a bigger piece of art.

How do we, as social workers, respond respectfully to cultural differences? How do we make use of beliefs, native healing practices, and cultural rituals that honor who our clients are but that may differ from our own? What is needed from social workers in order to provide end-of-life and bereavement care in a multicultural context?

In order to develop the understanding, skills, knowledge, and attitudes needed to provide end-of-life and bereavement care in a multicultural setting, the social worker needs to recognize that his or her individual view of reality is always socially constructed, does not account for all the phenomena of life, and should not take precedence over a client's view of reality. There are always multiple ways in which an individual understands and makes sense of her own life and each person is unique in how she may respond to life's challenges such as illness and death (Braun, Pietsch, and Blanchette 2000).

As social workers providing end-of-life care in a multicultural environment with a commitment to decreasing cultural misunderstanding and misinformation, we have to embark on a personal journey to create a new consciousness about differences. This is the only way we can then promote change at the institutional and societal levels.

How and when does one begin this personal journey? It begins when a person decides to examine the various roles of culture, race, ethnicity, religion, gender, and sexual orientation that define one's identity. Such a self-evaluation process—to know who we are and why we feel, think, and behave in certain ways—is a lifelong undertaking.

WHAT IS CULTURE?

Culture is a complex term, meaning different things to different people. As we embark on a discussion of multiculturalism in end-of-life care, it is important to define culture. Sujata Warrier says the following about the word: "Culture refers to the shared experiences or other commonalities that groups of individuals—based on race, ethnicity, sexuality, class, disability status, religion, age, immigration, or other axes of identification—have developed in relation to changing social and political contexts" (1998:3).

As this definition suggests, culture is not static, stable, or fixed (Warrier 1998, 2000). Rather it is fluid, multifaceted, often changing, and contains contradictory elements. Culture is often transmitted unconsciously. Changes in culture occur at different rates. For example, changes in technology and economics (material culture) occur faster than changes in other components of culture like family and religion. Culture influences the way one views the world, life, and death, and how one is going to respond to life challenges.

The term *culture* is also widely used to refer to religious groups (e.g., the culture of the church), specific regional groups (e.g., the culture of the American South), and specific institutions (e.g., the military). Each of these groups has explicit or implicit rules of conduct and a language that includes a set of symbols associated with the group (Braun, Pietsch, and Blanchette 2000).

There are variations among individuals of a same culture, for example: levels of education, class differences, religion, rural vs. urban environments, acculturation levels, and so forth. Individuals may also identify with more than one culture and may adopt beliefs, traditions, and behaviors of other groups and cultures. Thus, culture is the mix that makes an individual who he or she is. If we use this simple definition, then, there is no room for stereotyping because each person will have a unique and different culture. But "to say that as human beings we don't share similarities is to deny our basic humanity. Yet, to say that we are all the same—or color blind—is to deny the unique fabric of our lives that defines who we are and our worldview" (Hendrix 1999:9).

The traditional definition of culture, however, has frequently been conflated to include race and ethnicity. But culture is not limited to race and ethnicity. When we refer to culture in the context of ethnicity and race, it has to be understood within the history of oppression in the United States. Within this context, we are really speaking of power, dominance, and subordination. But other social, cultural, or religious groups that are not necessarily ethnic or racial groups—for example, women and gays and lesbians—have also been systematically discriminated against based on their gender, sexual orientation, or religion.

Not all ethnic, racial, or cultural groups have been victims of discrimination or oppression. But many have. For example, in the United States we have witnessed the oppressive treatment of Native Americans, the slavery of Africans, and the historical consequences and impact of such dehumanizing system on people of African descent, Jews who were barred from entering this country to escape the Holocaust, the Japanese internment camps, and the Chinese Exclusion Act of 1882, to mention a few.

Ethnic groups that have traditionally been devalued by the mainstream culture encounter serious health access problems, often live in underserved communities, and face limitations in the quality of end of life care. Hence, discrimination, coupled with economic inequality and a history of oppression are important features of many ethnic and racial groups whose individual members find themselves battling within the healthcare system.

Terry Cross (1995–96) observes that "to work toward culturally competent and family-centered practice, professionals need to acquire knowledge about the impact of a culture's history on families. That history includes the history of each individual's relationship with the mainstream culture, the federal government, and the helping professions."

DEVELOPING A CONCEPTUAL FRAMEWORK FOR MULTICULTURAL WORK IN END-OF-LIFE CARE

Hence, every individual has a culture, comprising values, beliefs, and traditions. "Our received culture dictates, to a profound degree, how we respond in any given situation, on conscious and unconscious levels. How we behave toward people who are different from us is a learned behavior. No one is born with prejudice or born racist" (Hendrix 1999:9). Hendrix reminds us that from our earliest experiences we were taught, either explicitly or implicitly, from those people who took care of us and in whom we trusted, usually our families. We learned from them who it was okay to be with and with whom not to associate. Usually it is through these first experiences that we begin to develop our biases, prejudices, judgments, and assumptions about people who are different from us.

Thus, through socialization, families and institutions in our communities form our cultural frameworks. Some of these institutions include the family, schools, churches, the media, social clubs, and so forth. At a personal level, the challenge we have is to identify the past teachings, biases, misinformation, and conditioning embedded in our cultural frameworks that promote division and separation among us. As social workers, we have to uphold the principle of social justice by challenging the many forms of discrimination, which unfortunately, are all too prevalent in today's health-care system.

Can we talk about cultural differences in health care without talking about health access problems, underserved communities, limitations in the quality of end-of-life care for underserved populations, and social justice? Can we leave out talking about how race matters in health care, especially in care at the end of life? The literature is replete with many examples of how race factors into inadequate or substandard end-of-life care.

For example, in an editorial in the *New England Journal of Medicine*, Freeman and Payne (2000) state that "a growing body of compelling and disturbing evidence points to inferior medical care for black Americans, even if they are on an equal economic footing with whites." In a study about racial differences in the treatment of early-stage lung cancer, Bach et al. (1999) found that blacks are less likely to receive surgical treatment than whites, and they are more likely to die sooner than whites. Another study shows that black and Hispanic patients receiving palliative care at a major urban teaching hospital are less likely than white patients to be able to obtain commonly prescribed pain medicines, because pharmacies in predominantly non-white neighborhoods are significantly less likely to stock adequate supplies of opioids than are pharmacies in predominantly white neighborhoods (Morrison et al. 2000). According to Morrison et al., this finding, together with reports (Cleeland et al. 1997; Todd, Samaroo, and Hoffman 1993; McDonald 1994) that nonwhite patients are significantly less likely than white patients to receive prescriptions for analgesic agents, suggests that members of racial and ethnic groups are at substantial risk for the undertreatment of pain (see chapter 19).

In another survey that mirrors Morrison et al. study, the *Detroit News* surveyed two hundred of the seven hundred retail pharmacies in Michigan's Oakland, Macomb, and Wayne counties and reported that filling prescriptions for painkillers is much easier in suburbs than poorer communities (Kurth, Chambers, and Patterson 2002). The *Detroit News* survey found that just one in five drug stores in poor communities stock OxyContin or morphine, opioids prescribed to alleviate severe pain for those with cancer or other terminal illnesses. "Morphine is available in more than half of the suburban pharmacies, while 87 percent of them carry OxyContin" (Kurth, Chambers, and Patterson 2002). These findings underscore national worries about the delivery of health care to the poor and contradict claims from the industry that pain relief is equally available to all.

A survey conducted by the Commonwealth Fund (2001) about racial disparities in the quality of care for enrollees in Medicare managed care, found that Hispanics are less likely than whites or African Americans to receive important preventive services, in particular, cancer screening (Schneider, Zaslavsky, and Epstein 2002). Compared with the total population (17 percent), a significant large proportion of Hispanics age fifty and older (30 percent) have never been screened for colon cancer. Schneider, Zaslavsky, and Epstein (2002) report that African Americans were less likely than whites to receive breast cancer screening (62.9 percent vs. 70.2 percent), diabetic eye exams (43.6 percent vs. 50.4 percent), beta blockers (64.1 percent vs. 73.8 percent), and mental illness follow-up (33.2 percent vs. 54.0 percent).

Ayanian et al. (1999) report that among patients with chronic renal failure who wanted a transplant, blacks remained significantly less likely than whites to have been referred for evaluation and significantly less likely to have been placed on a waiting list or to have received a transplant within eighteen months after the start of dialysis therapy. They state that even among patients who said they were very certain that they wanted a transplant, blacks were substantially less likely than whites to have been referred for evaluation (62.8 percent of black women vs. 83.6 percent of white women, 62 percent of black men vs. 83.2 percent of white men) and were substantially less likely to have been placed on a waiting list or to have received a transplant within eighteen months after the start of dialysis therapy (44.2 percent vs. 71.4 percent and 45.4 percent vs. 70.8 percent, respectively). These racial differences remained significant after adjustments for patients' preferences, sociodemographic characteristics, the cause of renal failure, and the presence or absence of coexisting illness.

Whittle et al. (1993) showed that white patients consistently underwent cardiac procedures (cardiac catheterization, PTCA, and CABG) more often than black patients. They report that their data, coupled with the results of other studies, suggest the existence of race-related inequities in the healthcare system. Although they cannot establish the extent to which subtle or overt racism underlies racial differences in the use of cardiac procedures, they believe that inadequate health education, differences in patient's preferences for invasive management, delivery systems that are unfriendly to members of certain cultures, and overt racism may all play a part (Whittle et al. 1993).

Along with all the data that point out racial disparities in the access to treatment and the quality of health care for people of color and poor people, we also find evidence of the barriers people of color face in accessing and receiving hospice services. One study found that hospice admission criteria, especially the primary caregiver requirement, were identified as impeding access for blacks (Gordon 1996). The same study showed that Hispanics faced the most access and service problems and were the most underserved. Hospices identified problems in serving Hispanics as language, reimbursement, and severity of illness issues (Gordon 1996). Brenner (1997) reports that according to information available from the National Hospice and Palliative Care Organization (1995) hospices served a patient base that was 85 percent white, 15 percent nonwhite. Hospices were staffed by personnel who were 90 percent white, 10 percent nonwhite. Sixty-five percent of all patients served were covered by Medicare; 7 percent of all patients were covered by Medicaid; 70 percent of all patients were sixty-five years old or older; 78 percent of all care provided by all hospice programs was provided to persons with cancer; and AIDS care represented 4 percent of the total persons cared for by hospices. Brenner argues that based on these statistics "it is clear that hospice has been relatively successful in serving middle-class, elderly white persons with cancer who have family members available and willing to care for them at home. Hospices as a whole have not been successful in providing access to *end of life care* [emphasis added] to persons and illnesses which diverge from this basic profile" (Brenner 1997).

In light of this disturbing evidence, how do we start changing the current healthcare paradigm to make it more responsive and equitable to all people? In order to insure that the diverse dying patients are appropriately cared for, it is important to understand how systems in our society are structured in ways that perpetuate health disparities. A theoretical framework might be helpful in analyzing the complexities of human and race relationships and cultural differences. Keep in mind that this is an exhaustive topic, and this will not even begin to address the magnitude of this social phenomenon.

I will use systems theory to analyze the racial relations in our society. This theory provides the basis for understanding how a society is organized and how it maintains balance through social mechanisms. This theory is but one way to analyze social and ethnic relations. Given the complexity of human relationships and identity politics, other approaches for the study of this topic are recommended.

The first social exchange we have is with our parents or with the caretakers who raise us. The family, in whatever form, constitutes a social "system." Thus, we will use the "micro" or "personal" level to refer to the person or individual in that system. It is at this level where the transformation process to affect change begins. It is at this level where consciously or unconsciously, intentionally or unintentionally we manifest prejudice or bias and maintain attitudes and feelings about the superiority of one group (usually whites) and the inferiority of other groups (usually people of color). The personal or micro level refers to the individual's beliefs, values, prejudices, and assumptions.

We said before that in order to understand and accept other people's realities and cultural differences we have to begin a process of self-exploration, and I would add, self-healing. Racism or any kind of oppression hurts both the oppressed and the oppressor. But how can we begin to heal these wounds? One way of doing it is through embracing *multiculturalism*.

Valerie Batts (1998) defines multiculturalism as the process of *recognizing*, *understanding*, and *appreciating* differences as well as similarities. These steps do not happen necessarily in order or simultaneously. They can overlap at any time. These steps are not a mere exercise of knowledge. Each one of them involves *thinking* (because the mind has to work with the information and misinformation it has about differences), *feelings* (because the heart has to undergo transformation), and *behavior* (because the process cannot take place only in the heart and mind). When the transformation begins, our behaviors and practices start to change.

As we engage in this transformation process, the questions to ask ourselves are: How do I identify myself racially, ethnically, and culturally? When was I first aware of my own culture? What is the first memory I have of someone dying in my family? What were the rituals, practices, or behaviors that my family observed at that time? Do I observe some of these rituals and practices? How important are they for me now? As we examine our cultural formation, we can also use these questions to explore our patients' racial/ethnic and cultural identifications.

Other questions for practitioners are: What aspects of my cultural background strengthen my work in end-of-life care? When was one of the first times that I noticed someone who was different from me? What did I notice? Who was present when this happened? What did the people who were present say about that person? When was one of the first times someone made assumptions about me based on a cultural identifier? When was one of the first times I made assumptions about someone based on a cultural identifier? What stereotypes about another person or people have I accepted without having the right information about that person or those people?

What aspects of my cultural background present challenges to my work in end-of-life care? As these questions are explored, we will be defining our personal cultural frameworks and enhancing our ability to work with and take care of diverse clients. These are crucial questions to explore if we want to have a multicultural perspective in end-of-life care that is responsive to the cultural and medical needs of our dying clients.

The "mezzo" or "interpersonal" level includes the family, community, school, hospital, and so forth. At this level, behaviors based on conscious or unconscious assumptions about self and others are expressed through interpersonal manifestations of racism, or classism, or anti-Semitism, or a range of other "isms." At the mezzo level we ask: How do I interact across differences? How do others interact across differences? What are the values of my family and my community? What are the values of other communities, cultures, and groups with which I interact? How do these values influence the way I interact with people of diverse cultural and/or ethnic background and the way they interact with me? What are the values of the organization or agency I work for or the organizations/agencies I interface with in my practice? How can I advocate for those who are least able to advocate on their own behalf? When I faced a challenging cross-cultural or cross-ethnic situations in my practice, what were the factors that contributed to the challenge? How did I handle the situation? Were there any conscious assumptions on my part about the person or persons involved in the situation? Were there unconscious assumptions about me and/or others that were brought up to the consciousness as a result of this situation?

The "macro" or "institutional" level refers to major institutional systems that form our society. The macro level also includes laws, policies, procedures, and practices. These institutional systems with their laws, policies, and practices influence the society in which we live. These systems include religion, health care, education, the military, and law. Many times the laws and policies that support these systems help perpetuate social injustice.

When we find the racial and ethnic disparities in end-of-life care that have been reported, we realize that multicultural end-of-life care implies more than an individual provider's adoption of a multicultural approach for caring for and supporting a person and their family through the final stages of that person's illness and bereavement. It also requires that institutional systems undergo substantial transformation. This transformation begins with the social worker's looking at the policies, laws, practices, rules, norms, procedures, and values that function to the advantage of one group and the disadvantage of others who are dying. It requires a deliberate institutional effort to provide training that heightens awareness of institutional barriers. It also requires that hospices and end-of-life care programs increase the cultural diversity of their staffs and improve their outreach and services to communities of color. As social workers, social activists, and community organizers, we need to consider how to stimulate interest in underserved communities and how to develop partnerships in these communities to work toward increased and more appropriate end-of-life care. We need to help empower people to act on their own behalf. As a result, the end-of-life programs serving these communities may look a bit different from the more traditional model.

In order to understand the interconnections and complexity of racial and ethnic relations and how they play out in end-of-life care, it is necessary to look at issues at the micro (personal), mezzo (interpersonal), and macro (institutional) levels. As Kirk and Okazawa-Rey point out, "oppression is a group phenomenon, regardless of whether individuals in a group think they are oppressed or want to be in a dominant position. Men, as a group, are advantaged by sexism, for example; white women, as a group, are disadvantaged. Every form of oppression—sexism, racism, classism, heterosexism, anti-Semitism, able-bodyism—is rooted in our social institutions such as family, education, religion and the media. Oppression, then, is systemic and it is systematic. It works through systems of inequality as well as the dominance of certain values, beliefs, and assumptions about people and how society should be organized. These are institutional and ideological controls" (1998:3).

Thus, race, ethnicity, class, gender, sexual orientation, age, culture, education level, religion, immigration status, and disability have been used to deny, restrict, or limit access to essential human services, including health care. One of the tenets of the social work profession is to pursue social change, particularly with and on behalf of vulnerable and oppressed individuals and groups of people. Thus, social workers can pursue social change in health care by carefully analyzing the systems in which they work, challenging those organizations and institutional systems that are oppressive, and advocating for policy making that brings about social change, justice, and equality.

APPLYING A MULTICULTURAL FRAMEWORK TO AN END-OF-LIFE SITUATION

The following real case example presents different issues that can arise in a multicultural end-of-life care setting. The scenario can be analyzed from a number of perspectives: as a patient, as a social worker, as a nurse, as a home health aide, as a manager/administrator, as a community member.

CASE EXAMPLE

An eighty-five-year-old white female patient was dying from lung cancer with metastasis to the bones. She was bedbound and no longer able to care for herself. She lived with her sister, who was also elderly and frail and unable to assist her. Because she needed twenty-four-hour care, she decided to utilize the private duty services of the agency that provided her home hospice care.

Her twenty-four-hour care required three eight-hour shifts of attendant care providers known as home health aides (HHAs). African-American HHAs filled two of the shifts. Soon after the attendant care started, the patient told the social worker that she only wanted white HHAs because she was "terrified by the black HHAs." The social worker, who was Latina, inquired about the care and treatment that she was receiving from the African-American HHAs. The patient had no complaints with their care and treatment but was fearful because of experiences she had with African Americans while living in an inner-city neighborhood. The social worker inquired about these experiences, and the patient replied, "Nothing really, just what I have seen."

The social worker discussed this with the white nurse case manager who felt that the patient had the right to make such requests as she was paying for the service and was "on her deathbed." He said to the social worker, "You're not going to change her attitude. She's dying!" The issue was discussed at case conference without resolution. Not satisfied, the social worker brought the issue to the chair of the Multicultural Committee, who suggested that the social worker speak to the director of the private duty department.

After full consideration of the issues, the director decided that: (1) the patient could not be granted her request as that would put the agency at risk for being sued by African American employees for racial discrimination; (2) the director would inform the African American HHAs about the patient's feelings and give them the choice of staying on the case or being reassigned; (3) the patient would be informed of the nondiscrimination clause in the home healthcare contract and be given the choice and provided the assistance to transfer to another local hospice agency. The nondiscrimination policy was expanded to include this type of situation and published in the agency newsletter.

This scenario brings up issues at the micro, mezzo, and macro levels. The request to change HHAs came from the patient's personal (micro) cultural framework that shows feelings, values, beliefs, prejudices, stereotypes, and biases against black people. But let us look at the implications of this request at the mezzo/interpersonal level: The nurse case manager as well as the social worker also analyzed the request from their own personal experiences and through the lens of their races. Could race have determined their different responses to the situation? How does one (the supervisor) handle the interpersonal problems a situation like this creates between the members of the interdisciplinary team and the members of the hospice program? How did the HHAs feel about this racist request? Should the request be honored given that this person was dying and she was paying for the services? What implications would honoring the request have had on the racial and ethnic relations within the interdisciplinary team and the other diverse staff in the hospice program? Was the agency abandoning the patient by offering transfer to another agency?

At the macro level: What are the institutional issues the administrator was facing? Did the administrator handle the problem in a way that was sensitive to both the patient and the HHAs? What policies, practices, and procedures were in place at this institution to guide the administration's response to the situation? What could have been the institutional implications of any response to this situation? In what ways does this situation mirror the racial tensions and dynamics that characterize a society where color still divides even at the end of life?

The patient was informed about the decisions, and she decided to stay with the agency and the same HHAs. One of the HHAs decided to be reassigned, and the other stayed on the case. The HHA who stayed on the case was able to work well with the patient and had the opportunity of being asked for forgiveness. Although this issue divided the hospice agency across racial lines, eventually, and after several conversations, it brought the nurse case manager and the social worker closer as they had to work through their own cultural differences. The agency's multicultural committee was able to work with the administration to develop a nondiscrimination policy that would include patients' special requests. As the social worker involved in this case, I felt satisfied with the outcomes, although I recognize that this was a very sensitive, difficult, and painful process for many people. One of the factors that determined the positive result was the willingness of the many players, including the administration, to look at the personal, interpersonal, and institutional sides of the issue and examine the values, principles, policies, and procedures of the institution in order to consider the implications for the patient, the employees, and the agency.

GUIDELINES FOR MULTICULTURAL END-OF-LIFE CARE

Let us focus now on the relationship between the practitioner and the patient. What is needed in order to provide end-of-life care that is responsive to the medical and cultural needs of our diverse clients? Effective multicultural end-of-life care includes an awareness of cultural aspects of pain and symptom management, cross-cultural assessment, cross-cultural communication, spiritual diversity, cross-cultural grief and bereavement, and the use of interpreters. Given the scope of this chapter, we will only discuss cross-cultural assessment, cross-cultural communication, and the use of interpreters.

CROSS-CULTURAL ASSESSMENT

One of the most important elements of a successful intervention and a patient-centered practice is assessment. When doing cross-cultural psychosocial assessments of patients who are at the end of life, the social work practitioner has to be mindful of the following: the cultural identity of the individual; the cultural factors related to the person's psychosocial environment; the cultural elements of the relationship between the individual and the healthcare provider; and the cultural explanations of the individual's illness (DSM-IV, Outline for Cultural Formulation, Appendix G, p. 897).

When we talk about the cultural identity of the patient, we are talking about how the person identifies him/herself. Does the patient identify with more than one culture? What is the patient's degree of acculturation? In other words, how close is the person to the native culture or to the host culture? If the patient is an immigrant, when did the patient immigrate to the United States? It would be important to assess how acculturated are other members of the family and if the different levels of acculturation present any conflicts in the interaction with the patient and family. Also, what are the patient's language preferences and writing and reading skills?

The cultural factors related to a person's psychosocial environment are important. Hence we identify stressors in the local environment, the role of religion, and the patient's support systems (what is the role of family and what family does the patient identify with?). We also assess the food preferences and prohibitions, and the patient's economic situation (is the income adequate to meet the patient's needs?). The cross-cultural assessment should include the patient's reliance on traditional healers and remedies. In many cultures, people seek and use alternative therapies, or traditional healers and remedies before seeking care from Western doctors. Some people may use a combination of both Western medicine and alternative healing systems at the same time, as in the case of Juan and Lola. This is understandable, inasmuch as traditional healers share the same language, culture, and belief system as the patient. They are usually in the neighborhood where the patient lives and may charge less than Western doctors for services. It is important to ask patients if they are taking herbal medications or medications from their country of origin, and ask what the purpose and effects of these treatments are. Some prescription drugs and herbal medicines taken in combination may have toxic effects that can be avoided.

Cross-cultural assessments have to take into consideration the cultural elements of the relationship between the patient and the social worker or the healthcare provider. It is important to notice differences with respect to culture, religion and social status and the impact of these differences on communication and in negotiating an appropriate relationship. A nurse colleague who works in a nursing home once told me about the cultural and religious clashes that occurred with a group of nurse assistants who were Catholic and wanted to say the rosary to some of their dying non-Catholic patients. While the action was well intentioned, the non-Catholic patients and other staff saw this as insensitive and imposing.

As we negotiate an appropriate relationship and provide health care, we have to be very careful with stereotyping clients. Tervalon and Murray-Garcia (1998) tell us about an African American nurse who was caring for a middle-aged Latina woman several hours after the patient had undergone surgery. A Latino physician on a consult service approached the bedside and, noting the moaning patient, commented to the nurse that the patient appeared to be in great deal of postoperative pain. The nurse summarily dismissed his perception, informing him that she took a course in nursing school in cross-cultural medicine and "knew" that Hispanic patients overexpress "the pain they are feeling." Although it is good to attend cultural competence trainings and learn about the ethnic populations we work with, it is more important to attend to the clues (in this case the moaning) as a part of the patient's present reality.

It is also important for social workers and any healthcare provider to notice how patients interface with different cultures as they navigate the healthcare system and how this experience can be extremely frustrating, even traumatic. There is a dynamic interaction between the culture of medicine and health care, the personal culture of the practitioner, and the culture of the patient and his/her family. For example, "in the end of life, many people are in a mood of separating, in a reflective mode, searching for meanings. That is very different from what a busy clinician is doing." Kreier writes, "To Arthur Kleinman, M.D., the Harvard psychiatrist and anthropologist who is one of the leading thinkers in the field of cross-cultural health care, every encounter between a physician [we would say "clinician"] and a patient is a cross-cultural experience, because the "illness experience" of the patient is different from the "disease process" that is the natural province of the physician [clinician]" (Kreier 1999). The cultural divide is intensified when, in addition to the terminal illness, patients and their caregivers are dealing with racial, ethnic, religious, age, and gender differences.

Cross-cultural assessments should always include the cultural explanations of the individual's illness. This includes the identification of predominant idioms of distress through which a need for support is communicated. For example, many Latinos will use the expression "*ataque de nervios*" (panic attack) when they are going through an intense emotional experience. A Latino patient may have, or feel like having, an *ataque de nervios* when a terminal diagnosis is disclosed to him/her. Likewise, some Latinos may feel like having or have an *ataque de nervios* if they know that a close relative is close to dying or has died. This may be their way of trying to cope with the experience and what they may be saying is that they need support. This can be a signal for social workers to know what would be considered appropriate support in the context of the relative's life.

Other people may explain an illness episode as someone possessing spirits, or *mal de ojo* (evil eye). The assessment should also include any local illness category used by the individual's family and/or community to identify the condition or symptoms. For example, in El Salvador and Nicaragua many people use the word *vasca* for nausea, whereas in other Spanish-speaking countries they use the same word as in English.

In order for the care to be patient-centered, no matter what the culture of the patient is, the practitioner has to elicit specific information from the patient about how he or she understands the illness, that is, the patient's illness explanation. This information will help the practitioner to organize the strategies for clinical care and will assist patients and families in making more useful judgments about treatments.

EXPLANATORY MODELS OF ILLNESS

Illness explanatory models are the different ways patients, families, and practitioners explain a specific illness episode. There may be two kinds of explanatory models: that of the patient and family, which are informal descriptions of the illness; and that of the practitioner, which is the medical explanation of the disease. The patient's and family's explanatory models often contain contradictions and shift in content. They are anchored in strong emotions and feelings that are difficult to express openly. Therefore, they have enormous clinical significance. Sometimes the patient's or family's explanatory model is in conflict with that of the provider. When this happens, negotiation skills are necessary to find a satisfactory resolution to the conflict (Kleinman 1988). This was certainly the case of Juan and Lola.

When the practitioner does not take into consideration the patient's and family's explanation of the illness, it may signal disrespect to the patient and family. The disregard of relevant psychosocial dimensions of care has adverse repercussions in the patient-provider relationship, and undermines the foundation of care, which is communication and trust (Kleinman 1988).

Western medicine explains illness in terms of microbes and biochemistry. In many other cultures, illness comes as the result of physical, emotional, or spiritual imbalance, fate, or the will of God. Some cultures believe that health and illness are a balance between hot and cold. Cancer may be considered cold while infections are considered hot. Some Southeast Asians share related beliefs that imbalances between yin and yang contribute to illness in terms of hot, cold, and winds (Keovilay, Rasbridge, and Kemp 2000).

In her book *The Spirit Catches You and You Fall Down*, Ann Fadiman (1997) explores the clash between a small county hospital in Merced, California, and a refugee family from Laos over the care of Lia Lee, a Hmong child diagnosed with severe epilepsy. Lia's parents believed that spirits had possessed the child and were the cause of their daughter's seizures. Some Asian cultures believe that illness is a punishment for past transgressions. Lia's doctors believe in a biological etiology as the cause of Lia's illness, and this view guided their treatment plan. Lia's doctors and her family could not agree on the cause and treatment of Lia's illness. Fadiman provides poignant examples of the "collision" of these two cultures—the Western medicine and the Hmong culture. Without blaming the Western medical model or the Lee's parental and cultural practices, she explores how these two disparate cultures and divergent views have an uneasy and very difficult coexistence and demonstrates the harm and danger that can happen because of ethnocentricity from both cultures. This true story is an excellent example of how different explanatory models can be in conflict as they try to make sense of a medical situation.

Fadiman poses eight questions that were developed by Kleinman. These questions are recommended for the assessment and explanation of the patient's and/or family's illness. The practitioner can also answer them to identify the commonalities and differences in understanding and giving meaning to the patient's illness process. (These questions can be modified and made more personal depending on your relationship with the client.)

- What do you call the problem? (You can also say: Tell me what you understand about your medical condition.)
- What do you think has caused the problem?
- Why do you think it started when it did?
- What do you think the sickness does? How does it work? How does it affect your body?
- How severe do you think the sickness is? Will it have a short or long course?
- What treatment do you desire? What are the most important results you hope to receive from this treatment? (You can ask: How do you want your condition to be treated?)
- What are the chief problems the sickness has caused?
- What do you fear most about the sickness?

Comparing and contrasting the patient's and the practitioner's answers helps to understand the differences in values, beliefs, and illness constructs and provides an opportunity for intercultural exchange, cooperation, and understanding.

Let us now return to the case of Lola and Juan. What would we need to know beyond their culture or their race? First, we would want to ask what was their major cultural identifier? How did they define themselves? What was their income level, and how did that play into the use of *curanderos*? What had been their experiences of discrimination in the past and in what ways might they have been excluded from end of life care? What was their illness narrative? Did it agree with that of their families or their healthcare providers? What was the reaction of the family to the illness? What role did religion play in their lives? Did the family and church support their choices given that both Juan and Lola had AIDS, a highly stigmatized disease? What was the ethnicity and race of the social worker and other healthcare professionals and how did that enter into the mix? How did the institution respond to their going against orders to receive alternative medicine? Were they considered noncompliant? Were they labeled as difficult or untreatable? What kinds of social supports did they have, and to what degree did their decisions strengthen or undermine these supports? Where did they live and did they have access to needed medications? These are but only a few of the questions that could be included in a cross-cultural assessment.

CROSS-CULTURAL COMMUNICATION

A European-American hospice nurse is caring for a Chinese patient who has stomach cancer. During a home visit, the nurse gives instructions to the patient about how to take the pain medication. When the nurse asks the patient if she understands how to take the medication the patient nods in approval. The next day, the nurse is called to the patient's home because her pain is out of control. When she looks at the patient's mediset she notices that the patient has not been taking the medication on schedule. The nurse is baffled. She thought that the patient had understood how to take her medications.

Communication is more than words. When two people communicate, a number of factors influence the interaction—language, personality, interpersonal perception, emotions, class, and culture, among others. Culture and communication are inseparable. Cross-cultural communication involves the principle of recognizing how culture influences what we are, how we act, how we think, and how we talk and listen (Dodd 1989). In the example mentioned above, the patient was probably indicating that she had heard what the nurse had said and not necessarily that she had understood. Expressing confusion or lack of understanding or simply saying, "No, I don't understand," to a white healthcare provider might well be embarrassing for Asian patients who are deferential in relationships to authority. A recommended strategy with any patient who speaks limited English is to ask the patient to repeat to you what you have explained.

When educating patients/families about pain medications, it is important to remember that for Latino or Chinese patients, it is better to use the word "opioid" than "narcotic." Narcotic is often synonymous with drug addiction and has a bad association. It is also important to assess the literacy level of the patient. Find out what language the patient is literate in, and if English is your common language, make sure that you speak at a level that will be understood.

Many theories and communication models are used to explain cross-cultural communication patterns. One that is often referred to in the cross-cultural communication literature is the "High/Low Context Cultures Model." However, one should exercise care about theories that explain communication patterns. Many of these theories have been used to stereotype cultures or individuals from different cultures. Here we use them only as a point of reference to understand cultural differences. The high context (HC) or low context (LC) cultures framework can be used as a global pattern to understand cultural differences. *It should not be used to stereotype or predict behavior for a whole group of people or to categorize specific individuals.* There are always differences among individuals in the same cultural group: religion, urban/rural background, economic status, exposure, time spent living with other cultural groups, acculturation level, proximity to other cultures, education, language, occupation, and so on. Also, although the words "high" and "low" describe context patterns, they do not indicate the superiority of one framework or the other. "High" does not mean better or more, "low" does not mean less or worse.

Individuals from HC cultures place a lot of emphasis on the group rather than the individual. Individuals from a HC culture will consider the collective (family) for a medical decision rather than rely on the individual alone. Many Latino and African American patients may think that it does not make sense to establish advance directives. They may think that when the needs arise the family will be able to make the decision for them. For many practitioners, this dimension of cultural differences can be problematic because it clashes with the American (low context culture) medical value placed on patient autonomy and self-determination.

The values and communication patterns in HC cultures are important to know when cross-cultural communication occurs between HC patients and LC healthcare providers. An explanation to healthcare providers about deference to authority will help a caregiver understand the reluctance of patients from HC cultures to question the healthcare professional, the reluctance of such patients to establish sustained eye contact with an individual perceived to be an authority figure, and the reluctance to say "no" to avoid embarrassment. In cultures where social workers, doctors, and nurses are perceived as authority figures, the individual may be reluctant to ask questions about his/her illness, about prognosis, treatment and even what a prescribed medication is for. I have talked to many Latino patients who after seeing their doctors do not have an idea of why they have been sent to radiology or asked to take a certain medication. When I ask them why they didn't ask the doctor, they simply say, "The doctor knows what he [or she] is doing." There is reluctance to question the physician even for information purposes.

Conversations about the management of symptoms are challenging, given that English and the healthcare language are low-context—the verbal message is explicit, one spells things out exactly, the message is carried more by words than by nonverbal means. Whereas the communication in high context cultures is characterized by the high use of nonverbal communication (voice tone, facial expression, gestures, and the like), the verbal message is more implicit—the context is more important; the conversation is indirect and where one talks around and embellishes the point. I remember an on-call nurse in a hospice program who told me how inpatient she becomes with Latino and Asian patients because they always wanted to give her every single detail of a situation instead of getting to the point. Families from some cultures—Latino, Filipino, Chinese, or Vietnamese, for example—might communicate in a circuitous fashion, not addressing feelings or specific matters directly. In these cultures it may also be inappropriate to address issues of diagnosis, prognosis, death, and funeral planning explicitly. Many cultures do not permit the disclosure of diagnosis to the patient. The issue of informed consent is complicated, as a healthcare provider must balance respect for cultural values about nondisclosure with the patient's right to adequate information to make decisions about treatments and medical care. Care providers must assess the patient's and family's values and communication and decision-making styles, and be willing to discuss death, dying, and grief openly before speaking frankly to the patient about end-of-life care. Taboo words like "death," "dying," "funeral," and sometimes even "cancer" can have adverse repercussions in the caregiver-patient relationship and can cause the patient and family to refuse care by the provider.

In cross-cultural communication at the end of life it is important then, to:

- Recognize that disclosing the prognosis of an illness and "truth-telling" empowers some, while for others it may cause hope to be lost and may hasten death.
- Ask specific questions of the patient and family about their beliefs and practices. Explore alternative methods such as herbal medicines, traditional healing practices, privacy, modesty, and physical touch.
- Build a supportive, trusting relationship based on honesty and mutual respect.
- Facilitate the negotiation of cultural understanding in provider-patient relationships, listen to the patient's stories, solicit their illness narratives and explanatory models, and build partnerships.

THE USE OF INTERPRETERS

Language barriers can lead to a number of communication problems, including miscommunication, misinterpretation, misdiagnosis, overtreatment, or undertreatment. When the provider and patient do not speak the same language, end-of-life care becomes more challenging. The provider may experience lower levels of empathy. The rapport needed for developing trust may be more difficult to achieve. The patient may feel less confident and resist self-disclosure.

When organizations are not able to staff programs to serve the diverse linguistic needs of their client populations, the use of interpreters and other interpretation services is necessary to bridge the communication gap. These services usually present other challenges. For example, organizations may utilize other paid staff from the organization to do the job of the interpreter. But these staff members are not usually trained to be interpreters and/or are not trained to address death, dying, and bereavement issues. They just happen to speak the language of the patient.

When the provider does not know how to use an interpreter, the relationship with the patient may get lost in the interaction. The patient's words may be translated but the meaning is lost.

Often, untrained staff, phone interpretation services (these may be very expensive and present an economic burden on the system), family, or friends (here there is a risk of relationship reversal) are used as interpreters. When family and friends are used, they often filter out the information that they think the patient and family should not know, or they may not know medical terminology. Therefore, it is important to advocate for trained interpreters. The sad reality in our hospitals, nursing homes, home health agencies, and inpatient hospices, however, is that interpretation services are usually provided by untrained staff.

Sometimes untrained staff can be detrimental to the work other members of the care team are trying to do with the family. I remember a Chinese patient I was assigned to in our palliative-care team, a thirty-eight-year-old man with metastatic pancreatic cancer. He was married and had three school-age children. His mother lived with the family and was the primary caregiver as the wife had become the breadwinner. The home care team comprised a Chinese nurse, a Chinese home health aide (HHA), and me, a Latina, as the social worker. After extensive chemotherapy, the oncologist informed the patient that his cancer was no longer responsive to the treatment and they could only provide him comfort care. He did not disclose the news to the family but indicated to the nurse that he was ready to talk to his wife and mother. Not having enough experience in discussing end-of-life issues with terminally ill patients, the nurse asked me to facilitate the conversation but she preferred to be a witness rather than the interpreter. I asked the HHA to interpret for me and I briefly informed her of what we were going to discuss. The meeting started, and after discussing some practical issues I asked the wife about her understanding of the husband's condition at this point. The answer I got from her was not related to my question. It was rather her question about a community resource. After I provided the information about the community resource, I asked her the same question about her husband's condition. Once again, the wife answered with another question. Noticing my confusion, the nurse, who had been observing and listening, intervened and told the HHA that she was going to interrupt the interpretation. The HHA left and the nurse informed me that the HHA was feeling uncomfortable talking so *directly* about dying. Therefore, she was not really interpreting what I was saying.

This experience showed me that when we are going to discuss sensitive end-of-life issues with a patient whose culture and language is different from our own, we have to make sure that the interpreter is comfortable with the subject and discussion entailed. We should not assume that speaking the same language guarantees an appropriate interpretation.

If medical interpreters are available, the following guidelines are necessary to facilitate the work with them and the dying patient (adapted from Trainer 2000):

- Spatial arrangements: determine where you will be sitting in relation to the patient and the interpreter.

- Negotiate how much time you will need for the visit, consult, or counseling session, taking into consideration that interpretation may require extra time.
- Always ask if the patient comes from a rural or urban area.
- Think about the different roles of the interpreter: Is the interviewer, a "tool" or mouthpiece, a cultural broker, an advocate, a clinical partner?
- Assess the interpreter's comfort level when discussing end-of-life issues.
- Confirm the issue of confidentiality with the interpreter and reassure the client.
- Provide background context, medical history, and the purpose of the interview to the interpreter before you start the session.
- Use simple language and pause between sentences to give the interpreter an opportunity to translate every word.
- Empower your client by giving him/her your undivided attention. Talk directly to the client, not the interpreter. Do not look back and forth from the interpreter to the client. Do not say "please tell So and So such and such." The interpreter is just a voice who should translate all that is said. Avoid a three-way conversation.
- If the client and interpreter start talking to each other, ask for interpretation of that conversation; do not be left out.
- Avoid medical jargon.
- Use as many descriptors as you can to assess pain.
- Ask for a cultural interpretation and explanation of the problem.
- Interpreters are usually bicultural as well as bilingual; they can be a source of information about the culture, customs, and worldview of the client.
- Encourage the interpreter to inform the practitioner of any cultural differences that may lead to misunderstandings or lack of compliance with the prescribed treatment. Respect the interpreter's suggestions but do not allow him/her to take over.
- If possible, encourage the same interpreter to continue working with the same client throughout the case.
- Validate the client's understanding by asking for brief summaries. Important ideas could be lost during the translation.
- While working with an interpreter, the practitioner's cultural sensitivity is under scrutiny and this may make the practitioner nervous. Practice will bring acceptable comfort levels. Mutual respect between practitioners and interpreters is necessary for a successful intervention.
- Keep in mind that most interpreters also play the role of advocates. In the case of highly emotional situations, the interpreter's assistance can be very helpful.

CONCLUSION

After Juan's death, Lola continued seeing her doctor, and, to this day, she continues using primarily Western medicine to treat her illness. Lola continues to use some home remedies, but she is very cautious about the remedies she tries. She doesn't think that her belief system failed her, but rather that the healer's treatments were not appropriate and effective for her and her husband's HIV condition. She realized that there might be conditions that will not respond to traditional healing. She is very grateful to her doctor for having helped her through one of her most difficult medical experiences, but she strongly believes that God made it possible for her to survive the crisis.

As the United States becomes more multiethnic and multiracial, the provision of end-of-life care to diverse populations will become the norm rather than the exception. We are challenged by factors that go beyond the diverse cultural needs of our clients: by a scarcity of resources, a growing demand for services, a healthcare system that insists on a containment of costs, medical staff not well trained in pain and symptom management, and by increasing client populations in inner city settings with dual (medical and substance abuse or mental illness) and triple (medical, substance abuse, and mental illness) diagnoses. All these factors demand an even greater ability to stay focused on a client's individual and specific biological, psychological, social, and cultural end-of-life-care needs. In order to do this, we must treat every patient as a unique individual who is allowed to define his or her culture and community. We must ask the patient about his or her community's response to death and dying, health and healing. We can determine the patient's worldview and value system by adding cultural questions to our assessments (Trainer 2000). We have to remember that respect for patient dignity and self-determination involves respect for cultural differences (Altilio 2000).

In Lola and Juan's case, their doctor responded in a culturally sensitive manner, showing respect for their decision to try a faith healer in spite of her belief that the healer's treatment could be detrimental to her patient's health. The doctor did not blame them when they got sicker. Instead, she was there to support and treat them again. As end-of-life-care practitioners, we have to recognize that the perception of all events is filtered through the lens of a person's culture, race, ethnicity, gender, and religion. Every provider of end-of-life care needs to recognize, understand, and appreciate cultural differences as well as similarities and racial/ethnic factors that may undermine access to best care and best practices. This is the only way we will be able to serve the needs of our diverse patients.

REFERENCES

Altilio, T. 2000. Western aspects of the health care/patient/family: Experience informed by culture, gender and age. Workshop presentation, Beth Israel Health Care System, New York.

American Psychiatric Association. 2000. *Diagnostic and Statistical Manual of Mental Disorders (DSM-IV)*. 4th ed. Washington, DC: American Psychiatric Association.

Ayanian, J. Z., P. D. Cleary, J. S. Weissman, and A. M. Epstein. 1999. The effect of patient's preferences on racial differences in access to renal transplantation. *New England Journal of Medicine* 341(22): 1661–1669.

Bach, P. B., L. D. Cramer, J. L. Warren, and C. B. Begg. 1999. Racial differences in the treatment of early-stage lung cancer. *New England Journal of Medicine* 341(16): 1198–1205.

Batts, V. 1998. Modern racism: New melody for the same old tunes. *EDS Occasional Papers.* Cambridge, MA: Episcopal Divinity School.

Braun, K. L., J. H. Pietsch, and P. L. Blanchette. 2000. *Cultural Issues in End-of-Life Decision-Making.* Thousand Oaks, CA: Sage.

Brenner, P. R. 1997. Issues of access in a diverse society. *Hospice Journal* 12(2): 9–17.

Carter, M. A., and C. M. Klugman. 2001. Cultural engagement in clinical ethics: A model for ethics consultation. *Cambridge Quarterly of Healthcare Ethics* 10(1): 16–33.

Cleeland, C. S., R. Gonin, L. Baez, P. Loehrer, and K. J. Pandya. 1997. Pain and treatment of pain in minority patients with cancer: The Eastern Cooperative Oncology Group Minority Outpatient Pain Study. *Annals of Internal Medicine* 127:813–816.

Cross, T. 1995–96. Developing a knowledge base to support cultural competence. *Family Resource Coalition Report* 14(3–4): 4.

DeSpelder, L. A., and A. L. Strickland. 1992. *The Last Dance: Encountering Death and Dying.* Mountain View, CA: Mayfield.

Dodd, C. H. 1989. *Dynamics of Intercultural Communication.* 3d ed. Dubuque, IA: William C. Brown.

Fadiman, A. 1997. *The Spirit Catches You and You Fall Down: A Hmong Child, Her American Doctors, and the Collision of Two Cultures.* New York: Farrar, Straus & Giroux.

Freeman, H. P., and R. Payne. 2000. Racial injustice in health care. *New England Journal of Medicine* 342(14): 1045–1047.

Gordon, A. K. 1996. Hospice and minorities: A national study of organizational access and practice. *Hospice Journal* 11(1): 49–69.

Harvard Graduate School of Education. 2002. HGSE faculty and researchers release definitive six-volume series on the new wave of immigration. Press release.

Hendrix, L. 1999. Intercultural competence: Working to get along and help each other. *Alzheimer's Association of Greater San Francisco Bay Area Newsletter* 1:9.

Johnson, C. J., and M. G. McGee, eds. 1991. *How Different Religions View Death and Afterlife.* Philadelphia: Charles Press.

Keovilay, L., L. Rasbridge, and C. Kemp. 2000. Cambodian and Laotian health beliefs and practices related to the end of life. *Journal of Hospice and Palliative Care Nursing* 2:143–151.

Kirk, G., and M. Okazawa-Rey. 1998. *Women's Lives: Multicultural Perspectives.* Mountain View, CA: Mayfield.

Kleinman, A. 1988. *The Illness Narratives: Suffering, Healing, and the Human Condition.* New York: Basic Books.

Kreier, R. 1999. Crossing the cultural divide. www.ama-assn.org/sci-pubs/amnews/pick_99/fadd0125.htm.

Kurth, J., J. Chambers, and D. Patterson. 2002. Painkiller drugs scarce for the poor. *Detroit News,* 27 October.

McCormick, E. 2000. Asians will soon be the biggest group in SF. *San Francisco Examiner,* 3 September.

McDonald, D. D. 1994. Gender and ethnic stereotyping and narcotic analgesic administration. *Research Nurse Health* 17:45–9.

Morrison, R. S., S. Wallenstein, D. K. Natale, R. S. Senzel, and L. L. Huang. 2000. "We don't carry that": Failure of pharmacies in predominantly nonwhite neighborhoods to stock opioid analgesics. *New England Journal of Medicine* 342(14): 1023–1026.

Nakao, A. 2000. Bringing culture into medicine. *San Francisco Examiner,* 16 April.

Ness, C. 2001a. 100-year high in California's percentage of foreign-born. *San Francisco Chronicle,* 6 August.

———. 2001b. West is most multiracial area in U.S. *San Francisco Chronicle,* 30 November.

Schneider, E. C., A. M. Zaslavsky, and A. M. Epstein. 2002. Racial disparities in quality of care for enrollees in Medicare managed care. *Journal of the American Medical Association* 287(10): 1288–1294.

Tervalon, M., and J. Murray-Garcia. 1998. Cultural humility versus cultural competence: A critical distinction in defining physician training outcomes in multicultural education. *Journal of Health Care for the Poor and Underserved* 9(2): 117–125.

Todd, K. H., N. Damroo, and J. R. Hoffman. 1993. Ethnicity as a risk factor for inadequate emergency department analgesia. *Journal of the American Medical Association* 269:1537–1539.

Trainer, T. M. 2000. Cultural suffering: Added distress for ethnic minority cancer patients. Paper presented at the Psychosocial Oncology 2000 and Beyond conference, Vancouver.

U.S. Census Bureau. 1999. Table 8: Race and Hispanic origin of the population by nativity: 1850 to 1990. www.census.gov.

——. 2000. Projections of the resident population by age, sex, race, and Hispanic origin: 1999 to 2100. www.census.gov.

——. 2001. Table 1: Population by race and Hispanic or Latino origin, for all ages and for 18 years and over, for the United States: 2000. www.census.gov.

Verdin, T., and A. C. Genaro. 2000. Minorities are now the majority in California. *San Francisco Examiner*, 30 August.

Warrier, S. 1998. From sensitivity to competency: Clinical and departmental guidelines to achieving cultural competency. In *Improving the Health Care Response to Domestic Violence: A Resource Manual for Health Care Providers*, ed. C. Warshaw and A. L. Ganley, 3–10. New York: Family Violence Prevention Fund.

——. 2000. Domestic violence: cultural competency in the health care setting. Workshop presentation.

Whittle, J., J. Conigliaro, C. B. Good, and P. Lofgren. 1993. Racial differences in the use of invasive cardiovascular procedures in the department of Veterans Affairs Medical System. *New England Journal of Medicine* 329(9): 621–627.

23

MARGINALIZATION AT THE END OF LIFE

SHIRLEY OTIS-GREEN AND CHRISTIAN B. RUTLAND

ALTHOUGH IT is a universal event, and nearly universally feared, death is often experienced as a shock in Western societies. Despite the reality that we all will die, most actual deaths are perceived as unexpected and somehow unfair. Perhaps it is precisely this unpredictability that leads us to fear death, and by extension, to distance ourselves from those who are dying. Those with illnesses or conditions that seem most unpredictable (and therefore most frightening) are most at risk to become marginalized. Here we will use the concept of marginalization to indicate the emotional and physical "distance" we keep from characteristics or behaviors (and all too often, the individuals and groups) that we find fearful.

Because we all will die, we are all at risk for eventual marginalization regardless of previous status or access to resources. End-of-life decision making is challenging for most members of society. People facing the end of their lives are asked to make literally life-and-death decisions regarding their health care with individuals they are likely to view as strangers, and to do so without sufficient time or information. Those with impaired capacity, limited communication skills, or other challenges are then especially vulnerable at the end of life. The current healthcare system is in flux and has proven to be difficult to navigate for the dying under the best of circumstances. It is not surprising, then, that the system is especially problematic for those with special limitations.

The majority of those dying will interface with a fragmented system of health care that limits access and resources for those who are most at need; the population that social work has historically served. This chapter will focus upon those who struggle with diminished decision-making capacity (whether from mental illness or cognitive impairment) or who have a history of substance abuse. We will illustrate issues of marginalization by nature of race, culture, gender, and class with case examples.

In the literature on acculturation, the term *marginalized* is used to describe those who are neither assimilated into the majority culture, nor still comfortably identified with their historical culture (Berry 1993; Dona and Berry 1994). Similarly, in the sexual orientation literature, Taywaditep (2001) uses this term to include those who are both disenfranchised from the mainstream culture and the gay culture at large. These culturally homeless individuals fall between groups and are among the most stigmatized and disempowered of all. For the purpose of this chapter, *marginalization* will be viewed not as a static descriptor to indicate membership in a particularly disenfranchised group, but rather as a more dynamic term indicating more universal situational risk factors. Developing a perspective that identifies marginalized individuals or populations as existing along a continuum reminds us of the complex and dynamic nature of these interrelationships.

Stigmatization is the most damaging aspect of the tendency to marginalize. Prejudices and assumptions limit opportunities and access to important resources and services. Many exacerbating factors can increase or decrease the degree of stigmatization that a patient will experience. Individuals may be marginalized by nature of race, ethnicity, culture, gender, age, economic status, ability level, or health condition. As we grow nearer to the end of our life, depression, dementia, and disabilities often further compound marginalization conditions. Disenfranchised populations are subjects of further distancing, victimization, and exploitation in the current healthcare system (see chapters 22, 24, and 25).

Models for Western health care have historically been based upon principles of autonomy, self-reliance, individualism, and independent decision making. But not all members of our society have the capacity or the power to apply these principles. Many of these values are in direct conflict with cultural values of interdependence (as for many African Americans) or generational deference (as in many Asian families). Many cultures encourage group decision making and weigh the impact of a patient's healthcare decision upon the family unit as a whole (Congress and Lyons 1992). Conflict is inherent in a medical system that views certain perspectives as valuable and other perspectives as "foreign." This ethnocentric tendency of the medical system further contributes to the marginalization of many.

Incidents of institutionalized racism cause many to view the medical system with skepticism. The Nuremberg Doctors Trial (1946–47) and the Tuskegee Study of Untreated Syphilis in the Negro Male (1932–73) remind us of how diligent healthcare professionals need to be to safeguard the interests of the most vulnerable (Dunn and Chadwick 1999). Adding further complexity to this is the way that financial factors sway healthcare recommendations for the less privileged.

Marginalized groups have long had the attention of the social work profession. Social work has its roots in religious traditions that sought social reform for the disenfranchised members of society: those suffering with mental illness, who were homeless, who were incarcerated, religiously persecuted, poor, or members of underrepresented populations. The profession of social work was formed in recognition and in response to the needs of the persistently underserved (Bloom 1990). Those with limited resources, those for whom literacy is impaired, those with beliefs not of the mainstream, those who are newly immigrated, those who are developmentally disabled or who suffer from serious mental illness, are at increased risk to become even more marginalized as death approaches.

Dying is in itself a marginalizing process. The actual biology of dying further separates the dying person from others. Dying is accompanied by numerous losses of function. More energy is required to engage in previously valued tasks with a resultant disengagement from life events. People can no longer work or participate in community functions. Eventually, they no longer attend church, mosque, or synagogue. They may be hospitalized or institutionalized, further distancing them from family and friends. Gradually most individuals turn inward and cease to show interest in others' activities. The societal implications of this physical isolation and psychological withdrawal are well documented (Nuland 1994).

Those for whom death will occur following a lengthy illness have an opportunity to begin to prepare for this inevitability. For others, death occurs suddenly from accidental events that arise unexpectedly. Others will face death as the result of violent acts perpetrated upon them (Shai and Rosenwaike 1988). The range of these experiences is not equally distributed. Those of certain disadvantaged ethnic groups, those with more limited access to resources, those with less formal education, or those for whom English is not a primary language are more likely to face an earlier, more unexpected and often more violent end to their lives (Borum, Lynn, and Zhong 2000).

The medical management of many previously fatal conditions has also improved, resulting in a rapidly escalating number of frail elderly. There are increasing survival rates for those with serious developmental disabilities. American demographics indicate population increases through immigration, resulting in language and value differences that further complicate care throughout the continuum of illness (Hopp and Duffy 2000). The field of bioethics has evolved in recognition of the complexities of just such situations (Davis 1996). Though the faces may have changed over the decades, the need for advocacy for the most vulnerable has not. As Emily Friedman noted at the turn of the millennium, "part of what society expects of [health care] is that we will protect those whom it has forsaken" (2000:9). She further reminds us that health care is valued in society because of the "decency, kindness, and compassion of the people who work in health care and offer sanctuary to the helpless" (2000:9).

The societal implications of this marginalization can last for decades following a death. Disenfranchised grievers are at greater risk to suffer from the effects of complicated bereavement (Corless 2001). The literature from the gay and lesbian community indicates that bereaved partners and parents who attempt to hide their grief are at greater risk to suffer depression and anxiety following the death of their loved ones than are those for whom grief can be more openly acknowledged (Gochros, Gochros, and Fischer 1986). Similarly, those who grieve a death by suicide (Quinnett 1987) often struggle with the additional burden of shame and questions of culpability, again decreasing the probability that their grief will be shared and supported. Early pregnancy loss, whether through miscarriage (Limbo and Wheeler 1987) or following an abortion (Panuthos and Romeo 1984), is also associated with isolated grief. Additionally, all healthcare workers need to be sensitive to the immense cultural variations that exist in the expression of grief (Hebert 1998).

Humans are social beings who thrive best when in relationship to others, yet historically death-avoidant behaviors served an adaptive benefit for survival. Until recently, causes of death were seldom clearly identified. It was adaptive to be cautious around the dying, in that the cause of this tragedy might still be present (e.g., communicable diseases could decimate entire communities). This creates a conflict when people encounter the dying. There are complex philosophical, spiritual, and existential implications of this tension as people struggle to be with those with whom they are intimate while self preservation urges flight from death and the dying.

The balance of this chapter will concentrate on several special circumstances that further increase the vulnerability of those facing the end of their lives.

THE EFFECTS OF DIMINISHED DECISION-MAKING CAPACITY

As we have noted, healthcare delivery in the United States is based upon a model that values autonomy in decision making. Those for whom shared decision making is important (such as many ethnic groups), and those who have diminished capacity for independent decision making (owing to either transient or chronic conditions) are at increased risk to become marginalized. Decision-making "capacity" is based upon a clinical assessment that determines an individual's ability to make meaningful health care decisions. It is most helpful to think of capacity as "decision-specific," with the goal being to preserve autonomy whenever possible (Abbas and Dien 2001).

Capacity is distinguished from the concept of "competence," which is a legally defined term for those in need of a court-appointed surrogate decision maker. Those who are too young, too old, too confused, too sedated, too frightened, too debilitated, too agitated, or too overwhelmed face tremendous burdens within our current healthcare system (Christopher 2001). As this list makes evident, having "impaired or diminished" capacity regarding decision making is not something that affects only certain groups (Swerdlow 2000), but something that has or will play a role for most of us at some point in our lives. As infants we were all dependent upon surrogate decision makers for our care, and we will likely be again at various times in our lives. Yet most of us are ill prepared for those moments.

Unfortunately, loss of cognitive functioning is not unusual at the end of life. Decision-making capacity might be limited for a variety of reasons. Yet even those who are chronically and severely impaired usually possess some ability to express certain preferences (Morrison and Zayas 1998).

It is the responsibility of the medical social worker to complete a psychosocial-spiritual assessment to assist the healthcare team in helping the individual communicate and comprehend information necessary to establish preferences when possible. Even individuals with serious cognitive impairment may be able to nominate a surrogate decision maker or healthcare proxy agent (Mezey et al. 2000). Many of the most marginalized groups are the least likely to have completed advance directives for health care. Assigning a surrogate decision maker is the most important element of these directives, and encourages family discussion regarding end-of-life wishes (see chapter 37).

Autonomous decision making is especially difficult for those for whom English is a second language. Although there is legislation requiring certain healthcare facilities to make interpreter services more readily accessible (for example, State of California Health and Safety Code 1990), the majority of patients still rely on family or friends to act as translators for most daily healthcare interactions. A further complicating factor is the tendency to use noncertified interpreters, who are too often not medically trained staff (such as housekeepers), to assist in spontaneous medical conversations with the patient (Baker et al. 1996; see chapter 22, this volume). Cultural factors regarding the value of privacy and respect for elders add another dimension to this situation. The implications of these issues for informed consent can be monumental.

CASE EXAMPLE

Mr. Chang is a sixty-seven-year-old Chinese man being evaluated for prostate cancer surgery. A scheduling conflict resulted in the certified interpreter's having only a limited time available to assist with the delivery of this information. Mr. Chang continued the conversation with his twenty-nine-year-old daughter acting as his interpreter. Meeting with the family later, the social worker learned that his daughter had felt too embarrassed to tell her father about the possibility of impotence and incontinence and now feels guilty because she suspects that his depression following treatment might be related to these problems.

People with severe psychiatric disorders are at increased risk for marginalization, perhaps owing to their seemingly unpredictable (and therefore more frightening) behavior. Except in limited circumstances, most individuals are quite functional and may not require an unusual level of social work support when dealing with end-of-life issues. Though many cancer patients develop clinical depression, this is treatable and most can be actively involved in their healthcare decisions even with advancing illness (Meyerowitz et al. 2000).

Numerous psychiatric diagnoses include diminished capacity. Many of these diagnoses, such as schizophrenia, acute mania, and pervasive developmental disorders, will be known before the diagnosis of a potentially terminal disease. Social work will be crucial to the initial assessment and in coordinating the necessary psychiatric regimen with any new treatment being considered. Should the individual decompensate behaviorally, social work may be required to coordinate urgent psychiatric consultation, either on an inpatient basis or with the patient's regular psychiatric caregivers (see chapter 18).

Offering palliative care to those with serious mental illness challenges the treating team to address care planning and vigilantly assess patient adherence (Goldenberg, Holland, and Schachter 2000). Coping with patient reluctance to undergo treatment recommendations can be especially taxing for the team, which often benefits from ethics board consultations in particularly difficult situations (Candilis and Foti 1999). Limiting the numbers of professionals involved in caregiving, striving for continuity within the healthcare system, and consciously addressing environmental factors that exacerbate symptoms (limiting interruptions, being more diligent regarding unexpected noises, and the like) are all strategies to diminish perceived environmental threats.

Cognitive impairments such as dementia (occurring gradually over time) and delirium (usually with a more acute onset) may not be diagnosed until well into end-of-life care, posing unique complications (Burgener 1998). Because of the nature of their assessments and the time spent with patients, clinical social workers may be among the first to recognize these potentially dangerous conditions and recommend appropriate consultation and diagnostic workup. The treating team can easily miss the signs of early dementia until a patient is already struggling with decision making and self-care. Social workers may not only be instrumental in initiating a diagnostic workup, but will certainly be required to set up the numerous resources necessary for the protection of an individual with diminished capacity.

Hypoactive delirium can also easily be missed or mistaken for depression. The social worker may be the first to recognize that the patient's affect is not only blunted and slow, but also confused, disoriented, and not tracking properly. Because the pharmacological treatment for depression can actually worsen the symptoms of a hypoactive delirium, it is urgent that this condition be promptly recognized. The alert social worker may be the initiator of a vital diagnostic workup. Hyperactive (or agitated) delirium is diagnostically more easily assessed, but social workers may be required to set up transitional care as a resolution, or this potentially life-threatening condition may be prolonged.

Delirium at the end of life may be treatment induced or the result of organic changes from the processes of worsening illness. Families are especially disturbed by cognitive changes in a loved one who is dying, feeling that they are losing the person they know. Skilled assessment is needed to determine potentially reversible conditions while still providing for necessary symptom management. This condition is not uncommon for many dying patients, yet is all too often undertreated.

Social workers may be most important in their role in ethics-driven consultation teams in assisting in the establishment of "substituted" judgment for those for whom decision making is most severely compromised. For those patients who are unable to offer this level of capacity, a "best interest" judgment may be indicated (usually through a consensus of "reasonable others"). While the Patient Self-Determination Act (passed by the U.S. Congress in May 1991) encourages health care organizations to address decision-making issues earlier in the process of the provision of care, this value of future focused planning is not shared by all cultures (Fung 1994). Thus, many individuals face decisions regarding end-of-life care without advance planning.

CASE EXAMPLE

Anna is a seventy-eight-year-old woman suffering from chronic obstructive pulmonary disease following more than sixty years of active cigarette usage. Her spouse and only daughter died some decades ago. Anna served in Vietnam and periodically reports flashbacks and a history of post-traumatic stress disorder. Past hospitalizations have prompted psychotic episodes that gradually resolved upon return to her studio apartment near her church. Additionally, she has diabetes and recently was found to have recurrent breast cancer. Long-standing borderline personality traits have left Anna isolated from friends and family. The social worker was called by nursing and told that the patient would not stay in the hospital because she has no one to care for her beloved dog. She threatened to leave the hospital against medical advice. The social worker was able to mobilize the church community to provide emergency "respite care" for Anna's dog and address her distrust of the medical system. Consistency in support and clarity in communication throughout the duration of her hospitalization was important for her to accept medical recommendations regarding her care.

SPECIAL CHALLENGES: ETHNIC, RELIGIOUS, CULTURAL, AND SOCIOECONOMIC INFLUENCES

The dominant ethnic, religious, cultural, and socioeconomic groups exert tremendous influence regarding the values, delivery, and access to health care in America (Crawley et al. 2002). Many who are incarcerated, in foster care, or who are otherwise facing curtailed freedoms also struggle with serious disabling conditions that affect their care and decision making at end of life (Ross 2001). In these groups, there is an overrepresentation of persons who communicate in a language other than English, who are of various ethnic and racial subgroups, and who have limited access to resources.

Although hospice is recognized as offering the "gold standard" in end-of-life care, only a small percentage of patients and their families access this service (Stuart 1999). Current trends demonstrate that the typical hospice patient is a middle-class, white adult with insurance who is actively dying from cancer and has a designated caregiver available (Brenner 1997). Even the most privileged may find significant barriers in timely access to needed end-of-life services (Dahlin 1999). In recognition of these problems, specialized hospices have been developed to meet the needs of those with AIDS and for children. Numerous studies have reviewed the many barriers faced by those seeking hospice support (Johnson 1998). These include deterrents to timely access to hospice (Gordon 1995), cultural and institutional barriers (Reese et al. 1999), a lack of minority access to hospice referral (Haber 1999), underrepresentation of those with dementia (Hanrahan and Luchins 1995), late referrals (Johnson and Slaninka 1999), and problems associated with Medicare hospice-benefit restrictions (Sontag 1992).

Being poor at the end of one's life creates many logistical hurdles to optimal health-care access in America (Hughes 2001). Transportation may be limited; lack of adequate insurance coverage can limit healthcare options; neighborhood pharmacies may not carry needed medications; family caregivers may face competing obligations that limit their ability to meet patient needs. Those who are homeless have additional logistical challenges that may be compounded by substance-use disorders, cognitive impairments, or mental illness (Morse 2000). Facing the end of life with limited resources challenges a healthcare system that has limited access and serious gaps in coverage. Those who lack adequate insurance coverage are susceptible to earlier deaths from otherwise treatable conditions. Lacking adequate access to prescription medications limits one's quality and potentially quantity of life.

CASE EXAMPLE

Juan is a thirteen-year-old son of divorced Spanish-speaking immigrants. He has widely metastatic sarcoma with advancing multiorgan failure. His parents are concerned about his increasing sedation and the subsequent diminishment in his ability to participate in coherent communication. They disagree with the medical team's recommendations regarding aggressive symptom management. His family has no insurance and has had difficulty managing his care at home. They have brought Juan to the hospital in hope of further treatment. Their local pharmacy does not normally carry the prescribed opioids owing to concerns about theft, and they have angered Juan's father when he attempted to get refills from them. His father believes that they question his motives for the heavy use of the opioids suspecting that he is illicitly selling the drug for profit. Juan's mother had used recreational substances during pregnancy with Juan and blames herself for his illness. She has voiced a fear that God is punishing her for her "sinful past" and has told her family that she believes that Juan's death will be "awful" as a consequence. Juan's family has asked that the medical team withhold information about his prognosis, and, up to this point, they have reluctantly complied with this request.

The medical oncologist has referred Juan and his family to the social worker for assistance with homecare management. Following a comprehensive psychosocial-spiritual assessment, the social worker has identified other healthcare professionals who can offer assistance to this distressed family, while assisting with the many concrete needs facing them. The chaplain is an especially important member of the team and agrees to follow the family throughout the remainder of Juan's illness. The social worker provides pain management education and supports the family in obtaining the necessary medications while addressing the myths that undermine their confidence in accepting opiates for Juan's pain. Compassionately, the social worker begins to explore the family's reluctance to communicate more openly with Juan regarding the possibility that he may die from his disease, recognizing that his mother's guilt, and father's anger, further contribute to Juan's isolation.

ADDICTIONS

Addiction medicine currently uses the term *substance use disorder* to diagnose anyone who has struggled with drug-induced dysfunction, whether from alcohol or other substance usage (American Psychiatric Association 2000). It is important to distinguish physiologic dependence from addiction, for both patients and many professionals confuse these two terms. Properly prescribed pain medications are extremely unlikely to result in addiction for those without a preexisting substance-use disorder (Portenoy 1998): there are many strategies that are useful in safeguarding against relapse for those with such a history.

For those whose substance use disorder is in remission, the term *recovered* or *in recovery* is used (Emrick 1994). Participants of Alcoholics Anonymous and other twelve-step programs may also have attained a state of *sobriety* as opposed to simply *abstaining* from substances. There are many successful nonparticipating abstainers who consider themselves also recovered. There is an ongoing debate within the field of addiction medicine regarding the merits of abstinence versus harm reduction, with both approaches having their proponents and detractors (Wodak 1998).

Those with a remote history of substance use, those actively using drugs, and those currently in recovery all face additional challenges within the healthcare system at end of life. Yet those most at need for skillfully trained pain-management and addiction specialists often lack adequate resources to have their needs met. Often they lack insurance or face other barriers to access. The patient may conceal a history of substance use in an attempt to minimize the stigmatization anticipated by those in health care. Deliberately withholding information about the use of certain substances believed to be viewed prejudicially can compromise certain treatment plans and have potentially dire consequences.

CASE EXAMPLE

Akira is a twenty-seven-year-old Japanese male who was seen by the social worker in urgent care less than four months after receiving high-dose chemotherapy and the development of recurrent fungal infections. In the assessment interview, the social worker learned that Akira had returned to his previous habit of marijuana and cigarette smoking almost immediately upon discharge from his initial treatment. He had been reluctant to inform his healthcare team of this because he was afraid that they would no longer provide for his care. Only in subsequent interviews did the social worker discover that Akira was also using alcohol to cope with his fears of recurrence. The social worker arranged for a family conference to reassure Akira about his access to ongoing care and to outline a behavioral contract regarding substance use including an evaluation by an addiction specialist. The social worker provided counseling to address his fears and to educate Akira about the potential consequences of his behavior and later referred him to a Cancer Survivors Support Group held in his community.

People with histories of a substance use disorder who are no longer actively using drugs or alcohol and who are in recovery may have undertaken serious self-evaluation, and as a result may have evolved more effective coping mechanisms that replace the maladaptive ones of drinking and substance usage (Schulz and Chappel 1998). Those in recovery have typically acknowledged their problems and have attempted to make amends to those they may have harmed, minimizing the regrets they confront at end of life. Many will also have a large and caring support system. Further, most successful participants of twelve-step recovery programs have developed spiritual awareness that allows the key aspects of recovery, acceptance, and serenity to guide them through end of life issues (Chappel 1998). Because of the intensity of this work, people in recovery may be better equipped to face end of life than others with an addiction history.

CASE EXAMPLE

Robert was a sixty-two-year-old physician who, despite twenty-six years of sobriety, could never escape the addiction of tobacco. He would ultimately die from lung cancer, but did so sober and without fear. After learning his prognosis, he increased his attendance at AA meetings and doubled his sponsoring of those new to recovery. He spoke often in the meetings, but only of the gratitude he felt for the gifts he had received from twenty-six years of sobriety. He was surrounded by his AA friends and family and approached his death with dignity, grace and a serenity that was inspiring to all who knew him.

Many people are able to stop using substances by simply abstaining from usage and reap great benefits as a result. However, because they may not have undergone the self-evaluation of those in recovery or have developed the latter's extensive support system, the abstainer may struggle more with depression and anxiety than those in recovery when confronting end of life. This puts abstainers at greater risk to relapse when confronted with serious stressors. Should relapse occur in either the abstainer or in the person in recovery, it is useful to help by reinstating sobriety. Though some abstainers may want to try twelve-step approaches when confronted with the end of their lives, insisting that they do so will likely prove counterproductive. Recidivism complicates end-of-life issues, so strategies designed to support the patient through this difficult period are necessary. Regular visits, consistency with clinicians, mobilization of the patient's support systems, and identifying sponsors can all be helpful.

People who meet the diagnostic criteria for a substance-use disorder and who are still actively using drugs and or alcohol can face further complications (Passik and Portenoy 1998). Both populations pose special challenges to any caregiving team (Wartenberg 1998). The complications from the direct or primary effects of multiple substances of abuse are many and can include sedation, agitation, confusion, disorientation, delirium, and death. Also, withdrawing from substances about which the caregivers may not have inquired or been informed can pose potentially life-threatening consequences. Though less imminently dangerous than the previous complications, the secondary effects that active substance use can have on judgment, insight, and impulse control can lead the patient to make poor decisions regarding treatment and disposition. In addition, affective instability and behavioral disruptiveness are frequently seen in those still actively using. Two case examples are illustrative.

CASE EXAMPLE

Carl is a twenty-year-old man with a poor prognosis of lymphoma who underwent bone marrow transplantation. He acknowledges that he struggles with addiction, has previously used multiple substances, and relapsed after learning of his diagnosis. After the transplantation process, the patient became extremely angry and demanding. He had numerous friends smuggle cigarettes into his room despite the use of a nicotine patch, and he frequently left the unit unattended and without medical clearance to smoke "whatever he wanted." He contended that because he was going to die anyway, he had no intentions of staying sober, and in fact, intended to use every drug he could access after discharge. Carl frequently threatened to leave the hospital against medical advice. A multidisciplinary team effort was required to help him stay long enough to stabilize sufficiently to be managed realistically as an outpatient. A medication contract was initiated to monitor Carl's medication use. The social worker was instrumental in reconnecting this man with others from his former recovery program. The detailed provision of outpatient resources, including the possibility of hospice, also helped Carl realize that he had choices other than continued substance abuse to cope with the end of his life.

CASE EXAMPLE

Joseph is a forty-year-old Armenian male whose leukemia is expected to respond very well to chemotherapy and bone marrow transplantation. While in the hospital, he is extremely sarcastic and labile in mood. He demands very specific medications, doses, and routes of administration, such as intravenous opioid analgesics and benzodiaza-pines/tranquilizers. When carefully questioned about substance use, he vehemently denies a problem, insisting he is simply unique and knows more than the doctors. His behavior escalates remarkably until he receives significant doses of morphine and Ati-van. His behavior brings into question whether or not he is capable of undergoing the rigors of transplantation. Attempts at education are initially rebuffed. A multidisciplin-ary treatment meeting is held, and harm-reduction strategies are recommended to assist Joseph through the transplant. Once implemented, he rapidly deescalates and is calm and more ready to proceed, agreeing to participate in a methadone maintenance pro-gram. The social worker then provides education and support for this patient, explain-ing that he will need a detoxification program after the transplant, and they agree to coordinate this at discharge.

In the first example, it was important to help the patient maintain sobriety. In the second example, the use of harm reduction involved a monitored medical adminis-tration of agents designed to prevent withdrawal and to prevent escalation of the addictive behaviors (such as a methadone maintenance program). Again, social work-ers are likely to be involved with arranging for such a disposition, and for making an accurate and up-to-date list of referral resources available. The social worker is also alert to the fear, anger, and anxiety that underlie this self-harming behavior.

Whether a patient with a substance use disorder is actively misusing substances or not, pain control can be an especially complicated issue (Savage 1998). Most substance abusers, regardless of their status, will have increased tolerance to, and therefore increased need for, analgesic medications. This increased tolerance is sometimes mistaken for drug-seeking behavior and can set up needless power struggles with the treatment team as the patient approaches the end of life (Stimmel 1998). Social workers can play an active role in preventing these conflicts by providing education and serving as a patient advocate, reminding the treatment team of the special needs of this population. Advocacy and education regarding the etiology of the patient's pain, disease status, prognosis, and so forth are helpful to assist the staff in understanding the patient's need for aggressive pain and symptom management regardless of substance use history (see chapter 19 for further discussion). Unfortunately, many healthcare professionals are reticent to treat associated symptoms such as anxiety, depression, or insomnia for these patients. This is further complicated by the resistance of patients and families to use potentially abusable medications out of fear of initiating a relapse to substance abuse. Additionally, there are likely misconceptions regarding pain management that the social worker can address.

Family caregivers of patients with serious substance abuse are likely to have developed a large array of protective coping strategies (Liepman 1998). These can become especially problematic when facing decision-making conversations at end of life. Informed consent requires direct and open communication among affected parties, and those with a lifetime of deferred decision making and cloudy communication styles will find the medical team's attempts to engage in these difficult conversations especially challenging (White and Fletcher 1990). Caregivers may also have complex reactions to the use of opioids and potential side effects such as sedation or confusion, and be reluctant to give these medications to family members with histories of or current substance-use disorders. This further challenges home care at end of life.

Effective end-of-life management for those with a history of substance abuse will likely be further complicated by a multitude of comorbid medical problems. Assisting a patient through a myriad of chemically induced consequences to achieve a "peaceful passing" takes a skilled and committed team of professionals. Just such a story is recounted in a powerful *Family Medicine Commentary* piece that offers mentorship regarding the value of learning to "save a death" when one can no longer "save a life" (Frank 1995:233). Scott Frank, a family practice physician, recounts his interactions with Jack, a patient with a long history of alcohol and nicotine use coupled with multiple medical problems (including cirrhosis, emphysema, lymphedema, and hypertension). Dr. Frank supported Jack through several cycles of relapses and recoveries until Jack developed squamous cell carcinoma and recognized that his life was nearing an end. Jack's last weeks were devoted to healing the relationships that had been strained through the years of substance abuse. Frank writes, "In medical school we were taught to always ensure that our patients die a 'Harvard death'—with all of their electrolytes in balance. Since then, I have learned to help patients die a 'family practice death'—with all of their psychosocial issues in balance" (1995:233).

Learning to accept people's choices and offering a willingness to share nonjudgmentally in their journeys creates a powerful legacy not just for patients and their families, but also for professional care-providers (Frozena 1991).

CLINICAL IMPLICATIONS

Traditional social-work skills are helpful in working with those who are marginalized at the end of life. Creating a therapeutic relationship with those who are facing increasing isolation and alienation is essential. Assisting in legacy-building tasks such as life reviews or the creation of an "ethical will" can be some of the most meaningful work one engages in. As patients approach their deaths, there are often windows of opportunity for significant life changes. Social workers can support the person and family as they engage in existential struggles to make meaning of their lives. Being attuned to culturally relevant narratives can be very helpful to patients and their families during this challenging time. Assisting in the creation of meaningful rituals is of increasing importance as death approaches. Advocating for necessary health care, the relief of burdensome symptoms, and assistance with the daunting array of logistical and financial nightmares faced by so many are important elements of the comprehensive psychosocial care plan.

The social worker in a medical setting is part of an interdisciplinary team of healthcare professionals who seek to provide optimal care within a limited resource frame. Often it is the role of the social worker to mentor for others the clear communication, collaboration, and consultation skills necessary to build an effective and cohesive team (see chapter 8).

It typically falls to the social worker to assist the team in problem solving, and this is best done from a strengths-based perspective. These skills are needed for both the professional staff and the families being worked with. Advancing illness invites nimbleness in the frequent reprioritization of plans and redistribution of resources. Worsening health may lead to concerns about disfigurement, disability, dependence, distancing from others, and eventually death. Each of these milestones offers opportunities for understanding, support, and education. Assisting others in accepting ever-changing limitations, fostering a positive sense of self, enhancing struggling support networks, and helping to create meaning as a patient approaches death can seem overwhelming. Compassion fatigue and professional burnout may result, if care is not taken to work within a clear system of boundaries and balance (see chapter 44 for further discussion).

Social workers may well find themselves with opportunities to educate their colleagues about the specific populations that their program serves (Garfield, Larson, and Schuldberg 1982). In-services, grand rounds, and other venues can be used to build cultural sensitivity, offer communication skill-building, and address those at the margins of society. Many healthcare professionals report a lack of formal education to intervene adequately with death and dying concerns and are especially challenged by the complexities of recognizing and intervening when patients are marginalized.

Because of the importance of obtaining clear information from the patient and family, comprehensive psychosocial-spiritual assessments are vital (Otis-Green et al. 2002). Individual, couples, and family counseling strategies are all helpful in working with the dying, as are the use of support groups. Structured psycho-spiritual-educational groups that assist the dying with meaning making can be especially useful (Breitbart 2001).

In situations where the language of the clinician and the patient or family differ, a comprehensive assessment requires competence in the use of skilled interpreters and accessible translators (Fung 2001). Social workers can be strong advocates that tools be made available in the languages needed by one's patient populations. Yet in a time of cost-containment, such resources may be among the first cuts unless we voice their importance.

Self-reflection and sensitivity to working with those we identify as different from us are essential (Midwest Bioethics Center 2001). As professionals working with those facing the end of life, we do well to personalize our recommendations by "practicing what we preach." If we advocate for our clients/patients to complete advance directives and wills, we would be wise to have addressed these issues for ourselves. This not only gives the social worker the opportunity to examine more authentically the barriers that facing these issues raise, but also reminds us that death does not distinguish between *them* and *us*. Arbitrary barriers that distance us from those we serve are problematic in social work, yet no more so than in work with those who are marginalized and are dying (see the introduction to this volume).

RESEARCH CONSIDERATIONS

All too little is known regarding the needs of those who are marginalized at the end of life. A review of the research regarding marginalization and end-of-life care reveals that social workers have written little in this area despite its central importance to the mission of social work. Further work is needed if we are to assert our historical mandate to advocate for the needs of the most vulnerable in society.

To provide truly evidence-based practice, we need to better understand the complex interface of ethnicity, social class, and illness in regard to issues such as decision making, treatment adherence, definitions of quality of life, and communication with the healthcare team (Meyerowitz et al. 1998). Furthermore, we need to explore the complexities of assimilation and immigration factors as they relate to concepts of race and ethnicity (Hern et al. 1998).

Preliminary research in areas such as understanding the timing of Do Not Resuscitate (DNR) orders, how frequently these orders are written, and the degree of patient involvement in DNR decisions indicates that ethnic and social factors are very influential (Thompson et al. 1999). However, it remains unclear whether these differences are due to patient preferences or clinician characteristics. Further research is needed, inasmuch as ethnic variability is too often collapsed without adequate substratification to identify meaningful cultural differences within groups.

Professionals who deliver end-of-life care face limitations in their training and understanding of the psychological, social, and spiritual domains of people who are dying. This severely limits a professional's usefulness. For those working in palliative care, skills based on "being with" rather than "doing for" are most essential (Cutcliffe et al. 2001).

Additionally, further research is needed to understand better cultural variables regarding preferences around dying (location, who is present, pain-control and sedation tolerances, and so forth), and to identify factors likely to be desired in improving the death experience for patients and their families (Klessig 1998).

POLICY IMPLICATIONS

Social workers have historically been at the forefront in addressing the needs of the underserved. Joining State Pain Initiatives that advocate for changes in end-of-life care can be a positive step in increasing access to care for those most vulnerable. Considerable attention is needed to remedy the multitude of barriers currently blocking access to needed care (Gordon 1996). Ethical problems arise when we consider the lack of access faced by so many in obtaining needed end-of-life services (Aroskar 1985). Having faced delayed or limited access to needed care for a loved one has important implications for the bereaved (Wyatt, Ogle, and Given 2000) and for society at large.

Descriptions of a "good death" typically include the desire to experience a supported death in one's home environment. Yet the literature is clear that the ability to achieve this is less likely for certain populations (Grande, Addington-Hall, and Todd 1998). Public policies that support family caregiving could influence the cultural and financial gaps that currently restrict access to desired outcomes for so many (Mahoney 1998). Those with severe, persistent mental illness or who have debilitating developmental disabilities are particularly vulnerable regarding limited care options at the end of life (Lesage and Morissette 1993).

Gender and ethnic issues emerge in the area of pain and symptom management (Bonham 2001). Women are less likely to receive adequate analgesia than are men. This undertreatment of pain is compounded further if the woman is older or a member of an ethnic minority, non-English speaking, or suffering from cognitive impairments. This discrepancy in care is even more pronounced if the patient has the misfortune of having pain while residing in a nursing home. It is difficult to tease out the reasons for this systematic undermedication for pain relief, yet these larger societal inequalities are in need of rigorous social work attention (Lynn, Schuster, and Kabcenell 2000).

Disparities in healthcare service delivery to minority patients underscore that healthcare providers are themselves underrepresentative of the populations that they serve (West 2001). Educational materials are seldom developed specifically for each of the audiences they are intended to serve. Often materials that are simply translated into another language are inadequate for the cultural variations that exist within broad generalized groupings such as "Latinos" or "Chinese." Additionally, we need to be mindful of the needs of persons with limited English proficiency and be aware of the need to assess for low literacy in whatever language the person normally speaks.

The ethical implications of legislation such as the Patient Self-Determination Act (1991) raise important questions for the profession (Ulrick 1994). Such legislation is passed only with the majority culture in mind, with the result that the values and beliefs of other groups are ignored. Minorities still face many barriers in the completion of advance directives (Baker 2002). Advocacy is needed to ensure meaningful access to health care if we are to truly implement the goals of such legislation. Public debate still rages regarding living wills, Do Not Resuscitate orders, euthanasia and the withholding or withdrawing of medical interventions (O'Keefe and Crawford 2002). The effects of marginalization and the consequent distrust, distancing, and isolation that result from disempowerment from medical care further complicate these issues.

The Institute of Medicine report *Improving Care at the End of Life* outlines the policy and politics of dying in America (Field and Cassel 1997). The authors enumerate the various pathways for dying, identify healthcare systems in need of restructuring, discuss accountability and quality concerns, explore the need for legal and fiscal reform, and offer education and advocacy directions necessary in order for true reform to occur. Specific suggestions for how to create meaningful change at an institutional, state, and federal level are presented. The implementation of these changes remains a task for us all.

As Walter Schuman so aptly observed more than a decade ago, "We need to create communities that will support and nurture the helpless and embrace them as one of us . . . to provide intensive caring units for them, not only with high-tech medicine but also with soft-touch, human contact" (1991:545). In *Dying Well*, Ira Byock writes passionately of his attempt to change the culture of dying in his community of Missoula, Montana, in order to embrace those who are traditionally abandoned as they face the end of life. Through novel use of the arts, music, and literature, members of this community are bridging the gaps that have long separated disadvantaged ethnic and religious groups. Traditionally, shared narratives of dying are important teaching tools (Moules and Amundson 1997), and culturally relevant stories can be powerful metaphors for social change (Cohen 2001).

PERSONAL AND PROFESSIONAL IMPLICATIONS

Cumulative experiences of caring for the terminally ill take a toll upon the caregivers, be they personal or professional. Our training has seldom adequately prepared us for the implications of compassion fatigue. Recent social movements have led to the development of continuing education for social workers, nurses, and physicians who work in end-of-life care to address this gap. Professional programs such as EPEC: The Project to Educate Physicians on End of Life Care and ELNEC: End of Life Nursing Education Consortium are national examples of this trend. Post-masters' certificate programs in end-of-life care such as those offered by Smith and New York University address the need for social workers seeking advanced training in this area. Recognition that "death is not necessarily an enemy" or indicative of a "failure" in medicine requires an ethical as well as cognitive reframing of the experience (Strouse 1995). Professional organizations and publications are recognizing the need for support in this regard. Shared testimonials regarding the impact of caregiving are no longer unusual in the professional press (Wittenberg 1996). It is imperative that those involved in this work appreciate the impact that their support can have on the dying as well as for the survivors. How a person ultimately dies leaves a legacy for all involved. Appreciating the importance of this work will assist the interdisciplinary team in remembering the life that ended with greater respect and dignity.

The added responsibilities in working with those facing the end of life are compensated by added gratification. The dying have many lessons to teach about living. We are witness to dying done by experts and have opportunities for vicarious learning that can influence our own approaches to death. The dying remind us of the importance of living authentically, mindful of our priorities and of the importance of relationships in our life. The few weeks surrounding a person's death can be suffused with meaning and are often remembered by those involved for decades to come. It is humbling to realize that how individuals die can influence the bereavement experience for so many. We are privileged to share in this potentially transformative journey.

Those facing the end of life are often stigmatized and marginalized. It is the responsibility of all social workers to recognize their concerns and to advocate and support them: a mission reflective of and basic to the core of social work values.

REFERENCES

Abbas, S. Q., and S. Dien. 2001. Mental capacity assessment of terminally ill patients. *European Journal of Palliative Care* 8(6): 250–252.

American Psychiatric Association. 2000. *Diagnostic and Statistical Manual of Mental Disorders.* 4th ed. Washington, DC: American Psychiatric Association.

Aroskar, M. A. 1985. Access to hospice: Ethical dimensions. *Nursing Clinics of North America* 20(2): 299–309.

Baker, D. W., R. M. Parker, M. V. Williams, W. C. Coates, and K. Pitkin. 1996. Use and effectiveness of interpreters in an emergency department. *Journal of the American Medical Association* 275(10): 783–788.

Baker, M. E. 2002. Economic, political and ethnic influences on end-of-life decision making: A decade in review. *Journal of Health and Social Policy* 14(3): 27–39.

Berry, J. W. 1993. Ethnic identity in plural societies. In *Ethnic Identity: Formation and Transmission Among Hispanics and Other Minorities,* ed. M. E. Bernal and G. P. Knight, 271–296. Albany: State University of New York Press.

Bloom, M. 1990. *Introduction to the Drama of Social Work.* Itasca, IL: F. E. Peacock.

Bonham, V. L. 2001. Race, ethnicity, and pain treatment: Striving to understand the causes and solutions to the disparities in pain treatment. *Journal of Law, Medicine and Ethics* 29:52–68.

Borum, M. L., J. Lynn, and Z. Zhong. 2000. The effects of patient race on outcomes in seriously ill patients in SUPPORT: An overview of economic impact, medical intervention, and end-of-life decisions. *Journal of the American Geriatric Society* 48:S194–198.

Breitbart, W. 2001. Spirituality and meaning in supportive care: Spirituality- and meaning-centered group psychotherapy interventions in advanced cancer. *Supportive Care in Cancer* 10(4): 272–280.

Brenner, P. R. 1997. Issues of access in a diverse society. *Hospice Journal* 12(2): 9–16.

Burgener, S. C. 1998. Quality of life in late-stage dementia. In *Hospice Care for Patients with Advanced Progressive Dementia,* ed. L. Volicer and A. Hurley, 88–116. New York: Springer.

Byock, I. 1997. *Dying Well.* New York: Riverhead.

Candilis, P. J., and M. E. Foti. 1999. Case presentation: End-of-life care and mental illness: The case of Ms. W. *Journal of Pain and Symptom Management* 18(6): 447–450.

Chappel, J. N. 1998. Spiritual components of the recovery process. In *Principles of Addiction Medicine* (2d ed.), ed. A. W. Graham and T. K. Schultz, 725–728. Chevy Chase, MD: American Society of Addiction Medicine.

Christopher, M. 2001. Innovations in assessing and expanding decision making capacity. *State Initiatives in End-of-Life Care* 12:3–5.

Cohen, J. 2001. *Farewell, My Friend: An Interfaith Conversation on Caring at the End of Life.* Missoula, MT: Missoula Demonstration Project.

Congress, E. P., and B. P. Lyons. 1992. Cultural differences in health beliefs: Implications for social work practice in health care settings. *Social Work in Health Care* 17(3): 81–96.

Corless, I. B. 2001. Bereavement. In *Textbook of Palliative Nursing*, ed. B. R. Ferrell and N. Coyle, 352–362. New York: Oxford University Press.

Crawley, L. M., P. A. Marshall, B. Lo, and B. A. Koenig. 2002. Strategies for culturally effective end-of-life care. *American College of Physicians–American Society of Internal Medicine* 136(9): 673–679.

Cutcliffe, J. R., C. Black, E. Hanson, and P. Goward. 2001. The commonality and synchronicity of mental health nurses and palliative care nurses: Closer than you think? *Journal of Psychiatric and Mental Health Nursing* 8:53–59.

Dahlin, C. M. 1999. Access to care. *Hospice Journal* 14(3–4): 75–84.

Davis, A. 1996. Ethics and ethnicity: End-of-life decisions in four ethnic groups of cancer patients. *Medical Law* 15(3): 429–432.

Dona, G., and J. W. Berry. 1994. Acculturation attitudes and acculturative stress of Central American refugees. *International Journal of Psychology* 29(1): 54–70.

Dunn, C. M., and G. Chadwick. 1999. *Protecting Study Volunteers in Research.* Boston: CenterWatch.

Emrick, C. D. 1994. Alcoholics anonymous and other 12-Step groups. In *Textbook of Substance Abuse Treatment*, ed. M. Galanter and H. D. Kleber, 351–358. Washington, DC: American Psychiatric Association.

Field, M. J., and C. K. Cassel, eds. 1997. *Approaching Death: Improving Care at the End of Life.* Washington, DC: National Academy Press.

Frank, S. H. 1995. A family practice death. *Family Medicine* 27(4): 232–233.

Friedman, E. 2000. Making choices: Meanwhile, back at the ranch . . . serving some of the most vulnerable people among us. *Health Forum Journal* 43(6): 6–9.

Frozena, C. L. 1991. The craft of the nurse. *Home Healthcare Nurse* 9(2): 51.

Fung, E. 2001. Using an interpreter effectively. *Hemaware* 6(5): 58–59.

Fung, L. 1994. Implementing the Patient Self-Determination Act (PSDA): How to effectively engage Chinese-American elderly persons in the decision of advance directives. *Journal of Gerontological Social Work* 22(1–2): 161–174.

Garfield, C.A., D. G. Larson, and D. Schuldberg. 1982. Mental health training and the hospice community: A national survey. *Death Education* 6:189–204.

Gochros, H. L., J. S. Gochros, and J. Fischer. 1986. *Helping the Sexually Oppressed.* Englewood Cliffs, NJ: Prentice-Hall.

Goldenberg, D., J. Holland, and S. Schachter. 2000. Palliative care in the chronically mentally ill. In *Handbook of Psychiatry in Palliative Medicine*, ed. H. M. Chochinov and W. Breitbart, 91–96. New York: Oxford University Press.

Gordon, A. K. 1995. Deterrents to access and service for blacks and Hispanics: The Medicare hospice benefit, healthcare utilization, and cultural barriers. *Hospice Journal* 10(2): 65–83.

——. 1996. Hospice and minorities: A national study of organizational access and practice. *Hospice Journal* 11(1): 49–70.

Grande, G. E., J. M. Addington-Hall, and C. J. Todd. 1998. Place of death and access to home care services: Are certain patient groups at a disadvantage? *Social Science and Medicine* 47(5): 565–579.

Haber, D. 1999. Minority access to hospice. *American Journal of Hospice and Palliative Care* 16(1): 386–389.

Hanrahan, P., and D. J. Luchins. 1995. Access to hospice programs in end-stage dementia: A national survey of hospice programs. *Journal of the American Geriatric Society* 43:56–59.

Hebert, M. P. 1998. Perinatal bereavement in its cultural context. *Death Studies* 22(1): 61–78.

Hern, H. E., B. A. Koenig, L. J. Moore, and P. A. Marshall. 1998. The difference that culture can make in end-of-life decisionmaking. *Cambridge Quarterly of Healthcare Ethics* 7:27–40.

Hopp, F. P., and S. A. Duffy. 2000. Racial variations in end-of-life care. *Journal of the American Geriatrics Society* 48:658–663.

Hughes, A. 2001. The poor and underserved. In *Textbook of Palliative Nursing*, ed. B. R. Ferrell and N. Coyle, 461–466. New York: Oxford University Press.

Johnson, C. B. 1998. Hospice: What gets in the way of appropriate and timely access. *Holistic Nursing Practice* 13(1): 8–21.

Johnson, C. B., and S. C. Slaninka. 1999. Barriers to accessing hospice services before a late terminal state. *Death Studies* 23(3): 225–238.

Klessig, J. 1998. Dying the good death: Death and culture. *Annals of Long Term Care* 6(9): 285–290.

Lesage, A. D., and R. Morissette. 1993. Residential and palliative needs of persons with severe mental illness who are subject to long-term hospitalization. *Canada's Mental Health* 8:12–17.

Liepman, M. R. 1998. The family in addiction. In *Principles of Addiction Medicine* (2d ed.), ed. A. W. Graham and T. K. Schultz, 1093–1098. Chevy Chase, MD: American Society of Addiction Medicine.

Limbo, R. K., and S. R. Wheeler. 1987. *When a Baby Dies: A Handbook for Healing and Helping*, 36–74. La Crosse, WI: Resolve Through Sharing.

Lynn, J., J. L. Schuster, and A. Kabcenell. 2000. *Improving Care for the End of Life: A Sourcebook for Health Care Managers and Clinicians*. New York: Oxford University Press.

Mahoney, J. 1998. An update on efforts by the hospice community and the National Hospice Organization to improve access to quality hospice care. *Hospice Journal* 13(1–2): 139–144.

Meyerowitz, B. E., S. C. Formenti, K. O. Ell, and B. Leedham. 1998. Ethnicity and cancer outcomes: Behavioral and psychosocial considerations. *Psychological Bulletin* 123(1): 47–70.

Meyerowitz, B. E., J. Richardson, S. Hudson, and B. Leedham. 2000. Depression among Latina cervical cancer patients. *Journal of Social and Clinical Psychology* 19(3): 352–371.

Mezey, M., J. Teresi, G. Ramsey, E. Mitty, and T. Bobrowitz. 2000. Decision-making capacity to execute a health care proxy: Development and testing guidelines. *Journal of the American Geriatrics Society* 48(2): 179–187.

Midwest Bioethics Center. 2001. Healthcare narratives from diverse communities: A self-assessment tool for healthcare providers. Kansas City, MO: Midwest Bioethics Center.

Morrison, R. S., et al. 1998. Barriers to completion of health care proxies: An examination of ethnic differences. *Archives of Internal Medicine* 158(22): 2493–2497).

Morse, G. A. 2000. On being homeless and mentally ill: A multitude of losses and the possibility of recovery. In *Loss and Trauma: General and Close Relationship Perspectives*, ed. J. H. Harvey and E. D. Miller, 249–261. Philadelphia: Brunner-Routledge.

Moules, N. J., and J. K. Amundson. 1997. Grief—an invitation to inertia: A narrative approach to working with grief. *Journal of Family Nursing* 3(4): 378–393.

Nuland, S. B. 1994. *How We Die*. New York: Random House.

O'Keefe, M. E., and K. Crawford. 2002. End-of-life care: Legal and ethical considerations. *Seminar for Oncology Nursing* 18(2): 143–148.

Otis-Green, S., R. Sherman, M. Perez, and P. Baird. 2002. An integrated psychosocial-spiritual model for cancer pain management. *Cancer Practice Supplement* 10(1): S58–S65.

Panuthos, C., and C. Romeo, C. 1984. *Ended Beginnings: Healing Childbearing Losses*. South Hadley, MA: Bergin & Garvey.

Passik, S. D., and R. K. Portenoy. 1998. Substance abuse disorders. In *Psycho-Oncology*, ed. J. Holland, 576–586. New York: Oxford University Press.

Portenoy, R. K. 1998. *Contemporary Diagnosis and Management of Pain in Oncologic and AIDS patients*. 2d ed. Newtown, PA: Handbooks in Health Care.

Quinnett, P. G. 1987. *Suicide: The Forever Decision.* New York: Continuum.

Reese, D. J., R. E. Ahern, S. Nair, J. D. O'Faire, and C. Warren. 1999. Hospice access and use by African Americans: Addressing cultural and institutional barriers through participatory action research. *Social Work* 44(6): 549–559.

Ross, H. 2001. End-of-life care issues need culturally sensitive approaches. In *Closing the Gap: A Newsletter of the Office of Minority Health,* 10. Washington, DC: U.S. Department of Health and Human Services.

Savage, S. R. 1998. Principles of pain treatment in the addicted patient. In *Principles of Addiction Medicine* (2d ed.), ed. A.W. Graham and T. K. Schultz, 919–944. Chevy Chase, MD: American Society of Addiction Medicine.

Schultz, J. E., and J. N. Chappel. 1998. Twelve step programs. In *Principles of Addiction Medicine* (2d ed.), ed. A.W. Graham and T. K. Schultz, 693–706. Chevy Chase, MD: American Society of Addiction Medicine.

Schuman, W. H. 1991. Hospice care for the living dead: Mental illness and our practices of care. *Nursing and Health Care* 12(10): 544–545.

Shai, D., and I. Rosenwaike. 1988. Violent deaths among Mexican-, Puerto Rican- and Cuban-born migrants in the United States. *Social Science and Medicine* 26:269–276.

Sontag, M. 1992. Hospice values, access to services and the Medicare hospice benefit. *American Journal of Hospice and Palliative Care* 11:17–21.

State of California Health and Safety Code. 1990. Senate Bill 1840, Chapter 672, Section 1259.

Stimmel, B. 1998. Prescribing issues and the relief of pain. In *Principles of Addiction Medicine* (2d ed.), ed. A.W. Graham and T. K. Schultz, 961–966. Chevy Chase, MD: American Society of Addiction Medicine.

Strouse, W. S. 1995. Letters to the editor: A near perfect death. *Family Medicine* 27(8): 488.

Stuart, B. 1999. The NHO Medical Guidelines for Non-Cancer Disease and local medical review policy: Hospice access for patients with diseases other than cancer. *Hospice Journal* 14(3–4): 139–154.

Swerdlow, P. S. 2000. Use of humans in biomedical experimentation. In *Scientific Integrity* (2d ed.), ed. F. L. Macrina, 73–100. Washington, DC: ASM Press.

Taywaditep, K. J. 2001. Marginalization among the marginalized: Gay men's anti-effeminacy attitudes. *Journal of Homosexuality* 42(1): 1–28.

Thompson, B. L., D. Lawson, M. Croughan-Minihane, and M. Cooke. 1999. Do patients' ethnic and social factors influence the use of do-not-resuscitate orders? *Ethnicity and Disease* 9(1): 132–139.

Ulrick, L. P. 1994. The patient-self-determination act and cultural diversity. *Cambridge Quarterly of Healthcare Ethics* 3(3): 410–413.

Wartenberg, A. A. 1998. Management of common medical problems. In *Principles of Addiction Medicine* (2d ed.), ed. A. W. Graham and T. K. Schultz, 731–740. Chevy Chase, MD: American Society of Addiction Medicine.

West, J. 2001. Recruitment and retention critical to minority health professionals. In *Closing the Gap: A Newsletter of the Office of Minority Health,* 10. Washington, DC: U.S. Department of Health and Human Services.

White, M. L., and J. C. Fletcher. 1990. The story of Mr. and Mrs. Doe: "You can't tell my husband he's dying; it will kill him." *Journal of Clinical Ethics* 1(1): 59–62.

Wittenberg, J. 1996. Profiles in caring: An interrupted death. *American Journal of Hospice and Palliative Care* 10:15–19.

Wodak, A. 1998. Harm reduction as an approach to treatment. In *Principles of Addiction Medicine* (2d ed.), ed. A. W. Graham and T. K. Schultz, 395–404. Chevy Chase, MD: American Society of Addiction Medicine.

Wyatt, G. K., K. S. Ogle, and B. A. Given. 2000. Access to hospice: A perspective from the bereaved. *Journal of Palliative Medicine* 3(4): 433–440.

24

LESBIANS AND GAY MEN AT THE END OF THEIR LIVES: PSYCHOSOCIAL CONCERNS

BRUCE THOMPSON AND YVETTE COLÓN

All individuals' life experiences contribute greatly to the complexity and uniqueness of the end-of-life issues that we all face. These experiences, as much as anything, shape our desires and beliefs about health, illness, death and dying. The Diversity Committee advocates recognition, acceptance and support of its recommendations concerning individuals' experiences with race; historical oppression; war and its aftermath; cultural, religious and spiritual practices; affectional orientation; discrimination and poverty. The true meaning of diversity (especially as it affects the end of life) is as much about these unique, view-shaping experiences as about the narrower, yet more common concept that focuses on ethnicity or religion. —Last Acts Coalition 2001

JUST AS interest in end-of-life care has increased over the past several decades, so has an emphasis within social work and other helping professions on diversity, including diversity of sexual orientation (Appleby and Anastas 1998). Attention to cultural differences in the negotiation of tasks related to death and bereavement has become a benchmark in the design of both policy (Irish, Lundquist, and Nelsen 1993; Koenig 1997) and direct service interventions (Dowd et al. 1998; Kawaga-Singer and Blackhall 2001; Koenig and Gates-Williams 1995). However, it is surprising that there is very little in the literature on end-of-life care that focuses specifically on the particular concerns and treatment considerations of lesbians and gay men. It is the intention of this chapter to provide a beginning conceptual framework for social-work interventions related to end-of-life issues for lesbians and gay men.

It should be noted at the outset that the vast literature on AIDS has expanded our understanding—both anecdotally and empirically—of what may be helpful to individuals and families who are confronting death (Aronstein and Thompson 1998; Benson and Brookman 1998; Cadwell, Burnham, and Forstein 1994; Dilley and Marks 1998; McKusick 1988; Shernoff 1999; Sadowy 1991). The AIDS literature has also been helpful in beginning to articulate health-related behaviors and policy issues related to end-of-life care for gay men.

Except for the National Lesbian Health Care Survey (Bradford and Ryan 1988), there are not a great deal of data on lesbian health-related behavior (Roberts and Sorenson 1999). Many studies suggest that lesbian, gay, and bisexual people do not seek routine medical services because of a fear of homophobia (Eliason and Schope 2001; Martinson, Fisher, and DeLapp 1996; Hitchcock and Wilson 1992).

In 1999, Saulnier reported on a community survey of lesbian and bisexual women that suggested that a provider of high quality, lesbian-sensitive services is someone who (most important) is a competent practitioner; has a positive attitude toward a women's female partner and the lesbian community; and is sensitive to social issues of concern to lesbians. Despite progress that has been made in increasing access to sensitive and appropriate gay and lesbian healthcare services, lesbians' utilization of high-quality physical and mental health services is hindered by long-standing provider biases (Stevens 1996; Peterson and Bricker-Jenkins 1996; Stevens and Hall 1992). The disclosure of sexual orientation to providers is difficult for lesbians and may result in withdrawal of support and increased stigma (Matthews et al. 2002; Klitzman and Greenberg 2002).

It is important to begin by considering multiple developmental perspectives in conceptualizing the needs of lesbians and gay men dealing with end of life issues. Normative, age-specific tasks related to developmental stages (adolescence, midlife, old age) as they intersect with tasks related to the end of life, of course, require attention. It is also useful to look at stages in the development of lesbian/gay identity and at the social and historical context of an individual's identity development. Where is the individual along the continuum of integration and consolidation of his or her gay/lesbian identity versus internalized homophobia and conflict about being gay/lesbian? It is obvious that a lesbian adolescent with a terminal diagnosis will bring different developmental issues and sense of self to dealing with the end of her life than will an older lesbian who has a partner and adult children from her partnership. Similarly, an older gay man who is dying and who has lived a closeted lifestyle (or disavowed a gay identity) may have very different concerns regarding his sexual orientation at the end of life than would a younger man who has formed his identity within the historical contexts of gay liberation and the AIDS epidemic. Appleby and Anastas distinguish between traditional and new gay culture in discussing gay/lesbian identity: "Unlike traditional homosexual culture, the new culture publicly affirms rather than conceals identity. It confronts society with gay and lesbian sexuality and demands equal rights rather than seeking to win tolerance by neutralizing moral indignation. The new gay culture is concerned not just with affirming the rights and the legitimacy of being gay; it is also, and equally, concerned with working out ways of living as a lesbian or gay man in society" (1998:92).

This distinction between traditional and new (postliberation) lesbian/gay culture is a useful one, perhaps even accounting for this beginning exposition of particular concerns for lesbians and gay men at the end of life. And the concept of lesbian and gay identity—as a source of both conflict and joy, as both disavowed and embraced—is a central developmental cornerstone of this exposition.

It is also useful to think of the developmental phases usually involved in death. Pattison (1978) has delineated the acute crisis phase, the chronic living-dying phase, and the terminal phase, each with its own specific challenges. Pattison also proposes that learning about one's imminent death sets up four possible "trajectories" of expectation, which then determine the stressors and tasks confronting the dying individual and others involved. They are: (1) expecting a certain death at a known time (acute terminal illness or accident); (2) expecting a certain death at an unknown time (chronic terminal illness); (3) expecting an uncertain death but a known time when certainty will be established (illnesses which are waiting on biopsy or organ availability); and (4) expecting an uncertain death at an unknown time (progressive chronic illness eventually leading to death). Rando provides a framework for assessing the stressors and coping particular to these phases, as well as some suggestions for psychosocial interventions (1984:199–225).

The imminence of death presents the individual with changes in biopsychosocial functioning. Such changes can lead to a diminishment and constriction of the self and the suffering that such constriction can entail (Charmaz 1983). Such changes can also lead to a psychological and spiritual transformation of self, an enlightened and expanded self, and the use of the imminence of death as an opportunity for growth (Coward 1990, 1995; Fryback 1993; Hall 1998; Steeves and Kahn 1987). Rizzuto suggests that being close to death results in a revisiting and reworking of psychologically important relationships, resulting in changes and growth at the end of life. She states, "Approaching death may bring the last occasion for a new encounter with the objects of the past: these cover the entire course of the dying person's life, and give the last occasion for further acceptance or rejection of aspects of the primary objects and others that have remained painfully discordant with the sense of self" (1979:78).

Rizzuto also makes the case that, for most people, the final representation of God comes in contemplating their own imminent deaths (1979:8). In fact, an extensive literature has emerged in recent years that presents anecdotal accounts of the experiences of people who are dying, usually written from a perspective of spiritual-psychological transformation and consolidation (Byock 1997; Groopman 1997; Callahan and Kelley 1992; DeHennezel 1997; Singh 1998). This literature, while providing insightful accounts of a wide range of people who are at the end of life, does not usually focus on lesbian or gay individuals, except occasionally presenting a gay man who is dying of AIDS. However, Phillips does capture very poignantly the experience of lesbians and gay men who, in facing death, may confront a loss of self and a sense of abandonment by God: "A gay identity, with or without being infected with HIV, may be seen as a cause, result, or major symptom of God's withdrawal of love" (1994:100). She stresses the importance of integrating spiritual concerns into psychotherapy at the end of life. Of course, some very informative accounts of the experiences of gay men and lesbians confronting death can be found in the works of gay and lesbian writers such as May Sarton's *A Reckoning: A Novel* (1978) and Mark Doty's *Heaven's Coast: A Memoir* (1997).

Over the past decade, theoretical and empirical publications have advanced our understanding of lesbians and gay men at adult stages of development—midlife and old age. Building on the pioneering works of Kelly (1977), Kimmel (1978), Berger (1980, 1982a, 1982b), Poor (1982), Lee (1987), and Friend (1991), the current literature on midlife and old age may provide ways of thinking about end-of-life concerns for gay men and lesbians. This literature examines themes common to both lesbians and gay men and looks at differences and distinctions between them (Kimmel and Sang 1995; Reid 1995; Humphreys and Quam 1998). In general, the literature presents a predominant view of older lesbians and gay men as aging "successfully" (Friend 1991), having exceptional ego strength and resilience as a result of the process of coming out and adapting, even in the context of a predominantly homophobic culture. Friend

(1991) calls this "crisis competence" and Berger (1980) calls it "mastery of crisis." J. D. Reid aptly summarizes the research on older lesbians and gay men:

> Taken together, the available literature suggests that the stereotypes of lonely, alienated, and despondent older lesbians and gay men are incorrect. Rather, what emerges is a picture of older gay men and lesbians who are active, selectively engaging in interests and activities of their choosing. There is, apparently, considerable variability in how the lesbian or gay man has adapted her or his identity to varying contexts of discrimination. Some older gay men and lesbians prefer to keep their sexual orientation private, while others are open and highly engaged in public organizations and activities. These data underscore the reality of unique and individual adaptations as a result of different developmental experiences and personal needs (1995:227).

Successful aging for gay men and lesbians may be associated with a range of circumstances (Bradford, Ryan, and Rothblum 1994; Cruikshank 1990; Ehrenberg 1996; Quam and Whitford 1992). For example, not surprisingly, Lee (1987) in his longitudinal study of gay men ranging in age from fifty to eighty, found higher life satisfaction in those men who were healthier, wealthier, and more socially involved. He also found that some older gay men found that the avoidance of coming out publicly was viewed as adaptive and stress-avoidant. On the other hand, Friend (1991) found less "successful" aging when the individual internalized and conformed to homophobic images, resulting in "living in the closet," usually with shame and self-loathing, or "passing" in a heterosexual lifestyle or marriage.

The literature on gay and lesbian adult development raises questions about how the adaptive and resilient characteristics of gay men and lesbians at midlife and in old age will be useful at the end of life. Are gay men and lesbians presented with particular challenges at the end of life? Therese Rando suggests that all people facing imminent death will experience stress, intermittently more severe depending on the course of illness and other events; she outlines a range of defenses, from primitive to more mature, used to cope with this stress. She points out both the adaptive and maladaptive aspects of defense—for example, regression, which can be seen as very primitive if it results in giving up, can also be seen as adaptive if viewed as the individual's ability to surrender enough to accept necessary care (1984:251–266).

We also know that homophobia frequently results in particular insensitivity within institutional systems, including legal, social service, and medical care systems (Kelly 1977; Berger 1982; Poor 1982; Reid 1995). These are the very systems that usually become most critical at the end of life. Lesbians and gay men may have a particularly difficult time coping with stress at the end of life if they experience the systems that are providing their care as insensitive, discriminatory, or punitive. On the other hand, as suggested by Friend (1991) and Berger (1980), they may bring a resilience and competence to end-of-life tasks, in terms of both psychological adaptation and negotiating difficult systems of care. Indeed, data on gay men with AIDS suggest extraordinary psychological resilience as measured by low rates of mood disorders and psychiatric distress. Healthier psychological functioning in gay men with AIDS has been associated with the following variables: having a confidante, receiving excellent medical care, having extraordinary personal resources (intelligence, education, interests), and being in psychotherapy (Rabkin et al. 1993).

Many, perhaps most, philosophical, spiritual, and psychological systems of thought conceptualize the end of life as presenting the individual with some challenge related to the dichotomy of integration/consolidation and disappointment/despair (Erikson 1986; Carni 1988; Byock 1996; Rinpoche 1992). Such conceptualizations posit some individual responsibility, within physical and emotional capacity, for "dying well" (Smith and Maher 1991; Weisman 1988); at the same time they suggest some degree of determinism, that is, that dying well may be the outcome of generally favorable dispositional and environmental factors over the life span. For example, Erik Erikson (1963) concludes his developmental framework by arguing that having a sense of integrity over despair amounts to being able to put one's final stamp of approval on one's life as the one and only life that one could have lived (Erikson 1963). Other developmental theorists have suggested that the adaptations required of gay men and lesbians in the coming-out process and in the establishment of a positive homosexual identity are prognostic of successfully meeting the challenges of aging (Francher and Henkin 1973; Kimmel 1978; Friend 1991; Reid 1995). From this perspective, it would make sense that the ego strength and psychological well-being that can be brought to the tasks of aging well might also be brought to the dying process. Later in his own life, Erikson theorized that the attainment of integrity in old age was accompanied by the virtue of wisdom, "an informed and detached concern with life itself in the face of death itself" (1982:6).

However, because not everyone dies old, facing death may entail making meaning of one's life in the context of whatever developmental stage at which one confronts death. For younger people who are dying, this might mean approaching developmental tasks at an "accelerated pace" (Andrews 1981), or it might mean "skipping" to the stage of integrity versus despair (Carni 1988).

In a well-constructed exploratory investigation, Merriam, Courtenay, and Reeves point out in their sample of mid-life, HIV-positive gay men that facing death resulted in a convergence of developmental tasks. This usually included revisiting "identity versus role confusion" and redefining the self; at the same time, it also entailed dealing with all of the other tasks of adult development—intimacy, generativity, and integrity. They concluded for this sample that coming to terms with intimacy and generativity were helpful in resolving issues of identity and ego integrity (1997:226).

Most religious institutions equate facing death with finishing the unfinished business of life and with letting go into whatever follows death, whether nothingness or some form of continuation (Johnson and McGee 1998). For many religious traditions that believe in a life after death, one's destination is determined in large part by how one has adhered to doctrine and by how one has negotiated dying. Unfortunately, in many cultural and religious traditions, the experience of death for a gay man or lesbian, as well as the experience of bereavement for their loved ones, may be characterized by lifelong struggles related to the doctrinal condemnation of homosexuality. This condemnation is a unique form of external and, consequently, internalized oppression. The ability to put one's stamp of approval on a life that has been experienced as condemned or marginalized may require tremendous internal resources, even for those who, when less vulnerable, were able to live with self-esteem and some objectivity about negative social attitudes. For those who have been ambivalent about their homosexuality or have viewed their life as "not chosen" or "flawed" by homosexuality, the efforts at consolidation at the end of life may be fraught with desperation.

CASE EXAMPLE

Matthew, age fifty-two, lived in rural New England with his partner, forty-two-year-old Paul. They had been together for twenty years when Matthew was diagnosed with quickly progressing lung cancer and was given six months to live. Matthew's Lutheran family lived in Minnesota, and, like them, Matthew was very organized. Without Paul's help, he made all of the arrangements for his funeral and established a trust so that Paul would inherit some money from his good investments; a life insurance policy would pay the remaining mortgage. Paul and Matthew had developed a good life "out of the mainstream," designing and distributing furniture for sale in fine retail stores. They were very proud of their house and garden and content to be alone. They had a close friendship with a lesbian couple from the next town, but otherwise did not have many friends. Although they were out to both of their families, contact was sporadic by phone; usually once a year, in person, both of them would visit his family separately—mostly to not have to deal family members' homophobia.

As Matthew's condition worsened, Paul became very depressed. He couldn't imagine life without Matthew, but was not very helpful most of the time in comforting him or meeting his basic needs. Paul was referred by the hospice nurse to a gay social worker in a nearby city. The focus of the work was on Paul's sense that he was also dying as Matthew approached the end of his life. Paul became increasing labile, unable to work, and frightened. With the help of antidepressant medication, he was eventually able to talk in the sessions, resume his work, and talk more about his sadness directly with Matthew.

Just before Matthew died, Paul was able to comfort him and to realize that life would never be the same without him. With the help of his lesbian friends, Paul was then able to arrange the funeral and cremation that Matthew wanted, even though the family objected and wanted Matthew's body returned to Minnesota. When the family contested Matthew's estate plan, Paul was able to secure the services of a lawyer and to prevail. Paul continued to use weekly therapy for two years after Matthew's death, during which he continued to feel very sad, lost, and directionless. He eventually decided to leave the country and to live in a small city where he could continue the business that he and Matthew had created.

The social worker's role with Matthew and Paul initially was to help them to appreciate the differences in their personal styles as they adjusted to the shock of the diagnosis. This approach at first seemed time-consuming, but it was essential to all the work that followed. Matthew was more able to take Paul into account in his almost obsessive approach to dealing with practical issues; gradually, he was able to talk in the sessions about his feelings about dying and his worry and regret about leaving Paul alone. Paul was gradually able to be more emotionally available and comforting to Matthew. Paul did get depressed over the six months leading up to Matthew's death, and he needed extra support from the social worker in dealing with Matthew's demanding and dismissive family. In the following two years, the social worker provided a relationship within which Paul could work through his grief, as well as address some long-standing depression, social isolation, and low self-esteem. His move to the city was seen as a breakthrough, and the social worker was able to offer him several referrals to continue the work he had begun; the worker also left the door open should Paul want to touch base in the future.

CASE EXAMPLE

Carmen was a forty-seven-year-old woman who had been living with HIV for twelve years when she was diagnosed with lymphoma. She lived in a large city with her partner of ten years and had been able to find sensitive, attentive doctors who managed her HIV adequately with a variety of medications. With her diagnosis of lymphoma, however, Carmen had to find a new set of doctors and was apprehensive about disclosing her sexual orientation to them. Carmen worked for more than twenty years as an administrative assistant in a small manufacturing company; her employers were very accommodating, and she had been able to adjust her work schedule and take time off to attend to her medical needs. Carmen completed her advance directives many years before with the help of her partner Lisa, a legal secretary. They both had tenuous relationships with their families of origin, who were homophobic and not supportive of Carmen and Lisa's commitment to each other. The two women, however, had a large circle of very supportive lesbian, gay, and heterosexual friends who helped whenever they were needed. As Carmen became more anxious about her worsening illness, Lisa, who had continued to work full-time, began to experience caregiver fatigue; she began supportive psychotherapy to help her, as much as possible, cope with Carmen's illness and eventual death. Carmen joined her in therapy for several months, and they were able to work on their feelings of guilt, Carmen's for being a "burden" to Lisa, and Lisa's for being the "healthy one in the relationship." Ultimately, Lisa took a leave of absence from her job; during the last few months of Carmen's life, they spent all their time together, traveling when they could and enjoying their relationships, with each other and with their closest, most devoted friends.

As a caregiver to someone with a limited life expectancy, Lisa first contacted the social worker for help and guidance. Because she and Carmen could not rely on their families for support, Lisa believed that she alone was responsible for all of Carmen's needs. The social worker helped her clarify Carmen's practical and emotional needs and identify appropriate responsibilities. The social worker assisted Lisa in feeling more comfortable asking friends for help and saying no to unreasonable demands made by family and her workplace. With Lisa's help, Carmen had taken care of legal matters; the couple had already communicated their wishes through their wills and advanced directives. Once Lisa was able to get help and take time for herself, she and Carmen could spend time together attending to their emotional concerns. At Lisa's request, the social worker saw them as a couple to help them sort out their feelings of guilt and anxiety; when the planned couple sessions ended, they were able to use what they had learned together to weather several medical crises. The social worker continued to see Lisa individually to help her face the challenge of redefining her identity and building a new life.

CASE EXAMPLE

At seventy, Peter had lived his entire adult life in the gay neighborhood of the city, priding himself on his independence and hard work. He had many friends and many former partners and had always been considered charming and handsome. He made his living supervising the construction of set designs for a local television station. He had mutually supportive relationships with his extended family, particularly with one sister who lived nearby. Until his stroke, which left him unable to walk and unable to talk very clearly, he did not experience life as difficult in any way. Things had come easy to him once he came out after military duty in the 1950s; he was happy to live through gay liberation, and he had never felt the need to be very introspective. He had enjoyed trips to the country, hiking and fishing; he also enjoyed meeting his friends at the gay bar and hanging out.

When his mother became sick ten years earlier, she was placed in a nursing home, where she died after two years. Around this same time, one of Peter's best friends died of AIDS in a hospice. Peter resolved then that he would never go to what he called a "death camp." But his sister was not able to care for him, and he was not able to be on his own. At first, after he was placed in the nursing home, some of his friends came to visit. Then he asked them not to come around so much; he felt that it was too burdensome for them and he was embarrassed about his current condition. He was also worried about homophobia on the part of some of the nursing home staff. When Peter was referred to the social worker by a nurse, he was very despondent and angry, and he talked about wanting to die as soon as possible. In the initial meeting with the social worker, he asked if arrangements could be made to hasten his death.

The social worker's role with Peter was complicated from the beginning. In the first session, the worker needed to assess quickly for suicidal intent, given the seriousness of Peter's request for wanting help to end his life. Peter's aphasia made it difficult to understand him and caused him much frustration. The worker established through a mental status exam that Peter was clear in his thinking and that there was no delirium, dementia, or psychotic features. It was then a matter of trying to establish enough alliance to begin to understand what was motivating his request. It was very important in this initial meeting to provide a safe enough environment for Peter to come out to the worker if he wanted to. The worker simply stated that it must be very difficult to be forced by circumstances to be so dependent and to live in such a regimented environment. Peter began to describe how hard it was for him to be in the military in the 1950s, and he was then able to talk about being a very independent person after that experience. He eventually came out to the worker in the session and began to be less anxious and enraged. The worker was able to see Peter twice a week at the beginning of the work and was able to obtain his agreement to meet with his sister and with two of his best friends, and Peter was able to share his concerns with them. The worker also arranged for a consultation for medication, and he was prescribed an SSRI; the worker also requested that Peter's physician order speech therapy, which resulted in somewhat clearer and less anxious communication. As Peter began to feel better over several months of work, he began to look forward to his sessions as well as visits from friends and to be less self-conscious about his speech. For the worker, what started out as a very unsettling crisis, a request for help with self-termination, turned into ongoing work characterized both by insight-oriented therapy and by case management. It also resulted in the worker's helping the nursing home begin to include material on sexual orientation in staff training programs. Supportive work with Peter continued until his death nine months later from a second stroke.

CASE EXAMPLE

Blanche was a sixty-five-year-old woman who was diagnosed with lung cancer during a breakup with her partner of ten years. Owing to financial difficulties, Blanche continued living in the apartment she shared with Laura, a situation she acknowledged as "complicated and uncomfortable." Laura took care of Blanche during the year she received both radiation and chemotherapy treatments. When Blanche completed treatment, she moved into a small apartment on her own and was able to remain friendly with Laura. For most of her life, Blanche was ambivalent about being a lesbian and lived a fairly closeted life. The breakup with Laura was, in part, about her inability to cope with Laura's comfort and openness about being a lesbian. She was geographically and emotionally distant from her family, who did not know about her relationships with Laura or other women. Blanche had some close friends who were lesbians, but she had never been part of a gay or lesbian community. During her illness, she had not been able to disclose her sexual orientation to any of her healthcare providers, feeling that such information was not relevant. She had little social support, and when her cancer spread she sought out a lesbian-friendly psychotherapist for help with several issues: coping with her illness and potential death, exploring her ambivalence about being a lesbian and strengthening her relationship with Laura. She and Laura had known each other for twenty-five years and had been partners for ten. Blanche finally came to see the value in their ongoing friendship. She struggled with developing advance directives. Ultimately, the only document she completed was her healthcare proxy, naming Laura as her agent. Although she remained very private about her personal life and maintained her independence as long as possible, Blanche reached out and made connections with other cancer patients and began to enjoy time with old friends who came to visit. She declined hospice care and received much of her care from a home health agency.

Blanche had been given a referral to a social worker when she was first diagnosed with lung cancer, but she did not begin psychotherapy until she had been in treatment for several months and felt severely depressed and unable to make decisions. Her goal in therapy was to cope better with her illness and living situation. Initially she found it difficult to talk about her ambivalence about her sexual orientation and her relationship with Laura. The challenge of therapy was to help Blanche see that although she did not see herself as part of any "community," she was indeed connected to others in different ways and could access help. She was able to value her continued relationship with and connection to Laura, despite their troubled history. The therapy was slow, taking into account Blanche's resistance to exploring emotional concerns. Although Blanche did not accept a referral to a cancer support group, with the social worker's encouragement she began to attend educational events offered by the cancer program at her hospital and began to socialize with other patients whom she met there. The social worker provided nonjudgmental support for Blanche's struggle to maintain her independence and her choice not to get hospice care.

CASE EXAMPLE

At age thirty-five, John was the most accomplished member of his very enmeshed Puerto Rican, Catholic, immigrant family. They idealized him for being a high school teacher in the city where they lived; he was particularly known for taking good care of Puerto Rican immigrant children. His family was in denial about his homosexuality, and John colluded with this denial, not wanting to upset his parents. When John's AIDS medications began to fail and he could no longer work, he moved home to a unit in the family tenement. This return home resulted in his family's confronting his homosexuality and his illness at once. As time went on and his physical condition deteriorated, conflicts began to emerge in the family about what kind of funeral to plan. John became increasingly angry with his mother for her insistence that he see a priest for confession. He also felt that his gay lifestyle was a mistake, leaving him at the end of his life with few friends and leaving a legacy of shame for his family. He was less and less able to take pleasure in his many professional accomplishments, and he regretted that he had never had an intimate partner. He also regretted that his family loved him for his accomplishments but could not love "his soul."

In the last year of his life John was able to use weekly therapy sessions with a gay-identified social worker (in the office, in the hospital, and finally at home). He was able to talk about his lifelong conflict and self-loathing about being gay and looked forward to his sessions, but was not able to feel less regretful about his life. At the very end of his life, somewhat delirious from medication and dementia, he agreed to see a priest for confession. At the small, Catholic funeral service, most of the family were still inconsolably distraught.

The social worker's role with John (and his family) was to help preserve a sense of himself, which could include the accomplishment of his ambition to become a teacher and to have a life of his own, separate from his enmeshed family. Within a very strong alliance, in the beginning of the work John was able to use therapy to discuss his lifelong struggle around his homosexuality. He was able to value himself more for "giving it my best shot" and to feel less guilt and shame. However, as his medical condition worsened and he was forced to move home, the struggle between adult consolidation and regression became more pronounced. John was very torn between appreciating and renouncing his gayness, and as a result he was not able to take much pride or pleasure in any review of his adult life. It was very difficult for the worker to be seen by the family and, eventually by John himself, as the repository of their ambivalence and shame. This was further complicated by John's compromised cortical functioning. This case is a reminder that end-of-life care can be very emotionally challenging, necessitating extra attention to both countertransference and to care for the caregiver (Davidson and Foster 1993; Shernoff 1995; Dane and Chachkes 2001).

PRACTICE GUIDELINES

In working with the gay and lesbian individuals and their families, the practitioner's role is to bear witness, to validate and support, and to provide a safe space for the individual, the couple, and/or the family to talk. In whatever setting, the worker's comfort in moving fluidly between psychodynamic and systemic interventions may be essential, at times focusing on individual issues and at other times focusing on the needs of the couple or the whole family. The transference and countertransference issues can be complex, determined in part by the clinician's comfort with homosexuality and his or her feelings about death and dying. The gay or lesbian practitioner may have particular difficulty working with issues of shame, doubt, and despair in the individual or in the family, and may need to rely on extra supervision. The non-gay clinician may not be familiar with the challenges presented by internalized homophobia and may make the mistake of either overdiagnosing or minimizing such issues. The sexual orientation of the therapist may not be as important as knowledge about and respect for homosexual lifestyle and the ability to be empathic.

If the individual is dying from a "socially undesirable" illness (AIDS, hepatitis, even cancer to some extent), issues of shame and guilt about both the illness and the perceived behaviors that led to the illness may be very central to the tasks of dying. The inability to be self-forgiving may or may not be resolvable. Indeed, it may be held on to as a way of making some final meaning of a conflicted life. It can be very difficult for the practitioner to let go of his or her own need for the individual to work it through. It can also lead to complicated grief and mourning for loved ones, even before the actual death. It is not unusual under such circumstances for survivors to be left a legacy of complicated mourning (Rando 1984; Worden 1991), particularly if they have not been able to alleviate or have contributed to the individual's self-loathing. Such circumstances can also result in the experience of disenfranchised grief (Doka 1989) for the survivors if they feel they cannot talk about what caused the death.

It can be helpful to take an approach that focuses on the strength that has allowed the dying person to embrace, to whatever extent it has been possible, an alternative life. The central task of psychological life is to achieve a balance of separateness and connection to others through various combinations of work, love, and play. A theoretical orientation that combines ego psychology, object relations, and attachment theory may provide the clinician with the framework for seeing the strength that is required to accept homosexuality as one's natural form of sexual and intimate expression. For many years in the history of psychiatry it was thought that if one's homosexuality was ego-syntonic (unconflicted) it indicated more primitive psychopathology; that is, if one's homosexuality was conflicted, it was indicative of more structure and therefore more treatable. This view has lost favor with most schools of developmental thinking, though it still does hold sway within some psychoanalytic and "conversion training" programs (Socarides 1968; Haldeman 2001; Drescher 2002). It is not surprising that gay men and lesbians might be suspicious of psychosocial interventions, not knowing the orientation of the practitioner or the practitioner's training. It may be helpful for the practitioner to find a way of indicating her respect for the choices and the struggles that have been required to maintain self-respect and find a place in the world as a gay man or lesbian. If this is not done, there may be no alliance within which to do the work at hand.

Lesbians and gay men have particular interests in documenting their preferences regarding advance care planning and end-of-life care (Stein and Bonuck 2001). It is crucial for lesbians and gay men to understand their legal rights and take definitive steps to implement them. Because of cultural and social biases, both lesbians and gay men in committed relationships are at a disadvantage compared to married heterosexuals. According to the Human Rights Coalition (HRC 2002), lesbian, gay, and bisexual employees are not entitled to unpaid leave under the Family and Medical Leave Act to care for seriously ill same-sex partners. The HRC also notes, "Many children of same-sex couples are permitted to have only one legal parent of each sex. . . . The non-biological or non-adoptive parent may be unable to continue to raise the child if the biological or adoptive parent dies while the child is still a minor." Same-sex partners must have signed legal documents such as a healthcare proxy, durable power of attorney, and living will in order to ensure that their wishes be followed. Even with these legal documents, however, lesbians and gay men have no guarantee that their wishes will be followed.

Each state takes different views about the rights of gay and lesbian parents regarding the custody of minor children. The law fails to accommodate the needs of gay and lesbian parents under the best of circumstances; the right of a surviving partner to continue to care for minor children can be challenged when gay and lesbian parents die. The importance of filing appropriate legal documents in this situation, in consultation with an attorney experienced in lesbian and gay family issues, cannot be overemphasized.

It may be helpful to facilitate some discussion with the dying person and with the loved ones about their particular views about life after death. Both cultural differences and cohort differences regarding this can be very important, and the source of tremendous conflict. Older generations of many cultural and religious traditions believe that if the gay man or lesbian does not regret his or her life—or even confess the sinfulness of it—the afterlife will be one of suffering and torment. The gay/lesbian dying patient, perhaps more psychologically vulnerable under the circumstances of dying, may have worked very hard in life to establish a system of beliefs that does not result in eternal condemnation, and may need an ally against the family's powerful pull in this direction. Creating the space for all parties to talk about this, individually or together, can be immensely helpful. Of course, it is potentially an area of intense feeling and conflict and the practitioner will need to be knowledgeable as well as appropriately neutral/nonjudgmental. For example, when parents view their child's homosexuality as a failure of their parenting, helping both parties let go and say goodbye and forgive each other is frequently part of the work. Parental self-blame is often based in cultural and religious beliefs that are frequently barely conscious, but can be tormenting because of their interference with both parties' expression of forgiveness and love.

CASE EXAMPLE

Annie, age sixty-five, was looking forward to retiring soon from an academic career that had been very gratifying; she was highly regarded as the only African American faculty member at her small university. She considered herself a good teacher and was well liked by students and colleagues over the years. She and her partner, Sarah, had been in a relationship for twenty years; they had a wide circle of friends and were close with their extended families. They had traveled for pleasure and seen many parts of the world. When Annie's cancer was diagnosed, it was heartbreaking for both of them. They informed their friends and relatives and had small dinners as Annie's energy allowed.

Annie was hospitalized for the last three weeks of her life. Sarah visited for long periods daily and was very involved with the medical team, advocating for Annie's comfort. They were able to talk about their good life together and about their mutual belief that they would meet again in another life. At Annie's memorial service at the university, Sarah thanked Annie's colleagues and both of their families for the love and support that they always received as a couple, particularly in the last months of Annie's "wonderful life."

This last vignette is important as a reminder that the end of life for gay men and lesbians does not always entail interpersonal conflict or the resolution of old psychological issues. Gay men and lesbians also have "good" deaths, where the letting go of life and the existential understanding of impermanence have their own comforts.

CONCLUSION

It is characteristic of modern life for individuals to assume and even to expect more ownership of the psychological and social nature of the entire life span. From this perspective, the state and the church are seen as having less and less control and responsibility over the ways in which people face end-of-life issues. This has obvious implications for large and complex contemporary social issues, including the relative responsibilities of the family (filial) and the society for the health and well-being of its older and medically vulnerable members. Such paradigmatic shifts in social policy provide a context for individual preferences and decision making both about practical matters concerning the end of life and about the intrapsychic and interpersonal meaning of life's end. Therefore, it may be important for end-of-life-care practitioners to consider whether there are expectable and predictable existential and practical concerns for gay men and lesbians who are confronting death.

It is clear that the cultural, political, educational, and legal changes that have occurred over the past thirty years have made life different for gay men and lesbians than before. In many ways, these changes have made life easier and less dangerous. However, the gains that have been made are uneven and not universal. Gay men and lesbians still are the victims of oppression, perhaps more so in some cultures or in some geographic areas that equate gay rights with secular deterioration of the human family. This unfortunate perspective can be particularly bitter for the gay man or lesbian who is confronting the end of life. The inability of one's partner to have visitation rights when one is hospitalized is one of the most glaring examples of institutionalized oppression. The ability of one's partner's family of origin to stake a claim on property and possessions is another. The expectation that homosexuality is not an aspect of life to be appropriately eulogized is another.

It is well known that all of these practices are not uncommon. We are only at the beginning of the transformation of gay and lesbian life. Perhaps more thought about the vicissitudes of end-of-life care issues will contribute to this transformation.

REFERENCES

Andrews, P. 1981. Developmental tasks of terminally ill patients. *Journal of Religion and Health* 20:243–252.

Appleby, G. A., and J. W. Anastas, eds. 1998. *Not Just a Passing Phase: Social Work with Gay, Lesbian, and Bisexual People.* New York: Columbia University Press.

Aronstein, D. M., and B. J. Thompson, eds. 1998. *HIV and Social Work: A Practitioner's Guide.* New York: Haworth.

Benson, J. D., and J. Brookman. 1998. Present in the balance of time: The therapist's challenge. In *The UCSF AIDS Health Project Guide to Counseling: Perspectives on Psychotherapy, Prevention, and Therapeutic Practice*, ed. J. W. Dilley and R. Marks, 335–352. San Francisco: Jossey-Bass.

Berger, R. 1980. Psychological adaptation of the older male homosexual. *Journal of Homosexuality* 5:161–175.

Berger, R. M. 1982a. *Gay and Gray: The Older Homosexual Man.* Champaign: University of Illinois Press.

———. 1982b. The unseen minority: Older gays and lesbians. *Social Work* 27:236–242.

Bradford, J., and C. Ryan. 1988. *The National Lesbian Health Care Survey*. Washington, DC: National Gay and Lesbian Health Association.

Bradford, J., C. Ryan, and E. Rothblum, eds. 1994. National lesbian health care survey: Implications for mental health. *Journal of Consulting and Clinical Psychology* 62(2): 228–242.

Byock, I. R. 1996. The nature of suffering and the nature of opportunity at the end of life. *Clinics in Geriatric Medicine* 12(2): 237–252.

———. 1997. *Dying Well: Peace and Possibility at the End of Life*. New York: Riverhead.

Cadwell, S. A., R. A. Burnham, and M. Forstein, eds. *Therapists on the Front Line: Psychotherapy with Gay Men in the Age of AIDS*. Washington, DC: American Psychiatric Press.

Callahan, M., and P. Kelley. 1992. *Final Gifts: Understanding the Special Awareness, Needs and Communications of the Dying*. New York: Bantam.

Carni, E. 1988. Issues of hope and faith in the cancer patient. *Journal of Religion and Health* 27:285–290.

Charmaz, K. 1983. Loss of self: A fundamental form of suffering in the chronically ill. *Sociology of Health and Illness* 5(2): 169–195.

Coward, D. 1990. The lived experience of self-transcendence in women with advanced breast cancer. *Nursing Science Quarterly* 3:162–169.

———. 1995. The lived experience of self-transcendence in gay men with AIDS. *Oncology Nursing Forum* 18:857–863.

Cruikshank, M. 1990. Lavender and gray: A brief survey of lesbian and gay aging studies. *Journal of Homosexuality* 20:77–87.

Dane, B., and E. Chachkes. 2001. The cost of caring for patients with an illness: Contagion to the social worker. *Social Work in Health Care* 33(2): 31–51.

Davidson, K. W., and Z. Foster. 1995. Social work with dying and bereaved clients: Helping the workers. *Social Work in Health Care* 21(4): 1–16.

DeHennezel, M. 1997. *Intimate Death: How the Dying Teach Us to Live*. New York: Vintage.

Dilley, J. W., and R. Marks, eds. 1998. *The UCSF AIDS Health Project Guide to Counseling: Perspectives on Psychotherapy, Prevention, and Therapeutic Practice*. San Francisco: Jossey-Bass.

Doka, K. 1989. *Disenfranchised Grief: Recognizing Hidden Sorrow*. New York: Lexington.

Dowd, S. B., V. L. Poole, R. Davidhizar, and J. N. Giger. 1998. Cultural implications of various cultural and religious groups in the death and dying process. *Hospice Journal* 13(4): 48–56.

Drescher, J. 2002. Sexual conversion ("reparative") therapies: History and update. In *Mental Health Issues in Lesbian, Gay, Bisexual and Transgendered Communities*, ed. B. E. Jones and M. S. Hill, 71–91. Washington, DC: American Psychiatric Press.

Ehrenberg, M. 1996. Aging and mental health: Issues in the gay and lesbian community. In *Gay and Lesbian Mental Health: A Sourcebook for Practitioners*, ed. C. J. Alexander, 198–209. New York: Haworth.

Eliason, M. J., and R. Schope. 2001. Does "don't ask, don't tell" apply to health care? Lesbian, gay, and bisexual people's disclosure to health care providers. *Journal of the Gay and Lesbian Medical Association* 5(4): 125–134.

Erikson, E. 1963. *Childhood and Society*. New York: Norton.

———. 1982. *The Life Cycle Completed: A Review*. New York: Norton.

Erikson, E., J. M. Erikson, and H. Q. Kivnick. 1984. *Vital Involvement in Old Age*. New York: Norton.

Francher, J. S., and J. Henkin. 1973. The menopausal queen: Adjustment to aging and the male homosexual. *American Journal of Orthopsychiatry* 43:670–674.

Friend, R. A. 1991. Older lesbian and gay people: A theory of successful aging. In *Gay Midlife and Maturity*, ed. J. A. Lee, 99–118. New York: Haworth.

Fryback, P. B. 1993. Health for people with a terminal diagnosis. *Nursing Science Quarterly* 6:147–159.

Groopman, J. 1997. *The Measure of Our Days*. New York: Viking.

Haldeman, D. C. 2001. Therapeutic antidotes: Helping gay and bisexual men recover from conversion therapies. *Journal of Gay and Lesbian Psychotherapy* 5(3–4): 117–130.

Hall, B. A. 1998. Patterns of spirituality in persons with advanced HIV disease. *Research in Nursing and Health* 21:143–153.

Hitchcock, J. M., and H. S. Wilson. 1992. Personal risking: Lesbian self-disclosure of sexual orientation to professional health care providers. *Nursing Research* 41(3): 178–183.

Human Rights Coalition. 2002. The state of the family: Laws and legislation affecting gay, lesbian, bisexual and transgender families. www.hrc.org/familynet/documents/SoTF.pdf.

Humphreys, N. A., and J. K. Quam. 1998. Middle-aged and old gay, lesbian and bisexual adults. In *Not Just a Passing Phase: Social Work with Gay, Lesbian, and Bisexual People*, ed. G. A. Appleby and J. W. Anastas, 245–267. New York: Columbia University Press.

Irish, D. P., K. F. Lundquist, and V. J. Nelsen. 1993. *Ethnic Variations in Dying, Death, and Grief*. Washington, DC: Taylor & Francis.

Johnson, C. J., and M. G. McGee, eds. 1998. *How Different Religions View Death and Afterlife*. Philadelphia: Charles Press.

Kawaga-Singer, M., and L. J. Blackhall. 2001. Negotiating cross-cultural issues at the end of life: "You got to go where he lives." *Journal of the American Medical Association* 286:2293–3001.

Kelly, J. 1977. The aging male homosexual: Myths and reality. *The Gerontologist* 17:328–332.

——. 1980. Homosexuality and aging. In *Homosexual Behavior: A Modern Reappraisal*, ed. J. Marmor, 176–193. New York: Basic Books.

Kimmel, D. C. 1978. Adult development and aging: A gay perspective. *Journal of Social Issues* 34:113–130.

Kimmel, D. C., and B. E. Sang. 1995. Lesbians and gay men at midlife. In *Lesbian, Gay and Bisexual Identities Over the Lifespan: Psychological Perspectives*, ed. A. R. D'Augelli and C. J. Patterson, 190–214. New York: Oxford University Press.

Koenig, B. A. 1997. Cultural diversity in decisionmaking about care at the end of life. In *Approaching Death: Improving Care at the End of Life*, ed. M. J. Field and C. K. Cassel, 363–382. Washington, DC: National Academy Press.

Koenig, B. A., and J. Gates-Williams. 1995. Understanding cultural differences in caring for dying patients. *Western Journal of Medicine* 163(3): 244–249.

Klitzman, R. L., and J. D. Greenberg. 2002. Patterns of communication between gay and lesbian patients and their healthcare providers. *Journal of Homosexuality* 42(4): 65–75.

Last Acts Coalition. 2001. Statement on diversity and end-of-life care. www.lastacts.org/files/publications/Diversity1.15.02.pdf.

Lee, J. A. 1987. What can homosexual aging studies contribute to theories of aging? *Journal of Homosexuality* 13:43–71.

——, ed. 1991. *Gay Midlife and Maturity*. New York: Haworth.

Marshall, C. F. 1991. Lifespan development, spirituality and facing mortality: Role of HIV status and exposure to death in the spiritual and psychological development of gay men. Ph.D. diss., Wright Institute Graduate School of Psychology.

Martinson, J. C., D. G. Fisher, and T. D. DeLapp. 1996. Client disclosure of lesbianism: A challenge for health care providers. *Journal of Gay and Lesbian Social Services* 4(3): 81–94.

Matthews, A. K., Peterman, A.H., Delaney, P., Menard, L., and D. Brandenburg. 2002. A qualitative exploration of the experiences of lesbian and heterosexual patients with breast cancer. *Oncology Nursing Forum* 29(10): 1455–1462.

8 CLINICAL PRACTICE ISSUES IN END-OF-LIFE CARE

McKusick, L. 1988. The impact of AIDS on practitioner and client. *American Psychologist* 43(11): 935–940.

Merriam, S. B., B. C. Courtenay, and P. M. Reeves. 1997. Ego development in the face of death: How being HIV Positive affects movement through Erikson's adult stages of development. *Journal of Adult Development* 4(4): 221–235.

Pattison, E. M. 1978. The living-dying process. In *Psychosocial Care of the Dying Patient*, ed. C. A. Garfield, 133–168. New York: McGraw-Hill.

Peterson, J., and M. Bricker-Jenkins. 1996. Lesbians and the healthcare system. *Journal of Gay and Lesbian Social Services* 5:33–48.

Phillips, J. M. 1994. The psychotherapist as spiritual helper. In *Therapists on the Front Line: Psychotherapy with Gay Men in the Age of AIDS*, ed. S. A. Cadwell, R. A. Burnham, and M. Forestein, 81–110. Washington, DC: American Psychiatric Press.

Poor, M. 1982. The older lesbian. In *Lesbian Studies*, ed. M. Cruikshank, 165–173. Old Westbury, NY: Feminist Press.

Quam, J. K., and G. S. Whitford. 1992. Adaptation and age-related expectations of older gay and lesbian adults. *The Gerontologist* 32:367–374.

Rabkin, J. G., R. Remien, L. Katoff, and J. B. Williams. 1993. Resilience in adversity among long-term survivors of AIDS. *Hospital and Community Psychiatry* 44(2): 162–167.

Rando, T. A. 1984. *Grief, Dying and Death: Clinical Interventions for Caregivers*. Champaign, IL: Research Press.

Reid, J. D. 1995. Development in late life: Older lesbian and gay lives. In *Lesbian, Gay and Bisexual Identities Over the Lifespan*, ed. A. R. D'Augelli and C. J. Patterson, 215–240. New York: Oxford University Press.

Rinpoche, S. 1992. *The Tibetan Book of Living and Dying*. New York: HarperCollins.

Rizzuto, A. 1979. *The Birth of the Living God*. Chicago: University of Chicago Press.

Roberts, S. J., and L. Sorenson. 1999. Health related behaviors and cancer screening of lesbians: results from the Boston Lesbian Health Project. *Women and Health* 28(4): 1–12.

Sadowy, D. 1991. Is there a role for the psychotherapist with a patient dying of AIDS? *Psychoanalytic Review* 78(2): 199–207.

Saulnier, C. F. 1999. Choosing a health care provider: A community survey of what is important to lesbians. *Families-in-Society* 80(3): 254–262.

Shernoff, M. 1995. Conclusion: A therapist's journey. In *The Second Decade of AIDS: A Mental Health Practice Handbook*, ed. W. Odets and M. Shernoff, 301–307. New York: Hatherleigh Press.

——. 1999. Dying well: Counseling end-stage clients with AIDS. In *AIDS and Mental Health Practice: Clinical and Policy Issues*, ed. M. Shernoff, 109–126. New York: Haworth.

Singh, K. D. 1998. *The Grace in Dying: A Message of Hope, Comfort and Spiritual Transformation*. San Francisco: HarperCollins.

Smith, D. C., and M. F. Maher. 1991. Healthy death. *Counseling and Values* 36(1): 42–48.

Socarides, C. 1968. *The Overt Homosexual*. New York: Grune & Stratton.

Steeves, R. H., and D. L. Kahn. 1987. Experience of meaning in suffering. *Image: The Journal of Nursing Scholarship* 19:114–116.

Stein, G. L., and K. A. Bonuck. 2001. Attitudes on end-of-life care and advance care planning in the lesbian and gay community. *Journal of Palliative Medicine* 4(2): 173–190.

Stevens, P. 1996. Lesbians and doctors: Experiences of solidarity and domination in health care settings. *Gender and Society* 10:24–41.

Stevens, P., and J. M. Hall. 1988. Stigma, health beliefs and experiences with health care in lesbian women. *Journal of Nursing Scholarship* 20:69–73.

Weisman, A. D. 1988. Appropriate death and the hospice program. *Hospice Journal* 4(1): 65–77.

Worden, J. W. 1991. *Grief Counseling and Grief Therapy: A Handbook for the Mental Health Practitioner*. New York: Springer.

25

PALLIATIVE CARE FOR PEOPLE WITH DISABILITIES

GARY L. STEIN AND LUCILLE ESRALEW

PEOPLE WITH disabilities and their families need informed, committed, and compassionate social workers and other healthcare professionals to assist them in navigating difficult healthcare issues, especially when confronting life-threatening illnesses. This community has been largely ignored in the current dialogue on end-of-life care and healthcare decision making. Many professionals in mainstream healthcare organizations lack awareness of the issues facing people with disabilities and their families and surrogates. Likewise, staff working in public agencies and community organizations who serve the disability community are often uninformed about the nature, ethics, and legality of complex health decisions involving their clients. These concerns are even more significant as the population of individuals with disabilities—especially those residing at state-run developmental centers and community group facilities—becomes elderly and requires specialized services.

People with disabilities are a diverse community with a range of cognitive and physical limitations and with different needs for assistance. Many, especially those with disabilities such as cerebral palsy, muscular dystrophy, brain injury, or mild cognitive impairments, have the capacity to make their own decisions. These individuals usually reside independently in the community, with a support system that may include case managers, personal care attendants, family and community advocates, and vocational and residential services. They usually need information on their service options when confronting life-threatening illness, especially on hospice and palliative-care services, assistance in documenting their preferences through advance directives, and support in navigating their way through complex healthcare systems.

Others with disabilities lack the capacity to make their own health decisions. These individuals are the focus of this chapter. Their health-related decisions are made by surrogates, primarily parents and other guardians, who act in their child's or ward's best interest and need information and support in selecting the most appropriate health care. Although an individual may lack decisional capacity in many situations, he or she may have some limited capacity to make some decisions or intermittent periods of limited capacity. Social workers and others on the healthcare team are critical in providing the information and guidance to help individuals express their preferences for care, in whatever limited ways. For example, individuals may have an opinion about whether or not to have a particular medical treatment or procedure, or what type of religious or spiritual support they desire during the course of their illness. A case-by-case approach is suggested.

Many people with disabilities who never had capacity (sometimes called the "never-competent") and who do not have a family member or other close person as guardian, receive guardianship services from state agencies. State guardians and case managers, who may be committed to serving their wards well, often encounter very high case-loads, have varying degrees of knowledge about end-of-life and palliative care, and are constrained by policy mandates that impact significantly on the delivery of appropriate, high-quality end-of-life care.

This chapter will consider mental health issues for people with disabilities at the end of life, as well as access to palliative-care services, the standards for end-of-life decision making for people with cognitive disabilities, policy constraints on state guardians, and recommendations for service providers and policymakers.

MENTAL HEALTH ISSUES

Clients with life-threatening illnesses need a range of supports to deal with the pain, discomfort, anxiety, fear, and depression that can further degrade the quality of their remaining time. Those who have intact cognitive skills can benefit from supportive counseling, which may be available through community-based mental health clinics or private practitioners. There are a growing number of clinical social workers, psychologists, and counselors who are skilled and comfortable in working with adults with physical and/or intellectual disabilities.

Supportive counseling presumes the client's ability to verbalize thoughts and feelings. Furthermore, counseling presumes the ability to understand the value of talking about one's concerns. For those with sufficient capacity, counseling can provide clients an opportunity to build coping skills, manage stress, and problem solve.

Individuals who are nonverbal or minimally verbal may benefit from expressive modalities such as art or movement therapies. Generally, the less verbal the client, the more likely it is that clinicians will rely upon environmental manipulations and behavioral techniques. Clinicians can train clients to cope better with stressors by teaching them to use relaxation techniques such as progressive relaxation, visualization, and deep breathing. Other individuals benefit from sensory relaxation, including listening to music, aromatherapy, or massage. Clinicians can train family and staff to encourage the client to use these techniques and to provide assistance when needed.

Similarly, clinicians should provide support to family and staff who act as caregivers. Parents and siblings struggle with their loved one's illness and care. In addition, support staff at the client's work site, as well as staff at the group home or developmental center, may have functioned as surrogate family members and developed strong attachments to the client. These individuals also need help in coping with the eventual loss of someone important to them. To the extent that support staff can process their reactions to their client's serious illness, the client benefits. Clinicians may offer time-limited sessions for support persons to process their own feelings of grief and responsibility. It is not uncommon for family or staff to express the belief that they have somehow "failed"—had they been more vigilant in providing care, the loved one or client might not be dying.

CASE EXAMPLE

Thomas is a thirty-two-year-old, moderately retarded male who is currently in the hospital and on a ventilator following complications from spinal stenosis. He has a poor prognosis. The day program staff has been working with Thomas for the past ten years. Recognizing the need for staff to have a forum to express their feelings, the agency director invited a mental health professional to lead a staff support group, providing staff the opportunity to process their thoughts and feelings regarding this client's situation, as well as the experiences of other clients with severe or chronic illness and debilitating conditions.

Clients may also experience a grieving process to the extent that they are aware that there are tasks they once accomplished that they no longer have the strength or ability to perform. It is not uncommon for the dying individual to become acutely aware of decreasing abilities, lost opportunities, and the anticipation of leaving behind significant relationships. Anger and sadness may occur as clients work through the stages of their own grief. However, if anger, sadness, fear, or regret becomes so overwhelming that feelings disrupt ability to function, the person should be evaluated by a mental health clinician.

The mental health goals for the client with life-threatening illness are to reduce or eliminate suffering, promote comfort, maintain dignity, and assure an optimum quality of life for the time remaining. Sometimes, clients can be helped to fulfill religious, cultural, or family expectations.

Psychiatrists may help alleviate the burden of excessive guilt and depression with medication. The purpose of medication is to afford the individual some relief from overwhelming anxiety or sadness and allow the client to use remaining time more comfortably. There are short-acting anti-anxiety medications and antidepressants that are useful in reducing overwhelming anxiety or depression. In addition to increasing disability, depression is potentially lethal. People with disabilities who have a terminal illness and feel hopeless are at risk of committing suicide. It is a mistake for clinicians to think that a preexisting disability—whether physical or intellectual—precludes individuals from attempting suicide. In addition, individuals who are seriously ill may lack the energy, strength, or motivation to maintain their usual schedule of work, recreation, or other in-home activities. Clinicians should help their clients find options for meaningful activity to the extent of their interests and capabilities.

The client's primary care physician and psychiatrist should work together to calibrate the client's medication regimen. When individuals with serious illnesses have a preexisting psychiatric disorders, signs and symptoms of the disorder may be exacerbated by physical illness. Additionally, because a terminal illness may interfere with the metabolizing and absorption of medications, medication dosages may require adjustments.

States have different models for the delivery of mental health services. For example, New Jersey has a Medicaid-funded program that provides on-site clinical services (at home or day programs) to meet the needs of clients who could not access traditional community-based mental health services. Caregivers may be interested in locating clinicians who can modify existing service delivery and provide in-home sessions. Provider agencies may be helpful in identifying practitioners who are willing to make home visits or who are within an easy commute from the client's home.

Unfortunately, there are well-meaning family members and staff who believe they are protecting individuals with disabilities by not fully sharing information regarding prognosis. We suggest that individuals who have some understanding of the impact of their illnesses have a moral right to know their situation unless there is a compelling reason not to tell them. Individuals who are cognitively impaired need to have information that will help them understand what is happening to them. The focus of intervention may be less a matter of advance healthcare planning and more a matter of helping clients make the most of every day.

Some workers are focused on "the living" and on a sense of their efficacy as service providers. It may be frustrating, saddening, or deflating for them to work with someone who they know will die soon. In anticipation of their client's demise, they may visit the dying person less frequently. They may find it difficult to stay with someone who is dying, unsure of what to do and what to say. Families often struggle with similar feelings of helplessness.

It is important for clients with disabilities to have significant others present. Without such presence, clients may feel abandoned at the very time they need support. It is important for healthcare professionals to examine their own reactions to the imminent death of clients who they have cared for and with whom they have bonded. Sometimes workers do not consider how their personal reactions to illness and death influence reactions to their clients (see chapter 15).

CASE EXAMPLE

Stephanie is a fifty-one-year-old female with cerebral palsy. She had successfully survived a bout with breast cancer three years before, for which she received surgery and chemotherapy. She has recently been diagnosed with ovarian cancer, which is advanced and has metastasized. Her physicians estimate that she has about six months to live. She consulted with trusted physicians and family members and decided that she will not pursue the suggested course of chemotherapy. She decided to call a "circle of friends" meeting of those closest to her, including support staff, to discuss how she wants to be supported in her remaining time. She is very clear that she wants to remain in her home as long as possible and to remain pain free to the extent possible.

Clients should feel cared for, supported, and, to the extent possible, enabled to come to terms with "unfinished business." Clients may wish to reunite with lost family members, make amends with individuals with whom have had a falling out, and generally "repair" or "undo" problems with existing relationships. Even clients with limited cognitive abilities may wish to complete unfinished business. Overall, health-care providers should strive to assure that their clients' final days are as comfortable as possible—free of pain and suffering, filled with dignity, and in accord with their cherished values.

ACCESS TO PALLIATIVE CARE

The provision of palliative-care and hospice services for people with disabilities seems uncontroversial, but comfort care has and continues to be largely unavailable for this community. Few palliative-care staff have experience in providing services to people with disabilities and workers of residential facilities and service organizations serving the community are largely unfamiliar with the range of comfort care options available for those with life-threatening illnesses. Change requires a cultural shift in the intro-duction of these services into the community and a new awareness among palliative-care, hospice, and disability-services staff.

Resources are becoming available. For example, New Jersey Health Decisions, a citizen-based bioethics organization that focuses on palliative care and healthcare decision making, is developing a community-based Disability Ethics Network to assist in end-of-life and other healthcare situations, community and staff education, and a working group to promote new service models and polices to promote hospice and palliative care. NYSARC, a New York State-based service organization serving persons with mental retardation and developmental disabilities and their families, published a guidebook on improving end-of-life care for older people with intellectual disabilities and their families. Its recommendations include strategies for hospice and bereave-ment services and education about advance healthcare planning (NYSARC 2000). In addition, the Volunteers of America plans to disseminate the NYSARC training man-ual through a website, networking, a national conference, and replication through an Oklahoma demonstration project.

ASSESSING DECISION-MAKING CAPACITY

Before palliative-care and hospice services may be made available to people with disabilities, social workers and the healthcare team must carefully determine the ca-pacity of the individual with the disability to choose this care before consulting her surrogate. If decision-making capacity is lacking, the team should consider the appro-priate standards for surrogate decision making by family members or other private guardians or by public guardians.

The capacity to make healthcare decisions has been defined as the ability to un-derstand information about a proposed care plan, appreciate the consequences of a decision, and reach an informed decision. Unlike competency, which is an "all or nothing" judicial determination, capacity is specific to the decision at hand (Miller 1995:73–75).

People with disabilities cannot be presumed to lack capacity for making healthcare decisions (Midwest Bioethics Center 1996). An assessment of capacity should be made by a mental health professional experienced in working with people with developmental disabilities; determinations of incapacity should generally be subject to a second consultation. In addition, because people with disabilities are occasionally prescribed many medications that affect behavior and cognition, care must be made to assure that lack of capacity is not due to adverse side effects. Even those individuals found to lack capacity to make complex decisions about end-of-life care, such as whether or not to forego life sustaining medical treatments, might be able to make some less critical choices about their care. J. E. Beltran summarizes the dilemma in assessing decision-making capacity: "There is a need to balance protection from harm with the patient's right to self-determination. This balancing requires skilled listening, the proper level of advocacy from caregivers, and pragmatic models of shared decision-making" (1996:19).

STANDARDS FOR HEALTHCARE DECISION MAKING

Two standards for surrogate decision making are most applicable to situations involving people with disabilities—substituted judgment and best interests (Beauchamp and Childress 1994). The substituted judgment standard is appropriate for surrogate decision making when there is some reliable prior evidence of a person's values and preferences to guide their healthcare and life choices. In essence, the surrogate attempts to stand in the shoes of the individual: what decision would the person make if she had the capacity to do so? This process entails the consideration of preexisting advance directives or written documents such as a living will, oral directives made by the individual, religious or spiritual beliefs, or prior medical decisions. This standard should be applied only to those individuals with sufficient cognitive functioning to have expressed their personal wishes.

The best interests standard is appropriate to use for individuals who have very limited cognitive abilities, who never had the capacity to express their personal interests (the never-competent), or for whom there is little reliable or credible evidence of prior wishes. The main criteria in the best interests analysis is the quality of the patient's life with a particular treatment, generally without taking into account the person's preexisting disability. The decision maker will balance the risks and burdens of treatment choices and options against the benefits of treatment, consider the possibilities of restoring functioning to an acceptable level, and seek to alleviate pain and suffering through the provision of palliative care. The best interests should be considered from the perspective of the individual being protected, not from the interests of other family members, the facility or institution caring for the person, or society at large to be free from the costs or burdens of providing care.

Beltran (1996) and Martyn (1994) propose a broader approach for decision making, a standard of best respect, similar to the best interests standard, with healthcare choices made by a team rather than an individual surrogate. The proponents of best respect suggest convening those individuals most familiar with the patient's life and values for an informed dialogue that results in a consensus on treatment decisions. This consensus-building should occur within the context of the patient's community of care, which may be a developmental center, community group home, or independent living arrangement. It should be the responsibility of an institutional ethics committee or other comparable body to convene the relevant parties—which may include family members, friends, or other supportive caregivers, as well as the interdisciplinary team caring for the individual (Beltran 1996). In the best respect model, physicians offer "objective" information about the patient, including diagnosis, prognosis, available treatment choices, and quality of life issues. Subsequently, the "search for subjective information . . . [examines] what the person has communicated in the past about her own life and its pleasures, pains, dignities, indignities, and dependencies. Second, the group should consider what this information tells them about the subjective value of life to this patient. Finally, given what has been shared, [a determination would be made on] which decision best respects the individual expression of this unique individual" (Martyn 1994:204).

SPECIAL ISSUES INVOLVING PUBLIC GUARDIANS

Ethical and legal principles in most states (with the exceptions of New York State and Missouri) permit family and other private guardians to withhold and withdraw life-sustaining medical treatments, such as artificial ventilation, nutrition, and hydration, from wards with disabilities who suffer from terminal illnesses (Martyn 1994; Capron 1992). However, for those people with developmental disabilities who lack capacity and for whom no family member or friend is available or willing to serve as guardian, a unit of state government assumes guardianship. These public guardians are often constrained by laws and policies in their abilities to direct medically appropriate care, with limits on do-not-resuscitate (DNR) orders, the provision of hospice care, and withholding or withdrawing medically inappropriate life-sustaining care.

For example, New Jersey policy guidelines provide detailed instructions for DNR orders before a state guardian may approve them. Furthermore, guardians may not approve the withholding or withdrawal of life sustaining medical treatments, even in end-of-life care situations where such actions are medically indicated and may be necessary to curtail needless pain and suffering (State of New Jersey 1999). In 2002, a state-designated task force developed new proposed regulations that encourage the provision of hospice and palliative care and permit DNRs, hospice care, and the withholding or withdrawal of life sustaining medical treatments if approved by a state-designated ethics committee and the director of the State Bureau of Guardianship Services (State of New Jersey 2002). It is anticipated that these new guidelines will become effective in 2003.

Similar procedural protections to allow public guardians to forgo life-sustaining treatments for their wards have been proposed for action by state legislatures across the country. Under this proposal, care may be withheld or withdrawn when a patient's condition falls into one of the following categories:

1. A persistent vegetative state lasting for twelve months;
2. A terminal illness with uncontrollable pain;

3. An advanced stage of a terminal illness with severe and permanent deterioration; or

4. For treatment withdrawal only, when the burdens of continuing care outweigh the medical benefits (McKnight and Bellis 1992).

Access to hospice and palliative-care services, as well as freedom from unhelpful and burdensome treatments, should be available to people with disabilities as medically indicated; their status as a ward of a family member or the state should be irrelevant to the provision of comfort care. Assuring that the disability community has access to palliative care requires the removal of outdated legal and policy barriers that deny or curtail access to these services.

RECOMMENDATIONS TO PROMOTE ACCESS TO PALLIATIVE CARE

EDUCATION

- Staff of public agencies and private organizations serving people with disabilities should be trained in the special needs of people with disabilities for advance healthcare planning, options for hospice and palliative care to manage life-threatening illnesses, and special concerns in providing and consenting to care.
- People with disabilities and their families and other surrogates need information and guidance on their rights to make informed healthcare decisions and on the availability of hospice and palliative care to manage pain and distressing symptoms, as well as on psychosocial and spiritual distress.

CLINICAL PRACTICE

- Mental health practitioners with training and experience in caring for people with developmental disabilities should be available to assess carefully the abilities and residual abilities of individuals to make healthcare decisions and plan for their future care, including the appointment of healthcare surrogates.
- People with disabilities should be provided education and guidance—when appropriate, based on assessed capacity—to make their own healthcare decisions and arrange their future care, including the appointment of healthcare surrogates.
- Mental health services—including counseling, behavioral and expressive modalities, and pharmacological treatments—should be available to clients with disabilities and their caregivers.

POLICY BARRIERS

- Laws and policies governing the care of state wards should be based upon the medical and service needs of the individual and not on the individual's status as a state ward.
- Outdated laws and policies governing the care of wards with life-threatening illnesses should be revised to promote access to hospice and palliative care and permit the withholding or withdrawal of unhelpful or burdensome life-sustaining medical treatments.

- Institutional and specially designated ethics committees should be developed to assist in making decisions regarding DNR orders and the withholding or withdrawal of life-sustaining medical treatments or other futile care. Ethics committees should assist in mediating and resolving conflicts regarding patient care that arise among patients, families and surrogates, the healthcare team, and administrators.

REFERENCES

Beauchamp, T. L., and J. F. Childress. 1994. *Principles of Biomedical Ethics.* 4th ed. New York: Oxford University Press.

Beltran, J. E. 1996. Shared decision making: The ethics of caring and best respect. *Bioethics Forum* 12:17–25.

Botsford, A. L., and L. T. Force. 2000. *End-of-Life Care: A Guide for Supporting Older People with Intellectual Disabilities and Their Families.* Albany, NY: NYSARC.

Capron, A. M. 1992. Substituting our judgment. *Hastings Center Report* 22:58–59.

Hollins, S. 1995. Managing grief better: People with developmental disabilities. *Habilitative Mental Healthcare Newsletter* 14:3.

Martyn, S. R. 1994. Substituted judgment, best interests, and the need for best respect. *Cambridge Quarterly of Healthcare Ethics* 3:195–208.

McKnight, D. K., and M. Bellis. 1992. Forgoing life-sustaining treatment for adult, developmentally disabled, public wards: A proposed statute. *American Journal of Law and Medicine* 18:203–232.

Midwest Bioethics Center and University of Missouri-Kansas City Institute for Human Development Task Force on Health Care for Adults with Developmental Disabilities. 1996. Health care treatment decision-making guidelines for adults with developmental disabilities. *Bioethics Forum* 12:S/1–7.

Miller, T. E. 1995. Advance directives: Moving from theory to practice. In *Quality Care in Geriatric Settings*, ed. P. R. Katz, R. L. Kane, and M. D. Mezey, 68–86. New York: Springer.

State of New Jersey, Department of Human Services. 2002. N.J.A.C. 10:48B: Decision making for the terminally ill.

State of New Jersey, Department of Human Services, Division of Developmental Disabilities. 1999. Circular 37.

Worden, W. 2002. *Grief Counseling and Grief Therapy: A Handbook for the Mental Health Practitioner.* New York: Springer.

26

CLINICAL PRACTICE WITH GROUPS IN END-OF-LIFE CARE

AMANDA L. SUTTON AND DANIEL LIECHTY

DRAWING FROM years of anecdotal experience in facilitating support groups for patients facing cancer, AIDS, and other life-threatening illnesses as well as for caregivers and the bereaved, we find it more and more evident that participating in support groups is an efficient and effective method of receiving support when facing the specialized issues at the end of life. Being a member of a group gives an opportunity to decrease isolation and meet others who are confronting similar situations, which normalizes intense feelings and reactions. Mutuality develops among the members and is based on this commonality of external events. This helps to decrease the stigmatization and isolation that members often experience, whether they are suffering from an advanced illness, are caregiver to an ill person, or are grieving. Mutuality occurs whether the group takes place face-to-face, over the telephone, or via the Internet. Recent research identifies and confirms the benefits gained by participation in a support group. Members' coping skills are thereby enhanced, as is their quality of life (Taylor et al. 1986; Spiegel 1989; Vugia 1991).

Basic social work values, philosophy, and education are naturally congruent with group dynamics and process (Kurland and Salmon 1999). Social workers have an impressive history in assuming pioneering roles in the promotion of group work (Roy and Sumpter 1983). Much of this work has been documented in the growing professional literature found in the intersection of two different areas of clinical social work practice: group work and end-of-life/palliative care/hospice/death and dying literature. Social workers interested in practicing group work in end-of-life care should acquaint themselves with the specific contributions of each of these knowledge bases. This chapter will outline and integrate the most salient features from each knowledge area and provide a sketch of best clinical practice of group work in end-of-life care.

DIFFERENTIATING SUPPORT FROM PSYCHOTHERAPY GROUPS

While end-of-life issues can be brought up and worked on in psychotherapy groups, the focus of this chapter will be on support groups led by professional facilitators. Important distinctions among these types of groups affect leadership roles, member's expectations, and the dynamics of the group.

PURPOSE OF THE GROUP

In the support modality, the purpose of the group is to bring together individuals who have a shared experience brought about by an external event (death of a child, chronic obstructive pulmonary disease, partners of end-stage Alzheimer's patients, and the like) with the express purpose of giving members an opportunity to ventilate their feelings about the experience, problem-solve, and build a community of support and mutual understanding. In psychotherapy groups, members enter the group because they have personal issues that they want to work on which have to do with their psychological makeup (social phobia, anger management, chronic anxiety, and so forth). Members of psychotherapy groups seek more deliberate and profound change in their behavior and aspects of their identity. Most end-of-life groups are *not* psychotherapy groups.

LEADERSHIP

Leaders of a support group view their roles as those of facilitator and educator. A support-group leader's expertise lies in her knowledge of group process, and her primary goal is to achieve a sense of safety. She does not view herself as an expert in feelings or the experience of the external event that has brought the group together. Although support groups can have a therapeutic effect on the life of the members, they are not therapy groups. In psychotherapy groups, the leader is an expert in group process and sees her primary role as promoting internal as well as external change in each of the individual members. In support groups, external change is encouraged and problem solving promoted. When members are able to make internal shifts, they are supported and celebrated, but this change is not seen as the primary goal of the group or the role of the leader.

GROUP DYNAMICS

Because psychotherapy and support groups have different goals, the rules and expectations of each vary. In the beginning phase, the membership depends on the leader to set a tone of safety and lend structure. The foundation for safety is created by the leader initiating a discussion of the rules and expectations of the group. Once initiated by the leader, members often contribute their own rules and expectations. When the rules are not just followed but also owned by the membership, they become norms. Once the group develops its own cohesive identity, members depend on one another for support and education as much, if not more, than the leader. At this point, the leader often takes a secondary role and much of the group content and process comes from the membership. Members are encouraged by the leader and each other to share as much or as little as they wish. The leader can resume a primary role when needed by the group. This usually occurs when issues arise that are difficult for the members to process, such as conflict or the death of a member. Creating a social network outside the group is also promoted and members can participate in the group as much or as little as they choose. In psychotherapy groups, a hierarchical system exists with the leader, who is seen as the expert. She has influence over the content and process of the group. Members are discouraged from socializing outside the group, and each individual member has insight-oriented goals. The content of the group is about helping individual members understand the underlying causes of their behavior. Members are expected to participate actively in their own insight and the insight of their fellow members.

BENEFITS OF SUPPORT GROUPS

Facing the uncertainty of a terminal diagnosis and the emotional, physical, and spiritual challenges at the end of life can be overwhelming. Often patients report their inability to speak with loved ones about their conditions for fear of causing emotional duress. Many caregivers admit not verbalizing their despairing feelings because they do not want to lose hope. When patients and caregivers find themselves in support groups with other "like" members, these barriers are removed, and members are able to share their feelings openly and honestly. This shared community allows individuals to focus on their own emotional needs without the fear of affecting loved ones negatively. Often this milieu is the first and only opportunity participants have to focus on themselves without putting the needs of loved ones first. Having the opportunity to articulate and explore taboo subjects decreases the somatic and emotional symptoms of stress that often accompany an advanced diagnosis or increased caregiver responsibilities or grief (Cella and Yellen 1993). Although similar benefits are derived from seeking help from an individual therapist, both experience and research has demonstrated that some very important processes occur only, or occur best, in a group setting (Yalom 1995; Rando 1993). The following section will outline the benefits of participation in a support group.

SOCIAL SUPPORT

The need for connection is especially strong in times of high emotional, psychological, and spiritual stress (Cohen and Willis 1985). During the course of an illness, caregiving, or grief experience, there are many times when individuals feel alone and disconnected from the rest of the world. They sense that no one understands their experience and may tend to withdraw into further isolation and despair. This withdrawal compounds their feelings of difference and segregation from the "healthy," "happy" real world. There is an underlying expectation in North American culture of stoicism, autonomy, and independence. Although these values and belief systems can be helpful in motivating individuals to cope with crisis, they also discourage seeking the support and help of others. In recent years, support and self-help groups have emerged as a socially acceptable mechanism for gaining support and assistance during a crisis while still maintaining independence and autonomy.

NORMALIZATION

When tragedy strikes an individual in the form of facing an advanced diagnosis, caring for a loved one who is dying, or grappling with the reality of life in the midst of grief, the world has turned upside down. Patients, caregivers, and the bereaved report "not acting like themselves" or "feeling crazy." Participation in groups with "like" individuals gives the opportunity for the individual suffering to witness others suffering similarly. To have experience validated by a professional is comforting, but having experience confirmed by a fellow survivor is much more meaningful. Watching others move through different emotional stages can present a view of what to expect as well as hope for recovery. Witnessing fellow group members struggle week after week with multiple challenges of advanced illness and loss confirms that this event is occurring in the midst of life and not apart from it.

REMOVAL OF STIGMA

We live in a mainstream cultural climate that privileges youth, beauty, success, wealth, health, power, control, coupledom, and sex. Terminal illness, loss, and death directly contradict the optimistic cultural values of youth, vitality, beauty, health, and success (Wolf 1992). Advanced illness, caregiving, and grief greatly affect an individual's ability to live up to these superficial standards; individuals are often left feeling shamed, judged, separated, and stigmatized by the greater community (Goffman 1986; Neuberg, Smith, and Asher 2000). We have learned from many of the liberation movements that a key element in maintenance of social stigma is that stigmatized people internalize the stigma and view themselves as socially tainted (Goffman 1986). If an individual is able to exist in a group of others who do not recognize and internalize the same stigma, she can recognize her own investment in the stigmatization process. People who no longer view themselves as socially tainted are well on the way to removing the stigma and combating the stereotype. The shame no longer "sticks," since an internalized sense of stigma is a necessary ingredient in the social perception of stigma (Miller and Major 2000). Once a person is able to examine her sense of stigma and is able to converse about it freely with others, the stigma attached to such circumstances begins to dissolve (Goffman 1986). A support group is an optimal environment to gain reflection and perception on the internalized stigma of being ill, dying, caregiving, or being bereaved.

SUBSTITUTE/EXTENSIONAL FAMILY HOLDING ENVIRONMENT

Regardless of culture, many individuals seek satisfying primary emotional needs within the family (Edwards and Demo 1998). At times of crisis, these needs are often more acute. Coping with illness, dying, and death does not occur in isolation. Each member of the family is affected by the event to varying degrees. Depending on many variables, family members are more, or less, able to deal with the increased needs. A support or self-help group can provide the patient, caregiver, or bereaved with an additional opportunity to have emotional needs met by a community who cares, without the limitations of being an equal participant with equal needs in the disease process or grief journey.

MUTUAL AID

Patients, caregivers, and the bereaved who have participated in support groups each report the benefit of giving as well as getting support. Research has shown the strong human desire to give support and be supportive to others (Wasserman and Danforth 1988). Imparting knowledge and assuming the role of teacher allows the patient with advanced illness to feel she has something to offer. This is particularly important when the illness process has taken away function and ability. Giving support, helping to problem-solve, and teaching coping skills allows the caregiver to experience a sense of mastery in the midst of feeling wildly out of control. The bereaved person is able to share her experience and guide others. She is able to report her progress and accomplishments and demonstrate to newer members that recovery is possible.

POOLED KNOWLEDGE AND RESOURCES

The collective wealth of a group is greater than the sum of its individual parts. Group members contribute their individual information, resources, and problem-solving skills to the collective knowledge base of the group. Each member is able to utilize these resources and is then more equipped to cope with the physical, practical, emotional, and spiritual challenges of advanced illness and grief. The pooled knowledge and experience of the group is a valuable asset to the group leader, as it relieves the facilitator of feeling she has to be solely responsible for maintaining up-to-date information about community resources and advances in medical treatment.

SHARED PERSPECTIVE

Shared experience creates shared perspectives. As clinical social workers, we face the daunting task of "tuning in" to the emotional needs of the client. We know a client's experience only when she shares it with us. In a group, there can be a mutual understanding of shared experiences when members talk to one another. If the group is for those with advanced illness, each member of the group shares the reality of what it is like to be a person with advanced disease. Although the experience of each member is not the same, the group shares a collective understanding of what it is like to be a person who is ill or caregiving or bereaved.

PSYCHOEDUCATIONAL COMPONENT

For most individuals, their knowledge of illness, dying, and grief happens during the experience itself. A cognitive understanding of what to expect helps to relieve anxiety. For the caregiver and patient, it is helpful to understand what to expect as disease progresses and symptoms increase or change. For the bereaved, recognizing the phases and stages of the grief can offer a framework to normalize the experience. This educational component is greatly enhanced in a group setting. Like the collective resources, members bring their knowledge and experience to the group. Each member is able to benefit from the rich discussion.

SPIRITUAL CONNECTION

Humans are social by nature. There is a growing recognition in the field that we are spiritual beings as well. It stands to reason, therefore, that our sense of spirituality will also have a strong communal quality (Canda and Furman 1999). Often there is a "group spirit"—a sense of spiritual unity and blending available in a group setting that goes beyond the psychosocial element. This experience of spiritual unity and blending can be beneficial across the psychological, social, spiritual, and even physical spectrum (Levin 2001). Recognition as a member of a group—something greater than oneself—is a spiritual awakening in itself. This reality can be especially helpful to the bereaved, patients, and caregivers inasmuch as it allows them to feel that their circumstance has less to do with punishment or failure, but that the experience is linked to something greater than themselves.

GETTING OUT OF THE HOUSE

As terminal illness progresses, caregiving responsibilities increase. As the debilitating symptoms of grief set in, individuals find themselves spending more time at home. Like the fading iris of a movie camera, many report their homebound experiences as feeling as if the world is getting smaller. Participation in a group—sometimes on the phone or on the Internet (see chapter 27)—allows the homebound person to remain with the world outside although her body is unable to go there. For caregivers or the bereaved, the support group offers a powerful motivating force for continuing to "get out of the house" and take some time away from their loved one and family in order to reflect on their own experiences. The group experience becomes a doorway back into a normal social life with people who understand.

GROUP FORMATION CONSIDERATIONS

Group work with people facing advanced illness, their families, and the bereaved is a dynamic and growing area of practice. Recent years have seen an explosion of programs due to their cost effectiveness, clinical value, and their economic benefits for agencies, medical practices, and institutions.

SETTING

A support group can occur in any space (including virtual space) where there is enough room for the leader and its members to have adequate privacy to share openly without interruption. Depending upon the population of the group members, special considerations might have to be made.

For patient support groups, the leader must take into consideration what symptoms a patient might experience that would inhibit her participation in the group. It is impossible to plan for all obstacles for patient participation, but if members' comforts are considered, they are more likely to make the effort to come. Usual considerations for the patient facing advanced disease would include room temperature control; access for people with physical disabilities; water and tissues; comfortable chairs; well-ventilated air; and a quiet, calm, and private setting that allows for intimate discussion.

Caregivers and bereaved individuals value having their physical needs met, but they are also concerned with practical issues that can affect their participation in the group. Patient care, childcare, and work responsibilities leave the caregiver with little time for a support group that draws them away from home demands. These new demands often carry over into the bereavement experience. When possible, having a support group for children and patients at the same time opens up time for caregivers or bereaved people to care for themselves without feeling they are ignoring their new responsibilities or taking time away from work (Silverman 2000).

Although it is true that support groups can take place in a variety of settings, the location of the group will have meaning to the potential members and the institution housing the group. When the support group occurs within the confines of a medical setting, it is important to explore how this might affect the content of the group, the role of the leader, and the members' perceptions of what they can and cannot discuss in the group.

For patients, some common concerns might be:

- How openly can I discuss my treatment, especially if I disagree with it?
- What if I am considering alternative options?
- Will being in the medical environment bring up sensory reminders of receiving treatment?
- What if further treatment is denied?
- If denied, can I still attend the group and will I still feel comfortable returning to the setting?

For caregivers, some common concerns might be:

- I am not satisfied with the pain management my wife is receiving. Can I raise these issues in the group?
- Will I feel comfortable asking for support about how to advocate for my wife?
- Can I still attend the group if my loved one is no longer receiving treatment there?
- The leader is a representative of the institution; how will this affect her role in the group?

For the bereaved, some concerns might be:

- What will it be like to return to where my loved one died?
- What will it be like to return to where my loved one received treatment?

During the planning stages of the group, it is equally important to explore the expectations the institution has for the group. If the medical setting sees the group as a tool to help patients comply with treatment, they will want the purpose of the group to be to educate members about how to cope with treatment as prescribed as well as to receive emotional support to deal with the side effects of treatment. The leader can prepare the members and clarify expectations. The clarification of expectations and purpose can help to minimize dropouts. Often by including the institution in the plans, the group gets the support needed to maintain and promote a healthy environment.

When the setting is not medical, the leader still needs to discover the expectations of the host institution. It is helpful for the leader to consider these expectations when formulating the group's purpose and content. If the purpose and content meet the institutional mandate, the institution is more likely to promote the group to potential members as well as to offer assistance and resources. It is in the leader's best interest to explore with potential members how they view the institution and what effect they think it will have. For example, when a bereavement group is meeting at a local church, will members feel comfortable discussing their lack of faith or spiritual crisis? Will members expect that everyone will be Christian? There is no right institution to house a specific group, but where one is housed will have meaning to the members and affect the content.

GROUP COMPOSITION

Of equal importance to location is the membership of the group. Each collection of individuals has implications for the content and process of the support group. In an optimal environment, decisions about size and composition should be dictated by the special needs of the potential members. However, because group composition can change quickly and frequently, leaders do not always have this luxury. Instead, they must think about ensuring the life of the group beyond individual membership. For this reason, a leader must consider the following compositional components when formulating a support group for patients, caregivers, or the bereaved.

HETEROGENEOUS GROUPS

Heterogeneous groups are made up of members who are different—illness types, illness stages, treatment choices, type of relationship, gender, age, and so forth. The advantage here is that members can learn from one another through their differences. For instance, group members who doubt their ability to face challenges and survive change can find inspiration from their fellow survivors (Herman 2001). Sometimes the diversity of a group can impede group cohesion and the mutual-aid process. In the beginning of a patient support group, it is common for some members to hope secretly that they do not belong in the group for "patients facing advanced illness" or for some caregivers to wish that their loved one is not sick enough for them to need the "taking care of the terminally ill" group. When aware of the potential to "not want to belong," the group leader can raise this reality for discussion. This action of processing will often point out the similarities that bridge individual differences. Members also compare themselves and their disease states with one another. When a member becomes weaker or dies, it raises fears of mortality. Certain members who are doing well with treatment might want to avoid this topic or focus on recovery. For this reason, it is helpful for leaders to consider this factor and bring it up with potential members during the screening process. The leader can then steer these members to more homogeneous stage-specific groups—for example, "recently diagnosed" vs. "advanced illness"—thereby avoiding a potential conflict in the group.

HOMOGENOUS GROUPS

Homogenous groups are made up of individuals who have something in common. Most support groups have some level of homogeneity, in that members are brought together because of a shared external event—death of a loved one, HIV, or children of cancer patients. The advantage of this type of group is that when people feel they have something in common, they are more likely to feel understood.

Most groups have both heterogeneous and homogeneous aspects to their compositions. No group is fully heterogeneous or fully homogenous. Diversity exists in all groups. However, as the support group movement has gained momentum, individuals are demanding that groups be formed according to the following homogeneous considerations:

DIAGNOSIS-SPECIFIC GROUPS. Diagnosis-specific groups include groups of a general diagnosis (for example, cancer of any type) to very particular diagnoses, such as breast or testicular cancer, AIDS, COPD, MS, or other specific diagnosis (Magen and Glajchen 1999; Dean 1995). Individuals facing an illness, and their caregivers, often prefer to join a group where the treatment and issues discussed will be specific to their diagnosis. For brain-tumor patients facing cognitive impairment or caregivers of Alzheimer's patients who wants to learn how to grieve the loss of their "whole" parent, individuals feel more comfortable discussing difficult topics with others they feel will understand "firsthand" what the experience is like.

ILLNESS STAGE–SPECIFIC GROUPS. Specifically for those contemplating palliative care options or termination of treatment, patients and family members want to be able to speak about concerns without being afraid of scaring another member who is not at the same place. Being a member of a homogeneous end-of-life group can bring comfort and ease not found in a more diverse patient or caregiver groups (Klass 1988; Silverman 2000).

BEREAVEMENT-SPECIFIC GROUPS. Certain individuals feel more comfortable when they are in a group where the other members have experience with a specific type of grief. This has particular relevance for individuals who have had a child die (Mahmani, Neeman, and Nir 1989), or had their loved one die as a victim of a violent crime, or had their loved one die as a result of suicide (Klass 1988; Silverman 2000).

AGE-SPECIFIC SUPPORT GROUPS. Children's support groups take place in both medical and nonmedical settings (Bacha, Pomeroy, and Gilbert 1999; Ablin 1993) Dying children generally suffer from a small group of diseases, with various forms of cancer being most common (see chapter 17). There is also a growing awareness of the need for children's support groups related to caregiving, grief, and bereavement issues (Klass 1988; Bendor 1990; Moore 1996; Beckmann 1999; Doka 2000; Silverman 2000) as well as adolescent groups (Baxter and Stewart 1998; Silverman 2000) and elder support groups (Cohen 1999). When group membership is formulated by age, it allows the leader and the group to focus on the impact of developmental issues on illness, dying, death, and bereavement (Herman 2001). Meeting with peers is particularly important for the adolescent. Illness, caregiving, and grief can increase isolation at a time when peer relationships are of primary importance. Being in a group with other teens suffering and coping with similar issues can normalize and validate the experience as well as raise self-esteem.

SPECIAL-POPULATION GROUPS. There is a growing awareness that the special needs of developmentally delayed or disabled people in relation to issues of grief and loss requires special concern. This is a new area of specialization among grief counselors, and includes the use of group work (McDaniel 1989; Rothenberg 1994). It is evident that illness, dying, death, and bereavement occur in all populations. Those suffering from mental illness as well as those who are incarcerated could benefit from the support and mutual aid of a group to address the special needs that arise when facing the end of life within the confines of these unique settings.

SPECIFIC CULTURAL/ETHNIC/SHARED-VALUE GROUPS. Values and beliefs are the lenses through which individuals see the world. Cultural and ethnic ideals have tremendous impact on personal identity and on the ways patients, families, and the bereaved understand and make sense of experiences and of decision-making processes. Facing death or grief often leaves individuals feeling as if they do not know what to do or how to act. Being a part of a cultural or ethnic community and sharing in the specific end-of-life rituals, can answer some of these questions by giving a sense of structure at a time when life seems overwhelming or unknown. Joining a support group with members who share the same values, beliefs, culture, and ethnicity has the potential to advance the group cohesion. The leader should take into consideration how the cultural norms and values will affect the content and format of the group (discussion or task-focused groups) thereby ensuring participation and enhancing safety (Herman 2001).

GENDER-SPECIFIC GROUPS. Whether patient, caregiver, or bereaved, men and women process experiences differently; it is therefore more beneficial, at times, to be in a group with others who process experiences similarly (Martin and Doka 2000). Further logic behind having gender-specific groups is that in gender-segregated groups, members may feel free to discuss and share issues they would feel reticent to explore in the presence of members of the opposite sex (Baldry and Walsh 1999; Sharp, Blum, and Aviv 1993; Gilbar 1991). Often men prefer a group with a planned agenda and set time frame. Psychoeducational groups have proven effective where part of the group is spent hearing a lecture and the other part of the group is spent in discussion (Herman 2001; Silverman 2000). The leader can look to the group composition to inform the content and format that will be most effective.

CAREGIVER SUPPORT GROUPS. The term *caregiver* applies to any individual who is involved in any way with the care of a dying individual. There is great diversity in the membership of caregiver groups: active caregivers, long-distance caregivers, relatives, friends, community members, and the like. Caregiver support groups are formed in recognition that family members and members of the close social network need support no less than the dying person. Caregiver support groups may be diagnosis specific or general in nature. One of the leader's most prominent tasks is the encouragement of ventilation of a full range of feelings about the shared experience. Because caregiving is such a daunting and exhausting responsibility, many caregivers feel relief when they anticipate their loved ones' death; however, they experience these feelings as unacceptable and inappropriate, and consequently they suffer guilt and shame. It is imperative that the leader reinforce that many feelings arise during the experience of caregiving and that they are all normal and valid. Caregivers also need help taking time to care for themselves and to process their own experiences. For many, the support group is the only time they take for themselves (Chesney, Rounds, and Chesler 1989; Hayes et al. 1998).

In end-of-life caregiver groups, the leader is often asked to maintain the duality of hope in the midst of despair. Such groups struggle with how to go on living when someone they love is dying. The leader should encourage the members to redefine hope even as the situation changes, and to allow the group to sit in the hopelessness when needed. There may be a strong educational component to the group where members learn about the illness, methods of coping with stress and anticipated grief, and the practical skills of end-of-life patient care.

BEREAVEMENT GROUPS. Bereavement groups are an integral part of end-of-life-care practice (Buell and Bevis 1989). Bereavement groups take place in both medical and nonmedical settings. In medical settings, such groups are often part of a hospice program (though not restricted only to families of hospice patients) because a functioning aftercare program is mandated by Medicare regulations for hospices (Zastrow 2001; Lattanzi-Licht et al. 1998). In nonmedical settings, bereavement groups are often attached to community agencies and religious institutions. Institutions such as funeral homes increasingly sponsor bereavement groups and bereavement aftercare (Weeks and Johnson 2000; Wirpsa 1998; Bolton and Camp 1989). The content of a bereavement group is similar to a caregiver group. The leader assists the members in telling their individual stories of their loved ones—the illness and the death. It is important that the leader and the group members know and use the names of the deceased people. As in a caregiver group, a key function for the leader is to help the membership express and articulate the full range of feelings about the illness and death, as well as grief and recovery.

The work of grief is to examine and mourn the many roles the loved one played and the different aspects of the relationship that are now missed. Individual grief work is usually not completed during the course of the group as grief does not have a specific timeline (see chapter 6). The other key goal of the group is for the leader and members to help one another explore how each member will go on living without their loved one and how their lives will change. One of the most stunning benefits of participating in a bereavement group is that the members help one another see how they have made individual changes—both large and small. For many members, participation in the support group is often the first sign that a recovery and healing process has begun (Klass 1988; Silverman 2000).

GROUP STRUCTURE

A support group can be either open-ended or time-limited. Giving the group a structure informs members what is expected of them in terms of a commitment. It also reinforces the message that the group has been planned with special considerations to ensure their safety and comfort.

OPEN-ENDED GROUPS. This classification implies that the group is ongoing, with no end date. Since the experience of advanced illness and caregiving is unpredictable, attendance problems can be frequent. The open-ended group provides an opportunity for individuals to receive the support they need without feeling they cannot meet their commitments. Members can be a part of the group for as long as they wish and drop out when they no longer need the group. The leader is free to use her discretion about adding new members.

TIME-LIMITED GROUPS. In this type of group, members commit to meeting for a contracted period. No new members are admitted. Often the structure of this type of group is comforting, for the group provides a safe haven at a time when everything else is up in the air. Group cohesion and feelings of safety are often expedited because members do not have to anticipate any type of change once the structure has been put into place (Herman 2001). Time-limited groups help the bereaved individual mark the passage of time and reflect on changes. Being afforded an opportunity to plan the ending, bereaved people can regain a sense of control as well as experience a loss and ending that is not devastating.

MEMBER SELECTION

Whenever possible, leaders should contact potential members in order to determine if the group is going to be helpful to the individual and if the individual is going to be asset to the group. Screening interviews are mutually beneficial and can occur on the telephone or in person. They allow the group member to meet the leader, ask questions, and voice any concerns or apprehensions about the group. The support group leader can use this opportunity to learn about the particular needs of the individual member and begin a therapeutic alliance. Linking group members' similarities and facilitating group cohesion can also occur in this initial meeting by raising shared situations or themes to be discussed in the group.

There are several tasks to accomplish during the screening interview (Herman 2001):

- Assess if the member's need for the group falls within the purpose, goals, and objectives of the group.
- Rule out individuals with conditions that could compromise the health of the group or put other members in danger: gross delusions or distortions of reality; active substance abuse; acute psychosis; or active homicidal or suicidal tendencies or serious character pathology.
- Learn about the potential member's illness and/or grief history as well as her current situation.
- Explain the purpose of the group and basic rules.
- Lay out the terms of the member contract (number of sessions, closed or open group, day and time, etc.)
- Give a thumbnail sketch of what the group might be like and general topics to be discussed.
- Clarify myths and misconceptions of support groups.
- Describe the role of the leader.
- Refer to appropriate services and supports when it has been determined that certain issues fall beyond the scope of the group (long-standing family conflict, history of alcohol abuse, premorbid mental health problems, and the like)

Typical questions to be explored are:

- What are your expectations of and for the group?
- How do you see the group being helpful to you?
- What do you see as being challenging about participating in this group?
- What concerns do you have about joining the group?
- What do you think you could contribute to the group?
- Have you had other support group experiences? If yes, please describe.
- What will it be like for you to hear others with similar experiences?
- What will it be like for you to hear others with different experiences?

Potential group members might display or reveal other qualities that might negatively affect the group process:

- Inability to listen to others
- Tendency to judge others or feel that their way is the only "correct" way
- Inclination toward sharing too much information too quickly
- Complete lack of empathy

Support group leaders need to trust their instincts. If at any point during a screening interview the thought comes up that a potential member is not suitable for the group, the leader should not be afraid to deny membership. This action not only preserves the health of the group, but also ensures that the individual is referred to services that are appropriate to her specific needs.

GROUP RULES

In order for members to feel comfortable disclosing their end-of-life concerns, safety needs to be established. The first step in creating a safe environment is the formulation of group rules. By collaborating with members on the development of the rules, the leader clarifies expectations of how members should act in the group. Potential members are put at ease by realizing that there is a code of behavior for all to abide. The leader can introduce the idea of rules during the screening interview to answer any individual questions or concerns; however, a group discussion of the rules and their exceptions is crucial to moving members beyond following the rules, to owning them. Reaching consensus on the group rules is often the first step toward members assuming responsibility for the group. In an ongoing group, when new members join, it is helpful to have a seasoned group member explain the norms and rules of the group. This reinforces the commitment of the seasoned member as well as models the idea that individuals are more than just participants of a group, but members of a support community.

Every group has its own rules, but the following is a framework for where to begin the discussion.

CONFIDENTIALITY. It is imperative to define the boundary of information that members will discuss in the group and share with outsiders versus the information members will only discuss within the confines of the group. With this standard, members can make informed choices about how they want to participate in the group. Most members would not take issue with sharing medical information or practical resources with people outside the group; however, within the privacy of a support group, members reveal feelings and aspects of themselves that they may not want to share with the outside world. For this reason, it is helpful that the majority of information shared in the group stays only in the group. This rule applies to the membership as well as the leader. It should be clarified that there is an important exception to this fundamental rule. When a group member shares information about wanting to hurt himself or another person, this falls outside the boundary of confidentiality. The leader has the responsibility to divulge the information and get the group member the help that he needs.

ATTENDANCE. Group members agree to an attendance policy. The policy will differ depending on whether the group is ongoing or time-limited. Implicit in the agreement is the idea that individuals make a commitment to join a support community and will be counted on to attend and be supportive of the other members. Individuals dealing with end-of-life concerns are often unable to attend regularly. It is for this reason that they are asked to commit to informing the leader when unable to attend. This way they can maintain a connection with the group when absent.

PATIENCE WITH GROUP PROCESS. It takes time for strangers to come together and form a supportive community. Members can initially feel awkward, question whether they belong, and feel uncomfortable about sharing their stories publicly. After a few sessions, individuals usually begin to feel known, supported, and able to support others. No matter how similar people's experiences are, everyone is still unique. It is necessary for members to maintain patience with one another, for everyone grows and changes in her own time. The group leader should encourage members to speak when they are having difficulty with the group process. Usually if one person is having an experience in the group, another is sharing the same sentiment but unable to express it. Once raised, work can be done to resolve the situation.

RESPONSIBILITY. The group leader can establish from the first meeting that members have a responsibility to make the group their own. Clarifying the role and expertise of the leader can help dispel the myth of "leader as expert." Instead, members realize the leader's role is to provide expertise in group process and facilitation and it is their role to provide the expertise in the experience of illness, caregiving, or grief.

MUTUAL RESPECT. Support groups are made up of individuals with opinions, beliefs, and value systems. These unique qualities affect decision making and the creation of solutions. Although it is helpful to hear the experiences and advice of others, each person is entitled to make his or her own choices. No decision is right and no decision is wrong. The leader must emphasize that members do not have to agree with another's choices, but they do have to respect an individual's right to choose. A significant way of showing respect to fellow group members is to refrain from interrupting another's story, philosophizing, or moralizing.

STAGES OF GROUP DEVELOPMENT

Although each group has unique components, most groups progress through similar developmental stages that can be generalized (Wasserman and Danforth 1988). Awareness of these stages allows the leader to anticipate needs and direct the leadership role toward meeting the overall goal of ensuring and sustaining a healthy, productive group environment. In time-limited groups, the phase model is more delineated, with one stage occurring and the next following. In open-ended groups, phases are more subtle and can occur simultaneously or in fits and starts.

STAGE ONE: ORIENTATION/TOGETHER AS INDIVIDUALS

At this stage, the group is coming together physically, but emotionally, psychologically, and spiritually it is still a collection of individuals (Corey 2000). The group atmosphere is often polite. Members tell their stories and proceed with caution, choosing not reveal too much information too soon. It is evident that members pay close attention to one another and try to decide if they fit in. For some members there can be hesitation, for by belonging to a group the reality of their situation is heightened.

In the beginning, the membership usually calls for the group leader to step in and take charge. In order to set the foundation for a safe environment, the leader should restate the group's purpose. "We are here tonight because every member of this group has had a child die." If the group's purpose can be stated clearly and directly, it models for the members that it is permissible to discuss difficult, sometimes "taboo" subjects in a direct manner. Stating the purpose lets group members know the shared experience that has brought them together. It also defines the work of the group. The leader can restate the policies and open a discussion for members to tailor the rules to the specific needs of the group, thereby letting the members take ownership. By introducing herself and clarifying her role, the leader sets the tone that this group will be run by a professional facilitator who has clear goals and expectations for herself (Walsh, Hewitt, and Londeree 1996). The leader can also clarify her respect for members' individual choices, opinions, knowledge, and abilities. Restating these observations encourages members to be active participants in the group's process and progression as opposed to passive. It also reinforces the expectation that each individual is ultimately responsible and capable of her own healing and recovery.

It is helpful if the leader reviews the guidelines for how members introduce themselves to the group, such as, "Tell us your name, your loved one's name, a little about their illness, and why you wanted to join a support group." This structure assists members in putting their thoughts together at a time when their nervousness about being in the group can leave them feeling frazzled. The leader can recognize the potential anxiety of group members and give them credit for attending the group despite any trepidation (Herman 2001). Offering this encouragement highlights members' strengths. It is important to ask for participation, but respect that some individuals are not yet ready to speak. Giving members the option to "pass" from a conversation if they do not want to speak normalizes the choice and sends the message that there are other ways to participate in the group beyond the verbal. A relatively silent member can be a powerful presence. The leader can also make a statement about her participation in the group, explaining that it might be stronger and more directive in the beginning while the group is forming and that once the group has established its identity and rhythm the directives and content will come from the members. This action highlights for members that the group belongs to them. It also reinforces the idea that the leader is always present if needed.

In this beginning stage, the group leader has two other important tasks to accomplish to facilitate the health of the group. As members are introducing themselves, the leader should listen closely and point out when members are discussing similar themes, feelings, or experiences. This skill is referred to as "linking." It helps to put members at ease by decreasing isolation, promoting the "all in the same boat" phenomenon, and building group cohesion (Shulman 1992). The group leader also wants to encourage members to ask questions of one another rather than have the leader be the sole focus of the group. She can encourage this by continuously scanning the faces of the group members and avoiding one-on-one sessions. Encouraging members to ask questions and get information from one another is a pivotal step in members taking ownership and responsibility for the maintenance of their group.

STAGE TWO: FORMATION/CONFLICT

As the group moves from the fragile coming together of individuals to a group with its own identity, members will tentatively begin to share ideas and feelings, particularly those related to perceptions and hopes concerning group goals and tasks (Corey 2000). Members progress beyond telling their story and indicate they want help with certain situations, advice from other members, support, and the like. Different members have different needs, and this diversity inevitably leads to disagreements and conflicts. Conflict is a natural component in the group development process and a sign of group growth. When conflict is allowed to arise in the group, it is evidence that members have developed a certain level of comfort to be able to share their differences.

In patient, caregiver, and bereavement groups, balance between hope and despair must be sought. Because of the unpredictability of illness, caregiving, and grief, individual members can fall on different places on the spectrum within moments. One week someone might feel more hopeful and the next feel despairing. A life-compromising symptom can appear with no warning. At the same time, a member can suddenly experience a reprieve from pain and be able to enjoy his morning walk. The constantly fluctuating experience leaves patients, caregivers, and the bereaved with changing needs. For this reason, it is difficult to create goals that will meet every individual need every week. The person who is experiencing crisis will want to ventilate her feelings, while the individual who is hopeful will not want to be brought down by another's despair.

When a conflict about what to discuss in the group arises, it is helpful for the leader to explain that conflicts are natural and potentially creative as a step toward building group cohesion (Rose 1989; Yalom 1995). The conflict can be likened to a growing pain—something that is uncomfortable but brings about the clarity that comes from difference. Often members will look to the leader to step in and intervene by giving nonverbal clues of distress—eye-rolling, arm-crossing, shifting in their seats, and the like. The leader can use his observations to broach the subject with the group, "I'm noticing that several people got quiet or shifted in your chairs when . . . and I'm wondering if there is a difference of opinion about what we want to talk about." The leader can use her feelings to model for members that it is difficult to discuss conflict: "I don't know about you, but sometimes when I feel there is a difference of opinion, I can get a knot in my stomach. What are you experiencing in the group when I raised the issue that we might have different opinions?" After members get an opportunity to discuss their different ideas, the leader can suggest that the group renegotiate the goals and expectations of what can be discussed. The renegotiation process can renew group commitment. The discussion can be framed by the leader as an opportunity to learn respect for one another's different preferences without compromising individual choice. The leader can also reiterate that members are expected to give as well as receive support.

Another type of conflict that can appear once the group has gained momentum is scapegoating. The dynamic of scapegoating is not a foregone conclusion, but can arise depending on the individual members and the dynamics of the group as whole.

This dynamic often occurs in the group unconsciously. Members are not aware they are participating in the process. Scapegoating—the tendency to single out one group member for particular criticism (as the source of the group's tensions) and (literal or figurative) ostracism by other group members (Girard 2001)—was given the most sustained treatment in the social work literature by Balgopal and Vassil (1983). Group cohesion can be built rather quickly by teaming up against a common "enemy." Scapegoating is a constant group temptation because it is effective in resolving tensions and creating a unified group. Often the member who is scapegoated has behavior in the group that is problematic (monopolizes group time, rejects help, displays hostility, or withdraws); however, scapegoating the member does not address the problematic behavior or the role it serves in the group. If a member repeatedly monopolizes the conversation, no one else has to reveal information or work toward achieving group cohesion. Scapegoating members is a way for the group to create "an illusion of work" rather than actually working on the difficult issues raised (Shulman 1992). By allowing the scapegoating to continue without intervention, the leader gives unspoken permission to avoid the real work. The leader must place her authority behind addressing the conflict and bringing the scapegoated member back. If no intervention takes place, members get the message that difficult issues are to be avoided. The message also engenders feelings that the group is not a safe place. Other members will understand implicitly—"I could be next"—and defer to more powerful members in fear of being scapegoated (Malekoff 1994; Anstey 1982).

The dynamic of dropping out of a group is a normal occurrence. It should not be interpreted as a sign of leader failure or an unhealthy group, unless it occurs consistently (Herman 2001). Support groups can be a beneficial way to deal with the multiple concerns that arise at the end of life, but they are not for everyone all the time. The leader needs to think about the effect of the member dropping out on the group as a whole. When someone drops out, it is important to contact the member, ask about the reason for leaving, and ask permission to share this information with the other members. It is imperative that the group has the opportunity to discuss what it means to them that the person left. The leader might have to dispel members' feelings that the group is somehow responsible for the premature departure.

STAGE THREE: CONSOLIDATION/RESOLUTION

At this stage of development, the tensions of conflict are largely resolved (Corey 2000). Members have come to see that the group is able to meet a wide spectrum of needs and that working through tensions can be a source of creativity. Members have found their roles and have become comfortable with expectations. This is the "high productivity," teamwork phase of the group. A supportive community has been established where members share feelings openly, problem-solve, challenge one another to meet individual goals, and are able to give as well as get support. Members are able to experience the mutual aid and supportiveness that healthy group cohesion offers.

Members will progress to a noticeably deeper level of communication, intimacy, and interaction. Confrontation, challenge, and disagreement continue but will be much more easily understood, accepted, and resolved. Group challenges, confrontations, and disagreements are most likely to lead to productive insight. Members may become vocal about how much they have in common as well how their multiple perspectives add richness to the group.

During this stage, the group is less dependent on the leader, unless an issue or experience arises where they need the leader's expertise and direction. The primary role of the leader is to help members articulate and explore the many facets of their feelings, as well as maintain the structure of the group. If the group is ongoing, this might be the time to think about bringing in new members. Especially with caregivers and patients, new membership is often necessary to maintain the health of the group, for medical crises can affect the ability to participate consistently. In order to avoid subgrouping of old and new members, the leader will want to prepare the old members for the inclusion of someone new into the community. It is helpful if the leader shares information about the new member and asks what it will be like to have someone different. Once the group is prepared, the leader can elicit the help of seasoned members in welcoming the new person and explaining the group rules, norms, roles, expectations.

STAGE FOUR: WINDING DOWN AND TERMINATION

Winding down and termination is an important and delicate phase for any group, but especially for groups dealing with end-of-life issues (Corey 2000). During this phase, conscious and unconscious feelings of anxiety about separation, fear of the unknown, concern about isolation and abandonment, sadness over the loss of contact with cherished group members, and anger at the arbitrary end date chosen by another are stimulated by the group facing its own impending end. For the patient facing death, the caregiver, or the bereaved, experiencing the complicated feelings caused by group termination can be especially powerful because the members are experiencing similar issues in their lives. If the leader is able to discuss this parallel process, members have the opportunity to talk openly about their complex feelings. It is often determined that the "planned ending" of the group gives members the chance to design and implement the kind of ending they would like for their group. Arranging the ending of the group is often a contrasting event to the lack of control each member faces in terms of planning his or her own death, or the dying of a loved one.

Leaders will notice in this phase of development a number of recurring themes and events. Members often begin to express appreciation for the help they have received from other members and the special role the group has played in their lives. For example, a member might say, "Thank you, that is really helpful, you understand perfectly where I'm coming from. . . . I just don't know what I'm going to do without you folks." Members might also begin to speak about avenues for maintaining contact with each other after the group. An alert leader will recognize such side comments as an indicator that the group is moving into the winding-down phase, even if the actual termination date is still weeks away. It is crucial that leaders explore the individual's as well as the group's feelings about ending. When this opportunity is not provided, members' feeling and fears of being abandoned and ignored are realized.

It can be helpful for members to make plans for continuing their support of one another outside the group. This can be a good idea, but it should not be seen as a Band-Aid to fix the needs left by termination. Members need to have the opportunity to discusses the specifics of what they will miss when the group is over before they problem-solve about how to meet those needs. Sometimes the group can serve as a rehearsal for loss, and include rituals for termination and grief.

Often the general tone and members' individual behaviors change as the group enters the winding-down and ending phase. Members may become periodically more pensive, less communicative, and more defensive with each other. This is to be expected. It is the group's way of asking for help from the leader. As in the beginning, when the group was not yet formed and did not yet have its own identity, the leader has the responsibility for providing the support and direction during the emotionally rocky time of termination. Members often feel vulnerable and do not have the same capacity to care for one another as they did during the middle phases.

One of the most crucial tasks during the termination phase is for leaders to encourage members to reflect on their individual growth and change throughout the life of the group. Members come to the group in one emotional place and leave in another. Regardless of whether their experience has been beneficial, or change has been noteworthy, something has occurred during their experience. When members have a difficult time articulating this, the leader can call on other members to reflect. One of the most powerful functions of a group is to act as a mirror in which members are able to see themselves reflected in the eyes of others. For the individual who is dying or facing the death of a loved one, seeing oneself reflected accurately can help maintain an evolving definition of hope. A plan and hope can act as transitional objects for members to hold onto when they are living their lives without the group. They can be soothed by the memories of the support and encouragement they received during the life of the group. It can be equally powerful for members to evaluate what was helpful about the group and what they would like to change or add for future groups. The activity of creating a "group legacy" marks their expertise as members and supports the idea that they have something to offer others.

The winding-down and termination dynamics are felt more strongly in time-limited groups, where the planned end date is an overt, visible reminder of the group's end. However, similar dynamics occur more subtly in ongoing groups. They may arise when a member of long standing chooses to leave, someone dies, the leader changes, or an individual chooses to attend only one group session. The leader should be aware of the significance and meaning of termination, endings, loss, separation, and grief and realize their presence even when they are not discussed openly. In ongoing groups, it is especially important for the leader to listen for opening to discuss these difficult feelings, inasmuch as the group structure will not always provide a natural opening.

DEALING WITH THE DEATH OF A GROUP MEMBER

The death of a member is a possible event in any group-work setting (Buelow 1994). However, it is likely to occur in support groups for patients who are facing advanced illness. This reality can be the unspoken white elephant in the room. When the group begins, members will often wonder to themselves, "Who will still be there when the group ends?" and "How will I handle it if someone dies?" When the death of a member actually occurs, individuals have different reactions that depend on the length of time the deceased member had been a part of the group, the role the deceased member played, the stage of group development at the time of the death, the level of intimacy exchanged within the group, and how the deceased person appeared and presented during the last session (i.e., if the death was very sudden and unexpected, or might have been expected based on the deceased member's recent physical presentation.) Members will have certain feelings when the deceased has been a role model and an inspiration as opposed to one who brought tremendous conflict into the group.

The death of a member demands that the leader respond in specific ways in order to ensure the health of the group. Usually if the members find out before the group begins, they will let the leader know, and plans can be made for how to inform the other members. If the leader is the first to be informed, it will be her responsibility to inform the group. The first step in preparing to tell the news is for the leader to ask herself the meaning of the death. Though facilitators are not members of the group, they do have a relationship with the deceased and, consequently, their own grief response. If the leader does not provide herself with the opportunity to examine her own grief, it may be expressed unconsciously in the group, and unexamined countertransference may lead to unconscious acting out (Gabriel 1991). Leaders are themselves subject to the same need to deny and repress mortality as others—it is the inevitable psychological need of any being that is simultaneously mortal and self-conscious (Liechty 2000). For this reason it is wise to understand these feeling before entering the group. In an ongoing group, it is important to inform new members that in the upcoming session, the death of a member will be discussed and it might be a difficult meeting for new individuals to attend. If the membership does not know before the group begins, the leader should watch to see if members notice that the deceased member is not there. If the group notices, the leader can raise that she has some "bad news." She can then inquire if the group wants to hear the news. This option gives the group some sense of control in that they can choose to hear the news or not. If an individual member is having a particular crisis, she can also let the group know and receive support for her concerns as well. If the group does not bring up that the member is missing, the leader can proceed by mentioning the "bad news" and query the group to see if they want to discuss it. The leader should recognize that whether the group notices the missing member gives information about the way in which the deceased member is viewed (or not viewed) in the group. This information can be used in helping the group to articulate their wide range of feelings about the death and the deceased member.

When the leader gives the news, it should be informative and succinct, "Fran died this morning." The leader should wait and observe the reactions of the group. The leader should not try to fill the silence, but instead witness it. After some time, the leader can recognize the silence and ask, "Can anyone put words to the silence in the room?" If no one responds, the leader can wait and respond, "It seems like we need to stay in the silence." Usually, someone will speak and begin to ask questions. The leader should respond and give information, but be economical. The emphasis should be on members' experiences rather than on the leader's trying to fill the space with information to avoid difficult feelings. Different members will have different responses. Some will have practical questions about the death, while others will want to talk about their feelings. If the deceased member was not beloved by the group, individuals might feel guilty for not appreciating the individual when he was alive. The leader can comment about the diversity of reaction and mention that there is not one appropriate response.

If it is evident that the group is not talking about the death or straying from topic, the leader can point this out. Further, the leader can share her response to model for members how difficult it can be to talk about dying. For some it will be easier to talk about reactions to the death individually. The leader can offer outside support but encourage individuals to bring the issues up to the group. In the next meeting, further discussion can take place. The leader can push for more responses now that members have had time to reflect. Keeping an empty chair in the group can promote discussion. If it does not, the leader can recognize that no one has mentioned the chair and ask if there are any thoughts about this. It can be an opportunity for the group to discuss the individual expressions of grief—including silence and individual, private reflection. Members might want to plan a special group ritual to memorialize the individual. Whatever ritual is chosen, it should be based on the experiences of the group as a whole as well as have meaning for the individual members (Herman 2001).

If processed openly and sensitively, the death of a member can have positive effect on the development of the group. When a member dies, it brings the issue of mortality into the center of group members' minds (May and Yalom 2000). This reality is something that leaders and members might choose to avoid, but are now unable to. The death is a reminder that extending oneself in trust and emotional intimacy entails the risks of pain and sorrow, and members may draw back from one another in the wake of the death. Having to acknowledge and accept death and mortality in a public place accelerates the intimacy felt between members. Similar to conflict, the death of a member can be a catalyzing event in the life of a group.

NEW TECHNOLOGIES: TELEPHONE AND ONLINE GROUPS

Within the last ten years, end-of-life groups have multiplied with the implementation of telephone and Internet-based support groups. Before the use of these technologies, involvement in groups was limited to patients, caregivers, and bereaved people who could leave the house, travel, and participate in a group at a given hour on a given day. Although groups met the needs of many individuals seeking care, many ruled themselves out of membership because they were homebound, unable to travel, or had time conflicts owing to treatment schedules, caregiving responsibilities, or work demands. For these individuals, support groups over the telephone or online can be a practical, cost-effective option (Colon 2001). These modalities might also be of use when the patient, caregiver, or bereaved person wants to maintain privacy and feels uncomfortable being a member of a face-to-face group. This might also be an option with more reluctant or uneasy members who can participate in the comfort of their own familiar surroundings rather than the impersonal environment of a medical setting or agency.

TELEPHONE GROUPS

In the beginning, it is important for members to state their names each time they speak. Clarifying names helps members learn one another's voices. Leaders should make a circular chart of the members and jot down some notes when individuals are speaking. This helps the leader to know who is participating and the specific issues each person is raising. As in a face-to-face group, the leader will want to link members' similarities and facilitate the problem-solving process. Rather than rely on visual cues to evaluate the experience of members, leaders must pay close attention to what is being said and how it is being said (tone, language choice, and inflection) (see chapter 27). The leader will have to ask direct questions and explore the different meanings of silence. Because the leader will have to query the members for clues as to the group experience, it is common for the leader to take a more active role. This is in contrast to a face-to-face leader who confines his active role to the beginning and ending stages as well when conflict arises.

Because members participate in telephone meetings from their homes, hospital beds, offices, etc, the boundaries of the group are less definitive (see chapter 27). Friends or family members may be present and interested in the subject matter. They may be tempted to join in to help their loved one. If this occurs, the leader must quickly state the purpose and the role of confidentiality of the group. The leader should politely ask the individual to leave the group immediately. Once the outsider is gone, the leader must explore with the group the meaning of the interruption. Feelings of safety are reinforced when members realize the leader is able to protect the security of the group and ensure privacy.

ONLINE GROUPS

Online groups can be gratifying for the leader because members are forthcoming about their experiences (see chapter 27). Taking the time to put feelings into written words is especially therapeutic. This process allows members to be reflective and insightful about their own experience and growth as well as to be helpful to others. The material shared is rich and potent. Because members are posting as the issues are occurring, they are not as defensive and much more "in the moment." Because of the online nature of the group, there is relative anonymity, and members do not anticipate the judgment or potential shame feared in a face-to-face group. Intimacy and group cohesion occur rapidly and often with little intervention or encouragement from the leader. However, this does not mean that the leadership role is not needed. On the contrary, because of the lack of visual and aural cues, leaders must help the group understand how members are feeling and how experiences are being processed. Use of language is important and revealing. If members post with all capital letters, it is implied that they are yelling at the membership; this action is felt very deeply. One of the leader's roles is to help members clarify what they mean when they are speaking. Many of us have experience writing, but do not have experience relying solely on the written word. Language can be stark and direct, and humor and sarcasm can be easily misinterpreted (see chapter 27). The group leader needs to be a strong presence to guide members through potential miscommunications. The leader must also monitor the frequency of member posts. The only way to make one's presence known online is to post. If certain members are more reluctant, it is hard to tell if they are there or not. Such uncertainty can erode trust. For this reason, leaders must encourage members to post regularly, however brief, in order to reinforce presence.

CONCLUSION

Participating in a support group, whether face-to-face, over the telephone, or via the Internet, has numerous advantages for those individuals experiencing the specialized concerns at the end of life. Once a cohesive group is formed, members benefit from being around others who are sharing the same external experience. Their intense feelings and responses are often normalized and supported, stigma and isolation are decreased, resources and knowledge are pooled, and the optimal opportunity exists for individuals to articulate and explore taboo subjects without feeling exposed or protective of family members. Leaders can ensure a successful group experience by careful planning and consideration about group location, setting, composition, member screening and selection, and formulation of group rules and expectations. Most groups move through similar stages, so that the leader's roles and responsibilities can be generalized. Facilitators are called upon to be more directive and active during the formation and termination as well as when conflict arises and when a member dies. Leaders who convey respect for the knowledge and expertise of the membership encourage the group to form its own identity, learn from one another, and be responsible for their own healing and recovery. The empowering opportunities found in end-of-life support groups can be equally life-renewing and hopeful for both member and facilitator.

REFERENCES

Ablin, A. R., ed. 1993. *Supportive Care of Children with Cancer: Current Therapy and Guidelines for the Children's Cancer Group.* Baltimore: Johns Hopkins University Press.

Anstey, M. (1982). Scapegoating in groups: Some theoretical perspectives and a case record of intervention. *Social Work with Groups* 5:51–63.

Bacha, T., E. C. Pomeroy, and D. Gilbert. 1999. A psychoeducational group intervention for HIV-positive children: A pilot study. *Health and Social Work* 24:303–306.

Baldry, E., and A. Walsh. 1999. Social and emotional support for women being treated for breast cancer: Social workers' involvement. *Australian Social Work* 52:37–42.

Balgopal, P. R., and T. V. Vassil. 1983. *Groups in Social Work: An Ecological Perspective.* New York: Macmillan.

Baxter, G. W., and W. J. Stewart. 1998. *Death and the Adolescent: A Resource Handbook for Bereavement Support Groups in Schools.* Toronto: University of Toronto Press.

Beckmann, R. 1999. *Children Who Grieve: A Manual for Conducting Support Groups.* Holmes Beach, FL: Learning Publications.

Bendor, S. J. 1990. Anxiety and isolation in siblings of pediatric cancer patients: The need for intervention. *Social Work in Health Care* 14:17–35.

Bolton, C., and D. J. Camp. 1989. The post-funeral ritual in bereavement counseling and grief work. *Journal of Gerontological Social Work* 13:49–59.

Buell, J. S., and J. Bevis. 1989. Bereavement groups in the hospice setting. In *Bereavement Care: A Look at Hospice and Community-based Services,* ed. M. E. Lattanzi-Licht, J. M. Kirschling, and S. Fleming, 107–118. Binghamton, NY: Haworth.

Buelow, G. 1994. A suicide in group: A case of functional realignment. *International Journal of Group Psychotherapy* 44:153–168.

Canda, E., and L. D. Furman. 1999. *Spiritual Diversity in Social Work Practice.* New York: Free Press.

Cella, D., and S. Yellen. 1993. Cancer support groups: The state of the art. *Cancer Practice* 1(1): 59–60.

Chesney, B. K., K. A. Rounds, and M. A. Chesler. 1989. Support for parents of children with cancer: The value of self-help groups. *Social Work with Groups* 12:119–139.

Cohen, M. A. 1999. Bereavement groups with the elderly. *Journal of Psychotherapy in Independent Practice* 1:33–41.

Cohen, S., and T. A. Willis. 1985. Stress, social support, and the buffering hypothesis. *Psychological Bulletin* 98:310–357.

Colón, Y. 2001. Telephone and online support groups. In *Cancer Support Groups: A Guide for Facilitators,* 81–94. New York: American Cancer Society.

Corey, G. 2000. *Theory and Practice of Group Counseling.* 5th ed. Belmont, CA: Wadsworth/Thomas Learning.

Dean, R. G. 1995. Stories of AIDS: The use of narrative as an approach to understanding in an AIDS support group. *Clinical Social Work Journal* 23:287–304.

Doka, K. J., ed. 2000. *Living with Grief: Children, Adolescents and Loss.* Washington, DC: Hospice Foundation of America.

Edwards, J. N., and D. H. Demo. 1998. *Marriage and Family in Transition.* Needham Heights, MA: Allyn and Bacon.

Gabriel, M. A. 1991. Group therapists' countertransference reactions to multiple deaths from AIDS. *Clinical Social Work Journal* 19:279–292.

Gilbar, O. 1991. Model for crisis intervention through group therapy for women with breast cancer. *Clinical Social Work Journal* 19:294–304.

Girard, R. 2001. *The Scapegoat.* Baltimore: Johns Hopkins University Press.

Goffman, E. 1986. *Stigma: Notes on the Management of a Spoiled Identity.* New York: Simon & Schuster.

Hayes, M. A., S. C. McConnell, J. A. Nardozzi, and R. J. Mullican. 1998. Family and friends of people with HIV/AIDS support group. *Social Work with Groups* 21:35–47.

Herman, J. 2001. *Cancer Support Groups: A Guide for Facilitators.* New York: American Cancer Society.

Klass, D. 1988. *Parental Grief: Solace and Resolution.* New York: Springer.

Kurland, R., and R. Salmon. 1999. Education for the group worker's reality: The special qualities and world view of those drawn to work with groups. *Journal of Teaching in Social Work* 19:123–137.

Lattanzi-Licht, M., J. J. Mahoney, G. Miller, and J. J. Maloney. 1998. *The Hospice Choice: In Pursuit of a Peaceful Death.* New York. Simon & Schuster.

Levin, J. S. 2001. *God, Faith, and Health: Exploring the Spirituality-Healing Connection.* New York: Wiley.

Liechty, D. 2000. Touching mortality, touching strength: Clinical work with dying patients. *Journal of Religion and Health* 39:247–260.

Magen, R. H., and M. Glajchen. 1999. Cancer support groups: Client outcome and the context of group practice. *Research on Social Work Practice* 9:541–554.

Mahmani, N., E. Neeman, and C. Nir. 1989. Parental bereavement: The motivation to participate in support groups and its consequences. *Social Work with Groups* 12:89–98.

Malekoff, A. 1994. Moments and madness: Humanizing the scapegoat in the group. *Journal of Child and Adolescent Group Therapy* 4:169–176.

Martin, T. L., and K. J. Doka. 2000. *Men Don't Cry . . . Women Do: Transcending Gender Stereotypes of Grief.* New York: Brunner/Mazel.

May, R., and I. Yalom. 2000. Existential psychotherapy. In *Current Psychotherapies* (6th ed.), ed. R. J. Corsini and D. Wedding, 273–302. Itasca, IL: F. E. Peacock.

McDaniel, B. A. 1989. A group work experience with mentally retarded adults on the issues of death and dying. *Journal of Gerontological Social Work* 13:187–191.

Miller, C. T., and B. Major. 2000. Coping with stigma and prejudice. In *The Social Psychology of Stigma*, ed. T. Heatherton, R. E. Kleck, M. R. Thebl, and J. G. Hull, 243–272. New York: Guilford.

Moore, B. 1996. Program profile: "I count too"—Supporting the children of the terminally ill. *Continuum* 16:18–20.

Neuberg, S. L., D. M. Smith, and T. Asher. 2000. Why people stigmatize: Toward a biocultural framework. In *The Social Psychology of Stigma*, ed. T. Heatherton et al., 31–61. New York: Guilford.

Rando, T. A. 1993. *Treatment of Complicated Mourning.* Champaign, IL: Research Press.

Rose, S. D. 1989. *Working with Adults in Groups.* San Francisco: Jossey-Bass.

Rothenberg, E. D. 1994. Bereavement intervention with vulnerable populations: A case report on group work with the developmentally disabled. *Social Work with Groups* 17:61–75.

Roy, P. F., and H. Sumpter. 1983. Group support for the recently bereaved. *Heath and Social Work* 8:230–232.

Sharp, J. W., D. Blum, and L. Aviv. 1993. Elderly men with cancer: Social work intervention in prostate cancer. *Social Work in Health Care* 19:91–107.

Shulman, L. 1992. *The Skills of Helping Individuals, Families, and Groups.* Itasca, IL: F. E. Peacock.

Silverman, P. R. 2000. *Never Too Young to Know.* New York. Oxford University Press.

Spiegel, D., and J. Spira. 1991. *Supportive-Expressive Group Therapy: A Treatment Manual of Psychosocial Intervention for Women with Recurrent Breast Cancer.* Stanford, CA: Stanford University Press.

Taylor, S. E., R. L. Falke, S. J. Shoptaw, and R. R. Lichtman. 1986. Social support, support groups, and the cancer patient. *Journal of Consulting and Clinical Psychology* 54:608–615.

Vugia, H. D. 1991. Support groups in oncology: Building hope through the human bond. *Journal of Psychosocial Oncology* 9:89–107.

Walsh, J., H. E. Hewitt, and A. Londeree. 1996. The role of the facilitator in support group development. *Social Work with Groups* 19:83–91.

Wasserman, H., and H. E. Danforth. 1988. *The Human Bond: Support Groups and Mutual Aid.* New York: Springer.

Weeks, D. O., and C. Johnson. 2000. *When All the Friends Have Gone: A Guide for Aftercare Providers.* Amityville, NY: Baywood.

Wirpsa, L. 1998. Death care giants team up with church: Relationship raises issues about church role in bereavement. *National Catholic Reporter*, 30 January.

Wolf, N. 1992. *The Beauty Myth.* New York: Anchor.

Yalom, I. D. 1995. *The Theory and Practice of Group Psychotherapy.* 4th ed. New York: Basic Books.

Zastrow, C. 2001. *Social Work with Groups.* 5th ed. Pacific Grove, CA: Brooks/Cole Wadsworth.

27

TECHNOLOGY-BASED GROUPS AND
END-OF-LIFE SOCIAL WORK PRACTICE

YVETTE COLÓN

Give sorrow words; the grief that does not speak
Whispers the o'erfraught heart and bids it break
—William Shakespeare, Macbeth IV:3

IN AN increasingly technological world, clinical work with the dying and their families no longer requires face-to-face contact. Many agencies and practitioners now use telephonic individual and group sessions, Internet groups, and online chat rooms that replace traditional in-home or in-office contacts. This chapter will consider and discuss the varieties of clinical support through technology that are available to patients and families dealing with end-of-life concerns. It will also explore the strengths of telephone and Internet support groups, including the capacity to participate more actively, the ways that self-disclosure happens earlier than in traditional groups, the loss of a group or individual client, and the challenges of "distance encounters."

The loss of a loved one is a profoundly traumatic event, affecting survivors in physical, emotional, and spiritual ways. Bereaved individuals often seek help and support through individual grief counseling, bereavement groups, and peer support groups. However, the expansion of the Internet has resulted in its increased use by the average person; more and more bereaved individuals are taking responsibility for their own emotional needs by using their computers to access online support groups and discussion forums.

It is no longer unusual for individuals to have personal computers and access to the Internet. Since the early 1990s, when the World Wide Web became available for public use, grieving persons have easily found diverse online bereavement communities, where there are now many support and discussion forums. For many years, clinical social workers and other mental health professionals have been involved in online discussion and support groups focusing on bereavement and end-of-life concerns. Patients, caregivers, and professionals have been able to connect with each other and carry on a conversation with anyone around the world without leaving their own communities. Those who live in rural areas, who feel inhibited by the prospect of participating in face-to-face individual or group therapy or those who are too physically limited by disability or caregiving responsibilities are still able to receive support. People with Internet access, but with no access to mental health services, now have a way to choose from a vast array of technology-based support. The demand for online services is high and online group participation continues to increase, especially for those who use the Internet to help them struggle with a major illness or major life event (Fox and Rainie 2002).

Most of the literature available on telephone and online support falls into the category of anecdotal, narrative experiences or sociological studies of computer-mediated communication. Several studies have used qualitative methods. Few studies have looked at clinical interventions or any results of participating in telephone or online bereavement therapy or support, as participant or practitioner. A systematic evaluation of group outcomes in technology-based support groups has yet to be done.

In a qualitative and quantitative analysis of a case management mode of intervention, in which an oncology social worker monitored sixty-nine newly diagnosed breast cancer patients by telephone for one year, Polinsky, Fred, and Ganz (1991) found that a telephone-based model proved to be highly effective and cost-efficient. McCormish et al. (1999) examined the effectiveness of a grief and loss therapy group for women enrolled in a residential substance abuse treatment program and found that the participants' mood, depression, and parenting skills improved over time. In studying the motivation for change among bereaved parents in a support group, Nahmani et al. (1989) emphasized the group's value in increasing communication between the bereaved couple. In a review of the literature about bereavement group interventions, however, Sharpnack (2001) identified many factors in past bereavement research that made it difficult to draw conclusions about specific groups.

Finn (1995) described a pilot project for an online support group and the advantages, disadvantages, and benefit to group leaders and participants. He noted that there has been little systematic evaluation of computer-based self-help groups and no research about their use as an adjunct to face-to-face support groups. Galinsky, Shopler, and Abell acknowledged that in 1997, technology was already beginning to play a small but important role in group practice and considered the benefits and problems of technology-based groups.

Stamm (1998) noted that mental health was ranked as the most common online telehealth consultation by the end of 1997. Mental health professionals have begun to explore the use of technology as a therapeutic and educational tool (e.g., Giffords 1998; Miller-Cribbs and Chadiha 1998; Cafolla 1999), but few studies have been rigorously evaluated. Meier (2000) stated that little is known about the ways that online communication affect clinical interventions.

In a study about computer-mediated support groups, Weinberg et al. (1995) noted that computer-mediated groups could serve those who are unwilling or unable to participate in a face-to-face group and discussed the advantages as well as limitations of this modality. Writing itself can be seen as therapeutic (Murphy and Mitchell 1998), as the online modality offers an instant outlet for emotions, creativity, and energy. In addition to factual information, group members can share memories, stories, photographs, poems, and coping skills to support each other and provide comfort. Group members can also reread archived postings to continue to get support and information at the times when they need it most.

TELEPHONE SUPPORT GROUPS

RECRUITMENT, SCREENING, AND ASSESSMENT

Cancer Care is a national nonprofit organization whose mission is to provide free professional help to people with all cancers through counseling, education, information and referral, and direct financial assistance. In 1994, while working at Cancer Care, I began facilitating an ongoing, long-term telephone support group for homebound cancer patients. Several years before, the agency served several clients who were interested in participating in a cancer support group, but who found it impossible to come into the office for group meetings. Because of their physical limitations, these clients had no other alternatives for social and emotional support. In a creative attempt to respond to the needs of homebound people with cancer, the agency created its first, and only ongoing, telephone support group.

Referrals to the telephone group came first from agency social workers, then from community social workers, who evaluated clients' interest in and need for a support group. Referrals included information about physical capabilities and limitations as well as existing support networks. Initial screening for the group began during the initial intake process and potential participants were put on a waiting list. They were contacted, screened further, and added to the group as space permitted. Attrition occurred when a participant died, terminated with the group, or improved in health enough to be able to use other resources. When contacted and assessed for the group, some clients removed themselves from consideration because they were too ill to participate, were not ready to explore their emotional concerns, or were uncomfortable using the telephone for group sessions. However, the majority of clients on the waiting list eventually joined the group. The group met weekly, then biweekly, for one hour for the seven years of its existence. The agency went on to expand this innovative service by offering many short-term telephone support groups for patients who were disabled or homebound, lived in rural communities, or were frail and unable to attend a face-to-face group.

A group facilitator can consider the number of clients in his or her caseload who could benefit from emotional support and socialization and can evaluate a client's interest in and appropriateness for a telephone support group. Clients who are isolated or unable to travel and who are able to speak about their emotional concerns can be considered for membership. Those who cannot verbalize their concerns, are not able or willing to discuss emotional issues, or who want only to socialize are excluded. The facilitator must assess motivation to participate in a telephone support group, and obtain background information about functional status, existing social support, telephone number, and emergency contact. Additionally, it is important to explain the focus of the group and how it works to all members. Facilitators can reassure and motivate clients by providing simple and direct answers to their questions.

As stated above, some potential group members may screen themselves out before the start of the group because they are not ready to explore their emotional concerns, are not ready for a support or bereavement group, or are uncomfortable using the telephone for group sessions.

FORMAT OF GROUP

Before any group applicants are contacted and the group begins, the facilitator must decide how often the group will meet and how long the sessions will be. If the group meets weekly, it can last for one hour. If it meets every other week or monthly, the facilitator can decide whether one and a half hours for each session will be sufficient. The focus of the group can be educational or supportive in nature; the facilitator must inform the group members of the structure and focus of the sessions, whether it will be open ended or whether each session will have a specific agenda.

PRACTICAL MATTERS

The size of the group is important. Having too many group members results in sessions that may be difficult to manage and the members will not be able to address and explore their concerns with enough time. Too few group members may leave everyone feeling unsatisfied or unsupported. Members can sometimes miss sessions because of medical concerns or caregiving responsibilities. Having ten to twelve members in any group ensures an adequate number of participants for each session and still allows time for focused discussion.

The cost of the group will vary depending on the size and telephone service used. The facilitator can conduct small groups, at minimal cost, by originating the calls to participants using the conference call feature found on many business telephones. Because the facilitator is placing the call, participants do not incur the cost of the phone call.

Telephone companies offer different services that make and maintain calls to participants with various charges per person depending on the level of service requested. If the group is conducted as a conference call using an outside service, the role of the operator is important. The operator will be the first person that each group member will have contact with at the beginning of each session. In this case, the facilitator must have a conversation with the operator to explain what the group is about, to stress confidentiality and noninvolvement in the operator's role, and to answer the operator's questions. Group members should be aware that the operator will not participate in the group, but needs to monitor the session occasionally to make sure there are no technical problems.

Depending upon the level of service that is used, an operator can use a "mute" mode with distraught or disruptive group members who can then hear the group discussion but cannot be heard by the others. The operator also can be notified automatically if someone is disconnected and the facilitator can contact the operator at any time during the session simply by pressing "o" on the touch-tone telephone. Facilitators may want to have a second phone line available in case of emergencies, so that they or the operator can retrieve any group member who has been accidentally disconnected.

The facilitator should provide written instructions and group guidelines prior to the first group or when a new member joins the group. With the group's permission, the facilitator can also provide a list of group members' addresses and phone numbers and encourage members to socialize by telephone between sessions, if this is part of the group contract. The facilitator can help participants differentiate between formal, structured, scheduled calls and informal, unscheduled, intermittent calls. Telephone group participants often develop personal relationships with each other and may wish to have contact outside of the group. In this case, the facilitator can request that group business be discussed only in the group sessions and remind the participants to maintain the confidentiality of the others in outside conversations.

If socialization and networking between sessions are encouraged, the facilitator and group members can send updated address lists, newsletters, articles, and other written information of interest to each other.

STARTING THE SESSION

Before the start of the group, each member is called and placed in the conference call feature of the facilitator's telephone or by the operator if an outside service is used. When all participating members are reached, the facilitator is connected to the call and the session begins. A first group session can be more formal, with introductions and a review of the group's purpose and guidelines. Subsequent groups can be informal, with the group members driving the session's agenda. The facilitator can choose to check in with each of the members to give them the opportunity to speak or to leave the group discussion open to issues that concern them during the session. Over time, the members will develop group norms and structure. The facilitator can guide them in developing a process and structure that is mutually beneficial. If the group is designed to be supportive in nature, the facilitator can help keep the members focused on their emotional concerns.

CONCERNS FOR FACILITATORS

Telephone therapy and support groups provide many benefits (Galinsky, Shopler, and Abell 1997; Rounds, Galinsky, and Stevens 1991; Shepherd 1987; Padach 1984). Group members can transcend physical or geographical limitations, receive support they would not have access to otherwise, have the opportunity to connect with others in similar circumstances, and discuss their concerns with a broader range of people than they would normally meet.

The use of the telephone can create a more comfortable atmosphere for clients who are in familiar surroundings during sessions, unlike the structured environment of a meeting room or therapist's office. Participation in sessions can remain consistent for members. Unlike participation in face-to-face groups, for example, a group member who cannot join a face-to-face group due to the constant demands of caregiving can count on the continuity of the group sessions. As long as a group member has access to a telephone, no matter where that telephone may be, they can continue to participate fully.

Telephone groups may provide group members relative anonymity that helps them feel more comfortable. It may allow participants to achieve closeness with others, facilitate self-disclosure, and help them cope with a difficult life event. Some participants in face-to-face groups may feel too inhibited to talk if they are faced with a number of virtual strangers at the beginning of the group. Without this social inhibition, group members feel more comfortable sharing their problems and worries. As a result, increased self-disclosure and bonding often occurs early in the group process, leading to deeper and more direct discussions. This level of intimacy will be different in long-term and short-term groups. When members know they will be able to participate in the telephone group together for a longer period, they will feel more comfortable exploring their emotional concerns to a greater degree rather than remaining focused on practical and concrete issues.

CLINICAL ISSUES

In telephone support groups, the facilitator and group members do not have visual cues that are present in a face-to-face group. This lack of face-to-face contact and visual cues can be problematic. The facilitator must then "listen" in a different way. Instead of picking up on visual cues, the facilitator must pay close attention to language, tone, inflection, pacing, and all the ways in which group members speak and relate to one another when they are well and coping adequately versus when they are ill or under stress. For example, when asked how they are feeling, group members who have trouble expressing their grief may say, "Fine." A facilitator may hear the pain or distress in their voices and draw them out a little more so that they can be supported and helped. The facilitator will need to be more active and sometimes more directive in the group to make up for the lack of eye contact and body language.

In a telephone support group, participants primarily discuss the emotional impact their own or their loved one's illness or death has had on them. If they are patients, they may discuss the problems of isolation and intimacy, changes in their relationships with family and friends, and changes in their self-image. Mortality, healthcare decision-making, and survival issues will be spoken of regularly. Families will relate coping strategies, problem solving, and the often overwhelming demands of caregiving. The bereaved will share profound pain and grief and the experiences of putting their lives back together after the loss of an important and integral person in their lives. Many of them will explore issues of helplessness, loss of control, and relearning coping skills. They will share strategies for improving communication with the healthcare team, advocating for themselves and the patient and finding the resources they need. They will share their courage and encourage others to persevere. A telephone group facilitator will promote group cohesion, provide structure and information, and encourage helping and supportive relationships among the members.

GROUP MANAGEMENT ISSUES

In telephone groups for patients, the death of a group member is a difficult experience for the members as well as for the facilitator. Due to physical limitations or geographical distance, members are often unable to attend a funeral or memorial service and as a result cannot participate in any of the social rituals that help them come to terms with the death. Sometimes the facilitator is the person who informs the group of the death of a member. The group members may find it immensely difficult to discuss the death and explore their feelings; the facilitator can support the members in over the course of several sessions and encourage them to share their feelings and relationship with the member who has died.

In many cases, the facilitator and members of a telephone group may not meet before the start of the group. Because of this, members may idealize the facilitator or project unrealistic demands upon her. Anger and frustration can be displaced onto the facilitator, who is seen as a representative of the medical system. The facilitator may never meet clients in a telephone group and know what they look like in person. In the absence of a mental representation of group members, the facilitator can sometimes overlook their concerns and see them instead as healthier or higher functioning than they really are. Several times during the course of a long-term telephone group for homebound cancer patients, the facilitator and group members discussed the idea of sharing photographs of each other. The group members always declined; after so many years of illness, they did not believe that photographs accurately represented who they were and they felt self-conscious about their physical state.

Active, verbal group members may want to take the role of cofacilitator or begin to dominate the discussions. In this case, the facilitator must redirect the conversation to the topic being discussed rather than singling out one or two members. It may become necessary to have a separate discussion with the dominant, often influential group member to discuss how that member can continue to help and support the group without taking over and excluding the less verbal participants.

In face-to-face groups, sessions are held in closed meeting rooms that offer privacy and safety. In a telephone support group, however, family members and others may be present or nearby during the session. They may be interested in a particular problem or moved to share information and pick up the telephone extension to talk with the group or the facilitator. As with any other interruption or crisis (for example, a hostile or disruptive group member), the facilitator must stop the group discussion immediately, state the purpose of the group, review the importance of confidentiality, and politely, but firmly, request that the nonmember leave the group immediately. Group members need to feel safe and believe that the facilitator will protect the integrity of the group.

ONLINE SUPPORT GROUPS

RECRUITMENT, SCREENING, AND ASSESSMENT

Anyone contemplating starting an online bereavement group or discussion forum must be familiar enough with email technology to feel comfortable communicating in this way. Previous participation in an open online end-of-life, mental health, or professional forum can help a facilitator understand and feel more comfortable with the process. All email exchanges between facilitator and group applicants should remain confidential. Participants should be required to respect the rules of confidentiality, commit to involvement for the duration of the group, and send a minimum number of messages each week. Anonymous groups, in which the identity and other information about the participant are not shared with the facilitator, should be discouraged. During the application and screening process, applicants should provide the following information to the facilitator: real name, address, and phone number; diagnosis and treatment information if the applicant is a patient, or the patient's information if the applicant is a caregiver or the date and nature of the patient's death if the applicant is bereaved; previous group and/or individual psychotherapy experiences; and topics and issues they wish to explore in the group. Screenings can take place by email or by telephone. Participants in an online group must be able to write and express themselves adequately in order to participate. This can be assessed via email responses to screening questions. Once participants are screened and accepted into a bulletin board or mailing list (see "Format of Groups" below), they have access to the group twenty-four hours a day, seven days a week for the duration of the group. At the start, the facilitator can create several discussion topics or provide general agenda items; the group members should be encouraged to create topics of their own as the group progresses. Members should be encouraged to send as many messages as they like, as long as the messages are on topic. The facilitator should try to monitor the group as much as possible; it is very important for the facilitator to log in at least once each workday in order to read postings or emails, respond to questions and concerns, and guide the group.

FORMAT OF GROUPS

Online groups can be conducted in three different ways: as a chat group, a bulletin board, or a listserv (mailing list). A chat group (or chat room) is a real-time exchange in which everyone is at his or her computer at the same time using a special program so that the entire group can communicate with each other. A bulletin or message board is a program or location on the Internet or other host in which participants can read and write messages at any time. Those messages are organized by topic and are posted chronologically. A listserv is a private email group in which each subscriber receives a separate copy, via email, of each message that is posted and can maintain ongoing communication with other list members who share a common concern.

PRACTICAL MATTERS

There are practical matters to consider in forming an online bereavement group. Facilitators must be knowledgeable about and comfortable with the technology they are using. They must also be knowledgeable about how people interact in text-based environments and be aware of issues involved in computer-mediated communication. They must be able to build a community, foster a sense of trust, and guide effective and therapeutic interactions among group members. The definition, role, and scope of responsibilities of the facilitator must be well thought out. A statement of format, guidelines, duration of group, and what is expected from participants can be sent out as an announcement. All email exchanges and postings to the group should remain as secure and as confidential as possible. The facilitator should have a stated policy for crises and emergencies experienced by the participants.

STARTING THE SESSION

The facilitator must decide, before any potential participants are contacted and before the start of the group, whether the group will meet as a chat group, a bulletin board group, or a mailing list group. A chat group more closely imitates a face-to-face support group in that there is a designated day and time when all group members are expected to participate and they are in the same virtual room together. A bulletin board or discussion group has the advantage of being able to organize discussions by topic as well as archiving all messages, but may be too time-consuming for all to read. Email or listserv groups are easy to participate in, because essentially the group occurs via the members' email. Group members do not have to log into a website or online bulletin board where the group takes place.

The duration of the group should be decided upon, and guidelines should be shared with participants. The facilitator may want to provide written instructions and group guidelines, by email, regular mail, or on a website, before the start of a time-limited group or when a new member joins an ongoing group. With the group's permission, the facilitator may also provide a list of group members with addresses and phone numbers and encourage members to socialize by telephone between sessions, if this is part of the group norm as envisioned by the facilitator. Any message to a bulletin board or mailing list group automatically will have the member's email address as well as the date and time of day the message was submitted.

CONCERNS FOR FACILITATORS

Facilitators must be aware that the physical and verbal cues on which they rely will be missing or different in an online group. The facilitator must pay close attention to language, engagement, and the ways in which group members write and express themselves. The facilitator must be more active and sometimes more directive in the group to make up for the lack of eye contact and body language.

Online support groups have the potential to provide many benefits to the participants. First, participants sometime develop personal relationships with each other and have individual contact outside of the group, sharing information and extending the network of support. Second, the level of intimacy and trust can be greater than telephone support because participants may feel more comfortable disclosing and discussing their concerns in writing. Finally, because there are no time restrictions, as there are in face-to-face groups, members of bulletin board groups can participate as much as they wish at times that are most helpful to them. This often occurs in the middle of the night for patients who are in pain or cannot sleep.

CLINICAL ISSUES

Schramm (1998) notes that there are basic elements in a psychotherapy group contract: regular and punctual attendance, confidentiality, participation, prohibition of physical aggression, responsibility for payment, extragroup boundaries, and completion of therapy. These are all elements that can serve as the basis for participation in online psychotherapy and support.

The text-based nature of the group environment presents a challenge. The written word can be stark and direct; humor and sarcasm can be misinterpreted easily and feelings can be hurt. Participants must be able to write effectively in order to get the maximum benefit from an online discussion. Group leaders must be skilled enough to facilitate the discussion, mediate conflict, and support all members through writing alone. Clinical supervision and knowledge of resources for conducting online support groups is critical.

In online support groups, the facilitator and group members do not have the visual or verbal cues that are present in a face-to-face group. Again, the facilitator must "listen" in a different way by paying close attention to language, the ways in which group members write, the ways in which they express themselves when they are feeling well and when they are upset or sick. The facilitator must be more active and sometimes more directive in the group to make up for the lack of eye contact and body language. If a facilitator does not send messages to the group on a regular basis, he or she is considered to be "absent" from the group.

Online groups also provide the facilitator with time to reflect on a response or an intervention prior to sending a message to the group. The asynchronous nature of online communication allows participants to consider and reflect on the work being done in the group in a way that does not occur in face-to-face groups, in which responses must be immediate in order to keep the process going.

GROUP MANAGEMENT ISSUES

Online groups can be time-consuming for the facilitator and for members because of the number of messages that must be read. The management of an online group requires not only clinical skills, but also some technical skills.

Additionally, the facilitator must be aware of the vast array of information, education, and support available on the Internet and has a responsibility to provide credible, reliable, and sound resources to group members. The facilitator also has the responsibility to raise questions about information that may not be sound. The Internet continues to grow exponentially and can be intimidating to navigate. The following questions are important to consider when looking for and evaluating information on the Internet:

- What is the purpose of the website?
- Are the mission and goals of the website clearly stated?
- How comprehensive is the website?

- What information does it contain?
- Where does the information come from?
- Is the information accurate and objective?
- Does the site provide timely and medically sound information or education?
- Are the website's content and links relevant and appropriate?
- When was the site created and updated?
- Are the website's contact information, privacy statement, disclaimers, linking policy, advertising policy, sponsors, and affiliations easily found and clearly stated?

A WORD ABOUT REIMBURSEMENT, LIABILITY, AND STATE REGULATIONS

Any agency or hospice can provide technology-based psychosocial end-of-life and bereavement groups in a cost- and time-effective way. A recent telehealth federal law (effective October 1, 2001) expands telehealth services covered by Medicare (Medicare 2002). Medicare reimburses clinical social workers for individual outpatient psychotherapy telehealth services. Private insurers vary in their coverage of technology-based services, but some insurers may reimburse clinical social workers for their telephone and online psychotherapy services. Facilitators should contact the appropriate organizations for information about Medicare, Medicaid, or private insurance reimbursement of telecommunication services.

The National Association of Social Workers recently added language about the use of telephones and computer technology to the latest version of its Code of Ethics, approved in 1996 and revised in 1999. For the most part, the Code of Ethics and the guiding principles of clinical social work are already spelled out in detail. The same things social workers do with clients in a face-to-face situation—providing competent services, maintaining confidentiality, explaining services, informing clients of the limitations and risks associated with such groups, securing informed consent—are equally important in a telephone or online setting.

Clinical social workers who provide technology-based services should consider licensure issues, particularly in the context of liability and the provision of services across state lines. It is important to review liability coverage for technology-based services with insurance carriers as well as licensing regulations with state boards of social work. It is just as important for facilitators to be aware of developing standards of practice, emerging licensing regulations, and the latest research.

It is critical to develop a plan for technology based-services. A simple proposal is vital, and should include a rationale for the service, benefits to the agency and to the client population, proposed budget, and a structured feedback and evaluation component. If an agency is not able to absorb all of the costs involved in creating and providing telephone or online services, outside funding sources can be approached. It is important to note that many important technology-based services hosted at major agencies (i.e., the American Pain Foundation's PainAid and Cancer Care's Online Group Program) were funded by outside sources.

SUGGESTIONS FOR FUTURE RESEARCH

Anecdotal reports suggest that patients who participate in telephone and support groups show a reduction in psychological distress and have better emotional functioning, improved attitudes, and a greater ability to cope (Galinsky, Shopler, and Abell 1997). Measurement tools similar to those used in traditional groups must be developed and used to quantify changes and improvements in mood and functioning during the course of technology-based group work. Most existing studies are based on small numbers of participants. Replicating these programs to include more participants of varied ages and ethnic backgrounds is important.

CONCLUSION

Technology-based groups can provide many benefits (Murphy and Mitchell 1998; Cafolla 1999; Weinberg et al. 1995; Padach 1984). The level of intimacy and trust can be greater because participants may feel more comfortable disclosing and discussing their concerns. Because there are no time restrictions, as there are in face-to-face groups, participants can send messages that are rich and meaningful. Social workers and mental health professionals (notably Colón 1999; Shopler, Abell, and Galinsky 1998; and Shopler, Galinsky, and Abell 1997) have written extensively about these benefits. More than ever before, online end-of-life communities are able to provide services to people who ask for support and information. As technology advances, technology-based services will become more accessible and affordable, giving clinical social workers the option of using them in their day-to-day practice.

REFERENCES

Cafolla, R. 1999. An introduction to the Internet for independent group practitioners. *Journal of Psychotherapy in Independent Practice* 1(1): 75–84.

Centers for Medicare and Medicaid Services. 2002. Revision of Medicare reimbursement for telehealth services. Program memorandum, October 1. http:/cms.hhs.gov/manuals/pm_trans/AB02052.pdf.

Colón, Y. 1999. Digital digging: Group therapy online. In *How to Use Computers and Cyberspace in the Clinical Practice of Psychotherapy*, ed. J. Fink, 67–81. Northvale, NJ: Jason Aronson.

Finn, J. 1995. Computer-based self-help groups: A new resource to supplement support groups. *Social Work with Groups* 18(1): 109–117.

Fox, S., and L. Rainie. 2002. Vital decisions: How Internet users decide what information to trust when they or their loved ones are sick. Pew Internet & American Life Project. www.pewtrusts.com/pdf/vf_pew_internet_health_searches.pdf.

Galinsky, M. J., J. H. Shopler, and M. D. Abell. 1997. Connecting group members through telephone and computer groups. *Health and Social Work* 22(3): 181–188.

Giffords, E. D. 1998. Social work on the Internet: An introduction. *Social Work* 43(3): 243–251.

McCormish, J. F., R. Greenberg, J. Kent-Bryant, et al. 1999. Evaluation of a grief group for women in residential substance abuse treatment. *Substance Abuse* 20(1): 45–58.

Meier, A. 2000. Offering social support via the Internet: A case study of an online support group for social workers. *Journal of Technology in Human Services* 17(2–3): 237–266.

Miller-Cribbs, J. E., and L. A. Chadiha. 1998. Integrating the Internet in a human diversity course. *Computers in Human Services* 15(2–3): 97–109.

Murphy, L. J., and D. L. Mitchell. 1998. When writing helps to heal: E-mail as therapy. *British Journal of Guidance & Counseling* 26(1): 21–36.

Nahmani, N., E. Neeman, and C. Nir. 1989. Parental bereavement: The motivation to participate in support groups and its consequences. *Social Work with Groups* 12(2): 89–98.

National Association of Social Workers. 1996. *Code of Ethics.* Washington, DC: NASW.

Padach, K. M. 1984. Long term telephone psychotherapy. In *Psychotherapy with Psychotherapists,* ed. F. W. Kaslow, 33–57. Northvale, NJ: Jason Aronson.

Polinsky, M. L., C. Fred, and P. A. Ganz. 1991. Quantitative and qualitative assessment of a case management program for cancer patients. *Health and Social Work* 16:176–183.

Rounds, K. A., M. J. Galinsky, and L. S. Stevens. 1991. Linking people with AIDS in rural communities: The telephone group. *Social Work* 36:13–18.

Schramm, M. G. 1998. No fine print: Part one—The basics of a group contract. *Self-Help & Psychology Magazine,* online edition. www.shpm.com/ppc/group/grnfine1.html.

Sharpnack, J. D. 2001. The efficacy of group bereavement interventions: An integrative review of the research literature. *Dissertation International, Section B: The Sciences and Engineering* 61(12-B): 6721.

Shepard, P. 1987. Telephone therapy: An alternative to isolation. *Clinical Social Work Journal* 15: 56–65.

Shopler, J. H., M. Abell, and M. J. Galinsky. 1998. Technology-based groups: A review and conceptual framework for practice. *Social Work* 43(3): 254–267.

Shopler, J. H., M. J. Galinsky, and M. Abell. 1997. Creating community through telephone and computer groups: Theoretical and practical perspectives. *Social Work with Groups* 20(4): 19–34.

Stamm, B. H. 1998. Clinical application of telehealth in mental health care. *Professional Psychology: Research and Practice* 29(6): 536–542.

Weinberg, N., J. D. Schmale, J. Uken, and K. Wessel. 1995. Computer-mediated support groups. *Social Work with Groups* 17(4): 43–54.

INTERNET RESOURCES

Consumer End-of-Life Resources

AARP End of Life Issues: www.aarp.org/endoflife
ACP-ASIM End-of-Life Care Patient Education Project: www.acponline.org/ethics/patient_education.htm
Aging with Dignity: www.agingwithdignity.org
American Pain Foundation: www.painfoundation.org
Bereaved Families Online: www.bereavedfamilies.net
Cancer Care, Inc., Special Section on End of Life and Bereavement: www.cancercare.org/BereavementandGrief/BereavementandGriefmain.cfm
Compassionate Friends: www.compassionatefriends.org
End of Life—Exploring Death in America: www.npr.org/programs/death
Finding Our Way—Living with Dying in America: www.findingourway.net
Grief and Loss in the Workplace: www.umich.edu/~fasap/health/grief
Grief Net: http://griefnet.org
Grief Recovery Online (English and Spanish): www.groww.org
Growth House—Improving Care for the Dying: www.growthhouse.org/death.html

HospiceNet: www.hospicenet.org/html/bereavement.html
KidsAid: http://kidsaid.com
PainAid—American Pain Foundation's Online Group Program: http://
    painaid.painfoundation.org
Partnership for Caring: www.partnershipforcaring.org/HomePage/index.html
WidowNet: www.fortnet.org/WidowNet

Professional End-of-Life Resources

American Medical Association EPEC Project: www.ama-assn.org/ama/pub/category/2910.html
Association for Death Education and Counseling: www.adec.org
Center to Advance Palliative Care: www.capcmssm.org
Center to Advance Palliative Care Manual: http://66.70.88.71/howtomanual
Community-State Partnerships to Improve End-of-Life Care: www.midbio.org/npo-about.htm
Hospice Foundation of America, Living with Grief: www.hospicefoundation.org/laterlife/
    grollman.htm
Innovations in End-of-Life Care: www2.edc.org/lastacts/archives.asp
Last Acts—A National Coalition to Improve Care and Caring at the End of Life:
    www.lastacts.org
Last Acts Statement on Diversity and End-of-Life Care: www.lastacts.org/files/publications/
    Diversity1.15.02.pdf
On Our Own Terms—Moyers on Dying: www.pbs.org/wnet/onourownterms/index.html
Oregon Health Sciences Center for Ethics and Healthcare: www.ohsu.edu/ethics
Project on Death in America: www.soros.org/death
Promoting Excellence in End-of-Life Care: www.promotingexcellence.org

Standards of Practice: Ethical Guidelines and Online Resources

American Counseling Association, Ethical Standards for Internet Online Counseling: http://
    aca.convio.net/site/PageServer?pagename=resources_internet
International Society for Mental Health Online, Suggested Principles for the Online
    Provision of Mental Health Services: www.ismho.org/suggestions.html
National Association of Social Workers, Code of Ethics: www.socialworkers.org/pubs/code/
    code.asp
National Board for Certified Counselors, The Practice of Internet Counseling:
    www.nbcc.org/ethics/webethics.htm

28

WORKING WITH FAMILIES FACING LIFE-THREATENING ILLNESS IN THE MEDICAL SETTING

SUSAN BLACKER AND ALICE RAINESS JORDAN

THE IMPACT of any life-threatening illness is experienced in profound ways, not only by the person diagnosed with the disease but also by family and loved ones. In the face of serious medical illness, families may experience intense emotional responses, possible financial strain, and new caregiving responsibilities. In addition, they must learn complex health information and establish relationships with health-care professionals. Adjustment requires psychological and social adaptation and learning to navigate the complexities of the healthcare system. A critical role of today's healthcare team is to assist the patient and her family in this process. As an integral member of the medical team, the social worker's role is to guide the family and patient through the system, encourage them to problem-solve actively, and assist them in accessing resources and supports. The social worker helps the patient and family to maintain hope, supports them in coping with the current crisis, and anticipates challenges that lie ahead (Zabora 1998; Taylor-Brown et al. 2001).

This chapter will explore the medical social worker's role in caring for the patient and family confronted by life-threatening illness. The key areas of family assessment in the context of palliative and end-of-life care will be explored, as will the interventions that social workers commonly use in working with family systems in this time of crisis, transition, and healing.

CONDUCTING A COMPREHENSIVE FAMILY ASSESSMENT

Working with families in today's fast-paced and complex healthcare setting is unique in significant ways from social work practice with families in other settings. Patients enter the medical system anticipating that they will encounter doctors and nurses, but they may be unclear or confused about the role of the medical social worker. The social worker must be able to introduce successfully her role on the interdisciplinary team, connecting this to the patient's medical care and goals, in order to intervene effectively.

Medical social workers typically become involved based on referrals or requests from another healthcare professional (most commonly nursing) or by a self-referral from the patient. In some settings, referrals may be generated during a psychosocial screening program with a high-risk or distress screening tool (Zabora 1996). Referrals to social work may be vague in nature. A member of the healthcare team may have noted that the patient exhibits signs that he is not coping effectively, has a history of mental health problems or nonadherence to medical treatment, or that there is a lack of support for the patient within the social situation.

The time available to assess the situation and to intervene with the patient and family is often limited. In the inpatient setting, there may be a host of limiting variables. At times this is may be a direct result of the patient's physical or cognitive condition and her inability to communicate or tolerate conversations of more that a few minutes. Individuals who have been admitted to the hospital are frequently transported from their hospital room to other parts of the facility for tests and procedures. Family members are often struggling to manage other demands in their lives and may not be present at the time the social worker and other members of the team are available to meet with them. The length of time that the patient is admitted to the hospital may be only a matter of days. Given the realities inherent in the healthcare setting, a focused identification of areas that need to be addressed is imperative for effective social work intervention. In the acute care environment, many interventions are short-term, often less than five contacts. Frequently when ongoing contact is warranted, telephone contact is the only means for follow-up.

Medical social-work practice is typified by its crisis-oriented nature. Often the worker has no previous history with the patient prior to the hospitalization or clinic visit before meeting the patient in response to an urgent request for services. Social workers often only receive a referral and become intensively involved with a family as the patient approaches his or her final months and weeks of life. Conducting a comprehensive assessment is essential in the process of identifying the patient and family's psychosocial needs and internal and external resources and in selecting appropriate interventions. The social worker must have a framework for quickly assessing who this family is, how they define their needs, and what can effectively be prioritized and addressed.

Taylor-Brown and colleagues have summarized the importance and focus of this assessment: "The developmental stage of a family's past losses and emotional cutoffs helps to focus interventions and potential outcomes. For example, the tasks and immediate needs of a family with young or adolescent children will differ from those of an aged retired couple. A family's communication style, crises management skills, role flexibility, decision-making process, and supports all influence how they adapt to and integrate life-threatening illness. Role disruption caused by illness may include changes in such areas as dependency relationships and decision making, which affect individuals and the family structure as a whole. Cultural and generational aspects further individualize the family and patient experience" (2001:15). Assessment involves examining the person in the context of their environment—not just in the medical setting but also at home, relating to those around them (Blum et al. 2001).

Information that contributes to the psychosocial assessment comes from many sources. In assessing the patient and family, the social worker should examine several interrelated areas (Weisman 1979; Germaine 1984; Wells and Turney 2001):

- Past and current medical situation
- Family structure, roles, and relationships
- Developmental stage of client and family
- Cultural values and beliefs
- Spirituality and faith
- Experiences with illness, disability, or death
- Coping history, strengths, and emotional responses
- Socioeconomic factors and resources

PAST AND CURRENT MEDICAL SITUATION

The social worker should begin assessing the family's psychosocial needs by first understanding the context of their history with the illness. A family confronted by a member's life-threatening illness is likely to have dealt with crises and losses at multiple points along the illness trajectory. It is important to understand this history to be able to help them in the present. Zabora (1997) observes that "to target interventions appropriately, one must understand the impact that the course of disease has on a patient's physical level of functioning." To begin to develop an understanding of the past, current, and future challenges that the illness and its treatment may impose on the family, it is important for the social worker to have a basic understanding of the significant medical problems of the patient. It is also important to assess how the individual's medical condition has affected the family. Understanding the present medical situation includes obtaining an understanding of the stage, or extent, of the illness or disability and the current medical goals of treatment. It is also important to consider current physical or psychological symptoms such as pain, fatigue, depression, and delirium and the effect that these are having on the patient and family's quality of life and the resulting caregiving needs.

Critical to the assessment is the determination of the patient and family's understanding of this information and its congruence with the information that has been delivered by the care team. Often it is when the medical team perceives that the patient or family is misinterpreting information that social work is consulted for assistance. The social worker must assess not only what has been understood, but also the barriers to communication and comprehension (including language and level of education) and the impact of her own feelings, coping mechanisms, and style on information processing.

Key questions for the clinician to consider are:

- What is significant to this patient's medical history?
- What is the current stage/extent of illness of the illness and what should be expected?
- What are the current goals of treatment?
- What are the patient's current physical or psychological symptoms (e.g. pain, fatigue, depression, delirium)?

- What is the patient/family's understanding and interpretation of this information?
- What are barriers to communication and understanding?

FAMILY STRUCTURE, ROLES, AND RELATIONSHIPS

In order to begin to work effectively with the family system, the clinician must identify what constitutes the family's constellation. In the patient's definition, this may include both family of origin and family of choice. During the process of admission to hospitals, the "next of kin" is often established, but the social worker should consider all family constellations, including same-sex couples, multigenerational households, fictive kin, and single or childless individuals. As the social worker identifies the key family members who are involved in the patient's life, he or she should also look for clues about the nature and quality of these relationships. Understanding the roles and responsibilities that each member has played in "health" and how these will be affected under the strain of "sickness" is important in order to be able to help the family in the process of adjustment.

CASE EXAMPLE

Mary G. was a thirty-eight-year-old businesswoman who was diagnosed with advanced colon cancer. During eleven months of treatment, she underwent two surgeries, radiation therapy, and chemotherapy to try to slow the growth of her cancer. She experienced remarkable weight loss, alopecia (hair loss), and significant fatigue from her treatments. She was unable to work for over eight months.

Mary was divorced, with no children. She was in a four-year relationship with David, a forty-year-old real estate broker. Mary and David were experiencing a number of conflicts in their relationship. They had had plans for marriage and children prior to her diagnosis. Since receiving the news of her diagnosis, Mary had become, in David's words, "distant, depressed, and disinterested in almost everything in her life." Mary described David as "expecting her to be happy all the time and to pretend like nothing is wrong." Mary also talked openly about feeling as if she "doesn't know who she is anymore." She felt that her life revolved around medical appointments and medications, and she missed her professional life and the routine of her job. David felt helpless and wished that everything could be the same in their relationship.

Mary and David were referred by their oncologist to the clinic's outpatient social worker. During the course of their five sessions, the social worker helped them to explore the strain in their lives and to consider how this was affecting their relationship. They were able to identify their individual coping styles and to consider how this affected each other. The social worker gently noted her observation of their avoidance of communicating around difficult issues and helped them to consider ways to open up to one another about their fears and hopes. Mary also arranged with her boss to create a newsletter for the business, allowing her to use her talents and feel that she was connected to her professional identity and her colleagues. She was able to continue this until a few weeks before her death.

The social worker's expertise in understanding the patterns and the nature of communication in families is critically important in end-of-life care. Assessment includes not only identifying patterns of communication but also developing an appreciation of the family's style of interpersonal interaction and relating given their unique social and cultural context. Often what is said, and what is not talked about, can reveal insight into the family dynamics. Similarly, who speaks for the family, and who the patient would like to include or exclude in conversations, can begin to reveal the nature of relationships and the dynamics of how the family works together.

A tremendous amount of information must be exchanged between the patient, family, and healthcare team. Early identification of the expectations of communication with the healthcare team is helpful as well, as is the identification of communication challenges within the family system. Considerations need to be given regarding confidentiality and the inclusion of family members following the patient's wishes.

Determining the patient's healthcare proxy or surrogate decision maker is important in anticipation that the patient at some point may no longer be able to communicate for himself or herself. Patients are often not aware of state laws outlining who in their lives would be legally considered their surrogate if they were not able to make medical decisions for themselves. It is common for the completion of an advance directive to be encouraged by healthcare facilities. Therefore, providing education about advance directives and dispelling common myths is often a very important intervention. Many families are comforted when faced with making decisions at the end of their loved one's life knowing that they are acting in direct accordance with their patient's wishes. The social worker's gentle and sensitive probing during assessment may encourage the patient and family members to communicate more openly about death and worries and fears about the process of dying. It is imperative to note, however, that the concepts of advance directives and advance-care planning are viewed with differing levels of comfort and acceptance in various ethnic or cultural communities.

CASE EXAMPLE

Angela was the mother of six devoted adult children. She had lived in a predominantly African American inner-city neighborhood all her life and had worked hard to support her family as a teaching assistant. Her husband, following a drug overdose, had died several years before on a respirator in a long-term care facility. She was adamant that she did not want to have life-sustaining measures if her breast cancer progressed. Although she expressed this concern to her medical team and completed an advanced directive, she shared with her physician that she was very uncomfortable discussing this with her children. Her physician assured her that he supported her wishes and felt that they were medically appropriate. As her disease worsened, the physician asked the patient if she would be comfortable participating in a family meeting to help her children understand and honor her wishes. She reluctantly agreed, and her family, suspecting the worst, cautiously agreed to attend. With fourteen family members in attendance, the social worker and the physician explained the purpose of advanced directives and the patient's specific requests. Several family members objected to the

Angela's desires, stating she was "giving up" if she was not resuscitated and hinting that they believed that the medical team might be discriminating against her because of her race and socioeconomic status. The patient maintained her position, and the physician explained the nature of her advanced illness and its likely course. The social worker also helped Angela to explain that she was appointing her eldest daughter to act as her proxy in the event that she became unable to speak for herself. A few weeks later, because of multiple brain metastases, she was admitted to the hospital for intermittent confusion and dehydration. In a second family meeting to determine the plan of care, the family was able to accept that although some of them might want more aggressive care for their mother, their mother did not want any life-prolonging measures. The patient was discharged to hospice, as had been her wish, where she died peacefully.

Key questions for the social worker to consider when assessing the family constellation, communication and the nature of these relationships are:

- How does the family define itself—both the family of origin and family of choice?
- What are the patient's wishes regarding confidentiality and the inclusion of family members?
- What roles have each member played in "health," and how will these be affected under the strain of "sickness"?
- How does this family work together in stressful times?
- What guides communication within this family?
- How do premorbid variables (e.g., presence of conflict, degree of cohesion) affect family coping and communication?

DEVELOPMENTAL STAGE OF CLIENT AND FAMILY

Illness can often affect a family in the face of other developmental and life challenges. An important aspect of assessing the family is to consider how the challenges associated with the illness and treatment (situational crisis) will affect the family, given its stage in the life cycle (developmental crisis).

Research indicates that the most commonly expressed concern by cancer patients is the impact of cancer on their families (American Health Decisions 1997). This is often described as a burden and is defined by patients in a number of ways. It may refer to the impact of a symptom on the patient's ability to participate in usual activities and family life. Fatigue, which is a more commonly reported symptom than pain among patients in the last months of life, profoundly affects quality of life and a patient's ability to function within the family. Burden may also relate to the financial strain that the illness has place on the family's resources, most commonly resulting from loss of income or medical care costs. Developmentally, the "burden" might be experienced in different ways. A young family, for instance, might become overwhelmed with the prospect of caring for an elderly parent while managing multigenerational tasks simultaneously, such as caring for an infant and working full time. By comparison, an older couple might not be concerned as much about conflicting responsibilities but might be realistically frightened about caring for an ill spouse during a time of increasing fragility and health concerns for both partners.

"Burden" may also be the individual's reference to the emotional impact of cancer. Clearly, the impact of being diagnosed with a fatal illness is difficult for patients and those who care about them. Many patients express guilt about the impact that their illness has had on those in their lives, about the changes that it has imposed on their family's normal routines and about the caregiving responsibilities that their loved ones have taken on. These collective worries can contribute to demoralization, depression, and anxiety. Caregivers, similarly, may experience emotional distress. Those who are not able to assume responsibility for their loved one's care may feel guilty that they have abandoned or failed their family member in some way. Alternatively, some family members, especially children, might become resentful of the forced changes in their lives because of their loved one's illness and feel selfish and guilty for experiencing this type of reaction.

Key questions for the worker to ask in order to consider the family's developmental stage include:

- How will the illness and treatment demands affect the family's developmental stage?
- What losses are typically associated with this life stage, and how will this crisis affect the family?
- To what degree does the patient/family experience the illness as a burden?

CULTURAL VALUES AND BELIEFS

Appreciating the cultural background of the patient and family is of paramount importance in the provision of quality psychosocial care. Cultural and social diversity includes racial or ethnic background, faith, and sexual orientation. Social workers should be aware of barriers that commonly exist within healthcare, including racism and homophobia, and how these systemic barriers may affect the individual patient and family's ability to access care and resources (Levine 2001).

It is imperative for the healthcare team to understand that culture is a lens through which individuals interpret and understand their experiences. Culture refers to "the integrated pattern of human thoughts, communications, actions, customs, beliefs, values and institutions of a racial, ethnic, religious or social group" (Cross et al. 1989).

Culture influences an individual's perceptions of the meaning of their illness, the healthcare system and professionals, and her beliefs about medical interventions. An individual's culture may also implicitly define caregiving responsibilities within the family, particularly those defined by gender roles. A patient and family's beliefs may shape what treatment options are or are not acceptable and, in final days of life, the rituals that are to be followed. Figure 28.1 illustrates this interplay.

Some cultural communities have a unique history of loss. Examples include traumatic deaths due to violence that have been witnessed in many inner-city commu-

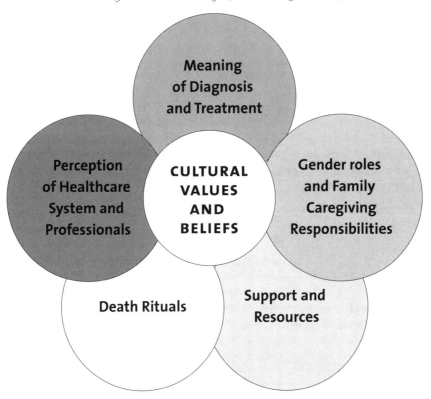

FIGURE 28.1 Cultural values and beliefs define the family's experience
Source: Weber and Blacker, 1997.

nities; deaths of multiple loved ones from AIDS as experienced by persons in the gay community; and loss of home, property, and personal safety as experienced by refugees from war-torn countries. How the individual or family has experienced these losses, and how they related this to their present situation, is important to consider in the assessment.

The worker can begin to understand the relevance of a patient and family's cultural background to the end-of-life situation by considering these questions:

- What is the identifiable "culture" (e.g., formal cultural or religious group beliefs, sexual orientation) of this family?
- How do this patient's and/or family's cultural values and beliefs contribute to their understanding, coping style, and psychosocial needs?
- How is terminal illness dealt with in the patient's culture? What values affect family caregiving, the use of medical technology, decision making regarding treatment, use of advance directives, truth-telling, and concerns about place of death?
- Are there conflicts between the patient's culture and values and those of their family?

- How do the cultural differences between the care team and the patient/family affect this situation?

SPIRITUALITY AND FAITH

Many patients struggle with questions such as "Why is this happening to me?" "What did I do to deserve to get this?" and "How can I live through this?" A patient may express this in many ways: "This is meant to make me stronger." "This is punishment—this is happening because I am a bad person." "This is fate and these are the cards that I have been dealt in life." "God won't give me more than I can bear." In order to cope, individuals create "meaning" or an understanding of their illness and its challenges. (Hedlund and Clark 2001) As Bailey (1998) points out, in order to maintain balance when confronting the crisis of life-threatening illness, the patient draws on every strength available: physical, intellectual, emotional *and* spiritual.

Given that the majority of Americans possess some faith or spiritual belief system, it is imperative for the social worker to identify how these beliefs contribute to or undermine the individual's/family's coping as part of the psycho-spiritual assessment. This includes determining the effect of illness on spiritual well-being (i.e., existential crisis) and the identification of a plan for insuring that spiritual needs are addressed and acknowledged in the process of care delivery. In the medical setting, social work and pastoral-care professionals often work closely to achieve this.

A number of tools have been developed to assist healthcare professionals in identifying the patient's spiritual needs. An example is the following model, developed by Dr. Christina Pulchalski (2002):

- F—Faith and Beliefs (e.g., Do you have spiritual beliefs that help you cope with stress?)
- I—Importance and Influence (e.g., What importance does your faith or belief have in your life?)
- C—Community (Are you a part of a spiritual or religious community?)
- A—Address/Action in care (How should this be addressed in your health care?)

CASE EXAMPLE

Betty L. was a sixty-nine-year-old, devout Methodist woman who was the sole caregiver to her seventy-eight-year-old husband. Robert was diagnosed with Alzheimer's disease, and she had cared for him in their home for more than three years. He had been exhibiting "strange behaviors" for almost six years but had refused to go to their family physician. He was hospitalized after a fall and treated for a fractured hip. During the hospitalization, he exhibited disorientation and aggressive behavior. At that time, the hospital's psychiatric consultation team was involved and a testing led to the diagnosis.

Betty had health problems of her own and had been having increasing difficulty managing Robert's care at home. She had refused home care in the past, stating, "For better or for worse, it is my job to be his wife." She also stated, "Something must be wrong with me. I shouldn't feel this way. I am a terrible person for feeling sorry for myself." The couple's two adult children lived three states away and visited infrequently, although they called Betty daily. Betty tried to minimize how badly their father was doing. She worried that they would pressure her to find a placement in a nursing home for Robert. She stated, "I couldn't live with the guilt if I ever did that to him. My mother was in one of those places and she was alone and frightened."

Robert was hospitalized after another fall, and a medical social worker met with Betty. Betty was obviously experiencing difficulty managing Robert's care—he was completely dependent on her for all activities of daily living and his cognitive ability more impaired. Both looked disheveled. During a conversation about the most viable and safe options for his ongoing care, Betty reiterated that she felt that as "a good Christian wife" she must honor her marriage vows "in sickness and in health." With Betty's permission, the social worker invited the hospital chaplain and Betty's local minister to help them consider this further. During their meeting, the chaplain suggested that perhaps her duty could be interpreted as finding the very best care for her husband. After considering this, Betty agreed to "at least look at a facility." Betty's two eldest children arrived, and supported the option of placement, as they felt that even with maximal home care supports, she could no longer care for him at home. They toured several specialty facilities, and Betty chose one just three blocks from their home. This facility was also appealing to her because her minister served on the board of directors and conducted prayer services for the residents. She visited Robert every day, and her health improved dramatically. She even became a volunteer, planning some of the holiday festivities for residents of the families and their families. Robert remained there for the next two and a half years, until his death.

Questions for the social worker to consider include in the assessment include:

- What meaning has this patient/family given to this illness?
- How do they define who/what is in control of or influencing this situation?
- How do spiritual beliefs contribute to the individual's/family's coping?
- How has this illness affected the patient and family's spiritual well-being?

EXPERIENCES WITH ILLNESS, DISABILITY, OR DEATH

A family's experience in coping with illness, disability, death, and other significant losses is often a predictor of how they will manage the current crisis. It is important for the team to appreciate that a family's perceptions and history with illness, disability, or even the death of other family members will affect their current experience. As a result, the patient and family may be very knowledgeable about treatment options or resources, presenting informed questions and actively engaging in the treatment plan. Alternately, the team might find that their efforts are being met, seemingly inexplicably, with an attitude of distrust or a strong reluctance to consider a specific care plan. With closer assessment, the team may learn the etiology. For example, unresolved grief or a negative experience with the medical profession may lead to a repetition of old experiences. The team may also discover that a lack of information sharing in the family may further contribute to misperceptions. Using this awareness and sensitivity, the team can then successfully adopt strategies that will best respond to the patient and family's concerns and needs.

Assessment should consider:

- What is this family's experience with loss, illness, disability, and death?
- What resources were accessed in prior situations that were perceived as helpful or not helpful?

Patients and family members will often recount past interactions with healthcare professionals. These histories are invaluable and can guide the healthcare team in their new relationship with the family. Attending to experiences can help identify misconceptions that may come into play in the present situation. Family/team meetings, coupled with proactive patient/caregiver education, help ensure that the past will not be repeated in the present. (Family meetings, or conferencing, are described in more detail later in this chapter.)

COPING HISTORY, STRENGTHS, AND EMOTIONAL RESPONSES

Gathering information about the presence of past or current mental health problems (such as premorbid personality or characterologic difficulties, depression, anxiety disorders, psychosis, or a history of substance abuse) is important in creating an effective care plan. Assessing how both the patient and those who are caregivers have utilized their own support systems (within their family, their faith, or social community) is essential to be able to build on their strengths. Assessment of coping strengths includes investigating the family's ability to access help and information, to communicate with healthcare team and skills to navigate the healthcare system. Assessing the patient or family member's ego strengths is also invaluable.

Patient and family members faced with life-threatening illness and death experience a range of emotions and responses, including shock, disbelief, sadness, and anger as well as intrusive thoughts or difficulty concentrating. For some patients, the diagnosis may trigger profound feelings related to other traumatic events or losses. Often family members become concerned about the patient's affect. Caregivers also commonly seek assistance for prolonged feelings of distress. Depression and anxiety are associated with reactions to the stress of a life-threatening diagnosis and its treatment (Payne and Massie 1998). Depression is diagnosed in healthy individuals by considering somatic symptoms, including changes in appetite, energy, and weight, making it more complicated to identify depression in the seriously ill patient (Abrahm 2000). In patients who commonly experience these symptoms as a result of their diseases or treatment side effects, it is very important to consider the psychological symptoms. These include feelings of helplessness and hopelessness, loss of self-esteem, anhedonia, dysphoric mood, and thoughts of death and suicide (Payne and Massie 1998).

Similarly, the somatic symptoms of sleep disturbance, loss of appetite, heart palpitations, and abdominal distress are often associated with anxiety. Therefore, the clinician should look closely at the patient or family member's affective presentation. Is the client experiencing recurrent unpleasant thoughts of the illness and death, disability, disfigurement and dependency on others? The anxious patient or family member is "characterized by overgeneralization and catastrophizing; negative outcomes seems inevitable, and patients view themselves as helpless in a hopeless situation" (Payne and Massie 1997:505). Supportive counseling, information sharing, problem solving, and mobilizing coping skills through brief therapy interventions often help to restore some sense of control and direction even in the setting of imminent death (Taylor-Brown et al. 2001). Depression and anxiety should be proactively assessed and, when identified, consultation for medications, in concert with supportive counseling, should be considered.

Taylor-Brown et al. (2001) note the importance of respecting the individual's protective coping mechanisms. Denial is often a concern for healthcare professionals, yet it needs to be carefully assessed and respected. Denial is usually defined as an unconscious process aimed at a threat that is perceived to be intolerable. In working with individuals with life-threatening illness, denying the full impact of the illness may at times be adaptive—allowing the individual to focus on aspects of living, not dwelling on dying. As Wood (1998) points out, denial often coexists with awareness. Jan, for example, was a patient with advanced liver cancer who was able to cope from day to day with her diagnosis. She refused to talk about death, and her concerns about her progressing illness, with her care team or her family. Upon further assessment, however, her social worker learned that she had completed a will and planned for the future of her teenaged children. She expressed that she hoped to see them grow older, to teach them the important life lessons that she had learned. She maintained this hope. "Hope can transcend reality, but hope does not equate with denial" (Hedlund and Clark 2001:309).

As Taylor-Brown and colleagues point out, "Awareness of dying does not have to be expressed to all members of the teams, nor do all patients and families express awareness through 'verbal' acknowledgement" (2001:14). In other instances, a patient may be perceived as denying what is happening to them, but may in fact have not been given adequate information. Any decision to challenge "denial" should be based in a thorough assessment of the nature, severity, persistence, and effect on coping (Vachon 1998). One must be mindful of how different cultures, genders, and individuals may express their realization of the dying process.

Key questions to address in this specific domain of the assessment include:

- Does this patient or family member have any past or current mental health problems or symptoms?
- Does this patient or family member have a history of alcohol/drug use?
- Does the patient/family member present with anxiety or depression?
- What supports have been helpful in the past when faced with difficult situations?
- How have this patient and family defined strategies for coping and accessed help?
- How do this patient and family define "hope"?

- How well are this patient and family able to communicate with the healthcare team and navigate the system?

SOCIOECONOMIC FACTORS AND RESOURCES

Assessing for the presence, or absence, of resources as well as for access to formal and informal supports is important in determining what interventions will be required to help the family manage the crisis. Screening for commonly experienced problems or barriers to care such as financial strain, low literacy level, lack of insurance or transportation, inadequate caregiving arrangements, or insufficient safety at home is essential.

The financial impact of illness and disability as well as caregiving demands are often underestimated. Many patients and families are concerned about the costs inherent in caring for their loved one at home or in a facility. Younger families might be worried that their employer will not be able to accommodate their requests for time off or that they will not be able to afford the additional help at home. Older couples might be concerned about the impact the high costs of caregiving will have on their savings for the surviving spouse. Understanding the patient and families' concerns about resources is critical to the psychosocial assessment.

The social worker also must assess the family's resources and the needs related to discharge. Discharge planning involves helping the patient and family plan where, and with what supports, optimal care can be provided. It is important to assess the patient and family's wishes and concerns related to the practical care that will be involved in the final days, weeks, or months of life, along with their ability to manage this plan.

Key questions to investigate in this domain include:

- What resources (formal and informal supports) does this family have to enable them to manage the demands of the illness?
- How is the patient/family managing the financial demands resulting from this situation?
- Does the patient want to remain at home and die at home?
- Is there a caregiver, or group of caregivers, who will be available to the patient until he dies?
- If the patient wants to die at home, do family members feel they can bear to live there after the death?
- If the patient is remaining at home, what needs to be initiated to help make this happen safely? What durable medical equipment needs to be obtained to maximize safety and comfort?
- What referrals for hospice and community support need to be initiated?
- If not, what kind of contingency plans need to be made (e.g., placement in a nursing facility or inpatient hospice, move in with children, hire private duty help)?

Assessment of these key areas will guide the team in determining how best to utilize resources such as hospice organizations, palliative-care programs, and home healthcare providers to help the patient and family achieve their goals for the end of life (Taylor-Brown et al. 2001).

PSYCHOSOCIAL INTERVENTIONS WITH FAMILIES

Social workers in the healthcare setting must draw on a variety of theoretical perspectives and be skillful in many interventions (Blum et al. 2001; Hedlund and Clark 2001). This section will review some of the most common interventions that social workers in the healthcare setting utilize to help patients and their families.

FAMILY COUNSELING AND FAMILY THERAPY

As the patient and family are confronted by the many of problems associated with a life-threatening illness, they are challenged to cope with the crises and losses associated with it (Wells and Turney 2001; Blum et al. 2001). To regain a sense of equilibrium, they must try to adjust or reorganize to manage the crisis. The worker's use of supportive therapy techniques including clarification, exploration, partializing, validating, and problem solving are critical skills in establishing a therapeutic relationship, developing a plan of intervention, and providing ongoing support to the patient and family (Taylor-Brown et al. 2001).

As has been discussed in the assessment section of this chapter, understanding a family's functioning prior to the illness allows the worker to understand how the illness has affected the family system. Identifying strengths and mobilizing resources are important in assisting patients and families as they cope with life-threatening illness and death. The degree of involvement and frequency of contact is a constant process of renegotiation. At some point in time, the social worker may find that the patient and family require increased intensive contact. This is commonly precipitated by the demands of the illness, changes in the patient's condition, increased demands of the caregivers, and challenges in decision making. "Family counseling is commonly used to enable families to effectively adapt to the changes illness imposes and to enhance effective coping. Family therapy may be needed when structural problems or preexisting problems in family functioning impede effective adjustment to the life-limiting illness or bereavement process" (Taylor-Brown et al. 2001:15).

As the patient's condition deteriorates, along with his or her ability to benefit from psychological interventions, the family becomes the focus of care (Loscalzo and Zabora 1998). In the final days of life, helping families to define how to say goodbye and to reassure their loved one that they will be remembered is typical of the very intense work that social workers do with families. Encouraging a process of collective life review and storytelling is often helpful for the family that has been able to resolve imminent practical issues and moved beyond a crisis state. Even if the patient is dying in an inpatient setting, engaging family members in ways that helps the patient to be comfortable may also be helpful as a way to increase a sense of control within an uncontrollable situation.

CASE EXAMPLE

Jonathan P. was an independent contractor in construction prior to being diagnosed with prostate cancer. Although his wife was aware of the severity of his diagnosis, he did not want to burden his eighteen-year-old son and significantly minimized his illness when talking with him. He continued to work through his treatment and would go to worksites even on days when he was fatigued and in pain. This continued for some time until eventually his disease progression and accompanying symptoms forced him to be hospitalized. The medical team was surprised at his son's anger with the initiation of hospice discussions and called the social worker to deal with the "difficult" young man. While counseling and educating the family, the social worker was able to help the patient disclose the severity of the illness to his son and to help the son understand that his father kept this from him out of love, pride, and protection. The son was then able to work with the team, and his anger dissipated.

FAMILY CONFERENCES

Another social work role is to assist the team in understanding the patient and family's goals of care, and to ensure simultaneously that they understand what has been communicated by the healthcare team. Family meetings, or conferences, are a helpful intervention to achieve this.

Family conferences are generally defined as meetings of a physician and other members of the healthcare team, relevant family members, and the patient to discuss issues germane to the patient's health. This intervention is consistent with the interdisciplinary focus of palliative-care practice and acknowledges that the unit of care is the patient, the family, and their support network. Reasons for holding family meetings include sharing information, gaining an understanding of family dynamics, affectively connecting with families, and reaching consensus regarding healthcare decisions. The focus of such meetings tends to be on providing medical information and advice (Kushner, Meyer, and Hansen 1989).

Healthcare professionals see family/team meetings as having a number of benefits. They present an opportunity to both gather and disseminate information efficiently. They can be an effective way for the team to present unified opinions and recommendations and to be present collectively in establishing a plan in concert with the patient and family. Family meetings or conferences are useful when a decision needs to be made, and they also decrease the possibility of miscommunication. It is also helpful to schedule regular meetings if it is anticipated that care goals will need to be reconsidered with some frequency or if there are tensions or conflicts between the care team and the family. This sends a clear message to the family that their concerns will be heard during a prearranged meeting with all of the key healthcare players. This also helps to contain the "chaos" that can develop if a family has multiple unofficial spokespersons or if members are having difficulty communicating with one another.

Results of research by Kushner and colleagues (1989) about the use of family conferences in the medical setting suggests that patients and families most desire a family conference when a hospitalization occurs for a serious medical illness; a new diagnosis of a serious illness is made; behavioral/psychological problems (such as depression) are present; and/or frequent visits have occurred without improvement in symptoms.

Despite the usefulness of family conferences, there are some challenges to overcome to ensure their effectiveness. Barriers that are most commonly cited by medical professionals, particularly physicians, include lack of time needed for meetings, lack of reimbursement for time (value implication), scheduling difficulties, and lack of training in facilitation/communication (Marchand and Kushner 1997). The social worker is often the team member who coordinates this meeting and may need to make a compelling case to other team members about the potential benefits of this intervention in order to overcome these barriers.

Despite the reality that variations of families meetings are relatively common in the inpatient setting, few healthcare professionals have been formally trained in how to optimize this intervention. As a starting place, it is helpful to identify a primary coordinator and facilitator for the meeting. There must be a clear and agreed upon identification of those individuals who are important to the patient in the decision-making process. A patient who is able to participate should identify key support persons. In the case of a patient who is unable to participate (e.g., one who is cognitively impaired or medically compromised), the role of the designated healthcare proxy/ surrogate decision maker must be respected. All members must be clear about the purpose of the meeting, and this should be stated as the meeting begins. Having a private space, with adequate seating, is important and sets the tone for the meeting. The healthcare professionals present should attempt to minimize interruptions (such as pagers sounding) whenever possible. All individuals present should be offered the opportunity to speak and ask questions (Blacker, Cohen, and Sormanti 2001; Weissman 2000).

CASE EXAMPLE

Gisela was an eighty-six-year-old Latina hospitalized for both congestive heart failure and chronic obstructive pulmonary disease. Although widowed, she had an extensive support system consisting of eight children, fifteen grandchildren, and dozens of concerned friends and community members. At any given time, there could be more than ten family or community members in Gisela's hospital room. As a result of a prior interventions by the social worker, the patient had designated her eldest daughter as her healthcare proxy during a previous hospitalization. However, the daughter was reluctant to perform the responsibilities of her role without the consent of the other family members. The physicians met with the daughter to discuss the medical futility of additional treatment and the initiation of hospice care. Although there were a few other family members present for this discussion, it was held unexpectedly during early morning medical rounds, when many of the family members were not in attendance. As word spread through the family and community about the discussion, family members became enraged and suspicious that information was being withheld from them. The social worker and the daughter contacted all of the family members for a family conference meeting at a time convenient for the family and team that evening. Those who were to attend were prepared for the meeting and were asked to prepare questions beforehand. These were given to the medical team ahead of time to optimize the time together.

During the meeting, the family members expressed their concerns and frustrations with the healthcare team. Strategies to improve communication were mutually developed. The physicians reviewed all the pertinent medical information and suggested a plan to all members at once. A plan for future communication was established and the family left the meeting feeling that their concerns had been validated and that a safe and reasonable plan of care had been developed for Gisela.

DISCHARGE PLANNING, CARE TRANSITIONS, AND REFERRALS FOR RESOURCES

Social work plays a critical role in coordinating the practical arrangements and planning necessary for discharge from the hospital and in helping the patient and family prepare for the challenges associated with increased caregiving needs. Social workers are also actively involved with care transitions that occur for those receiving outpatient care (Blum et al. 2001). Brad, in the case example below, illustrates the important role that the social worker plays in transitioning a patient from the hospital to hospice care at home.

CASE EXAMPLE

Brad was a thirty-five-year-old man preparing to return home after a prolonged hospitalization. He had been living with AIDS for four years. Over a period of ten months, he had experienced recurrent opportunistic infections, had lost more than sixty of his usual 165 pounds, and had become increasingly weak. All treatments to attempt to control his counts had failed. Brad decided that given the advanced stage of his disease, he did not want to receive aggressive treatment or to be hospitalized in the future. He opted to return home with hospice care and required a hospital bed, bedside commode, and a wheelchair, which would be coordinated through the hospice agency. The team perceived that his partner of ten years, Steve, was in complete agreement until later that afternoon when Brad's nurse paged the social worker. According to the nursing staff, Steve had been expressing concern about this plan and had even suggested that it was an error for Brad to return home.

The unit's social worker met with Brad and Steve to review the plan and to attempt to determine the nature of Steve's concerns. He denied any concerns in front of Brad, but an hour later, in the hallway, he asked that the social worker repeat the plan. The social worker shared with Steve that in her experience she had found that caregivers often confide in her that they are uncertain about what to expect about the dying process, and worry about their ability to manage the responsibilities of caregiving. She asked if these were concerns that he was experiencing. He shared with her that although he and Brad had lost many friends to AIDS, he had never been actively involved in the day-to-day care of a dying person before. The social worker provided him with more detailed information about what to expect in the final months, weeks, and days of life, including written information for caregivers prepared by the same hospice program. She also encouraged him to consider accepting the offers for assistance that he and Brad had received, but that he had declined, from Brad's sister and mother. Steve said that he felt pressure that he should be able to provide for everything that Brad needed on his own. The social worker stressed the importance of respite for caregivers. Brad had completed an advance directive naming Steve as his healthcare proxy. Therefore, she was able to assure him that he and Brad would remain in the position of decision makers, regardless of who they engaged as part of Brad's care team.

Steve called Brad's family and arranged for them to visit in three days time so that they could also meet the hospice nurse during the intake visit. Brad's mother agreed to be available to stay with them when they felt that his care needs had increased. By normalizing Steve's feelings, respecting his need to remain in control, providing concrete information and suggestions, and helping him create a plan for respite, she was able to facilitate the care transition for both men and address the distress that Steve was experiencing.

With the shift to ambulatory care, and emphasis on shorter lengths of stay for inpatients, the care needs of the patient at home have become increasingly complex. The types of therapies possible at home (e.g., pain pumps, suctioning, total parental feeding) have also become increasing complex. For the family caregiver, this can be both intimidating and overwhelming. Many families are maximally stretched in terms of their practical, financial, and emotional resources. It is difficult, if not impossible, for many families to meet the needs of the patient who requires constant supervision and assistance. Certainly the care team should initiate and maximize home care and community supports whenever possible. Hospice and palliative care is a critical part of addressing needs at the end of many patients' lives. Timely referrals to these services require thoughtful planning and reevaluation of the treatment plan and goals, as well as the inclusion of the patient and family in considering care options and education. Education and supportive counseling is an essential part of this process (Blum et al. 2001). Preparing family members for their caregiving responsibilities and providing education about resources is critical in discharge planning, and the team should consider how to achieve this goal. Use of family conferencing can be a key intervention in this process.

PREPARING FAMILIES FOR CAREGIVING RESPONSIBILITIES AT THE END-OF-LIFE: TEAM INTERVENTIONS

GOALS

- Provide information and establish communication
- Provide support for the patient and family or caregivers

- Addressing practical issues
- Adapt the physical environment and prepare caregivers to manage care

INTERVENTIONS

- Present clear information about what to do for pain and other symptoms
- Encourage the patient/caregiver to assemble a list of contacts, including on-call health-care professionals, family, and friends
- Clarify who will make decisions (identify surrogate decision maker) and clarify wishes
- Prepare family/caregivers for what to expect in the last weeks, days, and hours of life and what do when the death occurs
- Normalize a range of responses from patients and families
- Assist the family/caregivers with leave from employment, access to caregiving support and respite care
- Assist with plan for dependent children or other dependents
- Provide emotional support, and ensure a plan for ongoing emotional support and bereavement care
- Provide information about managing short and long-term finances (disability benefits, insurance) and other aspects of putting affairs in order
- Assist with plan for managing household tasks
- Assist with determining most suitable setting for care (e.g., patient's home or home of another family member, inpatient setting such as hospice)
- Arrange for all necessary medical equipment to maximize comfort and safety
- Provide education about managing personal care needs
- Empathize with the burdens that can be anticipated and help to identify particular stressors (Field and Cassel 1997; Taylor-Brown et al. 2001)

The social worker's role in securing resources and advocacy for supports is critical (Blum et al. 2001). The social worker assesses the impact of illness on employment, income, insurance, and medical benefits and recognizes that economic difficulties can be a source of suffering and distress for patient and family members. Navigating medical insurance and income entitlements often requires education of the patient and advocacy on his or her behalf. "Exploring resources, entitlements, and proactive financial and legal planning may restore some sense of control, provide options to be evaluated, and may reassure a dying patient that their family will be cared for" (Taylor-Brown et al. 2001:17).

SYMPTOM MANAGEMENT

Studies such as those conducted by American Health Decisions (1997) have shown that patients with advanced illness report a number of psychosocial concerns. In the face of a life-threatening illness and distressing physical symptoms, a patient often raises questions: "What does this mean?" "Will I be okay?" "Am I dying?" "What will dying be like?" "Will I suffer?" "Will my family be okay?" "Will they be able to handle this?"

One of the most commonly reported concerns is the fear of experiencing pain. Family members also rate this as a primary concern as well. Given the pervasiveness of this concern, proactive assessment and interventions for pain are critical in end-of-life care. When treating patients who are experiencing pain, however, the healthcare team must appreciate that pain is experienced on multiple levels. Fully assessing the quality and nature of the pain, as well as the thoughts, feelings, and meaning that both the patient and their caregivers attach to the pain, is necessary to being able to intervene effectively. Some cultural groups do not admit to suffering from pain, and this is also significant for the healthcare team to understand (see chapter 19 for further discussion of this topic).

Upon developing a treatment plan, the team must also be aware that for some patients the apprehension about pain medications is as relevant as the fear of pain. The identification of myths and misperceptions is an important part of the assessment process of all symptoms. Education about the nature and causes of the pain, the difference between tolerance and addiction, the multiple dimensions of pain, and how medications are used to treat pain is critical. (Altilio et al. 2001; see chapter 19 of this volume for more discussion.)

Social workers should actively participate in the assessment and management of pain and other symptoms such as dyspnea (shortness of breath) and anxiety by recognizing their multidimensional nature. A symptom may be experienced at a physical, social, psychological, and spiritual level (Ferrell et al. 1996). An intervention may occur at a practical or resource-oriented level. An individual with uncontrolled pain, for example, may be found through assessment of the problem to have been unable to fill a prescription for medications due to lack of insurance and financial concerns. This may also occur at a psycho-educational level. An individual or caregiver's fear and misinformation about pain medications or addiction may lead to reluctance to take the medication as prescribed. An appropriate team intervention for families in this situation includes providing education about the nature of the patient's pain, pain medications, and tolerance vs. addiction. The social worker may engage other team members to provide this education.

Social work interventions for treatment of symptoms often include the use of cognitive behavioral interventions with those who experience pain, anxiety, and dyspnea. These interventions are not a replacement for medical interventions, but rather, enhance the patient's ability to manage the effects of the symptoms and increase their sense of control.

Cognitive-behavioral interventions have been shown to be effective in reducing emotional distress and controlling physical symptoms such as pain and dyspnea and anxiety that patients may experience (Jacobsen and Hann 1998; Blum et al. 2001). A major strength of this treatment approach is that an intervention can be administered in a brief period and can be easily tailored to the individual (Blum et al. 2001). Family members can also be taught these techniques which can give the caregiver a powerful tool in which to feel useful and in control. Cognitive behavioral techniques are readily accepted by many patients and families, as the emphasis is on placing increased sense of personal control and self-efficacy. Cognitive-behavioral interventions include cognitive restructuring, contingency management, coping self-statements, distraction, bio-feedback, progressive muscle relaxation, systematic desensitization, hypnosis, problem-solving therapy, stress inoculation training, and guided imagery (Jacobsen and Hann 1998; Blum et al. 2001).

BEREAVEMENT CARE

The social worker's role does not end with the death of the patient. Grief is a highly personal and normal response to life-changing events—a process that can lead to healing and personal growth. It is universal, but its expression varies. Social work interventions in the acute care setting include assessing for "risk" of complicated grief reactions prior to the death, and providing education and initiating referrals for bereavement programs after the death. The reactions of children in the patient's life are often of concern for family members and warrant special attention.

Bereavement counseling and support groups may be available in healthcare settings or through churches and other community organizations. Hospice organizations provide bereavement follow up to the family/caregivers of their hospice patients, and many make these services available to the larger community. Bereavement groups or resources may be tailored to a particular bereaved group, such as parents whose children have died or family members of those whose deaths were caused by an act of violence or suicide; those who have suffered loss through a specific disease (for example, cancer or AIDS); or children who have experienced the death of a family member (Taylor-Brown et al. 2001).

Social workers in many institutions have led programs that offer memorial or remembrance services or rituals for surviving family members and for staff. Families are often very grateful for condolence notes or cards from the social worker, or from the team, that cared for their family member. Acknowledging the life of the patient, as well as the death, is important. This can be a very effective way to reach out to a bereaved family member and encourage him or her to make contact if further invention or support is warranted.

CONCLUSION

Psychosocial assessment and intervention during the final stages of the patient's illness should be available for all families and fully integrated as part of any care plan. Families should be the focus of care and partners in the process. Family members support the patient, assume caregiving responsibilities, engage in making treatment decisions, and are affected by discharge planning. Families are always accompanied by past losses and experiences with illness. Each family is unique in its cultural, social, and spiritual beliefs and in its ways of coping. Strengths of the family must be elicited and barriers to family functioning and coping addressed. The social worker plays a pivotal role in helping families facing challenges, whether they be in facing the reality of the patient's wishes, helping to make sense of the illness and treatment, advocating for the patient and family's psychological needs, accessing resources, or intervening through family conferences.

Interdisciplinary teamwork is essential to optimal outcomes for the patient and family. The role of the social worker in the healthcare setting is dynamic, and the ability of social work to improve the lives and care of the dying and their families is unique.

REFERENCES

Abrahm, J. 2000. *A Physician's Guide to Pain and Symptom Management in Cancer Patients.* Baltimore: Johns Hopkins University Press.

American Health Decisions. 1997. The quest to die with dignity: An analysis of Americans' values, opinions, and attitudes concerning end-of-life care. www.ahd.org/ahd/library/statements/quest.html.

Altilio, T., S. Otis-Green, and S. Blacker. 2001. Pain and palliative care: Skills for social work. Workshop presentation at the Association of Oncology Social Work Annual Meeting, Cleveland.

Bailey, S. 1998. Comprehensive spiritual care. In *Principles and Practice of Supportive Oncology,* ed. A. Berger, R. Portenoy, and D. Weissman, 717–731. Philadelphia: Lippincott-Raven.

Blacker, S., I. Cohen, and M. Sormanti. 2001. Family conferencing: A case example. Presentation at the Project on Death in America Retreat, Lake Tahoe, CA.

Blum, D., E. Clark, and C. Marcusen. 2001. Oncology social work in the 21st century. In *Social Work in Oncology: Supporting Survivors, Families and Caregivers,* ed. M. M. Lauria, E. J. Clark, J. F. Hermann, and N. M. Stearns, 45–71. Atlanta: American Cancer Society.

Cross, T. L., B. J. Bazron, K. W. Dennis, and M. R. Isaacs. 1989. *Towards a Culturally Competent System of Care.* Washington, DC: National Technical Assistance Center for Children's Mental Health, Georgetown University Child Development Center.

del Rio, N., and M. Okazawa-Rey. 2002. Cross-cultural social work assessment for clients at the end of life. ACCESS to End of Life Care.

Ferrell, B. R., M. Grant, G. E. Dean, B. Funk, and L. Ly. 1996. "Bone tired": The experience of fatigue and impact on quality of life. *Oncology Nursing Forum* 23(10): 1539–1547.

Field, M. J., and C. K. Cassel, eds. 1997. *Approaching Death: Improving Care at the End of Life.* Washington, DC: National Academy Press.

Geramine, C. B. 1984. *Social Work Practice in Health Care: An Ecological Perspective.* New York: Free Press.

Glajchen, M., D. Blum, and K. Calder. 1995. Cancer pain management and the role of social work: Barriers and interventions. *Health & Social Work* 20:200–206.

Hedlund, S., and E. Clark. 2001. End of life issues. In *Social Work in Oncology: Supporting Survivors, Families and Caregivers,* ed. M. M. Lauria, E. J. Clark, J. F. Hermann, and N. M. Stearns, 299–316. Atlanta: American Cancer Society.

Jacobsen, P., and D. M. Hann. 1998. Cognitive-behavioral interventions. In *Psycho-Oncology,* ed. J. Holland and W. Breitbart, 717–729. New York: Oxford University Press.

Kushner, K., D. Meyer, and J. P. Hansen. 1989. Patients attitudes toward physician involvement in family conferences. *Journal of Family Practice* 28(1): 65–68.

Levine, E. 2001. Special issues for gays and lesbians with cancer. In *Social Work in Oncology: Supporting Survivors, Families and Caregivers,* ed. M. M. Lauria, E. J. Clark, J. F. Hermann, and N. M. Stearns, 257–267. Atlanta: American Cancer Society.

Loscalzo, M. 1999. The COPE model: Its clinical usefulness in solving pain related problems. *Journal of Psychosocial Oncology* 16(3–4): 93–117.

Loscalzo, M., and K. Brintzenhofeszoc. 1998. Brief crisis counseling. In *Psycho-Oncology*, ed. J. Holland and W. Breitbart, 662–675. New York: Oxford University Press.

Loscalzo, M., and J. Zabora. 1998. Care of the cancer patient: Response of family and staff. In *Topics in Palliative Care*, ed. R. Portenoy and E. Bruera, 2:209–254. New York: Oxford University Press.

Marchand, L., and K. Kushner. 1997. Getting to the heart of the family conference: The resident's perspective. *Families, Systems & Health* 15(3): 305–319.

Miller, P., S. Hedlund, and K. Murphy. 1998. Social work assessment at end of life: Practice guidelines for suicide and the terminally ill. *Social Work in Health Care* 26(4): 23–26.

Munroe, B. 1993. Psychosocial dimensions of palliation. In *The Management of Terminal Malignant Disease* (3d ed.), ed. C. Saunders and N. Sykes, 174–201. London: Edward Arnold.

Payne, D., and M. Massie. 1998. Depression and anxiety. In *Principles and Practice of Supportive Oncology*, ed. A. Berger, R. Portenoy, and D. Weissman, 497–511. Philadelphia: Lippincott-Raven.

Pulchalski, C. M. 2002. Spirituality and end of life care. In *Principles and Practice of Palliative Care and Supportive Oncology* (2d ed.), ed. A. Berger, R. Portenoy, and D. Weissman, 799–812. Philadelphia: Lippincott Williams & Wilkins.

Taylor-Brown, S., S. Blacker, K. Walsh-Burke, G. Christ, and T. Altilio. 2001. *Innovative Practice in Social Work: Care at the End of Life*. Rev. ed. Chicago: Society of Social Work Leadership in Health Care.

Vachon, M. 1998. The emotional problems of the patient. In *Oxford Textbook of Palliative Medicine*, ed. D. Doyle et al., 867–880. New York: Oxford University Press.

Weber, G., and S. Blacker. 1997. Individual and cross-cultural diversity in the menopause experience. Paper presented at the Teaching to Promote Women's Health International Multidisciplinary Annual Conference, Toronto, July.

Weisman, A. D. 1979. *Coping with Cancer*. New York: McGraw-Hill.

Weissman, D. 2000. Fast fact and concepts #16: Conducting a family conference. End-of-Life Physician Education Resource Center. www.eperc.mcw.edu.

Wells, N., and M. Turney. 2001. Common issues facing adults with cancer. In *Social Work in Oncology: Supporting Survivors, Families and Caregivers*, ed. M. M. Lauria, E. J. Clark, J. F. Hermann, and N. M. Stearns, 45–71. Atlanta: American Cancer Society.

Zabora, J. R., and M. Loscalzo. 1996. Comprehensive psychosocial programs: A prospective model of care. *Oncology Issues* 1:14–18.

———. 1998. Psychosocial consequences of advanced cancer. In *Principles of Supportive Oncology*, ed. A. Berger et al., 531. Philadelphia: Lippincott-Raven.

29

HELPING THE BEREAVED

PHYLLIS R. SILVERMAN

THE BEREAVED have many needs. This chapter explores some of what is involved in meeting them, and it describes the range of helpers involved in this work and the factors that influence the bereaved as they become aware of their own needs. Because the needs of the bereaved change with time, it is important to see that available help may need to change as well. This chapter closes with a review of a range of programs that might be available to the bereaved in any given community and the role of the social workers in these programs.

Before a death, social workers are members of the hospice or palliative-care team that is typically part of the healthcare system. In working with the bereaved, they become part of a new team, which may be anchored only tangentially in the health-care system. On this new team, social workers function as consultants, referral agents, educators, and collaborators, as well as counselors to not only the bereaved but also to members of the larger community who have roles as caregivers to the bereaved.

HELPING

Help offered to the bereaved needs to be responsive to their changing situations and must recognize that there is no one way of coping with grief that leads to a better accommodation. The help offered, in part, is a reflection of how we as professionals understand the nature of bereavement. If we see grief as something from which people recover, then the goals of help will be to help mourners get over their grief and get on with their lives. If we recognize bereavement as a time of transition that leads to change, then help offered will take a longer view recognizing that this is not a time-limited condition. We also need to consider how mourners view their own grief. We need to ask what the attitudes, values, and beliefs that frame their responses are (Parkes et al. 1997). People who are grieving do not get over their grief, although with time the pain lessens. A variety of help, and a variety of helpers, may be necessary as the bereaved deal with all the issues facing them (Silverman 2000). Just as there is no one way to mourn, there is not one kind of help that makes grief come to an end. Help is not a matter of providing the bereaved with a clear formula for what to do. The goals of help will vary depending on what mourners feel they need at a particular time and where they are in their grieving process.

A good deal of attention usually is focused on helping the bereaved talk about how they feel. Early on in the grieving process, people may be too numb to examine their feelings or even to want to talk abut them. In the long run, however, recognizing and talking about feelings brings relief, but these are generally not sufficient to help with all that the bereaved are dealing with. Talking about feelings does not automatically lead to more effective ways of responding to the long-term impact of any given death. Appropriate help should provide mourners—both adults and children—with opportunities that are responsive to where they are in this process. Initially they may need a place to cry; with time, it may be easiest to talk about the person who died rather than to explore their feelings. As mourners become aware of their changing needs and differences in their daily lives, they need opportunities to learn new ways of thinking and acting on their own behalf in their changed worlds. If the dominant view in the community around them sees grief as something from which the bereaved will recover, they need to learn that this expectation rarely coincides with their experience. In fact, they face a complex process that involves their finding new opportunities that will help them look ahead. They may need to meet others who are bereaved to share coping strategies and to learn that they are not alone in what they are experiencing. Other helpers may offer alternate perspectives that help expand the bereaved's coping repertoire. It is important to facilitate their developing new possibilities, new cognitive skills, and new directions in their lives. This does not happen over the short term, nor is it a linear process. Ideally, those who are bereaved can move toward a more complex view of the way they relate to themselves and to others. In a sense, they find a new "voice" and a new ability to act for themselves and with others in their family, who are also mourning (see chapter 12).

WHO ARE THE HELPERS?

Implicit in grief work is that no one helper can meet the range of needs the bereaved experience. Most people, in addition, are not alone on this journey. Family and friends accompany them, and their ability to help must be considered as well. Who can best provide help will vary depending on the nature of the help needed at any given time. Clergy, funeral directors, and health and mental health professionals, including social workers, are among those who may have something to offer. As social workers it becomes important to keep the focus not only on what you can do for a mourning family, but also on where else in the community there are services or helpers who have something to offer. It is necessary to be aware of these opportunities and to be prepared to collaborate with these other services and with the bereaved and, as appropriate, make referrals, to become in some way an ombudsman or "ritual specialist."

One of the most important resources for those who are bereaved, regardless of their age or position in the family, is their own energy and imagination. Often the bereaved find themselves developing creative solutions and ways of being in the world that they would never have imagined for themselves prior to the death. The bereaved learn, if they did not know this before, that they need others from whom they can learn and that their willingness to develop and change eases the process of growth and accommodation (Silverman 1987, 2000).

OPENNESS TO HELP

Many factors can influence a mourner's ability to learn and to find the kind of help they seek. Several are discussed here. Gender differences can influence what kinds of help people seek and how they utilize it (Cook 1988; Martin and Doka 2000; Silverman 1988, 2000). Women and girls are generally more comfortable in acknowledging their need for others and reaching out to talk about what is happening and to process their reactions (Belle 1989). Younger boys have similar qualities (Silverman and Worden 1992). However, from the time they are teenagers, men seem less interested in processing what is happening to them. They are more likely to seek out others to share concrete activities or look for information about what they need to do. They often present themselves as if they should be able to manage by themselves (Boerner and Silverman 2002; Cook 1988; Silverman 1988). Some men find it easier to join a poker group, where they in fact do a lot of talking and sharing and learning, but would not choose to come together to simply talk about feelings (Campbell and Silverman 1996). When they do let themselves get involved, they find it very useful (Silverman 1987).

Gender is not the only factor that can influence an individual's receptivity to being helped or to seeking out help. Some families invite others into their lives, while others want to do as much as they can for themselves. There are families who close off their options and close their doors. Some people manage well in this closed context; others may suffer unnecessarily, with help just around the corner. It is rarely an "either-or" situation. There are many variations. For example, for some people, it may be easier to accept some forms of help from relatives than from professionals. Others may be more comfortable seeking assistance outside the family. Many bereaved find themselves sufficiently challenged by their grief that they are open to ideas and help they would not have considered before.

Antonovsky (1979) identified inner family resources that he associated with the ability to utilize help and with the family's adaptability. These include a basic flexibility in how the family views the world, its members' sense of connection to themselves and to each other, and how these come together in their psychological and social makeup. Both he and Reiss (1981) found that these qualities frame the sense of coherence that enables families, as well as individuals, to find means of coping that are affirming and adaptive. Families with this sense of coherence, in comparison to more closed families, have a perspective that allows them to give voice to their experience and to be more receptive to making the changes that are needed at this time in their lives. They may also be able to create resources where none exist. What help is provided, and by whom, therefore, has to be respectful of and compatible with the bereaved's style, which also may be influenced by their culture and ethnicity so that available resources are sensitive to the bereaved's worldview and that they consider appropriate help.

WHAT IS CHANGED?

There is always the need to learn more about the family and what changes are apparent as a result of the death. A key contributor to what has changed is the bereaved's relationship to the deceased. The role of the deceased in the lives of the mourners will effect how they experience the loss. In considering this aspect of the loss, the focus is on the need to find new ways of dealing with the little issues and details of daily living that are now different. Many of the bereaved may need help in recognizing that they cannot live life as before and they may need help in articulating exactly what changes are appropriate to consider. If the deceased was an intimate part of the mourner's daily life, the death will make a big difference. Thus, the death of a parent for dependent children or the loss of a spouse leaves a profound vacuum in their daily lives. Older, single children who lived with their parents may also find themselves facing a vacuum as they approach the future when one or both parents die (Osterweis, Solomon, and Greene 1984). When a child dies before their parents, this challenges the very order of the world as we know it. In the United States today, it becomes important to learn about the geographic proximity of where the deceased lived to those who are mourning. Friendship, a sense of connection, and care that were shared with the deceased, in spite of the distance that might separate them, can be lost. Thus the death of friends (Silverman 2000; Smith 2002) and siblings or elderly parents who lived at a distance can create other issues for the bereaved. Elderly widowed people who depended on the deceased for their ability to be independent have other needs now (Lund and Caserta 2002). We cannot ignore that in some families, the relationship to the deceased was complicated, ambivalent, and perhaps dysfunctional, and that death over time can be experienced as a relief. We meet many bereaved whose grief is not recognized by the larger society, as may happen with partners in a homosexual relationship, in cases of miscarriage, or when an extramarital partner dies. These mourners also need to have their experiences of grief and their relationship with the deceased legitimated and honored (Doka 2002a).

Change then, can be specific and very concrete, like managing money, or it can involve new ways of relating to important others in the family. For example, a newly widowed parent may need to learn how to be a single parent head of household. Bereaved parents whose child has died may need to learn to relate to each other in a very different way (Silverman 2000).

The need to learn is an integral part of the bereavement process. Most people do not recognize the amount and quality of the learning that is involved as they cope with their loss. It is acceptable practice when facing other life-cycle transitions, such as getting married or becoming a parent, to see the value of learning how to manage the associated changes. The same practice needs to be developed for the time after a death in our lives. A good deal of learning is involved as well. It is important to acknowledge that there is a need to learn new ways of living in the world, as well as new ways of dealing with difficult feelings. It is important, in this context, to look at people's learning styles. People learn in different ways, and the services they find useful will be those that match their learning style. Some rely on their intuition to guide them and take in new information as they find it. Others consciously seek out new information in an organized, systematic fashion. Some may use their sense of spirituality to make meaning and make changes. Others may use ritualized practices that are part of their religious or cultural orientation to accommodate and learn new roles. Social workers have to be aware of these different styles (Belenky et al. 1996) and adjust the pace and content of help they offer accordingly. An individual's learning style is related to where they are developmentally (see chapter 12). As a helper, it is important to know when to be concrete, when to generalize, when to draw on your own experience, and when to bring in that of others, as well as how to involve learners themselves in the very process of learning (Elbow 1973).

THE IMPORTANCE OF SOCIAL SUPPORT

Help for the bereaved is often couched in the language of support. It is essential to explore what we mean by support. The availability of connection and care makes it easier to learn and change, and to use the help that is available (Belle 1989; Sandlar et al. 1989; Silverman 1994, 2000; Vachon and Stylianos 1993). These are components of what we call social support. Support is a complicated concept that it is essential for all life to flourish. We are social creatures, and the need for others is essential to human life. To deal with the various vicissitudes and stresses of living, we must acknowledge the importance of relationships and the interdependencies among people that make a meaningful life possible.

In many ways, support is also synonymous with what we mean by help. While the nature of the support needed may change over time, the underlying need for support is constant. Cobb (1976) defined support as information leading people to believe that they are cared for, loved, esteemed, and valued. Stylianos and Vachon (1993) define support as a transactional process, requiring a fit between the donor and the needs of the recipient, and the particular circumstances of each.

Feeling supported is the result of being involved in a network with others with whom it is possible to communicate and with whom one shares a sense of mutual obligation. When people feel supported, they feel that they are being treated in a personal way, that they are talking to people who speak the same language, who offer suggestions about what to do, offer feedback about what is happening, and provide material help (Caplan 1976). Support is more than simply acknowledging that someone is having a difficult time. It also provides concrete things that can be helpful as well as new learning opportunities.

The availability of support, which means the availability of others, seems to be correlated with adaptive behavior. Recent research has demonstrated that support mediates stress and facilitates effective coping (Sandlar et al. 1989; Stroebe and Schut 2001; Folkman 2001). Adaptive behavior is the result of coping effectively with the stress so that it is possible to carry on with life. Some maladaptive behavior that can be dysfunctional is based on the nature of the stress (Belle 1989; Gottlieb 1981; Folkman 2001). Folkman (2001) notes that it is not possible to understand the value of support without looking at the context in which it occurs and the responses of the recipients.

She suggests assessing the social network in which the stress occurs and the available support within that network. A focus on the social network identifies actors in the network, their core relationships to each other, how they interact, and what help they provide (Gottlieb 1981). It also brings to the fore the compatibility of the learning styles of the bereaved and the support offered.

Folkman (1997) and Folkman and Moskowitz (2000) found that recipients of help who had a more positive approach to life and an acceptance of their need for assistance were better able to use the support offered after the death from AIDS of someone close to them. This is very similar to Antonovsky's concept of coherence, discussed earlier. There is a need to identify not only the actors in the situation but also their resources, attitudes toward help from others, and ability to respond to their own needs and the needs of others.

NEEDED HELP: CHANGES WITH TIME

This section matches the needs of the bereaved to appropriate helpers in the first months after the death. Shortly after a death, practical assistance may be most important, sustaining mourners so that they can survive through the first months and even the first year. The key helpers at this time may be family, friends, the funeral director, and clergy. A funeral, or an appropriate plan for the disposal of the body, has to be arranged, people have to be notified of the death, and the family has to prepare to be involved in what they consider appropriate religious and cultural rituals surrounding the death. In this context, again as a helper, it is important to ask the bereaved what traditions and practices guide the disposal of the body and their behavior at this time.

Help from family and friends is informal and spontaneous, and often responds on the spot to what is happening. These informal helping networks make it possible for the family to get through the first months. During this period mourners, still quite numb, often give the impression that they are fine. Because at this time most mourners do not in fact feel very coherent, their appearances can be deceiving. The most meaningful help is from those who can look beyond this surface impression and offer concrete help in meeting the family's daily needs, providing food, attending to the needs of various family members and generally functioning as "gofers" as they are needed. This can include making phone calls and helping implement funeral arrangements. Having familiar faces around can be very comforting. Each family has its own culture and traditions that dictate their expectations of support from others. In the same way, friends and nonbereaved family have their own sense of obligation about the importance of helping at this time. For example, in many communities—for example, Jewish or African American—it is understood, and sometimes ritually prescribed, that family and friends will be there to offer support and care. Some of these traditions have been transformed or lost as people are influenced by the larger American community, where the emphasis is on respecting people's privacy and keeping clear boundaries between those who are helping and the recipients. Even in the latter community, it is not that support or care is not available, but that it is offered with other constraints on what is considered appropriate.

One of the problems created by family and friends is their wish to make the mourners feel better. People are most helpful when they can just listen and try to hear what the bereaved are saying. Family and friends may benefit from receiving copies of the pamphlets and other written material that the family has received from, for example, the hospice or the funeral director to help them understand the bereavement process. The social worker, as consultant and collaborator, if present can help educate the family and friends to enhance the help they offer. Talking about the deceased may or may not be something the bereaved want to do. Friends and nonbereaved family members can educate the social worker about the traditions and customs that frame the bereaved's behavior. Some cultures value talking; others do not. In some cultures, especially the women, may wail or pull out their hair (Parkes et al. 1997). Most behavior at this time is reflexive, and for many this period is very vague in their memory. Most mourners are somewhat numb and the full meaning of the death has not become real for them. The bereaved cannot necessarily talk about their feelings in any depth, or with any perspective at that point in time.

Even if a death was anticipated, help is needed to notify family and friends about the funeral. Announcing an unanticipated death can be most difficult. When there are dependent children, telling them about the death is one of the most difficult things a parent, already experiencing a good deal of stress, has to do. Parents often need help in explaining to the children what has happened. They may have rehearsed some of this with the hospice social worker. However, when the death is sudden, they may have an even more difficult time. This needs to be done in a direct manner in language that is responsive to the child's ability to understand. Taking a child to the funeral is something that should be worked out with the child and with the clergy and funeral director, all of whom can help make it comfortable for the child.

Concrete assistance that helps the family maintain a sense of care and continuity is the kind of help most often provided by family and friends. Families need to eat, and bringing meals to a newly bereaved family may be just what they need immediately after the death. People may have difficulty functioning during this period. If there are dependent children, their needs cannot be put on hold. Offering to play with the children, or to baby-sit, can be very helpful. Again, this kind of help comes from other family members or friends whom the children know (Silverman 2000).

With support, people can often find their own solutions. For example, a widow described her sister's help: "My sister called every day the first month. She and a friend would come by occasionally and take me out for coffee and just let me talk. We talked about my fears of making it alone without my husband, we talked about my husband. I needed to work and they helped me work out how I could manage a job, a home and have some energy left over for my children. They were surprised after a while at my own ideas about what to do. I didn't know this part of me existed."

Being busy with other things can be very helpful. For many mourners, going to work is not only an economic necessity but also serves as a diversion. Going to school can serve the same purpose for children. Teachers and school personnel are a central part of a child's ongoing life and always part of children's helping network. In the lower grades, more often than not, children appreciate some recognition of what happened. Some schools have crisis teams to help staff and students deal with a death immediately after it happens. Often there is a community service that will provide consultation to the school when a sudden or traumatic death occurs. When hospice is involved, the social worker may already have a relationship with the school and can collaborate in helping the family get the appropriate support from it. Often the school is unaware that a death has occurred. As a social workers helping the family this is something that should be discussed with the children and their parent(s) to decide if, how, and when to inform the school.

HELP FROM CLERGY AND FUNERAL DIRECTORS

Rarely is there a funeral in this country that does not involve a funeral director. When the family has been served by hospice, often the staff work closely with funeral directors to help families make plans for the funeral (Weeks and Johnson 2000). In the period immediately after the death, many families find that the funeral director is an unexpected source of help. Funeral directors often distribute pamphlets on grief and on community resources for the bereaved. While families may not be ready to take in this information at the funeral, they have it when they are ready. Some funeral homes provide aftercare programs (Weeks and Johnson 2000) that are staffed by a social worker or other mental health professional or an experienced bereaved person who reaches out to those the funeral home has served. These programs can meet the need for counseling and for group support and can provide other services the family may need.

While the death may raise questions for the bereaved about aspects of religious theology, rarely is there a funeral where a clergyperson does not officiate. Religious traditions and rituals can be very important sources of comfort and support, regardless of whether or not the family is affiliated with a faith community. These rituals and traditions can give life some order in this chaotic time (Cook and Wimberly 1983; Gilbert 1993; Bouman 1993; Blackwell and Stern 2001; Brener 2001). Members of the church, mosque, or synagogue may also offer other kinds of help. At this stage, these tend to focus on the very concrete needs of the family. The "casserole brigade" organized from the bereaved's faith community or from the neighborhood can be a very real source of support, providing the family with food and helping them feel connected to their community.

Clergy can be very effective in providing support and being there to listen. However, members of the clergy are not necessarily exempt from feeling uncomfortable in dealing with a death. Just as sometimes neighbors or friends seem to stay away or avoid conversations about the person who died, so do clergy. Clergy too may need help with understanding what people are going through, to help them clarify their role, as provider of support and in helping the bereaved make sense of this death and death in general as part of the human condition. Clergy can also be helpful in developing programs in which members of their congregations can be available to help the newly bereaved in their congregation. Help can be one on one or in groups that bring the bereaved together to talk about their concerns. Some faith communities hire social workers to facilitate such groups, whereas others use trained volunteers.

HEALTHCARE PROFESSIONALS

The bereaved often experience problems with sleeplessness or lack of appetite. They may have little energy and, in general, lack a sense of well-being. With these symptoms they often turn to their physicians for help. Physicians may also need to be educated about the nature of bereavement and community resources that might help their grieving patients. Physicians often quickly prescribe sedatives or psychotropic drugs to help the bereaved cope with the physical tension and pain they are experiencing. In the short run these drugs may be very helpful, but over time physician needs to understand the fullness of the bereavement process and what other assistance is needed. They need to be aware of other resources in their communities. Some permit placing of program announcements and pamphlets about a program in their waiting room.

For those who were served by hospice, the contact does not end with the death. Families often appreciate this continuity. Hospice is mandated to provide bereavement services for one year following the death to families they have served (Lattanzi-Licht et al. 1998). Many hospices' bereavement programs are staffed by trained volunteers who visit the bereaved or reach out to them on the phone. Often the social worker supervises these volunteers. Some hospices offer time-limited individual counseling for their constituents. Some hospices send out information packets about bereavement; others offer support groups that reach out to the bereaved including those not served by the hospice. Given the specialized expertise of their professional staff, hospice often is a resource to their larger community as well.

It is becoming a common practice for families to seek out or be referred for mental health counseling. If people are still numb from the impact of the loss, this may be premature, and not a good time to start a new relationship. They may not yet be able to articulate how they feel or reflect on what is happening to them. Timing may be very important in how the bereaved use this type of service.

AFTER A WHILE, OTHER HELPERS ARE NEEDED

The bereaved often continue to need help for an extended period of time. Over time the numbness lifts, feelings become clearer, and the pain more palpable. Most family and friends, while still available, return to their own lives. Often family and friends begin to wonder how long this grief is going to last. Both they and the mourners begin to realize that they may not be able to meet the continuing needs of the bereaved.

Hospice bereavement programs are time-limited, mandated by law for one year. How extensive they are depends on the economic and staff resources of the hospice. It may overextend hospice resources to try to meet the needs of the bereaved in all the families they serve. As a result, hospice has begun to consider limiting their services to those who seem to be having the greatest difficulty. They are testing out various measures to identify those of their constituents who might be at greatest risk for making a poor adjustment to the death. They can then focus their attention on these families and provide less intense services to those with lesser needs. The dilemma is identifying those at risk. Relf (in press) reviews the literature on risk including the measures that have been developed and the research associated with them. Stroebe and Schut define a risk factor as "an aspect of personal behavior or lifestyle, an environment exposure or an inborn or inherited characteristic, which based on epidemiological evidence, is known to be associated with a health related condition considered important to pre-vent" (2001:350). Stroebe and Schut point to the methodological shortcomings of most research on risk factors. No definitive factors have been identified. They reviewed the research that considered personality traits, religiosity, gender, and age as variables associated with risk. Interpersonal variables such as available social support and kin-ship relationships have been considered as well. None of the studies seem able to reach a consensus. Relf (in press) noted that risk assessment and intervention have been conceptualized within a positivist paradigm that views the course of grief as predictable. An issue in assessing risk, which is a result of looking at grief in this linear model, in my view, is timing. When in the bereavement process is it appropriate to do such an assessment: two months, six months, or one year?

One key critical fact that puts a person at risk is a prior diagnosis of mental illness. C. M. Parkes, who pioneered the assessment of risk with the surviving families of those served at St. Christopher's Hospice in London, reminds us that "our ability to predict the course of grief will not be perfect. Too many unpredictable events and circumstances render such attempts very approximate" (1996:159). In addition there are those who are seen at risk who in the long run do well and others who are not identified as at risk who do not seem able to accommodate. Mourners can be in great pain for long periods of time but are not necessarily at risk. And, as noted earlier, there are always those we think we can help and who reject any efforts to ease their pain (Silverman 1987). Nonetheless, Parkes (1996) recommends this approach to max-imize the use of limited resources. It is important that the social work professional who has worked with the family prior to the death have input in the process of assessing risk, building on their clinical experience.

As the bereaved begin to realize that they need additional help, one of the dilemmas they face is in determining what kind of help they need and then finding this help in their community. Even counseling may not be sufficient to meet their various needs. In their role as counselors, social workers need to be aware of resources to complement the help they are already offering. Often a support group or a mutual help experience may be in order. These provide the opportunities for the bereaved to learn from each other. These are often listed in the local newspapers, libraries often have directories of services, and the Internet becomes a source of information as well. Hospice often is a community resource for information about other kinds of help.

It is not always easy to make a match between the needs of the bereaved and available services. There are good programs in various parts of the country that are not universally available in every community. Sometimes the bereaved themselves learn of these programs and approach a social work professional to help them develop a similar program in their community. The programs I discuss below can serve as models for the range of services that could be available in a given community. These programs provide new opportunities to facilitate the bereaved coping more effectively. The role of the social-work professional varies depending on the nature of the organization with which he or she is working. These programs for the bereaved can be found in freestanding agencies, a community center, or religious communities. They can be sponsored by an ongoing hospice or hospital. They can be part of national organization that has local chapters run by and for their members.

MUTUAL HELP:
BUILDING ON THE EXPERIENCE OF THE BEREAVED

Help offered by other bereaved people has a very special meaning to the bereaved. In groups and organizations of the bereaved, which I call mutual-help groups but that are more typically known as mutual-aid or self-help organizations, people who are grieving learn about the value of sharing their common experiences. Participants are provided with opportunities to learn new ways of coping or tricks of the trade—"This worked for me, maybe it would work for you?" Learning is easier when people speak the same language. In this situation, when someone says, "I understand," he or she really does. The bereaved no longer see themselves as the only ones with this experience. They see themselves reflected in the eyes of others. They no longer feel as isolated and vulnerable. There is an acceptance of each other's feelings and experiences. They provide each other with role models of what is possible. When the newly bereaved meet others who have survived a death, they get a sense of hope that they too can survive (Silverman 1977). In this way, their individual coping repertoires are expanded (Silverman 1978, 1980). Belenky and her colleagues (1997) observe that the learning in this context is made easier because of the collaboration that this setting encourages.

In a mutual-help setting, people learn how to live in an affirming manner in their new situation (Goffman 1963). There is always a mutuality that develops, so that participants move between roles, sometimes recipient and sometimes helper, in what is essentially a nonhierarchical setting (Borkman 1990; Riessman and Carroll 1995; Powell 1994: Apfel and Telingator 1995).

Several settings provide opportunities for this kind of learning. In its simplest form, this helping takes place in the informal exchanges of daily life as we share with and learn from others with similar experiences. In mutual-help groups or organizations, learning is often formalized (Silverman 1978, 1980, 1988; Lieberman 1993). Support groups and centers for bereaved children also provide opportunities for the bereaved to learn from each other (Flemings and Adolph 1986; Silverman 2000; Sandler et al. 2003).

A mutual-help organization is usually an incorporated group whose founders joined together to solve a common problem. Many long-established organizations started out as local community groups. Often these groups began when people who had a common loss met, sometimes by accident, and discovered how helpful they were to each other (Silverman 1978). For example, Compassionate Friends, an organization for bereaved parents, began in the early 1970s in a clergyman's office in a pediatric hospital in England, where a group of parents came together to talk about their grief after the death of their children (Stephans 1972; Klass 1988).

In mutual-help organizations, people are members, not clients. Members control policy, administration, and the nature of the help offered. These organizations depend on the volunteer energy of their members, who pay dues and donate their time to meet some of the administrative needs of the organization. Members not only provide support but also problem-solve together. Each organization develops strategies for coping that are based on the experiences of its members. In this setting participants are not constrained by professional roles that put boundaries between the person who is helping and the person being helped. Helper and beneficiary are peers, but usually those designated as helpers are veteran members who have successfully dealt with their own issues. Members learn that often they help themselves by helping others. They often stay with the organization for longer periods of time than they originally expected, moving between the role of helper and recipient into new roles depending on their needs and the situation.

These organizations provide many kinds of help: information meetings; scheduled support groups, or regular meetings that provide opportunities to share; a newsletter, telephone network, or hotline. In addition to group meetings, members also help each other as needed through informal exchanges on the telephone. When appropriate, many organizations are involved in political action, such as, for example, lobbying their legislatures for laws concerning drinking and driving. Newsletters and magazines provide people who cannot attend meetings with new information and the opportunity to share. This printed material is very effective for those who are not ready for a group, are not joiners, or who do not have services available in their local community. Many groups now have webpages through which they provide information and resources to a greater number of people. Mutual-help organizations also sponsor educational programs for professionals to help them understand the needs of bereaved families.

Professionals can serve as consultants and advisors to mutual-help organizations, but they do not set policy or determine what the helping program should look like. Some groups hire professionals to facilitate a support group they sponsor. In this case, the professional works for the organization. The group screens potential facilitators to be sure they are appropriate and appreciative and understanding of the nature of mutual help. Some organizations also train their own members to facilitate support groups.

Sometimes professionals can serve as collaborators with bereaved people, helping to organize a program or giving potential organizers encouragement and support (Silverman 1978, 1979). A good collaborator knows how to help people (in this instance the bereaved) mobilize their own resources and develop their own ideas, and knows when to move aside as the members take over (Silverman 1980). The bereaved often develop expertise from their own experience so that they have a greater understanding and more knowledge about the subject than trained professionals who have no personal experience with grief. Professionals who work with the bereaved, especially in a mutual-help setting, need to recognize that they are the students (Silverman 1978, 1985; McGovern 1997). For example, traditional theories about "letting go" were challenged by members of mutual-help organizations. Their experience had taught them that they remained involved with the deceased. From listening to their stories, professionals learned that grief is a life-cycle event from which people do not recover but to which they accommodate (Silverman 1986; Klass 1988).

The Self-Help Group Sourcebook (White and Madara 2002) lists thirty-two organizations that deal with bereavement. There is an organization for people whose relatives died in airplane accidents; there are organizations for the widowed, for bereaved parents, for parents whose children died of Sudden Infant Death Syndrome, for family and friends of murder victims, for family and friends of victims of drunk-driving accidents, and for those whose relatives committed suicide. In addition, there are many organizations that focus on particular conditions, such as the Candlelighter's Childhood Cancer Foundation, the Children's Brain Tumor Foundation, the Cystic Fibrosis Association, and the Muscular Dystrophy Association. Survivors of the September 11, 2001, tragedy have formed a variety of organizations to meet their various needs. The largest organization for the widowed is the Widowed Person's Service, sponsored by the American Association of Retired Persons, which reaches out to the newly widowed. It also provides services for those who have been bereaved for some time.

The groups listed in this directory are national, with local chapters in various parts of the country, and usually have resources for helping interested people organize new chapters. This number does not represent the many local groups doing similar work that are known only to people in their own community. A church basement or member's living room is the most common meeting place for most local groups or local chapters of national organizations. Most mutual-help organizations operate on shoestring budgets. The lifetime of these groups can vary, since at a local level they subsist on the passion of their members. It is this passion that drives their efforts and can make a difference in their community and in the lives of others like themselves. It is the energy and commitment of these bereaved people that empowers them and that has also informed and driven much of the innovation that is taking place in the field of bereavement.

SUPPORT GROUPS

Support groups are another form of mutual help, but differ in many ways from mutual-help or self-help groups (Yalom et al. 1988). A support group is a group of approximately ten people with a leader who is typically a mental health professional. The group meets on a regular basis to discuss issues that group members have in common. In structure if not substance these groups are very similar to those described earlier in this book (see chapter 26), for people are near the end of their lives. These groups differ from mutual-help organizations in that the professional is in charge and the members are not responsible for convening or continuing the group. Usually they pay a fee to the leader or sponsoring agency. These groups are offered by mental health professionals in private practice or by the staff of hospitals and hospices. Some funeral homes are now offering aftercare services, including support groups. Faith communities also sponsor groups for their members.

The role of the facilitator in a support group is to make it possible for people to feel comfortable by creating a supportive and safe environment, to be sure that everyone is heard, and to encourage people to share and learn from each other by asking questions that open up discussion. For a support group to be effective, it needs to be not only a place for people to share their pain, but also a place where they can learn how to look at their situation differently, how to think differently about themselves, and how to make a shift in the way they meet their own needs. The facilitator needs to understand group dynamics in order to help the group coalesce and to ensure that everyone participates. Unlike mutual-help groups, the facilitator often screens participants to ensure that they can benefit from this kind of help. Facilitators look for participants who can utilize or learn to utilize the opportunity to talk with each other about their losses, and who are not handicapped by major emotional or psychiatric problems. However, a word of caution is in order. There are limitations in our ability to predict who does well in a group. Facilitators need to be open to opportunities to reevaluate decisions and make needed changes. Both adults and children have a basic resilience and ability to grow and change as they deal with their grief. They may change in unexpected ways when involved in a group and meet others with whom they can share their experience.

When enough potential participants are available to form separate groups, groups are often organized by type of death (violence as opposed to natural causes), stage in the life cycle (children or the elderly), specific disease, or role in the family. For example, in some ways widowed parents of dependent children and parents with dependent children, one of whose children has died, have very similar needs, in that they need to learn about how their children grieve and how this changes their parenting. On the other hand, their needs are very different; the widowed are dealing with being single parents, and couples whose child died are renegotiating their relationship to each other.

Support groups can be a very meaningful way of helping children and adolescents, as well as adults. When the support-group model is used with younger children, discussion is usually accompanied by art activities and play (Zambelli and DeRosa 1992; Bacon 1996; Fleming and Balmer 1991).

One of the main distinctions between types of support groups is that some are time-limited, while others are more open-ended. Bacon (1996) describes the merits of open-ended as opposed to time-limited groups. Open-ended groups, such as those described below in children's bereavement centers, allow new members to join as they go along. Sometimes bereavement services that are offered by hospice sponsor open-ended groups. Members join as they are eligible. These groups have the stability of the agency or organization behind them, and this sustains the group as well.

An open-ended group is well suited to helping people over a long period of time as they find a way of living with their pain and beyond it. Yet the facilitator has to be sure to help the group members empower themselves to grow and deal with all the changes in their lives, and not use the group as a way of staying in the same place. Occasionally participants can use the group as an opportunity to lick their wounds. They feel supported in their pain but do not move beyond it. One way of keeping the sense of movement in the group is for the leader to develop questions related to a problem that a group member is experiencing. Old members can be helpful in brainstorming with new members to help them find alternative coping strategies. This process can become a regular part of the group. At some point people may need to graduate or move on to a different sort of group. This is true in mutual-help organizations as well. In mutual-help organizations, one option is for members to move into the role of helper. In support groups, the option is to form a group that focuses on moving on.

Another model combines a support group with an educational session. This is appropriate to a time-limited group. Each meeting begins with a didactic lecture on a topic of immediate concern to the group, such as an overview of grief, understanding children's reactions to loss, living in a single-parent household, dating, going back to work, and managing your money. The last session is open and in part is a farewell party. After each lecture, there is a coffee break, and then the group breaks up into small groups of no more than ten people each. The next hour is a support group with a trained facilitator, preferably someone who has dealt with a personal loss. If the facilitator is a trained mental health professional, then the group is best co-led by a person who has been bereaved. In the groups, participants talk about whatever is on their mind. Addresses are always exchanged, and participants are encouraged to continue to meet on their own afterward. Members of these groups often become permanent parts of each other's support network.

Among professionals, there is some discussion about how frequently support groups should meet (Jordan and Ware 1997; Bacon 1996). In my experience, it makes sense to meet every other week. Participants need time to process what happens in the group. Because the immediate consequences of bereavement clearly extend over a much longer period of time than was once thought, it may be appropriate to extend the meetings to be available for more of this time. Jordan and Ware (1997) suggest another meeting six months after the group ends, so that people can touch base and see what has happened and what else may be needed. This may not be as necessary if the group has been meeting and doing some of this on its own.

Caserta and his colleagues (1999) developed a self-care program called Pathfinders for elderly widows and widowers that employed both education and support. This grew out of research conducted by Lund and Caserta (2002) that indicated the elderly did not have good self-care habits once their spouses died. They formed groups that met together weekly to learn about taking care of their health needs. Over time it turned into a support group and an ongoing mutual-help experience that continued long after the formal program was over.

CENTERS FOR GRIEVING CHILDREN

Centers for grieving children use many of the techniques found in mutual-help organizations and in support groups. These centers are either freestanding agencies or part of hospice program designed specifically to meet the needs of bereaved children and their families. Typically they are supported by their own fundraising efforts and primarily staffed by specially trained volunteers, many of whom have had experiences with personal loss (Fleming and Balmer 1991; Silverman 2000).

These centers are growing in number throughout the United States and abroad. Their programming is designed to facilitate a mutual exchange of support and information for children and for their parents (Brabant 1993). Most centers do not charge a fee for service. Participants are invited to make donations as they can. While activities are focused on children, all the programs provide a simultaneous support group for parents or the children's guardians.

Although there are many variations in the way these centers deliver services, almost all of them are modeled after the Dougy Center, in Portland, Oregon. The Dougy Center extends supportive services to children, parents, or surrogate caregivers who are responsible for the child. It also actively consults with schools, communities, and parents around crisis situations (Silverman 2000). The Dougy Center's formal program consists of biweekly group meetings. There are concurrent groups for both children and their parents or caregivers. These are open-ended groups, with members staying as long as they need to. Children report that one of the most valuable parts of their experience in centers like Dougy is that they realize that they are not the only one who has experienced the death of a family member. They feel less alone and less different from their peers. When children decide that they are ready to move on, the closing circle that ends each session becomes a ceremony for saying good-bye. A child who is leaving is presented with a small pouch full of polished stones, with one unpolished stone. This rough stone is a reminder that there are always difficult moments in life.

In addition to its program serving the Portland community, the Dougy Center has developed the National Center for Grieving Children and Families. This center provides training for people who want to set up programs in their own communities, both in the United States and abroad. It publishes the *National Directory of Children's Grief Services*, which provides information on the location of programs in various parts of the United States and Canada; a skills-development training manual for volunteers; an activity manual; and handbooks about children whose family member was murdered or who committed suicide. It also has a series of guides for school administrators and teachers. Fees from training courses and sale of books help maintain the National Center for Grieving Children and Families. There are more than 150 similar centers throughout the United States.

For those of us who look for research evidence that supports the efficacy of this type of program for bereaved children and their families, the findings of Sandler and his colleagues (in press) do just that. In a carefully controlled experiment, they demonstrated the long-term value for bereaved children and their surviving parent of participating in a program based on the Dougy Center model. The outcome measures were extensive. Suffice it to say for now, compared to control families, both parents and children who participated in the program had a sustained sense of well-being and coped more effectively with day-to-day problems, while parenting skills were enhanced (see chapter 33).

PSYCHOLOGICAL AND FAMILY-CENTERED
COUNSELING AND THERAPY

Some bereaved people need more intensive care that focuses on their individual psychological problems. These problems often existed prior to the death, and the death may have brought them to the surface and exacerbated them. Sometimes it was the deceased who provided the stability to the family that is now missing. Therapy can become an opportunity to look at conflicted, ambivalent, or negative aspects of the relationship to the deceased that may impede the way mourners cope with their grief. Because rarely is there a single mourner, a family focus may be called for (Shapiro 1994, 2001; Nadeau 1998).

Raphael and her colleagues (1993) describe the range of psychotherapeutic interventions that can be used in helping the bereaved. They suggest that even the best-trained therapist or counselor needs additional training about the nature of the bereavement process. Raphael and her colleagues remind us that in order to avoid pathologizing grief, counselors should focus on the effectiveness of the family's coping styles. They should look for the family's positive problem-solving capacity and flexibility. The counselor should see himself or herself as enhancing these qualities and not focus primarily on family deficits and on what family members cannot do. They also recommend that many of the techniques therapists would use with bereaved clients who have a clinical diagnosis need to be modified.

Some mental health professionals make a distinction between counseling and therapy (Worden 2001). Webb (2002) refers to "therapy" as a process of help conducted by a mental health professional and "counseling" as the process of help that is provided by religious leaders and educational personnel. The professional training determines what name is given to the help offered, but the content and the goals of help may be similar. Shapiro (1994) reminds us that the goal of help, for the bereaved, is to enhance people's ability to cope with their grief regardless of who the helper is or what training he or she has had.

Most of the therapeutic approaches described below are relationally based, focusing on the mourner's relationship to self, to others in the family, and to the deceased (Silverman 2000; Shapiro 2001). One technique that encourages development and change is narrative therapy, as suggested by White and Epston (1990). Developing narrative is a basic way in which people organize their life experiences in meaningful ways, helping people understand and respond adaptively to what is happening to them (Neimeyer and Stewart 1996; Innovations 2002). White and Epston (1990) focus on helping people "re-story or re-author" their lives as a way of dealing with the changes they are experiencing. They do this by systematically asking their clients questions, building one on the other to clarify what it is they are experiencing. In this process clients can touch the problem, hold it, dissect it, and have a conversation with it. This makes it easier to think differently about what is happening in their lives, discover ways of reframing the meaning of what is happening, and thus rewrite their story. This process eases the way to making a shift in their view of themselves and others with whom they interact. White emphasizes the importance of externalizing problems, so that people are not defined only by their bereavement and grief.

Seligman (1995), building on the work of Beck (1979), describes a technique for externalizing and stepping back from the problem. This approach is part of cognitive behavioral therapy. Fleming and Robinson (2001) recommend cognitive behavior therapy as an effective tool to assist the bereaved reconstruct meaning. They see it as useful in helping the bereaved negotiate and renegotiate over time the meaning of the loss, which would include visiting and revisiting their relationship to the deceased. Fleming and Robinson see this as following on suggestions made by Silverman and Klass (1996).

Seligman's approach can be particularly helpful to parents, for example, who need to understand and react more effectively to their children's needs. This technique can be used in individual or group sessions, with adults and with children. Seligman talks about how people's explanatory styles (another way of describing meaning-making) affect behavior and may need to change. He recommends teaching parents to look initially at what is happening in smaller segments. He describes what he calls an ABC process—Adversity, Belief, Consequence. By breaking up what is happening, parents can see that the fact that "my husband died" is an *Adversity* that may or may not lead to the child's life being ruined. Making the assumption that a child's life is going to be totally spoiled is based on what *Beliefs* the surviving parent holds about what will happen as a result of the death. One choice is for the parents to believe that this will lead to a total catastrophe. By examining their beliefs—for example, "I can't raise my child alone"—and the *Consequences* of this belief—"I am helpless, everything is falling apart"—they can then test if the consequences would be different with a different belief. Another way of looking at the issue might be, "This is a serious challenge," and the consequences of this belief might be, "I need to learn how to be a single parent." These techniques could work with many bereaved people. It can energize them as they recognize their ability to problem-solve. Finding new direction is easier as people see an event as more specific and less pervasive—"I can do things. We all hurt. I'm not alone, we help each other." By learning to reason in this way, it is easier to examine the consequences of a particular behavior, and to see that there are choices to make that did not seem apparent before.

CONCLUSION

Many models engage and involve the bereaved and match help to their needs. Ideally, in any community there should be a continuum of help, including informal support, mutual-help groups, support groups, individual counseling, and group and family psychotherapeutic interventions. Shapiro (1994) sees therapy as an additional resource in a pool of community resources. Most bereaved people find that participating in a mutual-help organization, a support group, or a bereavement center program is sufficient to meet their needs. The role of the social worker shifts from clinician to organizer in the community, helping to develop new resources and developing collaborations with the bereaved.

REFERENCES

American Association for Retired Persons. 1999. *Widowed Persons Service: Directory of Services for the Widowed in the United States and Canada.* Washington, DC: American Association for Retired Persons.

Antonovsky, A. 1979. *Health, Stress, and Coping.* San Francisco: Jossey-Bass.

Apfel, R., and C. Telingator. 1995. What can we learn from children of war? In *Forgotten Children of the AIDS Epidemic,* ed. S. Geballe, J. Gruendel, and W. Andiman, 107–121. New Haven, CT: Yale University Press.

Bacon, J. B. 1996. Support groups for bereaved children. In *Handbook of Childhood Death and Bereavement,* ed. C. A. Corr and D. M. Corr, 285–304. New York: Springer.

Beck, A. T. 1979. *Cognitive Therapy and Emotional Disorders.* New York: International Universities Press.

Belenky, M. F., L. A. Bond, and J. S. Weisenstock. 1997. *A Tradition That Has No Name: Nurturing the Development of People, Families, and Communities.* New York: Basic Books.

Belenky, M. F., B. Clinchy, N. Goldberger, and J. Tarule. 1996. *Women's Ways of Knowing.* New York: Basic Books.

Belle, D., ed. 1989. *Children's Social Networks and Social Supports.* New York: Wiley.

Blackwell, G., and H. Stern. 2001. Providing spiritual support to family caregivers. In *Caregiving and Loss: Family Needs, Professional Responses,* ed. K. J. Doka and J. D. Davidson, 233–246. Washington, DC: Hospice Foundation of American.

Boerner, K., and P. R. Silverman. 2001. Gender differences in coping patterns in widowed parents. *Omega: Journal of Death and Dying* 3(43): 201–216.

Borkman, T. 1990. Experiential, professional, and lay frames of reference. In *Working with Self Help,* ed. T. Powell, 3–30. Silver Springs, MD: National Association of Social Workers.

Bouman, J. 1993. Jimmy died, call the church. In *Death and Spirituality,* ed. K. J. Doka and J. Morgan, 363–378. Amityville, NY: Baywood.

Brabant, S. 1993. Successful facilitation of a children's support groups when conditions are less than optimal. *Clinical Sociology Review* 2:49–60.

Brener, A. 2001. *Mourning and Mitzvah: A Guided Journal for Walking the Mourners Path Through Grief to Healing.* Woodstock, VT: Jewish Lights.

Campbell, S., and P. R. Silverman. 1996. *Widowers: When Men Are Left Alone.* Amityville, NY: Baywood.

Caplan, G. 1976. Family as a support system. In *Support Systems and Mutual Help,* ed. G. Caplan and M. Killilea, 200–220. New York: Grune & Stratton.

Caserta, M. S., D. A. Lund, and S. J. Rice. 1999. A self care and health education program for older widows and widowers. *Gerontologist* 39:615–620.

Cobb, S. 1976. Social support as a moderator of life stress. *Psychosomatic Medicine* 38(5): 314.

Connor, S. R. 1997. *Hospice: Practice, Pitfalls, and Promise.* Washington, DC: Taylor & Francis.

Cook, J. A. 1988. Dad's double bind: Rethinking fathers' bereavement from a men's studies perspective. *Journal of Ethnography* 17(3): 285–308.

Cook, J. A., and D. W. Wimberly. 1983. If I should die before I wake: Religious commitment and adjustment to the death of a child. *Journal for the Scientific Study of Religion* 22(3): 222–238.

Doka, K. J., ed. 2002a. *Disenfranchised Grief: New Directions, Challenges, and Strategies for Practice.* Champaign, IL: Research Press.

———. 2002b. *Living with Grief: Loss in Later Life.* Washington DC: Hospice Foundation of America.

Elbow, P. 1973. *Writing Without Teachers*. New York: Oxford University Press.

Fleming, S., and R. Adolph. 1986. Helping bereaved adolescents: Needs and responses. In *Adolescence and Death*, ed. C. A. Corr and J. N. McNeil, 97–118. New York: Springer.

Fleming, S., and L. Balmer. 1991. Group intervention with bereaved children. In *Children and Death*, ed. D. Papadatou and C. Papadatos, 105–124. Washington, DC: Taylor & Francis.

Fleming, S., and P. Robinson. 2001. Grief and cognitive-behavior therapy: The reconstruction of meaning. In *Handbook of Bereavement Research: Consequences, Coping and Care*, ed. M. S. Stroebe, R. O. Hansson, W. Stroebe, and H. Schut, 647–669. Washington, DC: American Psychological Association.

Folkman, S. 1997. Positive psychological states and coping with severe stress. *Social Science and Medicine* 45:1207–1221.

———. 2001. Revised coping theory and the process of bereavement. In *Handbook of Bereavement Research: Consequences, Coping and Care*, ed. M. S. Stroebe, R. O. Hansson, W. Stroebe, and H. Schut, 563–584. Washington, DC: American Psychological Association.

Folkman, S., and J. T. Moskowitz. 2000. The context matters. *Personality and Social Psychology Bulletin* 26(2): 150–151.

Gilbert, R. 1993. *Finding Your Way After Your Parent Dies: Hope for Grieving Adults*. Notre Dame, IN: Ave Maria Press.

Goffman, E. 1963. *Stigma: Notes on the Management of Spoiled Identities*. Englewood Cliffs, NJ: Prentice-Hall.

Gottlieb, B. H., ed. 1981. *Social Networks and Social Support*. Beverly Hills, CA: Sage.

Jordan, J. R., and E. S. Ware. 1997. Feeling like a motherless child: A support group model for adults grieving the death of a parent. *Omega* 35(4): 361–376.

Klass, D. 1988. *Parental Grief: Solace and Resolution*. New York: Springer.

Lattanzi-Licht, M., J. J. Mahoney, and G. W. Miller. 1998. *The Hospice Choice: In Pursuit of a Peaceful Death*. New York: Fireside.

Lieberman, M. A. 1993. Bereavement self-help groups: A review of conceptual and methodological issues. In *Handbook of Bereavement: Theory, Research and Intervention*, ed. M. Stroebe, W. Stroebe, and R. O. Hansson, 411–426. New York: Cambridge University Press.

Lund, D. A., and M. S. Caserta. 2002. Facing loss alone: Loss of a significant other in later life. In *Living with Grief: Loss in Later Life*, ed. K. J. Doka, 207–223. Washington, DC: Hospice Foundation of America.

McGovern, M. G. 1997. Bereaved families of Ontario. Personal communication.

Nadeau, J. W. 1998. *Families Making Sense of Death*. Thousand Oaks, CA: Sage.

Neimeyer, R., and A. E. Stewart. 1996. Trauma, healing, and the narrative emplotment of loss. *Family in Society* 77(6): 360–375.

Osterweis, M., F. Solomon, and M. Greene, eds. 1984. *Bereavement: Reactions, Consequences, and Care*. Washington, DC: National Academy Press.

Parkes, C. M. 1996. *Bereavement: Studies of Grief in Adult Life*. New York: Routledge.

Powell, T. 1987. *Self-Help Organizations and Professional Practice*. Washington, DC: National Association of Social Workers.

Raphael, B., et al. 1993. Counseling and therapy for the bereaved. In *Handbook of Bereavement: Theory, Research and Intervention*, ed. M. Stroebe, W. Stroebe, and R. O. Hansson, 427–435. New York: Cambridge Univ. Press.

Reiss, D. 1981. *The Family's Construction of Reality*. Cambridge, MA: Harvard University Press.

Relf, M. Forthcoming. Risk assessment and bereavement services. In *Palliative Care Nursing: Principles and Evidence for Practice*, ed. S. A. Payne, J. Skilbeck, and C. Ingleton. Buckingham, UK: Open University Press.

Riessman, F., and D. Carroll. 1995. *Redefining Self Help: Policy and Practice*. San Francisco: Jossey-Bass.

Sandlar, E., P. Miller, J. Short, and S. Wolchik. 1989. Social support as a protective factor for children in stress. In *Children's Social Networks and Social Support*, ed. D. Belle, 277–307. New York: John Wiley.

Sandler, I. N., T. S. Ayers, S. A. Wolchik, et al. 2003. The family bereavement program: Efficacy evaluation of a theory-based prevention program for parentally bereaved children and adolescents. *Journal of Consulting and Clinical Psychology* 71:587–600.

Seligman, M., K. Reivich, L. Jaycox, and J. Gillham. 1995. *The Optimistic Child*. Boston: Houghton Mifflin.

Shapiro, E. R. 1994. *Grief as a Family Process: A Developmental Approach to Clinical Practice*. New York: Guilford.

——. 2001. Grief in interpersonal perspective: Theories and their implications. In *Handbook of Bereavement Research: Consequences, Coping and Care*, ed. M. S. Stroebe, R. O. Hansson, W. Stroebe, and H. Schut, 301–327. Washington, DC: American Psychological Association.

Silverman, P. R. 1978. *Mutual Help Groups and the Role of the Mental Health Professional*. Washington, DC: National Institute of Mental Health.

——. 1980. *Mutual Help: Organization and Development*. Beverly Hills, CA: Sage.

——. 1982. The mental health consultant as a linking agent. In *Community Support Systems and Mental Health*, ed. D. E. Biegel and A. I. Naparstek, 238–249. New York: Springer.

——. 1986. *Widow to Widow*. New York: Springer.

——. 1987. Widowhood as the next stage in the life cycle. In *Widows: North America*, ed. H. Z. Lopata, 171–190. Durham, NC: Duke University Press.

——. 1988. In search of new selves: Accommodating to widowhood. In *Families in Transition: Primary Programs That Work*, ed. L. A. Bond and B. Wagner, 200–219. Newbury Park, CA: Sage.

——. 1994. Helping the bereaved through social support and mutual help. In *A Challenge for Living*, ed. I. B. Corless, B. B. Germino, and M. A. Pittman, 241–257. Boston: Jones and Bartlett.

——. 2000. *Never Too Young to Know: Death in Children's Lives*. New York: Oxford University Press.

Silverman, P. R., and D. Klass. 1996. Introduction: What's the problem? In *Continuing Bonds: New Understandings of Grief*, ed. D. Klass, P. R. Silverman, and S. L. Nickman, 3–27. Bristol, PA: Taylor & Francis.

Silverman, P. R., and J. W. Worden. 1992. Children's reactions to the death of a parent in the early months after the death. *American Journal of Orthopsychiatry* 62(4): 93–104.

Stephens, S. 1972. *Death Comes Home*. New York: Morehouse-Barlow.

Stroebe, W., and H. Schut. 2001. Risk factors in bereavement outcome: A methodological and empirical review. In *Handbook of Bereavement Research: Consequences, Coping and Care*, ed. M. S. Stroebe, R. O. Hansson, W. Stroebe, and H. Schut, 349–371. Washington, DC: American Psychological Association.

Stylianos, S. K., and M. L. S. Vachon. 1993. The role of social support in bereavement. In *Handbook of Bereavement: Theory, Research, and Intervention*, ed. M. Stroebe, W. Stroebe, and R. O. Hansson, 397–410. New York: Cambridge University Press.

Vachon, M. L. 1979. Identity change over the first two years of bereavement: Social relationships and social support. Ph.D. diss., York University.

Webb, N. B., ed. 2002. *Helping Bereaved Children: A Casebook for Practitioners*. New York: Guilford.

Weeks, O. D., and C. Johnson, eds. 2000. *When All the Friends Have Gone: A Guide for Aftercare Providers*. Amityville, NY: Baywood.

White, B. J., and E. J. Madara. 2002. *The Self-help Group Sourcebook: Your Guide to*

Community and Online Support Groups. 7th ed. Cedar Knolls, NJ: American Self-Help Clearing House.

White, M., and D. Epston. 1990. *Narrative Means of Therapeutic Ends.* New York: Norton.

Worden, J. W. 2001. *Grief Counseling and Grief Therapy: A Handbook for the Mental Health Practitioner.* 3d ed. New York: Springer.

Yalom, I. D., et al. 1988. Bereavement groups: Techniques and themes. *International Journal of Group Psychotherapy* 38(4): 419–446.

Zambelli, G. C., and A. P. De Rosa. 1992. Bereavement support groups for school age children: Theory, intervention, and case examples. *American Journal of Orthopsychiatry* 62(4): 484–493.

30

END-OF-LIFE BIOETHICS IN CLINICAL SOCIAL WORK PRACTICE

SUSAN GERBINO AND SHELLEY HENDERSON

ETHICS IS a branch of philosophy that concerns itself with human conduct and moral decision making. Ethics are principles that guide people in deciding what is right or wrong. It is not primarily concerned with getting people to do what they believe is right, but rather with helping them decide what is right (Arras and Steinbock 1995). Ethics asks whether an act, a social policy, or a practice can be morally justified. Often there are no clear answers to ethical problems.

End-of-life care is often fraught with ethical dilemmas—the need to choose between competing "goods" and competing "rights." A dying patient wants to stay at home to die; his or her family feels they can no longer manage the patient at home. Because we work with patients and families as our unit of care, both have claims to be cared for in the "right" way. Client self-determination and protection of life are core social-work values. These values may collide when a dying patient wants to kill himself.

Ethical theories are frameworks within which we can reflect on and evaluate the acceptability of our actions. The assumption is that ethical theory, codes of ethics, and ethical analyses are all tools that will help us make progress on these difficult issues (see chapter 9).

In the United States, much of the discussion around end-of-life decision making has been framed within by the context of the bioethics movement. American bioethics has emphasized a small cluster of middle-level values that are considered when analyzing ethical dilemmas. These values include autonomy, justice, beneficence, and nonmaleficence. These ethical principles frame and guide our discussion when considering ethical dilemmas. None of these principles trumps the others—there is no lexical ordering of the principles. Rather, each is considered, but when there is conflict between principles an attempt is made to make the decision through weighing the costs and benefits of each.

To this theory must be added our social work perspective. Social work considers the society in which the client lives and the history of the client's relationships, both with people and with institutions. Perhaps at no other time does life review predominate more than at end of life. Dying is often the catalyst for patients and families to look back at their lives, their accomplishments, their regrets, their ethical beliefs, and their values. Decision making at the end of life inevitably asks both patients and families to look at their ethical beliefs and to assess their values. It usually challenges the helpers to look at their own ethical beliefs and values as well.

THE PRINCIPLES

The principles of autonomy, beneficence, justice, and nonmaleficence are guides to analyzing complex cases. Autonomy is defined as "the exercise of your sense of values, independence, personal history, life, principles of behavior—who you are and how you exercise of your sense of values, independence, personal history, life, principles of behavior—who you are and how you live" (Dubler and Nimmons 1992:90). This definition encompasses all of the values, life experiences, and influences that make the individual unique. The social work value of self-determination is derived from autonomy. Informed consent is based on respect for autonomy. Its foundation lies in legal thought, which defends an individual's right to "determine what is done with his own body" (Arras and Steinbock 1995:44). A person must receive adequate and truthful information to be able to decide what to allow to be done to his or her body.

Beneficence is a fundamental tenet of medical practice derived from the Hippocratic Oath: the mandate to do no harm. Nonmaleficence is the command not to inflict pain.

The principle of justice involves concerns about equal distribution of resources and equal access to care. Justice issues bring attention to the risks and burdens of care and concerns for fairness, the rights of patients and clinicians and the duties of the corresponding parties. Justice issues involve the allocation of scarce resources. Medical futility becomes an issue when an intervention is deemed to produce no benefit and when the burden of the intervention outweighs the benefit.

As we strive to do what is best for our clients, we often grapple with ethical and clinical tensions. Edna S. is a client who presented us with many ethical/clinical dilemmas. At the crux of many decisions about end-of-life care is who decides. Deciding what is best for Edna S., a woman with a lifelong history of mental illness, is a complicated process. Embedded in our discussion of Edna S. are the concepts of autonomy and its corollaries, informed consent and self-determination. Decisional capacity, medical futility, and beneficence/nonmaleficence also come into play. To this we add the client's life narrative and the intersection of the client's world and the healthcare world.

CASE EXAMPLE

Edna S. was a sixty-five-year-old woman with breast cancer diagnosed in July 1991. At the time of diagnosis she was treated with surgery and chemotherapy. She had further chemotherapy in 1996 and in 1998. She was diagnosed with bone, liver, and nervous system disease in 2000. She was admitted to hospice on July 30, 2001.

Complicating her life and her cancer diagnosis was her lifelong diagnosis of schizophrenia—schizoaffective disorder with paranoia. At the time of admission, her psychiatric RN, whom she had known for seventeen years; the patient's brother; the hospice RN; and the hospice social worker were present. The patient had a sister and a mother who lived in the Caribbean. For health and financial reasons, they were unable to come to this country from their homeland to care for her. Her brother, who lived nearby, refused the role as the primary caregiver and healthcare agent. He was a loving and devoted brother but had long ago stopped trying to influence or take any responsibility for Edna S.'s behavior and care.

Although the patient's affect was bizarre and exaggerated, she was decisive and clear in her desire to choose hospice. She wanted to sign a DNR and was able to state without prompting that she did not want to be kept alive on machines. But her most urgent request was to stay home to die and not to be hospitalized. She was clearly psychotic and paranoid in certain realms of her experience, but she gave every indication that she was aware of her prognosis and was capable of making choices for her care. On the other hand, she reported in detail her paranoid struggle with a stalker who plagued her in the night. She frequently roamed the area outside her apartment and was a bother to her neighbors. She was well known to the police because of her neighbors' frequent complaints.

She had been able to live alone in the community because of the support she had received from the professionals in the community: the local visiting nurse service, the Department of Social Services, and the outpatient unit of a psychiatric hospital. Professionals who had known her for years agreed to continue to follow her professionally and advised that the hospice team accept her behavior. She could not change, and to ask her to try would simply invite an escalation of her symptoms. It was not difficult to predict that she would likely become more psychotic as her illness progressed, especially as the symptoms of her liver disease became an issue.

The ethical dilemma for the team was that she was a marginally controlled psychotic person with limited decisional capacity, without an advocate from her family or friends to serve as her healthcare proxy. Her loving but geographically distant family had been exhausted by her lifelong struggle with mental illness. Her only responsible advocates seemed to be the professionals who had long been her support.

Initially the patient was independent in her personal care. She was ambulatory but spent most of her time in bed watching TV. She was, however, unable to follow the advice of the team throughout her stay on the hospice program. She needed to assert control over every aspect her care, and when limits were set she became paranoid. She was unable to comply with medications, refused home health aid, and, in general, was a management and safety problem for the hospice team. As her physical condition deteriorated she became bedbound, and her mental state deteriorated due to her impaired liver function. Her acting-out behavior became almost impossible for the team to manage. She split the team with reports of deprivation from her nurse and her good reports about the understanding and empathic stance of the social worker. Until the splitting was recognized and interpreted to the team members, the effect was very disruptive.

Edna began to talk about resuming her chemotherapy. She called her primary doctor, who agreed to give her another course of chemotherapy, but she missed every appointment she scheduled. In the past, chemotherapy had exacerbated her psychotic symptoms. The deterioration of her mental state forced the team and other professionals to ask whether it would be possible to manage her care at home. Without family support, she needed twenty-four-hour home health care. But home health aides are not allowed to dispense medications if the patient is not self-directing. She would require the care of a licensed practical nurse in order to stay in her home.

At this point the ethics committee of the hospice convened. The psychiatrist and psychiatric nurse that had followed her for seventeen years were present. The decision was made to attempt to enlist the help of the family. Medically, it was clear that further chemotherapy was contraindicated because her condition was terminal. The committee recognized the option of admitting her to a terminal care facility, but she was still aware enough of her surroundings that she would have to be sedated. Moving her was clearly contrary to her life goal, which was to live in her own apartment in spite of her lifelong struggles. For this reason, the committee decided to do all that was possible to keep her at home. If the family could not help out, the hospice would provide continuous care with a licensed practical nurse for as long as they could. The goal was to make every effort to keep the patient at home until she died.

The principles of bioethics are dynamic and overlapping. They are stated as absolutes, but they are ideally practiced with a profound respect for all of the individuals involved, patient and professional. Therefore, the concept of autonomous decision making does not exist without the two moral rules of informed consent and truth telling (Levine 2001). Informed consent requires that the professional have an adequate understanding of the patient and be able to explain truthfully the treatment options available to them. The layperson cannot make treatment decisions without expert advice. Truth telling is as important for end-of-life decisions as at any other time. Fearful of taking away hope, medical professionals frequently struggle over advising when aggressive treatment should end and palliative treatment should begin. Without this courageous move, many patients and families are unable to access the supports, medical, emotional, and economic, that are available in palliative and end-of-life care.

Edna S. was clear that she wanted to die at home—a desire that would allow her to exercise her autonomy. She was also clear that she wanted as little interference in her day-to-day living as possible. This included her refusal of home health-aide services. She managed her fear of loss of control through attempts to split the hospice team. Although she was clear about her prognosis, she held out the hope that chemotherapy might give her more time. Her primary doctor was unable to tell Edna S. that the chemotherapy held little hope and was contraindicated at this time. He was concerned about her psychiatric condition and did not want to refuse her. Edna S. was herself ambivalent about treatment because she had some awareness of the disorganizing effect it had on her life. This ambivalence kept her from following through with the treatment, though perhaps the option of treatment was all she needed to maintain her fragile sense of self. As her medical illness progressed and she became less able to direct her life, the question of decisional capacity, an essential component of autonomy, was raised, and ultimately the ethic of care overrode the ethic of self-determination.

DECISIONAL CAPACITY

The right to determine one's medical care, even when those decisions may be unwise, is part of the principle of autonomy. However, autonomy rests on the presumption that the patient is competent. Because only a court has the ability to decide competency, many decisions at the end of life rest on the concept of decisional capacity.

Assessing decisional capacity at any time, but especially at the transition to end-of-life care, is a subtle and complex process. This assessment frequently requires balancing the emotional demands and pressures of the family to shield the patient from upset and the truth. It also requires the ability to make an adequate evaluation of the patient's decisional capacity. We are all, if nothing else, human. As a result none of us is truly autonomous nor are we capable of completely comprehending all of the risks or benefits of all treatment options. Yet, the principles of bioethics serve as a moral guide for the professional and should be followed as closely as possible.

Decisional capacity, according to Lo (2000:82), requires that

1. The patient is capable of making and communicating a choice.
2. The patient is capable of appreciating the medical situation and prognosis; the nature of the recommended care; alternative courses of care; and the risks, benefits and consequences of each alternative.
3. Decisions are consistent with the patient's values and goals.
4. Decisions do not result from delusions.
5. The patient uses reasoning to make a choice.

Ideally, the assessment of decisional capacity should be made over time. However, for many situations, a quick assessment in a detailed interview is required. A skilled social-work professional with good interviewing skills and experience at assessing decisional capacity should be able to make a determination about whether the patient understands her illness and prognosis. The interviewer should certainly be able to discuss advance directives and execute a healthcare proxy if one is not in place. More difficult is the discussion of DNR. There is never a time when this discussion is not difficult.

The discussion of the DNR should be incorporated into a detailed interview. The topic is not to be rushed or coerced. If there is uncertainty or confusion, the patient should be allowed to postpone the discussion while being reminded that the topic will be raised again in the future. The discussion can be introduced gently by inquiring about advance directives in general. A discussion of the healthcare proxy and substituted decision making is useful to introduce the notion of the patient's physical instability. The interviewer, who is an expert, is most helpful when advising the patient of the benefits and burdens of resuscitation. Patients and families also need to be advised of the consequences of their choice. This includes letting a terminally ill home care patient know the reality and usually the futility of a call to 911. The most important component to this discussion is the interviewer's exquisite attention to the emotional and physical vulnerability of the patient. This discussion requires the utmost respect for the dying person and his or her family.

The interviewer should be expert in psychosocial and medical issues at the end of life. Informed consent requires an honest explanation of benefits or limitations of any program that the patient is considering. They must understand and agree to the program before any medical care even an initial examination can precede. It is essential that the medical experts explain that aggressive treatment now has more burdens than benefit. The physician who is referring to an end-of-life program should try to communicate the prognosis, but there is no guarantee that the patient can hear what is being imparted. Denial is a powerful and adaptive defense.

The first circle of decision making is directed to the patient (Dubler and Nimmons 1992). This model is the ideal, although it may not always be culturally appropriate. But there are events in life, both temporary and permanent, that may require others to decide on our behalf and in our stead. This second circle of decision making is the healthcare proxy. George Annas (1991) provides us with this definition: "The heart . . . of all proxy laws is the same: to enable a competent adult (the 'principal' to choose another person (the 'proxy' or 'agent') to make treatment decisions for him or her if he or she becomes incompetent to make them. The agent has the same authority to make decisions that the patient would have if he or she were still competent. Instead of having to decipher a document, the physician is able to discuss treatment options with a person who has legal authority to grant or with hold consent on behalf the patient. . . . The agent must make decisions that are consistent with the wishes of the patient, if these are known, and otherwise that are consistent with the patient's best interests."

The goal of the healthcare proxy is to enable the agent to assess, when the patient lacks the ability to decide, the medical benefit and burden of any intervention and to make a decision based on knowledge of the patient's wishes. The more restrictions placed on the agent, the more ambiguity may arise at a time of crisis. Healthcare proxies can and should be revised regularly based on the life cycle of the person and his or her healthcare reality. It is also extremely important to notify the person who has been appointed as proxy and inform him or her of the patient's wishes and needs.

The third level of decision making is based on the need for others to decide for us. When a patient is deemed to lack decisional capacity, temporarily or permanently, and has not appointed a healthcare proxy, someone must make decisions for him or her. The person deciding for the patient will be a stranger. The stranger is likely to be a member of the healthcare profession, a doctor whose philosophy of care is not known to the patient, but mainly someone who does not know the principles and values of the patient. It is at this point that the ethicist most likely will become involved.

The ethicist is aided by two different standards to guide in decision making. They are "substituted judgment," what we believe the patient would want based on knowledge of his or her values and information about his or her life. The other is the "best interest" standard. This standard is implemented when the patient is a stranger and there is no access to personal information. The medical personnel must do what they deem "best" for this victim or anyone in a similar situation (Dubler and Nimmons 1992:126; see chapter 36, this volume).

In this case, as in most discussions of capacity, we, the practitioners, struggled between the poles of autonomy and protection. The question before us was whether Edna S. had capacity. Schizophrenia is not conclusive evidence of incompetence or lack of capacity to make specific decisions to refuse, direct, or accept medical care. Edna S. was able to understand the presentation of the hospice program and make clear her wishes not to be placed on machines. Yet her mental illness made it difficult for her to make choices about her day-to-day care and to follow the hospice plan of care.

The hospice team also wanted to "do no harm." Moving Edna out of her home to a terminal care facility while still aware of her surroundings would have violated the principle of nonmaleficence. Placing a home health aide or licensed practical nurse in her home once she began actively dying seemed justified by the principle of beneficence—to take positive actions on behalf of a patient.

What if the patient had signed off the hospice program to pursue aggressive chemotherapy? Could she have she understood the prognosis? We knew that she had liver metastases, and we were aware that previous chemotherapy treatments had exacerbated her psychotic symptoms. Although we may have thought this an unwise medical decision, Edna clearly understood that she was dying. If she had decided to pursue treatment, the principle of self-determination would have prevailed.

Edna S. never followed through with revoking hospice and pursuing chemotherapy. Instead, she remained within the hospice program. When she began to decline, however, it became clear that her decisional capacity was failing. She had no healthcare proxy. She had a family who cared about her but had no power or influence with her. Essentially, she was an unstable, isolated individual living alone in the community.

Edna S. was lucky to be well represented by her community of professional caregivers. They knew her for seventeen years and therefore were aware of her values, her difficult history, and her wishes. Using this knowledge, the hospice employed the standard of substituted judgment. Her desire to remain in the community and out of the hospital was paramount. A decision was made to use the services of a licensed practical nurse who was legally able to administer medications. This enabled Edna S. to die in her own home—safe and well cared for.

As stated earlier, justice issues can include a discussion of scarce resources and the benefits and burdens of care. The case of Mr. F. looks at issues of justice and the limitations of hospice care in terms of the services they can provide and the issue of aggressive treatment.

CASE EXAMPLE

Mr. F was a seventy-year-old male who was admitted to hospice with a diagnosis of AML. Mr. F. and his wife of forty-three years were the parents of four daughters. All of their children are married and had their own children. They all lived close by and were very involved. The family was Irish and Roman Catholic. Mr. F. had been the head usher of his church for fifteen years. He was also the retired fire chief in his community.

The initial diagnosis was made two years before his admission to hospice. Mr. F. had a bone marrow biopsy, but attempts to find a match for a bone marrow transplant had failed. The patient had been receiving transfusions once a month. Mr. F. signed a DNR upon admission to hospice and but also stated clearly that he wished to continue to receive transfusions. He was aware that his condition was terminal, but made it clear that wished to continue live every day that he could. Both he and his wife were very direct and pragmatic people. They had a good relationship and had no problem talking to each other about life-and-death issues. In every aspect of the work, the hospice team gauged their interventions to changes in Mr. F.'s emotional and physical needs.

During Mr. F.'s medical treatment in hospice, his need for transfusions was honored. In the first two months on hospice, he received weekly transfusion with two units of packed cells every other week. In March (the third month), it became clear that the transfusions did not last the entire week.

At this point, the team began to talk to Mrs. F. about the possibility that there would come a time when the transfusions might not be offered because they clearly were not "holding him." These were difficult discussions. His physician gently confronted the couple with an ethical dilemma. He was conflicted about using this scarce resource with such poor results. The patient was very clear that he wanted blood for as long as it was offered. The patient hoped he would improve enough to qualify for some experimental treatment. The primary physician indicated that he would continue the weekly transfusions until the family told him to stop. Although the patient would never say stop, he was able to accept the weekly limit.

Mr. F. became too weak to travel in the car and had to be transported to the hospital by ambulance in order to receive the blood. Within two days after receiving the blood, it was clear that these two units would not hold him for the week. In a very powerful moment on what would be the hospice team's last visit, the nurse said softly to Mr. F. that it seemed that the blood was just not holding him. There was not a dry eye in the room, including Mr. F.'s. But his response was, "I know, but I just want you guys to try to get me through April." Mr. F. died at home two days later.

This case demonstrates the twin pulls of justice and patient autonomy. The principle of justice involves concerns about equal distribution of resources and equal access to care. The issue becomes an ethical dilemma when the resources in demand are scarce—that is, when demand exceeds supply. Whether the demand is for organs, respirators, intensive care beds, smallpox vaccine, or blood, the need is emotionally and physically urgent, and not all in need will be satisfied. At the end of life we encounter an added limit to scarce resources: medical futility, and sometimes age.

Medical centers frequently set an age limit beyond which someone will not be considered for transplant.

At the end of life we encounter the benefit and limitations of programs such as hospice and palliative-care facilities. As devoted as we are to hospice and palliative care, we recognize the restrictions that apply to both programs. In effect, the patient and family must balance their decisions between benefit and burden when they choose the program that is right for them for end-of-life care. These limitations are also justice issues. Programs for end-of-life care place limits on aggressive treatment for terminal care.

Indeed, the case was further compounded by the complexity of medical futility, as the efficacy of the transfusions was also in question. Mr. F. was realistic about his prognosis but hoped that he might escape it. He clearly had decisional capacity, knew that the transfusions were not holding him as they had, but yet he wanted them to continue. What is fair to Mr. F.? What is the responsibility of the physician and the hospice program regarding the allocation of scarce resources? In this case, a compromise was struck—a weekly limitation coupled with ongoing care and counseling from the hospice team.

However, cases may not always allow for compromise. The allocation of intensive care beds and requests for chemotherapy, when no longer indicated, are examples of more complex situations. In those situations, the patient's wishes may be overruled in favor of the principles of justice and nonmaleficence.

THE ROLE OF CULTURE

In the United States, much of the discussion around end-of-life decision making in bioethics has been framed by the principle of autonomy. Recently, ethicists have begun to consider the social and cultural contexts of decision making at the end of life and the significant power differential that exists between patients and their providers.

The evidence from medical anthropologists has shown that the norm in many cultures is that patients should not be told their diagnoses and prognoses when the prospects for survival or recovery are poor (Michel 1994). It is also true that many cultures, among them Asian and Pacific Islander, have a more collectivist than an individualist approach to decision making (Ewalt and Mokuau 1995; McLaughlin and Braun 1998).

The case of Sun Li L. illustrates some of the difficulties inherent in helping patients and family when the principle of patient self-determination collides with culture.

CASE EXAMPLE

Sun Li L. was a thirty-nine-year-old Korean woman with progressive and severe multiple sclerosis. She was diagnosed with MS in the middle of college, with progressive illness over the past twenty years. She was virtually quadriplegic (some hand movements remained), blind, and had lost bowel and bladder control. She required two weekly enemas and needed to wear diapers. She had frequent painful urinary tract infections.

Her blindness had progressed over the past three years, starting in one eye and eventually both eyes. She stated that she felt trapped and claustrophobic. Right before her admission to hospice, she had increasing abdominal pain, progressive difficulties with swallowing, and the onset of shortness of breath. She was in substantial chronic pain. She was treated with antidepressants and high-dose opiates with only moderate efficacy. She began to state that she wished to stop eating and drinking. She was admitted to the hospice program with the plan to treat her pain aggressively in an effort to improve quality of life. A psychiatric consultation was also recommended by the referring hospital.

Sun Li was a patient in a palliative-medicine program. She could no longer travel to the program, but the hospice team worked closely with her primary physician and her other healthcare providers so that she had the benefit of both palliative care and hospice.

Sun Li was single and had never married. She lived in an apartment in the same building as her mother. Medicaid provided a twenty-four-hour live-in home health aide. She had a good relationship with her family, which also included a younger sister and an older brother who lived on the West Coast. Her father was deceased. Before her illness disabled her completely, Sun Li had worked as successful model and backup singer for a famous rock star. Her mother owned a nightclub, and the patient stated that her twenties were a "fun time" for her. She felt that she and her mother were "best friends," having worked together professionally. Her mother was the healthcare proxy.

Sun Li was alert and oriented and extremely articulate about her condition and wishes. Her major goal was to be as comfortable as possible under the circumstances. Her swallowing problems, which made it difficult to take some medications, frightened her. She clearly articulated her desire to be comfortable, even if it meant being made drowsy or unconscious. She stated her desire to avoid artificial nutrition and hydration. She wanted to stop eating and drinking, but told the staff she could not do this because her family would not understand. She took small amounts of food and fluid for comfort. She expressed frustration at not being able just to stop eating.

The psychiatric evaluation concluded that she was substantially cognitively intact. She had positive self-esteem and positive family and community relationships. She had decisional capacity and was able to make her own informed medical decisions.

Sun Li was able to establish a good connection with the hospice RN, MSW, and chaplain. She began having longer periods of relief from her pain and despair. Her emotional condition closely followed her physical state. She enjoyed listening to music and visits with family and was involved with current events and TV. She looked forward to a visit from her brother and his family. Before the visit from the brother, she reiterated her wish for help with quality of life and no life-prolonging interventions. She continued to express her fear about how she would emotionally manage further physical deterioration.

When her brother arrived, he told Sun Li that he had researched a new clinical trial for MS at a New York City hospital. He made an appointment for his sister and rejected any discussion of palliative and/or hospice care. Neither the patient nor her mother or sister objected. They told the hospice team that his male gender made him the head of the family and that he had the authority to determine the patient's treatment. The patient indicated to the hospice social worker that she did not want further treatment, but she was also clear that she would not go against his wishes. The brother refused to meet with anyone from the hospice or palliative-care team.

The patient did go for the consultation and was rejected for the clinical trial because of her advanced disease. Her brother continued to research possible treatments until she died several months later at home on hospice.

This case illustrates the complexities of cultural issues at end of life. Sun Li's ties to her family and respect for her cultural norms were extremely important to her. They preempted her stated wishes to stop eating and drinking and to choose palliative care instead of aggressive care. In this case, Sun Li's family was loving and very much wanted to do what was in her best interest. Her brother's intentions were honorable and in keeping with his beliefs that he should leave no stone unturned in the search for treatment for a beloved younger sister. We believed that she made an autonomous decision to defer to her brother's wishes. We are not sure if she would have actually followed through with entering a clinical trial if one had been found. We would have tried to help her make an authentic decision and supported her in whatever ways she needed.

AUTONOMY AND THE PATIENT SELF-DETERMINATION ACT

Given these cultural imperatives, it is important to examine the principle of autonomy and its corollaries: informed consent and patient self-determination. We recognize the cultural biases toward western individualist perspective. These two concepts of self-determination are the underpinnings of the Patient Self-Determination Act (PSDA), which was enacted in 1991.

The PSDA states that healthcare institutions that receive Medicaid/Medicare funding must provide written information to adult patients about state laws regarding advance directives. Advance directives can include a DNR order, a healthcare proxy, a living will, and durable power of attorney. The PSDA was passed in the hope that having these advance directives in place would provide greater clarity about patient's wishes, especially at the end of life.

The PSDA also came out of a basic mistrust of the healthcare system and the belief that physicians were making decisions for patients. Since the passage of the PSDA, one in four patients has executed advance directives, as against one in five prior to the legislation (SUPPORT 1995). In addition, the PSDA did not lead to higher rates of DNR or increased discussions with patients about DNR (Teno et al. 1997). These hopes were founded in the belief that all or nearly all patients have the same value systems and discounted the role of cultural differences. For example, in some cultures, there is distrust of the medical system to make decisions about scarce resources, based on historical discrimination. In other cultures, patients and families look to the physician to make the decisions about care.

The bioethics movement in the United States has made the same mistake by overly emphasizing autonomy. In the context of end-of-life care, it presumes the importance of advance planning and the "right" to withdraw or limit treatment (Koenig 1997). It also stresses "truth-telling"—the patient should know everything about his or her condition—and that the patient is the only legitimate decision maker about treatment or nontreatment. These precepts can often collide with the patient's cultural or spiritual values, where patients are to be protected from the "truth."

For many Americans, self-determination is seen as a freedom from group expectations, and self-reliance is viewed as a sign of strength. These values, however, often collide with other cultures. Koenig (1997), for example, challenges the notion of the emphasis on autonomy. She describes the "ideal" patient for such an ethical framework. We need to ask ourselves whether she is only describing the ideal white, Western, male patient. The "ideal" patient is one who:

1. Has a clear understanding of the illness, prognosis, and treatment options that is shared with members of the healthcare team;
2. Has a temporal orientation to the future and a desire to maintain "control" into that future;
3. Has the perception of freedom of choice;
4. Has a willingness to discuss the prospect of death and dying openly;
5. Has a balance between fatalism and belief in human agency that favors the latter;
6. Has a religious orientation that minimizes the likelihood of divine intervention or other "miracles";
7. And believes that the individual, rather than the family or other social group, is the appropriate decision maker (Koenig 1997:370).

When we look at this "ideal" patient profile and compare it to the varied cultural and spiritual beliefs of the patients with whom we work, we can see the inherent difficulties in using this framework in a multicultural world. In fact, there may be very few patients who fit this profile. Therefore, we must examine the assumptions that we often make about the patient/family's ability to engage in a dialogue about end-of-life decisions. We need to make sure that we are asking culturally and spiritually sensitive questions when working with patients and families.

African Americans differ from European Americans with respect to their willingness to complete advance directives and their desires for life-sustaining treatment (Garrett et al. 1993). Significantly more African Americans and Hispanics "wanted their doctors to keep them alive regardless of how ill they were, while more . . . whites agreed to stop life-prolonging treatment under some circumstances" (Caralis et al. 1993:158). A recent hospice study that looked at access and the use of hospice care by African Americans showed that a certain segment of the African American population preferred not to plan for death and their cultural belief systems opposed accepting terminality (Reese et al. 1999).

Where does this leave us in trying to help our patients make decisions? Michel (1994) has asked the following questions:

- Does the value of individual, autonomous decision making transcend cultural norms?
- The law governing informed consent?
- Is this approach truly respectful of who the patient is and the patient's preference? Are there ways to accommodate cultural differences given the moral imperative of respect for persons?

The first question Michel asks is essential to our discussion of Sun Li. Until her brother arrived, Sun Li seemed to place a high value on autonomous decision making. She had decided, with her mother's approval, to seek palliative and hospice care. We saw her as a highly articulate young woman with clear ideas about what constituted quality of life. Once her brother arrived, we saw a very deferential young woman. She did tell her brother what she wanted but was willing to try something new "for him."

As social workers we have been trained to respect cultural diversity, and we must struggle with these questions. One of the four senses of autonomy is authenticity (Miller 1995). Authenticity means that the decision the person is making is in keeping with his or her values. In short, the person is acting "in character." Was Sun Li's decision to defer to her brother an authentic decision? Perhaps it was, if Sun Li truly cared more about her brother's wishes than her own. However, she had been so clear about not wanting aggressive treatment. What about autonomy as free action—not the result of coercion, duress, or undue influence (Miller 1995)?

Hyun (2002) sounds a cautionary note about autonomy, authenticity, and culture. We felt that Sun Li's brother was caring, and indeed Sun Li had spoken about their close relationship over the years. Hyun (2002) is concerned about patients who transfer their decision-making authority to their families, especially about treatment decisions. While applauding recent efforts to respect values that may be dissimilar from Western cultural norms, Hyun insists that we must go farther than the cultural norms and look carefully at authenticity. Not all families are well intentioned, and not all decisions to defer to families are authentic.

These are very complex issues and our clinical assessments must be culturally sensitive as well as thorough. We must ask our clients how they define decision making around illness and who should be part of that process. Koenig delineates some culturally appropriate questions that can be helpful in our assessments:

- Is information about diagnosis/prognosis openly discussed in this culture? If not, how is information managed?
- Is death an appropriate topic for discussion?
- Is maintaining hope considered essential?
- How is decision making done? Is it shared with patient/family or delegated by the patient to someone else?

- How is quality of life vs. quantity of life weighted?
- Does the patient/family trust that the healthcare providers will act in their best interests? (1997:373)

She also suggests larger fundamental questions that must be addressed by bioethicists and others:

- What are the implications of respecting cultural or ethnic perspectives in bioethics?
- How will questions of diversity intersect with questions of justice?
- When patients and families disagree with providers' assessments of outcomes, how should such disputes be mediated? (1997:373)

We also need to make sure that the patient is not just going along with what is expected culturally. There is always the danger of rigid stereotyping and forgetting the unique individuality of each patient—his or her authenticity.

CONCLUSION

Quality end-of-life care for patients and families often rests on the decisions they make about ordinary and extraordinary care. We are all human, and we all have concerns about what will happen to us at the end of our lives. All of the questions that are raised at the time of diagnosis or at the end of life are the same. However, they are framed by the person's unique spiritual, cultural, economic, and emotional concerns. Philosophers teach us that a question is an answer in disguise. As social workers we are trained to listen with a "third ear." We expect the communication to be disguised and indirect at times. And we respect the individual and the ethical and moral mandate to tell the truth.

There can be no trust without the truth. Without trust there can be no integrity to the patient/doctor relationship. The medical profession is morally obligated to tell the truth and equally obligated to do no harm. Similarly, patients and families have the right to be told the truth and not be unduly harmed by the truth. The physician's ability or inability to tell the truth to both patient and family has played an important part in each of the cases presented in this chapter. It is essential that families be told the truth. Division in the family about end-of-life care and unrealistic expectations about treatment puts them at a bereavement risk.

While truth telling is often identified as the problem, it rarely is. The real problem is the ability to deliver the truth with sensitivity and awareness to who the patient and the family are and how they will receive the information. Social workers have always been aware of the need to know "who" the client is and the need to understand the family system. Recently, other disciplines have begun to recognize the significance of emotional factors in dealing with patients and families. This is the time when the true humanness of both medical professionals and patient meet. When the humanity of both parties is allowed to emerge each will have the foundation and language to discuss the medical reality that is present for one and in the future for the other.

The social-work code of ethics, with its emphasis on obligations to clients, colleagues, and agencies, serves as a template for all ethical decision-making processes. Bioethical decision making at the end of life is a complex web of medical/clinical information, social work values, legal issues, and patient and family values. For the most part these decisions take place primarily in hospitals, hospices, and nursing homes—where the interdisciplinary team approach is the model and where social work is not the primary profession. Social workers who are educated in the specialized area of bioethics are able to assume a position of expertise and influence the interdisciplinary medical team. The more social workers have the awareness and ability to identify ethical conflicts that arise in clinical practice, the more they are able to intervene appropriately in a crisis.

REFERENCES

Annas, G. J. 1991. The health care proxy and the living will. *New England Journal of Medicine* 324(17): 1210–1213.

———. 1993. *Standard of Care: The Law of American Bioethics*. Oxford: Oxford University Press.

Arras, J. D., and B. Steinbock, eds. 1995. *Ethical Issues in Modern Medicine*. Mountain View, CA: Mayfield.

Beauchamp, T. L., and J. F. Childress. 1994. *Principles of Biomedical Ethics*. 4th ed. New York: Oxford University Press.

Caralis, P. V., B. Davis, K. Wright, and E. Macial. 1993. The influence of ethnicity and race on attitudes toward advance directive and life-prolonging treatments and euthanasia. *Journal of Clinical Ethics* 4(2): 155–165.

Dubler, N., and D. Nimmons. 1992. *Ethics on Call*. New York: Crown.

Emanuel, E. J., and L. L. Emanuel. 1993. Decisions at the end of life: Guided by communities of patients. *Hastings Center Report* 23(5): 6–14.

Ewalt, P., and N. Mokuau. 1995. Self-determination from a Pacific perspective. *Social Work* 40(2): 168–175.

Garrett, J. M., R. P. Harris, J. K. Norborn, D. L. Patrick, and M. Danis. 1993. Life-sustaining treatments during terminal illness: Who wants what? *Journal of General Internal Medicine* 8:361–368.

Hyun, I. 2002. Waiver of informed consent, cultural sensitivity, and the problem of unjust families and traditions. *Hastings Center Report* 23(5): 14–22.

Jennings, B. 1991. Active euthanasia and forgoing life-sustaining treatment: Can we hold the line? *Journal of Pain and Symptom Management* 6(5): 312–316.

Katz, J. 1994. Informed consent: Must it remain a fairy tale? *Journal of Contemporary Health Law and Policy* 10:69–91.

Koenig, B. 1997. Cultural diversity in decisionmaking about care at the end of life. In *Approaching Death: Improving Care at End of Life*, ed. M. J. Field and C. K. Cassel, 363–382. Washington, DC: National Academy Press.

Levine, C. 2001. *Taking Sides: Clashing Views on Controversial Bioethical Issues*. 9th ed. Guilford, CT: McGraw-Hill/Dushkin.

Lo, B. 2000. *Resolving Ethical Dilemmas: A Guide for Clinicians*. Philadelphia: Williams & Wilkins.

McLaughlin, L. A., and K. L. Braun. 1998. Asian and Pacific Islander cultural values: Considerations for health care decision making. *Health and Social Work* 32(2): 116–126.

Michel, V. 1994. Factoring ethnic and racial differences into bioethics decision making. *Generations* 4:23–26.

Miller, B. L. 1995. Autonomy and the refusal of lifesaving treatment. In *Ethical Issues in Modern Medicine*, ed. J. D. Arras and B. Steinbock, 202–211. Mountain View, CA: Mayfield.

Quill, T. E. 1986. *Death and Dignity: Making Choices and Taking Charge*. New York: Oxford University Press.

Reese, D., R. E. Ahern, S. Nair, J. O'Faire, and C. Warren. 1999. Hospice access and use by African Americans: Addressing cultural and institutional barriers through participatory action research. *Social Work* 44(6): 549–559.

SUPPORT Principal Investigators. 1995. A controlled trial to improve care for seriously ill hospitalized patients. *Journal of the American Medical Association* 274:1591–1598.

Teno, J. M., J. Lynn, N. Wegner, et al. 1997. Advance directives for seriously ill hospitalized patients: Effectiveness with the Patient Self-Determination Act and the SUPPORT intervention. *Journal of the American Geriatrics Society* 45:500–507.

Veatch, R. M. 2000. *The Basics of Bioethics*. Englewood Cliffs, NJ: Prentice-Hall.

31

END-OF-LIFE CARE IN THE PRISON SYSTEM: IMPLICATIONS FOR SOCIAL WORK

SHEILA R. ENDERS

When you have an illness that will eventually cause your death, a door closes on what had seemed a future of endless possibilities. Everything may seem beyond your reach to you. Things once taken for granted are now uncertain, and new and unfamiliar issues arise. While others go about their activities and the business of the world continues, the road you travel may suddenly seem unfamiliar, its signposts poorly marked. —Lynn 1999

IT HAS OFTEN been said that death is the great equalizer: we all face death. For those in the free world, life forever changes with a life-limiting or terminal diagnosis. The doors to what is "future" are now limited.

Imagine that you are living in a nine-by-seven-foot space, the size of an average bathroom. The only furniture you have is a bed with a three-inch thick mattress, sheets, and a wool blanket. It is noisy; the sounds of steel doors, keys, and loud voices resonate. It is hot in summer and cold in winter. Two of you live in that space. You read or write letters. You watch TV or listen to the radio if you and your "roommate" can agree. You most likely eat your meals in your cell. There is no such thing as "alone" time. There is no privacy. You hope that your roommate complies when you ask him to turn his back while you change clothes or go to the bathroom. Imagine facing death, on that bed, in the context of a cell, in a space of forty to sixty square feet. Rather than blood-related family members being present, you have a cellmate and perhaps other inmate-friends who will help look after you. You must rely on the "system's" interest and ability to try to meet your physical, psychosocial, emotional, and spiritual needs while you are being punished. This is what it is like to die in prison.

My interest and experience with the correctional system began in 1992, when I was appointed to a legislatively mandated task force charged with exploring health care in the women's correctional institutions of the California prison system. The task force visited each of four women's institutions and gathered data through interviews with inmates and staff and through chart review. Based on the data collected, a five-year plan to improve the quality of health care for female inmates in California was developed.

As a member of the Department of Corrections AIDS Advisory Committee, formed in 1993, I helped investigate complaints of inadequate care, lack of access to medications, and discrimination within the prison system for people with HIV disease and AIDS. The committee then made recommendations to improve conditions for people with HIV/AIDS in California prisons.

Beginning in 1996, I participated in a three-year grant awarded by the Robert Wood Johnson Foundation to the University of California Davis West Coast Center for

Palliative Education and Research as part of the foundation's Promoting Excellence in End-of-Life Care campaign. I served as a team co-leader focusing on technical assistance for palliative-care education and end-of-life education for designated rural Northern California sites. I worked in simultaneous care for advanced cancer patients and as team leader for the provision of palliative-care education and technical assistance in developing an inpatient hospice program at the Central California Women's Facility (CCWF).

To these projects I brought experience as a medical social worker, including six years in hospice social work, fifteen years in clinical and social/behavioral research, and twelve years as faculty, program manager, and consultant for the University of California Davis/Sacramento AIDS Education and Training Center. I am certified as a clinical research coordinator through the Association of Clinical Research Professionals, having developed, coordinated, and/or supervised more than forty clinical trials in cardiology, HIV/AIDS-related disorders, and end-of-life care, and I have memberships on numerous HIV/AIDS and end-of-life committees, task forces, and boards.

While providing technical assistance for the staff and training hospice inmate-volunteers, I have heard many inmates verbalize their difficulties in communicating and expressing their healthcare needs. This was sometimes due to their lack of knowledge and understanding of an illness or disease or their fears of reprisal if they continued to seek information or help. Few had heard of or understood the meaning of advance-care directives. Although most inmates had seen the actual forms and some had actually completed them, those with limited reading skills lacked even a basic understanding of their purpose.

These experiences in the correctional setting led to my application and selection as a social work leader with the Project on Death in America Social Work Leader Awards Program. I was awarded a two-year grant that supports data collection and research at the Central California Women's Facility and the California Medical Facility, in Vacaville, to assist in developing a handbook using pictograms to assist people with low literacy skills or mild learning disabilities open dialogues with their medical care providers about end-of-life care and treatment decisions.

This chapter explores the role of the social worker in the correctional setting, an often ignored milieu with a flourishing numbers of aging inmates, many of whom are ill and will most likely die in prison. It examines some of the psychosocial challenges faced by social workers working with and advocating for change in the correctional setting, specifically change in end-of-life care and treatment. It presents strategies and examples of successful interventions for effecting positive change within the prison walls.

DEMOGRAPHICS

The "graying of America" applies not only to people living in the "free world," but also to the prison population in the United States (Harris 2000; Linder et al. 2002) As of December 31, 2001, the number of inmates in federal and state prisons and in local jails approached two million, according to Federal Bureau of Justice (FBJ) Statistics.

In 1999, the number of prisoners over fifty-five had doubled. Sixteen southern states in 1997 reported a 480 percent increase in the population of inmates over the age of fifty, while the total general prison population had grown by only 147 percent. It is anticipated that by the year 2030 more than one-third of U.S. prisoners will be over the age of fifty-five. Why is this happening? Cohn (1999), Beiser (2001), and Roberts (2001) suggest that "three strikes" legislation and "tough on crime" campaigns have led to the increase in the number of inmates who will age and die in prison. This is becoming a national crisis, but one that has received little attention.

According to the Bureau of Justice Statistics (2001), the numbers of incarcerated African Americans (3,535 per 100,000) and Hispanics (1,177 per 100,000) are disproportionately higher than Caucasians (462 per 100,000). The largest number of arrests and convictions occur among African American males, who also receive longer sentences than other ethnic groups. This results in the loss of male role models among minority groups. Two consequences of this are the creation of an unstable environment in the community that in turn leads to the cycling of more criminal activity, and a disproportionate number of African American males in the correctional system's aging population.

The aging of male and female inmates presents numerous challenges for the social work profession within the correctional healthcare system. It requires meeting the needs of a population whose health may already be at risk, given lifestyle choices such as drug and alcohol abuse, and whose previous access to health care consisted of emergency room visits. As the inmate population reaches middle and older age, health issues dramatically increase, and prisons are not currently set up to meet the needs of an increasingly aging population. Inmates, on average, are physiologically up to ten years older than their chronological ages (Aday 1994). In the "hostile and highly stressful atmosphere of a correctional facility, inmates age much faster than the general population" (Dubler 1998).

Health care today presents another paradox. People live longer because of medical advances. This often results in people living with five or six chronic illnesses that need close and costly monitoring by physicians who offer medicines and treatments to prolong life. Once an individual is incarcerated, the correctional system then becomes responsible for providing adequate health care. However, correctional institutions' budgets are strained; inmates distrust the quality of healthcare services; the correctional system distrusts the inmates; and there is an ongoing public outcry against inmates receiving adequate care when there are so many people outside of prison who do not have access to it. One California study (Vitiello 1997) found that the estimated average annual cost of maintaining a younger inmate is about $21,000, while caring for an older inmate costs the system about $60,000 per year. About one-third of older inmates now need substantial medical attention for one or more chronic illnesses.

To accommodate the needs of older inmates, it will be necessary to restructure the current healthcare system in prisons. As is true of people in the free world, inmates display a variety of disabilities. Inmates may have conditions that necessitate wheelchairs and require special accommodations, or they may be blind or deaf and require additional special assistance to function and navigate within the institutional setting.

Inmates need peer contact and support. As people age, the ability to cope with a faster pace of life becomes difficult; noise can be overwhelming; and feelings of vulnerability are enhanced. Each of these is an issue in the prison system. Social workers are challenged to develop the skills to tap into inmates' experiences that may have led to their choices, and to motivate inmates to learn about those behaviors that may result in failure or help them succeed in reaching their goals.

THE RIGHTS OF PRISONERS

The U.S. Supreme Court, in *Estelle v. Gamble* (1976), and the Seventh Circuit Court, in *Wellman v. Faulkner* (1983), found that the Eighth Amendment of the U.S. Constitution guarantees inmates a basic level of health care that is equal to the community "standard of care." However, the reality is that most people "in the community" are able to choose their own medical plans or coverage, and to choose a medical provider and hospital or other health facility. Inside the walls of a prison, there are no choices. Available clinical, social, and educational resources, medical providers, and, of course, security issues guide care and treatment, and they may not always meet the definition of either basic or adequate care (Cohn 1999).

Outside of prison, people face psychosocial challenges as they move into retirement and have fewer interactions with people. There may be an increase in fears of dying, disability, and deaths of family members, friends, colleagues, and even pets. There may be a reduction in physical ability, strength, and endurance; and if plagued by chronic, progressively debilitating illness, potential pain, helplessness, and fear of loss of independence (Florida Corrections Commission 1999). The impact of these conditions is greatly magnified in prison. Inmates often have a minimal sense of self-worth, and often their identities are based on how well they can control their environments.

Take a prison with inmates of many cultures and ethnic backgrounds and a basic tendency toward xenophobia; add a pinch of politically driven tightening of privileges; fold in a large dollop of lifelong lessons in mistrust and hatred; cook at 170 percent of design capacity; and top off with hot and humid summer months. Even the most bucolic of communities would be hard pressed to exist, much less thrive, in such an environment. Yet we ask this of prison inmates every day (Wilkinson and Unwin 1999).

In prison, security personnel and administration have total control over the environment. Inmates, under certain conditions, have total control over one another, in the manner of the "survival of the fittest." Social workers are challenged in this setting to identify, assess, and intervene humanely with inmates whose humanity may have long ago been shattered.

The same social-work assessment approaches used for a client in the free world are applicable to the prison setting. For example, it is necessary to have at least a basic knowledge of the cultural norms for each of the clients. However, it is also important to remember that cultural stereotyping is dangerous. Even among subgroups within a culture there are variations, and consideration must be given to making overgeneralizations about specific groups. It is possible to see contrasting cultural patterns within the same ethnic group. Specific attention must be paid to the individual cultural behaviors of inmates in order to understand his or her method of problem solving, coping, and receiving assistance. This is especially true for someone who is terminally ill or dying. The individual's cultural norms or acculturation patterns may contribute to the way decisions are made about medical treatment, pain, and symptom management as well as their psychosocial or spiritual needs.

Although an individual patient may have been born in the United States or become acculturated, he or she may wish to return to traditional cultural methods for treatment. Patients may defer to their elders for decisions about their medical care, even though they differ considerably from those of Western medicine.

The coping styles of different cultures may vary greatly as well. The ways in which patients and their medical providers interact may reflect differences in culture. For example, in the United States, the "dominant culture" places emphasis on and rewards autonomy and individualism. The patient is the person who makes the decisions, gives informed consent, and basically controls or drives the treatment process. Other cultures (e.g., Hispanic and Asian) rely on the family as a unit to make the decisions. Still others, including some Southeast Asian populations, defer decision making to the oldest male in the household, even if he is not related to the patient. There may also be cultural differences with regard to the way people approach the dying process, pain control, and death itself. Exploration of cultural values and beliefs, communication styles, and individual coping skills can improve efforts to provide quality at the end of life, even when it is not the quality for which the dominant culture strives.

Chances are, I believe, that if people in the general population were asked how they want to die, most would probably answer "in old age, fast, without pain, and in my own bed while asleep." In reality, most of us will get to old age, although not necessarily be in our own beds and asleep when we die. Many of us probably will live with a chronic illness or illnesses that will lead to progressive debilitation. Pain may or may not be an issue.

Most people wonder what kind of legacy they will leave behind. The general preference is to be remembered as a "good" or "kind" person, and imperfections are often forgotten or minimized. The longing to believe that life has meaning is intensified among the incarcerated. Serving time for acts that were "wrong," many prisoners fear that they will most likely be remembered for their faults, failings, or criminal acts, and not for their strengths.

For most inmates, a sense of dying or death begins when the metal doors shut behind them and their sentences begin. Death happens in many ways within the institution. Some inmates die by sanctioned execution. Some die at the hands of other inmates. Still others die of chronic, progressive debilitating diseases. For many inmates, their only previous experiences with death may have been in relation to their victim(s). Inmates, like most of us, fear dying alone, without the support of family or other loved ones, isolated from others and in pain.

Inmates are often incarcerated at, or transferred to, institutions far from their homes. Many men who have been the heads of their households leave damaged families behind. Often the spouses or partners of incarcerated men follow them by moving nearer to the correctional institution where the inmate is housed. Men are more likely to survive in the system by developing alliances with groups or gangs for protection and power. Visitation from family members may be limited by geographic distance, if there are families who are able and willing to visit.

Women traditionally commit fewer violent crimes, but are more likely to be involved in crimes of sex or drugs. However, the number of violent crimes committed by women is increasing, including murder as a result of domestic violence. Women in prison tend to develop relationships with each other, often becoming the "mothers" and "grandmothers" who look after each other and develop strong, family-like bonds.

Incarcerated women, however, experience great differences in visitation. Spouses, boyfriends or other family members are less likely to move away from their jobs, or to remove children from their schools to be nearer to the female inmates. Hence, female inmates are more likely to lose contact with their families and children. This is especially true if the woman is a single mother who had been the primary parent and support for the children. Older family members are left to take care of, and protect the children. Family networks are often destroyed.

Having toured most of the prisons in California, I have been struck by long lines of women and children standing in all kinds of weather and waiting for hours at a time to see an inmate in the men's institutions. More striking, however, was seeing the visiting area in the women's institutions often empty. There were no long lines, no children waiting to see their mothers, no mothers waiting to see their daughters. Men in our prisons outnumber women by such a large number that prisons are predominantly male institutions. Institutions for women are located in widely scattered areas of the state, far from neighboring communities, in isolated rural areas. Women tend to develop prison "families" from whom they receive nurturing and support, rather than rely on blood relatives.

When an inmate becomes ill and is transferred to an institution with a medical facility and offered access to a higher level of medical care, it creates another hardship for the family. With few assets to begin with, picking up and moving again may be prohibitive. Not only does the inmate lose his connection to the outside, but also the family may have greater difficulty in maintaining contact, especially if the inmate has a life-limiting or terminal illness and is unable to communicate as the condition progresses.

Aging and illness are also threats to the affected inmate. The ill inmate becomes more vulnerable, not only with custody staff, but also with his peers. Inmates who were once dominating members of the prison population become subordinate to younger, stronger inmates who take control. As inmates age and are not able to defend themselves physically, they often fall victim to intimidation or violence. Prison is a predatory society, and those who once were the predators eventually become the prey.

"What a dying inmate wants is not to be dying in prison. He wants out. Dying in prison is, in some sense, the ultimate mark of failure on your life. The greatest hope [for dying inmates] is to survive their illness until they finish their sentence, or to receive a compassionate early release, which happens in a few cases. They want to be cured, or let out to die. They don't want to die in prison" (Moss-Coane 1995). Inmates report dying in prison as one of their greatest fears (Byock 2001; Maull 1999a; Rideau 1999). They fear not only dying alone, away from any family or friends, but also dying without adequate pain control or other symptom management. Because large numbers of inmates are repeat offenders, the correctional system is less likely to pursue compassionate release or medical parole. Even if death were imminent, inmates would rather be transferred from a penal institution to an outside hospital just so it could be said that they died "free."

While I was providing technical assistance for the development of an onsite hospice in a women's institution, the warden asked, "So how do you know when the inmate is close to death so we can take them out to the hospital to die?" My response was, "The philosophy of hospice is to help the person remain in their home up to the death with adequate pain control and symptom management. Since this is the inmate's 'home,' they would die here."

The warden looked astonished and said, "But no one dies in here." The inmates and some staff confirmed these words. They reported that inmates might actually die during the process of transporting them from their cell or the infirmary, and are often transported outside the gates by ambulance and pronounced dead outside of the prison walls. The reasons for this may be based on several issues. It may be the institution's preference to move the inmate from the prison to an outside facility at the time of death so that statistics reflect a smaller death rate within the walls. It could be a way of avoiding the lengthy process associated with dying within the prison. This process includes identifying of the inmate, alerting the chain of command, fingerprinting the deceased, notifying relatives when available, and attending to the large numbers of forms that need to be completed by a variety of staff, including administrative, medical, and custodial. If the inmate dies at the hospital, much of this procedure falls on the hospital staff. They make the necessary death notifications and take care of much of the paperwork.

For the social worker, an essential component of effective and efficient healthcare delivery is to know what incarcerated patients want at the end of life in the event that they cannot decide for themselves. Inmates, by virtue of where they exist, have little to no choice or autonomy in their decisions, actions, or activities. They lack the power to control various parts of their bodies and their lives. In addition, the 1992 National Adult Literacy Survey reveals that 36 percent of inmates, compared with 26 percent of the general population, have at least one learning disability such as dyslexia or attention deficit disorders. These disabilities, on top of institutional and system barriers, compound the ability to access adequate medical or end-of-life care.

SOCIAL WORKERS AS FACILITATORS

Social workers play a pivotal role in working with incarcerated clients who are terminally ill or when death seems likely. The social worker's role is to facilitate discussion and interpret treatment options between the patient and the medical care team. These discussions can clarify treatment goals for the patient as well as the medical provider. Often these goals are not the same. The social worker's ability to assess, strategize, and intervene while gaining the trust and respect of the inmates and prison staff (medical and custodial) is particularly important within the confines of prison regulations.

The relationship between those charged with maintaining security in prisons and those who are imprisoned has long been characterized by mutual suspicion and distrust. Prisoners' distrust extends to medical personnel, who are generally perceived as not acting in incarcerated persons' best interests but as another arm of the prison system controlling their bodies and persons (Tillman 2000).

I have observed custody and medical staff making statements such as, "They're manipulative," "They're drug seeking," "They're scamming," or "They don't deserve. . . ." Certainly there are those who will "rip off the system," including cheeking pills to sell to other inmates. Drug availability on the inside is often better than on the streets. Although both custody and medical providers often believe that inmates exhibit strong drug-seeking tendencies, many inmates will forgo pain medications in order to stay alert and be aware of their surroundings.

During my observations of housing units in several California institutions, I saw inmates lying in their cells, reportedly too sick to report for their work assignments but afraid to seek medical care for fear of being hospitalized. If there is a need for hospitalization, inmates are removed from their "homes" and away from their supportive networks and prison "families." This fear is enhanced with a diagnosis of terminal illness. When hospitalization is an issue, the fear may be expressed as, "If I go in there, I ain't never comin' out."

HOSPICE AND PALLIATIVE CARE IN PRISON: THE ROLE OF SOCIAL WORK

Palliative-care programs or onsite prison hospices can give social workers the opportunity to assist inmates in processing their feelings as they face death. They can help assess whether an inmate's distress is a result of something coming from an internal source (pain, anxiety, fear, or depression) or from an outside source such as real or perceived intimidation. Social workers can advocate for and mobilize resources to make interventions while helping to resolve environmental internal stressors. Interventions may include the introduction of such techniques as meditation, relaxation, mental imagery, breathing exercises, or journal writing. Social workers by themselves may not be able to change the prison system. However, they can effect some transformation by developing mutually trusting relationships between the inmates and prison staff.

Giving inmates opportunities to serve as volunteers in providing care at the end of life for fellow inmates can change the culture of the institution. Even the most hardened criminal may come to terms with his or her own mortality, and even feel a sense of redemption, while helping others who are terminally ill.

CASE EXAMPLE

During one of the inmate volunteer training classes, a young man about twenty-five years of age who had been heavily involved in gang activities and was a self-professed killer of "more than I can count," started to speak. Reduced to tears, he talked about taking care of his first hospice patient. He said, "I have been involved in so much death, revenge for family and friends killed by rival gang members that I couldn't cry anymore. I got assigned to this guy, and I didn't think I would care too much about him either, just go in and do my job and go back to my yard. But as he was dying, he reached out and took my hand. He didn't say anything; he just looked into my eyes. When he died, I started crying and I cried for days. I cried for all of those I loved that had died and I cried for all of those that I killed. I cried for the families of everyone I killed and I felt so bad. I know I'm going to be here for the rest of my life, but this has changed me. I didn't think I could do this again, but I'm grateful that I have an opportunity to give something back for all that I took."

Similar feelings of gratitude for being able to give are common for inmates who participate in volunteer training and who sit vigil with the dying. Often they find, for the first time in their lives, that they have the ability to comfort and console. This is a powerful affirmation to inmates of their humanity, especially when they have only known violence or revenge. For these inmate volunteers, a softer side is worn with honor.

SOCIAL WORKERS AS CLINICIANS

Approximately twenty-five prison hospice programs have been, or are being, developed throughout the United States. Inmates often perceive hospice as another way that the system will deny life-saving care. Furthermore, prison administrators often view hospice as expensive and adding to the burden of cost for the system (Price 1998). Many inmates prefer to stay in their own cells, or on their own yard, for as long as possible because they fear that they will lose what little control they have over their own bodies and health care. Sometimes saying "no" to the system is the only control that a prisoner can exercise. The challenge for the social worker is to mediate and negotiate between the inmate and medical personnel, to explore distrust, and to facilitate a smoother transition to extended care or hospice.

Inmate volunteers can play an important part in building trust: as mediators along with social workers, as a companion or friend to someone who is dying, as someone familiar with the prison culture, and as a liaison to the social worker and security personnel. Each member of the treatment team must feel comfortable with the other members in order to ensure that the primary goals of treatment are met (Tillman 2000).

LOSS IS NOT NEW TO INMATES

Loss is an intense emotion and one that is ubiquitous to prison life. Even those who are charged with the responsibility for maintaining the medical care of inmates, regardless of what crimes have been committed, often exhibit negative attitudes and are, at times, void of compassion toward ill or dying inmates.

Older inmates may suffer from chronic heart problems, diabetes, high blood pressure, chronic liver disease, arthritis, and chronic obstructive pulmonary disease. Female inmates often have a history of gynecological problems and seizure disorders, especially if victims of sexual abuse and domestic violence. Inmates may take numerous medications on a daily basis. He or she may have difficulty hearing conversations and need stronger glasses to read or watch TV. Dental problems and gum diseases are prevalent. Many inmates have few or no teeth and do not have dentures to replace them. Many use canes, walkers, or wheelchairs to get around. Some show signs of dementia or early Alzheimer's disease.

For people outside of prison, Medicare and Medicaid or private insurance may help to defray the costs of medical care. However, inmates are not entitled to, or eligible for, these programs. The correctional system pays for inmate care, as well as for security escorts, transportation to and from the institution to a hospital, and for medical or mental health care services. With the additional costs of providing custody escorts and transportation for numerous trips to the hospital for aging inmates, care may cost twice that of someone with similar illness or illnesses outside of the prison walls.

Many inmates carry the effects of years of compounded losses. The effects may have begun in childhood with the loss of a parent, either through divorce or death; the loss of siblings, perhaps through violence; the loss of self-esteem due to abusive and neglectful treatment that may have contributed to chronic hopelessness. Violence is a way to alleviate the pain of loss.

Social workers need to help inmates understand the sources of their losses and how these losses and their anger connect. Once inmates are helped to understand the source(s) of their rage, they can deal with some of their underlying grief, learn ways to cope with loss, and ideally find ways to express feelings in a more socially acceptable way. "Compassion for inmates who are dying cannot be legislated or mandated, but humane and compassionate care for the dying can be facilitated" (Beck 1999).

To date, little attention has been paid to the grief and bereavement felt by inmates in most prisons. Some inmate hospice programs offer support groups or memorial services so inmate volunteers and inmate "family" members can begin working through their grief. Rituals such as reading from the Bible, lighting candles, and making quilts or creating other memorials pay tribute to past losses while inmates grieve the death of a fellow prisoner. Deaths occur in prison on a regular basis. Some deaths result from the violence that is part of prison life. A gang member dies at the hands of a rival gang, and that death is then avenged. An argument over drugs or money may result in death. A prison rape is reported, and the "snitch" becomes the next victim. There are "natural causes" of death, and of course there is execution. Inmates also experience losses in the form of deaths of family members.

Inmates also are not immune to losses outside of the prison. Inmates often report hearing of the death of a loved one such as a parent or sibling when a note is passed into the cell. One young woman told me that she learned of her mother's sudden and unexpected death when she found a note on the floor after the guards had come around to do a count of the inmates. It said, "Your mother died last night." There was no other information. She said, "I just got so angry. Why couldn't they just come and tell me to my face. I started to cry, and then I started to scream because my heart hurt so much. The guard came to my cell and just stared at me. I wanted to die too. I never thought I would be in here when my mother died. I should have been there with her, to take care of her. I have such a hole in my heart and there is nothing that will fill it back up." For her, bereavement work involved connecting the effect of rage with that of sorrow.

The correctional counselor monitors the level of supervision needed, work assignments, custody increase or reduction, maintenance of records and files, and recommendations for possible release. The requirements for this position may include a "general" knowledge of social and behavioral sciences and abnormal behavior patterns, "skill" in counseling individuals and groups, and knowledge of community resources. Social workers can and do fill these positions. However, most of these jobs are not filled by social workers, but by law enforcement and public safety officers who are less able to offer the psychosocial counseling needed at the end of life.

Social workers in the prison setting most often work to transition the inmate back into society once released from custody. Emphasis is placed on transporting the inmate back to their community of release, parole or probation officers and community resources such as housing and medical care.

When inmates become clients, the social worker is faced with the task of trying to develop a therapeutic alliance. Helping the "client" understand the root causes of his or her emotions (anger, anxiety, depression) can be very difficult, given that inmates are likely to act out rather than reflect. Inmates are often people for whom insight has been difficult. Creating an atmosphere of trust and understanding is challenging, as is sustaining the motivation to change. Not all inmates will want to talk with someone who is perceived to be a "systems" person. In prison, inmates are referred to as Mr. or Ms. to show respect, and custody is addressed in the same manner. Asking instead of telling shows respect. Inmates often respond favorably when treated with respect.

SOCIAL WORK ADVOCACY

To many, inmates represent the worst of the worst of humanity. In some instances, this may be true. However, not all who are incarcerated have done terrible things. Many inmates' crimes are a result of social structural disadvantages, or circumstances that, at any given time, might put many of us behind bars.

Think of the woman who has been battered for years and finds the courage to fight back. In protecting herself or her children, she kills. She is sentenced to life without possibility of parole. She took a life, but she also stopped the violence. She lost her life and her dreams of a family that will never be realized. Should she spend the rest of her days in prison? Prison is now referred to as a "correctional" institution. Society is led to believe that incarceration will "correct" the inmate's behavior and the inmate will be changed when he or she is released.

A mental patient, homeless, lacking the ability to access or stay in group care, stops taking his medication and begins to act out on the street. Complaints are made. The police investigate. The person becomes frightened and begins to strike out physically. It does not matter that he is out of control because of a chemical imbalance that is biologically based. Suppose he seriously injures or maybe even kills someone. Should he go to prison for circumstances he was unable to control? Should he go to prison because mental health treatment or facilities were lacking?

What of the person who commits crimes against property, never injuring anyone, but it is her third felony? That person now has "three strikes" and is remanded to life in prison. What of the teenager who commits a crime, is tried as an adult, found guilty, and sentenced to life in prison? Should these people be sentenced to live within the institutional setting for the rest of their lives?

Society will need to ask whether the crimes are worthy of serving a lifetime in a correctional setting. Should inmates be exposed to overcrowded conditions or to others who have committed horrific crimes? Is it better to release inmates if they are very sick, going to die, and no longer a threat to society? Should they die in prison because they are criminals? Are we prepared to treat the approximately three thousand inmates who die each year while in custody (Beck 1999; Radcliff 2000; Stolberg 2001)?

PALLIATIVE CARE THROUGH INTERDISCIPLINARY COOPERATION

Extending palliative care to inmates requires the cooperation of an interdisciplinary team including security and classification personnel. Palliative care is a way of offering relief of symptoms, especially pain to those who are terminally ill. The concept of pain within the prison is often looked at through the eyes of the "us" and "them" culture. Having the ability to withstand pain may be seen as a sign of strength for the inmate. Often, nursing staff as well as social-work personnel may have to assess the patient's pain based on nonverbal cues, such as frowning, moaning, tightening of the facial muscles, or clenching of fists. The inmate may not want to admit to having physical or emotional pain. This "tolerance" to pain may be a defense against vulnerability. It certainly contradicts the stereotype that staff often believe, that inmates will exhibit "drug seeking behavior" and have a higher incidence of drug abuse than people in the general population (see chapter 19).

Social workers are often called upon to help evaluate the patient's pain. Sometimes even the most powerful medications cannot relieve pain and more investigation is required to determine the source. Is the pain coming from a physical source, or an emotional one? Talking with the patient may help identify emotional sources for the pain. Relief may occur because there is another human being interested in what the inmate is feeling. Physical pain can be dealt with as effectively inside prison as outside, by medical personnel who have adequate training and knowledge. Social workers can be instrumental in teaching the patient ways to cope with emotional pain. Techniques such as imagery, relaxation, listening to music, and similar activities can be used to alleviate stress and gain power or control over pain.

SOCIAL WORKERS AS BROKERS

Social workers can maintain contact with interested family members. As with people in the free world, inmates often want to resolve outstanding conflicts prior to dying. An inmate may wish to contact members of his or her estranged family near the time of death in an attempt to reconcile. The social worker should attempt to contact the inmate's family members who may not have seen each other, either because of geography or because of family conflict. The social worker should also be prepared to assist the inmate in the event that family may not want to reconnect. If the family member chooses not to make the connection, his or her request is honored. This can be a very painful, emotional event for the dying inmate who is making his or her last attempt to bring peace and purpose at the end of life. The social worker can try to facilitate visitation with the inmate's prison "family." Chaplains are also available to offer spiritual assistance during these difficult times.

Laws vary from state to state, but basic factors influence or prohibit release from prison based on illness. Another advocacy role for the social worker is related to inmate release or parole. Medical parole offers a compassionate and practical response to dying inmates who are terminally ill and who pose little threat to society while on release. Determining an inmate's condition for medical parole is a delicate situation, however.

On one hand, inmate advocates might demand that an inmate be released because of his or her health. On the other side is the correctional system that will pay a large price if that inmate commits an offense once back in the outside community. Each state has the ability to grant medical parole with its own specific criteria. In a composite of basic criteria that must be met in all states, inmate-patients must:

- be in the final stages of a terminal illness and unlikely to recover prior to completing their minimum period of imprisonment;
- pose no threat to either themselves or society;
- have family members able and willing to care for them as they die;
- be certified as terminally ill by a physician, who has concluded that the applicant is debilitated or incapacitated and has severe restrictions with regard to self-ambulation or ability to care for himself or herself.

The parole board makes the decision to release, reviewing each case at least every six months, and decides whether to renew the grant of medical parole as well.

The process of applying for and being granted medical parole requires preparation on the part of the medical staff, social services staff, and prison administration. Social workers assist with the psychosocial assessment and offer a biopsychosocial assessment profile of the inmate to be released. Discharge planning is developed by the social work staff and presented to the parole board as part of the application package. If release is granted, the social work staff provides parolees in the community with extensive follow-up services including coordination of program interviews, family outreach, and support. Eligible inmates are provided both legal representation and social-work services at parole revocation hearings. The social worker's role here is to assist in transitioning care from the prison system to the outside once the inmate is released. This includes making contact with the inmate's family in preparation for the medical release. If the inmate is going to be cared for in a family member's home, the social worker can assist with arrangements such as transportation and referrals for medical care, hospice, and other community resources.

SOCIAL WORK AND HOSPICE CARE IN PRISON

Traditional hospice care does have a place in the prison setting. Logistics around security issues cannot be ignored. Appropriate palliative care should include pain control, symptom management, and attention to emotional and spiritual needs, but cannot sacrifice attention to prison policies and security concerns.

Educating both staff and inmates on the issues of advance-care planning and palliative care is essential. For providers of medical and psychosocial care in the prisons who feel inadequate in the skills of treatment, pain and symptom management, and emotional and spiritual issues, there are many community resources in palliative care and hospice that can offer continuing education programs or onsite services to meet these needs.

The development of telemedicine and its ability to assist in training and education can also improve the knowledge base on end of life, as well as break down institutional limitations. It is difficult for staff, whether custody or medical, to take time out of their day to attend any training. Telemedicine can be used for medical or psychosocial consultation on difficult cases or in efforts to train and educate staff. This can reduce the costs of educating staff in terms of educational materials, travel expenses, and pay for extra staff or overtime. Videotaping of sessions allows staff to be trained on a rotating basis or at their leisure, further reducing cost.

At the University of California Davis Medical Center in Sacramento, telemedicine is used to provide medical and other consultations throughout the greater Northern California region. This includes consultation to regional hospitals, emergency rooms, clinics, primary care networks, and research institutions, and to prisons that are linked with the telemedicine system. Clinical consultations can be conducted at multiple sites at the same time. For example, telemedicine clinical consultations have been used for evaluating and making treatment recommendations for HIV-infected and AIDS inmate patients. The University of California Davis West Coast Center for Palliative Care and Research staff, comprising a physician, nurse, and social worker, conducts clinical consultations with clinic staff for up to seven regional clinics simultaneously. Cases are presented and medical and psychosocial interventions discussed.

OFFERING COMPASSION

Inmate advocates who may be social workers often vote to offer compassionate release or medical parole to a dying inmate. Victims' rights advocates, on the other hand, want to see inmates remain behind bars. Whatever side of the argument, incarceration is punishment. Not providing adequate care for a dying inmate increases the punishment.

Fleet Maull, founder of the National Prison Hospice Association, writes, "Not knowing where to open on any level to one's own heart, one's sadness and regret and no way to reconnect with any real sense of being in relationship with others or a sense of community. There's no trust. . . . Your inner world is shame, the outer world is just a reflection of that coming at you. The community outside is just demonizing you. So you just go into a cocoon of armor and live in that place of armor and aggression. And that's what incarceration does to most people" (Maull 1998).

In most settings and on most days, social workers make a difference in someone's life. This includes working in hospitals, service agencies, and schools or through individual therapy. Social workers also develop public policy or advocate for change. The prison setting is a rich training ground to make a difference. Conflicted family dynamics, lower socioeconomic struggles, inability to establish and maintain personal relationships, lower literacy levels, and diminished problem-solving skills often are at the root of behaviors associated with criminal activity.

Social workers within the correctional system work in programs that deal with substance abuse, alcoholism, HIV disease and AIDS, lowered self-esteem, and domestic violence. Helping to develop a discharge plan for those who will be released is an important part of the inmate's future. A skilled social worker can elicit the core needs, wishes, and hopes of the individual and encourage successful completion of programs that will better the life course once an inmate is released.

The practice of social work within the correctional setting may seem overwhelming at first glance, and it can be. Yet, prison affords opportunities to provide services to one of the world's most vulnerable populations. The social-work clinician can assume a variety of roles in an effort to improve the quality of life through the journey of death for terminally ill inmates. Assisting in the resolution of family dynamics and conflicts, helping an inmate to complete unfinished business, and resolving spiritual and emotional issues can allow this disenfranchised population to die with some dignity.

Inmates need social workers who will advocate for their wishes, especially at a time when they are too sick or too uncertain to advocate for themselves. As for anyone who is dying, there are many emotional, spiritual, and existential tasks to complete. These tasks seem insurmountable for those who wish to have their lives account for something, but identify as a lifelong criminal, demonized by society.

The following story, as told by Tanya Tillman (2000), is a poignant reminder that sometimes the simplest of requests can make the most difference.

CASE EXAMPLE

"John," a fifty-five year old cancer patient, was referred on a Thursday afternoon for hospice services. On Friday morning, another team member and I went to assess the patient and discuss hospice care with him. We found him to be debilitated and fatigued, and although he could understand and communicate with us, he was simply too tired to engage in any meaningful discussion of hospice philosophy and the extensive questions and answers required in the intake process. It was evident that John had taken a dramatic turn for the worse in the past twelve hours, and we had little time to do anything meaningful for the patient unless we could identify his immediate needs. We asked him if there were one thing, anything, we could do for him at that very moment. He told us he wanted to see his brother-in-law who was also an inmate at our facility. All he could tell us was where this man lived in the prison and his "inmate nickname" and then he fell asleep.

I went back to my office with little to go on other than that I was looking for an inmate called "Face Maker" who lived in a neighboring dormitory.

A security colonel making his rounds in the medical facility stopped in my office to say hello and asked me if there were anything I needed or anything he could do for the program. With no more to go on than the information I gave him, in less than thirty minutes he had John's brother-in-law identified, located, pulled off his job assignment, and transported to the patient's bedside. Before he died, John was able to spend three hours with his brother-in-law, as he had requested.

Social workers provide guidance to improve people's lives in every stage of life and living, and throughout the process of dying and death. Social workers traditionally work to assess, advocate, problem-solve, intervene, and empower. Although the rewards of social workers for the work that they do with vulnerable populations are many, improving end-of-life conditions for terminally ill inmates may be viewed with skeptical eyes by those who believe they are undeserving.

Working within the correctional setting tests the social worker's resilience. The differences between working with people in the free world and those within the institutional setting can be dramatic. In the free world, interdisciplinary teams work with the patient and family to develop a plan of care based on the patient's wishes and goals. Inside the institution, the system's security needs are first and the patient's needs are secondary. For those with little experience in the activities of the correctional setting, it can be daunting to work within the context of these priorities.

It is crucial that social-service providers, custody, and administration learn to work together and understand one another's viewpoints. Social workers do not want custody to step in to intervene in a psychosocial situation any more than custody wants social workers to step in to resolve an institutional security issue. Taking the time to understand each other's goals and objectives within the context of the setting is of utmost importance.

THERE MUST BE AN ALTERNATIVE

Imagine that you are that inmate once again, isolated from all that you have known, vulnerable to the system taking care of you, and alone with your thoughts. Even though an inmate has committed a serious or terrible act, he or she should not be denied the opportunity to redeem him or herself. In most cases, nonjudgmental medical or psychosocial care can be performed more effectively when the clinician does not know the nature of the crime.

In discussions with people who have cancer or other life-limiting illnesses and their family members, many reveal that both the patient and caregiver feel isolated. When a terminal diagnosis is received, there is usually an outpouring of support from family, friends, colleagues, and neighbors. That support dwindles over time, as treatment progresses, remission may take place, and life resumes to some semblance of normalcy. People often are uncomfortable about asking, "How are you?" in case the answer is less than "fine," "doing well," or "feeling great." Most of us are uncertain of how to react if the response is "the cancer's back," "I'm having a bad day," or, "I'm dying."

Isolation occurs, and suddenly there's an elephant in the living room. People dealing with illness feel that they need to keep it to themselves for fear of burdening their loved ones. The term "good patient" refers to the phenomenon we often see in hospice. Patients will not tell their families or caregivers how they truly feel for fear of being a burden. They don't want to "bother" the doctor. Social workers, however, are often privileged by being allowed to help alleviate much of the "pain" of illness by affirming how difficult the situation must be. "This must be so hard for you," "I can't imagine what this must be like." One can never truly know what another person is going through, but can offer empathy and support by their presence and expression of caring.

This is true for terminal inmate-patients as well. They experience the pain of isolation resulting from their illness. They lose more control over their lives. Many believe that this is the "true punishment" for what they have done and why they are in prison. Nonjudgmental support offered by well-educated, knowledgeable, and compassionate social work staff can help support inmate-patients and encourage them in sorting through their feelings to complete end-of-life tasks.

CONCLUSION

Social work endeavors to help meet the basic needs of all people, focusing particular attention on empowering people in vulnerable life situations. Individuals who are incarcerated are among the most vulnerable populations. There is a paucity of written information about social work practice within the correctional setting. Involvement in policy development, analysis, and planning are areas in which social workers can make a tremendous difference.

Social workers identify the social context, obstacles, and barriers that get in the way of individual or community growth and development. Using strategies to overcome these barriers and obstacles, social workers can enhance a person's ability to address his or her own needs as well as influence social change. The profession seeks to promote social justice and social change with, and for, individuals, families, groups, organizations, and communities. Prisons are a microcosm of society, with elements of policy development, education and research, administration, political action, issues of cultural and ethnic diversity, and discrimination, poverty, and other forms of social injustice. Correctional institutions in general and end-of-life care in the prison setting in particular provide social workers with demanding yet unusually rewarding opportunities to apply the knowledge of social work theory and practice techniques proven to be effective in traditional settings. For social workers willing to take their skills to the limit, the correctional setting offers an uncompromising opportunity to effect a positive change within an environment where balancing conflicting perspectives and objectives is a constant challenge.

REFERENCES

Aday, R. H. 1994. Aging in prison: A case study of new elderly offenders. *International Journal of Offender Therapy and Comparative Criminology* 38:79–91.

Beck, J. A. 1999. Compassionate release from New York state prisons: Why are so few getting out? *Journal of Law, Medicine and Ethics* 27(3): 216–233.

Beiser, V. 2001. How we got to two million: How did the land of the free become the world's largest jailer? *Mother Jones*, 10 July.

Byock, I. R. 2001. Foreword: A handbook for end-of-life care in correctional facilities, Volunteers of America. www.dyingwell/grace2001.htm.

Cohn, F. 1999. The ethics of end-of-life care for prison inmates. *Journal of Law, Medicine and Ethics* 27(3): 252–259.

Craig, E. L. 1999. Prison hospice: An unlikely success. *American Journal of Hospice and Palliative Care* 16(6): 725–729.

Crawley, L. M., P. A. Marshall, B. Lo, and B. A. Koenig. 2002. Strategies for culturally effective end-of-life care. *Annals of Internal Medicine* 136:673–679.

Dubler, N. N. 1998. The collision of confinement and care: End-of-life care in prisons and jails. *Journal of Law, Medicine and Ethics* 26:149–156.

Estelle v. Gamble. 1976. 429 U.S. 97, 103–104.

Evans, C., R. Herzog, and T. Tillman. 2002. The Louisiana state penitentiary: Angola prison hospice. *Innovations in End-of-Life Care* 5(4): 553–560.

Florida Corrections Commission. 1999. Elderly inmates: 1999 annual report. www.fcc.state.fl.us/fcc/reports/fina199/1eld.html.

Flynn, E. E. 1992. The graying of America's prison population. *Prison Journal* 72:77–98.

Getz, A., and M. Mahony. 2001. Interview with Fleet Maull, founder of National Prison Hospice Association. www.youthhorizons.org/interview/fleet.html.

GRACE Project. 2001. Incarceration of the terminally ill: Current practices in the United States. www.graceprojects.org.

Griefinger, R. B. 1999. Commentary: Is it politic to limit our compassion? *Journal of Law, Medicine and Ethics* 27(3): 234–237.

Harris, K. 2000. The graying of our prisons. *Ottawa Sun*, 17 June.

Johnson, C. G. 1999. Commentary: A personal view on palliative and hospice care in correctional facilities. *Journal of Law, Medicine and Ethics* 27(3): 216–233.

Linder, J., S. Enders, E. Craig, J. Richardson, and F. Meyers. 2002. Hospice care for the incarcerated in the United States: An introduction. *Journal of Palliative Medicine* 5(4): 549–558.

Lynn, J., and J. Harrold. 1999. *Handbook for Mortals: Guidance for People Facing Serious Illness.* New York: Oxford University Press.

Mahon, N. B. 1999. Introduction: Death and dying behind bars—Cross-cutting themes and policy imperatives. *Journal of Law, Medicine and Ethics* 27(3): 215–216.

Maull, F. W. 1991a. Dying in prison: Socioculture and psychosocial dynamics. *Hospice Journal* 7(1–2): 127–142.

———. 1991b. Hospice care for prisoners: Establishing an inmate staff hospice program in a prison medical facility. *Hospice Journal* 7(3): 43–55.

———. 1998. Issues in prison hospice: Toward a model for the delivery of hospice care in a correctional setting. *Hospice Journal* 13(4): 57–82.

Moss-Coane, M. 1995. Prison hospice: An inside view. *NPHA News* 1(1): 1, 3.

Price, C. 1998. To adopt or adapt? Principles of hospice care in the correctional setting. *NPHA News* 6: 1–2, 11–12.

Radcliff, M. 2000. Dying inside the walls. *Journal of Palliative Medicine* 3:509–511.

Radcliff, M., and F. Cohn. 2000. Hospice with GRACE: Reforming care for terminally ill inmates. *Corrections Today* 2(3): 64–67.

Rideau, W., ed. 1999. *Angolite*. Angola: Louisiana State Penitentiary.

Roberts, F. H. 2001. Specialized healthcare in correctional facilities: The costs of caring for elderly, chronically sick and terminally ill inmates. www.correctionalnews.com/cn/archives/jf2001/feature3jf01.html.

Schmidt, S. 2002. Prison hospice serves up justice and compassion side by side. www.signonsandiego.com/news/uniontrib/sat/news/news_1in2hospice.html.

Seidlitz, A. M. 1999a. "Fixin to die": Hospice program opens at LSP-Angola. *NPHA News* 5(1): 3–5.

———. 1999b. FMC-Carswell: Doing "family" in a women's hospice. *NPHA News* 6:8–9.

Sheppard, D. 1999. Learning to love: Reflections of an inmate volunteer. *NPHA News* 6:4–5.

Stolberg, S. G. 2001. Behind bars: New effort to care for the dying. *New York Times*, 1 April.

Tillman, T. 2000. Hospice in prison: The Louisiana state penitentiary hospice program. www2.edc.org/lastacts/archives/archivesMay00/default.asp.

U.S. Department of Justice, Bureau of Justice Statistics. 2001. Summary findings, 31 December.

U.S. Department of Justice, National Institute of Corrections. 1998. Hospice and palliative care in prisons. Report, September.

Vitello, M. 1997. Three strikes: Can we return to rationality? *Journal of Criminal Law and Criminology* 87(2): 395–481.

Wellman v. Faulkner. 1983. 715 F.2d at 271.

Wilkinson, R. A., and T. Unwin. 1999. Intolerance in prison: A recipe for disaster. www.drc.state.oh.us/web/articles/article49.htm.

32

END-OF-LIFE CARE IN NURSING HOMES

MERCEDES BERN-KLUG AND KIM ELLIS

SOCIAL WORKERS employed in nursing homes encounter death and dying as part of everyday life. Of the more than two million deaths that occurred in the United States in 2000, 25 percent occurred in nursing homes (National Hospice and Palliative Care Organization 2002:5). Close to half of persons age eighty-five and older (the fastest-growing age group in the United States) die as a nursing home resident (National Center for Health Statistics 1996). These statistics understate the actual amount of dying in contemporary nursing homes, in that some nursing home residents complete their dying in the hospital or en route to the hospital and are not counted as "nursing home deaths."

This chapter begins with a discussion of the nursing home context, including demographic information describing nursing home residents and federal regulations affecting psychosocial care. The next section presents an overview of how social workers can be instrumental in helping to enhance the end-of-life experiences of nursing home residents, and their families, especially at key transition points in the nursing home stay. These include the admissions process, care plan meetings, hospitalizations, hospice care, and bereavement.

THE NURSING HOME CONTEXT

Nursing homes comprise a heterogeneous group. They can be public, private, or religiously affiliated. Their business status can be for-profit or nonprofit. They can be independent or part of a chain. They can care for fewer than ten people or more than five hundred. Krauss and Altman (1998) report that the majority of residents (66 percent) live in private, for-profit facilities. Research is needed to determine the extent to which the quality of end-of-life care varies by type of nursing home.

Field and Cassel (1997) note that contemporary nursing home care is for three categories of people: (1) those who are receiving weeks or months of rehabilitation or skilled services following a hospitalization and who are expected to return to community living; (2) those who are admitted with long-term care needs caused by advanced chronic health conditions and who will likely live months or years in the nursing home until they die; and (3) people who are admitted at the end of their life because their end-of-life needs exceed their resources for living independently in the community. In some cases, they remain only days or weeks before death.

The latter two groups are the focus of this chapter, with special emphasis on persons admitted to the nursing home for long-term care who will remain in the facility for many months or years until their death. Long-term care, then, "may be defined as assistance given over a sustained period of time to people who are experiencing long-term inabilities or difficulties in functioning because of a disability" (Kane, Kane, and Ladd 1998:4).

Other formal long-term care settings include assisted living facilities, residential care homes, and continuing care retirement communities. In some rural communities, hospital beds are considered part of the long-term care system in that certain beds are set aside for use by people with advanced chronic health conditions. Despite the increase in other institutional options, the nation's nursing homes provide 81 percent of formal long-term care (Krauss and Altman 1994).

Although nursing homes provide the majority of formal long-term care services, it is important to remember that most long-term care is provided "informally" at home, by family members and friends, most of whom are middle-aged and older women themselves (Kane, Kane, and Ladd 1998).

The need for long-term care in the nursing home is a function of physical and/or cognitive decline in health status in the context of exhausted or absent social support. In many cases, families willingly assume enormous financial and emotion costs to maintain their loved ones in the community for as long as possible. The nursing home stays of many are postponed for months, years and, in some cases decades, because of care provided by family and friends, often with the support of community services. In some cases, this informal care can prevent the need for a nursing home admission altogether.

As the individual's cognitive impairment, incontinence, or disability progresses, however, it may exceed the family's ability to provide care. Some people are admitted to nursing homes because they have outlived their support system, or their loved ones are not available to provide care because of their own health problems, geographic distance, or other life circumstances.

In 1999, there were 1.6 million nursing home residents in the 18,000 nursing homes in the United States, most (90 percent) of whom were sixty-five or older. Close to three-quarters (72 percent) of nursing home residents were women. Slightly more than half (57 percent) were widowed (Jones 2002). Today, about half of residents are age eighty-five or older, and more than half are cognitively impaired (Krauss and Altman 1996). In order for excellent care to be given, nursing home staff members need skills in communicating with people who are cognitively impaired. Staff also need skills in working with proxy decision makers such as family members. The high rate of cognitive impairment underscores the need for appropriate advance directives. Many nursing home residents also suffer from depression and/or dementia, which can complicate communicating about and delivering end-of-life care.

Keay and colleagues (1994) report that between one-third and one-half of people admitted to a nursing home die within a year. The provision of end-of-life care to nursing home residents is affected by both the characteristics of the residents and the characteristics of the nursing home. The context for the provision of care is affected by public policy, reimbursement regulations, and changing attitudes about what constitutes quality end-of-life care.

As a major provider of care for the dying, how well are nursing homes doing in delivering end-of-life care? There are no nationally representative data to answer that question, but we do have evidence from smaller studies. Hanson, Danis, and Garrett asked 461 family members of the recently deceased to comment on the end-of-life care their loved one received. They collected data describing deaths in hospitals, nursing homes, and at home. Almost all (91 percent) of family comments regarding hospice care were positive compared to 51 percent of comments describing nursing home end-of-life care. "Negative comments about terminal care in nursing homes emphasized poorly trained or inattentive staff and the remoteness of physicians. Several informants wondered if death was premature or suffering increased because of poor quality care" (1997:1341). This study suggests that of all death settings, the nursing home has the most room for improvement. Social workers—individually and as a profession—can be an important part of enhancing the quality of end-of-life in nursing homes.

On a daily basis, nursing-home social workers interact with residents who are approaching death, their family members, and fellow staff members. Social workers are trained in psychosocial assessment and care. These social work skills can be a crucial part of providing excellent end-of-life care to nursing home residents.

Federal regulations mandate that the nursing home facility "must provide medically-related social services to attain or maintain the highest practical physical, mental, and psychosocial well-being of each resident" (Code of Federal Regulations 2001:521). Federal regulations also require a full-time social worker in nursing homes with at least 120 beds, although the federal regulations do not require that the person in the social work position have a social work degree. Some state laws do require a degreed social worker in this position. (In 2001, the Department of Health and Human Services Office of the Inspector General began an investigation into a complaint signed by CSWE, NASW, the American Society on Aging, National Citizens Coalition for Nursing Home Reform, and other organizations regarding disregard of federal law requiring psychosocial care for nursing home residents by qualified professionals.)

The role of the nursing home social worker varies from state to state, and indeed, from facility to facility. The extent to which social workers are helping nursing home residents and families with issues and adjustments related to dying and death has not been well documented.

SOCIAL WORK INTERVENTION AT KEY TIMES OF TRANSITION

ADMISSIONS

In those cases in which nursing home care is the only option or the best remaining option, the admissions process often occurs within the context of a crisis. A turn for the worse in a decade long bout with chronic illness, a serious stroke leaving a person unable to care for herself, the advance of Alzheimer's disease or some other form of dementia, the unexpected death of the caregiver, can all lead to a nursing home admission. These crises are not just physical or cognitive crises; they are psychosocial crises as well.

Some family members report that the guilt they feel over the placement of a parent, spouse, or a child in a nursing home remains for years and sometimes forever. Forbes, Bern-Klug, and Gessert state that family members of nursing home residents with dementia reported that the decision to place their loved one in a nursing home was the most difficult decision they had ever made. "Nursing home placement was experienced as a violation of life-long values based in fidelity" (2000:253).

In the face of such anguish and disappointment, a trained social worker uses skills in interpersonal communication, validation, active listening, crisis management, and decision making to ease the transition into the new setting and situation. The social worker can articulate an understanding and recognition that the process of admissions can be extremely stressful for both the resident and the family. The social worker can offer help to residents and families by encouraging them to express their feelings— often mixed feelings—about nursing home care, and by putting residents and family members in touch with others who have been through the process. Social workers can share written resources about coping in the context of nursing home care. Many families perceive the entry into a nursing home as a cluster of major losses: loss of function; loss of independence; loss of care options; and a foreshadowing of the loss of life. Skilled social workers can offer important services to help residents and families cope with and transcend some of the fears related to these losses.

Not all nursing home admissions are cloaked in sadness and loss. For some residents and families, the move to the nursing home may be a welcome relief or represent arriving at a safe place. Some residents find that, despite their initial fears, their social interaction, nutrition, and personal hygiene improve once they move to a nursing home. Much depends on the nursing home and the physical and cognitive status of the resident, as well as the extent to which the family remains involved with daily life.

About one-third of the people admitted to nursing homes come directly from a private home, while 58 percent arrive from a hospital or a different nursing home (Sahyoun et al. 2001:2). Social workers can help socialize both the resident and the family to the nursing home by talking through issues, such as how often to visit, when to visit, and how to review social activities planned for residents and/or family members. It is helpful to have the social worker review the roles of key staff members in the nursing home and to clarify how physician visits are handled. The social worker should discuss the cadence of life in the facility (when meals are served, when activities are scheduled, and so forth), and talk about how to get information and resolve differences. This information is provided in the context of living in the nursing home, but clearly builds rapport for when the time comes to talk about dying in the nursing home.

The admissions process is not only the first time that the social worker spends one-on-one time with the family, but it may also be the only face-to-face time spent with the family unless family members are able to visit the nursing home during the day or the social worker is available in the evening. Family members who live out of town may be able to visit the nursing home only once or twice a year. The admissions process is an important opportunity to build rapport and assess the individual in the context of his or her family.

Admission processes vary from facility to facility. In some facilities, the social worker is responsible for the admissions process. In other facilities, a non–social work admissions counselor handles the process. Research conducted on hospices found that when social workers participated in the intake interview, there were advantages to the hospice as well as to the clients, including having more issues addressed by social workers in team meetings. Although there are no similar studies in the nursing home setting, it is likely that having trained social workers responsible for admissions in nursing homes may generate advantages to the facility and to residents as well.

Some facilities attempt to complete all of the admissions paper work in one sitting, while other facilities stagger the paperwork over days or weeks. In any case, there are many papers to review and sign—sometimes as many as twenty to thirty pages—including an admissions contract, insurance papers, Medicaid (Title XIX) forms, consent papers, agreements with pharmacies, selection of doctors, and private insurance forms. During the admissions process, end-of-life issues inevitably surface. The two most common issues are advance directives and funeral arrangements.

In 1990, with the enactment of the Patient Self-Determination Act (PSDA) (Public Law 101–508, Sections 4206 and 4751), the federal government began to require healthcare facilities that receive Medicaid or Medicare payment (including hospitals and nursing homes) to notify people upon admission that they are entitled to receive information on and have an advance directive. As part of the admissions process, the "responsible party" (the resident, or, if he or she is cognitively impaired, the family member or guardian) is asked if an advance directive is present or desired. Many people are unfamiliar with advance directives and do not understand the difference between a living will, a durable power of attorney for healthcare decisions, and a healthcare directive. Often the social worker provides education not only on the various options but also on the possible consequences of selecting one option over another. A skilled nursing home admissions counselor can help explain these differences and encourage the resident and/or family to discuss treatment preferences.

Kavesh (1994) observes that there are many issues to consider when advance directives are discussed in the context of long-term care. These include autonomy, self-determination, and the determination of decision-making capacity, as well as technical issues such as cardiopulmonary resuscitation, ventilator support, feeding tubes, and other treatment-related options that vary by medical condition.

Nursing home residents generally have the option of remaining with their community physicians or switching to the nursing home's medical director to oversee their care. Ideally, the resident, family, and physician should discuss the presence or absence of a written advance directive and should engage in an ongoing conversation about the resident's health status, prognosis, treatment preferences, and choice of a proxy decision maker. Social workers can encourage all parties to discuss, revisit, and document these issues. Social workers may find themselves striving to facilitate communication among unwilling or unavailable participants, be they family or staff.

Bradley, Perris, and Welte (1998) found that even after the enactment of the Patient Self-Determination Act (PSDA), less than half (36.7 percent) of the residents in six large nursing homes had at least one discussion concerning medical treatment wishes documented in their medical charts; 90 percent of people with a documented discussion had only one discussion, and it occurred during the first year of admission. Social workers can help assess and improve the way in which residents, family, and staff are educated about advance directives and the manner in which these documents and discussions are updated regularly. This should be done not merely for record keeping, but because an ongoing dialogue about end-of-life care can be useful preparation for the resident and the family.

In addition to asking about advance directives during the admissions process, nursing homes typically request the name of the preferred funeral home. This is to avoid confusion at the time of death, but it may come as a surprise to the family and resident. After all, it is not a question that one has much practice answering outside the nursing home context. For some, this question prompts little stress because they have already considered and perhaps made their final arrangement plans. Certainly the resident's or family's emotional response to the question provides the social worker with a wealth of information about the work that may lie ahead.

Social workers can help people understand local final arrangement options and costs (Bern-Klug, Ekerdt, and Wilkinson 1999). Workers can arrange for a panel of local funeral directors to talk with a group of interested family members, perhaps through the nursing home family council, if there is one. A representative from the local Funeral Consumers Alliance (www.funerals.org) can be invited to be part of the panel. Social workers can also encourage residents and families to talk with a representative of their faith community, if appropriate, about final arrangements. Also, social workers should have information readily available about local body- and organ-donation programs. Social workers should anticipate that talking about funerals may stimulate death anxiety for some residents and/or family members.

A successful admissions process is more than completing paperwork and sharing nursing home protocol. It is an opportunity to learn what the resident and family value and fear. It is also an opportunity for the social worker to plant seeds for later discussions about the end of life, including pain control, communication about prognoses, and the facility's attitude toward palliative care. It is a time for the social worker to establish himself or herself as a resource and as an advocate to help with the transitions associated with living and dying in the nursing home.

A successful admissions process leaves the resident and family knowing what to expect and whom to call as more information is needed. It leaves the nursing home staff better able to meet the care needs and expectations of this newly admitted person, and his or her family.

ASSESSMENT AND CARE PLAN MEETINGS

Federal regulations require that upon admission, every three months there after, and annually, every nursing home resident in a Medicaid/Medicare facility in the country

634 CLINICAL PRACTICE ISSUES IN END-OF-LIFE CARE

be assessed using a standardized instrument called the Minimum Data Set (MDS). Assessments are also required when there is a significant change in the resident's status, and upon return from a hospitalization. The MDS assesses cognitive, communicative/ hearing, vision, mood and behavior, psychosocial well-being, physical functioning and structural problems, continence, disease diagnoses, health conditions (including pain), oral/dental/nutritional status, skin, activities, medications, special treatments, and discharge potential.

Nursing homes are allowed some latitude in determining their own methods for completing the MDS. In some facilities, one person—usually a nurse—completes the form in consultation with other staff. In other facilities, the charge nurse, social worker, dietician, and other staff complete sections of the MDS for each resident.

Following the MDS assessment process, there should be a care plan meeting attended by key staff members, the resident (if cognitively able), and the family. According to nursing home advocates, "Both the assessment process and the care planning were established by the federal law as standards of good nursing home practice to achieve a resident's right to individualized care" (Burger et al. 1996:40). The social worker should bring any concerns about the resident's psychological, social, or spiritual challenges to the team meeting. Depression and anxiety are prevalent. Counseling services for the resident can be provided through the facility's social worker, a referral to an outside counseling group contracted by the nursing home, or through a counselor in the community that the resident retains (Beaulieu 2002:22). Some residents may need to be seen by a psychologist or a psychiatrist.

In those facilities in which care plan meetings take place, the social worker can facilitate discussions with the resident and family regarding changes in health status, updating advance directives, and ensuring that the team understands and respects the resident's wishes. The care plan meeting, although time-consuming, is an excellent venue for discussing the resident's status and prognosis, advance directive, palliative care concerns (including physical pain and emotional suffering), and issues related to the resident's and/or family member's concerns. Having these discussions can help to socialize the resident, family, and the staff to expect discussions on these and other important issues throughout the nursing home stay. Skills in active listening, decision making, values clarification, crisis management, and interpersonal communication are crucial for productive and compassionate care plan meetings. Unfortunately, not all nursing homes conduct in-person care plan meetings, and some do not make much of an effort to include residents and/or family members. Whether care plan meetings are a part of the nursing home's routine, the social worker should make sure that these critical issues are addressed with the resident and family.

The care plan meeting can be an important venue for discussing a change in prognosis or a change in care preference. If the resident has experienced a dramatic decline, serious accident, or acute event such as a heart attack or stroke, the team should discuss how the new situation affects the care plan, as well as the family.

But for many—if not most—nursing home residents, dying will not be signaled by a dramatic change or a noteworthy event. Indeed, the dying experience of most nursing home residents is cloaked in ambiguity. Increasingly, the nursing home culture is shifting to an awareness that the deaths of most residents are not preceded by clear signals of dying, especially if the resident does not have cancer. Nursing homes need to establish care plans to meet the palliative care needs of all residents, even those whose dying is ambiguous.

HOSPITAL TRANSFERS

Accidents, acute illness, and the effects of multiple chronic illnesses can all prompt a trip to the hospital. Advance directives that are in effect in the nursing home are not necessarily in effect en route to a hospital (consult your state law). Furthermore, in the heat of an emergency, the resident's advance directive may not accompany the resident to the hospital.

If the hospitalization is planned, special transportation or family may transport the resident. The advance directive can accompany the resident and be made part of the patient's chart in the hospital. Even when the advance directive is present, and even when it is consulted, it may be inadequate to address the situation. For example, living wills are generally invoked only when two physicians have documented that the person is "terminal." If that declaration has not been made, the living will is silent on care decisions. A durable power of attorney for healthcare decisions, which appoints a proxy decision maker, is generally more flexible and useful as an advance directive, especially when terminal status has not been determined.

Discussions about possible hospitalizations are important topics for care-plan meetings and between physicians and residents—or their proxy decision makers. The discussions need to include acceptable reasons for hospitalizations, and how to handle possible interventions that may be suggested in the hospital setting, such as ventilator support, or the insertion of a feeding tube. If they so chose, residents and families can arrange with the physician for a "Do Not Hospitalize" order, which will be communicated to the nursing home staff. Remaining in the nursing home can be especially important in the case of people who are approaching death, and should be considered a part of quality end-of-life care (Engle 1998).

Some authors and more than a few clinicians have argued that hospitalizing nursing home residents affected by dementia is more likely to harm than help them, as reported by physician D. Peter Birkett: "In acute care general hospitals, the confused are given tranquilizers; those liable to fall are put in restraints; those who do not choose to eat are tube fed; the incontinent are catheterized. These measures cause thrombophlebitis, pulmonary embolism, pressure sores, aspiration pneumonia, urinary tract infections, and bacteremia, each of which will, if diagnosed, be treated" (2001:210).

HOSPICE ENROLLMENT

Hospice services are available in the nursing home setting. In those facilities in which the administrator has a favorable opinion of hospice, residents are more likely to be enrolled in hospice (Jones, Nackerud, and Boyle 1997).

Medicare (or sometimes Medicaid) beneficiaries in nursing homes can receive federal payment for hospice services. The criteria for hospice enrollment include these points: the person is eligible for Medicare Part A; the doctor and the hospice medical director certify that the patient is terminally ill and probably has less than six months to live; the patient signs a statement choosing hospice care instead of routine Medicare covered benefits for the terminal illness; and care is received through a Medicare-approved hospice (for more information, refer to www.medicare.gov).

Medicare will pay for the hospice care, but it does not pay for room and board in the nursing home. Consequently, the nursing home resident will continue to pay out of pocket for nursing home care, or have care paid for by private long-term care insurance or Medicaid (a federal/state program that pays toward the costs of nursing home care for people who can document that they do not have the income and resources to pay for care).

If the person who is dying is being admitted, or readmitted to the nursing home after a hospitalization, a decision needs to be made whether to admit him or her as a regular nursing home resident (Medicaid or private pay), as a subacute patient (Medicare reimbursable), or as a hospice patient (Medicaid or private pay for general nursing home care including room and board, and Medicare for terminal illness-related care). The nursing home receives higher reimbursement for providing sub-acute care. While there is a financial incentive to facilities (and to families, if the resident is private pay) to delay hospice enrollment until the subacute days are exhausted, the needs of the resident should determine the type of care received.

The benefits of enrolling in Medicare hospice services as a nursing home resident can include payment for supplies and equipment related to the care of the terminal illness, such as pain medication (Medicare does not typically pay for prescribed medications otherwise), special mattresses that discourage bedsores, bereavement counseling (the family can receive bereavement support for up to one year after the death), access to volunteers and chaplain services, access to pain specialists, and extra nursing care, which allows the resident who is dying the opportunity for extra baths and personal services beyond those provided by the nursing home staff. Considering that dying nursing home residents average more than ten symptoms at any given time, the special expertise that hospice staff have with managing these symptoms can be an important asset to the resident, family and nursing home staff (Allegre, Frank, and McIntosh 1999).

Not all nursing home staff members are eager to see residents enroll in hospice. Some staff members feel they know the resident best and can provide the best care without the introduction of new people (hospice workers) for the last days or weeks of the resident's life. They do not perceive hospice to be beneficial to the staff, resident, or family. Other staff members welcome hospice personnel and recognize the expertise that hospice workers have in assessing and treating physical, psychosocial, and spiritual issues that can affect the process of dying. They see the hospice staff as an extension of the care that the nursing home staff can provide, not only to the resident who is dying, but also to the family. Some nursing home staff members realize they can improve their own end-of-life skills by observing and interacting with hospice staff.

The nursing home social worker can play an instrumental role in connecting the resident (or the family—if the resident has cognitive impairment) with hospice. The social worker can educate the family about hospice throughout the nursing home stay, and can encourage the family to let the physician know that they would like to discuss the option of hospice. The extent to which hospice can benefit the resident and family depends in part on the circumstances. Not all hospices are equally effective in the nursing home setting. Some nursing home directors of nursing or administrators find they must go through a number of hospices before they find one they can work well with.

The social worker may need to conduct formal and informal staff education about hospice. Nursing home staff members may not be familiar with hospice services or may have had a bad experience with hospice. Despite the potential benefits associated with enrolling nursing home residents in hospice, nationally only a small percentage of nursing home residents (and their family members) receives hospice benefits.

Although care for nursing home residents is increasing as a proportion of hospice case loads, only a small number of nursing home residents are enrolled in hospice care. "On average, less than 1 percent of residents per facility were identified as hospice beneficiaries. . . . Approximately 30.1 percent of homes reported having at least one hospice resident, and about 4.2 percent of facilities reported having 5 percent or more of their residents on the hospice benefit" (Petrisek and Mor 1999:284). In a study of nursing home residents in five states, Miller, Gozala, and Mor (2000) report that one-fourth of nursing home residents admitted to hospice had a cancer diagnosis and a length of stay of seven days or less. This short amount of time in hospice does not allow the resident, family, or nursing home staff time to develop the relationships needed for the most beneficial hospice care.

AFTER THE DEATH OCCURS: BEREAVEMENT CARE

As I was walking back down the hall, I noticed a man sitting in his wheelchair in the doorway of his room. I have seen this man over the past few weeks, but have never had a conversation with him. He was holding a page from the newspaper. It was the obituary section. He said to me, "read this—this one here about Larry. He was from here. He died last Friday. He wasn't feeling well and they sent him to the hospital last Wednesday or Thursday . . . I saw him the night before he left. Then he got there and he died. He's gone. He was my buddy. I'm going to miss him." He handed me the page and I read it.
                                                                    —Forbes n.d.

The death of a nursing home resident affects the family and the staff, and it affects fellow residents—especially roommates. Before the death occurs, the social worker can facilitate visits and other opportunities for expression among nursing home residents. After the death has occurred, some facilities hold an on-site memorial service. Others make arrangements to transport close friends to the funeral home. Some post the names of the deceased on the bulletin board, or print the names in the facility's newsletter. Other nursing homes have no formal method of letting surviving residents know about the death of a fellow resident.

If the person in the social service position is a BSW- or MSW-prepared social worker, it is likely that he or she has more formal education in dealing with loss, grief, and bereavement than any other onsite staff member. The social worker can be a resource not only to residents who are dying, their families, and other residents, but also to fellow staff members.

Social workers can connect people with bereavement resources in the community, and can also make available books, pamphlets, and videos about grief and bereavement (see, for example, www.lastacts.org for a wealth of resources). The social worker can offer an onsite support group for residents dealing with loss, including the death of a fellow resident. Workers can also organize one-time meetings or ongoing support groups for staff or family members.

In order for social workers to remain effective in nursing home settings, and indeed to grow in these settings, it is important to develop methods for addressing and honoring their own experiences of loss and grief as well as their own psychosocial needs (Hartz and Splain 1997).

THE CHALLENGES OF NURSING HOME LIVING AND DYING

Care provided in nursing homes varies from facility to facility, and can vary within a facility over time, during different shifts, and on different floors. The quality of care can be affected by a change in ownership or management. Providing excellent care in the nursing home setting is a challenge in the face of high resident-to-staff ratios, high staff turnover (among all levels of staff, from nurse aids to administrators), and lack of staff training—especially in end-of-life related issues.

The ways in which nursing home staff members perceive being evaluated by state surveyors may also contribute to substandard end-of-life care. The quality indicators that state surveyors use to assess nursing homes were designed with rehabilitation and maintenance of resident heath status in mind. Special provisions for residents who are dying were not incorporated (Matesa 2000). Therefore, when a dying resident experiences weight loss, bedsores, and dehydration—all conditions that can occur as part of dying—the nursing home staff may fear that they will be cited by state surveyors. This kind of systemic bind can be demoralizing to staff and can contribute to burnout.

S. S. Travis observes, "The resident approaching end-stage disease, has lost most of his or her compensatory mechanisms and is moving toward a time of terminal decline. This resident should not receive the same type of care as someone who needs restorative, rehabilitative, or curative care" (2001:284). The fact that nursing home residents are likely to be affected by dementia and/or depression as well as other multiple chronic conditions can complicate providing excellent care in general, and specifically at the end of life. Many nursing home residents are also socially vulnerable. They do not have family members or friends available. They are not connected in any way with people beyond the walls of the nursing home. Furthermore, not only are they isolated within the wider community, but they may also be experiencing social problems with staff members, fellow residents, and/or their roommates in the facilities in which they live.

For all these reasons, and more, the nursing-home social worker plays an instrumental role in helping to identify and meet the needs—especially the psychosocial needs—of residents who are approaching the end of life.

The nursing-home social worker role, however, is not well developed in many facilities. Some administrators and nursing directors lack familiarity with the skills and education of a social worker and assign duties that are not a good match for social worker skills. Social workers are educated using a biopsychosocial model and a person-in-environment model. The social work worldview may clash with those of other staff members who follow a medical model or who have not been trained to view the individual as part of the larger social context. The social worker may struggle with how to incorporate more of a social model for resident care. The social worker may have good ideas and intentions about how excellent end-of-life care could be delivered in the facility, but may lack the time or power to make needed changes. The social worker may need additional education in aspects of end-of-life care. High resident to staff ratios and high staff turnover compound these challenges.

On the other hand, the capable social worker in even a benignly mediocre nursing home can provide leadership far beyond his or her title. The social worker who is competent, confident, and compassionate can play a uniquely important role in the life of a resident and family. As one nursing-home social worker explained to her administrator, "for the resident and the family there is only one shot at a 'good death.' You can't go back and do it again. My job is to make sure that it is as good as possible. One family at a time, I can make a difference."

Research on the roles of the nursing-home social worker and how those roles can be strengthened to the benefit of residents and families who face dying in the nursing home setting is needed. Social workers have skills and education that can benefit residents and families, but we do not know the extent to which the application of these skills is encouraged or even allowed in nursing homes.

During admissions, care planning, hospital transfers, consideration of hospice, and in general, social workers should look for and create opportunities to talk with residents and families about their thoughts and wishes for end-of-life care; palliative-care protocols in the facility; the resident's and families' palliative-care concerns; how physical pain is assessed and treated; how psychosocial and spiritual issues are addressed; and how grievances are handled.

Throughout the nursing home stay, social workers can help residents and families identify and prioritize needs. Social workers need to be mindful of ethical, cultural, and spiritual issues discussed in other chapters of this book, which can affect nursing home resident's end-of-life experiences. They can provide referrals to other resources in the facility and in the community. Social workers can be instrumental in helping to identify resident strengths, including those strengths on the social work assessment and care plan (Beaulieu 2002). A strengths-based approach can help residents and families identify their capacities and build on their many years of experience in problem solving (Saleebey 2002). With seventy, eighty, and ninety years of experience in living, residents and family members have much to contribute to their own well-being in the nursing home setting.

The social worker can learn from residents and family members about what "peace of mind" means to them, and how peace of mind can be achieved in the nursing home setting. These discussions and the follow-up action surrounding the discussions can enhance the experience of living and dying in the nursing home setting.

CONCLUSION

The nursing home setting contains some of the most vulnerable people in our society. Typically, residents face multiple chronic conditions that are often compounded by depression or dementia. Residents are often socially as well as physically and cognitively vulnerable. Nursing homes have become dominant settings for dying. Because of the aging of the population and the trend toward institutionalizing people who are close to death, it is expected that the number and percentage of nursing home deaths will increase over the next decades (Teno 2002).

The nursing home has been called "heaven's waiting room" (Forbes 2001:41). Social workers in the nursing home setting encounter dying and death as part of daily life. With support, education, and encouragement, social workers may embrace the opportunity to help enhance the experience of dying in the nursing home setting. Social work skills are an excellent fit for the psychosocial end-of-life needs of nursing home residents and families.

REFERENCES

Allegre, A., B. Frank, and E. McIntosh, E. 1999. Hospice in the nursing home: A valuable collaboration. *Bioethics Forum* 15(3): 7–12.

Beaulieu, E. M. 2002. *A Guide for Nursing Home Social Workers.* New York: Springer.

Bern-Klug, M., D. J. Ekerdt, and D. S. Wilkinson. 1999. What families know about funeral-related costs: Implications for social work practice. *Health & Social Work* 24(2): 128–137.

Birkett, D. P. 2001. *Psychiatry in the Nursing Home.* 2d ed. New York: Hawthorne.

Bradley, E. H., V. Peiris, and T. Wetle. 1998. Discussions about end-of-life care in nursing homes. *Journal of the American Geriatrics Society* 46:1235–1241.

Burger, S. G., V. Fraser, S. Hunt, and B. Frank. 1996. *Nursing Homes: Getting Good Care There.* San Luis Obispo, CA: American Source Books.

Code of Federal Regulations. 2001. Public Health, 42 (Part 430 to End) Revised as of October 1, 2001. Washington, DC: U.S. Government Printing Office.

Engle, V. F. 1998. Care of the living, care of the dying: Reconceptualizing nursing home care. *Journal of the American Geriatrics Society* 46:1172–1174.

Field, M. J., and C. K. Cassel, eds. 1997. *Approaching Death: Improving Care at the End of Life.* Washington, DC: Institute of Medicine.

Forbes, S. 2001. This is heaven's waiting room: End of life in one nursing home. *Journal of Gerontological Nursing* 27(11): 37–45.

———. n.d. Unpublished field notes from the research project End-of-Life in Nursing Homes: Process and Outcomes of Care. NINR #R15NR04974.

Forbes, S., M. Bern-Klug, and C. Gessert. 2000. End-of-life decision making for nursing home residents with dementia. *Journal of Nursing Scholarship* 32(3): 251–258.

Gillick, M. R., N. A. Serell, and L. S. Gillick. 1982. Adverse consequences of hospitalization of the elderly. *Social Science and Medicine* 16:1033–1038.

Hanson, L. C., M. Danis, and J. Garrett. 1997. What is wrong with end-of-life care? Opinions of bereaved family members. *Journal of the American Geriatrics Society* 45:1339–1344.

Hartz, G. W., and D. M. Splain. 1997. *Psychosocial Intervention in Long-Term Care: An Advanced Guide.* New York: Haworth Press.

Jones, A. 2002. *The National Nursing Home Survey: 1999 Summary.* Washington, DC: National Center for Health Statistics.

Jones, B., L. Nackerud, and D. Boyle. 1997. Differential utilization of hospice services in nursing homes. *Hospice Journal* 12:41–57.

Kane, R. A., R. L. Kane, and R. C. Ladd. 1998. *The Heart of Long-Term Care.* New York: Oxford University Press.

Kavesh, W. N. 1994. Self-determination and long-term care. In *Patient Self-Determination in Long-Term Care: Implementing the PSDA in Medical Decisions*, ed. M. Kapp, 11–42. New York: Springer.

Keay, T. J., L. Fredman, G. A. Taler, S. Datta, and S. A. Levenson. 1994. Indicators of quality medical care for the terminally ill in nursing homes. *Journal of the American Geriatrics Association* 42:853–860.

Krauss, N. A., and B. M. Altman. 1998. Characteristics of nursing home residents—1996. *MEPS Research Findings #5.* Rockville, MD: Agency for Health Care Policy and Research.

Matesa, J. 2000. *Long-Term Care, Part IV: Developing Quality Indicators for End-of-Life Care in Nursing Homes.* Kansas City, MO: Midwest Bioethics Center.

Miller, S. C., P. Gozalo, and V. Mor. 2000. Use of Medicare's hospice benefit by nursing facility residents. http://aspe.hhs.gov/daltcp/reports/nufares.htm.

National Center for Health Statistics. 1996. *Vital Statistics of the United States, 1992.* Washington, DC: U.S. Government Printing Office.

National Hospice and Palliative Care Organization. 2002. *NHPCO Facts and Figures.* Alexandria, VA: NHPCO.

Petrisek, A. C., and V. Mor. 1999. Hospice in nursing homes: A facility-level analysis of the distribution of hospice beneficiaries. *The Gerontologist* 39(3): 279–290.

Sahouyn, N. R., L. A. Pratt, H. Lentzer, A. Dey, and K. N. Robinson. 2001. The changing profile of nursing home residents, 1985–1997. *Aging Trends* 4. Hyattsville, MD: National Center for Health Statistics.

Saleebey, D. 2002. *The Strengths Perspective in Social Work Practice.* 5th ed. Boston: Allyn & Bacon.

Teno, J. 2002. Now is the time to embrace nursing homes as a place of care for dying persons. *Innovations in End-of-Life Care* 4(2): 1–7.

Travis, S. S. 2001. Palliative care: A way of thinking, a prescription for doing. *Geriatric Nursing* 22(6): 284–285.

33

THE FAMILY UNITY PROGRAM FOR HIV-AFFECTED FAMILIES: CREATING A FAMILY-CENTERED AND COMMUNITY-BUILDING CONTEXT FOR INTERVENTIONS

CHRISTIAN ITIN, SUSAN McFEATERS, AND SUSAN TAYLOR-BROWN

THE FAMILY UNITY program for HIV-affected families provides a safe haven to address the dual foci of supporting and enhancing parents' parenting roles and supporting children who are coping with parental illness and, frequently, death by teaching them new ways to adapt to this painful reality. Programs that allow parents to act with integrity and to play an active role in planning for their children have the best chance of meeting the family's needs in a holistic manner (Gilbert 1999). Family Unity, a four-day retreat, has since 1996 provided a strengths-oriented, experiential, empowerment-based set of interventions, including recreational activities, adventure-based work, family rituals, and respite. These activities facilitate grieving and remembrance while enhancing the youths' connections to their families and the broader Family Unity community. By partnering with the families on an ongoing basis and inviting them to return annually, families become an integral part of the program's design and implementation. Family Unity is the main component of Together Everyone Achieves More (TEAM) services, a grant-funded program that provides year-round services to HIV-affected families.

The following case example provides an illustration of one such family—a composite based on actual participants—attending Family Unity for the first time.

CASE EXAMPLE

Rhonda is a thirty-one-year-old Latina woman who has four children. Both Rhonda and one of her daughters have AIDS. The first year that they were scheduled to come to Family Unity, a camp for HIV-affected families, they did not show for the bus because Rhonda became frightened about being at a camp where HIV is openly discussed. In the past, when she has tried to talk with her daughters about her illness, they have become very upset and cried or left the room. She felt as though she had failed as a mother.

Throughout the next year, her friends in the women's support group and her case manager encouraged her to attend camp. She feared talking about HIV because of earlier experiences. When Rhonda shared her diagnosis with some friends and her minister, they rejected her. Her minister's rejection was particularly painful because he had been very supportive of her earlier efforts to achieve and maintain her recovery.

When she finally arrived with her family at Family Unity, she was apprehensive yet hopeful about what would happen during the weekend. Rhonda was doing the best she could to care for her family while managing her own illness and her daughter's illness. Rhonda has been receiving HIV care since 1989, and her daughter, Angelique, has received HIV care since her birth in 1992. Rhonda believes that her husband, who died in 1993, infected her in the early 1980s. Recently, Angelique has been hospitalized repeatedly and is not doing as well as she was a year ago. Her three sons, Carlos (12), Roberto (13), and Juan (15), are HIV-negative and struggling with a variety of issues, including drug use, fighting, and poor academic performance. When Angelique was hospitalized for two weeks, Rhonda lived at the hospital because she was afraid Angelique's medications would not be given to her at the right times. The boys were left at home, largely on their own, and missed a lot of school during this time.

Rhonda is afraid to turn to neighbors for help because she fears that they will find out about their AIDS diagnoses and be mean to her family. She worries the most about passing before Angelique and feels that she is the only one who can care for Angelique. Rhonda does not have reliable family members to look after the boys. As they grow, she finds it increasingly difficult to manage them. She wants them to have a normal, carefree childhood. Instead, they are struggling and worrying about Angelique and her. She feels guilty about the loss of their childhood and blames herself. She worries about what will happen to them if she is not able to manage them and becomes overwhelmed when her case manager asks her to do permanency planning. Her main desire is to have her children stay together if she dies or is unable to care for them.

The first day at camp, Rhonda was quiet as she observed others openly talking about their lives. During the weekend, she began to open up and ask others for help in addressing her issues. She realized that many of her children's problems resulted from their fears that Rhonda was sicker than she really was at that time.

Equally, her children began to share their lives. Juan was so frightened that he frequently got into fights and was suspended from school repeatedly. He blamed himself for his father's death and had never expressed this to anyone before. He cried as he told his counselors about his worries. Other campers invited him and he agreed to join the twelve-step anger-management group at home by TEAM services, which was facilitated by two adolescents and two staff from Family Unity.

All of the children were apprehensive about the future. The weekend helped them form relationships with others who are confronting similar issues and begin building trust. The groundwork was laid for future work. When they returned home, they had community contacts to help them work on their individual and family issues as they wanted.

❈

THE JULY 2002 International Conference on AIDS in Barcelona called for long-overdue attention to children orphaned by HIV/AIDS, especially those in Africa, where the situation is particularly grave. There are estimated to be thirteen million orphans from HIV/AIDS, the majority in Africa, with 125,000 projected in America (Michaels and Levine 1992). At this time, the likelihood of dependent children of HIV-infected parents becoming orphans continues to be a reality, despite gains in medical treatment.

Few HIV/AIDS support services have been created to assist entire family systems. Historically, many of the first existing HIV support programs were created to offer assistance to gay men and their partners (Hackel et al. 1997). Often HIV/AIDS support programs are small, minimally staffed, and equipped to handle only the immediate needs of the individual infected with HIV/AIDS and provide support to caregivers such as in-home services or respite care. Many agencies provide services to individuals perceived as having urgent and immediate needs, such as financial assistance for food, medication, rent, and transportation. However, these services are often not able to handle the multiple long-term needs of child rearing families affected by HIV/AIDS (Hackel et al. 1997). To date, the services provided to surviving orphans are fragmented and short-term. Most of the time, relatives try to care for the orphans, but more information is needed about how these orphans and their new caregivers cope after the death of a parent. Anderson et al. (1999) reported that extended family members wish to care for surviving children and need support and resources in order to accomplish this.

Interventions are needed that approach the reality of HIV-affected families in which the surviving children can both cope with parental death and adapt to a new living situation. Responses need to be based upon a developmental perspective rather than waiting to respond at the time of parental death. Taylor-Brown (1999) calls for a community-based, developmental approach that maximizes the resiliency of family members confronting this situation. Developmentally, the death of a parent poses a major developmental challenge to the surviving children.

The existing literature addressing grief and loss in youth provides some helpful guidelines for assessing the developmental needs of grieving youth and is selectively addressed in this chapter. The majority of reported studies assessing children's grief and loss have focused on the experience of two parent families, predominantly Caucasian, middle or upper class families where the children have a surviving parent to help them navigate their losses. As noted earlier, HIV-affected families are drawn primarily from communities of color, living in poverty. Our experience suggests that the reality for HIV orphans is distinctively different from the reality of two parent families coping with parental illness and death. For single parent families, parental death is often more traumatic when there are inadequate arrangements made for stable living conditions for surviving children. For example, a young Latino was separated from all of his brothers at the time of his mother's death and two years later still does not have a stable housing situation because he refused to enter foster care as a fourteen year old. He has only intermittent contact with his siblings and his case manager still has not obtained health coverage for him.

The growing literature linking grief and trauma holds promise for refining our approach to HIV-affected youth and will be applied in future studies. Christ, Siegel, and Christ (2002) report that traumatic grief has been used to refer to conditions in children that manifest both grief and trauma. When trauma and bereavement symptoms are both present, it is advisable and often essential to address and at least partially resolve the trauma issues before the bereavement issues can be successfully processed (Christ 2000; Cohen et al. 2002; Pfefferbaum, Nixon, and Tucker 1999).

Today human services for HIV-affected families largely focus on whether permanency plans are made prior to parental death. There is limited attention to the viability of the new living arrangement or on attending to the biopsychosocial needs of orphaned children who live. Attention needs to be given to the coping and adaptation of surviving family members.

FAMILIES AFFECTED BY HIV/AIDS

Since the recognition of HIV/AIDS, much of the behavioral and social science research literature has focused on the impact of the virus on the infected individual. However, the effects of the disease extend well beyond those afflicted, reaching out and affecting the families who cope and care for a loved one with this incurable disease (Bor, Miller, and Goldman 1993). The difficulties, struggles, and adjustments that families face in coping with the impact of dealing with this highly stigmatized disease have not been fully understood (McFeaters 2000).

Parents living with HIV are surviving longer. They are confronting a number of challenges: from how to manage a chronic, life-threatening illness to helping their children cope with the realities of HIV disease while juggling the normal developmental issues that all families face. Children and adolescents in HIV affected families have unique developmental issues. They experience complex challenges ranging from watching a parent become sick to dying and, for many, experiencing multiple deaths. At the same time, parents cope with managing HIV in themselves and in some cases, in their children.

HIV-affected families need services that address developmental challenges that face all families and more. Their needs are multiplied because of the fact that most are families of color, living in poverty, in communities where they are heavily exposed to crime. For example, on her way to school in the morning an eleven-year old was raped at gunpoint. In her brief life, she has coped with her father's death, her mother's illness and this violent experience. Furthermore, many families also have to deal with current or previous substance abuse, domestic violence, mental illness, and other challenges, which complicate the normative developmental tasks of a family.

Social isolation resulting from a fear of stigma is one of the more challenging problems faced by families affected by HIV/AIDS. On the one hand, family members may draw a boundary between the family and others outside the immediate family system by not disclosing the diagnosis to more distant relatives, friends, close associates and others who comprise the social network (Bor, Miller and Goldman 1993). Low-income families may also live in close physical proximity to neighbors and institutions, where intimate interaction is prevalent and personal information or behaviors are hard to hide. An individual's diagnosis of HIV/AIDS can promptly become public knowledge, imposing shame and stigma on family relations, having a negative effect on identity and self-esteem (Dane and Miller 1992). Family members may therefore experience rejection by friends, the community, loss of jobs, and harassment (Powell-Cope and Brown 1992). Thus, the fear of stigma from HIV/AIDS in families can lead to isolation from extended family, friends, and others who might have been potential supports to the family.

According to Mellins and Ehrhardt (1994), families report stressors related to illness management, stigma associated with HIV infection, and multiple deaths due to AIDS. Compared with uninfected caretakers, HIV-infected parents reported more isolation and fewer financial and support resources. A painful psychosocial aspect of HIV/AIDS is the threat to the parent's ability to care for their children until they are ready to live independently as young adults. Moreover, some HIV-infected children and adults must cope with the anticipation of their own death while simultaneously mourning family members who have died (Boyd-Franklin, Drelich, and Schwolsky-Fitch 1995). This "out of season" loss is difficult for HIV-infected parents to address (Taylor-Brown 1998). Hence, anticipatory loss is an important issue for individuals and families coping with any terminal illness (Wolfelt 1983).

The impact of HIV/AIDS in families is complicated by other factors as well. By today's standards, the complexity and societal reactions to HIV/AIDS appear to be like no other disease. In all probability, families affected by HIV/AIDS face more complex problems in their adjustment to, and coping with, illness than families dealing with other chronic or life threatening illnesses (Bor, Miller, and Goldman 1993). When a family member dies of AIDS or commits suicide, the surviving family members may feel even more strongly that they have done something wrong in having a family member or friend die this way (Silverman 1994). Thus, families impacted by HIV/AIDS experience stigma, shame, ostracism, social isolation, and rejection, and therefore, complicated grief. They are in desperate need of supportive services that address the complicated factors associated with HIV/AIDS that greatly affect families multi-generationally. The strategies, adopted by infected mothers for themselves and their children, may not be congruent with textbook theory and call into question traditional models of coping behaviors (Mason and Korr 1999).

Adult caregivers are often the forgotten casualties of the AIDS epidemic (Kreibick 1995). Additionally, family members who are caregivers of orphaned children must address the psychological needs of both HIV-infected and uninfected children (Spiegel and Mayers 1991). In many HIV-affected families, the burden of caretaking falls on older extended family members, often grandmothers, who are now raising children and youth. Often these caregivers not only are coping with the loss of their adult child, but they must also take on the responsibilities of caring for surviving grandchildren. Their grief can often be complicated by feeling anger and resentment towards their child for leaving them with the unexpected demands of caring for grand-children at an unanticipated time in their own life cycle (Boyd-Franklin, Drelich, and Schwolsky-Fitch 1995).

Many times caregivers are angry at the unfairness of having to raise a second or even a third family due to HIV/AIDS. They often hold the anger within themselves and are fearful of expressing their feelings to their families for fear of making things worse. Even if a caregiver wants to work through the anger directly, it may not be possible to do so with the appropriate person. Additionally, the anger can often be complicated by unresolved grief that is difficult to resolve in the family (Kreibick 1995). These same feelings of loss, anger, and resentment can also be experienced by other newly appointed caregivers such as aunts, uncles, or close friends of the family (McFeaters 2000).

Children in these families are equally overlooked. Many serve as caregivers for their ill parents and siblings without community sanction or support for these roles. The family's experience of handling HIV disease affects school performance with many youth experiencing a decrease in school grades associated with the illness in the parent (Draimin et al. 1999). Adolescents are frequently left to their own devices while a parent is alive. During hospitalizations, many live on their own with a neighbor or a relative checking in on them.

The death of a parent affects the surviving family members in a variety of ways. The most apparent need of surviving children is to adjust to the premature death of a parent. The death leaves a gap caused not only by the lack of the dead parent's physical presence, but also by the part this parent played in framing and directing the family's life (Silverman 2000).

When a parent dies from AIDS, each child in the family loses life as she or he has known it. Siblings are frequently separated as relatives try to provide care. Recently, four surviving children ended up in the following living arrangements: two brothers were sent out of state five days after the funeral to live with an aunt, one daughter moved in with an older sister, and one daughter ran away and is living in a shelter for homeless adolescents. Not only did they lose their mother, but their sibling relationships were lost as well. Following a parental death, many have difficulty accepting the new caregiver's expectations of them and have difficulty adjusting to a new living situation while still in the immediate phase of grieving. The majority of orphans from poor families do not have the luxury of staying in their own homes immediately after death. Their family home is usually lost within the first week to a month, and far too many siblings lose contact with each other. The new caregivers often think that the children should behave similarly to children who have not had these challenges, which accelerate, if not obliterate, childhood as most people know it. Many caregivers also think it is better not to talk about the deceased, further isolating the children. The children, like their parents, often display remarkable resilience in the face of adversity. They are survivors and warrant more attention and direct support than they have received to date.

Finally, HIV/AIDS affected families must endure secrecy, stress and coping, a lack of social support, difficulty in communication and disclosure, responses to the illness, and changing structures and roles in families (Bor, Miller, and Goldman 1993).

For many, experiences with the social service and healthcare systems has been negative, complicating the desire and/or ability to access needed family services. Despite stigma and multiple losses, and despite the physical and social intensity of this disease, many children and their families manage not only to sustain themselves but also to thrive (Lloyd 1999).

EVOLUTION OF FAMILY UNITY CAMP

Family Unity had a very humble beginning. In 1995, few camps around the country were offering a camping experience for HIV-infected children and adolescents. At this time, many camps were afraid to incorporate HIV positive children due to the stigma and unfounded fear that HIV/AIDS might be casually transmitted. Double H Ranch in the Adirondack Mountains, one of Paul Newman's international network of camps for children who have life-threatening illness, welcomed HIV positive children to the camp. A mother whose son was going to Double H ranch for the immunology session commented to Susan Taylor-Brown, "Why can't we all go? We need a chance to have fun as a family." With this simple comment, the concept of Family Unity was born. It took two more years of planning and fundraising for the first families to arrive in 1997, and today 115 family members attend annually with fifty to sixty staff. The creation of Family Unity was a natural progression from the early support groups that were established for HIV-infected women and from groups for caregivers that the author began in 1990.

From the beginning, Family Unity has been a partnership among the families, the Family Unity staff, and the Double H staff. It is a dynamic process that responds to the emerging needs of the community. Our intent was to create a retreat environment that was respectful of families' cultures, assisted families in managing HIV, and its impact on the family, by specifically enhancing the families' ability to mobilize their energies in productive, as opposed to destructive, ways.

Family Unity builds upon the strong base of Double H Hole in the Woods Camp. Newman's vision was to create an environment where kids with life-threatening illnesses could have a camp experience just like any other kid and an opportunity to "raise hell" (Newman 2002). This vision provided the ideal foundation for Family Unity. From the opening night to the Sunday goodbyes, camp is designed to provide an array of opportunities for families to come together, selectively address HIV/AIDS-related issues in a supportive environment, and build powerful, sustaining family memories and supportive relationships with other families and staff.

Staff is drawn from the Double H staff, AIDS community, AIDS community service providers, social work programs in the area, and community members. Each group brings special talents to the weekend. From the start, members of the HIV/AIDS community have volunteered to staff the program. This helps to ensure that programming is responsive to the community of affected families and gives youth an opportunity to ask someone living with the virus what that is like. Frequently, children are afraid to ask their parents directly about the illness and find comfort in having frank discussions with other persons with HIV/AIDS. Equally, people with HIV/AIDS who volunteer as staff find giving back to the community enriching. They offer a variety of self-care workshops and offer support to the families during the retreat and throughout the year.

AIDS service providers gain from the opportunity to collaborate with families outside of their formal relationships. Nurses, art therapists, and case managers are part of the team. These informal interactions also help families feel more comfortable working with staff during times of stress. Specifically, children benefit from getting to know staff during camp. Too often they have limited, if any, contact with AIDS service providers in the community. Additionally, service providers in other community-based services volunteer for the weekend. Referrals to needed services are facilitated by the families' familiarity with staff from the referral agencies.

Undergraduate and graduate students collaborate with social-work faculty to offer a strengths-oriented partnership with families in a nonclinical setting. This provides an intensive and rich learning experience grounded in the approach of the program. Students are better equipped to implement a strengths orientation in their subsequent fieldwork settings, which helps community agencies to adapt a strengths-oriented approach. Despite social work's educational emphasis on empowerment practice and strengths-based orientation, a deficit orientation to clients is inherent in many approaches that are problem-focused. The deficit orientation is reinforced by the delivery of services that are framed in a reactive mode, responding in times of family crisis rather than offering preventive or developmental services to respond to the child's experience of death in a normative way.

Finally, over the years, community members who have heard about Family Unity have asked to be a part of the experience. Some are family members or friends of the professional staff. Their inclusion is very supportive to the professional staff member and broadens the volunteer's understanding of the work of the professional staff member. Some children of staff either attend as volunteers or are placed in the age-appropriate cabins to participate directly in the activities and camping experience. This furthers the reduction of the stigmatization associated with HIV/AIDS.

Staffing the program is an arduous and rewarding experience. For an intense and demanding weekend of service, the majority of staff does not receive compensation beyond a token gift of appreciation and the opportunity for continuing education. The majority of staff returns and their evaluations document their appreciation for the partnering with families and the benefit of immersion in the lives of HIV affected families coupled with ongoing training during the weekend. Because Family Unity is held over Labor Day Weekend, some staff experience scheduling conflicts. Staff are encouraged to return, and for every session to date most have done so, creating consistency.

PROGRAMMATIC DEVELOPMENT: INTERVENTIONS THAT ENHANCE FAMILY FUNCTIONING

The likelihood of premature parental death is approached from a developmental perspective that emphasizes strengthening coping and adaptation skills, decreasing social isolation, and providing support. The developmental approach emphasizes the strength of family relationships (Miller 1987; Watkins 2002) and integrates grief and loss in a context of supportive relationships that address the associated pain that children and families feel. Grief and loss issues are addressed in multiple ways during camp, with a focus on the importance of living life fully. Attention is given to creating a safe and supportive environment by emphasizing the importance of respecting each other and by preserving confidentiality when the families return home. This is handled symbolically throughout the weekend by the use of rituals (to be explained in more detail later in the chapter) that reinforce the weekend as an opportunity to open up issues for exploration and then close them at the time the program ends. Families are encouraged to continue working on the issues when they return home. Three key components that are examined in detail include legacy building, experiential interventions, and rituals.

LEGACY BUILDING

From the start, considerable effort has been focused on helping families create and preserve positive family experiences. Many families struggling with the realities of HIV do not have an opportunity for leisure activities that help provide sustenance during difficult times. Financial constraints also interfere with a family's ability to participate in community activities.

One of the most difficult and painful realizations for parents with HIV to face is the possibility that they will most likely die before their children become adults (Taylor-Brown and Wiener 1993). Creating a legacy for their children to remember them can help empower parents by providing them a way to leave a part of themselves behind for their children (Taylor-Brown and Wiener 1998). Family Unity weekend is rich with positive family experiences that are documented for each family. From the time they emerge from the buses, photographs are taken. Family portraits are taken and families participate in a picture-taking workshop.

The pictures are developed during the weekend and memory books are made. Initially, family books were developed. As children became orphaned, we found that siblings were rarely able to remain together, necessitating individual books for all. Beyond Family Unity, the pictures are used in the ongoing groups with youth to talk about their families as they combine narratives with the pictures.

In addition to family books, there is a master Family Unity book, and staff creates individual books. Every year, people bring their earlier books to share. A slideshow for the opening and closing ceremonies provides group history to old and new participants.

Extensive efforts to catalogue the pictures help make the pictures available in the future. Some families lose their possessions through evictions, family discord, or other means. As noted previously, siblings frequently are separated, and they want copies of the Unity pictures to preserve family memories. Yearly we have been asked to make reprints. Increasingly, digital photography and computer imaging are being used to aid this process (see chapter 13).

EXPERIENTIAL INTERVENTIONS

Traditional talk-based interventions, including cognitive, behavioral, psychodynamic, solution-oriented, and narrative, serve an important role in work with clients dealing with HIV/AIDS regarding the grief and loss issues experienced. However, for many clients, these are not sufficient. At the Family Unity retreat, a number of forms of experiential activities are utilized as a means of creating community, facilitating grief work, and aiding clients in enhancing their own resilience. This section will provide an introduction to the theoretical foundations for experiential work in general and attention to adventure-based practices in particular. Examples of how this form of practice is used at Family Unity will be explored, with consideration given to practice implications.

Experiential practice includes a range of nonverbal activities, such as various forms of expression (art, drama, dance), mind-body integration (yoga, massage, hypnosis, martial arts), horticulture, vocational, and activity-oriented (animal-assisted, recreation, and play). Adventure-based practice is one form of experiential practice, which includes the use of cooperative games, problem solving initiatives, trust activities, high-adventure activities (ropes courses, rock climbing, whitewater rafting) and wilderness expeditions such as backpacking, canoe expeditions, and dog sledding (Itin 1996). All forms of experiential practice rest on the use of what Dewey (1938) referred to as experiential learning. Although there are many models for experiential learning, Stehno (1986) identified four key elements in most models of experiential learning. A direct experience is had, then reflected upon, which then leads to an abstract conceptualization and future application. Most social workers, who engage in experiential practice, move beyond just experiential learning to the use of experiential education. Experiential education builds on the experiential learning process by using the transactional relationship between the client and worker and client and social milieu (as most experiential work occurs in a group context), and the reasons that the client, worker, and group are involved together (Itin 1999). Experiences are provided or utilized that build upon the transactional relationships that facilitate a purposeful change process.

With any experiential activity, including adventure activities, it is important to distinguish the level of the intervention. Activities can be aimed at various levels, from recreation to education, therapeutic development, and therapy (Itin 2001). Interventions at the level of recreation are aimed primarily at enhancing pleasurable feelings. At the level of education, the goal is to use an activity to introduce a new skill or concept. At the level of therapeutic development, the goal is to increase behaviors that are functional and to decrease or minimize those behaviors that are problematic for the client. At the level of therapy, the goal is utilize activities as a part of a meta-level change. It obviously takes increased skill on the part of the worker to engage a client in a form of experiential therapy. However, the engagement of clients in an activity at the level of recreation should not be considered one that does not require skill.

At Family Unity, experiential activities are most often aimed at the level of recreation and education. Participants are offered the opportunity to ride horseback or engage in arts-based activities. Clients make choices about their participation and the meaning of the activity. This does not mean that the activity may not have therapeutic value for the client. However, the activity is not directly introduced or facilitated by staff as a therapeutic intervention. There are some activities that are more utilized as a therapeutic intervention. Some of the rituals such as family boats and the "burden bag" focus on grief work (these are explained in more detail in the next section). They are introduced with specific and purposeful attention to providing an opportunity for clients to explore aspects of grief in a supportive setting. Individually, there are meta-level therapeutic processes led by staff who have more skills and experience, both with the client and with the activity.

Historically, the adventure activities are used at the level of recreation and education. Activities such as problem-solving initiatives and the ropes course are offered to clients, who engage in those activities on their own terms. There is little to no introduction of the activity, except for safety concerns, and there is minimal discussion after the activity, especially group-related processing. The activities provide the opportunity for the client to engage his or her own fears at a level he or she chooses. Most experience a sense of accomplishment, success, and mastery along with a level of thrill, excitement, and delight. However, before engaging in these activities, they often experience fear, nervousness, and doubt. We have grown to recognize the importance of using such adventure-based activities as a means of offering insights and therapeutic intervention for clients.

CASE EXAMPLE

Ellen was a thirty-nine-year-old woman, a longtime survivor of AIDS, who used the ropes course to demonstrate to herself, her own strength and commitment. She had come to the camp since the beginning in 1997, and yearly had experienced anxiety about her disease and its impact on her partner and children. This was expressed in a variety of ways from being unable to watch her children or partner traverse the ropes course, to having to leave the "Burden Bag" exercise because the emotions of other parents were overwhelming for her. She described Family Unity as one of the most positive experiences for her family and delayed major surgery last summer in order to participate because she openly stated that she needed the support of the community. At the same time, she freely admitted that it raised issues that were too painful to contemplate.

In 2001 she was able to tolerate watching her children and partner go through the ropes course. After a point, she decided she would go up while her family encouraged her from below. No one, including herself, thought that she would complete the course; any attempt was considered a success given her prior history with the ropes. At multiple points on the course, Ellen had the choice to go further or return to the ground. There is also a choice to go in a direction that was less physically demanding. She chose to go on the most challenging course despite the fact that her partner went the less physically demanding way and encouraged her to follow. She made comments such as, "I've made it this far," "I'm doing OK," and "I'm safe, aren't I?" At one point her partner was being more directive than supportive, and she responded, "I do not see you up here. Do I?" They both laughed at that. Ellen came down from the course on a "zip line" and expressed a healthy amount of delight on the descent and when on the ground. The "zip line" is a cable on a slight angle; riders go down on a pulley, allowing them to pick up a bit of speed and experience a falling sensation.

Staff provided a great deal of support in terms of validating her and the work she did. However, very little processing was done about the meaning of the experience. This was clearly a therapeutic experience for the client. However, it should also be clear from the description that the activity was not actively processed by the staff. Had the staff actively processed with her the ability to move through fear and realize she could master it, this would have moved the event from the level of recreation to that of therapy.

Currently, Family Unity is moving in the direction of experiential activities that are more intentional and therapeutic. Key staff are involved in ongoing training to acquire more skills in the purposeful use of adventure activities and experiential practice. The goal is to allow recreational, educational, and therapeutic activities to occur throughout the camp. The desire is not to remove the recreational aspects, but to make them more clinically focused to facilitate change. There are tremendous parallels between the grief and loss work and adventure activities. In moving through fear to a sense of mastery in an adventure activity, the work often enhances competencies that parallel what must be done in life in coping with the loss and grief in living with HIV/AIDS.

RITUALS

The use of rituals throughout the weekend is an important component of the camp. Rituals assist families in strengthening and building and/or rebuilding as ways of adapting to the impact of HIV/AIDS as well as in working through complicated grief (Boyd-Franklin, Drelich, and Schwolsky-Fitch 1995). The rituals of Family Unity have been designed to build safety and trust, to facilitate healing, and to create bonding among individual participants and families, while promoting a sense of community to allow for emotional expression.

Rituals also aid in creating and sustaining connections and support beyond the weekend. Many occur during the weekend experience. These rituals are constant and continuous, building on each other as the weekend progresses, and are often repeated year after year. Staff initiates some of the rituals and others are created out of the interactions that participants have with one another.

One of the first rituals of the weekend begins with an opening celebration. Remembering, honoring loved ones who have died, and celebrating being together are the focus. Family Unity is symbolically represented by the unwrapping of the Family Unity box. The box serves as a metaphor for the weekend where a safe environment is to be created and then rewrapped at the end of the session. During the weekend, safety and trust are created as participants are supported by staff and by other participants who share their experiences of HIV/AIDS (McFeaters 2000). The Family Unity box is filled with many other boxes containing a T-shirt from each year, wishes and hopes written by members at the last Unity meeting, angel cards, and a rose quartz.

Each item's relevance is discussed as it is found. The T-shirts provide an opportunity to remember a specific camping session. Memories are shared and cherished. Hopes and fears are shared, and then there is a transition to the angel cards, which offer inspiration. Finally, the rose quartz, which represents comfort, is presented. All members are invited to keep the quartz for a while during the weekend and encouraged to pass it on to another when they are finished. One year someone kept the rose quartz. At the closing, its absence was noted, and the wish was expressed that it help and comfort the person who had it throughout the upcoming year.

Family introductions follow the opening of the Family Unity box, and new families are welcomed. As the number of orphaned children has grown, staff or other family members stand with them during the opening so that an orphan does not feel alone. Honoring and remembering loved ones begins here. Everyone has an opportunity to offer the name of someone they would like remembered by the community. Families and staff share the names and anecdotes, frequently reminiscing about earlier Unity sessions. A tree was planted three years ago to signify lost members. Participants who have lost someone in the past year are invited to visit the tree after the closing to dedicate the names of loved ones who died. These names are recorded in the memory books that all campers and staff receive. This is typically a time of grieving by a subset of the group who are supported by families and staff in their expressions of loss. All activities are optional, respecting each person's self-determination. The opening is followed by a dance to facilitate connection and to promote bonding. This is strategically planned as a method of activity, not leaving participants emotionally open and vulnerable. It is a fun, lively event that participants and staff enjoy. It is clearly a community-strengthening activity.

A yearly activity that has become an important ritual of the weekend is early morning fishing with Max, the chief executive officer of Double H and cofounder of Family Unity. The early morning session has become special because it is a time of solitude, an opportunity to appreciate the beauty of the camp, coupled with an opportunity to spend time with Max, who is considered by many to be the heart of Double H. Max provides an open heart and a willingness to share the magic at Double H that anyone who has spent time there appreciates. Families openly appreciate his ongoing presence. Some of our more challenged youth and parents find early morning fishing the most soothing aspect of the weekend. As one young man said last summer, "I am just a boy who loves fishing with Max." While fishing, he has shared with staff his pain and frustration about his father's unwillingness to care for him and his mother's unavailability because of her addictions and her illness. He felt that he had been dumped at a relative's house, and he wished for a more direct connection to his immediate family. This opened the door to exploring ways in which he could build on his strengths and appreciate the connections he has created at Family Unity.

Community building is further fostered during meal times where participants share every meal. The sharing of food is a ritual that is universal in many cultures. For the last number of years, it has been customary for some of the Latino families to prepare a special meal toward the end of the weekend. The participants and staff look forward to this traditional meal.

Adults and older adolescents have historically gathered in a designated smoking area of the camp, where stories are shared and emotions are expressed. This activity allows catharsis, support, connection, and laughter in a very informal atmosphere.

Parents have instituted a nightly bingo game that starts after the children go to bed. Serious topics are mixed in with the fun of the activity. Similarly, the youth gather in their cabins for cabin chats that stretch into the night. As a group, they talk about concerns and how they are coping. Each participant has been given a memory book to write about his or her experiences and to add photographs of the weekend. Memory books are decorated binders that participants are given every year. Each memory book includes paper for participants to write their thoughts, feelings, and memories of the weekend. Photographs are taken through out the weekend, developed, and given to participants to add to their memory books. Lace, stickers, and theme paper are used to personalize the books. Many participants exchange phone numbers and addresses as a way to stay in touch and build support.

The "burden bag" exercise is a ritual that has been utilized for a number of years at Family Unity. It is used with all age groups to continue the facilitation of emotional expression during the camp weekend. It allows participants to identify feelings of grief and loss as well as the burdens they may be carrying. A canvas bag filled with rocks is used as a metaphor for the "heaviness or weightiness of emotions or life's burdens." As the bag is passed around the circle, each participant takes a turn talking about the feeling or word written on the rock he or she chooses, thus lightening the bag. When all group members have taken a turn and the bag is empty, facilitators then discuss the metaphor of "lightness of the bag" in the context of the importance of sharing and expressing feelings as a way to unload heavy emotions and burdens. The staff believe that heavy feelings can weigh individuals down if participants do not express them and unload them and the sharing of feelings with those whom they trust can thus help them to feel lighter and less overwhelmed (McFeaters 2000).

The "boat ceremony" is another ritual that begins on Saturday as individual families work together to collect natural artifacts (twigs, leaves, bark) from the grounds of the camp to create boats. On Saturday night, families carry their boats to the lakefront. Candles are distributed to camp participants, then are lighted and placed on top of the boats. The boats are gently pushed from the shore and illuminate as they float out into the water. This is often a time of silence, reflection, and remembrance. It is one of the most moving and meaningful components of the weekend, as well as one of the most emotional elements of the camp experience. Participants and staff often move to the campfire nearby and embrace as they sing softly.

On Sunday morning, a reflection service is held in a small nondenominational chapel on the grounds of the camp. The chapel is a small rustic building with a steep A-frame roof that is open twenty-four hours a day for reflection. Many colorful flowers are planted in front of the chapel, and the large carved-wood doors are welcoming. The pews of the chapel are always packed and individuals stand in the back and along the sides to share in their reverence. This ritual is designed to facilitate universal spiritual connections among all, rather than be a religious service. It is designed to provide participants with a context to reflect on the time spent together and in a larger camp community, as well as a time to process the emotional work completed over the weekend. For families, it is a time to honor the memories and share the meaning of the camp weekend.

The Family Unity director begins by saying "This is a time of reflection and a time to honor those that are with us as well as those who have passed." She speaks in a soft voice as she encourages anyone who is interested to share during this time. Participants of all ages take turns sharing. Some speak of those that have died; others share their gratitude for their families; others read poems, witness their faith, or sing spirituals. Some sit in silence as if they are in prayer, and others are tearful. The reflection service is always very moving and often emotional for participants and staff. The morning reflection also provides participants and families with a sense of community bonding, solidarity, and healing. The theme, "We all share a commonality that we have been touched by HIV/AIDS," creates a sense of unity and facilitates healing not only among individual family units, but also for all of the participants.

The weekend comes to a close with a closing ceremony in which the entire community participates. During this time, certificates of completion are given to families as they are called up one at a time and acknowledged for the work they have done during the weekend. The camp director speaks of special and significant moments that have occurred during the weekend. She reflects on lighter, more humorous moments. Participants laugh and add to her stories. In a more serious manner, she honors the bonds that have been created, and the community that has been built. She talks about the importance of needing one another and allowing for support in each other's lives. She encourages participants to stay in touch with one another. She also provides information regarding reunions and events to be planned through out the year to provide ongoing support beyond the camp weekend. The Unity box that had been opened at the beginning of the weekend is rewrapped, with new wishes and hopes inserted.

Hence, several of the final rituals are designed to assist families in creating ongoing support once the weekend has ended. They also convey the message that memories can be held over time, and unwrapped when needed. They offer a way of viewing the past as cumulative rather than as being marked by loss. The staff shares this explicit view that families need to be provided with ongoing support once the weekend has come to a close. This is based on the notion that families impacted by AIDS-related loss are often isolated and may not have a support network. The staff also believes that participants need to be encouraged to continue to support one another in the context of their families and to stay in touch with participants with whom they have become close.

There are several reasons why the use of multiple rituals are important for HIV-impacted families participating in retreat/camp environments. First, rituals create a sense of group bonding, support, and a feeling of strength from the greater group community (McFeaters 2000). Second, rituals assist in creating healing and celebration, and they help to acknowledge and honor the work families have completed as participants continue the grief work beyond the camp weekend and maintain the supports they have established (McFeaters 2000). Third, rituals assist families in working through complicated grief as ways of adapting to the impact of HIV/AIDS (Boyd-Franklin and Walker-Lockwood 1999). Fourth, rituals can serve as means of emotional release or catharsis, allowing survivors of HIV/AIDS to express their tears and grief openly (Boyd-Franklin, Drelich, and Schwolsky-Fitch 1995). Finally rituals assist participants affected by HIV to experience trust, acceptance, safety, support, an increased awareness and expression of feelings, and a sense of connection to one another and the community in participating in rituals throughout the camp weekend. None of these mitigates the multiple losses that these families endure, but each ritual strengthens participants' experiences of connection and continuity, both to the dead and to the living.

CONCLUSION

Family Unity operationalizes many critical social work practice concepts in work with multineed families (Kilpatrick, and Holand, 1999). The community-based, collaborative, and empowerment- and strengths-based interventions from the micro to the macro levels address challenges faced by the families affected by HIV by offering interventions at the individual, family, group, and community levels. Several interventions are provided to respond to the diverse needs of HIV-affected families. The very genesis of the program reflects the group focus; groups continue to be a major component within Family Unity as both families and youth participate in groups during the program and back in the community. During the retreat and throughout the year staff provide opportunities for individual counseling, support, and relationship building. Family work is facilitated though a number of rituals throughout camp and back in the community including several reunion dinners. The reunion dinners, the communal dinners at the retreat, the ceremonies involving the memorial boats, and remembrance all reflect the community focus on the program. Increasingly, the community focus is growing to include efforts to address the larger community in the Greater Rochester area.

By design, the possibility of premature parental death is approached as a reality for the children and adolescents from HIV-affected families. It is not denied, despite the challenges inherent is addressing this painful prospect. This approach lessens the toxicity of a life-threatening illness in a family member by assisting the families to find meaning together and helping to develop viable guardianship arrangements. Parents and children alike learn various ways of maximizing their time together while experiencing, firsthand, the caring community response by the Family Unity community. It is hard to capture the value of this for orphaned children. They relish being with families who openly share memories of their deceased parents. Parents see that children do survive and learn what has helped or not helped orphaned youth. Children are allowed to grieve in their own ways and at their own pace with the Family Unity community providing support and guidance along the way.

The focus on building trust and safety is especially helpful in reducing the isolation that often results from the stigmatization associated with the disease. Throughout the weekend, staff utilizes reflection, reassurance, empathy, and encouragement. They normalize and validate feelings, and they support and praise participants for what they have achieved over the weekend. They also assist participants in identifying the supports that are available in the community and encourage them to reach out and maintain connections with one another by exchanging phone numbers and addresses.

These approaches are further supported through the use of action-oriented, experiential approaches that help make mastery experiences possible. Traditionally, social workers have used active, community-oriented, experiential activities such as those in the settlement house and early youth-work movement. The Family Unity program is demonstrating how important these approaches are to address the real challenges that youth and family experience from the multiple traumas of coping with the stigma, loss, and grief of HIV/AIDS. Adventure-based practice provides young people and their families with the opportunity to enhance the skills associated with resiliency including reframing the experience, utilizing support, and developing relationships with significant people. Social workers need to utilize interventions that build upon youth's capacity through relationships (Watkins 2002). This approach facilitates the true empowerment of HIV/AIDS-affected families to make changes within the family as well as demand services from the larger community within which these families live.

The Family Unity program is not a panacea. It does not begin to address all of the complex needs of families living with HIV/AIDS. However, it does provide one important component: that of community support. It assists families in addressing the developmental tasks associated with all families as well as some of the grief specific work that HIV/AIDS affected families must cope with. Family Unity operates somewhat organically, just as a family does. As new needs, challenges, and opportunities present themselves, the youth, in concert with the staff, explore how to shape the program to meet them. One recent example of this process occurred as the program began to address the needs of the young people whose anger is often associated with the grief and loss of HIV/AIDS, poverty, racism, and other challenges. A staff person identified an anger management program based on a twelve-step process and presented it as an opportunity for the youth. They agreed to explore it and now the anger management group is a major part of the ongoing work born out of Family Unity. Another example of the macro-level interventions within an empowerment perspective has been the recent involvement of youth in legislative advocacy. They have begun arguing for additional services that can address the multiple long-term needs of families as well as addressing the social challenges of racism, poverty, unresponsive agencies, and inadequate child welfare policies. In 2002, a number of young people affiliated with Family Unity took part in a legislative breakfast at which they testified about their service needs before local and state legislators. They specifically addressed the policy gaps, including the lack of financial support for siblings to continue to reside together after the loss of a parent, the failure of judges to honor permanency plans developed by custodial parents, and the failure of case managers to provide the necessary services to ensure a successful transition after the death of the custodial parent. They have also spoken before a group of graduating social work students about what they want and need from social workers in terms of meeting service needs. This is the natural evolution of a program, which focuses on building capacities and leadership within clients.

ACKNOWLEDGMENTS

This work was supported by funding from the Project on Death in America, Open Society Institute, and Abandoned Infants Act, DHHS/Administration on Children and Families.

REFERENCES

Anderson, G., C. Ryan, S. Taylor-Brown, and M. White-Gray, eds. 1999. *Children and HIV/ AIDS*. New Brunswick, NJ: Transaction.

Bor, R., R. Miller, and E. E. Goldman. 1993. HIV/AIDS and the family: A review of research in the first decade. *Journal of Family Therapy* 15:187–204.

Boyd-Franklin, N., E. W. Drelich, and E. Schwolsky-Fitch. 1995. Death and dying: Bereavement and mourning. In *Children, Families, and HIV/AIDS: Psychosocial and Therapeutic Issues*, ed. N. Boyd-Franklin, G. Steiner, and M. Boland, 167–178. New York: Guilford.

Boyd-Franklin, N., and T. Walker-Lockwood. 1999. Spirituality and religion: Implications for psychotherapy with African American clients and families. In *Spiritual Resources in Family Therapy*, ed. F. Walsh, 90–103. New York: Guilford.

Christ, G. 2000. Impact of development on children's mourning. *Cancer Practice* 8:72–81.

Christ, G., K. Siegel, and A. Christ. 2002. Adolescent grief: It never really hit me . . . until it actually happened. *Journal of the American Medical Association* 288(10): 1269–1278.

Cohen, J., A. Mannano, T. Greenberg, and S. Padio. 2002. Childhood traumatic grief: Concepts and controversies. *Trauma, Violence, and Abuse* 1:307–326.

Dane, B., and S. Miller. 1992. *AIDS: Intervening with Hidden Grievers*. Westport, CT: Auburn House.

Dewey, J. 1938. *Education and Experience*. New York: Macmillan.

Draimin, G., I. Gamble, A. Shire, and J. Hudis. 1999. Improving permanency planning in families with HIV disease. In *Children and HIV/AIDS*, ed. G. Anderson, C. Ryan, S. Taylor-Brown, and M. White-Gray, 79–94. New Brunswick, NJ: Transaction.

Gilbert, D. 1999. Introduction. In *HIV-Affected and Vulnerable Youth: Preventative Issues and Approaches*, ed. S. Taylor-Brown and A. Garcia, 99–117. Binghamton, NY: Haworth Press.

Hackel, K., A. Somlai, J. Kelly, and S. Kalichman. 1997. Women living with HIV/AIDS: The dual challenge of being a patient and caregiver. *Health and Social Work* 22:53–62.

Itin, C. 1996. Adventure-based practice. In *Days in the Life of Social Workers*, ed. L. M. Grobman, 70–75. Harrisburg, PA: White Hat.

———. 1999. Reasserting the philosophy of experiential education as a vehicle for change in the 21st century. *Journal of Experiential Education* 22(2): 91–98.

———. 2001. Adventure therapy: Critical questions. *Journal of Experiential Education* 24(2): 80–84.

Kilpatrick, A., and T. Holand. 1999. *Working with Families: An Integrative Model by Level of Need*. Boston: Allyn & Bacon.

Kreibeck, T. 1995. Caretakers support group. In *Children, Families, and HIV/AIDS: Psychosocial and Therapeutic Issues*, ed. N. Boyd-Franklin, G. Steiner, and M. Boland, 167–178. New York: Guilford.

Lloyd, G. 1999. Introduction. In *HIV-Affected and Vulnerable Youth: Preventative Issues and Approaches*, ed. S. Taylor-Brown and A. Garcia, 1–4. Binghamton, NY: Haworth.

Mason, S., and W. Korr. 1999. Mothers with AIDS: Coping, support and ability to plan for their children. *Journal of HIV/AIDS Prevention and Education for Children and Adolescents* 3(1–2): 119–141.

McFeaters, S. 2000. Experiences of African American families at an AIDS bereavement camp: A descriptive study. Ph.D. diss., University of Maryland, Baltimore.

Mellins, C. A., and A. A. Ehrhardt. 1994. Families affected by pediatric acquired immunodeficiency syndrome: Sources of stress and coping. *Developmental and Behavioral Pediatrics* 15: S54–S60.

Michaels, D., and C. Levine. 1992. Estimates of the number of motherless youth orphaned by AIDS in the United States. *Journal of the American Medical Association* 268:3456–3461.

Miller, J. 1987. *The New Psychology of Women.* Boston: Beacon Press.

Newman, P. 2002. Actor and philanthropist. In *Right Words at the Right Time*, ed. M. Thomas, 232–234. New York: Atria Books.

Nord, D. 1996. The impact of multiple AIDS-related loss on families of origin and families of choice. *American Journal of Family Therapy* 24:129–144.

Pfefferbaum, B., S. Nixon, and P. Tucker. 1999. Posttraumatic stress responses in bereaved children after the Oklahoma City bombing. *Journal American Academy of Child Adolescent Psychiatry* 38:1372–1379.

Powell-Cope, G., and M. Brown. 1992. Going public as an AIDS family caregiver. *Social Science and Medicine* 34:571–580.

Silverman, P. 2000. *Never Too Young to Know: Death in Children's Lives.* New York: Oxford University Press.

Spiegel, L., and A. Mayers. 1991. Psychosocial aspects of AIDS in children and adolescents. *Pediatric Clinics of North America* 38:153–167.

Stehno, J. 1986. *The Application and Integration of Experiential Education in Higher Education.* Carbondale, IL: Southern Illinois University Touch of Nature Environmental Center.

Taylor-Brown, S. 1999. Summer camps for children, adolescents and families. In *Planning Children's Futures: Meeting the Needs of Children, Adolescents, and Families Affected by HIV/AIDS*, ed. S. Taylor-Brown, 51–55. Sheldon, CT: Annie E. Casey Foundation.

Taylor-Brown, S., and L. Wiener. 1993. Making videotapes of HIV-infected women for their children. *Families in Society* 1:468–480.

———. 1998. Talking to parents about creating legacy for their children. In *HIV and Social Work: A Practitioners Guide*, ed. D. M. Aronstein and B. J. Thompson, 339–347. New York: Haworth.

Watkins, M. 2002. Listening to girls: A study in resilience. In *Resiliency: An Integrated Approach to Practice, Policy, and Research*, ed. R. Greene, 115–132. Washington, DC: NASW Press.

Wolfelt, A. D. 1983. *Helping Children with Grief.* Muncie, IN: Accelerated Development.

34

SOCIAL WORK CONSULTATION TO MENTAL HEALTH WORKERS
SERVING CHILDREN AND FAMILIES AFFECTED BY DISASTERS

LISA ARONSON

I **HAVE** had the opportunity over the course of my career to serve as a social work consultant to indigenous social workers in Central America following Hurricane Mitch and in Turkey following the 1999 earthquake. I have also been enlisted as a consultant to a social service organization in India to help develop a manual to assist child survivors of the Bhuj earthquake of January 2001. My background work with acutely traumatized children and families at the University of California at Los Angeles prepared me to serve as a consultant to mental health practitioners within and outside the United States.

Social workers are often called upon to provide direct service or mental health consultation to individuals and communities following disasters. Although the case examples in this chapter arise primarily from international contexts and natural disasters, the concepts regarding acutely traumatized children and families facing sudden death apply to both direct service and mental health consultation and to both international and national disaster contexts. This chapter offers the social worker some essential tools to conduct effective direct service and consultation to local mental health providers assisting children and families in international and national disaster contexts. These tools include, but are not limited to, an understanding of the social impacts of disaster; the concepts of psychological safety—both the helplessness created by the sudden disruption of safety and the reconstruction of a sense of safety; the interplay of trauma and bereavement; and the significance of attending to sociocultural contexts.

THE IMPACTS OF DISASTER

Over the past two decades, natural disasters have taken the lives of three million people worldwide and adversely affected the lives of 800 million more (Weisaeth 1993). In developing countries, earthquakes, windstorms, tsunamis, floods, landslides, wildfires, and other calamities often cause widespread death, injury, and destruction, with large numbers of affected child survivors (Pynoos, Goenjian, and Steinberg 1995). Human-caused disasters, such as the terrorist attacks on the World Trade Center and the Pentagon on September 11, 2001, result in loss of life, loss of family members, exposure to graphic scenes of violence, and severe economic loss.

I will describe four disasters in some detail in order to give the reader a better appreciation for their massive effects.

HURRICANE MITCH, CENTRAL AMERICA

Hurricane Mitch, a category-five storm on the Saffir Simpson Scale, was the most deadly hurricane to strike the Western Hemisphere in the last two centuries, causing the deaths of more than ten thousand people between October 26 and November 4, 1998. Winds reached up to 200 miles per hour. Torrential rains fell at the rate of one to two feet per day, resulting in massive flooding and mudslides in the mountainous regions. Cash crops and food were largely wiped out. Hundreds of thousands of people were left without work. In Nicaragua alone, two million people were directly affected; 500,000 were left homeless and 4,000 died. Five villages were buried under several feet of mud (Goenjian et al. 2001).

While teaching in Tegucigalpa, Honduras, after the hurricane had ended, I heard vignettes from the mental health professionals of events they had witnessed. A nurse recounted that during the hurricane she attempted to return to her home. A high river made this impossible. She thought she saw the bodies of friends along with drowning cattle in the river's current as she waited to cross. Eventually she did return home, where her family waited, including her four-year-old daughter and her husband. Missing was her sister, the baby's caretaker. They presumed that she had drowned that morning, perhaps on her way to care for the baby. Upon returning to my hotel after a day of teaching, I heard several locals talk about more dead bodies that had been dug out of the mud bank bordering the now impotent thread of a river.

EARTHQUAKES, TURKEY

On August 17 and November 12, 1999, two earthquakes devastated the populated and industrial northwestern parts of Turkey. The Turkish authorities reported that more than 18,000 people had been killed and 49,000 injured. At least 1,268 aftershocks were reported following the original earthquakes. At the start of 2000, according to UNICEF, an estimated 200,000 people were housed in approximately 130 tented camps and prefabricated cities.

While in Turkey, I witnessed the devastation and the adaptation to it by the population. The evening before I was to meet with mental health providers in a tent city, I spent the night in a nearby city. I was staying in the only relatively tall building, which happened to be a hotel, left standing in the city. From my hotel room window, I looked out upon rows of once tall apartment towers that were now piles of flat discs, like cookies from a box that had been hurled from a high shelf. It was very painful imagining how many people had been trapped and wedged between the concrete floors. The next morning I arrived in the tent city. It had become a neighborhood with clotheslines, small gardens, flags, women sweeping their doorsteps, young men sipping coffee at a canteen, children arriving with a few books at the school, which was also in a tent. I was invited into a family's shelter. Inside, the family ate, slept, discussed, laughed, debated, cried, problem solved, and washed in the one large room that the tent provided. A Turkish carpet, a pot of tea, and a songbird enlivened the room. The father had gone to work in the city during the day, the children were at the school in the tent city, and the mother and oldest daughter were home. Their lives had become predictable and safe again in the tent. I later learned that many of the families in the tents had been offered homes in small apartment buildings that had recently been constructed. None had chosen to leave their tents.

EARTHQUAKE, INDIA

On January 26, 2001, the Bhuj earthquake occurred in Gujarat, India. This earthquake was one of the two deadliest earthquakes to strike India in its recorded history. The death toll was estimated at 19,727, and the number of injured at 166,000. Some 600,000 people were left homeless; 348,000 homes were destroyed, and an additional 844,000 homes were damaged. The Indian State Department estimated that the earthquake affected directly or indirectly 15.9 million people out of a total population of 37.8 million. More than 20,000 cattle were reported killed. Direct economic losses were estimated at $1.3 billion. However, other estimates indicate that losses may have been as high as $5 billion.

TERRORIST ATTACKS, UNITED STATES

In the terrorist attacks on the World Trade Center and the Pentagon on September 11, 2001, tens of thousands of people ran for their lives and were exposed to graphic scenes of death, violence, and destruction (see chapter 4). It is estimated that well over 100,000 people directly witnessed the events and that 422,000 people suffered post-traumatic stress disorder (Susser, Herman, and Aaron 2002). The attacks were followed by the imminent threat of further attacks, war, and bioterrorism (Yehuda 2002). At the World Trade Center alone, it is estimated that more than 2,700 people died.

INGREDIENTS OF PSYCHOLOGICAL SAFETY

Immediately following a disaster, interventions and support need to be focused on the affected area's infrastructure in order to protect the survivors' physical and mental health. Survivors require essential health and survivor measures: water purification; sanitation and the establishment of water systems; the reestablishment of schooling, communication, and public information; the establishment of networks of community workers; support to children in displaced families; and program preparation for the rehabilitation phase focused on children and the most vulnerable groups.

The social worker, using clinical skills specific to children, families, trauma, and bereavement, is a valuable resource to national and international governmental organizations and nongovernmental organizations as they work to restore psychological safety to the affected populations. In the national and international disaster context, the social worker can provide both direct service and consultation to the local mental health worker. Social-work consultation is particularly desirable in those situations where the local mental health workers are serving large groups of survivors and need clinical knowledge immediately and over time to provide direct service and training. The indigenous mental health workers are also in a position to educate paraprofessionals delivering service. "Trickle-down" theory of intervention is mobilized when a large public mental health emergency occurs and the mental health workers are unable to reach all of the affected survivors directly, relying instead upon paraprofessionals and others who are in daily contact with children. For example, the social work consultant can convey clinical knowledge to the indigenous mental health worker, who then advises others in contact with children and families (e.g., teachers and aides).

The social worker's first task is to understand what constitutes safety in order to appreciate fully the physical and psychological disruptions that a disaster entails. A feeling of safety ensues if psychosocial transitions are anticipated and prepared for. Conversely, massive losses for which we are unprepared often give rise to lasting difficulties in adjustment (Parkes 1997). If a breach in the state of safety occurs, an internal disruption, referred to as a "traumatic state," develops.

A key element of traumatic events is that they are unexpected and sudden. How does the lack of preparation inherent in a disaster affect the child and family? The principal goal of preparation is to help a child and family ready themselves for stressful events, changes, and new events. Preparation activates the individual's and family's protective mechanisms. The ultimate aim of preparation is not the avoidance of anxiety and distress, but the prevention of being overwhelmed by events. "Being prepared" means being empowered to know, predict, and prepare for future events. Preparation leads to maximum adaptation to change (Furman 1988). Lack of preparation is at the root of most maladaptive responses to stress (Parkes 1997).

Ordinarily, for a child, the caretaker is the agent of preparation. Ideally, a caretaker's tasks of protection and preparation continue throughout the child's childhood. If the caretaker has adequately prepared the child for an upcoming change or event, the child is less likely to be taken by surprise. If prepared, the child is less likely to feel overwhelmed, helpless, and powerless—feelings at the core of traumatization.

Joseph Sandler (1960) has proposed a "safety principle," a feeling of safety that is more than a simple absence of discomfort and anxiety. Much of ordinary everyday behavior can be understood as an attempt to preserve an internal and external level of safety. Sandler proposes that "safety signals" are feelings of being protected, as with the caretaker's reassuring presence or when our senses are in harmony with what we expect on the basis of our mental model of the external world. This safety feeling is maintained through regular and effective handling of quantities of incoming excitation by the caretaker and later by the individual.

The "ego," according to ego psychologists, or the "brain," according to neuropsychologists, counterbalances anxiety by heightening the safety feeling level, using whatever techniques it has at its disposal. Psychological mechanisms of defense, such as denial and ego restriction, are mobilized throughout a person's life to modify and control the perception of internal and external stimulation (Freud 1967). Neuropsychologists (Smith 2002) refer to the human brain's ability to exclude overwhelming or dangerous items from awareness. Selective perception excludes threatening items from awareness so that a person's sense of coherence can be maintained despite the realities and uncertainties of a situation (Smith 2002).

A further element of a sense of safety is basic trust. This basic trust is constituted during the earliest stage of childhood when a baby learns to rely on her primary caretaker. Throughout development, daily routines and social conventions keep anxieties at bay and establish patterns of expectation that allow people to interact without being overwhelmed. These everyday practices serve to renew basic trust continuously (Robben 2000).

In addition to these ingredients of safety, child developmental researchers have begun to catalogue protective factors that make up "resilience." Apfel and Simon (2000) have described characteristics that contribute to resilience: resourcefulness (which includes the ability to extract human warmth and loving kindness in the most dire of circumstances), active curiosity and intellectual mastery, flexibility in emotional experience permitting major affects and defending against overwhelming anxiety, the ability to evoke the memories of sustaining caretakers, the ability to find a purpose for which to live, the need and ability to help others, and the ability to maintain a sense of a civilized moral order. Smith (2002) has developed the concept of "salutary mechanisms," which serve as protective factors: hardiness, coping, social support, religion, happiness, humor and love, and selective perception.

Another factor that maintains a sense of safety and mitigates psychological morbidity is a prevailing sense of community and social life. If a community's health is disturbed, individual trauma may be aggravated. This can occur in communities where disaster victims greatly outnumber nonvictims and help necessarily has to come from the outside. In disaster situations, where relocation of victims may occur on a random basis, the old neighborhood ties and communality are destroyed (Erikson 1976). Furthermore, when a community is under stress, group regressive attitudes are mobilized, exaggerating ethnic and national identifications and historical shared anxieties. This group regression may facilitate psychopathology in individual members of the community (Ainslie and Brabeck 2003).

DISRUPTION OF SAFETY: TRAUMA AND HELPLESSNESS

Beginning in the 1980s, the diagnostic entity of post-traumatic stress disorder (PTSD) became increasingly refined. The working definitions of PTSD are encompassed by the Diagnostic and Statistical Manual of Mental Disorders (DSM) and the ICD-10 Classification of Mental and Behavioral Disorders: Clinical Descriptions and Diagnostic Guidelines (ICD-10). The central feature of PTSD in both nosologies is the exposure to an event that involves intense fear, helplessness, or horror (Fletcher 1996).

In the DSM IV, PTSD is characterized by three categories of symptoms: reexperiencing the traumatic event, avoiding stimuli associated with the trauma, and experiencing persistent symptoms of increased arousal. In ICD-10, PTSD is characterized by symptoms of unwanted reexperiencing of the traumatic event.

L. C. Terr has defined childhood trauma as "the mental result of one sudden, external blow or a series of blows rendering the child temporarily helpless and breaking past ordinary coping and defensive operations" (1991:11). According to Terr, trauma begins with events outside of the child that precipitate internal changes that are manifested in the following behavioral changes: strongly visualized or otherwise repeatedly perceived memories of the traumatic event; repetitive behaviors; trauma specific fears; and changed attitudes about people, aspects of life, and the future (Terr 1991).

Robert Pynoos, A. M. Steinberg, and I (1997) have detailed the intensive mental activity of the traumatized child during and following a traumatic event. The disruption of physical and psychological safety incites extreme mental activity. In this state of mind, a child registers the complexity of the traumatic event and experiences multiple traumatic moments within a relatively circumscribed situation. In addition, the child experiences changes in concern and foci of attention prior to and during the event, radical shifts in attention or concern when physical integrity is violated, and additional traumatic moments after the cessation of violence. He or she worries about the safety of significant others and returns to anxieties from prior traumatic experiences.

Not all children and families who have undergone a traumatic event suffer from PTSD. Direct exposure to the sudden violent event and a history of traumatization have been linked to the development of PTSD. However, some, but not all, of the symptoms that make up the diagnosis can be present in those who have a lesser degree of exposure and whose history does not include traumatization. From this point of view, it is worthwhile to consider that a spectrum of mental activity associated with a sudden violent event can exist in a child and caretakers and that reactions to traumatic events range from full-blown PTSD to varying degrees of mental activity associated with acute trauma.

RECONSTRUCTION OF A SENSE OF SAFETY

In a disaster context, the social worker consulting to local mental health workers or providing direct service can make use of a "trauma lens" to evaluate and treat acutely traumatized children and families. This lens includes the following concepts: sudden violent events have particular developmental impacts which depend upon the age of the child; secondary adversities often follow a traumatic event and exacerbate its effect; parenting capacities are challenged in the context of a traumatic event and its aftermath; bereavement in the context of a traumatic event is delayed because the child is preoccupied with the traumatic event until he regains a sense of security and power; a current traumatic event brings prior traumatic events to the surface; preexisting pathology can be exacerbated by the traumatic event; reminders of the traumatic event abound in the post-traumatic environment; there is the potential for ongoing regression and future psychopathology if the child's condition is untreated; and particular forms of mental activity occur during and following a sudden violent event that serve to restore a sense of power and security to the child.

The following case illustrates the use of the "trauma lens" in disaster relief work where death and injury were omnipresent (Aronson 2000).

CASE EXAMPLE

A concerned mental health worker brought me the case of seven-year-old Bulent, who had been trapped under rubble during the 1999 earthquake in Turkey. Bulent's parents and brothers died in the earthquake when their home collapsed. He had survived, after being trapped for fifteen hours under rubble. His leg injury required four surgeries, and more were anticipated. His paternal uncle and aunt became Bulent's caretakers. In their fifties, they had grown children of their own and were retired. Bulent was resistant to future surgeries. He clung to his aunt, he was demanding and could not wait for anything, and he was not eating well. His uncle was unhappy and unable to sleep. He worried that he could not properly care for his nephew and wanted to send him away to boarding school. The aunt and uncle were fearful about speaking to their nephew about the death of his parents and brothers, although they had brought him to the gravesites and brought gifts of flowers.

Bulent experienced secondary adversities and weakened caretaking, which directly resulted from the earthquake. Both may have influenced his physical and psychological recovery. These included his uncle's depression and feelings of being burdened, Bulent's serving as a reminder to the uncle of his dead brother, and his uncle's and aunt's difficulties coping with his bereavement due to their own grief as well as their uncertainty about his ability to absorb the facts of the deaths.

These challenges were multiple. To be reminded of his dead brother through Bulent's appearance challenged the uncle's caretaking. The feelings of being poor substitutes for his biological parents caused his uncle and aunt to reject him. Their mourning made them impatient with Bulent's focus on the anxieties arising from earthquake and entrapment. Their worries about his possible emotional fragility may have inhibited speaking frankly with him about his experience of the earthquake and the loss of his parents. Potentially, this new family formation could suffer from intrafamilial isolation.

Bulent was also reminded in the present of the experience of being trapped for hours. Waiting in the present for any amount of time triggered feelings and memories, the passivity inherent in medical procedures reawakened his feelings of helplessness, and separation from a caretaker in the present revived memories of the hours of being trapped alone in tremendous actual and subjective distress.

Bulent's earthquake experience had potential impact on his future psychological development. Presumably, Bulent had achieved independence in many areas of self-care, including self-sufficiency in bowel and bladder control, independence in eating, and the ability to reach out and obtain help when he required it. These functions were now psychologically attached to the memories of entrapment rather than remaining conflict-free. He had been unable to satisfy his hunger and could not obtain help through any of the methods he had developed. In addition, whereas his body had once been a source of pleasure, now, due to injury, it was a source of pain. As a result, it was possible that Bulent's body image was altered by the trauma, and instead of being associated with a seven-year-old's intense body pleasure and power, it was now associated with feelings of helplessness.

This case illustrates the interplay of trauma and grief. Bulent's aunt and uncle may have interpreted Bulent's reactions as grief-related rather than trauma-related. Looking at the reactions from a trauma perspective yields a very different understanding of his behaviors. For example, his demands and inability to wait may have resulted from fifteen hours of entrapment, and his clinging behaviors may have been attempts to insure that he would not be left alone again.

When the details of Bulent's earthquake experience were unearthed by the mental health worker and he and his new family began to understand his present anxieties, his aunt and uncle were more able to empathize with him. Similarly, the physicians were able to understand his resistance to medical interventions. In order for Bulent to participate in future medical procedures, he would need to understand that his fears might be linked to the passive experience of having been trapped. He may have associated aspects of the medical procedures with the entrapment, such as the loss of body activity that occurs under anesthesia, being without his parents in a vulnerable situation, as he was during the fifteen hours under rubble, and fears of losing consciousness, which may have occurred during the traumatic circumstance. Bulent's caretakers and the physicians, armed with information about the impact of trauma, could now help him differentiate the medical treatments from the traumatic events.

TRAUMA AND BEREAVEMENT

In a disaster, a child may witness the injury and death of a significant person. The particulars of how the death occurred will stay with the child, interfering with the normal mourning process. Because of the traumatic nature of the death, much of the child's mental activity is aimed at solving three tough problems of intense emotions and memories: those surrounding the death itself, helplessness, and personal life threat. The child who has witnessed the death of a significant person will suffer from persistent or episodic memories and thoughts of her own helplessness and fright; in particular, that she could have been harmed or killed herself. Mental images of how the loved one appeared, sounded, and behaved at the time of death and thoughts of what she could or should have done to prevent the death are details that may occupy the child. The memories which arise from a traumatic death are intrusive, not comforting, and are linked to troubling emotions of guilt, fantasies of retaliation, and a multiplicity of changed life circumstances. The child may also suffer physiological hyperreactivity. Triggers abound in the child's day-to-day environment.

Social workers need to know about traumatic bereavement. No matter what the

disaster context, there will certainly be children and family members who have witnessed the traumatic death of a loved one.

Traumatic bereavement may occur in many different contexts, from natural disaster
to political violence to interpersonal violence within the family or death by accident.
Contributing to traumatic bereavement in the child is the loss of a significant person
in the child's life in a sudden and unexpected way. The cases I will use to illustrate
traumatic bereavement derive from the contexts of family violence and accidents.
The concepts contained in these case illustrations can be applied to natural-disaster
situations.

CASE EXAMPLE

Rosa, age four, lost her mother in a fatal car accident during which she was in the
back seat, frightened for her own life. She witnessed her mother's mutilation, and
heard her mother scream as she had never screamed before. In the treatment context,
Rosa's play included recalling of the details of the accident with modifications that
provided her some emotional relief. For example, instead of the ambulance crashing
into their car at a high speed, Rosa, in play, placed a huge, not-to-be-missed speed-
ometer inside the ambulance, which the driver could not avoid seeing and as a result
slowed down. Or the driver, in her play, after striking their car, was severely admonished
by the police, cited, and incarcerated for life. Or her mother called to Rosa and Rosa
undid her seatbelt, leaped over the seat, and slammed on the brake with her hand in
time to avoid the oncoming ambulance. Another aspect of the play included having
her mother's head hit a soft pillow instead of the hard inside of the car, thereby preserving instead of crushing her mother's head. These aspects of play revealed the details
of Rosa's subjective experience and her fantasies and wishes that everything had come
out differently. In her play, her mother was not irrevocably damaged; Rosa behaved
heroically instead of feeling and being helpless; the ambulance driver did not strike
the car; and the ambulance driver was accountable for the accident, not Rosa or her
mother. The therapist did not have to evoke this play. All that was necessary was to
tell Rosa that she knew some of what she had seen and heard from Rosa's Daddy. Rosa
told her own story through the play.

At the beginning of the treatment, she was dominated by the details of how the
death occurred. Playing out and expressing the worst fears and moments through play
enabled her to find relief through her fantasy modification of the accident. Over time,
the trauma receded. She was then able to recall her mother before the accident, such
as the cuddles and the games they played instead of her mother's screams for help.
Slowly, she reconstructed her mother as she had been: whole, not mutilated; calming,
not frightening. Mourning was then able to proceed.

CASE EXAMPLE

Pat, age nine, witnessed his father kill his mother. In play, Pat was the good superhero
who tackled the evil supervillains as they invaded the treatment room in search of the

child and therapist. A war began, ongoing from session to session. Pat amassed, in play, powers over time that surpassed the evildoers. Symbolically, he overcame his father and saved his mother. Interwoven with this play were sessions about a protected animal in a faraway land, unable to be found or approached. His mother, like this animal, had been endangered, rare, and precious to him. He might have also, at the time of the attack upon his mother and afterward, wished to have been this animal.

The vivid memories of the traumatic event receded as he gained relief through his fantasies of power. The burden of the trauma lightened and relinquished its hold upon his mental activity. Gradually, Pat was able to describe how powerless he had felt during the murder and how afraid he had been for his own safety. The guilt he experienced about his inaction at the time was put into perspective as he considered his actual age and relative strength compared to his father's age and strength. As the trauma receded, Pat was able to describe his wishes that his mother be by his side. He was able to recall at will his mother's kindness, humor, and other characteristics. Mourning had begun after the traumatic state of mind receded.

CHILDREN WHO HAVE LOST SOMEONE UNEXPECTEDLY BUT NOT WITNESSED THE DEATH

Family members of the victims of the September 11, 2001, terrorist attacks on the World Trade Center and the Pentagon lost loved ones through a violent and unexpected event, that they did not witness. Despite not witnessing the death and not experiencing a life threat to themselves, the surviving family members may have experienced complications in their mourning process. This kind of death invariably involves a prolongation of the searching mode (which characterizes the preliminary phase of mourning), because in most cases no concrete indication of the person's death exists. Families waited for weeks and months hoping that their missing loved one would be found. Without the evidence of the dead body, family members awaited the return of their family member (Webb 2002; see chapter 4, this volume).

Unaccounted-for losses in natural disasters and political violence result in a suspended grief process that cannot begin until there has been some recognition or evidence of the reality of the death. This form of bereavement is referred to by a variety of poignant phrases: complicated bereavement, distorted mourning process, ambiguous loss, unelaborated mourning, frozen grief, and impaired mourning. In this condition, the child and the adult maintain the illusion that the former world will be returning because it was the safe world, and because there is no physical evidence to dispute its return.

During the Argentine "Dirty War" that raged from 1976 to 1983, citizens were "disappeared," never to return. The parents whose children had been abducted waited for their children to reappear. The family might preserve the child's room and possessions, and the mother might continue to change the sheets on a missing child's bed or prepare the child's favorite food so that he could enjoy it when he reappeared

(Robben 2000). On one hand, this provided hope. On the other, it prevented the task of mourning.

Under these conditions, the discovery of an article of clothing or the body confirms the physical reality of the death. A burial serves to locate the dead person in a gravesite. If no body or article can be found, funerary rituals can be helpful to initiate a grief process.

CHILDREN WHOSE CARETAKERS HAVE WITNESSED THE DEATH OF A LOVED ONE AND ARE TRAUMATIZED

In those situations where the child has not been exposed to a traumatic death, but the caretaker has been, the adult's level of emotion can generate powerful anxiety in the child. The adult's unavoidable mental preoccupation and physiological reactivity affect the adult's parenting. The parent seems altered to the child and is different than she was before. The parent's preoccupation can feel like a rejection. Information about the details of the death can introduce images to the child that threaten his intact image of the deceased. Often, the parent in this circumstance is so traumatized and absorbed with the mental activity typical of trauma that she is unable to recognize the impact of her state of mind on the child and upon her caretaking. The parent needs help in explaining to her child that she is very distressed while providing hope that she will be better with time.

CASE EXAMPLE

Joshua had not been present at the car accident, which had caused fatal injuries to his mother. Although his father had not witnessed the accident, he was sitting bedside at the hospital during his wife's coma before she was discontinued from life support. Over weeks the father observed his wife in her injured, severely altered condition. When he returned home in the evenings to care for Joshua, he was unable to discontinue the mental images of his wife. Contending with these intrusive images, he was unable to comfort Joshua. Joshua felt pushed away by his father, who had intentionally absented himself from his child so as not to overwhelm him inadvertently with details of the mother's condition. Joshua's father was helped to explain to his son that he was feeling very sad and that both he and his son were missing mommy. He was able to do this after he understood that he was staying away from Joshua for fear that he might overwhelm him with images of his fatally injured wife.

UNDERSTANDING THE SOCIOCULTURAL CONTEXT IN SOCIAL WORK PRACTICE WITH TRAUMATIZED CHILDREN

Every society has particular methods for restoring the psychological safety of its citizenry. Every society uses specific cultural symbols psychologically recruited by the group and the individual to express anxiety. Every society has distinctive family systems, distinct concepts of development, and unique methods of training its mental health workers. In order to be helpful, the social worker can prepare herself by understanding the culture she is entering through background reading and through listening to and asking questions of the indigenous mental health workers.

Following the 1999 earthquake, I was invited to speak to social workers at Hacettepe University School of Social Work in Ankara, Turkey. There, I saw how diagnosis and treatment are influenced by sociocultural factors. Because I grew up and was trained in the United States, I had had a lifetime of emphasis on the individual. A prevailing concept among developmental psychologists in the United States is that the traumatic event will stimulate helpless feelings in the individual causing him to regress to a childlike position. A related concept is that this step backward psychologically may interfere with an adolescent's task of developing an identity separate from his family and compromise his independent strivings. The Turkish mental health professionals disputed my view of the "separation-individuation" task of adolescent development and posited the Turkish view that the adolescent solidifies his sense of responsibility toward his family of origin during adolescence. These different views of adolescence shape the clinician's view of what is normal and what is pathological and may make an enormous difference to the clinician's assessment of the impact of a traumatic event upon a particular adolescent.

Following the earthquake in Armenia in 1988, mental health consultants found that the Armenian population manifested anxiety and fear specific to its culture. In particular, varied phobias appeared, which included fears of spirits, fears of Russians, and fears of Turks. The phenomena of illusions and "pseudo-hallucinations" disconcerted the first French teams who worked in Armenia. Children saw "spirits" and supernatural figures and heard the voices of the dead. The mental health practitioners worked with local anthropologists, teachers, nursery school personnel, and healthcare professionals in order to adapt their work to the cultural universe of Armenia (Moro 1994).

Following the earthquake in Gujarat, India, the Center for Environment Education, supported by the Indian Ministry of Environment and Forests, developed a manual, *Rebuilding Hope: An Educator's Guide to Helping Children Cope with Stressful Situations* (Pandya and Raghunathan 2001). In India, the educator is a valued guide for the child under all sorts of circumstances. This manual is rooted in the indigenous educators' understanding of Indian cultural attitudes toward stress and recovery. It emphasizes the restitutive functions of group support to individual recovery, the importance of providing a scientific rather than an astrological explanation of natural disaster, and the importance of parents tolerating temporary regressions in their children at times of stress. Through storytelling, creative writing, singing, plays, skits, role play, puppetry, arts and crafts, outdoor work, and caring for pets, the manual emphasizes "solidarity in distress" and the scientific understanding of earthquakes. The manual encourages the educator to reassure parents that coddling children who are suffering anxiety as a result of the earthquake will not lead to a decrease in the child's ultimate independence and resiliency.

The principles of safety and disruption of safety are culture-neutral. However, cultures vary from country to country, from locale to locale, from religion to religion, from class to class, from ethnic group to ethnic group. If the social worker understands the distinctive cultural emphases, symbols, belief systems, history, and mental health and educational systems, she will be effective, contributory, and deeply appreciated by the mental health workers attempting to address the needs of their distressed populations.

CONCLUSION

Throughout the educational and practice process, the social worker is equipped with the emotional, intellectual, and practical tools to serve in national and international disaster situations. Social workers play a pivotal role with vulnerable populations in the restoration of a sense of safety and the replacement of helplessness by a realistic feeling of effectiveness. With the additional understanding of the impact of trauma and bereavement on children and families, the social worker is equipped to provide direct service and advise indigenous mental health providers in disaster situations.

REFERENCES

Ainslie, R. C., and K. Brabeck. 2003. Race murder and community trauma: Psychoanalysis and ethnography in exploring the impact of the killing of James Byrd in Jasper, Texas. *Journal of Psychoanalysis, Culture, and Society* 8(1): 49–54.

Apfel, R. J., and B. Simon. 2000. Mitigating discontents with children in war: An ongoing psychoanalytic inquiry. In *Cultures Under Siege: Collective Violence and Trauma*, ed. A. C. G. Robben and M. M. Suarez-Orozco, 102–130. Cambridge: Cambridge University Press.

Aronson, L. 2000. Consultation to mental health providers in Turkey post-earthquake: Assisting children and caretakers exposed to a sudden violent event. In *Trauma Treatment Professionals' Training*, ed. A. B. Tufan, A. M. Aktas, and V. Duyan, 1–11. Ankara: Hacettepe University School of Social Work.

Erikson, K. T. 1976. Loss of community at Buffalo Creek. *American Journal of Psychiatry* 133:302–325.

Fletcher, K. E. 1996. Childhood posttraumatic stress disorder. In *Child Psychopathology*, ed. E. J. Mash and R. A. Barkley, 242–276. New York: Guilford.

Freud, A. 1967. Comments on psychic trauma. In *Writings of Anna Freud*, 5:221–241. New York: International Universities Press.

Furman, R. A. 1988. New perspectives on preparation. *Cleveland Center for Research in Child Development 1988 Workshop*, 1–11.

Goenjian, A. K., L. Molina, A. M. Steinberg, et al. 2001. Posttraumatic stress and depressive reactions among Nicaraguan adolescents after Hurricane Mitch. *American Journal of Psychiatry* 158(5): 788–794.

Moro, M. R. 1994. Earthquake in Armenia: Establishment of a psychological care center. In *Children and Violence*, ed. C. Chiland and J. G. Young, 125–159. Northvale, NJ: Jason Aronson.

Pandya, M., and M. Raghunathan. 2001. *Rebuilding Hope: An Educator's Guide to Helping Children Cope with Stressful Situations*. Ahmedabad, India: Centre for Environment Education.

Parkes, C. M. 1997. Normal and abnormal responses to stress—a developmental approach. In *Psychological Trauma: A Developmental Approach*, ed. D. Black, M. Newman, J. Harris-Hendriks, and G. Mezey, 10–18. London: Gaskell.

Pynoos, R. S., A. Goenjian, and A. M. Steinberg. 1995. Strategies of disaster intervention for children and adolescents. In *Extreme Stress and Communities: Impact and Intervention*, ed. S. E. Hobfoll and M. W. de Vries, 445–471. Amsterdam: Kluwer Academic.

Pynoos, R. S., A. M. Steinberg, and L. Aronson. 1997. Traumatic experiences: The early organization of memory in school-age children and adolescents. In *Trauma and Memory: Clinical and Legal Controversies*, ed. P. S. Appelbaum, L. A. Uyehara, and M. R. Elin, 272–289. New York: Oxford University Press.

Robben, A. C. G. 2000. The assault on basic trust: disappearance, protest, and reburial in Argentina. In *Cultures Under Siege: Collective Violence and Trauma*, ed. A. C. G. Robben and M. M. Suarez-Orozco, 70–101. Cambridge: Cambridge University Press.

Sandler, J. 1960. The background of safety. *International Journal of Psychoanalysis* 41:352–356.

Smith, D. F. 2002. Functional salutogenic mechanisms of the brain. *Perspectives in Biology and Medicine* 45(3): 319–328.

Susser, E. S., D. B. Herman, and B. Aaron. 2002. Combating the terror of terrorism. *Scientific American* 8:71–77.

Terr, L. C. 1991. Childhood traumas: An outline and overview. *American Journal of Psychiatry* 148(1): 10–20.

Webb, N. B. 2002. *Helping Bereaved Children: A Handbook for Practitioners.* 2d ed. New York: Guilford.

Weisaeth, L. 1993. Disasters: Psychological and psychiatric aspects. In *Handbook of Stress: Theoretical and Clinical Aspects* (2d ed.), ed. L. Goldberger and S. Breznitz, 591–616. New York: Free Press.

Yehuda, R. 2002. Current concepts: Post-traumatic stress disorder. *New England Journal of Medicine* 346(2): 108–114.

35

HEMATOPOIETIC CELL TRANSPLANTATION
AND THE END OF LIFE

IRIS COHEN FINEBERG

HEMATOPOIETIC CELL transplantation, more specifically known as bone mar-row transplantation (BMT) and peripheral stem cell transplantation (PSCT), may provide something ultimately sought in cancer care: cure. For some people, BMT and PSCT are first-line therapies intended to offer the best possible chance of long-term survival. For others, these treatments are desperate efforts to gain survival time when all other treatments have failed. Consequently, for some, choosing to have a transplant is truly a choice, one that requires extensive thought and consid-eration. For others, a transplant is not perceived as a choice but rather as the only alternative to certain death (Stevens and Pletsch 2002). Despite transplantation's being a long and intensive treatment fraught with many life-threatening risks and compli-cations, it represents a powerful source of hope for patients and their families. The success rates of transplantation vary widely, and transplantation is successful for treat-ing certain diseases at specific stages along the trajectory of illness and treatment (Harousseau and Attal 2002; Kusnierz-Glaz et al. 1997). This chapter focuses on the intersection of transplantation and death; numerous print and Internet sources provide further information about the details and complexities of transplantation (see the website list in the references).

The discussion of death in relation to transplantation is often brief and avoided by physicians and patients alike. Physicians are required to discuss with the patients the risk of death during the treatment consent process, but there is little other discussion of end-of-life (EOL) issues. As Snyder (1999) has suggested, several reasons may ex-plain this avoidance, including the focus on the possibility for cure, physicians' con-cerns about diminishing hope, and the generally young age of transplant patients. Unfortunately, although many patients live and benefit from transplantation, many also die (Crawford 1991). How and when this death occurs varies, influencing the reactions and needs of the people involved. Some patients die during the transplant process, others die of treatment related complications throughout the post-transplant period, and still others die of their diseases. The purpose of this chapter is to help social workers understand the numerous circumstances that may influence how pa-tients and families react to transplant-related death.

The chapter begins with basic information about transplantation as a foundation for understanding the setting in which patients and families face death. The brief description of the types, applications, and trajectories of transplantation provides a general view of an arena in which the details of biomedical technology and medical practices are constantly changing. Most of the discussion focuses on the contextual factors that may modulate how patients, family members, and staff experience transplant-related death. In addition to the specific challenges of treatment, some overarching characteristics of transplantation make it difficult. A primary characteristic is the continuous presence of uncertainty. From the very decision to pursue transplantation and onward, patients and families tolerate an ongoing uncertainty about what will be the obstacles and outcomes of transplantation (Haberman 1988). The uncertainty permeates the entire experience of transplantation. An additional challenging characteristic of treatment is its unfamiliar nature. Most people do not have a frame of reference, a point of comparison for imagining what it will be like to have the transplant experience. As a result, patients and families find the process difficult to conceptualize, even when they have read materials and discussed expectations (Haberman 1995). Clinical social workers' understanding of both the broad and specific challenges of transplantation should enable them to anticipate and address better the needs of patients and families.

BASIC INFORMATION ABOUT TRANSPLANTATION

Hematopoietic cell transplantation is the technical term for what the lay public knows as bone marrow and stem cell transplantation. Bone marrow transplants (BMT) allow the transferal of marrow, the substance in which cell production takes place. Bone marrow is a tissue in the center of the bones that serves as the manufacturing location for blood cells and an important part of the immune system. Bone marrow exists in different amounts in different bones, with the greatest accumulation primarily in the pelvic bones and secondarily in the sternum. In order to remove bone marrow for a transplant, a long needle is repeatedly inserted into the bone to remove the marrow. The marrow is stored in special bags and then transplanted into the patient through an intravenous (IV) line, a process similar to a blood transfusion. The transplantation enables the patient to receive a healthy, well functioning blood-cell producing system.

Peripheral stem cell transplants (PSCT), sometimes also called peripheral blood stem cell transplants (PBSCT), use a different procedure to capture and collect the critical components of the blood. After blood cells are made in the marrow but before they are fully developed, the body releases them into the bloodstream. These very young cells are called stem cells because they have not yet differentiated into the three specific blood cell types they will eventually become. In order to use stem cells for transplant, blood from a donor is filtered using a pheresis machine that separates the stem cells from the rest of the blood. The filtration happens in such a way that once the stem cells are removed from the blood, the rest of the blood is then immediately returned to the donor. The stem cells are collected in a bag and transplanted to the patient through an IV line.

TYPES OF TRANSPLANTS

Transplants are classified according to the relationship between the donor of the marrow/stem cells and the recipient (the patient) of those blood products. An *autologous* transplant is one in which the patient uses his or her own marrow or stem cells. A *syngeneic* transplant is one that takes place between identical twins, who inherently share the same tissue type. An *allogeneic* transplant is one in which a family member donates the marrow or stem cells to the patient. The donor is often a sibling but may be another family member. The donor is chosen based on a match between the donor and the patient's tissue type, a process called HLA-typing. In recent years, *"mini" allogeneic* transplants (also called non-myeloablative transplants) have been implemented using related donors but lower intensity conditioning regimens than traditional allogeneic transplants (Gurman et al. 2001). Since many people do not have a family member with a matched tissue type, they try to find a match in the rest of the population in order to have a *matched unrelated donor (MUD)* transplant. Matches are sought through national and international registries such as the National Marrow Donor Program (Confer 2001). Each type of transplant is associated with a different level of difficulty, length of hospitalization, risk, and set of possible complications.

No transplant is easy or free of the risk of death, but autologous transplants are considered the shortest, the least complicated, and the least dangerous. Like any type of organ transplant from one person to another, allogeneic or MUD transplants have the potential for rejection, with MUD transplants being the more risky. The type of transplant that a patient has determines the expected length of treatment, anticipated complications, and possible causes of treatment-related death. People having different types of transplants are therefore likely to be vulnerable to different EOL processes.

APPLICATIONS OF BLOOD AND MARROW TRANSPLANTATIONS

Transplantation has been applied as treatment for more and more illnesses since it began in the 1960s (Horowitz 1999). The treatment is primarily utilized to address hematologic malignancies, but it is also used for other malignancies, nonmalignant disorders, and immunodeficiencies. Hematologic malignancies include diagnoses such as acute leukemia, chronic leukemia, lymphoma, and multiple myeloma. Examples of other diagnoses treated with transplantation include breast cancer (Dicato 2002), small cell lung cancer (Rizzo et al. 2002), ovarian cancer (Bay et al. 2002), severe aplastic anemia (Myer and Oliva 2002), and severe rheumatoid arthritis (Verburg et al. 2002). Transplantation allows utilization of more intensive chemotherapy treatment that would otherwise be fatal to the patient, and for some diseases, it provides the replacement of a disordered marrow with a healthy marrow. Transplants are used to treat children and adults, with the oldest age limit expanding as transplant procedures develop. Some people in their sixties and seventies have received transplants, but eligibility depends on diagnosis, type of transplant and the overall condition of the patient (de la Cámara et al. 2002; Kusnierz-Glaz et al. 1997; Ringden et al. 1998).

The primary concept underlying transplantation is that it allows for the use of much higher doses and intensities of chemotherapy and radiation than would otherwise be possible. The high intensity doses of chemotherapy and/or radiation eradicate patients' own bone marrow, and the transplant replaces their system of blood cell production and immunity. In the case of autologous transplants, patients donate their own marrow or stem cells prior to the beginning of the conditioning (chemotherapy/radiation) for transplant. In allogeneic transplantation, the dual purpose of the high treatment doses is to attack the malignant disease and to eradicate the existing immune system to reduce the likelihood of rejection of the donated marrow or stem cells (Horowitz 1999). In a "mini" allogeneic transplant, lower doses of chemotherapy are used in the conditioning treatment before the transplant to promote some conflict between the donated marrow or stem cells and the disease cells, something called a graft-versus-tumor effect. The hope is that the transplanted system will generate an immune response to attack the disease. The advent of "mini" transplants has allowed the use of allogeneic transplantation for older and sicker patients since the doses of chemotherapy associated with the transplant are not as toxic as in a traditional allogeneic transplant (Kim 2002; Slavin et al. 2002).

TRAJECTORY OF THE TRANSPLANT PROCESS

The trajectory of a transplant begins with an intensive conditioning regimen involving chemotherapy and/or radiation. This pre-transplant period often takes seven to ten days, depending on the specific conditioning chosen by the medical team. The conditioning regimens vary based on which treatment protocols the institution offers for particular diagnoses. The pre-transplant period is followed by the transplantation day when patients receive the infusion of marrow or stem cells. This day is called Day 0 and serves as an important reference point for marking the post-transplant process using increasing numerals (i.e., Day $+1$, Day $+2$, etc.). The immediate period that follows Day 0 is the time when patients are most immunocompromised because the new marrow or stem cells have not yet engrafted into their system. This immediate post-transplant period is when patients are most vulnerable to life-threatening complications and most likely to feel actively side effects of treatment (such as nausea, diarrhea, mouth/throat sores, infections, kidney/liver problems, and fatigue). Within one to two weeks, there are usually signs of the marrow or stem cells engrafting in the patient. Once certain blood counts have reached sufficiently high levels, patients often slowly begin to feel better and to focus on their recovery. Those who have been inpatients for the transplant period may be allowed to leave the hospital at this point. Patients continue to be closely monitored medically and are usually required to have a family caregiver with them for several weeks to months following their initial transplant period. Patients follow multiple restrictions in the post-transplant period, including social contact limitations and dietary restrictions. The degree and length of restriction time post-transplant specifically vary from patient to patient but are shorter following autologous transplants than allogeneic and MUD transplants.

For patients who encounter serious complications during their transplant process, hospitalization in the intensive care unit (ICU) may be necessary for a portion of time, altering or ending the post-transplant trajectory. Patients and families usually have to become acquainted with an entirely different staff of healthcare providers than they have been with for several weeks on the transplant unit. In addition, the ICU environment is likely to be very different from that of the transplant unit. ICUs tend to be technology-oriented, fast-paced, equipped with small rooms, restrictive of visitors, lacking privacy and lacking facilities for immunocompromised patients. The emotional and medical intensity of ICU admissions contrasts sharply to the ongoing process of transplantation. The importance of the ICU in the transplantation trajectory is that it may be the end-of-life setting for many (Kroschinsky et al. 2002; McGrath 2001a). Admission to ICU harshly orients patients and families to the life-threatening situation of patients, a reality they may have minimized in order to endure the transplantation process. They are often shocked, overwhelmed, and very frightened by the admission.

CAREGIVERS

The healthcare team that cares for transplant patients usually includes many professionals from several disciplines. The core team often consists of transplant physicians, specially trained nurses, and clinical social workers (Kennedy 1993). However, several other people may be intimately involved with the patient and family—for example, clergy, dieticians and nutritionists, physical therapists, occupational therapists, art therapists, and music therapists (Gabriel et al. 2001; Griessmeier and Koester 2000). Often patients and families meet specialists, such as cardiologists and respiratory therapists, as consultation is needed for addressing treatment complications.

In addition to the healthcare team, it is important that patients have nonprofessional sources of support. For many patients, family members are closely involved in the treatment process (Grimm et al. 2000). "Family" is used broadly to include people whom the patients view as family, whether or not biologically or legally related. Many patients have friends, work colleagues, and perhaps fellow patients as part of their social support network. In the event that patients face death during or soon after transplant, who participates in the process varies greatly among individuals.

SETTINGS

Blood and marrow transplants are usually done on specially designed units within hospital settings (Cooper and Powell 1998). The units are equipped with air filtration systems and other mechanisms to minimize patients' exposure to infectious agents because patients are immunologically vulnerable during and following their initial transplant hospitalization. Traditionally, transplants have consisted of a lengthy inpatient hospital stay followed by close outpatient monitoring by the transplant team. During the inpatient stay, patients are usually required to spend some portion of time in a reverse isolation room that patients may not leave but visitors may enter. Protective isolation, used at the time that patients are most immunocompromised and vulnerable to infections, often requires visitors to wear gloves, facemasks, and gowns. Patients experience both a physical and emotional isolation (Cohen, Ley, and Tarzian 2001). There is some debate about the need for isolation, but most transplant centers continue to use it (Russell et al. 2000). Some medical centers have developed transplant programs that are primarily outpatient treatment using close monitoring by the healthcare team and family members (Grimm et al. 2000; Herrmann et al. 1998). For patients having the traditional inpatient transplants, hospitalization for the pre-transplant, transplant, and immediate post-transplant period typically lasts three to eight weeks, depending on the type of transplant. Autologous transplant admissions are usually the shortest. Transplant-related complications may cause patients to be hospitalized for many months. Once transplant patients have left the inpatient setting, healthcare providers depend on patients' family members and friends to assist with activities of daily living (e.g., transportation, food preparation, taking of medications) for several weeks to months while patients visit the healthcare team several times per week for outpatient monitoring. When working with patients having transplants, it is important to consider the setting and the familiarity of the setting to the patient and family.

Many people travel large distances to medical centers that offer transplantation (McGrath 2001b). As a result, there is tremendous disruption to patients and families' lifestyles. Those people from far away are usually required to stay near to the medical center for several weeks to months following the transplant (Grimm et al. 2000). Since patients need family caregivers to assist them during their post-transplant recovery, sometimes entire families move to the area of the medical center. Such moves often have marked impact on social, occupational, and financial realms of people's lives. People are often without extended kin or the customary social support structures in their lives. Families with children face additional challenges related to childcare, school changes, and children's adjustment to the illness and treatment. In the event that patients die during a transplant, the geographic dislocation has implications for the needs, coping, and adjustment of the family members.

IMPORTANT CONSIDERATIONS IN TRANSPLANT-RELATED DEATH

CAUSES AND TIMING OF DEATH

Death as the result of treatment and its side effects can occur at any time from the beginning of the transplant process to years later (Tabbara et al. 2002). I will broadly discuss a few causes of death in this section, but clinicians should pursue a more thorough understanding of these conditions through reading transplant texts and articles. The importance of understanding these causes is in realizing the EOL circumstances that accompany them. Some happen very quickly and require ICU admissions and life-support decisions. Others are more gradual, allowing longer periods for adjustment, discussion, and decision making. Furthermore, the timing of the death in relation to the illness trajectory, the life cycle, and the treatment trajectory is important for understanding the issues of death in transplantation.

CAUSES. Since transplant treatment involves high intensity chemotherapy and/or radiation, the toxicity of the treatment itself presents a risk. The toxicity to vital organs (such as lungs, kidneys, liver, and heart) may cause such severe damage that patients go into organ failure, commonly multisystem organ failure (Bonig et al. 2000). Demise from such toxicity may lead people to require intensive care treatment. Patients who have had allogeneic or MUD transplants are especially vulnerable due to the many medications, such as anti-rejection drugs, that they take for months or years. Another life threatening risk is non-engraftment. This occurs if the transplanted marrow does not assimilate into the patient's body and does not function to produce blood cells. The patient is left lacking an important part of the immune system, making him or her extremely vulnerable to infection.

Infection is one of the most dangerous threats to the transplant patient, even when engraftment has gone well (Barnes and Stallard 2001; Junghanss et al. 2002). Severe and/or systemic infections may also require treatment in the intensive care unit (Veys and Owens 2002). For example, fungal infections in the lungs are often life-threatening (Marr 2001). Patients can die of systemic infection, called sepsis, when the body is unable to fight the infection sufficiently. Another major cause of death is graft-versus-host disease (GVHD), a process by which the patient's body rejects and reacts to the donor's marrow or stem cells. This is one of the most dangerous complications that a patient can face, depending on the severity of GVHD and the timing of its development (Lee et al. 2002; Zecca et al. 2002). Finally, it is important to remember that transplant patients may die owing to relapse of their diseases.

TIMING IN RELATION TO ILLNESS. Depending on the illness, the timing of transplant-related death may be at different points in the illness trajectory. If the death takes place early in relation to time of diagnosis, patients and families may not have yet begun to adjust to the diagnosis. They may be still in shock about the illness when the death occurs, confounding the shock. Other patients and families have grappled with disease and treatment cycles for many years. Their lengthy illness careers may have strengthened their resolve to overcome the illness or it may have worn down their emotional and physical resources to cope with treatment. Below are specific examples of how diagnosis and the timing of transplantation may affect the end-of-life experience.

Patients with acute leukemia often are hospitalized on the day of diagnosis and undergo transplantation within a few months because the likelihood of success is highest if done early. The fast onset of the disease leaves patients with little time to adjust to the diagnosis and perhaps no opportunity to return home between diagnosis and transplant. Both patients and families are often in active "fight" mode, ready to do whatever is required in order to eradicate the disease. Unless the nuclear family has faced other serious or chronic illnesses among its members, it may be "fresh" to having life focused around the illness and treatment, thus having energy and optimism to bring to the situation. Death from such a transplant may still be in the context of the original shock of the diagnosis. Because the diagnosis flows directly into hospitalization and soon after into transplant and death, the entire illness event may feel like one unimaginable, surreal nightmare.

Patients with chronic leukemia face a different set of circumstances. People with chronic leukemia often do not feel symptoms of their disease and can progress with their normal lives, working and engaging in most of their usual activities. The disease can be often controlled with oral medications for months, and patients can continue their lives as if nothing has happened. They generally do not experience side effects or illness effects. For these patients, there is the difficulty of choosing when to have a transplant, since they enter transplantation feeling healthy and well, knowing that the transplant itself will make them ill. Although recommended earlier rather than later, there is no immediate urgency to having the transplant; furthermore, the treatment will make patients feel very sick and may kill them, when up until the transplant they may have felt normal. The decision to schedule the transplant may feel counterintuitive. However, if the disease is allowed to continue, it eventually converts to a more intensive and life-threatening form of disease that is far less responsive to any treatment. Thus, there is a window of opportunity during which transplant is useful and recommended. Patients with chronic leukemia and their families often struggle with the decision of when to have the transplant and often question this decision if the patient dies.

CASE EXAMPLE

Tiffany was a woman diagnosed with breast cancer in her mid-twenties who underwent mastectomy surgery with reconstruction followed by an autologous transplant. Within several years, Tiffany developed myelodysplastic syndrome, a preleukemic condition that can develop following certain chemotherapy regimens. Tiffany underwent an allogeneic transplant, facing numerous complications during her admission. She was able to return home after many weeks and began to strengthen as her post-transplant recovery continued. However, she was readmitted every few weeks, fighting complications that would arise. Tiffany maintained much anger about all of the illness and treatment she had had to endure during the recent years, and she did not want to discuss the possibility of dying. She continued to struggle with complications, always wanting to take the most aggressive treatment necessary. Upon her final admission, Tiffany developed organ failure. She consciously chose to be transferred to the ICU knowing she would be placed on a ventilator. She died within a couple of days on life support. She was thirty-three years old. For Tiffany, the long history of illness and treatment had motivated her to continue fighting for survival.

CASE EXAMPLE

Paul was a man diagnosed with Hodgkin's disease in his twenties who underwent an autologous transplant approximately one year after diagnosis. Within six months of transplant, the disease had returned, and Paul received radiation therapy to specific areas of his body where there was disease. Approximately four years later, Paul developed myelodysplastic syndrome due to his previous treatments. Within a few months of this new diagnosis, he underwent an allogeneic PSCT from a sibling. He persevered through the transplant and returned home. However, he experienced frequent readmissions due to complications. Within half a year of the allogeneic transplant, Paul was admitted for a severe infection. Given his physical condition and the information provided by physicians, he decided that more aggressive treatment would not change his nearing the end-of-life during the hospital admission. He chose to refuse antibiotics and not to be transferred to the ICU. He called his family and friends, telling them he anticipated that he would be dying later that day. Family and friends arrived throughout the day, and in the mid-evening, Paul died in his room, surrounded by those closest to him. For Paul, the long struggle with illness and treatment was worthwhile until the point he felt there was no more realistic possibility for survival. At that point, he wanted to control the circumstances of his death. He was thirty-four years old when he died.

TIMING IN RELATION TO THE LIFE CYCLE. Generally, transplantation is a treatment for a young population, people who were not yet expecting to die. Most commonly, patients are less than fifty years old, though at times people up to age seventy have received the treatment. These patients may be children, young adults, or midlife adults. For young children and their parents, there are particular issues in facing death at such an untimely period of life. For young adults, the injustice of the situation may dominate their experience. For young or middle-aged adults with young children, the focus often turns to the distress of leaving a partner (perhaps) but certainly of abandoning the children. The sense of opportunities that have been missed, concerns for who is left behind, feelings about a life that has not been lived, the unfinished projects and stories, are omnipresent for patients and for family members.

CASE EXAMPLE

Mandy was a forty-year-old married mother of two diagnosed with acute leukemia shortly after giving birth to her second child. She was immediately hospitalized for chemotherapy and possibilities for transplant were explored. Six months later, Mandy had an allogeneic PSCT from a sibling. Within two months of transplant, there was evidence of disease recurrence, demonstrating the aggressiveness of her disease. Mandy's husband and older child visited her regularly, along with other family members. Following the recurrence of the disease, the transplant staff made special arrangements to allow Mandy's baby to visit her regularly, although young children are not usually allowed in the protective transplant environment. Mandy authorized her physicians to try further treatments that were experimental and had little probability of saving her life. Her priority was to have as much time as possible with her children and family, especially her young baby. With the help of her husband, Mandy made a videotape of herself for her children. She and her husband strategized care plans for the children for when she died. Mandy died one year from the time of diagnosis, having left the hospital for less than a total of ten days during that year. Although she had wanted to go home many times, she persisted in pursuing any treatment options she was offered in the hope of having more time with her husband and children.

TIMING IN RELATION TO THE TRANSPLANT TRAJECTORY. Although physicians discuss the possibility of death as part of their consent process with patients and families, most people do not truly anticipate dying during their transplants. However, death can occur at any time, from early in the transplant process to years post-transplant. In many instances, patients' conditions can deteriorate very quickly in transplantation, as fast as hours or days. This is especially true early in the transplant process, when patients and families are intently focused on actively enduring treatment effects. Consequently, when fast changes occur in patients' conditions, many patients and families are not prepared. Patients may become incommunicative and be unable to provide direction as to what level of care they want pursued in response to the critical medical situation. Family members are often in shock, having to deal with a drastic swing from high hopes for cure to the probability of an immediate and technological death. Family members may need to make treatment-related decisions without having had any prior discussions with the patient about preferences and priorities. For some families, the medical condition dictates the options, leaving the family stunned at the pace of change and the harsh process by which their family member has been taken away from them by death.

The quick transition from being in the midst of care to being in serious danger can also occur months into the post-transplant period. For patients who are back at home (or in the local community) and focused on recovery, a serious complication may feel like a betrayal. Patients may be feeling quite well, doing more activities associated with normal life, requiring fewer appointments at the hospital for monitoring, and then a severe complication can reverse the gains. For both patients and families, this again requires a tremendous shift in mindset, from one of recovery and improving health to one of facing death and loss. By contrast, death during the post-transplant period may also be more anticipated and gradual. For example, patients may experience ongoing complications that lead them and their families to contemplate, over time, the possibility that they may die. Furthermore, relapse of diseases later in the transplant process may again offer more time for patients and families to anticipate the end of their lives.

CASE EXAMPLE

George was a thirty-four-year-old man diagnosed with acute leukemia and treated immediately with chemotherapy. Although he had six siblings, none of his family members had tissue types that matched his own. A search of the National Bone Marrow Registry successfully identified a donor who was willing and able to donate marrow for a transplant. George underwent a MUD transplant, encountering a few complications during his admission but enduring the treatment well overall. He was discharged from the hospital after five weeks and experienced slow but steady strengthening in his post-transplant recovery. Within half a year, he began to engage in part-time work and was starting to have more social contact with friends. His family lived very far from him, but he maintained close contact through telephone and occasional visits. Approximately eight months after the transplant, George was admitted due to a high fever and signs of infection. Within a day his condition had deteriorated, requiring him to be placed on a ventilator in the ICU. George was unconscious and progressively experiencing multiorgan failure. His family arrived within two days, shocked to see his condition after having recently seen him in increasingly strong health. By the third day, tests showed that George no longer had brain activity. A family conference with George's family members, the transplant physician, the ICU physician, the ICU nurse, and the transplant social worker included a review of the progression of events leading up to George's situation and clarified his current condition. Family members asked questions and expressed their shock at the fast pace of decline. Family members seemed to understand that George was dead by brain criteria and authorized the cessation of life support. The family and healthcare team gathered in George's ICU room and stayed together as the ventilator was turned off. Within a short time, George's vital signs ceased. The family expressed their despair over George's fast transition from wellness to death, especially at a point in time post-transplant, when he seemed to be progressively getting stronger.

FAMILY CONSIDERATIONS

One of the important considerations in transplantation is the social support network of the patient. Patients require social support throughout the hospitalization and recovery process, and for many family members, helping the patient feels like a significant contribution to the patient's care. Although patients are most often helped by family members who are biologically or legally related (i.e., parents, spouses, siblings), the term "family" will be used here more broadly to include those people whom the patient views as "family." For example, this may include partners, very close friends, and neighbors. Not all people have biological family members who are able or willing to help, and some people prefer to have care from their "chosen family" rather than biological family. Some people have built networks of friends and neighbors whom they view as family, either in addition to or instead of biological family members.

ROLES OF THE FAMILY. Regardless of who compromises family for a specific patient, that family has a vital role in the transplant process (Ho, Horne, and Szer 2002; Syrjala et al. 1993). Transplant requires the involvement of family caregivers in the care of the patient for an extended period, often months to years. The care involves a combination of physical care, practical assistance with basic activities (such as cooking and cleaning), emotional support, transportation, assistance with medications, and availability in emergencies. Family members often bear the frustrations and fears of patients. They may be taken for granted and often do not receive the social recognition of the practical and emotional strains that they bear. Family members experience additional strains of taking over the roles and duties that the patient had in the home, dealing with the financial impact of transplantation and negotiating with employers about time off and schedule flexibility (Zabora et al. 1992). Many family members try to be sources of emotional strength for patients, hiding their own fears and pain. For those who had primary caregiving roles, the death of the patient may lead to identity confusion and a sense of void due to the loss of caregiving roles.

VULNERABLE FAMILY MEMBERS. Certain family members may be especially emotionally and socially vulnerable, particularly in EOL situations. Children need to be informed about what is happening with patients, especially siblings, using language and concepts appropriate for their ages (Packman 1999). Developmentally disabled family members should also be included in the process thoughtfully, allowing them to participate in the treatment process and decision making to the greatest of their abilities. Socially, same-sex partners may be vulnerable if legal documents have not ensured their decision-making powers or if immediate members of the biological family do not recognize the partnership (see chapter 25). People who are not fluent in the dominant language used at the medical facility will need special assistance to ensure that they understand the treatment process and the condition of the patient. If needed, utilizing professional interpreters is preferable to family-member interpreters due to their objectivity and familiarity with medical and technical language (see chapter 22). Because the needs of vulnerable family members may be overlooked or ignored in end-of-life situations, social workers' assessment and advocacy skills are especially valuable in protecting and assisting these individuals.

THE DONOR. One family member who requires special care, especially in the event that the patient dies, is the blood or marrow donor. Being the donor in transplantation is an extremely personal investment with both positive and negative aspects. Donors experience painful medical procedures and disruptions in their lives such as numerous medical appointments and travel to medical facilities (Switzer et al. 2001). In contrast, donors have also reported feeling emotionally closer to patients because of the shared experiences and feeling better about themselves (Munzenberger et al. 1999; Switzer et al. 1998). Donors often have a sense of responsibility, hoping that their blood or marrow is "good enough" to save the patient. When the patient dies, donors may experience a sense of inadequacy and guilt. Some may feel that they have betrayed the patient and disappointed the surviving family members. Others may experience anger and resentment as part of their grief. The quality of relationship between the donor and patient may also affect the donors' reactions to patients' deaths. For example, a donor with a conflictual relationship with the patient may experience additional guilt and remorse if the patient dies.

SOCIAL ISOLATION OF THE FAMILY. Most transplant programs require that patients remain local to the medical center following the transplant for a period of several weeks to several months, depending on the type of transplant being done (Decker 1995). Consequently, for those people who are far from home, facing the death of the patient may occur in isolation from their natural social support system. Furthermore, the people "back home" who might be supportive have not witnessed the treatment with its intensity, side effects, difficulties, and day-to-day challenges (Baker et al. 1999). Those people do not have a first-hand point of reference to imagine what family members may be encountering during the treatment. This experiential divide may feel even more significant if patients die at the transplant center, away from home. The comforts of home that include the immediate home environment, the familiar community resources, the social support network, and the general sense of safety that people may feel at home are all unavailable to families facing the death of patients far from home. The medical center environment often offers some comforts such as an extensive group of staff members who have cared for the patients and accompanied families through the treatment, and other families who know firsthand about the difficulties of living through transplantation (Zabora et al. 1992). However, when families return home after the death of patients, they may grieve their loss in an environment that feels disassociated from their experiences and their deceased family members.

PATIENTS' PRIORITIES AND TREATMENT PREFERENCES

The lack of communication among patients, families, and healthcare providers about the possibility of death diminishes opportunities to address end-of-life issues effectively (Hickman 2002; McGrath 2002a, 2002b). One of the challenges in transplant-related death is that many patients and families have not discussed patients' priorities and preferences in regards to care decisions. When patients are unable to communicate, families may be left to struggle with difficult choices, especially about life-support decisions (Foster and McLellan 2002). Such struggles may include disagreement among family members and may also involve conflict with the healthcare team (Hickman 2002). Pain and symptom management, essential in transplantation and EOL care, requires understanding of patients' priorities and preferences to inform pain control decisions (Pan et al. 2001). Several strategies may help to promote communication. Advance directives and healthcare proxies are legal documents that facilitate communication about patients' wishes at the end of life. Family conferences are another communication tool. Integral to exploration of patients' and families' priorities and preferences is exploration of their cultural beliefs. Similarly, care providers should explore patients' and families' religious and spiritual beliefs.

PAIN AND SYMPTOM MANAGEMENT

Pain and symptom experiences accompany the process of end-of-life in transplantation. Attention to pain and symptom assessment and management has increased in recent years, acknowledging the importance of patients' experiences (Ferris, von Gunten, and Emanuel 2002; Loscalzo and Amendola 1990). Examples of symptoms in end-of-life are shortness of breath, bone pain, and the anxiety and distress associated with placement on life-support machinery. Assessment needs to focus not only on types and severity of symptoms but also on understanding what is most distressing to individual patients. Since pain and symptom management may include balancing positive and negative consequences of pain control interventions, understanding patients' priorities is essential (Steinhauser et al. 2000). For example, some patients may prefer to tolerate certain levels of pain in order to avoid being drowsy from pain medications. An especially challenging set of circumstances may arise when providing sufficient medication for pain relief may contribute to the death of the patient. It is on such occasions that knowledge about patients' priorities and preferences is essential for guiding families' and care providers' discussion and decision making (see chapter 19).

ADVANCE DIRECTIVES AND HEALTHCARE PROXIES

Advance directives and healthcare proxies are legal documents that help patients have a voice at a time when they are not able to participate in decision making (Fagerlin et al. 2002). Advance directives document people's preferences for various kinds of care. People may have specific views about what kind of medical interventions they do and do not want, where they would like to die, who they want involved in their EOL process, and what they fear or want most. For example, such documents may state wishes to be or not be placed on life support if the occasion arises. Healthcare proxies are documents in which people name a specific person to make healthcare decisions for them in the event they are unable to make decisions themselves. Aside from the legal power they hold, advance directives and healthcare proxies create excellent opportunities for discussion of patients' priorities and preferences between patients, family members, and healthcare providers. Social workers can provide such forms to patients and encourage them to discuss their priorities, with or without completing the documents. The discussion may be framed in the context of protecting the wishes of patients in the event they cannot communicate them at the crucial moment.

CASE EXAMPLE

Edward was a sixty-year-old man who was diagnosed with lymphoma and underwent an autologous PSCT. Although he tolerated the initial transplant period well, Edward had frequent readmissions to the hospital during the months following transplant. After his fourth hospitalization, Edward began to discuss the possibility of dying. Although his disease had not recurred, he felt that his body would not be able to overcome post-transplant complications. He verbalized his wish not be maintained on life support machinery if the occasion arose and signed a healthcare proxy form, naming one of his daughters as his proxy. During his last admission, Edward was admitted to the intensive care unit and attached to a ventilator. His adult children, though clear on his wishes not to be on life support, wanted to be sure that his condition was not reversible. His daughter, the named healthcare proxy, struggled with the decision to have him on the ventilator at all. On one hand, she knew her father did not want to be on a ventilator, but on the other, she was afraid of depriving him of an opportunity to survive. After three days, the children gathered at the patient's bedside, said their goodbyes, and permitted the healthcare team to stop the life support. The patient died within a few hours, surrounded by his children who expressed relief in knowing that they were able to honor the EOL wishes of their father.

FAMILY CONFERENCES

One forum for communication among patients, families, and healthcare providers is the family conference. Such meetings provide opportunities for people to discuss their understanding of information, ask questions, discuss decisions, and express anxiety and fears (Atkinson, Stewart, and Gardner 1980; Hansen, Cornish, and Kayser 1998). They may be especially important in families with an ongoing history of poor functioning and internal conflict. Who participates in a family conference may vary based on the topic of discussion, the immediacy of the situation, availability of participants, and relevance of the topic to team members. Conferences often include some of the core members of the interdisciplinary team, which usually consists of physicians, nurses, and social workers. Other members of the team, such as clergy, nutritionists, occupational and physical therapists, or recreation/music/art therapists, may participate as needed. Since transplant treatment is highly complex and tends to involve numerous people (the patient, family members and healthcare professionals), family conferences may be especially helpful for the smooth flow of information.

CULTURE

It is essential to explore and to try to understand patients' and their families' cultures. Everyone has a culture, whether dominant or minority. A person's culture includes numerous self-identifications, such as ethnicity, race, religion, nationality, and geographic origins. Cultural beliefs and traditions around death can be very powerful factors for patients and families (McKinley et al. 1996; Werth et al. 2002). For example, some cultures are strongly opposed to the discussion of death. In some cultures the performance of certain rituals during the dying process may be important to patients and families. Cultural sensitivity can best be demonstrated by taking the time to ask patients and families what is important to them and what concerns they have. Topics to discuss with people include what cultural traditions, values, and beliefs are relevant for them (Crawley et al. 2002). If you have some knowledge about a person's ethnic or racial self-identification and are familiar with some of the cultural concepts associated with that identification, consider asking in what ways those concepts are or are not relevant and important to that person and family.

RELIGION AND SPIRITUALITY

Religious and spiritual beliefs, whether or not they have been a central part of a patient's lifestyle, may play an important role when a patient and family face death

(Kaut 2002). Ties to organized religion may provide people with specific rituals that comfort them, religious leaders that may assist them, and a framework of faith within which to understand death. For some people, their relationship to organized religion may be more conflictual than comforting. People's spirituality may or may not be connected to religiosity. People's belief and connection to a spiritual force in the world is very personal and may or may not be attached to a formal religious structure. Given the importance of spirituality to many people's end-of-life experience, it is essential to explore patients' and families' beliefs (Puchalski 2002; see chapters 10 and 22, this volume).

CASE EXAMPLE

Sarah was a forty-four-year-old woman diagnosed with metastatic breast cancer without any prior diagnosis of cancer. Within a few months of diagnosis, Sarah pursued an autologous PSCT followed by radiation therapy. Sarah endured transplant with few complications and showed good progress in her post-transplant recovery. Divorced for many years, she was enjoying her adult children and starting to date. Her strong belief in Buddhism and her social connections to the Buddhist community in her area provided important sources of strength and inspiration for her. Within six months of transplant, the breast cancer began to progress and Sarah's physical condition deteriorated quickly. After careful consideration, Sarah decided that she did not want to die in the hospital. Because she needed intensive pain management and personal care, she chose to be at an inpatient hospice near her home. The hospice environment allowed her to bring many of her personal possessions to personalize her environment and make it as comfortable as possible. She was able to have her cat stay with her at the hospice, and friends and family could visit regularly. Sarah continued to practice her Buddhist faith and valued the opportunities to pray with members from her Buddhist community. She found tremendous peace in these practices and found them helpful in facing her nearing death. Sarah died peacefully at the hospice under the circumstances for which she had hoped.

BEREAVEMENT

FAMILY

Families of patients who die are likely to feel a deep sadness, and they may also experience anger. Other families may be less overwhelmed by the death, feeling comfort in the knowledge that the patient had tried all possible treatments available. Bereavement follow-up with transplant patients' families is often appreciated by the family members (Hedlund and Clark 2001). The lengthy treatment process allows long-term relationships to develop between family members and healthcare providers, and the shared experiences of witnessing the transplant process create a unique connection. Telephone calls to the family in the weeks following the patient's death may make family members feel cared for and not abandoned by the healthcare team. The calls may enable healthcare providers to assess the needs of the family members, allowing the provision of appropriate reading materials, referrals, or other interventions.

STAFF

Transplant teams are focused on helping people survive. They are dedicated and devoted to problem solving, addressing complications, and mediating side effects to keep patients alive. The relationships developed with patients and families may be very strong, a product of daily contact for months in the context of a life threatening illness. After a patient's death, staff must find a way to reconcile their adjustment to the death with the need to provide care for remaining patients who still need staff's optimism, strength, and encouragement in order to withstand the transplant process. While most healthcare providers may not formally discuss their grief reactions, social workers often provide informal emotional support to staff members following the death of patients. However, social workers also need to be aware of their own grief processes, both in relation to specific deaths and to the cumulative grief that occurs after working with many patients and families (Davidson and Foster 1995). Members of the transplant team need to incorporate positive coping strategies into their lives in order to face their grief and avoid burnout. Strategies may include reminiscing about patients with team members, focusing on the legacies patients have created, and engaging in life-affirming activities (see chapter 44).

THE ROLE OF SOCIAL WORKERS

Although there is little literature on the topic of death in transplantation, separate literatures exist on the roles of social workers in transplantation and in end-of-life care (Kennedy 1993; Kramer 1998; Monroe 1998). Witnessing patients' and families' experiences, being present with them, and not abandoning them at the end of life are critical aspects of the social work role. Provision of emotional support, psychoeducation, facilitation of communication, and provision of referrals and access to resources are also integral to the role. Much of what I know about transplantation and death is a culmination of many years of clinical social work practice with patients and families facing bone marrow and stem cell transplantation. Working in multiple medical centers has reinforced many of the universal themes noted in the chapter. Most importantly, it is the patients and families themselves who teach healthcare providers about the experience of transplantation and death. The critical task is to listen and truly absorb their teachings. The lessons learned provide tremendous inspiration and rejuvenation to social workers practicing in transplantation.

Although the information in this chapter provides a framework for understanding and helping patients and families who face transplantation and death, the most important sources of information are the patients, families, and professional caregivers directly involved in any given situation. Every patient is unique. The situational factors in transplant and end-of-life care are numerous and complex, making it especially important to view patients and families holistically and systemically. Regardless of what personal experiences social work clinicians have had, even with illness and death, they can never fully know the unique experience of another. Clinicians should never pretend, but should rather focus on learning about the particular experiences of each patient and family. Lessons from experiences with prior patients and families will be valuable information for helping others. Social workers' desire to understand and their willingness to witness and share the experiences of patients and families are very precious at a critical time in patients' and families' lives.

REFERENCES

Atkinson, J. H., N. Stewart, and D. Gardner. 1980. The family meeting in critical care settings. *Journal of Trauma* 20:43–46.

Baker, F., J. Zabora, A. Polland, and J. Wingard. 1999. Reintegration after bone marrow transplantation. *Cancer Practice* 7(4): 190–197.

Barnes, R. A., and N. Stallard. 2001. Severe infections after bone marrow transplantation. *Current Opinion in Critical Care* 7:362–366.

Bay, J. O., J. Fleury, B. Choufi, et al. 2002. Allogeneic hematopoietic stem cell transplantation in ovarian carcinoma: Results of five patients. *Bone Marrow Transplantation* 30(2): 95–102.

Bonig, H., D. T. Schneider, I. Sprock, P. Lemburg, U. Gobel, and W. Nurnberger. 2000. "Sepsis" and multi-organ failure: Predictors of poor outcome after hematopoietic stem cell transplantation in children. *Bone Marrow Transplantation* 25 (Suppl. 2): S32–S34.

Cohen, M. Z., C. Ley, and A. J. Tarzian. 2001. Isolation in blood and marrow transplantation. *Western Journal of Nursing Research* 23:592–609.

Confer, D. L. 2001. The National Marrow Donor Program: Meeting the needs of the medically underserved. *Cancer* 91 (Suppl. 1): 274–278.

Cooper, M. C., and E. Powell. 1998. Technology and care in a bone marrow transplant unit: Creating and assuaging vulnerability. *Holistic Nursing Practice* 12(4): 57–68.

Crawford, S. W. 1991. Decision making in critically ill patients with hematologic malignancy. *Western Journal of Medicine* 155:488–493.

Crawley, L. M., P. A. Marshall, B. Lo, and B. A. Koenig. 2002. Strategies for culturally effective end-of-life care. *Annals of Internal Medicine* 136:673–679.

Davidson, K. W., and Z. Foster. 1995. Social work with dying and bereaved clients: Helping the workers. *Social Work in Health Care* 21(4): 1–16.

de la Cámara, R., A. Alonso, J. L. Steegmann, et al. 2002. Allogeneic hematopoietic stem cell transplantation in patients 50 years of age and older. *Haematologica* 87:965–972.

Decker, W. A. 1995. Psychosocial considerations for bone marrow transplant recipients. *Critical Care Nursing Quarterly* 17(4): 67–73.

Dicato, M. 2002. High-dose chemotherapy in breast cancer: Where are we now? *Seminars in Oncology* 29 (Suppl.): 16–20.

Fagerlin, A., P. H. Ditto, N. A. Hawkins, C. E. Schneider, and W. D. Smucker. 2002. The use of advance directives in end-of-life decision making. *American Behavioral Scientist* 46:268–283.

Ferris, F. D., C. F. von Gunten, and L. L. Emanuel. 2002. Ensuring competency in end-of-life care: Controlling symptoms. *BMC Palliative Care* 1:5.

Foster, L. W., and L. J. McLellan. 2002. Translating psychosocial insight into ethical discussions supportive of families in end-of-life decision-making. *Social Work in Health Care* 35(3): 37–51.

Gabriel, B., E. Bromberg, J. Vandenbovenkamp, P. Walka, A. B. Kornblith, and P. Luzzatto.

2001. Art therapy with adult bone marrow transplant patients in isolation: A pilot study. *Psycho-Oncology* 10:114–123.

Griessmeier, B., and W. Koester. 2000. Between heaven and hell: Music therapy in the nowhere land of children's bone marrow transplantation. *Journal of Palliative Care* 16(3): 78–79.

Grimm, P. M., K. L. Zawacki, V. Mock, S. Krumm, and B. B. Frink. 2000. Caregiver responses and needs: An ambulatory bone marrow transplant model. *Cancer Practice* 8(3): 120–128.

Gurman, G., M. Arat, O. Ilhan, et al. 2001. Allogeneic hematopoietic cell transplantation without myeloablative conditioning for patients with advanced hematologic malignancies. *Cytotherapy* 3(4): 253–260.

Haberman, M. R. 1988. Psychosocial aspects of bone marrow transplantation. *Seminars in Oncology Nursing* 4:55–59.

———. 1995. The meaning of cancer therapy: Bone marrow transplantation as an exemplar of therapy. *Seminars in Oncology Nursing* 11(1): 23–31.

Hansen, P., P. Cornish, and K. Kayser. 1998. Family conferences as forums for decision making in hospital settings. *Social Work in Health Care* 27(3): 57–74.

Harousseau, J. L., and M. Attal. 2002. The role of stem cell transplantation in multiple myeloma. *Blood Reviews* 16:245–253.

Hedlund, S. C., and E. J. Clark. 2001. End of life issues. In *Social Work in Oncology: Supporting Survivors, Families, and Caregivers*, ed. M. M. Lauria, E. J. Clark, J. F. Hermann, and N. M. Stearns, 299–316. Atlanta: American Cancer Society.

Herrmann, R. P., M. Leather, H. L. Leather, and K. Leen. 1998. Clinical care for patients receiving autologous hematopoietic stem cell transplantation in the home setting. *Oncology Nursing Forum* 25:1427–1432.

Hickman, S. E. 2002. Improving communication near the end of life. *American Behavioral Scientist* 46:252–267.

Ho, S. M. Y., D. J. de L. Horne, and J. Szer. 2002. The adaptation of patients during the hospitalization period to bone marrow transplantation. *Journal of Clinical Psychology in Medical Settings* 9:167–175.

Horowitz, M. M. 1999. Uses and growth of hematopoietic cell transplantation. In *Hematopoietic Cell Transplantation* (2d ed.), ed. E. D. Thomas, K. G. Blume, and S. J. Forman, 12–18. Malden, MA: Blackwell Science.

Junghanss, C., K. A. Marr, R. A. Carter, et al. 2002. Incidence and outcome of bacterial and fungal infections following nonmyeloablative compared with myeloablative allogeneic hematopoietic stem cell transplantation: A matched control study. *Biology of Blood and Marrow Transplantation* 8:512–520.

Kaut, K. P. 2002. Religion, spirituality, and existentialism near the end of life: Implications for assessment and application. *American Behavioral Scientist* 46:220–234.

Kennedy, V. N. 1993. The role of social work in bone marrow transplantation. *Journal of Psychosocial Oncology* 11(1): 103–117.

Kim, H. 2002. Mini-allogeneic stem cell transplantation: Past, present, and future. *Cancer Practice* 10(3): 170–172.

Kramer, B. J. 1998. Preparing social workers for the inevitable: A preliminary investigation of a course on grief, death, and loss. *Journal of Social Work Education* 34:211–227.

Kroschinsky, F., M. Weise, T. Illmer, et al. 2002. Outcome and prognostic features of intensive care unit treatment in patients with hematological malignancies. *Intensive Care Medicine* 28:1294–1300.

Kusnierz-Glaz, C. R., P. G. Schlegel, R. M. Wong, et al. 1997. Influence of age on the outcome of 500 autologous bone marrow transplant procedures for hematologic malignancies. *Journal of Clinical Oncology* 15(1): 18–25.

Lee, S. J., J. P. Klein, A. J. Barrett, et al. 2002. Severity of chronic graft-versus-host disease: Association with treatment-related mortality and relapse. *Blood* 100:406–414.

Loscalzo, M., and J. Amendola. 1990. Psychosocial and behavioral management of cancer pain: The social work contribution. *Advances in Pain Research and Therapy* 16:429–442.

Marr, K. A. 2001. Antifungal prophylaxis in hematopoietic stem cell transplant recipients. *Current Opinion in Infectious Diseases* 14:423–426.

McGrath, P. 2001a. Caregivers' insights on the dying trajectory in hematology oncology. *Cancer Nursing* 24:413–421.

———. 2001b. Returning home after specialist treatment for hematological malignancies: An Australian study. *Family and Community Health* 24:36–48.

———. 2002a. End-of-life care for hematological malignancies: The "technological imperative" and palliative care. *Journal of Palliative Care* 18(1): 39–47.

———. 2002b. Qualitative findings on the experience of end-of-life care for hematological malignancies. *American Journal of Hospice and Palliative Care* 19(2): 103–111.

McKinley, E. D., J. M. Garrett, A. T. Evans, and M. Danis. 1996. Differences in end-of-life decision making among black and white ambulatory cancer patients. *Journal of General Internal Medicine* 11:651–656.

Monroe, B. 1998. Social work in palliative care. In *Oxford Textbook of Palliative Medicine* (2d ed.), ed. D. Doyle, G. W. C. Hanks, and N. MacDonald, 867–880. New York: Oxford University Press.

Munzenberger, N., C. Fortanier, G. Macquart-Moulin, et al. 1999. Psychosocial aspects of haematopoietic stem cell donation for allogeneic transplantation: How family donors cope with this experience. *Psycho-Oncology* 8:55–63.

Myer, S. A., and J. Oliva. 2002. Severe aplastic anemia and allogeneic hematopoietic stem cell transplantation. *AACN Clinical Issues* 13(2): 169–191.

Packman, W. L. 1999. Psychosocial impact of pediatric BMT on siblings. *Bone Marrow Transplantation* 24:701–706.

Pan, C. X., R. S. Morrison, J. Ness, A. Fugh-Berman, and R. M. Leipzig. 2000. Complementary and alternative medicine in the management of pain, dyspnea, and nausea and vomiting near the end of life: A systematic review. *Journal of Pain and Symptom Management* 20:374–387.

Puchalski, C. M. 2002. Spirituality and end-of-life care: A time for listening and caring. *Journal of Palliative Medicine* 5:289–294.

Ringden, O., M. Remberger, J. Mattsson, et al. 1998. Transplantation with unrelated bone marrow in leukaemic patients above 40 years of age. *Bone Marrow Transplantation* 21:43–49.

Rizzo, J. D., A. D. Elias, P. J. Stiff, et al. 2002. Autologous stem cell transplantation for small cell lung cancer. *Biology of Blood and Marrow Transplantation* 8(5): 273–280.

Russell, J. A., A. Chaudhry, K. Booth, et al. 2000. Early outcomes after allogeneic stem cell transplantation for leukemia and myelodysplasia without protective isolation: A 10-year experience. *Biology of Blood and Marrow Transplantation* 6(2): 109–114.

Slavin, S., M. Aker, M. Y. Shapira, S. Panigrahi, C. Gabriel, and R. Or. 2002. Non-myeloablative stem cell transplantation for the treatment of cancer and life-threatening non-malignant disorders: Past accomplishments and future goals. *Transfusion and Apheresis Science* 27(2): 159–166.

Snyder, D. S. 1999. Ethical issues in hematopoietic cell transplantation. In *Hematopoietic Cell Transplantation* (2d ed.), ed. E. D. Thomas, K. G. Blume, and S. J. Forman, 390–397. Malden, MA: Blackwell Science.

Steinhauser, K. E., N. A. Christakis, E. C. Clipp, M. McNeilly, L. McIntyre, and J. A. Tulsky. 2000. Factors considered important at the end of life by patients, family, physicians, and other care providers. *Journal of the American Medical Association* 284:2476–2482.

Stevens, P. E., and P. K. Pletsch. 2002. Ethical issues of informed consent: Mothers' experiences enrolling their children in bone marrow transplantation research. *Cancer Nursing* 25(2): 81–87.

Switzer, G. E., M. A. Dew, C. A. Magistro, et al. 1998. The effects of bereavement on adult sibling bone marrow donors' psychological well-being and reactions to donation. *Bone Marrow Transplantation* 21:181–188.

Switzer, G. E., J. M. Goycoolea, M. A. Dew, E. C. Graeff, and J. Hegland. 2001. Donating stimulated peripheral blood stem cells vs. bone marrow: Do donors experience the procedures differently? *Bone Marrow Transplantation* 27:917–923.

Syrjala, K. L., M. K. Chapko, P. P. Vitaliano, C. Cummings, and K. M. Sullivan. 1993. Recovery after allogeneic marrow transplantation: Prospective study of predictors of long-term physical and psychosocial functioning. *Bone Marrow Transplantation* 11:319–327.

Tabbara, I. A., K. Zimmerman, C. Morgan, and Z. Nahleh. 2002. Allogeneic hematopoietic stem cell transplantation: Complications and results. *Archives of Internal Medicine* 162:1558–1566.

Verburg, R. J., S. D. Mahabali, A. M. Stiggelbout, J. K. Sont, and J. M. van Laar. 2002. High dose chemotherapy and hematopoietic stem cell transplantation: A study of treatment preference in patients with rheumatoid arthritis and rheumatologists. *Journal of Rheumatology* 29:1653–1658.

Veys, P., and C. Owens. 2002. Respiratory infections following haemopoietic stem cell transplantation in children. *British Medical Bulletin* 61:151–174.

Werth, J. L., D. Blevins, K. L. Toussaint, and M. R. Durham. 2002. The influence of cultural diversity on end-of-life care and decisions. *American Behavioral Scientist* 46:204–219.

Wrede-Seaman, L. D. 2001. Treatment options to manage pain at the end of life. *American Journal of Hospice and Palliative Care* 18(2): 89–101.

Zabora, J. R., E. D. Smith, F. Baker, J. R. Wingard, and B. Curbow. 1992. The family: The other side of bone marrow transplantation. *Journal of Psychosocial Oncology* 10(1): 35–46.

Zecca, M., A. Prete, R. Rondelli, et al. 2002. Chronic graft-versus-host disease in children: Incidence, risk factors, and impact on outcome. *Blood* 100:1192–1200.

INTERNET RESOURCES

American Academy of Hospice and Palliative Medicine: www.aahpm.org
ABCD—Americans for Better Care of the Dying: www.abcd-caring.com
Blood and Marrow Transplant Information Network: www.bmtinfonet.org
Center to Improve Care of the Dying: www.gwu.edu/~cicd
Growth House: www.growthhouse.org
Leukemia and Lymphoma Society: www.leukemia-lymphoma.org
National Bone Marrow Transplant Link: www.nbmtlink.org
National Marrow Donor Program: www.marrow.org

36

ONCOLOGY

JOHN LINDER

SOCIAL WORK practice with cancer patients who have advanced disease requires a basic knowledge of medical oncology and a solid clinical social work foundation. Patients may first encounter an oncology social worker when cancer is suspected or positively diagnosed. The circumstances leading to such an encounter are usually undesirable and often unexpected.

Most people view cancer as an exogenous adversary, an enemy to be resisted and vanquished. Often cancer can be partially or wholly removed, which reinforces this perception of cancer as a foreign entity. Many people conceptualize having cancer differently than heart disease. These killers are respectively ranked as the number two and number one causes of death in the United States today. Patients treat a diseased heart as their own, a part that has worn out or is failing to function properly. Cleaning, replacing, repairing, or bypassing clogged arteries or leaking valves maintains the appearance of fixing a broken part that came as standard equipment. Similarly, organ transplantation, whether of the heart or other organ, mimics the installation of a used but serviceable replacement part, as one might do with a car or washing machine. In contrast, people view cancer as a deadly intruder, to be cut out or hunted down and destroyed. In fact, cancer is our body's own cells run amok.

This difference in perception is substantive. Patients frequently experience a cancer diagnosis, or even the suspicion of cancer, as an emotional emergency and so desire a speedy evaluation and the swift excision or initiation of therapy. However, their desires place them diametrically opposite healthcare practitioners, especially physicians, who know that a systematic diagnostic process with accurate findings usually results in the best treatment options. The regimen that most enhances a patient's chances for survival and cure is regrettably the most emotionally challenging for the patient and his or her family.

Some patients also feel shame or embarrassment at having cancer, and they view it as analogous to a diagnosis of parasites like lice or scabies. This may increase their reticence to disclose their diagnosis, which in turn can increase feelings of isolation and diminish social support. Social workers can help patients identify, understand, and express these feelings and can promote the importance of staying socially engaged.

Helping anxious patients and caregivers understand the purpose behind the seemingly plodding pace of diagnosis may afford social workers their first opportunity to serve the patient with cancer. Indeed, early in the process, physicians and the interdisciplinary healthcare team (including social workers) can do much to promote better patient understanding of the evolution of their disease and the medical response(s) to it. Such early efforts promote a stronger bond between patients, physicians, and the treatment team and can serve to establish the social worker as a valued resource for patients.

Some patients become utterly mired in the issue of detection, blaming themselves or others (often medical professionals) for not detecting a cancer in time, implicitly meaning "in time to cure me." However, it is important for them to know that very few cancers progress so quickly that a few weeks' delay in detection makes a significant difference in the outcome. A long process of precancerous cell changes precedes most cancers. The cancer itself has likely been present and growing for months or years, though undetectable using current technology.

Patients need to discharge the affect associated with this deadlock in order to move ahead. The anger, guilt, or blame that patients feel surrounding the impasse often masks the patient's acceptance/denial struggles and the grief, sadness, and anxiety that lie below the surface following a cancer diagnosis. Eliciting these feelings is a core social work function. By growing beyond this impasse, patients and families can refocus their energies on what can be done from this moment forward and can feel more empowered. The social worker promotes the appropriate expression of these powerful emotions, creates a safe environment for emotional expression, furthers understanding of self and disease, and facilitates the formation and enhancement of coping strategies. Early intervention with newly diagnosed patients helps them develop skills and learn strategies they can use throughout their illness.

CANCER BASICS

The term *cancer* is familiar to almost everyone; most people know someone who is living with it, has recovered from it, or has died because of it. However, the general population lacks accurate knowledge about many aspects of cancer, both medical and nonmedical. Cancers are technically divided between solid tumors (oncology) and blood-related or hematologic diseases (hematology). However, colloquially the terms *oncology* and *cancer* are often used interchangeably. This chapter follows the colloquial use of *oncology* unless otherwise noted.

The proliferation of mutant, malignant cells is the one characteristic common to all cancers. Cancer is not a single disease. In fact, more than a hundred conditions are called cancer, but different cancer types follow markedly different courses. Furthermore, the incidence of cancer is not distributed evenly across the population. Deaths from cancer occur disproportionately more often in older people. Various cancers differ in frequency from one geographic region to the next. Sometimes these differences seem to follow cultural lines, though this variation may be more closely linked with diet, daily routine, and geographic or environmental factors than with culture per se. However, with some cancer types, race or gender does predict incidence.

About 50 percent of all cancer patients will ultimately die from their disease. That number has fallen steadily since the 1930s, when fully 80 percent of patients with cancer succumbed (Lenhard, Osteen, and Gansler 2001). Three factors are credited with improved survival: education on general health, diet, cancer prevention and detection; improvements in technology and practice leading to earlier detection; and the timely delivery of increasingly effective treatments. This repertoire of treatments continues to expand, as it has for the past thirty years.

Cancer is more than an aggregation of malignant diseases, however. "Having cancer" describes an unpredictable process that unfolds for the patient and his or her entire social constellation. For the patient, the experience of having cancer precipitates a status passage that "may entail movement into a different part of a social structure; or a loss or gain of privilege, influence or power, and a changed identity and sense of self, as well as changed behavior" (Glaser and Strauss 1971:2).

"Receiving a (cancer) diagnosis can force an individual into an involuntary, irreversible, and undesirable status passage. It can also lead to numerous exits, besides that of (not having cancer). Part of the status transitions experienced by (people with cancer) involves accommodating to illness and alterations in identity." Though originally written by J. Lewis (1999) to describe status passages for a group of HIV-positive men involved in a research project, the simple substitution of "cancer" for "HIV-positive" transforms Lewis's words into an apt description of the lived experience of status changes brought about by having cancer. Self-identity, role, and status are destabilized by a cancer diagnosis and will remain so over the entire course of the disease. Patients and caregivers can have volatile reactions to a number of illness-related events, including the confirmation of a diagnosis, implementation of a treatment plan with its antecedent decision-making process, changes in the size or location of tumors, onset or relief of new symptoms or treatment side effects, or changes in key surrogate markers of disease state (for example, an increase or decrease in the prostate-specific antigen [PSA] numeric value in men with prostate cancer).

A cancer diagnosis early in the last century was often accompanied by the same type of ostracism, shame, and dread as an AIDS diagnosis in the 1980s and early 1990s. The public feared that cancer was contagious; few effective treatments existed. Cancer patients often heard the diagnosis as a death sentence, and most of them were right. Today effective treatments exist for many cancers. Malignancies that were nearly always fatal in the first half of the last century have much more favorable prognoses today. Testicular cancer is a good example. Metastatic testicular cancer (that is, cancer which had spread to organs distant from the testes), was 100 percent lethal well into the 1960s. Today, testicular cancer has an overall cure rate of 80 percent. Local disease, confined to one or both testicles, has a complete response (CR—no detectable disease after five years) rate of 99 + percent when treated.

But all cancers are not created equal. Cancer types grow at different rates. Moreover, the likelihood that a cancer will spread is a more important prognostic factor than the rate of growth. Some cancers are more likely to remain localized (confined to the organ or tissue of origin); examples include basal cell skin cancer and well-differentiated, low-grade breast and prostate cancers. Others are most likely to invade adjacent tissue and organs, for example head and neck cancer and cervical cancer.

Some cancers are highly metastatic, that is, likely to appear in organs or tissue distant from the site of origin. Examples include both small cell and non-small cell lung cancers and Burkitt's lymphoma, a non-Hodgkin's lymphoma afflicting both children and adults. Finally, the unpredictability of metastatic spread shown by many cancers is a source of consternation for patients and providers alike. Breast cancer and colon cancer, the second and fourth most commonly occurring cancers in the United States today (American Cancer Society 2001), are two cancers with highly variable metastatic potential.

Confusing things further, finding cancer in a particular part of the body does not mean it is that kind of cancer. Cancer found in the brain may well be lung cancer or colon cancer that has metastasized, or it may be true brain cancer originating in brain tissue. Patients find this very confusing. For instance, patients will say, "I had prostate cancer a few years ago and now I have bone cancer," when the bone cancer is actually recurrent, metastatic prostate cancer. Identifying the tumor type is medically highly desirable. Definitive diagnosis requires the analysis of a sample of the cancer tissue or tumor by a pathologist. And unfortunately, even tissue sample analyses sometimes yield inconclusive results.

Accurate cancer diagnosis facilitates selecting treatment options, offering a prognosis, and predicting the likely course the disease will follow, in much the same way that a doctor must know if an infection is viral or bacterial before prescribing an antibiotic (Holleb 1986; Lenhard, Osteen, and Gansler 2001).

Staging is another integral part of evaluating the patient. Staging describes the size of a tumor (T), the degree of regional lymph node involvement (N), and the extent to which the disease has metastasized (M). Taken together, this diagnostic information also provides the context for evaluating the relative effectiveness of competing treatments.

For example, a breast lump with no lymph-node involvement and no metastases would be described as $T_1N_0M_0$ breast carcinoma, or Stage 1 breast cancer. In all cases, the lower the number, the better the prognosis. The number after the "N" ("0" in this example) states how many local lymph nodes are involved. The number after the "M" (again "0" in this example) indicates the number of metastatic tumors (also called lesions) that have been located. Stage 1 indicates local disease with no lymph node involvement; Stage 2 denotes localized cancer with local lymph node involvement; Stage 3, metastatic disease; and Stage 4 indicates widespread visceral organ involvement.

A particular cancer may be especially sensitive or responsive to one type of treatment. Some, for instance, show great sensitivity to certain chemotherapies. Others are best controlled with radiation. Surgery is usually the primary treatment of choice for localized cancers, such as colon and breast cancer. Surgical removal of a cancerous testicle is routine. Treatment with chemotherapy or radiation prior to surgery, called *neoadjuvant* therapy, is indicated for some cancers. Following surgery, *adjuvant* therapy involving radiation, chemotherapy, or other treatments alone or in combination may be more effective in eliminating residual cancer and reducing the risk of recurrence than is surgery alone.

Sometimes two or more approaches offer substantially equivalent results. For in situ cervical cancer (local disease, no lymph node involvement, no metastases), surgery and radiation both offer a greater than 98 percent rate of cure (complete remission or CR; Holleb 1986). In such cases, the benefits and burdens of each treatment must be evaluated for each individual's circumstances and preferences.

How extensive the cancer is may also dictate the choice of treatment(s). A combination of therapies often yields the best results. Returning to the example of metastatic testicular cancer, the surgical removal of a testicle must always be followed with chemotherapy or the patient will die. With chemotherapy, 85 percent of patients can expect to be disease-free five years later and are considered cured. Finally, some cancers such as pancreatic and liver cancer remain resistant, or refractory, to all current anticancer therapies, rare surgical exceptions notwithstanding.

Surgery, radiation, and chemotherapy are the most common and widely used modes of cancer treatment. Bone marrow transplantation (BMT) and peripheral stem cell transplantation are less widely used, but are the primary treatment in some cancers, particularly hematologic (blood) disorders including leukemia and myeloma (see chapter 34). A number of new approaches are also in use or on the horizon: gene therapy (using genetic modification to combat cancer); radiosensitizing therapies that increase the effectiveness of radiation; anti-angiogenesis therapy that restricts the blood flow to tumors, essentially starving them to death; and drugs that cause cancerous cells to die as they try to replicate or that accelerate cancer cell death (apoptosis).

Despite everything that is known, on rare occasions the course and outcome of a particular individual's disease defies medical explanation and contradicts all reasoned expectation. These anomalies occur at both ends of the spectrum. A handful of those expected to die live instead, and may even have a complete response and be disease-free. Conversely, some diagnosed with curable or controllable cancer see their disease progress, and die despite proven therapy.

THE PHASES OF CANCER

Cancer's course divides roughly into two or three phases: (1) diagnosis, (2) treatment and the sequelae of treatment, and, for some, (3) a terminal phase. Taken together, these phases are sometimes described as the disease trajectory (see chapter 14). Each phase contains many emotionally challenging issues.

PHASE ONE: DIAGNOSIS

The individual's cancer journey may begin with a doctor's pronouncement of a diagnosis. However, many patients experience anticipatory anxiety prompted by unexplained changes in body or functional ability. These changes manifest in diverse ways, including shortness of breath or weight loss without good cause, blood in urine or stool, fatigue, jaundice, global or localized pain, changes in mental status from forgetfulness to inexplicable mood swings, and swelling of extremities.

Patients react to unexplained symptoms in varied ways: denial ("I'm not [gasp] short of breath"), fear ("I'm worried that my twenty-pound weight loss means something is wrong"), anger ("Stop pestering me to go to the doctor!"), resignation ("I probably have colon cancer; that's what my Dad died of"), or exasperation ("I haven't changed my routine or diet; I don't understand why I'm feeling so poorly"). The anxiety of uncertainty is transformed when a patient actually faces definitive news, at which time a different set of challenges emerges.

In the absence of symptoms, cancer may be discovered in the course of routine unrelated inpatient or outpatient procedures such as elective surgery, routine blood work, annual or pre-employment physicals or referral from an allied health professional.

The length and uncertainty of the diagnostic evaluation period can contribute to a number of problems; many of these problems are well suited to social worker intervention. For example, patients and families sometimes experience discord with the health system; a harried, bored, or thoughtless provider may treat an individual's most important diagnostic procedure in many years as just one more biopsy or bone scan. People unfamiliar with post–healthcare reform medicine and the changes wrought in the last decade may be intimidated by the health system. Differences in culture or primary language, financial disadvantages, inadequate resources (for instance, transportation or childcare), a lack of health insurance or paid sick leave, a low threshold for frustration, or an inability to negotiate complex phone systems can disrupt patients' emotional equilibrium and jeopardize treatment. The successful completion of required diagnostic procedures carries with it no guarantee that results will be communicated in a timely, compassionate, and confidential manner that can be understood by the layperson of average intelligence. Social workers can intervene effectively in each of these situations.

Patients and caregivers often feel overwhelmed by the daunting volume and importance of information to be mastered and its implicit emotional impact. Patients and caregivers sometimes mask their ignorance with feigned understanding, so it is important to have patients tell you what they understand of their disease or a particular treatment option. Avoid asking yes/no questions under these circumstances.

A diagnosis of cancer often precipitates a crisis of self-concept. Patients may question their roles and self-identity. How the disease will affect the patient's ability to fulfill roles as mother or father, spouse or partner, breadwinner, homemaker, neighbor, community member, church member, and so forth is uncertain, particularly when the cancer diagnosis is new. Beyond role, the individual's self-concept as healthy, or at least as a person without cancer, is shattered by the diagnosis. Patients require time, guidance, and support to synthesize a self-concept that incorporates the diagnosis and concomitant changes in functional status while allowing for a sense of well-being and expectation for the future. The disease or its treatment can result in a change in appearance (hair loss, bloated features, sallow complexion). Surgery may result in more invasive and permanent changes in body structure (mastectomy, colostomy, orchiectomy). These changes are significant affronts to most people's self-concept. Moreover, these changes may have implications for independence and intimacy and usually threaten self-esteem. Furthermore these changes arrive at a time characterized by diminished strength and endurance and heightened emotional vulnerability.

Reexamination and redefinition of the self continues through all phases of cancer.

Changes in functional status or treatment regimens, test results that show progression, remission, or stable disease, and familial or interpersonal events complicate the maintenance of a stable self-concept. Social work clinicians would do well to revisit the patient's evolving self-concept periodically, paying particular attention to transitional times for the patient or family.

Diagnosis has been identified as the second most effective phase for clinical intervention with cancer patients (Cwikel 1999). Empirically, the greatest change is attained through behavioral/cognitive interventions, though a number of modalities have demonstrated efficacy (Boynton 1994). Cognitive therapy, which works to identify and correct distortions in the reasoning process, can facilitate a shift away from unproductive behaviors and feelings. Strategies that enable the patient to reframe distressing perceptions and experiences are of great value. Behavioral tools that patients and caregivers can employ to reduce anxiety, promote restful sleep, maximize desired physical activity, decrease depression, and manage pain and other distressing symptoms are also helpful. These tools include progressive relaxation, guided imagery, self-hypnosis, meditation, and biofeedback. Expressive therapies will doubtless be useful for some patients or caregivers as well (Raymer 2002).

Helping patients and caregivers focus on one problem at a time, develop or maintain a variety of coping strategies, and assertively advocate can enhance or restore the patient's sense of power and control that has been eroded by disease. Helping patients identify and build on strengths is another key function for the social workers. At critical junctures in the course of diagnosis and treatment, a crisis intervention approach will likely be most appropriate (Raymer 2002).

This menu of interventions will continue to be useful as the disease course and the social worker/patient relationship unfold. Both the disease and the relationship are dynamic; reviewing social work interventions regularly will keep the relationship optimally helpful to the patient.

EDUCATION. Physicians and other medical providers often describe patients' eyes glazing over when the word "cancer" is first applied to patients. Subsequently, patients report poor recall of initial diagnostic conversations and are unable to provide comprehensive information to their families.

Patients and their caregivers need a great deal of information at the outset. What is cancer? What kind do I have? Where is it? How did I get it? What are my treatment options? What side effects will I get from treatment? What should I expect with this disease? Am I going to die? How do I get services in today's healthcare system? Why do I need permission to see specialists or have tests?

Educational interventions include enhancing patient/caregiver understanding of all relevant facets of cancer and health care. Asking patients what they know about their disease and how they feel right now is often the best place to start. This allows the social worker to assess how well the patient and caregivers grasp the scope and ramifications of the disease. With this knowledge, social workers can provide information directly and help patients identify other reliable sources of information that increase the patient's or family's knowledge base and restore or enhance a sense of mastery and control.

Social workers can also redirect patients back to physicians, who can revisit critical information that the patient or caregivers have not understood. The social worker fills an important role as a liaison between patients and physicians by helping to insure that true communication occurs. Patients usually need to hear information related to their diagnosis, treatment options, and prognosis from a physician, but social workers can help physicians speak in terms that their patients can understand. Because medical social workers understand technical medical language, they can help make physicians' explanations clearer to patients. Families need to learn how to get their questions answered; for example, rehearsing their questions with them in advance often helps. Simple, concrete suggestions can be of great help, such as suggesting that they make a list, bring it with them, write down responses, and check things off.

EMOTIONS AND COPING. Given the emotional magnitude of most cancer diagnoses, situational anxiety and depression are understandable, expected, and appropriate (see chapter 18). Recurrent assessment of the patient's emotional state is an essential element of competent social work practice, with particular attention to the intensity and duration of anxiety and depression. The presence of an identifiable situational link between disease-related events and feelings of anxiety and depression are one valuable tool in differentiating between normal and pathologic presentations. For example, the first acute episode of so-called air hunger, experienced when one feels unable to take in enough oxygen, universally provokes panic and profound residual anxiety. Moreover, just the anticipation of a recurrence of air hunger precipitates immobilizing anxiety and periodic panic.

These symptoms are serious but highly manageable. Fast-acting medication (usually liquid narcotic and/or liquid anxiolytic) coupled with behavioral training for patient and caregiver on how to breathe during episodes of shortness of breath can prevent or minimize the panic and should significantly decrease the incidence of air hunger over time. If these interventions reduce the sensation of air hunger but sustained anxiety and panic persist, an in-depth assessment of the patient and consultation with the physician, other members of the interdisciplinary team (including chaplaincy) and perhaps outside consultants (psychiatry) are advisable. And when no situational precipitant can be identified, additional assessment is indicated.

Similarly, intermittent depressed mood and flat affect related to a cancer diagnosis, treatment-related side effects or disease progression is a common, situationally driven and appropriate response. Likewise, depressed mood, anxiety, and sadness are consonant with the bereavement that follows a patient's death. When depression persists, increases in intensity, or is accompanied by increasing vegetative symptoms and/or suicidal ideation, a major depressive episode (patient or caregiver) or a complicated grief process (caregiver) is potentially underway. Again, these circumstances indicate the need for more extensive assessment as well as interdisciplinary and ancillary consultation. Pharmacotherapy will likely be beneficial and should be evaluated by the physician or consultant. Both during the disease process and in bereavement, the social worker should discuss the need to maintain a safe environment with the patient (when living) and caregivers (see chapter 18).

Involuntary hospitalization for suicidality is rarely indicated and universally complicates treatment for advanced cancer patients. While a majority of terminally ill patients discuss the wish to die, to be free of sickness or to have the dying process end, many of these references are oblique or symbolic and only a few are overtly suicidal. Nevertheless, all deserve a clinician's explicit and immediate attention focused on the circumstances triggering these thoughts and wishes. Often the patient is motivated by non-medical concerns (Back et al. 1996). In virtually all cases, viable strategies that stop well short of suicide can mitigate the expressed concerns. Examples include addressing unrelieved symptoms; increasing social, spiritual, or community support; facilitating dialogue between the patient and loved ones; and helping patients express their emotional distress. The social workers' finely tuned listening skills and professional resourcefulness are particularly valuable in these situations.

Finally, feelings of grief, loss, sadness, depression, and anxiety are ubiquitous in the diagnosis and treatment of cancer. Medicating patients prematurely to relieve these symptoms risks dampening or masking the feelings and retarding the process of coming to terms with cancer. An interdisciplinary approach to care, vigilant assessment, and vigorous advocacy help strike the balance that permits patients do the necessary work of coping while avoiding unproductive suffering.

RESOURCES. Patients often have practical needs, ranging from transportation and lodging during treatment to assistance accessing their health and financial entitlements. The social worker's comprehensive assessment should include these pragmatic needs. Social workers can identify resources that support activities of daily living, provide meal delivery or dietary consultation, or meet myriad other practical needs. The social worker serves as a concierge of the healthcare system: knowledgeable, focused, skilled at interpersonal interaction, someone who knows how to makes things happen. He or she facilitates much of the ongoing support and care of the cancer patient.

EMOTIONAL SUPPORT. Emotional distress is universal for patients and families coming to grips with a cancer diagnosis. While several studies suggested strategies for identifying patients at highest risk of emotional distress or who require immediate intervention, all patients and families clearly benefit from emotional support. (Holland 1999; Blum 2002; Roth 1997; Loscalzo and Jacobsen 1990; Zabora et al. 1990, 1997; Zabora and Smith 1991).

Gauging the patient and caregiver's emotional needs is an essential component of a comprehensive assessment. Social workers can explore the emotional impact of the diagnosis and the changes in personal and professional relationship that the diagnosis dictates or implies. They can also help patients and families express emotions constructively. Initially, individual intervention may be the most beneficial modality. However, a cancer diagnosis affects the entire psychosocial system, so facilitating opportunities for formal or informal family care conferences to share information and feelings can also be both powerful and beneficial. During diagnosis, these exchanges usually focus on establishing a common understanding of the disease, the patient's prognosis, and possible treatment options. These forums help identify changes required to the family system in order to meet the patient's treatment needs and compensate for functional limitations.

Group experiences that normalize the illness are another valuable tool in the social worker's toolbox. Local and web-based resources including peer and professionally facilitated discussions, support groups, and chat rooms (see chapter 27), as well as institutionally based resources, can be invaluable. The friendly visitor program, composed of postmastectomy peer survivors who have had reconstructive surgery or use prostheses, is one such resource (Silverman and Smith 1984). Contact with others leading fulfilling lives following a cancer diagnosis and treatment can bolster flagging spirits and strengthen tenuous self-esteem. Conventional or virtual support or educational groups and other contact with those facing similar challenges helps patients identify the strengths and coping strategies used by others.

Patients often build a strong relationship with their cancer-care specialists. The foundation for these relationships is laid during the diagnostic phase. An attentive, helpful, supportive, and upbeat staff in the cancer center or oncologist's office sets the tone for future interactions. While current research is equivocal on whether positive attitude translates into increased longevity, patients with more positive attitudes definitively report enhanced quality of life and sometimes reduced symptoms. This difference may be grounded either in perception and outlook or in experience. Regardless, social workers play an important role in helping establish this initial relationship.

The core transition occurring in the diagnostic phase is from a self-concept that does not include "I have cancer" to one that does. Some key elements support the development of a positive attitude in the face of a new diagnosis or challenging treatment. Good information leads to mastery, allowing patients to reclaim some control over their treatment if not their mortality. The social worker and other team members can help minimize isolation and calm patients' fear of abandonment. The social worker's relationship with the patient can safely contain the patient's anxiety and other powerful emotions. Being able to let one's guard down emotionally, confident that the social worker can both contain patient's or caregiver's messy feelings and will facilitate regaining composure allows emotional discharge while assuring a safe return to the business of daily life.

Once the diagnosis is confirmed and communicated, most patients face the issue of making treatment decisions.

PHASE TWO: TREATMENT

Determining the type and extent of the cancer enables the oncologist to identify the patient's treatment options. Treatment choices will depend primarily on these questions:

- What treatment goal (*cure* or *control* or *supportive/comfort care*) is appropriate for this patient's cancer type and disease stage?

- What treatment(s) constitute the current standard of care?
- Which best match the patient's preferences?
- Are clinical trials or investigational therapies available for this patient?

Occasionally, one particular treatment is clearly better than all others, easing the patient's task of weighing risks and benefits. More frequently, there are numerous treatment choices, each having unique risks and benefits. In these cases, patient preference plays a more prominent role.

Many factors complicate this scenario. Often physicians can only describe a range of possible outcomes and do not know which outcome this particular patient will have. Most of the treatments for prostate cancer, for example, carry a risk of erectile dysfunction and urinary incontinence. While the relative risk is usually known, an individual patient's outcome cannot be predicted. To make informed decisions, patients need to have sufficient understanding of the diagnosis, prognosis, and risks and benefits of each of their treatment options. But the emotional impact of coming to terms with a cancer diagnosis can impair concentration and logical thinking, often a number of family members or caregivers may be involved in selecting the treatment. Because some treatment benefits are time-sensitive, the urgency of decision making may be a factor as well. The therapeutic outcome of a clinical trial may also still be unknown, or a clinical trial may be designed simply to learn about the toxicity or efficacy of a new treatment. Such factors may cause a divergence of goals and expectations between patients, families, caregivers, and health providers.

Once a diagnosis is made the patient begins to absorb and understand the disease and its implications. The patient must decide how much of this information to share, with whom, for what purpose, and in what time frame. Depending on the extent and severity of both the disease and symptoms, the patient may feel a sense of urgency to adapt to this news. Some treatment options may have time-limited efficacy, so treatment decisions may be pressing. This situation is the antithesis of the hasty patient vs. methodical physician circumstance described during diagnosis.

Patients and caregivers frequently describe living with cancer as a protracted ride on a roller coaster. These ups and downs are present from diagnosis through treatment to cure, remission, stasis, disease progression, or death. These oscillations are brought on by weighing various treatment options, making treatment choices, anticipating and experiencing side effects, frequent fluctuations in functional ability or mood, and dealing with the uncertainty of potential improvement or decline. Patients and families experience feelings of elation, confusion, or disappointment as treatment results are monitored and interpreted, as the patient's functional status, appearance, treatment plan, and tumor size vary, and as his or her role at home and at work change.

Patients in the treatment phase of cancer respond most effectively to social work intervention, with behavioral/cognitive interventions having the greatest empirical efficacy (Cwikel 1999; see chapter 28 in this volume).

A broad base of support and numerous flexible coping strategies can smooth out some of the peaks and plunges. Social workers can help patients retain their equilibrium by providing the knowledge and understanding they need at each step, by facilitating communication between all parties, by providing a safe holding environment for patients' affect and anxieties, by offering perspective gained from watching many families cope with cancer, by alleviating distress, by facilitating problem-solving, and by empowering patients to exercise what control they retain. Many patients find comfort just in hearing the social worker accurately describe the roller coaster ride. Realizing that others have had a similar experience and have coped makes a difference.

While patient attitude has not been proven to affect overall survival, a positive attitude on the part of the patient is associated with higher quality of life and diminished side-effect impact (Weisman 1979; Zabora et al. 1990). Conversely, when patients approach cancer and its treatment with fear, despair, anger, and hostility, these attitudes are associated with lowered quality of life and more severe impact from side effects. With notable exceptions, most patients deal with their disease as they have dealt with other challenges in their lives. So social work practice involves assessing the given situation and relational dynamics, building on existing strengths, and minimizing the impact of entrenched deficits.

That said, life-threatening illness or impending death may act as a catalyst for transformation and for radically new behaviors by a handful of patients and caregivers. When these opportunities for change arise, an attuned practitioner can recognize and reinforce the newfound strengths. The social worker should cherish these experiences, as they represent profound healing amid the wreckage wrought by disease.

Another issue likely to arise as treatment proceeds is that patients and their families may place a disproportionate weight on test results that can rob patients of the opportunity to live each day as fully as possible. Looking forward with anxious expectation to a scan or blood test some weeks distant diverts attention away from how the patient feels right now and how the patient and family can get the most out of the current moment. Social workers can acknowledge the importance of test results while helping patients regain or maintain a focus on the present and the opportunities contained therein.

Rehearsing reactions to each of the possible results of a test or procedure may help patients discharge much of the emotion they may otherwise attach to a particular result, while developing sound strategies for coping with each possible outcome. Integral to such rehearsals is redirection to the present moment and its opportunities. An intervention that only fosters or reinforces the patient's rumination on outcome is collusive and counterproductive.

When the results indicate disease progression despite all therapy, patients enter a final phase in their disease process, the terminal phase.

PHASE THREE: TERMINAL CARE

The terminal-care phase marks a distinct and crucial transition in the disease course and the goals of treatment. Terminal care begins when viable disease-directed therapy is failing to produce beneficial effects or when patients opt to discontinue or demur proven or experimental disease-directed therapy and when the cancer will lead to the patient's death. The goals shift, focusing on support and comfort for the patient and their caregivers. Comfort is used here in the broadest sense, embracing relief through managing of physical symptoms as well as attending to the emotional, relational, and spiritual distress felt by patients, families, and caregivers.

Recognition of the transition to terminal care is a process that unfolds for people at different paces. The healthcare team, patients, and their families seldom come to this realization simultaneously. Often some member of the healthcare team first notices a patient's inexorable decline. Usually, this is someone with recent and sustained patient contact: home care providers, infusion-room nurses, clinic or inpatient staff, or pharmacists, for example.

The physician may have anticipated this moment for some time, yet may not be the first to recognize the patient's terminality. Physician contacts with cancer patients are intermittent, and their workloads predict they will be unlikely to dwell on or even recall the details of a case between visits from that patient. Furthermore, patients often put their most presentable self forward in clinic. They may, for example, believe or hope that in requiring less of their doctor's time they are less ill than others at the clinic. Physicians are busy and patients know it; by taking less of their doctor's time, they may feel they are repaying the physician for his or her care. At a more subtle level, patients may be concerned that taking too much time or placing too many demands on the physician will lead to abandonment. Further, the shorter the appointment, the less time is available to hear bad news.

Once the physician suspects that the patient is terminally ill, he or she may refer the patient to hospice, schedule a clinic visit or family conference to discuss this turn of events, delay dialogue and continue therapy uninterrupted, or simply reject or suppress his or her suspicion that the patient is dying and recommend additional curative treatment. Ordering additional tests or studies may be an appropriate medical enterprise, but it may also mask a physician's discomfort with talking about dying or a patient's or caregiver's resistance.

In any case, the social worker has a role at this time. Social workers, guided by principles of open communication and the patient's right to accurate and timely information, can assist in promoting dialogue, coordinating care, and providing a smooth transition to hospice care. Moreover, both social workers and nurses should raise the possibility of hospice care as appropriate. Often their frequent contact and different professional relationship with the patient and caregivers leads them to an earlier awareness of the patient's decline. They are ideally situated to recognize signs indicating a patient's terminal condition. As a part of the care team, the social worker can participate in family conferences or clinic visits, thereby helping to insure that patients, physicians, and caregivers emerge with a common understanding of the patient's condition and shared expectations regarding the goals of further care.

In each of these circumstances, social workers facilitate the expression of emotions. When, for example, a clinic visit has been scheduled to discuss a transition to hospice, patients need to know if this is likely to be the last time they see their physician and the clinic staff. Powerful relationships often develop over the course of treatment, and patients need to have the opportunity to reach closure with staff. These farewells are equally important to the job satisfaction and emotional well-being of staff. Failure to reach closure or to address impending death openly contributes to professional burn-out, particularly as these lapses accumulate.

The shift in the goals of treatment corresponds to changes in the patient's personal goals and activities. The patient's attention shifts to end-of-life tasks. While a number of models describe tasks common to the terminally ill, most reflect the experience of the dominant culture in the United States. Many other cultures have very different values and describe the tasks at life's end differently. Sensitivity to these differences is imperative in delivering care to diverse populations. Aware that these differences have significant implications for the delivery of care, social workers can help families discuss and delineate tasks specific to their culture, clan, or family. Pain control offers a pertinent example.

Adequate pain control is considered the cornerstone of good terminal care. Pain is measurable and can serve as an indicator of quality care. Moreover, pain is often listed as a core concern for patients with cancer. Effective protocols such as those promulgated by the World Health Organization, the Agency for Health Care Policy and Research, and the National Cancer Institute for the relief of pain are now broadly recognized and implemented. Most hospice home-care teams are vigilant regarding pain and act quickly to alleviate it. However, in some cultures, to attain eternal life one must be fully alert and unclouded by narcotic medications at the moment when life ends. For these patients, the relief of pain is much less important than clarity of mind. Consequently, these patients and their caregivers often refuse medications that could make the patient more physically comfortable. This culturally appropriate choice can cause hospice staff and other healthcare providers significant distress. The potential for problematic countertransference is substantial. Staff can feel inadequate, may worry that others, such as on-call personnel, other team members and outsiders alike, will criticize their care or judge it ineffective or negligent; and may even feel that the decision to forego pain medication, if made by caregivers, constitutes reportable abuse. Working with family or spiritual leaders and health provider colleagues, the social worker can help all parties understand one another's cultural and decision-making contexts.

CASE EXAMPLE

Mrs. James was a fifty-six-year-old African American who had been diagnosed with advanced, invasive, metastatic cervical cancer. Her husband of thirty-one years had died five years before from complications of diabetes and hypertension. Mr. and Mrs. James had four children: three adult daughters and a teenage son. Her son lived with Mrs. James; two daughters lived in the area and her eldest daughter lived about forty miles away. Her first and third daughters were married, and each had two children. Mrs. James particularly enjoyed time with her four grandchildren, and pictures of her family covered the living room walls.

Mrs. James's diagnosis was preceded by several weeks of cramping, abdominal discomfort, and occasional bloody vaginal discharge. When the pain became so severe that Mrs. James could not work, she sought treatment at the local teaching hospital's emergency room. She was admitted and received a comprehensive workup, resulting in a tentative diagnosis of cervical cancer. This diagnosis was based on the results of her physical examination, abdominal ultrasound, radiographies, and biopsy, which revealed invasive squamous cell cancer. Surgery was contraindicated because of extensive metastatic disease. Two of Mrs. James's daughters were with her when the medical oncology fellow and the attending physician confirmed the diagnosis and presented options for further treatment. The advanced nature of her disease meant that neither cure nor control of the cancer was a realistic treatment goal. While Mrs. James was offered chemotherapy, the physicians could offer no assurance she would benefit by feeling better or living longer, but would likely experience significant side effects from the treatment. The physicians told her she probably had less than six months to live and should put her affairs in order. The fellow recommended palliative care for Mrs. James; the term was new to her, like much of the information she received in this short time period. The physician explained that it meant focusing on her symptoms and keeping her comfortable, rather than on trying to cure her disease, and that hospice was the usual provider of palliative care. She remembered that her aunt had died at home a number of years before with hospice, so she accepted this treatment plan after talking it over with her daughters. The physician made a referral to a local hospice program.

Initially, this flood of bad news stunned both Mrs. James and her daughters. Prior to this hospital admission, Mrs. James had last seen a physician for a refractory bronchial infection eight years earlier. Once she and her daughters discussed this information with other family and friends, the two middle children said they felt the doctors were giving up on their mother too quickly and wondered if she was being offered inferior treatment because she is uninsured, poor, or black. These concerns were only referred to obliquely when one daughter asked the physician at the follow-up visit if there truly was no other treatment for her mother. The physician reiterated the advanced nature of Mrs. James's disease, her poor prognosis, and the offer of chemotherapy with the same caveats as before. The physician also offered a second opinion at a nonaffiliated institution and indicated that no other therapies were available at his institution. Because experimental treatment might be available elsewhere around the country, the family was also referred to the NCI website to explore this possibility further.

Mrs. James was admitted to hospice the day after her hospital discharge and was visited regularly by members of the hospice interdisciplinary team, including the nurse, social worker, chaplain, home health aide and a volunteer. Essentially bedbound since her discharge from the hospital, she needed assistance with bathing, eating, dressing, and transferring to the portable commode. She had intermittent severe cramping and was prescribed a substantial and steadily escalating dose of pain medication, consisting of slow-release morphine tablets to manage her constant, baseline pain, and liquid morphine, which is fast acting, for her severe episodic breakthrough pain. Mrs. James's persistent reports of pain indicated that her pain was not well controlled; her slow rate of medication usage suggested that the prescribed dosing schedule was not being followed.

Now, five weeks after discharge from the hospital, she was in a hospital bed set up in the living room of her modest apartment; the bed provided by hospice. She was most comfortable with her head slightly elevated, though she was increasingly unable to find any comfortable position. Many neighbors and friends stop by throughout the day so Mrs. James was seldom alone.

Before her hospitalization, Mrs. James was working an average of fifty hours a week cleaning homes. As an independent contractor, she had neither health benefits nor sick leave and could not afford to purchase health benefits for herself. She also had neither disability coverage nor social security. Mr. James worked as a custodian and handyman for a local convalescent hospital. While he had paid into the social security system, Mrs. James was too young to collect spousal survivor's benefits, and Mr. James's nursing home job provided no other retirement or survivor benefits. While Mrs. James's disabling cancer diagnosis and lost income now qualified her for Medicaid, approval was still pending.

Mr. and Mrs. James both had grammar school educations. They worked tirelessly, making many sacrifices, in order to provide educational opportunities and a better future for their children. Their eldest daughter was a credentialed high school teacher with a B.A. in English. The middle daughter, who is a certified nurses' assistant, worked flexible hours and was taking classes toward an Associate of Arts nursing certificate program. She provided most of the daily care for her mother and had been the most vocal about the treatment plan, which, she feared, kept her mother overmedicated. The youngest daughter, in her third year of college, was majoring in information technology. Mrs. James's son attended the local parochial high school, where his tuition was paid by an academic scholarship and supplemental support from his oldest sister.

For three decades, Mrs. James had been an active member of her church community and sung in its choir. Her minister and several members visited frequently and brought meals three times a week. Neighbors did her household laundry and grocery shopping.

The hospice nurse and the patient and her daughter each asked the social worker to visit. The nurse reported that the family was concerned that their mother had not been offered any treatment to cure or slow her cancer. The nurse also complained that the primary caregiver, the patient's daughter, was refusing to follow the plan of care. Mrs. James was worried about her son and wanted the issue of his guardianship resolved. He had uncharacteristically experienced disciplinary trouble at school twice since she fell ill, and his usually solid grades were slipping. Mrs. James's caregiver daughter feared her mother was being offered inferior health care.

DISCUSSION

In caring for the terminally ill, the social worker should start where the patient is. In this case, the "patient" is the patient/family system, which has five separate starting points: guardianship, Mrs. James's son's behavior, family concerns about Mrs. James's overall care, the primary caregiver's follow-through on the plan of care, and the socioeconomic and cultural context.

To establish which to deal with first, the social worker may have to triage these problems. Two factors must be weighed. The first is the urgency generated by Mrs. James's advanced disease, rapid decline, and very limited prognosis. The second has to do with resource availability. The social worker may have to reprioritize his or her caseload. For the James family, time is a luxury no one can afford.

Mrs. James's concern over guardianship is pressing. In many states, the most seamless transfer of guardianship occurs if the current and proposed guardians are both alive at the time of transfer, but given Mrs. James's advanced illness, that is unlikely to be the case. The social worker can start by asking Mrs. James if she has discussed her son's guardianship with him and the family. If there is general agreement, including the assent of the minor, guardianship should transfer with few complications, particularly because the biological father is already deceased. In other cases, biological parents who have been long absent through either divorce or separation can be problematic both to locate and to convince to waive custodial rights. This can be particularly vexing if the minor comes with tangible survivor income, like the survivor benefits Mrs. James's son receives from his father's entitlement.

Concern for her son's economic well-being is implicit in the issue of guardianship. His mother knows his modest Social Security income will not help him beyond high school, and the worker is well advised to remember the James's unswerving commitment to providing educational opportunities to their children. Mrs. James likely feels and needs to express her disappointment, guilt, or exasperation about not being able to provide that opportunity for her son personally. The social worker might relieve Mrs. James's concerns by suggesting potential sources of guidance and support for which her son may qualify. The choice of guardian may turn, for example, on which of his older sisters can best help him find and make use of programs to further his academic achievement.

Mrs. James is intent on implementing an acceptable plan to meet her son's need for adult guidance as he is emancipated. This process gives the social worker an opportunity to explore Mrs. James's feelings about missing the opportunity to see her son come into manhood, and may serve as a point of departure to examine a more global sense of loss associated with her death.

Skillful intervention may help her express her grief about missing many key events in her children's lives. She may want to review and celebrate important events that she and her family have shared. She may even want to create tangible objects to carry her influence and memory past her death into the future: video or audiotapes or letters to each of her children or grandchildren that mark some passage in their lives. This might include a letter to her son for his graduation from high school or college, his marriage, or the birth of his first child. These objects can extend the presence of a loved one well beyond their physical death and may bring the patient a greater sense of control or contribution. If families engage in these projects together, the project and the process become an occasion to celebrate and to grieve in the present, while creating a time capsule of memories for the future (see chapters 13 and 32).

The social worker might also use the issue of her son's guardianship to invite Mrs. James to reflect on her relationship with him and how he fits into the family. Bringing him fully into discussions of his mother's condition and how he and the family will be affected by her illness and death may help his bereavement and minimize any adverse impact her death could have on his emancipation. It is crucial to understand Mrs. James's perspective on her son's position in the family. If he is peripheral, does that derive from his age, his gender, or his disposition? Such an understanding can foster a mother/son or son/family dialogue that facilitates an appropriate guardianship plan and includes him more fully in his mother's dying process. This enhanced awareness may improve his academic performance by refocusing on his needs. Assessing his awareness of his mother's impending death and his feelings about it are important steps toward helping him give voice to his anger and sadness, rather than acting them out. Then his family, the school, and he can jointly develop a plan to get him back on track.

The issue of guardianship also provides the social worker with a good opportunity to approach the son. Finding out what he knows about his mother's illness and about the plan to transfer guardianship may allow him to ask questions and clear up any misunderstandings he has about what is happening to his mother or what will happen to him. Because he is a minor, any such discussion would require his mother's consent, as well as consultation with the proposed guardian and other family members, so that boundaries for such a conversation are clearly established. These preparatory conversations with adult family members will help the social worker respect family attitudes about how much or little information to share. However, the gravity of Mrs. James's condition and his age make his involvement highly desirable; the social worker must push to involve minor children appropriately, which at times will mean challenging adult family members' initial desire to limit children's involvement. Minors of all ages are profoundly affected by illness and death; efforts to shield them pose significant short-term and long-term risks to healthy development. Social workers are obligated to help adults understand these risks and work collaboratively to achieve age-appropriate and culturally sensitive involvement of younger family members.

These interactions with the family provide the social worker with opportunities to educate them about the risks and benefits of full disclosure with minors of various ages and developmental stages. Family dialogue can help identify the range of feelings he may be experiencing, such as terror, grief, anger, guilt, sadness, and a sense of injustice. However, it may be desirable to have some conversation with the son without other family in the room. If he and his mother have a relationship that would promote more thorough communication, perhaps she should be directly involved. However, normal teenage reticence often increases in the presence of others, whether peers or family.

In any case, to be effective the social worker needs to build a relationship with Mrs. James's son. Asking him about his interests and activities (sports, academics, hobbies, clubs, and the like) may help draw him out into more difficult topics. He may have concerns that he has not voiced, and asking him what is on his mind may let him lay out his own agenda. He may not understand the social worker's role; explaining a little about what the social worker does and how she can be helpful is usually a good idea. He may not understand why he is having a more difficult time than usual at school. Normalizing his questions and fears and discussing how unprepared, ignorant, or scared his classmates might be when confronted with his mother's illness may help him share his thoughts. His peers—indeed, some of his teachers—may not know how to treat him or talk to him. While building a relationship with adolescents usually takes time, how quickly the social worker proceeds depends on balancing the urgency of the situation and his need to know with the benefits of methodically laying a good relational foundation.

The social worker might also invite him to talk about his father's death: How did that affect him and his family? What role did he take in caring for or visiting his father? How did his classmates and friends respond? What feelings did his father's death evoke in him? Did he express those feelings, and if so, how? How were his feelings responded to? What helped him then? What was useless or even hurtful? These questions enable the social worker to discover how this young man has adapted to a previous significant loss and to assess for unresolved prior grief.

Including the family in this dialogue can also be helpful. He needs to be able to ask questions: "Where will I live?" "Will I have to change schools or leave this city?" "How will I be supported financially?" The social worker should prepare other family members for his potentially self-centered questions and place his concerns in a developmental context. By helping family members recognize that this is an unexpected disruption of his healthy emancipation process, the social worker may enhance their ability to sustain and assist him in that process. His mother's illness makes him different from his peers at a developmental stage when fitting in is usually highly prized.

The social worker might also identify and enlist other parental figures in his life, such as teachers, coaches, mentors, aunts and uncles, and people from church. The school may also have ways to enhance his coping, through counselors or advisors; at the very least, the school needs to know about the additional stresses in his life at this time. The social worker is well suited to coordinate support systems and empower key family members to make the most of these resources.

All four siblings will be orphaned by their mother's death, though the son may be at increased risk of feeling abandoned, helpless, confused, ambivalent, and uncertain about his future. Personality and family circumstance will make each individual's reaction unique, but the son's elevated risk factors include his age, developmental stage, birth order, and place as the sole surviving male in the nuclear family.

Once guardianship has been addressed, the social worker can turn to the family's concerns regarding the lack of treatment options being presented to their mother. This work begins with fact-finding. Is the nurse's report accurate? Which family members have voiced these concerns? Are there others who feel the same way but may not have spoken up? What is the basis for these concerns?

Answers to these questions will guide the social worker in formulating a plan before addressing the concern with the family. One might start with the nurse by finding out what she heard and from whom. The social worker might ask various family members what they know about Mrs. James's illness and discuss their feelings regarding their mother's treatment choices. The social worker is more prepared to respond helpfully when armed with a thorough understanding of the medical situation and the family's grasp of the diagnosis, prognosis, treatment plan, and specific concerns. If some fundamental misunderstanding about the nature and extent of their mother's illness is at the heart of family concerns for example, a family meeting with the physician, nurse, and social worker may best address their concerns.

If the concern is more clearly related to inequalities in our society's distribution of health resources, or the documented abuse of nonconsenting African Americans in medical experimentation, a different approach will be more helpful (Francis 2001; Freimuth et al. 2001; Roy 1995; Smedley 2002). Mrs. James's lack of access to routine primary care may well have contributed to her presentation with advanced disease. She or other family members may justifiably blame these systemic inequities for her death.

In that light, the issue of trusting the medical establishment globally and this health-care team specifically must be addressed. Staff should consciously examine whether race or socioeconomic status has affected the selection of treatment options. To the health consumer, each provider represents the larger healthcare system. Providers can easily take global concerns personally, so some defensiveness is a natural response. But it is neither therapeutic nor professional. Encouraging this family to air their grievances hand in hand with provider acknowledgment that the system has acted unethically and wrongly in the past may go a great distance toward repairing this relationship. If team-specific grievances or concerns are voiced, they must be dealt with in a straightforward manner. Most provider agencies have established grievance procedures, likely involving a patient advocate or ombudsman.

Patients deserve to know that they are free to voice their dissatisfaction, mistrust, and antipathy, whether the mistreatment is based on race, immigration status, educational attainment, gender, age, sexual orientation, or some other characteristic. Demonstrating awareness and sensitivity to past grievances in a nondefensive manner serves to lower the barriers that otherwise separate a patient, family, group, or clan from the healthcare system (see chapter 22).

Matching patients to staff based on race, gender, ethnicity, sexual orientation, or any other characteristic is likely a form of bigotry and segregation in its own right. However, when patients and caregivers see, hear about, or interact with interdisciplinary team members with whom they can identify or connect, a trusting and therapeutic patient/provider relationship will more likely develop. A diverse provider team reflecting the community being served helps assuage patients' misgivings and reservations and enhances patients' opportunity to ask how others have resolved these concerns. Regardless, it is essential to provide training in cultural identity, heritage, traditions, and culturally appropriate care to all providers (see chapter 22).

Sometimes an apparent adversarial reaction to a clinician or the team has more to do with being the nearest available target as a family attempts to come to grips with its anger or grief over a devastating diagnosis and prognosis. Some patients or caregivers never really catch up with the speed at which a disease progresses. People lash out at their healthcare providers in their struggles with the frustration, horror, and despair they experience as they or their loved one goes from healthy to dying to dead in short order. Understanding their helplessness and realistically recognizing one's own are crucial components of the social worker/client relationship.

For those working with terminally ill patients, the importance of being present cannot be overstated: presence alone can be profoundly therapeutic. Though offered from a spiritual care provider's perspective, Wayne Muller's exchange with a dying man speaks to the power of presence:

> Then, just before I left, he said, "You know, Wayne, I really don't understand most of what you say." He paused. "But I like your company and the sound of your voice." All the time I thought I was being wise and inspirational, it turned out Simon was soothed by my voice and my companionship. For my part, I rarely believe my companionship is enough, so I feel compelled to say clever and meaningful things. He wasn't interested. My company and my presence were enough. (MULLER 1996)

Showing up regularly, safely holding the strong, sometimes overwhelming emotions of the terminally ill and their families, validating the normalcy of those feelings, and echoing the powerlessness patients are experiencing is strong medicine. In the midst of this *bearing witness*, team members can offer tangible help by assisting in concrete ways with the physical, medical, psychological, spiritual, and resource-related needs that patients and caregivers have. While the experience of non-abandonment is seldom appreciated in the moment and may even be devalued or dismissed, its importance is most noticeable when absent and often most appreciated in retrospect.

Ultimately, in the face of fatal disease, health care cannot grant the one wish of patients and their families. We cannot restore health or indefinitely forestall death. The needs of the actively dying are few and tend to be less medical than psychosocial or spiritual. Care at this stage of illness is most effectively focused on comfort—palliation: the relief of suffering, preparation for the body's transition from a living organism to a lifeless vessel, and support for making meaning of one's living and dying. When physical symptoms are well managed as death draws near, most people turn their attention to the interpersonal, intrapsychic, and spiritual or existential realms.

At the same time, the family's concerns often focus on the ruthlessness of the disease and the emotional and practical havoc caused by its relentless progression. The patient and each family member will adjust to these challenging circumstances in a unique manner, often reverting to their own dominant style of coping when under stress. Social workers can assist by drawing attention to this process, helping individuals tolerate their own and one another's (often regressed) behaviors, manifested in response to the patient's unpredictable and rapidly changing condition. Spouses and others not related by blood may gain valuable perspective as they witness unfamiliar regressed behaviors rooted in the other's childhood or family of origin. Social workers on interdisciplinary teams are well suited to describe these interpersonal dynamics to their colleagues and suggest strategies to use and to avoid in working with particular patients and their families.

Validating and normalizing a range of emotions promotes coping. Individuals can draw strength from the realization that others have similar feelings though they may express them differently. Indeed, individual family members may recall similar circumstances that they have weathered successfully.

The fourth and final issue the social worker needs to address is the degree of family adherence to the plan of care, specifically the plan for the control of the patient's pain. This problem manifests in two ways: the patient continues to complain of unrelieved pain, and pain medication usage is not consistent with the current prescribed regimen. There is more medication left than there would be if the regimen were being followed.

The language social workers use here is critical. The question of whether or not a plan of care is being followed can be referred to in a number of ways: What pain management medications is the patient receiving? Is the plan being adhered to? Are the patient and family being compliant? For many people, the term *adherence* does not carry the same degree of judgment as the term *compliance*. Noncompliance sounds like someone is misbehaving. On the other hand, there are many reasons for not adhering to a plan of care. Some are without merit; some are well intentioned but ill advised, and others are completely sound and sensible. Discussing a family's implementation of a plan of care calls for the conscious and deliberate use of nonjudgmental language if the clinician wants to minimize defensiveness and learn what is being done for the patient's pain and why.

Medical personnel sometimes use language thoughtlessly, to the detriment of patient care and the provider/patient relationship. For example, we speak of patients failing treatment or therapy (see chapter 3). Patients do not fail therapy; therapy fails patients. Therapy can be ineffective, yield disappointing results, and fail to have the desired effects or produce a desired response. Sometimes we refer to people as their disease: "The lung cancer in room 204, bed 1." We mask bad news in euphemisms or technical medical shorthand: "disseminated, tumor, malignant, iatrogenic." Skillful social work intervention from diagnosis through treatment discussion and administration to outcome (cure, control, remission, unchecked progression, comfort care, death) involves the conscious and mindful use of language, especially language that does not blame, confuse, or mislead the patient or caregivers.

In Mrs. James's case, the treatment team wants to address the problems it perceives with the pain medications not being given in the doses or at the times prescribed, and the consequent pain the patient is experiencing. Until we ask, we do not know whether the patient and caregiver perceive this to be a problem.

The family may perceive, for example, that when the regimen is followed the patient is too drowsy or confused. Or someone in the family may have concerns about addiction. The patient or caregiver may believe that pain medication should not be taken if no pain is present. Perhaps the patient believes that suffering is or should be part of the living and dying experience. Someone in the caregiving group may believe the drugs hasten death, or fear that the patient's nausea or constipation, both potential side effects of pain medications, may be poorly controlled. The family may want their mother to be as independent as possible, and so have left her in charge of her own medications even though she may no longer be able to do this for herself. Whatever the reasons leading to the plan not being followed, it is essential to build a consensus based on Mrs. James's beliefs and concerns about how much pain she has and how best to manage her pain and administer medication (see chapter 19).

The inadequate treatment of pain is ubiquitous; the undertreatment of pain is well documented in the general population as well as in several subset populations to which Mrs. James belongs (women, ethnic minorities, older patients, and those of low socioeconomic status) (Field 1997, 2002). However, successful pain management is a high priority for hospice and palliative care providers, who are both skilled at managing pain in the home and attentive to patient autonomy regarding pain-control preferences. As long as a patient or family member is complaining of pain, or observation indicates that the patient's pain is poorly managed, the team has an obligation to work with patient and family to achieve the level of pain control the patient desires.

A lack of information is often at the root of misunderstandings about a patient's pain regimen. Patients and caregivers need to understand it takes two to five days for the patient to adjust to short-term side effects following an increase in the dosage. When patients and family members know, for example, that drowsiness is a usual and transient response to an increased dose, families are more likely to continue giving pain medication as prescribed. It is also helpful to explain the difference between physiological tolerance, psychological dependence, and addiction to patients and their families. Debunking the mythical connection between the administration of opioid narcotics, especially morphine, and the death event is a great comfort to caregivers as well. Though these events often occur closely in time, research suggests that no causal relationship exists between morphine and death (Pargeon 1999; Radbruch et al. 2002; Twycross 2002). By inviting and guiding patients and families to understand suffering at end of life, and by advocating for the best possible pain control in the family's context of cultural and spiritual beliefs, the social worker can help create an atmosphere most conducive to adherence.

If patient-centered care and autonomy are the standard of care, health providers must be prepared to accept decisions sharply divergent from their own. It is easy to start believing that one's own perspective rests on the highest moral ground. Teams do well to monitor themselves in this regard. Rigid convictions can produce paternalistic or authoritarian health care. An interdisciplinary team offers the benefit of both formal and informal exchanges between colleagues and the tempering of the individual practitioner's reactions and judgments by the team. Autonomy and patient choice are lost when the healthcare team harbors a preferred outcome and a belief in doing things one particular way.

In Mrs. James's case, the daughter who is acting as primary caregiver currently works in a skilled nursing facility and is training to be a nurse. The possibility for this combination to play mischief with Mrs. James's care is fairly high. As a student with no nursing experience and with minimal training in administering medications, the daughter's pharmacological education so far has likely included warnings about the power of some drugs, including morphine. She has also been exposed to the caution exercised when these drugs are administered, and warned of the risks of overdosing a patient. Moreover, her mother manifests many of the side effects associated with an overdose, including shallow breathing, some confusion, and somnolence. The daughter also works in a nursing home, where she may suspect that patients are kept medicated to control their behavior and minimize their demands. Because she is studying nursing and has significant nursing-home experience, her family may well defer to her because of her knowledge and experience, reinforcing her sense of responsibility and distorting her perceived ability to adapt the regimen effectively.

When a family member is a healthcare professional, that individual is at significantly elevated risk of trying to fulfill multiple roles, usually resulting in no single role's being done well. For the daughter in this example, a little bit of knowledge can be a dangerous thing. Her nursing-home experience does provide skills and a level of comfort with hands-on patient care. Taking on too much of that role robs her of the opportunity to be a daughter who is grieving her mother's illness and impending death. She will likely continue to provide the majority of care. However, the social worker can alert the team to this dilemma and encourage team members, particularly the nurse, to reinforce the caregiver's role as daughter. Perhaps the physician can emphasize the importance of meticulously following the prescribed regimen at the next clinic or home visit. Indeed, the physician can use this to build on the caregiver's interest in medicine and her ongoing nursing education, explaining the rationale for regular dosing and incremental titration of opioids. The physician can also address the challenges of being both a caregiver and the patient's daughter.

This team effort acknowledges the multiplicity of her roles, the significance of her contribution, and her paramount role as daughter. The team can relieve her of the responsibility for modifying the dosing regimen and elicit her support in its implementation. This strategy builds on her strengths and assures that first and foremost she gets to be a daughter losing her mother.

At the beginning of this discussion, a fifth starting point was enumerated. Socioeconomic and cultural considerations permeate each of the other four themes, and each has been discussed with a keen awareness of this patient and family's unique sociocultural and economic milieu.

Likewise, the starting points were discussed serially. In this and many other cases, social workers and provider teams will continually triage needs based on urgency, and most often will work on several issues simultaneously.

CONCLUSION

Mrs. James's illness raises issues that are integral to any good biopsychosocial assessment and plan of care. One is that the patient's need for intervention begins at diagnosis. The social worker may provide support, containment of affect, education, and a bridge to both material and therapeutic resources. The patient's and family's strengths need to be assessed and previous ways of coping with loss, illness, and grief identified. The social worker can help the patient and family advocate effectively, deal with complex choices, and understand the benefits and burdens of various courses of action.

The social worker also needs to assess the client's sociocultural context and family/support system, helping the team to understand particular individual choices and the values on which they rest. During the course of illness, the social worker provides ways for family members to express a broad range of feelings and for the patient to adapt to their changing role, function, and capacity. The social worker may offer individual, group, or family interventions aimed at helping family members understand and support one another. As was the case with Mrs. James, many tangible services, such as help with guardianship, insurance, her son's school, and referral to hospice, need to be provided by the social worker, who also advocates with the team in support of the patient and family.

Although the social worker tries to interpret the team's recommendations to the family, he or she may well be the target of the individual's or family's anger, grief, or helplessness. It is incumbent on the practitioner to be able to tolerate the feelings engendered by these projections. The capacity to absorb (and occasionally interpret) these powerful emotions can be one of the social worker's most important tools for helping. Moreover, modeling tolerance for strong affect can facilitate increased capacity to tolerate these emotions for the patient and family. The social worker needs to address all levels of the patient's and family's concerns and provide an empathic, supportive holding environment for the multiple relationships. The social worker needs to be mindful of the functional and dysfunctional roles that family members may play and help clarify what may or may not be working for the patient and family members. The social worker needs to be alert for family members (in this case Mrs. James's son) who may be marginalized or neglected. Likewise, the social worker does well not to rush to judgment about that apparent neglect or marginalization. Commonly, it is done with noble intent. In the James family, protecting the son from the onrushing calamity may be the well-intentioned yet flawed thinking behind limiting his exposure and involvement.

In the terminal phase of illness, the social worker bears witness, providing a relationship that does not abandon either patient or family. The social worker may play an interdisciplinary role with clergy, nurses, physicians, and other healthcare team members. It often falls to social work or nursing staff to inquire conscientiously of other team members the purpose and efficacy of life-sustaining, potentially death-prolonging therapies.

In summary, the social worker in oncology has to marshal the best of his or her skills to assess, advocate, support, and intervene on behalf of patients and their families. The social worker provides concrete referrals to resources in the health system and the broader community, often acting as liaison between medical professionals, various systems, and the patient and their family. This requires knowledge and understanding of the psychological, social, cultural, spiritual, and medical dimensions of patient and family care—and considerable self-knowledge and reflection.

ACKNOWLEDGMENTS

The research in this chapter is supported in part through a grant from the Project on Death in America's (PDIA) Social Work Leadership Development Award Program.

Additional support is provided by the University of California, Davis School of Medicine, Department of Internal Medicine, Frederick J. Meyers, MD, professor and chair.

REFERENCES

American Cancer Society. 2001. *Cancer Facts and Figures, 2001.* Atlanta: American Cancer Society.

Back, A. L., J. L. Wallace, H. E. Starks, and R. A. Perlman. 1996. Physician-assisted suicide and euthanasia in Washington State. *Journal of the American Medical Association* 275:919–925.

Blum, R. F., K. Kash, T. Myers-Navarro, L. Harrison, and J. C. Holland. 2002. Feasibility of screening for distress in the ambulatory cancer setting. Paper presented at the American Society of Clinical Oncology, Orlando, FL.

Boynton, K. T. 1994. Behavioral social work in the field of oncology. *Journal of Applied Social Sciences* 18(2): 189–197.

Cwikel, J. B. 1999. Social work with adult cancer patients: A vote-count review of intervention research. *Social Work in Health Care* 29(2): 39–67.

Field, M. J., and R. E. Berhman, eds. 2002. *When Children Die: Improving Palliative and End-of-Life Care for Children and Their Families.* Washington, DC: National Academies Press.

Field, M. J., and C. K. Cassel, eds. 1997. *Approaching Death: Improving Care at the End of Life.* Washington, DC: Institute of Medicine.

Francis, C. 2001. The medical ethos and social responsibility in clinical medicine. *Journal of the National Medical Association* 93(5): 157–169.

Freimuth, V. S., S. B. Thomas, G. Cole, E. Zook, and T. Duncan. 2001. African Americans' views on research and the Tuskegee Syphilis Study. *Social Science and Medicine* 52(5): 797–808.

Holland, J. 1999. NCCN practice guidelines for the management of psychological distress. *Oncology* 13 (N112a Suppl.): 459–507.

Holleb, A. I., ed. 1986. *The American Cancer Society Cancer Book: Prevention, Detection, Diagnosis, Treatment, Rehabilitation, Cure.* Garden City, NY: Doubleday.

Lenhard, R. E., R. T. Osteen, and T. S. Gansler. 2001. *Clinical Oncology.* Atlanta: American Cancer Society.

Lewis, J. 1999. Status passages: The experience of HIV-positive gay men. *Journal of Homosexuality* 37(3): 87–115.

Loscalzo, M., and P. B. Jacobsen. 1990. Practical behavioral approaches to the effective management of pain and distress. *Journal of Psychosocial Oncology* 8(2–3): 139–169.

Muller, W. 1996. *How, Then, Shall We Live?* New York: Bantam Books.

Pargeon, K. L., et al. 1999. Barriers to effective cancer pain management: a review of the literature. *Journal of Pain Symptom Management* 18(5): 5358–5368.

Radbruch, L., R. Sabatowski, F. Elsner, G. Loick, and N. Kohnen. 2002. Patients' associations with regard to analgesic drugs and their forms for application: A pilot study. *Support Care Cancer* 10(6): 480–485.

Raymer, M. 2002. Realistic short-term psychotherapeutic therapies at the end of life. Paper presented at the Third Joint Clinical Conference on Hospice and Palliative Care, New Orleans, LA.

Roth, A. J. K., L. Batel-Copel, E. Peabody, K. Weingard, H. I. Scher, and J. C. Holland. 1997. A rapid screening method to identify psychological distress in men with prostate cancer in ambulatory clinics. Paper presented at the American Society of Clinical Oncology, Denver, CO.

Roy, B. 1995. The Tuskegee syphilis experiment: Medical ethics, constitutionalism, and property in the body. *Harvard Journal of Minority Public Health* 1(1): 11–15.

Silverman, P. R., and D. Smith. 1984. Helping in mutual help groups for the physically disabled. In *Mental Health and the Self Help Revolution*, ed. A. Gartner and F. Riessman, 73–93. New York: Human Sciences Press.

Smedley, B. S., A. Y. Stith, and A. R. Nelson, eds. 2002. *Unequal Treatment: Confronting Racial and Ethnic Disparities in Health Care*. Washington, DC: National Academies Press.

Twycross, R. 2002. The challenge of palliative care. *International Journal of Clinical Oncology* 7(4): 271–278.

Weisman, A. 1979. A model of psychosocial phasing in cancer. *General Hospital Psychiatry* 1:187–195.

Zabora, J. R., C. G. Blanchard, E. D. Smith, et al. 1997. Prevalence of psychological distress among cancer patients across the disease continuum. *Journal of Psychosocial Oncology* 15(2): 73–87.

Zabora, J. R., and E. D. Smith. 1991. Family dysfunction and the cancer patient: Early recognition and intervention. *Oncology* 5(12): 31–35, 36, 38.

Zabora, J. R., R. Smith-Wilson, J. H. Fetting, and J. P. Enterline. 1990. An efficient method for psychosocial screening of cancer patients. *Psychosomatics* 31(2): 192–196.

PART IV

CONTEXT AND LEADERSHIP

INTRODUCTION: THE CONTEXTS OF END-OF-LIFE CARE

THIS SECTION brings together chapters that focus less on the dying individual and his or her family and more on systemic and contextual issues that effect practice with the dying. We have mentioned throughout the book that good practice is not measured simply by understanding the social worker–client relationship. It comes as no surprise to us, then, that the social contexts play an important role in assessing the quality of care, a point made most explicitly in this final section. The social worker must have and exercise other skills and develop new roles: evaluating and researching practice, implementing new programmatic ideas, becoming an agent of change, and getting involved in the political process.

From the inception of the profession, social workers have been active advocates for the underserved and the poor, and for those disenfranchised based on disability, age, social class, sexual orientation, and race. Over the years social workers have lobbied and worked to change laws that allowed child labor, discrimination, and limited funding for human services. Many of the "private" problems people have presented with have been located in "public" and societal practices that undermined their capacities for choice, autonomy, and human dignity. There are laws that govern how pain medication may be administered and which medications may be used. There are policies that define who has access to care and its financing. Many problems are rooted in aggressive treatments that treat the disease, but not the *person* with the disease. There is always an interface between societal problems and personal behaviors, between the way a system is organized and how people respond to it. Focusing exclusively on the clinical aspects of end-of-life care, in the narrowest sense, may not address the serious economic, ethical, and legal constraints at the local and federal levels in which individuals and families are embedded. The chapters in this section consider a variety of these issues.

Modern technology has created its own end-of-life problems, and some of the practices at this point in life are dictated by the legal system. Steve Arons, a lawyer writing from the perspective of the legal system, explains the relationship between the law and healthcare practices, looking at ethical issues in the practice of medicine as limited by the legal system. Arons helps the reader see the issues of advanced directives and physician-assisted suicide from a lawyer's point of view. This approach is very different from the way a social worker would approach and understand the problem.

Arons introduces the reader to the complexity of current laws that surround end-of-life care and the conflicting principles that underlie them.

Yet we cannot deal with the implications of what our patients wish without recognizing the other constraints on practice. We need to keep in mind, for example, that practitioners on the team who are licensed have the parameters of their practices dictated by the licensing laws of the state in which they practice. Ellen Csikai, from the viewpoint of a social worker, examines how issues related to advanced directives affect social work practice. Social workers need to be aware of state laws and the accompanying regulations that often dictate life-and-death decision making. These impact upon the patient and those caring for and about her. It is not only the laws that are important, but also the regulations that are written by various governmental bodies that support these laws and determine how they are implemented. Social workers need to consider how to be involved in the legislative process; what laws to support, what to work toward changing, how to become involved in developing and implementing regulations, and how they may influence what happens on a day to day basis with their clients.

Another point of interface between social institutions and the individual's right to death with dignity can be found in Jenny and John Dawes's chapter on dying in prisons. They address the private/public interface when people who are dying are incarcerated. A prison functions as what Erving Goffman (1967) called a "total institution," where there is little or no room for individual needs to be acknowledged or met. Goffman's concept of a total institution helps us understand institutions, not necessarily just prisons, that strip people of their identities. Entering a hospital for medical care, for example, requires that a person assume a new role in which behavior is primarily dictated by the needs of those who are treating and caring for him or her. In spite of any one hospital's efforts to make the setting more humane, hospitals are still organized so that those who work there can do their "work." This expectation extends to the way help is organized and how it is available. Any reader who has been hospitalized knows what it means to have to depend on others to meet one's needs, to be in pain, to feel helpless, as well to undertake the role of "patient," waiting patiently or impatiently for those needs to be met. Although the personal needs of the patients are important, meeting any one patient's needs is typically considered in the context of what makes the work of the staff most efficient. Hence the setting provides the context for what needs will be met by whom, and it orders the priorities for what needs to be done, when, and for whom. We begin to see why hospice is so important in providing home care where people can be more in charge of their lives. How much is the prisoner shaped by the institution in which he dies? Dawes and Dawes write of restoring human worth, choice, meaning, respect, and support for prisoners.

In many healthcare settings, the value of personalizing care to meet the emotional, cultural, and spiritual needs of people may not be recognized, in the interest of efficiency and saving money. Social workers have a crucial role to play in making the institutional setting more sensitive and responsive to the social, spiritual, and psychological needs of their patients. Esther Chachkes and Zelda Foster provide vivid examples of how social workers can exercise leadership in their chapter, "Taking Charge." They exhort the reader to see end-of-life care as an opportunity, even a mandate, to take leadership.

As we look at the big picture and consider how much assessment plays a part in clinical practice, it becomes clear that we might follow this same model in determining what role to play in advocating for changing systems to be responsive to the needs of patients and families. We need to develop assessment tools for looking at the larger contexts and making plans for appropriate interventions. This requires a return to our social work values, revisiting skills of community organization and community development, discarding those that may no longer be appropriate and building on those that are.

We can begin this type of assessment by looking at the organizational chart of the agency, at how the system is governed, who works in this setting, who makes decisions and where are they made. An institutional assessment also has to include: assessing the sources of funding for any institution, asking who benefits and who loses from such an arrangement, understanding the impact of financing on the kinds of care available, understanding the current legal policies that, for example, encourage or discourage patients and families from having advanced directives or, if they are unable to decide for themselves, having a healthcare proxy. Social workers need to understand the complex societal and legal restraints on pain management and assisted suicide. They need to analyze critically the way health care is financed and practiced, as June Simmons describes in her review of how end-of-life care is financed in this country.

Again there are legal questions: What laws govern resources that are available? For example, in Canada legislation is being introduced to extend palliative care coverage to home care, and the Canadian government is considering providing economic support to those who remain at home to care for the dying person. Assessment needs to understand the nation's priorities (Ferris et al. 2002). Would it be possible to advocate for family support of this sort in the United States?

Social workers need to ask what flexibility exists in any system, who their allies are, and how to effect change in this setting. They need to develop initiatives that can effect change without only using confrontation as a method. We have many methods in social work: relationships, brokering, and advocacy.

Social workers need to take leadership in providing end-of-life care for those who have been stigmatized or underserved, including those who, for example, may have committed heinous crimes. The assessment has to consider not only a holding environment for the patient and family, but also what a caring environment looks like in a particular setting, considering the community that is served. In asking how healthcare settings can become more responsive to individual and community needs, it is important to consider how to involve lay people or potential patients as partners in any of the planning.

Social workers must also assess the financial resources available to support quality end-of-life services as well as to understand who are its beneficiaries. Such an assessment also needs to include the social worker's willingness to be involved as a change agent, not only for her clients but also for herself. In their chapter on leadership, Foster and Chachkes observe that what social workers do *least* well is advocate for themselves: promoting what they have done, taking leadership roles and acting on their assessments of need, and bringing to reality their visions of what they have yet to accomplish.

Research findings become another element in an assessment of the contexts in which end-of-life care occurs. Social workers must be consumers of research to gain new knowledge about the needs of people are dying and the bereaved, but they must also be producers of knowledge. Betty Kramer and Mercedes Bern-Klug review the paucity of research emanating from social work. Research becomes critical in a human service and healthcare system that is advocating for evidence-based practice. We need to document the work we do and show its value. Kramer and Bern-Klug bring into focus the need and the support that is necessary to do this work, and the various qualitative and quantitative approaches that can be applied. There is no magic in doing research. Many practitioners need to overcome their discomfort with being involved in research and be alert to new work that is being done, often in partnership with other professionals. Social workers need to recognize that this can provide them with greater understanding of their clients and demonstrate the value of what they are doing, as well as provide direction for improving practice. It means stepping back with a critical eye and systematically looking at what is being done.

Social workers need to take leadership roles in program development. Chachkes and Foster provide many examples. Social workers must also be familiar with new program initiatives that solve some of the legal and social system problems associated with the end of life. For example, there are a number of innovative programs to help people make decisions about advanced directives. One of the better known is in La Crosse, Wisconsin (Hammes 1999; Hammes and Briggs 2002). The efficacy of this initiative has been researched and found to be very effective in expanding the population of people who have advanced directives in this small midwestern community.

Part of this assessment is to recognize the need to expand social workers' knowledge and skill base. Part of the assessment is to identify learning opportunities that can provide the means of dealing with this new understanding. This learning also has to include how to build new alliances to accomplish their goals. Betsy Clark, executive director of the National Association of Social Workers, describes her vision for what social work involvement in end-of-life care will look like in the future. She is represented here because of her extensive experience in working with people at the ends of their lives. She also stands as a reminder that we have an organization behind us to help with out advocacy work, to facilitate developing our voices for change.

This work puts an enormous burden on the person who becomes involved in it. We are asking a great deal of our readers. We began the book with a piece of our personal odysseys as we moved into this field. We end it with Irene Renzenbrink's personal story, which began as she grew from a young social worker in Australia. She soon learned the importance of being mindful of her own needs and what was needed in a helping system to sustain the helpers. She reviews the literature on self-care and the various labels that are being used for what she calls the need for relentless self-care. Renzenbrink teaches us the importance of what she has learned from the colleagues with whom she worked in Ireland: Mind yourself! And it is with these words that we end the book.

REFERENCES

Ferris, F. D., M. M. Balfour, K. Bowen, et al. 2002. *A Model to Guide Hospice and Palliative Care: Based on National Principles, and Norms of Practice.* Ottawa: Canadian Palliative Care Association.

Goffman, E. 1962. *Asylums: Essays on the Social Situation of Mental Patients and Other Inmates.* Chicago: Aldine.

Hammes, B. J. 1999. The lessons from Respecting Your Choices: An Interview with Bernard J. Hammes. www.edc.org/lastacts/archives/archivesJan99/printfeatureinn1(1).pdf.

Hammes, B. J., and L. A. Briggs. 2002. *Respecting Choices: Advanced Care Planning Facilitators Manual.* La Crosse, WI: Gunderson Lutheran Medical Foundation.

37

CURRENT LEGAL ISSUES IN END-OF-LIFE CARE

STEPHEN ARONS

T
HIS CHAPTER explores some of the most significant current legal issues in end-of-life care by examining the legal status of advance directives and physician-assisted suicide in the United States. The purpose of this chapter is to assist the clinician in understanding, but also in influencing, the legal decisions that increasingly will circumscribe the work of end-of-life caregivers.

It is not surprising that the law should be as pervasive a presence in end-of-life decision making as it is for virtually every other life activity. It is a staple of socio-legal analysis to point out that 170 years ago, Alexis de Tocqueville observed about the United States that sooner or later every political question becomes a judicial question. De Tocqueville's comment was not entirely negative, for the judiciary, more than any other public institution, attempts to make decisions based on established general principles applied to the particular facts of specific human conflicts. Power politics is surely part of law even in the courts, but it is not its entirety. The law, to put it simply, is commanded to apply reason to the exercise of power. This requirement in itself provides some protection to those who have right, but not might, on their side.

The legalization that de Tocqueville observed grinds on; and it may seem that not only politics but also virtually every personal, family, and community decision—even those that affect how we die—will sooner or later become a legal question. This too may not be entirely negative, since invidious discrimination, the erosion of privacy, savage economic inequalities, a sometimes arrogant medical technology, and devastating distortions in the allocation of healthcare resources are all too common; and since we live in a culture with a public discourse historically committed to ignoring death and dying. The influence of law in decision making about end-of-life care may be both protective and harmful.

How, then, should the role of law in end-of-life care be evaluated? How should clinicians and other caregivers understand the legal issues and try to influence the legal reforms currently being advocated? It will help to have an understanding of the legal perspective itself. That is what this chapter hopes to introduce. Clinicians who then seek to evaluate or to influence the intersection of law and end-of-life care—like the patients and families whose stories they know so well—will be at an advantage in legal and public policy discussions by virtue of also having reflected deeply, both personally and professionally, on experiences with death.[1]

In this work, the question must inevitably arise whether law is too blunt an instrument—too insensitive to the nuances of human interaction and too categorical a reflection of individual realities—to be used with the same effectiveness in dying as it is in living. In the rest of life the law provides reasonably well for guidance, protection, clarification, the reasoned channeling of power, and the settling of disputes. In many areas of medical care, too, law has been the vehicle whereby important protections have been provided to patients. The rise of the doctrine of informed consent and the resulting improvement in the balance of power within the doctor/patient relationship is a good example. But in the dying process, perhaps law cannot make things easier for some without making them harder for others, cannot make things more humane without making them more economically painful, cannot make an end-of-life decision more manageable without making it more a distortion of the realities on which it is based.

We may some day come to the conclusion, individually and collectively, that there ought to be a wall of separation between the law and our dying, that in a matter so profoundly personal and so deeply embedded in our most important relationships, state and federal legal regulation of dying has no proper place except to protect privacy and to ensure equal access to healthcare resources.

But for now we are stuck. Statutes and cases affecting how we die are being put on the books of the law at a breakneck pace. Whether it is to protect the vulnerable, to escape or impose professional liability, to advance a deeply held religious or cultural belief, to manipulate public policy on behalf of an interest group, or simply to find a way to ease the suffering and rationalize the process of death, almost everyone has turned to the law. Advance directives, do-not-resuscitate orders, state and federal regulation of pain management, family consent statutes, guardianships, terminal sedation, physician-assisted suicide—all are signposts along the road to the legalization of dying.

Fundamental ethical and cultural issues lie at the heart of legal interventions. They concern how we understand the human condition and how we constitute the individual's relationship to society. Sorting out these issues therefore requires that we take account of the legal principles of privacy and individual autonomy, and set them in the context of our basic constitutional assumptions about how courts should determine the legitimacy of state policies and the proper reach of legislative power. Legal struggles over end-of-life care appear to be grand conflicts of principle, but they also concern the mundane daily realities of individuals and their families who face dying. Together they take practical shape in advance directives, the regulation and practice of pain management, the legal status of physician-assisted suicide, and the potential "right to palliative care."

By looking at a few court cases and several reform proposals about these practical issues, we will examine the legal perspective and the way that its development in the next few years might affect end-of-life decision making in the United States. By exploring the current issues and forward edges of law's development, the discussion that follows may also help in evaluating the appropriateness and effectiveness of the law's burgeoning involvement in dying. In thinking about the role and effectiveness of law, it should be remembered that although it is the legal perspective that is being explicated here, the importance of legal doctrine lies primarily in the effects that it has upon all of those involved in end-of-life care decisions. What follows might therefore be read as a social worker's introduction to advocacy in the realm of the law and public policy of end-of-life care.

The next section of this chapter deals with advance directives and the expressed preferences of some people simply to be allowed to die. Here the basic tenets of the right to refuse or withdraw unwanted medical treatment are the focus. How well do advance directives protect the right to refuse, and are these rights properly balanced against contrary policies and protections claimed by the state to be in the interest of society as a whole? Critiques of the current shape of advance directives are reviewed, as are some possible reforms arising from those critiques. The section that follows deals with physician-assisted suicide, the putative right to palliative care and the ambiguity of terminal sedation. Here the focus is not only on being allowed to die, but also on hastening or perhaps even causing death. These issues put the rights of individual autonomy and the interests of the state under closer scrutiny. They require consideration of institutionalized medical and economic pressures, the realities of racial and ethnic discrimination, and the problems of unequal distribution of health care.

ADVANCE DIRECTIVES: CHANGING THE FORM AND CHALLENGING THE PROCESS

The core idea of advance directives such as living wills and healthcare proxies is to honor the autonomy and dignity of the individual by making it possible for each legally competent person, in conjunction with family and physician if desired, to express preferences and make decisions about medical care in advance of being rendered unable to do so by disease or injury. Incompetent persons, those who have lost consciousness or are otherwise unable to make their own healthcare decisions, retain these rights by means of advance directives. The advance directive protects the rights of autonomy and privacy in part by trying to ensure that an individual's healthcare decisions are truly voluntary and are accurately understood by caregivers. But the system of advance directives developed over the past twenty-five years seems not to work very well for very many people.

One legal scholar reached the following "inescapable conclusion" after studying the use and misuse of advance directives: "In far too many instances, patients' last days or weeks (sometimes even months) are filled with unnecessary pain and suffering and take place in settings or in the midst of interventions that are antithetical to their values and wishes."[2] A justice of the Missouri Supreme Court put the matter in his own state even more pointedly in a dissent from the well-known *Cruzan v. Harmon* case: "The Missouri Living Will Act is a fraud on Missourians who believe we have been given a right to execute a living will, and to die naturally, respectably, and in peace."[3]

The autonomy principle, as it is sometimes called, underlies not only advance directives, but also the more general legal requirement that no person may be subjected to any medical treatment without first giving informed consent. When a patient is subjected to such unconsented medical treatment, the law treats it as it would most other personal injuries or torts. An intentional, unwanted "touching" of this type is called a battery. Under the law, any competent adult may legally refuse unwanted medical treatment or have it withdrawn even if that treatment is life-sustaining. Some courts and commentators have based these legal requirements on the liberty or privacy interests protected by the U.S. Constitution and by many state constitutions. Others find them in the common law principles that make any unwanted, intentional touching a personal injury, or battery.

Wherever their origins, the rise of the autonomy principle and of its more specific rights regarding informed consent and refusal of medical treatment at the end of life have had significant effects on the doctor/patient relationship within and outside of healthcare institutions.[4] Whether these effects amount to a needed balancing of power between doctor and patient, an unnecessary and harmful polarizing of that relationship, or just another factor to be taken into account when trying to establish a collaborative relationship, is the subject of considerable debate in law and health care.[5] This ongoing debate is reflected as well in the state statutes that seek to define and regulate advance directives, in the frustration felt by those who judge the current generation of advance directives to be inadequate, and in the daily work of social workers advocating for clients and families in end-of-life situations.

There are two basic forms of advance directives controlled by state statutes: living wills, which are written by a competent individual to control healthcare decisions in the event of incompetence; and healthcare proxies or agents (durable powers-of-attorney for health care) who are appointed by individuals to make healthcare decisions if the patient becomes incompetent. The appointment of a proxy is often accompanied by oral discussion or written instructions about a patient's values and preferences. In general, both these forms of advance directives can be used to control medical decisions for patients who are expected to recover as well as for those who are near the end of life.

For those people who do not execute either of these advance directives, many states also have family consent laws or healthcare surrogate acts and, sometimes using the concept of "substituted judgment," control who can make certain healthcare decisions for a non-competent patient.[6] The variation among the situations covered and the procedures used in state laws governing advance directives is substantial, as is the way that each state's courts interpret its statutes. Some states have both living wills and healthcare proxy statutes. Others have only one form.[7] Advance directives usually include a patient's preferences about the use of resuscitation and the refusal or withdrawal of life support. They cannot direct any physician or healthcare institution to assist in a suicide or actively participate in hastening death where the use or termination of life support is not at issue. This is true even in Oregon, where the Death with Dignity Act provides a separate and specific set of conditions and procedures only for *competent*, terminally ill persons to request a physician's help in hastening death.

On the national level, the federal Patient Self-Determination Act of 1990 applies to virtually all healthcare institutions (which receive federal funds such as Medicare and Medicaid).[8] It creates no advance directives, no rights to refuse treatment, and no other substantive protections for people facing end-of-life care decisions. The federal act simply requires that each institution advise each of its patients about the state's advance directive laws and options and about the patient's rights under the state's law. The institution must also advise patients of its own policies about these matters. Unlike healthcare institutions, individual physicians are not required by the act to advise their patients of state law on these issues. It is clear that social workers too should become familiar with the particular laws regulating end-of-life decision making in the states in which they practice. These state laws may have a significant and sometimes un-expected influence on the advising, advocacy, mediating, or team participation in which social workers engage.

THE PROBLEMS

Critics have identified a number of factors that contribute to problems with these advance directives.[9] First, there are restrictions in many advance directive statutes about what kinds of treatment can be controlled by the living will or decided upon by the healthcare proxy. For example, only thirty-three states include permanent un-consciousness in the definition of conditions that qualify as situations in which life-support can be refused or withdrawn by living will or proxy decision. Thirty-three states also require that the dying of a comatose, terminally ill, pregnant woman be extended regardless of decisions she may have made in an advance directive.[10] There are also thirty-eight states that permit institutions and individual healthcare providers to refuse to comply with an advance directive. In some states refusal to comply must be based on strongly held religious beliefs or moral convictions; while in others no particular reasons are required, leaving the door open to physicians or healthcare institutions to trump a patient's expressed desires with decisions based on reasons of institutional policy, fear of liability, or medical judgment. Many states that allow non-compliance with advance directives require that providers facilitate the transfer of a patient to another provider, though this option may be of little practical use if it does not arise until an end-of-life situation.

Second, many state statutes are ambiguous, leaving room for medical and family conflict, disregard for patients' wishes, extended suffering and litigation, and making the job of the social worker more difficult. For example, the term *terminal illness* as used in many of these statutes may not include permanent vegetative state, severe Alzheimer disease, AIDS, or other severely debilitating conditions when a patient may "live" for weeks, months, or years with the aid of life-support. There may also be debate as to whether "hydration and nutrition" is a treatment that can be refused or simply an obligation on the part of the healthcare institution to provide adequate food and water to all patients. The *Cruzan* case, however, may have resolved this issue by declaring that the provision of artificial nutrition and hydration is a treatment and can therefore be refused.

Restrictive or ambiguous definitions of "terminal illness or condition" are also sig-nificant for another reason. The majority of states provide that physicians or institu-tions complying with advance directives for terminally ill patients are statutorily re-lieved of professional and legal liability for doing so. This is an important protection as far as it goes. But liability protections for complying may be insufficient to get reluctant doctors or institutions to comply with an advance directive in the absence of some legal liability for not complying.

It should be noted that the appointment of a healthcare proxy is thought of by some as superior to a written living will, because the restrictions and ambiguities of language may be avoided. But there are other ambiguities and risks in the use of healthcare proxies. As social workers in this area know all too well, the surrogate may not know enough about the patient's values and wishes, or the surrogate may unconsciously substitute his or her own values for those of the patient. There may be conflict between the surrogate and family members, or among family members, or with the attending physician. There may be problems of insufficient resources for certain kinds of care, or of emotional inability to cope with decision making about another's death. The emotional toll, feelings of guilt, or ambivalence experienced by surrogates who knowledgeably carry out a patient's will to the letter and with the agreement of all the family and physicians may be very great. All this may discourage the use of advance directives or contribute to their reputation as ineffective.

For both the living will and the healthcare proxy, the question also arises of whether it is ever possible to know well enough what a patient does or would want at the end of life. One way of reducing this problem is through the so-called values history as an adjunct to a living will or proxy appointment. It allows a person to express basic desires, fears, and general life values that would be of assistance in interpreting advance directives or in making end-of-life care decisions. The values history is not much in use, even among the minority of Americans who do create advance directives.[11] In part, this may be because people usually cannot predict how they will feel when faced with the termination of life. Working with an experienced social worker in preparing a values history might be helpful to a healthy person who is preparing an advance directive.

Third, these statutes may actually mislead individuals into believing that they have no rights to refuse treatment except those that are provided by the state statute itself. The right to refuse treatment clearly exists in common law and is arguably a substantive right held by individuals under the federal constitution, not simply a creation of state statutes. Thus a patient or doctor or institution may be misled if they think, for example, that certain life-support measures may not be refused or terminated unless power to do so is specifically granted in the state statute. Equally problematic may be the belief that only the strict standard of "clear and convincing evidence" can justify a refusal of life support under an advance directive. In fact, the patient or the proxy may be constitutionally entitled to have the advance directive carried out with a lesser degree of proof as to the non-competent patient's intentions.[12] The general question therefore arises as to whether some advance directive statutes, rather than advancing the principle of autonomy, may, in fact, unconstitutionally restrict autonomy and prolong the suffering of patients and their families.

Fourth, various "state interests" may be aligned against effectuating the autonomy of patients as expressed in advance directives. The legal term *state interest* simply refers to public policies that a state may legitimately adopt for the benefit of society as a whole. When such policies run counter to the interests or rights of individual patients, courts must use the Constitution to balance the two in some way. There are typically four categories of such state interests that are taken into account by courts in deciding conflicts over advance directives:

1. *Preservation of the sanctity of life* is a state interest that may be invoked as part of an effort to be sure that the intent of an advance directive is accurately perceived and is not overridden by a self-interested, overzealous, or insensitive surrogate, institution, or provider. The preservation of life argument also may be used simply to undermine individual autonomy—as it has been in the reproductive freedom cases—and to create a presumption in favor of medical treatment and the extension of dying in all cases.

2. *Maintenance of the ethical integrity of the medical profession* (EIMP) is a state interest based on the idea that public trust and the integrity of the doctor/patient relationship depend on the view that doctors are ethical only when they try to extend life, whatever the cost in suffering or indignity.[13] Following a patient's wish to be relieved of suffering by hastening an inevitable and imminent death is therefore regarded as medically unethical and a threat to the core ethics of the healthcare system as a whole and to the public image of doctors. This state interest may be based in part on the cultural belief that the death of a patient is a medical failure.

3. *The protection of innocent third parties* is a state interest that focuses on preserving the fetuses of dying pregnant women, or on extending the life of a patient whose wish to be allowed to die would leave a child without a parent or a family or without a loved one. The latter argument is not often made; the former—that a pregnant woman should be kept on life support in spite of an advance directive to the contrary—is found in many advance directive statutes.[14] A variation of this state interest–the protection of vulnerable persons from undue family, economic, medical, or social pressures–is found in arguments over physician-assisted suicide (PAS). The argument is that PAS is dangerously discriminatory and perhaps legally unacceptable because it exposes the most vulnerable patients to economic or social pressures to end their lives prematurely. This argument is particularly important to consider in view of the fact that many minority groups and poor persons, often with good reason, are suspicious of social services, health care, and general laws that are based on scarcity of resources or on racial or other forms of discrimination.[15]

This same state commitment to protect the poor, the disabled, and minorities might also conceivably be brought to bear as an argument for highly restrictive advance directives. The argument here would be that particularly high standards of proof about a dying person's original intentions should be required as a condition of honoring an advance directive. It might even be argued that advance directives should not be available at all for refusal or termination of life support. Both of these arguments would be based on a recognition of the pressures that might be felt by healthcare surrogates in situations of scarce healthcare resources or by disfavored minorities or disabled persons when drawing up living wills. The irony should be lost on no one, that a loss of autonomy in end-of-life decision making could be justified on a claim of protecting those people who already suffer from a loss of autonomy as a result of discrimination, poverty, or disability.

4. *The prevention of suicide* is a state interest based on the idea that refusing life-

sustaining treatment amounts to suicide, and that a state may legitimately adopt policies aimed at discouraging suicide and at forbidding assistance in committing suicide. Some state advance directive statutes and court decisions that limit physician liability for following an advance directive also declare that the patient who has died as a result of the advance directive's being carried out has not committed suicide and has not been aided in so doing. Since depression may play a role in a patient's adopting or a surrogate's carrying out of an advance directive, a more subtle version of the state's interest in preventing suicide might also be brought to bear to hinder the withdrawal of life support via advance directive. But the concern over depression and its relationship to suicide appears predominantly in legal arguments over physician-assisted suicide requested by competent patients.[16]

Many commentators see some or all of these state interests as weak in comparison to the right to refuse treatment or as improperly applied to end-of-life care decisions. But some versions of these state interests have been recognized by the courts in various states, and the effectiveness of advance directives and the power of the principle of individual autonomy have therefore been reduced.[17] Whether such a result is appropriate or not is a matter of debate. In some jurisdictions the balancing of one or more of these state interests against the right to refuse treatment may create a legal presumption in favor of treatment, so that *any* ambiguity about a patient's intent or advance directive may be resolved in favor of continued life support even when the quality of life is virtually nonexistent.

Advance directives have been adopted by fewer than 25 percent of Americans, and even well-organized efforts to increase their use and to encourage physician involvement in their creation have failed terribly.[18] The nonuse of advance directives may be a reflection of the problems identified above, in that advance directives may seem to be more trouble than they are worth in the eyes of many people. But nonuse could also be a result of a combination of other factors that might find expression in law:

- That life-threatening illness breeds dependence and depression, and weakens the claim for patient autonomy, a development that many doctors may accede to because it makes end-of-life decisions less personal and more medical.
- That there is a technological imperative in medical care, which, in effect, dictates that whatever can be done to extend a life should be done regardless of its economic, personal, or other consequences for patients or their families.
- That litigation about advance directives is to be feared above almost anything else but death itself, and that healthcare institutions and physicians will therefore be extremely reluctant to carry out any advance directive that would hasten a patient's death even by a few hours.[19]
- That discrimination and the complexities of a multicultural society and the challenges faced by disabled persons make advance directives suspect in the minds of many people whose experience with the healthcare system is often negative.[20]

At bottom, the nonuse of advance directives may also reflect the clash of paradigms between law and medicine and other therapeutic professions.[21] One professional paradigm claims always to defer to the client's expressed self-interest. Lawyers can therefore justify their work as enhancing a client's autonomy by providing legal representation that is based on the client's own decisions even if the outcome of that representation is regarded as negative by others or by the entire society. The other professional paradigm, perhaps typical of physicians and therapists, claims to determine through the profession's expertise what is objectively in the best interest of the patient's health. Doctors then justify their work not as enhancing autonomy but as improving the patient's condition as judged by medical standards, even if the outcome of the treatment is otherwise regarded negatively by patient or family. These paradigms are, of course, extreme statements of positions that few individual practitioners of either profession subscribe to completely. Nevertheless, this polarizing conflict between one-sided views of how doctors and lawyers work and think may distort the doctor/patient relationship and make advance directives more conflict-oriented than they would otherwise be.[22] The effect of these conflicts on social workers acting as advocates, ombudspersons, or members of ethics committees can be substantial.

THE LEGAL REACTIONS

Most of the problems with existing advance directives, the statutes that regulate them, and the nonuse of advanced directives by most Americans are the stuff of daily work for end-of-life care social workers. These problems are also topics for the voluminous legal scholarship and advocacy activities that have grown up over the past two decades. Among the most interesting of these current issues and actions in the law of end-of-life care are (1) testing the constitutionality of state statutes that impose undue burdens on the right to refuse treatment, (2) finding ways to enforce advance directives, (3) ensuring that due process safeguards are followed so that surrogate decision making in the absence of advance directives does not result in abuse of dying persons, and (4) creating what Ben Rich has called a "new generation" of advance directives. For end-of-life care social workers to have the influence that they should have on law and public policy, a basic understanding of the issues discussed briefly and commented on below would seem useful.

1. The *constitutionality* of *state advance-directive statutes.* Some state laws that "create" the forms of advance directives restrict the circumstances under which those advance directives can be used. But restricting the right to refuse treatment—a right upon which all advance directives may be based—may not be constitutionally acceptable. The answer to the question of whether restrictive advance directive laws are constitutional depends on whether the right to refuse treatment itself can be found in the U.S. Constitution. The leading case on the matter does not resolve the constitutional question, but *Cruzan v. Director, Missouri Dept. of Health*[23] strongly suggests that the right to refuse is a fundamental liberty right guaranteed to each person by the U.S. Constitution.[24]

Of particular importance to the work of end-of-life caregivers was Justice O'Connor's statement in Cruzan that carrying out a patient-appointed surrogate's decision "may well be required to protect the patient's liberty interest in refusing medical treatment."

This suggests that a state might be constitutionally forbidden to block the carrying out of the wishes of an incompetent patient's duly appointed surrogate, regardless of restrictions in the state's advance directive law. To put the matter another way, a state law that completely blocks appropriately made end-of-life decisions involving such things as withdrawal of nutrition and hydration or other life support might *itself* be unconstitutional. Litigation establishing the right to refuse treatment as a part of the individual liberty secured by the Constitution, and challenging the many state restrictions on advance directives, might thus bring a sea change to the ambiguous and often frustrating ways that advance directive statutes intervene in end-of-life care.

2. *Enforcing advance directives.* Justice O'Connor's statement about the potential constitutional obligation of a state not to unreasonably restrict or totally block advance directives has implications for enforcing advance directives when healthcare institutions or physicians are reluctant to carry them out because of state law or private conscience. But when such reluctance is based on a physician's or institution's medical judgment or personal disagreement with the patient, liability actions may be an effective way to encourage or compel the carrying out of advance directives.[25]

In a 1994 Michigan jury trial, a comatose woman who was put on life support in clear contravention of her advance directive recovered a substantial damage award from the hospital that had refused to honor the proxy's insistence on carrying out the patient's earlier expressed wishes. The patient later regained consciousness with severe brain damage. The proxy (the patient's mother and caregiver after discharge) sued the hospital for damages based on medical expenses and emotional harm arising after the patient's partial recovery, and for the injury suffered by the patient as a result of the unwanted medical treatment (referred to as the intentional tort of "battery"). The verdict in the Michigan case was challenged by the hospital, reviewed by the trial court, and the case eventually was settled after further negotiation.[26] But the trial court did rule that refusal to follow an advance directive and the consequent imposing of unwanted medical treatment did constitute a battery for which damages could be awarded. The case was not appealed, but it does suggest that personal injury legal actions may be available to enforce advance directives by holding liable those medical personnel who refuse to carry out an advance directive.[27]

In a related area, inadequate end-of-life pain management may be provided by a doctor or healthcare facility that fears that such pain relief might hasten the patient's death.[28] Even if there is no advance directive at issue or if the patient remains fully competent, the reluctance to treat pain adequately is an end-of-life problem of enormous magnitude that may be dealt with in part by legal action. A number of states have adopted legislation regulating, authorizing, or providing guidelines for the prescription of controlled substances for pain relief. In a few instances these laws include "safe harbor" provisions that protect doctors from liability if their prescription of adequate pain medication results in hastening a terminally ill patient's death, so-called double-effect euthanasia. The Bush administration appears to be working to defeat these provisions, a matter discussed in the next section of this chapter.

Even with these statutes, and because of the historic reluctance of the medical profession to adequately deal with pain, litigation similar to that being explored for enforcing advance directives may begin to emerge in the pain management area. An example is the 2001 California case *Bergman v. Eden Medical Center*, in which the family of a man dying from lung cancer and suffering excruciating pain sued under the law of "elder abuse" for grossly inadequate pain management. The patient's physician had provided virtually no pain medication while the patient was in the hospital, ostensibly because to do so would kill the patient. He discharged him five days after admitting him. The patient died a few days after discharge, and his family won a $1.5 million jury award based an elder abuse law claim that the doctor's conduct was reckless rather than merely negligent as would be required under malpractice law.[29]

3. *Improving due process guarantees.* Improving the carefulness and fairness that are required by law in making end-of-life care decisions will protect incompetent patients against abuse, with or without advance directives. Using appropriate hospital procedures to guard against abuse of patients by surrogates in the absence of advance directives was at the core of a Washington state case involving the withdrawal of a feeding tube. The patient had suffered a stoke at age thirty-seven and two years later remained severely disabled, with very limited ability to communicate through eye blinks and an eye-gaze board. There was conflicting evidence about whether or how much cognitive function he retained. The patient's father and sister, who had been appointed temporary guardians by the state, decided as surrogates that the patient's life support—a feeding tube implanted in his stomach—should be removed. After a meeting of the hospital's Ethics Committee and a neurologist's examination, permission was given and the tube was removed. Upon receiving written notice of the removal a day later, the patient's former wife, who had made regular visits to him in the hospital, came to visit him. She claimed to have communicated with him and to have learned that he did not want life support removed. A nurse's note in the medical record indicated something similar. In spite of this information having been given to the doctor and hospital staff, the tube was not reinserted for five days, and only then upon temporary court order. The patient was neither terminally ill nor permanently unconscious; and he had made no advance directive or any other indication, before or since his illness, of a desire to have life support terminated.

The ex-wife brought a tort action on his behalf against the medical providers. She sought a pre-trial ruling that additional due process requirements, established by the Washington Supreme Court for removal of feeding and hydration tubes from incompetent patients without advance directives, were required above and beyond the Ethics Committee's review. The trial court denied this motion. It ruled that the Washington Supreme Court's guidelines that a patient be found either terminally ill and incurable or permanently unconscious before a surrogate's decision could be effectuated *without a prior court hearing* did not apply to this case. The patient died before this ruling could be appealed.[30]

The case is significant because it illustrates the very real difficulties for even well-meaning surrogates and medical personnel trying to ascertain what an incompetent or marginally competent patient's desires would have been. This is especially important when there is no advance directive in place and there has been no discussion about the issue with the patient at any time. The case also illustrates both the importance and the difficulties of putting in place due process legal protections when end-of-life decisions are being made in the absence of reliable information about the patient's intentions or values. The Washington Supreme Court had generally required that court hearings, *or* reliable medical evidence of terminal illness or permanent unconsciousness, be provided before a surrogate's decision to terminate life support could be carried out. But in this particular case, these due process requirements were not followed, and various family members were left in doubt and conflict that compounded their grief.

There is, however, a further problem with due process guarantees and the legal proceedings that are sometimes necessary to enforce them. They take time, time that may be filled with suffering and grief. Due process protections should be balanced and favor neither the continuation nor the removal of life support; and they should not be cumbersome. Otherwise, situations like that in the Washington case may become more frequent, resulting in unnecessary anguish for everyone involved. Fortunately, it does not usually take very many successful lawsuits to change the behavior of institutions or caregivers.

Most cases discussed in the legal literature address advance directives that are ignored or undermined by medical providers or that are limited by state statutes. In such situations most observers believe that the courts should provide some enforcement mechanism or incentive for honoring the advance directive or patient intent. But as the Washington case above illustrates, it would seem to be equally important that the law defend patient autonomy by ensuring that great care is taken when a surrogate chooses termination of life support in the absence of reliable knowledge about the patient's views.

4. *Creating a new generation of advance directives.* This is perhaps the most direct and nonconfrontational method of reforming the limitations imposed by statute or created by the other shortcomings of advance directives. Although most of the preceding cases would benefit from social worker input, creating a new form of advance directive is one area in which the views and advocacy experience of end-of-life social workers could be most helpful. In supporting one new generation advance directive, the "medical directive," Ben Rich reached the following conclusion about the failure of first generation directives: "The next generation of advance directives will succeed where the others have failed. They will do so, in significant part, because they remedy the fatal flaw of the earlier versions—removal of the physician from a fundamental aspect of the professional relationship, which is to provide guidance, counsel, and moral support in planning for care at the end of life."[31]

The medical directive itself is based on the work of two physicians in 1989; and as analyzed by Rich, it combines the living will, the healthcare proxy, and the values history—all created cooperatively by patient and doctor prior to any need to use it. It would work like this. Physician and patient would together discuss and fill out the medical directive, which includes a kind of chart on which appear a half dozen medical situations ranging from the most dire to one's that most people would regard with ambivalence. Along the second axis of the chart would be a number of medical interventions. By discussing each scenario and intervention, the physician is able to learn of and help the patient formulate reactions to specific groups of possibilities. There is room to indicate where the patient feels ambivalent; and the whole process is complemented by the taking of some kind of values history (which may wholly or in part be completed by the patient at home with family members) in which the patient tries to provide more general and basic information about his or her attitudes or views about life, illness, independence, pain, mental abilities, medical treatment, and burdens on the family. The involvement of social workers with this process, while not mentioned specifically by Rich, might be helpful to the patient and to the physician, and might even make it more likely that medical directives would be drawn up in the first place.

Two things make the medical directive particularly significant legally. First, the entire document becomes part of the patient's medical record, providing thereby a deep, detailed, and comprehensive expression of the patient's views about end-of-life care that would be likely to be regarded by virtually any proxy, court, or medical care provider as clear and convincing evidence. Second, since the document is the product of a process in which the physician is extensively and cooperatively involved, it is unlikely that the physician would misunderstand, distort, or refuse to follow it. It should also be noted that if the physician discovers in the process of creating the medical directive that he or she would be uncomfortable carrying out the patient's wishes, the patient can seek another medical care provider well before there is need to use the directive.[32]

The medical directive is not without significant problems, however. It does not address the problem of patients' not knowing or being able to predict their wishes when confronted with the reality and finality of death. Nor does it address patient ambivalence. It is also worth asking whether it is realistic, in a world dominated by managed care and restricted Medicare benefits, that a physician would be able to take this kind of time with a patient, even with the aid of a social worker. Finally, it is possible that some physicians or healthcare institutions may, whether intentionally or just as a result of a clash between the culture of medicine and the culture of the patient, unduly influence a patient's decision making.

Because the medical directive constructively addresses so many of the legal limitations and so much of the medical and individual resistance to the use of advance directives, some version of it seems likely to move to the forefront of policy advocacy or legislative attempts to improve the way that law intervenes in end-of-life care. Moreover, since advance directives arguably involve letting patients die rather than causing them to die, strong resistance to improving their effectiveness is not likely. Still, for all four legal strategies mentioned above, there is a long way to go; and in the near future advance directives seem likely to remain limited in use and effectiveness.

THE MORE ASSERTIVE PATH: PHYSICIAN-ASSISTED SUICIDE, THE RIGHT TO PALLIATIVE CARE, AND TERMINAL SEDATION

The other major category of end-of-life care legal issues is physician-assisted suicide (PAS). The differences between advance directives and physician-assisted suicide are at once comforting and confusing, for as Yale Kamisar has stated in arguing for advance directives and against PAS: "When we must make tragic choices—choices that confront us when fundamental beliefs clash—we seek solutions that 'permit us to assert that we are cleaving to both beliefs in conflict.' As good an example as any is the way we have dealt with the law and ethics of death and dying. On the one hand, we want to respect patient's wishes, relieve suffering, and put an end to seemingly futile medical treatment. (Hence the right to refuse life-sustaining treatment.) On the other hand, we want to affirm the supreme value of life and to maintain the salutary principle that the law protects all human life, no matter how poor its quality. (Hence the ban against assisted suicide and active euthanasia.)"[33]

In 1997, the U.S. Supreme Court unanimously ruled in two cases that states *may* criminalize physician-assisted suicide without infringing on the constitutional rights of terminally ill patients who voluntarily request it. The ruling is closer to the beginning of the public and legal debate over PAS than it is to the resolution of that debate. It leaves open a number of issues of individual autonomy, state interests, the doctor/patient relationship, and patient abuse about which clinicians should be aware.

In order to understand the current legal issues related to PAS, it is useful first to review the 1990 Supreme Court case dealing with the withdrawal of life-sustaining treatment, *Cruzan v. Director, Missouri Dept. of Health.*[34] As a result of an automobile accident, Nancy Cruzan had been in a persistent, irreversible vegetative state for some time. Her parents, who were her co-guardians, sought to have her artificial feeding and hydration tube withdrawn so that she might be allowed to die from her injuries. According to her doctors, with the aid of life support Ms. Cruzan might have remained in a persistent vegetative state for another thirty to forty years. In this particular case, the enormous yearly expense of maintaining a person in a permanent vegetative state was born by the state of Missouri. The hospital refused to comply with the guardian parents' request without a court's permission. A court hearing ensued at which it was determined that although Ms. Cruzan had never written a living will or formally designated a healthcare proxy, there was sufficient evidence of her beliefs and desires from previous conversations with friends to justify withdrawing life-support legally.

The Missouri Attorney General appealed the decision. The state Supreme Court overruled the trial court, declaring that the state's interest in preserving life required "clear and convincing evidence" of Cruzan's wishes, and determining that such evidence had not been provided at trial. The trial court, in other words, had used a less demanding standard of proof than the state's highest court interpreted Missouri law to require. The case was then appealed to the U.S. Supreme Court, which ruled 5–4 that Missouri's policy of preserving life permitted it to impose upon Cruzan's parents the heavy burden of demonstrating "clear and convincing" evidence of Nancy's desire to exercise her right to withdraw life-sustaining medical treatment.

The Supreme Court acknowledged, at least for purposes of this case, that an individual has a constitutional, liberty-based right to refuse or withdraw unwanted medical treatment. The Court also acknowledged artificial nutrition and hydration to be a form of medical treatment. The Court made no distinction between competent and incompetent persons in recognizing this right to refuse medical treatment; thereby ruling, in effect, that with sufficient evidence of a patient's intentions while competent (in a living will or as presented by a surrogate), life support could legally be withdrawn from an incompetent patient.

The irony in this ruling was that Missouri's advance directive statute does not permit the use of living wills to terminate artificial nutrition and hydration.[35] In effect, therefore, the Court's ruling meant that (1) an individual's constitutional right to refuse treatment could be outweighed by a state's interest in preserving life unless the evidence of the individual's intention was overwhelmingly strong, and (2) there was almost no way to provide such overwhelmingly strong evidence, since Missouri's living will is unavailable for this purpose and the clear and convincing standard is so difficult for any surrogate to meet. Therefore, although the Court suggests that a constitutional right to refuse treatment might exist and could include the withdrawal of life support, the Court's majority reached a legal conclusion that Missouri state law would permit virtually no family to terminate life support for a patient in a permanent vegetative state because clear and convincing evidence is so difficult to provide. The result of *Cruzan* if applied to other states considering how to regulate termination of life support would be that—unlike in the abortion area—states would be left virtually on their own to decide how much more difficult the law would make it for individuals, families and caregivers to reach what many Americans regard as highly personal and private decisions.[36]

The *Cruzan* decision also shows how ideological or religious commitments can overwhelm the difficult, nuanced, and intimately personal decisions of end-of-life care. The Supreme Court required clear and convincing evidence of Ms. Cruzan's desire to *terminate* life support. The Supreme Court did not require clear and convincing evidence of Nancy's desire to be *sustained* in a vegetative state for years on life support. The four dissenting justices therefore pointed out that the Court's majority seemed more interested in establishing a right-to-life principle in law than in ensuring the *accuracy* of any decision about maintaining or withdrawing life support from an incompetent patient.[37] The importance of ideology over accuracy is further seen in the fact that after a second hearing on the Cruzans' request, the trial court decided that clear and convincing evidence was, in fact, presented. After hearing very little more evidence than it had heard at the first hearing, the trial court applied the clear and convincing standard of proof and authorized the removal of the feeding tube from Nancy Cruzan.

There was no appeal by the state. After years in which the Cruzan family's anguish was broadcast over the public megaphone of law and made into the subject of almost endless media attention and public debate, Ms. Cruzan eventually died. Several years later her father committed suicide, perhaps suggesting how painful it can be for families and caregivers when ultimately personal struggles are transformed into the stuff of ideological warfare.

THE CONSTITUTIONAL BACKGROUND

The two landmark cases dealing with physician-assisted suicide that came before the Supreme Court in 1997 are built in part on the ruling in *Cruzan*, and perhaps they continue the reign of categorical demands over personal problem solving. The first case, *Compassion in Dying v. Washington*, sought to establish a constitutional right for competent, terminally ill patients to voluntarily request and receive a willing physician's assistance in hastening death and making it more peaceful and dignified. The case was brought in the form of a claim that the Washington state statute criminalizing any form of encouraging or assisting suicide was unconstitutional insofar as it violated the asserted right of terminally ill patients to physician-assisted suicide. When the full U.S. Court of Appeals for the Ninth Circuit ruled on the case, it found the statute unconstitutional because an individual has a constitutional, liberty-based interest "in controlling the time and manner of one's death" which is not overcome by any of the state's legitimate interests.[38]

Judge Reinhart's majority opinion in the *Compassion in Dying* case rests on both *Cruzan* and the 1992 abortion case, *Planned Parenthood v. Casey*. He quoted *Casey's* description of liberty interests in general as involving "making the most intimate and personal choices a person may make in a lifetime, choices central to personal dignity and autonomy. . . . At the heart of liberty is the right to define one's own concept of existence, of meaning, of the universe and of the mystery of human life." Reinhart concluded "that *Cruzan*, by recognizing a liberty interest that includes the refusal of artificial provision of life-sustaining food and water, necessarily recognizes a liberty interest in hastening one's own death."

Reinhart then balanced this liberty interest against several state interests put forward by Washington in defense of its law criminalizing assisted suicide. He examined the state's interest in preserving life; preventing suicide; precluding the use of arbitrary, unfair, or undue influence on dying persons; protecting family members and loved ones; and maintaining the integrity of the medical profession.

After analyzing each interest carefully, Reinhart concluded that in the case of the Washington statute, each state interest was outweighed by the liberty rights of competent, terminally ill persons to control the time and manner of their own imminent death with a physician's assistance. The Reinhart opinion notes that a number of the state interests that were advanced to justify criminalizing PAS were the same ones discredited by the Supreme Court in the reproductive freedom cases. In considering the problem of undue influence on the elderly, the poor, the disabled, and minorities, Reinhart suggested that these persons might be as likely to be abused by the present system of inadequate medical care in general and end-of-life care in particular as they would be under a system of regulated physician-assisted suicide. He also noted that under the present healthcare system doctors already practice a covert form of voluntary physician-assisted suicide, primarily for well-to-do persons.

Reinhart also discussed the difference between persons on and off life support in their ability to gain a physician's help in dying, the intent of physicians when they prescribe pain medication that they know may also hasten death, and whether the cause of death for someone receiving a physician's assistance in dying is the doctor's action or the underlying disease or injury. Judge Beezer's dissent, reaching the conclusion that Washington's law criminalizing PAS should have been found to be constitutional by the court, is as thorough and articulate as the majority opinion. In fact,

Beezer's view ultimate prevailed in the case. The Circuit Court ruling in *Compassion in Dying*, that Washington's anti-PAS law violated the U.S. Constitution, was appealed. When the case reached the U.S. Supreme Court as *Washington v. Glucksberg*, Judge Reinhart's ruling was overturned.

The second case, *Quill v. Vacco*,[39] arose in New York, and was based on an equal protection claim. In *Quill*, the federal court of appeals in New York struck down a New York law similar to the Washington law invalidated in *Compassion in Dying*. The gist of the claim was that New York's ban on physician-assisted suicide treated differently two groups of patients who were in fact the same. Plaintiffs argued that those competent, terminally ill patients who were on life support had a right under New York and constitutional law to forgo or withdraw unwanted medical treatment and thereby to have a doctor's assistance in hastening their inevitable death. At the same time, the plaintiffs claimed that New York law prevented equally sick, competent, terminally ill patients who were not candidates for life-support from receiving the assistance of their doctors in hastening and making more peaceful their deaths (through self-administering prescribed drugs). The Second Circuit Court of Appeals agreed that under these circumstances withdrawal of life support and physician-assisted suicide were essentially the same thing, and struck down the New York statute as a violation of the Equal Protection Clause of the Fourteenth Amendment. The different but related claims of *Quill v. Vacco* and *Washington v. Glucksberg* (originally *Compassion in Dying v. Washington*) were ruled on together by the Supreme Court in 1997.

The Supreme Court unanimously reversed the two courts of appeals and upheld the laws criminalizing physician-assisted suicide in both New York and Washington State. The high court distinguished *Cruzan* as being a right-to-refuse-treatment case without implications for physician-assisted suicide. It distinguished *Casey*, the reproductive freedom case, as concerning a fundamental right that historically and constitutionally did not encompass a "right to die" simply because both procreation and dying are highly personal and important. The Court was therefore unwilling either to find or to create a constitutional liberty interest in "determining the time and manner of one's death." It ruled that there is no fundamental constitutional right to die.

Because the Court found no fundamental right to die in *Washington v. Glucksberg*, the state had only to show that under prevailing constitutional doctrine the challenged statute was "reasonably related to important and legitimate state interests." To put it another way, in order to justify its statute's constitutionality the state did not have to meet the much tougher test of showing that its interests were "compelling" and that its statute was necessary to achieve those interests. The Court's refusal to find the kind of fundamental constitutional right that Judge Reinhart's Appeals Court opinion had recognized was pivotal.

Having concluded that the state interests advanced had only to be rational, it became unnecessary for the Supreme Court to go into the same detail in analyzing the state interests as Reinhart had done. The high court therefore mentioned the preservation of human life, maintaining the ethics of the medical profession, and protecting vulnerable groups only briefly for the purpose of showing that they are important and legitimate. Chief Justice Rehnquist's opinion, citing what he saw as the experience of the Netherlands, also noted that a state may reasonably fear that permitting physician-assisted suicide will start it down the "slippery slope" to voluntary and perhaps eventually to involuntary euthanasia.

In the companion *Quill* case, the Supreme Court also found that there *is* a meaningful distinction between persons who are candidates for life support and those who are not. New York law could therefore treat the two groups differently without violating the principle of equal protection of the law. As Chief Justice Rehnquist put it, "when a patient refuses life-sustaining medical treatment, he dies from an underlying fatal disease or pathology; but if a patient ingests lethal medication prescribed by a physician, he is killed by that medication. . . . [Referring to *Cruzan*] our assumption of a right to refuse treatment was grounded not . . . on the proposition that patients have a general and abstract 'right to hasten death' . . . but on well established, traditional rights to bodily integrity and freedom from unwanted touching."[40]

The Court's decisions against physician-assisted suicide in both *Glucksberg* and *Quill* were unanimous; but the unanimity thinly masked a wide divergence in the thinking of the justices and opened up more legal and policy issues about end-of-life care than it resolved. There were five opinions from the nine-member Court. The members of the Court did agree on four principles: that they are unwilling to find a general right to assisted suicide in the Constitution, that the distinction between withdrawing life support and physician-assisted suicide is reasonable, that perhaps a future case might establish that the dying are entitled to adequate pain relief and palliative care, and that it is more appropriate for individual states to debate and make policy about physician-assisted suicide than for the Supreme Court to impose a single, constitutionally based view upon the nation. Perhaps thinking about the political and legal firestorm that its 1972 abortion decision had ignited, the Court's opinion ended by stating, "Throughout the Nation, Americans are engaged in an earnest and profound debate about the morality, legality, and practicality of physician-assisted suicide. Our holding permits this debate to continue, as it should in a democratic society."[41]

This last point is particularly important in view of the existence of Oregon's Death with Dignity Act. Passed by initiative in 1994 and reaffirmed in 1997, the Oregon statute permits physician-assisted suicide under certain specified conditions created with the intent of minimizing or eliminating many of the potential abuses that concern both the proponents and opponents of assisted suicide. The Oregon law allows physicians to prescribe a lethal medication for self-administration if requested by a competent, terminally ill patient who has been referred to counseling if the physician believes he or she suffers from depression or other mental impairment.[42] Two physicians must concur in the terminal illness diagnosis (less than six months to live); no physician may directly act to terminate a patient's life; no lethal prescription may be written until the patient is no longer suffering from any serious mental disorder; the patient must voluntarily request the physician's assistance twice verbally at least fifteen days before a prescription is written and once in writing at least forty-eight hours in advance; neither age nor disability qualify in themselves as terminal illness for purposes of the act.[43]

CURRENT ISSUES

As a result of the Supreme Court's clear ruling and ambivalent opinions in the *Glucks-berg* and *Quill* cases, a number of legal and policy issues related to physician-assisted suicide remain very much open to public debate, to further legal action, and to additional input from clinicians and other providers or beneficiaries of end-of-life care.[44] Taking up these issues, *Compassion in Dying*, which brought the *Glucksberg* case and is one of the foremost advocacy organizations working on end-of-life issues, has pursued a litigation strategy to complement its other work. One element of this strategy is based on a claim that state constitutional rights to PAS may exist even if a federal right does not. The first use of this strategy suffered a loss in 2001, when Alaska's Supreme Court ruled that the complex and difficult issues of PAS are "quintessentially a legislative matter."

Compassion in Dying has also pursued cases aimed at showing that the provision of adequate due process protections in any end-of-life decision-making process can prevent the abuse of the most vulnerable patients and families. If this can be demonstrated in situations involving advance directives and surrogate decision making, then due process guarantees may also alleviate some of the concerns raised about legislative or constitutional approval of laws permitting PAS. A third prong of the litigation and advocacy strategy being pursued around the country seeks to ensure that adequate pain management[45] is provided in end-of-life situations. It is in this area of law and policy that an issue of enormous magnitude has been joined.

In November 2001, the U.S. Attorney General issued an order declaring that physicians who prescribe pain medication with the intent of hastening the death of a patient will be subject to losing their licenses to prescribe substances listed in the federal Controlled Substances Act. Attorney General Ashcroft's action was an attempt to undermine or eliminate the Oregon "Death with Dignity Act," which provides a controlled environment in which physician-assisted suicide is available. But in addition to overturning, by federal fiat, a law duly enacted by the citizens of Oregon, Ashcroft's ruling could also inhibit the ability of doctors anywhere in the United States to prescribe adequate pain medication for terminally ill patients. Regulating the practice of medicine is a matter for individual states; and the federal claim of power to revoke a doctor's license to prescribe pain medication if the U.S. Attorney General disapproves of a doctor's motive for doing so, threatens the practice of medicine with a witch hunt.

Oregon challenged Ashcroft's order immediately in federal district court, where in April 2002, U.S. District Court Judge Robert Jones issued a permanent injunction against enforcement of the Ashcroft order. The court ruled that the Justice Department had exceeded its authority under the Controlled Substances Act by attempting to regulate the practice of medicine in Oregon. The Bush administration appealed Judge Jones's decision to the Ninth Circuit Court of Appeals. Briefs had been filed, but no date for the hearing had been set at this writing.

The case does not raise constitutional issues as Judge Jones decided it. But the Ashcroft order does threaten to overturn a legally adopted state law, and it may thereby run counter to the part of the U.S. Supreme Court's ruling in the *Glucksberg* and *Quill* cases that says that physician-assisted suicide is a matter to be determined by the voters or legislators of each state. In addition, whether one supports or opposes PAS, a greater concern to the provision of adequate end-of-life care is the chilling effect that Ashcroft's order, if upheld on appeal, might have upon the practice of medicine and the adequacy of pain management nationwide. Issues of pain management may be overwhelmed by the tactics adopted by the federal government to kill off legally regulated physician-assisted suicide. In fact, all the issues of end-of-life care may be lost in a continuation of the great culture war over reproductive freedom.

The actions of the federal government and the responses to it from around the country demonstrate the problems inherent in turning sensitive individual and family decisions about end-of-life issues into national political and ideological battles. A look at the *amicus* (friend of the court) briefs filed in *Oregon v. Ashcroft* makes the point.[46] Supporting the State of Oregon are not only patients and families whose end-of-life decisions would fall under the control of the federal government and whose deaths might be needlessly painful. A number of statewide organizations of physicians, such as the California Medical Association, which opposes PAS but sees the threat to medical practice in the Ashcroft order, have filed briefs. So, too, have statewide physicians' groups in New York and Washington, the American Academy of Pain Management, the American Geriatric Society, and several AIDS organizations. Groups supporting the Ashcroft order include the U.S. Conference of Catholic Bishops and a number of right-to-life and anti-abortion groups.

In the end, *Oregon v. Ashcroft* may wind up before the U.S. Supreme Court. If it does, it will be because the order does raise an important constitutional issue. That issue is likely to be the same one that the Justices only speculated about in the *Glucksberg* and *Quill* cases—whether a terminally ill person is entitled to adequate pain relief and other palliative care in the last weeks or days of life. If the matter does take this shape, it will be of crucial importance that social workers and other end-of-life caregivers bring their experience and wisdom to bear on the debate that will accompany the case.

Other unresolved end-of-life care issues of ongoing importance include:

1. *Right to palliative care.* A number of commentators have read the *Glucksberg* opinions to suggest that at some future point the Court might be amenable to finding a constitutional right to adequate palliative care. On the other hand, it has been argued that the Court's failure to adequately explore the clinical implications of its reasoning in the *Glucksberg* case—coupled with the relative lack of enforcement of legal restrictions on other forms of end-of-life conduct—means that the "the impact of the Court's decisions remains primarily in the hands of clinicians, patients, and families."[47]

If a right to palliative care came into being, it might be by a Supreme Court pronouncement or by legislative enactment. But in fashioning such a right, whether by legislative enactment or by constitutional litigation, decision makers would face questions about what specific provisions palliative care might include. There seems to be little argument about the importance of pain management and comfort care, and the availability of hospice care would seem to be essential even though its cost may be substantial.[48] A right to palliative care might also include the availability of terminal sedation; though that might raise the specter of misunderstanding patient wishes and of involuntary application. It has been suggested that abuse of patients might be a problem in terminal sedation to a greater degree than in PAS.[49]

Another important element of the right to palliative care might be a set of protections for the integrity of the doctor/patient relationship at the end of life, so that end-of-life care decisions reached fairly by doctor and patient would not be subject to extensive outside scrutiny in medicine, law, or politics. This might be especially important in view of the complexity and relational nature of end-of-life decisions. Finally, it must be kept in mind that an enormous part of the nation's healthcare expenses are attributable to the last six months of life, and that these resources are unevenly distributed largely on the basis of economic status. Taken together, these facts suggest that a right to palliative care that does not suffer from the same limitations and risks of abuse that both PAS and current end-of-life practices create, would not be easy to establish.

An economically equitable and generally available system of palliative care might in effect, though not in design, include the option of physician-assisted suicide in individual cases. This is already the covert case under the current healthcare system for individuals who have substantial resources and long-term relationships with their physicians. But removing the fundamental issues of PAS from direct constitutional or public policy debate and placing them beneath the surface of an agreed-upon need for universal palliative care might not be possible. The establishment of a right to palliative care might seem the most appealing of the legal strategies after *Glucksberg*; but many advocates on both sides believe that a more direct and open approach to PAS would be preferable. The danger is that in our desire to settle once and for all the unsettling ethical and legal issues of PAS, we may lose our best opportunity to create a practical and effective improvement in end-of-life care for everyone.

2. *Double-effect pain medication.* Part of the argument for approving PAS has been that it is already practiced covertly, primarily for people with access to the best medical care, through the prescribing of pain relief medication in doses so large that they may very well not only ease the pain of a dying person but also accelerate the dying. Should this double-effect medication be regarded as assisted suicide, or even active euthanasia, and be prohibited by law as Attorney General Ashcroft's aggressive actions suggest? Or should it be encouraged and protected as an incidental result of good medical practice? A number of state statutes deal with pain medication and physician liability.[50] The U.S. Congress considered weighing in on this issue in 1999 with a bill ironically called "The Pain Relief Promotion Act" that would have made it a federal felony under the Controlled Substances Act for a doctor to prescribe drugs for terminally ill patients "intentionally . . . for the purpose of causing death." The bill was intended to thwart the Oregon PAS law. But it might equally have exposed doctors to the chilling effect of potential criminal liability for humanely seeking to end their patients' worst pain and suffering through double-effect pain relief.[51] Though the bill was not enacted, its underlying principles animate Ashcroft's efforts to limit the practice of medicine and the provision of end-of-life care according to the views of the Bush administration.

3. *Terminal sedation.* Some members of the Court in the PAS cases suggested that although assisted suicide might be banned by a state, a patient suffering extreme pain and anguish near death might still have recourse to terminal sedation. The idea seemed to be based on the belief that terminal sedation is more like "letting someone die" than it is like "causing someone to die," a distinction vital to the Court's approval of a right to refuse medical treatment and its disapproval of physician's causing death through PAS. But David Orentlicher, among others, has raised the issue of whether the Court properly understood the nature of terminal sedation. Writing in a 1997 article,[52] Orentlicher pointed out that terminal sedation includes not only sedating a patient to unconsciousness, but also withdrawing feeding and hydration. Taken together, he argues, these two steps amount to active intervention by the physician who therefore "causes" the patient's death sooner than it would otherwise have happened. Orentlicher calls this "slow euthanasia" and suggests that by implicitly approving it, the Court has opened the door to more of the kinds of abuses that were discussed in *Glucksberg* than PAS itself would. However this medical, ethical, and practical debate is eventually resolved, it is clear that in the near term terminal sedation will remain a covert reality for some and an urgent question of law and public policy for others.

4. *The slippery slope.* One of the strongest continuing arguments against PAS has been the concern that if assisted suicide for the competent, terminally ill patient is approved, there will be no legally principled or practical way to stop it from eventually being extended to people who are not terminally ill, who do not have access to good palliative care, or who are in some way disfavored by society and therefore judged not worthy of continuing life.[53] The power of the slippery-slope argument may lie partially in the deep psychological and cultural ambivalence toward death that affects us all.[54] This is a central theme of Robert Burt's powerful and unsettling book, *Death Is That Man Taking Names.*

A particularly nefarious form of this potential abuse could be against the large number of disabled persons in the United States. It could be argued, of course, that if protections like those built into the Oregon Act can be effective, there is no reason why terminally ill, disabled persons should not have the same rights and access to humane treatment as others have.[55] Also included in the slippery-slope argument should be concerns about similar pressures placed on dying patients by family, economic circumstances, availability of alternative medical care, or social or medical discrimination. Some would also suggest, as Judge Reinhart did in *Compassion in Dying,* that many of the abuses to which the slippery-slope argument refers are already inherent in a healthcare system that woefully misallocates resources according to economic status, race, ethnicity, and even gender.[56]

5. *The role of the medical profession.* The Court in the PAS cases claimed that a state may properly enact laws that criminalize PAS for, among other reasons, protecting the ethical integrity of the medical profession (EIMP). The argument holds that if physicians become takers of life as well as healers, they might lose the public's confidence and the doctor/patient relationship might be eroded. The AMA and some other professional healthcare associations have been most adamant about this. On the other hand, Justice Stevens's concurring opinion in *Glucksberg* pointed out that EIMP

might be equally eroded by forbidding physicians to follow their patient's treatment decisions or by not providing patients adequate "medication to ease their suffering and make death tolerable and dignified."[57] Few contest the importance of protecting the doctor/patient relationship, but there seems to be little agreement about either the nature of that relationship or how to protect it. There are significant differences of opinion about physician-assisted suicide within the medical profession, and between many practitioners and their professional organizations. There is therefore at least a possibility that organizational opposition to PAS may soften, just as opposition to reproductive freedom began to shift forty years ago.

6. *The misallocation of healthcare resources.* The United States is notorious among Western nations for inequalities in its healthcare system. While many people have health insurance, nearly 43 million people do not. The quality of available health care seems to depend heavily upon one's wealth and income, with the rich getting the best care in the world and the working poor often getting virtually none. One of the arguments for legalizing and regulating PAS is that it is currently and covertly available on a voluntary basis mostly for the wealthy; while at the same time the dislocation of healthcare resources means that many poor and underinsured people must either suffer the pain and anguish of dying without adequate palliative care or be consigned to terminal sedation against their own wishes or those of their families.[58] Indeed, a number of commentators concerned about the end-of-life medical abuse of the poor and racial and ethnic minorities have argued forcefully that even with legally enforced regulations such as those in Oregon, there is no place for legalized PAS until healthcare system resources are made more equal.[59]

Some commentators have gone even farther, condemning the current healthcare system and illustrating the irony of making PAS the only health care guaranteed to the poor. Yale Kamisar writes, "The moral issue of our day is not whether to enable or prevent a few individuals' dying in the comfort of their home in the presence of private physicians. The moral issue of our day is whether to do something about our immoral system of care, in which treatment is dispensed according to a principle best characterized as that of economic apartheid."[60]

A balanced comparison between law, medicine, and culture in Holland and the situation in the United States makes it clear how important the nature of a healthcare system is to the decision about whether approving PAS is an acceptable public policy.[61]

7. *Individual autonomy, rational control of dying, and the rights of self-determination.* Although the *Glucksberg/Quill* court was unwilling to find in the Constitution a generalized right to physician-assisted suicide, the fundamental question of what rights each of us holds at the end of life is not closed. It is not closed because the Court may yet find a similar right in a different set of circumstances. It is not closed because the public's concern for privacy, liberty, and self-determination in matters of great personal, spiritual, and familial importance has not disappeared with the Court's rulings. It is not closed because these are questions about the relationship of individuals to their government. Questions about the nature of self have been the lifeblood of democratic concerns and individual self-definition since before the Constitution was written. The voluminous output of scholarly books and articles about PAS and end-of-life care is testimony to the depth, complexity, and staying power of the issue.[62]

The context for this debate over autonomy at the end of life lies in a culture founded on the great and abstract principles of individual self-determination and constitutionally limited government powers. Certainly that context entitles each of us to participate in deciding the relative reach of government and individual power in end-of-life decisions. It is also true that almost from the beginning, the culture of individualism has had to struggle toward equality and to search for meaning through the forming of communities and the establishing of the norms that define them. Certainly that struggle is about how each of us ends our lives as well as how we live them. And along with these principles are, or should be, the facts[63] about medicine and health care, about the erosion of autonomy with old age and illness, about the interdependence of doctor and patient, the limitations and imperatives of technology, and the dark underside of human nature. Certainly that not only entitles us to address these issues, but also demands that we do so carefully and that we balance principles with facts, letting neither law nor medicine corner the market on truth. Finally, both public debate and private reflection about PAS are infinitely more complex and difficult because they concern life's most mundane fact and most profound mystery, death. There is much need for humility here.

The role of law in end-of-life care is becoming more pervasive. Its adequacy to the task of reflecting both the extremely personal nature and the fundamentally public implications of decisions about end-of-life care is as open to debate, as are the particular issues that law tries to resolve. As one legal scholar has put it, "we have the reason of beneficence, as well as the reasons of autonomy, why the state should not impose some uniform, general view by way of sovereign law but should encourage people to make provision for their future care themselves . . . [or to] leave decisions in the hands of their relatives or other people close to them whose sense of their best interests—shaped by intimate knowledge of everything that makes up where their best interests lie—is likely to be much sounder than some universal, theoretical, abstract judgment born in the stony halls where interest groups maneuver and political deals are done."[64]

But we must also recognize that the healthcare system is, at present and with the sanction of law, anything but equitable. In a society that has historically favored the autonomy of some at the expense of others, perhaps it is a condition of achieving autonomy that we first use law to end discrimination in health care. In dying it is perhaps the same as in living—no one can be free unless we are all free.

To some of us, it seems that the technology of medicine and the imperatives of treatment are rapidly outstripping our individual, collective, and legal abilities to arrive at ethical end-of-life care decisions with which we can live, and die. It may seem also that law is indeed too blunt an instrument to address the complexity of such decisions, and that these decisions are better left jointly to patient, doctor, and family in a system of adequate and equitable health care. From these perspectives, it would seem the wisest course to allow individuals, families, and their physicians to arrive collaboratively at decisions specific to each person's dying. That seems preferable to sweeping away gradual, often painful learning about these matters with a set of reductionist rules, prohibitions, and permissions adopted by courts or legislatures rushing to reassure us that we need not come to terms with death and suffering.

At some point in the future we will figure these issues out as a society. For now, it is hard enough to confront them in one's own practice, family, or life. We should be willing to shoulder the responsibility—even the legal responsibility—for these difficult decisions on a case-by-case basis, even if we do not yet have a road map of what is forbidden and what is required. But we can neither make these decisions nor accept personal responsibility for them if the law occupies the regulatory field and renders humility and privacy irrelevant, and equity and compassion unattainable.

Perhaps no group of professionals is better suited to help improve the quality of end-of-life care and decision making—whether by individuals, families, and caregivers or in legislative committees, court hearings, and public discourse—than are the social workers who are reading this book. By experience, training, and temperament, those whose daily work touches virtually all aspects of end-of-life care can bring to the multi-faceted discussion of end-of-life issues a real-world knowledge that is often missing from the ideological, doctrinaire, or institutionally self-interested debates on this topic. For that reason, the underlying theme of this chapter has been to assist the clinician in understanding and thereby in influencing the myriad legal and public policy decisions that affect dying in America.

To enter into this fray may at first strike the clinician as a daunting and draining effort that does not hold much hope of aiding in the difficult daily work of supporting individuals and families in making life's most difficult and personal decisions. But this is a heavily and increasingly legalized society, and that fact has two important implications for social workers engaged in end-of-life care. First, the law already circumscribes much of the work in end-of-life care, and therefore the interaction between social workers and law is inevitable. That interaction can be a matter of frustration, confusion, and adversarial anger; or it can become an opportunity for informed and constructive collaboration. Second, much of the law affecting end-of-life care and decision making is too blunt, too brittle, or too detached from reality, and has no hope of becoming otherwise unless persons of experience and sensitivity participate in changing it.

To put the matter more simply, public policy and law are much in need of the experience, knowledge, and perspectives that social workers engaged in end-of-life care are uniquely able to provide. The avenues for providing this assistance are many: as advocates for change in institutional settings, as members of ethics committees, as outspoken and reflective participants in the profession, in work with sympathetic lawyers, legislators or other healthcare professionals, as witnesses or friends of the court in legal proceedings, and perhaps most important of all, as empathic and nonpolarizing participants in a society that at least aspires to conduct an informed and constructive public discourse. Neither the manner nor the content of social worker participation in the law and public policy of end-of-life care can be prescribed here. What can be prescribed is that this participation should take place, that there is not only an opportunity but also a need—perhaps even an obligation—for those most familiar with and reflective about end-of-life care to make themselves heard.

NOTES

1. A deeply humane, thoughtful, but troubling discussion of our ambivalence toward death and how this affects everything from medical practice to legal policies and principles can be found in Robert Burt's book *Death Is That Man Taking Names: Intersections of American Medicine, Law and Culture* (University of California Press, 2002).

2. B. A. Rich, "Advance Directives: the Next Generation," 19 *Journal of Legal Medicine* 1 (1999), p. 17. See also *Means to a Better End: A Report on Dying in America*, published in November 2002 by Last Acts. The report indicates that although 70 percent of Americans want to be able to die at home surrounded by friends and family and in little pain, the reality is that 70 percent of Americans die in hospitals or other institutional settings, alone and in considerable, unnecessary pain. The report is available at www.lastacts.org/scripts/la_tsko1.exe?FNC=BetterEndHome_Ala_newtsk_laxlike_html.

3. *Cruzan v. Harmon*, 760 SW2nd 408 at 442 (Mo. 1988), Welliver, J. dissenting. The majority of the Missouri court held that Missouri could constitutionally require a very demanding "clear and convincing evidence" standard for honoring a non-competent patient's previous orally expressed desire not to remain in a persistent vegetative state. Cruzan had no living will. But the majority opinion of the Missouri Supreme Court implied that the state's living will statute was constitutional, even though by its own terms it could not be used to terminate artificial food and hydration. This catch-22 undoubtedly annoyed Justice Welliver, in whose view the living will statute was unconstitutional because it violated the right of individuals to refuse or to terminate unwanted medical treatment.

4. For a critical discussion of the autonomy principle, positioning it in the history and philosophy of the Enlightenment and using Freudian theory to raise questions about the contradictions imbedded in autonomy as applied to end-of-life care, see Robert Burt, "Self-Determination and the Wrongfulness of Death," 2 *Journal of Health Care Law and Policy* 177 (1999).

5. See, for example, Susan Channick, "The Myth of Autonomy at the End-of-Life: Questioning the Paradigm of Rights," 44 *Villanova Law Rev.* 577 (1999).

6. The term "competent" or "non-competent" refers to the legally judged ability of a person to make healthcare decisions. It may involve questions of whether the patient is conscious or in a coma, severely or mildly developmentally disabled, a child or an adult, and so forth. The idea of decisional capacity is itself the subject of legal and medical disagreements. For a review of some of these issues, see Barry R. Furrow et al., *Health Law* (2d ed.), chapter 16 C and F. For a discussion of the use of advance directives for mental health care by those with mental illness, see R. Fleishner, "Advance Directives for Mental Health Care: An Analysis of the Statutes," *Psychology, Public Policy, and Law* 4(3): 788–804 (1998).

7. To get an overview of state-by-state provisions, or to find out how a specific state is interpreting its advance directive laws, consult *The Right to Die Law Digest* (recently retitled the *End of Life Law Digest*), a quarterly loose-leaf service put out by the Partnership for Caring. For specific situations that you may confront, there is no substitute for consulting a knowledgeable attorney about how to navigate these sometimes murky waters.

8. 42 U.S.C.A. sec. 1395 et seq.

9. What follows is based in part on the work of David Orentlicher, "Trends in Healthcare Decision-making: The Limits of Legislation," 53 *Md. Law Rev.* 1255 (1994), which provides a thoughtful and thorough critique of many aspects of advance directive legislation. See also Edward J. Larson and Thomas A. Eaton, "The Limits of Advance Directives," 32 *Wake Forest Law Review* 349 (1997).

10. For a discussion of the issue, see section B, "Incompetent Pregnant Women" in Radhika Rao, "Property, Privacy, and the Human Body," 80 *B. U. Law Rev* 359 (2000). See also

End of Life Law Digest, published by the Partnership for Caring and available at www
.partnershipforcaring.org.

11. See B. A. Rich, "The Values History: A New Standard of Care," 40 *Emory Law Rev.* 1109
(1991).

12. The question of what is and what is not misleading depends on the unresolved issue of
the strength of the right to refuse treatment under common law and the federal constitution. *Cruzan* decided that a state may impose the "clear and convincing evidence"
standard when there is *no* advance directive in place *and* the question is whether to
withdraw artificial feeding and hydration from a person in a persistent vegetative state.
Missouri's living will statute expressly excludes the withdrawal of life support from its
terms, which in itself may unconstitutionally limit the right to refuse treatment. In a state
in which a validly appointed healthcare proxy is prevented from ordering the withdrawal
of life support by a "clear and convincing evidence" requirement, such a denial might
also be unconstitutional. On the difference between statutory and constitutional bases for
advance directives, see David Orentlicher, note 9 above. See also "Critique of Living Will
Statutes," pp. 129–132 in Arthur S. Berger, *Dying and Death in Law and Medicine: A
Forensic Primer for Health and Legal Professionals* (Praeger, 1993).

13. For a complete discussion of EIMP, see David Kalt, "Death, Ethics, and the State," 23
Harvard Journal of Law and Public Policy 487 (2000).

14. See note 10, above.

15. See Patricia King and Leslie Wolf, "Empowering and Protecting Patients: Lessons for
Physician-Assisted Suicide from the African-American Experience," 82 *Minn. Law Rev.*
1015 (1998).

16. On the issue of depression and physician-assisted suicide, see L. Ganzini and M. Lee,
"Psychiatry and Assisted Suicide in the United States," *New England Journal of Medicine,*
June 19, 1997.

17. Like the principle of individual autonomy and the right to refuse treatment, these state
interests appear again along with some others in the debate over physician-assisted suicide.

18. The SUPPORT study can be found at "A Controlled Trial to Improve Care for Seriously
Ill Hospitalized Patients," 274 *Journal of the American Medical Association* 1591 (1995).
For two excellent discussions of the implications of the study, see Rich, note 2 above, and
Burt, note 1 above.

19. There is little basis for the fear of liability where advance directives are concerned. Only
one case has been recorded in which a doctor was alleged to have improperly terminated
life support, and the doctor won the case. Only a few cases have been brought, and with
little success, for failure of a doctor or healthcare institution to follow an advance directive.
See *Health Law,* p. 884.

20. Different subcultures may have different understandings and fears—born of their own
experiences of discrimination as well as of their cultural values—about medical care in
general and end-of-life issues in particular. This is a major issue for the availability of
health care, for advance directives, and for physician-assisted suicide. To explore this topic
further, see Patricia King and Leslie Wolf, "Empowering and Protecting Patients," note
15 above. For a discussion of the problems faced by disabled persons in end-of-life medical
care, see Shoshana Kehoe, "Giving the Disabled and Terminally Ill a Voice: Mandating
Mediation for All Physician-Assisted Suicide, Withdrawal of Life Support, or Life-
Sustaining Treatment Requests," 20 *Hamline J. Pub. Law and Policy* 373 (1999). The article
focuses primarily on PAS, but its approach is highly relevant to the way that advance
directives are designed and used.

21. For an insightful and sweeping history of the culture of medicine, the shift away from
physician control of death, and the search for rational control of death by autonomous
individuals, see Burt, note 1 above.

22. For an extraordinarily sensitive and thoughtful exploration of the doctor/patient relation-

ship and the inadequacy of thinking of it as simply a bipolar power struggle, see Eric Cassell, *The Nature of Suffering and the Goals of Medicine* (Oxford University Press, 1991).

23.   497 U.S. 261 (1990). The *Cruzan* case allowed the state of Missouri to impose a "clear and convincing evidence" standard—one that is very difficult to meet—on a surrogate seeking to withdraw artificial feeding and hydration from a vegetative patient on the basis of a patient's earlier-stated desires. Justice O'Connor voted with the majority on this decision, but agreed with the four dissenters that the right to refuse treatment is, beyond the *Cruzan* case, a general liberty interest found in the federal constitution.

24.   Expressed as a federal liberty interest, the right to refuse medical treatment is often referred to as the "right to die," a more inclusive term that has unfortunate and misleading connotations. For a discussion of the most recent U.S. Supreme Court cases on end-of-life rights—the 1997 *Glucksberg* and *Quill* cases—see the section of this chapter headed "The More Assertive Path."

25.   The reluctance of doctors and healthcare institutions to comply with advance directives may be based on a belief that healthcare professionals know better than patients, their families or surrogates what constitutes appropriate treatment. In some instances, however, it is the individual conscience of the practitioner that is the source of resistance. Such conscience should, of course, be respected by law without compromising the patient's right to refuse treatment. That is perhaps why many advance directive statutes require that when conscience is the issue, the physician or institution must help find another. The practical effectiveness of such statutory requirements is in doubt, especially where a patient might be constitutionally entitled to refuse life support but is not entitled to do so according to the advance directive statute.

26.   The Michigan case, *Osgood v. Genesys Regional Medical Center*, is reported in the *End of Life Law Digest* (formerly the *Right to Die Law Digest*).

27.   There are few cases in this area. Though there is substantial possibility for developing tort actions for refusal to follow advance directives, they are fraught with complications, such as how to measure the damages suffered by one whose "life" is prolonged by life-support specifically rejected by an advance directive. See John Donahue, "Wrongful Living: Recovery for a Physician's Infringement on an Individual's Right to Die," 14 *J. Contemporary Health L. and Policy* 391 (1998).

28.   A thorough exploration of the nature and possible remedies for inadequate pain management can be found in Ben Rich, "A Prescription for the Pain: The Emerging Standard of Care for Pain Management," 26 *Wm. Mitchell Law Rev.* 1 (2000). On the relationship of pain management to PAS requests, see Boscom and Tolle, "Responding to Requests for Physician-assisted Suicide: These are Uncharted Waters for Both of Us," *Journal of the American Medical Association*, July 3, 2002.

29.   It is beyond the scope of this chapter to explore in detail the current legal issues in pain management and how they relate to advance directives, but in addition to the articles in note 28 above, two sources may be useful to those who wish to pursue the topic further: the pain project website of Compassion in Dying (www.compassionindying.org), the organization that represented Mr. Bergman in the California case mentioned in the text; and the congressional testimony and other work of David Joranson of the Pain and Policy Studies Group of the University of Wisconsin, which can be found at www.medsch .wisc.edu/painpolicy/index.

30.   A complete description of the case and its significance can be found in Kathryn Tucker, "Surrogate End-Of-Life Decision-Making: The Importance of Providing Procedural Due Process," 72 *Wash. Law. Rev.* 859 (1997).

31.   See Rich, note 2 above at p. 23. The importance of using law to reinforce or re-create the collaborative relationship among patient, physician, family, and other caregivers at the end of life is supported by the work of Dr. Eric Cassell and Dr. Ira Byock and legal scholars Robert Burt and Harvey Teff. See Eric Cassell, *The Nature of Suffering*, note 22

above; Ira Byock, "The Nature of Suffering and the Nature of Opportunity at the End of Life," *Clinics in Geriatric Medicine* 12, no. 2 (May 1996); Robert Burt, note 1, above; and Harvey Teff, *Reasonable Care: Legal Perspectives on the Doctor/Patient Relationship* (Clarendon Press, 1994).

32. Rich, note 2 above, makes a number of useful criticisms and suggestions about the medical directive. As originally conceived, the medical directive asks patients to indicate their treatment preferences but always uses the phrase "if medically reasonable." The term, Rich points out, is ambiguous and might allow a physician to substitute his or her judgment for that of the patient under some circumstances. There is also the problem of the rarely seen relative who emerges at the last moment to throw the family into turmoil by contesting what the patient has decided upon in the medical directive. The suggested response would be to send copies of the medical directive, at the time of its writing, to friends and relatives who would thereby be on notice of the patient's intentions. Rich suggests that the process envisioned here is likely to increase the percentage of patients who have advance directives even though some individuals will simply find it too uncomfortable to participate in such a process while they are still healthy.

33. Yale Kamisar, "Against Assisted Suicide—Even a Very Limited Form." Statement to the U.S. House of Representatives Judiciary Committee of Oct. 7, 1995 at www.house.gov/judiciary/2172.htm, pp. 11–12. The statement contains a powerful argument against PAS on the basis of the so-called slippery slope argument.

34. 497 U.S. 261 (1990).

35. See text at note 3, above, for the dissenting view of one Missouri Supreme Court justice who regarded the Missouri living will statute as a sham.

36. At least two other states, New York and Michigan, also require clear and convincing evidence of a patient's prior, competent decision before life-support can be terminated.

37. The dissenters' criticism of the Court's majority–for using the Cruzan family's tragic loss to bolster the legal power of a state's right-to-life policy–presumably applies to the Missouri attorney general as well. Known for his views against abortion, the attorney general had appealed a trial court's initial ruling that was favorable to the Cruzans. When the case returned to the trial court with the clear and convincing standard of proof in place, the trial court again reached a decision in favor of the Cruzans even though the difference in evidence presented in the two hearings was barely noticeable. The Missouri attorney general did not appeal this second ruling, perhaps demonstrating thereby that he was more concerned with advancing anti-abortion legal principles than with the fate of Nancy Cruzan and the suffering of her family. The matter is significant because it suggests that legal and policy arguments over physician-assisted suicide may be intertwined for both sides with the issue of choice in reproductive matters.

38. The various opinions provide articulate and thoughtful discussions of the issues. The Court of Appeals final decision is *Compassion in Dying v. Washington*, 79 F3d 790 (1996). The District Court opinion in the same case is reported at 850 F. Supp. 1454 (1994). The quotations in the text are drawn from 79 F3d 790.

39. The Court of Appeals decision is *Quill v. Vacco*, 80 F3d 716 (1996).

40. 521 U.S. 793 (1997).

41. *Washington v. Glucksberg*, 521 U.S. 702 (1997). A robust public debate about end-of-life care may be appropriate, but if some part of end-of-life-care decision making is in fact constitutionally based—that is, if individuals do have some kind of fundamental right to palliative care or to be free of the suffering imposed by aggressive, life-at-any-cost, medical treatment—then no majority-backed legislation can eliminate those constitutional rights.

42. See Ganzini and Lee, "Psychiatry and Assisted Suicide," note 16 above.

43. See the *Oregon Revised Statutes* sections 127.800–.897 (1995) for additional regulations and requirements. Statistical information about the early operation of the Death with

Dignity Act are reported in *American Medical News*, March 12, 2001, and are the subject of a critical editorial in the March 19, 2001, edition.

44. Rebecca Dresser, "The Supreme Court and End-of-Life Care: Principled Distinctions or Slippery Slope?" in *Law at the End of Life*, C. Schneider, ed. (University of Michigan Press, 2000).

45. See *Bergman v. Eden Medical Center* at note 19 above.

46. The list of amicus briefs and links to them can be found at the Compassion in Dying Advocacy web site, www.compassionindying.org.

47. See Robert Burt, "The Supreme Court Speaks: Not Assisted Suicide but a Constitutional Right to Palliative Care," *New England Journal of Medicine*, Oct. 23, 1997, p. 1234. A discussion of the need for improved end-of-life medical care as a substitute for approving PAS can be found in David Pratt, "Too Many Physicians: Physician-Assisted Suicide After *Glucksberg/Quill*," 9 *Albany Law J. of Science and Technology* 161 (1999).

48. On the promise of hospice care, see Zuckerman and Wollner, "End of Life Care and Decision Making: How Far We Have Come, How Far We Have to Go," in *The Hospice Heritage Celebrating Our Future*, Corless and Foster, eds. (Haworth Press, 1999).

49. See David Orentlicher, "The Supreme Court and Terminal Sedation: Rejecting Assisted Suicide, Embracing Euthanasia," 24 *Hastings Constitutional Law Quarterly* 947 (1997), suggesting that "terminal sedation serves fewer of the purposes of right-to-die law while posing a greater threat to patient welfare."

50. See the *End of Life Law Digest* (formerly *Right to Die Law Digest*), which lists state statutes and updates cases that interpret them.

51. See "Caring for the Dying: Congressional Mischief," *New England Journal of Medicine*, Dec. 16, 1999, p. 1923.

52. Orentlicher, "The Supreme Court and Terminal Sedation," note 49 above.

53. The Washington State case dealing with the failure to provide adequate due process before terminating life support of a patient without an advance directive (mentioned earlier in the text) sought to impose safeguards for termination of life support that would have reduced the likelihood of such abuses and thereby reduced the power of the slippery slope argument. It is no accident—and it is a tribute to the integrity of Compassion in Dying— that the attorney who represented the patient (through a guardian) in the Washington case was also counsel for Compassion in Dying in the two PAS cases before the U.S. Supreme Court in 1997.

54. See Burt, note 1, above. See also, Yale Kamisar's statement to the U.S. House of Representatives Judiciary Committee, note 33, above.

55. For a discussion of the problems faced by disabled persons in end-of-life medical care and a proposal to use mediation in certain PAS settings, see Shoshana Kehoe, "Giving the Disabled and Terminally Ill a Voice: Mandating Mediation for All Physician-Assisted Suicide, Withdrawal of Life Support, or Life-Sustaining Treatment Requests," 20 *Hamline J. Pub. Law and Policy* 373 (1999). See also King and Wolf, note 20, above.

56. There are also those who argue against legalizing PAS for fear that the "slippery slope" effect will ultimately undermine even the right to refuse treatment. The fear of legalizing euthanasia is often cited by opponents of the right to refuse treatment.

57. For a thoughtful discussion of the use and misuse of the EIMP argument and ways to advance this important interest, see Kalt, note 13 above. For an in-depth discussion of the doctor/patient relationship itself, see the works at notes 1 and 22 above.

58. See the 2002 report of Last Acts, "Means to a Better End" at note 2 above.

59. See, for example, King and Wolf, note 20 above.

60. See Kamisar, note 33 above, at p. 17.

61. Such a balanced and eye-opening comparison can be found in "A Dozen Caveats Concerning the Discussion of Euthanasia in the Netherlands," chapter 6 in Margaret Battin,

The Least Worst Death: Essays in Bioethics on the End of Life (Oxford University Press, 1994).

62. In addition to the works already mentioned in these endnotes, see more philosophical works such as Ronald Dworkin, *Life's Dominion* (Knopf, 1993); Dworkin, R. G. Frey, and Sissela Bok, *Euthanasia and Physician-Assisted Suicide* (Cambridge University Press, 1998); and Robert Burt, *Taking Care of Strangers* (Free Press, 1979). For a literary compendium of thoughts about death and dying, see *The Grim Reader,* ed. Maura Spiegel and Richard Tristman (Doubleday, 1997).

63. See Susan Wolf, "Pragmatism in the Face of Death: The Role of Facts in the Assisted Suicide Debate," 82 *Minn. Law Rev.* 1063 (1998).

64. Dworkin, *Life's Dominion,* p. 213.

38

ADVANCED DIRECTIVES AND ASSISTED SUICIDE: POLICY IMPLICATIONS FOR SOCIAL WORK PRACTICE

ELLEN CSIKAI

Mrs. A, an eighty-year-old woman who lived alone, was found unconscious by her neighbor one morning. The neighbor checked on her daily because her only family, a daughter, lived three hundred miles away. Mrs. A was diagnosed as having had a massive stroke with little chance of any meaningful recovery. The daughter was contacted and traveled to come in to the hospital. Because of the daughter's responsibilities of a full-time job and three children and Mrs. A's inability to travel, they visited infrequently. When the physician asked the daughter if Mrs. A had an advance directive, she did not know. They also had never discussed Mrs. A's wishes if this type of situation were to arise. The daughter was visibly upset by Mrs. A's condition and was unable to make a decision, voicing concern about "killing" her mother if medical treatment was discontinued. The social worker, as part of the team, was called upon to intervene with the daughter.

O**NLY WITHIN** the last three decades has a concern arisen regarding protecting individuals' rights in end-of-life care situations, especially as medical advances have created situations whereby individuals may be kept alive almost indefinitely. Individuals, while still competent, need to be able to express their treatment preferences if in terminal or "hopeless" medical situations at a future time, so that they do not languish in a conditions that they would deplore or create situations that may cause conflict or anguish for their families. Advance directives meet this need and have been widely sanctioned under federal and state law beginning with the California Natural Death Act in 1976.

The Patient Self-Determination Act of 1990 was the first national or federal attempt to educate individuals about advance directives and increase use. Another attempt to insure that end-of-life matters remain in individuals' own hands has been through the passage in the state of Oregon of the Death with Dignity Act (1994), which makes provisions for the practice of physician-assisted suicide. While still highly controversial, other states (such as Michigan and Washington) have and are likely to continue to consider ratification of similar statutes as the public demands a "choice in dying." However, despite this legislation, evidence exists that usage rates are as low as 4–15 percent (Cantor 1998; High 1993; VandeCreek and Frankowski 1996) and that even if an advance directive exists, it may not be followed by family members or healthcare professionals (Cantor 1998).

This chapter focuses on both advance directives and assisted suicide, including definitions of the salient aspects of the issues and policies surrounding them, and the roles and responsibilities of social workers in working with individuals and families to maximize self-determination and quality of life.

FEDERAL AND STATE POLICIES REGARDING ADVANCE DIRECTIVES

The Patient Self-Determination Act (PSDA) (Public Law No. 101–508, 1990), became effective December 1, 1991, and was aimed at promoting the use of advance directives. According to Ulrich (1994), this act gave recognition to the pluralistic and democratic ideals of the United States in the ways individuals choose to live their lives and to die.

The PSDA required that all persons who are admitted to or utilize healthcare services that are Medicare and Medicaid providers, such as hospitals, nursing homes, and in-home health care, be asked if they have an existing advance directive. When one is produced, it is placed in the medical chart/record. Patients also must be informed of their right to formulate an advance directive, if they do not have one. The most important feature of the law is that education is to be provided both face-to-face with individuals and to the community at large about what advance directives are and how to go about formulating one. Most institutions responded to the law by developing pamphlets to be handed out upon admission to the healthcare facility/service, and further questions were delegated to usually social services or clergy. The PSDA also required that the Department of Health Human Services conduct a national campaign to inform the public about advance directives (Sugarman et al. 1993). An assumption about increased education was that if individuals had sufficient information, they would then complete advance directives (LaPuma, Orenlicher, and Moss 1991). This was quite naive, inasmuch as it failed to recognize that people in acute crises cannot always process new knowledge. Often people whose lives are at stake may use denial as a healthy way of coping, but denial does not allow new information in. Additionally, many patients are uneducated and may speak a variety of languages, so this important information may not be accessible.

The potential benefits of the PSDA were thought to be many. Intangible benefits for individuals could include increased autonomy through the expression of medical preferences, decreased suffering as undesired treatments would not be utilized, and offer emotional comfort in the perception of not being a burden to family or loved ones (financially or emotionally). For healthcare workers a benefit was expected in that individuals will have already considered some difficult situations and have specified desired care in an advance directive. For hospitals, the PSDA was expected to reduce costs of care (Sugarman et al. 1993). However, this has not been substantiated (Teno, Nelson, and Lynn 1997). As stated, the time of admission to a health facility is likely not the most appropriate time to ask about and discuss advance directives, for individuals may be too ill to participate in such discussions.

All fifty states have now passed statutes protecting the use of advance directives, although the form of advance directives may vary. California was the first state to enact a "Natural Death Law" in 1976. Although this first statute was stimulated by Karen Ann Quinlan's father, who pursued judicial means to authorize the removal of life supports from his daughter, this law would not have actually applied in her case. The law only covered incapacitated individuals whose death is imminent (which constitutes a small percentage), not those experiencing a prolonged dying process, the fear of many (President's Commission 1982).

The final impetus for the protection of patients rights and for passage of the PSDA was the case of Nancy Cruzan in Missouri. Cruzan was in a persistent vegetative state without hope of recovery after an auto accident. Her parents wished to remove life-supporting treatments and allow her to die. They stated that their daughter would not have wanted to live in such a condition and that it was not consistent with her values. Although in this case the individual's wishes were not made explicit prior to her injury, a surrogate who knew her was able to express them. The courts would never have been involved had an advance directive been in place. This case also points to the importance of surrogates in directing the care of those who become incapacitated and cannot make decisions about their own medical treatment.

One difficulty in each state having separate laws regarding advance directives is that individuals may need to formulate a separate directive for each state in which they may possibly receive medical treatment. This may become cumbersome but essential for patients from rural areas transferring across state lines for treatment in larger cities or for transplant patients that must transfer out-of-state to large transplant centers.

THE NATURE OF ADVANCE DIRECTIVES

Advance directives are intended to extend individuals' autonomy to a time when they become incapacitated or incompetent due to a debilitating illness/condition. The advance directive forms utilized are as varied as the individuals themselves. There is little uniformity in the information contained within each document, which has further contributed to considerable confusion in attempting to enforce them among medical clinicians, even if they are aware that the documents exist.

Probably the oldest type of advance directive in use is the living will. Living wills are considered "instruction directives" that may specify the type of treatment that an individual wants or does not want to receive (President's Commission 1982). In these, individuals express basically only one directive: that if terminally ill and permanently incompetent, the individual would want all medical treatment withdrawn. These older forms are often ambiguous and vague, especially when discussing treatment using terms like "extraordinary" and "heroic." Additionally, the situations often specified are not likely to raise ethical concerns about whether to continue with treatment when there is no hope of recovery as many other unspecified conditions would (Culver

1998). This type of document may even be one that is handwritten on a sheet of paper by the individual himself and may be used currently by many individuals especially those without access to formalized documents.

Individuals may name someone to speak on their behalf. These are "proxy directives." The named persons are expected to assure that individuals' directives, if any, as specified in the document are carried out. As not all situations are specified, they then are entrusted to use substituted judgment or the best interest standard to make appropriate decisions regarding medical treatment. One of the possible difficulties with this alternative is that named surrogate decision makers may not be aware that they are to serve as surrogates and further may not have discussed individuals' wishes for treatment with them (Culver 1998). The President's Commission in 1982 recommended that a better form of advance directive may be one in which a surrogate decision maker is named and combined with statements of individuals' wishes. This allows individuals broader control in decision making.

Culver (1998) has suggested seven characteristics necessary for useful advance directives:

1. Instructions specified should correspond as closely as possible to questions that are most likely to arise in the care of seriously ill, incompetent persons.
2. Instructions should be clear.
3. Future states should be anticipated.
4. Instructions should include whether individuals would want the advance directive followed if there was some small chance of a partial or full recovery or if recovery seemed remote.
5. Attention should be paid to the withdrawal of various types of life support if individuals were in a situation where they would want treatment stopped.
6. Attention should be paid the withdrawal of invasive types of life-sustaining treatment, such as nutrition and hydration.
7. Advance directives should only be completed by individuals who thoroughly understand the content and the implications of their instructions.

In 1998, the Council on Ethical and Judicial Affairs of the American Medical Association made several recommendations in response to increasing concerns over the seemingly ineffective utilization of advance directives in formulation, access, understanding, and use in health care settings. Among these recommendations included the use of both advisory and state statutory documents. Advisory documents may include worksheets used to record preferences that will inform physicians and others of patients' wishes. Physicians should directly discuss end-of-life preferences with patients and their proxies ahead of time if possible and assist in filling out such worksheets. This activity should not be delegated to another member of the healthcare team. Central repositories for completed advisory documents should be established to allow access particularly in emergency situations, and that doctors' orders sheets should be used to document preferences so that "covering" healthcare professionals may also have access to patients' preferences if they do not know the patients. When advisory documents are used in conjunction with the state's statutory model form (often contained in the statute itself) patients' wishes may have the greatest chance of being made known and respected. In the management of end-of-life care treatment, individuals must be given an opportunity to define what they mean by comfort care in the context of their own illness and personal values (Quill et al. 1998).

DISCUSSIONS ABOUT ADVANCE CARE PLANNING AND FORMULATION OF DIRECTIVES

According to K. W. Goodman (1998), the overall goal of completing advance directives is that preferences are expressed about end-of-life care to caregivers, family, and others, so that self-determination is preserved. In reaching this goal, however, what may be more important is the process that occurs in eliciting these preferences. For example, if this process improves communication between providers and individuals, and between individuals and their families, there can be great benefit. Advance care planning is a much broader activity than constructing a formal living will or designating a power of attorney for health care. The overall goal of advance care planning is to ensure that medical care is directed by the patients' preferences when patients are unable to participate in decision making themselves. A more specific goal is the improvement of health care decision making processes, such as facilitating shared decision making among patients, surrogates, and providers and encouraging individual and public dialogue about issues of death, dying, and decisional incapacity. Another specific goal is the improvement of patient outcomes, such as patient well-being and reducing concerns about creating burdens for families and significant others (Teno, Nelson, and Lynn 1994).

However, "advance care planning requires that both clinicians and patients do what they are strongly disinclined to do: to think and talk about circumstances in which health declines, curative measures fail, and the process of dying and the ultimate fact of death must be confronted" (Rich 1998:627). The Study to Understand Prognoses and Preferences for Outcomes and Risks of Treatments (SUPPORT), a two-year study of patients with life expectancies of six months or less, was completed in 1994 (SUPPORT Investigators 1995). The study revealed numerous inadequacies in patient–physician communication and in physicians' knowledge of patient preferences regarding CPR and timing of DNR orders. Notably, patients who died spent at least ten days in an intensive care units and were in moderate pain at least one-half of the time, according to their families. The study also included an intervention phase aimed at improving communication by the provision of timely information about prognosis, documenting patient and family preferences and understanding of the disease and prognosis and utilizing a nurse help carry out necessary discussions, including arranging and convening meetings with patients and families (all of which required the permission of the attending physician). Surprisingly, the outcome of this phase revealed no improvement in patient–physician communication or other indicators used: timing and incidence of DNR orders written, physicians' knowledge of patients' resuscitation preferences, number of days spent in an ICU, receiving mechanical ventilation or comatose prior to death, and reported level of pain. Recommendations of the study were that there should be not only increased interaction between patient and physician, but also more proactive measures, such as increased community education regarding advance directives, to improve the commitment of individuals and society may be needed (SUPPORT Investigators 1995).

A major reason for elderly individuals not completing advance directives is that they simply put off decisions or defer to others (High 1993). When should discussions about advance directives occur? Who should initiate and be responsible for discussions about advance directives? Who else should be involved? According to one study (Johnston, Pfeifer, and McNutt 1995) of groups of outpatients and physicians in primary care offices, 91 percent of patients agreed that these discussions should occur before individuals become extremely ill, and 84 percent agreed that they should take place while healthy. A majority of these respondents also indicated that discussions should occur in the physician's office prior to hospitalization. Both patients and physicians believed that the physician is responsible for initiating such discussions. A majority of patients ranked as closest to them a spouse or significant other, children, parents, siblings, friends, clergy, or lawyers, and indicated that these should be brought into discussions of advance directives. According to these patients, the content of the discussion should include life-sustaining treatments, health status at the time of discussion, survival chances and likelihood of full recovery, and effects of treatments on the family. The physicians felt that discussion of chances of survival was more important than that of discussion of patients' overall health status at the time that advance care planning is taking place (Johnston, Pfeifer, and McNutt 1995).

One suggestion for making advance care planning more meaningful and more useful is the inclusion of a "life values history" or profile in discussions and documentation (Cantor 1998; Schonwetter et al. 1996). What may sound like a simple process may be very complicated indeed. Items in a values history include the recording of individuals' judgments of the importance of independence, being mentally alert, and the use of life-sustaining measures during a chronic or terminal illness. Cantor proposed a format that uses case scenarios with a list of options from which individuals would choose. For example, "my attitude toward a permanently unconscious state, confirmed by up-to-date medical tests, showing no hope of ever regaining consciousness: 'intolerable—I prefer death'; 'tolerable'; 'tolerable, so long as insurance or other non-family sources are paying the bills'" (1998:649). In most documents, however, responses are open-ended out of necessity, which may serve to complicate further the completion of directives by individuals. Discussing life values in addition to life-sustaining treatments requires additional time, which may limit the use of this strategy. While limitations seem inherent in incorporating any discussion of life values in advance care planning, communication and understanding of end-of-life care treatment preferences may be facilitated by such interaction (Schonwetter et al. 1996).

The American Medical Association's Council on Ethical and Judicial Affairs recommended that physicians be involved in two key phases in the process of advance care planning: structuring the central discussion and "after patient reflection, cosigning and insuring that a completed document is recorded in the medical record"

(1998:673). Physicians should make discussions of end-of-life care preferences a standard practice (Rich 1998). However, some have lamented the reluctance and the limited ability of physicians to discuss issues of death and dying with their patients. Reasons for not discussing end-of-life care preferences are not clear. Whether they do not fully appreciate the appropriateness of advance directives (Morrison, Morrison, and Glickman 1994) or simply forget (Dexter et al. 1998) or they are not prepared to acknowledge futility in certain medical situations, or that they have not examined their own feelings and beliefs about their own death, are all possible explanations. Goodman (1998) believes that the problem is not with the documents or policies themselves, but with poorly trained professionals. Training in effective communication and in the ethical, psychological, and legal aspects of death and dying must take place in order for the documents to have the greatest impact. One current educational initiative for physicians is sponsored by the AMA: The Education for Physicians in End-of-Life Care (EPEC). This "train-the-trainers" program covers a wide variety of subjects related to end-of-life care, including discussion of gaps in end-of-life care, legal issues, models of end-of-life care, communicating bad news, advance care planning, "whole" patient assessment, pain and symptom management, physician-assisted suicide, medical futility, withholding/withdrawing medical treatment, depression/anxiety/delirium, and the last hours of life. This curriculum is not required; however, physicians do receive continuing medical education credit for completing the course. Little incentive to complete the course exists for many older physicians, whom may especially benefit because of the absence of end-of-life care content during their medical school training.

PHYSICIAN-ASSISTED SUICIDE: THE ISSUES AND DEBATE

In both the acts of voluntary active euthanasia and physician-assisted suicide, the intention is to hasten or cause death of a competent person who has consented to the act. The distinction is in the administration of the means of death. Acts of euthanasia involve the physician directly administering a lethal dose of medication causing death. In acts of physician-assisted suicide, the physician prescribes medication and instruction to the patients on how to self-administer the lethal dose (Asch 1996; Cohen et al. 1994; Emanuel 1994). Passive euthanasia is the withholding or withdrawing of life-sustaining treatment and is legally sanctioned through the enactment of an individual's advance directive or the decision of a surrogate decision maker.

Whether one is for or against physician-assisted suicide, the issue is likely to produce strong emotional responses. The arguments in favor of physician-assisted suicide appeal mainly to the concept of individual autonomy and individual rights. A right to refuse medical treatment is widely recognized and accepted in health care today, including in end-of-life care situations. If individuals have a right to decide what constitutes a good life and to end life when treatment is not consistent with that view of a good life (Emanuel 1994), then assisted suicide would not be ethically different from utilization of advance directives in withdrawing life-sustaining medical care.

Much of the strongest opposition to physician-assisted suicide centers on two themes: the Hippocratic Oath of physicians to "do no harm," which prohibits the prescription of lethal medication, and the notion of the "slippery slope." The "slippery slope" argument contends that allowing the voluntary choice of physician-assisted suicide could lead to coercion to choose that option. Thus, particularly vulnerable populations, such as the elderly and persons with AIDS (those not diagnosed as terminal), may not have a free choice at all (Csikai 1999a).

Even those who support physician-assisted suicide acknowledge that safeguards may be necessary such as psychological consultation to insure that a treatable depression does not exist and that the individual is of sound mind. Additionally, second opinions of diagnoses, and checks to make sure that individuals are fully informed (Gunderson and Mayo 2000) would be needed. One safeguard often proposed is the limitation of physician-assisted suicide to the terminally ill only. The public is well aware, through the media, of cases of patients whose suicides were assisted by Dr. Jack Kevorkian. Many of them were not terminal but suffered from chronic debilitating illnesses, such as ALS and multiple sclerosis. The restriction of physician-assisted suicide to the terminally ill is especially controversial, even for those who support physician-assisted suicide in general (Gunderson and Mayo 2000).

LEGISLATIVE EFFORTS AND SUPPORT FOR PHYSICIAN-ASSISTED SUICIDE

Currently, the only state to have legalized physician-assisted suicide is Oregon. The Oregon Death with Dignity Act was originally passed in 1994 but was not implemented at that time, pending the outcome of legal challenges, including in the U.S. Supreme Court. In 1997, the Court upheld the constitutionality of New York and Washington State laws banning physician-assisted suicide. The ruling kept the rights within each state as to legislation regarding this issue.

At least thirty-seven states have criminalized the act of assisted suicide through legislation. Several states, such as California, Hawaii, and Maryland, continue active debate. In November 1998, Michigan voters rejected a ballot measure to legalize assisted suicide (Medical Ethics Advisor 1999b). Efforts to push legalization in Michigan appear to have lost some strength with the conviction and incarceration in March 1999 of Dr. Jack Kevorkian after he performed an act of euthanasia that was videotaped and televised nationally on a segment of 60 Minutes. Before his conviction, Dr. Kevorkian assisted in more than a hundred deaths.

The controversy over physician-assisted suicide will likely continue as public favor of the practice continues to grow. In one study (Mauro 1997), 57 percent of Americans polled believed that physician-assisted suicide should be allowed. Additionally, over the past few years public opinion polls have found 52 percent and 69 percent in favor of assisted suicide and as many as 79 percent who supported the Oregon law (Medical Ethics Advisor 1999b). In 1998, one thousand adults were studied on behalf of the organization Compassion in Dying regarding legislation of issues related to assisted death. Many of the responses were favorable toward legalizing physician-assisted suicide. The majority thought that Congress should not be involved in regulating lethal drugs that could be prescribed by physicians. Further, 74 percent agreed with the statement, "People in the final stages of a terminal illness who are suffering and in pain should have the right to get help from their doctor to end their life if they so choose" (Medical Ethics Advisor 1999a:53). Overall, the public is supportive of the right to choose physician-assisted suicide.

Even though there is widespread disapproval of physician-assisted suicide by various professional associations/organizations, including the American Medical Association, the American Nurses Association, and the National Hospice and Palliative Care Organization, many studies have reported professional support for physician-assisted suicide (Asch 1996; Back et al. 1996; Cohen et al. 1994; Csikai 1999b). In a study of Washington physicians, a majority thought that physician-assisted suicide was ethical in some circumstances and that the practice should be legalized (Cohen et al. 1994). Several studies have reported that physicians would consider helping a terminally ill person with physician-assisted suicide (Bachman et al. 1996; Cohen et al. 1994). In fact, physicians in Washington had further indicated that they had provided lethal prescriptions to 24 percent of patients who requested it (Back et al. 1996). Seventeen percent of 1,139 critical care nurses surveyed reported that they had received requests to perform assisted suicide, and 16 percent of these nurses had engaged in the practice during their career (Asch 1996). In a study of 122 hospital social workers, 22 percent reported encountering requests to discuss assisted suicide with patients (Csikai 1999b), and of a sample of 110 hospice social workers, 38 percent reported such requests as well.

THE OREGON DEATH WITH DIGNITY ACT

In 1997, a measure to repeal the Death with Dignity Act went before Oregon voters and was defeated, thereby removing the final hurdle was cleared for implementation of the act (Miller 2000). During 1998, the first year of implementation of the act, twenty-three persons received prescriptions for lethal medication; fifteen died after ingestion. In the second year (1999), sixteen persons died after ingestion of lethal medications prescribed under the act. Five additional persons received prescriptions but died of their underlying disease prior to ingestion, and two were alive as of January 1, 2000. Although an increase occurred in the number of persons who died after ingesting lethal medications under the act, the number is small compared to the overall number of deaths that occurred in Oregon during the same period (Chin et al. 1999; Sullivan, Hedberg, and Fleming 2000). Opponents' fears do not appear to have been realized in the first years of the practice in Oregon. Reasons for choosing this option were related to the desire for control over their own deaths and not because they were uneducated, poor, uninsured, had other financial concerns, or were receiving inadequate end-of-life care. Three-quarters of the patients requesting assistance in dying were enrolled in hospice programs at the time and palliative care was available to all patients (Sullivan, Hedberg, and Fleming 2000). Previously documented reasons for requesting physician-assisted suicide have been identified as future loss of control, being a burden, being dependent on others for some or all of personal care, loss of dignity, being restricted to bed more than 50 percent of the time, and experiencing severe depression or depressed mood (Back et al. 1996).

Guidelines for the Oregon Act are extensive. A terminally ill individual (prognosis of six months or less) may request assisted suicide from a physician. A second physician must confirm the diagnosis and prognosis and then a fifteen-day waiting period ensues. The request must be oral and followed by a written request as well as a second oral request. At this point, then a prescription for lethal medication may be given (usually barbiturates taken by mouth). Mental health consultation is not required, but can be requested by either physician. Notification of the family is not required (Miller 2000).

PROFESSIONAL POLICY:
CLIENT SELF-DETERMINATION IN END-OF-LIFE DECISIONS

The National Association of Social Workers (2000) has addressed the responsibilities that social workers have in assisting individuals with end-of-life decisions in the policy statement "Client Self-Determination in End-of-Life Decisions." According to this policy, client self-determination is defined as "the right of the client to determine the appropriate level, if any, of medical intervention and the right of clients to change their wishes about their treatment as their condition changes over time or during the course of their illness" (NASW 2000:41). This assumes that the individual is mentally competent to make health care decisions.

The focus of the policy suggests that individuals should be able to choose what care they deem most appropriate for themselves at the time of serious illness and impending death. The social work value of self-determination fits with the utilization of advance directives and even with the arguments in favor of physician-assisted suicide. "NASW does not take a position concerning the morality of end-of-life decisions, but affirms the right of the individual to determine the level of his or her care" (NASW 2000:42). This policy also outlines the appropriate roles for social workers in end-of-life decision making. These include providing information necessary for an informed choice and exploring alternatives, helping individuals express thoughts and feelings, and helping individuals and families to deal with grief and loss issues. Also, social workers should encourage involvement of family, friends, and significant others in decision making, and provide ongoing support to these individuals. Indeed the social worker needs to offer "emotional and tangible assistance" to families in the bereavement process (NASW 2000). Regarding assisted suicide, the policy further elaborates that social workers are free to choose whether to participate in discussions according to their own beliefs and values. The professional obligation exists that if a social worker is unable to discuss such issues, then the individual should be referred to a competent colleague who can address end-of-life issues. Where assisted suicide is illegal, it is not appropriate for social workers to "deliver, supply, or personally participate in the commission of an act of assisted suicide when acting in their professional role" (NASW 2000:44). If physician-assisted suicide is legal, social workers may be present during the act if requested by the patient. Finally, NASW (2000) calls for state chapters to encourage their membership to participate in local, state, and national level committees/task forces to study issues of end-of-life care and to be actively involved in education and research regarding end-of-life care issues.

SOCIAL WORK INTERVENTION IN END-OF-LIFE CARE

In response to the PSDA, healthcare institutions have developed procedures whereby information is provided to patients upon admission and presence of an advance directive is to be documented. In many instances, the information is provided through brief pamphlets explaining the patients' rights under state law to formulate a directive. This, as can be imagined, could leave much to be desired, especially as admission personnel are not appropriately trained in the meaning and importance of having an advance directive. If patients have further questions, institutions generally have protocols regarding which department within the facility is to be consulted. Social services or pastoral care departments often respond to requests for information or to discuss advance directives with patients and families. Social workers may also be consulted throughout a patient's hospital stay to discuss end-of-life care and advance directives. Often this occurs prior to a risky medical procedure or surgery, which may arguably be most stressful and least appropriate time for patients and families to discuss such important issues.

In the discussion regarding advance care planning, patients and families should discuss such issues related to end-of-life care and their personal values regarding life and how they wish to die. It is during this conversation that a request for information or discussion about physician-assisted suicide may arise. Social workers are also asked by patients to discuss either euthanasia or assisted suicide (Csikai 1999a), which seems natural since social workers are often the professionals that patients and families look to for exploration and discussion of the meaning of various treatment options, as well the person to whom their hopes, fears, and other concerns are brought. Social workers must be prepared for such discussions by assessing their own values regarding particularly controversial end-of life care practices and options for care, as well as knowing the legal and financial aspects of each option.

Perhaps the biggest impact that social workers can make in the area of advance care planning is in engaging patients and families in dialogue about end-of-life care and how to achieve quality and meaning at the end of life. In public opinion research conducted by the National Hospice Foundation (NHF) in 1999, more than one out of every four American adults are not likely to discuss issues related to a parent's death even if the parent is terminally ill. Additionally, fewer than 25 percent of Americans have thought about how they would like to be cared for at the end of life and put these wishes in writing. Although 36 percent of the respondents reported that they had told someone about how they would like to be cared for at the end of life, further results from focus group discussions revealed that they often viewed that a passing comment about how they wished to die was equal to informing loved ones of their wishes (NHF 1999). As revealed by the SUPPORT study (SUPPORT Investigators 1995), too, an intervention by a professional (in this case a nurse) aimed at examining patient/family wishes in a terminal situation when already in the acute hospital setting may be too late. Planning for the end of life should begin before encountering the situation, when it may become an emergency and when emotions are running high. Encouraging discussion and use of advance directives (even though few people may complete them) may lead to a better understanding of individuals' wishes by families, providers, and the individuals themselves. These discussions need to include as many of the patient/client family members and significant others (as the patient identifies them) as possible and thus may serve to empower all involved in the process.

Social workers' advocacy skills are important here as well in insuring that patients' wishes are carried out. Among the most important service for people who are terminally ill is that there is someone to be sure that patients' wishes are enforced (NHF 1999). Patients and families often may have fears related to prior experiences with death and dying with friends and family members and possibly in situations where preferences for care were not solicited by providers and wishes were not followed. Also important was emotional support for patients and families and an opportunity for patients to put their lives in order (NHF 1999), both of which fall under the particular skills and values of social workers. Policy development is also an important domain for social workers who must advocate for changes in policy that maximize individuals' abilities to express preferences access to resources for end-of-life care.

Specifically, when a patient asks about hastening death or assisted suicide, the social worker must fully explore the meaning behind the request. Rather than put forth an emotional reaction that may shut down communication, individual, family, community, and cultural concerns about dying should be examined. This exploration may actually decrease the risk of suicide if individuals can express their concerns and understand the options available to them (Miller and Hedlund 1996). Mental health professionals are taught that suicidal ideation is an indicator of depression or impaired judgment and that when these individuals wish to die that treatment should be sought. Evaluation of depression in terminally ill individuals is difficult, inasmuch as symptoms are often similar to normal reactions to the possibility of death and the dying process, such as sleep disturbances, fatigue, poor concentration, weight loss, and preoccupation with death (Quill et al. 1998). With the possibility of legalization of assisted suicide in other states in addition to Oregon, social workers may need to design, test, and then teach different ways to evaluate depression, competence, and judgment in individuals who request assistance in dying (Miller 2000).

To prepare for requests to discuss assisted suicide, social workers can ask themselves the following questions to clarify their positions and values on the issue. "Would I be able to assist a patient in accessing the means for assisted suicide?" "Can I, in good conscience, continue to care for a patient requesting assisted suicide?" "What are the competing ethical, professional, and legal factors that must be considered before responding to a request?" "How far-reaching are patients' autonomy rights?" "Does the practice of assisted suicide violate respect for persons, harm society, or harm social workers?" (Kopala and Kennedy 1998). Depending upon this self examination, social workers may choose to intervene with individuals and families that have questions about hastening death or assisted suicide or to refer such individuals and families to other professionals who are comfortable with discussion of these issues. A problem may occur, however, if few professionals exist that are knowledgeable and willing to discuss issues, which may be the particular case in rural environments.

When an advanced directive is enforced, a situation is present whereby patients are not capable of making decisions for themselves due to their life-threatening or terminal medical condition. At this time a decision often must be made as to whether to continue or withdraw life-sustaining treatments, for there may be no or little hope of meaningful recovery. If the patient has clearly stated a preference in an advance directive, then there virtually is no decision to be made by the family or medical professionals. The patient's preference must be followed. Often family members disagree with the patient's preferences in light of the patient's imminent death if the advance directive is followed, but must be able to respect the wishes of their loved one. Social workers are often in a position to assist families in doing so. Removal of life-prolonging or life-sustaining treatment in a terminal situation is considered passive euthanasia and is sanctioned by the use of advance directives. Often this action is referred to, even by clergy, as "letting nature take its course." Passive euthanasia is not physician assisted suicide. Social workers must understand and be able to communicate this distinction not only to families, but also to health professionals who lack an understanding of this concept and may have personal difficulty accepting the need to withdraw life support from a patient.

One of the many demographic changes that are affecting the dynamics of end-of-life care is that people are living longer and many now face a range of chronic illnesses. Some of these illnesses, such as congestive heart failure and chronic obstructive pulmonary disease, often have acute episodes that require hospitalization and rehabilitation, which may include the assistance of home health care or nursing home care. Social workers in each of these settings can capitalize upon these opportunities to engage families in discussion about how they would wish to handle the terminal phase of their chronic condition and initiate a discussion about advance care planning. Acute medical episodes may certainly present as crises for the individual and the family, and a state of disequilibrium undoubtedly will occur. The use of crisis intervention can provide a "turning point" and an opportunity for individuals and families (Roberts 2000). The social worker should help the family respond to possible changing dynamics resulting from stress and different coping styles in response to the medical crisis (Shulman and Shewbert 2000). Additionally, focus can be placed on the quality of the individuals' and families' lives in between episodes rather than on fear about when the next episode will occur.

An awareness of cultural diversity in end-of-life care planning is very important, especially in relation to information regarding a terminal illness and who may be involved in decision making about medical treatment. Patient autonomy, the right of individuals to make informed decisions, is widely accepted in America. However, examination of the attitudes of various ethnic groups toward this notion revealed that Korean Americans were less likely than African and European Americans to believe that the patient should be told about diagnosis, terminal prognosis, or that the patient should make decisions regarding life-sustaining technology. Korean and Mexican Americans were more likely to believe that only the family should be told the truth;

however, increased acculturation of the family increases the likelihood that they will share the autonomy model with African and European Americans (Blackhall et al. 1995). Patients should be asked whom they want to involve in discussions and decision making about their illness and end-of-life care treatment, especially as there is much diversity within ethnic groups.

Just being asked to complete an advance directive may also be a sensitive ethnic/cultural issue. This may have to do with how ethnically diverse populations view what it means to do so. For example, in one study of 139 African Americans, Hispanics, and whites from a general medical clinic setting, 10 percent of African Americans and only 2 percent of whites felt that an advanced directive would mean giving up (Caralis et al. 1993). A significantly lower prevalence of advance directives among African Americans and Hispanics than whites has been reported, which may be due to their preference toward more aggressive treatment (Kahn 1994) and to continue life-prolonging treatment regardless of the severity of their illness (Caralis et al. 1993). In focus groups of African Americans and Hispanics, lack of trust and suspicion of the healthcare system was discussed frequently as having an influence on attitudes of African Americans toward the use of advance directives. This often included a suspicion of the physician's candor regarding the severity of the illness. Both African Americans and Hispanics also indicated a lack of awareness of the existence of an option to complete advance directives (Hauser et al. 1997).

Yet another point of impact for social workers in end-of-life care is as members of interdisciplinary teams in healthcare settings. As the liaison between the patient, family, and other healthcare providers, social workers can help team members understand patients' and families' fears, hopes, and wishes regarding end-of-life care treatment. As social workers assess and intervene on multiple levels, information gained regarding patients' values, pressures, preferences should be shared with the team (Smokowski and Wodarski 1996). Helping other professionals understand the context of the situations faced by patients and families and providing a broad systems perspective is particularly important. Social workers can arrange family conferences to discuss advance care planning stressing the importance of involvement of all the health professionals involved, especially physicians. Behaviors such as active listening, exploration, and use of empathy can be modeled in an effort to increase the use of these skills among professionals encountering difficult conversations with patients. Social workers should not only execute their own advance directives and engage their loved ones in discussion about end-of-life care, but should also encourage team members to do the same in order to heighten self awareness and sensitivity to others (Soskis and Kerson 1992).

Social workers have a significant educational role in advance care planning and end-of-life care practices. Part of the Patient Self-Determination Act has mandated that healthcare facilities provide education to the community regarding the importance of advance directives. Social workers should be involved in planning community seminars with local organizations such as NASW local chapters or the local AARP group or may be invited speakers at such seminars. Social work departments may also be engaged in education within their own facilities so that a greater comfort level in discussion of end-of-life care is achieved. In a study of social workers on hospital ethics committees, both social workers and committee chairs expected that social workers should have greater involvement in educational activities than was occurring, which points to an opportunity for social workers to take the lead in this area (Csikai and Sales 1998). Social workers should engage professionals in their particular service area within the hospital or in their agency around certain issues, such as pain management, withdrawal of tube feedings, or physician-assisted suicide and the implications of each of these issues in the care of patients. These discussions bring out deeply held emotions that may have previously impeded effective work with patients who need a great deal of support and intervention at the end of life. Such dialogues can be helpful if structured by the social worker and if they occur after a particularly traumatic or emotionally charged situation involving difficult end-of-life care decision making or death of a patient, again making capitalizing on an opportunity for growth.

In summary, social workers need to participate in all aspects of advance care planning and issues related to assisted suicide at the clinical, advocacy, and policy levels. As the population continues to age, these issues are becoming increasingly important to both examine and intervene in their implementation. Involvement must not only occur on an interpersonal level with patients, families, and providers including clinical intervention, but also on organizational, community, and societal levels in terms of policy and education in order to fulfill our professional mission of enhancing the lives (and deaths?) of all people.

REFERENCES

American Medical Association, Council on Ethical and Judicial Affairs. 1998. Optimal use of orders not to intervene and advance directives. *Psychology, Public Policy, & Law* 4(3): 668–675.

Anderson, J. G., and D. P. Caddell. 1993. Attitudes of medical professionals toward euthanasia. *Social Science & Medicine* 37(1): 105–114.

Asch, D. A. 1996. The role of critical care nurses in euthanasia and assisted suicide. *New England Journal of Medicine* 334(21): 1374–1379.

Bachman, J. G., K. H. Alcser, D. J. Doukas, R. I. Lichtenstein, A. D. Corning, and H. Brody. 1996. Attitudes of Michigan physicians and public toward legalizing physician-assisted suicide and voluntary euthanasia. *New England Journal of Medicine* 334:303–309.

Back, A. L., J. I. Wallace, H. E. Starks, and R. A. Pearlman. 1996. Physician-assisted suicide and euthanasia in Washington. *Journal of the American Medical Association* 275(12): 919–925.

Blackhall, L. J., S. T. Murphy, G. Frank, V. Michel, and S. Azen. 1995. Ethnicity and attitudes toward patient autonomy. *Journal of the American Medical Society* 274(10): 820–825.

Buchanan, A. E., and D. W. Brock. 1992. *Deciding for Others: The Ethics of Surrogate Decision Making.* New York: Cambridge University Press.

Cantor, J. 1998. Making advance directives meaningful. *Psychology, Public Policy, & Law,* 4(3): 629–652.

Caralis, P. V., B. Davis, K. Wright, and E. Macial. 1993. The influence of ethnicity and race on attitudes toward advance directive and life-prolonging treatments and euthanasia. *Journal of Clinical Ethics* 4(2): 155–165.

Chin, A. E., K. Hedberg, G. K. Higginson, and D. W. Fleming. 1999. Legalized physician-assisted suicide in Oregon: The first year's experience. *New England Journal of Medicine* 340:577–583.

Cohen, J. S., S. D. Fihn, E. J. Boyko, A. R. Jonsen, and R. W. Wood. 1994. Attitudes toward assisted suicide and euthanasia among physicians in Washington State. *New England Journal of Medicine* 331(2): 89–94.

Csikai, E. L. 1999a. Euthanasia and assisted suicide: Issues for social work practice. *Journal of Gerontological Social Work* 31(3–4): 49–63.

———. 1999b. Hospital social workers' attitudes toward euthanasia and assisted suicide. *Social Work in Health Care* 30(1): 51–73.

Csikai, E. L., and E. Sales. 1998. The emerging social work role on hospital ethics committees: Social workers' and chairs' perspectives. *Social Work* 43(3): 233–242.

Culver, C. M. 1998. Advance directives. *Psychology, Public Policy, & Law* 4(3): 676–687.

Dexter, P. R., F. D. Wolinsky, G. P. Gramelspacher, W.-H. Zhou, G. J. Eckert, M. Waisburd, and W. M. Tierney. 1998. Effectiveness of computer-generated reminders for increasing discussions about advance directives and completion of advance directive forms: A randomized, controlled trial. *Annals of Internal Medicine* 128:102–110.

Emanuel, E. J. 1994. Euthanasia: Historical, ethical, and empiric perspectives. *Archives of Internal Medicine* 154(5): 1890–1901.

Goodman, K. W. 1998. End-of-life algorithms. *Psychology, Public Policy, & Law* 4(3): 719–727.

Gunderson, M., and D. J. Mayo. 2000. Restricting physician-assisted death to the terminally ill. *Hastings Center Report* 30(6): 17–23.

Hauser, J., M., S. F. Kleefield, T. A. Brennan, and J. Fischbach. 1997. Minority populations and advance directives: Insights from a focus group methodology. *Cambridge Quarterly of Healthcare Ethics* 6:58–71.

High, D. M. 1993. Why are elderly people not using advance directives? *Journal of Aging and Health* 5(4): 497–515.

Johnston, S. C., M. P. Pfeifer, and R, McNutt. 1995. The discussion about advance directives. *Archives of Internal Medicine* 155:1025–1030.

Kahn, K. L. 1994. Health care for black and poor hospitalized Medicare patients. *Journal of the American Medical Association* 271:1169–1174.

Kopala, B., and S. L. Kennedy. 1998. Requests for assisted suicide: A nursing issue. *Nursing Ethics* 5(1): 16–26.

La Puma, J., D. Orentlicher, and R. J. Moss. 1991. Advance directions on admission: Clinical implications and analysis of the Patient Self-Determination Act of 1990. *Journal of the American Medical Association* 266:402–405.

Medical Ethics Advisor. 1999a. Americans say, "Keep your laws off my body." *Medical Ethics Advisor* 15(5): 52–53.

———. 1999b. Increase in debates, state bans don't change central fact: It's coming (1999). *Medical Ethics Advisor* 15(5): 49–51.

Miller, P. J. 2000. Life after death with dignity: The Oregon experience. *Social Work* 45(3): 263–271.

Miller, P. J., and S. Hedlund. 1996. Oregon's assisted suicide law: A different perspective. *American Journal of Hospice and Palliative Care* 13(3): 26–53.

Morrison, R. S., E. W. Morrison, and D. F. Glickman. 1994. Physician reluctance to discuss advance directives: An empiric investigation of potential barriers. *Archives of Internal Medicine* 154:2311–2318.

National Association of Social Workers. 2000. Client self-determination and end-of-life decisions. *Social Work Speaks.* Washington, DC: NASW Press.

National Hospice Foundation. 1999. National public opinion research: Baby boomers fear talking to parents about death. Press release.

President's Commission for the Study of Ethical Problems in Medicine and Biomedical and Behavioral Research. 1982. *Making Health Care Decisions.* Washington, DC: U.S. Government Printing Office.

Quill, T. E., D. E. Meier, S. D. Block, and J. A. Billings. 1998. The debate over physician-assisted suicide: Empirical data and convergent views. *Annals of Internal Medicine* 128(7): 552–558.

Rich, B. A. 1998. Personhood, patienthood, and clinical practice: Reassessing advance directives. *Psychology, Public Policy, & Law* 4(3): 610–628.

Roberts, A. R. 2000. An overview of crisis theory and crisis intervention. In *Crisis Intervention Handbook: Assessment, Treatment, and Research,* ed. A. R. Roberts, 3–16. New York: Oxford University Press.

Sabatino, C. P. 2000. *End-of-life Care Legal Trends.* Washington, DC: ABA Commission on Legal Problems of the Elderly.

Schonwetter, R. S., R. M. Walker, M. Solomon, A. Indurkhya, and B. E. Robinson. 1996. Life values, resuscitation preferences, and the applicability of living wills in an older population. *Journal of the American Geriatrics Society* 44:954–858.

Shewchuk, T. R. 1998. Completing advance directives for health care decisions: Getting to yes. *Psychology, Public Policy, & Law* 4(3): 703–718.

Shulman, N. M., and A. L. Shewbert. 2000. A model of crisis intervention in critical and intensive care units of general hospitals. In *Crisis Intervention Handbook: Assessment, Treatment, and Research,* ed. A. R. Roberts, 412–429. New York: Oxford University Press.

Smokowski, P., and J. Wodarski. 1996. Euthanasia and physician-assisted suicide: A social work update. *Health and Social Work* 23(1): 53–65.

Soskis, C. W., and T. S. Kerson. 1992. The Patient Self-Determination Act: Opportunity knocks again. *Social Work in Health Care* 16(4): 1–8.

Sugarman, J., N. R. Powe, D. A. Brillantes, and M. K. Smith. 1993. The cost of ethics legislation: a look at the Patient Self-Determination Act. *Kennedy Institute of Ethics Journal* 3(4): 387–399.

Sullivan, A.D., K. Hedberg, and D. W. Fleming. 2000. Legalized physician-assisted suicide in Oregon: The second year. *New England Journal of Medicine* 342(8): 598–604.

SUPPORT Investigators. 1995. A controlled trial to improve care for seriously ill hospitalized patients: The study to understand prognoses and preferences for outcomes and risks of treatments. *Journal of the American Medical Association* 274(20): 1591–1598.

Teno, J. M., H. L. Nelson, and J. Lynn. 1994. Advance care planning: Priorities for ethical and empirical research. *Hastings Center Report* 24(6): S32–36.

Ulrich, L. P. 1994. The Patient Self-Determination Act and cultural diversity. *Cambridge Quarterly of Healthcare Ethics* 3(3): 410–413.

VandeCreek, L., and D. Frankowski. 1996. Barriers that predict resistance to completing a living will. *Death Studies* 20:73–82.

39

END-OF-LIFE CARE IN PRISONS

JOHN DAWES AND JENNY DAWES

THIS CHAPTER discusses how the dignity and worth of all people and the importance of human relationships can be reflected in practice in end-of-life care for prisoners. This will be a continuing and more common issue for social workers to address as long as imprisonment rates and length of sentences continue to increase. End-of-life care is primarily viewed as occurring when a prisoner's health is such that their death is anticipated. However, it is recognized that prisoners' lives can end in other ways, often sudden and traumatic.

SOCIAL WORK'S PROFESSIONAL VALUES

Social work is a normative profession that affirms a belief in our common humanity. While social workers may choose to be postmodernists in regard to other "truths" (Dawes 2002a; Ife 1997:84–92; Thompson 1995:15–16), they must not retreat from a belief in the dignity and worth of all human beings (Australian Association of Social Workers 1999; National Association of Social Workers 2002). "The primary mission of the social work profession is to enhance human well-being," and core values are the "dignity and worth of the person" and the "importance of human relationships" (NASW 2002). Social work believes that people can aspire to a better life and, when ill, are entitled to receive a high standard of medical care and palliative care as they approach death. This belief includes prisoners, although social work has experienced discomfort in accepting mandated and/or involuntary clients (Barber 1991; Rooney 1992; Ivanoff, Blythe, and Tripodi 1994; Trotter 1997). Several authors have argued that prisoners should be eligible for quality end-of-life care and have considered appropriate mechanisms to ensure this (Dawes 2002b; Maull 1991a, 1991b, 1998). This chapter will assume a basic eligibility of prisoners to quality palliative care, although this remains a highly contested view (Dawes 2002b), and will discuss issues that may arise in the provision of such care and what social workers may be able to do to ensure that prisoners receive good care.

THE UNIQUE ROLE OF SOCIAL WORKERS IN PRISON SETTINGS

Many, and perhaps most, correctional officers have attributed the causes of crime and the individual pain and misery of crime for offenders, including the difficulties of adjustment to prison, as being entirely the result of actions by offenders or their personal weaknesses and failures to cope (Liebling 1992). Put another way, prisoners import into prison their sources of distress. Social workers employed in the criminal justice system, especially in prisons or preparing pre-sentence reports for courts, may have inadvertently contributed to this position. This has occurred because social workers have not only dealt with "cases," that is, individuals, but have also tended to look for the causes of an individual's crime within the individual himself or herself, often using a medical metaphor (e.g., criminal behavior is a sickness) as the basis of communication (Shulman 1984:4). This has come about by a reliance on "psychologistic practice models" (Barber 1991:1). These approaches are reductionist because they fail to make the link between personal troubles and the wider community and the institutions that surround the individual (Barber 1991:1).

It is suggested that an analysis that claims that social workers are focused only on the "inner functioning" of their clients is simplistic and does not accord with the current realities of social-work perspectives that link the prisoner to his or her environment. An ecological perspective, when applied to prisons, provides a framework for understanding the stresses and strains of imprisonment and a richer field for practice than does relying upon psychological and problem-solving approaches exclusively. Social workers are best placed to link prisoners to their families and to the community (Sheldon 2000:493; Oliviere 2001:239). One problem that has plagued prison governance for years is correctional officers filling "posts." Correctional officers regard themselves as working in positions that need to be filled to maintain safety in prisons (Findlay 1998:459; Willmott 1997:333; Day 1983:36). These posts are based upon and "locked" into a known geographical area in the prison, for example, a guard post, a sally port, a wing, or a cellblock. Therefore, correctional officers do not have the organizational capacity to be flexible in their responses to prisoners (even if they wish to) and to focus on an individual rather than the group. It is suggested that this fundamental difficulty with correctional officers will never be overcome, despite many well-meaning and ingenious efforts (for example, case management, unit management, and privatization) in many jurisdictions. Indeed, life for correctional officers will become even more group-focused as crowding increases and governments reduce operating budgets together with continuing demonization of offenders in the political discourse (Mahon 1999).

Social workers are ideally placed to work more flexibly within prisons. At the Louisiana State Penitentiary, "social workers are on site 24 hours per day to work with the patient and his family" (Tillman 2000:519). They do not fill "posts" like correctional officers, and they can legitimately focus on individual dying prisoners and their families. Hayes describes changes in the Louisiana prison system that reduced suicides to just one "in almost 12 years and 57,091 admissions" (1995:452) in a system that had been plagued by difficulties and was poorly regarded. One aspect of the agency's strategy, suggested to Hayes by a prison warden, was the placement of "social workers back in the cell blocks."

Social workers operating in the cellblocks are able to note the impact of status changes and life transitions on prisoners (including coming into prison, health crises,

bereavement, breakdown in relationships, and other losses, including receiving a terminal diagnosis) and to work with prisoners to assist them in coping with these transitions, understanding them, and, except for death, moving on. An existential perspective, aimed at assisting the prisoner "recognize suffering as part of the ongoing
process of life—for human growth and realization of meaning" (Krill 1986:182), can
be grafted onto the other work undertaken by social workers. Self-forgiveness is an
important part of human growth, and moving out from "denial" may create the necessary conditions leading to self-forgiveness and seeking the forgiveness of others before death.

Looking beyond the inner functioning of the prisoner, there are interpersonal processes that social workers may be able to address. These include individual racism,
minority status, being the victim of bullying, taboos, and issues to do with discussions
about deaths of significant persons and communication between different groups of
staff. Shulman (1984:4) notes the value of being aware that clients interact with others
at many levels. With this awareness about prisoners, the social worker may act as a
mediator and/or advocate for the prisoner (Ezell 1994:41–42; Shulman 1984:8), encouraging a climate where staff is more open with prisoners and reasons are given for
decisions.

There is another role that social workers can play. Judith Lee (1994:12) states that
"social work *can* assist people who are oppressed in empowering themselves personally, interpersonally, and politically towards liberation." For some prisoners the word
"liberation" may have at least two meanings. The first, obvious, and sometimes most
problematic and elusive meaning is that of freedom from captivity or release from
prison. This is increasingly unlikely for many prisoners who receive very long sentences and are likely to die in prison. Liberation also has a second and more difficult
meaning. Some prisoners appear to come to terms with their sentences, have forgiven
themselves, and demonstrate a quiet dignity and sense of purpose as they go about
their daily business in prison. Lee (1994) would probably suggest that such prisoners
are empowered and that the social worker's role is to contribute to this kind of empowerment through skill and knowledge at every opportunity. In prison this has occurred through drama, art, undertaking a university degree, religion, caring for native
animals, and, for a small but growing group of prisoners, working as hospice volunteers.

SIMILARITIES BETWEEN PRISON AND
PALLIATIVE-CARE SOCIAL WORK

Social workers in corrections and palliative care share some similarities in their workplace environments, which are often hierarchical and dominated by the other professionals' imperatives. Corrections emphasizes containment, and medical treatment,
although usually provided, is delivered within the constraints of the correctional system. Social workers must operate in a secondary setting with other team members
who may not share their beliefs about the dignity and worth of all people and who
may be more authoritarian and directive in their work with patients and prisoners.

A number of social workers have written about the unique role of social work in palliative care (George 2000; Oliviere 2001; Ryan 1996; Sheldon 2000). Sheldon (2000:492) suggests that, in the United Kingdom, social work in palliative care is becoming recognized as a specialist area. Her study, while small, identified thirty-three themes in the social work role in palliative care, grouped into six categories. There was a focus on family relationships and enabling family communication (Sheldon 2000:493). Related to this task was the ancillary work of managing anxiety—family, other hospice professionals, and the worker's own stress (Sheldon 2000:495). George (2000:268), writing in the Australian context, makes the powerful point that allied health professions such as nursing and physiotherapy are firmly based in the health sciences. Social work, in contrast, is based in the social sciences and humanities. Social work, then, can bring a different, nonmedical perspective to the field of "medicalized" death. Although social work is in a marginalized position in palliative care, George (2000:277) exhorts social workers to develop personal understandings and positions on the ethical issues that arise in social work practice in palliative care.

In a slightly older Australian study, Ryan surveyed fifty-three social workers employed in hospice and palliative care and 134 service directors of these programs to assess their utilization and perception of social workers. The service directors returned 120 replies (Ryan 1996:49). Most services did not employ a social worker (seventy-seven, or 64 percent) with forty-one (34 percent) doing so. The seventy-seven services employed a variety of other staff (twenty-two grief counselors; twenty-two pastoral care workers; ten counselors; nine psychologists; four welfare workers; eleven others, mainly nurses; and twenty-five classified as "none of the above." The majority of those agencies employing social workers were very positive about social work and the skills and knowledge applied by social workers (Ryan 1996:51).

The thirty-seven social workers (thirty-three females and four males) reported particular problems they encountered: overlap and blurring of roles (ten); skepticism of social work's contribution (nine); role conflict with nurses (six); role conflict with pastoral care workers (four); and lack of training and omnipotence of nursing staff (Ryan 1996:51). Ryan concludes that his findings suggest that "social work may have to fight hard to have a core, distinct role in multi-disciplinary palliative care teams in Australia" (1996:52). He identifies key areas for contribution by social work:

- Articulating and ensuring attention to psychosocial factors in patient care
- Direct service delivery with patients and their families
- Contributing a specialist knowledge of community resources
- Being involved with the selection, training, placement, ongoing support, and supervision of hospice volunteers
- Involvement in the education of other disciplines and the community and bringing a psychosocial focus to this
- Contributing to hospice policy and planning, evaluation, and research (1996:48).

Social workers involved in end-of-life care in prisons can adapt all of these community roles, and they form a useful reminder of the worth of their daily contribution of professional skills.

According to Oliviere (2001:237), social workers occupy an "eccentric" or off-center position "at the interface between the wider society and the patient's family system." Social workers in corrections may also perceive themselves as operating at such an interface at some distance from what is seen as the core work of their organization. In prisons and palliative care, both are uniquely positioned to help the person at the end of life by mediating meaningful beneficial connections between the person and appropriate social systems, although the efforts of social workers helping prisoners at the end of their life may attract less social approval. However, both forms of social work have the same core—the valuing of a human being. This is manifest in a belief that it is not appropriate to abandon people at death and in facilitating a "good death." Dame Cicely Saunders (Thompson 2002:28) says that "a good death is a person's *own* death." The self-determinism inherent in this statement is that a person is entitled to die in his or her own way and is congruent with social work's belief in self-determination.

DYING ALONE

Although dying "is an inherently lonely state, because it is irreversible, relentless, incomparable in its finality and because social support typically comes from persons, albeit empathetic, not experiencing dying" (Berger et al. 2000:69), it is mainly the understanding and committed company of others that offers amelioration. Prisoners, however, are at risk of experiencing both care from unsympathetic others and dying alone.

Being left to die alone is perhaps the ultimate rejection a person can experience, the antithesis to good end-of-life care. The challenge of preventing this may be easier to overcome once a prisoner is cared for within a recognized palliative care program. However, this will not necessarily remove the fear of rejection engendered for a prisoner by his knowledge that many prisoners do die alone, often in distress, even though he may be in an institution with hundreds of other people nearby. This is an extremely important matter for prisoners (Tillman 2000:518), and its significance was recognized in Australia during the Royal Commission into Aboriginal Deaths in Custody.

The RCIADIC was established in 1987 following a rapid increase in Indigenous deaths. It inquired into ninety-nine Aboriginal deaths in detail from January 1980 until May 31, 1989, and considered the wider context of those deaths. This included comparisons with non-Aboriginal deaths in the same period. The RCIADIC found that "Aboriginal people do not die at a greater rate than non-Aboriginal people in custody," but added, "what is overwhelmingly different is the rate at which Aboriginal people come into custody compared with the rate of the general community" (Johnston 1991, vol. 1, Findings 1.3.1 and 1.3.2; for a more detailed discussion of the RCIADIC see Dawes 2002a). The RCIADIC also paid particular attention to whether a prisoner died alone. Many of the 152 prison deaths were sudden and lonely and in distressing circumstances. Another sixty-three excluded deaths were in hospital, which the RCIADIC assumed meant the person did not die alone. However, this is not necessarily true. It is also possible that, being prisoners, these people did not find everyone around them was an empathic carer. More certain is that they were strangers to them.

TABLE 39.1 ALONE AT TIME OF DEATH

STATUS	INDIGENOUS	NONINDIGENOUS	TOTALS
Alone	13	105	128
With others	3	31	34
Totals	16	136	152

Includes self-inflicted deaths, homicides, accidental deaths, and deaths from natural causes (e.g., heart attack, cancer)

Sources: Biles, McDonald, and Fleming 1992; Dawes 1997.

The possibility of dying alone is discussed in another study. Dawes (1997) examined nineteen deaths from natural causes in the South Australian state prison system. One prisoner had a heart attack in the front seat of a prison truck while with an officer and another prisoner. Four deaths occurred in dormitory accommodation and eight in hospitals, but a significant number, six deaths, occurred in single cells. It is also possible that some of the other prisoners died without anyone being alert to what happening for them, particularly if a prisoner's life ends suddenly. Usually this is unexpected, and often it is traumatic. In such situations, there may be little care that can be given for the prisoner whose life has come to an end, but much that may help those affected. For example, a young man, recently imprisoned, attempted suicide in his cell. He was transferred to hospital where he remained on life support until his parents arrived. The hospital social worker contacted the correctional agency as an advocate for the parents who wanted to see their son's cell and to discuss his death with staff. In the absence of a protocol for this, their visit was facilitated personally by John Dawes in his role as chief executive officer, but using his social work skills. They seemed to find the visit helpful.

One role for social workers is to advocate that, where prisoners' physical or mental health is frail, they are more closely cared for and monitored. If such care cannot be given in situ by appropriate providers who are also able to access further support, then removal to a prison medical facility or to an external hospital or hospice offers some hope that the prisoner will not be left alone (Lattanzi-Licht, Mahoney, and Miller 1998:132).

Of course, prisoners who are receiving palliative care in their own cells—that is, decentralized care, called by Maull the "scatter-bed" approach (1998:62)—may still die alone. Social workers' voices can advocate for such prisoners to be moved to a hospice if possible and appropriate or for volunteer prisoners to assist through the long night hours. Dying with supportive and caring staff and volunteers present is an important statement of the worth and individuality of the prisoners. Reducing the numbers of prisoners who die alone in their cells should be a policy choice for all decent prison systems.

THE ISSUE OF ADVANCE DIRECTIVES

As well as the issue of dying alone, another concern regarding end-of-life care in prisons relates to the increasing prevalence of advance directives in the United States, the United Kingdom, and Australia (and in other developed Western countries). Frail and/or elderly people may be encouraged to consider making various "advance directives," particularly a "do not resuscitate order" (DNR). Sometimes a DNR is a condition of entry into a hospice program—although in the United States less than "one third of dying persons use hospice care" (Friedman, Harwood, and Shields 2002:73; see chapters 37 and 38, this volume).

DNRs manifest the particular challenges of providing appropriate end-of-life care to prisoners. A person living in the community is more likely to have access to the support of a loving family and friends and to be confident that a completed DNR is not giving approval to caregivers to provide less than adequate care. But in a prison, with limits on funding and resources, getting enough appropriate care can be difficult. Deficiencies in care can be interpreted by prisoners as being devalued as a human being. In such an environment, completing a DNR may be seen by the prisoner concerned as giving approval to the authorities to provide a lesser standard of care (Parker and Paine 1999; Maull 1998:68). This may be heightened in some cases by prisoners' awareness that their crimes have created the desire in others (such as victims' families) to see the prisoner's life end.

Social workers alert to prisoners' concerns may be able to reassure the prisoner that she or he will receive appropriate care and to act to ensure blockages to receiving appropriate services are minimized (Shulman 1984:5–7). When advance directives do not apply, then medical and nursing decisions will be made by the prison hospice care staff where prisoners are wards of the state, for example, in Louisiana (Tillman 2000:516), and by relatives or an agent, if available, in other jurisdictions if the prisoner is incompetent.

DUTY OF CARE

The end of life in prisons presents other issues, some not dissimilar to deaths in other public institutions or in a workplace. Those in charge of them may have a legally constructed duty of care. The processes by which this is supposed to be enacted may require internal formal reporting and perhaps investigation. In addition, there may be external accountability mechanisms that activate the involvement of third parties, including police and lawyers. In Australia, deaths in custody and in any public institutions are subject to an investigation under the auspices of the coroner for the relevant state. Similar provisions apply elsewhere. This may lead to an inquest, an open court hearing, to determine what led to the person's death. Social workers involved may be called as witnesses. Awareness of these possible consequences can impinge on end-of-life care in both positive and negative ways, for example, motivating authorities to pay attention to providing adequate care, but also creating an anxiety that sometimes results in rigid enforcement of intrusive procedures. Social workers who are conscious of their roles as advocates can view any inquiry as an opportunity that might produce an improvement in service delivery.

STRUCTURE AND ORGANIZATION OF SERVICE

There are several possible ways in which end-of-life care for prisoners can be provided and social work skills are helpful in assessing this. A terminally ill prisoner may be able to be cared for within the prison, either in his or her own cell or in a medical facility within the prison. This is one policy choice (Dawes 2002b). It is also possible that a community hospice (or some other palliative care provider) may deliver services into the prison. A prisoner may also be moved to care outside the prison, either into a hospice or other facility in which some palliative care is provided, or to his or her own home or a friend's and have the appropriate care delivered there.

Although it might be preferable to have the full range of options and allow the prisoner to make an informed personal choice (Lattanzi-Licht, Mahoney, and Miller 1998:231), this seems unlikely, but it does suggest a possible goal for service development. Consideration would need to be given to the advantages and disadvantages of each option (Dawes 2000b). These will vary with the particular circumstances of each prison and its community.

Similarly, the location of care for each prisoner offers advantages and disadvantages that will differ for each individual. Social workers are well placed (Oliviere 2001) to assist in this because taking a holistic approach to end-of-life care means balancing the need to deliver appropriate medical/nursing services against the prisoner's social/ psychological needs. For instance, transferring a prisoner outside the prison involves leaving a place, people, and routines that may have become very familiar. Fellow prisoners and prison officers may have become sources of social support. This can be a substantial loss for a long-term prisoner, despite the sense of personal "failure" and fear of dying inside, described by Maull (1991a, 1998) as a "double whammy."

However, the social worker may find the prisoner has very limited choice or none, because of availability or official policy. The work is then to find the choices that can be made (or developed) within the prescribed limits to enable the prisoner to have as much quality of life as possible. If the prisoner leaves the prison, the role may become more about facilitating connections to significant friends left behind and supporting these friends, including in their bereavement.

In any context, the social worker will be dealing with a number of other people. Even where a formal well-integrated multidisciplinary team has not developed, social workers can find opportunities to form supportive connections, develop skills, and utilize strengths. Respect for others, a social work value, also means recognizing that someone else may be the appropriate person to provide aspects of care, for example, the prison chaplain, perhaps because that it is the prisoner's choice and not one's own.

FRAMING THE WORK

The challenges in providing end-of-life care in prisons should not obscure the fact that such a time provides the opportunity to make life-changing differences as it is a time of existential crisis for all those closely involved (Caplan 1990:28). Thus, it may also be confronting to the social worker involved, perhaps for personal reasons that may need to be dealt with through support, supervision, and self-care (see chapter 44).

According to Berger et al. (2000:69), "the fundamental elements of appropriate care . . . for terminally ill patients should include substantive communication with a competent doctor; appropriate psychosocial support; sensitivity to cultural, philosophic, and spiritual needs; regard for personhood; respect for the patient's valued interpersonal relationships; and an individualized plan of care."

Keeping these in mind, it may also be useful, in providing end-of-life care for prisoners, for social workers involved to consider adopting the framework of intervention set out in the mission statement of St. Christopher's Hospice in London (Saunders 2002:24). As well as providing the imprimatur of a leading service to what the social worker is attempting to achieve, this structure may help facilitate discussion, liaison, and support with external palliative-care services for whom these are likely to form well-accepted aspects of service. It is pertinent to note that Dame Cicely Saunders, so instrumental in the founding of St Christopher's, was originally a medical social worker.

These are:

- To affirm life; not to hasten death but to regard it as a normal process
- To respect the worth and individuality of each person for whom we care
- To offer relief from pain and other distressing symptoms
- To help patients with strong and unfamiliar emotions. To assist them explore meaning, purpose, and value in their lives. To offer the opportunity to reconcile and heal relationships and complete important personal tasks
- To offer a support system to family and friends during the patient's illness and bereavement.

It is worthwhile considering some aspects of each in the prison context:

1. *To affirm life: not to hasten death but to regard it as a normal process.* The challenge for all those involved in end of life care in prisons is to achieve some sense of "normal" death in the gendered, non-normal world of a prison with its skewed age and social profile (including no children), controlled environment, and unusual physical surroundings. But the issue is really about enabling the person to live out their remaining time as much as possible in ways that they wish and to die with as much peace as possible. Assisting the prisoner maintain connection with fellow prisoners, supportive staff, and visitors, together with day-to-day life in the prison, can form a significant part of this. A social worker should ask: Who is the person connected to? And who should this prisoner be connected to? The prisoner may also wish to be protected from some others, and he or she may need some support about this choice.

2. *To respect the worth and individuality of each person for whom we care.* Respect for the inherent worth and individuality of each person for whom we care is part of the value base of social work. But holding to this belief does not necessarily make the work easy, as many writers from a medical and nursing perspective attest (Lehmann

1983:38; Norman and Parrish 1999a:1–2, 1999b:654; Day 1983:35–36; Willmott 1997: 334). Some of the people for whom we care have behaved in ways that shake our belief in humanity and that can easily come between our clients and us as we struggle to support them. There is no easy way to address this. We each have to make our own resolution and ongoing commitment. It is worth remembering that, no matter how wicked the crime or crimes, the person is more than a prisoner. There is a chance for social workers to get to know more of the person's story—a person who happens to be a prisoner. People, including prisoners, cannot die appropriately when huge "chunks" of their life story remain untold or when desired opportunities for reconciliation with families and friends (and perhaps even with victims) are denied to them. This could occur through writing letters or having personal messages passed on.

The social worker could also explore with the prisoner how she or he might die if they were free citizens in the community. This might provide some helpful clues in further personalizing care. An element in this may be to enable the prisoner, should he or she wish, to make some choices about funeral arrangements and the disposal of possessions, however meager. This can form an expression of power and control in a situation and an environment where these are quite limited and enable the person to insure inclusion or recognition of those significant to them. There is a real possibility, in the prison context, that some people's grief will be disenfranchised (see Doka 1989). For example, a long-serving South Australian prisoner killed himself just prior to release. An apparently lonely man, he had no known friends outside the prison system, and his family had not been in contact for years. After his death the family arranged the funeral but refused to allow prisoners and staff to attend. His fellow prisoners did contribute to a wreath, and a memorial service was held at the prison. Social workers are well placed to intervene in such situations to promote the well-being of those most affected.

In the prison context, it can be even more important to facilitating a peaceful death that conditions are created that encourage a prisoner to speak about the positives in his or her life and have these affirmed. However, because of the correctional environment and its constraints, affirming life and the positives in prisoners' lives may not be the choice of other staff or prisoners—they are involuntary associates and can partially opt out of participation (see Findlay 1998:460). The social worker may want to advocate for staff and prisoners who cannot cope (Lattanzi-Licht, Mahoney, and Miller 1998:81–81).

3. *To offer relief from pain and other distressing symptoms.* Narrowly interpreted, offering relief from physical pain and other distressing symptoms is the work of physicians and nurses. The social worker's role can be conceived as peripheral if pain is narrowly defined. In medicalized settings, a focus on psychological and physical care often takes precedence (Oliviere 2001:238), but pain in its broader meaning may include acute awareness of being in the "graceless" (Maull 1991:179) environment of a prison, often shut away from family and friends and being subject to the capriciousness of institutional life. This conception provides the scope for the social worker's unique skills, for example in engaging "family" in its wider sense, in assisting prisoners as they come to the end of their life.

4. *To help patients with strong and unfamiliar emotions.* Loss, fear, anger, depression, resentment, guilt, powerlessness, loneliness, ambivalence, anxiety, regret, shame, and despair are not uncommon emotions at some time to most human beings. As a person comes to the end of life, he or she may be strongly present in reflecting on the current situation and where life has led. Prisoners are no different, nor those closely involved with them, including other prisoners (Maull 1991). The challenge presented to the worker is to try to facilitate the expression of such emotions and the thoughts connected to them, so nonphysical pain, a barrier to communication, is reduced. This is pertinent when opportunities to do so may be especially limited, something that can be particularly true of secure institutional settings (Maull 1991).

Although this may be familiar work to many social workers dealing with end-of-life care, the prison context may inhibit such work. Prisoners have an additional acculturation in the expression of emotion, which may vary somewhat between institutions and with how long the person has been there and his or her perceived status among peers. Creative work, such as the use of music and various forms of art, may facilitate expression, especially if verbal communication presents difficulties. However, those involving themselves in their circle of care and concern may include people who remain part of that culture or linked to it. Providing sufficient privacy may be a challenge and respectful sensitivity must be exercised to ensure the prisoner's best interests prevail.

5. *To offer a support system to family and friends during the patient's illness and bereavement.* Many factors will affect the capacity of prison systems to offer support for family and friends as a prisoner approaches the end of life. Correctional agencies see themselves as legally mandated to work with unconvicted prisoners on remand and convicted prisoners under sentence. For such agencies to offer support to a dying prisoner's family and friends constitutes a major extension of their role. However, such a role is increasingly being forced on correctional agencies because they are confronted with providing care for an aging prisoner population serving longer sentences as governments respond to calls for harsher sentences (Dawes 2002a, 2002b).

In hospice care, the family includes all those in loving relationships with the person who is dying, who offer support, regardless of blood or legal ties (Lattanzi-Licht, Mahoney, and Miller 1998:29). Thus, in the prison context, prisoners, prison staff, and others involved over time in supporting the prisoner may well be considered "family." For example, in a comprehensive biography of the last Australian prisoner to be executed, Richards (2002:294, 369) describes the Catholic chaplain's twice saying mass for the condemned man. On each occasion a young prison officer chose to participate along with Ryan and take communion. The first was two days before Christmas 1966 and the second was at 7:00 on the morning of the execution on February 3, 1967. Ryan had been convicted of shooting and killing a prison officer in a daring escape from Pentridge Prison in Melbourne, Victoria.

Although it may be possible to recognize individuals of such a "family" network and offer them help, including during their bereavement, there may be others, friends and members of the prisoner's family, who are affected and would like to be more involved, but who face a multiplicity of barriers. Some correctional agencies have responded positively to the challenge of overcoming some of these by providing accommodation near prison hospices for stayovers by family and friends. Where this is not possible, community groups may be able to offer support through the provision of affordable accommodation nearby for prisoners' families and friends. Many prisons are located far from towns and cities and do not attract the interest of concerned citizens through a support group. These agencies may have to consider the provision of accommodation on prison property for such purposes. During the 1970s, Ararat Prison in Victoria, Australia, provided a flat for use by families of long-term prisoners who had traveled interstate to see their prisoner relatives. Such a facility could easily be used for relatives of a dying prisoner to stay over and thus be able to spend more time with that prisoner.

Other prison systems, for example Angola (Louisiana State Penitentiary), provide for extended visits for relatives of prisoners receiving hospice care (Tillman 2000:521). Indeed, at Angola, family, including children, are allowed to remain with the dying prisoner around the clock. Where there is no family, prisoner volunteers may be able to be "a companion and friend to the dying patient" (Tillman 2000:518). If there is no one, including other prisoners, then the social worker and other staff may, indeed should, provide the gift of human presence at death.

WHEN LIFE ENDS SUDDENLY

Many deaths in prisons are not from terminal illness. These other deaths may be unexpected and traumatic, thus making considerable demands on intrapersonal and system resources and complicating the grief of survivors. Outcomes for them and the organization are likely to be better if protocols are already in place. The preceding discussion can provide some guidance for their development.

Perhaps the greatest challenge for some social workers in prisons in some countries is the issue of end-of-life care for prisoners who are executed by the state. Involving oneself in this act may be personally confronting and present the greatest challenge to social work values about end of life care (see Richards 2002).

CONCLUSION

Good service delivery of end-of-life care in prisons is in its infancy, but social workers are uniquely placed to make a significant contribution to its development. In this socially isolated, structured, and contained environment, it offers a special opportunity to model the importance of valuing each person as long as he or she lives, respecting him or her in death, and, in its aftermath, finding ways to sustain life's losses with courage and dignity rather than acting out through destructive behaviors.

REFERENCES

Australian Association of Social Workers. 1999. Code of ethics. www.aasw.asn.au.

Barber, J. G. 1991. *Beyond Casework*. London: Macmillan.

Berger, T., F. Rosner, J. Potash, P. Kark, and A. Bennett. 2000. Communication in caring for terminally ill patients. *Journal of Palliative Medicine* 3(1): 69–73.

Biles, D., D. McDonald, and J. Fleming. 1992. Research Paper No. 7, Australian deaths in custody, 1980–88: An analysis of aboriginal and non-aboriginal deaths in prison and police custody. In *Deaths in Custody Australia, 1980–1989*, ed. D. Biles and D. McDonald, 107–136. Canberra: Australian Institute of Criminology.

Caplan, G. 1990. Loss, stress, and mental health. *Community Mental Health Journal* 26(1): 27–48.

Dawes, J. 2002a. Losses and justice: An Australian perspective. In *Loss and Grief: A Guide for Human Service Practitioners*, ed. N. Thompson, 174–189. London: Palgrave Macmillan.

———. 2002b. Dying with dignity: Prisoners and terminal illness. *Illness, Crisis and Loss* 10(3): 188–203.

Dawes, M. J. 1997. Dying in prison: A study of deaths in correctional custody in South Australia, 1980–1993. Ph.D. diss., Flinders University of South Australia.

Day, R. 1983. The challenge: Health care vs. security. *Canadian Nurse* 79(7): 34–36.

Doka, K., ed. 1989. *Disenfranchised Grief: Recognizing Hidden Sorrow*. New York: Lexington.

Ezell, M. 1994. Advocacy practice of social workers. *Families in Society* 1:36–45.

Findlay, I. 1998. Managing terminally ill prisoners: Reflection and action. *Palliative Medicine* 12:457–461.

Friedman, B., M. Harwood, and M. Shields. 2002. Barriers and enablers to hospice referrals: An expert overview. *Journal of Palliative Medicine* 5(1): 73–84.

George, J. 2000. The allied health professions and death. In *Death and Dying in Australia*, ed. A. Kellehear, 257–283. South Melbourne: Oxford University Press.

Hayes, L. 1995. Prison suicide: An overview and guide to prevention. *The Prison Journal* 75(4): 431–456.

Ife, J. W. 1997. *Rethinking Social Work: Towards Critical Practice*. South Melbourne: Longman.

Ivanoff, A., B. Blythe, and T. Tripodi. 1994. *Involuntary Clients in Social Work Practice*. New York: Aldine de Gruyter.

Johnston, E., ed. 1991. *Royal Commission Into Aboriginal Deaths in Custody*, vols. 1–5. Canberra: Australian Government Publication Service.

Krill, D. F. 1986. Existential social work. In *Social Work Treatment: Interlocking Theoretical Approaches*, ed. F. J. Turner, 187–217. New York: Free Press.

Lattanzi-Licht, M., J. Mahoney, and G. Miller. 1998. *The Hospice Choice: In Pursuit of a Peaceful Death*. New York: Simon & Schuster.

Lee, J. A. B. 1994. *The Empowerment Approach to Social Work Practice*. New York: Columbia University Press.

Lehmann, A. 1983. Nursing's last frontier: Our Canadian prisons. *Canadian Nurse* 79(7): 37–39.

Liebling, A. 1992. *Suicides in Prison*. London: Routledge.

Mahon, N. 1999. Death and dying behind bars. *Journal of Law, Medicine & Ethics* 27(3): 213.

Maull, F. 1991a. Dying in prison: Sociocultural and psychosocial dynamics. *Hospice Journal* 7(1–2): 127–142.

———. 1991b. Hospice care for prisoners: Establishing an inmate staffed hospice program in a prison medical facility. *Hospice Journal* 7(3): 57–82.

———. 1998. Issues in prison hospice: Toward a model for the delivery of hospice care in a correctional setting. *Hospice Journal* 13(4): 57–82.

National Association of Social Workers. 2002. Code of ethics. www.naswdc.org/pubs/code/code.asp.

Norman, A., and A. Parrish. 1999a. Working and learning in a controlled environment. *Nurse Education Today* 19(1): 1–2.

———. 1999b. Prison health care: Work environment and the nursing role. *British Journal of Nursing* 8(10): 653–656.

Oliviere, D. 2001. The social worker in palliative care: The "eccentric" role. *Progress in Palliative Care* 9(6): 237–241.

Parker, F., and C. Paine. 1999. Informed consent and the refusal of medical treatment in a correctional setting. *Journal of Law, Medicine & Ethics* 27(13): 240.

Richards, M. 2002. *The Hanged Man: The Life and Death of Ronald Ryan.* Carlton North, Victoria: Scribe.

Rooney, R. 1992. *Strategies for Work with Involuntary Clients.* New York: Columbia University Press.

Ryan, M. 1996. "Walking a minefield": Findings from a survey of social workers in Australian hospice and palliative care programs. *Australian Social Work* 49(3): 47–54.

Saunders, C. 2002. The philosophy of hospice. In *Loss and Grief: A Guide for Human Service Practitioners,* ed. N. Thompson, 23–33. London: Palgrave Macmillan.

Sheldon, F. 2000. Dimensions of the role of the social worker in palliative care. *Palliative Medicine* 14:491–498.

Shulman, L. 1984. *The Skills of Helping Individuals and Groups.* 2d ed. Itasca, IL: F. E. Peacock.

Thompson, N. 1995. *Theory and Practice in Health and Social Welfare.* Buckingham, UK: Open University Press.

———, ed. 2002. *Loss and Grief: A Guide for Human Service Practitioners.* London: Palgrave Macmillan.

Tillman, T. 2000. Hospice in prison: The Louisiana state penitentiary program. *Journal of Palliative Medicine* 3(4): 513–524.

Trotter, C. 1999. *Working with Involuntary Clients.* St Leonards, New South Wales: Allen and Unwin.

Willmott, Y. 1997. Prison nursing: The tension between custody and care. *British Journal of Nursing* 6(6): 333–336.

40

SOCIAL WORK END-OF-LIFE RESEARCH

BETTY J. KRAMER AND MERCEDES BERN-KLUG

AS HAS been evident throughout this volume, there is urgent need to improve practices and policies relevant to end-of-life care. Research provides an essential avenue for evaluating the current state of services provided at the end of life and for determining what practices and policies are most likely to have a beneficial impact at all levels of care. Although research on dying persons, their families, and end-of-life care has grown dramatically in recent years (George 2002), there is general agreement across disciplines that the paucity of scientific knowledge relevant to end-of-life constrains efforts to improve care practices and policies significantly (Cohen, MacNeil, and Mount 1997; Corner 1996; Ferrell and Grant 2001; Pickett, Cooley, and Gordon 1998). Although the unique perspectives and training of social workers to effect change and address inequities in service systems across the life course and in a wide variety of settings have the potential to make important contributions to enhancing end-of-life care, the social work literature is limited in this area.

The purpose of this chapter is to discuss essential issues relevant to social work end-of-life research. We begin this chapter by articulating four fundamental assumptions about social work end-of-life practice and research. We will discuss the conceptual challenge of defining "end of life" and highlight the scope of social work end-of-life practice and research. We articulate three primary research roles that social workers may adopt, and we conclude by suggesting areas of inquiry that represent research needs in the field.

ASSUMPTIONS

Assumption 1: Social work conceptual frameworks can contribute to end-of-life research in medical and nonmedical areas.

Social work curriculum covers a wide range of theories that address issues of power, culture, strengths, interpersonal dynamics, and psychological, biological, and social development. Diverse conceptual frameworks and theories can enliven and broaden the scope of the current end-of-life literature, which is primarily concerned with medical issues. Social work's emphasis on psychosocial issues, transitions (both on a personal level and between care systems), family dynamics, and serving people who are disenfranchised or marginalized are assets to end-of-life research.

In addition to practice and research centered on the person-in-environment frame-work, Robbins, Chatterjee, and Canda (1998) have suggested that social workers de-velop familiarity and expertise in applying other theories that adopt a broad definition of human behavior. They remind us of the valuable contributions to social work practice and research possible through systems theory; conflict theories; theories of empowerment; theories of assimilation, acculturation, and bicultural socialization; psychodynamic theory; life span theories; theories of cognitive and moral develop-ment; symbolic interaction; phenomenology, social constructionism, and hermeneu-tics; behaviorism, social learning, and exchange theory; and transpersonal theory. These theories have much to offer social workers engaged in end-of-life research, and suggest domains for investigation that are not elaborated in current literature.

Assumption 2: Social workers have vital and unique roles related to end-of-life care.

Interdisciplinary teams are considered an essential standard for quality care of the dying; social workers are core members of these teams. The social work role includes addressing (for the individual and the family, as well as for the team) psychosocial issues such as suffering, loss, anxiety, guilt, remorse, fear, gratitude, meaningfulness, and hope. Social-work team members have communication skills and training in crisis management and decision making. Workers are knowledgeable about community programs and resources available to support the individual and the family. Part of being an effective social worker is being an effective advocate, ever cognizant of the inappropriate use of power and of social justice issues. Social workers learn, and can teach, how to effect change at the micro, meso, and macro levels. These attributes and others facilitate excellent end-of-life care, in the context of teamwork.

When social workers work with individuals and families outside of a healthcare team context, and indeed outside of a medical context, they draw upon this set of skills as well. As will be noted, given the scope and breadth of practice, social workers are in the unique position of helping individuals and families address grief, crisis, and traumatic loss in multiple and varied settings not traditionally addressed by other professionals.

Assumption 3: It is the responsibility of the social work profession to articulate its role and document its effectiveness.

Social work research lags far behind what our colleagues in medicine and nursing have initiated to document the role of various professions in care of the dying, to illuminate deficiencies in care, and to identify and test innovative strategies for im-proving care. An exhaustive search of the literature conducted for another project revealed nearly four hundred articles that addressed a broad range of topics relevant to social work and end-of-life, palliative care, and grief work. Analysis revealed that the vast majority of publications were discussion pieces or descriptions of programs and services. Only 24 percent of the published manuscripts were empirical studies. Although discussions and descriptions are useful for stimulating thought and providing details about services, they are not sufficient. Social workers have the responsibility to determine and to demonstrate that what they contribute to end-of-life care is nec-essary and of value.

Assumption 4: Inattention to research constrains social work's ability to improve care.

The absence of social work research has the potential to diminish professional standing and to constrain the profession's ability to improve care. The ultimate reason to engage in research is to improve services and to enhance care (Ferrell and Grant 2001; Richards, Corner, and Clark 1998). The deficiencies in care of the dying, especially physical care, have been well documented (Meier, Morrison, and Cassel 1997). The most rigorous study conducted to date, the Study to Understand Prognoses and Preferences for Outcomes and Risks of Treatments (SUPPORT), was a $28 million project that enrolled more than nine thousand patients with life-threatening illnesses in five U.S. teaching hospitals over a four-year period. SUPPORT demonstrated deficiencies in provider/patient communication of treatment preferences, overreliance on aggressive treatment, poor control of pain, and limited responses of physicians to interventions designed to increase discussions of patient preferences (SUPPORT Principal Investigators 1995). Another study that looked at care in various settings documented end-of-life care deficiencies (Hanson, Danis, and Garrett 1997). Drawing upon a representative sample of bereaved family members of older adults who died in multiple settings, deficiencies were reported in healthcare provider availability, communication skills, and availability and quality of in-home care (Hanson, Danis, and Garrett 1997). These and many other studies document that there is enormous room for improvement in how care is provided to seriously ill persons and their family members.

Although the deficiencies are well known, gaps in research limit the understanding of evidence-based solutions for addressing them. The Institute of Medicine's 1997 report on improving care at the end of life notes the paucity of research in general and an absence of a scientific foundation of practice, and it concludes that "much remains to be learned about how people die and how reliably excellent and compassionate care can be achieved" (Field and Cassel 1997:235). Drawing upon insights gained from working with people facing end-of-life issues in multiple settings, social workers have numerous and important opportunities to enhance care and to contribute to the growing body of knowledge relevant to end-of-life care.

WHAT IS "END-OF-LIFE"? A CONCEPTUAL CHALLENGE

As we attempt to discern the roles and functions of social work in end-of-life care and hence in end-of-life care research, we should acknowledge the conceptual ambiguity around this term. There is no consensus regarding what is meant by the term *end of life*. In the research literature, the term is used in many ways. In the practice context, "end of life" may be operationalized in many different ways depending, in part, upon what the setting has to offer and who is served. Examples of terms and concepts that are used synonymously include dying, actively dying, having a terminal diagnosis, and having a health condition that responds poorly or no longer responds to curative care. As is evident then, "end of life" may mean the last hours of a person's life, the last days, the last months, or the last years.

As we begin the twenty-first century, we are faced with more—rather than less—ambiguity about who could—or should—be considered to be "at the end of life."

This ambiguity about when the socially constructed (and medically implemented) dying role takes over from the sick role or the chronically ill role has yet to be fully articulated. We have arrived at a point in human history when informed people can legitimately hold different opinions about whether someone is "at the end of life." As more people survive into old age with multiple chronic conditions, some of which are progressive, this ambiguity will become even more commonplace. The ambiguity is not limited to older adults with multiple chronic conditions. It can affect any age group when the person's health status is seriously impaired and he or she is at higher risk for death, but the time of death is highly uncertain, and further treatment is possibly warranted.

This ambiguity about determining health status at the end of life can spill over to ambiguity about the time of death. Indeed, for the leading causes of death, it is difficult to determine when any one person will likely die, although they may be quite sick. Joanne Lynn comments on this ambiguity in describing the sample from the SUPPORT study: "Thus, very few SUPPORT patients could readily be classified as 'dying' in the sense that they—or anyone—would have found it appropriate to accept death and be treated for symptoms at home. Instead, they were thought to have a substantial chance to leave the hospital and to do well for a while if treatment were successful. Most of our patients were in the "middle muddle" of prognoses, bad enough to be at risk of death but good enough to hope for longer survival with the appropriate treatment" (Lynn et al. 2000:S218).

Whether the person's status is ambiguous or he or she is in the "middle muddle," social workers are often involved in addressing the psychosocial, financial, and re-source issues that are sure to arise. As we will discuss, the potential for social workers to address end-of-life related concerns are pervasive across a wide variety of settings.

SCOPE OF SOCIAL WORK END-OF-LIFE PRACTICE AND RESEARCH

Social work research in end-of-life care should optimally address the varied domains and wide scope of social work practice. While end-of-life care is commonly thought of as being provided in healthcare settings, social work's role and potential impact moves beyond medical settings, as shown in figure 40.1. Social work is the most broadly based profession in relation to the multiple settings where practitioners provide services to persons with life threatening conditions or to those who have experienced deaths in their social networks, or traumatic losses in their lives. There are few social work contexts in which practitioners do not interact with clients and their family members who are experiencing loss, grief, and/or trauma (Kramer 1998).

Examples of the scope of settings in which social workers may confront end-of-life issues include child welfare and family service agencies, schools, court systems, mental health agencies, employee assistance programs, crisis centers, homeless shelters, nursing homes, day and adult day centers, senior centers, community based substance abuse and health agencies, hospitals, and hospices. Although not traditionally discussed as an end-of-life care issue (outside of the context of persons with life-threatening con-

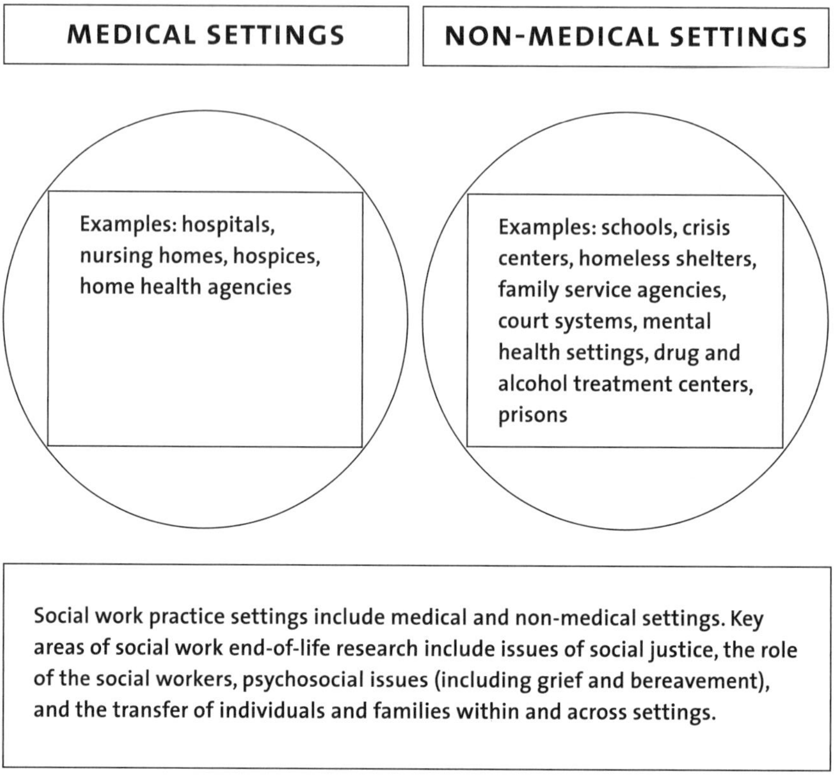

| MEDICAL SETTINGS | NON-MEDICAL SETTINGS |

Examples: hospitals, nursing homes, hospices, home health agencies

Examples: schools, crisis centers, homeless shelters, family service agencies, court systems, mental health settings, drug and alcohol treatment centers, prisons

Social work practice settings include medical and non-medical settings. Key areas of social work end-of-life research include issues of social justice, the role of the social workers, psychosocial issues (including grief and bereavement), and the transfer of individuals and families within and across settings.

FIGURE 40.1 Social Work End-of-Life Research Arenas
Source: Weber and Blacker 1997.

ditions), active or passive suicide is also encountered by social workers in varied settings.

Tasks that social workers may undertake relevant to end-of-life care are as varied as the settings in which they are employed. Social workers may assist with preparation about dying and dealing with the death, assisting clients who are confronting multiple losses, and addressing grief and bereavement. End–of-life issues reach beyond the time of death. A case in point is the school social worker who provides counseling and other supportive services to students, parents, and teachers following the death of a student or teacher who has been sick, or following a sudden death due to an accident or acute illness. School social workers may also address end-of-life issues associated with terrorism, community violence, or natural disasters. When a serious diagnosis is present, the social worker can begin preparing people for the death. But in many cases, school social workers may be more actively involved is helping people cope with trauma, grief, or bereavement associated with multiple losses.

SOCIAL WORK RESEARCH ROLES

There are three fundamental research roles that social workers who are committed to enhancing end-of-life care may engage in: the research consumer, the contributing partner, and the creator and disseminator of knowledge (Williams, Tutty, and Grinnell 1995).

THE RESEARCH CONSUMER

Social workers have an ethical responsibility to consult the research literature. Reading the work of others can help provide perspective on one's own practice, can help alert the worker to emerging issues, and can provide practitioners with guidance when they are not sure how to handle situations. Numerous studies document the deficiencies in the training of social workers to provide end-of-life care (Berzoff 2001; Christ and Sormanti, 1999; Dickinson, Sumner, and Frederick 1992; Kovacs and Bronstein 1998; Kramer 1998; Sormanti 1995). Palliative care fellowships and advanced practice certificate programs provide some training to address gaps; however, all practitioners will need to keep up with advances in the field and be mindful of the findings from the latest research.

Competent and responsible practitioners need to be able to weigh the benefits and drawbacks of different interventions, justify why a particular intervention was selected, and inform their clients about the benefits and limitations of alternative options. The field is changing rapidly, and it is necessary to review periodically the emerging and growing body of literature. Because excellent end-of-life care is interdisciplinary, social workers should stay abreast of the literatures in the areas of medicine, nursing, psychology, and other fields related to the worker's scope of practice. As Williams, Tutty, and Grinnell note, "Consuming research findings—reading with understanding in order to utilize findings—is the most important research role a social worker can play" (1995:18).

There are several resources to facilitate keeping up with developments in the literature.

Appendix 1 provides examples of some of the key journals that publish in the area of end-of-life care. It is useful to determine if there have been "special issues" of social work and other journals devoted to information in this area (e.g., see *The Gerontologist* 42 [2002], Special Issue on End-of-Life Research: Focus on Older Populations, or the special issues on end-of-life care in recent issues of *Smith College Studies in Social Work* and *Health and Social Work*). Watch for the charter issue of a journal published by Haworth Press, *Social Work in End of Life Care Practice*, scheduled for spring 2005. As one means to promote attention to this area, it would be useful to write to journal editors to request that they consider a special issue if they have not done so already. Most social work health organizations have developed special resources in the area of end of life. Consulting web sites and journals may reveal useful information to the research consumer.

CONTRIBUTING PARTNERS IN RESEARCH

Social work practitioners may become contributing partners to someone else's research project in a number of ways. There may be researchers interested in conducting investigations at the agency or organization where the social worker is employed, who request staff participation in designing or implementing the study. For example, Betty J. Kramer is currently conducting research at a community agency that provides interdisciplinary care to older adults with advanced chronic disease. Kramer approached the agency and shared her interests in understanding how the team members care for older adults and their family members at the end of life, and the role of social workers in that process. She asked the agency what they might be interested in understanding from a research project on this topic. Staff interests have been integrated as part of the study, and practitioners are assisting in data collection efforts.

Sometimes social workers identify a research project of interest, but they feel that they do not have the skills or resources to carry it out. In these situations, they might consider seeking out a researcher with an interest in the subject area. Practitioners can check with their local colleges or universities for a social work faculty member or doctoral student interested in the area of research. The social worker might also present the research idea to the agency's administration to discuss the possibility of bringing in an outside researcher. In all of these situations, social workers must communicate their needs and observations for research to be most meaningful. Drawing on their insights gained from working with people facing end-of-life in multiple settings, there are many opportunities for social workers to make important contributions to address deficiencies in care and to contribute to the growing body of knowledge relevant to end-of-life care.

KNOWLEDGE CREATORS AND DISSEMINATORS

Although many practitioners would not conceptualize what they do as research, most are continuously engaged in the process of collecting and analyzing data and observing the nexus between policy and practice. Social workers routinely collect assessment data, analyze them, implement a plan for action, and analyze the results. They engage in participant observation, noting the impact of services and the impact of policies on the lives of individuals and families. They bear witness to the suffering of others and are confronted with the challenges and barriers of helping to alleviate that suffering. They have ongoing opportunities to observe the effects of their interventions and to note what works and what does not. Their vantage point allows them to see where the rubber hits the road in terms of service provision. Their observations and insights can be used as the impetus for research projects that may lead to improvements in end-of-life care or may be used as the basis for a case study to be shared in the literature with other practitioners and researchers. Unfortunately, all too often, these observations go undocumented and are never disseminated for consideration by others. With the proper training and awareness, social work practitioners can learn to conduct their own research projects and can form partnerships with researchers for collaborative studies.

Naturally, there are challenges and potential barriers that prevent practitioners from formally documenting and disseminating their practice experiences. Ferrell and Grant (2001) note several barriers for direct service research in palliative care, such as limited funding, the perception that research will interfere with demands of client care, the challenge of conducting research in sensitive areas, ethical concerns about conducting research with vulnerable populations, and balancing demands of research with awareness of client needs and confidentiality.

Each situation must be weighed individually, although there are strategies that may help the social worker in addressing these barriers. Before embarking on a research project, it is essential to consult and then carefully assess the research literature in the subject area to determine what is already known about the topic. If the research project is to be published, it is important for the author to know how his or her study builds on the knowledge base, and how it fills specific gaps in the literature. Manuscripts that do not address these issues are not candidates for publication. By reviewing the literature carefully, it becomes clear how other researchers have approached the topic. This will provide useful ideas for implementing the study. It may be useful to consult with other practitioners or researchers who are familiar with the literature. They may offer guidance for how to address issues that are of concern, and can help put the research topic into perspective.

It is important to be realistic about what can be accomplished within the scope of other responsibilities and to design and implement research that is relevant to improving care (Ferrell and Grant 2001). Securing outside funding can be time-consuming. Partnering with an established researcher in the beginning may enhance the chances for success in securing funds. It may be useful to know that multiple rewrites are par for the course in preparing proposals for funding and in preparing manuscripts for publication. Most manuscripts are rewritten many times before they are submitted for publication, and once they are accepted, they may be rewritten again after comments from journal reviewers are received.

If a social work practitioner chooses to engage in research, it is mandatory to follow the guidelines established in the agency or organization for the protection of "human subjects" (i.e., people invited to participate in research). Social workers in healthcare settings need to be aware of the HIPPA (Health Insurance Portability and Accountability Act of 1996) regulations; compliance is mandatory as of April 2003 (see www .hhs.gov/ocr/hipaa).

Last, social work researchers are needed in the field in general, and particularly in the area of end-of-life issues. Social work practitioners need to commit themselves to advanced training and doctoral education to learn the skills and techniques necessary to plan and conduct rigorous research projects that can move the field forward.

RESEARCH NEEDS IN SOCIAL WORK AND END-OF-LIFE CARE

National leaders in social work and end-of-life care recently declared the urgent need for research that documents the roles and contributions of the profession and evaluates programs, policies, and interventions to improve care at the end of life. At the first national Social Work Summit on End-of-Life and Palliative Care held in March 2002, identifying a research agenda was one of the top ten core categories identified that needed to be addressed in the immediate future (Blacker, Christ, and Bloom 2002).

In conjunction with the Project on Death in America Social Work Leaders program, Betty J. Kramer is currently conducting a project to frame a set of national research priorities for social work in end-of-life care. Although the agenda is by no means set, several factors should be taken into consideration to guide future research. These include established priority areas, methodological limitations of prior research, and underdeveloped domains of research that are relevant to the social work profession.

ESTABLISHED PRIORITY AREAS

Research in social work and end-of-life care should not be done in isolation of the work that is being done by other professionals. It is essential that new studies build on prior research and that they address critical needs in the field. As suggested by Morrow-Howell and Burnette (2002) "social workers must attend to interfacing and overlapping areas with other social, behavioral, and biomedical sciences" in advancing the research agenda. As such, it is important to take into consideration the priority areas that have been identified more generally in the field and also to consider unique areas of professional commitment and the development of knowledge specific to the provision of social work.

Several research priority areas identified by the Institute of Medicine (IOM) are clearly relevant to the concerns addressed by social workers. General areas identified in the report (Field and Cassel 1997) include understanding and evaluation of treatment of the physical, cognitive, and emotional symptoms at the end of life, and the need for social, behavioral, and health services research. The following list details specific needs articulated in the IOM report that are particularly relevant to the social work profession.

- Development, use, and refinement of reliable, valid, and practical symptom assessment tools and measures for studying the prevalence and severity of psychological symptoms in patients with advanced disease and for evaluating interventions appropriate for such patients
- Comparison and evaluation of nonpharmacologic therapy options for cognitive and emotional symptoms.
- Extent and severity of physical, emotional, financial, and other adversities experienced by people dying from common diseases
- Spiritual growth and other valued experiences at the end of life
- Attitudinal, organizational, legal, cultural, and other factors that impede the application of existing knowledge and principles of care
- What people want as they approach death; what is meaningful to their families and others close to them
- How the care and support that is valued can be effectively and efficiently organized
- Benefits and costs of interdisciplinary expertise
- The effects of different care processes and structures (home care, hospice care, nursing home)
- The impact of various financing arrangements on patient well-being and access to care

- Efficacy and appropriateness of therapies for grieving survivors
- The role of social support and the relationship between caregiver experience and social and demographic characteristics
- Cultural, emotional, and affective aspects of perception of symptoms, attitudes, behavior, and decision making

Additional topics recently identified as end-of-life care research priorities include those identified by particular interest groups, including psycho-oncology, calling for research in psychological issues related to genetic risk and testing, symptom control (anxiety, depression, delirium, pain, and fatigue), and management of the psychological aspects of palliative and end-of-life care (Holland 2002); intensive care unit (ICU) research to uncover problems and overcome barriers (Rubenfeld and Curtis 2001), prevention of medical errors (Myers and Lynn 2001); and need for measures to examine quality of care and quality of life of patients diagnosed with life-limiting illness (Teno, Byock, and Field 1999). George (2002) echoes many authors in this book, noting that insufficient attention has been paid to psychological and spiritual issues, the prevalence of psychiatric disorder and the effectiveness of the treatment of such disorders among dying persons, provider and health system variables, social and cultural diversity, and the effects of co-morbidity on trajectories of dying.

CONCEPTUAL AND METHODOLOGICAL ISSUES

As we move forward and contemplate potential contributions that need to be made, we should be mindful of the limitations of prior research. In a recent review of research on end-of-life care, death, and dying, George concludes, "Both conceptual and methodological advances are high priorities for future research. Conceptually, the most important task is for the field to establish one or more definitions of dying that are used across studies. Other conceptual needs include (a) distinguishing among quality of life, quality of death, and quality of end-of-life care, (b) identifying appropriate outcomes in addition to consumer satisfaction, and (c) enlarging explanatory models to link preterminal states and characteristics with parameters of the dying process. Methodologically, the highest priority is longitudinal studies that cover longer segments of time than those in research to date" (2002:96).

It is essential that the research methods chosen fit the questions being asked. Qualitative methods are ideally suited to research that is "exploratory or descriptive, that assumes the value of context and setting, and that searches for a deeper understanding of the participants' lived experiences of the phenomenon" (Marshall and Rossman 1994:38). As a newer field of inquiry, much must be explored before adequate measures can be developed. Taxonomies of quality end-of-life care have been developed from the medical "expert" perspective rather than those of patients and families (see Bowman, Martin, and Singer 2000). Qualitative approaches will provide rich understanding of the experiences of the dying and their family members, and of service and organizational issues. In the early stages of researching a topic in particular, resources may be better utilized supporting interpretive methods to understand issues of concern more fully. Qualitative studies are needed to uncover the needs and preferences of patients and families and to bring multiple voices to understanding the complex issues confronted at the end of life.

Quantitative studies are needed as well. The facts and insights that can be gleaned from numbers are important, and they help to explain variations across settings and in outcomes of care. Quantitative studies help to shed light on the prevalence of problems; they allow researchers to test explanations; and they provide a powerful means to evaluate interventions and programs. Many benefits may be derived from mixed methods studies (Padgett 1998), and many social work researchers advocate for a multimethod approach to enhance the richness of data available to understand complex issues (Bernstein and Epstein 1994; Combs-Orme 1990; Grinnell 1997; Padgett 1998).

UNDERDEVELOPED RESEARCH AREAS

The opportunities for research, given the needs in the field, are vast. Social workers could make important contributions to understanding how best to prepare and assist the informal and formal support systems of those facing the end of life. Such support systems would include family members, close friends, fictive kin, and formal care providers in both medical and nonmedical settings. This would include attention to ways to enhance the communication dynamics between people who are facing death and their loved ones, and to understanding family conflict at the end of life. Because of social work's expertise in working with individuals, families, and groups around the time of crisis, we have a strong foundation on which to build better awareness of family-based interventions applicable at the end of life. Examples of questions that have not been adequately addressed include: What types of interventions are most effective in supporting family needs in divergent settings? What are families' perceptions of end-of-life care in various settings such as the hospital, nursing home, or at home? What are the processes that produce ethnic/race, socioeconomic status, or gender related differences in families coping with and reacting to the death of a family member? What type of support do families need during and after the death of a family member, and who can provide this support? (Stahl 2000).

Social work research is needed to document the effects of the environment on the experience of living and dying with a terminal condition. Environmental research includes the physical and social environments that affect how individuals and families experience the end of life. Given that many people undergo transitions between settings at the end of life (e.g., home to hospital to nursing home), there is much that needs to be learned about the consequences of these transitions and the quality of life, quality of care, and quality of death in various settings (Stahl 2000). With better descriptions of the environment, we can begin to design and conduct research that includes manipulating characteristics of the environment and testing environmental interventions.

There is opportunity for social work research that addresses ethical issues confronted by individuals, families, and systems as the end of life draws near. Research on ethical issues is particularly germane when the end-of-life experience involves people who cannot speak on their own behalf, such as infants, children, and people of all ages who lack mental competency or are incapacitated. Ethical issues arise in the context of who gets access to care and what type of care is provided. Healthcare professionals encounter new ethical challenges with the introduction of new medications, diagnostic tools, and treatment options. Availability of technology does not automatically mean it is appropriate to use in all cases. This will continue to be an important area of end-of-life research.

Social work researchers and practitioners should play a far more active role in policy development and policy analyses. Many local, state, and federal laws and regulations affect the experience of dying, for example, Medicare and Medicaid regulations governing hospice, state guardianship laws, state assisted-suicide laws, insurance regulations, and state or local regulations specifying burial practices. Morrow-Howell and Burnette's (2002) review of social work–authored publications showed that there has been minimal attention to policy analysis. Social workers often see the effects of state and federal policies in the lives of people. If research efforts focus only on those receiving services, then those already denied services because of policies will be further neglected. Policy evaluation and analysis is essential to enhancing care at the end of life and research in this area will allow social workers to engage in public policy dialogues and debates. Social workers must remain engaged in evaluating the impact of current policies and in promulgating better policies, especially when the deleterious effects of the laws and rules fall disproportionately on the most vulnerable and disenfranchised people in society.

Another clearly underdeveloped research area includes evaluation research and the testing of interventions. In many areas of social work specialization, clear gaps exist in interventions research. Although the very nature of the profession is to implement interventions to enhance quality of life, social workers have not adequately addressed the development and testing of psychosocial interventions (Morrow-Howell, Burnette, and Chen 2001) to address the pain and suffering documented so clearly in the literature. There is particular need for evaluation studies of culturally, gender and age relevant family and/or caregiver interventions, nonpharmacological treatment interventions, and studies to examine the efficacy of bereavement interventions in divergent settings and with different age groups.

As we sit at the forefront of this area of inquiry, it is an exciting time because there is so much that social work researchers may do to enhance knowledge and shape the development of programs and policies that will affect care at the end of life for a great many people. At the University of Wisconsin, Betty J. Kramer has developed a framework of ten areas of end-of-life social work that is used in social work education efforts. Appendix 2 includes a summary of these ten topic areas, with examples of potential research that is needed. So little is known in this field, and, as this appendix illustrates, there is opportunity to illuminate understanding of multiple issues and at many levels of practice.

SUMMARY

This chapter serves as a call to the social work profession to take a much more serious and active role in the development and dissemination of knowledge that may be used to enhance care at the end-of-life. The scope of practice is vast, cutting across multiple service settings, problem areas, age groups, and diverse populations; the needs for improvement in care are great. It is the responsibility of the social work profession to articulate and document its role in end-of-life care. While all competent practitioners should keep abreast of developments in the field, there is much promise in opportunities for practitioners and researchers to join efforts to make research more meaningful and productive. As a relatively new field of inquiry, there are largely underdeveloped areas of inquiry and tremendous opportunity for social workers to bring a holistic perspective to end-of-life care research in divergent settings.

APPENDIX 1: JOURNALS THAT ROUTINELY CARRY ARTICLES RELATED TO END-OF-LIFE ISSUES

American Journal of Hospice and Palliative Care
Clinical Journal of Pain
The European Journal of Palliative Care
Hospice Journal
Hospice Magazine
Innovations in End-of-Life Care (online international peer-reviewed journal, found at www.edc.org/lastacts)
International Journal of Palliative Nursing
Journal of Hospice and Palliative Nursing
Journal of Pain and Symptom Management
Journal of Palliative Care
Journal of Palliative Medicine
Journal of Psycho-oncology
Journal of Psychosocial Nursing
Midwest Bioethics Journal
Omega: Journal of Death and Dying
PAIN
Palliative Medicine
Progress in Palliative Care
Supportive Care in Cancer

CRITICAL AREAS OF END-OF-LIFE CARE	EXAMPLES OF AREA CONTENT	EXAMPLES OF POTENTIAL AREAS OF INQUIRY
1. The social work role and perspective on EOL care	A. Context: What is EOL care and its relevance to social work (functions and roles of social workers in multiple settings relevant to EOL) B. Definitions and goals: Palliative care, hospice care, trauma response, crisis intervention C. Functions and roles of social workers on interdisciplinary EOL care teams D. Potential contributions of social work in EOL care (biopsychosocial, life span, and strengths perspectives—anything that talks about unique perspectives taken by the social work profession that is transferable to EOL issues) E. Professional self awareness (any content on rationale for why social workers must be self-aware and reflective in general sense, the value of this and potential impact on professional practice) F. Recognition of potential challenges (e.g., strain, stress, burden, or burnout) in social work practice that is transferable to EOL care	1. EOL care needs assessments relevant to wide variety of settings of social work practice 2. Descriptive studies of social work roles and outcomes sought in wide variety of settings 3. Descriptive studies of the social worker's role in interdisciplinary involvement and related outcomes 4. Implementation and evaluation of organizational strategies to provide staff support (Ferrell and Grant 2001) 5. Studies to identify "best practices" of social work in multiple settings with diverse populations
2. Comprehensive culturally, gender, and age-relevant psychosocial assessment at the end of life	A. Functional B. Physical C. Psychological/emotional D. Social E. Spiritual F. Assessment of suicide risk	1. Development and testing of assessment instruments for use in multiple EOL contexts 2. Descriptive studies to understand from the client and family members the outcomes they seek in terms of physical, psychological, social, and spiritual well-being 3. Development and testing of quality of life instruments for use in palliative care (Ferrell and Grant 2001)

(continued)

CRITICAL AREAS OF END-OF-LIFE CARE	EXAMPLES OF AREA CONTENT	EXAMPLES OF POTENTIAL AREAS OF INQUIRY
3. Social work assessment and intervention with diverse family forms and informal caregivers facing EOL care	A. Assessment of family constellation, roles, functioning, structure, relationships, communication, knowledge, and resources in cultural context B. Family needs, burdens, strengths, and competencies (physical, psychological, emotional, social, and spiritual) in cultural context C. Coping strategies and support systems D. Process, goals, and methods of family meetings and conferencing in EOL care E. Process, goals, and methods of family counseling in EOL care F. Mobilizing new or existing family, system and community resources to provide support (Ferrell 1998) G. Culturally, gender, and age relevant family and/or caregiver interventions	1. Descriptive studies to enhance understanding the challenges facing diverse family forms at the EOL 2. More in-depth understanding of family needs and desired outcomes for quality EOL care and congruence with client expressed needs and outcomes 3. Studies to document the presence and nature of family conflict at the end of life and strategies for addressing this conflict 4. Studies to understand, address, and respond to family conflict 5. Evaluation studies of culturally, gender, and age-relevant family and/or caregiver interventions 6. Exploratory studies to enhance understanding of cultural variation in perspectives on optimal EOL care 7. Exploratory studies to understand barriers to communication at the end of life between family members 8. Interventions to overcome barriers to communication
4. Differential diagnosis and treatment in EOL contexts	A. Depression B. Anxiety C. Delirium D. Dementia E. Substance-related disorders	1. The role of age, race, gender, sexual orientation and income on the identification and treatment of symptoms 2. Descriptive studies to understand better prevalence and patterns at the end of life across diverse populations and age groups 3. Evaluation of nonpharmacological treatment inter-ventions

(continued)

CRITICAL AREAS OF END-OF-LIFE CARE	EXAMPLES OF AREA CONTENT	EXAMPLES OF POTENTIAL AREAS OF INQUIRY
5. Communication with patients, families, and other care providers	A. Definition and goals of communication in EOL care B. Factors influencing communication in EOL care with attention to communication needs/issues among persons who are gay, lesbian, transgender, or bisexual C. Common communication barriers and traps in EOL care D. Communication skills essential to EOL care E. Skills for delivering bad news and ways to facilitate integration of bad news F. Truth telling in cultural context G. Discussion of options and changing goals of care with patients and family members H. Facilitation skills for communicating how client/family or others are informed about prognosis and course of illness I. Presenting cases so professionals will listen J. Communication issues among health and social service providers	1. Descriptive studies of what social workers are doing to facilitate communication at the end of life 2. Studies of barriers to communication between family members, patients, and professionals, including goal clarification and weighing treatment options 3. Exploratory studies of cultural variation in communication needs and preferences and how they differ between clients and their support systems and/or family caregivers 4. Studies of communication experiences and preferences among pediatric populations 5. Studies to investigate how social workers can facilitate individual and family final arrangements (funeral and body disposition) that are meaningful and match the available resources
6. Commonly experienced symptoms along continuum of illness and symptoms near time of death	A. Common symptoms 1. Shortness of breath (dyspnea), cough 2. Nausea and vomiting 3. Dehydration 4. Weakness and fatigue 5. Dysphasia, dry mouth, and hiccups 6. Bowel-related symptoms: constipation, diarrhea, obstruction and ascites (abdominal bloating) 7. Urinary tract disorders (incontinence, retention)	1. Studies to explore the emotional/psychosocial response to symptoms and/or treatment as reported by clients and family members across the life span 2. Development and evaluation of teaching programs to educate social workers in enhancing quality of life at the end of life, and helping individuals and family members prepare for the death 3. Studies to determine how best to work with individuals and families when the prognosis is ambiguous.

(continued)

CRITICAL AREAS OF END-OF-LIFE CARE	EXAMPLES OF AREA CONTENT	EXAMPLES OF POTENTIAL AREAS OF INQUIRY

	8. Pressure ulcers, tumor necrosis, fistulas (skin integrity)
	9. Weight loss and loss of appetite
	B. Familial emotional/psychosocial response to symptoms and treatments (IV fluids, tube feeding, symbolism of food and hydration as caring)
	C. Social worker's role in symptom management (to include working with significant others and the impact of illness on patient body integrity, functioning, and dependency issues)
	D. Signs and symptoms of imminent death and planning for death
	  1. Near-death anxiety/restlessness
	  2. Death rattle
	  3. Symbolic communication vs. confusion
	  4. Near-death awareness and near-death experience
	  5. Altered mental status (specifically related to "dying" experience, not global dementia or delirium)
	  6. Preparation for death and after-death care and grieving rituals (culturally relevant body disposition wishes, desires and needs of family at time of death, decisions about organ or body donation, facilitating grieving process at time of death)
		4. Descriptive studies that examine the social worker's role in symptom management
		5. Evaluative studies of the effectiveness of social work involvement in symptom management

7. Pain, distress, and suffering management	A. Definitions for various forms of pain and suffering B. Risk factors for psychosocial, spiritual, and existential distress	1. Development of methods for assessing pain in persons who are nonverbal or confused (Ferrell and Grant 2001)

(continued)

CRITICAL AREAS OF END-OF-LIFE CARE	EXAMPLES OF AREA CONTENT	EXAMPLES OF POTENTIAL AREAS OF INQUIRY

	C. Barriers to pain relief and management related to healthcare professionals, healthcare system, patients, and families (including fear of hastening death)
	D. Assessment of pain and suffering and discrepancy between patient, family, and healthcare provider/team member's assessment
	E. Principles of addiction and tolerance
	F. Pharmacological management of physical pain and related side effects
	G. Nonpharmacological and social work interventions and complementary therapies and indications for their use across the life span for responding to and managing distress, pain, and suffering and enhancing quality of life at the end of life:
	  1. Psychoeducational programs for patients and family
	  2. Cognitive behavioral interventions
	  3. Crisis intervention
	  4. Distraction
	  5. Play therapy
	  6. Counseling
	  7. Reminiscence and life review
	  8. Use of complementary therapies
	  9. Environmental interventions
	  10. Online interventions (telephone and Internet)
	  11. Advocacy with team and healthcare system
	  12. Culturally specific interventions
	  13. Group work
		2. Testing of culturally and age relevant interventions for responding to and managing distress, pain and suffering and enhancing quality of life at the end of life
		3. Development and evaluation of educational programs to address the barriers of pain relief and management related to healthcare professionals, healthcare systems, clients, and family members

(continued)

CRITICAL AREAS OF END-OF-LIFE CARE	EXAMPLES OF AREA CONTENT	EXAMPLES OF POTENTIAL AREAS OF INQUIRY

8. Loss, grief, and bereavement	A. Definition of terms (grief, bereavement, mourning)
	B. General relevance of grief issues to social work practice
	C. Understanding loss, grief and bereavement in relation to multiple practice and population-specific issues
	D. Types of grief (anticipatory, uncomplicated, complicated, staff grief)
	E. Current theories of grief, mourning and bereavement (Stage, process, and task theories and models)
	F. Common manifestations and cultural variation of grief
	G. Assessment of grief, including assessment components for cross-cultural grieving
	H. Critique of the "grief work hypothesis"
	I. Culturally, gender, and age-appropriate interventions and practice guidelines for working with people across the life span who are grieving or bereaved (e.g., grief counseling, play therapy, music, bibliotherapy, group work, storytelling, use of rituals, what not to do or say, etc.)
	J. Funerals and burial rituals
	K. Recognition of professional grief
	  1. Professional understanding of their own grief and loss issues and how that may affect work with clients
	  2. Compassion fatigue
	  3. Self-care issues and strategies
		1. Studies to understand the experience of loss, grief, and bereavement in multiple practice and population-specific settings
		2. Evaluation studies to examine the efficacy of bereavement interventions in divergent settings and with different age groups
		3. Studies to uncover the role of social workers on interdisciplinary teams relevant to grief work with other professionals
		4. Testing of approaches to facilitate staff grief (Ferrell and Grant 2001)
		5. Studies to help workers better address sudden death (nondisease), such as accident, homicide, natural disaster, terrorism, and suicide, with people of all ages

(continued)

CRITICAL AREAS OF END-OF-LIFE CARE	EXAMPLES OF AREA CONTENT	EXAMPLES OF POTENTIAL AREAS OF INQUIRY
9. Ethical and legal issues	A. Overview of ethical and legal principles, issues, and dilemmas confronted in EOL context (e.g., prolongation of life, double effect, futility, informed consent, withholding/withdrawing treatment, confidentiality, paternalism, breach of duty, foreseeability) B. Assisted suicide C. Euthanasia D. Medicalization of dying E. EOL decision making F. Advanced directives and promoting their effective use in culturally sensitive ways G. Competency, capacity, and guardianship H. Laws relevant to family medical leave, advance directives, durable power-of-attorney, healthcare proxies, guardians, withholding and withdrawing of treatment, out of-hospital DNR orders, pain management I. Legal issues that impact EOL concerns among gay, lesbian, bisexual, or transgender persons J. Social workers' role on ethics committees and in ethical decision making K. Equity (accessibility to care, justice, ethnic and racial disparities regarding access to care)	1. Descriptive studies of how individuals and families from different ethnic and cultural groups understand ethical decisions 2. Intervention studies of teaching social workers to identify, assess, and address ethical issues in end-of-life care 3. Descriptive studies of the types of EOL-related cases brought to hospital/nursing home ethics committees 4. Studies to develop and test assessment protocols to determine decisional capacity for healthcare-related treatments 5. Studies that gauge the extent to which advance directives are useful—and in what ways—in making health-related treatment decisions 6. Review of state guardianship laws 7. International comparative studies of how EOL ethical and legal issues common in the United States are constructed in other countries

(continued)

CRITICAL AREAS OF END-OF-LIFE CARE	EXAMPLES OF AREA CONTENT	EXAMPLES OF POTENTIAL AREAS OF INQUIRY

10. Healthcare systems, policy, and advocacy	A. Changing healthcare systems and impacts of managed care
	B. Process and skills of case management
	C. Process and skills of discharge planning
	D. Payment for EOL care and access to care
	  1. Medicare and Medicaid
	  2. Reimbursement issues and impact of financial strains on patient/family
	  3. Other community resources and entitlement programs appropriate to EOL
	E. How the organizational and agency context affects practice
	F. Nexus between policy and practice
	G. Advocacy at local, state, and national levels
	  1. Protection of patients' dignity, confidentiality, rights and access to care
	  2. Advocacy issues, strategies, and methods (e.g., removing barriers to quality care; addressing gaps in service; helping survivors and families secure the protection of existing laws; working for any changes needed in organizations, programs, policies, and legislation; making changes and engaging in advocacy efforts)
		1. Studies that examine challenges persons experience in navigating various healthcare systems at the end of life
		2. Studies to examine the barriers associated with transitions for one site of care to another and the social worker's role in facilitating those transitions
		3. Descriptive studies to uncover organizational and healthcare system variables related to favorable versus poor outcomes
		4. Studies addressing cost/benefit analysis of social work intervention
		5. Studies of economic factors as clinical variable affecting care and patient outcomes
		6. Studies of ethnic and socioeconomic disparities in EOL care access and quality of care
		7. Provider perception of patient/caregiver socioeconomic status and the clinical implications
		8. Policy analysis of availability and uses of life insurance, inheritance laws, and custody issues
		9. Descriptions of how care systems are organized to provide end-of-life care (Lynn et al. 2000)

REFERENCES

Bernstein, S. T., and I. Epstein. 1994. Grounded theory meets the reflective practitioner: Integrating qualitative and quantitative methods in administrative practice. In *Qualitative Research in Social Work*, ed. E. Sherman and W. J. Reid, 435–444. New York: Columbia University Press.

Berzoff, J. 2001. *Developing and Evaluating Post-masters Curriculum in End of Life Care.* Dallas: Council on Social Work Education.

Blacker, S., G. Christ, and B. Bloom. 2002. Designing an agenda for social work on end-of-life and palliative care. Executive summary of the Interactive Workshop Report (draft) from the Social Work Summit on End-of-Life and Palliative Care, March 20–22, 2002.

Bowman, K. W., D. K. Martin, and P. A. Singer. 2000. Quality end-of-life care. *Journal of Evaluation in Clinical Practice* 6:51–61.

Christ, G., and M. Sormanti. 1999. Advanced social work practice in end-of-life care. *Social Work in Health Care* 30(2): 81–99.

Cohen, S. R., C. MacNeil, and B. M. Mount. 1997. Well-being at the end of life: Part 2 — Research for the delivery of care from the patient's perspective. *Cancer Prevention Control* 1(5): 343–351.

Combs-Orme, T. 1990. The interface of qualitative and quantitative methods in social work research. In *Advances in Clinical Social Work Research*, ed. L. Videka-Sherman and W. J. Reid, 181–188. Washington, DC: NASW Press.

Corner, J. 1996. Is there a research paradigm for palliative care? *Palliative Medicine* 10(3): 201–208.

Dickinson, G., E. Sumner, and L. Frederick. 1992. Death education in selected health professions. *Death Studies* 21(4): 1–16.

Ferrell, B. R., and M. Grant. 2001. Nursing research. In *Textbook of Palliative Nursing*, ed. B. R. Ferrell and N. Coyle, 701–709. New York: Oxford University Press.

Field, M. J., and C. K. Cassel, eds. 1997. *Approaching Death: Improving Care at the End of Life.* Washington, DC: National Academy Press.

George, L. K. 2002. Research design in end-of-life research: State of science. *The Gerontologist* 42:86–98.

Grinnell, R. M. 1997. *Social Work Research and Evaluation: Quantitative and Qualitative Approaches.* Itasca, IL: F. E. Peacock.

Hanson, L. C., M. Danis, and J. Garrett. 1997. What is wrong with end-of-life care? Opinions of bereaved family members. *Journal of the American Geriatrics Society* 45:1339–1344.

Holland, J. C. 2002. History of psycho-oncology: Overcoming attitudinal and conceptual barriers. *Psychosomatic Medicine* 64(2): 206–221.

Kovacs, P., and L. Bronstein. 1999. Preparation for oncology settings: What hospice social workers say they need. *Social work in Health Care* 24(1): 57–64.

Kramer, B. J. 1998. Preparing social workers for the inevitable: A preliminary investigation of a course on grief, death and loss. *Journal of Social Work Education* 34(2): 1–17.

Kramer, B. J., and G. Christ. 2002. Developing a social work research agenda in end-of-life care. Paper presented at the Project on Death in America Social Work Leaders Retreat, Lake Tahoe, California.

Lynn, J., H. R. Arkes, M. Stevens, et al. 2000. Rethinking fundamental assumptions: SUPPORT's implications for future reform. *Journal of the American Geriatrics Society* 48(5): S214–S221.

Marshall, C., and G. Rossman. 1994. *Doing Qualitative Research.* 2d ed. Thousand Oaks, CA: Sage.

Meier, D. E., R. S. Morrison, and C. K. Cassel. 1997. Improving palliative care. *Annals of Internal Medicine* 127:225–230.

Morrow-Howell, N., and D. Burnette. 2002. Gerontological social work research: Current status and future directions. *Journal of Gerontological Social Work* 36(3–4): 63–79.

Morrow-Howell, N., D. Burnette, and L. Chen. 2001. Research priorities for gerontological social work: Setting a national agenda. Paper presented at the Society for Social Work Research Annual Meeting, Atlanta.

Myers, S. S., and J. Lynn. 2001. Patients with eventually fatal chronic illness: Their importance within a national research agenda on improving patient safety and reducing medical errors. *Journal of Palliative Medicine* 4(3): 325–332.

Padgett, D. K. 1998. *Qualitative Methods in Social Work Research: Challenges and Rewards.* Thousand Oaks, CA: Sage.

Pickett, M., M. E. Cooley, and D. B. Gordon. 1998. Palliative care: Past, present, and future perspectives. *Seminars in Oncology Nursing* 14(2): 86–94.

Richards, M. A., J. Corner, and D. Clark. 1998. Developing a research culture for palliative care. *Palliative Medicine* 12:399–403.

Robbins, S. P., P. Chatterjee, and E. R. Canda, eds. 1998. *Contemporary Human Behavior Theory: A Critical Perspective for Social Work.* Boston: Allyn & Bacon.

Rubenfeld, G. D., and J. Randall Curtis. 2001. End-of-life care in the intensive care unit: A research agenda—Comment. *Critical Care Medicine* 29(10): 2001–2006.

Sormanti, M. 1995. Fieldwork instruction in oncology social work: Supervisory issues. *Journal of Psychosocial Oncology* 12(3): 73–87.

Stahl, S. M. 2000. End-of-Life Research Conference Proposal: National Institute on Aging/ National Institutes of Health. Working paper.

SUPPORT Principal Investigators. 1995. A controlled trial to improve care for seriously ill hospitalized patients: The Study to Understand Prognoses and Preferences for Outcomes and Risks of Treatments (SUPPORT). *Journal of the American Medical Association* 274:1591–1598.

Teno, J. M., I. Byock, and M. J. Field. 1999. Research agenda for developing measures to examine quality of care and quality of life of patients diagnosed with life-limiting illness. *Journal of Pain & Symptom Management* 17(2): 75–82.

Toseland, R. 1994. Commentary: The qualitative/quantitative debate—Moving beyond acrimony to meaningful dialogue. In *Qualitative Research in Social Work*, ed. E. Sherman and W. J. Reid, 453–458. New York: Columbia University Press.

Williams, M., L. M. Tutty, and R. M. Grinnell. 1995. *Research in Social Work: An Introduction.* 2d ed. Itasca, IL: F. E. Peacock.

41

FINANCING END-OF-LIFE CARE

JUNE SIMMONS

THE EFFECTS of life-threatening illnesses are many. One of them is the awareness that dying is real and perhaps imminent, an insight that permits the opportunity for a life review and for attention to unresolved family issues in a way that "having time" does not. The kind of health care received and its effectiveness in allowing freedom from pain and other disruptive symptoms while remaining mentally alert are crucial for making the most of the end of one's life. Choices available are unfortunately limited by the nature of healthcare reimbursement as well as by the frequent lack of knowledge of the available end-of-life care options. It is important for social workers to be knowledgeable about all of these issues in order to counsel and advocate best for their clients in this last phase of life. As Marilyn Moon and Cristina Boccuti write, "The Medicare program, which serves people age 65 and older and those with disabilities, is the most important source of health insurance for Americans at the end stages of their lives. Therefore, its rules regarding methods and levels of payment and covered benefits have a strong impact on end-of-life care" (2003).

This chapter reviews healthcare approaches and payments and their implications for practice. It considers individual choices as well as some of the issues in accessing care for the uninsured.

AN EVOLVING ISSUE: TRANSFORMATION OF PATIENT NEEDS

The term *end-of-life care* is of recent origin. The transformation in medical care to extend life has been a major factor. Death soon after the diagnosis of a terminal illness was the usual course in the past. Dramatic new medical interventions now give many patients prolonged time to live with an extended course of disease. The phrase *chronic illness* is now a regular part of the medical discourse. In the past, care often produced a cure or death came soon after.

We have seen a dramatic expansion of the lifespan — it has doubled in this century. The lifespan has increased by 2 percent per year for the last several decades, while at the same time the disability rate has dropped by an almost equal rate. As a result, both life and the healthy years are longer. When decline begins, it is a longer, slower slope. The timing of death has become more difficult to predict. The most dramatic example is seen in patients with heart failure. Whereas previously heart failure often resulted in sudden death, now "on the day before death, the median prognosis for patients . . . is still a 50% chance to live six or more months" (Lynn 2000:2508).

There has also been a shift in medical epidemiology in which the needs of patients and the circumstances faced by families have changed. We now have many ways to try to save patients, and few frameworks for determining when the treatment is worth the suffering and expense it may bring. Health professionals have been trained to treat the disease trajectories. High-technology solutions have been developed to extend life, and medicine has focused its training on cure. Medical education is just beginning to address how to care for patients palliatively through the end stage of life.

We have developed a hospice benefit, but most health insurance excludes coverage for essential but noncurative palliative-care services. Both medicine and the payment mechanisms to support it have traditionally focused almost exclusively on cure and on the extension of life, rather than on the alleviation of suffering and quality of life. According to Ira Byock, M.D., a noted end-of-life-care reformer and scholar, "Pain and other sources of physical distress among the dying are being inadequately controlled or even addressed, resulting in unnecessary suffering at the end of life. This occurs across the spectrum of healthcare settings, including many of our nation's most prestigious medical institutions" (2001:1123).

Issues of poverty and barriers to access to care take a different shape at the end of life. There are tremendous disparities in access to care for the poor and uninsured in America, so that access to timely diagnoses and aggressive treatments can be difficult. But at the end, when it is clearly end-of-life care, Medicaid covers this benefit in most states. For the elderly, who constitute the largest portion of end-of-life care, Medicare provides the hospice benefit, whether in traditional Medicare or in managed care arrangements. In addition, for many with extended illnesses, they can qualify for Medicare after eighteen months of qualifying for disability despite their ages. For those with no coverage, laws require emergency rooms to admit patients in need of care and hold hospitals responsible for discharging patients with inadequate care plans. As a result, the poor may actually have more access to care at the end of life with greater equity than at other phases of health care. However, economically disadvantaged ethnic minorities often fear that referral to hospices is another way of withholding curative care on a racial basis.

CHANGING END-OF-LIFE POLICY AND PAYMENT

Starting in the mid-1970s, America began to grapple with the issue of death in the public policy forum. The care resources to extend treatment and life, coupled with the introduction of paramedics and intensive care units, led to new ethical and care dilemmas never really faced before. With new medical tools, the question of how much care should be administered and for whom first arose. The first major policy effort was an attempt to reach societal consensus on ethical and legal guidelines for when it was appropriate to stop treatments that could be viewed as unwanted or even burdensome. Karen Ann Quinlan's case brought this issue to the fore when her parents asked that she be removed from a ventilator (see chapter 37). Gradually, court rulings led to the right of competent patients and families of incapacitated patients to be able to refuse life supports if the suffering outweighed the benefits of treatment. Until this time, insurance and the law forced continuing treatment and life support. If insurance benefits and personal resources were exhausted by extended care, the individual became Medicaid-eligible and still had access to inpatient care. There was almost no coverage for any care unless it was curative.

Another cultural shift in the early 1970s was the seminal work of Elisabeth Kübler-Ross, who helped Americans to realize that dying was a reality and a phase of life with rich potential value. She laid the groundwork for understanding a "good death" and healthy grieving. She noted that patients were dying in hospitals and often beholden to unwanted interventions, even though they wished to die at home in peace, not tethered to equipment and free of pain.

A related contemporary development was Dame Cicely Saunders's approach to end-of-life care in Britain, which influenced the nascent American hospice movement. In hospice there is no cure, only loving support and relief from pain and other suffering. As a result, the first hospices in America were volunteer organizations working closely with physicians and receiving no reimbursement from insurance. Pioneers worked to create the right for patients to choose to die at home with proper pain relief and strong emotional support for the family and the patient. This movement was so effective and so valued by families that it lobbied for and eventually won the establishment of the Medicare hospice benefit we know today.

CURRENT FINANCING

MEDICARE

It has been estimated that end-of-life care represents 10–12 percent of all healthcare spending. Private insurance covers costs in end-of-life care, but this chapter focuses on Medicare for several reasons. Medicare is the largest health insurance plan in the country and the strongest data source for looking at this issue, since so many deaths in America occur within the older population: 2.3 million people, for example, died in 1997, and 80 percent were Medicare beneficiaries at the time of death. Twenty percent of these Medicare beneficiaries were also Medicaid-eligible. Approximately 25 percent of the entire Medicare budget is spent on care in the last year of life (Hogan et al. 2000; Saphir 1999), and 40 percent of that is spent in the last thirty days of life (Lubitz and Riley 1993). The average cost of care per person is $26,000 just from Medicare. This is six times the cost of the average Medicare beneficiary (Hogan et al. 2000). However, the older old (eighty-five and over) have a cost one-third lower than those sixty-five to seventy-five. Investment of our national resources at this level merits understanding whether the care is appropriate and desired. While the rate of uninsured and underinsured in America is at shocking levels, the older and the disabled populations and those who are "poor enough" have good coverage for end-of-life care. This certainly does not solve the problem, but it does shrink the issue a great deal relative to other sectors of healthcare needs.

UNIQUE CHARACTERISTICS OF MANAGED CARE
FOR PAYMENT REFORM

Medicare benefits can be received through the standard Medicare program or a managed care organization. Most of health care in America now is within the managed care structure. Although this has resulted in some controversy and much mistrust of the healthcare system due to the changes in relationship and coverage this has caused, it is an important trend. Not all managed care organizations are alike, and some of the major nonprofit systems are exemplary.

The advantage of Medicare for end-of-life care is that if it is in a fully integrated system, patients and families may have more flexibility in how they cover care needs. Kaiser Permanente provides one example of a large fully integrated managed care system with nonprofit values. Later in this chapter, I will give other examples of new trends in end-of-life care through programs that offer flexibility, rather than try to pull together the terrible patchwork of funding streams that traditional Medicare brings, since it pays separately to each site of care and each provider. The potential value of managed care, when well managed and not for profit, is that it can integrate funding streams, resulting in greater flexibility in adapting healthcare systems to the changing needs of patients and families identified in this chapter.

On the other hand, many managed care systems have come to be viewed with suspicion, given the profit motive. These deep and powerful controversies are still at play, although somewhat reduced by intervening legal rulings and settlements and growing experience.

Two portions of the Medicare benefit that are very closely involved in end-of-life care are home health and hospice care. Out of the trillion-dollar Medicare budget, home health amounts to only $29 billion and has been cut back drastically in recent years. Hospice, the program we would expect to significantly assist in this stage of life, represents a mere 1 percent of the Medicare budget (Miller, Gozalo, and Mor 2000; National Hospice and Palliative Care Organization 2001).

HOSPICE

Hospice was devised, fought for, and won as the new "best practice" approach to end-of-life care in the mid-1980s (Byock 2001). It was designed to provide a way to allow patients the choice to die at home and to receive emotional, spiritual, and supportive care along with highly skilled palliative care directed at keeping patients alert and free from pain, nausea, weakness, and shortness of breath to the extent possible. Hospice has been a very successful program, serving well those that are able to access it. As a result, most Medicaid programs and many private insurance plans have adopted it as a benefit as well. Nonprofit hospices are active fundraisers and strive to assure access to the uninsured as well.

We find excessive regulations in long-term care and strict utilization controls in acute care that prevent the use of insurance dollars for supportive care. Medicare itself was designed with a congressionally mandated focus on restoration and rehabilitation, and the regulations reflect this focus. As a result, state surveyors are likely to cite nursing homes for failure to treat conditions that frequently accompany the dying process, such as stopping eating and withdrawal. Nursing homes for years have had to fight to avoid being cited as deficient in care for not aggressively treating patients whose natural course would be to die peacefully in accordance with the patient's and family's wishes. As a result, only 1 percent of nursing home patients receive hospice care (Petrisek 1999).

BARRIERS TO HOSPICE CARE

Friedman, Harwood, and Shields (2002) note that there are many hospice programs and that through Medicare, Medicaid, or employee-sponsored health insurance, most insured people have nearly full coverage for hospice care. Yet less than one-third of dying persons use hospice care. There are many barriers identified in their study, including physicians' difficulty in accepting death, their lack of education in end-of-life care, and their concern at "abandoning" care of their patient at such an important time, since hospice often provides its own new care team upon admission.

Hospice admission by regulation must require the physician to certify that a patient is likely to die within six months. This is medically very difficult or even impossible with most patients and most diagnoses. In addition, a hospice referral requires a discussion between physician and patient regarding the imminence of death, for the patient will be required to relinquish his or her right to curative benefits under hospice. These kinds of requirements make hospice a difficult referral for the physician to make.

Patients and families often do not know about or understand hospice. It is important for social work professionals to understand these barriers and to be well informed in order to advocate for appropriate use of the hospice benefit when it is available and appropriate.

Referrals to hospice have increased, but they tend to be much too late for the program to bring full benefit. Even though the hospice benefit is for up to six months, the median stay is only twenty-nine days (National Hospice and Palliative Care Organization 2001). One study noted that 15.6 percent of the patients died within seven days of admission (Field and Cassel 1997:40–41).

ECONOMIC BURDEN

Insurances of all types combined do not cover all end-of-life costs. The cost of health services is a dramatic obstacle to the achievement of widespread improvement of the quality of end-of-life care. This is manifested in several important trends. One is the shocking disparity in insurance coverage in our country. Currently more than forty-four million Americans are uninsured, and another fifteen to twenty million are underinsured (Higginson and Edmonds 1999). Approximately two-thirds of nursing home residents are on Medicaid, generally because their savings were used up paying for uncovered care. While Medicaid has gradually allowed some waivered programs to provide care at home, most of these patients are forced to enter the nursing home in order for care to be paid for. The Olmstead Act of recent years is supposed to change this fact, but reality lags behind policy at this time.

COSTS TO CAREGIVERS

Healthcare expenses are growing rapidly and both insurers and employers are struggling with these dramatically rising costs, increasingly seeking to shift costs to the individual. Many working families are thus faced with medical bankruptcy when a family member has a significant and disabling injury or illness. The SUPPORT Study documented the severe impact on family resources—29 percent of the families reported loss of the major source of income, and 31 percent lost most or all of their family savings.

In addition to deductibles and co-pays, these impacts hinge on the significant costs of "out-of-pocket" services, the term we use for needed care that insurances will not pay. These usually include such things as medications, transportation, in-home care providers, and other special needs. Long-term care insurance was developed in the late 1980s and early 1990s to address this issue, but it has only recently matured to have value and remains expensive, especially for older purchasers who are most aware of their need for it.

In addition, informal caregiving is a huge hidden subsidy to the system. The monetary value attributed to informal care given by families and others has been estimated at approximately $196 billion, which is more than the combined costs of the home health and nursing home ($32 and $83 billion) budgets (Arno, Levine, and Memmott 1999). Approximately twenty-six million Americans provide care to loved ones, and the average care provided is eighteen hours a week over four and a half years. This trend is expected to grow dramatically. Many leave their work, resulting in lost wages as well as reduced retirement and social security benefits. In addition, recent studies have noted significant emotional and health impacts from this continued stressful circumstance. This results in higher use of health services, as well as a 63 percent higher mortality risk compared with noncaregivers (Schulz and Beach 1999). Business pays the tab as well, with the productivity losses and increased absences and insurance costs rolling up to as much as $29 billion per year nationally (National Alliance for Caregiving 1997).

CURRENT TRENDS

While hospice remains deeply valued and many continue to work to open access to this important program through professional and community education, a new movement has also begun: that is, the move to palliative care. Defined earlier in this chapter, this new movement seeks to define a domain that complements hospice. Many patients do not and will not access hospice or will enter hospice much too late to realize full benefit of its unique clinical resources. In addition, end-of-life care can now encompass a much longer period than six months for many progressive conditions (up to a year or two), well beyond the time permitted by hospice regulations.

It is clinically artificial to draw such an abrupt line between curative care and supportive care. Hospice regulations require that each patient relinquish their traditional Medicare benefit and, as such, access to continuing efforts at cure. Palliative-care programs encompass both cure expertise and symptom-control expertise, which have great value throughout the course of care, thus removing the requirement to draw such an abrupt and complete line in the clinical sand. This also means that to enter hospice, the patient and family may have to begin care with a new care team and give up their trusted and known care team at a critical point, whereas with palliative care they simply receive expanded services and new experts in their care. Unfortunately, there is currently almost no payment for palliative care as such.

These dichotomies in care choices drawn by the hospice program are very disruptive aspects of the payment system that are a poor fit with the natural needs of patients and families. They also create ethical and emotional dilemmas for the professionals who have cared for them and do not wish to abandon them at this critical point in their lives. Hospice is excellent for many, but for those for whom it is not right or comes too late because of regulatory and emotional barriers, we need new solutions.

Much more appropriate, many now think, is to bring the clinical resources of the hospice team to the curative arena. This is what we call the care movement, whose elements were defined earlier. It is both a clinical specialty and a movement. The movement takes many forms and is burgeoning across America. It can be a consultation team within the acute medical setting. It can be a unit within a medical center. It can be an alternative home care program. Payment structures need to be developed to address it (Byock 2001).

BARRIERS TO PALLIATIVE CARE

Unfortunately, most palliative-care services and programs are not covered by insurance because they are so new. And although they can comfortably accompany a full and aggressive treatment program focused on possible cure, they bring tremendous clinical expertise to the amelioration of symptoms resulting from both the disease and the treatment regimens. This is crucial to quality life at the end of life. Yet financing has not yet caught up with this key trend and lags behind as the evidence is gathered to establish the efficacy of this approach to end-of-life care. As Ira Byock notes, "Treating patients with advanced illness and complex needs has become a fiscally risky business because of decreasing Medicare and Medicaid reimbursements, the Balanced Budget Act of 1997, prospective payment arrangements and lack of adequate risk adjustments in managed care, as well as in long-term care. Cost shifting on a local basis can place physicians, hospice providers, health maintenance organizations, and long-term care institutions at odds over the care of high-cost cases. Pervasive cost cutting has made quality improvement efforts difficult to implement" (2001:1125).

BEREAVEMENT SUPPORT

One of the strengths of hospice is its inclusion of a requirement that each program provide social work support during the dying process and up to one year of bereavement support for the families of the deceased, usually provided by social workers. No other healthcare payment resource offers this, and it is important to advocate for its inclusion in the palliative-care programs as they evolve. In general, healthcare finance asks families to provide care but does not consider providing this kind of supportive care to them, even though this can be a crucial turning point in their lives and a time when care is needed. Bereavement support outside of hospice is still either provided on a voluntary basis through volunteer hospices or other similar organizations or occasionally addressed as a mental health benefit if the needs are psychiatric and great. This is an important area for social work program development and for advocacy for sources of funding to make it sustainable.

INNOVATIONS IN CARE

All across America, clinical innovators are finding funding to test important new approaches to solve these crucial problems in end-of-life care. Since traditional healthcare financing does not yet address these innovations, foundations and government-funded research initiatives are paying to test proposed solutions. These initiatives are occurring in a variety of settings. The most freedom to innovate in this way is in fully integrated managed care settings where it is possible to move funding to preferred sites of care to determine best methods and costs of care. Many view managed care with mistrust, yet, on the other end of the spectrum, the fully integrated value-based system holds promise as a laboratory for establishing best practices in systems not burdened in the same way with "silo financing" and conflicting financial incentives.

A very innovative effort in this regard has occurred under the leadership of Richard Brumley, M.D., medical director of Home Health and Hospice in the Tri-Central member service area of Kaiser Permanente of Southern California. Dr. Brumley noted that a significant percentage of deaths were occurring in the intensive care unit of the hospital and sought to offer broadened choice to patients and physicians. Many patients and physicians were not prepared to move to the hospice alternative. Focusing on cancer, congestive heart failure, and emphysema patients, Dr. Brumley won support to move some funding to testing a new palliative-care home program. (In another setting, all the providers and payment structures would be separated, and it would be impossible to move the funding to the service the patient needed.) Physicians continued ongoing care of their patients but could also refer them for palliative home care in this program under the Kaiser Permanente benefit. They did not have to face the issues in hospice noted earlier, and yet could access many of the same enriched resources.

With rigorous research underlying the work (provided by Partners in Care Foundation), Dr. Brumley offered a combination of hospice-skilled nursing, the full interdisciplinary team of hospice, and physician home visits. In addition, twenty-four-hour access to a hotline in which an RN with the full record of the patient was available to guide patients through their off-hours crises. Care plans anticipated likely crises and lined up readily available solutions so that families and patients could address these upsetting episodes of pain and fear immediately and easily. Social work and spiritual support were provided as well to help families think through the care and support needed over the inevitable course of the illness.

The research demonstrated that having these very practical supports and expanded clinical resources available allowed patients to receive care otherwise not available. As a result, they avoided emergency room visits and hospitalizations and had other enhancements in care that resulted in a greatly enhanced care experience for all as well as a lowered cost of care. This important program has now been adopted in several other Kaiser Permanente locations and was recently acknowledged by the Vohs Awards, which Kaiser Permanente gives each year to acknowledge the outstanding nationally recognized quality improvement program. This program illustrates the unique advantage fully integrated value-based managed care systems can provide in evolving health care to meet changing needs and adapt to changing medical care resources over time.

CONCLUSION

Medical care in the United States continues to strive to address the development of the ideal models of care for end-of-life care. The nature of dying has changed dramatically over the course of the last fifty years, the kinds of medical intervention available have multiplied, and the needs of patients and families have changed. Healthcare financing was designed to bring people access to care. We have learned, as the needs for care and the kinds of care have changed, that it is difficult for healthcare financing to adapt and evolve quickly enough to match payment to current need. As a result, many are unable to access crucial care, and significant suffering occurs.

It is essential for social workers to understand end-of-life care financing and programs in order to educate patients, advocate for individuals needing care, and engage in meaningful participation in the ongoing movement to improve end-of-life care and the associated financing resources as we continue to move ahead.

REFERENCES

American Geriatric Society. 1997. Measuring quality of care at the end of life: A statement of principles. *Journal of the American Geriatric Society* 45:526–527.

Arno, P. S., C. Levine, and M. M. Memmott. 1999. The economic value of informal caregiving. *Health Affairs* 18(2): 182–188.

Byock, I. 2001. End-of-life care: A public health crisis and an opportunity for managed care. *American Journal of Managed Care* 7(12): 1123.

Ferris, F. E. D., and I. Cummings, eds. 1995. *Palliative Care: Towards Standardized Principles of Practice*. Ottawa: Canadian Palliative Care Association.

Field, M. J., and C. K. Cassel, eds. 1997. *Approaching Death: Improving Care at the End of Life*. Washington, DC: National Academy Press.

Friedman, B., M. K. Harwood, and M. Shields. 2002. Barriers and enablers to hospice referrals: An expert overview. *Journal of Palliative Medicine* 5(1): 73–81.

Gage, B., and T. Dao. 2000. Medicare's hospice benefit: Use and expenditures, 1996 cohort. http://aspe.hhs.gov/daltcp/reports/96useexp.htm.

Higginson, H., and P. Edmonds. 1999. Services, costs, and appropriate outcomes in end-of-life care. *Annals of Oncology* 10:135–136.

Hogan, C., J. Lynn, J. Gable, J. Lunney, A. O'Mara, and A. Wilkinson. 2000. *Medicare Beneficiaries' Costs and Use of Care in the Last Year of Life: Final Report to the Medicare Payment Advisory Commission.* Washington, DC: Medicare Payment Advisory Commission.

Knaus, W. A., J. Lynn, J. Teno, et al. 1995. A controlled trial to improve care for seriously ill hospitalized patients. *Journal of the American Medical Association* 274:1591–1598.

Last Acts Task Force on Palliative Care. 1998. Precepts of palliative care. *Journal of Palliative Medicine* 1:109–112.

Love, A. A. 1999. Law curbs nursing home evictions. Associated Press, 25 March.

Lubitz, J., and G. Riley. 1993. Trends in Medicare payments in the last year of life. *New England Journal of Medicine* 328(15): 1092–1096.

Lynn, J. 2000. Learning to care for people with chronic illness facing the end of life. *Journal of the American Medical Association* 284:2508.

Miller, S. C., P. Gozalo, and V. Mor. 2000. Use of Medicare's hospice benefit by nursing facility residents. Center for Gerontology and Health Care Research, Brown University. http://aspe.hhs.gov/daltcp/reports/nufares.htm.

Moon, M., and C. Boccuti. 2003. Medicare and end-of-life care: Last Acts financing committee report. www.lastacts.org/files/poublications/medicare.pdf.

National Alliance for Caregiving. 1997. Family caregiving in the United States: Findings from a national survey. www.caregiving.org/conttent/reports/finalreport.pdf.

National Hospice and Palliative Care Organization. 2001. Facts and figures on hospice care in America. www.nhpco.org.

National Hospice Organization. 1993. *Standards of a Hospice Program of Care.* Alexandria, VA: National Hospice Organization.

Petrisek, A. C., and V. Mor. 1999. Hospice in nursing homes: A facility-level analysis of the distribution of hospice beneficiaries. *Gerontologist* 39:279–290.

Saphir, A. 1999. The third way: Palliative care gives providers a chance to treat chronic conditions better while lowering costs. *Modern Healthcare,* 12 April.

Schulz, R., and S. R. Beach. 1999. Caregiving as a risk factor for mortality: The Caregiver Health Effects Study. *Journal of the American Medical Association* 282:2215–2219.

Zerzan, J., S. Stearns, and L. Hanson. 2000. Access to palliative care and hospice in nursing homes. *Journal of the American Medical Association* 284:2489–2494.

42

TAKING CHARGE:
SOCIAL WORK LEADERSHIP IN END-OF-LIFE CARE

ESTHER CHACHKES AND ZELDA FOSTER

LEADERSHIP IN end-of-life care requires that the social worker be assertive, be willing to influence others, and be able to use her expertise to deliver a substantive contribution to both the provision of services and policy development. Social work is a profession that has historically struggled with issues of professional self-esteem and identity, particularly within centralized and hierarchical organizations. Its professional socialization favors mediation, negotiation, and consensus. This has often operated to place social workers in less prominent positions, supporting the ideas and programs promoted by others while down playing their own. Embracing a leadership position, therefore, requires that social workers examine their feelings, thoughts, and values about taking charge and facing any cynicism about their ability to effect change. Assuming a leadership role also demands an understanding of the skills and competencies, including political skills, required to produce change in bureaucratic human-service organizations.

The experience of the authors has emphasized how clinical experience and the truths that emerge influence practice. Both Zelda Foster and Esther Chachkes, each in her own professional and personal way, moved from practice knowledge to leadership activities. Zelda Foster's leadership in the hospice movement and Esther Chachkes's leadership in organizing the social work response to the HIV/AIDS epidemic are examples of clinically based leadership. Through mentorship and collegiality, as well as the juxtaposition of personal, professional and societal forces, they took leadership to develop new programs. They are joined by many others and by members of the National Association of Social Workers, the staff of Gay Men's Health Care, and other community-based organizations. Each social worker must find the path that can best impact systems and influence change in the work environment and other professional arenas.

Social work networks need to broadcast and legitimate practice models and highlight significant programs and expertise. Social workers need to recognize the leaders who created models of excellence. Some of the work of these leaders will be described in this chapter as examples of the range of contributions one can make to the field.

BACKGROUND: SOCIAL WORK IN HEALTHCARE SYSTEMS

Medical social work has a long history, which begins at the turn of the twentieth century. Concerns about the living conditions of the medically ill and the connection between social conditions and the delivery of medical care prompted Dr. Richard Cabot and other physicians (Cabot 1915) to advocate for the establishment of a social work department, under the leadership of Ida Cannon, at the Massachusetts General Hospital in Boston. Dr. Cabot was convinced that medical and social factors were interrelated, and he believed that the teamwork of doctor and social worker was the foundation for good medical care. Working from a public health perspective, he understood the role of community organization and patient advocacy, now the identified functions of the social worker. He also understood the differences between neighborliness, charity, and professional interventions and advocated an approach that supported professional, social, educational, and preventative activities. However, despite his concern with the patient's social situation, Cabot's interests were not as rooted in social welfare and reform as they were in a concern about proper diagnosis and the influence of the individual patient's social condition on medical compliance. Social workers at that time adhered to the prevailing belief that the social worker's primary role was to assist the doctor with the social interventions that became part of good medical care.

Since the early 1900s, medical social work has been an established profession within the healthcare system. However, the profession has remained an ancillary provider of service, and one with lower status than that of doctor. This may be attributed in part to the predominance of women in the profession and to its identification with vulnerable and poor populations (Lewis 1981). Despite this dynamic, many important advances must be noted. Social work schools were developed, offering graduate degrees. Inspired leaders and academics contributed to social work research and to a developing knowledge base in psychosocial issues. Social work found representation in policy formulation. And healthcare settings until recently were the largest employers of social workers in the country.

EVOLVING SOCIAL WORK ROLES

Over the years, social work roles have shifted, and various skills have been promoted at different times as intervention modalities developed and strategies evolved. Counseling and mental health skills, advocacy and community organization skills, and administrative skills have been central. Their centrality has depended upon how the major functions of the profession have been defined. In more recent years, the profession has maintained several important functions within the healthcare system. These include discharge planning as well as psychosocial assessments and counseling to facilitate coping and adaptation to illness and disability. The enduring and central role of social work, however, is that of psychosocial clinician. Social work services provide value to institutions. They allow institutions to carry out their mission for quality care by addressing the psychosocial distress of patients and families in a holistic context.

CURRENT ROLES

Social workers are present in many settings, fulfilling a multitude of roles and employing multiple skills. The setting, to a large extent, shapes how these roles and skills are sought, defined, and expressed. There is no doubt that social work is a profession that involves many roles, and that each social worker carries a wide array of functions even within a specific setting. Competing priorities are often determined by the needs of the population served, the employing institution's goals, and a social work–defined mandate. For example, the discharge-planning role mandates a quicker transition from hospital to community and therefore diminishes the focus of the clinical counseling to help patient and family manage this transition. Social workers need to consider new models for short-tem counseling to fit this arrangement.

For institutions providing end-of-life care, the role of the social worker is central. When illness reaches its terminal phase, psychosocial and emotional turmoil intensify as patients and families try to cope with the drastic changes in their lives. Supportive help is often necessary to enable people to organize their lives, to manage the impact of this phase of the illness, and to maintain as much functioning and quality of life as possible. The patient and family are called upon to tolerate the limitations imposed by the illness, to develop compensatory defenses, and to organize the psychosocial environment to facilitate coping and management. Clinical social work entails helping people to understand, integrate, and use information, mourn losses, and maintain a positive view of themselves when illness has shattered their sense of self and undermined their self-esteem. Clinical social workers help people resolve conflict around caregiving roles. They help with conflicts in interpersonal relationships that are the result of stress at its maximum, when people feel vulnerable and out of control. Clinical social work also helps people manage issues of dependency and emotional reactions such as depression, anxiety, fear, and anger—powerful emotions that frequently accompany terminal illness.

To accomplish all of this, the full repertoire of social work modalities is employed, including individual therapies, behavior modification, family treatment, group therapies, crisis intervention, and stress-reduction interventions such as guided imagery, hypnosis, assessment of pain and pain management, and other stress-management techniques. In addition to these clinical interventions, social workers provide the range of historic social work activities targeted to strengthen the environment of care by identifying and linking people to community resources and protective support systems. These are traditional roles, ones that reflect social work knowledge and skill that continue to hold great significance as palliative care gains momentum in the health-care environment and as care shifts from aggressive treatment to supportive care. Social work, with its knowledge and experience in treating the person in the environment, promotes a holistic approach to quality psychosocial care at the end of life.

ZELDA FOSTER'S LEADERSHIP IN END-OF-LIFE CARE

In the mid-twentieth century, the care of the dying was relegated to a neglectful detachment in the face of cure-oriented and aggressive treatment philosophies. Social workers often felt alone in serving a population that had lost status and promise. During the 1960s, along with other reform movements, the hospice movement rose out of a deeply motivated reform agenda (Wald, Foster, and Wald 1980). It grew outside of established organizations and mainstream medical care. Zelda Foster, as a young social worker in the late 1950s, was working in a Veteran's Administration Hospital, with patients who had what were then fatal illnesses such as Hodgkin's disease, leukemia, and malignant melanoma. She was intensely moved by their isolation and by the silence and the false reassurance that surrounded them. As she challenged this imposed silence, she was met with bewilderment and sometimes hostility from the staff of the hospital ward. Her director, Sylvia Clarke, supported her, and subsequently with her help and that of Grace Field, Zelda wrote of her experiences (Foster 1965). Dr. Cicely Saunders, the founder of both the international hospice movement and St. Christopher's Hospice in London, along with Florence Wald, the dean of the Yale School of Nursing at that time and a major force behind the hospice movement in the United States, read her article and invited Zelda to a Yale conference in 1966. The leaders, who wanted to reform dying in America, shared their experiences and ideas about treatment and care and developed a passionate resolve to make changes where possible (Foster 2001; Saunders 2001).

In the ensuing years, there has been a complex history of the development of hospice and palliative care. It has involved many legislative, philosophical, political, scientific, and institutional struggles and has led to changes in how care is delivered at the end of life. For Zelda, the experience brought lifelong relationships with Dr. Saunders, Florence Wald, and other leaders of the hospice movement, the co-founding of the New York State Hospice Association, a national role in this arena in the Veterans Administration, and a current role as faculty in two post-master's programs funded by the Soros Foundation's Project on Death in America.

It is only in recent years, with the incorporation of hospices into hospital settings and the advent of palliative-care initiatives, as well as with the support of various foundations and organizations such as the Soros Foundation, the Robert Wood Johnson Foundation, and the United Hospital Fund, that care for the dying or end-of-life care has become a focused and even compelling establishment mission (O'Connor 1999). Nursing schools, medical schools, medical centers, and most recently social workers have received funding, supported by foundations and other organizations, to change the culture of death in America by developing curricula and educational programs on end-of-life care, serving as faculty scholars, doing research, establishing demonstration programs, and assuming leadership roles.

Hospice legislation has emphasized a multidisciplinary approach to end-of-life care and mandates social work as a core profession. Furthermore, healthcare organizations, in general, are better attending to the needs of dying patients, encouraged to do so by both the legislation that requires advance directives and the patient-centered standards of care promoted by the Joint Commission on Accreditation of Healthcare Organizations (2000) and the Omnibus Budget Reconciliation Act of 1986. These mandates identify social work as a core profession and affirm and legitimate a solid social work presence. They have aided in the expansion of the social work role to new areas for practice. These include clinical interventions in pain and symptom management, end-of-life decision making, advocacy for navigating the healthcare system, psychoeducational programs for patients and families that are culturally relevant, and targeted group-support programs for bereavement, grief, and coping with traumatic events. Social workers, valuing interdisciplinary cooperation and collaboration, have been influential in promoting team meetings and family conferencing as well as in stimulating a multidisciplinary dialogue within their institutions.

BARRIERS

Social work's ability to hold and develop these roles is now becoming a critical concern because of current forces within healthcare organizations that seek to redefine what best promotes psychosocial functions. Over a twenty-year period, changes in reimbursement methodologies for medical centers, as well as the advent of managed care, have demanded cost-effective practice and bottom-line economies. New patient-focused care programs are being designed that often result in the decentralization of social work departments. Without the support of a social work department, the social worker is left to fend alone among other more powerful professionals who are establishing their roles in this new climate (Davidson and Foster 2003). Nurses and others are claiming much of the domain associated with social work expertise. Social workers are caught in the bind of fulfilling institutional demands while losing autonomy and professionally defined functions. This creates for social workers, social work departments, and agencies the difficult task of identifying, clarifying, and negotiating an appropriate function within the institution. Social workers need to recognize and promote ways in which the institution can enhance its status, market share, and funding. Despite this difficulty, social workers have influenced their roles within organizations by assertively examining the systems in which they are working to determine how to construct relevant and satisfying roles and to understand the barriers that work against this.

There are barriers from within the profession as well. Many social work practitioners identify with their employing institutions or fields of practice and may have a greater alliance with the larger professional community than with the field of social work. In the past, social work contributions have melded into more general interdisciplinary efforts. Often social workers in leadership positions are associated with the programs with which they play central roles while seemingly disassociated from their social work identification and participation in the profession. Spokespersons in public and policy development forums, and in the media, are frequently not identified as social workers. Identification primarily as psychotherapists also minimizes the broader social work function. In addition, social workers with PhDs may not be identified as social workers unless their MSWs are also listed.

This seems to be less true of nurses and physicians, who tend to remain visible and allied with their disciplines and educational and research environments. Often their leadership roles are fully promoted and recognized by their professional organizations. An important dilemma for social workers is how to make an interdisciplinary programmatic contribution while explicitly advancing social work–based initiatives and recognition. The relevance of social work's professional organizations and schools of social work to making explicit the issues facing practitioners is key to advancing social work roles and practice (Rank and Hutchison 2000; Berkman 1995).

Professional organizations, despite the efforts of some, are not sufficiently inclusive and embracing, nor are they able to compensate for losses in social worker's functions both in the field and in the esteem held by the public. It is therefore essential that social workers continue to exert leadership by presenting their innovative programs nationally so that there is strong social work visibility and recognition. Professional organizations should be encouraged to promote the profession, to articulate the voices of its members, and to gain membership in governmental and advocacy arenas where policy is developed. It is imperative to engage social workers in leadership positions not directly associated with social work. Professional organizations need to continue to reinforce their sponsorship of emerging networks, publicize examples of practice excellence, and promote media recognition as well as visibility in academic, political, and professional circles.

ADVANCING LEADERSHIP

As part of the Smith College School of Social Work Post-Master's Program in End of Life Care, advanced practitioner students are required to take a seminar on leadership in end-of-life care. Zelda Foster and Esther Chachkes have successfully taught this seminar. In the course, emphasis is placed on examining each student's practice with a view toward identifying expert roles and leadership opportunities. Frequently these advanced practitioners diminish their own clinical expertise and minimize their innovative work. Some report feeling oppressed by a lack of administrative and professional support. A cycle often develops that further erodes their autonomy and influence.

As these participants have begun to look at their practice and at the forces within their organizations, they have identified opportunities to influence change. While acknowledging that domain conflicts, administrative lack of support, and value differences continue to exist, patterns of self-blame and defeatism are challenged. In this course, practitioners are challenged about their lack of assertion and professional self-regard. Students are encouraged to join emerging networks both in the Smith program and within social work at large that demonstrate ways of promoting recognition and visibility. These become a new source of strength and validation.

Each returning class also has to complete a final project in the second year of the program. The projects for the returning class of 2001 demonstrated the results of leadership initiatives that direct practitioners can take when responding to patient care needs. One social worker, for example, developed a spirituality assessment tool; another, through her own experiences of grief, helped a counseling center to recognize the complexity of grief reactions that she titled, "loving two people at one time." A third student and her classmate developed a new curriculum for end-of-life care that was funded and incorporated into a master's-level program and for which they received PDIA funding. Another student instituted a formalized family conferencing program with physician attendance in an ICU unit of a cancer hospital. Yet another developed an interdisciplinary peer-supervision group that became mandated throughout her cancer center. Seven others wrote publishable papers, and many presented at national conferences. Two developed innovative programs for brain tumor patients and for patients in intensive care units. A number of graduates now teach in schools for social work, and many supervise staff and social work students.

Other examples of leadership were reflected in the development of Internet-based support groups. These creative approaches reflect how direct practitioners, using their clinical expertise, can move beyond the case to make systems change. It was essential for participants to be recognized and to have their work validated so that they could free up creativity and imagination to exert new leadership.

ESTHER CHACHKES'S LEADERSHIP IN PROMOTING END-OF-LIFE CARE

As Zelda Foster moved from case to cause, Esther Chachkes exerted her leadership in the development of palliative care at the New York University Medical Center. To achieve leadership, she had to assess systems, including opportunities and obstacles. She needed to assess social work influence in new and changing mandates dispassionately. She had to articulate core values, analyze changing concepts of treatment, broker formal and informal barriers, and facilitate change within and outside the institution. Further, she needed to examine her place in the organization and to search out opportunities that could be garnered with colleagues who shared a mutual stake. For her, as for Zelda, passionate beliefs about the value of one's experience, a willingness to risk sharing convictions, and the capacity to join and enlist others were essential to taking leadership.

In 1997, in response to the growing demand for end of life services, the NYU Medical Center received a small grant from the New York State Legislature to begin developing a palliative-care program. Because Esther Chachkes, the director of social work, had been a strong advocate for establishing palliative-care services, she was given the responsibility to coordinate this program. She convened a task force and a plan was completed. Key supporters from medicine, nursing, and hospital administration were invited to be members. It took a year to overcome institutional barriers related primarily to philosophical differences and to define the role of primary-care physician and palliative-care physician. Perhaps it was easier for these medical issues to be mediated with a social worker in a leadership position rather than a physician. Social work leadership established a kind of neutrality that facilitated conflict resolution. In 1998, the first component of the program, the Palliative Care Consultation Team, began providing services to a handful of patients. In discussion with hospital administration, Esther requested that leadership of the program now be taken over by a physician dedicated to the team. She would remain a member of the Palliative Care Committee and be active in a more informal role, but she recognized that the program's survival needed medical and administrative leadership. It was her political assessment that in order to protect the integrity of the program within the hierarchical context of the hospital, she would need to "pass the baton" to a more senior administrative person while still maintaining an influential presence on the team. By 1999, the program was in full force with a training component, increased referrals, and a full team that included a chaplain and a full-time social worker. Social work has remained a core component of the program, and social work leadership has continued to help incorporate and institutionalize a psychosocial and family-oriented approach.

EXPERTISE SHOULD ADVANCE PRACTICE

No matter how small the intervention or potential impact, each practitioner must find her or his voice and be willing to take a first step toward taking leadership in end-of-life care. A pivotal aspect of leadership is the examination of the relevant social work expertise that lends itself to a more substantial contribution.

Innovative social work practice in end-of-life care appears in many settings, as a creative and meaningful response to patient and family needs. Creativity is fostered by the fact that many of social work's functions and skills are also universal across settings and fields of practice, and thus social work services are highly adaptive to diverse populations and systems. At times this strength might give the appearance of generality and accommodation. The challenge for the profession is to maintain flexibility and transferability while embracing the expertise intrinsic to special areas of practice. End-of-life care has a knowledge base, defined roles, and specific skills and interventions that can be systematically learned and practiced. Some of these are shared with other professions. However, the attention to the complex interrelationships that characterizes how people function in their environments is unique to social work and is a central aspect of its domain. In addition to helping the patient and family, the social worker's role within the institution serves the organization by both promoting its societal mission and addressing its bureaucratic needs so that patients can use services appropriately and patient satisfaction remains high. Social workers establish linkages and relationships between community-based organizations and more traditional healthcare delivery systems so that services are patient/family and community focused within and across settings and beyond episodes of treatment.

Psychosocial clinical social work has been the foundation and central contribution of social work. Helping ill and dying patients and families is rooted in individual and group theories and practice. Specialized skills in family work, treatment of children, and bereavement and grief work are also essential. Knowledge of cultural and spiritual issues is highly regarded. The helping arenas have widened as counseling is offered in many kinds of groups and in a variety of settings and agencies. Social workers are expected to have specific expertise regarding various diagnoses and treatments. Opportunities for social work contributions present themselves in every aspect of care.

Two current concerns in hospice service delivery serve as a case in point. One is the low percentage of minority groups utilizing hospice care, and a second is the late referrals to hospice and to palliative-care programs. These two examples illustrate how the social worker's understanding of the role of racial and cultural factors, barriers in accessing healthcare systems, and outreach skills can be marshaled to foster timely and appropriate services. Macro-level issues such as discrimination and historic misuse of research for oppressed populations, as well as micro-level issues, are essential to addressing hospice utilization.

Other roles for social workers, such as educator, researcher, manager, administrator, and marketing expert, add value to the institution's ability to deliver high-standard services and programs. Social workers increasingly sit on ethics committees and often provide leadership on these committees. The social work perspective on end-of-life decision making provides the ethics committee with knowledge about executing advance directives, particularly as this is most successful when counseling addresses interpersonal dynamics. Even if social workers do not sit formally on an ethics committee, they are often part of ethics consultation teams and offer assistance in the resolution of complex situations through mediation and clinical expertise.

It is equally important that social workers engage in additional activities such as interdisciplinary education, employee staff support and wellness programs, and interdisciplinary team development. All of these activities can lead to a fruitful and personally gratifying professional life. Social work skills in communication, program planning, and relationship building can help to extend activity beyond the setting and can reframe traditional functions, including community outreach (which for the organization is marketing and public relations). Social workers play a vital role in identifying and developing services for specific populations. Psychoeducational counseling, including via teleconferencing, represents new and evolving opportunities. Social workers are being called upon to participate in quality-improvement activities such as standard setting, establishing competency measures, clinical pathways, and outcome research. Research, teaching, presenting, publishing, and network development are absolutely necessary for social work practice to move beyond direct service so that learned experience can be transformed into conceptual and scientific frameworks as well as program and policy development (see chapter 42).

SOCIAL WORKERS AND THE COMMUNITY

Social workers have a historical and current commitment to the place of community in supporting and assisting patients and families. While information and referral services have value, there are evolving definitions of community and continuity of care that go beyond providing information and facilitating referrals. These allow for partnerships, shared services, outreach, and, in general, fewer boundaries between institutions, encouraging a reduction of divisions and fragmentation. The development of these linkages falls readily into an area of social work strength and mission and into the social work perspective of the person-in-environment.

As other professional groups are also beginning to claim the domain of community, it is now time for social work to be proactive, connected to its history and its ready access to community agencies and programs. Traditional networking skills and a historic commitment to continuity of care should enable social workers to link more comfortably with other organizations.

One example of such a partnership program is the Doula to Accompany and Comfort Program established by the NYU Medical Center and the Jewish Board of Family and Children's Services (JBFCS). This unique program began in 2000. It enables well-trained volunteers to provide emotional support for dying people who have limited family support systems. It emulates maternity doula care, which provides emotional and physical support for mothers during labor and birth. Doulas are trained at JBFCS and placed at NYU Medical Center to provide service, and they are supervised in both settings. Recently the program expanded to train doulas so that they can help patients and families understand the function of healthcare proxies, thereby facilitating communication among family members and with physicians, nurses, and other relevant healthcare personnel. After piloting the program at NYU Medical Center, it has moved to other hospitals and nursing homes.

SOCIAL WORK CONTRIBUTIONS

Although there are many dynamics that create barriers to social work leadership in end-of-life care in healthcare settings, there are also outstanding and impressive examples of social work's contributions. There is a rapidly evolving and catalytic development of social work–sponsored programs and talented practitioners and a current explosion of energy and purposeful direction. An integrated knowledge base has also emerged. New practitioner-led networks are encouraging readily accessible information sharing. And practitioners are looking to collegial and professional support to provide a platform for ideas and practice models. Many examples of innovative practice models exist.

Cancer Care has developed comprehensive and extensive psychosocial programs providing a wide array of services. This social work agency also developed technological approaches to supervision and education, including teleconferencing across the United States.

Professional organizations such as the Association of Oncology Social Work have enabled social workers to have an ongoing forum for shared ideas, concerns, and contributions. Similarly, the National Hospice and Palliative Care Organization (NHPCO) social work section has produced extensive material dealing with competency, practice standards, and outcome measures (Raymer 2001) and has lobbied and advocated for standards at the national level.

The Soros Foundation's Project on Death in America has provided more than thirty social work leadership awards. This effort, led by Professor Grace Christ, has resulted in a burst of new and strengthened initiatives directed toward advancing social work practice in education, organizational development and research (Christ and Sormanti 2000).

Among many outstanding projects is the development of a social work network in end-of-life care in addition to the establishment of a continuing education program (Christ 2001). Terry Altilio, an expert in the role of social work in pain management, has established a Listserv, a network designed to link social work specialists in the sharing and discussing of the multidimensional aspects and issues related to end-of-life care (Altilio 1999, 2001).

Schools of social work are benefiting from PDIA grants, and Joan Berzoff of the

Smith College School of Social Work and Barbara Dane of the NYU School of Social Work are leading important post-master's fellowship programs. These programs are also linked to agencies such as Cancer Care, which provides clinical supervision to the Smith students nationally. Numerous agency practitioners have been funded and continue to be funded to change the culture of dying for people in prisons, in nursing homes, in pediatrics, and among the disenfranchised. These leaders are sharing their work, creating new areas of knowledge, and inspiring the work of others, as the Project on Death in America has acknowledged. In fact, this book is yet another example of leadership in end-of-life care.

It is crucial to identify these initiatives as illustrations of the current state of the art. These give visibility, status, and recognition to the profession. Moreover, each further step provides empowerment and a new groundwork upon which to build future endeavors.

ROLE MODELS

Social work has many role models who demonstrate achievement and new possibilities. These include Matthew Loscalzo, who has written extensively and contributed to the knowledge base on coping with pain and the psychosocial impact on pain management (Loscalzo and Bucher 1999). Esther Chachkes, early in the AIDS epidemic, established social work programs and a strong social work response that led the establishment of a palliative-care program at the NYU Medical Center. Zelda Foster coedited *The Hospice Heritage* (Corless and Foster 1999) and, with Kay Davidson, wrote on the stresses and satisfactions of social workers in end-of-life care (Davidson and Foster 1995, 2003). Myra Glajchen directs the Palliative Care Institute at Beth Israel Medical Center in New York City (Glajchen 2001). Susan Gerbino provides staff support to a number of hospice programs (Gerbino 2001). Phyllis Silverman's pioneering work in the creation of the widow-to-widow program continues her studies of continuing bonds and children in grief. Grace Christ has published extensively on children and bereavement and further demonstrates expertise in this area.

These leaders, with a deep commitment to clinical practice, a sense of personal and professional confidence, and a belief in their competencies, were able to negotiate the bureaucratic structures and hierarchies of their institutions to promote their achievements. Their personal attributes include passion and commitment, which are important aspects of leadership.

Other leaders in end-of-life care have less visible social work roots but are significant as role models. Karen A. Davie, former president of NHPCO, is one example of a person who used her social work background to attain an important institutional and public policy role. Other examples are Mary Lambyak, CEO of the Suncoast Hospice of Florida, and Bernice Catharine Harper, president of the Foundation for Hospices in Sub-Saharan Africa. There are many other noteworthy leaders. It will be important to continue to embrace them as members of the social work profession and to encourage their ties to social work.

SUMMARY

It is increasingly evident that health care remains fragmented and too often lacking in its biopsychosocial mission. An expert panel at the Institute of Medicine concludes, "Health care today harms too frequently and routinely and fails to deliver its potential benefits" (Institute of Medicine 2001). It further states, "For too many patients, the health care system is a maze and many do not receive the services from which they would like to benefit." These trends have had a negative impact on social work in the current marketplace. The overall environment in health care is creating an unfavorable work environment for social work and perhaps even the loss of social work in health as a positive vocational choice. A recent study by the John A. Hartford Foundation analyzed the loss of social work jobs (NASW 2001) and reported significant losses of social work positions in selected hospitals. Paradoxically, an article in the same newsletter described a California assembly committee hearing, decrying the "crisis of social worker shortage."

Through the work of various social work networks, important projects and new initiatives have made significant inroads in end-of-life care. More foundation funding is likely as leaders emerge and success encourages more success. The networks are uniting social workers in many fields of practice—gerontology, pediatrics, oncology, hospice care, and others—fields that do not often collaborate as part of the end-of-life continuum of care. As further networking and collaboration occurs, this enhances the status of social workers and increases empowerment and internal affirmation of the value and contribution of social work to the provision of quality patient care. It offers the potential of spreading to other areas of health care and acting as a model for strengthening a social work base, which can offer direction and purpose in a healthcare system.

Over the next decade, the healthcare system will need to be revamped to encourage collaboration among professionals and to make patient needs and preferences the centerpiece of care. This may be difficult to achieve, but the social work contribution to this mission is vital. To ensure a role in an evolving healthcare system and to insure quality end-of-life care to patients and families, the social work profession will need to assume a greater and more confident leadership role, one that is comfortable with assertiveness and power and with demonstrating a willingness to risk and to affirm its expertise.

REFERENCES

Altilio, T. 1999. Building a pain management program: Background and basics. *Oncology Times Supplement on Oncology Pain Management* 14(5).

———. 2001. Social work network in palliative and end of life care. Listserv.

Berkman, B. 1995. The emerging health care world: Implications for social work practice and education. *Social Work* 41(5): 541–549.

Blacker, S., and A. Rainess. 2000. How community resources can help relieve anxiety. *Primary Care and Cancer* 20(9): 27–30.

Cabot, R. 1915. *Social Service and the Art of Healing*. New York: Moffat, Yard and Co.

Christ, G. 2001. Annual report, Social Work Leadership Development Awards, Project Death in America.

Christ, G., and M. Sormanti. 2000. Advancing social work practice in end of life care. *Social Work in Health Care* 30(2): 81–99.

Clark, D. 2001. A special relationship: Cicely Saunders, the United States, and the early foundations of the modern hospice movement. *Crisis & Loss* 9(1): 15–30.

Corless, I., and Z. Foster, eds. 1999. *The Hospice Heritage: Celebrating Our Future.* New York: Haworth.

Davidson, K., and Z. Foster. 1995. Social work with dying and bereaved clients: Helping the worker. *Social Work in Health Care* 21(4): 1–16.

——. 2003. Balancing satisfaction and stress in social work. In *Dying, Death and Bereavement: A Challenge for the Living* (2d ed.), ed. I. Corless, B. B. Germino, and M. A. Pittman, 313–328. New York: Springer.

Foster, Z. 1965. Social work management of fatal illness. *Social Work* 10(4): 30–35.

——. 1979. Standards for hospice care: Assumptions and principles. *Health and Social Work* (4)1: 118–127.

——. 2001. A crossroads. *Illness, Crisis & Loss* 9(1): 42–49.

Gerbino, S. 2001. Personal communication about staff support groups in five Westchester hospices.

Glajchen, M., D. Blum, and K. Calder. 1995. Cancer pain management and the role of social work: Barriers and interventions. *Health and Social Work* 20:200–206.

Institute of Medicine. 2001. *Crossing the Quality Chasm: A New Health System for the 21st Century.* Washington, DC: National Academies Press.

Joint Commission on the Accreditation of Health Care Organizations. 2001. Standards of care. www.jcaho.org.

Lewis, H. 1981. The emergence of social work as a profession in health care: Significant influences and persistent issues. In *Proceedings of the Third Doris Siegel Memorial Colloquium, New York, April 9, 1981.* New York: Mount Sinai Hospital Medical Center.

Loscalzo, M., and J. Bucher. 1999. The COPE model: Its clinical usefulness in solving pain-related problems. *Journal of Psychosocial Oncology* 15(3–4): 93–117.

Monroe, B. 1998. Social work in palliative care. In *Oxford Text of Palliative Medicine* (2d ed.), ed. D. Doyle, G. W. Hanks, and N. McDonald, 867–880. New York: Oxford University Press.

National Association of Social Workers. 2001. *NASW Newsletter.*

O'Connor, P. 1999. Hospice vs. palliative care. In *The Hospice Heritage: Celebrating Our Future,* ed. I. Corless and Z. Foster, 123–137. New York: Haworth.

Rank, M., and W. Hutchison. Leadership within the social work profession. *Journal of Social Work Education* 36(3): 487–502.

Raymer, M. 2001. NHPCO social work section chair. Drafts of the Social Work Assessment Tool; Impact of Social Work Services on Hospice Outcomes; Competency-Based Education for Social Workers.

Saunders, C. 2001. Social work and palliative care: The early history. *British Journal of Social Work* 31:791–799.

Wald, F., Z. Foster, and H. Wald. 1980. The hospice movement as a health care reform. *Nursing Outlook* 28(3): 173–178.

43

THE FUTURE OF SOCIAL WORK
IN END-OF-LIFE CARE: A CALL TO ACTION

ELIZABETH J. CLARK

I N NOVEMBER 2002, Last Acts, a national program supported by the Robert Wood Johnson Foundation, released the first state-by-state "report card" on care for the dying in this country. In the study, *Means to a Better End: A Report on Dying in America Today*, each state received a letter grade on eight key elements of palliative care. The findings showed that most states did poorly on most criteria. When asked to rate the healthcare system's ability to provide emotional support for the dying and their families, 46 percent of those responding said that the system did only a fair or poor job (Last Acts 2002a).

Care of the dying occurs across the lifespan and across various settings, including hospitals, nursing homes, hospices, prisons, and individual homes. Social workers are trained to provide psychosocial support to individuals and families experiencing significant life transitions, and the common values, knowledge, and skills of social work are applied to specific situations. In end-of-life care, social workers take the lead in providing essential emotional and social services to the dying and bereaved. Yet, social workers report gaps in end-of-life care education, and recent studies of social work curricula, including postdegree training, have documented that existing educational programs have not been adequate in providing social workers with the competencies needed to work with people who are dying and bereaved (Christ and Sormanti 1999).

The role of social work is still being defined within modern health care, and specifically with regard to facing advanced illness and end of life (Institute of Medicine 2001; Brown et al. 2001). The future of social work in end-of-life care cannot be discussed without first looking at trends that will affect that future. Several trends will be important as the profession of social work endeavors to assure and offer excellent end-of-life care for all individuals. These trends include the aging of our population, the impact of managed care, increased racial and ethnic diversity with concomitant increased disparities in health care, and increased emphasis on and need for cultural competency.

AGING OF THE POPULATION

The first of the baby boomers will reach sixty-five years of age within the next decade. While the helping professions have long been aware of this aging phenomenon, most professional groups and the vast majority of health and mental health agencies are not prepared to handle the increased need for services that will result. This may be particularly true for end-of-life-care services.

Almost 2.5 million Americans die each year, and the majority of these deaths are in people over age sixty-five (Cassel and Foley 1999). The last century witnessed the transition from deaths due to acute illness to deaths caused by chronic conditions. Medical discoveries and technological advances have helped people live longer, despite diseases that once would have been likely to cause earlier death. Heart disease and cancer are today's leading causes of death, but, with progressive aging, many more individuals will die deaths complicated by or caused by neurobiological diseases such as Alzheimer's disease or Parkinson's.

As more people live to older ages, the need for expanded health and mental health services, including end-of-life care, is certain. People over sixty-five already use a disproportionate amount of healthcare services. When coupled with the fact that the fastest-growing segment of the population is the group over age eighty-five, the impact on health systems, family caregiving, and long-term care is understandably significant.

Almost all of the helping professions report a shortage of professionals trained in the care of the older adult. Social work is no exception. The National Institute on Aging (1987) projected a need for fifty thousand social workers trained in gerontology by the year 2000, with an additional twenty thousand needed by 2010. Less than 10 percent of that number is currently available (O'Neill 1999a). Additionally, only a small percentage of social work faculty and students report having an interest or expertise in working with the elderly (CSWE/SAGE-SW 2001). An added impediment is that social workers who choose the field of aging are among the lowest-paid in the profession (NASW 2002).

THE IMPACT OF MANAGED CARE

Much has been written in the social work literature about the problems resulting from managed care—problems such as decreased quality of services, lack of access to care, reimbursement issues, and lack of coordination of services (Davidson, Davidson, and Keigher 1999).

Managed care will continue to influence health care, including end-of-life care and the provision of social work services. Managed care already has changed the way health and mental health services are delivered in this country, and almost all social work specializations and practitioners have been affected by the changes. First of all, the locus of practice has shifted from costly inpatient settings to outpatient services. Although this shift is consistent with the cost reduction goals of managed care, it is not consistent with the long-term pattern in social work employment. Under managed care, there are also limitations on the types and amount of services that can be offered or will be covered by the managed care plan. This has the effect of controlling the number and types of providers in the marketplace and has resulted in the narrowing of the demand for clinically trained social workers (Davis 1998).

Another concern is that social work education is highly dependent on the availability of unpaid field placements in community agencies and programs. Since managed care is based on generating revenue, students may be seen as an economic burden both because of their inability to charge for services rendered and because the time required for their supervision cannot be billed to third-party payers. A significant reduction in the number of available field placement opportunities for social work students would threaten the existing model of social work education (Vandivort-Warren 1996).

Many of the current methods and skills being taught in schools of social work—brief therapy, short-term interventions, intensive case management, an emphasis on prevention, and outcomes measurement—are compatible with the prevailing managed-care model. Yet, there is a large cohort of experienced social work practitioners who were taught differently and who still rely on long-term practice models and do not routinely use outcomes measurements to document the efficacy and cost-effectiveness of their interventions. This group will require intensive retraining and ongoing education for their practices and skills to remain relevant in today's managed-care environment.

In end-of-life care, the profession of social work faces many challenges related to managed care. The first is a lack of understanding about the relevance, importance, and scope of the social worker's role in chronic illness, palliative care, and hospice. This is linked to limited reimbursement and lack of coverage for social work services in many care plans. Social workers have demonstrated effectiveness and cost-savings in hospice programs (Reese, Raymer, and Richardson 2000), but in many settings, social work services are seen as "value added," meaning that they would be nice to have, but not essential. This makes social workers an easy target when trying to trim costs.

If the uniqueness and value of social workers are not recognized, decision makers will assume that their roles and functions can simply be tagged onto the duties of a nurse or, in the case of some hospices, relegated to the clergy. Other institutions or agencies mistakenly believe that social work services in end-of-life care can be handled by volunteer-led support groups without professional oversight or input. Social workers recognize the complexity of the issues in end-of-life care and contend that compassion without competency is not sufficient.

To provide quality end-of-life care, social work must be included. Social workers have to demonstrate and validate their specific skills and contributions not only to health/mental health care but also to managed care. The profession needs to present a unified agenda to address these issues in the classroom, in the agency, in the community, and in the political arena.

DISPARITIES IN HEALTH CARE

America is becoming increasingly multiracial and multicultural. The period from 1990 to 2000 represented the largest population growth in American history, with a dramatic increase in people of color from 20 percent to 25 percent (Perry and Mackum 2001). While the profession of social work has had extensive experience with issues of diversity, the magnitude of the demographic shift heightens the diversity currently confronting social workers.

Two phenomena related to diversity have affected the social work profession since its inception. First is the large proportion of minority populations that the profession serves. Second is the pervasiveness of poverty and social problems among these populations (Diaz 2002). These concerns contribute significantly to health disparities, regardless of how this concept is defined—lack of access to care, inability to purchase or obtain care, receipt of substandard care, or lack of culturally sensitive care.

Currently, forty-four million people in the United States are uninsured, 84 percent of whom are workers and their dependents (Freeman and Reuben 2002). An additional thirty-one million of the non-elderly are estimated to be underinsured for catastrophic illness.

As a society, we know very little about the health of immigrant populations, but we have a fairly clear understanding of barriers to health care that immigrants face. These include fear of jeopardizing eligibility for citizenship, fear of government, and fear of authority figures such as physicians (Clark 2001). Disparities in immigrant health care are related not only to public health but also to civil rights.

Similarly, little data can be found concerning the health status of rural Americans. The only current data are concentrated on Appalachian counties in the eastern part of the United States. Rural Americans tend to be older, poorer, less educated, and more likely to be uninsured than their urban/suburban counterparts. Rural communities have higher rates of chronic illness and disability and report poorer overall health status than their urban neighbors (Intercultural Cancer Council 2002). Residents from rural areas generally have less contact and fewer visits with physicians and lower levels of preventive care.

It is to be expected, then, that these disparities in the healthcare system extend to end-of-life care for many groups in our population. Unequal access to hospice and palliative care is a major obstacle for most minorities (Scott et al. 2002). These issues are compounded even further when marginalized populations such as prisoners, the chronically mentally ill, nursing home residents, and persons with substance-abuse problems are considered. There is only limited knowledge about the healthcare preferences of people from marginalized groups, and initiatives to enhance their care at the end of life are new (Christopher 2001).

BUILDING CULTURAL COMPETENCY

The Code of Ethics for the profession of social work charges social workers with the ethical responsibility to be culturally competent (NASW 2000a). *Cultural competence* "refers to the process by which individuals and systems respond respectfully and effectively to people of all cultures, languages, classes, races, ethnic backgrounds, religions, and other diversity factors in a manner that recognizes, affirms, and values the worth of individuals, families, and communities and protects and preserves the dignity of each" (NASW 2000a:11).

To be culturally competent requires a high level of self-awareness, professionalism, and knowledge. It also requires ongoing education about diversity and new populations. In addition, the profession must redouble its efforts to recruit and train a diverse group of social workers not simply for the delivery of social services, but also to increase avenues for acquisition of culturally competent skills by all social workers (NASW 2000b:60).

Training specific to cultural and ethnic differences regarding palliative care and end-of-life care in special populations is essential for social workers. Topics to be considered include the meaning of the illness experience and suffering, communication styles, patterns of decision making, the role of the family, acceptable methods of symptom management, use of nontraditional therapies, issues of trust, and specific religious beliefs and rituals.

BUILDING COMPETENCY FOR END-OF-LIFE CARE

The groundwork for establishing competency in end-of-life care has been laid by numerous researchers and groups. In the late 1980s, the Robert Wood Johnson Foundation funded a multiyear randomized study of deaths in American hospitals. The Study to Understand Prognoses and Preferences for Outcomes and Risks of Treatment (SUPPORT) involved nearly five thousand dying patients. It included sophisticated prognostic tools and trained nurse facilitators, yet patients died in poorly controlled pain, their advanced directives—if they existed—were not followed, and family needs were frequently unaddressed (SUPPORT 1995).

In response to SUPPORT, the foundation launched a professional and public engagement campaign called Last Acts. The Last Acts Coalition now has close to a thousand partners (Last Acts 2002b) and has sponsored numerous projects and grants to increase professional education, promote institutional change, and create public engagement around the topic of death and dying.

Last Acts (1997) also defined and promoted the following concept and precepts of palliative care:

> Palliative care means taking care of the whole person—body, mind, spirit—heart and soul. It looks at dying as something natural and personal. The goal of palliative care is that you have the best quality of life you can have during this time.
>
> 1. Palliative care respects the goals, likes, and choices of the dying person;
> 2. Palliative care looks after the medical, emotional, social, and spiritual needs of the dying person;
> 3. Palliative care supports the needs of the family members;
> 4. Palliative care helps gain access to needed health care providers and appropriate care settings; and
> 5. Palliative care builds ways to provide excellent care at end of life.

These precepts describe for health professionals five areas that are key to delivering high quality care at the end of life. They provide an excellent starting point, and the precepts have been adopted by numerous professional associations and institutions.

Since 1997, fourteen medical specialty societies as well as the Joint Commission on Accreditation of Healthcare Organizations (JCAHO) have endorsed or adopted a set of Core Principles for End-of-Life Care. Similarly, in 1999 the Nursing Leadership Consortium on End-of-Life Care brought together twenty-three specialty nursing organizations with the goal of advancing the nursing profession's commitment to improve care at end of life (American Association of Critical-Care Nurses 1999).

Like the professions of medicine and nursing, there has been much activity in establishing and advancing the social work role in end-of-life care. In 1999, the Project on Death in America (PDIA) created the Social Work Leadership Development Awards in order to identify and strengthen leaders from the social work profession to develop the necessary organizations, networks, educational initiatives, practice guidelines, research agendas, and policy directions. The awards promote the visibility of social workers committed to end-of-life care and enhance their effectiveness as academic leaders, role models, and future generations of social workers (Project on Death in America 2002).

In 2001 the Society for Social Work Leadership in Health Care delineated the core competencies that inform social work practice in end-of-life care (Brown et al. 2001). These included practice competencies (knowledge, skills, and attitudes) as well as a description of social work roles and functions in end-of-life care: completing psychosocial assessments; developing comprehensive psychosocial treatment plans; participating as a member of the interdisciplinary team; and psychosocial interventions with individuals, families, groups, organizations, and the community.

In early 2002, the Social Work Summit on End of Life and Palliative Care brought together thirty professional social work associations representing more than 160,000 practicing social workers. Cosponsored by the Last Acts Provider Education Committee, the Duke Institute on Care at the End of Life, and the Soros Foundation's Project on Death in America, the summit had the goal of forming a coalition of national social work organizations and experts to enhance and elevate end-of-life care training, practice, education, research, and policy for the social work profession. One outcome was the development of a consensus statement and social work "priority map" for palliative care, end-of-life care, and grief work (PEG) (Stoesen 2002).

The work of the summit is being carried forward, in part, by a national collaborative project that has the intent of shaping both the public policy and social work practice dimensions in the care of the dying. Funded by the Open Society Institute's Project on Death in America, the initiative is spearheaded by the National Association of Social Workers, the largest professional organization for social workers in the world. Titled "Building Social Work Practice and Policy Competencies in End of Life Care," the project will utilize multiple strategies to develop and disseminate national social work standards for PEG and to expand and formalize mechanisms for information transfer and continuing education for the broader social work community (O'Neill 2003).

A CALL TO ACTION

If social work is to claim to be a core profession in end-of-life care, we must be able to articulate the basis for that central position, and the profession must assume a highly visible leadership role. This will require commitment and concerted and integrated activities at all levels of social work: education, practice, research, professional associations, administration, and policy.

To facilitate further dialogue and to encourage a collaborative action plan for the profession of social work, a beginning list of challenges is presented here.

EDUCATION

- Incorporate end-of-life issues in both undergraduate and graduate social work curricula and in continuing education programs.
- Contribute to public education about end-of-life issues beginning in elementary and middle schools.
- Develop cultural competency training tools for end-of-life care.
- Prepare a group of social work specialists to act as clinical role models for students, beginning professionals, and experienced clinicians moving into end-of-life care.
- Support interdisciplinary educational efforts to increase competency of all health/mental health professionals in end-of-life care.

PRACTICE

- View palliative care, end-of-life care, and grief work as a continuum and assure continuity of care.
- Promote an interdisciplinary care model to address better the complex problems surrounding end-of-life care.
- Strengthen social work clinical competencies and specialty skills to ensure quality end-of-life care for all populations, especially the vulnerable and marginalized.
- Modify and refine existing interventions to be applicable across practice settings and age groupings.
- Determine ethnic and culturally sensitive variations for interventions in end-of-life care.
- Participate on institutional ethics committees dealing with end-of-life issues.
- Develop methods for improving communication and decision making in end-of-life care.

RESEARCH

- Promote the development of a social work research agenda on end-of-life issues.
- Ensure that social work researchers are included on national panels that review and award research grants.
- Develop better measurement tools to assess effectiveness of end-of-life interventions.
- Promote clinical guidelines that are evidence based for optimal end-of-life care for patients and families.
- Publish and disseminate social work research findings in interdisciplinary journals.

PROFESSIONAL ASSOCIATIONS

- Endorse the Last Acts Precepts of Palliative Care (listed earlier in this chapter).
- Establish national standards of social work practice for end-of-life care across settings of care.
- Collaborate with other professional disciplines to implement a paradigm shift in end-of-life care.
- Disseminate social work end-of-life care standards to educational programs, professional associations, and legislative and regulatory bodies.
- Develop a national credentialing process to ensure social work competency in end-of-life care.
- Provide a clearinghouse to disseminate best social work practices in end-of-life care.
- Conduct a public awareness campaign regarding the important role of social work in end-of-life care.
- Facilitate collaboration and resource sharing specific to end-of-life care among social work organizations.

POLICY

- Ensure that legal and regulatory barriers do not hinder excellent psychosocial care at end of life.
- Advocate for access to, and reimbursement for, social work therapies and interventions that will promote the highest quality of life for the dying and bereaved.
- Work to eliminate disparities in end-of-life care for all populations, the majority and the marginalized.
- Seek social work certification or credentialing that provides consumer protection.

ADMINISTRATION

- Build infrastructures that promote the philosophy of palliative care.
- Formulate workplace practices and policies sensitive to appropriate end-of-life care and bereavement.
- Strive to achieve a culturally diverse workforce for offering end-of-life services.
- Strengthen community-specific efforts and direct resources toward these efforts to improve end-of-life care.
- Establish methods for patient and family feedback regarding needs and services.
- Develop evaluative tools to ensure staff accountability in the provision of care.
- Provide adequate continuing education opportunities so staff can remain current about advances in end-of-life care.

SUMMARY

Currently, there are more than 600,000 professionally trained social workers practicing in this country. Clinically trained social workers are the largest providers of mental health services (O'Neill 1999b), and in many rural and medically underserved areas, social workers are the only mental health providers available. Social workers can be found in all clinical settings caring for persons who are chronically ill, dying, or bereaved. They have an ethical obligation to offer competent services and to work on all levels to ensure not only quality of life, but also quality of dying.

REFERENCES

American Association of Critical-Care Nurses. 1999. Designing an agenda for the nursing profession on end-of-life care. *Report of the Nursing Leadership Consortium on End-of-Life Care.* Aliso Viejo, CA: American Association of Critical-Care Nurses.

Brown, S., S. Blacker, K. Walsh-Burke, G. Christ, and T. Altilio. 2001. *Care at the End of Life.* Chicago: Society for Social Work Leadership in Health Care.

Cassel, C. K., and K. M. Foley. 1999. Principles for care of patients at the end of life: An emerging consensus among specialties of medicine. www.milbank.org/endoflife.

Christ, G., and M. Sormanti. 1999. Advancing social work practice in end-of-life care. *Social Work in Health Care* 30(2): 81–99.

Christopher, M. 2001. Approaches for patients from marginalized groups. *State Initiatives in End-of-Life Care* 12.

Clark, E. J. 2001. Unequal burden: Care disparities. *NASW News* 46(9): 2.

Council on Social Work Education/Sage-SW. 2001. *A Blueprint for the New Millennium.* New York: CSWE.

Davidson, T., J. R. Davidson, and S. M. Keigher. 1999. Managed care: Satisfaction guaranteed . . . not! *Health & Social Work* 24(3): 163–168.

Davis, K. 1998. Managed health care: Forcing social work to make choices and changes. In *Human Managed Care,* ed. G. Schamess and A. Lightburn, 409–424. Washington, DC: NASW Press.

Diaz, L. 2002. Cultural competence. Practice update from the National Association of Social Workers.

Freeman, H. P., and S. H. Reuben. 2002. *Voices of a Broken System: Real People, Real Problems.* Bethesda, MD: National Cancer Institute.

Institute of Medicine. 2001. *Improving Palliative Care for Cancer.* Washington, DC: National Academy of Sciences.

Intercultural Cancer Council. 2002. Cancer facts. www.iccnetwork.org.

Last Acts. 1997. The precepts of palliative care. www.lastacts.org.

——. 2002a. *Means to a Better End: A Report on Dying in America Today.* Washington, DC: Last Acts National Program Office.

——. 2002b. Fact sheet. www.lastacts.org.

National Association of Social Workers. 2000a. *NASW Code of Ethics.* Washington, DC: NASW Press.

——. 2000b. Cultural competence in the social work profession. *Social Work Speaks: NASW Policy Statements 2000–2003,* 59–62. Washington, DC: NASW Press.

——. 2002. Social work income 2. *Practice Research Network: Informing Research and Policy Through Social Work Practice* 1(6). Washington, DC: NASW Press.

National Institute on Aging. 1987. *Personnel for Health Needs of the Elderly Through the Year 2020.* Bethesda, MD: Department of Health and Human Services, Public Health Service.

O'Neill, J. V. 1999a. Aging express: Can social work keep up? *NASW News* 44(2): 3.

——. 1999b. Profession dominates in mental health. *NASW News* 44(6): 1, 8.

——. 2003. End-of-life project underwritten. *NASW News* 48(1): 1.

Perry, M. J., and P. J. Mackum. 2001. Population change and distribution: 1990–2000. www.census.gov/prod/2001/c2kbr0.

Project on Death in America. 2002. www.soros.org/death.

Reese, D., M. Raymer, and J. Richardson. 2000. *National Hospice Social Work Survey: Summary of Final Results*. Alexandria, VA: National Hospice and Palliative Care Organization.

Scott, C. K, D. Hughes, M. Doty, B. Ives, J. Edwards, and K. Tenney. 2002. *Diverse Communities, Common Concerns: Assessing Health Care Quality for Minority Americans*. New York: Commonwealth Fund.

Stoesen, L. 2002. Role in end-of-life care examined. *NASW News* 47(5): 4.

SUPPORT Principal Investigators. 1995. A controlled trial to improve care for seriously ill hospitalized patients: The study to understand prognoses and preferences for outcomes and risks of treatment (SUPPORT). *Journal of the American Medical Association* 274:1591–1598.

Vandivort-Warren, R. 1996. *CSWE/NASW Report on Preparing Social Workers for a Managed Care Environment*. Washington, DC: National Association of Social Workers.

44

RELENTLESS SELF-CARE

IRENE RENZENBRINK

We in this work are somehow missing an outer layer of skin and must take care to renew ourselves.
—Dame Cicely Saunders, founder of the modern hospice movement

SEVERAL YEARS ago, Robert Hockley, a valued Australian friend and colleague in the loss and grief field, died of cancer in his early fifties. Because we were living on different continents while he was dying, he wrote me a farewell letter. In it, he urged me to practice "relentless self-care," for he felt that those of us who work with dying and bereaved people are extremely vulnerable to stress and illness and therefore need to take better care of ourselves.

Over the past thirty years I have worked in various high-stress areas of social work, including end-of-life care in home, hospice, and hospital settings and in adult and pediatric intensive care and oncology units. I also worked as a social worker in the funeral industry for many years and was involved in community recovery following mass shootings in Australia and New Zealand.

Although the word "relentless" might seem rather dramatic, it does describe the reality of social work practice in many settings and, in particular, the area of grief, death, and bereavement. Dealing daily with intense emotion can be extremely challenging and may even be dangerous to health and well-being. In 1987, Dr. Robert Fulton, the founder of the Center for Death Education and Counseling at the University of Minnesota, issued the following warning to caregivers of the dying: "The time might not be too far distant when signs are posted over the entrance to terminal care wards that read, The Surgeon General of the United States has determined that the care of the terminally ill may be detrimental to your health" (1987:256).

Today, in many countries throughout the world, cuts to healthcare budgets have left many workers with heavier workloads and lower job satisfaction. It is not uncommon to hear social workers complain about having to do "more and more with less and less" or about increasing numbers of "quicker and sicker" discharges. Services in the community have not kept pace with the complex care needs of patients who choose to die at home. Family support may not be readily available, and benefits for caregivers are often inadequate or nonexistent. (A recent decision by the Canadian Government to ensure that Canadians "can provide compassionate care for a gravely ill or dying child, parent or spouse without putting their jobs or incomes at risk" will no doubt set a new benchmark in palliative-care service provision and significantly reduce caregiver stress in that country, at least.)

Increased pressure in a climate of diminishing resources can result in higher levels of disillusionment, burnout, and compassion fatigue. High staff turnover and absenteeism can be costly in human and economic terms, as standards of patient and family care and staff morale suffer. Significant advances in the study of occupational stress in the healthcare field over the past two decades have led to greater recognition that the "well-being of the workforce is a prerequisite to the well being of the patient" (Firth-Cozens and Payne 1999).

This chapter focuses on the stress and grief associated with the care of dying and bereaved people and the ways in which social workers cope with pressures in their work. Research findings, theoretical perspectives, and the practice wisdom of leaders in the field of grief, bereavement, and trauma can provide both an intellectual framework and an emotional safety net for social workers who face the pain of loss on a daily basis.

Many terms in use today describe different aspects of the helping relationship and varying degrees of severity and stress in care giving situations. Some are *occupational stress* (Vachon et al. 2001), *burnout* (Freudenberger 1975), *compassion fatigue* and *secondary traumatic stress* (Figley 1995), *psychological trauma* (Herman 1992), *transference and countertransference* (Pearlman 1995; Valent 2002), *empathic strain* (Raphael 1984), and *vicarious traumatization* (Pearlman 1995).

These terms refer to concepts that have arisen in various fields of practice, including health care, crisis and disaster situations, domestic violence, and traumatic bereavement. The stressors experienced by both helper and client may be related to the nature of the critical events themselves, the client or patient's account of their experience, factors within the workplace, and the unique personal and professional issues for the worker involved.

In this chapter I will describe and discuss these concepts and their implications for social work practice in end-of-life care for the student, the new graduate as well as the more experienced practicing social worker.

Drawing on an understanding of grief and bereavement theory as well as deeper philosophical perspectives, I will also explore such concepts as *the wounded healer* (Nouwen 1972), *the intimate stranger* (Fulton 1974), *the inner bereaved child* (Raphael 1984), *caregiver grief* (Papadatou 2000; Remen 1998), and *soul pain* (Kearney 1996). This latter group provides an even richer, and perhaps less medically oriented source of enlightenment about our role as helpers in the area of death, severe loss, and bereavement.

Finally, I would like to offer some ideas about "best practice" in the area of staff support and strategies for the promotion of greater well-being and reduced stress. I hope that my contribution to this book will encourage social workers to practice "relentless self-care" at a personal and professional level and to insist on the development of appropriate policies and procedures at an organizational level.

BURNOUT

Burnout is the result of prolonged job stress and appears to be more prevalent among those who enter the helping professions with high ideals and expectations. It is characterized by a sense of powerlessness and inability to achieve work goals related to the nature of the work itself or to hierarchical pressures and constraints (Valent 2002). A commonly used definition of burnout, developed by Maslach (1993) is "a syndrome of emotional exhaustion, depersonalization, and reduced personal accomplishment that can occur among individuals who work with people in some capacity."

Studies of burnout have been conducted with many occupational groups, including doctors, nurses, teachers, emergency services personnel, and, to a lesser extent, social workers. Burnout in healthcare settings is correlated with youth and inexperience, high expectations, heavy workload, lack of support, lack of autonomy or participation in decision making, frequent direct patient contact, and severe patient problems. It is also manifested in psychosomatic complaints, frequent illness, and impaired performance on the part of the worker (Firth-Cozens and Payne 1999).

Veninga and Spradley (1981) concluded from their studies that "the modern workplace can devastate lives, destroy hopes, and deplete energy." Their research showed a lowered resistance to illness and a host of health problems, including allergies, backaches, headaches, insomnia, depression, and overuse of drugs and alcohol among workers subjected to prolonged stress.

Burnout can also be caused by an imbalance or lack of reciprocity in relationships with patients and employers. At the interpersonal level, there may be constant giving to patients and families with little thanks in return. In end-of-life care, dying patients and their families are understandably more preoccupied with their own needs and can hardly be expected to nurture the staff. This is not to say that the work does not bring its own rewards and satisfactions, or that patients and families are not grateful for the care they receive. It is just that staff cannot, or should not, expect to be supported by their patients.

At the organizational level, there may even be a "violation of the psychological contract" (Schaufeli, Enzmann, and Girault 1993) when managers and supervisors are particularly unsupportive or even cruel. Unfortunately, administrators in end-of-life care services do not always have the clinical background or capacity for empathy that is required to manage staff working in such a sensitive area. Employees expect to be treated with respect and to have their efforts acknowledged and rewarded. When this does not happen, reciprocity is "corroded" and disillusionment and negativity begin to set in.

Social workers in end-of-life care may be particularly susceptible to burnout because they tend to be "feeling" people who are caring and thoughtful. Trained to focus on the whole person rather than on the disease, the social worker in end-of-life care will be more concerned with the emotional and social impact of the illness than on pain and symptom control, the traditional domain of medical and nursing staff.

Taught to adopt a nonjudgmental and sympathetic listening approach, the social worker is expected to be empathic and compassionate. He or she may develop particularly close and meaningful relationships with terminally ill patients and their family members. In the early years of operation of the palliative care unit at Royal Victoria Hospital, Montreal, the social worker's position was thought to be one of the most stressed because everyone else in the multidisciplinary team felt that they were able to do what the social worker did, that is, talk to patients and families about the impact of the illness on their lives.

Social work activities may be more difficult to measure or define in a tangible way, and "successes" often remain invisible. In end-of-life care, profound and complex helping encounters requiring great therapeutic skill and sensitivity often go unrecognized, or, worse, are dismissed by colleagues as "just a little chat." In his book *What Dying People Want* (2002), David Kuhl admits that learning to listen and "bear witness" to the patient's personal experience of illness was much more difficult than simply gathering information about the illness, or, as he puts it, "being a detective."

Role blurring can be a major source of stress in end-of-life care. Although the combined skills and knowledge of different team members can enhance patient and family care, the reality is often quite different. Unfortunately, rivalries, tensions, and politics are all too common, even in this special area of work. The difficulties may even have increased over the years since other disciplines such as nursing and medicine have adopted a more holistic, person-in-situation approach, and place greater emphasis on developing effective counseling and communication skills.

Social workers and chaplains are still more likely than other members of the multidisciplinary team to "sit with" the distress and "be with" a dying patient rather than actively engage in problem solving. Despite this more passive role, good social workers also understand that active practical help with legal, financial, or housing matters is vitally important. Attending to practical matters can significantly reduce the patient's anxiety as well as build confidence and trust in the worker. Greater emphasis on tasks can at times provide the social worker with some respite from the more emotionally charged counseling issues such as family conflict, anticipatory grief, and "unfinished business."

However, because some workers may use the practical tasks as a shield, good supervision is needed to help the social worker find the right balance in her workload and case planning. If the worker defends against the pain of involvement too much, the patient might be deprived of the level of intimacy and personal understanding that he or she needs in the last days and weeks of life.

It is therefore important that social workers, together with their less task-oriented colleagues such as chaplains and volunteers, understand and recognize the value of simply "being there" for patients and families. They need to clarify and state their roles and responsibilities within the multidisciplinary team, recognizing that at times they might be able to make a more useful contribution in supporting or debriefing the nurses rather than only in aiming to work at the bedside with patients.

Selection of a primary focus of intervention for each member of the team can also be helpful. It not only reduces stress in staff through sharing of the load, but it also avoids unnecessary duplication of effort. There is nothing more harmful or exhausting for patients than to be asked by all members of the "helping" team about their feelings or the meaning of their illness. Lateral thinking, flexibility, and sensitivity are required here.

Mary Vachon's landmark studies of occupational stress (1994, 1998) have suggested a number of strategies to prevent burnout in nurses and other occupational groups.

These include developing a sense of competence, control, and pleasure in one's work, having a personal philosophy of death and illness, and lifestyle management and stress-relieving activities such as meditation, good nutrition, and exercise. In particular, Vachon emphasizes the importance of analyzing sources of stress and fatigue and of distinguishing between personal and professional variables. Sometimes individuals blame themselves for things that are really faults in the system or, conversely, blame the organization for problems that are personal.

It is also important to understand one's reasons and motivation for choosing to work in hospice or end-of-life care (Vachon 1978). Some people may be drawn to working with the dying and the bereaved in order to resolve some of their own unconscious fears or past losses. They may even be motivated by a need to gain mastery and control over death. Careful staff selection and the appointment of mature staff with a capacity for maintaining a healthy balance in their lives have been found to be important. Staff will also need an ability or willingness to explore the "big questions" about life, love, and death and, ultimately, to find some meaning in the suffering they witness.

COMPASSION FATIGUE

Compassion fatigue and secondary traumatic stress are synonymous terms introduced by Charles Figley et al. (1994) to describe the stress resulting from helping or wanting to help a traumatized or suffering person. A "natural consequence of feeling compassion or deep sympathy towards those who are stricken by misfortune," compassion fatigue can result in physical and emotional exhaustion with adverse effects on the caregiver's own health and well-being.

The difference between burnout and compassion fatigue may be best understood in terms of "who suffers," although the "emotional exhaustion" described in the burnout literature is barely indistinguishable from compassion fatigue. The patient suffers when a burned-out caregiver becomes cynical and detached, while the worker is the one who suffers when he or she continues to provide compassionate care to patients to his or her own detriment. But in actuality, both the patient and worker suffer in either case.

In compassion fatigue, the suffering of the helper mirrors the pain of those being helped. To quote Figley (1994), "The professional work centered on the relief of the emotional suffering of clients automatically includes absorbing information that is about suffering. Often it includes absorbing that suffering as well." Signs of compassion fatigue include dread of working with certain clients, intrusive images, loss of hope, and outbursts of anger and frustration. There is the same loss of energy and increased susceptibility to illness that are found in burnout, but perhaps less anger, disillusionment, and criticism of an inhospitable or inflexible system. The "problem" tends to be located in the individual caregiver.

In the same way that being "forearmed is to be forewarned" in relation to burnout, knowledge about compassion fatigue and the consequences of constant giving out can help workers to recognize the danger signs. It is also important to share the load and accept that the standard of care may not always be as high as one would wish.

This is not a suggestion about lowering standards so much as learning to live with what is sometimes described as "the good enough death." Just as people do not live perfect lives, so, too, will their deaths be marked by struggles, imperfections, and even disappointments.

VICARIOUS TRAUMATIZATION

The term *vicarious traumatization* (Pearlman and McCann 1990) is often used synonymously with compassion fatigue and refers to the "transformation of the helper's inner experience as a result of empathic engagement with the client or patient." The concept of vicarious traumatization has been developed mostly in relation to therapists who work with victims of sexual abuse, domestic violence, and particularly horrifying and traumatic experiences. Workers in these fields of service have reported intrusive images, nightmares, and negative attitudes such as cynicism and suspicion.

Repeated exposure to the darkest side of humanity can leave workers feeling angry, powerless, and disillusioned. These reactions have much in common with burnout and earlier conceptualizations of countertransference that referred to the "activation of the therapist's unresolved or unconscious conflicts and concerns" (Pearlman and McCann 1990).

Perhaps the feature of vicarious traumatization that best distinguishes it from the phenomena of burnout and compassion fatigue is the degree of disruption to the therapist or caregiver's view of self and the world. Loss of faith in the essential goodness or trustworthiness of people can severely affect the therapist's own relationships and quality of life. The reactions mirror the reactions of victims of violence and can leave the caregiver feeling paralyzed, vulnerable, and helpless and suspicious (Pearlman and McCann 1990).

While end-of-life care is not usually associated with trauma and violence, there may well be terminally ill patients who will relive or revisit past experiences of violence and feel especially vulnerable to intrusive investigations, interventions, and treatment. There is also a great deal of traumatic stress that is rarely acknowledged in palliative care. The sight of emaciated bodies, uncontrolled bleeding and diarrhea, sounds of struggling for breath, screams of pain, distortions and grimaces, and agitation—all of these can be deeply disturbing and distressing for patients and families and for even the most experienced staff.

Ted Bowman (1999) makes a useful distinction between burnout, compassion fatigue, and vicarious traumatization. He explains that burnout is a state of fatigue or frustration when goals of caring are not achieved, while vicarious traumatization involves a transformation of the helper's inner experience as a result of empathic engagement with traumatized individuals. Compassion fatigue, on the other hand, is the stress resulting from helping or wanting to help, a natural consequence of compassion. Antidotes for burnout, vicarious traumatization, and compassion fatigue must therefore address both the stress and the demoralization aspects.

On the subject of the related concepts of *transference* and *countertransference*, it is probably enough to say that social workers need to use supervision and even therapy to understand the connections between their own experiences and those of their patients and clients. Transference is a psychoanalytic concept that refers to the "the reliving of past interpersonal relations in current situations" (Fiscalini 1995). It is a fundamental tool in psychoanalysis and psychoanalytic therapy because it allows patient and therapist to bring material from the past into conscious awareness to prevent the patient from repeating history in a destructive way.

For example, the patient may "transfer" to the therapist some of the thoughts and feelings they have about their own parent, and in a countertransference reaction, the therapist may begin to have strong parental feelings toward the patient who presents very much as "the child." Self-awareness on the part of the therapist is all-important in these situations. There is relevance for end-of-life care here because dying patients and bereaved family members may be extremely vulnerable and susceptible to being rescued or exploited or in danger of being "killed" with kindness as staff relive their own experiences.

Joan Berzoff offers the view that countertransference is ubiquitous to any helping relationship and offers a way into the patient's subjective experience. If the social worker does not *feel* what the patient is feeling, then she may be shutting down an avenue for empathy and connection. She also points out that in current psychoanalytic thinking, countertransference is no longer seen as something that should be left outside the consulting room, but rather as something valuable that gives the therapist access to the patient's subjective experiences.

Raphael, Lindy, and Wilson (reported by Valent 2002) use the term *empathic or countertransference strain* to refer to the stress that follows exposure to clients' traumatic events. Again, this concept seems to be closely related to vicarious traumatization. However, they distinguish between two types of "strain" that correspond with intrusive and avoidance features of posttraumatic stress disorder (see the section on Traumatic Stress). While the intrusive kind of empathic strain is characterized by "loss of boundaries, over-involvement, and reciprocal dependency" with clients, the other, more avoidable type includes withdrawal, numbness, intellectualization, and denial.

These concepts are closely related to the understanding of defenses against anxiety in social systems developed by Isobel Menzies-Lyth following studies of nurses in hospital wards (Hirschorn and May 1999). For example, the routine practice of nurses waking up patients to give them their sleeping pills was interpreted as a way of avoiding personal connections with patients, which might otherwise cause the nurses anxiety or grief. Social workers and other staff may use endless meetings, case conferences, data collection, and report writing in the same way.

PSYCHOLOGICAL TRAUMA AND HEALING

In many ways Judith Herman's seminal work on psychological trauma and recovery (1992) provides a backdrop for the development of the concepts outlined so far, all of which have been derived from an understanding of stress, coping, and the impact of intense emotional experiences. Herman presents an analysis of many different types of trauma, including sexual and domestic violence and the impact of war. Studies of soldiers in combat have been particularly influential in shaping our understanding of trauma and stress at a personal and societal level.

Although it was accepted that soldiers suffered from "shell shock" and "war neurosis" after World War I and World War II, the term *post-traumatic stress disorder* (PTSD) did not appear until the 1970s. For decades it was thought that soldiers who experienced severe mental distress or who "broke down" after periods of combat were "moral invalids, unsuited to military service. It was finally recognized that even the strongest minds could be affected after long enough intense exposure" (Herman 1992). Opposition to the Vietnam War was a catalyst in this recognition. As long as a war is considered noble and glorious, the suffering of soldiers is seen as a necessary sacrifice that must be endured. The view that the Vietnam War was no longer legitimate facilitated greater recognition of the profound distress of veterans.

It is interesting to note that Abram Kardiner, the American psychiatrist who is credited with formulating the first outline of the traumatic syndrome, was a man with a history of damaging childhood experiences of violence, poverty, and neglect. After being analyzed by Sigmund Freud in Vienna, he returned to New York in 1922 to work with war veterans, acknowledging that his own "ceaseless nightmare" from childhood helped him to identify with the veterans' plight (Herman 1992).

Today PTSD is listed in the American Psychiatric Association publication *Diagnostic and Statistical Manual of Mental Disorders* (DSM) as "the development of certain characteristic symptoms following a psychologically distressing event that is outside the range of normal human experience" (Parkinson 2000). As Herman points out, it is not so much that the traumatic experience is rare or extraordinary, but rather that it overwhelms ordinary adaptations to life. The common denominator of all psychological trauma is described as "intense fear, helplessness, loss of control and fear of annihilation." Other reactions include feelings of powerlessness, increased anxiety and vulnerability, intrusive images and thoughts, nightmares and sleep disturbances, shame, regret, anger, blame, guilt, and bitterness (Parkinson 2000).

Although at first it might seem inappropriate to bring the history of psychological trauma into this discussion, I have always felt that there are important parallels and implications for end-of-life care and staff support. We certainly see the kind of trauma reactions listed above in terminal cancer and HIV/AIDS patients, and also in people who have been severely injured. Patients often refer to their feelings of powerlessness and helplessness and express fears about dying in pain, or "rotting away" or even about "drowning in their own blood."

While some terminally ill patients may be accommodated in private rooms in sensitively designed, freestanding hospices and palliative-care units, many patients will spend their last days in larger wards where they may see and hear their fellow patients in their dying hours and days. In a world where the experience of death is less common, these sights and sounds can be shocking and distressing not only for the patients and families but also for staff. It is often said that the extraordinary becomes ordinary for staff engaged in this kind of work, but can it ever really be "ordinary"? The cumulative effects of daily critical incidents are often imperceptible but have a way of catching up with us.

While doctors and nurses bear the brunt of exposure, social workers can also be severely affected by the sights, sounds, and smells associated with terminal cancer and other disfiguring or degenerative conditions. It could even be argued that their "person-in-situation training" encourages them to think even more about the complex human being in the bed rather than the disease entity, leaving them less defended than their medical and nursing colleagues.

Social workers may develop reluctance about entering the wards or the rooms of dying patients and retreat into their office to do paperwork and phone calls to protect themselves. These are issues that can be raised in supervision. In home visits there is even less protection. The other side of the coin, of course, is the sense of being a guest in a patient's home and privy to some very special hospitality and opportunities for meaningful observation and conversation. Patch Adams deplores the loss of the home visit and says, "When doctors gave up the house calls they gave up the gold" (Adams 1993).

Military metaphors are often used in hospitals, particularly in end-of-life care. Medical staff might say "we have lost the battle" or "we are winning with this treatment" or that the patient "has a lot of fight left in him." It is as if we are waging a war against diseases, a war against death. In the same way that soldiers were once labeled as morally weak, social workers and other staff who display signs of stress and compassion (battle?) fatigue may be labeled "weak" or "unsuited to the work." Furthermore, the same camaraderie and sense of common purpose that sustained soldiers and helped them to get back to the frontline is also the key to survival for social workers and their colleagues in stressful areas of work such as intensive care.

During the world wars it was found that strong leadership helped soldiers to feel safe and bonded as a group. Perhaps the decline in the status and authority of doctors as the "rightful" leaders of healthcare teams might be contributing to higher levels of stress and uncertainty in today's system. In the 1970s, doctors were still being referred to as "captains of the ship." They led ward rounds, chaired meetings, made final decisions about treatment or discharge, and had a sense of ownership in relation to their colleagues, referring to them as "my nurses" or "my social worker." This authoritative style has now given way to a more collaborative and egalitarian one, particularly in hospice care.

Perhaps we have ignored the suffering of staff in highly charged life-and-death settings in the same way that the plight of soldiers was ignored for so long. The suffering is minimized because the work is seen as a noble, higher calling. It is interesting to see that "debriefing," once an operational term used by military organizations and later emergency services, is now widely used in hospitals and crisis work. It is simply a structured conversation or meeting, an opportunity for those involved to talk about their roles and reactions to critical events, thus reducing anxiety and minimizing the risk of developing more complicated psychological and physical problems. It also reassures participants that they are not alone. It is not a panacea or a magic wand, nor does it take away all pain and distress in one session. It is merely a starting point that acknowledges the reality of a crisis. Unfortunately, overly enthusiastic mental health professionals can also misuse debriefing. I remember a minister from a disaster-affected community in New Zealand protesting about the many debriefing offers flooding in after a mass shooting in his parish. Exasperated, he said, "If anyone else offers to debrief me I'll take my trousers off!"

Having worked not only in hospitals and hospices but also in a funeral company where I was called upon to assist families following suicide, homicide, industrial accidents, and road deaths, I began to see the grief, stress, and trauma that these various settings had in common. My involvement in community recovery following two mass shooting incidents in Melbourne in 1987 led to an interest in disaster management, and, once again, the language and issues resonated with all my previous social work experiences. I saw the potential for healing and harm minimization in all of these different settings. Debriefing, support, counseling, mutual-aid approaches, and camaraderie can become the kind of "companionship in adversity" to which the Archbishop of Canterbury referred in an address to the people of Hungerford, England, following the mass shooting in that village in 1987. He spoke about the kind of companionship that "breeds not bitterness but warmth, a warmth which in due time embraces not only who shared the adversity but also the neighbour, the newcomer, the visitor or passerby, the stranger" (Runcie 1987). Sometimes I think that social workers and other helping professionals fail to see that together with our colleagues and the people we are called upon to serve, we are, in fact, a community, an order of companionship in adversity in which we can draw strength from one another.

Herman (1992) also refers to traumatic stress in abused and oppressed women and other minority groups and advocates for the use of mutual-aid and self-help approaches in overcoming a sense of powerlessness. Given the powerful hierarchies that exist in healthcare organizations today and the ways in which entire social work departments have been dismantled or placed under threat, the social work profession may need to develop even more effective political strategies to protect their own and their clients' interests.

If we, as social workers, accept that the "personal is political," according to the slogan made famous during the women's movement, then strategies for dealing with burnout, compassion fatigue, and vicarious traumatization must address powerlessness as well as other sources of stress and demoralization. Opportunities for debriefing, supportive counseling, supervision, ongoing education, and participation in leave-taking rituals will be important. Submission writing and lobbying management and government leaders about needed reforms may also be part of our responsibility to our clients and ourselves.

CAREGIVER GRIEF: "PRIVATE SHADOWS"

In recent years, the concept of caregiver grief has been highlighted by Dani Papadatou (2000), a professor of clinical psychology in the Faculty of Nursing, University of Athens, following research with nurses in pediatric oncology and intensive care units. She uses the term *private shadows* to describe the grief of caregivers who are exposed to multiple deaths and whose grief has tended to go unnoticed. Kenneth Doka (1989) would use the term *disenfranchised* to describe this grief that has not been recognized or validated. However, it was Robert Fulton (1980) who first referred to the often intense and hidden grief of staff in nursing homes who were not "legitimately bereaved" yet sometimes grieved more deeply over a patient than the patient's own relatives did.

The losses that Papadatou identified in the nurses studied included the loss of a close relationship with a particular patient; losses related to identification with the pain of family members; the loss of one's own unmet goals and expectations; past unresolved losses or anticipated future losses; and the death of self or confrontations with one's own mortality. She found that nurses fluctuate in their reactions towards the deaths of their patients, oscillating between "experiencing" and "avoiding" according to Stroebe and Schut's Oscillation Theory (Papadatou 2001). She sees this fluctuation as healthy and adaptive, allowing staff to find meaning and to integrate the losses into their life and work. In recent years, nurses have become more involved in the assessment of psychosocial stressors, family counseling, bereavement care, and what is known as reflective practice. Clinical nurse specialists in palliative care do not have the same hands-on role that generalist nurses once had. This change from a task focus to a person-centered approach may well add to nurses' experiences of stress and grief.

The losses described above could apply equally to social workers, although the tradition of individual supervision in social work might in some way serve as a buffer to stress. Social workers may be more accustomed to sharing their personal reactions to a death with their supervisors and colleagues and will also benefit from being involved in bereavement follow-up activities. Although nurses have always used their "handovers" for sharing information and for mutual support, the focus has tended to be more on the patient than on the nurses themselves. However, as cost containment, managed care, and dismantling of social service departments continue, supervision is becoming merely administrative, if it is offered at all.

GRIEVING AS A SELF-CARE STRATEGY

In her popular book *Kitchen Table Wisdom* (1998), Dr. Rachel Naomi Remen suggests that staff burn out not because they do not care but because they do not grieve. She notes, "the expectation that we can be immersed in suffering and loss daily and not be touched by it is as unrealistic as expecting to be able to walk through water without getting wet." Grieving as a strategy for self-care is rarely, if ever, mentioned in the stress-management literature, but in end-of-life care it makes a great deal of sense. Staff may need to take their leave of special patients and families through attendance at funerals, acknowledgement of the death at bereavement review meetings, or memorial booklets kept in the ward. Enlightened hospices with comprehensive bereavement follow-up services usually include grief support programs for staff. Even if there are no formal staff support activities, the knowledge that families will continue to receive the support they need will also reduce staff anxiety and feelings of responsibility after a period of intense involvement.

INTIMATE STRANGERS

Robert Fulton's (1986) concept of the "intimate stranger" highlights another dilemma for the professional caregiver. He warns of the danger of becoming a surrogate relative or friend in the emotionally charged atmosphere of end-of-life care. In his words, "Think what we ask ourselves as caregivers to do: offer succor to the dying, attempt to ease their pain; attend to their psychological and social problems; and in addition, aspire to minister to their spiritual needs and concerns. We strive to accomplish all this, moreover, as virtual strangers. This is to my mind, an extraordinary undertaking. We must recognize that we are strangers to the overwhelming majority of our patients, albeit intimate strangers" (Fulton 1986:151).

Close encounters with the dying and the bereaved can be very meaningful and satisfying. Sometimes they may even appear to be more important than relationships with family and friends in the real world. It is not uncommon for these real-life relationships to suffer as more and more time is invested in work. Once again, it is through supervision and interactions with vigilant and caring team members that such overinvestment can be named and guarded against.

Dr. Balfour Mount, a pioneer of palliative care in Canada, once said that professionals in this field face a unique dilemma, because they are always forming a relationship with a patient while at the same time preparing for the relationship to end (Kingsbury 1978).

THE WOUNDED HEALER

It was Henri Nouwen, a Catholic priest who was born in Holland in 1932 and died in Canada in 1996, who popularized the concept of the wounded healer and traced it back to its biblical foundations (Ford 1999). Nouwen believed that our own woundedness and experiences of suffering can be a source of healing and compassion for both ourselves and others. Although he wrote *The Wounded Healer* with ministers in mind, the concept of the wounded healer has great relevance for all helping professionals, including social workers. Not surprisingly, many of us enter the caring professions in an attempt, perhaps not always conscious, to make sense of our own experiences of hardship and suffering. Nouwen speaks about the "professional loneliness" of ministers who are "often more tolerated than required." Social workers can also find themselves at the "edge of events" in hospitals and even in hospice/palliative-care settings, although here there is usually a greater emphasis on the personhood of the patient than in acute settings where the diseased body is the central focus.

The Irish palliative-care physician Michael Kearney also writes about loneliness and soul pain in his book *Mortally Wounded* (1996). He defines soul pain as "the experience of an individual who has become disconnected and alienated from the deepest and most fundamental aspects of himself or herself." Using poetry, dream work, and guided imagery, he works with dying patients at a deeper, soulful level, which he calls "depth work." Although cure for the disease is no longer possible, Kearney believes in the potential for healing to occur in the midst of the suffering and tries to help patients to find the hidden "treasure" in their experience. The concept of soul pain also has relevance for staff who may have become alienated from their deeper selves and assumed a more mechanical, superficial role in their work. Perhaps there are elements of soul pain in burnout and compassion fatigue. Nouwen also holds the view that something valuable and beautiful can emerge from the struggle and the loneliness: "But the more I think of loneliness, the more I think that the wound of loneliness is like the Grand Canyon—a deep incision in the surface of our existence which has become an inexhaustible source of beauty and self understanding" (Nouwen 1979:84).

THE INNER BEREAVED CHILD

Beverley Raphael (1984) writes eloquently about the pain of identification with the suffering of others. In addition to her concept of "empathic strain" (see Compassion Fatigue), she has also contributed to the field the concept of the "inner bereaved child," or "that part of us that is reawakened when we share someone else's loss and attempt to comfort and console them. In her book The *Anatomy of Bereavement* she writes, "While compassion allows us to empathize with the distress of others and to offer them comfort and consolation, it may also bring distress for us proportionate to the severity of their loss, the closeness of our identification with their situation and the degree to which our own earlier pain has been revived" (Raphael 1984:404).

It is important that we acknowledge our vulnerability and the identification we inevitably develop with certain patients and families. Whether it is because the patient is our own age, reminds us of a close relative or friend whose death we dread, or reminds us of our own cultural background, it is important to be aware of the bonds we are developing and the connections we are making. Sometimes our own needs and unfinished business can get in the way.

ANAM CARA (SOUL FRIEND)

When I had an opportunity to live and work in Ireland to assist some Irish hospice and palliative-care organizations to develop their bereavement services, I came across the writings of Irish poet, philosopher, and scholar John O'Donohue (1997, 1999). His books are treasure troves of Celtic wisdom and spirituality, inspiring and encouraging reflections on every aspect of human existence. In the Gaelic language *anam cara* means soul friend, "a person to whom you could reveal the intimacies of your life in a friendship which represents an act of recognition and belonging." The relationship between a social worker and a dying patient or grieving relative may at times take on an *anam cara* quality, or, as the renowned philosopher and existentialist Martin Buber would say, the sacredness of an "I-Thou" encounter. According to Buber, "I-Thou is the primary word of relation. It is characterized by mutuality, directness, presentness, intensity and ineffability" (Friedman 1976:57).

O'Donohue also refers to the modern tendency to use the language of "psychologese," perhaps another name for psychobabble. He particularly dislikes the use of the words "processing" and "dealing with" in relation to our inner experiences and feels that these terms lack sacredness and depth. We process peas and beans, he says, and a deal is a business arrangement or something that is done in a casino. Social work today abounds with examples of language that distances us from the essential nature of our task. Risk assessment, outcome measures, competencies, and even the term *psychosocial* can trivialize and oversimplify very complex and unique human experiences.

MINDING YOURSELF

Instead of saying, "Take care," the Irish say, "Mind yourself" or "Mind how you go." I offer the following suggestions to social workers everywhere in the hope that they will use them to "mind themselves" and practice "relentless self-care."

1. *Use supervision.* Supervision is a time-honored tradition in social work practice, and it tries to combine administrative, professional development, and support functions. Essentially, supervision is offered to social workers in the service of the client and is not meant to be a substitute for personal work or therapy. Even in the most supportive agencies there may be reluctance on the part of the worker to expose personal vulnerability for fear of being judged inadequate; however, a good supervisor will be able to create a safe place for sharing of both personal and professional struggles and will acknowledge strengths. Use supervision, insist on it, and if it is not available in your workplace, find it outside or create peer supervision groups in your institutions.

2. *Consider therapy.* Sometimes supervision and the support of caring colleagues, family, and friends is not enough. Therapy with a qualified and skilled psychotherapist can be a great help in healing our woundedness. Elisabeth Kübler-Ross urged workers in this field to "empty their pools of pain and negativity" in order to be truly effective helpers. In the same vein, Malcolm X, the black revolutionary leader, once said, "only people who have experienced a revolution within themselves can reach out effectively to help others." In my own life I found the help of a psychoanalyst profoundly helpful in sorting out many personal difficulties and in coming to terms with the cumulative effects of many losses and changes. It is probably unlikely that the "pools" of negativity are ever completely emptied—perhaps they are more like potholes and have a tendency to fill up again!

3. *Discover your values.* Life without "guideposts to meaning" can be very bleak. Even if a social worker does not have a particular religious affiliation or perspective, it is difficult to see how anyone could survive, let alone thrive, in the work of caring for dying and bereaved people without a source of spiritual sustenance and renewal. Most people working in end-of-life care would acknowledge the need for a strong sense of the positive growth, transformation, and healing that comes from struggling to overcome adversity. Many people in this field gravitate toward nature, regularly replenishing themselves in and near the sea, mountains, lakes, trees, and gardens. They use secular or religious prayer, meditation, art, poetry, and music to connect with the divine and with the mystery and wonder of the universe.

4. *Develop support programs.* Social workers working in the field of loss and grief and end-of-life care need knowledge, self-awareness, and, above all, support. It is often

said in social work that we use ourselves as a tool. That tool needs to be cherished and nurtured as well as taught. If not, we will become hardened, and we will begin to defend ourselves against the pain of loss and grief. We will distance ourselves from clients at a time when they are at their most vulnerable and in need of authentic, honest, and compassionate care.

The Victoria Hospice Society in British Columbia is one of the few services in the world with a staff support policy, committee, and designated budget. With approximately eighty full-time staff and several hundred volunteers, the Victoria Hospice Society has introduced a variety of staff support activities. These include availability of professional counseling on a short-term basis, fireside chats, staff retreats, formal presentations about handling stress and grief, and a regular newsletter. They also have a weekly draw from a "treasure chest" where a staff member might win a massage or a book voucher.

5. *Balance.* Maintain a healthy balance between home and work responsibilities and find creative, life-giving activities and relationships outside as well as inside the workplace. At work, try to find some respite from individual and family counseling through involvement in teaching, writing, group work, volunteer training, community development projects, and supervision. Avoid emotionally draining meetings or interviews at the end of the day if possible.

6. *Stress management.* Try to analyze and understand sources of stress at home and at work. Ask yourself whether the job really matches your personality, needs, and experience. Maintain good habits such as regular physical exercise and good nutrition, and try to get enough sleep. Be with people with whom you can laugh and play. If the system you work in is damaging your health and well-being, it might be best to leave rather than try to reform it, unless you can find powerful allies.

7. *Grief and mourning.* Recognize your need to grieve and mourn for patients who have died in your care and participate in memorial activities as you feel the need. Cry when you need to, if that is your way of expressing yourself. But don't panic if you can't cry—there are many ways to grieve.

8. *Education.* Continue your education about end-of-life care and about experiences of grief, trauma, stress management, staff support, healing, and any other topics that awaken your interest. It always helps to know that your reactions are normal and to engage the intellect. A few post-master's continuing education programs have begun to address these needs for colleagueship and mastery of new knowledge, skills, and self-reflection, including the Smith College School of Social Work and NYU School of Social Work.

9. *Teamwork.* Remember that you are not alone. As a member of a social work department and of a multidisciplinary team, you can draw on the strength and wisdom of colleagues. At the Royal Children's Hospital in Melbourne, we used to meet in the canteen for "cappuccino therapy" every morning. Of course, it requires time and an open, caring work culture to develop trust and camaraderie with colleagues. Phyllis Silverman's report on the first widow-to-widow program in Boston was entitled, "If you will lift the load, I will lift it too." Ideally, this is the way we should work in teams.

10. *From the personal to the political.* One of the most effective ways to avoid

burning out is to make a difference. I have always gained enormous satisfaction from my community-development and social-action activities. Moving from the personal to the political can mean advocating for changes at a hospital, community, or governmental level. Through lobbying, writing submissions, and setting up new services such as self-help groups and education programs, you can translate what you are learning as a caseworker into social change. Join forces with others who have a vision for how things can be done differently and for the better—don't forget to stop and look at the big picture now and then!

A PERSONAL AND PROFESSIONAL REFLECTION

In writing this chapter, I have had the opportunity to reflect on my life as a social worker and some of the changes that have taken place in the field since I was a student. The social work curriculum at the University of Melbourne in the late 1960s did not include any subjects that dealt with the pain and stress of repeated exposure to human suffering. In retrospect, it was my philosophy studies that gave me some of the emotional and spiritual armor I needed to cope with the onslaught of deprivation, damage, injury, disability, and misery to which I was exposed. We were babes in the wood in the sixties, barely out of high school, with passionate idealism and Bob Dylan and The Beatles to sustain us.

One of my first fieldwork assignments as a social work student was to visit the asylum where my beloved Dutch grandmother spent the last weeks of her life when she was suffering from advanced dementia. I was horrified by what I saw there. The stewed lukewarm tea was passed around in a tin bucket with milk and sugar already added, denying individual preferences developed over a lifetime. The place had that instantly recognizable institutional smell, and I vividly remember the sounds of screaming and moaning, a terrible place for a precious life to end. Not one of my teachers or supervisors asked me about my personal reactions to this assignment. Nor did anyone think to ask me why I chose alcoholism as a topic for my first social work essay, although it was undoubtedly an attempt to save, or at least, better understand my father, whose addiction to alcohol was very damaging to our family life. In fact, the quality of supervision was sadly lacking in my last two student "placements." One supervisor actually painted her fingernails during our sessions! The other, a social worker in a mental health clinic, wrote a final report about my performance as a student that read more like a diagnostic statement about my psychopathology than an evaluation of student learning.

My first job as a social worker was away from home in a large Sydney teaching hospital. Although my father had suddenly died of lung cancer during my last year of social work studies, I was thrown into a cancer ward and expected to sink or swim. Unfortunately, I sank. I can still remember the horrifying sight and smell of an entire row of patients with tracheotomies. It was my job to "place" these poor people, to find nursing homes for them to die in, because the hospital at that time did not have a palliative-care unit. It was like a scene out of *MASH*. There was no supervision, no support, just a tearoom where the social workers ate "Sao" crackers with jam or vegemite (a favorite Australian snack), drank cups of tea, and laughed and talked about what they did at the weekend. As a newcomer, I felt utterly alone, and after four difficult and frightening months, I left. I did a lot of comfort eating and one day actually feigned illness to get out of work by putting baby powder on my face because I was too ashamed and confused to admit that I was falling apart. I will always be grateful to my dear childhood friend, Lynda Campbell, who came all the way to Sydney to accompany me back to Melbourne. It took us three days instead of the usual eight hours to drive back in a baby Fiat that was overheating and leaking oil at the same time—an experience that bonded us for life! Lynda now teaches social work at our alma mater.

This was a tough early lesson about the importance of support and supervision and about dealing with one's own grief in order to be an effective helper. It was at this time that I began to search for better ways of caring for the dying, the bereaved, and those forgotten people, the professional caregivers. Although we were taught about "detached concern" and "controlled emotional involvement," we were not taught about coping with grief, trauma, or, for that matter, how to practice relentless self-care.

A few years later I had an opportunity to work in an oncology unit in another large teaching hospital, this time in my hometown, Melbourne. I must confess that I was drawn like a magnet toward Dutch families, in particular those with a father who was dying of cancer. I had a strong motivation to help them. Above all, I wanted them to communicate with each other in an open, honest, and meaningful way, to say, "I love you, thank you, and goodbye." As Dame Cicely Saunders once suggested in an interview in *Time* magazine, we all need to do this if we possibly can. With the help of a good supervisor, I began to realize that this urgency represented my own unfinished business. My father had died in a great deal of pain and turmoil, and I wanted to undo some of the damage that his death represented. We must be very careful not to impose our own needs and wishes on vulnerable families. When we have a particularly intense involvement with a family in crisis, it is important to ask ourselves, "Who, or what does this remind me of?" and to discuss this with someone we trust.

In the early 1970s I discovered the writings of Elisabeth Kübler-Ross. Not only did she highlight the needs of dying and bereaved people, but she also validated the experiences of caregivers, whom she felt were "limping behind in the stages" just like the patient's family members. In her book *Working It Through*, she urges caregivers of the dying and the bereaved to "work through" their own grief issues: "We must come to grips with the many deaths, the little deaths we encounter every day and the big deaths that mark important passages in our lives or we can never truly help another person fully. The reason is simple. The work will be too threatening. Too many of one's own buttons will be pushed if these intensely personal issues have not been resolved" (Kübler-Ross 1982:26).

There have been many times through the years when I have felt the loneliness to which Henri Nouwen refers in *The Wounded Healer*, or, as Irish author Marian Keyes would say, "this sensitivity is like carrying around an extra limb." I have participated in some appalling ward rounds and multidisciplinary team meetings in hospitals and even in hospices, where patients and families were the objects of derision and laughter.

I have been accused of lacking a sense of humor and of being too thin-skinned. Having been on the receiving end of such a meeting as a patient myself, I have always been acutely sensitive about them.

After that first disastrous job experience, I became terribly disillusioned about social work and felt more and more depressed while trying to make sense of some of the wounds in my life. I was hospitalized for a short time in an adolescent psychiatry unit and will never forget the humiliation of being interviewed (interrogated is how it felt) by a group of doctors and other professionals in white coats about my "symptoms." Instinctively, I held something back, tried to maintain a sense of self that was more dignified. I didn't feel safe, and certainly not respected or heard. As soon as the "interview" was over, I ran into the garden, sat under a tree, and sobbed. Soon after, I signed myself out. It was a painful yet illuminating experience. I learned that some help is actually more harmful than helpful.

For more than twenty-five years, I have been involved in the development of hospice and bereavement services. Robert Fulton once described the hospice movement as a counterrevolutionary movement that "takes its stand against a secularized, impersonal, utilitarian and increasingly hostile world" (1986:155). He also saw hospice as part of the women's movement, insisting that "the human virtues of love, sympathy, and human compassion be recognized in a world that is all too callous and brutal." We have made extraordinary progress. The achievements certainly compensate for some of the struggles and sacrifices, although sometimes I fear that we are sliding backward and that the values that Fulton articulated are being ignored.

I have had some recent personal experience of the healthcare system and "medigoround," as I have heard it described. Four years ago I was diagnosed with Wegener's granulomatosis, a rare and incurable autoimmune disease that has caused irreversible damage to my nasal bone structure and sinuses. I have had blood tests, chest x-rays, and CT scans and suffered unpleasant side effects from the treatment. But the worst of it has been the indifference of healthcare personnel, with the notable exception of one physician. Although I am well, there is always a chance that the disease will progress and cause more damage. I am learning to live with that. The change in my appearance has been distressing. I grieve for the way I used to look and feel somewhat betrayed by my body. I often think about my dying friend's letter. Never give up on relentless self-care, Rob said. I try to heed his parting words and now live a more creative and less stressful life with the full support of a loving partner. I enjoy writing, teaching, and conducting workshops on loss, bereavement, and especially about "relentless self-care" in many places throughout the world.

Patch Adams believes that creativity is a vital ingredient in wellness: "Creativity is one of the greatest medicines ever. . . . Creativity is essential nourishment. . . . It is the very soul of our self worth." In his book, *Gesundheit!* (1993) Patch describes his vision for a more humane healthcare system and how he and his friends have established a unique hospital in West Virginia. The film made about his life and work, *Patch Adams*, starring Robin Williams, is a must for every helping professional interested in enlightened patient care. Perhaps not surprisingly, the number-one topic about which he is asked to write or present workshops is burnout. In the book he tells a very moving story about the two weeks he spent in a locked ward in a psychiatric hospital after trying to kill himself. It was in his freshman year at college, and he had reached a very low ebb after breaking up with his girlfriend and after his favorite uncle and surrogate father committed suicide. Patch describes this time in the hospital as "the turning point in my life—a spiritual awakening to the power of love." It was the love of family, friends, and fellow patients that helped him the most, but he had to learn to accept that love. Elisabeth Kübler-Ross also says "to live well basically means to learn to love."

I've come a long way since my student days, but at heart I'm still the Beatles fan I was forty years ago. My hopes, dreams, and ideals are firmly intact, and I still believe in the words of that well-known Beatles song, "All you need is love."

Mind yourself!

REFERENCES

Adams, P., and M. Mylander. 1993. *Gesundheit!* Rochester, VT: Healing Arts Press.

Barger, N., and L. Kirby. 1995. *The Challenge of Change in Organizations: Helping Employees Thrive in the New Frontier.* Palo Alto, CA: Davies-Black.

Berger, A., and P. K. Portenoy, eds. 1998. *Principles and Practice of Supportive Oncology.* Philadelphia: Lippincott-Raven.

Bowman, T. 1999. Promoting resiliency in those who do bereavement work. *Lifeline* 27.

Corr, C., and D. Corr, eds. 1983. *Hospice Care: Principles and Practice.* New York: Springer.

De Boulay, S. 1985. *Changing the Face of Death: The Story of Cicely Saunders.* London: Religious and Moral Education Press.

Doka, K. 1989. *Disenfranchised Grief: Recognizing Hidden Sorrow.* New York: Lexington.

Figley, C. 1994. *Compassion Fatigue: Coping with Secondary Traumatic Stress Disorder in Those Who Treat the Traumatized.* New York: Brunner-Mazel.

———, ed. 2002. *Treating Compassion Fatigue.* London: Routledge.

Firth-Cozens, J., and R. Payne, eds. 1999. *Stress in Health Professionals: Psychological and Organizational Causes and Consequences.* New York: Wiley.

Fiscalini, J. 1995. Transference and countertransference as interpersonal phenomena. In M. Lionells, J. Fiscalini, C. H. Mann, and D. B. Stern, *Handbook of Interpersonal Psychoanalysis,* chap. 26. Hillside, NJ: Analytic Press.

Ford, M. 1999. *The Wounded Prophet.* New York: Doubleday.

Freudenberger, H. J. 1975. Staff burn-out. *Journal of Social Issues* 30(1): 159–165.

Friedman, M. 1976. *Martin Buber: The Life of Dialogue.* Chicago: University of Chicago Press.

Fulton, R. 1986. In quest of the spiritual component of care for the terminally ill. Paper delivered at the Yale University School of Nursing.

———. 1987. The many faces of grief. *Death Studies* 11:243–256.

Herman, J. 1992. *Trauma and Recovery.* New York: Basic Books.

Hirschorn, L., and L. May. 1999. Stress in the nursing department. In *Stress in Health Professionals: Psychological and Organizational Causes and Consequences,* ed. J. Firth-Cozens and R. Payne, chap. 13. New York: Wiley.

Kearney, M. 1996. *Mortally Wounded: Stories of Soul Pain, Death and Healing.* New York: Scribner.

Kingsbury, K. 1978. *I Want to Die at Home.* Melbourne: Jenkinson Press.

Kübler-Ross, E. 1982. *Working It Through.* New York: Simon & Schuster.

———. 1991. *On Life After Death.* Rutland, VT: Celestial Arts.

Kuhl, D. 2002. *What Dying People Want.* Toronto: Doubleday.

Maslach, C. 1993. Burnout: A multidimensional perspective. In *Professional Burnout: Recent Developments in Theory and Research,* ed. W. Schaufeli, C. Maslach, and T. Marek, 19–32. Washington, D.C.: Taylor & Francis.

Nouwen, H. 1972. *The Wounded Healer.* New York: Doubleday.

O'Donohue, J. 1997. *Anam Cara: A Book of Celtic Wisdom.* New York: HarperCollins.

———. 1999. *Eternal Echoes: Celtic Reflections on Our Yearning to Belong.* New York: HarperCollins.

Papadatou, D. 2000. A proposed model of health professionals' grieving process. *Omega* 41(1): 59–77.

———. 2001. The grieving health care provider: Variables affecting the professional response to a child's death. *Bereavement Care* 20(2): 26–29.

Parkinson, F. 2000. *Post-Trauma Stress.* London: Fisher Books.

Pearlman, L., and L. McCann. 1990. Vicarious traumatization: A framework for understanding the psychological effects of working with victims. *Journal of Traumatic Stress* 3(1): 5.

Raphael, B. 1984. *The Anatomy of Bereavement.* New York: Basic Books.

Remen, R. N. 1998. *Kitchen Table Wisdom.* New York: Berkeley.

Runcie, R. 1987. Archbishop of Canterbury: Transcript of address to the people of Hungerford, August 1987. Berkshire Social Services Department.

Schaufeli, W. B., D. Enzmann, and N. Girault. 1993. Measurement of burnout: A review. In *Professional Burnout: Recent Developments in Theory and Research,* ed. W. B. Schaufeli, C. Maslach, and T. Marek, 199–212. Washington, DC: Taylor & Francis.

Sprang, G., and J. McNeil. 1995. *The Many Faces of Bereavement.* New York: Brunner-Mazel.

Stamm, B. H. 1997. Work-related secondary traumatic stress. *PTSD Research Quarterly* 8(2): 1–6.

Vachon, M. 1978. Motivation and stress experienced by staff working with the terminally ill. *Death Education* 2:113–122.

———. 1994. *Occupational Stress in Caregivers of the Critically Ill, Dying, and Bereaved.* New York: Hemisphere.

———. 1998. Caring for the caregiver in oncology and palliative care. *Seminars in Oncology Nursing* 14(2): 152–157.

———. 2001. The nurse's role: The world of palliative care nursing. In *The Oxford Textbook of Palliative Nursing,* ed. B. Ferrell and N. Coyle, 647–659. New York: Oxford University Press.

Valent, P. 2002. Diagnosis and treatment of helper stresses, traumas and illnesses. In *Treating Compassion Fatigue,* ed. C. Figley, 17–37. London: Routledge.

Veninga, R., and J. Spradley. 1982. *The Work–Stress Connection.* Toronto: Ballantine.

CONCLUSION

WE BEGAN this book with personal and compelling narratives by professional helpers, describing their own experiences with illness, death, dying, and bereavement. We have learned through this process that it is through one's own lived experiences that the greatest knowledge and wisdom may be found. This is a theme that we deemed most important to this book. It underscores the fact that in working with the dying and their families, as well as with the bereaved, it is important to integrate the personal with the professional. The professional who is working in this area is always informed by the personal, and acknowledging this and understanding it is critical to good professional practice; the chapter on respectful death sets a context for the book. We owe respect to the families we serve and to the dying member of that family, as well as to ourselves. And therefore we conclude the book with the Irish admonition to "mind yourself."

We have learned a good deal from its many contributors in the course of writing and editing this book. We have come to respect the role of social workers in end-of-life care. We see that they are drawn to the field, in part, because it allows them to bear witness at one of life's most intimate moments. Our colleagues—social workers, nurses, and physicians—come to this field with a desire to support dying individuals and their families in ways that reflect how they lived. Social workers speak of their work with the dying as some of the humblest and yet most spiritual moments of their lives. There are vital lessons that the dying teach us, and there is great value in hearing these anew. Dying people and their families live with uncertainty and ambiguity, and they help us to do the same. As social workers, we cannot take away suffering. But we can witness it, and this then enables us to act as guides, as communicators, as collaborators, and as guardians of our clients' wishes.

We are committed to practicing with values in accordance with the ethical principles of the profession, particularly as we consider the needs of the disenfranchised. Yet the contexts in which we work with the dying, especially in medical settings, often devalue and marginalize the people whom we serve—and the profession of social work itself. The ways in which clinical practices, medical hierarchies, entitlements, and even interdisciplinary teams are constructed mirror issues of power and powerlessness in the larger society. The allocation of resources such as hospice or palliative care are often based on power arrangements. Likewise, many conflicts between the

Western values of autonomy and independence and the more interdependent values of many other worldviews are unconsciously played out in the field of end-of-life care. We have tried to demonstrate that although death is always an individual and relational event, it also occurs within political, cultural, and social contexts. Because dying is also about access to resources, social workers are always in the foreground of trying to deal with disparities in the provision of care for the dying, whether based on immigrant status, mental illness, substance abuse, status as a prisoner, age, income, or race.

The various chapters in this book remind us that clinical work with the dying does not take place in the fifty-minute hour. It requires the capacity to be present fully, and therefore to stand still. Paradoxically, it also requires a great deal of activity: in interdisciplinary collaborations, leading family conferences, stimulating multidisciplinary dialogues, and advocating for equity in care. We have learned from the contributors to this book that this means more than sitting in a room; it means becoming active listeners. This is what is required of us if we are to be a companion on a journey, a champion for their dying person's needs, an advocate for death with respect and dignity, deftly handling interpersonal challenges, negotiating impasses, and finding ways to support dying individual and their families' strengths.

One of the questions we asked is this: How do we social workers remain on the front lines of death, dying and bereavement, actively listening, confronting some of the most complex legal and ethical issues in this country, supporting and empowering individuals and families, and still remaining open enough to face our own mortality at the same time? This takes courage and fortitude. It also takes self-care. Work with the dying can be lonely, and so it is even more essential that forms of renewal be found to sustain one's sense of hope and purpose. In writing the introduction to this book, we tried to reflect on the range of chapters in the book and what they have to teach. We now see them as a whole, and they point to our obligations and the value of what we as social workers can contribute to this area of practice. We have an obligation to ourselves, to the people we serve, and to our profession. Sometimes renewal and care for the social worker come from doing a job well and reaching to create new initiatives and new partnerships within the community that will change the culture of dying in America.

We have begun a dialogue between the contributors to this book and its readers. It is an opening conversation that we all must continue, professionally and personally, as we move through the years. It is literally a matter of life or death.

INDEX

Abramson, J. S., 165
Acute stress disorder, 376–77
Adams, P., 856, 865–66
Addictions, 469–73, 567, 718
Adjustment disorder, 368–69
Advance directives: conflicts between wishes of patient and family, 270; in context of long-term care, 632; cultural differences in use of, 455; discussions of, opportunities, unwillingness, 765–67, 771–75; education issues, 552–53, 774–75; failures to accompany patient to hospital, 635; family's or physician's unwillingness to comply with, 136, 762; federal and state policies, 762–63; forwarded by Cruzan case, 763; for gays and lesbians, 493; healthcare proxies and proxy directives, 597, 598, 635, 688–89, 733–34, 764; immunity for healthcare providers complying with, 176; inclusive, 603; information as part of nursing home admission process, 632; inmates' lack of understanding of, 610; legal issue of enforcement, 739; living wills, 176, 635, 733–34, 763–64; Medicare requiring query as to, 762–63; need arising along with medical advances, 761; need for separate directives for different states, 763; for nursing home

patients, 629; for prisoners, 784; purposes, types, characteristics, difficulties, and benefits of, 175–76, 732–34, 762–64, 765–67, 771–72; recommendations by AMA, 764–65, 766–67; stating patient's preference, 773; transplant patient (with case example), 688–89; values history as adjunct to, 735, 742, 766
Advance directives, legal issues: *Bergman v. Eden Medical Center*, 740; constitutionality of state statutes, 738–39; enforcement, 739; improving due process guarantees for incompetent patients, 740–41, 748; injury from unwanted treatment as "battery," 739; new generation of, 741–42; protection for doctors for double-effect euthanasia (pain relief hastening death), 739–40
Advance directives, problems with: absence of legal liability for noncompliance, 734, 735; ambiguity as to ability to refuse "hydration and nutrition," 734–35; ambiguity as to "terminal illness or condition," 734; factors behind nonuse by most Americans, 737; failure to address unpredictability or ambivalence of patient at end of life, 742; fear of litigation, 737; ideological influ-

ences of right-to-life principle, 744; ignorance, conflict, or value-substitution on part of healthcare proxy/surrogate, 735; incorrect belief regarding refusal or termination of life-support measures, 735; legal presumption in favor of treatment, 737; opposition to, by "state interests," 735–37; physicians or healthcare institutions unduly influencing patient's decision making, 742; polarizing clash of legal versus medical paradigms, 737–38; requirement of "clear and convincing evidence" to refuse life support, 735; restrictive state statutes, 734; unconstitutional restriction of autonomy, prolonging suffering, 735
Adventure-based experiential practice, 651–53, 658
African Americans: advance directives, lower prevalence of, and suspicion of health care system, 604–5, 774; disparities in quality of health care, 444–45; disproportionate numbers incarcerated, 611; expressions of bereavement/grief/mourning, 258; impeded access to hospice care, 445; impeded access to routine primary care, 715; percent under hospice care, 417;

415; innovative program of Kaiser Permanente, 822–23; Last Acts Coalition concept and precepts of, 842; medical education only beginning to address, 816; need for, 411, 414, 415, 418–19; origin of term, 412; physicians melding with families' strength, 58; in prisons, through interdisciplinary teams, 620–21; problems with interdisciplinary teams, 168; providing empathy, compassion, sharing of suffering, xxv–xxvi, 34–37; providing "holding environment," 39; providing personal connection, xx; question of legal right to, 749–50; question of terminal sedation and physician-assisted suicide, 750, 751; reports on, 413; similarities to prison work, 780–82; social workers' inadequate preparation for, xix–xx; social workers' role in, 268, 409, 419–21, 422; team specialization, 412; trend toward, 820–21; typical programs and comprehensive model, 412; *see also* Hospice care; Pain and symptom management
Panic attacks, air hunger, 703
Papadatou, D., 857–58
Parkes, C. M., 143, 255, 580
Parkinson, F., 855
Partners in Care Foundation, 822–23
Passive euthanasia, 767, 773
Pathfinders self-care program, 585
Patient's Bill of Rights (American Hospital Association), 152
Patient Self-Determination Act (PSDA), 467, 476, 603–6, 632, 633, 733–34, 761, 762
Pattison, E. M., 483
Payne, R., 444
Pellegrino, E., 163
Peripheral stem cell transplantation. *See* Transplantation

Personal experience, suggested questions to explore patient/caregivers perspectives, 125
Petrisek, A. C., 637
Phillips, J. M., 484
Phillips, S., 27–28
Photographs and albums, 326, 650, 655
Physician-assisted suicide: as adjunct to adequate pain management at end of life, 748; arguments against, 178, 768; arguments for, 768–69; autonomy, self-determination, and rational control of dying, 752–53; comparison to euthanasia, 177, 767; *Compassion in Dying v. Washington*, 745; concern over depression and relationship to suicide, 737; constitutional background, 744–47; description of, 389; as discriminatory and legally unacceptable, 736; double-effect pain medication and potential criminal liability, 750; due process protections, 748; ethical issues, 177–79; gender issues in decision making, 218; Kevorkian, J., 768; leading to legislation, 137; legal issues confusing, 742–44; mistrust of clinicians by minorities, 384; as option in palliative care, 750; Oregon's Death with Dignity Act, 218, 389, 747, 748, 761, 768, 769–70; *Oregon v. Ashcroft*, state versus federal authority, 748–49; polls indicating public favor, 768; professional support and reports of patient requests for, 769; *Quill v. Vacco*, 746–47; role of medical profession, 751–52; as "slippery slope," 751, 768; U.S. Supreme Court ruling on criminalization, 743; *Washington v. Glucksberg*, 746, 748, 751–52; *see also* Suicide
Physicians: approaches on interdisciplinary teams, 163–66; few certified in palliative care, 8, 158; help for

bereaved, 579; medical profession's ethical integrity (state interest), 736; protecting patients from truth of diagnosis, 304; reluctance to "abandon" patients to hospice care team, 819, 821; sharing of responsibility by, 165; use of term "discipline," 162–63; *see also* Medical culture
Piaget, J., 234
Pietà of Michelangelo, 139
Planned Parenthood v. Casey, 745
Play with ill children, 332–33
Poetry: as communication with lost loved ones, 21–22, 40–41; as request to be remembered, 242; as spiritual expression, 188–89; usefulness of, 73
Popkin, M. K., 368, 369
Postadults, 349
Post-traumatic stress disorder (PTSD), 85, 376–77, 665–66
Potash, J., 786
Power issues: on interdisciplinary teams, 100; for professional organizations, 162
Power of attorney for healthcare, 176, 217–18, 635, 733; *see also* Advance directives
Prayer, 196, 259, 399, 430–31
Pregnancy loss, association with isolated grief, 464
Preparatory play with ill children, 332–33
The President's Commission for the Study of Ethical Problems in Medicine and Biomedical Research, 177, 180
Prisons, end-of-life care in: advance directives, 784; advantages of social workers in cell blocks, 779–80; advocacy of amelioration of prison and sentencing systems, 619–20; aging and ill falling victim to intimidation or violence, 614; aging prisoner population serving longer sentences, 610–12, 788;